THE CALIPH AND THE IMAM

THE CALIPH
AND
THE IMAM

THE MAKING OF SUNNISM
AND SHIISM

TOBY MATTHIESEN

OXFORD
UNIVERSITY PRESS

OXFORD
UNIVERSITY PRESS

Oxford University Press is a department of the University of Oxford.
It furthers the University's objective of excellence in research, scholarship,
and education by publishing worldwide. Oxford is a registered trade mark of
Oxford University Press in the UK and in certain other countries.

Published in the United States of America by Oxford University Press
198 Madison Avenue, New York, NY 10016, United States of America.

CIP data is on file at the Library of Congress.

ISBN 978–0–19–068946–9

DOI: 10.1093/oso/9780190689469.001.0001

Printed by Sheridan Books, Inc., United States of America

Acknowledgements

A ny book that covers as big a ground as this one, tracing the development of Sunnism and Shiism across centuries and regions, accrues many debts. First and foremost, I owe a debt of gratitude to the many people who shared their knowledge and experiences with me during fieldwork. Then, I owe a debt to the many scholars who have contributed to the different disciplines and subfields that I draw on for this book, from religious and Islamic studies to Middle East and South Asian Studies, history, anthropology, sociology, and political science. The extensive notes and bibliography at the end of the book acknowledge that large body of scholarship, and the aim of the book is to bring sometimes disconnected literatures into closer conversation with each other.

I furthermore thank the numerous people and institutions that have supported me throughout the research and writing of this book. At the Middle East Centre of St Antony's College, and the wider University of Oxford, where I held a five-year Senior Research Fellowship and where the idea for this book first emerged, I thank Walter Armbrust, Stephanie Cronin, Faisal Devji, Roger Goodman, Louise Fawcett, Edmund Herzig, Homa Katouzian, Margaret MacMillan, Adam Roberts, Philip Robins, Ahmad al-Shahi, Avi Shlaim, Michael Willis, as well as Eugene Rogan, who encouraged me to write about as big a topic as this. Amongst Oxford's outstanding community of younger scholars, I had stimulating and fun conversations with Kathrin Bachleitner, Maziyar Ghiabi, Andrew Hammond, Susann Kassem, Raphaël Lefèvre, Ceren Lord, Rory McCarthy, Emanuel Schäublin, Manal Shehabi, and Anne Wolf. For research support, I thank Caroline Davis and all the staff of the Middle East Centre and St Antony's College, Mastan Ebtehaj and Maria Luisa Langella of the Middle East Centre Library, Debbie Usher of the Middle East Centre Archive, Lydia Wright of the Oriental Institute Library, and the staff at the Bodleian Library (as well as of the British Library and the Institute of Ismaili Studies in London).

My agent Felicity Bryan envisioned that this book would fill an important gap in the literature. She sadly could no longer see it go to print. It was

George Lucas in New York who then pushed it forward and was a reassuring presence throughout the writing process. I am indebted to him and to my editor Tim Bent of Oxford University Press US, who saw the potential of the book and whose many comments improved it considerably. At Oxford University Press UK, I thank Cathryn Steele, who took the lead in the final stages of production, as well as Luciana O'Flaherty, the copyeditor Martin Noble, the publicist Anna Gell, and the whole production and marketing team. I am also grateful to Catherine Clarke, Michele Topham, and everyone at Felicity Bryan Associates. My meticulous research assistant Dominic Gerhartz helped especially with the references and finalising the manuscript for production.

Matteo Legrenzi brought me to Ca' Foscari University in Venice for a Marie-Curie Global Fellowship. He has been a great supporter and a true gentleman. At Ca' Foscari, I thank Laura Burighel, Silvia Zabeo, and the Department of Philosophy and Cultural Heritage. This project has received funding from the European Union's Horizon 2020 research and innovation programme under the Marie Sklodowska-Curie grant agreement No. 888063 on *Sunni–Shii Relations in the Middle East (SSRIME)*. At Stanford University, I thank Lisa Blaydes and the Abbasi Program in Islamic Studies for hosting me as a Visiting Fellow in 2022, and Larry Diamond, Farah El-Sharif, Haidar Hadi, Matthew Lynch, and Hesham Sallam for their collegiality and support. At the University of Bristol, I thank Martyn Powell, Benedetta Lomi, David Leech, Jon Balserak, Rupert Gethin, Gavin D'Costa, and Rita Langer for welcoming me so warmly.

Over the years, several universities, institutes, and research networks invited me to speak, work through my ideas, and receive useful feedback: Aarhus University, Australian National University, the Middle East Study Group at Birkbeck University (London), Doha Institute for Graduate Studies, European University Institute in Florence, German Institute of Global and Area Studies in Hamburg, George Mason University, IREMAM Aix-en-Provence, Rice University in Houston, University of Bern, American University Beirut, Oxford Centre for Islamic Studies, UCLA, Maison des Sciences de l'Homme—École Pratique des Hautes Études in Paris, Project on Middle East Political Science (POMEPS) at George Washington University, and the SEPAD Project at Lancaster University. At the Central European University in Budapest, I profited from comments by Osman Dincer and Harith Hasan al-Qarawee, and at Aligarh Muslim University in India from comments by Professors Irfan Habib and Syed Ali Nadeem

Rezavi. I am grateful to Toby Dodge, Ali Ansari, Daniel Neep, and the participants of a workshop for a Festschrift in honour of Charles Tripp at the LSE.

Several colleagues have read parts of the manuscript related to their area of expertise, and some have provided extensive feedback. I thank Usaama al-Azami, Rahaf Aldoughli, Andrew Arsan, Mohammad Ataie, Metin Atmaca, Ayşe Baltacıoğlu-Brammer, Gabriele vom Bruck, Houchang Chehabi, Juan Cole, Stephanie Cronin, Louise Finn, Denis Hermann, Helen Lackner, Charles Melville, Eugene Rogan, Adrian Ruprecht, Christian Sahner, Cyrus Schayegh, Rainer Schwinges, and Charles Tripp. The Fellows of the *TOI: Bringing in the Other Islamists—comparing Arab Shia and Sunni Islamism(s) in a sectarianized Middle East* project led by Morten Valbjørn and Jeroen Gunning at Aarhus University provided feedback on several draft chapters. I thank Morten, Jeroen, as well as Courtney Freer, Fanar Haddad, Raphaël Lefèvre, Ben Robin D'Cruz, and Younes Saramifar for their valuable comments. I further want to acknowledge conversations with Rainer Brunner, Faisal Devji, Toby Dodge, Richard Drayton, Werner Ende, Mark Farha, Nelida Fuccaro, Simon Fuchs, Gregory Gause, Hamza al-Hasan, Samuel Helfont, Fouad Ibrahim, Raihan Ismail, Abbas Kadhim, Shruti Kapila, Laurence Louër, Ali Khan Mahmudabad, Ussama Makdisi, Renad Mansour, Mary-Ann Middelkoop, David Motadel, Anees al-Qudayhi, Reinhard Schulze, Guido Steinberg, Sami Zubaida, and Max Weiss. Nassima Neggaz and Naysan Adlparvar kindly shared their publications with me. For support over the years, I thank Ulrike Freitag, Kai Hafez, Laleh Khalili, Marc Lynch, James Piscatori, Madawi al-Rasheed, Morten Valbjørn, and Charles Tripp.

I am especially indebted to the many people that helped me during fieldwork, opened their homes to me, and guided me along the way. In Beirut, I thank Khaled Abdallah as well as Rabih Dandachli, Bassel Salloukh, and Sa'dun Hammada. In Lucknow, I thank Ali Khan Mahmudabad and his father Suleiman, the Raja of Mahmudabad. They hosted me during Muharram 2019, my last research trip before Covid-19, and were so generous with their time, knowledge, and hospitality. I am grateful to them and everyone in Mahmudabad, Lucknow, Hyderabad, and elsewhere who helped me navigate my way around India, especially Ovais Sultan Khan in Delhi and Syed Ali Nadeem Rezavi and Ruquaia Hussain at Aligarh University. In Iraq, I thank Hayder al-Khoei and S. Salih al-Hakim and the staff of the al-Kalima Centre for Dialogue and S. Jawad al-Khoei of the Al-Khoei Institute, as well as Alaa al-Bahadli, and in London Yousif al-Khoei and the Khoei

Foundation. Many more people helped me in Najaf and Karbala, especially the staff of the Abu Fadl al-Abbas shrine. In Albania, I thank Hajji Dede Edmond Brahimaj and Arben Sulejmani for introducing me to the history and culture of the Bektashis. And I am indebted to the many people who helped me during earlier language study and research trips, in the Gulf especially to Abd al-Nabi al-Akri, Jasim Hussayn, Habib Al Jumaa, Mahdi Salman, and Jafar al-Shayeb.

On a personal level, I thank Maria for more things than I can possibly list here. Her love gave me the strength to weather the pandemic and finish this book. That its publication coincides with the birth of our first daughter is an indescribable joy. This book is dedicated to them both. I thank Claudia Honegger for her encouragement, and for kindling my interest in the *longue durée*. And I thank Edna and José Anibal and everyone at the Sitio for being such gracious hosts during the final stages of writing, and Robi and Joana for welcoming me in the Bay Area.

So, this book would not have been possible without the support of a great number of people. Yet, they are in no way responsible for any mistakes or shortcomings others may find in this book, or for its approach and conclusions.

Contents

PART IV. REVOLUTION AND RIVALRY, 1979–

List of Plates

List of Maps

Note on Spelling and Transliterations

This book largely employs the transliteration guide of the *International Journal of Middle East Studies* (IJMES) without, however, providing full transliteration. Transliteration has not been employed for personal names, place names, and organisations following accepted English spelling. Since the book discusses different periods and regions in which Arabic, Persian, Turkish, Urdu, and other languages predominate, it was not always possible to adopt the locally most prominent spelling. For the sake of consistency and coherence, and to make the narrative easier for the reader, Arabic spelling has been adopted for terms and names that would otherwise have to be spelled several times in different ways (like Ali al-Rida, or Imam Rida, instead of Reza). The same goes for Ottoman names that have largely been rendered according to Arabic transliteration. Prominent figures are spelled according to their most prominent transliteration, or the system dominant in their country. So: Mohammad Reza Shah, Saddam Hussein, etc.

Given the *longue durée* approach of the book, another difficulty has been to remain true to geographical denominators as they were used in the different time periods, without, however, confusing the reader by employing several terms for the same geographical area. This has led to a somewhat anachronistic use of terms like Iran, Iraq, Syria, and the like, which should not indicate that these terms had the same meaning in earlier centuries as they would after the establishing of the relative nation states. They often did, however, carry a certain meaning and roughly delineated similar geographical areas, unlike other terms (the term Pakistan, for example, is therefore not mentioned before the twentieth century). The specialist reader who may see this as a problem is asked to forgive any shortcomings resulting from it to facilitate readability and accessibility for a general audience.

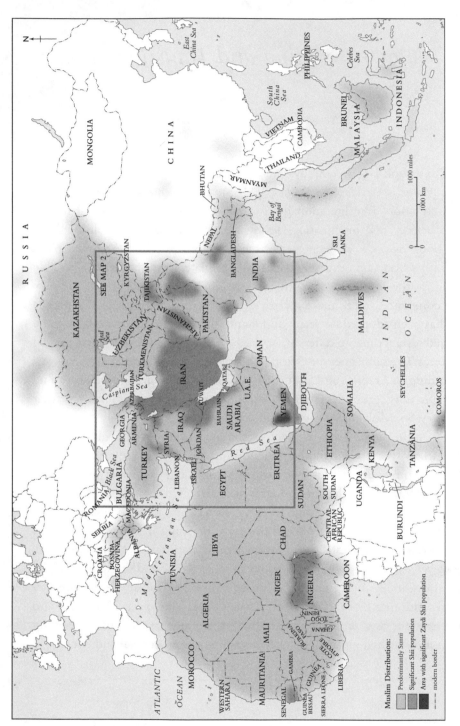

1. Map of wider Islamic world indicating Sunni and Shii populations

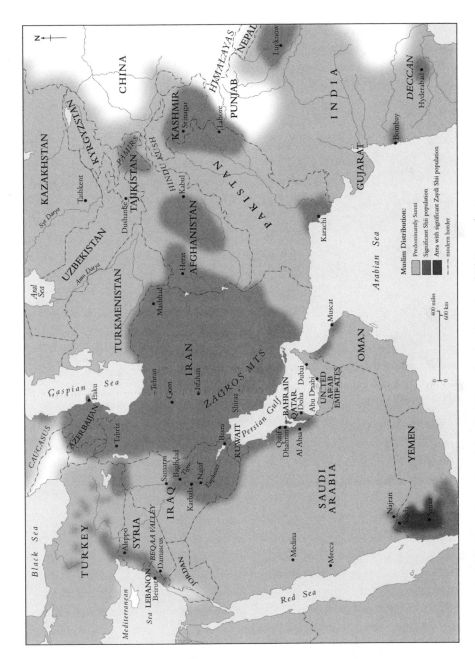

2. Map of Middle East, Central, and South Asia indicating Sunni and Shii populations

Prologue
From Karbala to Damascus

The midday sun struck the gilded dome built over the grave of Hussain, grandson of the Prophet Muhammad, blinding anyone who dared to look up at it. It was the spring of 2019. I was sitting inside the shrine, located in the holy city of Karbala in Iraq, attending the 'Spring Martyrdom' Conference, intended to promote and celebrate Hussain as a universal figure. I was among a few dozen guests and hundreds of visitors, all gathered at a site which, over centuries, has been both a place of fervent worship and heavy fighting. Here took place the massacre of Hussain and his followers in the Battle of Karbala in the year 61 of the Islamic calendar (680 AD) at the hands of an army sent by the Umayyad Caliphate based in Damascus. The shrine was often contested between competing powers espousing Sunnism and Shiism. It was ransacked by Wahhabi zealots in 1802, and bombarded by Saddam Hussein's tanks during the short-lived Shii uprising of 1991. (Plaques around the shrine commemorate the latter event, indicating the bullet holes still visible in the marble walls.) After the US-led invasion of 2003, it became a symbol of a new-found Shii self-consciousness, and when the so-called Islamic State (IS) declared a Caliphate in Northern Iraq and eastern Syria in 2014, it vowed to turn to rubble the 'idolators' and 'tomb worshippers' holy sites at Najaf and Karbala. In response, tens of thousands of Iraqi Shia, urged on by Iraq's senior Shii cleric, took up arms to defeat IS. (As I entered the shrine, some of these Shii paramilitaries were still celebrating their victory in front of it.) Karbala is thus to many the birthplace of the Sunni–Shia split, and epitomises how Sunni and Shia have been at odds ever since.

That morning in 2019, on the podium in front of Hussain's grave, Sunni and Shii dignitaries praised Hussain as a unifying figure. Given the polarisation and violence of recent years, this was remarkable. Hussain is of course

an especially important figure for Shia, who see him as an Imam, the rightful
political and spiritual successor to the Prophet Muhammad. Less known,
however, is that Sunnis and Sufis likewise hold Hussain in high regard and
feel he was wronged. Karbala and many other shrines associated with the
Family of the Prophet Muhammad constituted not only Shii sites of memory, but similarly places where adherents of various confessions and faiths
could come together without focusing on differences. The symposium
offered the hope of celebrating this inclusive heritage of Islam. And it served
as a corrective to standard narratives of perpetual Sunni–Shia strife.

The question of the nature of relations between Sunnism and Shiism preoccupied me long before that conference in Karbala, and indeed since I first
started engaging with the Middle East and the wider Islamic world in the
aftermath of 9/11 and the Iraq War of 2003. Before the Iranian Revolution
of 1979 and the 2003 invasion of Iraq, the terms 'Sunni' and 'Shii' were little
used outside of specialist literature.[1] Yet within a few months of the invasion,
Western media and politicians invoked them to explain the conflict in Iraq,
and much of the region's ills. The US Army was not being attacked by Iraqis
but rather by 'insurgents' in the 'Sunni triangle', or followers of a 'firebrand
Shii cleric'.[2] Many argued that the two sides had resented and fought each
other for nearly 1,400 years. The description of Iraq as sectarian served both
to deflate blame from the American-led administration, and in a circular
logic, to legitimise reshaping Iraqi politics along sectarian lines.[3]

Simplistic narratives of binary opposites, of Islam and the West, of Sunni
and Shii, made me wary. I decided to dig deeper and over years of research,
fieldwork and countless conversations with people across the Islamic world
realised that Sunnis and Shia indeed have had a long and complicated relationship but that standard narratives fall way short of explaining it. It took
centuries for Sunnism and Shiism to develop. Neither the coherence of the
two nor the dividing line between them were always clear, nor always
conflict-prone.

My first stint learning Arabic abroad was years ago in Cairo, where I
visited many of the sites that were the legacy of the tenth/eleventh century,
which has been termed the 'Shii Century', when the Shii Fatimids reigned
from Cairo (and Shii powers reigned in Iraq and the Gulf region). I came to
realise that Sunni–Shia relations played out across a much wider geographical area than often assumed. While the Arab world is often associated with
Sunnism and Iran with Shiism, Shiism played a much larger role in the

history of the Arab world (and of the Eastern Mediterranean, Central Asia, and the Indian subcontinent) than commonly assumed (as did Sunnism in Iran). The next speaker up on the podium, an Egyptian poet, a graduate of al-Azhar University—perhaps the most prominent seat of Sunni religious learning—who recited a verse lamenting the martyrdom of Hussain and extolling how much Egyptians honour Hussain, demonstrated this. Many Egyptians believe that in 1153, the Fatimids had transferred the head of Hussain to Cairo. There they interred it and would hold mourning processions for his martyrdom and celebrations for his birthday. They also founded al-Azhar University as a Shii institute of learning. The Sunni rulers that deposed the Fatimids in 1171 restructured it as a Sunni University, and in modern times it has facilitated Sunni–Shia dialogue. Although their Sunni successors vowed to suppress the Fatimids' legacy, it lived on in the built environment, and in popular culture. Egyptian Sufis still gather at the Hussain mosque in Cairo to celebrate Hussain's birthday, singing and dancing ecstatically.[4]

How intertwined the history of Shiism and Sunnism is was made even more explicit by the next speaker up on the podium, Baba Mundi, the leader of the Bektashi Sufi order with its headquarters in Albania. Although some Sufis are staunchly Sunni, most trace their spiritual lineage to the Prophet through Ali, his son in law, founding figure of the Shia, and father of Hussain. Some Sufis, like the Bektashis, are therefore considered pro-Shii (although they long allied with Sunni rulers).

Baba Mundi was in Karbala to sing the praises of Hussain, and to celebrate Karbala's firm place in the minds and hearts of Sufis, and those of Balkan Muslims more generally. A few months after the Karbala conference, I joined him and tens of thousands of Bektashis on a journey up Mount Tomor in Albania to visit a shrine set up for Abbas Ibn Ali, a half-brother of Hussain, who had died fighting alongside Hussain at Karbala and for whom another major shrine exists in Karbala. The days-long festival exemplified that Karbala could mean different things to different people at different times (fire played an important role, for example, and alcohol flowed freely).[5] Many more shrines and rituals further afield link themselves to Karbala and the Family of the Prophet in locally specific ways. Other examples include the Ali shrine in Mazar-i-Sharif in Afghanistan, 'discovered' several centuries after Ali's death and where many Central Asian Muslims, Sunnis and Shia, believe Ali is buried (though most Shia outside Afghanistan believe he is buried in Najaf, 80 kilometres from Karbala). Indian Shii dynasties built replicas of the Imams' shrines, and brought memorabilia associated with them to their cities to serve as a focus of popular piety. The re-enactment of the Imams' suffering, and pilgrimage to these sites, have made the cultural memory relevant in the present, and have linked Shia, and many Sunnis, to Karbala in myriad ways.[6] What I grasped from these and other interactions with Sufis was that Sufism was especially important as a counterpoint to simplistic accounts of Sunni–Shia relations because Sufis often disregarded doctrinal or legalistic dividing lines as defined by the clergy.[7] And I realised how important and emotionally compelling key sites of memory like Karbala and Damascus were.

After the battle of Karbala, the remains of the Family of the Prophet slain at Karbala and the wives and children that had been spared in the battle were brought before Yazid, the Umayyad ruler, in Damascus. So was the head of Hussain (it was, as noted, later moved to Cairo, while his body was interred in Karbala). The Umayyads, a family that was part of the old Meccan aristocracy and had initially fought against the Prophet Muhammad but then embraced the message of Islam, saw themselves as the rightful rulers of Syria and the wider Muslim community and the successors to the Prophet—in other words, as Caliphs. They stood in sharp opposition to Ali, whom Shia see as the first successor to the Prophet and their first spiritual and political leader, or Imam. It was from Damascus that they organised the campaigns against Ali in the mid-seventh century that became known as the First Muslim Civil War. Unsurprisingly, Shia detest the Umayyads, though many Sunnis also regret their quarrels with Ali and Hussain (although some Sunni Revivalists of the modern period lionise them).

As an Arabic language student in the 2000s, I spent many a hot afternoon in the quiet and cool courtyard of the Umayyad Mosque in Damascus, marvelling at the depictions of a lush paradise garden around the courtyard, and the past glory of the Umayyad Caliphate. Earlier European travellers and Orientalists, Westerners studying the 'Orient's' cultures, religions, and societies, and whose crucial roles in deepening Islam's divides I will discuss throughout, too, long admired it, and equated it with mainstream Islam. Nevertheless, the longer I spent in Damascus, the more I noticed that Shii pilgrims, from Iran, Lebanon, or the Gulf States, would also visit the Umayyad Mosque and nearby shrines associated with the Family of the Prophet, such as the Sayyida Zaynab shrine—located some six miles to the southeast of Damascus—where Shia believe that Zaynab, a granddaughter of the Prophet Muhammad and daughter of Ali, is buried. Zaynab, and other survivors of the Karbala massacre were brought to Damascus and held captive by Yazid in the Umayyad Mosque in Damascus, where Zaynab allegedly gave a speech condemning her brother's murder and held the first mourning ceremony (Sunnis generally believe she is buried in the Sayyida Zaynab mosque in Cairo). Like Hussain, Zaynab is central to Shiism, yet is a notable descendant of the Prophet, and a powerful female figure for Sunnis, too.[8] In Damascus was thus commemorated the greatness of the Umayyads alongside the founding story of Shii suffering—the tragedy of Karbala and the ways in which the Umayyads, who had taken over the mantle of the Prophet and proclaimed themselves Caliphs, treated the Imams and their kin and followers.

That Sunnism and Shiism, and indeed the pre-Islamic past (the site of the Umayyad Mosque was previously a basilica dedicated to John the Baptist), could be commemorated in the same space, and in others dotted around this ancient city, was testament to a shared heritage and lived reality of Islam and Middle Eastern religiosity more broadly. At other times, however, these sites of memory were appropriated by competing powers. They represented both what one scholar termed an 'architecture of coexistence', and the emotionally compelling and competing narratives of Sunnism and Shiism.[9]

Over the nearly two decades that I spent engaging with the people of the Middle East and the wider Islamic world (including while researching a PhD and earlier books on Sunni–Shia relations) I encountered many examples of coexistence, ambiguity, and polarisation. Shrines in the post-Ottoman world and on the Indian subcontinent, and Muharram processions in India, attended by Shia and Sunnis, are examples of the former.[10] Mourning the death of Hussain and his Companions in battle and atonement for not having saved Hussain could assert Shii difference[11] and Sunnis sometimes criticised Shia for it.[12] But these could likewise become inclusive festivals at which Sunnis invoked Hussain.

Sunni Revivalists I engaged with in North India and Saudi Arabia, on the other hand, strongly refuted Shiism (they called it a 'deviant sect', or not part of Islam at all) and warned me against going to Shii areas with wild rumours of Shii practices, and that it was not possible to trust Shia because they might perform dissimulation (*taqiyya*)—to which over the centuries Shia sometimes have been forced to resort to for self-preservation. This was a common trope in anti-Shii polemics even if it was much less frequently used than these polemics made Sunnis (and many Orientalists) believe.[13] Many Shia I met held similar prejudices towards 'Wahhabis', a term some applied widely to Sunnis. While they want Sunnis to accept them as a valid branch of Islam, most Shia believe that they constitute a chosen group of Muslims.[14] On both sides, prejudices and conspiracy theories exist.[15]

But these issues did not lead to conflict in and of themselves. As I and some of my colleagues have long argued, sectarian identity is most salient when political powers instrumentalise it.[16] This was evident in many of the countries that I visited during my research. In Bahrain, Sunnis and Shia have long lived side by side, joining in Muharram processions, and Leftist movements. Sunni–Shia tensions stem from the island's history as a province of Iran and then its conquest by a Sunni ruling family in the eighteenth century and the disenfranchisement of its Shii population; a pattern that entrenched itself under British protection. After the Iranian revolution, the Shia's pent-up resentment intersected with the appeal of the revolution, and Gulf rulers' fear of a region-wide Shii rising. Many Lebanese have long tried to transcend the limits of sectarian identity as institutionalised under the French Mandate, a system symbolised by the huge posters of political leaders and the flags of sect-based militias and parties on streets across the country, but to little avail. In Syria, the Baath party's nationalist rhetoric positioned itself against that colonial legacy, rendering sectarian identity officially a taboo. The regime's ubiquitous informants wanted to stamp out all talk of difference, while relying on the support of non-Sunnis, who dominated the highest echelons of the state, and the security services that policed the country. In Iran, the Shii clerics in charge officially embraced Islamic unity and its Sunni minority. But Shiism and a sense of ethnic superiority were so pervasive, and so coupled with the ambition to become a major power, that I understood why its Sunni and Arab neighbours feared its revolution, and why Sunni Iranians feel like second class citizens.

And in Iraq, a country in which centuries of Ottoman rule and then the British had enshrined Sunni supremacy, competing cultural memories, rooted in the many sites across the country associated with the early split, like Karbala, were reconstituted after the US-led intervention brought to power the first Shii-led government in a millennium. When a civil war engulfed Iraq shortly afterwards, the Americans and their allies as noted quickly blamed 'ancient hatreds', rather than their own lack of post-invasion planning, while simultaneously institutionalising ethno-sectarian divisions in ways reminiscent of French and British imperial policies. The conference in Karbala was an example of Shii empowerment, unthinkable pre-2003, and while it reached out to Sunnis, it did so from a position of strength.

Despite the overwhelming evidence, both historically and contemporary, that it is the interaction of doctrinal tensions with political ones that lead to conflict, many still see Sunnism and Shiism as perpetually at loggerheads and invoke 'Sunni' and 'Shii' as catch-all terms to explain division and bloodshed in Muslim societies. The notion that 'ancient hatreds' divided Sunni and Shii and that the two were polar opposites throughout Islamic history, persists, not least in public debate and amongst decision-makers (and amongst scholars working on especially polarised periods or places, and who are unaware of contrasting examples). Some argue that doctrinal debates a millennium ago explain violence today. Others solely focus on the impact of the modern state and the interventions of regional and global powers, or see sectarian conflict as purely a product of material struggles, often refusing to take history seriously and make connections with previous periods, or to engage with doctrinal debates.[17] It is against these simplistic notions that reduce Sunni–Shia relations to conflict and doctrinal tensions, or that argue that history and doctrinal debates don't matter, that I chose to write *The Caliph and the Imam*. It is not a history of everything that happened between Sunnis and Shia since the Prophet Muhammad's death in 632, and in some chapters the narrative emphasises certain regions more than others. (The early period, though covered in some detail, is given less weight than developments after 1500.) Nonetheless, it is the first history of Sunni–Shia relations from the seventh until the early twenty-first century based on extensive fieldwork and a thorough synthesis of existing scholarship from different disciplines in major research languages.[18]

Its approach is twofold. It firstly shows that it is vital to understand how Sunnism and Shiism developed chronologically and doctrinally, and how earlier periods shaped later ones. History matters, and only by understanding the early and middle periods can we understand how later ones constituted themselves with reference to them. And secondly, it highlights that only a global perspective that studies connections across the Nile to Oxus region, the land mass from North Africa and the Eastern Mediterranean to the Indian subcontinent, from the Arabic- and Turkic-speaking worlds to the Eastern parts of the Persianate one, and linking that to European and American Empire, can do justice to the subject.[19] For it is across this temporal and geographical reach that Sunnism and Shiism constituted each other, something that studies focusing solely on one period or region, like the Middle East, miss.[20] It takes intra-Islamic debates and contestations seriously all the while placing them in their social, political, and historical contexts. This is not meant to exoticise and essentialise Islam. Rather, the book traces how developments in the Islamic world interacted with wider ones such as: the Crusades and the Mongol conquests, early modern state formation, the discovery of the sea route to Asia, the beginnings of Empire and capitalism, the print revolution, the emergence of the modern state and colonialism, independence, and eventually, the attempt to remould societies through foreign intervention in an age of American hegemony.

Because the first few centuries of Islam are foundational, and were invoked in later periods, and because many Muslims draw inspiration and guidance from it, Part I starts with the *Formation of Sunnism and Shiism*. The different ways in which Sunnis and Shia saw and remembered the early period shaped distinct confessional cultures, even if in lived reality, much was shared.[21] Political support and patronage was key in the development and spread of Islam's main branches. But early Muslim rulers seldom embarked on a wholescale eradication or conversion of others (and even if they would have wanted to, their grip over society and territory was too weak).

From about 1500 onwards, however, the centrality of religious identity for legitimisation and state formation led to mass conversions and a stronger interest in people's beliefs, as I will show in Part II, *The Shaping of Muslim Empires*. Although Shiism originated amongst Arabs, and was over centuries not primarily associated with Iran, from the early modern period onwards, Sunni–Shia relations became intertwined with Iran's position in the Islamic world. And connections between the Middle East, Central Asia, and the Indian subcontinent, increasingly a major arena of Muslim intellectual life, intensified.

As I will show in Part III, the arrival of European Empires and the modern state proved transformative and led to more Western interest in Islam. Orientalists focused on textual doctrinal debates and conflicts in the first centuries of Islam. By translating polemics and law texts, they entrenched divisions that hitherto played little role in people's lives, especially on the Indian subcontinent, where Britain ruled over large Sunni and Shii populations. (They argued, for example, that Sunnis were not supposed to attend Muharram and the colonial state eventually organised separate Muharram processions for Sunnis and Shia.) Sunni and Shii became legal categories that were reinforced in interactions with the state. Since they largely engaged with Sunnism, Orientalists based their view of Shiism on what Sunnis said.[22] The Sunni version of history, of Caliphs and Sultans, of the schools of jurisprudence and of great scholars, was written down in official histories and recited in the Great Mosques. Despite much diversity within Sunnism, its historical narrative became the establishment's view. Shii views and books, with their opposed assessment of the early period, were marginalised and kept out of Sunni collections or destroyed. Sunni books referred rarely to Shiism, and if they did it was in a negative way.

The few Shii informants and communal leaders that cooperated with Empire did not manage to break that master frame, although they played a role in institutionalising Shiism alongside Sunnism. The first Orientalist conference on Shiism was only held in 1968.[23] Orientalists often saw Sunnism as equivalent to the Church and Shiism as a 'sect'.[24] But these comparisons raised more questions than they provided answers, and uncritically employing terms and concepts from the study of Christianity (and Judaism), made little sense. Equating Islam with Sunnism missed the complexity of Islam and marginalised Shiism (and left Sunnism undefined).[25] The terms ta'ifa (sect), or ta'ifiyya/sectarianism, often used in this context, are derogatory and misleading.[26] In contrast, I refer to Sunnism and Shiism as the two main branches of Islam, each made up of several madhahib, schools of jurisprudence. For Sunnism and Shiism constitute competing claims over the correct interpretation of Islam and both see themselves as at the centre of Islam, not at its margins.[27]

Religious identity thus became associated with specific countries and with the institutions of the modern state. After the 1979 revolution in Iran, it became also tied to international relations, as I show in Part IV, *Revolution and Rivalry*. The Shii symbolism of the revolution was obvious (it gained pace during Muharram and a Shii cleric became its figurehead).[28] And yet its ambition was pan-Islamic and Sunni Islamists were initially thrilled by it. Generally, however, Iran's revolution and the reaction to it exacerbated the Sunni–Shia divide in hitherto unimaginable ways and connected it directly to regional and global politics, especially to the American quest to isolate revolutionary Iran and remake the Middle East.

Invoking the Sunni–Shia divide uncritically has done great harm. By misunderstanding the history of Sunni–Shia relations and the legacy of rulers using religion for political ends, many have contributed to the very tensions that have been tearing apart the Middle East and Muslims in general. It is against that misunderstanding that I wrote *The Caliph and the Imam*.

So, what really is the relationship between Sunnism and Shiism, and how did the two come into being? That is where we must start.

PART I

The Formation of Sunnism and Shiism, 632–1500

The split between what became Sunnism and Shiism, and the groups that straddled their boundaries, started with a dispute over who should lead the community of Muslims after the death of the Prophet Muhammad, and whether that person had to be one of his descendants or not. Sunnis accept Abu Bakr, Umar, Uthman, and Ali as the four 'rightly-guided' Caliphs (the so-called Rashidun Caliphs), the successors of the Prophet Muhammad, and Shia believe that Ali was the successor chosen by the Prophet, and that his and Fatima's descendants are the legitimate leaders, or Imams, of the Muslim community. Sunnis derive their name from Sunna, Arabic for tradition, which in an Islamic context refers to the summary of all the deeds and sayings of the Prophet Muhammad, which should provide a model for Muslims to follow. The *People of the Tradition and the Community, Ahl al-Sunna wa-l-Jamaa*, thus denotes Sunnis, while Shia derive their name from the Arabic *Shiat Ali*, the *Party of Ali*. Sunnis embraced the Caliphate and Shia the Imamate as the ideal type of political leadership.

It took centuries before the terms 'Sunni' and 'Shii' came to delineate cohesive religious communities. During the beginnings of Islam these categories did not exist, nor were the terms widely used. They only developed gradually over time, as many other branches and movements were repressed or died out, and two major consensuses coalesced around 'Sunnism' and 'Shiism'. Even later, people subsumed under these categories did not necessarily have more in common than some core historical narrative and agreement on popular practice (and a dislike of the relative other branch of Islam). The early period is crucial because the conduct and sayings of the Prophet, and for the Sunnis his Companions and for the Shia the Imams, are meant to guide Muslims. A disagreement about what that guidance precisely was, how it should be interpreted, and who is a trustworthy narrator of those early events, led to the development of different schools of jurisprudence. Sunnis developed four legal schools that can on specific questions be further apart than they are from the Shia, while the three main Shii legal schools likewise have major disagreements, not least on which Imam to follow. But on a most basic level, Shia wanted Ali and his descendants to succeed the Prophet Muhammad as Imams, while Sunnis thought authority should lie with the Caliphs.

Based in Damascus, the Umayyads were the first of the Sunni Caliphate dynasties and ruled from 661 to 750. The Umayyads were strong rivals of Ali and his offspring, who Shia consider the legitimate rulers of the Muslim community. The Umayyads were defeated by the Abbasids in the mid-eighth century, who established a new Caliphate based in Baghdad in 750. The political power of the Abbasids varied over time and in the later period waned. The Abbasids' relationship with the Alids and early Shiism was complicated and ranged from suppression to accommodation. In the tenth century, the 'Shii Century', they even ruled nominally on behalf of a Shii political dynasty. Simultaneously, the Fatimids established the only Shii Caliphate ever to exist in Cairo. That over the first few centuries of Islam not only Sunni but also Shii dynasties ruled, allowed for the patronising of scholars of both branches of Islam, and the further codification of Sunni and Shii schools of law, and positioned Shiism as Sunnism's main challenger.

Sunni–Shia relations were profoundly affected by the Crusades. As part of the Muslim counter-mobilisation, Shii rulers were supplanted by Sunni ones. Still, state power was often weak, and Muslim rulers accepted populations of different belief if they paid taxes and accepted the ruler's authority. Missionaries travelled far to convert people, but entire populations were generally not converted by force in short time frames. Confessional ambiguity was widespread, even though scholars tried to more clearly delineate the boundaries between the schools, and bring in rulers on their side. This intensified when the Mongols conquered large parts of Eurasia in the thirteenth century, and put the last Abbasid Caliph to death. In the Middle East, their advance was only checked by the Mamluks of Egypt, who styled themselves as protectors of Sunnism and successors of the Abbasids.

In the context of new ruling dynasties converting to Islam and legitimising their rule Islamically, Sunni and Shii clerics wrote books of political theory that were also a refutation of the relative other branch, shaping Sunnism and Shiism and their stance towards each other.

This early and middle period of Islam needs to be well-understood not just because it is when the split happened and when Sunnism and Shiism became codified, but because in later periods, from the early modern Empires to Muslim revivalist movements, many sought to legitimise themselves by referring to it. They are thus especially relevant not just because this is where the original split happened, and where Sunnism and Shiism gradually formed themselves in conversation and competition with each other, but because later conflicts crystallised around competing visions of the past.

I

After the Prophet

According to Muslim tradition, Muhammad was born in Mecca around 570 into the Banu Hashim, a subsection of the tribe of Quraysh. Since he was an orphan, he grew up in the household of his paternal uncle, Abu Talib, a chief of the Banu Hashim. In his mid-twenties, he married an older, wealthy woman, Khadija, with whom he had several children, of whom the daughters Zaynab, Umm Kulthum, Ruqqaya, and Fatima survived, leaving him without a male heir. Around the age of forty, Muhammad received his first revelations, which kept occurring until his death.[1] He then pronounced himself openly as the Prophet of God and started to convince people around him to join his cause.

Khadija was the first to believe in the Prophet's vision, but there is some disagreement as to who the first male Muslim was, a debate that is of relevance to our story. In the first biography of the Prophet's life by Ibn Ishaq (died around 767) and edited by Ibn Hisham (died around 833), Ali, the son of his uncle and former protector Abu Talib, is the first male Muslim, after whom came a liberated slave of the Prophet, Zayd bin Haritha, and then Abu Bakr. Given that Ali and Abu Bakr became rivals over Muhammad's succession and foundational figures for Sunnism and Shiism, this is crucial. According to the same biography, Ali was only ten years old when he became a Muslim. When Abu Talib had fallen into debt, Muhammad in turn agreed to take Ali into his own family and raise him. Ali married his daughter, Fatima, hence becoming his son-in-law as well as being his cousin.[2]

The bonds between Ali and the Prophet were thus strong. While the earliest sources cite Ali as the first male Muslim, other sources claim that Abu Bakr had become a Muslim before Ali. The historian al-Tabari (839–923), who offers competing narratives in his monumental *History of Prophets and Kings*, simply states that 'there is a difference of opinion among the early scholars'.[3]

More partisan Sunni authors tried to resolve this dilemma by saying that although Ali was indeed the first male convert, he was also young and the first child to accept Islam, with Zayd bin Haritha the first freedman and Abu Bakr the first free adult male to accept Islam. According to this logic, it counted more if one accepted Islam as an adult male than as a child (or a former slave or a woman).[4]

It's critical to make one thing clear: the sources for the early period of Islam, both for the period of Muhammad's life and the immediate aftermath, when the decisive splits happened, are contested. They were mainly compiled from the eighth and ninth centuries onwards, so in hindsight and often from confessional or dynastic viewpoints. There is a tendency in Western academic scholarship to be critical of the classical accounts of early Islamic history and of the Muslim sources for it.[5]

Muslim scholars working within the Islamic tradition do not necessarily share that scepticism of the sources, at least not those from within their school (though Sunnis and Shia disagree about which sources are trustworthy on the early period). Nonetheless, everyone acknowledges that the early history is key, not just because it is where the original split happened, but because Muslims are supposed to structure their life according to the precedents set by the Prophet and his Companions (for Sunnis), and the Prophet and the Imams (for Shia). The following account is based on those sources, even if they reflect the divisions over legitimate authority in the Islamic community. They say little about social and cultural history, the subaltern classes and illiterate masses, and women (with the notable exception of women of the Prophet's household), and since they were often written by religious scholars, probably emphasise doctrinal difference more than ordinary Muslims would have done.[6] But anyone who wants to write about the earliest period of Islam needs to use them and recent scholarship has attempted to be source-critical while still trying to utilise them.[7]

The debate about the first male Muslim after the Prophet is such a case where the sources would have been written down in the eighth century, when the rival factions, some of whom would later be called 'Sunni' and 'Shii', were coming into being and codifying their version of the early history of Islam. As these groups disagreed over whether Abu Bakr or Ali should succeed the Prophet, the question of who the first male Muslim was became crucial.[8]

Apart from precedence in Islam, the excellence of the contenders was a factor. Sunni writers lauded Abu Bakr for his knowledge, wisdom, and unique qualifications that in the eyes of his supporters made him a sound choice for the succession. They claimed that Abu Bakr's actions were exceptionally worthy because of his advanced age, and that his knowledge was therefore greater, and he was thus a better choice as Caliph.[9] Proponents of Ali, on the other hand, would emphasise his spiritual knowledge and his youthfulness.[10]

In general, even though a small group of people adopted Islam and became committed Muslims, the people of Mecca and the elders of the Prophet's own tribe of Quraysh were initially not receptive to the call to Islam. Muhammad was protected by his uncle, Abu Talib, and by his marriage to Khadija, but when both died in 619 his situation became precarious.[11] Muhammad and his earliest supporters then left to a town that would later be called Medina, in what came to be known as the *hijra*, the emigration and marks the start of the Muslim (*hijrî*) calendar. In Medina, Muhammad was more successful in establishing himself as a political and spiritual leader. After fierce battles with the Meccans, the Muslims took Mecca in 630, and much of Mecca and the Quraysh accepted Islam. The Prophet's days in Mecca were numbered, though, and as Islamic historiography tells us he would die in Medina in 632.

After the Prophet Muhammad's death, a dispute over his succession erupted. Most Muslims argued that the Prophet's successor should be elected by the community's elite based on merit. They would later become the Sunnis. Others—who would become known as the Shia—believed that Muhammad had designated his cousin and son-in-law Ali as his successor, and that henceforth Ali's offspring should lead. This, in essence, is the origin of the Sunni–Shia split.

Muhammad's sons all predeceased him, and upon his death his closest male relative was Ali. A group of Muslims favoured Ali, and while Ali is recognised by all Muslims as having been an important Companion of the Prophet, he was not immediately chosen as his successor. Instead, other Companions of the Prophet became his successors (in Arabic *khalifa*, from which the anglicised term 'Caliph' is derived): Abu Bakr, Umar, and Uthman. They ruled the Muslim community during the first period of conquests, when Islam spread from the Arabian Peninsula to North Africa, the Levant, Iraq and Iran, and beyond.

For the Shii view that Ali should have naturally succeeded the Prophet, speaks the general importance of dynastic succession in the cultural context of the time.[12] The supporters of Abu Bakr and his successors thought that the Caliph should come from the Quraysh, the tribe of the Prophet, but not necessarily from the branch that the Prophet hailed from, the Banu Hashim, and that henceforth the Quraysh, especially those from Mecca, despite having previously fought the Prophet, would hold a special and powerful position amongst Muslims.[13]

As outlined above, Abu Bakr had been one of the first to adopt Islam, was one of the most prominent Muslims in the early Meccan period, and accompanied the Prophet from Mecca to Medina. The Prophet had also married Abu Bakr's daughter Aisha, binding the two families together. Most Sunnis believe that Abu Bakr was elected at a meeting at Saqifa, while others thought that he was designated by the Prophet himself.[14]

As Caliph, Abu Bakr (11–13/632–634) fought the so-called *ridda* wars (or Wars of Apostasy) against dissident tribes that refused to pay tribute and allegiance to the Muslims after Muhammad's death (and by winning them, Abu Bakr established his and the Quraysh's authority). Under his reign, Islam spread. But because he was from the old aristocracy, his election alienated others.[15] The later Shia saw in him a usurper who took power with the help of several Companions, including his successor, Umar bin al-Khattab.[16]

According to Sunni tradition, the Prophet's property was not supposed to be inherited but spent as charity (there is a saying of the Prophet narrated by Aisha to that effect). The Shia, on the other hand, maintain that the Prophet not only designated Ali as his successor but also left his personal property to him and Fatima, and their offspring. The Shia hold it against Abu Bakr that he refused Fatima the oasis of Fadak as inheritance after the death of her father, which they say had belonged to the Prophet and been promised to her.[17] Abu Bakr sought to follow the precedents set by the Prophet, but when it came to the Prophet's family, that aim met with a problem. During the Prophet's lifetime they held a special place in the community, and there were Quranic verses referring to that special position. In Abu Bakr's time, however, the political expediency of a Caliphate led by the Prophet's Companions, and the need to maintain the privileged status of the Prophet's family, started to clash.[18] To avoid confusion, and possibly to prevent Ali or another challenger from taking over the Caliphate, Abu Bakr chose Umar as his own successor before his death.[19]

Umar had also been close to the Prophet, who had married Umar's daughter, Hafsa. Under Umar's Caliphate (13–23/634–644), the Muslims conquered Iraq, the first Iranian provinces, and Egypt, solidifying the new polity and sustaining the Arab tribes that had become the military backbone of the Islamic state. These were dangerous times and Umar was assassinated in 644 in the mosque of Medina.[20] He had made some concessions to the Banu Hashim, and gave Ali several of Muhammad's estates to administer, while withholding the Fadak oasis mentioned above. He also regularly consulted with Ali.[21]

Unlike Abu Bakr, Umar did not appoint his successor, and after Umar's death, a consultative assembly (*shura*) of six convened to choose the next Caliph (though Umar had apparently chosen the members of the *shura*). They were Abd al-Rahman bin Awf, Sa'd bin Abi Waqqas, Uthman, Ali, and Zubayr (with the sixth, Talha, returning to Medina only after the election had been completed). Ali was a member of the council and a candidate, but lacked support, and the leaders of the Quraysh backed Uthman. The council chose Uthman, who would rule for twelve years until his assassination in 656.[22] Despite being side-lined, Ali pledged allegiance to Uthman. Shii authors intensely contest the succession from Umar to Uthman, while Sunnis defend it.[23]

As a wealthy member of the Meccan aristocracy, Uthman was an important early Muslim, and as a sign of his trust the Prophet had first married his daughter Ruqayya to him, and after she had died also another of his daughters, Umm Kulthum.[24] During the reigns of Umar and Uthman, tensions within the Islamic community rose to the surface, between the Arab tribes that had driven the expansion of Islam, the descendants of the first Muslims that had supported Muhammad in Mecca and Medina, and the old aristocracy of Mecca that came under the leadership of the Banu Umayya branch of the Quraysh. The Umayyads had initially fought against the Prophet Muhammad and the early Muslims. They then embraced Islam, and took over the leadership of the community, symbolised by figures such as Abu Sufyan and his sons Yazid and Muawiya, who spearheaded the military conquest of Syria and would rule there henceforth.

Under the Umayyad Uthman, they managed to expand their power at the expense of the early supporters of Muhammad. A few years into his reign, members of his family controlled all major governorships. Opposition to him and this practice emerged in places such as Egypt and Iraq. In Kufa, on the banks of the Euphrates and 100 miles south of Baghdad, where an encampment for the conquering Arab troops had been set up, the opposition to Uthman's policy of distributing property to his appointees, and to the policy of his governor, developed into support for his rival, Ali, and turned Kufa into a bastion of proto-Shii pro-Alid sentiment.[25] Endeavours to reach a peaceful agreement failed. While Ali had previously pledged allegiance to Uthman, opposition to the Caliph now rallied around Ali.

Because of their kinship ties, Ali tried to mediate between Uthman and the opposition. But he was unsuccessful because Uthman relied on the advice of his Umayyad kin.[26] The opposition, backed by tribal forces and early Companions, as well as Aisha and Ali, laid siege to his palace in Medina, and after Uthman refused to accede to their demands, killed him in June 656.[27] With Uthman's violent death, tensions between the different forces broke out into the open.[28]

Now, the circles that had opposed Uthman and the Quraysh/Umayyads pushed through the election of Ali and, in 656, to the joy of his supporters, Ali became Caliph. He was not elected by a *shura* of the earliest Companions or backed by the Quraysh, the formal procedure for succession as laid down by Abu Bakr. Instead, Ali declared that he was the legitimate successor to the Prophet and gained public recognition for this. While the exact wording of his first sermon as Caliph is difficult to determine, Shii historiography claims he rebuked the Muslims for having previously turned away from him and the Family of the Prophet, the *Ahl al-Bayt*, and argued that true religious guidance could only be found through them. This alienated his enemies, but further bound his followers to him. The irregularity of his election paved the way for more infighting.[29]

Ali probably had no hand in the murder of Uthman, yet some of those who may have been responsible became Ali's supporters, and he had to rely on them to secure his rule.[30] The supporters of Uthman claimed that he was the legitimate ruler, and that a new Caliph should be elected in a free election. While most Muslims, including what would later be called Sunnis, eventually accepted the Caliphate of Ali as one of the four Rashidun Caliphates, staunch Uthman supporters refused to recognise Ali.[31] In a clear break with the reign of Uthman, Ali replaced most governors, thereby undermining the Umayyads, who had held key governorships.[32]

Ali moved the capital of the Caliphate to Kufa (in present-day Iraq) from the Arabian Peninsula, to which it was never to return. The centre of gravity of Islamic history thus shifted, Kufa remained a centre of pro-Alid sentiment.[33] But Ali faced numerous rebellions and the years following Uthman's murder saw the first civil war (*fitna*) in Islam.[34] A key challenge to his reign was a rebellion by members of the Quraysh, especially Talha and Zubayr, who claimed the Caliphate, and who were supported by Aisha, the Prophet's wife and daughter of Abu Bakr. Mecca, where prominent Qurayshis went

from Medina, now became their base. Talha, Zubayr, and Aisha had been key
in the opposition to Uthman, but now that they moved against Ali claimed
to avenge Uthman's death.[35] Although these Quraysh had first reluctantly
pledged allegiance to Ali, they then broke their oath and rebelled against
him. In 656, they fought a losing battle against Ali's forces, in which many
challengers, including Talha and Zubayr, were killed. Aisha had been present
at the battle, sitting on a camel and pushing the soldiers on (hence it became
known as the 'Battle of the Camel'). After her defeat, she was escorted to
Medina.[36] It was the first time a Muslim army faced a Muslim army. It was
not going to be the last. Ali ordered that the opponents captured in the battle should not be killed or enslaved, as non-Muslim opponents would
have been.[37]

Opposition did not subside, however. Ali had won that round of fighting,
but the governor of Syria, Muawiya bin Abi Sufyan, a relative of the assassinated Uthman, emerged as Ali's most formidable challenger. Muawiya
demanded that Ali hand over the murderers of Uthman, claiming blood
vengeance, and perhaps even saw Ali as complicit in the murder.[38] After an
arbitration attempt had failed, the armies of Muawiya and Ali clashed at the
Battle of Siffin south of Raqqa on the river Euphrates in the summer of 657.
Sensing the victory of Ali's Iraqi troops in what was a bloody and prolonged
engagement (some chronicles speak of tens of thousands of troops on both
sides), one legend goes, some of Muawiya's troops attached religious texts,
perhaps copies of the Quran, to their lances, raising them into the air.[39] This
had a strong impact on many of Ali's troops, who forced him to stop the
fighting and seek arbitration with the enemy. Arbitration was supposed to
be carried out by a delegate from each side at a future date to settle the
dispute peacefully, and the two armies separated and went home. Ali agreed
to mediate. But some of Ali's soldiers soon concluded that they had sinned
in pushing Ali to agree to arbitration, and now argued that appointing men
as arbitrators was sinful because authority should only rest with God or his
designated representative—in this case, Ali—and they petitioned Ali to
resume the fight against Muawiya. When Ali refused, they seceded from him
and subsequently became known as those who went out (*kharaja min*) from
the community, as Kharijis, creating, in effect, the third major branch of
Islam besides Sunnism and Shiism.[40]

The arbitration process did not lead to an agreement and tensions with
Muawiya resumed. Ali's participation in the arbitration, moreover, damaged
his reputation.[41] With the rise of the Kharijis, he was now facing opposition

from two sides. And while he fought a war against the Kharijis and killed many of them, it was ultimately a Khariji who would kill him in 661. After their forceful appearance and crucial role in the first civil war, the Kharijis would play a more limited role. One group of those who rejected Ali's agreement to negotiate with Muawiya later became known as Ibadis, named after the founder of their school of jurisprudence, Abdullah Ibn Ibad. Part of the general movement that rejected Ali's arbitration, Ibadis in later periods and to this day object to being labelled as 'Kharijis', largely because of the negative connotation the term has. They managed to attain political control in parts of North Africa and Oman, where the Ibadis developed a separate legal school and established an independent political tradition based on a rotating leadership amongst leading families, but would be marginalised elsewhere.[42] Overall, the historiography of the first *fitna* became highly contentious as later Islamic collective identity defined itself in relation to it (with the alleged heresy of the Kharijis being one of the few things on which Sunna and Shia could agree).[43]

After Ali's death—by a poisoned sword and while praying in the Great Mosque at Kufa—the legend goes that his body was buried in secret by his family and closest associates in Najaf, for fear that his Umayyad or Khariji enemies could exhume and desecrate it. The tomb in Najaf was only 'rediscovered' two centuries later, and then soon became a popular pilgrimage location, especially for Shia.

Given Ali's role in the civil war, and as a critic of the three preceding Caliphs and the founding figure of the Shia, it took Sunnis a while to accord Ali similar status to his caliphal predecessors. In fact, in the first centuries of Islam, there were anti-Ali sentiments across what would become Sunnism, although these anti-Ali positions gradually faded out of mainstream Sunnism, once the notion of the four Rashidun Caliphs was firmly established. Shia called those that actively opposed Ali and the subsequent Shii Imams *Nasibis* (pl. *Nawasib*).[44]

As the shrine of Ali grew in importance, attracting more visitors and scholars, and eventually turning Najaf into a major centre of Shiism, Sunni authors also cast doubt on the location of Ali's shrine to undermine Shiism more generally. Some even claimed that the tomb contains the remains of a viciously anti-Shii figure and that Shia are visiting a figure they despise.[45] Several other places, including a shrine in Afghanistan (Mazar-i-Sharif/ Balkh), were put forward as burial sites of Ali.[46] Another Sunni theory holds that he was interred in the governor's palace in Kufa, or that he was transported to Medina and buried near his wife Fatima's grave.[47] Some took a middle ground. In a book on Ali's life and death, for example, the Sunni scholar Ibn Abi al-Dunya (d. 894) included many Shii sources, perhaps in part because without them a book on Ali would not have been complete.[48] And Shii authors defended the authenticity of the Ali shrine in Najaf.[49]

The so-called party of Ali, the Shia, would mourn the death of Ali and consider his and Fatima's sons and descendants, the *Ahl al-Bayt*, the legitimate leaders of the Muslim community. Shia think that divine knowledge was handed down via Muhammad to Ali and then to his offspring, the Alids, an anglicised version of the Arabic term *Alawi*, especially to those men they revere as Imams.[50] Shia would disagree amongst themselves about the precise number and lineage of those Imams. But they agree that most of them were persecuted and even killed on the orders of Sunni Caliphs, and they also think that the Prophet and the Imams are infallible.[51]

Sunnis would by and large pledge allegiance to the Umayyad Caliphs based in Damascus, who claimed to be the official successors to the Rashidun Caliphs. Some Sunni authors argued that the order of succession meant that Abu Bakr was the worthiest, and Ali the least (of the four Rashidun Caliphs), as Ali had been criticised especially in Umayyad historiography. But eventually, the belief in the justness of the Rashidun Caliphs, including Ali, became central to Sunnism.[52] If it is with Ali that the original split takes shape, he is also a unifying figure. For Ali pledged, however reluctantly, allegiance to the first three Caliphs accepted by Sunnis, and refrained from criticising Abu Bakr and Umar (while criticising Uthman primarily during the latter part of his reign, when Sunnis are also critical of him).[53] That symbolism of Ali can be seen in the appropriation by of Ali's sword, the *Dhu l-Faqar*. The origin of the sword is disputed. According to the biographical literature, it belonged to a Meccan who was killed in a fight against the Muslims at the Battle of Badr in 624. Thereafter, it is believed to have been one of the swords of the Prophet, who gave it to Ali during the Battle of Uhud of the same year.[54] Shia see this as yet another sign that the Prophet had designated Ali as his heir, and Sunnis also believe that the sword then belonged to Ali. Upon his death, it was handed over to his sons Hasan and Hussain, but after Hussain's death at Karbala in 680 there are conflicting stories. Subsequent Sunni and Shii rulers sought to gain possession of the sword, which they hoped would imbue them with legitimacy.[55]

The question remains as to when exactly the split started to be about ideas rather than political rivalries. Some argue that Ali saw himself as rightful successor to Muhammad and started to lay the foundation for Shiism. Shia moreover argue that his special charisma made him particularly worthy, in other words that the split was both political and ideational from the start.[56] This is difficult to accept for Sunnis, who recognise Ali as Caliph but see Shiism as a misinterpretation of his and his descendants' role. Sunnis argue that, by including Ali amongst the Rashidun Caliphs, they honour him and protect him against unfair accusations from his adversaries and false adorations from his admirers.[57] Early and medieval Sunni authors went to great lengths to prove that Shiism had misappropriated Ali.[58]

Black legends sought to present Shiism in a bad light. One such theory claims that Abdallah Ibn Saba, a Jew who converted to Islam in the seventh century and became an early Alid supporter, introduced Jewish messianic ideas into Shiism. Ibn Saba became a figure against whom many sought to delineate what they saw as the righteous interpretations and histories of Islam and was supposedly executed for his beliefs. His story is a recurrent theme in anti-Shii polemics, which, through Ibn Saba, try to link Shiism to Judaism, and in works by Shii authors, who see in him someone who went too far in his admiration for Ali.[59] Still, whether the Caliphs were supposed to be both political and religious leaders is debated, even though the political and the religious element were not easily separated in Islam's early period. The Sunni tradition, and with it many Orientalists, eventually depicted the Caliphs as primarily political authorities.[60]

With Ali assassinated in 661, his arch-rival Muawiya was able to expand his power, ruled as Caliph from 661 to 680, and institutionalised the Umayyad dynasty in Damascus.[61] One of Ali's sons, Hasan, became the second Imam of the Shia. Seen as a rival for power, Muawiya rallied his troops against Hasan and his supporters. In the face of overwhelming might, Hasan capitulated in front of Muawiya. This was feted by supporters of the Umayyad cause, who thought this undid the Sunni–Shia split as it was just beginning.[62] Hasan then retired to Medina, and gave up the open challenge against Umayyad authority, although his supporters continued to visit him and the Shia believe that he was the first of the descendants of Ali as Imams that was pushed aside. For Sunnis, Hasan, who had also backed Uthman when his palace was under siege, exemplifies a middle-ground position.[63]

As noted, Hasan's younger brother and successor as the third Shii Imam, Hussain, chose a different approach. After the death of Muawiya in 680/60,

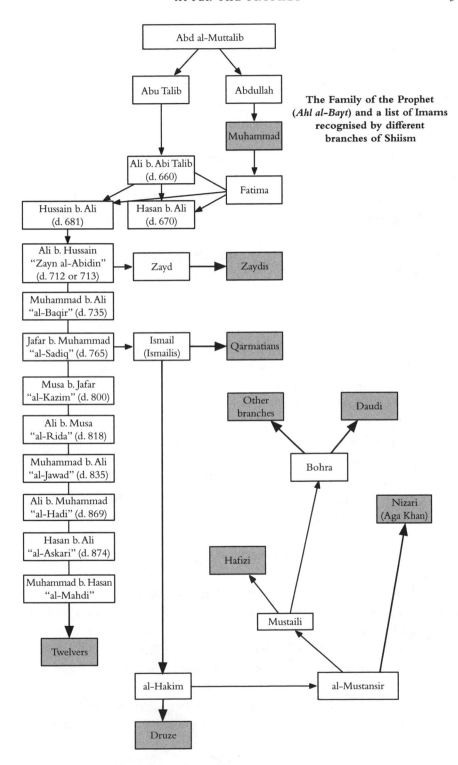

The Family of the Prophet (*Ahl al-Bayt*) and a list of Imams recognised by different branches of Shiism

Hussain and his followers refused to pledge allegiance to his son and successor as Umayyad Caliph in Damascus, Yazid I (d. 683). The Umayyads then waged a punitive military campaign against Hussain and his followers. Hussain went from Medina, where the Alids had been living, to Mecca, and shortly afterwards to Kufa, the former seat of Ali's Caliphate, at the invitation of pro-Alid Kufans. Meanwhile, one of Hussain's emissaries, Muslim, started a revolt in Kufa, which was repressed by the governor and forces loyal to Yazid. On his way to Kufa, word reached Hussain that the situation there had changed, and that he would not be welcomed. He seemed willing to return to Medina, but a convoy of Kufan riders loyal to Yazid hindered him from doing so and escorted him with the order to neither let him return to Medina nor let him reach Kufa.

A few days later, an army loyal to Yazid made up largely of Kufans emerged near a place called Karbala, not far from the Euphrates, where Hussain and his followers had been resting. According to the legend, Hussain had only about seventy men with him, as well as women and children, while Yazid's army numbered several thousand men. Hussain again refused to swear the oath of allegiance and prepared for battle. In the morning of 10 Muharram, after he had held the morning prayer, Hussain's group was attacked from all sides, first with arrows, and then in a sword battle. All the men, including of course Hussain, were killed and their bodies buried, and their heads were cut off and sent to Damascus for Yazid to examine and display. The women and children, however, including Hussain's son Ali, were spared and escorted to Medina. This is an important detail, for as noted it was the women, such as Zaynab, who would start the mourning for Hussain, and it was Ali bin Hussain, the so-called 'Zayn al-Abidin' (adornment of the worshippers), who became the next Imam. It was through him that the line of Imams continued.[64]

The problematic nature of the sources puts in doubt linear narratives of the Umayyad period (661–750). The standard accounts, such as those by al-Tabari as related by nineteenth-century Orientalists may still be the ones in textbooks and most well-known.[65] And yet, as noted, these accounts may contain much later addition.[66] The basic tenets of the story, however, are largely accepted by Sunnis and Shia, i.e. that major battles occurred and that Hussain was killed. Many Sunnis also think that Hussain was facing injustice, and Sunni scholars have criticised the Umayyads for this.[67]

In fact, even though early Shii historiography focused on the life stories of the Imams, these stories were often also present in accounts of Sunni authors, and their qualities were often also praised, although not to the extent that Shii authors would.[68]

Soon after the death of Hussain in 680, many Kufans felt regret for having first invited and then slain the Prophet's grandson. A group of 'repentants' began to form and, after the death of Yazid in 683, started to agitate in public, vowing revenge. In Mecca, a former supporter of Hussain, Ibn al-Zubayr, refused to pledge allegiance to the Umayyads and established a counter-Caliphate. He managed to extend his influence into Iraq, and the nobles of Kufa switched allegiance from the Umayyads to Ibn al-Zubayr, which benefitted the proto-Shia. A first group sought to avenge Hussain, and several thousand vowed to fight a Syrian army in 685 at Resaina but were defeated. On their way to battle they had stopped at Karbala to mourn Hussain at his grave.[69]

The next Alid rebellion was led by Mukhtar bin Abi Ubaid Thaqafi. Vowing to avenge Hussain, he tracked down and killed many of those involved in the Karbala battle. He led his rebellion nominally on behalf of a descendant of Ali, who, however, unlike Hasan and Hussain, was not a descendant of Fatima, but of a woman from the tribe of Hanifa, Muhammad Ibn al-Hanafiyya. Mukhtar thought that the latter was the Mahdi, the Messiah. Eventually, however, he was defeated, though not without a last defiant stance in the face of overwhelming military might and dying hero-ically in battle.[70] Mukhtar incorporated many non-Arab Muslims into his movement, for which later Arab authors criticise him. Shia cherish him as one of the few early Shii military heroes, and even though Shia did not agree with his choice of Mahdi, he may have introduced a messianic elem-ent into the nascent Shii community. At the same time, his doctrinal views did not become mainstream and were later seen as controversial even by Shia. It may be his relatively peripheral position that meant that Sunni and Shii authors largely agreed in their representation of his revolt.[71]

As the Islamic empire expanded in the seventh and eighth centuries, the question of how to treat newly conquered populations indeed arose. The four Caliphs had similar views about the superiority of Arabs, having grown up in Arabia, and the Arabs seemed a chosen people because of the Prophet Muhammad's revelations in their midst, and the prominence of Arabic as the language of the Quran. Shia, however, would later depict Ali as less inclined to Arab supremacism. While many Arabs refused to marry their daughters to non-Arabs, even if they had become Muslim, various early Shii legal traditions rejected the supremacy of Arabs in marriage.[72] It is worth remembering, however, that the protagonists of the early split, and the Imams themselves, were Arabs (with a few exceptions such as Salman al-Farisi, an Iranian Companion of the Prophet). Only now that Persians, Turks, and many others converted to Islam, Sunnism and Shiism became characterised by ethnic, tribal, linguistic, and regional diversity.

Numerous rebellions now claimed to defend the rights of the Alids to rule. Some scholars argued that some of these revolts, like those in Kufa, pitted early Muslims of relatively low tribal status against tribal leaders, with Shiism giving ideological cohesion to a sort of class rebellion.[73] Most of these uprisings were repressed, and were later written out of the standard histories of Shiism for being 'extremist', but they infused Shiism, initially a movement defending the Alids, with a somewhat aristocratic character, with an anti-establishment one.[74] That dichotomy, standing, on the one hand, in opposition to the status quo, while defending the *Ahl al-Bayt* because of their blood ties to the Prophet, characterised early Shiism.

Sixty-one years after the death of Hussain, grandson of the Prophet, in the Islamic year 61 (680), the grandson of that Hussain, Zayd bin Ali, after whom the Zaydiyya, a sub-branch of Shiism, is named, again revolted (as we had seen, the Islamic lunar calendar starts with the emigration, *hijra*, of the Prophet Muhammad and his followers from Mecca to Medina, which is the equivalent of 622 in the Christian calendar). Zayd had lived in Kufa for ten months, and many had revered him as an Imam. From Kufa, the heart of the pro-Alid movement, he revolted against the Umayyad Caliph, Hisham Ibn Abd al-Malik (r. 724–743), on 6 January 740, with 200 men. On the second day of heavy street fighting, he was shot by an arrow and killed. Secretly buried by his followers, Zayd's body was exhumed by the Caliph's men, his head sent to court, and his body left to rot on display in Kufa before it was burned (or so the tradition goes).[75] Once again, a descendant of the Prophet had been slain by the Caliph's soldiers, and his surviving followers would not forget who had killed him, and whom amongst the Kufan Shia had not supported him.

Zayd was the son of the above-mentioned Ali 'Zayn al-Abidin', the son and successor of Hussain, and fourth Shii Imam and the half-brother of Muhammad al-Baqir, whom the rest of the Shia accepted as the fifth Imam, and to whose offspring they trace the later line of Imams. It was with Zayd and at the time of Muhammad al-Baqir that the pro-Alid movement experienced its first major rift.[76] Zayd apparently thought that the first two Caliphs, Abu Bakr and Umar, were elected legally, although he thought that

Ali would have been the preferable candidate.[77] Therefore, Zayd refused to curse the first two Caliphs. This led to a split between adherents of Zayd and those of Muhammad al-Baqir and his sons.[78] Zaydis went as far as calling the other Shia *rafidi,* rejectionist, for their refusal to acknowledge the early Caliphates, aligning themselves with Sunnis on this point.[79] For their acceptance of the Rashidun Caliphs, Sunnis saw Zaydis as the 'least bad' of the Shia, or even as non-Shii.[80] The term *rafd,* however, also means the rejection of the Imamate of Zayd (and favouring Muhammad al-Baqir and subsequent Imams instead). Supporters of Zayd seemed to first have used it to denounce those who did not support Zayd. *Rafida* then became a widely used Sunni slander against Shia in general.[81]

Zaydis argued that worldly power mattered, and that only those descendants from the *Ahl al-Bayt* who attained it, and who fought for their position as Imam, were worthy (as opposed to the 'mere' spiritual authority that Shii Imams after Ali retained).[82] The founding figure of Zaydism is thus a classic hero who rose up against unjust rule, and the principle that the leader of the community should rebel against unjust rulers (*khuruj*) became key in Zaydism.[83] This shows how much in flux Shiism was in the early period, and how the question of who amongst the *Ahl al-Bayt* had a rightful claim to rule was still contested.

Idris bin Abdallah (d. 791), who had participated in Alid rebellions and claimed to be an Alid, was a case in point. He fled to North Africa, where he founded a dynasty that took his name, the Idrisids, who would rule from 788 to 985. Their descendants would go on to found Fez and play a crucial role in Islamising Morocco, where later ruling dynasties also legitimised themselves with reference to descent from the Prophet.[84] In sum, these early Alid rebellions failed, but pro-Alid movements found safe havens in areas outside Caliphal control (or were careful not to display their beliefs too openly under Caliphal rule).

Not long before his death in 632, the Prophet had made one last pilgrimage to Mecca, and on this occasion had told his followers that God had given the world two things, the Book (the Quran) and the Sunna (the example of the Prophet, also called the Tradition), while according to another source he had said that God had given his Book and the *Ahl al-Bayt* as safeguards. In conjunction, these elements—Quran, Sunna, and the *Ahl al-Bayt*—shaped Islam after the Prophet. Debates about the content and hierarchy of these

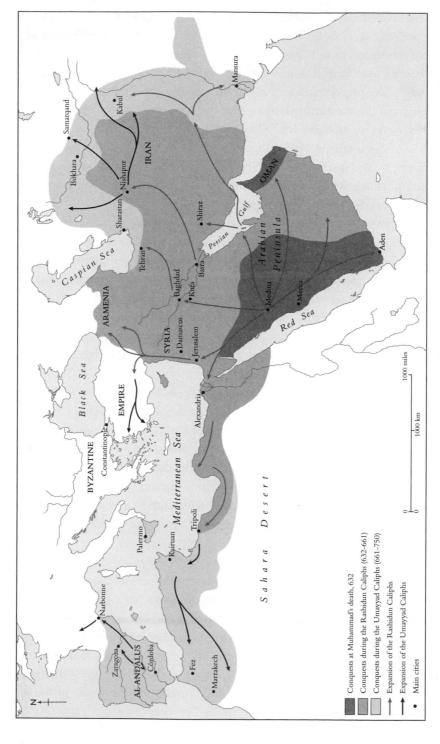

3. Early Muslim conquests and caliphates, ~750

three elements formed the essence of the disagreements between Sunna and Shia.[85]

The concept of 'Sunna' came to stand for the words and deeds of the Prophet. For later Sunnis, it also generally encompassed the Sunna of the earliest Muslims, and therefore of the Rashidun Caliphs. It became the second source of Islamic jurisprudence after the Quran.[86] Simultaneously, the concept of the *Jamaa*, of the Muslim 'community', developed in opposition to the various 'schisms' that in the community's view diverged from the original teachings. The very term *Ahl al-Sunna wa-l-Jamaa* (the People of the Tradition and the Community), which denotes Sunnism, only reached its coherence through delineation towards Shiism and other movements.[87]

Sunnism became codified in four major Sunni schools of jurisprudence (Shafii, Maliki, Hanbali, Hanafi) and two major schools of thought (Maturidism and Asharism). A third major school of thought, the rationalist and philosophical Mu'tazila, was important from roughly the ninth until the eleventh centuries, when it was gradually repressed alongside Shiism. For much of Islamic history, these schools of law and thought defined what was acceptable and what was not. The schools of law were founded in the eighth and ninth centuries, in the late Umayyad and early Abbasid periods, but their founding figures did not carry out official functions for the Caliphates, and instead sought to collect and systematise knowledge about the Prophet's message and life. By the eleventh century, the legal schools had become consolidated.

This established the dominance of jurists over religion, law, and the emerging scholarly and religious institutions, with the political realm largely left to the Caliphs. Jurists formulated a system of jurisprudence that was to guide Muslims as closely as possible in accordance with the Quran, seen as the direct word of God as pronounced by the Prophet, and the Sunna.[88] The most important Sunni Hadith (lit. saying) collections became the cornerstone of Sunni jurisprudence and religiosity. Sunnis trace the Hadith to the Prophet's Companions, who remembered His sayings and deeds. To define whether a Hadith is authoritative or not, scholars compiled extensive biographies of the narrators, establishing their trustworthiness. This was especially important when Hadith contradicted each other on a specific issue. The most authoritative Sunni Hadith collections, often referred to as the Six Sound Collections (though there are more than six collections used by Sunnis), were compiled during the mid- to late ninth century. Their compilers were probably originally Persian-speaking, testament to the spread of Islam to the East, to Iran and Transoxania, and to the contribution of Persian-speakers to Sunnism.[89] And once Sunnism became more firmly established, the traditions of Shii-leaning narrators were seen as lest trustworthy.[90]

The formation of Sunnism, like of Shiism, was a drawn-out process that started with the founders of the legal schools and the Hadith collectors, but took several centuries to become widely recognised and institutionalised.[91] The term 'Sunni' was not used widely until the fourth/tenth century, when Sunnis reached a consensus under which many strands of early Islam could be subsumed, while some, such as the Shia, were so different that they could not.[92] Key doctrinal positions, such as the ideas that Sunnis accept the first four Caliphs and Shia only the Caliphate of Ali, developed over time, and some adopted a middle ground.[93] Even the Shia did initially not unanimously condemn or reject the legitimacy of Umar, Abu Bakr, and Uthman, as we have just seen in the case of the Zaydis. After all, Ali had pledged allegiance to them, even if reluctantly.[94] And the Sunni schools spent much time delineating themselves vis-à-vis one another, and their relationship with Shiism could vary. In theology (*ilm al-kalam*), that is, outside of the field of law, cross-fertilisation between the different branches of Islam was especially strong. Here, Sunni and Shii scholars could at times debate theological and philosophical questions, for example the importance of reason versus revelation, without constantly referring to their differences.[95]

The oldest school and the one with the most followers is that of Abu Hanifa (d. in Baghdad in 767). Abu Hanifa denounced groups he deemed heretic and was nuanced in his assessment of proto-Shiism. He refused to reject any of the Companions of the Prophet and to decide between Uthman and Ali, which as we've seen was an early and basic delineator of differentiation. His school was elaborated by his disciples and, having originated in Iraq, was the school favoured by the early Abbasid Caliphs. The *hanafiyya* quickly spread to Syria and to the Eastern Islamic lands and became the school of jurisprudence in the largest and longest-lasting Muslim-ruled states, of the Saljuqs, Ottomans, Mughals, and many others.[96]

The second school was founded by Malik Ibn Anas (d. 795). He was born in Medina and lived and died there, and the essence of his school is that the period that the Prophet and the early Muslim community spent living in Medina constitutes an especially important example that should serve as guidance for Islamic law. He collected Hadith and wrote the earliest compendium of Islamic law to have survived, emphasising Quran and Sunna and, in cases where there was disagreement, analogy and the consensus of the scholars of Medina. The second Abbasid Caliph, Abu Jafar al-Mansur (d. 775), had approached him with a proposal to establish a legal school that would unify the legal practices of Muslims. His school was to spread in North Africa and Spain, and it remains the dominant school in the Maghreb, as Northwest Africa is known, today.[97]

One of Malik's students was Muhammad Ibn Idris al-Shafii, after whom the third school is named. Al-Shafii was born in Palestine around 767 and died in Cairo in 820. He sought to standardise the use of the sources of jurisprudence and emphasised the importance of the Sunna next to the Quran. His school is seen as more open to discussions with Shiism, and over the centuries scholars versed in both Shafii and Shii law crossed the borders between the two.[98] Al-Shafii's tomb in Cairo became a popular place of visitation and was expanded by Sunni rulers after the end of the Fatimid reign in the late twelfth century. The Shafii school spread across the Islamic world, not least to Egypt, Iraq, the Hijaz, Yemen, and Khorasan (northern Iran), and to Southern India and Southeast Asia.[99]

The fourth Sunni school is that of Ahmad Ibn Hanbal (780–855, d. in Baghdad), who fought against what he saw as innovations that were introduced after the time of the Prophet and the Companions by returning to the Quran and the Sunna.[100] Ibn Hanbal worked on a canon of authoritative Hadith in order to best reflect the Prophet's sayings and deeds, so that later generations of Muslims could live accordingly. He espoused a literal reading of the Quran and Hadith, and any practice that could not be traced to the earliest Companions was considered an innovation to be rejected.[101] For Ibn Hanbal and subsequent scholars of his school, the Shii view on the Companions, and on the authenticity of the Hadith, was impossible to reconcile with their quest for certainty around the Prophet's traditions.[102] He may initially have been critical of Ali's Caliphate—at the time some only saw the first three Caliphs as legitimate—and may have seen Ali as the 'fourth best' of the Rashidun Caliphs. But he may have wavered on this point because of the implication this would have had for the Sunni position that all the Companions of the Prophet are to be honoured. He eventually included many of Ali's sayings in his Hadith collection and standardised the idea of the Rashidun Caliphs, including Ali, as Sunni doctrine.[103] Hanbalism became especially strong in Iraq, Syria, Palestine, and the Arabian Peninsula. It was fully constituted and then instrumentalised by the Abbasids during the tenth and eleventh centuries, but it had fewer adherents than the other three schools, and often became a vehicle for the expression of localised grievances against the status quo. It did not become the official school of any major state until the eighteenth century, with the rise of the neo-Hanbali Wahhabi movement on the Arabian Peninsula and hence had little need to adapt to the realities of long-term rule over religiously mixed populations. It is his school that has taken the strongest stance against Shiism.

Sunni and Shii positions hardened around opposing views on the Companions of the Prophet, especially the Rashidun Caliphs and Aisha. Aisha, who had led the opposition to Ali's Caliphate, transmitted many of the Prophet's sayings and deeds accepted by Sunnis. Hadith transmitted through her became key in Sunni jurisprudence, and in the argumentation that Abu Bakr, her father, was the legitimate successor to the Prophet.[104] She is cherished by Sunnis as the daughter of the first Caliph and the favourite wife of the Prophet. Shia, however, think Abu Bakr usurped the place of Ali and loathe Aisha for her activism against Ali, and do not accept Hadith transmitted by her. While she was one of the most important women in early Islam, she was attacked by Shia to enhance the standing of those she fought, like Ali and Fatima. Sunnis are in a delicate position as they, too, generally do not approve of Aisha's activism against Ali, whom they regard as the fourth Caliph. Charges of adultery by Shii authors in attacks on her are sharply rebuked by Sunnis, however, who invoke a Quranic verse that they say proves her innocence.[105]

Given the seriousness of the charge and the ways in which it undermines perceptions of her family's honour, attacks on Aisha's moral integrity aroused Sunni feelings. Ritual cursing of her and the first three Caliphs, became a way for Shia to assert their identity. Sunnis were outraged, and Sunni rulers sought to stand up to this. The Caliph al-Mutawakkil (d. 247/861), for example, ordered the execution of a man accused of cursing Abu Bakr, Umar, and their daughters, the Prophet's wives Aisha and Hafsa.[106] Partly in reaction to Shii accusations, defence of key figures of the Rashidun period, such as Aisha, became central to Sunnism.[107] Given their dislike of Aisha, Shia glorified the two other key women of early Islam, Khadija and Fatima (although they are also well-regarded by Sunnis).[108] Sunna and Shia thus embraced different personalities of the foundational period, a preference reflected in naming. Most Islamic names are accepted by all Muslims, such as Muhammad, or Ali, which despite being a favourite name of Shia is common amongst Sunnis. But others carry more specific sectarian connotations and Shia would, for example, avoid Abu Bakr and Umar, common names amongst Sunnis.[109]

The consolidation of the legal schools coincided with dramatic political changes. Opposition to the Umayyads, who had established their reign in Syria in the mid-seventh century, grew over time. In Syria itself, the early Shia made little inroads, and Ali was not favoured by many because of his fight against the Umayyads.[110]

The movement that was eventually to overthrow them in 750 were the Abbasids, who took their name from Abbas, the Prophet's uncle. The Abbasids would move the capital of the Caliphate to Baghdad, which had previously been only a small settlement, shifting the centre of gravity of Islamic history yet again.[111] They would rule for the next 200 years, and retain their position as Caliphs until 656/1258. While this seemed to suggest that they claimed to rule based on their relation to the Prophet, this was a claim that was only to emerge forcefully after they had taken over the Caliphate. Who exactly made up the *Ahl al-Bayt*, and was therefore imbued with special spiritual and political authority, was contested. For the Shia, the *Ahl al-Bayt* came to mean only those who were descendants of Muhammad through his daughter Fatima's marriage with Ali. Abbasid missionaries were vague about who exactly was the saviour figure and what branch of the Prophet's family he would come from so that their call could resonate with the various groups that wanted the *Ahl al-Bayt* to regain political control. The Abbasid movement was formed through an alliance between descendants of Abbas and Abu Hashim, the son of Muhammad Ibn al-Hanafiyya (Ali's third son), on whose behalf al-Mukhtar had led his failed revolt.[112]

The Abbasids thus supported Alid rebellions against the Umayyads.[113] When the Abbasids finally came to power in 750, some Shia supported their claim to have a hereditary right to rule.[114] The Abbasid's insistence of the importance of ties to the Prophet also strengthened the claim of the Alids, whose blood ties to the Prophet were stronger, and which resonated with Arabian tribes accustomed to hereditary leadership.[115] The Alids became the Abbasids' main competitors for the allegiance of Muslims, and Abbasid policy towards them oscillated between co-optation and repression.[116] Alid support for the Abbasids was short-lived and, in 762 and 786, they rebelled against the Abbasids.[117] The Abbasids now proclaimed that the descendants of Abbas took precedence over the descendants of Ali and Fatima.[118] This in turn sharpened the Shii understanding of who did and who did not belong to the *Ahl al-Bayt*.[119]

Eventually, however, with some exceptions, as discussed below, the Abbasids would move away from that closeness to Shiism, not least because they felt threatened by it, and ally themselves with proto-Sunni clerics and support the codification of Sunnism.[120] They agreed with the Shia in their negative views of the Umayyads and the positive portrayal of Ali, but developed different narratives of the first civil war and the subsequent period. Ultimately, the Abbasids would, in their own interest, emphasise the continuity and righteousness of the first Caliphs to present themselves as successors of the Rashidun Caliphs, and Shia the right to rule of the Alids. A 'healthy' veneration of the Alids was seen favourably, as opposed to outright rejection of them or their deification (the latter a feature that Sunnis and mainstream Shia ascribe to 'extremist' Shia). This went hand in hand with Abbasid attempts to adopt the rationalist philosophical Mu'tazila to incorporate and contain proto-Shii sentiment.[121]

The Abbasids severely restrained the Alids, and Shia even accuse them of poisoning several Imams.[122] Stories of martyrdom of the Imams and other early Shii figures came to constitute an important feature of Shiism.[123] But relations were more complex than that. Such a crucial figure as the Fifth Abbasid Caliph Harun al-Rashid (766–809), whose court and person figure in some of the *A Thousand and One Nights* tales, for example, suppressed Shia who rebelled against him and ordered the destruction of the Hussain shrine in Karbala and ordered the arrest of the seventh Shii Imam, Musa al-Kazim, while the latter was on pilgrimage to Mecca. He then had him sent to Basra and Baghdad, where he found a residence for him, which Shia claim was a form of house arrest. And when Musa al-Kazim died in 799, some Shia claimed that he was killed on the Caliph's orders.[124] On the other hand, it was al-Rashid who 'rediscovered' the tomb of Ali in Najaf and had the first dome built over it.[125]

The Abbasid Caliph al-Mamun (r. 813–833) embraced a core concept of the Mu'tazila, the createdness of the Quran, which went against the belief of other Sunnis that the Quran had always existed. The debate centred around the question whether the Quran, as the word of God, existed outside of God, or whether it was synonymous with God. The Mu'tazila argued the former and decoupling the text of the Quran from the personality of God allowed it to develop a system of linguistics to interpret the text in novel ways. al-Mamun also declared the superiority of Ali over Abu Bakr and Umar, appeasing the Shia and enraging Sunni traditionalists. His actions were an attempt to position the Caliph as the ultimate arbiter of Islamic norms over and above the clerics.[126] It seemed as if the tables had turned in the Alids' favour.

Al-Mamun summoned Ali al-Rida, whom the Shia revere as the eighth Imam, to Khorasan, present-day Iran, to where al-Mamun had moved his court. al-Mamun then seems to have designated Ali al-Rida as his successor, possibly because he held apocalyptic beliefs about the end of the Abbasid dynasty, or to appease the Shia.[127] This was cited by non-Shia as evidence that he, al-Rida, could not have seen himself as a Shii Imam, for how could he have accepted to become a successor to a Sunni Caliph, and therefore to someone other than a Shii Imam? Shia, on the other hand, argued that he was coerced to do so, and subsequently poisoned.[128] In any case, the succession never took place. But it shows that not just the meaning of Sunnism and Shiism, even the boundaries between the two, were far from fixed (and had the succession taken place, might have developed in entirely different ways).

Whether of natural causes or not, Ali al-Rida died in 818 in Tus in Khorasan. On al-Mamun's orders, he was buried next to the tomb of al-Mamun's father, the former Caliph Harun al-Rashid, who had died on a trip to Khorasan a few years earlier. Thus, the eighth Shii Imam, who was designated to become Caliph after al-Mamun's death, was buried next to a Caliph known for anti-Shii acts, and for building the first dome over Ali's grave. Ali al-Rida's tomb would become a Shii pilgrimage site and the only grave of a Shii Imam in Iran, known as Mashhad, which literally means 'place of martyrdom'.[129] Over subsequent centuries, it would play an important role in strengthening Shii allegiances in Iran, as would the myth that Hussain Ibn Ali had married Shahrbanu, the daughter of the last Sassanid Shah, Yazdegerd III (632–651), and that their offspring, including the fourth Imam Ali 'Zayn al-Abidin', and all subsequent Imams were thus both descendants of the Sassanids and of the Prophet. By the ninth century, Shii sources asserted that link, and a shrine in Rayy in her honour would become a popular pilgrimage site.[130]

Eventually, struggles over the definition of Sunnism and Shiism grew fiercer. With its emphasis on reason, and its de-emphasis of the Sunna, had the Mu'tazila become dominant in Sunnism, it may have led to better relations with Shiism. Some proponents of the Mu'tazila argued that Ali was the most excellent of the Companions, while accepting the Caliphate of Abu Bakr, and the 'Sunni' order of Caliphs.[131] But the Mu'tazila was opposed, and eventually defeated by the Hadith-focused schools. The Caliph al-Mutawakkil (r. 847–861), retracted the idea of Ali's supremacy, and persecuted those advocating the createdness of the Quran.[132] And that some

Mu'tazili ideas lived on in rationalist Shiism and in some Zaydi and other texts on the margins of the Sunni world ended up heightening rather than lessening tensions between Shiism, Zaydism, and non-Mu'tazili Sunnism.[133]

Another key figure in eradicating the Mu'tazila was al-Ashari (d. 324/925–6), a former adherent of that school who became the key Sunni doctrinaire of his age, and who also had no love lost for Shiism.[134] He was one of the founders of the heresiographical genre, in which authors gave brief, deprecative descriptions of the various 'sects' of Islam, inspired by a saying attributed to the Prophet Muhammad that His community would be divided into seventy-three groups (firaq), of which seventy-two would go to hell and only one would be saved. This saying, generally accepted by Sunna and Shia, and interpreted by both as proof of their special status and the fallacy of others, led authors to describe the falsities of other groups to highlight the merits of one's own.[135] That Asharis would in subsequent centuries themselves become the victims of purges, exemplified that the struggles over the definition of Sunnism were still under way.

The rise of Shii dynasties in the tenth and eleventh century, the so-called 'Shii Century', changed the parameters of the debate. It boosted Shiism, which adapted to a situation of political power, and became more clearly defined, which in turn led to the development of rival Shii strands.[136] It also forced Sunnis to seriously engage with Shiism, and write more detailed refutations.[137] Let us first return to the Zaydis. The Zaydis had split off from the rest of the Shia after the death of the fourth Imam in the eighth century, and followed Zayd bin Ali, from whom they take their name. Zaydis then started a propaganda campaign and established three separate states: one in the Daylam region by the Caspian Sea in Iran; one in Yemen; and one in North Africa, of which the Yemeni one was the most durable.

The first Zaydi state was established near the Caspian Sea by al-Hasan Ibn Zayd (d. 844) and lasted until the twelfth century.[138] Its most prominent leader was al-Hasan al-Utrush (d. 917), who wrote a detailed compendium of law.[139] Apart from the namesake of the movement, Zayd bin Ali, the prominent Hijazi scholar al-Qasim Ibn Ibrahim (785–860), elaborated the Zaydi theory of the Imamate and delineated it from the Sunni Caliphate and the Imamate of other Shia.[140] He and other early Zaydis adopted and developed Mu'tazili ideas.[141] The rulers of the Zaydi state near the Caspian Sea seem not to have embraced the teachings of al-Qasim but his grandson propagated al-Qasim's teachings there, which led to a falling out with its rulers and forced the former and some of his supporters to flee to Yemen.[142] With their help, Imam al-Hadi (d. 911), the grandson of al-Qasim, established Zaydism in Yemen. Imam al-Hadi's writings form the basis for what would become known as the Zaydi-Hadawi school of law.[143] An exchange of ideas took place between the Zaydis of Yemen and Iran until the decline of the latter in the twelfth century, when the Yemeni one became the principal Zaydi state.[144] Remaining Zaydis in Iran largely embraced the spiritual leadership of the Yemeni Imams and, in the first half of the sixteenth century converted to Twelver Shiism.[145]

Zaydis insisted that their community be ruled by a descendant of the Prophet with strong qualifications. Unlike amongst other Shia, the position of Imam was not hereditary, and each new contender had to claim the imamate by both emphasising his learnedness and piety, and proving, at least potentially, his military prowess.[146] By definition, there were times when there were competing contenders to the Imamate.[147] Zaydis ascribed many canonical works to Zayd bin Ali (although their authenticity was later put in doubt).[148] While Twelver Shia and Zaydis are critical of Sunni Hadith collections, they differ in the kind of Hadith they use for jurisprudence, as Zaydis do not recognise the later Shii Imams as authoritative.[149]

Families claiming descent from the Prophet put forward candidates for the Imamate that were then selected by senior scholars, notables, and tribal leaders, who pledged allegiance to the new Imam. They played an important balancing role in North Yemen's tribal system and were invited by a tribe to come and live amongst them in a protected enclave to perform religious and judicial functions.[150]

Even more so than Zaydis, Ismailis would shape the Shii Century. They had split off from the rest of the Shia after the demise of Jafar al-Sadiq in 765. Al-Sadiq, the sixth Imam recognised by all Shia except the Zaydis, was a towering figure and even regarded as an authoritative transmitter of Hadith by Sunnis. The founding figures of the Hanafi and Maliki schools of jurisprudence, Abu Hanifa and Malik bin Anas are said to have studied with him in Medina (anti-Shii Sunni authors dispute this). Jafar al-Sadiq was a crucial figure who introduced key elements of Shii doctrine (including the very status of the Imam) and systematised the Shii school of law. Giving his centrality in the formation of Shiism, it was at times called the 'Jafari' school.[151] But since the Imams were still alive and could guide the Shii community directly, Shiism was not yet codified like the Sunni schools.

After Jafar al-Sadiq's death a disagreement emerged about his succession. His oldest son, Ismail, who seemed like his father's and his supporters' preferred candidate, predeceased his father (little is known about him, and both his birthday and time of death are disputed, as it was used in debates about the validity of his succession). Some claimed that the designation of Ismail was valid, and that the Imamate had passed on to Ismail's descendants (those would become known as the Ismailis). Many of al-Sadiq's followers had expected Ismail to be his successor, and it was conceptually difficult to change the notion of a designated succession, even though the successor had died.[152] But others could not accept this reasoning. They argued that Ismail's younger brother, Musa al-Kazim, should be the next Imam. Just as the rift with Zaydism, this one was irreversible.

Succession continued to be a problem. Formal designation of a successor usually took place when an Imam approached death, and was pronounced to a small circle of confidants. At times, this was done to evade persecution of a successor, a sign of Shii suspicion towards the powers of the day. Both the eighth Imam (Ali al-Rida, d. 818) and the ninth Imam (Muhammad al-Jawad, d. 835) left single male heirs who were only seven years old at the deaths of their fathers. The tenth Imam, Ali al-Hadi, was only a boy, yet most of his father's followers accepted him as Imam.

When al-Mutawakkil (r. 847–861) became Abbasid Caliph, he sought to tighten the reins of power and moved against the Alids. As noted, he broke with the pro-Mu'tazilite position of the earlier Abbasids, and instead turned to the Hanbalis and other traditionists for support, which positioned him against the Shia.[153] He ordered the renewed destruction of Hussain's shrine at Karbala (after his predecessor Harun al-Rashid had ordered the destruction of the mausoleum in c. 787, it had been partly rebuilt by followers of the Imams) and urged the tenth Imam, Ali al-Hadi, to move from Medina to Samarra in Iraq, close to the Abbasid court. When Ali al-Hadi arrived in 848, he was confined to his house. Unable to personally interact with his followers, he communicated with them through representatives. After a period in Medina, in which the Shii Imams directly interacted with their followers, the last two Imams then faced much more difficult circumstances. Shii sources claim Ali al-Hadi was poisoned on the orders of the Caliph. His house in Samarra was then turned into a shrine patronised by later Sunni and Shii rulers.[154] The site attained even larger importance when it also became the burial place of the eleventh Imam, al-Hasan al-Askari, who died there in 874.

Al-Hasan al-Askari is said to have had a young son, Muhammad, who disappeared, throwing the Shii belief system into disarray. The Shia had hitherto seen themselves as a special community led directly by the Imams, whose word was law, and who were seen to varying degrees as spiritual and political leaders, and divine guides. What precisely the beliefs of the earliest Shia were, however, is still debated, on the one hand because of the general nature of the sources, and the secretive nature of early Shiism, and on the other hand because what may have been widespread beliefs in early Shiism of the semi-divine status of Ali and the Imams, whose teachings were confined to a small circle of followers, were later labelled as '*ghuluw/ghulat*', 'extremist'. After the last Imam's disappearance, however, not only was all subsequent political rule in theory illegitimate, but the very role of the Imams as spiritual guides had to be rethought. This was a problem, for the Imams' leadership was key to attaining salvation. To overcome it, Shia argued that the last Imam, Muhammad 'al-Mahdi', had not died but instead gone into a state of seclusion, and would re-emerge on the Day of Judgment. Initially, four 'ambassadors', some of whom had been representatives of the previous Imams, were said to be able to communicate with him, but after the last of those died (probably in 941), Shia believe the Imam went into the Major Occultation and ceased direct communication with his followers. It is only now that the term 'Twelver Shii', in the sense of limiting the number of Imams to twelve, emerged, and made sense. And it is now that Shiism developed into a scripturalist religion, and that it positioned itself against other branches of Shiism that did not fit Twelver Shiism as it was now being defined.[155]

The Baghdadi mystic Muhammad Ibn Nusayr al-Namiri (d. 883), was a close associate of the tenth and eleventh Imams. His followers came to believe that he was entrusted with secret knowledge about God and that he had become the gate through which believers could attain full knowledge of God's revelation. Implicit here was the idea that Ali had already been a God-like figure and that he had passed on divine knowledge through the Imams to Ibn Nusayr. Ibn Nusayr's beliefs were characterised as extremist and dismissed, including by the eleventh Imam, Hasan al-Askari, and later Twelver Shia. To describe them as not more than a sect following one man, Ibn Nusayr's followers were called Nusayris. Members of the group would, however, use different terms as a self-description, and from the late nineteenth century become known as Alawites.[156]

Alawite missionaries were successful in Iraq, Syria, and the Levantine coastal area, where they rivalled Ismailis and Twelver Shia, but benefitted from the generally Shii atmosphere. The Hamdanids, a local ruling dynasty who embraced and supported Twelver Shiism, had taken control of Aleppo in 944 and turned it into an intellectual centre, patronising, for example, Al-Mutanabbi and Abu Firas, two of the most celebrated Arab poets of all times.[157] Born in Kufa, al-Mutanabbi moved to the Hamdanid court, and wrote poems praising the ruler. Some of the best-known poems in the Arabic language, still anthologised, studied, and recited by Arabs regardless of religious background, were produced by a Shii poet praising a Shii ruler, further evidence of the constituent role Shiism played in Arab history.[158]

From Hamdanid Aleppo, Alawite ideas spread across the region, eventually gaining a foothold in the mountains on the Syrian coast.[159] At the height of the Shii Century, Alawism was a significant religio-political force, even if adherents outside the Syrian mountains were gradually incorporated into other Shii strands. In the regions in which it did take hold, Alawism may have been seen as the local variant of the wider pro-Alid movement. Alawites and Twelver Shia in Syria only separated into distinct groups once a more legalist Twelver Shiism developed in the Shii areas of Jabal Amil and the Bekaa (Alawites did not develop a written legal corpus).[160] The confusion amongst Twelver Shia about the precise situation after the disappearance of the twelfth Imam led some to embrace Alawism, Zaydism, and Ismailism, with their continuing line of Imams.[161]

The difficulties to agree on a single line of Shii Imams, the disappearance of the twelfth Imam, and Messianism, provided ample ammunition to critics. Sunnis argued that, if it was true that God wanted the community to be led by the *Ahl al-Bayt*, why had He not made them stronger, more successful politically, and ensured that their line be continued for longer? They reasoned that the Shii claim was undermined by the Shii Imams' lack of political success. These attacks, and competition over leadership of the broad pro-Alid movement, led to a stronger delineating of Sunnism and Shiism, and of the three main Shii schools of jurisprudence, Zaydism, Ismailism, and Twelver Shiism, against strands that claimed the same origin.[162] Zaydis, for example, would become especially critical of core tenets of Twelver Shiism.[163]

When Twelver Shiism reinvented itself after the disappearance of the twelfth Imam, the Sunni legal schools served as an example. The Twelver Shii, or 'Jafari' school of jurisprudence, developed a distinct spiritual tradition and political theory, and an elaborate legal corpus.[164] Its clerics claimed to stand in as representatives of the twelfth Imam until his reappearance.

The Caliphs maintained that the alms tax, *zakat*, should be paid to them and then centrally distributed to the poor. Given the Shii distrust towards the early Caliphs and Sunni-dominated states, their clerics argued instead that *zakat* should not be paid to the state but to the clerics as the representatives of the Imam.[165] The result was a community-centred political economy of piety, in which a special religious tax, amounting to one-fifth of one's annual surplus income, funded the religious and social welfare infrastructure of the clergy. This allowed Shiism, and its clergy, to survive periods of Sunni reassertion.[166]

Just as Twelver Shiism was consolidating itself, so did Ismailism, and differentiated itself from the former. Ismailis spread their ideas through missionaries and were boosted by two rival Ismaili dynasties, the Fatimids in North Africa and the Qarmatians in Eastern Arabia and the Syrian steppe, who emerged in the early tenth century.[167] The two dynasties disagreed over the line of Ismaili Imams. Ismail's son Muhammad (c. 738–?), the Ismaili Imam, had gone into hiding to avoid persecution by the Abbasids, and left Medina first for southern Iraq and then for Khuzistan in Iran. With Muhammad bin Ismail, a period of concealment started for the Ismaili Imams. Once in Iran, he seemed to have despatched his own missionaries to neighbouring regions. His death date is not known, but may have been some time in the late eighth or early ninth century, during the Caliphate of Harun al-Rashid (768–809). As pointed out, al-Rashid arrested Musa al-Kazim, the Shii Imam, and sent him to Iraq.[168]

When Muhammad bin Ismail died, many of his followers denied that he was dead and thought he would instead reappear as the Mahdi. This became the position of the Qarmatians. The Fatimids, on the other hand, stuck to a defined line of Imams, and claimed themselves to be the Imams of that line.[169] In the ninth century, Ismaili agents and missionaries spread across the Islamic lands. These well-organised and disciplined missionaries were successful, and in a few decades managed to gain adherents from their strongholds in Iran and southern Iraq to regions such as Yemen, Bahrain, Syria, Khorasan, Transoxania, Sind, and North Africa. Both Fatimids and Qarmatians sought to draw these networks to their side.[170]

The Fatimids first succeeded in mobilising the Kutama Berbers of Eastern Algeria, with whose help they captured Raqqada in Tunisia and surrounding territories. From there, they moved eastwards and conquered Egypt.[171] At its height, the Fatimids ruled from their capital at Cairo over the area from present-day Morocco to Syria, the Hijaz and Yemen, as well as Sicily and

Malta, and established the only Shii caliphate ever to have existed. The Fatimids were Imams, religious leaders over those Ismailis that accepted their leadership, and Caliphs in the political sense, rulers over a largely non-Ismaili population.[172]

The Qarmatians, on the other hand, gained ground in Iraq and Eastern Arabia, where for two centuries their strongholds were the islands of Bahrain, the port of Qatif, and the oasis of al-Ahsa. Their reign deepened the Shii affiliations of the population, which had supported earlier pro-Alid movements.[173] In Sunni historiography, all sorts of mischief is ascribed to them.[174] The most serious charge is confirmed by different accounts, which is that during an attack on Mecca in 930, they murdered scores of pilgrims, and then stole the rectangular black stone, the Kaaba, that sits at the centre of Mecca's Grand Mosque. The Kaaba was already a site of pilgrimage in pre-Islamic times and during the Prophet Muhammad's time became the focus of the Hajj pilgrimage, one of the pillars of Islam, accepted by Sunna and Shia. The Qarmatians are alleged to have transported it across the Arabian Peninsula, only to return Islam's most holy artefact to the Hijaz after the payment of a large ransom.[175] This shocked the wider Muslim community. Sunni writers have used it to denounce the alleged treachery of Shia more generally and link the Shia in Qatif and al-Ahsa to the Qarmatians to denigrate them. Shii historians, on the other hand, are proud of the long local history of Shiism in what they term the 'Lands of Bahrain' (Bahrain, Qatif, and al-Ahsa).[176]

The Fatimid Caliphs, who ruled Egypt from 969 until 1171, built the old city of Cairo and founded the aforementioned Al-Azhar University. They claimed both spiritual and political leadership and sought to establish a Shii alternative to the Abbasid Caliphate. They minted gold coins that became standard currency in the Islamic Mediterranean and around the Arabian Peninsula, bearing only the names of the Fatimid Caliphs (and not those of the Abbasids).[177] The Fatimids had assumed the title of Caliph in opposition to the Sunni Abbasid Caliphs, and their missionary networks and outlining of what it meant to be Ismaili and rule a state according to Ismaili teachings meant that non-Shia defined their position towards Shiism more concretely.[178] They also established suzerainty over Mecca and Medina, which the Abbasids and their governors in Egypt had previously formally controlled, and in whose name the Friday prayer in Mecca had been read. But this changed from 969 onwards, when it was read in the name of the Fatimid Caliphs—important for their legitimisation.[179]

The Fatimid state organised Shii processions and rituals, and Shii inscriptions praising Ali became ubiquitous across Cairo. In 1153, the Fatimids had the head of Hussain transferred from Askalon in Palestine (then under threat by the Crusaders) to Cairo, where they interred it near the palace next to the remains of earlier Fatimid Caliphs. As noted, the Hussain mosque with the mausoleum for Hussain's head became a popular site of visitation for Sunnis and Shia.[180] The Companions, especially those seen as the first three Caliphs by Sunnis, were publicly cursed.[181] The Fatimids established a legal code that resembled Sunni ones in organisation but differed on content. Codified in a massive legal work by the senior cleric of the Fatimid era, the *Qadi* al-Numan, it refused to accept traditions derived from the first three Caliphs revered by Sunnis, instead only accepting traditions of the Prophet and the *Ahl al-Bayt*, a synthesis of earlier Shii and Zaydi law, but on a grander scale, fit for purpose to rule over large populations.[182]

Central to the Fatimids' belief system, which emphasised seven pillars of Islam, was the guardianship of the Fatimid Imams.[183] In general, Fatimid public processions and the founding and expansion of mausoleums fostered adherence to the *Ahl al-Bayt*, an adherence that survived their reign.[184] Popular practices, such as the visitation of *Ahl al-Bayt* shrines in Cairo, had predated the Fatimids, although Shii visitors had at times been harassed by the authorities. But their rule strengthened these practices and deepened a 'Cult of Saints' and visitation of tombs, and the Fatimids expanded shrines around those tombs. Many of these buildings could be appreciated and visited by Ismailis, Twelver Shia, and Sunnis alike.[185] And despite the institutionalisation of Ismaili rituals and law, and continued missionary activity abroad, however, the Fatimids did not convert the mainly Sunni and Christian population.[186]

But in the Fatimid-ruled Levant, a missionary movement that proclaimed the Fatimid Caliph al-Hakim as a God-like figure gained pace in 1017 and continued when al-Hakim disappeared near Cairo in 1021. These beliefs in the divinity of al-Hakim eventually went beyond what was acceptable to the other Fatimid Ismailis, and were suppressed in Egypt. But in the Levant, they led to the emergence of the Druze, who derive their name from one of these missionaries, al-Darazi. Another key figure, Hamza bin Ali bin Ahmad, organised the movement and his writings, together with those of other early Druze, serve as the Druzes' doctrinal canon. After being suppressed in Egypt, it gained converts in Syria over the coming two decades. Its leader then closed the gate to conversion in 1043, after which it was technically no longer possible to become or cease to be Druze (though in practice there were exceptions). Beliefs became guarded by a clerical caste, and acquired a mysterious aura. The Druze belief system emerged from the wider Ismaili sphere, but through its emphasis on the divinity of the Imams, and the transmigration of souls, and ideas of God, also constituted a departure from it.[187] Since after 1043 they no longer sought to proselytise, they were less threatening to regional powers, and at times presented themselves as Sunni Muslims in interactions with Sunni rulers.[188]

In the Maghreb, resistance to the Fatimids and Ismaili missionaries grew. al-Hakim had alienated Sunnis by ordering the public cursing of the Prophet's Companions, then forbidding it when he faced resistance, only to reintroduce it again later. He established a foundation for the training of Ismaili missionaries, and set up a separate Sunni institution with scholars of the Maliki school of jurisprudence, which was becoming the key Sunni school in the Maghreb. But as Fatimid control weakened, Maliki clerics instigated mobs against Ismailis, and Ismailism ultimately almost disappeared from present-day Tunisia, Eastern Algeria, and Western Libya, where the Fatimid movement had once originated, and the Maliki school asserted itself in turn. Shii influence waned or was subsumed into Sunni popular religiosity.[189]

In the first half of the twelfth century, Maliki jurists settled in Alexandria, and petitioned the Fatimids to change inheritance law, which differs substantially between Shiism and Sunnism, from Ismaili to Maliki law (the request was refused). At times, Shafii, Maliki, Twelver Shii, and Ismaili judges adjudicated inheritance cases according to their schools, and, in Alexandria, Sunni law colleges were set up.[190] Despite this, resistance to the Fatimids amongst Sunnis in places like Alexandria increased.[191] In 1137, a Sunni minister apparently tried to depose the Caliph with clerical help.[192] The Fatimid polity was troubled by famines, administrative problems, and military insurrections from the 1060s onwards. While the last Fatimid Caliph was in office until 1171, Fatimid power diminished and was undermined by succession disputes, and the breakaway and resistance of largely Sunni populations.[193] And the Fatimids' Sunni successors would try to erase their legacy, and Sunni clerics would mobilise against Twelver Shia and Ismailis in Upper Egypt.[194]

Some of the popular Shii practices instituted by the Fatimids, however, like the Birthday of the Prophet, remained part of popular culture.[195] When and by whom these celebrations of the Birthday of the Prophet were first practised is still debated. What is clear, however, is that over much of Islamic history, Sunnis and Shia observed it, albeit Sunnis often as a celebration and Shia as a ritual of lamentation. Some argue that their embracing by Sunnis was a way to incorporate the devotional rituals so vividly displayed by Shia into a ritual associated with the Prophet (rather than with Hussain). And even though Sunnis could mourn Hussain alongside Shia at Ashura, in other contexts they started celebrating his demise.[196]

The travelogue of Nasir Khusraw, the famous mid-eleventh century traveller, for example, describes the general atmosphere of the 'Shii Century', and how the Ismaili states in Eastern Arabia and Egypt were threatened by Sunni powers. Khusraw, an Ismaili, could travel across the Islamic lands and encounter Shii communities, from the Levantine coastal area to Cairo, Najd, and Arabia.[197] In the central Arabian region of Yamama, for example, he came across the Zaydi Banu 'l-Ukhaydir dynasty, who ruled Yamama from 253/867 until the mid-fifth/eleventh century.[198]

Many Ismailis and Zaydis later became Twelver Shia.[199] The Buyids (934–1055), the other major Shii dynasty of note, originated in the Caspian Sea, then under the control of Zaydi Imams, and may have been Zaydis themselves. They then assumed power in Baghdad, upended Abbasid Caliphal rule, and became Twelver Shia. They outwardly maintained the Abbasids' rule yet wielded real power themselves, and turned Baghdad into a centre of Shiism. The Caliphate—in the Umayyad and the early Abbasid periods, the Caliph was still religious and political authority—lost in importance.[200] That a Shii dynasty could pro forma maintain a Sunni Caliph points to the complexity of Sunni–Shia relations even as doctrinal boundaries were being established more clearly.

The Buyids patronised Twelver Shiism at a time when its key doctrines were just being formed and canonised, and when it was under pressure from Ismailis, Zaydis, and Alawites.[201] Twelver Shii scholars now developed an elaborate corpus of jurisprudence and foundational texts. Scholars such as Muhammad bin Ali Ibn Babuya (or Babawayh) al-Qummi (d. 991) and Shaykh al-Mufid constituted Twelver Shiism vis-à-vis the other schools, wrote refutations of them, and systematised Shii Hadith collections. Shaykh al-Mufid wrote extensively in defence of the Imamate of Ali and his descendants and outlined the legal differences between Shia and Sunna.[202] The different ways in which Sunni and Shii scholars arrived at specific rulings were formulated more clearly (even if Sunni and Shii scholars often agreed on specific rulings).[203]

Sunni jurisprudence is primarily based on four sources (*usul al-fiqh*): Quran, Hadith, *qiyas* (analogy), and *ijma'* (consensus). The first two are sources, and analogy is a methodology (one uses evidence from the first two sources to come to conclusions about a subject that is not directly mentioned in them). Consensus is the result of interpretation of the first two sources, as well as of rulings made by analogy, and posits that where there is agreement amongst the key scholars there is no need to go back to the sources to infer new rulings.[204] As noted, the development of jurisprudence based on these sources was a gradual process. Al-Shafii introduced the idea that everything that could reliably be seen as having been a tradition during the time of the Prophet could not be rejected categorically.

Shii jurisprudence also accepts the Quran as the key basis. But some Shii scholars argued that when the Quran was canonised, a process that most scholars basing themselves on Sunni historiography date to the period of the Rashidun Caliphs, to Abu Bakr and especially Uthman, the compilers altered, or 'falsified', the Quran to erase references to Ali and the *Ahl al-Bayt*. Some claimed that only certain words were changed. To support this, they cited Shii Hadiths of the Imams. Others argued that the text was the same, but that the order of the verses had changed, and that comments by Ali were ignored, and that only the Imams knew the right order. Shii sources gave Ali a much more important role than Abu Bakr and Uthman in the compilation of the Quran, with some arguing that his was the authentic version. These views were probably widespread amongst early Shia, and the latter position adopted even by key clerics in later periods, for a wholescale denouncing of these ideas put Shii scholars at odds with the Hadith of the Imams. But with the establishment of a more centralised Shiism under the Buyids, and in order to deflate Sunni criticism and be taken seriously by Sunnis, Shii scholars declared that the Quran that by then existed in book form was exactly the one that had been handed down to Muhammad, abolishing in the Shii mainstream the notion that the Quran had been falsified.[205] Even though this remained a popular trope in anti-Shii heresiography, Sunna and Shia thus largely agree on the most importance source of Islamic law: The Quran.

But they established different ways to interpret it (*tafsir*). That key Shii doctrines are not explicitly referred to in the Quran, and neither is the all-important succession to the Prophet, also stands in contrast to Hadith of the Imams. Some Shii scholars tried to resolve this not by saying that the Quran was falsified, but by arguing that it was impossible for the Quran and the

Hadith not to agree, because the Prophet himself had stated that Muslims should be guided by both.[206] Only two or three Quranic verses could, if interpreted from a Shii perspective, give support to the Shii interpretation of the succession. They refer to the love and respect for the *Ahl al-Bayt*.[207] These are 33:33, in which the *Ahl al-Bayt* are referenced (one of only two occurrences of this term in the Quran, the other dealing with the family of another prophet), and 42:23, which refers to kinship.[208] Two interpretations developed, one more Sunni, the other more Shii. Shia understood *Ahl al-Bayt* in this case to refer to Muhammad, Fatima, Ali, Hasan, Hussain, and their descendants. Sunnis interpreted *Ahl al-Bayt* as referring primarily to the wives of the Prophet Muhammad, including Aisha. Some extended this to include his daughters, including Fatima, as well as Ali, and their sons Hasan and Hussain, but not their offspring.[209]

Early Sunni Quran commentators argued either that the terms used in the Quran did not refer to the descendants of the Prophet or that love for his family was not wrong and could take place in a Sunni context as long as it did not involve the idea that his descendants or their representatives should lead the community. The nominally Sunni Quran commentator al-Thalabi (d. 427/1035) for example, stated that, if love for the *Ahl al-Bayt* was the only thing distinguishing a Sunni from a Shii, then he, too, was a Shii. He sought to integrate love for the Prophet's family into Sunnism, thereby depoliticising it, and without denigrating the other Companions of the Prophet or elevating the *Ahl al-Bayt* above other Companions (he referred to Shia as rejectionists and attacked them in commentaries on other verses).[210] Faced with this situation, Shii exegesis developed methods to deduce the hidden meaning of the text, partly through the interpretative powers of the Imams. But after the disappearance of the twelfth Imam Shii scholars produced Quran commentaries that interacted much with the ideas and methodologies of Sunni Quran commentators.[211]

Another debate surrounds the second source of Islamic law after the Quran, the Hadith. As noted, Sunnis compiled Six Sound Collections during the ninth century. In polemics directed at a Sunni audience, Shii authors also used these Hadith collections.[212] In legal discussions, however, Shii scholars relied on Hadith transmitted through the Imams, who the Shia believe are infallible and transmitted the Prophet's message most authoritatively.[213] Shii Hadith was systematised in the ninth and tenth centuries in four canonical books (which serve a similar function amongst Shia as the Six Sound Collections do amongst Sunnis). Hadith from these collections are then compared with Shii books on the biographies of the narrators.[214] Much like in the Sunni schools of jurisprudence, this led to a focus on Hadith at the expense of other sources of jurisprudence. For a century after the Minor Occultation (874), a scripturalist, Hadith-focused, and anti-rationalist school became dominant in Shiism. It argued that because the Prophet and the Imams had laid down the rules of what was right and what was wrong, the role of the clerics should be minimal and not include the methods used by the Sunni jurists at the time, especially independent reasoning (*ijtihad*).[215] It played a major role in systematising Shii Hadith scholarship but was eventually challenged by the rationalist Usuli school.

Ali's Hadith collection, the *Nahj al-Balagha*, collected and disseminated by al-Sharif al-Radi (970–1015/16), is foundational for the Shia, and since he was such an important Companion of the Prophet has also been used and commented upon by Sunni scholars (though others have doubted its authenticity).[216] Jafar al-Sadiq, the sixth Imam of the Shia, is also deemed an authoritative Hadith transmitter by Sunnis.[217] But Shii scholars claimed that Sunni Hadith traditions have been altered to undermine the position of the *Ahl al-Bayt* and Shiism, by inserting negative references about the *Ahl al-Bayt* and taking out positive ones.[218] This makes Shii scholars doubt some of the foundations upon which Sunni scholars base their jurisprudence.

This similarly applies to the two other main sources of Sunni jurisprudence: consensus and analogy. For Shia the period in which new Hadith could be promulgated continued as long as the Imams were alive and communication with them was still possible, so until about 941, while for Sunnis it ended with the death of the Prophet and his Companions.[219] The first systematic works on Shii sources of jurisprudence were disseminated from the eleventh century onwards, substantially later than the earliest Sunni works of jurisprudence.[220] A rationalist school within Shiism, led by figures such as Shaykh al-Mufid and Sharif al-Murtada, now established the principles of the sources of jurisprudence as the dominant mode of inferring rulings and side-lined the traditionists.[221] Shaykh Abu Jafar al-Tusi (d. 1067/8), systematised Shii law in a comparative law book that was modelled on Sunni legal scholarship. This *Kitab al-Khilaf (Book of Difference)* focused on the contested subjects between the different schools of jurisprudence, first giving the opinions of Sunni authors and then the 'correct' Shii interpretation. It outlined in detail opinions on rituals (such as prayer), practices, taxes, and other questions.[222] His *oeuvre* was a response to Sunni criticism that Shii jurisprudence was deficient.[223]

Since the consensus of Sunni jurists runs counter to Shii beliefs, Shia did not think more scholars agreeing on something made it truer, as Sunnis do. For if consensus was a valid source of jurisprudence, how could the majority not have accepted Ali as the Prophet's successor?[224] Shia also do not use analogy except under specific circumstances, arguing that it leads to uncertainty, and often use 'evidence of reason' (*dalil al-'aql*) as the fourth source of jurisprudence.[225] The Shii rationalists argued that independent reasoning can be used to infer rulings that are not found in the other sources.[226] While the Imams lived amongst the people, Shia were in no need for it, for the words of the Imams were law. Thereafter, Shii scholars adopted reason as a key source of jurisprudence.[227]

Sunni scholars used independent reasoning in the formative period of Sunnism. After the establishment of the legal schools it had often been claimed that the so-called 'door of *ijtihad*' had been closed. According to this view, interpretation of the sources considering factors outside of the four bases of Sunni jurisprudence mentioned above was no longer valid, and Sunnis settled major questions by consensus. That standard narrative of Sunni legal history has been challenged, however, and legal positions could shift over time.[228]

In addition, legal texts did not necessarily dictate social practice. Islam, as other religions, is characterised by a discrepancy between religious law and lived reality. Famous examples are the celebration of Sufi poetry and music, the production and drinking of wine, or the pictural representation of people, even though all three are supposedly proscribed by both Sunni and Shii law. An excessive focus on law has led to a narrow and distorted understanding of Islam.[229] During the early centuries, the overwhelmingly rural population was much less aware of doctrinal difference and led lives influenced by a plurality of religious practices not condoned by scriptures.[230] Customary law played an important role, and the ease with which Shia could, for example, pretend to be Sunnis throughout much of Islamic history, complicates things considerably.

But differences in jurisprudence shaped the self-understanding of Sunnism and Shiism, and led to different views on political theory, prayers,[231] inheritance and divorce, funerary practices,[232] and pilgrimage that shaped practices of the everyday. The experience of Shia living under Sunni rule entrenched some of these differences.[233] Shia, for example, did not accept rulings made by the Caliph Umar, which became binding for Sunnis, on marriage[234] divorce and slavery.[235] The position of the *Ahl al-Bayt*, and the fact that descent from the Prophet happened through his daughter Fatima, whom Shia think should have inherited the Prophet's possessions, may explain why, according to Shii law, women can inherit based on their blood relation to the deceased, unaffected by their gender.[236]

The patronage of rulers in the Shii Century allowed for the codification and application of these and other matters of Shii law at a time when Shiism was thrown into a crisis by the disappearance of the twelfth Imam. The Buyids sponsored Shii scholarship and ritual practice. But they did not suppress Sunnism, and as noted ruled nominally on behalf of the Abbasid Caliphs, who remained spiritual authorities, even if they were often no more than figureheads, confined to their palaces.[237] They did not abolish the Caliphate or declare a counter-Caliphate, though the idea was raised at the time, and technically remained 'appointed' governors of the Abbasids. A reason for this might have been purely practical—most of their subjects and troops were Sunnis. At the same time, they might not have had much of a choice, for Twelver Shiism was still being codified, and it may have been difficult to find a suitable Shii candidate for the position of Caliph (and since the Buyids were not from an Alid background, they would not themselves have been eligible, as opposed to the Fatimids, who as Alids claimed to be both Caliph and Imam). And submitting to the Fatimid Caliphate in Cairo would have meant giving up autonomy.[238] In fact, the Shii dynasties, and the different branches of Shiism, had far from harmonious relations, although tensions with Byzantine limited hostilities. But when the Buyid ruler Adud al-Dawla (d. 983) proposed an alliance against Byzantium to the Fatimid Caliph al-Aziz Billah, the latter was not interested. Adud al-Dawla then signed a treaty with Byzantium instead.[239]

The Buyids expanded the shrines of the Imams (including of the seventh and ninth Imams in Kazimiyya) and founded Shii institutes of learning. Hussain's grave in Karbala, which had been as noted a site of worship in the ninth century but had then been destroyed on the orders of the pro-Sunni Caliph al-Mutawakkil, was refurbished and became frequently visited again. Adud al-Dawla built the first substantial shrine over Ali's grave and was buried there himself.[240] This coincided with the publication of the first pilgrimage manuals as visiting the graves of the Imams and other members of the *Ahl al-Bayt* in the Hijaz, Iran, Iraq, and Syria became part of Shii ritual practice.[241] As the countless shrines dotted around the Islamic world attest, shrine visitation became a major expression of Muslim popular religiosity.[242] And of course Sunnis and Shia agree that the pilgrimage to Mecca

(Hajj/Umrah) is a pillar of Islam. That non-Shii Muslims, too, held the Alids and descendants of the Prophet, Sayyids or Sayyidas, in high regard may in many contexts have limited the Shii connotation of reverence for the *Ahl al-Bayt*, and turn it more into a part of mainstream Muslim religiosity.[243] Shia practices of shrine visitation were especially similar to those of Sufis.

The term Sufi indicates *one who wears wool* and originated with a group of Companions of the Prophet and other early Muslims who dressed in rough wool to show their asceticism and dedication to the faith, in opposition to the more elaborate and luxurious clothing that started to become fashionable amongst the Muslim upper classes. The earliest Sufis wanted to go beyond the adherence to the rituals as laid out by the Prophet Muhammad, and engage in additional prayers, and other rituals, to focus on inner spiritual development. In pursuit of the path towards truth, Sufis would live ascetically, and renounce worldly possessions. Most Sufis adopted the Quran and the Sunna as the basis for proper conduct but argued that they contained hidden meaning, and that it took special spirituality and knowledge to access that. In the ninth, tenth, and eleventh centuries, Sufis in Basra and Baghdad, as well as in Nishapur and the upper Oxus, wrote foundational works. While the early texts were written in Arabic, Persian increasingly became important for Sufism, as it expanded eastward, and incorporated pre-Islamic intellectual traditions. From early on, some Sufis were deemed especially knowledgeable, and teacher–pupil relationships facilitated the path to spiritual advancement. These were initially loose arrangements, which became more formal by the tenth century, with the pupil receiving a sort of licence from his teacher after passing the initiatory stages of the Sufi path. By the twelfth and thirteenth century, these relationships had developed into orders that would spread across the whole Islamic world, from Morocco and al-Andalus, to Southeast Asia. Named after the Sufi way, these *tariqas*, or paths, would adopt the names of their founding figures, and become tight-knit and resourceful networks. Sufis argued that in principle, everyone could reach spiritual accomplishment, if properly disposed and guided.[244]

As noted, Shia believe that the Imams had access to the inner meaning of the Prophet's message, and so some Sufis developed Shii leanings and regarded the Shii Imams as important transmitters of spiritual knowledge. Other Sufis would become anti-Shii. Whilst all the Sufi orders shared some foundational texts, organisational structure, ultimate ambition of reaching spiritual purity, and ritual practice, their position on the Sunni–Shia question could diverge considerably. When Sunni traditionalists sought to discredit Sufis, they would accuse them of Shii tendencies. They would point to the similarity between the Sufi notion that a spiritual guide can mediate between the believer and God, and the Shii view that the Imams were such guides. Sufis and Shia use the same term to refer to the ideal spiritual leadership (*wilayah*). But while Shia see the Imams as related to the Prophet by blood and want them to be political leaders, for Sufis the *walis* are men chosen because of their spirituality and knowledge (though in reality many emphasise a lineage going back to the Prophet, even if it can be spiritual and does not have to be a blood lineage).[245]

Scripturalist Shia, too, could be harsh towards what they saw as Sufi transgressions, such as when they supported the indictment against a famous early Sufi, al-Hallaj, who was executed in Baghdad in 922. What drew the ire of Shii scholars was that al-Hallaj was well versed in Shiism and had according to some accounts been a Shii, then developed his own doctrine, including an idea of the Mahdi different from Shiism. The indictment of al-Hallaj came at him from a Shii point of view in a Sunni court.[246] Shiism and Sunnism delineated more clearly what was acceptable and what was not, and directed their ire not just at each other, but also at those outside the two emerging consensuses. When Sufis started to build major shrines for their foundational figures and visit them, Sunni traditionalists, especially Hanbalis, saw this as blasphemous, and denounced it (even though some Hanbalis were Sufis themselves).[247] While its relationship with Sufism is thus complex, Hanbalism positioned itself as a staunchly anti-Shii social movement, capitalising on Sunni anxiety during the Shii Century.

Like the Fatimids, the Buyids, too, institutionalised Shii public festivities. During Ashura, markets were closed and the population urged to participate. Another commemoration, Ghadir Khumm, was even more explicitly Shii, since it commemorates what Shia believe was Ali's designation as the Prophet Muhammad's successor. While travelling, according to Shii tradition, the Prophet is supposed to have taken the hand of Ali at a stopover near a pond called Ghadir Khumm on the caravan route between Mecca and Medina and there designated him as his successor. The Shia base Ali's right to rule on Hadith claiming that the Prophet designated Ali as his successor during the incidents described above. Sunnis by and large accept these Hadith as valid, but do not see Ghadir Khumm as a designation of Ali.[248] Shia point to the fact that versions of this are included in Sunni Hadith collections.[249] The public celebration of this day under the Buyids and the Fatimids signified a new Shii self-consciousness. These rituals were condemned by Sunnis in Baghdad, above all by Hanbalis, who would organise counter-festivals such as a Day of the Cave, *Yawm al-Ghar*, celebrating the day on which the Prophet took refuge in a cave with Abu Bakr.[250]

Hanbalis clashed with Shia and the authorities after the Buyid takeover in the 930s. They established a moral police to enact the Quranic notion of 'enjoining good and forbidding evil', and sought to stop visitation of the Imams' shrines, in response to which the Caliph al-Radi (r. 322–9/934–40) issued a decree in 323/935 condemning Hanbalis. After the arrest of a prominent Hanbali, his supporters were accused of setting fire to the market of the Shii al-Karkh quarter in Baghdad. A Shii mosque also became a scene of hostilities. Destroyed under the Caliph al-Muqtadir, it was rebuilt in 328/9 (939/40) and then partly destroyed by Hanbalis a year later, because of which some Hanbalis were arrested, and the mosque placed under guard. Crowds were cheered on by Hanbali preachers.[251] Hanafi Sunnis living in the largely Shii al-Karkh quarter, on the other hand, rarely participated in clashes.[252]

Hanbalis combined the doctrinal refutation of Shiism and the Mu'tazila with direct action against them and the Buyid-Abbasid polity. Hanbalis such as Ibn Batta (917–997) authored Sunni professions of faith or creed,[253] while Shia such as Ibn Babawayh (d. 991) wrote the first Shii creeds.[254] These creeds articulated what a believer had to embrace to be accepted as either Sunni or Shii. The Shii ones referred to the Imamate of the *Ahl al-Bayt*, and the Sunni ones the justness of the Rashidun Caliphs and the notion that the Companions of the Prophet should not be criticised, entrenching the positions at the heart of the Sunni–Shia divide.[255]

Tensions between Hanbalis, Shia, and Mu'tazila continued in early eleventh-century Baghdad. A key Shii cleric, Shaykh al-Mufid, for example, was twice made a scapegoat and temporarily banned from the city.[256] Competition could range from people from predominantly Sunni and Shii quarters building walls around their respective quarters in order to protect themselves against each other (the project was self-funded and the Shia seemed to have started it after they were ordered not to perform Ashura) to Sunni and Shii runners being cheered on by their respective factions in official sports competitions.[257] Political polarisation, doctrinal differentiation, and social conflict went hand in hand, as schools of jurisprudence became categories through which other socio-political divisions, such as struggles between urban quarters, or political rivalries, were expressed.[258]

As I have shown, the dividing line between Sunnism and Shiism took several centuries to form, and even when it was laid down in creeds and texts of law, in lived reality, and popular religiosity, and in more spiritual and philosophical writings, or Sufism, that line could be hard to find, let alone implement. Nonetheless, the rise of Zaydi, Twelver Shii, and Ismaili dynasties and the establishment of the only Shii Caliphate in history in the tenth and parts of the eleventh century, which have become known as the Shii Century, were a dramatic reversal of fortune for Shiism. The backing of Shii dynasties facilitated the institutionalisation of Shii ritual practice and the codification of law and doctrine, and the move from tight-knit communities centred around the Imams, to codified branches of Islam that could reproduce itself. The generally Shii atmosphere allowed all Shii strands to flourish, but the different branches and dynasties spent much time fighting one another, and no grand Shii alliance occurred. Instead, divisions within Shiism, between Twelver Shia, Ismailis, Zaydis, Alawites, and Druze became entrenched.[259] The Shii Century helped Shiism spread but did not lead to a Shii International.

The four Sunni schools of law had become established, and while there were still fundamental debates over the coming centuries about what it meant to be a Sunni, the basic tenets of the faith, and how it distinguishes itself doctrinally from Shiism and Ibadism, had become clearer, partly in response to the Shii political challenge. Given the weakness of the polities, sectarian identities and doctrine were seldom imposed on whole populations. An adherence to the *Ahl al-Bayt* deepened just as the foundation stones for many *Ahl al-Bayt* shrines were laid. Sectarian identity was, however, increasingly invoked for the purpose of political legitimisation. The identity politics of the Shii Century lead to a backlash expressed in Sunni terms. In Baghdad, Hanbalis would present themselves as defenders of Sunnism and allies of pro-Sunni Abbasid Caliphs. Soon, wielding sword and pen, Sunni rulers and clerics would push back against Shii powers, first in Iraq and then in Egypt and Syria.

2

Sunni Reassertion and the Crusades

When the Sunni Saljuqs took Baghdad in 1055, it symbolised the start of the end of the 'Shii Century', and when in 1171 Saladin deposed the Fatimids in Egypt, the last of the major Shii dynasties was supplanted by Sunni rule. From then on, until the rise of the Safavids in Iran in 1501, Shiism would cease to be the religion of the political powers of the day, with a few exceptions such as under a Mongol ruler and local Shii rulers. This period has been termed the 'Sunni Revival', or, in the words of a major historian of the Islamic world, 'The Victory of the Sunni Internationalism', for the rulers that took over power in Egypt, Syria, and Iraq legitimised their rule by delineating it from that of their predecessors, replaced institutionalised Shiism with institutionalised Sunnism, and connected their Sunni-led states.[1] Whether much of what rulers did can be described as 'Sunni' is debatable (as noted, the Shii Century likewise did not mean that Sunnism disappeared, or that top-down conversion was enforced, and lead to divisions amongst Shia). These rulers were Sunni, but the Sunni–Shia divide was not necessarily more significant than other fault lines, not least the dividing lines between the Muʻtazila and other Sunnis, for example, as struggles over the definition of Sunnism continued.[2] Muslims, both Sunni and Shii, were moreover confronted with the Crusaders, who conquered and occupied parts of Palestine and the Levant from the eleventh to the thirteenth century.

The First Crusade had started after Byzantine Emperor Alexios I lost territory to the Saljuq Sultan of Rum, Kilidsch Arslan I, and sought the help of fellow Christian powers in Europe. The Saljuqs were a leading family of a Turkic tribal federation that had largely converted to Hanafi Sunnism in the tenth century at the instigation of Sufi missionaries. Pope Urban II mobilised Christian Europe from 1095 onwards, culminating in the conquest of Jerusalem in 1099 and the establishment of a Christian settler state in the Levant. For two centuries, relations between Europe and the Middle East became dominated by the Crusades, religiously legitimised wars that shaped mutual perceptions, and profoundly affected religious and political dynamics. The last Crusader outpost fell in 1291, although smaller Crusades and Christian orders on Mediterranean islands tried for centuries to 're-conquer' the Holy Land.

At the outset of the First Crusade, Egypt was still ruled by a Shii Caliph, and Shii dynasties ruled parts of Syria, where much of the population espoused Shiism in one form or another. When the last Frankish possessions fell two centuries later, however, the Fatimid Empire had vanished, Turkic and Kurdish rulers were asserting Sunnism across Syria, Iraq, and Egypt, and Shiism was marginalised. Amidst the Crusades then, the Shii Century gave way to a Sunni reassertion. Much scholarship on the Crusades tends to focus on Christian–Muslim dynamics, seeing these two categories as homogeneous.[3] But Intra-Islamic relations between Sunni, Ismaili, or Twelver Shii rulers were as important as relations with the 'Franks'.

And on the Christian side, similar processes were under way. The Byzantine Emperor Alexios I had initially asked the Catholic Pope for help, and the various Christian denominations in the Levant were broadly sympathetic to the cause. Once the Catholic Crusaders had established the Kingdom of Jerusalem, they set their sights on the religious practices and doctrines of the Byzantines and Levantine Christians to integrate them into the Catholic Church and stamp out 'heresy' amongst them, much to the chagrin of Eastern Christians. The Orthodox Church was effectively taken over by the Catholic Church for the high period of the Crusades, and the centre of the Orthodox world, Constantinople, ransacked by Crusaders in 1204. While some Eastern Churches such as the Maronites eventually submitted to Rome, the Orthodox patriarchs re-established their authority after the defeat of the Crusaders at the hand of Saladin at the Battle of Hattin in 1187.[4] The confessional question remained alive amidst religiously legitimated war.

The threats of the Crusaders at times lead to greater Muslim unity. At other times, Sunnis would accuse Shia, Ismailis, Alawites, and Christians of cooperating with the Crusaders, casting doubt on their loyalty, narratives that would resurface in later periods. According to these narratives, the initially swift success of the Crusaders in taking Jerusalem is blamed on the collusion of Shii powers such as the Fatimids. That it took so long for Muslim forces to gather and expel the Crusaders is then explained with reference to divisions amongst Muslims.[5] The Muslim Holy War against the Crusaders, the *Jihad*, thus took place amidst rivalries between Sunni and Shii rulers.

At the end of the tenth and the beginning of the eleventh century, Buyid Shii rule was challenged by people like Mahmud Ibn Sebuktegin, the founder of the Ghaznavid dynasty in Afghanistan and Eastern Iran. He presented himself as defender of Sunnism and supporter of the Abbasid Caliphs and led campaigns into the Indian subcontinent. He waged war against Hindu kingdoms, and ended Ismaili rule in Multan in Sind, where Ismailis had established a mini-state around 958 on behalf of the Fatimids. Mahmud moved against them with force in 1005–6. Initially, he made their last ruler a tributary, but a few years later directly annexed the area and massacred the Ismailis.[6]

In Iran and Iraq, Mahmud launched a campaign against the Buyids and 'heretics' he believed to be associated with them, fighting Twelver Shia and Ismailis. When he took over control of Rayy from the Buyids in 1029, he burned the library and executed or expelled 'heretics' from the city. In a pronouncement to the Abbasid Caliph al-Qadir (r. 381/991–422/1031), he presented this as a success of Sunnism over the Shiism of the Buyids, whose allegedly weak rule he blamed for the spreading of 'heresies'. Al-Qadir in turn awarded him honorific titles for his defence of Sunnism, and Ibn Sebuktegin would become glorified in poetry as a Sunni hero and implanter of (Sunni) Islam in South Asia.[7] Ibn Sebuktegin was not the only ruler who through the dissolution of libraries and burning of manuscripts tried to establish the doctrinal views and historical narratives of his side and eliminate competing, often Shii, ones.[8]

As Ibn Sebuktegin presented himself as the defender of Sunnism, the Abbasid Caliph al-Qadir, still nominally under Buyid rule, took measures to strengthen the Caliphate and assert Sunnism. The Buyid ruler Baha al-Dawla, who had instated al-Qadir, had taken up residence in Shiraz, leaving al-Qadir more room for manoeuvre in Baghdad.[9] The Abbasids' embrace of Sunni traditionalism was as much a religious as a political strategy.[10] Al-Qadir had issued a decree in 1017 prohibiting discussions of Shii and Mu'tazili doctrines, recognising the Companions and the order of the first four Caliphs and banning criticism of Aisha and Muawiya. He made the Hanbali school official doctrine and together with the Hanbalis of Baghdad set up festivals for Sunnis to rival those of the Shia and encouraged the veneration of the Companions. His policies were continued by his successor al-Qaim (1031–75).[11]

The Hanbalis of Baghdad rallied around these pro-Sunni Abbasid Caliphs and, during the time of al-Qadir and al-Qaim, rose in prominence, which led to renewed doctrinal tensions and clashes with Shia.[12] There were also occasions on which Shia and Hanbalis cooperated to achieve political goals, although the chronicles would then describe this as a 'miracle'.[13] More often, the chronicles would depict the situation in Iraq like Ibn al-Athir: 'discord broke out in Wasit between the Sunnis and the Shiites, as is their normal practice'.[14]

Tensions also rose between supporters of different Sunni schools, who competed for government office, patronage, and popular support.[15] Nishapur, a key city in Khorasan, emerged as an especially important centre of scholarship and trade in the eleventh and twelfth centuries, and one in which, as in Iraq, the advocates of all Sunni schools of law, as well as Sufis and Shia, could actively proselytise. That could lead scholars to learn from and interact with each other, as in the case of al-Thalabi, who incorporated Sufi and Shii interpretations of the Quran. But Nishapur also became famous for the intense rivalries especially amongst the different Sunni schools, and in particular the Shafii and Hanafi ones.[16]

As part of his overall policy of discrediting Shiism and undermining the Fatimids, al-Qadir claimed that the Fatimids were not Alids, so essential to Fatimid legitimacy.[17] Their genealogy was vulnerable because they claimed there were several 'hidden imams' in the line between them and Muhammad bin Ismail, the son of Ismail with whom, as noted, the split from the Twelver Shia began, whose names they would not reveal. Non-Fatimid genealogists were not impressed. The Sunni Egyptian scholar al-Suyuti (d. 911/1505), for example, did not include the Fatimids in his *History of the Caliphs*, because he considered their claim to the Caliphate fraudulent, and because they had cursed the Companions.[18] He only briefly discusses the Fatimids under the heading 'the impious dynasty of the House of Ubayd', which is the way the Fatimids were described by those who denied them Alid lineage.[19]

Other North African historians such as Ibn Khaldun and al-Maqrizi, on the other hand, were more nuanced.[20] Indeed, al-Maqrizi (1364–1449), the probably most important source for the history of the Fatimids, dismissed attacks on Fatimid genealogy and doctrine, and encouraged his readers to see the doctrinal charges against the Fatimids as slanders by their enemies.[21]

Ibn Sebuktegin and al-Qadir started the replacement of Shii with Sunni rule amidst struggles over what it meant to be 'Sunni'. This intensified under the Turkic Saljuqs. The adoption of Sunnism by Turkic and Kurdish tribal groups, and their rule over large Muslim-inhabited regions, shifted the balance of power in favour of Sunnism, and broadened ethnic and linguistic diversity in the central lands of Islam.[22] Of course, ethnic ascriptions such as Arabs, Turks, Kurds, Persians, and Uzbek simplify heterogeneous groups that have only in later historiography emerged as fixed categories. In general, Turkic here means that they originally spoke variations of Turkic languages, rather than notions of 'purity' of lineage or blood (the same would apply to the other terms). As mentioned above, Saljuq advances would spark the First Crusade. By the early eleventh century, the Saljuq Tughril had conquered Nishapur and nearby cities, began to construct an empire, and in 1055 drove the Buyids out of Baghdad. Saljuq successor states would remain influential in the region for centuries.[23] Sectarian tensions surfaced before and after the Saljuq takeover. In 1053, for example, Turkish troops set fire to the markets in the largely Shii al-Karkh quarter after Sunni–Shia clashes during Muharram.[24]

After the Saljuqs had taken control of Baghdad, rival leaders sought to instrumentalise sectarian identity to rally substantial parts of the population around them, and garner support. The Turkish military leader al-Basasiri, who had Shii leanings, organised resistance to the Saljuqs after the deposition and imprisonment of the last Buyid leader, al-Malik al-Rahim. His rival, a Sunni leader, who had allegedly invited the Saljuqs to Baghdad, also invoked sectarian loyalties. With Fatimid support, al-Basasiri then managed to briefly take over Baghdad, and had the Fatimid Caliphs praised from Baghdad's pulpits. A Shii Caliph was thus briefly praised from the seat of the Sunni Caliphate before Sunni rule was re-established (as noted, the Buyids never established a Shii Caliphate, or abolished the Abbasid one, which now allowed the Abbasid Caliphs to align themselves with Turkic Sunni military elites instead).[25] Initially, Tughril seems to have entered Baghdad in 1055 under an agreement with the Abbasid Caliph, and presented himself as a defender of Sunnism, and of the Caliph. But when the Saljuq armies approached the city, the Abbasid Caliph intervened with Tughril on behalf of al-Malik al-Rahim, the last Buyid Amir. In time, the Abbasids would come to resent too direct Saljuq control.[26]

While the Saljuqs did not repress Shiism wholeheartedly, public life became Sunni. The Shii call to prayer, which specifically referred to Ali as the legatee of God, was replaced with the Sunni one, and Shii graffiti were painted over. A prominent Shii leader was killed and the house and books of the well-known Shii cleric Abu Jafar al-Tusi, who had played such a crucial role in codifying Shiism in previous decades, were burned. Al-Tusi himself had to leave the city and went to Najaf, where he became one of the first Shii clerics to teach near the shrine of Ali. The Shii al-Karkh quarter, which was not much affected by the initial Saljuq conquest, was attacked and Hanbali preachers roamed the streets proclaiming that 'heretics' should convert, urged on by senior officials. When Shia in al-Karkh tried to hold public Ashura processions, Sunnis mobilised against it.[27]

The figure that epitomises the Saljuqs' sponsoring of Sunnism was their Wazir Nizam al-Mulk (1018–92). Nizam al-Mulk founded a Shafii school, or *madrasa*, the Nizamiyya, while others established Hanafi *madrasas*. By the early thirteenth century, pan-Sunni teaching institutions were established in Baghdad that taught all the four Sunni schools—and entirely excluded the Shia.[28] The spreading of *madrasas* in this period was not only a state-organised effort to produce cadres for the 'Sunni' revival. Private donors, too, endowed *madrasas*, and the administrators and clerics had some autonomy in running the institutions. The wider spread of the *madrasa* system did lead to a clearer delineation between Sunni schools of jurisprudence on the one hand and, through the pan-Sunni teaching institutions, of what was Sunni and what was not. They were primarily meant to influence Sunnis, but implicitly undermined Shiism.[29]

Since Ismailis still retained state power in Egypt and strong transnational networks, they constituted a direct threat, and were singled out. Al-Ghazali (1058–1111), the foremost Sunni scholar of Baghdad, wrote an anti-Ismaili treatise at the request of the new Abbasid Caliph al-Mustazhir to undermine missionaries propagating the Fatimids.[30] Al-Ghazali and others opined that Ismailis were non-Muslims and could be killed.[31] A crucial scholar at the Nizamiyya *madrasa*, he wrote the *Revival of the Religious Sciences*, a detailed manual about religious practice.[32] By further outlining the 'proper' conduct of Sunni Muslims and penning treatises against the Ismailis, al-Ghazali gave ideological backing to the political project of the Saljuqs, and to the wider Sunni Revival.[33] After the overthrow of the Fatimids in 1171, Ismailis lost the support of a major state, and the centre of gravity in the Ismaili world shifted to Hasan al-Sabbah and mountain fortresses such as Alamut in Northern Iran. The population in that area may have been largely Shii before the Ismaili takeover. A split amongst Ismailis over succession after 1094 had led to two distinct branches, one tied directly to the Fatimids in Egypt, and the other, later called the Nizari Ismailis, centred around Alamut. The fall of the Fatimids increased the relative importance of the Nizari Ismailis, and their statelet at Alamut ensured Ismaili survival.[34]

Even though the Fatimids had sharply delineated themselves from Twelver Shia, the anti-Ismaili sentiment directed against them also affected the other Shia.[35] This can be seen in Nizam al-Mulk's *Book of Government*, one of the most famous examples of the Islamic Mirror of Princes genre. The book preceded Machiavelli's *The Prince* by four centuries, but has been compared to it because it covers similar ground. It is replete with references to the alleged threat posed to the ideal Sunni ruler by 'heretical' sects, especially Ismailis.[36] He argues that they should be dealt with harshly in order to protect the realm, and that one should be wary of 'employing men of perverse sects and evil doctrines', and cites Sunni leaders like Ibn Sebuktegin, who massacred Ismailis, as good examples.[37] Al-Mulk's distinction between Ismailis and Twelver Shia is primarily semantic.[38] He portrayed critics of Aisha as heretics and enemies of the state.[39] Some Shii authors in turn toned down criticism of Aisha, for fear of retribution.[40]

Still, even the architects of the Sunni Revival could personally adopt nuanced policies. Nizam al-Mulk and the Saljuq Sultan Malik Shah themselves gave their daughters to Shii notables in marriage, appointed Shii Wazirs, and maintained local Shii rulers so long as they paid tribute.[41] Turkish soldiers listened to tales about Ali, and Shii officials could bribe Sunni *ulama* to state that they were Sunni not Shia if they faced trouble.[42] The early Saljuqs may even have originally been influenced by Ismailism, and there are reports of individual rulers courting conversion to Shiism for political gains.[43] Indeed, the Saljuq period in Iran saw not only the reassertion of Sunnism but also the entrenching of Sufism and Shiism.[44]

The rulers of Tabaristan, the Bavanids, for example, acted as Saljuq vassals but sponsored Twelver Shiism. And they, too, proved pragmatic. After the Alids and their Shii followers in the town of Astarabad had attacked Shafiis and their *Qadi* in 1159, the Shii ruler took the side of the Shafiis, cancelled the Alids' pensions, and reinstated the Shafii *Qadi*.[45] Despite the Sunni atmosphere, the Saljuqs and other rulers of this period were opportunistic actors whose tendency to side with one school over another was temporarily and spatially specific.[46] They institutionalised Sunnism more strongly but they did not instigate a whole-scale purge of Shiism.

Indeed, some Shii authors published works that relied on Sunni Hadith and Quran commentaries to bolster the Shii argument. The Iraqi Ibn al-Bitriq (d. 600/1203), for example, wrote polemical works that formed the basis for larger volumes that collected all Sunni Hadith supporting Shii claims for the *Ahl al-Bayt*'s right to rule.[47] Rayy, an important trading town near modern-day Tehran, was home to most major Islamic schools.

Shii influence had been strengthened through the Caspian Zaydis, and the Buyids, who ruled the area in the late tenth and early eleventh century. When Ibn Sebuktegin conquered the area, however, in 1029, he, as noted, persecuted Ismailis and other Shia, and burned their libraries. The Saljuqs, who took over Ray in 1041, adopted a more equitable policy, favouring Hanafi and Shafii Sunnism, but persecuting Shiism less harshly. Political tensions and doctrinal debates divided the city into three major urban regions: One each inhabited primarily by Hanafis, by Shafiis, and by Shia.[48] In the second half of the twelfth century, different Saljuq rulers vied for supremacy, and sought to play out these three major groups against each other, leading to urban violence and further polemics.[49]

In 1160, a local Shii convert to Sunnism anonymously published an anti-Shii tract. *The Vices of the Recusants/Rejectionists*, the latter employing the pejorative term rejectionist for Shia, circulated widely and rapidly, and was read out and discussed at public gatherings in the city.[50] A few years later, it spurred the local Shii scholar Abd al-Jalil Razi Qazwini to react by publishing his *Defects of the Malefactors (Sunnis) in Refutation of the 'Vices of the Recusants'*, generally abbreviated as *Kitab al-Naqd*. An assertion of Shiism, it sought to build bridges with Sunnis, especially Hanafis, who remained prominent in Rayy, and the rationalist schools of thought, hoping that pro-Alid sentiments amongst Sunnis could lead to a rapprochement (while criticising the Hanbalis). The book was sponsored by the leader of the Alids in Rayy, and showed how even limited sources of patronage allowed for the continuation of inner-Islamic debates after the upending of Shii rule. The *Kitab al-Naqd* asserted Shii doctrine and political theory in a Persian more accessible than that of classical theological works to give lay Persian-speaking Shia arguments in debates with Sunnis.[51] Rayy became a microcosm for the wider struggles for leadership in Islam.

As noted, Ismailis were treated especially harshly in this period, but they would also fight back. Both Malik Shah and Nizam al-Mulk died in 1092, the former probably poisoned, the latter stabbed. While theories abound and both are suspected of having had a hand in each other's murder, many believe Nizam al-Mulk's death was the work of an Ismaili assassin. Other theories blame the Abbasids or even a conspiracy between them and the Ismailis.[52]

The deaths of these two central figures and the lack of a clear succession plan gave the Abbasid Caliphs the opportunity to re-establish authority, and, in order to differentiate themselves from the Sunni-minded Saljuqs, they did this by emphasising pan-Islam and seeking a rapprochement with the Shia.[53] These efforts culminated in the project of the Abbasid Caliph al-Nasir (1180–1225), who moved against the Saljuqs and sought to unite the different Islamic schools under his leadership. To that end, he maintained good relations with Sufis and Shia, appointing Shii officials and renovating Shii shrines. He even engaged Ismailis, who had been anathema because of the political and doctrinal threat they posed and their assassinations. But after the downfall of the Fatimids, and a pro-Sunni turn amongst the Nizari Ismailis, whose leader Rukn al-Din Hasan III (r. 1210–21) publicly converted to Sunnism and invited Sunni clerics to visit the fortress at Alamut, a temporary alliance was possible.[54]

Al-Nasir sought to strengthen the position of the Caliph as spiritual and political leader of all Muslims, and to do so also had to secure the allegiance of Baghdad's large Shii population. He is, for example, mentioned in an inscription as the protector of the Shii sanctuary at the al-Askari shrine in Samarra, where the twelfth Shii Imam, allegedly disappeared.[55] Sunni writers sometimes accused him of having Shii inclinations. To boost his legitimacy, he circulated a work on Hadith written by himself and integrated Sunni and Shii youth into chivalry youth.[56] This gave greater visibility to these groups, which had long played a significant role in Baghdad. While they were often organised in separate Sunni and Shii youth organisations, they at times served to lessen communal tensions by leading mixed ceremonies.[57] Al-Nasir's attempt to free the Caliph from political tutelage, and establish a pan-Islamic Caliphate was ultimately cut short by the Mongols, who in the first decades of the thirteenth century conquered more and more of Eurasia from their original strongholds in Central Asia.[58]

The legacy of al-Nasir's ecumenical tendencies can be seen in the built environment, and in a pilgrimage guide he commissioned that included sites across the Islamic world without attribution to different confessions. It incorporated the shrines of the *Ahl al-Bayt* as well as sites associated with the Companions most detested by Shia. The guide was compiled by the traveller al-Harawi (d. 1225), who left graffiti at the many shrines that he described in his book. He was confessionally blind when leaving his mark or recording specific sites: he wanted to include them all.[59] Many of these sites originated in the Shii Century, but were later patronised by Sunni rulers. In Aleppo, for example, *Ahl al-Bayt* shrines were built by the Twelver Shii Hamdanids, who as noted had taken control of Aleppo and the Jazira in 944. One of their Amirs, Sayf al-Dawla (d. 967), during a daydream in

351/962–3 apparently rediscovered a tomb said to belong to a little-known (and disputed) son of Hussain and had a mausoleum built over it.[60]

Despite the originally Shii context in which this shrine and others were founded, later Sunni dynasties, including leading figures of the Sunni Revival, expanded and supported them. This may have been done to appease Shii populations and to claim the *Ahl al-Bayt* for Sunnism.[61] A mausoleum related to the Battle of Karbala was erected on a hill outside the old city of Aleppo, commemorating a stone on which Hussain's head is said to have rested after it was severed from his body.[62] This shrine complex was built during the reign of al-Salih Ismail (569/1174–577/1181) as a collaborative Sunni–Shia effort, and inscriptions include a list of all the twelve Shii Imams with their titles, a Sunni invocation of the Rashidun Caliphs, and the names of Sunni rulers who supported the project (including Saladin and his successors).[63] In sum, Sunni rulers patronised *Ahl al-Bayt* shrines, which became pan-Islamic sites of worship and collective memory, while Shii notables and Alids remained key in their foundation, management, and upkeep.[64] And besides, Sunni rulers established new sites in honour of Companions of the Prophet, more recent Sunni scholars, or Old Testament Prophets.[65]

That such Sunni patronage of *Ahl al-Bayt* shrines occurred during the Sunni Revival undermines—yet again—simplistic and antagonistic narratives about the nature of Sunni–Shia relations and may have been designed to achieve unity amongst Muslims against the Crusaders.

For the rise of Turkic Sunni dynasties was deeply intertwined with the Crusades. Throughout the eleventh century, Turkmen warriors and nomads such as the Saljuqs of Rum (Konya) and the later Ottomans established principalities in northwest Iran and Anatolia, further converting their populations to Islam. A militant spirit grew amongst them that focused on fighting the Christian Byzantine Empire and expanding the realm of Islam. Sufis combining elements of Sunnism and Shiism flourished in this milieu and were key in that fight.[66]

Shii powers, too, fought against the Crusaders. The Hamdanids in Aleppo and the Banu Ammar in Tripoli were on the frontline, and the Fatimids, who initially controlled Jerusalem, spearheaded the effort against Byzantium and the Crusaders after some initial hesitation. Usama Ibn Munqidh (1095–1188), the scion of a local Shii ruling family from Shaizar (Casarea) in Syria, the Banu Munqidh, wrote a famous autobiography detailing his interactions with and fights against the Crusaders.[67]

How complex the situation was can be seen in the Levantine port city of Tripoli. The Shii Ismaili Banu Ammar, who took over control of Tripoli in 1070, patronised Shiism and established a large library. Originally of North African Fatimid origin, the Banu Ammar tried to safeguard their autonomy through shifting alliances with the Fatimids, the Abbasids, and the Crusaders.[68] Already before that, many of Tripoli's inhabitants were Shia. The travel writer Nasir Khusraw visited in 1047, finding that 'the people of this city are all Shiites, and the Shiites have built nice mosques in every land'.[69]

When the Crusaders first appeared outside the gates of Tripoli, its rulers agreed to pay a large ransom and send guides and provisions. But after the Crusaders attacked Tripoli again, the Banu Ammar refused to cooperate. In return, Tripoli was put under years-long siege from 1101/2 until 1109, and in the process of which the Crusaders built a fortress next to the old town. Fakhr al-Mulk Banu Ammar then appealed for help to Sunni rulers in Damascus and Baghdad rather than to the Fatimids in Cairo. The inhabitants of Tripoli, on the other hand, wrote letters of appeal to the Fatimids, who sent a fleet and reasserted control. The Fatimids considered Fakhr al-Mulk's appeal to Sunni rulers an act of treason, and so he had to live out his life at Sunni courts, and some of his family was arrested. In any case, Fatimid assistance was not enough to prevent Tripoli from falling to the Crusaders in 1109 and Shii and Sunni authors alike portrayed Fakhr al-Mulk as a hero.[70]

The Aleppan Hamdanids became a tribute-paying Byzantine protectorate from 969 onwards, and in subsequent decades oscillated between them and the Fatimids.[71] In 1015, the Fatimids conquered Aleppo but left nominal control of the city to the Twelver Shii Mirdasids (1024–79/80), who had to navigate the complicated political landscape of the time. In 1070, they had the prayer read in the name of the Abbasid Caliph al-Qaim and of the Saljuq Sultan Alp Arslan, but the inhabitants of Aleppo, still mainly Shii, disapproved. After the defeat of the last Mirdasid by a local Saljuq, the town was no longer strong enough to resist Crusader attacks and sieges.[72]

It is in this context that the judge and head of the Shii community in Aleppo, Ibn al-Khashshab, in 1100 travelled to Baghdad to rally the Abbasid Caliph against the Crusaders. Aided by local Sufis and merchants, he organised a demonstration in the Caliph's mosque during Friday prayer. The Caliph was apparently furious but promised help, although substantial military support did not materialise. A Shii leader thus spurred a Sunni Caliph into action in the face of the Crusader threat. Ibn al-Khashshab would continue to organise Aleppan resistance, and he, too, has been painted a hero in Arab historiography, not least for his role in a crucial 1119 battle between Aleppans and the Crusaders of Antioch.[73] Yet Ibn al-Khashshab was an outspoken enemy of Ismailis, and legitimised their mass execution in Aleppo in 1113 on the charge that they had cooperated with the Crusaders. In turn, an Ismaili assassinated Ibn al-Khashshab in 1125.[74]

Subsequent rulers would embark on a double-pronged campaign to defeat the Crusaders and strengthen Sunnism against Shiism. Already Imad al-Din Zangi, ruler of Mosul, and founder of the Zangid dynasty, who took Aleppo in 1128, built Sunni *madrasas* and Sufi lodges to spur moral renewal and defeat internal 'heresies'. His son Nur al-Din, who succeeded him as ruler of Aleppo in 1146, at the outset, appeased the Shia of Aleppo, according to one source allowing the Shii call to prayer and visiting a local Shii shrine. Shortly thereafter, however, he would ban the call and suppress the Aleppan Shia. In 1157, then, he would quell a Shii revolt just as he was fighting the Crusaders. When a previous ruler had tried to build a Sunni *madrasa* in Aleppo in 1122, Shii resistance managed to halt the project, and some Shia burned down the building. But under Nur al-Din, Shii resistance was broken, and several Sunni *madrasas* were built. Half a decade after Aleppan Shia called upon the Sunni Caliph for help, they were themselves purged by a new Sunni ruler. During the reign of Nur al-Din's son, al-Salih Ismail, the Aleppan Shia were still able to make their support for the ruler contingent on him accepting the Shii prayer. But the prominence of Shiism waned, although a small community survived and maintained charitable endowments.[75]

Nur al-Din was an integral figure of the Sunni Revival. In 1154, he captured Damascus, and then ruled over much of Syria, and was accepted as ruler by his relatives in Mosul as well. He now set sights on the remaining Crusader outposts, and on the Fatimids.

Talai Ibn Ruzzik, a Twelver Shii who had become Wazir of the Fatimids in 1154, reached out to Nur al-Din to establish an alliance against the Crusaders, but Nur al-Din was not interested.[76] The Fatimid Caliph then struck an alliance in 1167 with the Crusader King Amalric.[77] In his description of the negotiations between the Kingdom of Jerusalem and Egypt, William of Tyre, the twelfth-century chronicler and Crusader historian, discusses the beliefs of the Fatimids, emphasising the divide between them and the Abbasids.[78] He thought that Shiism was closer to Christianity than Sunnism (although he does not explain why it would be closer, except emphasising the alleged 'superstitio' of the Sunna).[79] Perhaps it was the idea of the Messiah. His writings give a rare insight into how the Crusaders saw inner-Islamic dynamics. He explains the visit of a Fatimid delegation and a suggestion of a treaty with the Crusader leaders with the rivalry between Fatimids and Saljuqs.[80] When Fatimids and Saljuqs occasionally allied themselves against the Crusaders, William thought that it was the threat of the Crusaders, and disdain for them, that brought them together.[81]

His portrayal of the Fatimids is sympathetic, but the Crusader views of the Ismailis would deteriorate after Ismailis assassinated Crusader leaders and lost power.[82] In the fanciful stories of the Crusader historians, and in Sunni heresiography, they became hashish-smoking, blood-thirsty killers of dubious beliefs. They described Ismailis as *Hashishi*, using a term, which was probably a pejorative reference to Syrian Ismailis that invoked low-class people of lax morals rather than actual hashish smokers, to describe them as *assassins*.[83]

Nur al-Din would eventually send an army to Egypt, led by Saladin, one of his officers from the Kurdish clan of the Ayyubids (the name by which his heirs would come to be known), who would soon take power. Saladin first appointed himself Fatimid Wazir in 1169, expanding his control over the state apparatus and slowly but surely replacing Ismaili rituals, prayers, and judges with Sunni ones. He ended the Fatimid reign from within even if he, at least nominally, accepted the suzerainty of the Fatimid Caliph. Two years later, in 1171, Saladin used the death of the Fatimid Caliph to abolish the Fatimid Caliphate. Friday prayers now honoured the Abbasid Caliphs in Baghdad, the Sultan Nur al-Din, and the Rashidun Caliphs. Simultaneously, Saladin established more Sunni *madrasas* and supported Sufis, who were important in the Jihad against the Crusaders. One Sunni law college was established near the mausoleum of al-Shafii, a popular site of visitation that Saladin expanded, further symbolising the connection between the new rulers and Sunnism.[84] A Sunni *madrasa* was built on the site of the old Fatimid palaces, while many Fatimid buildings were reappropriated.[85] Initially primarily supporting Shafiism, the Ayyubids then moved towards a pan-Sunni policy of supporting all four schools.[86] Saladin had a group of jurists teach Sunni law at the Hussain shrine in Cairo, to where the Fatimids had moved what they believed to be Hussain's head. He appropriated the Hussain shrine to disassociate it from Shiism, but veneration of Hussain continued.[87] And the widely accepted shrine visitation that the Sufis practised and propagated, constituted another form of state-sanctioned Islamic practice, and contributed to the spread of Sufism.[88]

When Nur al-Din died in 1174, Saladin marched on Damascus and became ruler of Syria and Egypt. In the 1180s, he further expanded his realm, paving the way for the formation of a large Muslim army that would move towards the Frankish possessions in the Levant, conquering Jerusalem in 1187. The Muslim conquest of Jerusalem was the most significant defeat of the Crusaders, and would lead to the third Crusade 1189–92, a joint effort of England, France, and the Holy Roman Empire to retake Jerusalem (although unsuccessful in that endeavour, the campaign consolidated the Crusader states in Cyprus and along the Syrian coast).[89] In Damascus and after establishing control over Aleppo in 1183, Saladin took a more appeasing stance towards Shia than his predecessor Nur al-Din.[90]

The heirs of Saladin, who died in 1193, the Ayyubids, ruled over Egypt and the Western Fertile Crescent until Mamluk soldiers overthrew them in the mid-thirteenth century. The Mamluks were the slave soldiers of the last effective Ayyubid ruler of Egypt. Since Saljuqs and Mamluks were of Turkic origin, and Saladin a Kurd, these ruling classes faced an ethnic barrier with the largely Arab population, a barrier that a sponsoring of Sunnism was meant to overcome.[91] Shii-leaning populations did not feature prominently in this ruling bargain.

In Sunni-minded historiography, intra-Islamic divisions have been blamed for the initial failure of the Muslims to repel the Crusaders.[92] But sectarian identity did not dictate alliance formation. Some Twelver Shia and the Fatimids were fighting proactively against the Crusaders but there were also Shia and local Sunni rulers that sealed truces or temporary alliances with them.[93] The legendary leader of the Ismailis in Syria, Rashid al-Din Sinan, for example, maintained good relations with the Crusaders because he saw them as lesser enemies than Nur al-Din and Saladin. The Syrian Ismailis clashed with the Crusader order that controlled the Krak des Chevaliers fort and to whom they had to pay tribute, and in 1173 sent an emissary to King Amalric to seek a formal rapprochement. But the Crusaders, who would have lost revenue under this arrangement, had nothing of it and killed the Ismaili emissaries.[94] William of Tyre reported that, in 1173, the Syrian Ismailis offered to convert to Christianity in return for tax exemptions, which contributed to his positive portrayal of the Ismailis at the time.[95] This promise of conversion, however, is dismissed by pro-Ismaili historians as fiction. In any case when both Ismailis and Nur al-Din and his successors, the Zangids, came under attack by Saladin, the former foes forged an alliance against him. When the Ismaili dynasty fell in 1174, Ismaili assassins tried to kill Saladin. After being unsuccessful twice, they made common cause with him to fight the Crusaders.[96]

In the Levant, the disappearance of Sunni rule, first through the Fatimids and the Buyids and later through the Crusades, gave Shii-leaning communities space to consolidate themselves. Local Shii historiography maintains that Arabs in the hills behind Tyre, especially from the Amila tribe, pledged loyalty to the Alids from the 650s onwards. The Amila tribe, which had entered the area before the Muslim conquests, gave the surrounding area its name—Mount Amil, Jabal Amil, the hills south of Mount Lebanon.[97] Nasir Khusraw, the travel writer, described the inhabitants of Tyre in 1047 as 'mostly Shii', though he also noted a Sunni judge in town.[98]

They, as well as Druze and Alawites, were minor players in the unfolding struggle. For significant periods, they nominally came under Frankish rule, but retained some autonomy. Fearing pan-Islamic loyalties however, the Franks were keen to cut off communication of the mountain communities, such as the Twelver Shia in Jabal Amil, and the Druze, with Damascus.[99] The mountain communities were quick to switch sides when Frankish rule became tenuous. There is not much evidence of Shii resistance to Frankish rule in Jabal Amil and Shia from Palestine also fled to Jabal Amil.[100] A Damascus chronicle of the 1150s mentioned that Muslims from Jabal Amil were soldiers of the Franks.[101] The Shii inhabitants around the Tebnine/Toron Crusader castle, an important waypoint on the road from the port of Tyre to Damascus at the heart of Jabal Amil, seem to have lived in harmony with the Franks, something the Sunni travel writer Ibn Jubayr denounced in 1184.[102] Ibn Jubayr, critical of Shiism and Ismailism, praised Saladin instead.[103] That local communities would come to terms with Crusader rule was the norm. The Crusader elites were linguistically, religiously, and ethnically detached from the bulk of the population. The people that lived in the towns, administered the possessions, and worked on the fields of the Crusader principalities were generally left to their own devices if they paid tribute (even the various local Christian Churches largely survived the Crusades with their specificities intact).[104]

Saladin seized Jabal Amil in July 1187, and accepted a local Shii, Husam al-Din Bishara, who patronised Shii scholars, as chief. From 1187 up until 1291, when Tyre surrendered to the Mamluks, Jabal Amil was semi-autonomous between the Franks on the coast and Damascus. At times, Shia seem to have attacked the Franks, at others joined forces with them.[105] Shia were the majority in Jabal Amil, the Beqaa valley, and in parts of Mount Lebanon that later became Maronite. They would periodically suffer repression, but develop a learned tradition.[106] In the Kisrawan hills between Beirut and Byblos, Shiism found some adherents, and Alawite missionaries proselytised in the mountains behind Latakia and Tartus and into the Kisrawan.[107] Some Alawites were killed during the First Crusade, others came nominally under the control of Crusader principalities along the Syrian coast.[108] In the first half of the thirteenth century, a new Alawite leader, al-Makzun al-Sinjari, reinvigorated the community, and delineated its boundaries more clearly.[109]

While Twelver Shiism and Ismailism spread far and wide, not least towards Iran and the Indian Subcontinent, Alawites and Druze would only survive in these Syrian coastal regions. With their beliefs that depart from what was becoming Sunni, Twelver Shii and Ismaili mainstream, they would likely have been suppressed had they inhabited more central locations or been subject to states that were investing more resources into the homogenisation of religious beliefs of its subjects. After the Shii Century, the Crusades allowed them to entrench themselves.

Slowly, the whole region was coming to terms with the fact that, instead of being a passing phenomenon, the Crusaders were religious fanatics intent on staying in Jerusalem and the Levant. Both Sunni and Shii rulers fought against them to varying degrees, with the Fatimids, from whom the Crusaders initially took Jerusalem in 1099, initially taking the lead. Ultimately, Sunni rulers such as Saladin would defeat the Fatimids and the Crusaders, and so the period has by Sunni historians been described as a second golden age of Muslim power, and Nur al-Din Zangi and Saladin as heroes. These Sunni sources also downplayed a Shii presence especially in Syria before the Sunni Revival, and suppressed Shii sources or narrators.[110] Some argued that strengthening resolve against external enemies should also involve the punishment or conversion of those deemed heretic, like Ismailis and Shia. As such, a reversal in fortunes saw Sunnism in ascendance over Shiism (and as noted largely ended the political aspirations of the Ismailis).

The Crusades lead both to Sunni–Shia unity and polarisation. What had been remote mountain regions and peripheral coastal areas were transformed into religious and ideological battlegrounds, contested by the

Fatimids, the Crusaders, Ismaili, Druze, Twelver Shii and Alawite missionaries, and the Sunni Zangids and Ayyubids, and later Mamluks and Mongols. As Muslims and Christians in the Southern Mediterranean came to terms with a wave of religiously legitimised conquests, they outlined more sharply what they deemed correct belief and what they saw as heresy.[111]

The Sunni re-centring in the face of external threat and internal contestation undermined Shiism ideologically and institutionally. A set of Sunni beliefs, traditions, jurisprudence, views of history, became institutionalised to produce Sunni jurists and texts. Sunnism henceforth had the means and intellectual capability to denounce other interpretations of Islam and keep them outside of the Sunni consensus, and to reproduce itself.[112]

After the defeat of the last Crusader outposts in the thirteenth century (Tripoli, the last major Crusader state, fell in 1289) by the Sunni Mamluks, Sunni rulers desired to punish those whom they deemed to have cooperated with the Franks. And eventually, a new force would emerge from the steppes of Central Asia. This new power set sights on the seat of Sunni spiritual authority—the Abbasid Caliphate in Baghdad—and many Sunnis regarded it as an existential threat. Some Shia, in contrast, sensed an opportunity to regain the patronage of a major power.

3

Polemics and Confessional Ambiguity

The expulsion of the Crusaders coincided with dramatic political changes, and the emergence of a new invading force: the Mongols. Their conquests of Iran, Anatolia, and the Eastern Arab lands in the thirteenth and fourteenth centuries reshuffled the cards between Sunnism and Shiism, and Sufism (and eliminated the Ismailis as a major political force). They upended pre-existing institutions and political arrangements and the Middle East became polarised between two major powers, Mongols on the one side, and Mamluks, who portrayed themselves as defenders of Sunnism, on the other. It is in the context of that rivalry that Sunni and Shii clerics penned some of the most elaborate, and vicious, polemics against the relative other side. At the same time, everyday religiosity was often confessionally ambiguous.[1]

By the 1250s, both the seat of the Sunni Caliphate, Baghdad, and the Ismaili stronghold, Alamut, were sacked by the Mongols, then still non-Muslims, and many of their inhabitants put to the sword. The end of the Abbasid Caliphate gave Shiism more room to flourish. Put succinctly, while the centre of Sunnism, Baghdad, was ravaged by the Mongols, the intellectual centre of Shiism at the time, Hilla, submitted to the Mongols and was consequently not devastated.[2] Sunnis were quick to blame Shia for collusion with the Mongols. And as some Mongol rulers started to patronise Shiism, Sunni scholars penned the most thorough anti-Shii polemics to date.[3]

The Mamluks were, as noted, initially slave soldiers of Turkic origin who converted to a nominally Sunni Islam. The term *Mamluk* refers in Arabic to 'one who is owned'. And while their political fortunes would carry them very far from these origins indeed, the term stuck. They conquered the last

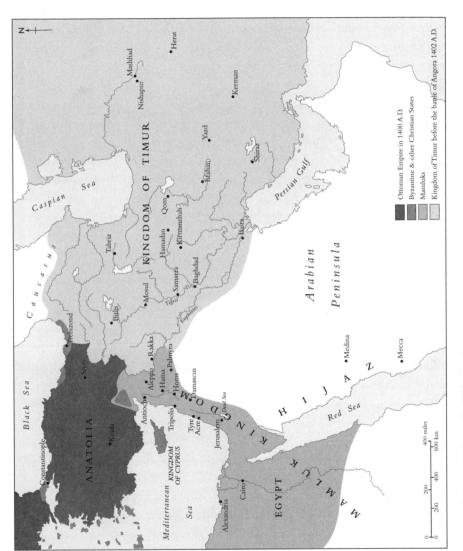

N

Black Sea

Constantinople

ANATOLIA
Konia

Mediterranean
Sea

Antioch
Aleppo Rakka
Hama Palmyra
Tripolis Homs
Tyre Damascus
Acre
Jerusalem

Sivas

Trebizond

Bidis

Mosul

Tabriz

Samarra
Tigris
Baghdad

Euphrates

KINGDOM OF TIMUR

Caspian Sea

Nishapur

Mashhad

Herat

Kerman

Qom
Hamadan
Kirmanshah
Isfahan
Yazd

Shiraz

Persian Gulf

Basra

Caucasus

KINGDOM
OF CYPRUS

MAMLUK KINGDOM

Dead Sea

Alexandria

Cairo

EGYPT

Red Sea

H I J A Z

Medina

Mecca

Arabian
Peninsula

Ottoman Empire in 1400 A.D.
Byzantine & other Christian States
Mamluks
Kingdom of Timur before the battle of Angora 1402 A.D.

0   200   400 miles
0   200   400   600 km

4. Mamluks and Mongols (Ilkhanate), c. 1400 AD

Crusader outpost, and in the mid-thirteenth century overthrew Saladin's heirs, the Ayyubids, whose dynasty's legitimacy in part rested on Saladin's role in the fight against the Crusaders. After two centuries of Crusader control, the Mamluks re-established Sunni rule in the Levant. Simultaneously, the Mongols made inroads into the central Islamic lands. In 1258, Hulegu, a grandson of Genghis Khan—whose reign established the full extent of Mongol power—captured Baghdad, hitherto centre of the Sunni world and which would henceforth be ruled by subsequent Mongol dynasties.[4]

The Mongols, who quickly established control over Iran, Iraq, and much of the Eastern Islamic lands, rivalled the Mamluks, with their base in Cairo and control over much of Syria. The two powers clashed in Syria, which the Mongols invaded repeatedly (and where they executed the last Ayyubid ruler). To bolster their legitimacy, the Mamluks, starting with Sultan Baybars, welcomed refugees from the Abbasid family and invested them as Caliphs in Cairo from 1261 onwards. Once in Cairo, the Caliph's first act was to hand over all executive power to the Sultan. This symbolised the Mamluks' claim to be the new, legitimate Sunni rulers, supported by Caliphal authority, even though the role of the Abbasids was symbolic, and they were not recognised beyond Egypt.[5]

The Mamluks ruled over the most significant sites for Sunnis and patronised Mecca, Medina, and Jerusalem. Sultan Baybars established a judicial system with a judge each for the four Sunni schools of law. This was a departure from previous policy: under the Fatimids, the Twelver Shii and the four Sunni schools had occasionally been used in the legal system alongside the Ismaili one, and under the Ayyubids the Shafii school was prominent. The Mamluks entrenched a legalistic Sunnism based on the four schools that excluded Shiism.[6] This may have contributed to the Mongols' disdain for dynasties that legitimised themselves through reference to a Caliph, and may have made them more open to look for alternative Islamic sources of authority, such as Shiism.[7]

Mongols and Mamluks were military elites that hailed from the Eurasian Steppe. Both were converts to Islam—or in the process of conversion, in the case of the Mongols—and ruled over largely sedentary, and by now predominantly Muslim populations from whom they were ethnically and linguistically alienated. Their religious policies, patronage of religious scholarship and sites, and dedication to the Islamic cause, varied considerably, however, but were all meant to bring some cohesion to the populations under their control, and strengthen bonds of loyalty. The Mamluks settled and made Cairo their capital. They were slaves who had been brought as children from outside of the territory of Islam, and been converted as part of their education. Once they had taken political control, they espoused Sunnism, and legitimised their wars against Mongols, Crusaders, and Shia religiously, and encouraged Christian conversions to Islam.[8]

When they embarked on their epic conquest of Eurasia in the early thirteenth century, the belief of the Mongols had been syncretistic. Initially, Mongol rulers had been Shamans, Buddhists, Christians, or generally 'flexible' in their religious beliefs, and had patronised different Holy Men. Christian missionaries tried, but ultimately largely failed, to convert Mongols to Christianity. Initially seen as a major threat, in the late thirteenth century, as the Mongols were defeating the foremost Sunni powers, views of the Mongols in Europe and amongst the Crusaders became more favourable, although a grand alliance between the Crusaders and the Mongols never transpired, and the Mongol incursions into Syria coincided with the waning of Crusader influence.[9] Initially a coalition of different nomadic groups, the Mongols allied with each other for the sake of conquest. After the death of their Great Khan, Möngke, in 1259, they split into four rivalling branches, and much of their energy was consumed with in-fighting. The Ilkhanate, and the Golden Horde branches, are most relevant for the Islamic world. Hulegu Khan inherited the Middle Eastern part (Iran, parts of Iraq, Azerbaijan, Armenia, parts of Afghanistan and Anatolia) of the Mongol Empire after Möngke's death, and he and his successors became known as the Ilkhans (meaning subordinate Khans, indicating their initial deference to the central Mongol Khan Möngke). The Golden Horde, a separate Mongol Khanate, would try to undermine the Ilkhanate's Middle Eastern Empire, and in that endeavour even temporarily allied itself with the Mamluks. Rule over largely Muslim populations spurred their engagement with Islam. They conquered vast territories, establishing courts in numerous places, but remained semi-nomadic.

Sufis had long been active amongst the Mongols, and inspired some conversions. Mahmud Ghazan Khan (d. 1304) was the first major Mongol ruler of the Ilkhanate branch to convert to Islam in 1295.[10] Amongst the so-called Golden Horde Khanate, it was Özbek Khan (1313–41), who adopted Islam as state religion. Officially Sunni, he also employed Twelver Shia at court.[11]

When the Mongols converted, the question as to which branch of Islam to embrace posed itself. Given their rule over large Muslim populations and the former seat of the Sunni Caliphate, this was a crucial question, and one most pertinent to the Ilkhans that ruled these areas. Hanafi, Shafii, and Shii scholars tried to convince the Mongols of the superiority of their school of jurisprudence, a process that intensified under the Ilkhan Uljaytu (r. 703–716/1304–16).[12] Uljaytu's religious identity shifted over time. He is said to have embraced Christianity, Buddhism, Hanafi, and Shafii Sunnism before turning to Shiism in 1310.[13] This may have been influenced by the Shii scholar ʿAllama al-Hilli (1250–1325), and would draw the ire of Sunni scholar Ibn Taymiyya.[14] The two sought to strengthen the boundaries between adherents of the different schools and spur the powers of the day into action on their side. To understand how they came to play the role of sectarian identity entrepreneurs we'll turn to how the Mamluks established their rule in Syria and the Levant, and what this meant for the non-Sunni populations there.

In the Levant, Maronites, Druze, Alawites, and Shia were integrated into the Mamluk realm without much difficulty. They had become as we've seen quite resilient throughout the Crusader period and were sufficiently established to cope with Mamluk authority. Clan chiefs were skilled at interacting with imperial authorities and, in the case of the Druze, for example, often claimed to be Sunni. At the same time, most day-to-day interactions of commoners in rural contexts were with members of the same community, and a local elite dealt with taxation and other administrative matters.[15] In the Kisrawan district, located northeast of Beirut, the mixed population had not rebelled seriously against the Franks, and its loyalty was hence suspect after the Frankish withdrawal in 1291. The Mamluks undertook three campaigns in the Kisrawan, in 1292, 1300, and 1305 at a time of intense rivalry with the Mongols.

The 1292 expedition was a disaster. Returning from a victorious campaign in Armenia, Sultan al-Malik al-Ashraf dispatched a part of his army to the Kisrawan because of the help that the Kisrawanis had allegedly given to the Franks. Locals decimated his troops.[16] The cause for the 1300 campaign—in the context of the Mongol invasion of Syria—was that Mamluk soldiers defeated by the Mongols were attacked by Kisrawanis on their way back from the front. This time, the Mamluks won, killing many Kisrawanis.[17] Some returning soldiers may have told Ibn Taymiyya what had happened, and he in turn gathered support for the campaign.[18]

Born in Harran into a Hanbali clerical family, Ibn Taymiyya was socialised in the Hanbali milieu of Damascus.[19] He was accused of heresy and interrogated just before the Mongol invasion of Syria in 1299/1300.

During the invasion, however, and the siege of Damascus, he rallied rulers and population against the Mongols, and mediated between them and the Damascene.[20] He then issued anti-Mongol fatwas in which he argued that the Mongols, who had started to convert to Islam, were not properly Muslim and not implementing Islamic rule, and should therefore be fought. Ibn Taymiyya established a link between the alleged treachery of the Mongols and the fact that some of their supporters were Shia.[21]

The Mongols under Ghazan Khan, who had embraced Islam, were themselves legitimising their campaign in Syria with reference to Islamic and Mongol forms of legitimate warfare and rule, and after Mamluk forces had desecrated mosques in 1299 during an incursion into territory held by the Ilkhanids, obtained a fatwa legitimising war against the Mamluks.[22] Tensions with the Mongols continued for years, but in 1303, a Mamluk army defeated the Mongols near Damascus. This allowed the Mamluks to embark on another campaign to the Kisrawan in 1305.

Who exactly the targets of the campaigns were remains debated (modern Lebanese historiography tends to use confessionalised narratives to stake political claims in the present).[23] Maronite historians, for example, see the campaigns as evidence of the Maronites' resistance against 'foreigners', in this case the Mamluks.[24] Druze chieftains and possibly Alawites, Maronite Christians, and perhaps Twelver Shia and Ismailis indeed resisted the Mamluks.[25] But Shia and Alawites are specifically mentioned as targets in 1305: 'They killed and seized all the Nusayris [Alawites] and renegades they encountered, and other heretics, and cleared them out of the hills.'[26] No Alawites and only few Shia survived in the Kisrawan, where settlement by Sunnis and Maronites was encouraged.[27]

Ibn Taymiyya seems to have participated in these expeditions as a sort of scholar-warrior. The governor of Damascus, Aqqush al-Afram, sent Ibn Taymiyya and the leading Shii notable of Damascus, to negotiate the peaceful surrender of the Kisrawanis and, when they refused, the army moved in.[28] Ibn Taymiyya issued a fatwa legitimising punitive measures, although it is not entirely clear when it was written, and he seems to equate Alawites with Twelver Shia and generally rallies against Shiism.[29] The text preceding Ibn Taymiyya's fatwa on Alawites epitomises the mood at the time: 'Their affairs were unknown to most people during the occupation of the coastal lands by the vanquished Crusaders; but when Islam returned they were uncovered.'[30]

That the region was strategically located between Beirut, Damascus, and Tripoli—between the region's most important harbours and its political centre—probably propelled the Mamluks to take military action. Members of the military and bureaucratic establishment pointed to the political sedition of the Kisrawanis as reasons for the expeditions. But piety-minded *ulama* emphasised their religious deviance as reasons for these campaigns.[31]

Ibn Taymiyya's fatwa had a long afterlife, and was frequently invoked by later anti-Shii movements. But the authorities, both before and long after Kisrawan, found a modus vivendi with Shia, Druze, and Alawites and employed them for tax collection (and the Kisrawanis were given the opportunity to submit to the authority of the Sultan before the campaign).[32] In addition, there is not much evidence in Alawite historiography of difficult relations with the Ayyubid and Mamluk rulers before these campaigns, and little reference is made to Alawites in Ayyubid and Mamluk chronicles, suggesting that the Sunni rulers' attitude towards them must have ranged from indifferent to cordial.[33] The 1305 campaign was led by the Druze Buhturid emirs, who were assigned tax farms in the area. Their beliefs would obviously have been anathema to Sunnis, even if Druze lords sometimes presented themselves as Sunni.[34] And the aforementioned governor of Damascus, Aqqush al-Afram, would eventually defect to Iran, where he became governor of Hamadan for Uljaytu, the Mongol ruler who would convert to Shiism.[35] Some Ismailis, too, regained possessions and were given tax farms, and for a while would have been the overlords of Alawites. Ismailis were even used by the Sunni Mamluks to assassinate Mongol foes.[36] The Mamluks thus frequently engaged with populations whose beliefs they officially despised.

It was against these policies that Ibn Taymiyya railed.[37] He tried to use tensions in the Kisrawan to drive the Mamluks into a larger campaign to eradicate beliefs that he deemed incompatible with Sunnism.[38] In a letter to Mamluk Sultan al-Nasir Muhammad in Cairo, he explained that the campaign should be the first step in a holy war against the 'hypocrites in Syria, Egypt, the Hijaz, Yemen and Iraq' that would eventually strengthen the Sultan and (Sunni) Islam.[39] Preachers should be dispatched to educate deviant villagers, with harsh punishments reserved for those who continued to advocate the 'wrong' message. After blaming the rise of the Mongols on Shiism, he elaborates on the heretical views of the Shia.[40] In Ibn Taymiyya's eyes the enemies of Sunnism were the enablers of the Franks and the Mongols.[41] He claimed to have uncovered the secret connections between theological heresy, political mobilisation, and external support. Unlike previous polemicists, however, Ibn Taymiyya engaged with Shii sources.[42]

That Ibn Taymiyya agitated not just against Shiism, but against certain aspects of Sufism, too, caused him trouble with the authorities, and he had to leave Damascus for Cairo just after the Kisrawan campaign. There, he was imprisoned and put on trial on charges of anthropomorphism (the debate about the exact nature of God, and his attributes), a long-standing dispute between the three main Sunni schools of thought, the Mu'tazila, the Asharis, and the Maturidis, similar in intensity to the debate about the createdness of the Quran mentioned above. As noted, when the Caliph al-Mamun had sought to impose the views of the rationalists, Ahmad Ibn Hanbal resisted.[43] Ibn Taymiyya, as a Hanbali, reasserted and elaborated this position, which went against what by that time had become the Ashari Sunni consensus. This caused an uproar and led to him being persecuted, which in turn led him to elaborate his position at public trials and in written tracts.[44] He was jailed six times for a total of over six years.[45] In fact, while Damascus was an important centre for Hanbalism, Hanbalis were resented by the elites of the other schools, and by Sufis.[46] Controversial Hanbali positions widened that gap. Rivals could accuse others of heresy, and socio-religious elites tried to bring the rulers in on their side. Shia were sometimes the victims of this, but others were, too, including, in the end, Ibn Taymiyya himself.[47]

Because of Ibn Taymiyya's trial, and periodic repression against Shiism, some have argued that the Mamluks established a kind of Inquisition.[48] They repressed an Alawite rebellion in 1318 and may have at times collected special taxes from Alawites and Ismaili leaders.[49] They executed several Shia in the 1300s, often for cursing the Companions.[50] In 1363, the authorities in Damascus denounced Shii doctrine and vowed to stop the spreading of Shii practices such as temporary marriage and the cursing of the Companions—by force if need be. We know little about the immediate reasons for this edict, and its application seemed to have been limited.[51] Shams al-Din Ibn Makki al-Amili (the suffix denoting that he was from Jabal Amil) (734–786/1333/4–84) is the most celebrated Shii scholar to have been executed in Mamluk Syria. But he seems to have become a victim not just of doctrinal disputes but of personal rivalries and political intrigues. He had in fact studied under Sunni scholars and in his heresy trial even claimed to be a Shafii.[52]

Nonetheless, the Mamluks did not have a single religious policy, or one approach towards Shiism (and instead of following Ibn Taymiyya's advice of embarking on a wholescale campaign against Sufism and Shiism even put him on trial for his views about God).[53] Despite reports of heresy trials across Mamluk domains, few were executed, and there was no formalised body akin to the Inquisition in Europe a century later. Ibn Taymiyya was no Torquemada, not for a lack of wanting, but for a lack of support from the political leadership, and other Sunnis.[54] Instead of repressing them, the state relied on the cooperation of non-Sunni elites for tax collection and basic administration. At the same time, the Mamluks could not officially condone their practices if they did not want to undermine their *raison d'état*, which was a Sunni Muslim one.[55] Within that general framework, there was much room for manoeuvre.

Other examples can easily be found. In Damascene *madrasas*, for example, the occasional student could include Shiism in his curriculum and go on to deliver lectures and issue fatwas.[56] In Damascus, a relatively small but visible Alid community enjoyed social prestige. One of these families administered the Bab al-Saghir cemetery, near one of the gates to the old city, where key figures from early Islamic history, and some of the remains of the martyrs of Karbala, and the *Ahl al-Bayt*, are buried.[57] They were formally organised as a sort of guild, with an intermediary, the *Naqib al-Ashraf*, representing their interests. The office of *Naqib al-Ashraf* was established under the Abbasids and, by the third/ninth century, many major towns had a formal organisation for the Alids, which kept a genealogical register to authenticate claims to Alid descent. Not all openly Shii, as descendants of the Prophet the Alids had an affinity towards Shiism.[58]

Shii sympathies did not prevent one from going about one's life as usual in medieval Damascus, if they were not expressed too openly, say, by walking into the Umayyad Mosque, denouncing the Companions, and then repeating this in front of a judge (which happened on occasion).[59] Men with Shii sympathies could reach high office, but these sympathies could be invoked by competitors to hasten their downfall.[60]

So long as Shii chiefs in Jabal Amil respected Mamluk rule and Shii clerics refrained from attracting too much attention, the Mamluks did not interfere. With Shiism in Aleppo, Damascus, and Kisrawan in retreat, Jabal Amil became the Shii centre in the Levant, bolstered by an influx of Shii families and relative independence. Jabal Amil had been strategically significant to the Franks, with their focus on Palestine and the coast, but was a backwater for the Mamluks.[61] The Kisrawan was taken over by Druze lords and Maronite leaders.[62] Shia continued to live in the Beqaa, although Sunni chiefs were dominant until the late fifteenth and early sixteenth century.[63]

In the coastal cities of Beirut, Tripoli, and Sidon, Sunnism was strengthened by an influx of Sunni Turkmans and a decline of Ismailism. Druze chiefs supported this process, and maintained good relations with the Mamluks.[64] Formerly a centre of Shiism, Mamluk Tripoli became an important port town, whose market and fortifications were expanded, and a centre for Sunni scholarship.[65] The Kisrawan campaigns—so central to the story of the Sunni–Shia divide because of their later appropriation—was not especially representative of Sunni–Shia relations, and would not have been so consequential had they not occurred amidst tensions with the Mongols.

The Mongol ransacking of Baghdad in 1258 and the downfall of the Abbasid Caliphate had been traumatic for Sunnis. Baghdad, for centuries the political and spiritual capital of Sunnism, which is said to have had a million inhabitants, was partly destroyed. Hulegu Khan (c. 1215–65) led the Mongol forces westwards into Iran and Iraq. Initially the Il-Khan, vice or subordinate Khan, of the great Mongol Khan Möngke, he would found the Ilkhanid dynasty that was going to govern the Mongols' Middle Eastern possessions. Möngke ordered Hulegu to move westwards to destroy and subjugate the Muslim powers, specifically the Lurs of southern Iran, the Ismailis of Alamut, the Abbasids in Baghdad, and the Ayyubids in Damascus and Mamluks in Cairo. He would defeat all but the Mamluks. At the head of one of the largest armies ever assembled, he moved East. The elimination of Ismailis as an independent political force had been a specific request by Möngke, owing to previous hostility between the Mongols and the Ismailis, and Hulegu subdued one Ismaili fortress after another, many of whom surrendered without a fight, until he reached their last holdout, Alamut. That was put under siege in late 1256, and when it fell, most of its inhabitants were killed, and much of its comprehensive library, destroyed.[66] Thereafter, Ismailis largely faded from public view, although small groups of believers and several lines of Imams survived in secret.

Before even approaching Baghdad, Hulegu thus dealt a near-mortal blow to one of the hitherto most powerful Shii movements in its last stronghold: Ismailism. But that did not stop Sunnis from developing conspiracy theories about an alleged Shii–Mongol alliance. They developed soon after the Mongol conquest of Baghdad in 1258. In this context, a conspiracy theory, at the centre of which stood an alleged traitor with questionable beliefs—the Shii Wazir Ibn al-Alqami—proved soothing.[67] It consisted of the following elements: In 624/1256, the troops of the Caliph violently suppressed an uprising in the Shii al-Karkh quarter of Baghdad, a move that was said to have enraged Shia in high office (apart from the Wazir, the governor of Erbil was a Shii, too). Indeed, the inhabitants of al-Karkh are supposed to have complained to Ibn al-Alqami, who is from then on said to have started hating the Caliph.

The Mongol leader Hulegu Khan, who led the campaign, had two Shii advisors, Nasir al-Din al-Tusi and Shams al-Din al-Juwayni. Al-Tusi is said to have played a role in predicting for Hulegu that nothing bad would follow the conquest of Baghdad, whereas one of his Sunni advisors had prophesied catastrophic scenarios if the Caliphate were to fall, while al-Tusi simply said Hulegu will replace the Caliph.[68] Al-Tusi, whose father had been a Twelver Shii, had lived for years with the Ismailis at Alamut, where he may have himself become an Ismaili. There he wrote an account of his spiritual journey with Ismaili overtones, and a famous book on ethics. Twelver Shia argue that he wrote his Ismaili-influenced works under pressure from the Ismailis, while Ismailis and Ismaili-sponsored scholarship argues he was a genuine Ismaili.[69] The Ismailis then sent him to negotiate with the Mongols when they approached Alamut. But al-Tusi joined the Mongols instead, who then took Alamut, and killed most inhabitants.

Under Mongol patronage, al-Tusi went on to establish the Maragha observatory, the at that point probably most advanced astronomical observatory in the world, and a seminary where astronomers, mathematicians, theologians, jurists, and poets would come to study and write (for which he is renowned in the history of science).[70] That he now abandoned Ismailism for Twelver Shiism made little difference to Sunni polemicists, who, rather than as *Nasir al-Din* (Supporter of Religion), referred to him as '*Nasir al-Ilhad*' (Supporter of Heresy).[71]

And Ibn al-Alqami, who advocated a passive policy towards the Mongols, was supposed to have advised the Caliph to weaken the army and maintained contact with the Mongols, from whom he demanded to become governor of Baghdad. When Hulegu stood before Baghdad, Ibn al-Alqami was sent to negotiate with him. In the belief that Ibn al-Alqami had reached an agreement with Hulegu over his position, the Abbasid Caliph al-Mustasim left the city with his entourage to meet Hulegu, only to be killed by the Mongols.

The city was ransacked. The chroniclers describe massacres and the death of thousands of inhabitants, and the burning and looting of large parts of the city. Claims of hundreds of thousands casualties abound in Islamic historiography. While they may have been inflated, the siege and subsequent sack of one of the largest cities in the world by one of the largest armies ever assembled surely brought about death and destruction of epic proportions, and the fall of the Caliphate became a cornerstone of Sunni communal memory.[72]

According to the conspiracy theory, the house of the Wazir, and the houses of Jews and Christians, were spared (the shrines of the Shii Imams Musa al-Kazim and Muhammad al-Jawad as well as the graves of the Caliphs were, however, also destroyed). Shortly after he indeed became Mongol governor of Baghdad, Ibn al-Alqami died, which most chroniclers present as divine punishment and others as a retribution by Hulegu for his treason against the Caliph.[73]

Hulegu's Shii advisors were accused of having advised him to kill the Abbasid Caliph al-Mustasim, with the argument that had he been allowed to live, Mongol rule would be tenuous.[74] A delegation of Shii scholars from Hilla convinced the Mongols to spare Hilla, then the centre of Shiism, and the two Shii shrine cities of Najaf and Karbala from being plundered by pledging allegiance to Hulegu and sending him gifts.[75] And when Hulegu asked Iraq's Muslim scholars to answer the question as to whether a just but unbelieving ruler was better than an unjust believer, only the Shii scholar Radi al-Din Ibn Tawus (1193–1266) dared to answer, arguing that a just ruler, whether or not he was a believer, was better, and prepared a fatwa to that effect (the other scholars eventually signed alongside him). Hulegu was therefore much pleased with Ibn Tawus, and allowed him to leave to Hilla with a large entourage, and then appointed him head of the Alids in Iraq.[76] According to Sunni historians, Ibn al-Alqami, and/or the Shii governor of Erbil, Ibn Salaya, sought to establish a Shii, or 'Fatimid', Caliphate after the killing of the Abbasid Caliph. However, Ibn al-Alqami was a Twelver Shii and not an Ismaili, and Ibn Salaya was eventually killed by the Mongols.[77]

The Ibn al-Alqami myth spread fast. Contemporary chroniclers noted it as a matter of fact. Early Mongol chroniclers discussed it when they tried to rehabilitate Ibn al-Alqami. We will never know for sure if Ibn al-Alqami betrayed the Caliph. Given the Mongol military might, the army they amassed outside Baghdad's walls may well have surpassed 100,000 men, and the speed with which they conquered much of Eurasia, blaming the fall of Baghdad on one Shii official offered an easy way out for Sunni chroniclers, instead of focusing on Mongol power or the deficiencies of the Abbasid polity.[78] That the Mongols destroyed the most important Shii sites (alongside Sunni ones), even though they had them rebuilt later, problematises the

'Shii conspiracy' narrative.[79] And for all that's been written about Ibn al-Alqami's alleged support of Shiism and treachery, he, in fact patronised scholars that are not easy to categorise as either Sunni or Shii.

In Syria, to which Hulegu turned his attention next, just as in Baghdad, Shia, or Shii-leaning individuals, and Sufis, were accused of collaborating with the Mongols. A Damascene Shafii judge, for example, had led a delegation to Hulegu and, after the latter had conquered the city in 658/1260, was appointed chief judge. His apparent action against Sunnism was explained with his alleged embrace of the Sufism of Ibn 'Arabi (1165–1240), and with Shii leanings.[80] Ibn Arabi, who hailed from al-Andalus but had settled in Damascus, played a major role in systematising and popularising a philosophical strand of Sufism that became popular in the Mongol Empire and beyond but that was despised by Sunni puritans.[81]

Hulegu initially sought to continue from Syria via Palestine to Cairo, but the death of Möngke in late 1259 required him to return to attend the council deciding the Mongol Empire's future (those negotiations came to nothing and led to the splitting of the Empire into four rivalling branches, of whom Hulegu's was one). He took with him much of the Mongol army, leaving the remaining outposts vulnerable. The Mamluks took advantage of the situation, sealed a passive alliance with the remaining Crusaders at Acre, and routed the Mongol army at Ayn Jalut on 3 September 1260.

After the Mamluks took Damascus a few days later, a number of 'rejectionists' were executed for collaborating with the Mongols, although the most important collaborator had been a Sunni Ayyubid prince (which led a furious Hulegu to execute the last Ayyubid ruler of Syria, who was in his captivity, effectively ending the dynasty that had played such a prominent role in the Sunni Revival).[82]

Amidst these political upheavals, Shii scholars refined their arguments, and often did so by using Sunni sources, and modelling their works on Sunni ones. The Ibn Tawus brothers exemplified this. Radi al-Din Ibn Tawus, whom we have got to know above as the Iraqi scholar who issued a fatwa legitimising Hulegu's rule, was born in Hilla into a prominent Shii family and married the daughter of the Shii Wazir Nasir bin Mahdi (d. 1220). Well acquainted with the political elite, including the Caliph, he did not hold an official position until after the Mongol invasion, when Hulegu appointed him leader of the Alids. Ibn Tawus built a large library that contained many Sunni works, and used them to try and convince Sunnis of Shii positions, such as, for example, that the Prophet had addressed Ali as Commander of the Faithful, implying Ali's elevated position over Abu Bakr, Umar, and Uthman. He also accused Sunni Quran commentaries of anti-Shii bias.[83]

These arguments were refined by al-Hilli and, together, these scholars systematised Shii Hadith scholarship, introducing a four-tiered classification of Hadith, ranging from sound to weak, that was influenced by Sunni Hadith scholarship.[84] This scholarly endeavour must be placed in its political context, as converting the Mongols was at stake when al-Hilli came of age. Born in Hilla, he studied with members of his family, with the Ibn Tawus brothers, and with Sunni scholars, and would become known under his nickname 'Allama al-Hilli (the very learned one from Hilla).[85] Al-Hilli would go on to systematically outline Shii dogma and jurisprudence in an anti-Sunni work and wrote a crucial Shii creed, which outlined what a believer had to accept to be considered a true Shii, especially the Imamate of the Twelve Imams.[86] al-Hilli became one of the key advisors of the Mongol ruler Uljaytu and provided written answers to his questions about Shiism.[87]

Uljaytu asked Sunni and Shii scholars to debate jurisprudence and political theory at court, where Shia claim they were able to outsmart their Sunni counterparts. Uljaytu may have visited Ali's shrine and embraced the notion that the *Ahl al-Bayt* constituted the ruling tribe of Islam, a perception that resonated with Mongol perceptions of tribal hierarchies, according to which rulers should be descendants of Genghis Khan, and seemed useful as the Mongols sought to solidify their reign over Mongols and conquered Muslims.[88] The argument seems to already have convinced Uljaytu's predecessor, Ghazan Khan, his older brother, who held the *Ahl al-Bayt* in high esteem and is said to have visited the shrines in Najaf and Karbala in 1303, endowing hostels for Sayyids and pilgrims, and improving the canals.[89]

Uljaytu probably encouraged his entourage to convert with him, although not all did so. Sunni sources emphasise that his conversion, symbolically marked by changing the call to prayer and minting new coins, led to dissent. Mamluk circles despised Uljaytu because of his embrace of Shiism and because he attempted one last failed invasion of Syria.[90] Sunni hardliners such as Ibn Taymiyya were outraged. By abolishing the Abbasid Caliphate, wreaking havoc in Muslim lands, and then adopting Shiism, the Mongols had, in Ibn Taymiyya's view, combined all the gravest possible sins at once. He and al-Hilli girded for intellectual battle.

As the protégé of the Ilkhan, al-Hilli wrote several well known works, including a polemical work that refuted the Caliphate, and defended the

Imamate. This book, *Minhaj al-Karama fi Ma'rifat al-Imama* (The Way of Dignity, concerning the Knowledge of the Imamate), was dedicated to Uljaytu and must have been written sometime between his conversion in 1310 and al-Hilli's death in 726/1325. The context of Uljaytu's conversion after his predecessors had abolished the Caliphate made this example of Shii scholarly assertiveness intensely provocative.[91]

A copy soon reached Damascus, where it provoked Ibn Taymiyya to pen his refutation of Shiism, the multi-volume *Minhaj al-Sunna al-Nabawiyya fi Naqd Kalam al-Shi'a wa-l-Qadariyya* (The Way of the Prophetic Sunna concerning the Criticism of the Words of the Shia and the Qadiriyya).[92] It is arguably the most important, and substantial, book ever written by a Sunni scholar against Shiism, and a continuation of his life-long struggle against what he called innovations in Islam.[93]

The book is structured as follows: Ibn Taymiyya takes on a Shii argument, introducing it with 'and the rejectionist said', before refuting it in detail. At times, he digresses from the topic to condemn Shii practices and provoke al-Hilli, whom he calls a 'liar', and whose book he calls *The Way of Remorse* (*Nadama*) instead of *The Way of Dignity* (*Karama*).[94] He took issue with al-Hilli's closeness to the Mongol rulers, accusing the Shia of cooperating and taking 'unbelievers' as Imams, and specifically refuted the Imamate, certain conceptions of prophethood, and the designation of Ali as the successor to Muhammad.[95]

Ibn Taymiyya's polemic is, like the Shii polemics using Sunni sources, an example of intense engagement with the Other.[96] On the question of the infallibility of the Prophet, which al-Hilli seems to advocate, there was disagreement but also cross-fertilisation.[97] Some have even argued that Ibn Taymiyya's engagement with al-Hilli influenced his thinking about the ideal Islamic state and his view of God.[98]

Like Sunnis before him, Ibn Taymiyya used historical examples and theological arguments to undermine al-Hilli's defence of the Imamate, for example the notion that all the Imams except Ali did not rule, which undermined the Shii idea that the Imams needed to exist to fulfil a particular function. He compared the Imams' achievements with those of Sunni rulers, and the first three Caliphs, and argued that the latter had expanded, administered, and secured the territory of Islam. While he praises Ali, he argues that his reign was plagued by civil war and Caliphal weakness, implicitly undermining the Shii focus on Ali. He emphasises that Hasan and Hussain are respected in Sunnism as well.[99] But he takes aim at the succession of the

Imams who were children and indulges in the story of the twelfth Imam, refuting al-Hilli's argument that the theory of the Mahdi was referred to in a Hadith of the Prophet.[100] Ibn Taymiyya argues that the eleventh Shii Imam, Hasan al-Askari, did not have any children and, even if he did, the child would not have reached maturity and could hence not be an Imam, and that it was irrational to believe that the Mahdi could live for centuries (Shia believe that the Imam is alive and in hiding). This was one of the most difficult points for Shia to respond to.[101]

Ibn Taymiyya accepts the Shii notion that most of the Imams, especially the first six, were knowledgeable and virtuous, arguing that 'in what these (Shii imams) did of the good and in what they called for of the good, they are thus imams who shall be taken as models therein'.[102] But he argues that this applied to many early Muslims, some of them more knowledgeable and virtuous than the *Ahl al-Bayt*, and that they should serve as role models in their appropriate fields. And if a ruler exercised authority and ensured basic security in his realm, he did not have to be infallible to deserve obedience.[103]

Ibn Taymiyya took comfort in the fact that, simply put, Sunnis were the majority of Muslims, and that there were numerically more Sunni scholars than Shii scholars and that the former's consensus was more significant.[104] To him, the Sunnis, the 'People of the Tradition and the Community', are those who live according to the tradition, the Sunna, as opposed to those who follow the *Ahl al-Bayt* (the Shia). And the Sunnis are 'the community', the mainstream of Islam, as opposed to dissident movements, such as the Kharijis, and are characterised by continuity from the time of the Prophet. They therefore form a middle ground in terms of doctrine that allows for the integration of different opinions and interpretations. The case of Ali is such a point, in which the 'People of the Tradition and the Community' adopted a middle ground between the Kharijis (who first supported but then killed Ali) and the Shia, the partisans of Ali. In his critique of Shiism, he thus perhaps defined the People of the Tradition and the Community more clearly than ever before.[105]

One of his key considerations was to stop the visitation of tombs and all pilgrimages apart from the one to the Hijaz.[106] He was opposed to Sufi and Shii shrines, not least those at the al-Baqia cemetery in Medina. Ibn Taymiyya claimed that these mausoleums were an innovation that had emerged under the Buyids and Qarmatians and that Hadith legitimising pilgrimage to these sites were falsified.[107] At the time, Medina had Zaydi rulers and Shii *ulama* were prominent in the city. The Hijaz was a cosmo-politan crystallising point of wider debates, and one where pilgrims inter-acted. Control, both political and ideological, of the Hijaz, was important. Ibn Taymiyya denounced the influence of Shiism in Medina in a special treatise, arguing that the people of Medina had been freer from 'innovations like the Shia' than any other region important in early Islam.[108] The Hijaz, so crucial for Muslim rulers' legitimation, had come under Mamluk control in the 1260s. The Mamluks initially accepted the Zaydi rulers, who had much local support.[109] But in the second half of the fourteenth century, this became an embarrassment for the Mamluks, who strengthened Sunni clerics there and pressured the rulers to renounce Zaydism, which they did.[110] Ibn Taymiyya's attacks on shrine visitation and Sufism, on the other hand, would as noted lead to his final imprisonment in the citadel of Damascus, where he died in 1328 (and mainstream Sunni scholars could defend certain practices of visitation).[111]

In their attempt to use Sunni literature to bolster Shii claims, al-Hilli and other Shii scholars quoted the Quran commentary by al-Thalabi, which is why Ibn Taymiyya tried to rid Quranic exegesis of pro-Shii tendencies.[112] While he could not accuse al-Thalabi, a Sunni, of being a heretic, he accused him of being a sloppy scholar, an example of what could go wrong if some-one not well versed in Hadith adopted an encyclopaedic approach.[113] Ibn Taymiyya's writings were collected and systematised by his students and disciples, such as Ibn al-Qayyim (d. 1350), who were likewise anti-Shii.[114] One of them, Ibn Kathir (d. 1373), sat on a council that sentenced an Iraqi Shii to death for cursing the first three Caliphs and the Umayyads.[115] His multi-volume universal history, *Book of Beginning and End*, tells a Sunni version of Islamic history and seeks to rehabilitate the Umayyads, delegit-imise pro-Alid accounts, and invokes the Ibn al-Alqami myth.[116] By the end of the fourteenth century, the hardline Sunni position against Shiism was firmly established, even if still fairly ineffective in getting rulers to enact it.

The Mamluk-Mongol rivalry spurred Sunni–Shia polemics that hardened the distinction between Sunnism and Shiism. The Mongols abolished the Abbasid Caliphate, which as noted had found a modus vivendi with Shiism, and one Mongol ruler briefly embraced Shiism. But the traditionalism advocated by Ibn Taymiyya left little room for accommodation. Clerics such as al-Hilli and Ibn Taymiyya sought to influence the rulers to adopt their views of history and political order. By engaging systematically with the

Shii arguments, Ibn Taymiyya standardised Sunnism and set the tone for later polemics. But Ibn Taymiyya would not become a mainstream figure until the eighteenth/nineteenth century. Only then did Ibn Taymiyya become a sort of godfather for the Salafis (those emulating the path of the *Salaf al-Salih*, the righteous ancestors, often interpreted to mean the first three generations of Muslims).[117] His writings on Shia and Alawites, invoked ad infinitum in the modern period, are referenced surprisingly little before then.[118] Al-Hilli's position under Uljaytu was more secure, and he became a towering figure in Shiism. Later Shii scholars saw in al-Hilli an archetype of a politically active scholar of Shiism's rationalist school, as opposed to the more philosophical and esoteric interests of other Shii scholars.

Further illustrating their closeness, Uljaytu had al-Hilli's remains buried in a new tomb complex for himself.[119] Some suggest that this tomb was supposed to house the remains of Ali and Hussain, which Uljaytu planned to exhume from Najaf and Karbala and relocate there. This never happened, of course, and the tomb became a mausoleum for Uljaytu, adorned with Shii inscriptions.[120] An anecdote links this period to the next. At the opening of Uljaytu's tomb complex (before his death), on Uljaytu's right sat a guest of honour: Shaykh Safi al-Din (d. 1334). Safi al-Din was the founder and name giver of a new Sufi order that was fast rising in importance, the Safavids. The downfall of the Abbasid Caliphate allowed confessionally ambiguous Sufi orders like the Safavids to flourish (it was not until the fifteenth century that they would become outspokenly Shii).[121] Unlike the Safavids two centuries later, however, Uljaytu did not convert the bulk of Iran's population to Shiism, and Uljaytu's successors adopted Sunnism. The Mongols' open embrace of Shiism was but an interlude, but one that facilitated the spreading of Shii ideas.[122] Some Sunni sources state that Uljaytu became a Sunni again towards the end of his life, possibly on his deathbed. This might have been a way to bestow legitimacy in Sunni eyes on his son and successor, Abu Said, who was a Sunni, abolished the Shii call to prayer, and minted new coins.[123]

To be accepted as Islamic monarchs Uljaytu, Abu Said and subsequent Mongol rulers patronised Mecca and Medina. There, claimants to local rule would at times try to obtain support from the Mongols against Mamluk-backed rivals. One such claimant obtained a military force from Uljaytu in 1316, amidst Mamluk difficulties in the Hijaz, and a possible common Shii link. The attempt was cut short by Uljaytu's death later that year.[124] Despite their symbolic rivalry in the Hijaz, Abu Said opened peace negotiations with the

Mamluks, which led to the Mamluk-Mongol peace treaty of 1323, a rapprochement sometimes explained with their common adherence to
Sunnism.[125]

The two sides could make peace after all, and the pragmatic Mongols
embraced those religious leaders that most suited their worldly ambitions,
and the Mamluks seldom followed Ibn Taymiyya's advice of embarking on
a Jihad against heresy at home. Instead, Ibn Taymiyya himself was put on
trial to determine whether his beliefs constituted heresy, and would end his
days locked up in the Damascus citadel—first with pen and paper, which he
used to reassert his controversial positions and annoy the authorities even
further, and then without.

That this most famous of Sunni polemicists would eventually fall because
of the influence of Sufis is telling of how powerful and well-institutionalised
Sufi orders had by then become and how intertwined the relations between
Sunnism and Shiism were with Sufism. In fact, although harsh polemics
became more widely produced and disseminated, confessionally ambiguous
Sufi orders flourished. This was a point not lost on Sunni authors. Ibn
Khaldun, the fourteenth-century historian, argued that Ismailism, which
had not that long ago lost its grip on power in North Africa, and the strand
of Sufism represented by Ibn Arabi, the famous Sufi of Andalusian origin
who had died in Damascus, and whose ideas were fashionable at the time,
were similar in their doctrine of the Mahdi (Messiah). It was not a compli-
ment when he stated that 'the Sufis thus became saturated with Shia theories' and that 'the fact that [the Sufis] restrict [precedence in mysticism] to
'Ali smells strongly of pro-Shia sentiment'.[126]

Some argued that Sufism adopted traits from Shiism when the latter
came under threat during the Sunni Revival.[127] Reverence for Ali and the
Ahl al-Bayt was widespread amongst Sufis in Iraq, Iran, Khorasan, and
Anatolia. This does not mean, however, that these Sufis believed in what had
by that time been defined by the clergy as Twelver Shii doctrine, such as the
notion of the return of the Hidden Imam, but that they thought that, first
of all, the Prophet Muhammad had special charisma and knowledge and
that, after him, Ali, too, was imbued with special charisma and esoteric
knowledge that he then passed on to his descendants.[128] Most Sufis therefore trace their spiritual lineage to the Prophet through Ali, who was a key
figure in the writings of the earliest Sufis.[129] But despite their spiritual
reverence for Ali, most Sufis at the time would probably have accepted the
Sunni view of the Rashidun Caliphs.[130]

The abolition of the Abbasid Caliphate by the Mongols gave room to Sufi orders, beliefs, and popular practices that did not fit into normative and legalistic understandings of Sunnism and Shiism as propagated by clerics like al-Hilli and Ibn Taymiyya. Neither Mongol nor Mamluk or local Saljuq rulers seriously imposed one confession on their subjects. Alid loyalty and devotion to the *Ahl al-Bayt* were accepted far into the Sunni spectrum, and termed 'good Shiism' by Sunnis (as long as it did not defy the notion of the Rashidun, for instance).[131]

This coincided with a challenge by short-lived dynasties of different religious persuasions, especially in Central Asia and Eastern Iran, of central political authority after the death of Abu Said, the last Ilkhanid ruler, in 736/1335.[132] Some were ambiguous in their religious identity or changed it repeatedly. Others such as the Sarbadars in Khorasan (738–789/1337–81), the Marashis in Mazandaran (from around 760/1358–9 to the second half of the tenth/sixteenth century), and the Mushasha in Khuzistan (ca. 840–1092/1436–1681) openly espoused Shiism.[133] Many were successors to the Ilkhans and some of them, like the Jalayrids, who ruled Azerbaijan and Iraq from 1340 to 1410/32, displayed allegiance to Shiism and Sunnism. Their coins contained no references to the Imams but instead to the Sunni Caliphs, and one of their rulers, Shaykh Uvays (r. 757–776/1356–74), is praised as being both 'knower of the knowledge of Ali' and 'equal in justice to Umar'.[134]

The Sarbadars, who ruled parts of Khorasan in the fourteenth century, were a militant Sufi order that was first Sunni and then adopted a Shiism with strong expectations of the return of the Mahdi. While this may have amounted to little more than minting new coins, their enemies still used their Shii turn to legitimise campaigns against them, and their reign was eventually ended by the mighty Timur, also known as Tamerlane or Timur the Lame, in 1381.[135] The Shii Marashi rulers in Mazandaran were, like the Sarbardars, Shii Sufis (they were related to the Safavids by marriage).[136] Others such as the local Zaydi Sayyid dynasty of the Kar Kiya in Biya Pish (East Gilan) and Daylam on the Caspian Sea helped the Safavids in their rise to power.[137]

From 1370 onwards a new central authority was established under Timur, who conquered and raided vast territories, and whose successors are referred to as Timurids and went on to rule Central Asia and Eastern Iran until 1507. Many Timurid rulers patronised the shrines of locally important saints, which were a focus of popular religiosity.[138] Timur himself was most likely associated with the Naqshbandi Sufi order, the most anti-Shii of the Sufi orders, but he and his successors also expressed allegiance to the *Ahl al-Bayt*. He claimed descent both from Genghis Khan and Ali and employed many Shii soldiers. In campaigns against Shii rulers, he claimed to defend Sunnism, and punished them for cursing the Companions of the Prophet, but also accommodated with Shii rulers that submitted to him.[139] He exiled the founder of an important Sufi order with Shii leanings, the Nimatullahi order, Shah Nimatullah Wali. But he did so probably more because he saw him as a potential political threat than for doctrinal reasons, and he also posed as a defender of the *Ahl al-Bayt* and the Shia during his conquest of Syria.[140] Timur is thus associated with contradictory actions, and religious identity seemed to have been more a political tool rather than a driving force for him. The Turko-Mongolian custom that still played a significant role in his reign, lost in importance under his successors in favour of Sunnism.[141]

His son and successor, Shah Rukh (r. ca. 811–850/1409–47), is credited with strengthening Sunnism over earlier Mongol rites, including through the establishment of Sunni *madrasas* and patronising of Sunni Sufi orders.[142] He stylised himself as an Islamic ruler and tried to be recognised as Caliph over the entire Muslim world, in which he was challenged by the Mamluks, who, as noted, hosted the descendants of the Abbasid Caliphs.[143] Like his father he also showed allegiance to the *Ahl al-Bayt*. And while he occasionally attacked Ismailis, he did not fully suppress Shiism.[144] Shah Rukh and his family patronised three major shrines: two Alid ones and a third for a Hanbali Sufi. The latter was the shrine of Abdullah Ansari (d. 1089) at Herat, which became the centre of Timurid rule in the fifteenth century. Ansari had been an important teacher, Hanbali traditionist, and Sufi—a rare combination.[145] Although as a Hanbali he himself had been opposed to shrine visitation, Ansari's grave became the focus of local piety, and he became something of a patron-saint of the city. Associating themselves with Ansari strengthened the Timurids' claim to defend Sunni traditionalism (Shah Rukh expanded the shrine and encouraged visitation to it).[146]

Shah Rukh and his family also supported the shrine at Mashhad of Ali al-Rida (Reza in Persian), whom we have got to know as the eighth Shii Imam, whom the Caliph al-Mamun had asked to come to Khorasan and appointed as his successor, and the shrine in Mazar-i-Sharif in honour of Ali Ibn Abi Talib, where, as noted, many Central Asian Muslims, and other

Sunnis, believe Ali is buried.[147] We have seen how the Ali shrine in Najaf has long been a major site of pilgrimage and devotion. The location of a grave for Ali in Mazar-i-Sharif was allegedly revealed around 1135–6 to a mystic at the time of the Saljuq Sultan Sanjar. While it is far-fetched that Ali's body was transported all the way from Kufa to Afghanistan without anyone noticing for centuries, that place may have been a pre-Islamic pilgrimage site, and it seems plausible that the discovery narrative surrounding the shrine of Ali was supposed to give Central Asia a major Islamic pilgrimage site. It would then be promoted as an alternative burial place to the Ali shrine in Najaf not just by Central Asian Muslims but also, as noted earlier, by Sunni polemicists, who sought to undermine the Shii focus on Najaf by claiming that Ali was not buried there.[148] But with Ali, first Imam of the Shia and fourth Caliph of Sunnis, at its centre, the shrine allowed for much shared devotion. It was under Shah Rukh's great-grandson, Hussain Mirza Bayqara (r. 875–912/1470–1506), the Timurid ruler of Herat and wider Khorasan, that the Ali shrine in Mazar-i-Sharif was expanded. He allocated funds to the shrine in a *waqf* and promoted it as a major pilgrimage destination and an alternative to the Hajj.[149]

The shrine at Mashhad, too, had already emerged as an ecumenical site of pilgrimage in the late tenth century.[150] Shah Rukh himself went on pilgrimage to Mashhad, and other members of his dynasty were buried and crowned and sought spiritual power there before military campaigns.[151] It was at the command of Shah Rukh's wife, Gawhar Shad, that the Friday Mosque and large ceremonial halls were added to the shrine, enhancing its grandeur and reach.[152] This was also important economically, as new endowments, irrigation systems, and infrastructure projects revitalised whole regions.[153] And it epitomised the confessionally ambiguous milieu of Timurid Central Asia.

Whatever their face value, coins, too, were sometimes expressions of such ambiguity. They had of course long been used to determine a ruler's identity with some success, given that they often contained a confession of faith that would allow some conclusions about sectarian allegiance. But rulers that were nominally Sunni at times minted coins containing Shii references in territories inhabited by Shia.[154] The coins of the Timurid ruler Abu al-Qasim Babur (d. 1457/861), who ruled Khorasan in the late 1440s and the 1450s, bore Shii slogans on one side and Sunni ones on the other.[155] It has long been argued that the two rival Turkmen dynasties that largely ruled fourteenth- and fifteenth-century Iran (and with whom the Timurids were intermittently at war but also intermittently allied) associated themselves either more with Shiism (the Black Sheep/Qara Qoyunlu in Iraq and Western Iran) or more with Sunnism (the White Sheep/Aq Qoyunlu dynasty with their capital at Tabriz in Northern Iran).

It is probably true that the Black Sheep dynasty, especially under Jahan Shah (r. c. 1439–67), who was initially a vassal of the Timurid Shah Rukh but then increasingly independent, patronised Shiism. However, Jahan Shah, too, minted coins with Shii slogans on one side and Sunni ones on the other. His brother, Aspand, supported Twelver Shiism as governor of Baghdad from 1433 to 1445. Another descendant of the Black Sheep dynasty would flee to India in 1478, where he, as we will see, would found a Shii ruling dynasty.[156] But both the Black and White Sheep dynasties maintained relations with nominally Sunni and Shii Sufi orders.[157] And while Sunni chroniclers accused the *Black Sheep* of nefarious beliefs, scholars are still debating their confessional identity.[158]

The point is that many figures and movements in the fourteenth and fifteenth century combined mysticism, millenarianism, and charismatic leadership, and did not subscribe to narrow definitions of Sunnism or Shiism as laid down by the clerics. Another such figure was Fadlallah Astarabadi (740–796/1339/40–94), whose writings mixed esoteric Shiism with Sufism. He was executed by Miranshah, a son of Timur, after a clerical death sentence. While incorporating Shii ideas, his writings did not openly contradict Sunni doctrine on most points, and his execution was likely more a result of political disagreements rather than religious ones.[159]

The above-mentioned Nimatullahi order, on the other hand, exemplifies how confessional ambiguity slowly gave way to a more explicit sectarian identity, in this case a Shii one. Its founder, Shah Nimatullah Wali, claimed descent from the fifth Shii Imam, Muhammad al-Baqir. Born in Aleppo in 1330, he then went to Mecca and afterwards lived in Transoxania and then in Mahan near Kerman, where he died in 1431.[160] Despite himself having had trouble with Timur, and being exiled by him, Sufi orders like the Nimatullahis played a crucial role in fifteenth-century Timurid Iran, as their networks cut across regional and ideological divides.[161] The nominally Sunni founder of the order venerated Ali as a spiritual figure. The master who initiated him into Sufism in Mecca was a Shafii from Yemen, Abdullah al-Yafii (d. 768/1367), and he himself quoted anti-Shii figures as authorities on Hadith. In subsequent centuries, the order would adopt a more Shii identity and establish close relations, including through marriage, with the Safavids.[162] Shah Nimatullah invented a woollen crown with five corners for the Prophet Muhammad, Ali, Fatima, Hasan, and Hussain, which was later expanded to twelve corners to indicate devotion to the Twelve Imams and became the model for the Safavid twelve-pronged headgear, the Qizil Taj.[163]

Similarly, the Kubrawi Sufi order, founded in the mid-twelfth century, was confessionally ambiguous.[164] This was especially so with one of its off-shoots, the Nurbakhshiyya, which emerged in the first half of the fifteenth century. Muhammad Nurbakhsh (795–869/1392–1464/5), whose father claimed descent from Imam Musa al-Kazim and hailed from Eastern Arabia, was initiated into the Kubrawi order during studies in Herat, but then claimed to be the Mahdi and wrote a treatise criticising the Twelver Shii view of the twelfth Imam. In Kashmir, the order established a long-lasting presence, as we will see (there, some even prayed according to Sunni custom—with their hands folded—in the winter and according to the Shii way—with hands hanging loose—in the summer). Nurbakhshi, who were frequently suppressed and fell out with the Safavids in the early sixteenth century, remained influential across the Eastern Islamic lands. Eventually, they played down their views on the Mahdi and adopted standard Twelver Shii beliefs.[165]

Another example is the Shii Mushasha dynasty in fifteenth-century Khuzistan, whose founder also claimed to be the Mahdi. When his first teacher in Hilla tried to have him excommunicated and executed, he pretended to be a Sunni Sufi to escape persecution. They somewhat counter-intuitively sacked the shrine of Ali in Najaf and, when the Safavids came to power, the latter initially moved to repress them. Relations between the two only improved in the late sixteenth century, after the Mushasha had brought their beliefs more in line with what by then had become mainstream Twelver Shiism, and when the Safavids needed their political support.[166] The Ismaili Imams also began to be based in Anjudan, Iran, from the fifteenth century onwards, facilitated by a general pro-Shii trend and the fact that, after the destruction of their fortresses by the Mongols, Ismailis presented themselves as 'just' another Shii-leaning Sufi order and maintained close relations with some of them.[167] Shii influence thus spread through Sufi orders centred around the spirituality of Ali.[168] But not all these openly embraced Shiism. And there were plenty of clerics, poets, and historians who were later claimed by Sunna and Shia, either because their identity may have really been ambiguous, or because in parts of their work they may have been more inclined towards one side and more to another in other parts. Pro-Alid statements could be juxtaposed with references to the validity of the Rashidun Caliphs, and it is difficult, if not impossible, to decide retrospectively whether their views were actually so ambiguous, whether they were concealed to protect themselves, or whether they constituted a veneration of the *Ahl al-Bayt* without acceptance of Shii political claims.[169]

Whatever the complications of its politics, this period saw serious intellectual engagements. In some areas of learning, such as grammar, logic, rhetoric, philosophy, mathematics, medicine, or astronomy (the latter symbolised by al-Tusi's Maragha observatory, which hosted scholars of different confessions), Sunni, Shii, and Ismaili scholars transmitted knowledge and learned from each other without focusing on sectarian boundaries.[170] Clerical biographical dictionaries compiled over the coming centuries would often go to great lengths to try to prove that a historical figure belonged to a specific school. But a striking number of scholars were hard to classify. Another example was a scholar, who spent much of his life preaching at the Shii shrine of Musa al-Kazim in Baghdad, and is 'defended' by Sunni authors by pointing out that he also frequented the tomb of Ahmad Ibn Hanbal.[171] Another scholar studied in Hanbali circles and spent much of his life teaching Hanbali law, but was eventually beaten and expelled for allegedly holding Shii views, and then wrote an anti-Sunni work.[172] Other examples included, for example, the famous historian al-Tabari, the historian and geographer al-Masudi, or the philosopher Ibn Sina (Avicenna), to whom are variously ascribed pro- and anti-Shii statements, even though, or perhaps because, these figures were not partisan and nuanced in their assessment.[173] Ibn Abi al-Hadid was a Sunni scholar who received patronage by the infamous Shii Wazir Ibn al-Alqami to write a multi-volume commentary on the *Nahj al-Balagha,* Ali's Hadith collection, which he dedicated to his patron.[174]

When it came to debates about the apocalypse, or the occult sciences, there was little that differentiated nominally Sunni from Shii scholars.[175] The canonisation of a liturgy for the *Ahl al-Bayt* from Timurid Herat in Safavid Iran is another example. The *Rawdat al-Shuhada,* an Alid martyrology that focuses largely on Hussain, was composed at the court of Sultan Bayqara in Timurid Herat, and then became the key basis for sermons and passion plays of the Karbala tragedy in Iran after the Safavid takeover. Shia have long claimed that its author, Kashifi (c. 830–910/1426–1504/5), was a Shii, and it is pro-Alid and partly based on Shii sources. But Kashifi was likely a Naqshbandi Sunni, who admired the *Ahl al-Bayt* from a Sunni perspective.[176]

In fact, strongly Sunni Sufi orders like the Naqshbandiyya also expanded. A founding figure of the order, after whom it is named, Baha al-Din Naqshband Bukhari (718–791/1318–89), received patronage by Central Asian rulers, who supported a shrine complex around his tomb in Bukhara. Naqshbandis retained a strong influence on Timurid rulers and their successor states.[177] Since they emerged in a region with a marginal Shii presence, they had no major quarrels with Shiism at the outset. Yet since the Naqshbandiyya is unique amongst Sufi orders in that it traces its spiritual lineage to the Prophet back through three chains, one of them, which in time came to be the most important one, through Abu Bakr, made it especially averse to Shii attacks on Abu Bakr.[178] Its anti-Shiism intensified when the order spread to Herat in the fifteenth-century amidst Sunni–Shia tension there and competition with some of the pro-Alid Sufi orders mentioned above that were slowly becoming more openly Shii.[179]

Abd al-Rahman Jami (817–898/1414–92), the poet and Naqshbandi mystic, epitomises this. He and other Naqshbandis were elegiac defenders of the *Ahl al-Bayt*, who, they argued, had been misappropriated by Shiism.[180] Sultan Hussain Bayqara, who had an interest in Shiism and expanded the Ali shrine, was apparently encouraged by a Shii cleric to include the names of the Imams in prayer and on coins, and the Sultan may have seen this as an affirmation in the line of the local allegiance to the *Ahl al-Bayt*. However, he may have been dissuaded by Jami and other Sunnis from doing this.[181] Still, Jami endorsed the 'discovery' of the Ali shrine at Mazar-i-Sharif, despite himself having just returned from a visit to the Ali shrine in Najaf on the way to the Hijaz. Jami was trying to get Hussain Bayqara to prevent Shia from 'discovering' more graves associated with descendants of the Imams in the area. His endorsement of the Ali shrine may have been a way to limit that practice and claim the *Ahl al-Bayt* for Sunnism.[182] In a poem written for the ruler, Jami refuted Shiism.[183] The anti-Shii turn of the Naqshbandis thus came at a time when a ruler considered adopting Shiism. Unlike many other Sufi orders, the Naqshbandiyya emphasised adherence to Islamic law and Hadith.[184] This emphasis on the Sunna and on the order's lineage through Abu Bakr intensified after the rise of the Safavids in Iran.[185]

While Central Asian Muslims of all backgrounds held the *Ahl al-Bayt* in high regard, there were always those who sought to enforce the boundaries between Sunnism and Shiism. Polemicists sought to affirm the differences between Sunna and Shia precisely because this was not the lived reality at the time, and because these boundaries were not clear to everyone. Their views were not yet imposed on large populations. Al-Hilli and Ibn Taymiyya shaped Shiism and Sunnism, respectively, and their writings had important afterlives. But they were unsuccessful in their immediate political aims. Neither Mamluks nor Mongols were interested, nor had the means, to enforce doctrinal views across vast territories and dispersed, religiously diverse, populations, and the rulers of Central Asia were more than happy to sponsor different forms of Islam. In time, however, the polemics, a result of intense engagement with the other side, did lead to a sharpening of the Sunni–Shia divide.

In the fifteenth century and especially the sixteenth century, a few decades after the start of the Catholic inquisition in Europe, and simultaneous with the Reformation, however, a new kind of state, more powerful and with an ambition to enforce doctrines more thoroughly across specific territories, emerged in the Islamic world. This was epitomised by two rival dynasties that based their legitimacy on two competing interpretations of Islam, one Sunni and the other Shii. Both emerged out of this confessionally ambiguous milieu; the House of Osman, which rose to prominence in the aftermath of the Crusades, and would found the Ottoman Empire and proclaim a renewed Sunni Caliphate, and the Safavids, the Sufi order that derives its name from its founder Safi al-Din Ishaq (d. 1334), who we met sitting at Uljaytu's right when the latter opened his mausoleum. At that point, Safi al-Din, though seen as a semi-divine leader by his disciples, was still a Sufi leader like others of his age, and may have still self-described himself as Sunni if pressed on this point. His descendants, however, would embrace Shiism, and take almost the whole of Iran with them, reversing, forever, the fortunes of Shiism, and the parameters of Sunni–Shia relations. Their states would also be profoundly different from the ones discussed so far.

PART II

The Shaping of
Muslim Empires,
1500–1800

In the sixteenth century, several new Muslim Empires consolidated themselves: Ottomans, Safavids, Uzbeks, and Mughals. They differed from the political entities that had preceded them—from the early Muslim rulers, from Umayyads and Abbasids, to subsequent ones, such as Mamluks and Mongols— because they embraced new forms of military organisation and weaponry, administration, and trade. Moreover, in contrast to the preceding periods, they adopted a more exclusive confessional identity to legitimise their rule, rally against enemies, forge alliances, and foster a cohesive ideology. The Muslim Age of Confessionalisation shared similarities with the Christian European one. These were not yet nineteenth-century 'Empires' and states that penetrated most aspects of people's lives.[1] Nonetheless, each one ruled over vast territories, and ethnically, linguistically, and religiously diverse populations that they shaped to varying degrees. Their military successes were driven by gunpowder. It was first discovered in China in the ninth century, and after their invasions of China was then employed by the Mongols in their conquest of the rest of Eurasia discussed above. The technology that had helped the Mongols bring down the Abbasids was now employed by new Muslim empires to conquer and control the formerly Mongol domains.[2]

The Ottomans espoused Hanafi Sunnism and the Safavids Twelver Shiism to secure their rule at home and abroad. Their rivalry lasted from the start of the sixteenth century until the early eighteenth century, when the

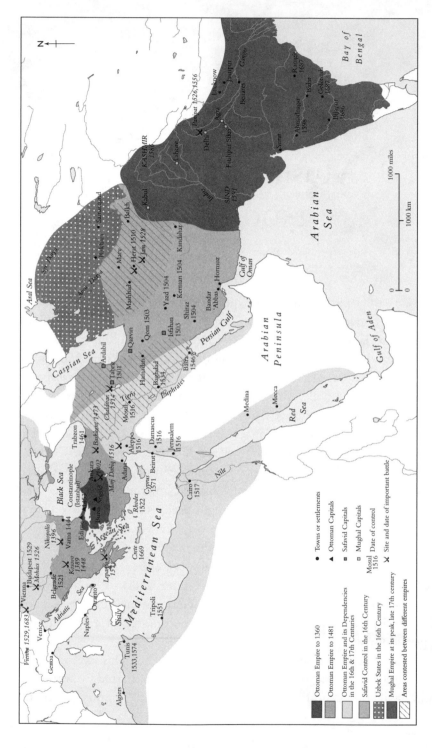

5. Major Muslim Empires (Ottomans, Safavids, Mughals and Shaybanid Uzbeks)

Bay of
Bengal

Ranipur
1637

Ishtir

Golconda
1687

Ahmadnagar   Bijapur
1598   1686

Surat

Arabian
Sea

Jaunpur

Banares   Ganges

Lucknow

Delhi   Fathpur Sikri
1556

Agra

KASHMIR
1586

Lahore

SIND
1591

1000 miles

1000 km

Panipat 1526, 1556

Samarqand

Kabul

Balkh

Bukhara

Marv   Herat 1510

Mashhad   Jam 1528

Kandahar

Kernan 1504

Yazd 1504

Shiraz
1504

Hormuz

Bandar
Abbas

Gulf of
Oman

Arabian
Peninsula

Aral Sea

Syr Darya

Amu Darya

Qazvin

Qom 1503

Isfahan
1503

Persian Gulf

Caspian Sea

Ardabil

Tabriz
1501

Hamadan

Basra
1546-?

Red
Sea

Medina

Mecca

Chaldiran
1514

Mosul
1516,?

Baghdad
1534

Tigris

Euphrates

Damascus
1516

Jerusalem
1516

Nile

Cairo
1517

Aleppo
1516

Beirut

Trabzon
1461

Marj Dabiq 1516

Adana

Cyprus
1571

Black Sea

Constantinople
(Istanbul)
1453

Ankara
1402

Bursa

Nikopolis
1396

Kosovo
1389

Varna 1444

Edirne

Aegean
Sea

Rhodes
1522

Crete
1669

Vienna 1529, 1683

Budapest 1529

Mohács 1526

Belgrade
1521

Lepanto
1571

Mediterranean Sea

Venice

Otranto

Naples

Genoa

Sicily

Tunis
1533, 1574

Tripoli
1551

Algiers

Adriatic

N

• Towns or settlements

▲ Ottoman Capitals

■ Safavid Capitals

□ Mughal Capitals

Mosul   Date of control
1516

✕ Site and date of important battle

▨ Ottoman Empire to 1360

   Ottoman Empire to 1481

   Ottoman Empire and its Dependencies
   in the 16th & 17th Centuries

   Safavid Control in the 16th Century

   Uzbek States in the 16th Century

   Mughal Empire at its peak, late 17th century

⧄ Areas contested between different empires

Safavids were overthrown (while the Ottomans would survive until the early twentieth century). Through mass conversions to Shiism, the Safavids, albeit weaker and ruling over a smaller territory than Ottomans and Mughals, achieved a greater degree of ideological cohesion.[3]

The association with major early modern states transformed Sunnism and Shiism, and their relationship. Elites on both sides tried to delineate more clearly what was Islamic and what was not and to subvert the other. This made the lives of Shia in the Ottoman Empire and Sunnis in Iran harder, as they were suspected of sympathies for a foreign power. Many Iranians were forcibly converted to Shiism. The two sides fought devastating wars, and border regions such as Kurdistan and Iraq were in a state of war for much of the sixteenth century.[4]

As rulers stylised themselves as religious and political authorities, they used sectarian identity, now closely tied to state identity, to undermine rivals and repress domestic dissent.[5] Espousing a rival branch of Islam from their neighbours allowed for more independence, and alliances further afield, as in the case of the Safavids, and Indian Muslim dynasties (who were not interested to submit to the Ottoman Caliphate).

These empires symbolised the high period of the 'Persianate world', as Persian as well as various forms of Turkish became languages of the court and imperial administration (with Arabic in use in religious circles and Arab provinces). This facilitated interactions across borders and confessional divides. But that interaction also led to a larger awareness of sectarian difference, and polemics in Persian.

Of Turkic origin, with Persian as the language of the court, and a source of patronage for fortune seekers from other Muslim realms, the Mughals, as we'll see, were intimately tied to developments in the Ottoman, Safavid, and Uzbek realms. They became the wealthiest and most powerful Muslim dynasty ever to exist, leaving behind a remarkable legacy in the built environment, in art, and in poetry (as did the Safavids and Ottomans). Their reign is known for confessional tolerance. Nevertheless, several Mughal rulers embarked on confessional projects of their own, and from their base in Northern India, faced a range of semi-independent Muslim States in the Deccan plateau in the southwestern part of the Indian subcontinent, some of which embraced Shiism so as not to have to submit to Mughal authority.

Despite a stronger alliance with one interpretation of Islam, many early modern Muslim rulers could accommodate others, especially when acquiring new territory or populations. Their still often tenuous rule allowed for such flexibility, especially if they retained support amongst a core group of the same confession. These states were still not fully subjugated by European Empires, or fully dependent economically. And yet, European influence deepened.

By the eighteenth century, Muslim powers faced increasing European encroachment. Europeans first emerged as traders and then in the form of the overseas trading companies that established early fortified settlements along the coast (Europeans further refined the use of gunpowder technology). The discovery of the sea route from Europe to Asia via the Cape of Good Hope (and the discovery of the Americas) led to the gradual loss in importance of the overland Eurasian 'Silk Road', which had crossed the Muslim territories of Central Asia and been the economic backbone of the Muslim Empires. This brought first the Portuguese and Italian city states and then the Dutch, French, English, and others into contact with the Muslim Empires. The shift to the sea route, increasingly controlled by European powers, foreshadowed a power shift. The East India Company established a presence along those coastal areas, and conquered much territory on the Indian subcontinent, and signed treaties with rulers along the Arabian Sea and Indian Ocean. It also increasingly ruled directly.

As a result, Muslims fostered new links, especially between the Indian subcontinent and the Middle East. Just as European princes sealed alliances with other princes along confessional lines after the Reformation, so did Muslim rulers, and reformers. And the Christian states sought to form alliances with Muslim states against the one Muslim power that was a real threat to them: the Ottomans. The beginnings of an inward turn in Sunnism, to the sources and early period of Islam, coincided with the beginnings of Empire. And in Shiism, the fall of the Safavids, and the rise of the shrine cities of Najaf and Karbala as centres of Shiism in the eighteenth century, funded in part by Indian Shii money, led to similar debates. In sum, Sunnism and Shiism, and their relationship, were profoundly transformed. Lived reality could still be confessionally ambiguous. Yet Muslim Empires had tied sectarian identity to specific territories and now, attempts at unity coincided with the emergence of sect-centric revivalist movements that were convinced of their own superiority, and wanted to suppress the other.

4

The Age of Confessionalisation

In the fourteenth and fifteenth centuries, clerics delineated boundaries between Sunnism and Shiism more clearly, and encouraged rulers to enforce what they considered the right belief. Yet, popular piety, Sufi orders and folk reverence for the *Ahl al-Bayt* were little affected. Rulers, many of Turco-Mongol origin, like Timur and his successors, patronised Sunnism and Shiism. Ottomans and Safavids emerged in this milieu, and owed much to it. But they would also radically transform it. Despite their common origin these two dynasties would spearhead a Muslim Age of Confessionalisation.

The Ottomans rose to power in late thirteenth-/early fourteenth-century Anatolia during the wars against Byzantium in the aftermath of the 'high period' of the Crusades, when various Muslim powers drove the Crusaders out of the Levant and subsequently turned their attention to Constantinople. After the fall of the Saljuqs, the Ottomans vastly expanded their realm, conquering Constantinople in 1453. Like the Safavids, who derived their name from Safi al-Din Ishaq (d. 1334), the Ottomans derived their name from their founding figure, Osman Ghazi (d. 1324 or 1326).[6] The Ottomans would establish one of the largest, most powerful and long-lasting Muslim empires and one that ruled over large Christian, Jewish, and Shii populations.[7] The official religion of the state became, as noted, Hanafi Sunnism but, as we will also see, many across the empire revered the *Ahl al-Bayt* and espoused religious practices deemed unorthodox by Sunni clerics. In fact, Sufi orders and holy men had played a key role in converting Turks to Islam and were held in high esteem and supported by the Ottomans.[8]

The Safavids themselves were one of many such Sufi orders, and emerged out of the confessionally ambiguous Sufi milieu described in the previous chapter.[9] Founded by Safi al-Din Ishaq (d. 1334) in early fourteenth-century northwestern Iran, in a small city called Ardabil, it slowly became Shii, a process that was completed under the leadership of Shaykh Junayd (d. 1460), who gathered an army to establish an independent polity.[10] Most of Junayd's followers were Turkmen from Anatolia, an area the Ottomans claimed as well. The Ottomans themselves had suffered a major setback in the Battle of Ankara (1402) at the hands of Timur, during which the Ottoman Sultan Bayezid I was captured and died in captivity while his troops were routed. But Timur in turn died three years later, and his successors struggled to hold his vast possessions together, whereas the Ottomans, after an initial civil war amongst Bayezid's sons, managed to reconquer territory lost to Timur and vastly expand their possessions in Europe.[11]

Relations between Ottomans and Safavids were complicated. By the mid-fifteenth century, the Safavids had become a threat in a region vital to the Ottomans, with the Turkmen tribesmen caught between the two sides.[12] The first serious confrontations between Ottomans and supporters of the Safavids now ensued. At the same time, because of the Safavids' large Anatolian following, and keeping in line with a policy of supporting Sufi orders, the Ottomans also made annual payments to the Safavid order in the fifteenth and intermittently in the sixteenth centuries. Sultan Murad II (r. 1421–44, 1446–51) still received Junayd at his court, although he later asked him and his disciples to leave Ottoman territory.[13]

Junayd's son Haydar (d. 1488) continued his father's policies and came into more serious conflict with the Ottomans, who saw an assassination attempt against Bayezid II (r. 1481–1512) in 1492 as inspired by the Safavids and cut off the stipend and started to persecute their followers.[14] Haydar encouraged his supporters to wear a red, twelve-pleated tuque headdress (in honour of the Twelve Imams), that had previously been worn by supporters of the Nimatullahis, which gained them the designation Qizilbash (red head).[15] These Qizilbash soon gained a reputation of being fiercely loyal to the Safavids, and of being excellent warriors. With their help, Haydar's son Ismail was able to defeat the last White Sheep ruler and seize their capital Tabriz in 1501, proclaiming himself Shah. Ismail is said to have written a poem that asserted 'whoever recognizes the Twelve Imams, it is proper for him to wear the red/crimson' hat like the Qizilbash.[16] Many of Ismail's supporters saw him as a sort of holy figure, as both worldly and spiritual leader, not unlike some of the millenarian movements of preceding centuries. What precisely the beliefs of the Qizilbash were is still debated, as, opposed to the more text-based Shiism of the clerics, they left few sources on which we could base our analysis. But suffice it to say that their ideas of ideal leadership, popular religiosity, and the position of the Safavid leaders would eventually come to be at odds with the Twelver Shiism outlined by the clerics. For now, however, the Qizilbash allowed Ismail to make Shiism the state religion of Iran and start a large-scale conversion campaign. This gave the new, foreign dynasty a legitimising ideology that differentiated Iran from the Sunni Ottomans and Uzbeks, with whom the Safavids were soon at war. Shah Ismail sent emissaries to the Ottoman Empire to propagate the Safavid message and persuade Qizilbash to move to Iran to join the Shah's army.[17] The Safavid propaganda was well-organised by leaders of the order dispatched across Anatolia (and the Balkans, Iraq, and Syria), who recruited new followers and arranged ritual practice.[18] Some Ottoman Qizilbash came to see the Safavid Shahs as both spiritual and political leaders, even paying taxes to them and serving in their armed forces.[19]

The Ottomans initially did not react strongly. But a revolt by pro-Safavid Qizilbash in Ottoman Anatolia in 1511 spurred them into action. This occurred amid tensions within the ruling house of Osman, and Selim I (r. 1512–20) used the Qizilbash rebellions as a pretext to depose his father with the support of the Janissaries. The Janissaries, who were mostly Christian prisoners of war or converts recruited at a young age and technically slaves of the Ottoman household, were the elite troops of the Ottomans. Another Sufi order with strong Shii tendencies, the Bektashis, discussed in the introduction, accompanied them as chaplains, lived in the barracks, and educated new Janissaries. These Shii leanings did not stop them from being loyal to the Ottoman household, however, or from fighting against the Safavids. In fact, soon after the Janissaries had helped him ascend the throne, Selim attacked the Safavids.[20] To the Ottomans, the Safavids were a challenge because they originated in what was now Ottoman territory and had much support there, initially more so than for religious reasons. Qizilbash became the backbone of the Safavid military, and enforcers in the new state, and the Ottomans worried most about Qizilbash risings in Anatolia.

While the Qizilbash provided military muscle, in order to staff the judiciary and convert the population, the Safavids encouraged the immigration of Arab Shii scholars from Jabal Amil, Iraq, and Bahrain. These clerics attained high office and reformulated Shiism as a religion of state. Given their origin in territories ruled by Sunnis, these clerics were well-versed in both Shii and Sunni traditions and could engage with the Safavids' Sunni subjects, and legitimise the rivalry with the Ottomans by penning polemics.[21] Ali al-Karaki (1464–1533), from Jabal Amil, became the key ideologue behind the Safavid conversion campaign and their highest religious official.[22]

He composed an anti-Sunni treatise and made the cursing of the first three Sunni Caliphs compulsory.²³ Shii rule was symbolised by adding a third element to the call to prayer, the *Shahada*, the testimony, which is the first sentence that anyone wishing to become a Muslim has to say, and is the first pillar of Islam: 'There is no god but God (and) Muhammad is the messenger of God.' These first two testimonies refer to God and Muhammad, but during the Safavid Era, a third one praising Imam Ali's guardianship was introduced, with the muezzin following this by saying 'I bear witness that Ali is the friend of God.' Adding the third *Shahada*, initially disputed amongst Shia, now became widely accepted, and symbolised Shii rule.²⁴

In newly conquered territories with large Sunni populations such as Tabriz and Herat, strongmen enforced the public cursing as a ritual of humiliation and a test of loyalty. Enforcers spied on Sunnis to see if they would curse the Caliphs and, if they refused, enforce harsh punishment up to the death penalty.²⁵ This practice drew the Ottomans' ire, not least because the list of those cursed sometimes included Abu Hanifa, the founding father of the Ottomans' school of jurisprudence, and even the Ottoman Sultans themselves. As Shah Tahmasp (d. 1576) wrote to his Ottoman counterpart, Suleiman II:

> We in the God-protected realms have ordered that the ritual disavowers and indigent darvishes and the multitude of people who have been chanting the curse of the enemies of the family of the lord of the prophets and the sayyid of the guardians of the faith through cursing in the heart and aloud, from this day should count you and your followers among the accursed Bani 'Umayya, Bani Marwan, Barmaka, and Bani 'Abbas [whom they curse] in the markets, quarters, mosques, academies, and from the pulpits.²⁶

Although no longer enforced from Ismail II onwards, the cursing of the Caliphs remained part of popular culture. Umar, who was Caliph at the time of the Islamic conquest of Iran, and, unlike Ali, was sometimes portrayed in Iranian-Shii narratives as having discriminated against Iranian Muslims, was criticised especially. On the anniversary of the day Umar was killed (*Umar Kushan*), for example, replicas of Umar were paraded through the streets and denigrated (there was even a shrine for his killer). Unsurprisingly, these practices enraged Sunnis.²⁷

Much of the population in Iran's cities had been nominally Sunni, although there were some largely Shii cities and regions ruled by local Shii dynasties such as Gilan, Mazandaran, Khuzistan, and Sabzavar and the cities of Ray, Varamin, Qom, and Kashan. In the largely Sunni cities, a Shii elite, often Sayyids, had worked in government, and had received privileges for their service. Together with the Qizilbash, these Shii elites were early supporters of the Safavid state. The Safavids also re-employed parts of the old Sunni administrative elites, but some Sunni clerics and notables left Iran to Ottoman, Uzbek, or Mughal territory, and others continued to hold their beliefs in private. Those who did not emphasise their sectarian affiliation could remain unharmed, though accounts of executions of Sunni clerics and notables abound. Less well-connected Sunnis at times paid a sort of protection fee to Shia to attest their Shiism. Lower-class Sunnis, who could not afford this, were targeted most systematically for conversion, and if they resisted, could be killed.[28]

This went hand in hand with the repression of Sufi orders. For once in power, the Safavids, who themselves originated as a Sufi order, saw the other orders, with their strict hierarchy and disciplined following as rival sources of religious and political authority. They first targeted Sufi orders with a distinct Sunni identity (Qadiris and Naqshbandis), while those with a more Shii identity (Nimatullahis) were tolerated, and their leaders either co-opted or marginalised.[29] Some of the Shii-leaning orders would now emphasise the centrality of Ali and even the twelfth Imam.[30] The Nimatullahis, for example, increased veneration of Ali in rituals and prayer.[31] The same holds true for the Dhahabi order, which, from its inception in the fifteenth century as a breakaway group of the Kubrawi order, was strongly Shii.[32] Naqshbandis would instead flourish in the Ottoman, Mughal, and Uzbek domains, and in their original strongholds such as Bukhara, Samarqand, and Herat, bolstered by Sunni refugees from Iran.[33] Naqshbandis became significant anti-Safavid and anti-Shii ideologues and interlocutors between the Sunni-led empires, which intensified the Safavids' hostility towards them.[34]

To speed up conversion, Shii Friday prayer leaders were appointed across Iran.[35] Previously, many Shii clerics had argued that in the absence of the twelfth Imam, any government was ultimately illegitimate, and rejected congregational Friday prayers. Some Shii clerics now argued that, for the first time in centuries, a legitimate government had taken power and was to be supported.[36] A similar debate revolved around the question of warfare. Shia had seldom followed calls for Jihad issued by Sunni Caliphs (who were at times quite content to collect a special levy from them instead). It was only in the Safavid state that a Shii political authority mobilised its population in a Jihad and that Shii clerics, the representatives of the Imam, legitimised it.[37]

Like the Friday prayer, however, this remained contested. The close association between Shii scholars and politics and the introduction of new practices were not unanimously accepted, with some Shii scholars criticising their peers.[38] But these critics did not manage to halt these practices, nor prevent the association of other clerics with the Safavid state.[39]

Shii clerics also further codified and systematised Shiism, oversaw further conversions, and disseminated treatises to convince Sunnis of the validity of Shiism.[40] Muhammad Baqir al-Majlisi (1627–99 or 1700), catalogued Shii Hadith traditions in his monumental *Bihar al-Anwar*, which would eventually take 110 volumes to print it in full. It was meant to represent Shii beliefs and practices and act as a source for the education of future Shii scholars.[41] Apart from Arabic, Shii works were now translated into and written in Persian to reach a wider audience.[42] The Safavid period coincided with the consolidation of Persian as the language of high culture and scholarship far beyond Iran, especially on the Indian subcontinent.[43] Familiarity with Persian facilitated interactions between Ottoman, Safavid, and Mughal domains.[44] Ottoman Sultans wrote poetry in Persian, while Turkish was the native tongue of the Safavids and the Qizilbash, and the court language, though in formal diplomatic correspondence with each other, the Ottomans would generally use Ottoman Turkish and the Safavids Persian.[45] Non-Arab Clerics would still use Arabic for major religious works, including for polemics, not least to show their familiarity with the language of the Quran, but would choose Persian or Ottoman Turkish to reach a wider audience. A common Persian high culture facilitated myriad engagements, including personal, economic, and political ties and cultural (including literary) interactions.[46]

There was no ideological, cultural, or linguistic 'iron curtain' between Safavid and non-Safavid domains, though political rivalries, geographic boundaries, and separate intellectual and educational centres fostered a distinctiveness. In parts of the Islamic sciences and in philosophy, a profound engagement continued. Even the Shii clerics discussed above borrowed from Sunni Hadith scholarship. Poetry, art, and liturgy were fields shared across the Persianate world (the most renowned of the Persian miniature painters, Behzad, whose paintings are seen as iconic of the period, for example, was initially patronised by Timurid and Uzbek rulers in Herat, before moving to the Safavid court). The Sufi themes that pervaded miniature paintings in the fifteenth century took on a more explicitly Shii-Sufi

form in the sixteenth.[47] Moreover, exactly what percentage of the population converted to Shiism during Safavid rule is still debated, as it was a
gradual process, so that even by the early eighteenth century there was still
a significant Sunni population, and Sunnis could hold high office.[48]

Yet the conversion of the bulk of the population in the heartland of the
Persianate world meant that people across that world were deeply affected.
For the Safavid period shaped a new Shii self-understanding and cultural
identity that reflected political power. This was expressed, for example, in
the publication of popular literature collections that included anti-Sunni
jokes, fostering a more assertive popular Shii identity that presented Shia as
wiser, more refined, and more pious, and less prone to dogmatic stupidity,
hypocrisy, and false piety than Sunnis.[49]

This new self-consciousness was displayed during Muharram processions,
which became occasions of state.[50] After the Safavids had made Isfahan their
capital in 1591–2, they would take place on Isfahan's new, purpose-built
central square, the epicentre of Safavid symbolic power, where European
travellers and diplomats also attended.[51] Pilgrimage to Shii shrines became
another central element of the new popular religiosity. Initially, the shrine at
Ardabil of Shaykh Safi al-Din, the founder of the Safavid dynasty, became a
well-frequented site of pilgrimage. Shah Tahmasp (d. 1576) expanded that
shrine and had two magnificent carpets woven in its honour. Signifying the
rising influence of Britain, and its fascination with the 'Orient', one of these
carpets was in the nineteenth century brought to the Victoria and Albert
Museum in London.[52] Also on display in the museum is a sword by Shah
Tahmasp on which his whole lineage dating back to the *Ahl al-Bayt* as well
as a Surah from the Quran are engraved. This lineage was important in the
Safavids' quest for legitimacy, for at some point during the fifteenth century,
they discovered (others would say invented) a genealogical link to the seventh Shii Imam, Musa al-Kazim.[53] This allowed the Safavids to patronise the
shrine of Imam Rida at Mashhad as a sort of ancestral heritage.[54] For the
shrine of Imam Rida was the only tomb of a Shii Imam that would remain
permanently under their control. The graves of the other Imams were all in
territories that were contested between Safavids and Ottomans (as in Iraq),
or controlled by the Ottomans (as in Medina). Let us now turn to the
Ottomans.

After conquering Constantinople, the city named after the fourth-century
Byzantine Emperor Constantine, in 1453, the Ottomans moved to bind the

faraway provinces of their empire closer to what would become their new capital, which gradually acquired the name Istanbul. A process of centralisation went hand in hand with the empire's greatest military successes and its assertion as a world power. This process, which mainly involved enhanced taxation and conscription, as noted, led to fierce opposition in the periphery amongst groups such as the Qizilbash.[55] Having taken Constantinople, the Ottomans claimed the title 'Caesar of Rome' to indicate that now that Byzantium was theirs they were also heirs to Roman sovereignty.

The Habsburg family, who were rising amongst Europe's aristocratic families to become one of the most important houses, had long established their base in Austria but by the sixteenth century ruled large parts of Central Europe and called themselves Holy Roman Emperors (i.e. both the secular head of Christendom and the heir to Roman sovereignty). This in turn spurred the Ottomans, who would compete with the Habsburgs for control of the Balkans, to emphasise their claim as Caliphs to suzerainty over all Muslims. The relationship between the Ottomans and their two main enemies, the Habsburgs and of course the Safavids, was thus a dialectical one. Faced with Christian and Shii enemies, who styled themselves as both political and religious leaders, the ideological dimension of these rivalries served to strengthen the general Muslim aspect (in the rivalry with the Habsburgs) and the specifically Sunni aspect (in the rivalry with the Safavids) of Ottoman rule.[56] This coincided with the expansion of Ottoman territory and the incorporation and conversion of new, non-Muslim populations, including in the Balkans. These new populations would, from the second half of the sixteenth century onwards, be pushed to convert to a specifically 'Ottoman Sunni Islam'.[57]

In this context, the Ottomans institutionalised a hierarchical and well-organised clergy (with up to 1,000 employed by the state at a time). Hanafism became the official school of jurisprudence and was applied across the Empire.[58] These scholars legitimised war against the Safavids and the repression of the Qizilbash, thereby enhancing their own status and proclaiming their Sunni authority.[59] A similar hierarchically organised clergy developed in the Safavid realm.[60] The consolidation of a religious and bureaucratic class and a refashioning of state legitimacy contributed to a sharper delineation of Sunnism and Shiism.[61]

Scholars from both sides sought to extend the notion of Jihad to war against fellow Muslims, which was theoretically not allowed—Jihad had previously been reserved to the expansion of the territory of Islam, such as in the early Muslim conquests, or defence against non-Muslim invaders, such as during the Crusades. As we have seen, Shia had seldom made use of the principle. The Ottomans therefore had to get clerics to legitimise war against the Safavids, and vice versa. In the build-up to the Battle of Chaldiran in 1514, the first major engagement between the Ottomans and the Safavids, these Ottomans scholar-bureaucrats agreed that the war was not only legally valid but an obligation. Two of the most senior Ottoman clerics, Nureddin Hamza Sarigürz, and Kemalpashazade, argued that fighting the Safavids was a duty for every Muslim because the Safavids were apostates. While Sarigürz justified the harshest measures against the Safavids and their supporters on Ottoman soil, Kemalpashazade claimed that the latter should only be confronted if they were rebelling or trying to secede (later fatwas would expand this distinction to allow the Sultan to come to an arrangement with the Ottoman Qizilbash, while still fighting the Safavids).[62]

Denouncing the Safavids as heretic thus served practical purposes, giving ideological cohesion to the war effort and regulating war booty (legitimising enslavement of opponents and confiscation of their property), and asserting one's own orthodoxy.[63] The texts would list the allegedly deviant acts of the Safavids such as the cursing of Abu Bakr, Umar, and Aisha, declaring them 'infidels and heretics. To kill them and to destroy their communities is an implicit and essential obligation for all Muslims [...] the Sultan of Islam is authorized to kill their men and to distribute their property, women and children among the defenders of religion.'[64] Fatwas and polemics, some of which were written by Sunni refugees from Iran, further galvanised anti-Safavid feelings.[65] These polemics targeted the Qizilbash (in this context meaning the Safavids), their supporters (primarily in Iran), and those Iranians who had converted to Shiism. The fatwas also stated the unbelief (*kufr*) of the Qizilbash.[66]

In letters to Shah Ismail I before Chaldiran, Selim I reiterated these allegations in offensive language, challenging him to the battlefield.[67] It would be a decisive victory for the Ottomans. Selim I expanded the realm. Shah Ismail I, whose army had been vastly outnumbered, would never lead his troops into battle again. Any major expansionary plans, including the further spread of Shiism beyond core Safavid realms, were abandoned.[68] In military terms, the rivalry was decided—the Ottomans had won. This meant that the position of the Ottoman Qizilbash could be rethought. Those that did remain loyal to the Safavids either migrated to Iran or started to refashion this allegiance in a more original Sufi sense, towards the Safavid Sufi order as a spiritual authority, rather than towards the Safavid state as political authority. This only worked to a certain extent, however, as the lines between the two principles had become blurred, and the Ottomans remained suspicious.[69]

In the wake of the campaign against the Safavids, Selim I turned his attention to the Mamluks of Egypt, the other major Muslim power on the Mediterranean. The Ottomans had already fought several wars against the Mamluks in the late fifteenth century, because of territorial conflicts and because the Mamluks were the Ottomans' major rivals for the claim of leadership of Sunnism, as they were still controlling the Hijaz and an Abbasid Caliph lived at their court.[70] They were initially neutral towards the Ottoman-Safavid rivalry, but when tensions heightened after Selim's ascension in 1512 and the declaration of war on Iran, the Mamluks took a pro-Safavid stance.[71] This, however, gave the Ottomans the pretext to move against them with full force. They legitimised it with fatwas stating that—though Sunni—the Mamluks had lost all legitimacy by siding with the Safavids, and could be fought.[72]

The Ottomans defeated the Mamluks throughout 1516–17 and took over Syria, Egypt, and the Hijaz.[73] In Egypt and Syria, where the large towns had long-standing Sunni religious traditions and a preference for the Shafii and Hanbali schools, the Istanbul-trained Ottoman Hanafi clerics faced resentment. Relations amongst clerics from the different Sunni schools of law, and between Arabs and Turks, were not free of friction, but political stability under Ottoman rule led to prosperity and development of the great cities, and secured the all-important pilgrimage routes, which helped smooth the transition.[74]

As part of their campaign against the Mamluks, and to secure the Hijaz, the Ottomans pushed further into the Arabian Peninsula. In Yemen, they encountered the Zaydi Imams, and in the East, they intermittently ruled over Sunni tribal groups and Twelver Shii sedentary populations.[75] What started as an Ottoman reaction to the Qizilbash rebellions and the establishment of the Safavid state thus led to massive territorial gains. Within a few years, the Ottomans had driven back the Safavids, massively enlarged their Empire by incorporating Mamluk domains, and now stylised themselves as the archetypical Sunni Muslim rulers, legitimised by control over the Hijaz.

The Sharifs of Mecca, who governed the Holy Places, accepted Ottoman suzerainty. The Ottomans had already in the fifteenth century used the title of Caliph, but to little effect. In the Sunni theory of the Caliphate, the

Caliph had to be a member of the tribe of the Prophet, Quraysh (the Mamluks did not claim to be Caliphs themselves, but instead hosted descendants of the Abbasid Caliphs in Cairo). Despite not being Quraysh, the Ottomans captured the last Abbasid Caliph in Cairo upon their conquest of the city, who, according to the Ottoman narrative, transferred the title of Caliph and a number of relics said to have belonged to the Prophet Muhammad, and later the Umayyad and Abbasid Caliphs, including the Mantle of the Prophet, to Selim I (they were then displayed in the Topkapi Palace, the residence of the Ottoman Sultans).[76] Ottoman clerics did not find elegant ways around the lack of Qurayshi descent, but nonetheless justified the Ottoman Caliphate. With the incorporation of Mecca and Medina and massive territorial gains, Ottoman claims to the Caliphate gained in substance.[77] The Ottomans used this in their rivalry with the Habsburgs, and the Safavids, who they portrayed as rebelling against the one rightful Islamic ruler.[78] They sought to portray themselves as defenders of Sunnism, and as spiritual leaders of all Muslims, giving especially Shii-leaning Sufis enough room to feel part of the system.[79]

Suzerainty over the Hijaz brought symbolic and economic benefits. It was a major source of revenue and afforded the power to regulate pilgrimage. The Ottomans were suspicious of Shii pilgrims, and at times of heightened tensions with the Safavids would sometimes ban Iranian pilgrims (though for most periods they did not).[80] And for Sunni pilgrims from Central Asia, travel across Safavid domains could be challenging. Still, the Hajj resulted in much grass-roots Sunni–Shia interaction.[81] As cosmopolitan cities, Mecca and Medina were open to all Muslims, including Shia, who could debate issues of the day. Shia were able to visit and teach in the Holy Places, and sometimes even became prominent under the protection of the Sharifs, but generally faced restrictions. An old Shii community in Medina was tolerated, even if it was socially outcast and economically disenfranchised.[82] After one scholar had encountered Shia in Mecca, he compiled a treatise against them and read it out aloud at the Grand Mosque. Interest was allegedly so great that, fourteen years later, handwritten copies had reached the Maghreb, Transoxania, Yemen, and India.[83]

After Selim's death in 1520, Suleiman I, who was to reign for forty-six years until his death in 1566, further expanded the empire. In Europe, he became known as 'Suleiman the Magnificent', in large part because of the potency of his military. In the Ottoman Empire, however, he was the 'law-giver', suggesting that his most important legacy was the establishment of a legal order based on Hanafi Sunnism.[84] Suleiman expanded a court system that paid closer attention to peoples' beliefs and religious practices. This went hand in hand with the expansion of the clerical class, who were given more power to enforce Sunnism. Qizilbash rituals and communities were a preferred target, and some of the court cases are reminiscent of witch trials in early modern Europe.[85] The state encouraged denunciations of suspected Qizilbash, and countless Ottoman imperial decrees ordered the suppression and expulsion of suspected pro-Safavid Qizilbash.[86] This was no Inquisition as in the Catholic Church with a centralised decision-making body and an organised structure across the realm. But the state did pay more attention to peoples' beliefs, constructed more and larger mosques, and enacted new laws about mosque attendance.[87] Suleiman's Imperial Sunnism is symbolised by the Suleimaniyya Mosque in Istanbul and other mosques and public buildings conceived by Mimar Sinan (d. 1588), the most iconic of Ottoman architects, which shaped Istanbul and many provincial cities across the Empire.[88]

Under Suleiman's leadership, the Ottomans took the Hungarian capital of Buda in 1526 and laid siege to Vienna in 1529. The Ottoman army was thus engaged in Europe, which is partly why Suleiman initially exchanged polite diplomatic notes with the Safavids. But by the 1530s, he would turn against them.[89] His aim was to establish Ottoman control over the passes linking Iran with eastern Anatolia and Georgia by conquering Armenia and Kurdistan and to expand towards the Persian Gulf by capturing Iraq. The success of this campaign would contain the Safavids militarily and surround them with (largely Sunni) enemies.[90]

Baghdad changed hands three times between 1508, when the Safavids under Shah Ismail took the city from the White Sheep dynasty, and 1638, when the Ottomans definitively consolidated their rule. For both sides, Iraq was part of a sacred topography with sectarian overtones.[91] The more the Safavids legitimised themselves with Twelver Shiism, the more important Iraq became: Safavid links to the shine cities were emphasised, and patronage of the shrines of the Imams increased.[92]

From 1533 onwards, in turn, the Ottomans pushed into Iraq and took Baghdad, a campaign to which they sought to ascribe a Sunni identity. The Ottomans, for example, inscribed the names of Abu Bakr, Umar, and Uthman into the walls of mosques they encountered. Upon arriving in Baghdad, Suleiman visited the grave of Abu Hanifa, the founder of the empire's official school of jurisprudence. The tomb had allegedly been destroyed by the Safavids upon their conquest of the city in 1508. Suleiman's first act was to order the construction of a tomb, a mosque, and a *madrasa* in honour of Abu Hanifa, highlighting the state's association with Hanafism. The reconstructed tomb of Abu Hanifa and the continuation of Ottoman patronage reinforced its location at the centre of the largely Sunni Adhamiyya quarter, which is on the opposite side of the Tigris from the largely Shii Kazimiyya quarter that includes the shrines of two Imams. The tomb of Abu Hanifa was destroyed again in 1623 when Shah Abbas I took the area and reconstructed yet again after the final Ottoman conquest in 1638 by Murad IV.[93]

While the Ottomans regarded Shii religious practices and Safavid funding of Shii shrines and clerics with suspicion, they renovated the shrines of the Imams in Kazimiyya, Najaf, and Karbala, established new fresh water supplies for Najaf and Karbala, and built pilgrims' lodgings. They also maintained the system of financing the shrines through endowments, even if that meant accepting Iranian patronage of the shrines.[94] A renowned Shii poet, Fuzuli, for example, who had been employed by the shrine of Najaf and had written odes praising the Safavids, was kept on, awarded a special stipend, and started praising the Ottomans instead.[95]

In newly conquered territories, the Ottomans initially collected fewer taxes than the Safavids and invested in infrastructure to win over the population.[96] At times, Ottoman rival princes even tried to use the Qizilbash to their advantage. Both Empires supported dissident princes of the other side (the Ottoman princes Murad and Bayezid and the Safavid prince Alqas Mirza are the most famous ones). Alqas Mirza allied himself with Sunni notables from Shirvan in the eastern Caucasus who rebelled against Safavid and Shii control. He sought Ottoman help, raised the possibility of returning to Iran as an Ottoman client, and may have converted to Sunnism.[97]

The Safavid Shah Ismail, on the other hand, supported Murad, who at the Safavid court donned the Qizilbash cap.[98] A few decades later, the Safavids initially supported Bayezid's ambitions to the Ottoman throne but, when the opportunity arose, were quick to hand him over to a certain death in return for better bilateral relations.[99] The Ottomans were most pleased with Shah Tahmasp for this; it was a major factor in peaceful relations between 1555 and 1578.[100]

The Ottoman state seems to have continued to interact with and issue property deeds to known supporters of the Safavids.[101] When Ottoman armies occupied frontier regions, some Qizilbash found employment with the Ottomans, sometimes after having converted in public, sometimes without having done so.[102] Frontier populations, and their rulers, could switch sides, too. Kurds, who lived along the Ottoman–Safavid frontier, are a case in point. The rulers of the Emirate of Bitlis were first pro-Ottoman, then switched to the Safavids, then again to the Ottomans, before reverting to the Safavids. The late sixteenth-century Kurdish Emir Sharaf al-Din Khan Bidlisi, who Shah Ismail II initially appointed as head of all Kurds in Iran, later became a major Ottoman military commander.[103]

In support of Sultan Suleiman's campaign against the Safavids in 1554–5, the last campaign of the first Ottoman–Safavid War (1532–55), the new Shaykh al-Islam (from 1545), Abu s-Suud Efendi (d. 1574), issued anti-Safavid and anti-Qizilbash fatwas. While condemning the Safavids and legitimising war, he did so in less alarming terms than during the first anti-Safavid campaigns (referring to an important distinction in Islamic law about warfare and Jihad, he did not decree the fight as a duty for every Muslim, the strongest way in which a Jihad can be declared, but rather as simply permissible).[104]

After this campaign, the two sides signed the Peace Treaty of Amasya in 1555 in which they recognised each other's legitimacy, and the Ottomans finally accepted the Safavids as Twelver Shia and Muslims. The Ottoman Sultan proposed that Shii pilgrims would not be prevented from visiting Mecca and Medina and the tombs of the Imams in the Hijaz and Iraq if the Shah banned the cursing of the Companions.[105] The treaty was followed, as noted, by two decades of improved relations.

However, the new Ottoman ruler, Murad III, again went to war with the Safavids in 1578. To the Ottomans, the weakness at the heart of the Safavid polity after the death of Tahmasp in 1576, was too big a chance to miss.[106] Ottoman clerics reiterated the unbelief of the Safavids and the obligation for war against them and described Safavid propaganda in Shirvan, which had remained predominantly Sunni, as a breach of the Treaty of Amasya.[107] The first expedition lasted until 1588 and resulted in territorial gains for the Ottomans, after which a peace treaty in their favour was signed in Istanbul in 1590, which again included the ban on the cursing of the Companions.[108]

Shiism provided a potent legitimising ideology for the Safavids domestically, but limited their reach abroad, and gave the rivalry with their Sunni neighbours a confessional element. These neighbours were often tribally organised and included the Lezgis of the Eastern Caucasus, the Afghan and Baluchi tribes of Kirman and Sistan, and, prominently, the Uzbeks to the

East, with whom the Safavids were embroiled in a struggle over the spoils of the disintegrating Timurid Empire.[109] Ottomans and Uzbeks even maintained a secret correspondence in the early sixteenth century to coordinate anti–Safavid action.[110]

The Turkic Uzbeks claimed descent from Genghis Khan and, in the fifteenth century, started to conquer more territory from their base in Khwarazm, the oasis region near the river Oxus, culminating in the rule of Muhammad Shaybani Khan (r. 905–915/1500–10).[111] Between the fourteenth and the seventeenth century, various descendants of Genghis Khan had ruled Central Asia, which deepened the hold of nominally Sunni Islam, and the Chaghatay language.[112] Religious identity became a common denominator between the otherwise linguistically and ethnically diverse rulers and populations. In the early sixteenth century, Timurid rule over Khorasan ended in the face of Uzbek conquests. Like their Timurid predecessors, Uzbek rulers patronised the *Ahl al-Bayt*, performed pilgrimage to Mashhad, and were buried and crowned there. Shaybani Khan initially stylised himself as both political and religious leader and, upon his conquest of Herat in 1507, had himself praised in Friday prayers as *Imam of the Age* and *Caliph of the Merciful*.[113] That his claims resembled those of Ismail I, intensified their rivalry, which crystallised itself in competition over control of the shrine city of Mashhad, the burial place of Imam Rida.[114]

Despite their reverence for the *Ahl al-Bayt*, and influenced by Sunni Sufi orders such as the Naqshbandiyya, the Uzbeks developed a disdain for political Shiism and its incarnation in the Safavid state. A prominent Sunni cleric, historian, and polemicist, Fadlallah Ruzbihan Khunji (1455–1521), who would become one of Shaybani Khan's advisors, epitomises these changing times. Initially a court historian to the nominally Sunni White Sheep dynasty in Tabriz, he fled after Ismail I took the city in 1501.[115] His first destination was Kashan, where he wrote a long refutation of al-Hilli's book on the Imamate, which already drove into action Ibn Taymiyya two centuries earlier, and epitomised how powerful an outlining of the Shii argument it was.[116] He then found patronage at the court of Shaybani Khan.

Close to the Naqshbandiyya, Khunji venerated the *Ahl al-Bayt* and, when performing the pilgrimage to Mashhad together with Shaybani Khan, is said to have accused the Shia of putting more emphasis on cursing the Companions than on venerating the *Ahl al-Bayt*.[117] At the court of Shaybani Khan, Khunji wrote a historical work with the aim of spurring the Uzbeks into action against the Safavids[118] and would later write a manual for kings that was an elaboration of Sunni political theory (it vilified the Safavids but recognised Shiism as a school of Islam).[119]

Khunji connected diverse Sunni trends and dynasties: he worked for the White Sheep state and, after a visit to Egypt, lauded the Mamluks as defenders of Sunnism (before their alliance with the Safavids), then entered the service of the Uzbeks and praised them and the Ottoman Sultans.[120] He refined Sunni political theory against the backdrop of the Safavid challenge and sought to spur different powers into action against them. His works were to be extraordinarily influential in the Sunni Persianate sphere from Central Asia to the Indian subcontinent. His reverence for the *Ahl al-Bayt* did not prevent him from enforcing boundaries between Sunnism and Shiism.

Khunji's and Shaybani Khan's ambitions were soon shattered, however. The Safavids under Ismail I defeated the Uzbek army at the Battle of Marv in 1510, killing Shaybani Khan, which stopped the Uzbeks and divided them.[121] Ismail I took Mashhad and Herat and continued patronising the shrine of Imam Rida (as did his son and successor, Shah Tahmasp).[122] The different Uzbek leaders, though rivals, maintained some cooperation in the face of the Safavid enemy. They took over more parts of the Timurid Empire to the East, defeating Babur, then a local Timurid ruler, in the Battle of Gijduvan in 918/1512. Babur then sought Safavid support, for which he had to accept Safavid suzerainty and impose Shiism in his domains. The Uzbeks legitimised their campaign against him with sectarian arguments and would drive him out of Central Asia. Few would have at that time thought that he would become the legendary founder of the mighty Mughal dynasty in Northern India.[123] (More about him in the next chapter.)

Thereafter, the Uzbeks challenged the Safavids again in Khorasan, which over the coming decades saw five invasions by the Uzbeks and counter-attacks by the Safavids.[124] The region suffered, and massacres were committed by both sides. The new Uzbek leader Ubayd Allah Khan legitimised a renewed campaign on Mashhad in 1529–30 in a letter to Shah Tahmasp with reference to his duty to reverse the corruption of the people by the Safavids' Shii teachings.[125] The Uzbek letters drew sharp responses from Safavid letter writers in 1532 that contained anti-Sunni polemics and defences of Shii principles of legitimate rule.[126]

In the second half of the sixteenth century, the Uzbeks were weakened by infighting, but by the 1580s, when the Safavids were themselves weakened due to their second war with the Ottomans and domestic problems, the Uzbeks attempted to retake Khorasan. Shortly after Shah Abbas' coronation, a polemic between Uzbek Sunni clerics and Shii clerics from Mashhad reiterated the sectarian arguments above. To undermine Safavid authority, the Uzbeks sought to refute Shiism and present Sunnism as the only valid form of Islam (they apparently reacted to a letter by Shii clerics spurring the Safavids into action over Mashhad). The polemic was meant to legitimise Uzbek control over Mashhad with religious arguments. The Uzbek clerics argued that Shia were heretics so the Uzbeks could confiscate their and the shrine's property, but also praised the Imams in order to legitimise control over Mashhad.[127] The letters spurred further Sunni–Shia debates, including a famous one in India.[128] In Safavid chronicles, depictions of the Uzbek conquest of Mashhad in 998/1589–90 include grim details about Uzbek massacres, executions of Shii clergy, and plundering of the shrine.[129] When the Safavids under Shah Tahmasp reconquered Khorasan, they in turn unleashed violence against Sunnis.[130]

As Ottomans, Safavids, and Uzbeks legitimised their empires and wars with religious arguments, different powers in Europe, which were themselves fighting and allying with one another with renewed religious vigour in the context of the Reformation and Counter-reformation, became more interested in and involved with the Muslim Empires. The competition between Muslim powers and their rivalries with European powers, which were themselves engaged in confessionalised rivalries with each other, contributed to the sharper delineation of confessions in Christianity and Islam.

This era of 'Confessionalisation', a term which has its origin in the term confession, the pronunciation of one's faith in public, was initially coined by historians of early modern Europe to describe a renewed commitment to confessional identity in Europe after the Reformation, and the link between religious identity and early modern states, but can also be applied to the Middle East.[131]

For the Age of Confessionalisation shared key features around the Mediterranean even if there were crucial differences between Islam and Christianity. For a start, unlike Protestantism, which challenged Catholicism, Sunnism, and Shiism had for centuries developed in dialogue and competition with each other, had been used in inter-state rivalries, and had experienced reform movements and movements to assert doctrinal boundaries. But like in Europe, religious identity and specifically confessional identity became key to early modern state formation and legitimisation in Muslim contexts.[132] In addition, heightened awareness of sectarian difference after the Reformation left Europeans more attuned to sectarian difference in Islam and to the ways in which this could be exploited. Prior to the Reformation, Christian authors looked for 'schismatics' amongst Muslims and found them in the ranks of the Shia, after the Reformation, authors sought to compare Christianity and Islam against the backdrop of this confessional split.[133]

Most Europeans learned about differences between Sunna and Shia through interactions with the Ottomans, thus adopting the Sunni point of view.[134] Stefan Gerlach, a Lutheran chaplain to the Habsburg embassy in Constantinople during the 1570s, for example, largely related Ottoman officials' views on the difference between Sunnism and Shiism.[135] On one occasion, the Austrian ambassador even objected to being seated next to the Safavid ambassador on the grounds that the key Ottoman cleric had issued a fatwa ranking the killing of a supporter of the Safavids (Qizilbash) higher than the killing of seventy infidels (i.e. Christians).[136]

The Ottomans' rivalry with Europe and the gradual loss in importance of the overland route from Asia after the discovery of the sea route via the Cape of Good Hope (as well as the discovery of the Americas) was the wider context. Throughout the sixteenth century, Venice, the Vatican, Portugal, and Russia tried to ally with the Safavids against the Ottomans, who were the main threat to most European powers. While a grand alliance was not forthcoming, and Europeans and Safavids intermittently made peace with the Ottomans, these interactions influenced European views of the Ottoman–Safavid and Sunni–Shia rivalry and spurred their interest.[137]

During the sixteenth century, the Portuguese expanded their footholds in Hormuz, the wider Persian Gulf, and along the Indian Ocean to Goa, on the middle of the western Coast of India, where they founded the Estado da Índia. Portuguese travellers and naval commanders became more aware of the complexity of Islam and particularly of Shii states' rivalry with the Ottomans, as they were looking for alliances with Safavid Iran and the Shii states in the Deccan (which were close to and had relations with the Estado da Índia) against the Mamluks and the Ottomans. From their base in Hormuz, the Portuguese established forts in Bahrain and Qatif, major centres of Shiism in the Persian Gulf, where their presence rested on a fragile alliance with Iran. Portuguese sources of this period are thus favourably disposed towards Shiism and Shii dynasties.[138] This relationship, too, was in part based on anti-Ottoman sentiments, not least in the Gulf, where the

Ottomans expanded their presence in the sixteenth century to check Portuguese advances.[139]

The Portuguese perception of the Safavids would change, however, as they became competitors. By the seventeenth century, the Portuguese feared a Safavid-Deccani alliance to take over their Estado da Índia. They saw the Safavid-Deccani alliance as based on Shiism (and compared it to the relationship between Catholic states in Europe). By that time, however, the Deccani rulers had in part reverted to Sunnism, and political and military relations between the Deccan and Safavid Iran were feeble, so the Portuguese over-estimated the significance of sectarian identity in Muslim alliance formation.[140]

More interactions with Iran led to more interest, and European visitors to Iran started describing Shii rituals and beliefs.[141] A history of the Ottoman-Safavid rivalry published in Italy in the late sixteenth century favoured the Safavids as potential allies, emphasised the religious dimension of the rivalry, and saw the wars between the two powers as an opportunity for the Christian princes of Europe.[142] Trade of the Dutch East India Company with Iran led to a certain amount of cultural transfer and to the development of Persian Studies in the Netherlands in the seventeenth century.[143]

Missionaries and Christian orders also expanded their activities in Iran. They were interested in the history of Islam—again, to better refute it and to convert Muslims. Inevitably, this led to counter-reactions and the strengthening of doctrinal positions on the Muslim side (for example when a Catholic polemic published in Iran led to a forceful Shii response in the seventeenth century).[144] France's foreign policy, on the other hand, was mainly shaped by the Bourbons' rivalry with the Habsburgs, and it thus sought alliances with the Habsburgs' arch-enemy, the Ottomans. As a result, its official interest in Iran was less pronounced than that of other European powers. Nonetheless, a marginalised group in France called the Dévots advocated a pro-Catholic foreign policy that should ally with the Habsburgs and would look for an alliance with the Safavids against the Ottomans. Catholic missionaries travelled to Iran in the sixteenth and seventeenth centuries and described it as more susceptible to missionary activity and a potential ally for European powers because of its Shii identity. As a result, the French encouraged the study of Persian.[145] A member of an Iranian mission to Spain published a book in Spanish on Iran after converting to Catholicism, under the pen name Don Juan of Persia, and his account of the rise of the Safavids emphasises the religious dimension.[146]

This activity reached its climax under the Safavid ruler Shah Abbas, who reigned for more than four decades, from 1587 to 1629, a period that epitomises the high period of Safavid power and cultural refinement. He masterminded the new capital Isfahan, for which he employed thousands of Armenian Christian artisans, who established themselves in the New Julfa quarter of Isfahan, and allowed Christian missionaries in.[147] This led to favourable descriptions in Christian circles. Some missionaries wrote histories of Islam that appreciated the Shii point of view.[148] A Dutch scholar incorporated Persian and Shii sources into his early-eighteenth-century history of Islam[149] and French Protestants wrote histories of Iran that outlined Shii beliefs and rituals.[150]

Nonetheless, negative accounts of Ottoman and Iranian rulers persisted. By the eighteenth century, 'Oriental Despotism' had become a fixed term to describe the politics of the Muslim Empires, in juxtaposition to Enlightenment Europe. Fascination and alienation went hand in hand.[151] The Sunni–Shia question and the Ottoman-Safavid rivalry even entered popular fiction, as for example in the *Letters Writ by a Turkish Spy* and in Montesquieu's *Lettres Persanes*.[152]

The Ottoman-Safavid conflict thus became entangled with the struggle between the Ottomans and European powers, and European expansion to Asia, and a subject of interest in Europe. At the same time, neither Ottomans or Safavids fully allied with European powers against the other, and the Ottomans, for example, remained officially neutral in the largest struggle amongst European powers in the seventeenth century: the thirty years war.[153] But the perception gaining ground in Europe was that Sunnis were the mainstream Muslims, and Shia a movement on Islam's fringes, except in Iran.

Shah Ismail I's successors Tahmasp (r. 1524–76), Ismail II (r. 1576–7), and the above-mentioned Shah Abbas slowly downgraded the religious element of Safavid leadership. According to some sources Ismail II played with the idea of reintroducing Sunnism, stopped the cursing of Abu Bakr, Umar, and Uthman to please the Ottomans, and rewarded Iranian Sunni notables who had not adopted Shiism.[154] He appointed a Sunni, Mirza Makhdum Sharifi, who was influential at court, to the highest religious office. But Ismail II soon died under suspicious circumstances, and Mirza Makhdum fled to

Ottoman territory, where he was welcomed with open arms, and composed an anti-Safavid polemic. The book was handed to the Ottoman Grand Wazir Sinan Pasha and Sultan Murad III in 1580, coinciding with a renewed war with Iran. This episode is puzzling: A Sunni scholar was sufficiently close to the Safavids to gain the trust of a new Shah and to then be appointed to high office. In palace intrigues, however, he lost out and, eventually, became a legitimiser of the rivalry on the Ottoman side.[155] Like Khunji's anti-Shii polemic, this one drew a response from a Shii scholar working at the Mughal court, whom we will get to know in the next chapter.[156]

This interregnum notwithstanding, after the initial period of conquest and revolutionary fervour, legalistic Twelver Shiism gave the Safavid Shahs a sense of stability that the messianism of the Qizilbash could not. In fact, some of the Qizilbash beliefs and ritual practices were now labelled 'extremist'.[157] The clerics, now so vital to the legitimisation of the state, further developed the theory that the qualified jurist was the deputy of the Imam on Earth and could therefore wield real power.[158] Even though the Qizilbash had of course initially brought the Safavids to power, they had become too powerful for the taste of the Safavids, and were increasingly replaced by new forces in the military. This facilitated better relations with the Ottomans, who could now worry less about the loyalties of Ottoman Qizilbash.[159] The definition of what it meant to be a Shii in the Safavid Empire was thus reshaped at the same time as the definition of what it meant to be a Sunni in the Ottoman Empire, i.e. in the context of state consolidation and sectarianised inter-state rivalry.[160]

Shah Abbas and his successors supported Shii scholars and the shrines at Karbala, Najaf, and Mashhad, and turned the new capital Isfahan into a centre of Shiism.[161] For its splendid mosques, bazars, and squares, Isfahan became known as 'half the world' (nesf-e jahan), and the city's main square 'image of the world' (naqsh-e jahan), because its beauty was thought to be unrivalled and so many of the world's riches and wonders could allegedly be found there. On the square Shah Abbas built a new congregational Friday prayer mosque, which symbolised the self-confidence they felt in holding Friday prayers in the absence of the Imam. The mosque epitomised the royal Shiism of the Safavids, and a Persian-Shii style of mosque architecture. It was a highly symbolic departure from the old Friday Mosque of Isfahan that had been established soon after the arrival of Islam. Substantial work on it dates to 1051, when Isfahan became the capital of the Saljuq empire, and their Sunni-minded Wazir Nizam al-Mulk ordered the construction of a domed chamber. While it was also patronised by later Shii rulers, including Uljaytu, and the Safavids added Shii elements to it, Shah Abbas built a new Friday mosque more closely associated with his own dynasty and with Shiism, rather than with the Sunni Saljuqs, and one that like other mosques in Iran was a visual counterpoint to Ottoman ones.[162]

New Shii seminaries and *madrasas* attracted clerics and philosophers from across the Shii world, turning Isfahan, for centuries a centre of Sunnism, into the intellectual centre of Shiism.[163] Qom, which had been one of the few centres of Shiism in Iran before the Safavids, with its shrine for Fatima, the daughter of the seventh Imam, Musa al-Kazim, and sister of the eighth Imam, Ali al-Rida (Reza), also increased in importance.[164]

Although the Ottoman-Safavid rivalry eased and the Ottomans reasserted control over the Turkmen Qizilbash tribes, the securitisation of Shii and pro-Alid groups in the Ottoman Empire was difficult to reverse. Apart from the Qizilbash in Anatolia, the Ottomans ruled over substantial Shii populations in Iraq, the Levant, and the Arabian Peninsula. As a Sunni Empire and Caliphate that ruled over much of North Africa, the Middle East, and the Balkans for centuries, the Ottomans' success depended on ensuring the allegiance of diverse populations, sometimes by force, at others by giving religious and ethnic communities autonomy and co-opting their leaders.[165]

At times, the Ottomans used anti-Shiism and repression, at others, they sought to channel pro-Safavid religious and political movements away from the Safavids. The Qizilbash were repressed and resettled in newly conquered territories such as Bulgaria or Cyprus, and partly reintegrated into the system.[166] Once their immediate threat had waned, it became important to prevent Qizilbash from migrating to Iran to forestall the depopulation of Anatolia. One way to integrate Qizilbash and pro-Safavid elites was by recognising their claims to descent of the Prophet.[167] Another was through the Sufi orders. Sufis were involved in the Ottoman effort to establish a new public Islam.[168] Sunni-minded Sufis in the Ottoman Empire, such as the Naqshbandis, would publicly emphasise their devotion to the *Ahl al-Bayt* and lament the martyrdom of Hussain to prevent the *Ahl al-Bayt* from being monopolised by Shiism.[169] Other orders that the Ottomans promoted had strong Alid features and traced their spiritual chain to Ali through a line of Shii Imams.[170] Some of these Sufi orders were torn between the two powers, and sought to play up their Shii leanings in dealings with the Safavids, and their Sunni ones when engaging the Ottomans.[171]

The most famous example are the above-mentioned Bektashis, named after Hacci Bektash, a thirteenth-century Sufi. Not trained as a cleric, he stood in a tradition of local holy men and wandering dervishes, whose poetry contained strong Alid motives.[172] In the fourteenth and fifteenth centuries, the Ottomans supported Bektashi lodges, especially under Sultan Bayezid II (r. 1481–1512), who fostered the editing of Hacci Bektash's writings and hagiographies, which unified the order and refocused it on a shrine complex built in his honour. When the Ottomans repressed some Shii-leaning Sufi orders in the face of the Safavid challenge, not only was the Bektashi order not repressed, it was strengthened further, and put in charge of educating the Janissaries, the elite military force of the Ottoman household.[173]

The Janissaries adopted Bektashism as a warrior ethos and in military ceremonies would invoke not only the eponymous founder but also Ali, and the other Imams, and Janissary documents could praise the Imams and the Ottoman Sultan.[174] This allowed the Ottomans to transform the pro-Alid sentiment in the Empire from a challenge into a backbone of support. The Ottomans even appropriated the iconography of Ali's legendary sword, *Dhu l-Faqar*, for the Janissary corps' insignia.[175] The original of the sword had probably disappeared by then, but the Ottomans created many replicas— including for use in Janissary processions, thereby further popularising it.[176] To many a clear Alid symbol, with Shii overtones, some of the replicas were produced with Sunni references, such as the names of the Rashidun Caliphs.[177]

The Ottomans thus appropriated an Alid symbol, and many nominal Sunnis strongly identified with the *Ahl al-Bayt*, especially with Ali. Histories of Islam written by Ottoman Sunnis, including by Naqshbandis, epitomised that allegiance to the *Ahl al-Bayt*.[178] Some of the earlier Sultans incorporated Alid motifs when they stylised themselves as millenarian leaders.[179] Alid symbolism was widespread in visual culture, ritual practice, and literature. Shii narratives of the supernatural qualities of Fatima and of the charisma of Ali, for example, were included in an illustrated book produced for the Ottoman court.[180] Ottoman rulers sponsored Ashura celebrations in places such as Cairo in an effort to counter overtly Shii mourning processions,[181] even if they occasionally banned it in Iraq.[182] The problem was thus less the beliefs or practices of particular religious groups per se. Rather, it was trans-national connections to a rival Empire and the shifting definitions of 'ortho-doxy' that determined the toleration of one religious group and the rejection of another. And the Ottoman Caliphs did not see a contradiction in having their main military force carry Ali's sword on their flags and being trained by an Alid Sufi order, even if, or perhaps because, their main Muslim enemy were the Shii Safavids. For it allowed the Ottomans to portray themselves as all-encompassing Muslim leaders and incorporated pro-Alid milieus into the Ottoman mainstream.

The fatwas mentioned above were useful to deal with the Qizilbash threat and to legitimise war against the Safavids, but the Ottomans were much less rigorous in applying them towards their Shii subjects, especially outside of Anatolia. In theory, the excommunication of the Qizilbash and the Safavids, legitimised both killing them as well as those who had friendly relations with them (like the Mamluks of Egypt). Qizilbash captured in wartime could be sentenced to death.[183] The fatwas were commissioned by the Sultan or other officials, and the polemics were often dedicated to the Sultan and endorsed anti-Safavid policies.[184] At times, the Ottoman state did distinguish between 'Qizilbash' and Shia.[185] One fatwa states that Qizilbash pretend to be Shia yet are not, facilitating their excommunication (rather than of Shia in general).[186] On the other hand, the polemic by the Persian Mirza Makhdum, whom we have got to know as the Sunni cleric appointed by Ismail II, equated the Safavids with Shiism and attacked Shiism.[187] Fatwas and anti-Safavid polemics continued to be produced in the early seventeenth century, including by senior Ottoman clerics.[188] But Qizilbash persecution was not systematic. Nonetheless, the vilification of Qizilbash, the Safavids, and Shiism more generally, in Ottoman chronicles, where Ottoman actions against the Safavids were framed as a defence of Sunnism, influenced Ottoman cultural memory. Ottoman elite understandings of the right kind of Sunnism were formed in this context and in time would be embraced by wider parts of the population.[189] From the mid-sixteenth century onwards, manuals on correct (Sunni) religious practice circulated around the Empire, while similar manuals outlining correct (Shii) practice spread in Iran.[190]

Sixteenth-century Ottoman clerics defined heresy with a view to both the Safavids and their supporters on Ottoman soil. By doing so, they reasserted Ottoman Sunnism as the new norm and a source of legitimacy. In some of their argumentations, they linked back to the anti-Shii and anti-Ismaili polemics of the eleventh and twelfth centuries discussed above.[191] The anti-Qizilbash fatwas could be used to imply that marriages amongst Qizilbash were void. Whilst we do not know to what extent this was enforced, Sunni–Shia marriages were denounced and officially prohibited, and extremely rare at this point.[192]

Still, it is important to remember that these fatwas were primarily invoked if Shia rebelled or were accused of crimes. If they did not, the fatwas would likely not be applied at all. One should therefore not see the fatwas or the polemics as shaping the daily lives or religious practices of Ottoman subjects, or to argue that all Shia or Qizilbash in the Ottoman Empire were marginalised or repressed. After all, large Twelver Shii, Qizilbash, and other pro-Shii populations survived centuries of Ottoman rule with their beliefs intact, something that more than any other argument points to the limits to how far the state was willing to go in the enforcing of Sunnism. Some Ottoman writers tried to advocate greater harmony and a more nuanced view of Shiism and the Ottomans appointed Shia to high-ranking positions.[193] In coastal Syria, for example, the Ottomans appointed Shii notables and feudal lords as tax farmers and local officials. These Shii elite families were not generally referred to in sectarian terms in the sixteenth century, despite the Ottoman rivalry with the Safavids. On the contrary, their problems with the Ottoman state escalated in the late seventeenth century, at a time when, as we'll see, the Ottomans and Safavids achieved a rapprochement. This was related to taxation and local power dynamics rather than to the Ottoman–Safavid rivalry or the anti-Qizilbash campaigns, and the Ottomans only associated Shii elite families with the Qizilbash when they needed a pretext to move against them. In fact, amongst the first tribal leaders to offer allegiance to Selim in 1516 so that he could 'implement Islamic order and establish justice' was a member of the Shii Harfush family from Baalbek, which took over control of the Bekaa valley around this time.[194]

The Ottomans likewise ruled over Shii populations in the Hijaz, where as we have seen there was a small Shii community in Medina, and in Eastern Arabia. The islands of Bahrain, the port city of Qatif on the coast of the Persian Gulf, and the oasis of al-Ahsa had been Shii for centuries, at least since the Ismaili Qarmatians established themselves in the area around 900. It may have been under successive local dynasties that conversion from Ismailism to Twelver Shiism accelerated.[195] From the fourteenth century onwards, when the Shii Jarwanids ruled the lands of Bahrain, a caste of local Twelver Shii clerics developed.[196] On the mainland, in Qatif and al-Ahsa, most rulers were Sunni, but much of the sedentary population was Shii.[197] Bahrain, Qatif, and al Ahsa developed a specific Shii tradition, in which local clerics and notable families, who were prominent in their villages and urban quarters, would wield social authority, and where mystical trends of Shiism flourished. These Shii communities were closely tied to the shrine cities of Karbala and Najaf, a connection that Ottoman rule intensified. But especially Bahrain also maintained close relations with nearby Iran. Traders, pilgrims, and clerics would move between Eastern Arabia, Iran, and Southern Iraq with ease, facilitated by the smooth waters of the Persian Gulf, and the relatively short distance to places such as Najaf via Basra.[198]

The region then became embroiled in the rivalry between Ottomans, Portuguese, and Safavids (as we've seen the latter two would at times be in alliance against the Ottomans). The Ottomans technically controlled Basra, al-Ahsa, and Qatif from the mid-sixteenth century onwards. Basra was to remain nominally Ottoman, with local tribal forces in control, while also serving as an important port for Iran.[199] They retained sovereignty over al-Ahsa and Qatif until 1670, when they lost it in a revolt of the local Bani Khalid tribe, who was mainly Sunni but on good terms with Shia. The Ottomans saw local Shia with suspicion and limited interactions between Qatif and the Hijaz in the second half of the sixteenth century for fear of Safavid subversion through the pilgrimage route.[200]

But as Shii Ottoman émigrés rose to high office in Iran, Shii clerics could face difficulties in the Ottoman Empire. One mid-sixteenth-century travel account of a Shii cleric from Jabal Amil, who became the highest-ranking cleric in Iran, shows that fear of repression in the Ottoman Empire may have contributed to his emigration. And yet, before going to Iran he was able to travel unharmed across Ottoman territory and visit the shrine cities in Iraq and interact with relatives and notables there.[201] Another cleric from Jabal Amil, who was executed in Istanbul in 965/1558 for espousing Shii beliefs, has become prominent in Shii cultural memory. Yet his story is equally complicated. He had studied in centres of Sunnism and was employed by the Ottoman state in Istanbul as a cleric working in the Shafii Sunni tradition. His fate was sealed by several interconnected factors, including that he had drawn the ire of Ottoman officials. As such, his execution was the exception rather than the rule in the Ottoman treatment of Shii clerics.[202] Still, the notion that Shii clerics were persecuted by the Ottomans but employed by the Safavids bound Arab Shii communities more closely to Iran and entrenched their anti-Ottoman sentiment.[203] At the same time, the fact that Jabal Amil had one of the highest concentrations of mosques in the Ottoman Levant and that Shia were able to establish religious schools that served as regionally important centres of Shii learning bears witness to

Ottoman coexistence with Shiism (though Shii mosques would have received less support from the state than Sunni ones, or none at all).[204] Twelver Shia, Qizilbash, Alawites, and others resorted to the same courts as other Ottoman Muslims[205] and were mostly described as Muslims in Ottoman sources.[206]

In some surveys, however, they were classified as 'other Muslims' or, in the case of Alawites and Druze, as 'non-Muslims'.[207] The Ottomans sought to continue a special Mamluk-era tax on some Alawite men, but abolished a similar tax on the Ismailis. It continued to be collected from Alawite-inhabited districts until at least the end of the eighteenth century and is the closest to a special sectarian tax levied by the Ottomans on a Shii group. The tax could, however, be amended in times of hardship and was later subsumed under other levies. In the early sixteenth century, the Ottomans apparently collected a special tax from Shia going on pilgrimage from Damascus to Najaf but it was abolished once Iraq became Ottoman. Unlike the non-Muslim populations, Shia did not face major financial disadvantages because of their beliefs. And the state was perfectly happy for Alawite, Shii, and Druze overlords to collect taxes.[208] Unlike Christians and Jews, which were considered *dhimmi* (non-Muslims protected under Islamic law) and had to pay a special tax, this did not apply to Ottoman Shia. The various Christian denominations, and the Jews, collected taxes and practised personal status law amongst themselves. This became known as the millet system, from the Arabic word *milla*, which indicates a religious community, and was sometimes used to indicate that a religious community was akin to a 'nation', another connotation of the term.[209] Ottoman Shia were not organised according to this system and nor, it seems, were Alawites or Druze.[210] This is a significant distinction, one that we will take up later.

Let us briefly return to Iran. In the early seventeenth century, Shah Abbas I (1571–1629, r. 1587–1629), whom we have got to know as the founder of Isfahan, expanded Iran's territory again. He recaptured Mashhad and Herat from the Uzbeks in 1599. Mashhad, as the only burial place of a Shii Imam in Iran, became Iran's main pilgrimage site, and eclipsed Herat, the former political and cultural capital of Khorasan.[211] The Safavid Shahs made the pilgrimage to Mashhad, expanded its shrine, covering its dome with panels of gold, and were buried there. Shah Abbas, a frequent visitor, even walked there from Isfahan in 1601.[212] Mashhad replaced Ardabil as the Safavid's holy city, and the move signalled a move away from a focus on the Safavid order and towards Twelver Shiism, a move that had already been under way in previous decades, and had started during the long reign of Shah Tahmasp I (r. 1524–76).[213] In the Persian Gulf, Shah Abbas took territory hitherto held by the Portuguese through the Kingdom of Hormuz such as Bahrain in 1602, Qeshm in 1608, and Gombroon (which is today known as Bandar Abbas, meaning 'Port of Abbas') in 1614, with Hormuz itself falling in 1622.[214] Direct Safavid rule strengthened Shiism in Bahrain and linked it further to Iran, which likewise had an impact on the adjacent coastal areas of the Shii port town of Qatif, with its strong trade, family, and religious ties to Bahrain.[215]

In 1603, Shah Abbas, emboldened, attacked the Ottomans, who, embroiled in yet another war with the Habsburgs and weakened by internal rebellions, had to cede Caucasian and Iranian provinces to the Safavids. In 1623, he then took over Baghdad and had Friday prayers held in honour of the Imams and Sunni mausoleums destroyed. A few years later, the Ottomans reconquered Iraq and restored these same mausoleums, claiming to liberate the city's Muslim (read Sunni) population. Indeed, Iraq and its shrines became symbolic battlegrounds in this struggle for geopolitical dominance, and every new intervention was justified with the repression of one side against the relative other. A final peace treaty was negotiated in 1639 (again, the Ottomans insisted on a clause prohibiting the cursing of the first three (Sunni) Caliphs).[216] The Safavids had lost Iraq forever and had given up on territorial expansion.

From 1639 until the downfall of the Safavids in 1722, thus, Ottoman–Safavid relations were much improved.[217] Diplomatic correspondence became increasingly polite, as the Ottomans elevated the Shah in status.[218] The two courts exchanged elaborate gifts that shaped common aesthetic sensibilities and visual culture.[219] The Ottomans accepted Safavid patronage of the Iraqi shrines and allowed more Iranian pilgrims and burials near the shrines, and official Ottoman documents dealing with the shrines and Iranian pilgrimage do not discuss the Sunni–Shia question.[220] For the Safavids, peace with the Ottomans protected them from a possible alliance between their Sunni neighbours. And so the Safavids did not take advantage of major military defeats of the Ottomans in Europe, such as the defeat in 1683 after the second Ottoman siege of Vienna.[221]

The waning influence of the Qizilbash in Iran relaxed the Ottomans' anxiety. Once both imperial centres lost interest in them and some became integrated into pro-Shii Sufi orders accepted by the Ottoman state, they were rarely referred to in the government correspondence. The Qizilbash continued traditions more associated with the Ahl al-Baytism and Alid loyalty of the fifteenth century, and possibly earlier traditions related to fire worship and local holy men (fire continued to play a role in many of the pro-Alid movements around the Eastern Mediterranean and Anatolia).[222] They also maintained connections to Iraq. Bektashi lodges existed near the shrines of the Imams and in the major cities of Iraq. Patronised under Ottoman, then Safavid, and in the seventeenth century again Ottoman control, these Sufi lodges served as a conduit and meeting place for pilgrims from Ottoman and Safavid domains.[223]

Alongside the more ideational reasons that we have been discussing, and which, for the real-world consequences their ideas had, could at times push leaders into confrontation, economic interests could be both drivers and limiters of conflict. For one, control over silk-producing provinces such as Azerbaijan, Shirvan, and Gilan as well as access to shipping routes in the Persian Gulf and the Caspian Sea were crucial drivers of the confrontation.[224] At the same time, silk and other trade from Iran to Europe had to largely cross Ottoman territory, which was a key factor in the betterment of relations in the late sixteenth and early seventeenth century.[225] During times of war, both sides suffered economically.[226]

The Safavid polity was always weakest at its periphery, where Sunni tribes resented central authority. In the early eighteenth century, it was those forces that would overthrow the Safavids, spurred on by military weakness, increased taxation, and renewed efforts at conversion to Shiism.[227] Both the Ottomans and the Safavids faced encroachment by European powers. In 1718, Austria and the Ottomans signed the Peace Treaty of Passarowitz, and the Ottomans were just dispatching a mission to Isfahan in 1720 to conclude an agreement that would have shipped Persian goods to the Austrian Empire duty-free when the Afghans started invading Safavid territory. Sensing Safavid defeat, Peter the Great of Russia led his armies along the Caspian coast in the summer of 1722. The formal justification was an attack on Shirvan led by Sunni Muslim tribes from Daghestan a year earlier in which Russian merchants were killed along with several thousand Iranian officials and other Shia. The latter were accused by these Sunni tribes of mistreating Sunnis. The rising had a sectarian component and was associated with anti-Shii discourse, though that must be understood in the context of oppressive rule over a largely Sunni population at the periphery of the Empire.[228] The Ottomans wanted to check this Russian advance in their backyard, and respond to calls to aid Sunnis in the Caucasus. They thus decided to enter the scramble for the collapsing Safavid Empire.[229] On 15 May 1722, Grand Vizier Ibrahim Pasha and the Divan came up with a plan of action that reinvoked sectarian arguments to legitimise war. After almost a century of peaceful relations, the senior Ottoman cleric again sanctioned war, stating that Iranians were apostates.[230]

The Safavid capital of Isfahan was ransacked by the Afghans later in the same year, and the Ottomans occupied Tabriz in 1724, the city the Safavids had taken from them in 1501.[231] The Afghan revolt against the Safavids was legitimised by fatwas from Sunni clerics in Mecca that Mirwais, the father of their leader, Mahmud, had obtained on an earlier visit to the Hijaz. Upon their entry into Isfahan, the Afghans, under Mahmud, forced the last Safavid Shah, who had just surrendered, to ride at the tail end of thousands of Afghan troops, which were preceded by twelve soldiers cursing Shiism, a symbolic mockery of the Safavid practice of praising the twelve Shii Imams. The end of the dynasty that had converted Iran to Shiism, and posted cursers of the Sunni Caliphs across the Empire, could hardly have been more symbolic, and humiliating.[232]

The rise of the Safavids and their adoption of Shiism as state religion transformed the nature of Shiism, and despite the administrative and military problems that led to the Safavids' downfall, the conversion of Iran was going to be permanent. Shii communities outside Iran became influenced by Safavid Shiism (for example passion plays during Muharram and large processions).[233] Practices that had hitherto been held in private or only at certain localities were increasingly practised across the Shii world, differentiating more strongly the everyday lives of Shia from that of Sunnis.[234]

The rivalry became so vicious precisely because both dynasties emerged in the pro-Alid Sufi warrior milieu of fourteenth- and fifteenth-century Anatolia, and competed over the allegiance of the same populations. For let us not forget that many Ottoman Qizilbash saw the Safavid Shahs as both spiritual and political leaders, paid taxes to them and served in their armed forces.[235] In the Ottoman Empire, a process of state centralisation, consolidation, and expansion abroad, as well as the challenge by the Safavids and their supporters on Ottoman soil, was intertwined with a strengthening of Hanafi Sunnism as the *raison d'état*.

Even though both sides used different interpretations of Islam to undermine the other and legitimise wars, it would, once again, be a mistake to reduce the conflict to religion. To the Ottomans, the Safavids were simply a challenger too close to home, stemming, as they did, from the same tribal areas that were the backbone of Ottoman support. Sectarian identity did not determine the two Empires' relations with other Muslim powers such as the Mamluks in Egypt (whom the Ottomans defeated even though they were Sunni) or the Mughals of India. Indeed, the Ottomans had been at war with the largely Sunni predecessors of the Safavids, the White Sheep Turkoman dynasty, who had sealed an alliance with Venice against the Ottomans because they felt threatened after the Ottoman conquest of Constantinople, and they remained suspicious of the Safavids' Sunni successors in the eighteenth century. The Sunni Mamluks were defeated and their territories annexed by the Sunni Ottomans, while the Shii Safavids 'only' suffered territorial losses and survived for another two centuries.[236]

A process akin to the confessionalisation in Europe, thus played out across the central Islamic lands in the early modern period. That the sectarian aspect was a product rather than the cause of the Ottoman–Safavid rivalry made it no less real to those affected by it. It left lasting scars in the multi-ethnic and multi-religious borderlands, chiefly in Anatolia, the Caucasus, Iraq, and the Persian Gulf, and, in the context of the rivalry with the Uzbeks, in Khorasan. In these frontier zones, local communities had to choose sides. With state-identity tied to sectarian identity, Shia in the Ottoman Empire became suspected of disloyalty, much like Sunnis in Safavid Iran.[237] The Safavids' mass conversion meant that many Sunnis either had to convert or were expelled, whereas the Ottomans, ruling over much larger territories, came to terms with Shii groups and integrated them into pro-Ottoman Sufi orders, while repressing those deemed sympathetic to the Safavids.

The top-down conversion of Iran to Shiism, with enforcers posted across the country, or the hunt across the Ottoman Empire for alleged supporters of the Safavids shaped the lives of ordinary people. And the Safavids did much to entrench the idea of Iran as a territory with a distinct sectarian identity separate from the neighbouring, largely Sunni domains.[238]

As Marshall Hodgson, the major historian of the Islamic world put it, 'Islamdom was now sharply and definitively divided into Shii majority and Sunni-majority, each unprecedently intolerant of the presence of the opposite minority.'[239] Clerics wrote polemics and justified wars against rival empires with the argument that they had deviated from true Islam. But the two sides frequently did make peace, toned down their sectarian rhetoric, and were pragmatic. Frontiers were porous and could shift, and invasions could be reversed, and trade and the movement of people, including pilgrims, continued.

The respective interpretations of Islam that the two dynasties embraced, Hanafism and Usulism, became the most widespread schools within Sunnism and Shiism, respectively, well-suited for early modern administration and legitimisation, and capable of coming to terms with each other. This was also evident on the Indian subcontinent, where the Mughals embraced Hanafism and the Shii states Usulism.

5

Muslim Dynasties on the Indian Subcontinent

Sunnism and Shiism also flourished on the Indian subcontinent, where Islam spread in numerous ways: by way of the Sufi orders through their wandering Derwishes and missionaries; by way of conquest from Anatolia, Iran, and Central Asia, with the armies that moved from there down into Northern India and established political dynasties; and by way of the sea, through traders who brought Arabian horses from the Persian Gulf to the Malabar coast.

Amidst political upheaval in other parts of the Islamic world, the wealthiest and most populous Muslim-ruled states emerged on the subcontinent, which fast became a key arena of Muslim intellectual and cultural life. How did the spreading of Sunnism and Shiism to the Indian subcontinent, and the emergence of Muslim dynasties, transform the relationship between the two? And was there a specifically Indian Muslim experience in which sectarian identity was less relevant, as is often claimed? Let us recapitulate.

Mahmud Ibn Sebuktegin, founder of the Ghaznavid dynasty in Afghanistan and Eastern Iran, discussed above, led the first major invasions into the Gangetic plain from his base in Afghanistan. He established a pattern of Turkic military incursions and set up Sultanates in Northern India. As noted, Sebuktegin presented himself as a defender of Sunnism and the Abbasid Caliphate, and suppressed Ismailis. On the Indian subcontinent, however, he is primarily remembered for spreading Islam.[1]

The successive Turkic or Mongol dynasties that were to establish Sultanates in Northern India were mostly Sunni Hanafi, and some developed close relations with Sufis. But because the populations they conquered, and parts of their army and bureaucracy, were so diverse, representing India's many ethnicities and religions, they were never in the position to act like the

Safavids in Iran. Muslims called the area beyond the Sindu/Indus river 'al-Hind', which in time became the term 'Hindu' to denote the amalgam of non-Muslim religious traditions. Mass conversion of al-Hind's population, even if it had been on the table, was not in the cards.[2]

Alliance-formation with local elites was therefore vital and required a pragmatic approach. Given the sheer scale of the land, and its agrarian economy, it meant that Indian Muslim rulers, not unlike the Ottomans, were dependent for the collection of taxes on the cooperation of local elites, whatever their religion may be.[3] Although they were of Turkic origin and Turkish dialects retained some importance, Muslim rulers spoke and wrote Persian. Their origins in Central Asia, their use of Persian, and the constant influx of migrants from Islamic lands further West, from Central Asia and Iran, kept the Indian subcontinent connected to the central Islamic lands, where the relationship between Sunnism and Shiism was, as noted, being reformulated. While these rulers were all Persianised Turks that linked themselves back to the Mongol legacy of Central Asia, only the dynasty founded by Babur in the sixteenth century would be called 'Mughals'.

The religious policies of the Indian Muslim rulers, and the Mughals especially, are multifaceted. Most embraced Sufism in one form or another. As should be clear by this point, Sufism escapes easy categorisations. Some Sufi orders, such as the Naqshbandis, so influential here, were pronouncedly Sunni. Others, in this context the Nurbakhshis, though fewer in number, were Shii. The Chishti order, founded by Muinuddin Chishti, who died in 1236, was nominally Sunni, but revered the *Ahl al-Bayt*. As noted, Sufis share a respect for and allegiance to the *Ahl al-Bayt* and often to Ali, whom they see as especially charismatic and knowledgeable.[4] Ismailism, for example, spread here through association with Sufi orders such as the Suhrawardis.[5]

The first of the large Muslim states in Northern India was the so-called *Delhi Sultanate*. In the late twelfth century, the Saljuqs and Ghaznavids, the dynasty founded by the above-mentioned Sebuktegin and named after their base in Afghanistan, Ghazni, where he had died in 1030, began to lose their hold over Khorasan and Afghanistan. One of their former client states, based in Ghur, conquered more territory in Khorasan, and, like the Ghaznavids beforehand, attacked the Ismailis in Multan. Multan, where Ismailis had lived semi-autonomously since the tenth century under local rulers, had become one of the few bases for Ismailism after it was repressed elsewhere.[6] The Ghurids, as they became known, were initially criticised for their religious beliefs. To be accepted more widely, they embraced Sunni Hanafism, and established the Delhi Sultanate in Northern India, which lasted over three centuries, from 1206 to 1526. At the height of its power in the fourteenth century, the Delhi Sultanate ruled over much of the Indian subcontinent.[7] The Qutub Minar, Delhi's famous minaret, symbolises the Sultanate's ambitions of Islamic statehood, and the built environment around it the Indianisation of Islamic architecture, and indeed of Islam itself.

The Delhi Sultanate proved a haven for people fleeing from the Mongol conquests and destructions in other parts of the Muslim world. In 1229, the Abbasid Caliph bestowed a robe of investiture on Shams al-Din Iltutmish, the Sultan of Delhi from 1211 to 1236, symbolically linking the Delhi Sultans to the central Sunni institution in Baghdad. Iltutmish patronised both Hanafi and Shafii legal traditions—although, as we'll see, the Hanafi school would eventually become the dominant Sunni school of jurisprudence in Northern India. On an official level, the warrior dynasties that established themselves in Northern India were keen to present themselves as orthodox Sunnis, and as legitimised by the Sunni Caliphs. But the Sultanate also provided the umbrella under which Sufism flourished, as the Abbasid Caliphs were overthrown by the Mongols. Not all Delhi Sultans directly supported Sufism and some of the early ones even sought to marginalise it. In the provinces, however, wandering Sufis and Sufi lodges became the focus of popular piety.[8] The central government and the Sufi leaders in Delhi would each send out representatives to provincial towns, where these two networks could overlap, leading to an impression that Sufism was the official Islam. The senior Sufi in Delhi at the height of the Sultanate's power was Nizam al-Din Auliya (1238–1325) of the Chishti order. Delhi Sultans and early Mughals patronised his shrine. Other Sufis venerating the *Ahl al-Bayt* flourished alongside it.[9]

Relatively stable Muslim rule and the prosperity and means of patronage of the Delhi rulers attracted Sayyids, descendants of the Prophet, especially in the wake of the Mongol conquests. Delhi Sultans such as Muhammad bin Tughlaq (r. 1325–51) encouraged Sayyids to migrate to counter-balance clerics and Sufis as religious–ideological legitimisers of his reign. Most were Sunni, but some were Shia. In general, their emphasis on descent from the Prophet and genealogical purity enhanced the position of the *Ahl al-Bayt* in the Muslims' imagination.[10] Infighting amongst Sunnis and bin Tughlaq's interest in philosophical discussions, during which some Shia became the Sultan's favourite courtiers, strengthened Shiism. It is ironic that we owe some of the earliest descriptions of a Shii presence in Delhi and in the coastal trading communities to Ibn Battuta, whose fourteenth century travelogue is amongst the most famous in the Islamic world. Originally from Morocco, he was able to travel in the fourteenth century for twenty-four years from West Africa to China, finding patronage at the courts of Muslim rulers, including in Delhi, conversing in Arabic, describing things that were foreign, but also familiar to him.[11] Often seen as an example of closer connections across the Islamic world, his account is also an example of a Sunni worldview with a bias against Shiism, and whenever he recounts a Shii presence in the many places he visits he denounces them as *rafidis*, ('rejectionists'), perhaps to prove his Sunni credentials.[12]

Along the Western coast, Islam arrived with traders from the Arabian Peninsula and elsewhere as part of the Indian Ocean trade. Under the Delhi Sultanate, Ismaili Shia settled in Delhi, but after an uprising in 1237, many were killed and expelled and settled in Sind and Gujarat.[13] The number of Twelver Shia increased under Muhammad's successor, Firuz Shah Tughlaq, in the second half of the fourteenth century. Although official histories denounce them, they were able to proselytise, and al-Hilli's books, for example, were now read here, too.[14] When Timur, whom we have got to know in the context of Central Asia, invaded the Indian subcontinent in 1398 and weakened the Delhi Sultanate, Shii intellectuals moved to the courts of provincial Muslim dynasties.[15] Eventually, the Delhi Sultans would be supplanted by the Mughals.

The Mughals stemmed from the cultural, political, and religious milieu of Central Asia, but were pushed out by the rise of the Safavids and Uzbeks. Babur had come to power at the age of twelve in a small Central Asian principality. His family had been Sunni Hanafi and followers of the Naqshbandi Shaykh Khwaja Nasiruddin Ubaydullah (1403–88), who was crucial in spreading the Naqshbandiyya in Central Asia.[16] As noted, in this period, the Naqshbandiyya was positioning itself as a Sunni order that adhered to Sunni norms and laws, and became more anti-Shii as the Safavids were rising to power in Iran. Naqshbandi influence over the new Islamic Empire-in-the-making of Babur gave the order entirely new prospects. Babur's Naqshbandi background made him intuitively suspicious of Shiism. But ethnic and political differences between Babur's branch of the Mongols, and the Sunni Uzbeks, who were the main rivals of the Safavids in Central Asia, and also allied with Naqshbandis, initially led Babur to seek help from the Safavid Shah Ismail.[17]

Babur had to pay lip service to the sovereignty of the Shah and even wore the twelve-pointed headgear to denote that he was a follower of Shah Ismail and a Shii. Safavid assistance helped Babur to capture, at least briefly, Samarqand in 1511, an important trading hub on the silk road and a crucial step in his future career. Samarqand was a bastion of the Naqshbandis. But now, coins were struck and prayers read in honour of the Shah, and included the Shii declaration of faith. Acceptance of Babur was short-lived, and soon, the city rebelled against what was seen as Iranian–Shii control.[18] The Safavids' repression of Naqshbandis elsewhere must have been a sore point, and that Babur, a Naqshbandi and inheritor of Timurid legitimacy, cooperated with the Shii Safavids must have worked to his disadvantage here. The Uzbeks in turn rallied Sunni troops and opinion by declaring the Safavids and Babur's forces heretics.[19]

Expelled from Samarqand, Babur seized Kabul in 1512, where he initially stayed as governor, and then crossed the Khyber Pass and moved south into the Indian subcontinent. In the late 1520s, Babur conquered much of Northern India and, after defeating the previous rulers of Agra, made the city his capital. Unlike these rulers, who had supported the Chishtis, Babur patronised the Naqshbandis.[20] Perhaps owing to his own experience in Central Asia, however, he counselled his son and successor Humayun to 'ignore the disputations of the Shia and Sunnis, for therein is the weakness of Islam'.[21]

The rivalries of Central Asia, between the different Sufi orders and between Sunnism and Shiism, were transplanted to a new realm. The ties that bound the Mughals to the Ottoman, Safavid, and Uzbek Empires were economic, military, intellectual, religious, and social. The Mughals employed migrants from Iran, even as Mughals and Safavids were at loggerheads over control of Afghanistan.[22] The Indian subcontinent's natural resources ensured that economic ties flourished despite political rivalries with all these domains (although the least with the remote Ottomans).[23]

After Babur died in 1530, political factionalism and challenges beset the realm. Humayun was temporarily driven out of power, with an Afghan leader, Sher Khan, emerging as his main rival. Like his father, Humayun sought assistance from the Safavids. In July 1544, he arrived in Qazvin, which was then still the Safavid capital, seeking the support of Shah Tahmasp. The latter pressured his guest to convert to Shiism and, with little other

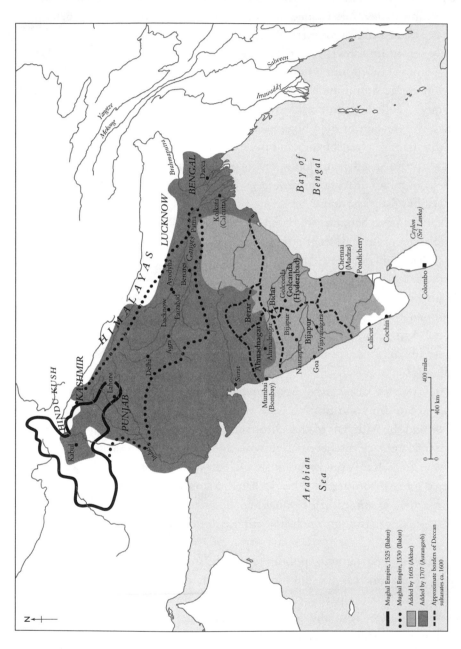

6. Muslim rule in India, 1500–1800

Mughal Empire, 1525 (Babur)
Mughal Empire, 1530 (Babur)
Added by 1605 (Akbar)
Added by 1707 (Aurangzeb)
Approximate borders of Deccan
sultanates ca. 1600

options left, believing that Shii Safavid soldiers would have refused to serve him if he did not do so, Humayun converted. In 1545, a joint Safavid-Mughal force marched on Afghanistan. Despite having just nominally converted to Shiism, Humayun reaffirmed the Naqshbandis' tax-free land holdings, which helped him assert his authority in Kabul. But it would take another ten years for Humayun to conquer Delhi.[24] There had been troubles in his army between Sunni and Shii divisions, and some of the territories they conquered, like Afghanistan, were strongly Sunni, with the population and local clerics resenting the Shii symbolism used by his army. Once in Delhi in 1555, in the interest of imperial policy and influenced by Sunni advisors, Humayun refrained from invoking Shii symbolism until his death a year later.[25] But Shii influence at the heart of Mughal power persisted.

The son of Humayun and Hamida Banu, a Persian Shii and daughter of a scholar in the Mughals' service, would become the next Emperor. His name was Akbar (r. 1556–1605), *The Greatest*, and he would be the most famous of the Mughal rulers, often remembered for his tolerant rule, even if his early years in power witnessed sectarian killings and persecution.[26] His first prime minister, Bairam Khan, was a descendent of the quasi-Shii Black Sheep tribal federation that had ruled parts of Iran before the Safavids. Bairam Khan had been instrumental in helping Humayun reconquer Northern India and Akbar establish his rule. After initially keeping him in power, Akbar removed him from office amidst allegations that he appointed Shia to key positions.[27]

Akbar consolidated Mughal rule over large non-Muslim populations. In the first years of his reign, he embraced Chishti Sufism and made the pilgrimage to the shrine of the founder of the Chishtiyya in Ajmer.[28] In 1571, he moved the capital from Agra to Sikri, a town a few dozen kilometres further west, where another prominent Chishti Sufi resided. After further conquests in Gujarat, he had a new capital built here, which he named Fatehpur ('city of victory') Sikri, one which symbolised the eclectic religious policies of his reign. As part of the new city, Akbar built a massive mosque in whose courtyard initially also lay the residence and later the much-visited shrine of the Chishti Sufi, a testament to the intimate relationship between Chishti Sufism and the Mughals. The mosque itself and other parts of the city also contain elements of Hindu and Buddhist architecture, the former a reflection of Akbar's Hindu alliances.[29]

In the heart of the city was a forum, opened in 1575, where Akbar had representatives of different religions and confessions debate each other.

Previous Muslim rulers occasionally hosted such debates, but Akbar's were more institutionalised. He had received religious training from Sunni and Shii clerics. They now affirmed their positions in public, which entrenched the respective positions, and emboldened the Shia, who in India would previously have been cautious of voicing their opinions publicly for fear of reprisals.[30]

In 1579, after having allowed Hindus and Christians, including missionaries, to join the debates, which shocked the Muslims, Akbar declared that he would be the final arbiter on religious matters.[31] He developed a syncretistic religio-political plan to usher in an era of Universal Peace between religious factions in which Hindus held the same social status as Muslims and abolished special taxes on non-Muslims.[32] He was influenced by Abu'l Fazl, who wrote Akbar's biography, one of the most famous texts of the period, in which this new syncretistic religious and political project, the *Din-i Ilahi*, Religion of God or Divine Faith, is described as the ultimate achievement of his reign.[33] Akbar called himself *Commander of the Faithful* and *Imam of Islam and the Muslims* and later Mughal historians even called him *Caliph*. He appropriated Sunni and Shii notions of just rulership to dismiss both the Ottoman Sultan's claim to the Caliphate, and the Safavids' nominal over-lordship. This assertion of Mughal independence was a significant departure, as Akbar's predecessors had still had to occasionally accept the Safavids' supremacy in return for military support (and the Delhi Sultanate had still sought Abbasid investitures).[34] Sunni and Shii clerics were dismayed and rebelled in unity, though they did not manage to halt his new policies.[35]

While the Din-i Ilahi's influence waned with Akbar's death in 1605, he had set a precedent. Akbar and subsequent Mughal rulers positioned them-selves as great Muslim leaders in their own right, separate from and above Safavids and Ottomans. To this end, they adopted an ecumenical policy of giving different faiths and confessions freedom of religion and employment, including at court, and so Shia of Persian origin became a sort of bureau-cratic aristocracy. Sunni chroniclers sometimes invoked this to accuse Akbar of pro-Shii tendencies.[36]

Such accusations could be used to bring down competitors. The official history of Akbar's reign describes one such official, who had been Akbar's tutor and who because 'of his "lack of bigotry and his broadmindedness" was called a Shii in India and a Sunni in Iran. In fact, he was journeying on towards the serene city of universal tolerance and so the zealots of each sect used to censure him.'[37] In the wake of Akbar's father's return from Iran, and continuously thereafter, scores of Iranian immigrants found a new home, and patronage at court. In India they were held in high regard because of their cultural capital as 'Persians', whether they were ethnically Persian or not, for their superior command of the Persian language and cultural refinement. Some were Sunni, others Shii. The latter would compete with the mostly Sunni entourage of the rulers originally from Central Asia.[38]

Local and regional rivalries could thus become connected to histories of animosity in Central Asia and Iran.[39] The larger notion of descent from Timur, and Central Asian notions of kingship and warrior ethos were key to Mughal legitimacy.[40] Yet so was alignment with the Persianate world, which consisted of two lines, one linking Northern India and the Deccan to Iran, in which Shiism was strong, and a Sunni one linking the Mughal capital via Afghanistan to Bukhara and Samarqand. Shifting alliances along these axes, and moving from one to the other as a source of legitimacy and support, could involve a sectarian statement, as the early Mughals had to realise.[41] This was not just a replica of the Ottoman–Safavid and Uzbek–Safavid rivalries, but they shaped some of the debates and factions here, and had driven some to the Indian subcontinent in the first place.

The influx of Persian speakers strengthened Persian as the language of high culture, commerce, and diplomacy at the Mughal court, at the expense of other languages (including the original mother tongue of the Mughals, Chagatai Turkish).[42] This facilitated conversations across the wider Persianate world. The Mughals, for example, had courtiers read key Persian works on poetry and morals such as those of Nasir al-Din Tusi (d. 1274), the famous astronomer and cleric, who had written this book while at the Ismaili mountain fortress of Alamut before making common cause with the Mongols in their conquest of Baghdad. His and other Persian works were not chosen for their confessional stances, which were implicit and ambiguous, but for providing a general moral framework that lay outside the control of the Sunni clerical establishment. And still, in this general Persianate culture, Shii themes were (omni-)present.[43]

Mughal intellectuals also intervened in wider Sunni–Shia debates.[44] When Sunnis fleeing Safavid policies obtained patronage at Indian Muslim courts, they clashed with Shii officials. One of them, for example, wrote a polemic intent on purging the influence of Shiism in Mughal India.[45]

Two intellectual heavyweights stand out: Nurullah Shustari and Ahmad Sirhindi. Shustari was a Shii official employed under Akbar and his son

Jahangir (r. 1605–27). Until the early part of Akbar's reign, many Shia remained silent about their beliefs, or pretended they were Sunnis. In the liberal climate of his later reign, however, this would change.[46] Shustari and other Shia argued that because Akbar was a just ruler who tolerated religious difference, Shia could openly profess their beliefs.[47] The case of the Ismailis of Gujarat illustrates this well. Here, a branch of the Ismailis whose spiritual leaders resided in Yemen, were known as Bohras. Initially on good terms with Hindu and Muslim rulers, they were persecuted in the fifteenth and sixteenth centuries by the Sunni Sultans of Gujarat. They were forced to practice dissimulation, and some converted to Sunnism, dividing the Bohra community into a Sunni and an Ismaili Shii one. Relations could become hostile, preventing intermarriage and other social relations, and even leading to the assassination of the other group's leaders. They also tried to get rulers to repress the other side.[48] They, for example, sought Akbar's intercession in their succession disputes and protection against bigotry of local officials. After Akbar received the leader of the Tayyibi Bohras, he instructed his officials in Gujarat to grant them religious freedom and appointed Shii officials there, which led to a counter-reaction amongst Sunni Bohras.[49]

Shustari symbolises a similar shift to a more open proclamation of Twelver Shiism. He originally hailed from Shustar in Khuzistan, a borderland in southwestern Iran near Iraq that was affected by the Ottoman–Safavid conflict. He studied and worked in Safavid Iran but left for India in 1585. He found patronage in Akbar's court and was initially appointed *Qadi* in Lahore, where he ruled according to Sunni jurisprudence.[50] But he became increasingly vocal about his Shii beliefs.[51] He wrote three polemics, one of which countered an anti-Safavid and anti-Shii polemic written by the Sunni Iranian exile Mirza Makhdum Sharifi, who had defected to the Ottomans.[52] The other anti-Sunni polemic was a rebuttal of Khunji's refutation of al-Hilli. As noted, Khunji was the key Persian Sunni ideologue of his time.[53] Despite his prominence amongst some Sunnis on the subcontinent, the Mughal elite largely did not embrace Khunji's elaboration of Sunni political theory, because he had chastised Babur for allying with the Safavids in his campaign in the heartlands of Central Asian Sunnism.[54]

Finally, Shustari wrote an encyclopaedia of Shii scholars and their works, in which he claimed historical personalities, including many confessionally ambiguous Sufis, for the Shia, and highlighted the Shii contribution to Islamic history and scholarship, and showed Shia that they could now be outspoken about their beliefs.[55] But after the death of Akbar and the accession of his son Jahangir in 1605, the mood in the Empire changed, and Shustari fell out of favour. It might have been one of his anti Sunni polemics that aroused the ire of the ruler, who had him so severely flogged that Shustari died.

Yet, paradoxically, Jahangir's reign is equally known for Shii influence, and his wife, Nur Jahan, was a Shii.[56] She was the daughter of a senior Iranian Shii official under Akbar, Itimad al-Daula, who stayed on under Jahangir. Al-Daula, Nur Jahan, and her brother constituted a powerful Shii circle at court.[57] In his memoirs, Jahangir praised the rule of his father for his tolerance and contrasted it with the sectarian atmosphere in Ottoman, Safavid and Uzbek domains and he commissioned a Shii to write a book on the art of government.[58]

In 1619, Jahangir also had the prominent Sunni Sufi Sirhindi arrested shortly after he started circulating his ideas in letters his disciples spread.[59] They included denigrating statements about Hindus and Shia, and described the religious atmosphere at court under Akbar and to a certain extent Jahangir as too tolerant, writing that 'the harm of being in the company of a heretic exceeds that of being in the company of an infidel; and the Shia are the worst of the heretics'.[60] Sirhindi had already written an anti-Shii polemic, around 1587, in response to the rise of Shiism in India and to the polemic between Uzbek and Iranian clerics over the status of Mashhad discussed above.[61] Sirhindi was about to emerge as a rival source of author-ity, and his outspoken anti-Shiism was an embarrassment to the Emperor, whose favourite wife was as noted Shii. His arrest may have been a result of Shii influence, but Jahangir's punishing of the figureheads of a new Shii and Sunni assertiveness could also have been an attempt to suppress sectarian discord.[62] Sirhindi, whose stature in South Asian Islam was later touted by Muslim revivalists, founded a new sub-branch of the Naqshbandiyya (its name, Mujaddidi, referred to a belief shared by Sunnis and Shia, that every century will see the rise of a renewer of the faith. Sirhindi was seen by his followers as that person, in fact even as *Mujaddid Alf-i Thani*, 'renewer of the second millennium of Islam', which started during his lifetime.[63] Naqshbandis were crucial in the Sunni Revivalism on the Indian subcontinent. Sirhindi reshaped the Naqshbandiyya by emphasising political action, worldly piety, and adherence to Sunni norms even more, and the Mujaddidi–Naqshbandis would also become popular in Central Asia and the Ottoman Empire.[64] Sirhindi and his followers were appalled by the Shii assertiveness of Shustari and the circles at court. As noted, Naqshbandis had been influential under the early Mughals but were marginalised under Akbar and Jahangir. But in the later years of Jahangir's reign and under his successors, they reasserted their position as partners of the Mughals, and as defenders of Sunnism.[65] Sirhindi is a case in point. After a year in prison, he was released, and gained influence at court. His later writings are milder on the Shia, but his order would remain staunchly anti-Shii, and would influence subsequent Mughal rulers.[66]

A mixed picture thus emerges of the Mughals with regards to religion. On the one hand, they were heirs to the Naqshbandi-Hanafi milieu of Timurid Central Asia coupled with an adherence to the *Ahl al-Bayt*.[67] On the other hand, they embraced Sufi orders such as the Chishtiyya that were less focused on outer conformity with Islamic laws. Which Sufi order they allied with had consequences for Sunni–Shia relations. And thirdly, they allied at times with the Safavids, married Shia, employed Shia at court, even tolerated Shii rituals, and had their bureaucrats read works on morals written by Shia. And Ismailis, who had been repressed by earlier Indian Muslim rulers, and became marginalised across much of the Middle East and Central Asia, flourished. The Mughals' tolerance for Shiism made them sensitive to outright attacks on Shiism. Mughal rulers sought to stand above and not take sides, not least because their largest religious 'problem' was how to rule over large non-Muslim populations.

Nonetheless, the period witnessed a growing Shii assertiveness, spurred by the Safavids, that was symbolised by clerics such as Shustari, the open practising of Shii rituals and the conversion of local dynasties to Shiism. Perhaps because of their delicate position, Mughal chronicles are largely silent on Sunni–Shia relations, or Shii rituals. But Shii rituals must have taken place especially after the end of Shii dissimulation. European travelogues describe Muharram processions in Agra and Lahore from the seventeenth century and in Delhi from the eighteenth century, involving not only Shia but Hindus and Sufis, too—which drew the ire of conservative Sunnis.[68] As in Central Asia and Anatolia, reverence for the *Ahl al-Bayt* had already spread through Shii-leaning Sufi orders such as the Nurbakhshis, and some Sunnis preferred Ali over the other Rashidun Caliphs, which facilitated Shia proselytising.[69]

Embracing a particular sectarian identity proved exceptionally useful for rulers wishing to assert their independence, including from the Mughals, or supplant a previous or neighbouring ruler and rival. In Kashmir, for example,

Shii-minded Sufis such as the Nurbakhshis and Shii rulers had been significant since the fifteenth century. The rise of the Safavids and of local Shii dynasties on the Indian subcontinent in the sixteenth century made them pronounce their faith more openly and led the Nurbakhshi leadership to dispatch missionaries.[70] The order gained patronage from the Shii tribe of the Chaks, who ruled Kashmir for large parts of the sixteenth century.[71] In certain areas, much of the population and the local rulers became Shii, though most Muslims remained Sunni as Sunni Sufis countered Shii influence.[72] The power of the Chaks was broken by Mirza Haidar, who allied with the Mughals. He supported Sunnism and punished Shii Sufis, destroying their places of worship in 1543, legitimised by a fatwa from Hanafi clerics against the Nurbakhshis.[73] In 1550, Mirza Haidar was himself overthrown and killed, leading to the resurgence of the Shii Chaks. Under Mirza Haidar, mentioning the Shii Imams' names had been forbidden. Now the prayer was recited in their name and the Chaks rebuilt previously destroyed structures.[74] Some Shii rulers even had the prayer read in the name of the Safavids rather than the Mughals.[75]

During Akbar's reign, a Sunni *Qadi* in Kashmir sentenced an outspoken Shii to death. Riots followed, and a Shii official in turn had that *Qadi* assassinated and that Shii official was then executed by Akbar. Sunni–Shia tensions overlapped with struggles for political control, as Sunni leaders and clerics helped Akbar establish control.[76] When the Chaks fell in 1586, Kashmir came under direct Mughal rule (the governors they appointed were Sunni and Shii). In other words, Akbar, whom we have gotten to know for his ecumenical policies, here used Sunni resentment towards the Chaks to legitimise the incorporation of Kashmir into his realm. He even settled Safavid defectors there.[77] The situation was so sectarianised that when Shustari, the key Shii cleric of the period, and then still a Mughal official, visited Kashmir in 1591 to investigate complaints over the revenue system, it pushed him to pen his polemics.[78] Tensions in Kashmir continued under subsequent Mughal rulers, fuelled by a growing Shii assertiveness and the influx of Naqshbandi missionaries.[79]

Further south, in the Deccan Plateau, Muslim dynasties likewise embraced Shiism. Here, a dynasty of Iranian origin established the Bahmani Kingdom (1347–1526), ruling first from Gulbarga and later from Bidar (in present-day Karnataka state). They were officially Sunni, but lay the ground work for the spreading of Shiism. They patronised the shrines in Najaf and Karbala, employed Sunni and Shii Iranians, and Sufi orders such as the Nimatullahis, who straddled the lines between Sunnism and Shiism, spread.[80] In the late fifteenth/early sixteenth century, the Bahmani Kingdom disintegrated into smaller successor states, three of whom embraced Shiism. The ruler of one of them, Yusuf Adil Shah,[81] had come in touch with Shiism through visits to Iran. He had promised to promote Shiism if his political fortunes allowed it. Given that much of his military and his Muslim subjects were Sunnis, his counsellors advised against it. Nonetheless, after hearing of the success of the Safavids, he proclaimed Shiism state religion in 1502. The Friday prayer was read in the Shii way, although the cursing of the Companions remained forbidden and Sunni governors were allowed to have the prayer read in the Sunni way. Some Bijapur notables and rivalling dynasties soon rallied Sunni opinion to undermine the Adil Shahis. They prepared for a Jihad legitimised by Yusuf Adil Shah's imposition of Shiism, which forced him to flee and, later, to revert to Sunnism.[82]

Adil Shah's son, Ismail, who assumed the throne in 1510, was too young initially to rule (he was ten). Still, when Ismail, who an Iranian Shii foster aunt had brought up, was old enough, he became more assertive. He again made Shiism the state religion, at least symbolically, but did not impose it on his subjects.[83] He had the Friday prayer read in honour of the Safavids and ordered his army to imitate the Safavid custom of wearing twelve-pointed caps.[84] The Safavids were revered as overarching religious authority, although that relationship was mostly symbolic.[85]

Ismail's son, Ibrahim Adil Shah, abandoned all those practices, embraced Sunnism and local customs, and dismissed Iranian Shia at court.[86] While this led to a rupture in diplomatic relations with the Safavids, the latter refused to join an alliance against Bijapur.[87] Ibrahim's son, Ali Adil Shah, who took the throne in 1558, again reverted to Shiism. Emulating Safavid practice, he employed Iranians to curse the first three Sunni Caliphs and enforce Shiism.[88] Sectarian identification lent cohesion to the rivalries at court. There were loosely defined groups, one made up of those who had come from abroad, many of whom were originally Shii Iranians. Then there were local Deccanis, who had recently converted to Sunnism. As elsewhere, it was not the categories of 'Sunni' and 'Shii' per se that defined the groups or set them against one another, but the intertwining of sectarian identity with struggles for power and patronage and an early modern world of Muslim diplomacy, in which shifting sectarian allegiances could provide external support.[89] Several Safavid missions to Bijapur throughout the sixteenth century, for example, encouraged the Deccan rulers to strengthen Shiism.[90]

After Bijapur again abandoned Shiism in favour of Sunnism in 1583, Shah Abbas of Iran sent a mission in 1594 to convince the then ruler of Bijapur, Ibrahim, to revert to Shiism, to no avail.[91] Nonetheless, Iran and Ibrahim Adil Shah II, the new Bijapur ruler who took over in 1580 and ruled for over forty years, maintained cordial diplomatic relations. This helped the ruler of Bijapur to keep the Mughals at bay. Shah Abbas even intervened to prevent the annexation of Bijapur by the Mughal Jahangir (Bijapur was eventually integrated into the Mughal Empire in 1686).[92] Mirroring the nominal alignment of the Shii rulers with the Safavids, those Adil Shahi rulers who adopted Sunnism had the prayer read in honour of the Ottoman Caliphs (something the Mughals never did). But relations with the remote Ottoman Empire remained generally limited.[93] And Sunni and Shii rulers in the Deccan could seal alliances or oppose each other, a process further complicated by frequent switches of sectarian allegiance within ruling dynasties, and intermarriage between them.[94]

The second Bahmani successor state was Ahmadnagar, where the son of a Hindu convert working for the Bahmanis established the Nizam Shahi dynasty in 1490. Burhan Nizam Shah I, who ruled until 1554, was converted to Shiism by an Iranian, Shah Tahir Husayni. The latter was a Nizari Ismaili Imam who claimed to be a Twelver Shii to avoid persecution. He was initially invited to join Shii scholars at Shah Ismail Safavi's court, but he soon fell out of favour and fled to escape a death sentence issued at the request of Twelver Shii clerics. Husayni then joined Nizam Shah's court as a religious advisor, and that is where he converted him, despite himself being an Ismaili, to Twelver Shiism, which paved the way for friendly relations between the Nizam Shahis and the Safavids. Some Sunnis rebelled, and subsequent Nizam Shahi rulers again reverted to Sunnism. Their territories were eventually annexed by the Mughal Shah Jahan in 1633.[95]

Shii scholars patronised under the Nizam Shahis moved to the realm of the Qutb Shahis, the rulers of the third major Bahmani successor state, whose new capital, Hyderabad, was founded in 1591 near their old fort. The city was named in honour of Ali (Haydar, meaning 'lion', being one of Ali's common associations).[96] According to the Shii view of the city's history, the Qutb Shahis decided that their old capital had become too congested. They wanted to leave their imprint by building a new capital, one with a large square, *souqs*, and splendid buildings reminiscent of Iran. At its heart, their Iranian architect envisioned the Charminar, the monument that has come to symbolise Hyderabad.[97] With four towering minarets (Charminar

literally means 'four minarets', and each one is 160 feet high), it is replete
with Shii symbolism. The mosque that is built on the top floor of the
Charminar, like many other Indian Shii buildings, features the number
five—referring to the Prophet, Fatima, Ali, Hasan, and Hussain. But to connect the city even more clearly to the lives of the Imams, the rulers sought
and obtained relics allegedly having pertained to the Prophet or the Imams,
over which small shrines were built that serve as sites of visitation.[98]

Persianate influence was strong not just in the built environment but also
in poetry and rituals.[99] Muharram in Qutb Shahi Hyderabad was ecumenical, centred around Ashurkhanas, communal halls built for this purpose
and sponsored by the elite, and the recitation of poems praising the *Ahl al-
Bayt* fused Sunni Sufi and Shii devotional piety. The architecture of
Hyderabad, and the poetry eulogising the *Ahl al-Bayt* were a cultural and
syncretistic highpoint.[100]

That support for Shiism was lost when the Deccan States became integrated into the Mughal Empire. Sectarian identity played a role in Deccan-
Mughal relations, but, typically, not in a clear-cut way. While sectarian
affinity between Shii officials employed by the Mughals and the Deccan
dynasties is at times invoked in the chronicles, it was probably limited. A Shii
general, Muhammad Baqir, even led the Mughal armies against the Qutb
Shahis in 1629.[101] Nonetheless, some of the campaigns, especially the final
ones led by Aurangzib, the Sunni-minded son of Mughal ruler Shah Jahan,
and later one of the longest-reigning and most infamous rulers himself,
were by chroniclers legitimised by the Iranian, and Hindu alliances of the
Deccan rulers. Aurangzib, who ruled for nearly fifty years (1658–1707), is of
paramount importance. Already during a campaign he led against the Qutb
Shahis in 1656, and which his father then aborted, he showed his Sunni-
mindedness, arguing that they should be suppressed because they had deviated from the true (Sunni) faith and allied with the Safavids.[102] He finally
succeeded in conquering their fort in 1687. But unlike during the Ottoman–
Uzbek–Safavid rivalries, where clerics supported sectarianised wars against
other Muslim powers, his own senior clerics, who felt no love for the Shia,
accepted the Deccan Shii rulers as Muslims and thus refused to endorse the
campaign, arguing that war between Muslim states was illegal.[103]

After the annexation of the Deccan States, some of the buildings in
Hyderabad associated with the Qutb Shahis, and with institutionalised
Shiism, were looted, and the Shii call to prayer banned.[104] The assertion of
Mughal authority over the Deccan States meant that the public religiosity

associated with the Mughals, which by now had become more Sunni Hanafi and Naqshbandi, gained in strength at the expense of other Sufi orders and Shiism.[105] Aurangzib conquered vast territories, consolidated the Empire, and supplanted the religiously liberal atmosphere of Akbar and Jahangir. He brought back Naqshbandi influence and codified Sunni Hanafi law to be used across the realm (a century and a half before the Ottomans were to embark on a similar project). The production of this manual of Islamic jurisprudence, the *Fatawa Alamgiri*, constituted a massive form of state patronage for the Sunni clergy, with many scholars from across the Islamic world working on the collection for years.[106] Common adherence to Hanafism did not lead to much more contact between the Ottoman and Mughal Empires, however, as letters from Aurangzib indicate that he did not recognise the Ottomans' claims to the Caliphate (instead seeing himself in that position).[107]

Aurangzib was the last of the Mughal emperors to rule fully independently, and who defeated the Shii-leaning states of the Deccan and Hindu rulers. He was later idolised by Sunni Revivalists, reviled by Hindu nationalists, and regarded with caution by Shia.[108] His Sunni affiliation was born out of his personal experience. As prince, Aurangzib was governor of Gujarat. There he had had to deal with the challenge of a millenarian movement— the Mahdavi movement—and the Bohras. He repressed the Ismaili Bohras and became close to leading clerics of the Sunni Bohra faction, one of whom he would appoint as the Empire's highest judge. Aurangzib even presided over an interrogation of the Ismaili Bohra leader, whom he then executed.[109]

Aurangzib's Sunni-mindedness may have been reinforced by the fact that another son of Jahangir, Shah Shuja, governor of Bengal, and a rival of his to the throne, was pro-Shii. And yet another brother as well as his foremost rival, Dara Shikoh, received support from Ismaili Bohras. Both these rivals were unsuccessful, and Aurangzib had Shikoh executed, justifying it with his allegedly heretical inclinations.[110] Yet, Shah Shuja's governorship in Bengal, to where he brought Shii officials, strengthened Shii influence there.[111] As elsewhere on the Indian subcontinent, most Muslims in Bengal were Hanafi Sunnis, and had converted in large numbers from the early thirteenth century onwards. But as in the other Indian Muslim principalities, there had been a Shii elite, and Shii practices were popular amongst recently converted populations.[112] Aurangzib appointed a Shii as new governor, or Nawab, of Bengal, although how open he was about his beliefs is not known.

Once at a safe distance from Aurangzib, and in charge of vast revenue, he became both more autonomous, and more openly Shii. This coincided with a waning of Mughal central authority after Aurangzib's death in 1707. Aurangzib's successor Bahadur Shah, who ruled for only five years, is ascribed Shii leanings. In 1710, he had Ali described as legatee of the Prophet in Friday prayers alongside references to Abu Bakr, Umar and Uthman. This may have been intended to fuse Sunni and Shii notions of political authority to strengthen Mughal authority. But it led to a backlash from Sunnis, and in Lahore, one of the largest cities of the Empire, and its former capital, to a revolt and the lynching of a preacher.[113] The decision was revoked, and the Emperor deposed. In the subsequent decade, opposition to a group of influential Shii brothers at court coalesced around a faction of Sunnis of Central Asian origin, which ultimately deposed them and helped Muhammad Shah, the last of the Mughals, to the throne.[114]

In the early eighteenth century, Bengal was thus ruled by semi-independent Shii governors. As elsewhere Iranian Shia found employment at court and the rulers and merchants sponsored Shii *madrasas*, patronised Shii clerics and festivities, such as Muharram, for which they endowed whole villages, and built vast Shii communal halls specifically designed to honour the Imams, the largest of which is 680 feet long.[115] But Bengal was also the site of the East India Company's first factory in the early seventeenth century, and would become the site of its first major military conquests. In 1757, the East India Company beat the forces of the Nawab, who were nominally defending Mughal territory, in the battle of Plassey, after which it annexed Bengal. Courtly patronage for Shiism dried up, though some patronage for Shii institutions by wealthy individuals and Shii influence in religious practice persisted. Company officials would be petitioned by Sunni and Shii factions to draw them in on their side.[116] Territories under Company rule became areas where Sunni and Shii missionaries competed. The rise of the Company in the eighteenth century coincided with and contributed to the gradual waning of Mughal central authority, as provincial dynasties attained semi-independence from the Mughals, and came under British influence.[117] Apart from Bengal, a second Shii dynasty established itself in Awadh, a Mughal province in Northern India in what is today Uttar Pradesh, and a third, at Hyderabad, now Sunni-led, reasserted its independence from Delhi.

In Hyderabad some institutions directly associated with the Qutb Shahis were repressed, and the city declined in importance for a few decades.

It re-emerged as a vital economic, cultural and political centre under the Asaf Jahis, the Nizams of Hyderabad, who were mostly Sunni. Yet Shii notables, some of whom migrated there from other princely states, held prominent positions in the city, and Shii influence lived on in the city's Muharram ceremonies, which continued to be patronised by Shii elites and the Nizams.[118] The Nizams gave much room to Shii cultural expressions, and patronised some of them, facilitating harmonious Sunni–Shia relations.[119]

Embracing interpretations of Islam that differed from the Hanafism and Sufism of the Mughals, or in the case of Hyderabad, from the Shiism of their predecessors, was a way for these local dynasties to assert their independence. The most striking case is Awadh. Mir Muhammad Amin had come to the Mughal court in Delhi from Nishapur in Iran in 1708 and had gained in prominence as a protégé of Shii circles at court. The last Mughal Emperor Muhammad Shah then appointed him governor of Awadh—still a Mughal province—in 1722, and named him *'Burhan al-Mulk', Proof of the Realm*.[120] This was the same year the Safavids were deposed in Iran, and Shiism lost state support.

In their stead, the new Shii rulers of Awadh now started to support Shiism.[121] In 1739, Nadir Shah, who had declared himself Shah of Iran in 1736, attracted by the Mughals' vast riches and hearing of their military and political weakness, gathered a huge army, took Lahore, and moved towards Delhi. Upon hearing of Nadir Shah's advances, Burhan al-Mulk joined the Mughal Emperor to defend Mughal domains. After being routed and captured by Nadir's troops, however, he became an intermediary between the two sides. In some chronicles he is accused of having urged Nadir Shah on to take Delhi, rather than accept a cash tribute by the Mughal Emperor. Burhan al-Mulk then died under suspicious circumstances, possibly of a suicide to not be held responsible for the subsequent devastating sack of Delhi.[122]

With Nadir Shah in effective control of Northern India, at least for a moment, Burhan al-Mulk's nephew, Safdar Jang, courted Nadir Shah to appoint him to the governorship of Awadh. Nadir Shah then recommended him to Emperor Muhammad Shah, who remained nominally in charge and confirmed Safdar Jang as governor of Awadh, founding a hereditary dynasty. Nadir Shah decided to return to Iran, in part to deal with the Ottomans. Nonetheless, the Nishapuri dynasty was now in control in Awadh, and the image of the Mughals irrevocably shattered.

After Burhan al-Mulk's death, Safdar Jang is said to have hired thousands of Nadir Shah's Shii Qizilbash cavalrymen from the withdrawing army, many from the same Turkmen tribes that had brought the Safavids to power. These warriors would settle in Awadh, form a key part of its army, and bolster its Shii identity.[123] Safdar Jang, who died in 1753 and his son Shuja ud-Daula, who ruled Awadh until 1775, occasionally helped the Mughals militarily. A turning point was the Battle of Buxar in 1764, when after a last combined attempt to uproot the East India Company from Bengal, which as noted the Company had taken in 1757, the troops nominally under Mughal leadership suffered a humiliating defeat. Shuja ud-Daula's troops abandoned the other pro-Mughal forces, including those of the Emperor, though they continued to resist further Company incursions northwest into Awadhi territory. Eventually, Shuja ud-Daula surrendered, and was reinstalled as governor of Awadh.[124]

Thereafter, Awadh's rulers came ever more under Company influence and became more independent from the Mughals. They signed treaties with the Company, and its representative at court got involved in day-to-day administration.[125] The symbolic break with Mughal sovereignty was the coronation in 1819 of Ghazi al-Din Haydar as King of Awadh.[126] On a Shii holiday the crown was placed on the ruler's head by the senior Shii cleric in Awadh, after which the new king embraced the Company representative, then ascended to the throne.[127] None of the other Indian local rulers that were becoming more independent of the Mughals went as far as Awadh, rupturing any semblance of subservience.[128] This allowed the Company to establish more direct control over politics and the economy in Awadh.[129] In religious affairs, and the ways in which patronage was handed out, however, the Awadhi rulers could do as they pleased.

They transformed their capital Lucknow through lavish mosques, arches, exquisite palaces along the river Gomti, and huge *Imambaras*, mourning houses for the Imams, which are a specific South Asian form of Shii religious buildings that fulfil important social functions.[130] The Nawabs were amongst the wealthiest rulers on the Indian subcontinent, and the world. By the mid-nineteenth century, Lucknow had several hundred thousand inhabitants, and visitors from Europe described it as one of the grandest cities in the world. William Russell, correspondent of *The Times*, who visited Lucknow in 1857, would write: 'Not Rome, not Athens, not Constantinople; not any city I have ever seen appears to me so striking and so beautiful as this.'[131]

It was here that the courtly Shiism of the Safavids, and of the Deccan States, was reformulated for a Northern Indian context as a religion of state.

The rulers turned Lucknow into a Shii centre, expanded its seminaries, libraries, and mosques, and built replicas of the Imams' original shrines in a distinctively Awadhi style. These shrines allowed the masses to connect more directly with the *Ahl al-Bayt*, since pilgrimage to the original shrines was only possible for a few. The rulers brought Shii scholars into the administration, and in the 1790s built an impressive-looking Friday prayer mosque. As discussed earlier, holding Friday prayers indicated the rulers' and clerics' self-confidence in the justness and religiously legitimated nature of their rule. Initially, many Indian Shii clerics opposed them for fear of alienating Sunnis—most of the Muslim population. But the holding of Shii Friday prayers in the name of the Nawabs provided the ideological legitimisation for independence from Mughal suzerainty.[132]

Muharram processions were occasions of state, in which the mourning of Hussain was, at the same time, an assertion of worldly power and a form of proselytising.[133] They attracted large crowds, as Shii influence spread to the lower classes, and led to stronger cross-class connections. But as the cursing of the Caliphs became more prominent, it alienated Sunnis, and led to a sharper division between Sunnism and Shiism.[134]

Aspiring clerics studied in the shrine cities of Iraq, and upon their return staffed the judiciary and new religious institutions. One of them, Sayyid Dildar Ali, would come to epitomise Awadhi Shiism. He arrived in Iraq as an Akhbari, as noted, the scripturalist Hadith-focused school of Shiism, then became an Usuli, and would play a key role in making the rationalist Usuli school, with its emphasis on the public role of the clerics and their independent reasoning, dominant in Awadh. His intention was to break the influence of Sunni and Shii Sufi leaders in Awadh, and empower a clergy-centred Shiism. He refuted anti-Shii polemics and wrote treatises against Akhbaris and the kind of popular Sufism that straddled confessional lines.[135] He and other clerics developed close ties to the state, controlled alms and became landowners.[136] Under the Mughals, as noted, religious education had been set up in an ecumenical way, incorporating the philosophical tradition of Isfahan and the wider Persianate world, epitomised by Mir Fath-Allah Shirazi. Originally from Iran, he was employed at the court in Bijapur under both Sunni and Shii rulers of the dynasty, after which, in 1583, Akbar, aware of his Shiism, entrusted him with organising the educational system for the entire Mughal realm.[137]

The *Dars-i Nizami*, as it was called, was then further developed by clerics of the Farangi Mahall, a building complex in Lucknow.[138] These Sunni clerics initially maintained good relations with the local Shii rulers and clerics, who studied with them.[139] In the eighteenth century, the *Dars-i Nizami*, with its focus on logic, philosophy, and rational argumentation, was challenged on the Sunni side by a more literalist and traditionalist education, and on the Shii side by a more self-consciously Shii clergy.[140] Hanafi Sunnis of Farangi Mahall served in senior administrative functions, the judiciary, and as Muftis under the Nawabs. However, from the 1840s onwards, Shii clerics pushed for a Shii-led judicial system.[141] And after developing closer ties with the shrine cities in Iraq in the eighteenth and early nineteenth century, Shii clerics established seminaries in Lucknow, separating Shii education from the Farangi Mahall.[142] Once the Nawabs emphasised their Shii identity, key Sunni clerics emigrated to Sunni-led princely states, and embraced a more forceful Sunni identity that included a rejection of Shii rituals.[143] The decline of Mughal patronage, and the rise of Shii dynasties, undermined the charitable foundations that had funded Sunni educational and religious institutions.[144]

In Lucknow and the smaller townships across Awadh, the rulers' support of Shiism, spurred many elites to convert to Shiism. After the annexation of further territories in Northern India by the Company, and the ending of Sunni rule in those places, Shii proselytising sponsored by Awadh also increased in Company-ruled territories, which alienated Sunnis.[145] Sayyids, too, were pushed to espouse Shiism.[146] Descendants of the first three Caliphs—Abu Bakr, Umar, and Uthman, referred to as 'Shaykhs'—were more inclined to Sunnism, though a few of those also converted.[147] Some Sayyid families that ruled local townships in Awadh converted to Shiism, such as the rulers of Mahmudabad. Others remained nominally Sunni, while sponsoring Muharram processions and hiring Shii preachers.[148]

As in the rest of the Indian subcontinent, however, Shia remained a minority of Muslims. The Awadhi polity rested on an alliance with Sunnis, from the judiciary to the landed gentry, the administration and the military. The more exclusivist the Usuli Shii clerics became, the more anti-Shii the emerging Sunni Revivalist movements turned. Since Shiism in Awadh was the religion of state, Sunnism here had an insurgent quality. Even Sufi orders with Shii affinities could develop anti-Shii tenets in the face of Shii assertiveness.[149] Despite strong rivalries amongst different Sunni Revivalist movements, they all saw Shiism as a threat. And they were all, in one way or another, inspired by Shah Wali Allah Dihlawi.

Shah Wali Allah was born in Delhi in 1703, where his father was the principal of a *madrasa* and initiated him into the Naqshbandiyya. In 1730/1, he went on Hajj and studied Hadith in the Hijaz. He links the religious legacy of Mughal India and the Naqshbandiyya, to the debates on the Arabian Peninsula.[150] In Medina, he studied with Hadith scholars who blended Indian, North African, and Hijazi intellectual traditions.[151] It was here that he came across the works of Ibn Taymiyya, the strongly anti-Shii thirteenth/ fourteenth century scholar. Muhammad Ibn Abd al-Wahhab, the founder of the Wahhabi movement, had also briefly studied in Medina with an Indian Naqshbandi Shafii, who came from the same circles as Shah Wali Allah's teachers. Two key figures of eighteenth-century Sunni Revivalism, Shah Wali Allah and Ibn Abd al-Wahhab, came of age in a similar milieu, and may even have sat in front of the same teachers. It was here that a Sunni Revivalism centred on the Hanbali school and one centred on the study of Hadith and the networks of the Naqshbandiyya converged, with Shiism as a common enemy.[152]

The two came from a different intellectual tradition, but that did not stop their detractors from calling Shah Wali Allah and other Indian clerics who had studied in the Hijaz 'Wahhabi'.[153] Shah Wali Allah emphasised the importance of the first two Caliphs (not least over Ali), referred to Shia as 'rejectionists', and translated Sirhindi's *Radd-i Rawafid*, the famous anti-Shii polemic mentioned above that was originally written in Persian, into Arabic. He tried to convince Sufis that they had inflated the position of Ali and sought to limit, though not to ban outright, Shii practices during Muharram. He was less extreme in his anti-Shiism than the real Wahhabis, and in general refrained from direct attacks on Shia, and praised the *Ahl al-Bayt*.[154]

Despite these nuances, however, the Muslim revivalism he set in motion turned virulently anti-Shii. Given the Company's rapid takeover of Indian Muslim princely states, Shah Wali Allah sought to turn to Islamic tradition to resist British imperialism. His disciples organised a Jihad against both the British and 'polytheists', i.e. Hindus, and Shii influence. Shah Wali Allah and his followers resented the influence of Shii officials such as Safdar Jang, the above-mentioned Nawab of Awadh who became Wazir of the Emperor Ahmad Shah from 1748 until 1753, and other Shia in government and the judiciary.[155] In that sense, they gave ideological expression to political rivalries between so—called 'Iranis', often Shia with Iranian origin, and 'Turanis', often Sunnis of Central Asian origin, and with ties to Afghanistan and the Naqshbandiyya (though that did not preclude alliances of convenience, and Sunni Afghan mercenaries, for example, would fight on different sides in eighteenth-century India's myriad wars, including on the side of Shii Iranis).[156] Another important Shii was Najaf Khan, one of the Mughals' last and most talented generals.[157] During his tenure from 1779 to 1782, Delhi witnessed Sunni–Shia tensions. When a Naqshbandi Shaykh criticised the Shii processions during Muharram he was assassinated by an Iranian Shii.[158] As the state was often directly or indirectly associated with Shiism, these movements presented their cause as a defence of Sunnism against Shiism.[159] They were allied ideologically to Mughal successor states that, in contrast to the Shiism, Sikhism, or Hinduism of other states, embraced a Sunni Revivalism tied to the Naqshbandi networks. The most important of these were the Rohilla Afghan rulers of Rohilkhand, which in many ways became the Sunni counter-part to nearby Shii Awadh. That the Nawab of Awadh, in conjunction with Company troops, defeated them in 1774/5, and incorporated Rohilkhand into Awadh, fuelled ethno-sectarian animosity.[160] Several Sunni Revivalist leaders either were from families that had converted to Shiism or had grown up or spent time in Shii-ruled territories, and rebelled against that experience.[161]

Sayyid Ahmed Barelvi, for example, was born in 1786 in territory that had come under the rule of the Nawabs of Awadh. He advocated direct action against the British, and against Shii rituals sponsored by Awadh's rulers. His was a protest movement against a perceived decline of Sunni power, and the rise of British imperialism and Shiism. After a severe confrontation with Shia, Sayyid Ahmed and hundreds of followers went on the pilgrimage to Mecca in 1821, where he may have encountered the teachings of Ibn Abd al-Wahhab. The voyage led to his adherents being labelled 'Wahhabis' in India, even though he, like other Indian Sunni Revivalists, largely came from the Naqshbandi not the Hanbali tradition. He was then active in Peshawar, Punjab, and Kashmir, where he led an anti-Sikh Jihad, with the ultimate aim to move against British domains and Shii-ruled Awadh, but was killed with his followers in 1831 in Kashmir.[162]

Shah Wali Allah's son and intellectual heir, Shah Abd al-Aziz, who died in 1824, wrote several polemics against Shiism, the most famous of which is the 'Gift for Twelve Shia', *Tuhfat-i ithna 'ashariyya*.[163] In twelve chapters, one each for the number of Imams recognised by Shia, he rebuts core Shii beliefs.[164] Shah Abd al-Aziz sets out why Shia are a threat and argues that the rise of the Safavids had boosted Shiism and influenced Sunnis.[165] He wavered on the question of whether or not Shia were Muslims, arguing that those who denigrated the Companions were apostates. Like his father, he sought to counter the widespread notion that Ali was better than the first three Sunni Caliphs. Instead, they propagated the idea that the first two, Abu Bakr and Umar, whom Shia attack, had been exceptionally good Caliphs. Over time, the lionising of Abu Bakr and Umar became a mainstay of Sunni identity in South Asia.[166] A return to extensive and literalist study of the Hadith, the deeds and sayings of the Prophet, can be traced to Arabic scholars of the late fifteenth and early sixteenth century, and Indian scholars of the sixteenth and seventeenth centuries.[167] These ideas were further developed on the Indian subcontinent by Naqshbandis and the Ahl-i Hadith (People of the Hadith), who saw themselves as heirs to Shahs Wali Allah and Abd al-Aziz, as well as to the Salafism of the Arabian Peninsula.[168] The Ahl-i Hadith saw Shiism, with its different way of studying Hadith, as a threat to the certainties they hoped to gain from the Hadith.[169] Printing would accelerate processes that were already under way, and intensify the literalist interpretation of the sources.

Pro-Alid Sufi songs, the colourful Muharram processions attended by Sunnis and Shia and many others, poetry, and the syncretistic religious policies of the Great Mughals such as Akbar epitomised the ecumenical legacy of Indian Islam. That ecumenical Muslim culture was in part spurred by the Muslim's minority status, and a sense of belonging to a supra-confessional Persianate world. But the Shii dynasties in the Deccan and in Awadh, Shii identity entrepreneurs like Shustari and Dildar Ali, and Sunni Revivalists such as Shahs Wali Allah and Abd al-Aziz, the more sectarian turn of Mughal rulers such as Aurangzib, and the arrival of British imperialism, also set in motion more antagonistic processes. Competing dynasties espousing Sunnism or Shiism supported separate Sunni and Shii revivalisms. This gave wider traction to debates that may otherwise have remained more localised, and allowed them to resonate beyond the Indian subcontinent. The networks of the British Empire, which was extending its control over the Indian subcontinent and the Middle East (a term a British official would invent in 1901 to indicate its position within the Empire), facilitated wider interactions across that Empire and beyond. As in other parts of the Islamic world, a turn towards the fundamentals of Islam in the face of Empire, meant revisiting the sectarian question, and whereas Muslim unity was always an avowed goal so was the purging of alleged unbelief and 'improper' Muslim practices.

6

Reform and Reinvention in the Eighteenth Century

The eighteenth century witnessed massive political and economic transformations: the disintegration of several Muslim Empires, the rise of European powers, and the adoption of sectarian identity by some rulers and movements, and the rejection of sectarian division by others. How did this impact the meaning and relationship of Sunnism and Shiism?

The decline of the Safavids and the waning of Mughal power displayed the weaknesses of the Islamic Gunpowder Empires, and constituted a major rupture. Post-Safavid rulers embraced Sunnism, and one of them, Nadir Shah—who of course sacked Delhi in 1739 and helped install the rulers of Awadh—even tried to do away with Sunni–Shia division once and for all. But shortly after, Sunni Revivalists challenged the Ottomans, and attacked Shiism and Sufism. This, in turn, led to a revitalisation of the Iraqi shrine cities, where, no longer serving the Safavid state, the Shii clergy expanded its base and reformulated Shiism. When Iran's rulers reverted to Shiism again, which they did in the 1750s, and started to rely again on the legitimisation of the clergy, the latter went ahead, but also became political players in their own right.

An increasing European presence and growing economic, political and military penetration led more and more Muslims to reason that in order to counter this Islam needed to reinvent itself. Some argued that only a renewed focus on the scriptures and early history of Islam could provide guidance, and emphasised a narrower sectarian identity. Others thought that Sunni–Shia unity was necessary. The dialectic and tension between these approaches would preoccupy the Islamic world as it entered the modern age.

In 1722, the Afghan Mahmud, who as noted was a Sunni, defeated the Safavids and conquered Isfahan (and as also noted, during the sack of

Isfahan, Mahmud humiliated the last Safavid Shah and mocked his Shii allegiance). Despite his rhetoric of common Sunni opposition to the Safavids, the Ottomans did not ally with him. After his death, his cousin Ashraf declared himself Shah in 1725 and asked the Ottoman Sultan to recognise him and withdraw Ottoman forces from previously Safavid territories by trying to play on Sunni solidarity. His argument, as laid out in a letter by Sunni Afghan clerics, was that, since Shia were heretics, they did not enjoy land ownership rights, so the land he had just conquered was technically ownerless and dutifully his. And he wanted to be accepted as an independent ruler. The Ottomans, however, responded by declaring war on Ashraf.[1] Some Ottoman clerics were sympathetic because of the Afghans' Sunni identity, but the highest of them argued that the Afghan leader could be declared a rebel just for claiming that he had authority independent of the Ottoman Sultan-Caliph.

As we've seen throughout this story, playing on sectarian solidarity had its own limitations and pitfalls. The Ottomans dispatched troops to Iran but were routed near Hamadan amidst reports that an Afghan delegation had managed to convince Sunni Ottoman soldiers not to fight against fellow Sunnis. Because the Ottomans were nominally fighting Ashraf with the aim to restore the Safavids as puppet Shahs to power, Ashraf put to death the last Safavid Shah, Sultan Hussain, whom he was holding captive, in 1726. Shortly thereafter, Afghans and Ottomans signed a peace treaty in which the Afghans acknowledged the Ottoman Sultan's supremacy. For their part, the Ottomans and the Russians signed a peace agreement dividing up the northern Safavid lands and then pledged limited support to the son of Shah Sultan Hussain, Tahmasp II, who sought to regain Safavid territory.[2]

Indicating that sectarian hostility could be reversed if political expediency demanded it, the Ottomans would over the next two centuries host and pay stipends to descendants of the Safavid dynasty, as a sort of insurance policy.[3] In the territories the Ottomans gained in the old frontier regions, they reemployed members of the Sunni notable families that had served under previous dynasties.[4] In contemporary chronicles, the Afghan victory was described as a victory for Sunnism, and the disunity of the Safavids (and parts of their Georgian Christian soldiers) as a loss of Shiism.[5] Indeed, Isfahan, previously the Safavid capital and a centre of Shiism, was dealt a heavy blow. The endowments that had supported the Shii clergy were largely put to different uses, and many scholars migrated to the shrine cities in Iraq or to India.[6]

Twelver Shiism was sufficiently institutionalised, however, for most Iranians to remain Shii, and many clerics remained in Iran. In addition, Shiism flourished in Eastern Arabia, Jabal Amil, Iraq, and, as noted, in India.[7] In Iran itself, there was a common anti-Safavid feeling amongst Sunnis, especially in the frontier regions, but other divisions were just as important.[8] Afghan rule was undermined because of disagreements between the Afghan rulers in Isfahan and their relatives in Afghanistan, not because of Sunni–Shia difference. And when the new strongman Nadir Shah started to fight the Sunni Afghans, he did so initially with many Sunni troops.

In this, Nadir Shah stands out. He was from the Afshar tribe and started out as a military leader supporting Tahmasp II, who sought to regain the Safavid possessions from the Afghans. The Afshars had been one of the Turkmen tribes that had originally brought the Safavids to power, and his family had been Shii. He, too, displayed Shii leanings. When he conquered Mashhad in 1726, still nominally on behalf of Tahmasp II, Nadir Shah ordered the refurbishment and expansion of the shrine of Imam Rida, and used Shii language to denounce the Ottomans in 1732. But when he pro-claimed himself Shah, he professed to be a Sunni.[9] In his first speech as Shah in 1736, he said that the country would henceforth revert to Sunnism and argued that sectarian difference had caused bloodshed between Iran and the Ottoman Empire, and that it was time for Islamic unity. To that effect, he proposed that Iranians adopt the Jafari school of jurisprudence, named after Jafar al-Sadiq, which would be structured like the four Sunni schools. What this Jafari school was supposed to entail, however, never became entirely clear. For Iranian and Shii audiences, Nadir Shah seemed to advocate that Shiism would exist more or less as before, but that, for the sake of peace with the Ottomans, one should refrain from the Shii rituals most objection-able to Sunnis. Outwardly, to facilitate a settlement with the Ottoman Empire, he tried to present it as a shift from Shiism to Sunnism that involved the abandonment of core Shii doctrines and rituals.[10]

Nadir Shah sent letters to the Ottoman Sultan stating that Iranians were returning to the Sunnism they had espoused before the Safavids, calling it 'the clear faith which has been inherited by the People of Iran'.[11] Iranian clerics travelled to Istanbul to discuss the idea. Nadir Shah sought the appointment of an Iranian pilgrimage leader and a column in the Kaaba akin to the columns of the four Sunni schools, amongst other demands. In return, he would ban Shii practices offensive to Sunnis.[12] Agreement was reached on all matters except the religious ones, which the Ottomans refused.[13]

Still, Nadir Shah forbade the cursing of the first three Caliphs and the Companions of the Prophet, and the mentioning of 'Ali the friend of God' in prayer.[14] Religious objects contained the names of the Rashidun Caliphs and of the *Ahl al-Bayt*.[15] Nonetheless, the Ottomans demanded from Nadir Shah a complete acceptance of Sunnism and the superiority of the Sultan and, when they declared war against him in 1742, the senior Ottoman cleric issued a fatwa against the Jafari school.[16] In a last attempt to save his proposal, Nadir Shah convened Sunni and Shii scholars from realms under his control at the shrine of Ali in Najaf.[17] On his way to the meeting, Nadir Shah visited both the Shii Imams' shrines (Musa al-Kazim and Muhammad Taqi) as well as the tomb of Abu Hanifa in Baghdad. He then proceeded to Karbala, where he performed the circumambulation of the shrine, to which his wife donated substantial funds. In Najaf, he ordered the dome of the shrine of Ali to be gilded.[18] A prominent Sunni Shafii cleric from Baghdad, Abdullah al-Suwaydi, was sent to the conference by the Ottoman governor of Baghdad, wrote a detailed account, and co-signed an ecumenical statement after the conference.[19]

That statement referred to the coexistence between the different schools and recognised the Jafari school, yet was so ambiguous that both sides could interpret it differently. Nonetheless, the perhaps most serious attempt at formal Sunni–Shia rapprochement to date, as al-Suwaydi put it, 'brought joy and happiness to the Sunnis. Nothing like it has occurred through the ages.'[20] The Ottoman leadership, however, would only make peace with Nadir after he completely abandoned his project and reneged on his demands in a letter to the Sultan that explicitly started with a praise of the Rashidun Caliphs and a denunciation of the Shii practices of the Safavids.[21]

Clearly, Ottoman-Iranian rivalry was about more than sectarian difference. The Ottoman Sultan-Caliph was not interested in accepting a fifth school of jurisprudence, which would become a vehicle for Iranian influence, even if that school would have been stripped of its anti-Sunni features and would have smoothened relations with Sunnism. The Ottomans had found a modus vivendi with Shiism, and did not want to risk undermining their Sunni credentials by recognising it further. Indeed, beyond al-Suwaydi's document, it did not leave much of a legacy. And, just like other ecumenical initiatives discussed in this book, this one, too, was political from the outset, an attempt by Nadir Shah to undermine latent claims to the throne by the deposed Safavids, and provide the ideological blueprint and legitimacy for an Empire with Iran at its core, but one that was supposed to extend far beyond. For Nadir Shah expanded his realm and incorporated many more non-Shii subjects.[22] Nadir's early military successes against the Afghans had been spearheaded by Sunni soldiers. As his realm expanded all the way to India, he substantially enlarged his army (to 350,000 in 1747) by recruiting Turkmen, Uzbek, Afghan, Baluch, and Kurdish tribesmen, most of them poor Sunnis, in order to offset the largely Shii infantry and cavalry, many from the old Qizilbash tribes, that still had loyalties to the Safavids.[23] Nadir Shah sometimes organised separate divisions according to ethnic and religious origin, and encouraged rivalries, all the while suppressing public displays of sectarian factionalism.[24]

A new Islamic Empire, centred on Iran, Central Asia, and Northern India, controlling the sea routes along the way, and on good terms with the Ottoman Empire, legitimised by pan-Islam, and a strong military and administration, may have withstood European pressure longer. Nadir Shah of course plundered Delhi in 1739, shattering the image of the Mughals as Islam's most powerful dynasty, taking their most cherished and valuable treasures, and hastening the decline of that dynasty and the ascent of the East India Company and Mughal successor states like Awadh.[25] Instead of establishing a new Empire, however, Nadir Shah retreated from Delhi with his loot to deal with the Ottomans, who as noted were not impressed with his proposals. Though he effectively ended the prospects of two of the mightiest early modern Muslim Empires, the Safavids and the Mughals, he failed to institutionalise a more lasting polity, or bring about Sunni–Shia rapprochement and an accommodation with the Ottomans, and was eventually killed by his own troops in 1747.

The political instability after Nadir Shah's death was overcome in the 1750s by the Zands, a tribal dynasty founded by Karim Khan Zand. They installed descendants of the Safavids as puppet Shahs, or ruled directly. Karim Khan Zand was not known for his piety, and claimed to derive his legitimacy from being a representative of the people. This was a far cry from Safavid claims to divine kingship, though Karim Khan reverted to the Safavid practice of using Shii symbolism, sponsored Shii rituals, and continued patronage of Shii religious institutions. It was under his reign that Shii clerics that had fled after the Safavids' demise started to return.[26] Karim Khan expanded the southern city of Shiraz and developed the ports in the Persian Gulf. As part of this endeavour, he sealed alliances with Arab tribal groups across the Persian Gulf. Some of these were Shii, such as those around Basra. Many others were Sunni, and some, urged on by the Zands, settled along the Iranian coast, where local Sunni rulers ruled nominally on behalf of the dominant power in Iran. Connections across the Persian Gulf, and the movement of people, goods, ideas, and arms, hence increased.[27]

The Zands also integrated more firmly the mixed Shii and Sunni Northern provinces of Azerbaijan. After Karim Khan died in 1779, the Zands declined, and the Qajars, who had been rivals to both Nadir Shah's Afshars, and the Zands, replaced them both, emerging as the new ruling dynasty of Iran (until the 1920s). Aga Mohammad Khan Qajar, its founder, made Tehran his capital in 1786, and upon his coronation wore the royal sabre of the Safavids, styling himself both as a successor of the Safavids and a defender of Shiism. Over the coming years, he and his troops conquered the rest of Iran. After Qajar's death in 1797, his successors gave clerics important roles in administration and public life.[28] Ottoman and Persian rulers again legitimised themselves with reference to Sunnism and Shiism, respectively. But both came under increasing European influence. And a new movement vowed to fight against both the Ottomans and Shiism.

The founder of this movement was Muhammad Ibn Abd al-Wahhab, whose legacy looms large, and who played an extraordinarily important role in imbuing Sunni Revivalism with an anti-Shii bent. He was born in 1703 in a small town in Najd, in the centre of the Arabian Peninsula, into a family of religious scholars. Following the family tradition, he set out as a young man to travel and study. He first went to Medina in the West, then to the Eastern oasis of al-Ahsa, and finally to Basra, the port town on the Northern tip of the Gulf. There, he encountered Shia and Sufis that performed a wide range of religious practices, which seemed blasphemous to him. It was on these sojourns that the essence of his ideology crystallised itself. In Basra, a town with many Shii inhabitants then nominally under Ottoman control, he was expelled for preaching against the religious practice of the locals.[29] Upon his return to Najd, Ibn Abd al-Wahhab disseminated a treatise outlining his views and started preaching.[30]

Central to Ibn Abd al-Wahhab's message was the idea of the unity of God (*tawhid*) and the belief that any religious practice that could be seen as elevating other people to divine status should be denounced and abolished, and those committing these alleged heresies could be excommunicated (*takfir*). Even if the latter thought of themselves as devout Muslims, they could be killed and expropriated if they refused to join the call. Ibn Abd al-Wahhab's ideas found some resonance in Najd, but were rejected even by his own family and the official religious scholars in Najd (his brother would write a famous refutation of his ideas).[31] Because of his insistence on *tawhid*, his followers called themselves *al-muwahidun*. The similar sounding term *Wahhabiyya* or *Wahhabis* was initially mainly used by opponents of the movement to discredit it as a sort of sect that follows the example of its founding figure, but has become widely used.[32]

Earlier empires and states had of course used their version of Islam to justify war against opponents or persecute perceived heretics. The Wahhabis went further, however. Unlike earlier local rulers, or the multi-confessional empires, they were deeply interested in the personal beliefs and rituals of their subjects, and were keen to reshape them profoundly. They sought to abolish the visitation of graves and holy sites, apart from the one to the Kaaba in Mecca, and singled out Sufism and Shiism, for whom visitations of other sites are crucial, as exceptionally heretical.[33] In his writings on Shiism, Ibn Abd al-Wahhab based himself on Ibn Taymiyya, discussed above in relation to the campaigns of the Mamluks against the Alawites (Nusayris) of the Kisrawan, and the struggles with the Mongols. Just as Ibn Taymiyya had denied the Mongols protections as Muslims, arguing that they were not upholding the rule of Islam and should be fought, Ibn Abd al-Wahhab argued that those that claimed to be Muslims but did not follow the path of *tawhid* had to be fought. Like for other Hanbalis, the Shii view on the Companions and the authenticity of Hadith was deeply troubling to Ibn Abd al-Wahhab and impossible to reconcile with the quest for certainty around the Prophet's legacy. Hanbalis espoused a literal reading of the Quran and Hadith, and any practice that could not be traced to the pious ancestors was considered an innovation, and to be rejected.[34] Ibn Abd al-Wahhab therefore called Shii criticism of the Companions 'the destruction of the basis of religion, because its base is the Quran and the Hadith'.[35] He must have found attempts to bring together Shiism and Sunnism such as the one by Nadir Shah deeply troubling.[36] While he was a Hanbali, he and his later followers also rejected the notion that once a consensus had been established within a school of jurisprudence, a reinterpretation of the sources was no longer needed. For it was the Wahhabis' reinterpretation of the sources, and a selective appropriation from the Hanbali tradition, that made their ideas so explosive, and so revolutionary.[37]

In 1744, he sealed an alliance with a provincial ruling family, the Al Saud, which gave ideological cohesion to the Al Saud's political project and political backing to the Wahhabi mission.[38] On the Arabian Peninsula, a good number of local emirates had long competed. They were usually able to form a stronghold in one oasis and ally with surrounding tribal confederations. Raids on neighbouring oases were frequent, as resources were scarce. These emirates retained local support, and a strong sense of togetherness but they would generally not have an ideology that people from outside their group could subscribe to.

That, however, was precisely what Ibn Abd al-Wahhab and his descendants, the Al al-Shaykh, achieved. By embracing the message of Ibn Abd al-Wahhab, the Al Saud family gained a decisive advantage over its rivals: an ideology that turned tribal allies into fighters for a cause higher than blood bonds, local loyalties, or spoils of war (although these certainly helped). The alliance was beneficial for Ibn Abd al-Wahhab, too, for without the backing of a local ruler he may well have remained a peripheral figure, or been killed. Instead, he became the spiritual leader of a major political force, and helped the Al Saud establish what has been termed the first Saudi state.[39]

The Saudis were now able to confront their rivals. To the East was the Bani Khalid tribe that ruled over the predominantly Shii city of Qatif and the religiously mixed oasis of al-Ahsa. Primarily Sunni, some of its branches may have adopted the Shiism so prominent in the urban setting of Qatif, Hofuf, and Mubarraz, and the surrounding villages and oases. To the North, in Hail, the Rashidi Emirate, allied to the Ottomans, proved to be their most formidable enemy; and to the West, the Hashemite Sharifs of Mecca ruled over the Hijaz, nominally on behalf of the Ottomans.[40] Theirs was a rebellion against the Ottomans, under whom, as shown above, confessional ambiguity and substantial autonomy of religious communities went hand in hand with a state-sponsored Hanafi Sunnism and Sufism. Ibn Abd al-Wahhab and his followers, on the other hand, denounced all who did not embrace their puritan version of Islam that sought to emulate the life of the Prophet and his earliest Companions (*al-Salaf al-Salih*), including many Sunnis, as non-Muslims (for their embrace of the *al-Salaf al-Salih* they have been called Salafis). They also applied this to the Ottomans.

In turn, the official Ottoman clergy and Sunni and Shii clerics in many of the regions that Ibn Abd al-Wahhab had visited on his 'study tour', such as the Hijaz, al-Ahsa, and Basra, all now under attack from the Saudi-Wahhabi forces, denounced them.[41] Indeed, in the late eighteenth century, on a journey to the region, the Danish traveller Carsten Niebuhr noted that numerous interlocutors, from Zaydis and Twelver Shia to Sufis and Ibadis, worried about the spectre of the Wahhabis.[42] He and other European travellers sensed that an important movement had arisen on the Peninsula.[43]

By the time Ibn Abd al-Wahhab died in 1792, he had founded a religious movement with committed disciples. Some of his sons and other disciples further developed Wahhabi doctrine and deepened its anti-Shii impetus.[44] When the Wahhabis raided al-Ahsa and Iraq in the 1780s, 1790s, and 1800s, then under Ottoman control, they aimed to put these ideas into practice. They destroyed mosques and mourning houses in al-Ahsa and Qatif, but ultimately did not kill or expel all Shia, and allowed the latter to live if they did not practise their faith openly.[45] In 1802, however, the Wahhabis attacked Karbala, looted the city, destroyed the Hussain shrine, and killed thousands. The leading Shii cleric of the city only survived by hiding in an attic.[46] The Wahhabis also laid siege to Najaf for a year, initially unsuccessfully, but in further raids in 1806 and 1810 managed to conquer the city, loot the shrine's treasures, and destroy Ali's tomb.[47]

These raids resonated far and wide. They were an affront to the Ottomans, who nominally ruled over Iraq, and caused consternation amongst Shia from Iraq to India. The Saudi ruler Abdulaziz Muhammad Al Saud, under whose leadership the Wahhabis sacked Karbala, was assassinated in 1803. Some argued that the assassin was a Shii seeking revenge for the killing of his family at Karbala. Others claimed that he was a Kurd from near Mosul, and that he may have been sent by the Ottomans.[48] The raids would remain reference points in Shii historical memory ever since, and entrenched the hostility between Wahhabism and Shiism.[49]

Equally traumatic to Shia was when, in 1803 and 1805, the Saudi-Wahhabi forces conquered Mecca and Medina and destroyed historic buildings such as the domes above the shrines of the *Ahl al-Bayt* in the al-Baqia cemetery. These raids into Southern Iraq, and the Hijaz, came as such a shock to the Ottomans that they urged Muhammad Ali, the semi-independent Pasha of Egypt, who had taken power after the French occupation, and was modernising his army, to deal the Wahhabis a final blow. Egyptian troops expelled the Wahhabis from the Hijaz in 1812/3. Together with infighting amongst the Al Saud, this led to the collapse of the polity (the Saudi ruler was executed in Istanbul in 1818, and the Wahhabi heartlands in Najd were ransacked). In the coming decades, parts of the movement regrouped, and regained political control of Central Najd and parts of Eastern Arabia, during which time they again repressed Shiism, but would be crushed again, by the Rashidis, the local allies of the Ottomans, and would not re-emerge in a major way until the early twentieth century.[50]

The Wahhabi raids led to a Shii counter-mobilisation. The first religious scholars had settled in Najaf in the eleventh century. The number of scholars and students was small, however, and Najaf in a poor state. Hilla was for centuries the more important centre of Shii scholarship in Iraq.[51] But in the eighteenth century, after the collapse of the Safavids and amidst weak Ottoman control, the shrine cities developed at a rapid pace. Many clerics moved there from Iran, where they had been losing patronage, and India, where new Shii-led states needed clerics to staff the bureaucracy. Others came from Bahrain, al-Ahsa, and Qatif, to escape political instability and Wahhabi raids. The raids accelerated the movement of people from the border regions between the Arabian Peninsula and Iraq. They settled near cities like Najaf and Karbala, major pilgrimage and market towns, which brought them into closer contact with Shii clerics, who converted these tribesmen that had only had a vague sectarian affiliation. Shiism in Iraq, which had been predominantly urban, was gaining a significant tribal element.[52]

The raids had exposed the vulnerability of the shrine cities, and the conversion of tribesmen was one way to prepare against any future attacks. Conversion was further boosted by intermarriage between Sayyids and leading tribal families and by a policy of tribal settlement that began in 1831, when the Ottomans re-established direct rule over Iraq (until then, a group of Ottoman governors called Mamluks had ruled Iraq with a fair degree of autonomy, and their ineffectiveness facilitated the Wahhabi raids).

Over the course of the nineteenth century, therefore, old Iraqi tribal confederations and new tribes arriving from the Arabian Peninsula, settled, and converted to Shiism (those that stayed nomadic into the twentieth century often remained Sunni). Many of the large tribal confederations spanning the Arab East gained Shii subsections. Even those that remained nominally Sunni at times revered the *Ahl al-Bayt* and participated in Muharram ceremonies. Shiism gave sedentarised tribesmen, for whom the charisma of Ali and the bravery of Abu Fadl al-Abbas in the battle of Karbala proved appealing, a new sense of togetherness. The Ottomans, who sought to increase tax revenues and agriculture, indirectly spurred this process. When they relied on Shii clerics as intermediaries, they further increased their visibility. Together with an end to the ban on public Shii rituals that had been in place under the Mamluks, and was now revoked by the new governor of

Baghdad, a Bektashi, this reversed the fortunes of Shiism. Shii mourning processions and passion plays were held openly, including in Baghdad, and many buildings dedicated to the mourning of Hussain were erected, contributing to the visibility of Shiism.[53]

Eastern Arabia underwent a similar process. The port city of Qatif had been Shii since the ninth century, and further inland, the oasis of al-Ahsa, had long had a Shii presence (as well as of all four Sunni schools). Wahhabi raids here had similar consequences. Some tribal confederations in al-Ahsa converted to Shiism in the eighteenth and nineteenth centuries, as the Wahhabis, the Ottomans, and the Bani Khalid vied for influence. The Shia of Qatif, al-Ahsa, Bahrain, and the growing Shii community in the newly established port city of Kuwait all strengthened their links with Najaf and Karbala, as scholarly and trade networks overlapped.[54] Shia from Iran, Bahrain, and al-Ahsa also migrated to the emerging port town of Kuwait, where they established good relations with the Kuwaiti ruling family. Their cosmopolitan background secured them a prominent role in regional trade networks, and in Kuwaiti politics.[55]

Bahrain had been part of the Safavid realm since the start of the seventeenth century where as noted earlier Bahraini clerics held high office. This strengthened Shiism on the islands and, to a lesser degree, in Qatif and al-Ahsa.[56] After the demise of the Safavids, control over Bahrain became contested and institutionalised Shiism lost support.[57] In 1783, the Maliki Sunni Al Khalifa from the Utub tribal federation conquered the island. They rendered much of the population landless and turned the local Shia into serfs on the farms that the Al Khalifa and their Sunni tribal allies usurped as spoils of conquest, or employed them as pearl divers. A social division between tribal Arab Sunnis and largely sedentary Shia 'Baharna' resulted, and antagonistic feelings based on these memories of conquest between these two groups became spatially enshrined—the old Safavid administrative centres declined, and were replaced by new, Sunni-dominated ones, as Bahrain came under Saudi-Wahhabi influence.[58] This change in fortune for Shiism in Bahrain, al-Ahsa, and Qatif led many Shia, including aspirant Shii clerics, to emigrate towards Iraq or Iran.[59] There, these clerics from Eastern Arabia, who were confronted with Sunni rule in their places of origin, and whose religious tradition had retained a strong mystical and scripturalist element, engaged in doctrinal debates with clerics from Iran. Many of these clerics were Akhbaris, which at this point suited Shia under Sunni rule better than Usulism.[60]

Akhbaris and Usulis disagreed over the position of clerics as interpreters of tradition. After the downfall of the Safavids in the 1720s had dispersed Shii clerical authority, the debate intensified. Akhbaris argued that the textual tradition had to speak for itself, while Usulis thought that constant reinterpretation by capable senior clerics allowed the faith to adapt to changing circumstances. The Akhbaris, who as scripturalists argued that only the Quran and the Hadith could be accepted as the basis of Islamic law, bore similarities with the Hadith-focused movements amongst Sunnis. But Akhbaris disagreed with many of these Sunni movements, and with the Usulis, in the use of independent reasoning (*ijtihad*) in the interpretation of the sources, which they likened to speculation, accusing Usulis of following Sunnis on this point. Many key clerics of the Safavid realm had been Usulis. Akhbaris had remained prominent in Eastern Arabia. Now scholars of the rivalling schools converged on the shrine cities. The Iranian Wahid Bihbihani, the leader of the Usuli camp, moved to Karbala in the 1760s, where Yusuf al-Bahrani, the Bahraini leader of the Akhbari camp, already resided. Bihbihani confronted the Akhbaris head-on, and after al-Bahrani's death in 1772, asserted his position. Bihbihani walked the streets with a gang of enforcers who would execute people professing to be Akhbaris, leading to their marginalisation.[61]

A third Shii movement was founded by Shaykh Ahmad al-Ahsai (1753–1826), who had been born into one of those tribal families in al-Ahsa that converted to Shiism. As noted earlier, the al-Ahsa oasis was frequently raided by the Wahhabis, and the ensuing political uncertainty may have contributed to his emigration.[62] His mystical ideas, which involved him claiming to have access to special spiritual knowledge, and be able to communicate with the Imams, were anathema to the rationalist Shii clerics. But his movement, called the 'Shaykhi Movement', swiftly gained in prominence, leading to a backlash of the Usuli clerics, who excommunicated them. At the insistence of the Usuli clergy of the shrine cities, the Sunni Arab Ottoman clergy of Baghdad even joined in excommunicating a spiritual heir of Shaykh Ahmad al-Ahsai.[63]

After Bihbihani's death, his students, many of whom were Iranians, would emerge as the most important clerics in the Shii world, cementing Usuli dominance. An eighteenth-century Shii reform movement, seeking to employ reason to deal with the challenges of a changing world, paved the way for the position of Shii clerics in politics. At a time of debates over the meaning and leadership of Sunnism, a similar struggle within Shiism was won by the Usulis.[64] Usulism was boosted by the support of Awadh's senior Shii clerics, and their distribution of funds in the shrine cities in favour of the Usuli clergy. Patronage by the Shii dynasties of India and Iran was key. In 1790, the chief minister of Awadh funded a canal to change the flow of the river Euphrates and bring more water to notoriously dry Najaf. The canal opened in 1803 and, as water supply became more stable, the city's population grew and Najaf attained newfound importance. At the same time, reduced water levels elsewhere, namely around Hilla, caused residents of that area to settle along the new canal.[65] The Wahhabi raids then led Shii donors to fund protective walls around Najaf and Karbala.

The rulers of Awadh sent enormous sums to Iraq, initially through Iranian trading houses with outposts in Lucknow and the shrine cities, and then through the networks of the British Empire. The East India Company thrice extracted ten million rupees from the rulers of Awadh to finance wars (the first two in 1816 and the third in 1825). These loans were never repaid, but a part of the interest was henceforth dedicated to the shrine cities. Because of this so-called Oudh Bequest, the Company and British officials in India and Baghdad became involved in Shii politics.[66] Improved water supplies, facilities and security, together with faster transport and communication connections, led to growing numbers of pilgrims and closer ties between the shrine cities and far-flung Shii communities.[67] Technically under Ottoman administration, the shrine cities developed more or less autonomously.[68]

Further conversions meant that by the late nineteenth century, there would be more Shia than Sunnis in the Ottoman provinces that would come to constitute Iraq.[69] This alarmed the Ottomans. But they were unable to reverse this process. In fact, Ottoman policies alienated the tribes and led them to further embrace the message disseminated from the shrine cities. In Karbala, for example, Ottoman/Mamluk control was tenuous, and the Sunni governors in the city even tolerated the cursing of the first three Caliphs. Only when local gangs tried to take over full control in the 1830s and 1840s did the Ottomans occupy the city, leading to bloodshed.[70] This contributed to Karbala's decline relative to Najaf, which submitted peacefully to more direct Ottoman rule.

Despite Southern Iraq becoming more Shii, and more closely related to the shrine cities, in a small area in the very south of the country, migrants from Najd, the Wahhabi heartland, started to settle. The town, Zubayr, grew around the tomb of Zubayr, a Companion of the Prophet who had died fighting Ali, and became a centre of Sunni scholarship.[71]

North of Baghdad in primarily Sunni areas, the Imams' shrines in Kazimiyya and Samarra emerged as symbols of a new-found Shii self-consciousness. When the prominent Shii cleric Muhammad Hasan Shirazi moved from Najaf to Samarra in 1875, Ottoman officials feared the spreading of Shiism in Sunni areas. They opened new Sunni schools in Samarra, one in cooperation with the Naqshbandiyya, and appointed a Sunni to head the shrine.[72] Occasionally, Iran would intervene with the Ottoman authorities to complain about Ottoman anti-Shii activities.[73] And Iraqi Shii notables themselves could petition the Ottoman authorities successfully if Shia were provoked by Sunni clerics with the support of local Ottoman officials.[74]

Even though Shia now paid more attention to Kazimiyya and Samarra, Najaf and to a lesser extent Karbala became the centres of Shiism, with strong connections to the Persian Gulf, Southern Iran, Eastern Arabia, Jabal Amil, and, by way of the Indian Ocean, to Bombay and the Shia of the Indian subcontinent. The contributions of Shii ruling families were increasingly complemented by those of Shii landowners and traders profiting from the Indian Ocean trade. The senior clergy expanded a system of representatives in Shii communities to collect taxes and provide religious guidance.[75] Pilgrimage and the practice of burying the dead in Najaf in the vast 'valley of peace' cemetery boosted these connections. Corpses had long been transported to Najaf in relatively small numbers from Iraq, Iran, and the Gulf (and a few from India), but these numbers increased throughout the nineteenth century.[76]

If the fall of the Safavids in 1722 had undermined institutionalised Shiism, the consolidation of the Qajars in Iran reversed that. Especially the second Qajar ruler, Fath Ali Shah, who reigned from 1798 to 1834 patronised the shrine cities of Iraq, as well as Qom and Mashhad.[77] The Qajars sponsored public Shii processions and invited foreign diplomats to witness them.[78] But unlike the Safavids, who had spiritual authority of their own, the Qajars relied, at least partially, on the goodwill of the clerics, who according to Shii political theory held authority in the absence of the Imam.[79] The Qajars therefore had to prove their religious credentials. A key scholar, for example, legitimised the Qajars' declaration of defensive Jihad after Russian incursions, but upheld the overall argument that temporal authority was illegitimate. The same applied to Friday prayers, which, according to some clerics, should not include a prayer for the Shah.[80] Still, large communal Friday prayers, implying the justness of Qajar rule, became commonplace.[81] And Qajar rule entrenched Shiism as the national religion of Iran. In some ports on the Persian Gulf, where Sunnis had constituted large proportions of the population, that share declined throughout the nineteenth century.[82] Later Qajars such as Nasir al-Din Shah, who reigned from 1848 to 1896, popularised a royalist Shiism and, again, like the Safavids, built specific sites for the public display of Shii rituals under royal auspices. The most famous of these, the Tekyeh Dowlat, built in the 1870s adjacent to the Qajar Palace in Tehran, was a large arena, modelled on European concert houses, specifically, the Royal Albert Hall, that impressed Nasir al-Din Shah on his tour of Europe, in which thousands of spectators found space. Nowhere was the incorporation of Shiism into the theatrical representation of the modernising state more prominent.[83] Nasir al-Din Shah saw himself as the 'Sultan of the Shiites', and sought to portray himself as protector of Shia outside of Iran. In this endeavour, he succeeded symbolically, for example by visiting the shrine cities in Iraq in 1871 on his first foreign visit. He also published a travelogue of his trip to the shrine cities of Iraq, which became ever more familiar to Iranians. He promised major expansions of the shrines, and in a goodwill gesture towards the Ottomans to fund an expansion of Abu Hanifa's shrine in Baghdad (which the Safavids, in contrast, had destroyed to humiliate the Ottomans). At the same time, however, his attempts to gain extraterritorial rights for Shia in Russia, or Afghanistan (Herat), failed, as did his attempts to expand his jurisdiction over non-Iranian Shia in the Ottoman Empire.[84]

In Iran, Shii themes had for centuries been depicted on murals, paintings, and other objects.[85] This intensified under the Qajars, who through their patronage of art, such as portraits of royals and depictions of Shii themes, shaped a visual culture that familiarised a mass audience with the tragedy of Karbala.[86] And through their funding of mosques and shrines across Iran, they further developed a distinct Iranian-Shii architectural style.[87] They sponsored Shii scholarship, financing, for example, the first printings of key Shii works written under the Safavids.[88] A type of passion play marking the martyrdom of Hussain they popularised also spread beyond Iran.[89]

Tensions with the clergy surfaced when some Qajars embraced the mystical movements discussed above, as when one Qajar prince founded a branch of the Shaykhi movement in Iran,[90] or when they patronised some of the Sufi orders that had been repressed by the Safavids.[91] Usuli clerics tried to repress these movements, portraying themselves as defenders of Shii orthodoxy.[92] Senior clerics assumed ever more authority, facilitated by the increasing centralisation of Shii clerical leadership in a small number of clerics resident near Iraq's shrines and in Qom. This process went hand in hand with the expansion of these Shii centres, and with the growth of tele-graph lines that allowed faster communication with followers in Iran and India. The clergy still benefitted from royal patronage from India and Iran. But, after the downfall of the Safavids had broken the link between clergy and state, they had become more independent owing to rising amounts of religious taxes from other Shia.[93] In Iran, the shrine in Mashhad, for example, had had a large endowment since the Timurid era. Endowments allowed their custodians, often clerics, considerable autonomy, and to employ thou-sands of people. Many Iranian clerics thus became large landowners, and influential politically.[94]

To confront the ideological challenge from Wahhabism and Shiism, the Ottoman state strengthened the Hanafi establishment, and allied even closer with Sunni-minded Sufi orders such as the Naqshbandis. In the seventeenth and eighteenth centuries Naqshbandis expanded in the Ottoman Empire, especially amongst Kurds in the frontier zone between the Ottoman Empire and Iran.[95] Their emphasis on adherence to Sunni norms appealed to Ottoman elites.[96] The rise of a local sub-branch of the order is associated with Mawlana Khalid Baghdadi (1776–1826), a Kurd from Shahrazur. In 1809, he travelled overland to Delhi, where he was initiated into several Sufi orders, including the Mujaddidi Naqshbandiyya founded by Sirhindi. He was then urged to return to his homeland to propagate the order. Back in Kurdistan, he established the Naqshbandi-Khalidi sub-branch of the order, which would become influential across the Ottoman Empire.

This was part of a wider Sunni Revival. It connected the Indian subcon-tinent's Sunni Revivalism with its anti-colonial and anti-Shii element to the Middle East. That the predecessor of the Naqshbandi leader that had initi-ated Khalid into the order in Delhi had been killed by a Shii in the context of sectarianised late-eighteenth-century court intrigues had strengthened the anti-Shiism of the Naqshbandis in Delhi, and may have influenced Khalid. Anti-Shii statements are ascribed to him, and he is said to have encouraged his followers to end each prayer with a denunciation of Christian powers and Shia Iran. As a Kurd from the frontier region, Qajar Iran and its sponsorship of Shiism was a very real and immediate concern. But as a Persian speaker he had connections to Iran, and tried to strengthen the order there, too. Under his successor Shaykh Taha (d. 1853), even members of the Qajar ruling family and other Shia were accepted into the order.

One of them was Abbas Mirza, who had been governor of Azerbaijan and emphasised the need for Sunni–Shia unity.[97] This showed that Naqshbandis could tone down hostility towards Shiism if circumstances demanded it, for example when proselytising in largely Shii areas such as Azerbaijan.[98] Khalid spent the last years of his life in Damascus, establishing the order there and in other parts of Syria and Iraq. Here, it rivalled long-established Sunni Sufi orders such as the Qadiriyya, whose founder's shrine in Baghdad had been expanded by the Ottomans. The late Ottoman state saw the Naqshbandi-Khalidi order as a bulwark against Iranian and Shii influence, and against Salafism, and facilitated its expansion, especially in its Arabic-speaking provinces.[99] These developments led the Ottomans to pay more attention to Iraq, and to expand further into the Arabian Peninsula, thereby becoming more involved with Shiism and Zaydism. The Ottomans saw Shiism as a threat, but wanted Ottoman Shia to accept the authority of the Ottoman Sultan-Caliph.

The rise of the Wahhabis and the Ottoman reaction also affected the Southern parts of the Arabian Peninsula: Yemen and Oman. Unlike the central regions of the Arabian Peninsula, these southern coastal regions had been the subject of much imperial interest, and had long been integrated into Indian Ocean trade, lying at a crucial node between East Africa and the Western Coast of India. Yet their mountainous hinterland had also allowed for the Zaydi and Ibadi Imamates to survive and consolidate themselves, and prevented their incorporation by larger (Sunni) powers.[100] Zaydis had, as we have seen, split off from other Shia after the death of the fourth Imam, Ali bin Hussain (Zayn al-Abidin), and, unlike the later Ismailis and Twelver Shia, chose to follow Zayd bin Ali and his successors as Imams. The Ibadis are the only surviving branch of the Khariji movement, the third major strand of Islam besides Sunnism and Shiism (formed when the Kharijis rebelled against Ali Ibn Abi Talib, and one of them killed him).

Zaydis developed a political theory of the Imamate that stated that any descendant of the Prophet who was both brave, pious, and knowledgeable about religious law could become Imam, but that he should also be the most erudite of his generation. If the current Imam was found to have violated the law, an aspiring claimant should be able to take power away from him.[101] Patrimonial succession was in principle disapproved of, though it did happen in modern times. While various powers strove for influence amongst Zaydis in North Yemen, and at times deposed an Imam (such as an Ismaili dynasty), Zaydi Imams usually ruled.[102] Zaydism had developed as a separate school of jurisprudence akin to the four Sunni, the Twelver Shii and the Ismaili schools. It was based on the Quran, on reason and consensus, and on Zaydi Hadith.[103] Although Sunni Hadith collections were used by Zaydi scholars, they were often deemed to be weak because they were compiled by people who had an interest in downplaying the position of Ali and the Shii Imams (here, Zaydis agree with Shia).[104] But as a small community, and to a greater extent than other Shia, Zaydi scholars encouraged the study and, at times, application of other schools of jurisprudence as well, especially Sunnism. Over time, this brought Zaydism closer to Sunnism in matters of law.[105]

In the first centuries of Islam in Southern Yemen, the Sunni Maliki and Hanafi schools were prominent, but by the tenth century the Shafii school became dominant.[106] As the least hostile of the four Sunni schools towards Shiism, Shafiism was the least criticised by Shii clerics, contributing to relatively harmonious Shafii–Zaydi doctrinal relations.[107] Their main differences relate to political theory, not ritual practice or jurisprudence. Even when they came under Zaydi rule, Shafiis would generally not see the Zaydi Imams as spiritual and political leaders, as Zaydis would.[108] In contrast to Twelver Shiism, Zaydism places less emphasis on shrine visitation, and forbids prayers asking the Imams to intervene on one's behalf, but values pilgrimage to nearby Mecca, which up until the fifteenth century, at times had Zaydi rulers.[109] The rule of Sunni dynasties in the South of Yemen, such as under the Ayyubids, curtailed Zaydi influence in the South and forced Zaydis to cultivate relations with Sunnis (some Zaydi Imams would even take a Sunni turn and praise the Rashidun Caliphs).[110] The Wahhabis tried to expand into Yemen from the 1800s onwards, and some Shafii Sunnis may have been sympathetic to them, but they were ultimately unsuccessful.[111]

Further up the coast of the Arabian Sea, in Oman, similar dynamics were at play. Sunni Muslims in the Dhofar mountains and on the Southern coast were primarily Shafiis. But in the mountains of Northern Oman the Ibadis, the only surviving branch of the Khariji movement—as noted, the third major strand of Islam besides Sunnism and Shiism—established an Imamate. The Ibadi Sultans of Muscat had in the sixteenth century come under Portuguese tutelage, and together with the Portuguese expanded their realms. They also came under Iranian control, such as in the 1730s and 1740s, when Nadir Shah expanded Iran's Navy and reach in the Persian Gulf.[112] But after Nadir Shah's downfall, the Sultans of Muscat asserted their independence from Iran, consolidated and expanded their influence upwards towards the Gulf, and towards East Africa, becoming a regional naval power, and establishing ties with Britain.

The Saudi–Wahhabi forces had also set their sights on expanding towards Oman. In the late eighteenth century, they had sent the works of Ibn Abd al–Wahhab to Oman, demanding of its people submission to its teachings. Ibadis worried that the Wahhabis would not see them as proper Muslims, and might treat them harshly. Together with local Sunni tribal groups, the Wahhabis started raids on Oman and smaller Emirates along the Gulf coast. The ruler of one of them, Ras al–Khaima, swore allegiance to the Wahhabis, and there were sympathies in others. An Omani attempt to subdue Bahrain in 1801 led its Al Khalifa rulers to call for Wahhabi help, which repelled the Omanis, but brought Bahrain closer into the Saudi–Wahhabi orbit. Faced with increasing threats by the Saudi–Wahhabi forces, and some factions of Omani tribes and some of the Emirs declaring allegiance to them, the rulers of Muscat signed a protection agreement with Britain in 1798. Military support from Britain, and the repression of the Wahhabis in the 1810s by an Ottoman–Egyptian army stopped the Wahhabis.

The agreement with Britain moreover ended Omani ambitions in the upper Gulf, where Britain signed similar treaties with local rulers instead.[113] But it facilitated a branch of the Omani ruling family to establish themselves as Sultans of Zanzibar on the East African coast, increasing their territory and adding major economic resources. The Sultans of Zanzibar ruled over a population that at times included much of latter-day Kenya, and that was largely Sunni. And although they sponsored Ibadism, their reign was characterised by religious tolerance, not only of Sunnism but also of Shiism, to which some traders from the Indian subcontinent that settled in their domains, adhered.[114] After having at times had a rotating, and elected Imamate, the Al Bu Said dynasty would from the mid-eighteenth century onwards become Oman's (and Zanzibar's) hereditary Sultans.[115]

In Yemen, however, Sunni Revivalism, Ottoman imperialism, and the Zaydi Imams were increasingly at loggerheads. The Ottomans had established a presence in Yemen in the sixteenth century, when, as noted, they conquered the domains of the Mamluks of Egypt after the latter's alliance with the Safavids. Attuned to seeing the region through a sectarian lens in the context of the rivalry with the Safavids, Ottoman officials viewed political fragmentation and sectarian factionalism between Zaydis, Shafiis (and Ismailis) as in their interest. The Ottomans, for example, maintained good relations with Ismaili chiefs and gave them tax farms to undermine the Zaydi Imams (while despising their religious beliefs in private).[116]

The spiritual leaders of this branch of the Ismaili movement, the Mustailis, centred around Najran and neighbouring regions, had long resided in Yemen. In the sixteenth century, however, two developments caused a split. On the one hand, Ismailis in Yemen suffered from anti-Ismaili Imams and the Ottoman invasion. At the same time—as noted—the Mustaili Tayyibi Ismaili Bohra community in India grew and flourished under Mughal rulers such as Akbar. Many Indian Bohras split away from the leaders in Yemen to have more say over their community's finances and spiritual leadership. This led to a decline of visitations and revenue from India to Yemen, and undermined the Ismaili leadership there.[117] Henceforth, Ismailis in Yemen would play a subordinate role, while Indian Ismailis would reorganise, and become involved in the Indian Ocean trade.

Ottoman writers had described the sixteenth-century conquest as a victory of the righteous Ottoman Sultan's 'forces of Islam', the 'people of the Sunna', over the 'heretical' Zaydi enemies, the 'sect of Satan'.[118] In an account by the Mufti of Mecca and Hanafi professor at Sultan Suleiman's college of the four Sunni schools of jurisprudence, fallen Zaydis go to hell, while Sunnis enter paradise and Zaydi tribesmen are described as treacherous.[119] He argued that Sunnis in Aden were naturally opposed to Zaydis, and denounced an alleged alliance between Zaydis and the Portuguese against the Ottomans.[120] The Ottomans conquered largely Shafii Lower Yemen with relative ease, but had trouble bringing the Zaydi Imamate in Northern Yemen under their control. They expanded Sufi shrines such as the shrine of Mocha's founding saint to counter the Zaydi Imams.[121] But they were eventually pushed out in 1636. A new dynasty of Imams led the northern tribes against the Ottomans and, when the latter were expelled, consolidated their power and gained possessions in Lower Yemen.[122] The first Ottoman period in Yemen thus ended with a reinvigorated Zaydi Imamate that engaged in the burgeoning Indian Ocean trade and transformed into an early modern state.

The division into Upper and Lower Yemen had been a key feature of Yemeni politics for centuries, with Zaydis generally living in Upper Yemen, and Shafiis in the South. In the seventeenth and eighteenth centuries, however, the Imamate, which now became held by the Qasimis, conquered most of Yemen, incorporating large Shafii populations. Lower Yemen was a prized possession as it was more fertile, and its ports provided additional revenue.[123] Many northerners moved south as officials. This could increase tensions between northerners and 'original' southerners but also dilute boundaries. If many descendants of officials who moved from the North to the South were originally Zaydi, they now became Shafii.[124] Scholars of the two traditions were in dialogue with each other, and political opportunism, rather than rigid boundaries, characterised relations.[125]

Still, for guidance on religious matters, Shafiis continued to look to Shafii scholars. As the supreme scholar of the Zaydi state, the Imam sometimes tried to enforce Zaydi law in Shafii areas and appointed Zaydi judges and ordered the teaching of Zaydi texts in largely Shafii towns.[126] And in Lower Yemen, the Zaydi Imams employed Zaydi tribesmen as warriors and tax collectors, and subsidised these tribes with taxes collected, in part, in Shafii areas.[127]

The other main revenue came from the ports, and from a new commodity: coffee. This was especially so with the port of Mocha, which gave the coffee exported through it the name Mocca. By 1538, Mocha became a major harbour, in part due to the Ottomans, challenging Aden's long-standing position as Yemen's most important port and key node in Indian Ocean trade.[128] Proceeds from Mocha's port allowed the Qasimis to secure their rule.[129] Given the Qasimis' rupture with the Ottomans, Mocha started turning away from its more immediate neighbourhood, the upper Red Sea—Ottoman-controlled Egypt and the Hijaz—and more towards the Indian Ocean. The English and Dutch established factories at Mocha in the early seventeenth century as Yemeni coffee became a sought-after commodity, over which the Qasimis held a virtual monopoly. The port was mainly run by Zaydi elites, but the many foreign merchants, and Jews and Banyans, establishing themselves at Mocha to trade, gave the port town a cosmopolitan flair.[130]

Spurred by commercial and political success, the Qasimis sought to shift the Imamate from a rotating system to a dynastic model, a shift traditional Zaydi scholars from the Zaydi-Hadawi school were unwilling to sanction. The Qasimis therefore turned towards a group of clerics that questioned the very fundamentals of Zaydism at a time when similar debates were occurring in Sunnism and Shiism. These clerics, most prominently Ibn al-Amir (1099/1688–1182/1768) and Muhammad bin Ali al-Shawkani (d. 1834), argued that traditional Zaydi jurisprudence did not hold up under scrutiny and criticised the Zaydi Sunna tradition, which paid much respect to the narrations of the early Zaydi Imams. Like other Sunni Revivalists, they were concerned with the very methods and sources with which scholars derived specific legal rulings. They argued that religious law should be based primarily on the Quran, and secondly on the Hadith, and that on this latter point Zaydis needed to follow more closely developments in Sunni Hadith scholarship. They saw the traditional Zaydi legal tradition as too based on scholars' personal interpretations as opposed to the texts of revelation (Quran and Sunna). They also rejected much of the Zaydi theological tradition, by virtue of it being a branch of Shiism and subscribing to Mu'tazili principles, and abandoned the Zaydi theory of the Imamate that had stated that the Imam had to be a knowledgeable descendant of the Prophet.

These scholars blurred the lines between Zaydism and Shafiism and developed a reform Zaydism closer to Sunnism. In fact—and it is here that these scholars inspired Sunni reformists beyond Yemen—they rejected the strict adherence to any of the legal schools, Zaydi or Sunni, and argued that once the authenticity of the texts had been established it was the responsibility of the trained scholars to exercise *ijtihad*, personal interpretation based on the texts and reason, to come up with answers to pressing problems.[131]

The main cleric driving this process, al-Shawkani, would become the Qasimi Imamate's chief justice.[132] He rejected the idea that Zaydis should rise against unjust rulers and emphasised the need to obey the authorities of the day, replacing a key aspect of Zaydi political theory with a Sunni one. As this was the key principle invoked by competing claimants to the Imamate, al-Shawkani effectively legitimised Qasimi dynastic rule, and received much patronage in return.[133]

Al-Shawkani's enemies were quick to denounce him as 'Wahhabi'. It is true that he, and Ibn al-Amir before him, had welcomed the founding of a state to the North in which clerics played a key role, and supported some Wahhabi positions. They did not agree with them wholeheartedly, however, since Wahhabis had excommunicated Zaydis.[134] This was sensitive in Yemen, and a far cry from the approach of al-Shawkani, who, being from a prominent Zaydi scholarly background himself, sought to bring Zaydism more in line with Sunnism, but not excommunicate traditional Zaydis.[135]

On a core divisive issue between Sunna and Shia—the cursing of the Prophet's Companions—he remained firmer, declaring it unacceptable.[136] When he wrote a long treatise on the issue with the government's support, riots erupted in Sanaa and traditionalist Zaydi scholars penned counter-treatises. Cursing Companions of the Prophet turned into a form of protest. Traditional Zaydi beliefs and practices would fuel an opposition movement to a nominally Zaydi Imamate and a scholar who was born as a Zaydi but then legitimised the Sunnification of Northern Yemen.[137] This is ironic because Zaydism is the branch of Shiism least concerned with the cursing of the first three Caliphs. In fact, as noted, Zayd's apparent refusal to curse Abu Bakr and Umar on his deathbed had led to the original split between Zaydis and the rest of the early Shia.[138]

The Qasimi Imamate became plagued by internal rivalries, local rebellions, and a loss in revenue at the turn from the eighteenth to the nineteenth century.[139] Since coffee was now also produced in other areas, prices collapsed. Together with the loss of key ports, symbolised by the British East India Company's taking over of the port at Aden in 1839, and renewed Ottoman ambitions, this undermined the Imamate.[140] Competing claimants to the Imamate re-emerged and Yemen became contested between the Ottomans and the British.[141] Muhammad Ali Pasha, de facto ruler of Egypt still nominally linked to the Ottomans, conquered Taiz in 1837 after defeating the Wahhabis in Najd, but was pushed back by the British who were establishing themselves in Aden.

Ottoman expansion in Yemen over the coming decades, which as we will shortly see coincided with attempts to reform the Empire from within, faced many challenges. Given the distance from Istanbul, the geography, and the socio-political and economic situation of Yemen, Ottoman officials realised they could not establish a bureaucracy or as close a control over the population as in other parts of the Empire. Therefore, they governed Yemen largely based on tribal and sectarian difference.[142] The most critical question for the Ottomans was how to deal with the Zaydi Imams. When the Ottomans arrived, the Zaydi Imam al-Mutawakkil Muhsin moved North from Sanaa, from where he and other Imams would resist the Ottomans.[143] The Ottomans wanted to integrate the Imams into their system, yet suspected them of wanting to claim the title of Caliph or not accept the Ottoman Sultan's claim to the Caliphate. Opposition to Ottoman rule in non-Zaydi Shafii parts of Yemen, where the authority of the Imam was feeble, seemed less threatening because it did not go that far.[144]

Imperial confessionalisation thus reshaped Yemen. Already during their first occupation, the Ottomans had instrumentalised divisions between Zaydis, Shafiis, and Ismailis. When the Qasimi Imamate expelled the Ottomans in the seventeenth century, and founded a state funded by the export of coffee, it allied itself with clerics bent on bringing Zaydism closer to Sunnism to legitimise dynastic rule. Like Nadir Shah, the Qasimis became more Sunni after incorporating large Sunni populations. The legacy of al-Shawkani loomed large. Together with Shah Wali Allah, the main Sunni Revivalist from India, and Ibn Abd al-Wahhab, he would enter the canon of Sunni Revivalism as another foundational figure.

By the eighteenth century, Sunni and Shii reformists sought to apply reason to re-interpret the sources of Islamic law in the face of political and intellectual challenges. Within Shiism, a rationalist strand that promoted the centrality of the clergy became dominant. Najaf and Karbala emerged as major centres of Shii scholarship, pilgrimage, and financial flows. Sunni Revivalists claimed that a return to the early period and a revisiting of the sources, especially the Hadith, was needed to purify and strengthen Islam, and debated their ideas in the Hijaz. Some of these movements sought to invoke independent reasoning when interpreting the sources, and resisted the rigidity of the established schools of law. Sunni reformism gave rise to rationalist, open-minded, and ecumenical approaches, and simultaneously to exclusivist, sectarian, and inward-looking puritan ones (with Shiism emerging as a possible partner for the former strand, and enemy for the second).

People, capital, and ideas travelled with increasing ease, facilitated by new means of communication, transportation, and publication and the emerging networks of Empire that bound the Middle East closer to India. Indian Shii rulers financing the revitalisation of the Southern Iraqi shrine cities in the face of economic and political problems were just one example. The Wahhabi movement likewise resonated far beyond the Arabian Peninsula. The Ottomans, who had long come to terms with Shia that accepted Ottoman supremacy, tried to assert their control over Shii populations, and in that process spurred counter-reactions, for example the conversion of much of Southern Iraq to Shiism. Developments across the Islamic world became ever more intertwined.

Major Sunni–Shia ecumenical efforts coincided with the rise of explicitly sectarian movements, as Muslims sought to reform and reinvent their faith. After Nadir Shah tried to achieve Sunni–Shia unity, the Wahhabis were bent on eradicating all those they deemed unbelievers, under which category they included Shia.

Nadir Shah, the Zands, the early Qajars, the Ottoman Sultans, the Saudi-Wahhabis, the Ibadi and Qasimi Imams (as well as Mughal successor states on the Indian subcontinent and Afghan rulers) were early modern rulers that strongly identified with one interpretation of Islam, and used it to legitimise themselves, yet could accommodate others, especially when acquiring new territory or populations (even the Wahhabis ultimately did not fully implement their agenda). Their still often tenuous rule allowed for such flexibility.

These states were still not fully subjugated by European Empires, or fully dependent economically. And yet, European influence deepened at breathtaking speed. The sectarian question preoccupied Muslims just as European overseas trading companies, mercenaries, and diplomats became ever more omnipresent.[145] As these trading companies gained more economic concessions, and, increasingly, direct control over people and territory, with that engagement came more knowledge production about Islam.

PART III

Empire and the State, 1800–1979

In the eighteenth and the nineteenth century, the mighty Muslim Gunpowder Empires weakened and disintegrated. In their stead emerged a new kind of state that often came in the form of European rule over Muslim-majority territories, or in the form of a defensively modernising one like that of the Ottomans. That was transformative. For it reshaped every part of people's lives, including religion and sectarian identity. A sense of Muslim decline vis-à-vis European Empires gave impetus to new ideologies, and to revivalist movements.

The Muslim Gunpowder Empires had suffered from stagnant or decreasing economic revenue, and the need to spend more on warfare, including against well-funded and well-armed European overseas companies and states.[1] The Safavids were the first to go. After the Safavids it was the turn of the Mughals, whose Empire, as shown, had been one of the largest, wealthiest, and most envied. When European trading companies assumed more direct political control, most Muslims became subjected to direct or indirect European imperial rule (chiefly by Britain, France, Russia, and the Netherlands).

The British Empire was especially consequential for inner-Islamic relations. To put this into perspective: At the height of its power in the early nineteenth century, the Saudi–Wahhabis ruled over or received tribute from over two million people across much of the Arabian Peninsula. In contrast, by the end of that century, Queen Victoria was the head of state of over half the world's Muslims, ruling nominally over at least a hundred million Muslims, with British judges administering 'Anglo-Muhammedan' law across the Empire, a law that for the first time recognised the categories of

Sunnism and Shiism as separate before a court of a modern state.[2] A large part of the Empire's Muslim subjects lived in India, which fast became the source of immense wealth for the East India Company and Britain. After the establishment of a London–Bombay telegraph line that crossed Ottoman and Iranian territory, completed in 1864/5, and the opening of the Suez Canal in 1869, British possessions along the new sea route to India became even more important, and closer connected to each other.[3]

And as imperial rule became more direct, perceptions of Islam started to have real-life consequences, and reshaped Muslim societies in ways hitherto unimaginable.

Throughout the long nineteenth century, the Ottoman Empire, which ruled much of the Balkans and the Middle East, too, lost its most fertile provinces and began to crumble at its periphery. Faced with war and instability, and under pressure from and increasingly indebted to European powers, it reformed from within, adopting many of the facets of a European-style modern state, and made concessions to European powers, including in religious policy.

The European imperial state and the modernising Ottoman one not only saw religion differently; it altered the self-understanding of religious communities and relations between them. With its ambition to control the lives of its subjects—to regulate, categorise, delineate borders, identities and citizenship, issue passports, apply standardised laws, and garner loyalty, often by combining national and confessional identity—the modern state reshaped society.[4] It asked questions about sectarian affiliation in censuses, institutionalised sectarian difference in law and representative institutions, and its presence would be felt in every village and every urban quarter, even in remote areas that had hitherto had little regular interaction with state authority. Since so much of the Muslim world came under direct imperial control, the relationship with the modern state was a doubly difficult one, for that state was often associated with foreign control (and even in the Ottoman Empire, Iran, and Afghanistan, which remained nominally independent, many perceived reforms as foreign-inspired). The Safavids' successors, the Qajars, who endured until 1925 became known for their flamboyance and patronage of Shiism, but their state was a rudimentary one, and over time they were forced to hand over more and more concessions to foreign powers and businesses. Amidst state weakness, Europeans expanded their influence, as did the Shii clergy, channelling, in part, popular resentment against that influence (as did Sufi orders in the Ottoman Empire and

Sunni Revivalists in India). European penetration and a more intrusive state could lead to backlash that was often expressed in religious terms.

The new modes of communication and transportation that underpinned Empire, including mass printing, forged closer ties and a sense of common purpose between Muslims around the world, and at the same time fostered stronger, and novel, global confessional identities. They facilitated inter-actions between Sunni Revivalists in British-controlled Cairo and Muslims in India, ferried pilgrims from India to the Hijaz and Iraq, and transferred funds from Indian Shii rulers to the shrine cities in Iraq. The Aga Khans, for example, were active in pan-Islam all the while using the networks of the British Empire to tie Ismailis to one global community controlled by the central Imamate. In the Shii shrine cities, an increasingly centralised and hierarchical Shii clergy bound far-flung Shii communities closer to it and to each other, appointing representatives, collecting taxes, giving legal and spiritual guidance, and managing pilgrimage, all the while supporting the Ottomans on issues of common concern. And Salafism gradually became more influential in the Sunni religious field.

As the state sought to restructure society, it collected ever more informa-tion about its subjects, including their history and beliefs, and established intelligence networks that gathered local knowledge, and made it intelli-gible to colonial officials. In the process, information about local cultures and religions was collected on a vast scale, and categorised in novel ways.[5] Sunni, Shii, Ismaili, Druze, Alawite, and other markers of identity, now became lenses through which colonial officials reordered Muslim societies. European powers tried, for example, to intervene on behalf of non-Sunni Ottoman Muslims just as they did on behalf of Ottoman Christians and Jews. This undermined the centuries-old Ottoman policy of seeing non-Sunni Muslims simply as Muslims, and led to the institutionalisation of sectarian identity, for example in the coastal provinces of the Empire that would later become Lebanon. Sectarian identity started to be seen akin to ethnicity, and as the basis for political claims. After the disintegration of the Ottoman Empire, the French and British Mandates for Syria, Lebanon, and Iraq then established political systems on that basis.

Two ideas are crucial to understand how Empire affected Muslims. One is the idea of Sunni supremacism that implied Sunnism represented ortho-dox Islam and Shiism a schism, and that Sunni rule was the norm. The second is the 'mosaic' view, the idea that the peoples in the Muslim-majority world from the Eastern Mediterranean to the Indian subcontinent constituted a mosaic made up of religious and ethnic groups. Together, these ideas informed Empire and would shape new states, even if France and Britain would draw different conclusions from it.

Muslims reacted to this in numerous ways: one approach was Muslim unity, or pan-Islam, uniting Muslims against the divide-and-rule attempts of European powers. At the same time, Sunni and Shii transnational ties strengthened. Many of the national identities that emerged in the late nineteenth and early twentieth century, were, even if not always explicitly, tied to a sectarian identity. And the printing and the editing of classics, including polemics and law texts, by Orientalists and Muslims alike, transformed the meaning of religion altogether, undermining more ambiguous lived practices, and led to a more scripturalist Islam, in which sectarian boundaries were more rigidly enforced. Sunnism and Shiism emerged as starker and more rigid categories than they had ever been before. And gradually, Muslim clerics and laymen, dissatisfied with the secularising turn of the modern state, exemplified by the Turkish abolition of the Caliphate, and its impact on society, joined forces to form the first modern Islamist movements, with their aim of establishing a modern state according to Islamic norms. Although pan-Islam was often an avowed goal, Sunni and Shii Islamists established separate movements that would cooperate and learn from each other, but that would also lead to competing Sunni and Shii Islamist utopias, to separate but intertwined quests for an Islamic state.

7

British India and Orientalism

How did Empire reshape Muslim societies and what role did perceptions of Islam play in that process? This question can be answered by looking at how Orientalism was intertwined with British rule in India, where a large part of the British Empire's Muslim subjects lived.

Knowledge production on religion in the 'Orient', the generic term that vaguely denoted the lands to the East of Europe, and on Islam, started in the early modern period, but intensified in the nineteenth century, and led to the development of the academic discipline of Orientalism.[6] Informed by an Enlightenment view of history, religion was seen as backward, something to be overcome if conditions of 'modernity' were right, and invoked to justify why colonised peoples should remain colonised—the very trope of the 'civilising mission'.[7]

At the same time, the modern state recognised boundaries between religions more starkly, including by codifying religious law, and, in the most extreme circumstances, organising political systems accordingly. It turned religious groups into 'majorities' and 'minorities' and while claiming to give equality before the law to all citizens, started to become heavily involved in the regulation of religion, and thereby exacerbated pre-modern tensions and boundaries between religious groups.[8] Religion became an object of political struggles, and was transformed in the process. While some lay intellectuals and religious leaders, who spread their ideas in the new medium of print,[9] cooperated with Empire, others invoked a religious framework to resist it. Hence why religion, including Islam, could emerge as a language of protest against Empire, and a way in which Empire operated.

The tension between and simultaneity between Muslim unity and difference characterised this period. The idea of Muslim unity, of Sunnis and Shia coming together in pan-Islam, was one reaction to Empire. Another was the development of Sunni and Shii revivalisms and collective identities, and a

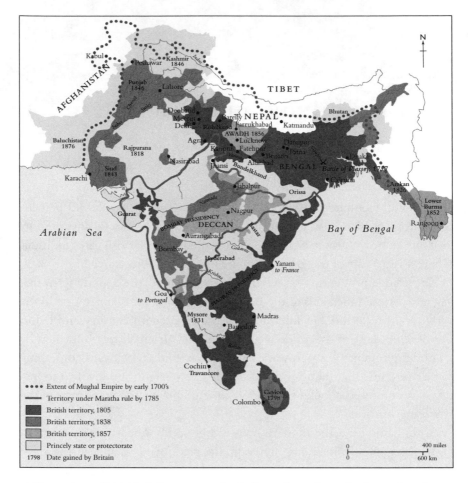

7. Expansion of British influence on the Indian subcontinent in the 18th and 19th century

much more widely understood, and institutionalised distinction between Sunnis and Shia (and Ismailis) that led to the formation of separate educational institutions, political associations, newspapers, and so on. Printing and the rapid transmission of information reinforced the idea of a unified Islamic world, but also connected Sunnis and Shia, and Ismailis across that world more closely to each other, and led to a sharper delineation between them. Orientalist knowledge production played an important role in the process.

As noted earlier, Crusader historians, Church historians, missionaries, diplomats, travellers, and early Orientalists generally conveyed the Sunni point of view, except for those by visitors to Iran or Shii-ruled states on the Indian subcontinent, who reiterated the Shii position.[10] This of course had led to some knowledge of Sunnism and Shiism during the Crusades, and in the Ottoman-Safavid context, as Europeans were looking for allies against the Ottomans. In the early modern period, the large-scale exploration and writing about extra-European history and society expanded dramatically, and was also always a way to shed light on developments back in Europe.[11] The above-mentioned eighteenth-century expedition led by Carsten Niebuhr, the Danish explorer and geographer, was a good example of a new-found interest in 'Oriental' religion. It was a product of the European enlightenment and Empire, and its mission was to gather historical context for a better understanding of the Bible. A focus on different manifestations of Islam was implied; and the sectarian milieu of Protestant Northern Europe attuned Niebuhr's eye to religious differences in the Middle East.[12] He visited Shii sites in Iraq, met with the Zaydi Imam in Yemen, detailed the Shii presence in the Persian Gulf, and the emerging Wahhabi movement. Niebuhr's account, which contains a section on 'the different sects of Mahommetans in Arabia', shows how European observers recognised sectarian boundaries, and how peoples in the region were, not least under the impression of the Wahhabis, keen to relate their confessional histories.[13]

The post-Reformation context led many authors to compare the split in Christianity with that in Islam. In the aftermath of the Reformation, and the confessionalised wars of the seventeenth century, some equated Sunnis with Protestants and Shia with Catholics, while others argued the opposite.[14] Some invoked the Sunni–Shia split to denounce Catholic-Protestant conflict in Europe.[15] A few Protestant authors wrote about Islam to criticise the Catholic Church.[16] Sunni Revivalists on the Arabian Peninsula or in India seemed to share with Protestantism a kind of Puritan utopia to which they sought to return. Johann Ludwig Burckhardt, the early nineteenth-century traveller from an important Basel Calvinist family, wrote: 'I think myself authorised to state, from the result of my inquiries [...], that the religion of the Wahabys may be called the Protestantism or even Puritanism of the Mohammedans.'[17]

I pointed out earlier why that did not make much sense, for Sunnism and Shiism had by that time already developed separately for centuries. Writings about Islam and the Orient became projections for struggles being fought out in Europe. Terms such as 'church' and 'sect' or 'orthodoxy' and 'heterodoxy' were applied to Islam. In this process, Sunnism became associated with the Church, and Shiism became a sect, a view that was informed by Sunni heresiography. These categories were sometimes promoted by Muslim authors themselves, for example by Turkish authors who described Ottoman Sunnism as the orthodox form of Islam, and the Ottoman Caliph as legitimate leader of Muslims.[18]

The first Islamic sources that Orientalists edited, translated, and printed were mainly Sunni, further entrenching the Sunni reading of Islamic history.[19] This started with the most basic narratives of the origin of the split. Most Western histories of Islam, for example, described Abu Bakr as the 'natural' successor to the Prophet because of his merits, adopting the Sunni narrative of succession to the Prophet.[20] The Shii argument was not taken seriously, from the question of whether Ali was indeed buried in Najaf to the intricacies of Shii theology and jurisprudence.[21]

Given that knowledge of Shiism in European universities was largely based on readings of Sunni sources, often acquired through contact with the Ottoman Empire, the few Orientalists writing about Shiism, such as the Hungarian Ignaz Goldziher (1850–1921)—a pioneer of Islamic Studies in Europe—had little exposure to Shii sources and produced negative accounts.[22] Goldziher called Shiism an unorthodox, sectarian movement with absurd ideas threatening the theosophy of Islam.[23] He included Shiism under the heading of 'sects'[24] and entertained the idea that it had a different Quran from Sunnis (a particularly offensive, and outdated, Sunni accusation against Shia).[25] He agreed with an earlier assessment by the German Islam scholar Theodor Nöldeke, who had called a Shii interpretation of the Quran 'a wretched web of lies and stupidities'.[26] Nöldeke admitted that he had only read parts of the book he was referring to, but nonetheless dismissed it out of hand because it emphasised that only the *Ahl al-Bayt* were really in a position to understand the Quran, as noted a core Shii tenet but one not accepted by Sunnis.[27] Orientalists also appropriated polemical terms such as *ghuluw* (exaggeration), which is used largely by Sunnis to describe groups that saw Ali and his descendants as god-like figures, or as almost equal to the Prophet.[28]

Orientalists divided Muslims into two camps: a mainstream Islam represented by the urban centres, where Sunni Caliphs ruled, and 'unorthodox', schismatic rebels at the periphery, described as a deviation from Islam. The rituals and public displays of Shiism were exoticised. British colonial fiction and memoirs depicted Shii rituals and beliefs as 'irrational' and 'bloody'.[29] Many saw the Sunni–Shia split in racial terms. Some emphasised the Arab

nature of Shiism until the Safavids' rise to state power.[30] Joseph Arthur
Comte de Gobineau, one of the founders of racial determinism, portrayed
Shiism as the continuation of ancient Iranian rites and as alien to Islam and
in opposition to the Arabs. As noted throughout, these views were simplistic
and erroneous.[31] The accusation of Shiism's foreignness and Persianness
appropriated older Sunni polemics but imbued them with modern racism.
Sunni Arab nationalists of the twentieth century would appropriate those
racialised stereotypes and associate Shiism with Iran, and as alien to the Arab
body politic, as we will see below. Christian missionaries in the nineteenth
century Levant, as well, posited that Shia had physiognomic features that
could prove their foreignness.[32] Similar racialised features were ascribed to
Shii Hazara in Afghanistan.[33] At times, Sufism, too, was attributed a
Persianness as opposed to the Arabness of (Sunni) Islam.[34]

Increasingly, some scholars worked with non-Sunni sources. Zaydi literature from Yemen, for example, acquired by European and American
Orientalists, served as a basis for the earliest scholarly accounts of Zaydism.[35]
French and Italians came into contact with Ibadism in North Africa, and
British and Americans wrote about Ibadism in Oman.[36] One of the first
translations of a Shii law book into a European language was undertaken
by a French diplomat so that European powers could better defend the
interests of their nationals in Iran's courts.[37] And we will see in the next
chapters how Europeans engaged with Shii-leaning movements in the
Ottoman Empire in the nineteenth century. But the master frame, the
belief that the region constituted of a mosaic of sects under Sunni leadership, remained intact.

Orientalism thus deepened the notion of Sunnism and Shiism as separate
categories, and though it developed an interest in Shiism saw Sunnism as
the mainstream version of Islam.[38] By primarily looking at texts, and some
of the old polemics, Orientalists imposed stark binaries where there previously had been more fluid relations and interactions, and where lived reality
was characterised by confessional ambiguity (as I noted in the context of
Muharram, for example). This applied to differences within Islam and
between 'World Religions' such as Islam, Indian religions, and Buddhism.[39]
This was especially so in the British Empire, which came to rule over more
than half the world's Muslims, most of whom lived in India. Given the ways
in which British rule in India informed imperial projects elsewhere, and
the importance of the Indian subcontinent for wider Sunni–Shia relations,
I will discuss this in detail.

Here, as shown, the East India Company (EIC) and later the British government ruled over Sunnis and Shia. Sunnis represented the vast majority of Muslims, but some of the ruling families that had formed treaty relationships with the EIC were Shii, and the most significant uprising against British rule—in 1857, termed a mutiny by the British and rebellion, revolution, or first war of independence by Indians—would have Shii-ruled Awadh at its centre. It was in India that strategies of imperial rule over Muslims were first developed, including through the codification of the Sharia. Patterns established there were then applied elsewhere, as many British overseas possessions, including those in the Persian Gulf and Southern Arabia, were administered by the Government of India. The Company had established outposts in India in the seventeenth century. Over time, it acquired its own possessions and fought major wars, which eventually led to more direct British rule. Given that the British Empire relied on the control of key ports along the way to India, the Company also established trading outposts on the Iranian coast, on the Southern coast of the Arabian Peninsula, at Aden and Muscat, and signed treaties with local rulers. Britain signed the first treaty with Gulf Arab Sheikhdoms, including Bahrain, in 1820, binding the islands that had a Shii majority but had in 1783 been conquered by a Sunni ruling family, the Al Khalifa, closer to it. It consolidated the position of the ruling clan, and checked the incorporation of Bahrain into the Saudi-Wahhabi realm. Ever greater British involvement meant that colonial administrators learned more about Shiism and witnessed the oppressive nature of Al Khalifa rule, without, however, putting in doubt their support (British officials argued that were it not for them, Bahraini Shia would fare even worse).[40]

Britain thus engaged with both Sunnism and Shiism, and, as we will see shortly, already under Company rule institutionalised a separate judicial recognition of the two. Britain would also become involved in the management of religious endowments and pilgrimage in a major way—not just the Hajj, which all Muslims undertook, but the Shii pilgrimage to Iraq and the management of funds for the upkeep of the Shii shrines there. As travel became cheaper and faster, more Indian Muslims went on pilgrimage to the Shii shrine cities in Iraq and to the Hijaz, and at times studied and lived there. More Iranians went on Hajj as well. From the 1850s onwards these sorts of pilgrimages became more affordable and less time consuming for wider sections of Muslim societies, and so the number of pilgrims increased exponentially. These connections were paramount not only for the development of Muslim reformism, and pan-Islam, for they led to interactions between pilgrims from various backgrounds, but also for increasingly global sectarian identities. The European Empires that ruled over large Muslim populations, such as the French, British, Dutch, and Russian Empires, facilitated pilgrimage, yet worried that it might be used to spread anti-colonial ideas, including pan-Islam, and controlled it tightly.[41]

1857 is generally seen as a watershed in the history of British India. Broad-based dissatisfaction with the heavy-handed tactics of British officials and the plunder of the country's wealth led to a mass rising, symbolically supported by the last Mughal Emperor, Bahadur Shah Zafar II. The uprising enjoyed support across India and amongst Sunnis and Shia. The Company had been gradually expanding its presence in the eighteenth and first half of the nineteenth century, invoking the alleged decadence and ineffectiveness of local rulers to justify annexation. Some territories had been administered directly, in others the previous rulers remained nominally in charge.

After the suppression of the 1857 Rebellion, British rule became more direct and pervasive and less tolerant of dissent. Direct rule of the British Crown over India, termed the British Raj, was established in 1858 and lasted until 1947. Several Indian princely states that became vassals were allowed to retain nominal independence. Hyderabad, ruled by the Sunni Nizams, though with a Shii presence, was the largest of them.[42] In the North, the Nawabs of Rampur, for example, originally Sunni Rohillas of Afghan origin who had converted to Shiism in the first half of the nineteenth century, supported the British in 1857 and were able to retain autonomy.[43]

Awadh, which was a centre of the rising, fared differently. As noted, the Company had played a key role in the proclamation of Awadh's rulers as 'Kings', but after the Company's resident had expanded his influence, in 1856 did away with the appearance of independence, and annexed the whole of Awadh that was not yet under its control.[44] The last ruler, Wajid Ali Shah, was deposed and imprisoned, the court dissolved.[45] The dislocation the deposition caused, and the symbolism of the annexation, fuelled the rising, and the Awadhi capital of Lucknow was held for a year by anti-British forces. In the middle of it, the son of Wajid Ali Shah, Birjis Qadr, again accepted Mughal sovereignty and supported the rising in the name of Bahadur Shah.[46] Wajid Ali Shah spent most of the uprising in confinement, though he was still nominally invoked and retained local support. Some of Awadh's Shii landlords supported the rising together with Hindu Rajas, in terminology invoking Shii and Hindu symbolism. Some Shii clerics joined

Sunnis, including a popular Sufi leader, in supporting the short-lived revolutionary government in Lucknow.[47] Others, including the most senior Shii cleric, however, refused to endorse the rising as a Jihad, like the Sunni rebel leaders did, arguing that it could only be proclaimed by a Shii Imam.[48]

For their support of the rising, Lucknow, the Awadhi ruling family, and their allies in surrounding townships were punished harshly. The Great Imambara was defiled, and the Shii Friday Prayer Mosque turned into a British military barracks.[49] The Shii clergy were marginalised, as the judiciary and the Shii seminary were largely dissolved. Eventually, however, the Shii elites would de-emphasise their involvement in the rising, and senior clerics and members of the ruling family would receive stipends.[50] The British established direct rule over Awadh (albeit with the same ruling family nominally in control). Some of the elites moved to the shrine cities in Iraq, where the funds from the Oudh Bequest, now administered directly by the British state, continued to fund Shiism. Through their engagement with the Nawabs of Awadh and their management of the Oudh Bequest, British officials became more familiar with Shiism.[51] The British involvement in distributing the funds in the shrine cities was so significant that it heightened Ottoman suspicions of Britain and Shiism in Iraq, as we will see later.[52]

A major legacy of the ninety years of direct British rule was the development of antagonistic Hindu and Muslim communal identities, and the eventual separate establishment of Pakistan and India in 1947 based on those identities. Some argue that this was an age-old antagonism that gained in strength under British rule, and others that British rule invented and strengthened these categories to divide and rule, reaching its climax in the decision to form two separate states upon independence. Direct British rule, and the rule of the Indian princely states that were in a vassal relationship with Britain, certainly contributed to the development of identity politics based on religion, ethnicity, and caste, and in some cases to the very creation of these categories.[53]

The debate is complicated by the fact that Muslim and Hindu nationalists claimed they were representing ancient communities, and that nationalist historiographies in India and Pakistan foster that understanding. Proponents of the Muslim national movement, many of whom were, ideologically speaking, successors of Islamic revivalism, saw themselves as defending Muslims against imperialism.[54] Proponents of Hindu nationalism likewise argued that they were defending an age-old community that had been treated unfairly first by Muslim rulers and then by the British.[55] But as noted, there was much overlap in lived reality between adherents of different religious communities, think of Muharram, and confessional ambiguity could characterise many people's lives.

Pan-Islamic and Hindu sentiments grew under British rule, but so did stronger, and more far-reaching, Muslim confessional identities amidst a further differentiation—institutionally and ideationally—between Sunnis, Shia, Ismailis, and others. This is a paradox at first sight only. British rule allowed for greater visibility of non-dominant confessions and an unhindered discussion of religious difference. This had certain precedents in the Mughal era, when Shia pronounced their faith more unreservedly in public disputations, but under the Raj, which claimed to allow for religious freedom, this intensified. As a minority of Muslims, albeit with pockets where they were nominally in control and had access to patronage, Shia proselytised and publicly performed Muharram across the subcontinent's cities, and built large mourning houses, mosques, and religious seminaries.[56] Urbanisation and the transformation of public space brought people from diverse backgrounds into closer contact.[57] In public squares, preachers from opposing sects and religions would debate each other in front of large audiences. New seminaries trained preachers for these public disputations, which popularised the arguments of older sectarian polemics, talking up the virtues of one's own confession and denigrating the other.

The disputations strengthened communal boundaries between religions and between Sunna and Shia.[58] In Lucknow, some Shia refined a type of poetry mocking Sunnis.[59] Some of the more sectarian preachers, one of whom was a convert from Sunnism, turned Muharram recitations and processions into more narrowly Shii events by, for example, cursing the first three Caliphs during the mourning sessions for Hussain. This led Sunnis to abandon the sessions, and to a court case for blasphemy.[60]

The arrival of mass printing, and mass literacy, was transformative. Previously, Islamic books had circulated in manuscript form, and their distribution had been limited. Mass-produced Qurans and Hadith collections changed the transmission, teaching, and interpretation of Islamic knowledge irrevocably, strengthening the literalist interpretations of widely available texts.[61] Print publications in the language of the Muslim masses, Urdu (no longer just in the Persian and Arabic of earlier periods, with a readership confined to the elites), popularised the core tenets of Sunnism and Shiism and provided transcriptions of some of the public disputations and concise versions of older polemics.[62] As shown above, Shah Abd al-Aziz's anti-Shii polemic *The Gift*, initially written in Persian, was frequently republished and translated into Urdu and Arabic, and shaped Sunni views of Shiism on the Indian subcontinent.[63] Given the fierceness of the attacks, and its rapid spread, it drew substantial responses from Shii scholars.[64] A scholar from Awadh, Sayyid Hamid Hussain (1830–88) wrote a voluminous response to a chapter of the book, in which Shah Abd al-Aziz had criticised the Imamate, the question of the succession to the Prophet that lies at the heart of the Sunni–Shia divide and that had been the core of the al-Hilli-Ibn Taymiyya polemic. This book, entitled *Abaqat al-Anwar*, came to embody the Shii point of view and provides sources for all the major Hadith used by the Shia to defend their view of the Imamate. It was published in various volumes in late nineteenth-century Lucknow and, in the late twentieth century, translated into Arabic in an abridged form and published in Iran. The descendants of the author became a prominent Shii scholarly family, and one of their descendants would migrate to Iran in the nineteenth century, a journey that was to have world historical consequences. But more about that later.[65]

These polemics, in print and in public disputations, sectarianised the Indian Muslim public sphere and hardened doctrinal and social divisions, spelling out more clearly where precisely the boundaries between Sunnism and Shiism lay.[66] Political support and patronage allowed the clerics of both sides to write polemics and ensured that their work would be printed, and translated. Yet Urdu, and new forms of poetry that were recited in public, could also become a language and poetic practice that would unite South Asia's Muslims regardless of their sectarian identity.[67]

In short, a sort of marketplace of public religiosity took shape, where competing religio-political groups asserted their position. By the late 1880s, some smaller Shii mosques adopted a Shii addition to the call to prayer (we previously discussed this in other contexts—it had become a way of asserting a Shii identity under Shii rule, such as in Iran and in Awadh, but was and is banned in many Sunni-ruled states). It stated that 'Ali is the legatee of God, and his Caliph without interruption', specifically denying the validity of the first three Caliphs accepted by Sunnis.[68] This led to conflict, and was a major departure from the confessionally more inclusive nature of Muharram rituals, during which Sunni nobles employed reciters for mourning sessions, which Sunnis and Shia attended jointly, and Sunni poets and clerics wrote eulogies for Hussain.[69]

Another way the colonial state recognised and sharpened communal identities was through censuses. The first British censuses of India did not ask for sectarian identity of Muslims, a situation the compilers lamented.[70] But from 1881 onwards, the India-wide census counted Sunnis and Shia separately because 'it was thought desirable to collect information as to the sects of the Mohammedan section of the population'.[71]

Indians first had to declare their religion and then, in the 1881 survey, in a subcategory, their 'caste, if Hindu; Sect if of other Religion', i.e. Sunni or Shia for Muslims.[72] The British Raj had played a major role in entrenching castes amongst Hindus by recognising them officially. It now recognised the categories of 'Sunni' and 'Shii' and 'Ismaili' as equivalents of caste amongst non-Muslims.[73] In these censuses, the number of those officially identifying as Shia was very small (in 1881, out of a total population of 220,654,245, 47,586,236 declared themselves as Sunni, 809,561 as Shia, and 2,535,349 Muslims did not specify a sect).[74] Some Shia, Ismailis, and others may not have recorded themselves as Shia, and the category Sunni did not do justice to the considerable Shii influence in material culture and popular piety. Others simply refused to embrace a sectarian category or were plainly unaware of the distinction between Sunnism and Shiism, until an official asked them about it.[75] A note from the 1891 census is revealing:

> For the less instructed of Muhammadans and especially amongst Sunnis, the difference between the two sects is little understood, and the enumerator had in general to ascertain the sect by a question as to how the hands were placed in prayer. Sunnis pray with one hand placed over the other in front of the body, Shias with both hands depressed by the sides.[76]

Asking this question sharpened sectarian boundaries. The 1901 census put it as follows: 'Taken as a whole the Shias are probably better educated than the Sunnis because the latter sect is the more numerous, and difference from it involves some knowledge of principles beyond those held by the masses.'[77]

In subsequent censuses, more Muslims specified their sectarian identity.[78] Shii communal representatives embraced the institutional logic of numerical recognition and representation. A newly formed Shia political conference petitioned the government in December 1909 to continue to list Shia separately in the upcoming decennial census, even if not all Shia had identified as such, as officials were thinking of abandoning these categories altogether.[79] It was one of many organisations that sought to represent caste and communal interests in the context of the census.[80] Ismailis and Ahmadis, a new movement founded by a pro-British leader, also wanted to be counted separately.[81]

By reshaping society according to a logic of communal representation the colonial state spurred the development of confessional institutions and representative bodies, and reinforced sectarian identity. Previously, the Dars-i Nizami schools trained both Sunni and Shii clerics and Mughal administrators. The Raj had little use for that type of education and after 1857 replaced it by English language schools for 'secular' education and by confessional schools for religious education. In the late nineteenth century, the British administration still supported joint Sunni–Shia ecumenical education, but by the early twentieth century started supporting confessional schools.[82] A sectarian differentiation of the educational system followed.

In response, Muslim elites founded educational institutions to combine 'traditional' and 'modern' sciences. Initially all-Muslim projects, they then became primarily associated with Sunnis, while Shia founded their own institutions, amidst a rise of Sunni Revivalism. The most famous of these was the Muhammadan Anglo-Oriental College in Aligarh in 1875. Intended as an all-Muslim university with strong Shii backing, some Shii clerics criticised what they perceived to be a Sunni and secular project in which clerics had little say. Tensions emerged in the departments dealing with religion and history and amongst students. Prayers would eventually be held separately.[83] The other key institution was Dar al-Ulum Deoband, founded in 1866 by the intellectual heirs of Shah Wali Allah and Shah Abd al-Aziz. It became the institutional centre of Sunni Islamic revivalism on the Indian subcontinent. Its relationship with Shiism fluctuated, but Deoband was generally perceived as critical of Shiism. Madrasas based on the 'Deobandi' model were set up across Northern India and later Pakistan and the borderlands with Afghanistan, and amongst Sunnis in Iran, in the late nineteenth and twentieth century, and further afield.[84] The Nadwat al-Ulama, where teaching in Arabic would become paramount, was established in 1892/3. Shia were initially involved in its foundation, but were later excluded after a meeting in 1895, during which three Barelvis, including their leader, Ahmad Raza Khan (1856–1921), had attacked the institution for closeness to Shia and Wahhabis. Once it moved into its grand buildings in Lucknow in 1898 on the north bank of the river, it became seen as a Sunni madrasa by Shia. It also established ties with Sunni reformists in the Arab world.[85] The Sunni Revivalist Barelvi movement, founded by Raza Khan as the *Ahl-i Sunnat wa Jama'at*,

The People of the Tradition and the Community, too, became important on the Indian subcontinent. It was Sufi-inspired and differentiated itself from Salafis. Nevertheless it was fiercely anti-Shii, and Raza Khan wrote anti-Shii treatises.[86] Another example was the Fara'idi movement in Bengal, founded by Haji Shariat Allah (d. 1840), a revivalist movement set upon 'purifying' Sunnism, including from the Shii influence that had spread under Bengal's eighteenth century Shii rulers.[87]

And in the princely state of Bhopal, the Sunni scholar Siddiq Hasan Khan, whose father was a convert from Shiism, and had written anti-Shii polemics, played a crucial role.[88] In 1871, he married the ruler of Bhopal, Jahan Begum, and helped rule the city, located in the central Indian state of Madhya Pradesh, until he was deposed by the British in 1885. The patronage of his wife gave him the resources to disseminate Salafi ideas, and crack down on Bhopal's small Shii community.[89] He introduced the teachings of the above-mentioned Yemeni scholar Muhammad al-Shawkani to a wider readership.[90] Khan's patronage was also important for the relatively poor Wahhabi scholars in Najd. Some of them came to study Hadith in Bhopal and Delhi in the late nineteenth and early twentieth century, and some Wahhabi books saw their first print runs here.[91] Siddiq Hasan Khan's books were in turn read across the Islamic world and influenced Arab Salafis.[92]

The annexation of Awadh in 1856, in contrast, had dealt a heavy blow to Shii scholarship, and Shii schools in Lucknow were closed. A few decades later, after growing disillusioned with the pan-Islamic institutions, Shii elites founded their own ones, beginning with the Madrasa Nazimiyya in Lucknow in 1889 and, in 1894, the Sultan al-Madaris. These schools combined the standard Twelver Shii curriculum of Iraq and Iran with the local Farangi Mahall tradition.[93] The Madrasat al-Waizin in Lucknow, founded in 1911 at the initiative of Sir Mohammad Ali Mohammad Khan Bahadur, the Raja of Mahmudabad, trained graduates of the other Shii colleges and prepared them for missionary work. It published widely and regularly in Urdu and English, and its English-language publications are amongst the first to promote Shiism in a European language.[94] As a result of Shia slowly moving away from Aligarh, the Shia College was established in Lucknow in 1917 with British support. Aligarh had become a centre of Muslim nationalism, and so the colonial state was keen to weaken it, for example by supporting separate Sunni and Shii institutions in its stead.[95]

The building of these Shii institutes of higher learning in the early twentieth century coincided with a period of decline and instability in the shrine cities in Iraq, exacerbated by the British invasion of 1914 and the drying up of the Indian fund that had hitherto financed students and scholars there, and the need to provide Shii education in India.[96] Shii elites and British officials now sought to portray India's Shia as loyal and not prone to rebellion, in contrast to some Sunnis (despite Awadh's prominence in 1857).[97] Political organisations likewise oscillated between unity and particularity. The All-India Muslim League (popularised as the Muslim League) was founded in 1906 as a pan-Islamic movement with the aim of uniting and representing all Muslims of the subcontinent. Muslim unity regardless of sectarian difference lay at its heart. Several of its early proponents, leaders, and financiers, such as the Aga Khan III, Imam of the Ismailis and founder president of the Muslim League, and the Raja of Mahmudabad, were Shia.[98]

These Shii elites did not see a contradiction in supporting ecumenical and confessional projects. The All-India Shia Conference (AISC) was set up in 1907 because some of the old Shii landed families had grown weary of Aligarh, and a political arm, the All-India Shia Political Conference (AISPC) was established as some Shii leaders feared their voices would not be heard in the Muslim League. The AISPC became the main institutional representative of Shia in India, its annual conferences a gathering for Shia and Ismailis from across the subcontinent.[99] It was complemented by social, cultural, and economic organisations set up to make the Shii community more self-reliant.[100]

As noted, it was not as if Sunni and Shii had been non-existent categories before British rule. Some people strongly self-identified as Sunni or Shii, and clerics such as Shustari, Dildar Ali, or Shah Wali Allah, had sought to enforce boundaries. But these categories had not become fixed in law, institutionalised separately, or categories through which one could stake political claims. They were not yet discussed widely in public disputations, or discussed in polemics printed en masse. And on a personal level, many sought to de-emphasise sectarian identity, chose not to pronounce it openly, or were simply unaware of the issue. It cannot be emphasised enough that in everyday lives, the boundaries of these identities remained fluid. Muharram rituals, to repeat, were shared religious and social experiences in which Sunnis and Shia (and Hindus) participated without broadcasting their sectarian differences. Still, they embodied the Indian Shii political legacy, and remained most prominent in those areas that at some point had been under the control of a Shii dynasty, as well as in the major urban centres of the Mughal Empire.[101]

It was here that direct British rule marked a break, and a major departure, that accelerated the confessionalisation of Indian Muslims, which then, ironically, crystallised itself around Muharram.[102] Attuned to a vision of difference based on the scripturalist scholarship of Orientalism, British officials, could, for example, argue that 'strictly speaking the Muharram ceremonies [...] should only be performed by Shias, but Sunnis of the lower classes commonly join in them'.[103] That vision also shaped their understanding of Muharram in Lucknow.

After a period of decline following annexation and the repression of the 1857 rising, Lucknow re-emerged as the capital of South Asian Shiism, and as the administrative centre for the reconstituted United Provinces, a focus of national politics, business, and migration.[104] This meant that the Sunni–Shia question, which was especially relevant in Lucknow, became a topic of national significance.[105] After 1857, the colonial state redesigned the urban environment. Previously, Muslims had buried their dead in small plots around the city, but British officials saw this as a health hazard, closed them, and allocated sites outside the city for burial. This led to petitions from Sunnis and Shia for separate graveyards, which spurred the municipality to indeed establish distinct graveyards.[106]

This was one example in which the state, by trying to regulate society more thoroughly, fostered divisions between Sunnis and Shia in tandem with sectarian identity entrepreneurs. Another was the Muharram processions. In response to Shii complaints that Sunnis participating in Muharram in Lucknow had diluted its essence and turned it into a 'carnival', the government in 1906 organised separate Sunni and Shii processions, with separate routes through the city and different 'Karbalas' at which the processions would end. As a result, they lost their ecumenical character. Sunnis included praises of the first four Caliphs, and Shia curses of the first three Caliphs. Riots in subsequent years led the local government to appoint an investigative committee. This committee argued that the Sunni practice was an innovation intended to provoke the Shia, that Sunnis could laud the Caliphs on other days, and that Shia should be discouraged from cursing the first three Caliphs.[107] Taking a sectarian stance was a way for new socio-political actors to assert their position and marginalise the more established, ecumenically minded ones such as the clerics of the Farangi Mahall.[108]

An example from a few decades later illustrates this point. After tensions during Muharram re-emerged in the 1930s, a new committee upheld the previous conclusions. In response, Sunnis argued that their practice of lauding the Caliphs could no longer be restricted and started a civil disobedience movement. In 1939, the municipal administration and its Congress members, who sought to play to majority Sunni opinion in light of national politics, allowed the Sunni procession in praise of the Caliphs. Shia then started a movement of their own, with tens of thousands, including members of the former ruling family and senior clerics, courting arrest for cursing the Companions. The state tried to enforce the ban again, but tensions resurfaced. This entrenched Sunni–Shia divisions across India. New popular forces openly defied the old clerical and political leadership and used the agitations to assert their leadership of increasingly separate Sunni and Shia communities.

On the Sunni side, a preacher whose father had led previous anti-Shii agitations, was central and established a Sunni school to train preachers to debate Shia in public. The Sunni emphasis on lauding the first three Caliphs, and at times even praising the killers of Hussain, was a departure of previous Sunni practice, and not universally accepted. Ultimately, however, the lauding and cursing of the Caliphs became yardsticks of more antagonistic Sunni and Shii identities, as well as of protest against government restrictions.

For Sunnis, embracing anti-Shiism became a way to assert a pan-Sunni identity, despite the many political and doctrinal divisions amongst Sunnis. And on the Shia side, the agitation affirmed a cross-class pan-Shii identity. At the same time, after the death of the most senior Shii clerics, new actors claimed leadership of the community through polemical engagement with Sunnis.[109] Princely states that were nominally independent and where the administration was run by 'native' officials also witnessed tensions. The Nawabs of Rampur, for example, were Shii and had patronised Sunni and Shii clerics, though the administration was mostly staffed with local Sunnis. When a new ruler dismissed much of his father's old administration in the 1930s, hiring Shii officials from outside the region, including as chief minister, this led to resentment amongst the old officials, which was expressed in sectarian terms, including in a polemic that included names of Shia who had allegedly profited from state favouritism.[110] In other places, such as in the Punjab, British rule led to a more open embrace of Shiism.[111] In the North-West Frontier Province, between Afghanistan and British-ruled territory that later became Pakistan, in the 1920s, the British administration intervened on the side of a Shii clan after its members had been evicted from its land by Sunni clans and a Naqshbandi leader. After British pressure, the Shia were able to return to their land. The British intervention, including the paying of stipends to Shii clans and the appointment of a political agent to them, then upset the Sunni clans.[112] The modern state intervened in confessional disputes, often at the instigation of Muslims themselves, and thereby often exacerbated tensions and deepened boundaries. It also sought to count, classify, and regulate correct religious practices. This was part of a larger process whereby people in the Raj became officially part of a community.

British officials and Orientalists encouraged the study of Hindu and Muslim law and religion, and translated and printed Indian chronicles. As pointed out, Shia were rarely mentioned in Mughal-era chronicles and if they were it was in a denigrating manner. Now these chronicles, inclusive of their anti-Shii bias, became seen as the 'authentic' history as 'told by India's historians'.[113] By studying communal identities, the British 'recognised' them and helped institutionalise Sunnism and Shiism separately. The perhaps most transformative aspect of the modern state was that communal boundaries would become delineated by law.

To understand the significance of what happened to Islamic law in the Raj, I'll compare it quickly with developments in the Ottoman Empire, in which legal reform was a key part of the nineteenth-century reform process. While historically, Sharia courts had been dealing with personal status law, criminal law, and other matters, the Ottoman legal reforms after 1839 led to a certain separation between so called Nizamiyya and Sharia courts. Technically, Sharia courts should henceforth only handle religious questions and personal status law. That separation was, however, not always of great significance, and both courts were to use a codification of Sunni Hanafi law, the so-called Mejelle.[114] That codification in itself was a major milestone, and served as the basis for the law of much of the post-Ottoman world.

As part of that reform process and under the pressure of European powers, members of religious minorities such as Christians and Jews saw improvements in their legal status. But this did not apply to Shia, who continued to be subject to Hanafi law. Ottoman courts never officially recognised Shiism or judged according to Shii law, and attempts by Shii clerics or the Qajars to have Shiism recognised in Ottoman courts, failed. That did not stop some Shia from resorting to Shii clerics when it came to personal status law even if they were not officially recognised. There was probably a tacit agreement whereby Ottoman officials would accept this arrangement, without, however, endorsing it openly. Hanafi judges were officially appointed across Shii-inhabited areas, but informally, the Ottomans must have been tolerating Shii judges.[115] Despite this flexible approach, Shiism never served as the basis of Ottoman law, and it is here where Ottoman confessional ambiguity reached its limits.

In such cases, more direct state involvement, as part of the modernising reforms of the second half of the nineteenth century, upset informal arrangements that had long glossed over potentially embarrassing identity juxtapositions. It was thus a major transformation when European Empires codified and institutionalised Sunnism and Shiism separately, and used both side by side (previously only Shii-ruled states had administered Shii law, Sunni-led states generally did not accept Shii law). And it is one that has previously not received much attention, especially when it comes to the comparison between India and the Middle East.

The three large European Empires in Muslim-majority countries—the Dutch, French, and British—all sought to employ a mixture of Islamic and 'customary law' (and learned from each other).[116] The British were the first to institutionalise Sunni and Shii personal status law separately in India, and later in Bahrain and Iraq. In the interwar period, the French did the same in Lebanon and Syria (although, unlike in India, where the judiciary was staffed by 'secular' lawyers trained in the British tradition, the courts in these countries would be staffed by clerics of the different religious communities). As relatively strong differences exist in personal status law amongst the schools of jurisprudence, and especially between Sunnism and Shiism, this separate institutionalisation was significant. Justified in a liberal imperial vein, arguably to give communities 'their rights', it normalised and legalised sectarian difference.

In the Mughal Empire, the judiciary had ruled according to a mixture of Hanafi law and local customs, which could vary by region. The compilation of Hanafi law under Aurangzib, the Sunni-minded Mughal Emperor, finished in the 1670s, was in many ways a precursor to the Ottoman codification of Hanafi law in the nineteenth century, and led to a certain standardisation of legal norms across the Empire. Religious difference between Muslims, Christians, and others, was acknowledged, but non-Muslims, most of the population, were judged in the same courts, invoking the same laws as Muslims, especially for commercial cases. Unlike later

British courts, Mughal courts generally did not try to define group membership and did not differentiate between Sunna and Shia.[117] Even Shustari, whom we have gotten to know as a key cleric advocating a stronger Shii identity, worked as a Sunni judge in Lahore.[118] I've noted that some of the Shii-run states in the Deccan and the North brought Shii clerics into the administration, but Hanafi law generally prevailed.[119]

From 1772 onwards, the East India Company claimed jurisdiction in civil and criminal matters over populations under its control and, regarding personal status law, started to judge Muslims and Hindus separately. This of course glossed over the differences within both groups when it came to law (the category of Hindu included many different groups, including Buddhists, Jains, and Sikhs). Initially, all those classified as Muslims were adjudicated in the same manner.[120] The EIC ordered the translation and editing of Islamic legal texts that could be applied as a Muslim code of law by Company officials. That transformed the nature of Islamic law, as Islamic judges had previously had much leeway in interpreting the sources and issuing judgments, and judges could come to different conclusions on similar cases when taking context into account. Now law moved into a more text-based, and standardised direction. Initially, most of the texts translated and used were Hanafi. Translations of Shii law texts were commissioned from the late eighteenth century and started to be applied from the early nineteenth century onwards. In 1805, British administrators published a *Digest of Mohummudan Law* that included some translations of Shii commercial law texts, and another one in 1825, which comprises, for the first time, translations of Shii law texts regarding inheritance.[121] Courts now recognised a distinction between Sunni and Shii.[122] This was likely a result of the Company expanding into Shii-inhabited areas or annexing previously Shii-ruled territories such as Bengal, to which the 1772 EIC edict originally applied.

A difference in jurisprudence between Sunna and Shia, which had never existed in India, not even in the Shii-ruled states (with minor exceptions), nor in the Ottoman Empire, was now established by British Orientalists and Company judges, in cooperation with local clerics and lawyers, to grant the 'sectaries' their rights, as they put it.[123] In some cases, Shii clerics pressed for this and were involved in the judiciary in territories under Company control. Shii clerics therefore at times depicted Company rule favourably because of its respect for Shii law.[124] It was another Shii cleric who had previously worked in a British court who in the early 1840s helped convince Awadh's rulers to replace Sunni law administered by ecumenically-minded

Sunni scholars with Shii law administered by Shii clerics. The Shii judiciary, however, only lasted until 1856, when Awadh was annexed.[125] This undermined the Shii clergy, who were no longer employed in large numbers, and furthered the separate institutionalisation of Sunnism and Shiism. Direct rule over Awadh meant that British officials now ruled over large Shii populations, and paid more attention to the codification of Shii law.[126]

A digest published in the 1860s included volumes on Hanafi and Shii law.[127] The British application of law glossed over religious differences and standardised law in novel ways. While Buddhists were seen as Hindus in juridical terms, and all Sunnis (also the less numerous Shafiis) were judged according to Hanafi law, 'Sunni', 'Twelver Shii', and then 'Ismaili' became separate categories of personal status law. The introduction of a manual that combined translated Islamic legal texts and precedents put it succinctly: 'The law administered in India with regard to Mahommedans is that of 1. The Soonees. 2. The Sheeas.'[128]

By the late nineteenth century, this became ever more pronounced. Until 1864, British judges were usually assisted by a Muslim scholar, but thereafter used translations of Muslim legal manuals directly.[129] In a handbook intended for use across British India, the Indian lawyer, and statesman Syed Ameer Ali whom we will hear more about later, emphasised differences between Sunni and Shii jurisprudence. His 1880 book was, tellingly, entitled *The Personal Law of the Mahommedans (According to All the Schools) Together with a Comparative Sketch of the Law of Inheritance among the Sunnis and the Shias.*[130] Through a mix of translations of legal texts and a collection of court cases that set precedents in the British common law tradition, British administrators, in conjunction with Muslim scholars, developed 'Anglo-Muhammadan law'. This was then applied in other British colonies with significant Muslim populations, and after independence, formed the basis for Muslim Personal Law in India and Pakistan.[131]

Differences in inheritance law could make choosing a religious affiliation appealing, depending on the situation. A further differentiation crystallised itself around religious endowments, on which Sunni and Shii views differed slightly. After an Indian Muslim lawyer who had studied Arabic at Cambridge translated Shii law books into English, a differentiation between Sunni and Shii endowments was recognised.[132] Under Company rule, some endowments, whose status was recast under Anglo-Muhammadan law, were simply taken over.[133] The Raj introduced major changes in 1863. Previously, huge endowments had served the upkeep of specific religious buildings, and trustees had considerable leeway. A second group of family endowments, off which a family would live, were used to sustain wealth over generations. The colonial state now argued that the latter were illegal and instead applied inheritance law that further subdivided property and affected the wealth of elite families.[134]

Endowments now became limited to religious purposes as laid down by Islamic law. As a result, some families established new ones to save their legacy and name, and did so in support of specific religious buildings such as mosques and mourning houses. That technical change led to more sect-specific endowments.[135] New communalist organisations tried to control these endowments. All-India Shia Conference delegates compiled lists of Shii endowments to ensure they were used for the purpose of the 'Shii community'. Some of the largest ones had previously been managed by descendants of elite families, and its funds could be repurposed for wider infrastructural and municipal projects. The All-India Shia Conference claimed that Shii endowments had been taken over by Sunnis (some of these Sunnis had been allies of the Awadhi rulers—and their role was previously not seen as a problem). Separate Sunni and Shii *waqf* reform movements culminated in the formation of separate Waqf Boards in 1936.[136] Allegations of corruption also led to an investigation of the Oudh Bequest. In this context, the British Resident in 1900s Baghdad tried to steer the funds away from Iranian clerics, who were perceived to be anti-British, and towards Indian ones, who as British subjects were seen as more loyal, as well as to Arab ones.[137]

Communities whose status was not immediately clear, such as Ismailis and Khojas, were forced to shed their confessional ambiguity. Many Khojas, for example, thought of themselves as Muslims, but in some respects followed Hindu law. This was no longer acceptable, and they had to choose. As one British judge paradigmatically put it, 'they cannot have it both ways'.[138] In pre-colonial times, Ismailis had at times concealed their beliefs to escape persecution. Some claimed to be Twelver Shia and others to be Hindus.[139] Khojas had sometimes claimed to be Sunni Sufis, and some argued that they had been Sunni since converting to Islam.[140] This exemplifies the ways in which the colonial state and communal identity entrepreneurs established more rigid notions of 'Hindu' and 'Muslim', and fostered a stronger differentiation between Sunnis, Twelver Shia, and Ismailis.[141]

Several lines of Imams claimed descent from the earliest Ismaili Imams. One line had in the eighteenth century reappeared in Iran and received religious taxes from Ismailis on the Indian subcontinent. After his predecessor was killed in Yazd in 1818 in what may have been a campaign instigated by Twelver Shii clerics, Imam Hasan Ali Shah became a senior Qajar official. He received the title Aga Khan by Fath Ali Shah Qajar (d. 1834), henceforth the title of the Ismaili Imams. Initially sent to re-establish order as governor of the restive Kerman province, he fell out with the new ruler, Muhammad Shah Qajar, and rebelled, and may have already been in contact with British officials. The Qajars relied on Britain to keep Russia from fully dominating Iran, and the British expanded their influence especially along the Iranian coastline. But Britain was wary of Qajar ambitions in Afghanistan, and of alleged Russian designs on India from the North, and expanded northwestwards from India, annexing Sindh and invading Afghanistan.[142] The Aga Khan's revolt was a convenient distraction for Britain that weakened the Qajars' prospects in Afghanistan. The Aga Khan was, however, defeated by the Qajar army in 1841, and then moved to Qandahar, Afghanistan, where he assisted the British at the time of their short-lived invasion of Afghanistan.[143] He started receiving a British stipend and settled in Bombay in 1848.[144]

The Aga Khan I took advantage of the metropolitan setting, and the new communication and transportation connections to bind far-flung Ismaili communities closer to his person. This worked in some cases, but not in others. For example, the Aga Khan wanted Khojas be recognised as Ismailis too, and collect taxes from them, something his predecessors had already tried in the 1820s. A lawsuit to that effect was filed in 1830 but then withdrawn. With the Aga Khan in India, the issue resurfaced. Tensions culminated in the 1866 Aga Khan case, in which his claims to be the heir to the old Ismaili Imams were fought out in the Bombay High Court. The Khojas who did not want to accept the Aga Khan, pay him taxes, and have him control communal property argued that they were Sunnis, and that the Aga Khan therefore had no rights to their allegiance or finances. But the Aga Khan won, and the Nizari Khojas became recognised as a community of 'Shia Imami Ismailis' (two groups of Khojas, one claiming to be Sunnis and another claiming to be Twelver Shia, refused to pay taxes to him and established their own organisations, claiming that their sectarian identity was different from his).[145] His successors became the hereditary Imams of one of the two main strands of Ismailism, and the institutions they would set up would support general Muslim and humanitarian causes, and distinctly confessional ones, and tie Ismaili communities to the central Imamate.[146] The preferences of inheritance of 'Khoja Mohammedans' subsequently became listed in Anglo-Muhammadan legal manuals, establishing a third legal category of Muslims beside Sunni and Shii: Khoja/Ismaili.[147] That some of the earliest Indian Muslim lawyers and high court judges were Shii and Ismaili ensured attention to Shii and Ismaili law.[148] Personal status law became crucial for Ismailis and led to the publication and translation of Ismaili law texts.[149]

Some Ismailis and Khojas took advantage of the opportunities offered by the British Empire, moving as traders between East Africa, Southern Arabia, the Persian Gulf, and India and founding confessional institutions and trading outposts along the way. The migration of Khoja merchants to Muscat, Oman, for example, dates back to the late eighteenth century, and Khojas would become influential here, in Zanzibar and elsewhere.[150] Prosperous and bound by religious law to donate one-fifth of their surplus income to the Imam for communal and charitable causes, the Khojas who became Twelver Shia as well as the Ismaili Daudi Bohras, established their own institutions and communal leaderships, and financed wider Shii causes, including in the shrine cities.[151] Print publications bound these communities to each other.[152] In places such as Zanzibar, under joint British-Omani rule, the institutional and legal differentiation between Sunni, Ismaili, and Twelver Shii Khojas was reproduced.[153] In South Africa, Indian Muslims similarly were organised according to sectarian and ethnic background.[154] Developments in India thus had repercussions across territories under British influence, including in the Persian Gulf, which was tied to India administratively and economically.

The movement of people and the networks of the Raj fostered a cosmopolitanism that suited the Age of Empire, but would become problematic in the Age of Nationalism. British residents in the Persian Gulf, including in Bahrain, for example, employed Persian-speaking Shia as interpreters and bureaucrats, boosting transnational ties of trading and administrative families.[155] Shia and Sunnis, Arabs and Iranians and others, moved across the Persian Gulf, and to other parts of the British Raj. In Bahrain, which as we've seen was in a treaty relationship with Britain since 1820, the general view of Shiism as unorthodox and pro-Persian, the communalist vision of the Empire, and the appropriation of the anti-Persian and anti-Shii views of the Sunni elites led British officials to institutionalise a criminal justice system that privileged Sunnis over Shia. The police force, largely made up of foreigners, including by Sunnis from other parts of the Empire, and the criminal justice system, staffed with British and Sunni judges, largely policed Shia villages and neighbourhoods seen as hotbeds of opposition to Al Khalifa rule (though Sunnis that rebelled were likewise suppressed). At the level of personal status law, separate courts for Sunnis and Shia, modelled on the Indian example but staffed with clerics, entrenched sectarian difference.[156]

The role of the British Empire in the very making of Sunnism and Shiism as separate legal, political and religious categories, and the relations between the two, can hardly be overstated. It wasn't that British colonial authorities simply chose one side against the other. As we have seen it was far more complicated than that, and Muslims themselves played an important role, too.

Britain undermined the various Islamic Gunpowder Empires, most directly the Mughals. Indian Sunni Revivalists blamed Britain for the extinction of Sunni power in India, and they feared that Britain and other European powers would do the same to the Ottomans. Britain's relationship with the rulers of Awadh, the managing of the Oudh bequest, and engagement with Shii princely families elsewhere, led to a familiarity with Shiism that contributed to the separate institutionalisation of Sunnism and Shiism. And the close relationship with Ismailis resulted in the creation of a third category: Khoja, and in some regions, other strands of Ismailism.

In Southern Arabia and Zanzibar, Britain protected the Ibadi Sultans from conquest by the Wahhabis of the Arabian Interior. The treaties with the rulers of the Persian Gulf, on the other hand, cemented Sunni rule but facilitated the rise of other city-states based around major Gulf ports, and the influx of religiously and ethnically diverse populations.[157] It also ensured that these polities, Bahrain, Kuwait, Qatar and the Trucial States, the later United Arab Emirates, would not become directly controlled by the Wahhabis. And in relations with Iran, it was primarily the attempts to limit Russian influence, and the desire to extract major concessions, that informed British policy, rather than a disdain for Shiism. British policy towards the Islamic world was primarily driven by national interest and profit, and the infamous divide-and-rule approach. Cooperation was the yardstick, rather than Muslim orthodoxy or heterodoxy.

Still, in the key Muslim territories of the British Empire, Britain would mainly engage with Sunni Muslim rulers (Sunnis were, after all, in the majority). This would become more pronounced once Britain expanded into the Middle East, and would culminate in the alliance with the Hashemites in World War I, and the eventual establishment of a Sunni-led monarchy in Iraq. The knowledge production that had emphasised that Sunnis had ruled historically, and that Shia were unruly rebels, would inform this pattern.[158] And the codification of Shii and Ismaili law, the close relationship of some of these elites with the British state, and a sense that a differentiation amongst Muslims did not harm British interests, led to a stronger differentiation between Sunnism, Shiism, and Ismailism.

This was no different in Afghanistan, which British officials saw as a strategic buffer zone between Russia, Iran, and British India. After the collapse of Nadir Shah's short-lived pan-Islamic Empire, one of Nadir's former commanders, Ahmad Shah Durrani, from 1747 onwards solidified his rule roughly in the territory of later Afghanistan, but also periodically conquered adjacent territories, all the way to Delhi, which Ahmad Shah sacked in 1757. Ahmad Shah and his successors, known as the Durranis, were Pashtus and Sunni Hanafis. They expanded the application of Hanafi law, built up a nascent Sunni clergy, and allied with pro-Sunni Sufi orders.[159] But they were also careful not to be seen as anti-Shii, and employed a group of Shii elite bureaucrats, the Qizilbash, whose name indicates their origin amongst the tribes that had brought the Safavids to power in neighbouring Iran two centuries earlier. Some had come to Afghanistan during Nadir Shah's invasion of Northern India, and stayed on (as did some Qizilbash in Northern India, who, as noted, strengthened Shiism there). Others were recruited directly by Afghan rulers in need of Persian-speaking bureaucrats. The thousands of Shii Qizilbash in Afghan government service highlighted that the Durranis tried to continue the ecumenical policy of Nadir Shah, and were keen to employ 'outsiders' that were not tied to local clan loyalties. Another reason for Ahmad Shah Durrani's absence of anti-Shiism was his ambition to incorporate Iran into his domain (he succeeded, for a while, to take Mashhad, and there paid respects to the shrine of Imam Rida, and invested a Safavid prince, Shah Rukh, as his 'vice-regent'). When he tried to ally with the Ottomans against Iran's new rulers, the Zands, he decried them as rebels, but not primarily because of their Shii identity.[160] The Zands, and then the Qajars, held firm in central Iran, however, limiting their westward push and the Durranis were most successful at expanding into Northern India, where they came into conflict with the East India Company, and with the Sikhs in the Punjab, with whom they fought several devastating wars.

By the nineteenth century the Durranis had lost control of the country amidst internal rivalries, the drying up of revenue from sporadic conquests and taxation from possessions on the Indian subcontinent. Simultaneously, their reliance on Persian-speaking and Shii Qizilbash bureaucrats, who though small in number wielded wide influence, led to resentment amongst other groups, especially Pashtu tribal elites, and conflict at court. This tension was political, but the Qizilbash's sectarian identity was invoked to undermine them.[161] In 1826, Dust Muhammad Khan, of the Muhammadzais, a subbranch of the Durrani confederacy, likewise Pashtuns, took control of Kabul, from where members of that dynasty would rule henceforth. In a development not dissimilar from Mughal India, Qizilbash families had intermarried with leading Afghan political dynasties, and various aspirants to the throne had Shii mothers or Shii wives. Dust Muhammad Khan, was one such example, and he relied on Qizilbash support in this push for the throne (leading his rivals to ally with Sunni families of Kabul). But once in power, he tried to downplay his Qizilbash connections and become more widely accepted, and in quarrels between Qizilbash and Sunnis often endorsed the latter.[162]

No longer able to expand their territory, Afghan rulers turned inwards, bringing provinces cut-off by mountain ranges and inaccessible in the winter under their control. They invoked Sunnism, and instituted a system of tribal and ethnic hierarchies, with Pashtuns at the top.[163] As Britain became more involved in Afghan politics, its officials explained Afghan politics and history by emphasising tribal and sectarian division and enmity. The Shii Qizilbash, for example, were seen as sources of potential Iranian influence, and thus as subversive, and they worried about Dust Muhammad Khan's Qizilbash mother, for example. But this was evidence less of Iranian influence and more of confessional tolerance of Durrani and early Muhammadzai rule, and it was in fact Dust Muhammad who tried to give the Afghan state a more Islamic identity, and one more closely tied to the Timurid political legacy of Central Asia, and its Sunni Revivalist and Naqshbandi milieus.[164]

Britain's ambition to shape the politics of Afghanistan, a country seen as vital to the security of British India, and to keep Russia and Iran at bay, led to the invasion of Afghanistan in 1839 and the defeat of Dust Muhammad, who had declared a Jihad first against the Sikhs, and then against the British. But the invasion was a disaster. Most of the anti-British fighting was done by Sunni Pashtuns but some Qizilbash of Kabul were instrumental in the anti-British Kabul uprising of 1841–2.[165] The British defeat led to the so-called 'Great Game', a proxy war between Tsarist Russia and the British, in which both sides sought to influence Afghan politics and draw current or aspiring rulers to their side. In 1878, worried about threats to India, British, and Indian troops invaded again, and in the aftermath, Britain extended its influence over Afghanistan, including over its foreign policy, even more. Britain supported the claim to the throne of Amir Abd al-Rahman Khan, who would receive a stipend and a steady supply of arms, with which he set upon building a stronger state, and one that became distinctly anti-Shii.[166]

The Hazara are an ethnic group, possibly of Mongolian origin, that converted to Twelver Shiism in previous centuries. Some argued they adopted Shiism at the time of the pro-Shii Mongol rulers of the early fourteenth century, with further waves of conversions following the Safavid takeover of Iran. This may also have been a way to differentiate themselves from Sunni neighbours (although there were also some Sunni sections).[167] The Hazara were largely tribally organised and lived in the Hazarajat, a region in the central highlands of Afghanistan. They had little in common with the urban-based Qizilbash bureaucratic elite, except Shii belief and the fact that they spoke a local dialect of Persian (although urbanised Qizilbash at times allied with rural, armed Hazara to bolster their position).[168]

At the outset of his rule, Khan invited Hazara chiefs to Kabul, emphasising Sunni–Shia unity and enlisting Hazara for military campaigns. He and his governors initially tried to limit Sunni–Shia hostility, after Sunnis had claimed that Shia were not proper Muslims, and had, for example, refused to give their daughters in marriage to elite Shii Qizilbash.[169] Except his rule would become associated with extreme anti-Shii measures. When a Hazara subsection, which was partly Shii and partly Sunni, rebelled, he strengthened the Sunni subsection against the Shii one.[170] He awarded properties to Sunnis fleeing Iran.[171] Habib Allah Khan, Abd al-Rahman Khan's son and successor, forbade members of the Shii Turi tribe living in Kurram from travelling via Afghanistan to pilgrimage in Mashhad. The argument was that their safety could not be guaranteed, but the Afghan government was also suspicious of a Pashtun (and Shii) tribe that had allied with Britain, and which it saw as under its own authority.[172]

After subduing other parts of the country, Abd al-Rahman Khan cast Hazara as rebels. Some submitted, but by 1892, Hazara in different regions revolted, and the Amir urged Sunni tribes from across Afghanistan to join in what he and Sunni clerics called a Jihad against unbelievers, which allowed for their enslavement and confiscation of property. Enticed by these prospects, around 100,000 soldiers mobilised to fight them; Sunni preachers were assigned to the units. Tens of thousands Hazara were killed, enslaved or forced to flee, and Hazara political and religious elites were summarily rounded up and executed or exiled. Many Hazara fled to Iran or to British India, especially to the Punjab, boosting the number of Shia there, and in 1904, a so-called Hazara Battalion was enlisted in the British India Army. This, in turn, increased the Afghan government's hostility towards Hazara even further.[173] Those who stayed were forced to convert at least outwardly to Sunnism, and the Amir appointed Hanafi judges and sent spies to observe whether Hazara were practising now banned Shii rituals such as Muharram. An anti-Shii Jihad, propagated in pamphlets and in mosques and bazaars, thus built a state closely associated with Sunnism, supported, at least tacitly, by Britain.[174] The Afghan state and its ruling elite became more Sunni. Sunni Hanafi education was expanded and Hanafi law enforced more thoroughly.[175] The Hazara that survived would play a peripheral role, as social segregation between religious groups divided tribal and rural communities.[176]

After hearing of the massacre against the Hazara, the Shah of Iran, at the instigation of a senior Shii cleric in Iraq, asked the British government for clarification. The latter in turn wrote to Amir Abd al-Rahman Khan, in response to which Qizilbash leaders described their situation favourably, to reassure the Shah. Simultaneously, and in keeping with the anti-Shii atmosphere at the time, however, Habib Allah Khan, the future ruler, had Qizilbash mourning houses turned into Sunni mosques, appointed Sunni Imams there, and forbade Shii practices.[177]

It points to the complexity of Sunni–Shia relations in Afghanistan, that many of the anti-Shii measures were recorded by Faiz Muhammad Katib, a Hazara, who became the official historian under Amir Abd al-Rahman Khan's successors, in his *History of Afghanistan* (though he had to add curses to descriptions of Hazara). For individual Shia, largely Qizilbash but also Hazara, could still prosper, and Qizilbash continued to be prominent in the cities, especially in Kabul.[178] Katib acted as a representative for Hazara interests with the government, yet also maintained relations with the Iranian embassy in Kabul. He had studied Sunni and Shii jurisprudence, including with one of Kabul's leading Sunni scholars of the time, before entering government service.[179]

Like the leaders of the Ottoman Empire and Qajar Iran, Afghan monarchs tried to reform their country in the face of growing imperial penetration, amidst resistance from the clergy. The Sunni clergy had expanded their power by supporting the anti-British Jihad (and the anti-Hazara campaign). They were key partners of the grandson of Amir Abd al-Rahman Khan,

Amir Aman Allah Khan, in the struggle for independence from Britain, achieved in 1919, and embraced the pan-Islamic cause.[180] But positions and alliances could shift. In 1929, Kabul witnessed a major Tajik-led rebellion by Habib Allah against the Aman Allah Khan. The rebels were supported by Naqshbandi clerics, who issued fatwas authorising the killing of Hazara. This turned Hazara into allies of the former regime, and Muhammadzai rule was soon re-established.[181]

In Afghanistan, British intervention and Sunni Revivalism thus contributed to a Sunni-centric and anti-Shii state building. The 1931 constitution enshrined Hanafi Sunnism as state religion, and state nationalism became tied to Sunnism and the ruling family.[182] In the mid-twentieth century Pashto nationalists, who were primarily Sunni yet included a few Shia, argued that ethnic nationalism could overcome sectarian divisions. But ethnic nationalism in a multi-ethnic country had its own perils, and the Shii Hazara and Qizilbash started to see themselves as ethno-sectarian groups in their own right.[183]

Apart from fears of Russian advance, another reason for British involvement was to limit the influence of the Qajars in Khorasan, where the latter invoked a need to protect Shia. The Afghan ruler of Herat did indeed enslave some Shia and sold them to the Khanate of Khiva, a Sunni-Naqshbandi state in present-day Uzbekistan. Its use of Persian Shia as slaves was apparently a way to gain revenue, foster loyalty, and instil fear. And when the Iranian army besieged Herat in 1837, local Sunni clerics declared an anti-Shii Jihad. Herat's eventual incorporation into Afghanistan was legitimised with its alleged Sunni as opposed to Shii identity.[184] Herat retained a Shii community and links to Iran, but the failure to achieve extraterritorial rights for its Shii population undermined Qajar ambitions to portray Iran as protector of global Shiism (the Qajars likewise failed to gain protection rights over Shia in Russia).

Tsarist Russia projected its influence into Iran and Central Asia and ruled over significant Sunni and Shii populations in the Caucasus since conquering them from Iran in the early nineteenth century. Russian officials, too, organised censuses asking for sectarian affiliation, and, to limit the connections of clerics with the religious centres in the Middle East, organised their education separately, and in the 1820s and 1830s established the position of a senior cleric each for Sunnis and Shia under state control. In 1872, Russia established separate 'spiritual departments' for Sunna and Shia. In a process not dissimilar from their British counterparts, Russian Orientalists and officials studied the difference in social structure, political allegiance, and jurisprudence between Sunnis and Shia, building on their experience with Sunni Tatars. Russian officials, too, compiled compendiums of Islamic law that outlined rules according to Hanafi law, as codified by the Ottomans and the Mughals, and studied Shii law books, which were readily available in the Caucasus, given its proximity to Iran. They did this to better monitor the workings of the local courts in which Muslim clerics retained wide authority over personal status law. Shii clerics dealt with cases involving Shia, and Sunnis with those involving Sunnis, while the district administration mediated in mixed disputes. When Sunnis rebelled under Naqshbandi leadership, the state worked with Shii clerics. At other times, Sunnis were portrayed as more loyal and obedient, and Shia as prone to rebellion since they distrusted temporal authority.[185] In sum, in the Caucasus, too, the categories of Sunni and Shii became frequently invoked by imperial officials, even if, on a popular level, pan-Islamic feelings, and ethnic nationalism, became more important markers of identification.

As this chapter has shown, the modern state reshaped people's lives, including their sectarian identities and the meaning of religion more broadly. Orientalism, and the recognition of sectarian difference in an imperial context, played a major role in that process. Together this would foster a stronger identification with sectarian identity alongside reinvigorated pan-Islamic identities. Empire, the institutions and logic of the modern state, printing, urbanisation, and faster connections contributed to a reconstitution of Sunnism and Shiism as more rigidly defined and separate categories. Identity entrepreneurs could invoke sectarian identity to make political claims, and legitimise their position, often in conjunction with Empire. Similar processes were at work in the Ottoman Empire, spurred by the growing influence of Russia, Britain, France, Austria, and Prussia.

8

Ottoman Reorganisation and European Intervention

In 1826 Sultan Mahmud II, issued a decree dissolving the Janissary corps, which, as noted, had been the Ottoman elite military force, and announcing the formation of a new army. The Janissaries had come to be seen as exemplary of the entrenched interests of the old system, and had in preceding decades always managed to fend off similar attempts to challenge their position. As on these previous occasions, when their position was challenged, the Janissaries rebelled, and marched on the Sultan's palace in Istanbul. This time, however, the Sultan was prepared. He crushed the Janissaries' revolt by shelling their barracks, killing thousands of them, ending their influence once and for all. This incident has often been cited as a symbolic break with the old order, and the start of a new era, and we will devote much of this chapter to the Ottoman transformations of the nineteenth century.

The Ottoman experience was so crucial because the Ottoman Empire was the most important major Muslim Empire to remain nominally independent, because it covered vast and strategic territories, and because with its claim to Sunni leadership through the Caliphate and rule over large Shii populations it was central to Sunnism and Shiism. The last century or two of Ottoman rule had long been described as a period of decline, turning that transcontinental Empire dominating half of the Mediterranean, and on the verge of conquering Europe, into an indebted and militarily weakened rump Empire in the nineteenth and eventually Turkey in the twentieth century. But that simplistic notion has been challenged by many scholars, not least because it overlooks and sidelines the dramatic reforms the Ottomans undertook. It is true that since the eighteenth century, European powers had extended their influence in the Empire, both economically and politically, won wars, and supported rebellions at its periphery and taken over some of its territory. They also exerted concessions for monopolies, major investments, and protections of foreign citizens and religious communities. This led to much soul-searching amongst Ottoman elites and prompted them to reorganise and centralise their state so that it could better resist European encroachment. Ottoman nineteenth century reforms were long described as 'Westernisation', focusing on the adoption of European forms of government and military organisation (and dress). But the reality was more complex. Ottoman elites also looked to their own history, to when the Empire was at the height of its power in the sixteenth and seventeenth century, and to Islamic history and norms, all the while studying the European experience. The result was drastic changes that could, however, also be reversed, and could at times be contradictory (and not all of which were followed through). The impact of these reforms was thus multifacetted. The most famous cornerstones are the New Order under Selim III (1789–1807), the reforms under Mahmud II (1808–39), of which the crushing of the Janissaries was a famous part, and the so-called Ottoman Tanzimat (Reorganisation) started symbolically with the Gülhane (Rosegarden) edict of 1839 under Sultan Abdulmajid I.[1]

Many changes, such as the reform of the army, were administrative and technocratic in nature but they often had wider repercussions. Because the Bektashi order was so heavily involved with the Janissaries, it was repressed alongside them and many of its lodges closed or destroyed. Sunni clerics denounced an order that for centuries had been part and parcel of the Ottoman social fabric (with millions of followers across the Empire) and a powerful symbol of the confessionally ambiguous lived reality of Muslim Ottomans. Some lodges were handed over to Sunni Sufi orders, whose leaders, together with the official Ottoman clergy, sentenced Bektashi leaders to death or exile. Others had to renounce Bektashi teachings and espouse Sunnism, and were vilified. Janissaries and Bektashis were cast as the antithesis of the reforming and centralising state, all the while Sunni-minded Sufi orders became its partners (though, they too, balked at some of its secularising aspects).[2] Attempts to impose conscription in turn led to friction with rural communities, including with Druze and Alawites (although an expanding and modernising army and state apparatus also provided them with opportunities).[3]

The Ottoman approach oscillated between an adoption of European forms of political and military organisation, and a reorganisation based on Ottoman and Islamic ones. Different Sultans and officials could favour one side more than the other but they all brought about a stronger state, introduced new notions of government, and fostered new ideologies and senses of togetherness. In the process, the Ottomans reshaped their policy towards the Shia of the Empire, and towards Iran. As shown above, the Ottomans had largely looked the other way when it came to the beliefs of Shii-leaning populations. But now, amidst the backdrop of increasing European imperialism, and the fostering of a more centralised and pervasive state, that state paid more attention to the beliefs of its subjects, and sought to investigate and shape them more strongly. That European powers and missionaries became more and more interested in non-Sunni Ottoman Muslims, made matters worse.

Catholic missionaries had already argued in the seventeenth and eighteenth centuries that the Druze and Alawites' allegedly tense relations with Sunnis made them more receptive towards Christianity.[4] Druze were known in Europe since Druze Emirs tried to ally themselves with Christian powers, and the exile of one of them at the seventeenth century Medici court in Tuscany.[5] The Druze had retained a distinct identity under Sunni rulers because conversion to the Druze faith was not technically possible. The main areas of Druze settlement were in modern-day Lebanon, where Druze Emirs attained political power and rivalled but also cooperated with Maronite Emirs. That Druze overlords ruled nominally at the behest of the Ottomans exemplified Ottoman practice, even if Druze often officially claimed to be Sunni. The Ottomans, aware of their limited authority, largely ignored the Druzes' religiosity. At some point, likely in the eighteenth century, Druze settled in the Hauran, where one of the mountain ranges would later be named Jabal Druze, Mount Druze. Druze rebelled mainly when the modernising state sought to enforce conscription and disarm them.[6]

The Druze case mirrored that of the Alawites, who, as noted, lived on the coast and in the mountain regions between Tripoli in the South and Antioch in the North, with a concentration around Latakia.[7] Alawites had resisted when the Ottomans took over the area in the sixteenth century, but to no avail. The Ottomans saw them as heretics but did not go out of their way to convert them to Sunnism and were more interested to tax them and prevent rebellions or raids on neighbouring areas. The Ottomans at times collected a Mamluk-era extra tax on Alawite villages. Described as Nusayris in times of crises, Ottoman documents usually referred to them as Muslims, and Alawite notables collected taxes and interacted with the state. Although Alawite communal memory, traveller accounts, and French officials claimed otherwise, most Alawites led lives not dissimilar from other rural Ottomans. The rise of tobacco production in the eighteenth century and the transformation of Latakia from a small port into a regional hub at the expense of Tripoli, provided new opportunities. With the rise of Latakia came more outside interest, symbolised by the opening of a French Consulate in 1788.[8] The French and others started to see Alawites as a cohesive religious group with designated leaders.[9]

Sunni Revivalism made itself felt, here, too. In 1824, a regional governor who had affinities for Alawites was killed by Sunnis of Latakia, who were apparently supported by a cleric from Tunisia, who invoked Ibn Taymiyya's fatwa on the Nusayris legitimising the killing of Alawites and the enslavement of Alawite women and children. The sudden appearance of Ibn Taymiyya, who had seldom been mentioned in Ottoman sources of previous centuries, symbolised the connections of a new era, in which Salafi-Wahhabism started to influence Sunnism more generally.[10] While some Alawites initially welcomed the occupation of Syria in 1831 by the modernising Sultans of Egypt, who promised equality before the law, they rebelled in 1834 and made common cause with the Ottomans. Their revolt was suppressed by the Egyptians, who were driven out in 1840/1 through a joint rebellion of Druze and Shia, armed by Britain.[11] Attempts at disarmament and conscription by Muhammad Ali, the Viceroy of Egypt, had fuelled the uprisings.

Alawites had long lived side by side with Ismailis, another example of a Shii community whose situation was profoundly transformed.[12] They shared popular religious practices at local shrines, and some Ismailis had converted to Alawism. The Ottomans appointed Ismailis as local leaders and tax farmers, including in Alawite areas, which could lead to tension.[13] Their sectarian identity was not considered a problem; only when Ismailis revolted in 1816–18 was their alleged heresy invoked. Over the nineteenth century, Ismailis abandoned their old castles, with more Sunnis and Alawites moving in, and relocated to Salamiyah, a region in which the Ismaili movement had first originated.[14] And, as we will shortly see, the situation of Twelver Shia, as well as Turkish and Kurdish Alevis (descendants of the Qizilbash), Yazidis, and other populations that venerated Ali, was also transformed, not least by greater European intervention.

By the mid-nineteenth century, European powers intervened directly on behalf of the Empire's Christians and Jews. They supported what they portrayed as Christian 'liberation' struggles in the Balkans and Greece against Turkish 'oppression', and fostered the hopes of other Ottoman Christians.

The loss of territories inhabited by Christians increased the Muslim share of the Empire's population, a development larger in scale than in Qajar Iran, but with similar consequences (its self-understanding thus became more Muslim and Sunni).[15]

Political and military intervention coincided with the influx of goods from industrialising Europe, upending long-standing economic ties and local industries, and enriching a new class of often Christian intermediaries in the trading centres and ports. Simultaneously, the Ottoman reforms of 1856 gave non-Muslims equal rights to Muslims and introduced the notion of secular Ottoman citizenship.[16] That these changes on the judicial level for Jews and Christians coincided with the ascent of a class of businessmen, Consuls and other intermediaries, who started constituting a kind of informal Empire, led to backlash from the Muslim population, whose provincial elites felt side-lined. This resentment contributed to clashes and pogroms in Aleppo against Christians in 1859 and in Damascus and Mount Lebanon in 1860. Their causes were largely economic, social, and political. Still, public opinion in Europe saw them as Ottoman suppression of Christians, and they were invoked to legitimise more European intervention.[17]

Capitulations that enshrined legal privileges of foreigners became more intrusive, as European powers asserted their political, military, and economic dominance, much to the resentment of Ottoman reformers.[18] Some now extended that legal protection to whole 'minorities', especially Christians and Jews.[19]

After the Russo-Ottoman war of 1877–8, which led to further Ottoman territorial losses, Britain effectively annexed Egypt and Cyprus, and France Tunisia from the Ottomans. This was facilitated by Ottoman indebtedness to European creditors and eventual bankruptcy. France held most Ottoman Public Debt and was the main investor in the Empire. As its economic interests expanded, so did its political ambitions.[20]

The French and British overseas trading companies, and the states, had long been rivals. Napoleon had portrayed his invasion of Egypt in 1798, shortly after the French Revolution, as a liberal imperialist venture. He planned to move from there to India, and was in contact with Indian leaders such as Tipu Sultan, but plans faltered after the British defeated the French in Egypt (and managed to largely keep France out of India).[21] France would withdraw from Egypt, but establish control over most of the rest of North Africa and other parts of Africa as well as Indo-China. And France projected its power further into the Eastern Mediterranean, and stylised itself as an alternative to Britain and Russia, and an ally of local Christians, who were organised in Eastern Christian churches. France embraced the Catholics amongst them, or those, like the Maronites, who had come to an agreement with the Catholic Church. Russia, in turn, protected Orthodox Christians.[22] Britain (and Prussia) forced the Ottomans to recognise a tiny Protestant community, and supported it, as well as smaller Christian churches like the Nestorians. But Britain, with its complicated sectarian make-up at home, its own Church, and tensions between Protestants and Catholics in Scotland and Ireland, and a much larger Empire that rested on alliances with non-Christian elites, had few obvious Christian allies in the Levant, but experience dealing with Muslims of all persuasions.[23]

Britain and France thus also started to become interested in the Empire's non-Sunni Muslims. By the late nineteenth century French military attachés and consuls argued that Alawites and Druze, too, could be potential French allies.[24] Britain forged ties with the Druze, as noted an offshoot of Ismailism that dated back to the late Fatimid period, and who had served as local rulers, as a counterweight to France's alliance with the Maronites.[25] Britain was wary of a full disintegration of the Ottoman Empire, for fear this might empower France or Russia.[26] Still, that great powers supported different 'sects' reinforced the notion that the Levant, a term that in Italian and French indicated the area in the East where the Sun rises (lever/levantare) and came to denote much of the Eastern Mediterranean, and in the twentieth century more specifically coastal Syria and later Lebanon, was made up of a 'mosaic' of religious groups.[27] Directly linked to that was the notion that protection of non-Sunni religious groups could pave the way for greater influence, something the Ottomans feared.[28] Missionaries exacerbated those fears and feelings of sectarian difference.

Missionaries took advantage of new means of communication and travel to counter other world religions such as Islam. Proximity to Palestine and an interest in Ottoman Christians brought them to the Ottoman Empire, where the above-mentioned reforms facilitated their activities.[29] Protestant ones from Europe and the United States strengthened, for instance, confessional difference between Middle Eastern Christians, and boosted conversions to Protestantism.[30] Missionaries realised that large-scale conversion of Muslims, especially of Sunnis and Twelver Shia, with their long history, established scriptural tradition and clergy, was not possible.[31] They saw non-Sunni Muslims, especially Alawites, Alevis, Druze, Ismailis, and Yazidis, who were simultaneously targeted by missionaries dispatched from the Shii shrine cities and by Sunni missionaries despatched by the state, as easier targets for conversion.

That missionaries recognised them as different from their Sunni neighbours strengthened their group identities (in Anatolia it also spurred Armenian nationalism, for example, which in turn influenced their Alevi neighbours). Since the state did not officially recognise non-Sunni Muslims as such, they, unlike Christians, were, as discussed previously, not accorded separate representation. When some converted to Christianity to escape military service, from which Christians, due to the protections, were exempt, this led to a backlash of Sunnis and Ottoman officials against converts, and the communities they originally belonged to.[32]

The first to proselytise systematically were American Protestants, who arrived in the hinterland of Latakia in the 1830s, and then English Presbyterians and Anglicans. By the 1870s, the American Reformed Presbyterian Mission operated dozens of schools.[33] French (and to a lesser extent British) consuls intervened on behalf of Alawite leaders and in local power struggles.[34] In the nineteenth and early twentieth centuries, 'Nusayris' elicited much interest from foreign missionaries, scholars, diplomats, and Ottoman officials alike.[35] From the 1870s onwards, as the Ottomans were paying more attention to the Alawite mountains, France (and Britain) claimed special ties to Alawites and took Alawite revolts as proof that this feeling was mutual, though there was scant evidence for that.[36] Secrecy around beliefs led to speculative writings based on Sunni heresiography. Orientalists, diplomats, and missionaries promoted the notion of a fairly homogeneous and delineable 'pays des Nosairis'. These writings, and the translation of Ibn Taymiyya's fatwas against them, solidified the belief that Nusayris were distinct from and on bad terms with Sunnis.[37]

British ties with the Ismailis expanded via India. In the late nineteenth century, Syrian Ismailis travelled first to Iran and then to India to enquire about the Aga Khan, who, as noted, was strengthening ties with Ismailis around the world from his base in Bombay, and claimed to represent the true line of Ismaili Imams. Some accepted him as Imam, which heightened Ottoman suspicions, and in the 1900s Ismaili leaders were put on trial for following a foreign Imam and British subject, and not accepting the authority of the Sultan-Caliph. That the British government had unsuccessfully intervened on the Ismailis' behalf increased Ottoman wariness of links between non-Sunni Muslims and European powers.[38] The Ottomans in turn sought to bind non-Sunni Muslims closer to it, in an attempt at 'defensive unity'.

Let us look at how this played out in the Levantine provinces of the Empire with large Christian and Shii-leaning populations. After communal violence in Mount Lebanon in the 1840s, the Ottomans, under pressure from European powers, established a system of sectarian representation, and a so-called Double Governorate, one headed by a Maronite Christian and one by a Druze even though the populations under their respective control were not homogeneous. In 1861, this became a sectarian quota system, at the heart of it lay the premise that sects, especially Maronites and Druze, were like ethnic groups—allegedly ancient and unchanging—and that boundaries between them were clear-cut and conflict-prone (even though population movements, conversions, and interactions in mixed villages and regions were the norm).[39] Notable families presented themselves as natural leaders and interlocutors of 'their' communities, which they sought to delineate from others.[40] Maronite activists, historians, and clerics argued, at times, that a Christian Maronite 'nation' was seeking independence from Ottoman rule akin to Christian nationalist movements in the Balkans and Greece.[41]

But in response to the violence of 1860, for example, Butrus al-Bustani, a Maronite convert to Protestantism, argued in a series of anti-sectarian texts that love of the homeland could allow for co-existence in Greater Syria.[42] Al-Bustani and other Christian intellectuals were part of the so-called Arab 'renaissance', the *Nahda*. They emphasised the idea that all Arabic-speaking peoples had crucial things in common, and advocated a separation of religion and state.[43] Many saw themselves both as Arabs and Ottomans, embraced the Ottoman reform project and joined the schools and military institutions of the Empire, while advocating for more Arab autonomy within the Empire.[44]

Their ideas were somewhat at odds with those of Sultan Abdulhamid II, who assumed the throne in 1876 and reigned until 1909. For he embodied an even stronger centralised state around himself as Sultan-Caliph and an Ottoman identity tied more explicitly to Islam, and, especially in his later reign, authoritarianism. His reign is important for inner-Islamic relations for he tried to unite Muslims behind the Ottoman state, and was wary of external recognition of Muslim difference.[45] He oscillated between pan-Islam and a strong defence of Sunnism, which involved, for example, urging Shii-leaning communities to adopt Sunnism to prove their Ottomanness. These communities became targets of a programme to 'educate' Muslims in the correct (Sunni) beliefs, and an expanded education system that propagated pan-Islam and loyalty to the state.[46] This especially affected the Alevis of Eastern Anatolia,[47] Yazidi Kurds,[48] and Alawites.[49]

Ottoman officials also targeted Alawites in Adana, Mersin, and Antioch, in what would become the Sanjak of Alexandretta. Here, many Alawites outwardly adopted Sunnism. From 1908 onwards, the Young Turks forced Abdulhamid to reinstate the Ottoman Constitution, and embraced a more strongly Turkish ethnic national identity. This spurred Arab autonomist desires and the political opening allowed those voices to be heard in public. The Young Turks saw Alawites in Alexandretta as potentially subversive because they spoke Arabic. Still, while Ottoman policy aimed at ethnic and religious assimilation, missionaries, and European powers, emphasised Alawite difference.[50]

The reforming Ottoman state lost territory to European powers, but also sought to strengthen its grip on other territories, especially in Arabic-speaking provinces. As noted, the Ottomans had responded to the Wahhabis, who with their conquest of the Hijaz undermined the Islamic legitimation of the Ottomans, by pushing further into the Arabian Peninsula. In 1849, they established a presence on the Red Sea coast and, in 1872, took Sanaa, gaining formal control over much of Yemen (excluding Britain's enclave in the South, at Aden).[51] The Ottomans feared that the Suez Canal (opened in 1869) and Britain's presence at Aden could lead to further British gains in the Red Sea, and threaten the Hijaz, so crucial to Ottoman legitimacy. This spurred new Ottoman conquests.[52] In 1871, the Ottomans established control over al-Ahsa and Qatif alongside Kuwait and Qatar. Their rule was tenuous but facilitated stronger connections of Shii communities and tribal groups with southern Iraq just as conversions to Shiism intensified there.[53] In Kuwait, Shii merchant families that had immigrated from Iran, Eastern Arabia or Iraq were important in state formation, and allied with the al-Sabah family, who nominally ruled on behalf of the Ottomans and relied on the support of the merchants (and on a Sunni–Shia, Arab-Iranian elite pact, with some Iranians of Sunni origin, and some Arabs of Shii origin).[54]

These Ottoman conquests, and the attempt to establish aspects of the modern state in far-flung regions, led to a closer engagement with Shiism. Imperial overreach and delusion, attempts at imposing new forms of government, and a sectarian vision, led to the disastrous Ottoman occupation of Yemen.[55] Ottoman authors had long blamed the Zaydi Imams for the country's backwardness and political strife, arguing that they were opposed to Ottoman notions of government.[56] The Ottomans wanted to expand Islamic education and promote the Sultan amongst Shafiis but not amongst Zaydis because proselytising amongst Zaydis had previously increased support for the Imam.[57] A government review from December 1890, on the eve of a major uprising, advocated 'gradually removing the sect of Zaydism from the minds of children' through state-sponsored primary schools staffed with Shafii teachers from Hudayda and Taiz.[58] Not all of these plans were implemented, but Ottoman rule strengthened institutionalised Sunnism, for example by Sunnis becoming Muftis of Sanaa (a position previously held by Zaydis).

Initially, the Ottomans shrugged off overtures by claimants to the Imamate suggesting an alliance.[59] But from the 1890s onwards, a new Imam (Muhammad bin Yahya, called al-Mansur) and major tribes rebelled.[60] The rising, which was strongest in the predominantly Zaydi Northern highlands, was driven by resentment at Ottoman attempts to disempower tribal leaders and tax them, as well as widespread famine. Al-Mansur called representatives of the Ottoman government unbelievers, on the grounds that they had violated the Sharia (through judicial reforms, and by allowing alcohol consumption).[61] This was a response to the previously discussed Ottoman plans to introduce a standardised court system, the Nizamiyya courts, across the Empire, which should hear all civil and criminal cases and adjudicate from 1879 onwards according to the Ottoman's codified Hanafi law compendium, a major aspect of Ottoman reorganisation. Sharia courts were to be relegated to dealing with family and personal status law.[62] This did not work in tribally organised Shafii and Zaydi Yemen, where codified Hanafi law was seen as an anomaly, and, after a few years, Sharia courts and informal tribal arbitration resumed.[63] Struggles over the application of law became symbolic battles between the Ottoman administration and the Imams.[64]

Al-Mansur's son, Imam Yahya Muhammad Hamid al-Din, expanded the rebellion in 1904.[65] In Lower Yemen, the Ottomans had been better at co-opting local strongmen and landowners. But the rebels took Sanaa in 1905, and even though the Ottomans landed new troops they only briefly managed to retake Sanaa—at a cost of many thousands of men, a disaster that led to the slogan that Yemen is the 'graveyard of the Turks' (that slogan was later expanded to include other invaders).[66] An expedition to punish the Imam failed, and the Ottomans, faced with enormous costs, agreed to negotiate. They seemed willing to accede to some of Imam Yahya's demands, and give him some judicial and religious autonomy. But his refusal to give up the title

of Commander of the Faithful, which, as noted, implied a challenge to the
Ottoman Sultan's position as Caliph, prolonged the fight.[67] The Ottomans
argued that the Zaydi identity of the Imam and his followers drove the
rebellion, and tried to use Shafii resentment towards the Imams to limit the
latter's appeal.[68]

After the 1891/2 uprising and, again, as part of a 1907 reform project,
Ottoman officials advocated partitioning Yemen along sectarian lines. The
Ottomans thought that a Shafii province would 'naturally' be predisposed
towards them as 'fellow Sunnis' and form a bulwark against the Zaydi highlands.[69] Some, though not all, Shafiis welcomed Ottoman rule, and Shafii
teaching, tomb visitation, and Sufi gatherings, which had been curtailed
under the Imams, flourished.[70]

The 1904–7 and 1911 uprisings, combined with wider changes across the
Empire, and the rise of the Young Turks, led to a policy shift. The Ottomans,
worried about the enormous costs of their occupation of Yemen, looked to
emulate British-style informal rule.[71] And so the Treaty of Daan of 1911
empowered tribal Shaykhs and the Imam. For the first time the Ottomans
formally sanctioned Zaydi religious authority in a part of Upper Yemen.[72]
The agreement stopped short of creating a separate Zaydi province, an
Ottoman governor-general nominally retained authority and the civilian
administration remained in Ottoman hands. But the Imam could rule
according to Zaydi law in domains under his control, and over Zaydis in
other provinces.[73] He would still refer to himself as Imam and often as
Commander of the Faithful, but the Ottomans were satisfied that this
applied primarily to Zaydis and did not amount to a rival claim to the
Caliphate.[74] The Ottomans retained control of majority Shafii areas.[75] In
Yemen, as elsewhere, sectarian identity, whose relevance grew as the state
tried to exercise more direct control, was becoming a way of articulating
political claims, and of dividing and ruling diverse populations.

The Ottomans' approach to Twelver Shiism, and Iran, was likewise transformed profoundly, in more ways than one. Instead of seeing Shiism only as
a threat, Ottoman officials started seeing it as an opportunity, both to reach
Sunni–Shia unity in the Empire and a rapprochement with Iran. This was a
major change from the tense Ottoman–Iranian relations of old. Iran faced
challenges similar to the Ottoman Empire. A series of military defeats had
also made the need for military reform plain. When the Qajars had come
to power in the late eighteenth century, the Ottomans initially refused to

recognise them as independent Muslim rulers because they would not accept the pre-eminence of the Ottoman Sultan-Caliph. But after Russia fought against both in the early nineteenth century, the two sides fraternised. Yet, the Ottomans then signed a peace treaty with Russia. This allowed Russia to focus on Iran and 'liberate' what it called oppressed Christian communities in the Caucasus, in the territories of later Armenia and Georgia. Its open advocation of Christian solidarity, furthered the connection between confessional identity and the self-understanding and foreign policy in the Muslim Empires. As a result of these territorial losses, Iran's population became less diverse, and more Shii, and Shii clerics legitimised the Qajars' declaration of defensive Jihad against Russia.[76] In turn, this Ottoman 'betrayal', as the Iranians saw it, led to the Ottoman-Qajar war of 1821–3, which the highest Ottoman cleric legitimised by arguing that the Iranians were apostates. But the 1823 Erzurum treaty ending those hostilities was the first to no longer emphasise sectarian division.[77]

Some Qajars, such as Crown Prince Abbas Mirza, who had been governor of Azerbaijan, and general in charge of the war with Russia, came away from this experience believing that better relations with the Ottomans, and Sunni–Shia unity, alongside military reform, were paramount.[78] In diplomatic negotiations, including in the lead up to the 1823 treaty, Iran asked for an end to the Ottoman ban on Sunni–Shia marriage; that Shii testimony in Ottoman courts, which was at times seen as less trustworthy, should be equal to that of Sunnis, and that disputes between Shia in Ottoman territory should be heard in a Shii court. The first two concerns were accommodated, but not the last, which would have constituted a protection akin to that granted to European powers, and the expansion of which to Muslims the Ottomans sought to avoid at all costs (the Ottomans cited fears that Iranian Shia would curse the Caliphs with impunity as a reason for refusal).[79]

After making peace with the Ottomans, Iran again turned on Russia. Russia had occupied not just Christian-inhabited areas of Georgia and Armenia, but also in what is now the Republic of Azerbaijan, where Shia appealed to Iran for help. Shii clerics pushed the Qajars towards a new war. The Qajars, too, had recently reorganised their army along European lines, but even that army was no match for the Russian one, and was routed. Iran had to sign the 1828 treaty of Torkmanchay which confirmed Iran's territorial losses of the 1813 Treaty of Golestan, and permanently placed the Caucasus—much of present-day Georgia, Armenia, and Azerbaijan—under Russian control. Iran lost up to a fifth of its revenue, and a tenth of its population and territory, and became indebted to Russia. The victorious Russian army even carried away artefacts from the shrine of Shaykh Safi, founder of the Safavid dynasty, in Ardabil. Russia insisted on a population transfer, and so some Armenian Christians moved from Iran to the Caucasus, and some Shia from the Caucasus to Iranian Azerbaijan.[80]

This was followed by the establishing of a harder border between Russia, Iran, and the Ottoman Empire, which led to more exclusive senses of belonging tied to a dominant ethnic and religious identity. This posed a dilemma for people along the border, who had to choose on which side their loyalties lay, and made states wary of cross-border connections. The Russians suppressed the influence of Iranian Shii clerics amongst Shia, and Turkish Sunni ones amongst Sunnis in the Caucasus. Secularising Shii intellectuals then sought to repress Shii rituals, and saw a sect-centric Shii identity and Sunni–Shia division as obstacles to be overcome amidst a rise of secularism, pan-Islam, and pan-Turkism.[81]

A harder Ottoman-Iranian border problematised the situation of Kurdish tribal communities and Iranian pilgrims and scholars in the shrine cities. When an international commission led by Britain and Russia surveyed the border in the 1850s and 1860s, Ottoman officials urged Sunnis along the border to declare loyalty to the Sultan and claimed 'ownership' of territories inhabited by Sunni Kurds, claims that were largely rejected by the commission, locals, and Iran, but would occupy the Ottoman imagination (and were invoked to seize said territories in 1905–11).[82] The border delineation indicated the new self-understanding of the modernising states.

Qajar reforms paled in comparison to Ottoman ones. The Qajars had a small central administration, and struggled to keep their country under control (some provinces were defying central authority for long periods). They brought in some Europeans to reorganise the state, especially the army, from where the man that would eventually overthrow the Qajars in 1925, would come.[83] But in essence, the Qajars relied on the selling of taxation rights for their income, and notables and the clergy wielded much power.[84]

The Ottomans undermined the Qajars' ambitions as protectors of global Shiism by, for example, limiting Iranian influence in Iraq. Here, the long-standing ambiguous policy towards Shiism was in the nineteenth century challenged by mass conversions to Shiism, some of which had been set in motion, like the rebellion in Yemen, by the Ottomans' own policies. The Ottomans initially used a mix of repression, counter-propaganda, and support of Sunnism, to try and contain the Shii wave. The antagonism was heightened by an Ottoman reliance on urban elites, and a mistrust of rural Shii tribesmen and Shia in the shrine cities, towards these urban elites and the state. Abdulhamid brought young Shia from Iraq to study in Istanbul to convert them to Sunnism, and, when he heard of Shii influence in the army, purged Shii soldiers or relocated them.[85] Ottoman officials recommended expanding Sunni education in Iraq, blaming Iranian and Indian patronage, and Sunni proselytisation for Shiism's success. They also argued that many were unaware of doctrinal minutiae, and thus easily swayed.[86] Iraqi Sunnis pushed the state to counter the conversions and so it appointed Sunni preachers in Shii areas and gave the head of the Naqshbandi-Khalidi lodge in Baghdad the funds to build a college in Samarra. Sufism, with its long history in Iraq and many important shrines, was supposed to counter Shiism and Salafism. Most were staunchly Sunni orders but some who had affinities to Shiism were also used to bind Shia closer to the state.[87] The Naqshbandis, supported across the Empire, became vehicles through which an Islamic identity, and the commercial interests of small merchants and urban notables against European economic penetration and political reforms, were expressed.[88]

The state also tightened control of Alid guilds, historically bases of Shii support.[89] When Shii pamphlets gained traction across the Empire, Shii books could be banned.[90] And the Ottomans ensured that only government-sanctioned presses printed copies of the Quran, and confiscated Qurans printed in Iran (and other areas such as Russia or Egypt) for fear they could undermine the state's religious authority (even though, as noted, their text was the same).[91] Ironically, after Ottoman sedentarisation policies had driven tribesmen to convert to Shiism, the taking over of endowments as part of centralising reforms undermined local Sunni religious institutions.[92]

When these measures failed, the Ottomans reached out to Shia. The idea of Muslim unity had of course been around for some time (think of Nadir Shah's Najaf conference in the mid-eighteenth century). In the late nineteenth century, it gained renewed traction, and was advocated by intellectuals and activists like Jamal al-Din al-Afghani (1839–97). He had advocated pan-Islam since the late 1870s and sought to win over Muslim rulers to his cause, an alliance between the three still more or less independent Muslim countries—the Ottoman Empire, Iran, and Afghanistan, an alliance for which Sunni–Shia unity was imperative.[93]

Al-Afghani, 'the Afghan', knew what he was talking about. He was an energetic political activist and publicist and throughout his life he claimed to be from Afghanistan, and to be a Sunni. But he was born in Iran and was probably originally Shii, and may have changed his identity because he thought that being from Iran would damage his ambition to become the figurehead of pan-Islam.[94] Indeed, while Afghanistan was trying to build a stronger state, and reform the judicial system with the help of Hanafi scholars from the Ottoman Empire and the Indian subcontinent, Amir Abd al-Rahman Khan and his government at times invoked Sunni–Shia unity (although, as noted, he would also embark on a bloody anti-Shii campaign). In 1886, for example, he commanded the Qajar governor of Mashhad for limiting festivities in the city celebrating the death of the commander of the forces that killed Hussain at Karbala, and emphasised the need for Sunni–Shia unity.[95]

Al-Afghani convinced Sultan Abdulhamid that pan-Islam could strengthen Muslim and Ottoman resolve against Russia and Britain, and lead to closer Ottoman–Iranian ties.[96] In 1892, the Sultan invited al-Afghani to Istanbul to work towards Sunni–Shia unity and gather the senior Shii clerics of the Empire.[97] Sultan Abdulhamid wrote in his memoirs:

> Islam must work toward the end of reinforcing its bonds. It would discover great profit were the Muslims found in China, India, Central Africa, and in the entire world to draw near one another. It is regrettable that we have not managed to reach entire agreement with Iran on this point. Moreover, we have every interest in drawing nearer so as to put an end to the games of the Russians and the British. In my palace at Yildiz, a celebrated man of science, Sayyid Jamal al-Din, gave me hope when he said, 'it is possible for the Sunnis to unite with the Shia to the extent that the former stand ready to prove their good will.' If what he told me can prove true, this would be of exceptional interest for Islam. The ambassador of Iran at Istanbul, Haji Mirza Khan, promised me his help in guiding this vast enterprise to a good conclusion. Jamal al-Din rallied certain ulama in Iran, in the same manner that he attracted to himself a number of high functionaries. Thus, if it is possible to arrive at a total accord with regard to the envisioned goal, a great step will have been taken and the two states will be much closer.[98]

Pan-Islamism gained traction amongst Ottoman officials, some former diplomats in Iran, and amongst Iranian exiles in Istanbul. They published about Sunni–Shia unity and argued, for example, that the split had been fostered by selfish rulers and not been in the interest of the earliest Muslims, and that neither Abu Bakr nor Ali would have approved of it (they focused on Ali as the fourth Sunni Caliph and first Shii Imam as a unifying figure).[99] Some blamed Ottomans and Safavids for having manufactured Sunni–Shia animosity to legitimise expansionist policies.[100]

After the many wars with Iran, and the assertiveness of the Empire's Shii subjects, a rapprochement with Shiism, and Iran, made sense. Even Cevdet Pasha (1823–95), the famous Ottoman statesman, former Ottoman justice minister and scholar, known for his strong stance against Bektashism and Alevism, who had praised the repression of the Janissaries, now argued that Sunni–Shia unity was needed to counter European-Christian influence. He thought it could be achieved by repairing the tombs of the *Ahl al-Bayt* in Medina and the shrines of Iraq, places important to Sunnism and Shiism, and by winning over Shii scholars to Sunnism and the Sultan.[101] Ottoman reformers with an Islamist bent advocated Sunni–Shia dialogue, while remaining doctrinally rigid and railing against groups seen as outside of the Twelver Shii mainstream, such as Bektashis, Alevis, and Ismailis.[102]

Ottoman officials hoped that a rapprochement with Shii clerics in Iraq would give them leverage in Iran and prevent the Shii clerics from being susceptible to influence from Iran and Britain. The Ottomans, for example, perceived Sunni–Shia unrest in Samarra in 1894 as inspired by Iran and when the British Consul in Baghdad sought to visit Samarra to ensure the safety of Indian Shii students there, suspected it to be an attempt to extend British protection to Shii clerics (Britain, as noted, claimed to have a say in Shii affairs and the shrine cities because of its rule over Shii populations in India and managing of the Oudh Bequest).[103] The same year, the group around al-Afghani wrote to Shii clerics in India, Iran, Iraq, and Central Asia, urging them to support pan-Islam and accept the Sultan's authority, in return for a stipend.[104]

Shiism was accorded more visibility across the Empire. The Ottomans redoubled efforts to patronise *Ahl al-Bayt* shrines in Iraq, the Hijaz, and Syria, and continued to facilitate (but also regulate and tax) pilgrimage to Najaf and Karbala.[105] They allowed large Ashura and Muharram processions in Iraq and in other parts of the Empire, such as in Cairo and Istanbul, where Iranian and Arab Shia, and Bektashis, worshipped together.[106] So popular were the processions in Istanbul that they were even included in the first European tourist guides on Istanbul. European travellers and early Orientalists visited them, for many a first encounter with Shii rituals.[107] Shii mosques and community centres operated openly in Istanbul.[108] Shii clerics oscillated between suspicion that the purifying ambitions of Sunni Revivalists and modernists would target them, and an embracing of pan-Islam under the leadership of the (Sunni) Sultan-Caliph.[109] While the growing acceptance of Shiism led to better relations with Shii clerics in Iraq, it did not significantly improve relations with Iran.

The Ottomans had, for example, grown wary of Iranian patronage for the shrine cities, and preferred to patronise them themselves.[110] They implemented checks at the Ottoman-Iranian border, and quarantined pilgrims from Iran, Russia, and India, arguing that they, and nomads straddling the border, constituted health hazards. Couched in the language of public health and modern administration, they sought to limit traffic from Iran, making the Ottoman-Iranian border harder.[111] They also enforced a longstanding policy prohibiting the marriage between Ottoman women and Iranian men (both Sunni and Shii), and tried to limit the ability of Iranian subjects to buy property around the shrine cities.[112]

The exiles in Istanbul, and some of the Shii clerics in Iraq, were major critics of Nasir al-Din Shah Qajar, who reigned since 1848, and who they saw as out of touch, despotic, and authoritarian, and blamed for the increasing European penetration and economic crisis. The exiles started advocating constitutional rule, and that some of them were dissident relatives of his made the Shah even more suspicious of where this was all heading.[113] In the so-called Tobacco Rebellion of 1891–2 this network outed the Shah as an autocrat subservient to foreign interests. Grand Ayatollah Muhammad Hasan Shirazi, who resided in Samarra, demonstrated the power of the clergy when his fatwa led ordinary Iranians to stop smoking tobacco in order to force the revocation of a concession sold to an English merchant.[114] While that show of force was not lost on the Ottomans, and may have been a reason for Abdulhamid's reaching out to Shii clerics, it made the Shah wary of the clergy and the exiled dissidents.[115] The two major nodes of the network on the Shii side, the exiles and the clerics, were thus outspokenly anti-Shah— hardly a recipe for diplomatic success.

Moreover, they had quarrels of their own, for some of the exiles were inclined towards Shii mystical movements that had been at loggerheads with the clergy, or were members of masonic lodges.[116] And the more the activities of this eclectic group increased, the more anxious the Shah grew about the Sultan's relationship with what he saw as a group of dissidents bent on undermining him.[117] The Sultan, who wanted to be accepted as leader of all Muslims, and the Shah, whose realm stood between the Ottoman Empire and the Muslims of Central and South Asia and who had little to gain and much to lose from having Shia submit to the authority of the

Sultan, failed to come to an agreement.[118] When a disciple of al-Afghani assassinated the Shah in 1896 the Ottomans arrested and extradited some of al-Afghani's confidants. Al-Afghani's direct involvement could not be established and the Ottomans refused to hand him over, but he remained under house arrest in Istanbul until his death the following year.[119] In the eighteenth century the Ottomans had rebuffed Nadir Shah's proposal for fear of undermining their own position and boosting Nadir Shah's standing. Now it was a Shah, who refused to endorse a project he saw as asserting Ottoman supremacy, and undermining his own.

The Qajars and the Shii clergy were increasingly at loggerheads. This culminated in the Constitutional Revolution in Iran from 1905 to 1911, in which Shii clerics played a key role, leading to the establishment of a short-lived parliament in the summer of 1906 to check the authority of the Shah. (The constitution had been ratified by Nasir al-Din's son and successor Muzaffar al-Din Shah, but when he died shortly after doing so in 1906, his successor disregarded it, leading to a political standoff that was resolved when the constitutionalists marched in Tehran, and the eleven year old Ahmad was declared Shah. He would be the last of the Qajar Shahs.)[120] The Qajars were naturally not pleased with that political role of the Iraq-based Shii clergy, but neither was Russia, which complained to the Ottomans about the Shii clergy's correspondence with Shia in Central Asia and the Caucasus.[121]

This highlighted the increased power and global connections of the Shii clerics and coincided with a renaissance in Shii learned society, with the shrine cities acting as a focal point for Shii reformists. They reacted to challenges from within (the Akhbari–Usuli rivalry and the challenge of mystical movements) and from without (Wahhabism, Ottoman reassertion, and, later, Empire and secular ideologies). This strengthened ties between Shia from Jabal Amil, Syria, the Gulf, Central Asia, and India with Iran and the shrine cities in Iraq, where the clergy became more hierarchically organised and better connected globally. Lay intellectuals worked with clerics to found new publications and institutions and establish a pan-Shii public sphere in which reformist ideas spread, and in which clerics could reinvent themselves for the modern age.[122] Pan-Islam was a stated goal of these Shii reformists, but they also forged a new Shii self-consciousness.

Print media and faster communication and travel spurred this Shii revival, alongside pan-Islamic, pan-Arab, and pan-Turkic senses of togetherness.[123] In the twentieth century, one strand of Arab nationalism would put its hopes in the Arab Revolt in World War I, and in Amir Faisal and the idea of a

United Arab Kingdom with its capital at Damascus. Another embraced Greater Syrian nationalism, or other localised versions of country-specific Arab nationalism, as I will show below. The tensions between these different approaches, and the different variants of Arab nationalism could be fierce, however. Others still, especially Maronites and Druze, advocated sect-centric local collective identities. But few Arab Sunnis would have thought of organising as Sunnis at this stage (seeing themselves part of larger, Ottoman, Arab, and Islamic wholes), and few Arab Shia initially made such claims.[124]

During the war, the Ottomans allied with Germany, not least because Britain, France, and Russia had so persistently interfered in the Empire and annexed parts of it. German Orientalists were thrilled by the alliance with the de facto spiritual head of Sunnism, and pushed the Ottoman Sultan-Caliph to declare a Jihad against Allied Powers. Just to be on the safe side, the Germans also sought the support of senior Shii clerics in Najaf, who reiterated Sunni–Shia unity in their fatwas.[125] Some Indian Muslims in the British army refused to fight the Ottomans, and in India, pro-Ottoman Caliphate feelings were galvanised by the Khilafat movement. But overall, the Jihad failed to spur a Muslim revolt in the colonial territories of the Allies. Most Indian Muslim elites, especially Shii ones like the Aga Khan, declared loyalty to the British (after the Government of India had assured them that the Holy places in the Hijaz and Iraq would not be attacked).[126]

At the start of the war, a newly formed Arab Bureau coordinated British Middle East policy and devised a plan for an Arab Revolt in the Ottoman Empire, Britain's counterpart to the *Jihad Made in Germany*. The British published articles on Ottoman anti-Shii activities in Najaf and Karbala and Sunni Arab anti-Ottoman leaders such as Ibn Saud and the Hashemite Sharif of Mecca, Hussein bin Ali, became valuable allies.[127] The revolt, nominally led by the Sharif of Mecca, started in early 1916. In return, Sharif Hussein was promised a United Arab Kingdom.[128] Britain and France then divided the Ottoman Empire between themselves under the Sykes-Picot Agreement, a secret treaty drawn up in early 1916, and subsequent treaties, which paved the way for Britain and France to assume direct control of the Arab East. The Ottoman defeat meant that after the war, its territories outside of what would become Turkey were divided between France and Britain.

According to the Sykes-Picot agreement, Syria and Mosul were to come under French control; Transjordan and central and southern Iraq under British control. The promises to the Arabs and the secret agreements contradicted one another. Arab hopes were high when Faisal, a son of Sharif Hussein, entered Damascus in October 1918, shortly after its capture by British troops, and declared an independent Arab government with the permission of British General Allenby. But the declaration of an Arab Kingdom on the back of the British Army raised French fears that the British were undermining the agreement. On the British side, there were Arabists, who had cooperated with the Hashemites and wanted to keep their promises. And there were those advocating direct rule and full incorporation into the British Empire. However, direct imperial rule was increasingly seen as a remnant of the past, including by that new world power that had proven so decisive to the war's outcome, the United States. And so a different sort of arrangement was found.

The notion that the peoples of the Middle East constituted a religious and ethnic mosaic unable to govern themselves, as the predominance of one group could lead to repression of others, and the pattern established through the interplay of local elites and informants, Orientalists, missionaries, colonial officials, and reforming Ottoman ones, of turning the identities of religious groups into something fixed and inherently political, served as the blueprint for the transformation of the Ottoman Empire's Arab provinces after World War I.

9

The Mandates

On a formal level, the Paris Peace Conference in Versailles 1919/20 lay the foundation for the post-war global order, and the reorganisation of the Middle East. Faisal, who attended the conference in 1919, was not granted recognition for the Arab Kingdom. But neither were the former provinces of the Empire simply annexed by the victorious European powers, as some in Britain and France had hoped. This was in part because the United States under Woodrow Wilson sought to reorder the world along national lines (spurred by the fear that Empire boosted the message of the other new global power, Bolshevik Russia, and its different vision of self-determination promoted by Lenin).[1] Still, France and Britain would gain control of those territories, and the ways in which they saw the populations that came under their rule, and recognised sectarian difference, developed largely over the preceding century, now shaped their policies, even if they would draw different conclusions from it.

The delegates to Versailles set up the League of Nations in Geneva and, as part of it, a mandate system to administer the former territories of the Ottoman and German Empires through a guardian power to prepare them for independent statehood. It was a compromise between old and emerging powers, and advocates of decolonisation that would recast and measure the collective identities of peoples in the region in new ways.[2] Upon returning from the Paris Peace Conference, Faisal called elections for a Syrian Arab Congress in May 1919, which was to meet with a delegation sent by Woodrow Wilson. Elected representatives from across Greater Syria demanded full independence and opposed the division into smaller states in a meeting with the King-Crane Commission on 3 July. The American King-Crane Commission enquired about aspirations for statehood. But without being able to deliver on its promises, the commission raised hopes and then disappointed many.[3]

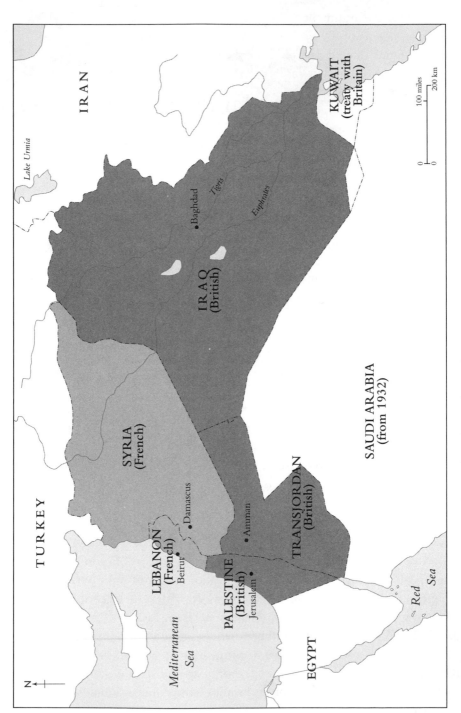

8. The post-Ottoman Middle East with British and French mandates, 1920s

To bolster the argument that Arabs were able to rule themselves according to the norms of the post-World War I international system, the Syrian Arab Congress drafted a constitution in March 1920, which specified the king to be a Muslim, but included commitments to freedom of religion. Rashid Rida, a well-known Sunni cleric, who was elected to the Congress as representative of Tripoli and in 1920 briefly became its President, signed off on the institutionalisation of religious difference and a largely secular 'liberal' constitution. It included provisions for each religious community to organise personal status law, pious endowments, and a council for the community. For every 40,000 citizens of a minority, one seat would be reserved in the House of Deputies. Islamic law was not stipulated as the main source of legislation.[4] Faisal's administration put in place a rudimentary state. Emotions were running high, as developments on the ground, and in diplomatic circles, increasingly diverged. Faisal's appeal was strongest in the region from Palestine to Alexandretta and from Beirut to Deir al-Zur, which in Arabic is called *Bilad al-Sham,* the Lands of Syria. The long-standing cultural affinity in this region had intensified in the late nineteenth century, and his administration then served as a catalyst for Syrian Arab nationalism.[5] But the French, wary of Britain's position and concerned that Arabic-speaking Christians of Mount Lebanon could ally with Faisal, would not tolerate an independent Arab Kingdom.[6]

French policy was shaped by its earlier engagement with the region. French Orientalists and officials had long invoked cultural difference to rule Muslim populations in North Africa. They highlighted the distinctiveness of 'Moroccan Islam' or 'Tunisian Islam', played up intra-Sunni and Berber-Arab divisions and portrayed Ibadis in Tunisia and Algeria as inherently different from other Muslims. Similarly, in the Levant, France ruled by emphasising ethno-sectarian difference. France clearly sided with the region's Christians, and advocated an alliance with non-Sunni Muslims. The latter was not a foregone conclusion, however.[7] Some in France advocated a slow withdrawal from the colonies and an internationalism not unlike that of Wilson, and Arabists such as Louis Massignon (1883–1962), one of the founding figures of French Orientalism, sympathised with Faisal. In his scholarship, he had defended the orthodoxy of Sunnism and the virtue of Sunni Sufism over Shiism. For him, Shiism and sectarianism had led the Islamic world astray and undermined Islam's unitary potential.[8] Massignon, who had converted to Islam during an earlier trip to Iraq, saw in Faisal an ideal representative of the Arabs and wanted France to honour war-time commitments and support both Sunnis and Christians. Massignon was involved in negotiating an agreement between Faisal and French Prime Minister Georges Clemenceau at the Paris Peace Conference in which France would recognise Syrian independence in return for acceptance of a less-intrusive French Mandate. But in January 1920, Clemenceau lost the elections, and the conservatives that won dismantled the agreement, and built a different sort of mandate.

Robert De Caix, France's other main negotiator, who had initially lost out to Massignon, was empowered by Clemenceau's defeat. De Caix was a former editor at one of France's main colonial reviews, *L'Asie française*, and a leader of the so-called *parti colonial*, which vowed to re-establish France's global position and incorporate new colonies. He argued that the best way to safeguard French interests in the Levant was work with non-Sunni communities and establish small states that would not challenge French dominance. He saw the large Arab state advocated by Faisal as a threat, not least to French colonies in North Africa, where Arabs could be drawn to an independent Arab Kingdom. Through relentless campaigning and by playing on French fears of losing out to Britain, De Caix succeeded to turn his vision into the basis for policy in the French Mandate for Syria and Lebanon.[9] While many Christians embraced the prospect of a French Mandate, others looked to Faisal, as did many Shia and Druze. Faisal galvanised emotions amongst Arabic-speaking peoples of different faiths. Despite being a Sunni monarch with much support amongst Sunni Arabs, Faisal was not exclusionary, and his administration pluralist.[10]

The San Remo Conference in April 1920 decided the future of the Ottoman provinces, and ended hopes for quick Arab independence. Britain and France were given mandates to formally administer the former territories of the Ottoman Empire that would not become Turkey, France the mandate for Lebanon, Syria, and Alexandretta, and Britain that for Mesopotamia (later Iraq) and Palestine (later Palestine and Transjordan).[11] In the face of overwhelming military might and abandoned by his British wartime allies, Faisal capitulated. Some of his military leaders refused to do so, however, and were in turn routed by the French forces at the Battle of Maysalun on 24 July 1920. That traumatic defeat became a point of reference for Syrian and Arab nationalism.[12]

On 25 July 1920, French troops entered Damascus and Faisal left for the UK. British officials then put him forward as 'candidate' for the Kingship of another state: Iraq. Faisal was going to gain a country and a crown after all, though not the one he had originally intended. Some of his aides joined him, while others went to Cairo, where they worked with the Syro-Palestinian Congress that continued to advocate the ecumenical ideal of Arab nationalism. Funded by a Lebanese Christian émigré, with the Christian Michel Lutfallah as President, the Sunni cleric Rashid Rida as Vice President, and Shakib Arslan, a Druze leader, its Secretary, the Congress lobbied the mandate administration in Geneva to grant the Arabs independence. Its representatives abroad saw themselves as Arabs first and not as representative of a particular religious community (and Shakib Arslan is indeed primarily known for advocating pan-Islam alongside Arabism). Shakib Arslan would become Arab nationalism's most prominent promoter in Europe and at the League of Nations in coming years (his Druze identity was never an issue, a testament to the anti-sectarianism of Arab nationalism at the time). In Geneva, however, they faced the better organised Zionists, who prevailed.[13] In Palestine, Britain would back Zionist immigration, adding yet another ethno-religious nationalist movement to the region, which fit the view of the Middle East as a 'mosaic', and further entrenched it. This undermined the cosmopolitan spirit of Arab nationalism and contributed to its transformation into a more exclusivist ethnic nationalism associated with the legacies and lived experiences of Sunni Arabs, that defined itself more and more against Zionism.[14]

The communalist vision of the region was now firmly established. In Iraq, the location of the original Sunni–Shia split, the shrines of the Imams, the seat of the most senior Shii clerics, and large Sunni and Shii populations, British policy was shaped by the experience of the war and Empire, and the view of Sunni supremacism. As discussed, British Orientalists and officials considered the Sunni view of history as the standard version. Long engagement with Shiism in India, Iraq, Iran, and Bahrain, as well as with 'heterodox' movements such as the Druze, Ismailis, Alawites, and Alevis meant, however, that Shii-leaning movements were not unknown in Britain either. As shown, these groups, like the Christians, now came to be seen as separate communities. This view of religious difference and group cohesion was consequential, even if Britain and France would draw different conclusions from it. As British troops occupied Iraq during the war, an ad hoc administration modelled on British India was put in place. Britain had issued a wartime declaration ensuring the safety of the holy places in Iraq (to reassure

Indian Shia and Iran).[15] After the capture of Baghdad by British forces in March 1917, the shrine cities were to become enclaves not under direct British rule, though that view quickly changed.[16] Initially, Sir Arnold Wilson sought to institutionalise an equal representation of Sunnis and Shia. He claimed that, unlike under Sunni rule, when Shia were referred to as 'sectaries', '[a]t the hands of the British Government Shiism is entitled on historical grounds to equal treatment with Sunnism instead of being regarded as a sect'.[17]

The British officials who built Iraq and saw and institutionalised Sunnism and Shiism separately were influenced by their experience in India, and by the separate rituals and processions they witnessed in Iraq.[18] They established separate judicial systems and religious classes in government schools for Sunnis and Shia based on Indian precedents. Anglo-Muhammadan law regulated most cases, but for personal status law cases involving a Muslim party Islamic law could be used by a 'native jurist' regarded by the people as a religious leader. While Sharia courts were, following Ottoman practice, primarily staffed by Sunni clerics, Shia could seek adjudication according to Shii law, and Shii jurists were officially employed, too (though the final decision had to be approved by a British judge).[19] In the Department of Education, confessionally separate religious classes were introduced (it would later be headed by a Shii minister).[20] The administration argued that the Ottomans had treated Sunnis preferentially when it came to religious endowments and projects, and the collection of taxes, including on Shii burials near shrines, and sought to redress this. The taxes that had hitherto been levied on Shii burials near the shrines were now used for the upkeep of those shrines. The British started to hold Sunni and Shii endowment accounts separately, without, however, institutionalising a separate Shii endowments department.[21] But why, given its long engagement with Shiism and the senior clerics in Najaf and Karbala, would Britain eventually build the Iraqi state largely with Sunnis, and leave a legacy of Sunni supremacism behind?

The answer is multi-facetted. In the post-war global order, dominated by Woodrow Wilson's emphasis on national self-determination, the mandates were supposed to amount to nation-building. Iraq was shaped by British officials, but with a local, 'native' government and head of state. In Iraq, the cheaper option of building a state with an Arab figurehead, favoured by the Arabists, won out over those advocating Indian-style direct rule.[22] British officials claimed to break with the Ottoman past and to create a modern state with representation of all parties, but it was built on the foundations of the old, Sunni-led administration, largely excluding the Shia. While British officials initially hoped to find some support amongst Shii clerics,[23] antipathy soon went both ways.[24]

As noted, some senior Shii clerics had supported the pro-Ottoman and anti-British Jihad during the war, but the most influential one, Ayatollah Yazdi, had not. Many Shia who had signed up with the Ottomans deserted after the first battles, and Ottoman conscription and heavy-handed tactics alienated many, leading to anti-Ottoman uprisings. In Najaf and Karbala, townspeople ousted the Ottomans and established self-governing regimes—without, however, becoming pro-British.[25] The Shii clerics' desire for independence made them suspicious of Britain. They had observed Britain expand its influence in Iran, and worried it would do the same in Iraq, and interfere with the finances and activities of the shrine cities.[26] In October 1917, the assassination of a British captain started off a major uprising in Najaf led by Shii clerics and tribal leaders. Initially focusing on local demands, the uprising's leaders soon demanded independence. In response, the British Army blockaded Najaf and hanged men deemed responsible in May 1918. This soured relations between the British and Najaf. Iran tried to intervene, as did some British officials in India, who worried pan-Shii feelings of solidarity might cause them trouble.[27]

The British administration also developed closer connections with Sunni tribal confederations such as the Unayza, and gave them preferential treatment over the Shii clerics, leading to even more tensions with the latter.[28] British officials saw urban areas, including Najaf and Karbala, as hotbeds of nationalist revolt and Shii clerics as 'troublesome' town-dwellers in contrast with the allegedly 'noble' tribal leaders of the countryside.[29] One of the most senior clerics from Karbala, Mirza Muhammad Taqi al-Shirazi, endorsed armed resistance that culminated in a major revolt in 1920.[30] Most of the fighting was done by Shii tribes in the south. But Sunnis also supported the uprising and Sunni–Shia religious and political meetings were held in mosques across Iraq. The Shii notable Jafar Abu al-Timman and his National Party fostered Sunni–Shia unity against the British (and his party in turn closed in 1922 and he exiled).[31] A poem by the Iraqi poet and Sunni Mufti of Mosul, Muhammad Habib al-Ubaydi, to overcome sectarian affiliation in the face of Empire, resonated widely:

> Do not talk of a Jafari or Hanafi
> Do not talk of a Shafii or Zaydi
> For the Sharia of Muhammad has united us
> And it rejects the Western mandate.[32]

British officials instead described Sunni–Shia cooperation directed against them as 'religious fanaticism'.[33] The 1920 revolt cemented British suspicions towards the Shia and was harshly suppressed.[34] Thereafter, British officials worked with the ex-Ottoman administrative and military elites, circles around Faisal, notables and tribal leaders, excluding the Shii clerics and the masses from power.[35] This was a continuation of Ottoman practice, which had largely relied on Sunni notables and elite bureaucrats.[36]

By 1920, Gertrude Bell, the famous Arabist who would become Oriental Secretary in Iraq, and played a crucial role in its creation, wrote that 'The Shi'ah problem is probably the most formidable in this country.' According to Bell, the Ottomans hadn't made use of a single Shia deputy and argued that unless power remained in the hands of the Sunnis 'you will have a mujtahid-run, theocratic state, which is the very devil'.[37] Bell and other British officials described the *mujtahids*, the most senior Shii clerics, as 'Persian' and an alien force, and as hindering the development of a modern Iraqi state and the integration of Shia into that state.[38] Their views were influenced by the old Sunni families of Baghdad, with whom they socialised.[39] Under the monarchy, many large landowners and urban notables were Sunnis, and controlled large parts of the economy. The social elite of Baghdad, too, was largely Sunni, as was the officer class, while the rank-and-file were largely Shii. In the cities, this domination was a legacy of Ottoman rule, which had relied on Sunni elites, and in the countryside by a certain dominance of Sunni tribes over Shii tribal peasants.[40] In time, British policies also empowered a group of Shii tribal Shaykhs and landowners. Yet, the 1920 revolt, which coincided with Faisal's arrival in Iraq from Syria, solidified the British turn towards Sunni elites, and towards Faisal, who was put forward as King of Iraq in late 1920/ early 1921. There remained the question of Iraq's precise borders.

Under the Sykes–Picot Agreement, Mosul came under the French sphere of influence. But in return for British withdrawal from Syria and the recognition of French interests, France gave up that claim to Mosul and was instead given a stake in a new oil company that was to explore oil reserves there.[41] These economic concerns coincided nicely (in the view of British officials) with political ones. Mosul and the largely Kurdish-inhabited areas in what would become Northern Iraq, where most of the population was Sunni (alongside Christian, Shii, Yazidi, and Ahl-e Haqq communities), were included in Iraq (rather than in Syria, or given autonomy). This was done partly to add more Sunnis to Iraq (something Faisal had allegedly lobbied for, fearing that without it elections 'would place Shia in a very strong position', a prospect that 'filled him with misgivings').[42] With Sunnis in charge and oil income from Mosul, British officials saw Iraq as a viable venture that could pay for itself. British officials that had lived in India and Cairo tried to give Iraq an Arab identity, even though a significant part of its population was Kurdish, and side-line the Shii clerics that many Shia saw as leaders, and then implant a King that had just been driven out of Syria but was originally from the Hijaz. For all the talk about authenticity, and Faisal's personal charisma and popularity, it was an endeavour built on shaky foundations.

While many Sunnis were quick to embrace the state as a way for personal advancement, the rupture between the British and the Shii elites was such that the Shii clergy banned Shia from state employment, seeing the state as illegitimate but above all protesting against Shii marginalisation.[43] Sunni dominance was a continuation of Ottoman practice, a product of British machinations and the legacy of Shii resistance. Shia had been discouraged by the Ottomans and community leaders from attending Ottoman schools. That there were few formally educated Shia now contributed to their underrepresentation.[44] Shii tribal chiefs opposed conscription for a national army because they feared Shii tribesmen would be recruited as foot soldiers serving Sunni officers. After more than a decade of political deadlock, a National Service Bill was passed in 1934, leading many Shia to enlist, though the officer corps remained largely Sunni (many of whom had served in the Ottoman army).[45] Britain would establish special army contingents of ethnic and religious minorities, a practice that would lead to a confessionalised view of repression, and mirror French practices in Syria.[46]

In theory, Faisal could have been a unifying figure. That he was a Hashemite, descendant of the *Ahl al-Bayt*, left a deep impression on British officials, who thought that this might make him acceptable to the Shia of Iraq.[47] The pedigree of the Hashemite family, who centuries ago had been Zaydi Shia, and ruled Mecca and Medina, was respected amongst large sections of the Arab Muslim East that had not yet come under the influence of their archenemies, the Al Saud and the Wahhabis.[48] Some Shia corresponded with Faisal when he was in Damascus and supported his campaign for the Iraqi throne, and Faisal met with Shii clerics in Iraq.[49]

He symbolically scheduled his inauguration ceremony on a Shii holiday in August 1921 and visited Shii processions, though his advisors were shocked that Shii actors associated the new Iraqi flag with the killers of Hussain rather than with Hussain himself.[50] Shii leaders hoped that the

Hashemites, under pressure by the Al Saud in the Hijaz, would be amenable to Shii interests and check the advance of the Wahhabis. When the Saudi tribal militia raided southern Iraq in 1922, the clerics organised a conference in Karbala to establish a Shii militia under Faisal's leadership.[51] But the British, who sought to limit interactions between Faisal and the clerics, discouraged him from visiting this conference, and the project faltered.[52] They also prevented Faisal from giving in to the clerics' demands for a treaty to formalise relations with Britain.[53]

Despite trying to portray himself as anti-sectarian and unifying, Faisal relied on the British and the largely Sunni officers and officials that accompanied him to Iraq from Syria.[54] And tensions between Faisal and the Shii clerics soon escalated. The latter, and many other nationalists, had given Faisal the benefit of the doubt, and hoped that he could lead Iraq into real independence. But Faisal's dependence on Britain undermined his relations with the clergy.[55] Once it became clear that they had different visions of a future Iraq and relations with Britain, tensions escalated. The senior clerics, led by Mahdi al-Khalisi, issued fatwas in June 1923 banning participation in elections. In return, al-Khalisi was arrested on the orders of Faisal and exiled to Iran. Other clerics joined him, hoping for a major reaction in Iraq. Instead, the role of the clerics declined.[56]

As suggested earlier, many Shia, including clerics and urban elites, had taken up Iranian citizenship as a form of protection or to escape Ottoman conscription. As noted, Najaf and Karbala were shaped by the interactions of Arabs, Iranians, Indians, and others, and pilgrims, students, and teachers resided there for long periods. While some clerics were Iranian, most Shia in Iraq spoke Arabic, saw themselves as Arabs and traced their lineage to Arab tribes. It was ironic that their Arab nationalist credentials would be put into question by Syrian bureaucrats and a King from the Hijaz. Arab clerics, such as al-Khalisi's family, that had taken Iranian citizenship were now subject to increased scrutiny on the part of Arab nationalist officials (and it was used to justify his expulsion to Iran).[57] Over the coming decades, the administration found a modus operandi with some Arab *mujtahids*, and tensions between Arab and Iranian clerics increased.[58]

The reciprocal privileges Iranian nationals had enjoyed under the Ottomans were revoked, as the Iraqi monarchy constructed its identity vis-à-vis Iran. This dealt a blow to places such as Karbala with a strong Iranian presence and that depended on pilgrims from Iran. Iran tried to uphold these privileges and its influence in Najaf and Karbala, but to little effect. Most Iranian citizens

either took Iraqi nationality or went to Iran.[59] The British and Iraqi adminis-
trations sought to regulate and limit pilgrimage from Iran, India, and elsewhere. Visa requirements and other administrative hurdles led to a decline in
the number of Iranian pilgrims, who visited the shrines in Iran instead. Qom
emerged as an alternative for Shii education, scholarship, and pilgrimage. Less
funds from India and Iran led to the relative decline of Najaf and Karbala. That
the shrines and *madrasas* depended on financial contributions and religious
taxes rather than endowments now made itself felt. Najaf had 8,000 or more
students at the turn of the century. By the 1950s that figure had dropped to
under 2,000, as many chose to pursue a secular education or study in Qom.[60]

The Sunni state elites and modernising Shii education officials sought to
widen secular education amongst Shia and weaken the seminaries. To accelerate that trend, and to include the Shia somewhat, the education ministry was
the only one that often had a Shii minister (in the beginning, it was even
headed by a Shii cleric). There were also attempts to set up a new faculty of
religious studies, the University of the *Ahl al-Bayt*, referring to the wider
Family of the Prophet, of whom Faisal and the Hashemites were a part, a nod
to the ecumenical potential of his reign. It was directly associated with the
monarchy and should educate Sunnis and Shia in theology. These projects
faltered but would inspire a new *madrasa*, the Muntada al-Nashr, in Najaf that
was recognised and in part funded by the state. Founded in 1935, it trained
generations of state-recognised Shii scholars and officials, seeking to combine
religious and secular education. But its close association with the state made
it suspect in the eyes of the traditional Najafi scholars, whose authority it
challenged, and who undermined it.[61]

These Shii officials had to contend with Sati al-Husri, the Director of
Education from 1923 to 1927, and the most powerful education official in
early Iraq. He was originally from Syria and a confidant of Faisal. Through
education, al-Husri sought to instil pan-Arabism into the populations that
found themselves in the new state. He doubted the Arabness of the Shia and
their allegiance to the state and sought to keep them out of government.[62]
As these ideologues put together a new nationalist curriculum, debates
crystallised around Islamic history.[63] Al-Husri and others accused Shia of
shu'ubiyya, referring to a reaction to the privileged status of Arabs under the
Umayyads by non-Arab Muslims, a common anti-Shia and anti-Iranian
theme.[64] Some Sunni Arab polemicists used the words 'Persian' and 'Shia'
interchangeably.[65] Al-Husri had already drawn the ire of Shii clerics because
of his secularising education policies, and he and his followers embarked on

a full-blown confrontation with Shia, which did much to inflame Sunni–Shia tension, and make Shia react as a group. Muharram processions, so powerful in invoking the early split and lament the death of Hussain, became another source of conflict, and were seen by Sunni Arab nationalists as an anomaly. The Iraqi monarchy sought to limit these processions, or ban them outright, to prevent interactions between Shia across Iraq. Many Shia, in turn, saw their policing as repression by a Sunni-dominated state.[66]

Despite his reliance on British and Sunni support, Faisal tried to include more Shia in his administration and counter their alienation.[67] In a memorandum written shortly before his death in 1933 on holiday in Switzerland, he denounced Shia marginalisation and prophesied a dire future should Iraqis not set aside 'the huge differences between the sects that is exploited by evil-doers'.[68] Such frankness led later Shii politicians to embrace him as an exemplary figure.[69] In fact, by the mid- to late 1920s, Shii leaders reversed course and abandoned their boycott, instead pushing for more representation. When Shii organisations and leaders asked for proportional representation and a share of political appointments and economic benefits, basing their claims on censuses detailing sectarian affiliation, such as the one in 1932, which confirmed Shia as Iraq's majority, this threatened Sunni elites.[70] Shii demands went largely unanswered, but their articulation set a precedent for later claims based on numerical strength, not unlike in British India, Syria and Lebanon, where censuses asking for sectarian affiliation strengthened sectarian identities as bases for political claims. After Faisal's death, and the ascension of his son and then his grandson, Shii political entrepreneurs and clerics concluded that their demands would not be met, and supported another rising in 1935, in which the senior cleric, Kashif al-Ghita, invoked Shii grievances. But the revolt was put down, and the position of the clerics as power brokers declined vis-à-vis that of Shii tribal leaders.[71]

The number of Shii ministers increased in the late 1940s and 1950s, but made up only 27.7 per cent of overall appointments under the monarchy (1921–58). The Shii tribal leaders, however, had by the 1950s become Iraq's largest landowners. In the past, these Shii tribal leaders had cooperated with clerics. Now, however, the tribal Shaykhs broke ranks with the clerics and embraced the state. Some were elected to parliament and became a sort of landed aristocracy. They joined their Sunni counterparts in benefitting from the state, only occasionally defending Shii constituencies, and their wealth and upward social mobility meant that some Sunnis started intermarrying with Shia. They spent more time in Baghdad, which became the focus of political and economic activity. The poor followed suit, and by the 1950s half of Baghdad's much enlarged population was Shii (up from only 20 per cent before World War I). Najaf and Karbala, long the focus of Shii economic, political, and religious ties, lost in importance, though that was partly compensated by closer connections of the shrine cities with Shii communities around the world.[72] More Shia found state employment in an expanding bureaucracy. Sunni elites ensured that the relative distribution of governmental positions did not change significantly by also hiring more Sunnis.[73]

Under the British Mandate, the three Ottoman provinces Basra, Baghdad, and Mosul became one country under Sunni dominance, with much of the Shii and Kurdish population marginalised. While the mandate itself officially ended in 1932, the treaty with 'independent' Iraq gave Britain much room to interfere and allowed the stationing of British troops. British influence would only be broken by the overthrow of the monarchy in 1958.[74]

France's policy in Lebanon and Syria shared similarities with the British approach in Iraq, but relied more on cooperation with non-Sunnis, who were recast as 'minorities', a term that only made sense now that new borders had been drawn, and that became widely used in the inter-war years.[75] Unlike Iraq, which the British Army controlled throughout World War I, the Levant remained under nominal Ottoman control, and, after the withdrawal of Ottoman troops, local notables and governors stepped in, many allied with Faisal's Arab Kingdom. French troops landed in Beirut in October 1918, and were largely welcomed by Maronite Christians. The French legitimised the mandate with a *mission civilisatrice* and a special relationship with the Maronite and Uniate Catholic Christians of the Levant, a connection that some even linked back to the Crusades.[76] When France was given the mandates over Lebanon and Syria at the conference of San Remo in 1920, and then ended Faisal's Arab Kingdom in 1920, the French created separate administrative units, each dominated by an ethno-religious group: the State of Greater Lebanon, the State of the Alawites, the State of Jabal Druze, the State of Syria, and the Sanjak of Alexandretta. The latter eventually became part of Turkey, Greater Lebanon was first ruled as a mandate (1920–43), and then became independent, while the States of the Alawites and Jabal Druze were eventually integrated into the Syrian Republic.[77] The French organised institutions by appointing representatives of religious communities, which ensured that 'sect' as a category would shape political life. This sectarian view of the Levant was meant to ensure the special position of Christians. As most Christians were Arabic-speaking, a reorganisation along ethnic or linguistic lines would have strengthened Arab nationalism. France was wary of Christian Arab nationalists and refused to grant special status to ethnic or linguistic groups such as Circassians and Kurds, who, it argued, were simply Sunnis.[78]

Maronite-dominated Greater Lebanon was largely rejected by Sunnis, many of whom wanted to be part of Syria. This was not primarily related to religious difference, but more to do with the affinities across the *Bilad al-Sham*, greater Syria, that had been strengthened in previous decades, and about which most Sunnis (and many others) felt stronger than about Lebanon. Tripoli, the largely Sunni port town and second major city in the new territory, became cut off from its economic hinterland in what would become Syria and declined further in comparison to Beirut, a continuation of processes set in motion in the late Ottoman period and the rise of Beirut as commercial entrepot precisely for the kind of integration into the European-dominated world market that had caused so much resentment then.[79] Sunni boycott of the Lebanese state, comparable to the Shii boycott of the Iraqi state, facilitated Maronite efforts to monopolise political control and secure the presidency of the republic.[80] French commercial interests led France towards a more proactive policy in the Levant, and Maronite leaders sought the inclusion of the fertile agricultural areas of Jabal Amil and especially the Beqaa into the new polity to make it economically viable. As these areas were largely inhabited by Muslims, the new polity, economically and politically dominated by Christians, gained a significant Muslim population, the poorest of whom were Shia, whom Maronite and Sunni elites saw as backward and with suspicion.[81]

Shii leaders found themselves in a delicate situation. The two regions of Shii settlement, the Beqaa Valley and Jabal Amil, had been part of different economic and political networks. At the end of the eighteenth century, the Ottoman governor Ahmad Pasha, nicknamed '*al-Jazzar*' ('the butcher'), had broken the power of Shii leaders and integrated Jabal Amil more into the Empire, but as a part of Sidon province, leading to a focus towards Palestine and the Mediterranean. The Beqaa, on the other hand, was politically and economically oriented towards Damascus. The two communities observed religious rituals differently, and there was no overarching religious or political representation as 'Shia'. And while Jabal Amil had a long tradition of religious scholarship (although the number of clerics in the nineteenth and

early twentieth century was small), less could be said of the Beqaa, despite
the Shii Harfush family ruling it semi-autonomously from the early sixteenth century to 1866.[82] That the Ottoman state had not institutionalised
Shiism separately may have prevented the formation of such overarching
religious bonds.[83]

Shia did not feel as attracted to France as Christians, nor were they as
enthusiastic about pan-Arabism as Sunnis. Yet, some Shii leaders from the
Beqaa were supportive of Faisal and held positions in his brief government,
spurred by their long-standing ties with Damascus (one of his senior aides
was a Shii from the Beqaa). Faisal visited the Beqaa in 1919 to lobby for the
Arab Kingdom and enlist troops. When the above-mentioned King-Crane
Commission visited the Beqaa, it received petitions supporting integration
with Lebanon, others with Damascus, and a few asking for an independent
Greater Lebanon. The commission wrote that most Shia, alongside almost
all Sunnis in the areas to be included in Lebanon, were against France as
mandatory power, as were many Muslims in what would become Syria
(Christians mostly favoured France).[84] And all of this was further complicated by the fact that even in regions where one group predominated,
others also lived there (Christians and Sunnis lived alongside Shia in the
Beqaa, for example, sometimes in mixed villages).

Faisal likewise courted Shii notables in Jabal Amil but due to local rivalries sought to walk a middle path and tried to persuade the French to give
Jabal Amil limited autonomy. Faisal's government, in a departure from
Ottoman practice, appointed Shii judges in Tyre and Sidon. But when the
French ended Faisal's government, Shia by and large threw in their lot
with the new Lebanese state and campaigned for positions in its bureaucracy. Shia of the Beqaa supported the 1925 Syrian revolt that had its
origin in Jabal Druze, which I will discuss below, in response to which the
French built up a rival clan of Shii leaders that had some support amongst
intellectuals from Jabal Amil.[85] Most Shia in Jabal Amil, on the other hand,
did not openly support the revolt. When French officials sought to pass a
new constitution in 1926, they relied on Shii votes in the Lebanese
Council (since Sunnis largely refused to be involved in drafting the constitution). To entice them the French administration in January 1926 recognised Shiism as different from Sunnism in personal status law.[86] This was
a consequential break with the past (and akin to the practices of the
British Empire, which had previously recognised Shiism in India, Bahrain,
Iraq, and elsewhere).

Confessionalised personal status law courts were welcomed by clerics, whose status they enhanced, though the most senior Shii clerics refused to join them for fear of losing independence (a move they could afford, as they had their own income from religious taxes).[87] People were reminded of their sectarian affiliation in interactions with the courts.[88] Cemeteries and endowments, which were increasingly organised separately for Sunnis and Shia, became another focus of identity politics.[89] The French Mandate officially recognised Shia as 'Jafaris', as opposed to the more denigrating term previously common across Lebanon, 'Metwalis', from the Arabic term wilayah indicating their allegiance (wilayah) to Ali.[90] Sunni leaders looked down on Shia because of doctrine and because of class and regional prejudices. Yet they opposed their separate religious representation, arguing that they should simply be seen as Muslim (which meant continued subordination to Sunni religious authorities).[91] For the mandate enhanced the status of the Sunni Mufti of Beirut to the Mufti of the republic, i.e. for the whole of Lebanon, who presided over the Supreme Islamic Legislative Council representing all Muslims, including Shia. It was not until the 1960s that Shii clerics would set up a separate representative body.

Some Shia thus embraced the new polity and saw in France a power that ensured religious freedom, while others resisted it. Many felt part of a larger Syrian and Arab body politic, but the focus of potential benefits and infrastructural investment now became the Lebanese state, and so many eventually pinned their hopes on the latter. Simultaneously, new publications sought to inscribe Shia into pan-Arab and pan-Islamic collective identities, and became a forum for pan-Shii debate that led to stronger bonds between Shia from across Lebanon and beyond.[92] As in Syria and Iraq, key debates revolved around education: Jabal Amil and the Beqaa had been marginalised under the Ottomans and benefited little from the rise of Beirut to commercial capital (in fact, not unlike Tripoli, the South suffered from a shift of port activity from Sidon and Tyre to Beirut), and state and missionary schools were located in Beirut and Mount Lebanon.[93] Private schools and charitable institutions had been largely Christian or Sunni, and so Shii ones now sought to remedy a lack of formal schooling amongst Shia. The first of these was established in Beirut in 1923, and like many later projects funded by Lebanese emigrants in Africa or the Americas.[94] Economic hardship and political uncertainties had led many Lebanese to emigrate over preceding decades, and they would now fund sect-centric activities back home.[95] The school and similar institutions instilled nationalism and notions of citizenship, alongside communal identity, into children. That private schools could write their own history textbooks facilitated this.[96] In the Shia case, this included detailed studies of Shii-majority regions in Jabal Amil published in new transnational Shii intellectual magazines.[97] Far from a unified nationalist narrative, like the one Arab nationalists sought to impose on Iraq, in Lebanon religious communities propagated competing visions of the past. Maronites and Druze had undergone this process earlier. After the formation of Lebanon, Shia and Sunnis also constituted themselves as a distinct religious community, although Sunnis were initially reluctant.[98] Eventually, however, Sunnis embraced the new state, and cooperated with Maronites. In Beirut, a Sunni bourgeoisie established a system of sectarian representation, with a leader at the top, who also sponsored confessional education, and social services. This clientelist system bound lower and middle-class Sunnis to their patrons, and vice versa, a process akin to the other communities.[99]

Between the passing of the constitution in 1926 and the French-Lebanese Treaty of 1936, Shii support was important for the Maronite-dominated state, given that Sunnis saw it as illegitimate. Shii leaders mobilised and voted for the treaty, which paved the way for Lebanese independence in 1943. Still, Shia remained on the periphery (parts of Jabal Amil were annexed to Palestine), and, when Sunni leaders decided to re-enter the political arena in the mid-1930s, Maronite elites relied more on Sunni leaders because of the importance of Sunnis in the main coastal cities, including Beirut, and because of their ties with the rest of the Arab world. Once Maronites shared power with Sunni leaders, Shii ones, with their powerbase in the rural hinterland, became an afterthought (symbolised by the National Pact of 1943 between Maronite president Bishara al-Khuri and Sunni prime minister Riyad al-Sulh, who had been a rival of the Shii leaders of Jabal Amil). The pact sought a balance between Lebanese and Arab nationalism, embraced primarily by Maronites and Sunnis, respectively, and it was agreed that, building on article 95 of the 1926 constitution, different sects should for a transitory period be represented proportionally across the state based on a previous census (it then became the permanent arrangement).[100] The very idea of a census asking for religious affiliation that listed Muslim sects separately was new (the Ottomans, as noted, did not differentiate between Muslims).[101] This reinforced confessional boundaries between Shia, Druze, Ismailis, and Alawites (as well as between Christian denominations). The position of speaker of parliament was reserved for a Shii, but this was a less important position than the presidency or the prime ministership, which went to Christians and Sunnis, respectively, reflecting the relative Shii weakness. In parliament, seats were fixed at a ratio of six for Christians and five for Muslims (here, no sectarian differentiation amongst Muslims or Christians was made).[102] Positions within state institutions were also allocated according to sect, and Lebanon became the archetype of a sectarian political system of which communal leaders profited.[103]

The French faced resistance on many fronts. Some rebelled against sectarian representation and the ways in which borders were drawn, others against colonial rule, and still others for economic reasons or in response to the stark violence unleashed by French Empire. The devastation and economic crisis brought about by the Great War and ensuing political changes affected livelihoods—a severe famine claimed hundreds of thousands of lives in rural areas such as Mount Lebanon.[104] Like in Iraq, uprisings occurred throughout the French Mandate. The most famous of these was the so-called Great Syrian Revolt of 1925, which started in Jabal Druze and spread to the Sunni urban populations of Damascus, Hama, and Homs.[105]

Mandatory authorities in turn relied heavily on repression and intelligence-gathering.[106] The security forces recruited amongst minorities and became paranoid that Germany and Britain were supporting rebel leaders, including such with a religious or separatist dimension.[107] During World War I, Britain had prevented the French from enlisting Sunni Arabs, whom it saw as supporters of their patron, Sharif Hussein. After the war and the dashing of hopes that Damascus would become the capital of an Arab state under the leadership of the Hashemites, Sunni landowners urged their allies and employees not to join the security forces. Troops from other regions, sects, or ethnic groups were used to subdue rebellions, which intensified sectarian polarisation. The *Troupes Spéciales* recruited heavily amongst Christians, Circassians, Ismailis, Druze, Armenians, and Alawites. In a mutually reinforcing process, the French considered these groups less sympathetic to the Arab nationalist cause and more trustworthy.[108] For Alawites, the army was one of the few institutions open for social advancement, and, since they were mostly from poor rural backgrounds, they could seldom buy themselves out of military service. That Alawites were used to put down rebellions in other parts of Syria deepened mistrust of Sunnis, who accused the former of conspiring with the French.[109] Equally consequential was that the French created a separate Alawite State.

When French troops landed in the Levant in 1918, they contacted Alawites, and a French intelligence report argued that due to hostility between them and the Ottomans circumstances were as favourable for military intervention in the Jabal Ansariyah (the 'Nusairi mountains') as in Lebanon (where Christians were thought to be well disposed towards France). During World War I, Turkish officials worried that Alawites, as Arabs, might ally with Faisal, who was in touch with Alawite leaders. But some of them were suspicious of Faisal and corresponded with the French in 1919 to achieve a separate political entity and rebelled against Faisal using French arms. Following Ottoman withdrawal, a power vacuum and demographic shifts led to a conflict between Alawites and Ismailis of Qadmus in 1919, challenging Ismaili chiefs, who had long ruled the area. After an Ismaili shot the son of an Alawite leader and refused to pay blood money, Alawite clans mobilised and ransacked Ismaili (and other) villages, driving Ismailis out of the mountains. The French then tried to interfere, which turned this local revolt, now led by the Alawite Shaykh Salih al-Ali who declared support for Faisal, into an anti-colonial rising. Al-Ali even received backing from Turkish Nationalists (the two sides spoke of a common Jihad against the French), who were keen to regain territories under French control. But after France and Turkey ceased hostilities in October 1921, their support to al-Ali ceased, which ended his prospects. It is noteworthy that neither Faisal nor Kemal Pasha (later Atatürk), the Turkish Nationalist leader, had a problem with al-Ali's sectarian identity (Faisal may even have promised Alawites autonomy).[110]

In contrast, the French strengthened Alawites that emphasised sectarian difference, and institutionalised Alawite autonomy in 1922. With Latakia as its capital, the Territoire/État des Alaouites encompassed the Mediterranean coastal area from today's northern border of Lebanon to the southern border of Turkey. Its borders were drawn to separate Alawite from Sunni populations and turn the former into a 'majority' of about 70 per cent. Alawites, however, lived predominantly in mountainous and rural areas and Sunnis and Greek Orthodox, and some Ismailis and Maronites, predominated in the cities. In Latakia, Sunnis formed the largest group, and Sunnis and Christians were large landowners (and Alawites at times peasants on their land). Some of the Sunnis had supported Faisal (whose administration briefly ruled the territory from Latakia) and would now support the anti-mandate Arab nationalist movement. The drawing of boundaries reinforced tensions between Alawites on the one hand and Sunnis and Greek Orthodox on the other, and even the French ultimately doubted the viability of the state.[111] The French, who had the final say, relied on local cooperation (the

French governor established a council with Alawite tribal leaders and notables). And Ismailis, too, started to be counted separately, and were able to judge according to Ismaili law, although the French did not deem Ismailis numerous or concentrated enough to be institutionalised or receive administrative autonomy.[112]

A sense of Alawite difference had intensified in the late Ottoman period because of more outside interest and pressure to convert to Sunnism or Christianity. Throughout the mandate, Alawites underwent a process of collective identity formation and transformations in juridical and doctrinal terms, adopted a new self-designation, and compiled the first communal histories.[113] The *History of the Alawites*, the first comprehensive history by a member of the community, for example, was published in 1924. Its author had been an Ottoman official, but appreciated French efforts to call the community 'Alawites' and no longer Nusayris, and give them autonomy.[114] French authors published extensively about the 'Pays des Alaouites' amidst a renewed Jesuit push to convert them to Christianity.[115] The first French governor of the territory published extracts on Alawite doctrine and history, presenting France as the saviour of this mountain people.[116] The commander of French troops in the region wrote a tourist guide for the state that emphasised Alawite difference.[117] A pro-French, bilingual Arabic-French newspaper, *El Alevy*, was established in 1923.[118] The term 'Alaouite' was supposed to win the French goodwill, and indeed symbolised to many, including to clerics, a step out of a past in which they had been stigmatised. Some sought to be called Jafari, and the period saw the start of a Twelver Shii-Alawite rapprochement.[119]

Influenced by Shii reformist and pan-Islamic trends from Jabal Amil and Najaf, Alawite clerics sought to reform their faith. The mandatory authorities claimed that Alawites had hitherto been discriminated against and, decreed in 1922 that they, akin to other religious communities, should be able to rule according to their 'confession' in personal status law cases and would no longer need to resort to Sunni judges. But Alawites, unlike Sunnis and Twelver Shia, had no scripturalist legal tradition (though informally their clerics adjudicated according to customary law). Reformist Alawite clerics approached the leading Twelver Shii cleric of Syria, Muhsin al-Amin, for help, who sent them Twelver Shii legal manuals for use in local courts and answered legal questions.

During studies in Najaf in the 1890s, Muhsin al-Amin saw that Shii education needed reform, and, when he settled in the Shii al-Harab quarter of old Damascus in 1901, he opened Shii schools that combined traditional and modern education.[120] As the de facto leader of the small Twelver Shii community in Syria, he strengthened bonds between Arab Shii communities but also advocated pan-Islam and Arab nationalism. He refused the position of Shii Mufti that the French sought to institutionalise, as Syria's Shia sought to be counted and treated simply as Muslims, with the partial exception of endowments, in contrast to Lebanon.[121] As Syrian Shii leaders made common cause with Sunnism, Shiism became more visible. After Shia of Damascus and the surrounding countryside had profited from a relative opening in the late Ottoman period, the French Mandate enabled public Shii rituals, including at the mausoleum of Zaynab outside of Damascus, where clashes with Sunnis prompted al-Amin to ban aspects of the processions offensive to Sunnis.[122] Al-Amin was one of many Shii clerics that even though challenged by new social groups, assumed new political roles. From the Tobacco Revolt and the Constitutional Revolution in Iran to community organisation and public sphere participation in India, to political leadership of anti-colonial resistance in Iraq, to Lebanon and Syria, where they engaged the state as communal leaders, clerics reinvented themselves and asserted their centrality in Shii politics, and many accepted certain aspects of representative government.[123] They invoked pan-Islam, but as public figureheads of Shii communities, also visibly asserted difference.

In 1936, Alawite leaders proclaimed to be Shii Muslims, outlining acceptable and unacceptable practices of belief. The move of Alawite students to Najaf in coming decades intensified this rapprochement.[124] In a pan-Islamic spirit, the Mufti of Jerusalem, Amin al-Hussaini, a key Sunni religious and political leader, recognised Alawites as Muslims.[125] This came at a time when Syrian nationalists and France negotiated a treaty that was going to temporarily end Alawite territorial autonomy. As some Alawites (and Druze) sought to be accepted as Muslim, Arab, and Syrian, others emphasised difference and wanted to retain territorial autonomy. Demonstrations in favour and against union were held in Latakia and Jabal Druze, where the prospect of a Syrian-French treaty likewise rekindled separatist and unionist ambitions. But as the French sacrificed Alawite and Druze separatism in negotiations with nationalists and the prospects of independent statehood for these statelets were waning, assimilationists gained the upper hand.[126] But separatism had lasting consequences, and some resisted being put under the authority of Damascus in 1936.[127]

By the late 1930s, Alawites had been recognised as Shia by senior Shii and Sunni clerics, embraced a new name, experienced administrative 'independence', become institutionalised separately in judicial terms, and started entering the armed forces.[128] Many Alawites remained in the mountains, or worked as farmers on the plains of central Syria, but in the 1940s and 1950s many others moved to Latakia, Tartus, and other urban areas along the coast, and to Damascus, which could lead to tensions with Sunnis and Christians in those cities.[129]

Alawites also lived further up the coast in Cilicia and Alexandretta, which were also a separate province under French Mandate but would eventually become a part of Turkey. While Cilicia was allocated to Turkey in the treaty of Ankara in October 1921, the Sanjak of Alexandretta remained autonomous under French Mandate until 1939. Some pro-French Alawites left Cilicia in 1921 to move to the Territoire des Alaouites. But most favoured Turkish rule and eventually espoused Turkish nationalism, in part because of state-led Turkification measures.[130] In Alexandretta, the primary French administrative division was between Turkish and Arabic speakers. Turks were not further distinguished along religious lines, but Arabs were subdivided into Sunnis, Alawites, and Christians, and organised separately. Alawites were the largest group of Arabs, representing 28 per cent of the population in 1936. Many of them, including landowners and poor peasants, initially favoured autonomy under French protection, as did some Christians. Sunni Arab landowners favoured union with Syria. And pan-Arab nationalists saw the unification of Alexandretta with Syria as a step in a struggle to unite the whole Arab world.[131]

This latter group was led by Zaki al-Arsuzi, who came from a middle landowning Alawite family in Latakia and whose father was an Arab nationalist in the late Ottoman period, for which he was arrested and resettled in Antioch. After studies at the Sorbonne, al-Arsuzi became an advocate of Syrian and Arab nationalism. He rejected France's sectarian policies that organised Sunnis and Alawites separately, and aimed to bind Arab Sunni, Alawite, and Greek Orthodox populations together under the banner of Arabism against the Turks. Arab nationalists resented the Turkifying policies of the Young Turks after 1908 and then the planned incorporation of Alexandretta into Turkey during the Alexandretta Crisis, which they, alongside other Syrian nationalists, saw as 'amputation' from a wider Syrian and Arab body politic. The nationalist movement in Damascus paid lip service to Alexandretta and welcomed refugees from the Sanjak. But the nationalist government in Turkey massively supported pro-Turkish organisations, and made it a cornerstone of negotiations with France and other powers. This led to Alexandretta's integration into Turkey in 1939 as 'Hatay province', the Turkish name for Hittite, as the region's inhabitants were recast as original Turks. Alawites could, in the 1938 plebiscite deciding the fate of the territory, register themselves as Sunni Arab, Alawites, or, the option encouraged by Turkey, as Turks.[132] Al-Arsuzi, on the other hand, alongside other Arab Alawites from Alexandretta, would move to Syria, where he would found a political movement, that would eventually merge with the one led by Michel Aflaq and Salah al-Din al-Bitar, to form the Arab Nationalist Baath Party. While the latter would eventually have to flee Syria, and were embraced especially by the Iraqi Baath, the Syrian Baath, in which Alawites would assume prominent roles, saw al-Arsuzi as a key founding figure and leading ideologue of the party.[133]

The last Shii-influenced community that the mandate transformed were the Druze. The early Arabic-language printing press in Ottoman Damascus had described Druze as backward and brutal and criticised their beliefs, urging the Ottomans to supress them. But by 1910, some Druze leaders, who were treated harshly by the Ottomans, came to be seen in Damascus as anti-Turkish resistance figures and supported by urban Arab nationalists.[134] Druze elites, especially a group around Sultan al-Atrash, became Arab nationalists and participated in the Arab Revolt in WWI.[135] Faisal assured Druze leaders that their region would retain some autonomy and special laws. The King-Crane Commission's visit to Jabal Druze also kindled hopes for autonomy here. Some Druze chiefs realised that a French occupation was likely and began corresponding with the French.[136] While the French intervention in Lebanon in 1860 had favoured Christians over Druze, French strategy after World War I also saw Alawites and Druze as potential allies that could be used to undermine the resistance of Sunnis, many of whom espoused Arab nationalism and were hostile to France.[137] This worked to a certain extent in the case of the Alawites, although, as noted, a major Alawite rebellion challenged the mandate. But amongst Druze, the policy backfired completely.

The French Mandate in Jabal Druze was, unlike in Damascus and Aleppo, not preceded by military occupation but by a formal agreement with Druze chiefs, who were promised a government according to local custom and with their participation. The first governor was a Druze chief, but after he fell ill, the French appointed a French one, Capitaine Gabriel Carbillet. He saw the Druze chiefs as corrupt landed aristocrats oppressing the peasantry, a perception that owed more to his vision of pre-revolutionary France than to the realities of Jabal Druze, and sought to break their power to liberate Druze peasants. He set out on a massive infrastructure programme for which he lacked the manpower, and so resorted to forced labour. Even captured Druze chiefs had to work on the road building projects, and the brutality of Carbillet and his staff alienated locals. Resentment culminated in 1925 in a rising led by Sultan al-Atrash. It quickly spread to other parts of the country and led to the country-wide so-called Great Syrian Revolt.[138]

French officials were keen to emphasise that this was a 'Druze revolt' rather than a Syrian one, while Syrian nationalists, claimed this was a nationalist rising for independence that proved the political maturity of the Syrian and Arab nation.[139] Druze leaders emphasised their Muslimness and Arabness, claims that were boosted by the Druze role in the Arab nationalist movement and the 1925 revolt.[140] The Arab nationalist and anti-imperialist propaganda that accompanied the revolt denounced France's sectarian policies by invoking the ideals of the French revolution.[141] Carbillet was removed and the revolt suppressed harshly (including by bombing Damascus). Most nationalist Druze leaders were killed or driven into exile (some were allowed to settle in the territory of Ibn Saud).[142] The French maintained the area administratively independent until 1936 (though like the Alawite territory it was re-established in 1939 until the end of the French presence after WWII).[143] The Druze were cast as a rebellious and warlike mountain people whose religious beliefs in reincarnation were said to make them even more fierce and irrational.[144] The French established a Druze court that adjudicated according to a mixture of Hanafi and Druze law, a practice that apparently dated back to late Ottoman times.[145] Given different rules of inheritance between Druze, Shia, and Sunnis, competing claimants could have recourse to a confessional court or to the general Syrian court for Muslims, which would rule differently and thus reinforce and problematise the sectarian identity of the deceased and their successors.[146] As in the case of the Alawite state, uncertainty over relations with Damascus led to a show of strength of unionists and separatists, and to rivalries over local government positions (the 1936 government appointed Faisal's former emissary to the Druze, though not a native of the region, as governor).[147]

France's open partisanship for Christians, symbolised by the establishment of Lebanon, their alliance with non-Sunni Muslims, and their strong opposition to Arab nationalism, forged a new sense of togetherness amongst the rest of the Syrian population, which became expressed through Arab nationalism.[148] As noted, the origins of Arab nationalism lay in the late Ottoman Empire, in an alliance between Arab Ottoman officers, bureaucrats, and urban notables of the mainly Sunni towns. The turn of the Young Turks towards Turkish nationalism galvanised Arab nationalism as a rivalling political project, and the simultaneous political opening gave it room to flourish. Arab nationalist circles supported Faisal, and when the French crushed his state, tensions were a given. The French Mandate then led to nationalist solidarity across classes, between the Sunni urban notables of Damascus, Aleppo, Hama, and Homs, and with other sectors of society. They formed the National Bloc that would lead peaceful resistance to the mandate. While the Arab nationalist glue that developed between them was not explicitly Sunni, and as noted, many of the early Arab nationalist ideologues had been non-Sunni, many Christians and some non-Sunni Muslims worked with the French and resisted attempts to be integrated into Syria under a National Bloc government, which reinforced the latter's Sunni identity. The key nationalist leaders used secular rhetoric, not least to counter the explicitly sectarian policies of the French. But that the movement's leaders and supporters were mainly Sunni and urban meant that a cultural affinity developed between the urban Sunni upper classes from which Alawites and others from the 'periphery' were absent. An urban–rural divide overlapped with a sectarian one.[149] And a sense that Sunnis of Syria were a numerical majority but marginalised politically gained traction.

The many problems of France in Syria and the political acumen of the National Bloc, as well as international pressure after France's brutal suppression of the Great Revolt and the bombing of Damascus in 1925, together with Britain's granting of independence to Iraq in 1932, led to the Franco-Syrian Treaty of Independence of 1936, which paved the way for actual independence in 1946.[150] Even though it was not ratified by the French parliament, it abolished the autonomy of the Druze and Alawite states, a major demand of Syrian nationalists, and ushered in a Syrian nationalist government.[151] A major confrontation between the National Bloc and the French authorities was directly related to France's sectarian vision. A reform of personal status law had been in the making for years, and, as we have seen, Christian and non-Sunni communities had been encouraged to administer their own personal status affairs since the start of the mandate. France increased the number of such communities, both amongst Christians and Muslims, to undermine the position of Sunni Muslims. The 1936 decree, which was supposed to be implemented in 1939, took this to a logical con-clusion. Sunni Muslims, who constituted the largest group, were effectively cast as but one Muslim community (the others being Alawites, Twelver Shia, Druze, and Ismailis) alongside Christian 'communities', who were all given their personal status law courts and powers to regulate their own affairs.[152]

In preparation for the decree, several studies were carried out and reports requested from various provinces about the application of personal status law. They were full of examples of Sunni *Qadis* informally delegating author-ity to Alawite and Shii clerics to deal with specific cases, practices said to have been in effect since late Ottoman times and to function largely fric-tionless.[153] The state now did away with that confessional ambiguity. Muslim clerics also found other aspects of the decree objectionable, including the acceptance of someone leaving one's religion, but the crux of the matter was political: Sunni clerics and notables, citing the census of the mandatory state, emphasised that Muslims were the *majority* in the country and could thus not be relegated to a status akin to a *minority*. The decree was meant to undermine the Sharia courts, which under the Ottomans had wide juris-diction over Muslims. This relegation of Sunni clerics to regulate succession and marriage amongst Sunnis caused uproar.[154] The charge was led by Syria's senior Sunni clergy, but Muhsin al-Amin, who had refused to be instrumentalised by the French authorities in this regard and did not accept separate Shii representation, joined his Sunni counterparts in arguing that Muslims could not be divided and could not be treated like other religious groups.[155] National Bloc politicians declined to enact the decree and resigned. With the government collapsed, France re-established separate states for Alawites and Druze after rekindling their separatist ambitions, but during World War II, as Syria and Lebanon became contested between Vichy and Free French governments, the powers of the mandate authorities diminished. France's imposition of a distinctively sectarian political and judicial system in Syria akin to Lebanon was ultimately not successful. For the last years of the war, Syria came under de facto control of British troops, and in 1946, Syria, including the formerly Alawite and Druze territories, became independent.[156]

These attempts to play off religious groups against each other had long-lasting consequences. Arab nationalist suspicion over the loyalty of Alawites and Druze, kindled by the French Mandate, lingered after independence.[157] Post-independence Syria was initially ruled by a small circle of Sunni fam-ilies, and open display of sectarian loyalties or difference, was now frowned upon and suppressed, which meant that Sunnism and Arabism became the new norm. A suppression of sectarian difference also meant the assertion of the majority.[158] The Druze court was recognised by the new Syrian government in 1948 and remained institutionalised separately.[159] All other Muslim communities, including Twelver Shia, Ismailis, and Alawites, however, were in juridical and official terms seen as Muslims, and had to use courts based on Sunni law for matters of personal status law.[160] A long-standing demand of nationalists and Sunni clerics, it would also suit Alawites, for as they became more prominent they no longer wanted to be seen as different by other Syrian Muslims. Alawite and Druze leaders seen as autonomist were dealt with harshly.[161] Many Druze and Alawites now joined radical nationalist parties such as the Baath, and the army.[162] Given the role of 'minorities' in the armed forces of the mandate, once the army entered politics in Syria from 1949 onwards, these officers would play prominent roles.[163]

The modern state sought to exert much greater control over populations and territory, and form all aspects of life.[164] In the Middle East that state recognised, legitimised, and institutionalised sectarian difference, and empowered communal leaders, who profited from the institutionalisation of sectarian politics. The British and French Mandates operated to this logic, yet treated Sunnis and Shia differently. The French, who ruled Lebanon and Syria in the inter-war period, were pro-Christian, and played up difference between Shii-leaning groups and Sunnis, which alienated Sunnis and fostered new senses of togetherness. Earlier accounts, which emphasised the persecution of Christian and non-Sunni Muslims by Sunnis, were invoked to justify 'protection' of minorities. Some cooperated with the French, but other members of 'minorities' supported Faisal's government and the wider Arab nationalist cause.

The British, on the other hand, based on long-standing ties and war-time alliances, had an affinity towards Sunni Arabs (though they were not willing to risk conflict with France for it). They abandoned Faisal in Damascus, but installed him as king in Iraq (and his brother in Jordan). These monarchs, and those in Britain's Gulf protectorates, were Sunni, and were described as 'authentic' and 'traditional' and a continuation of the 'natural' Sunni-led order of Muslim societies. Despite Britain's long relationship with the Shii rulers of Awadh and the shrine cities, the British view of Shiism in Iraq was negative because of the Shii clergy's previous anti-British stances. The adoption of Sunni biases towards the Shia, and the idea that Sunnis were more authentically 'Arab' and less problematic partners led, together with the clergy's reluctance to engage the British-led administration, to the marginalisation of Iraqi Shia. British rule also entrenched the rule of the Sunni Al Khalifa over Bahrain's majority Shia population.

As the French alienated most Syrians, so did the British in Iraq. In Syria, most of these happened to be Sunnis, and, in Iraq, most of them happened to be Shia. In both cases, the mandatory authorities relied on an alliance with 'minorities' of the population in the new territory, although that term was not pronounced in British discourse, and Faisal and his largely Sunni Arab nationalist supporters did not see themselves as a minority, but a region-wide majority. French and British writers had adopted Sunni biases towards Shia and 'unorthodox' populations, which were now invoked to legitimise at times contradictory policies, and to institutionalise difference, in Lebanon and Syria by empowering Christians, Druze, and Alawites and in Iraq by staffing the state primarily with Sunnis. In both countries, special units of the armed forces recruited from minorities were used to put down rebellions amongst people of other ethnicities and/or faith.

The mandate period profoundly transformed relations between religious groups. It was not that religious difference had not mattered previously. But it was now institutionalised in a new kind of state, one that established new borders and in which the question of sectarian coexistence had become distinctly political. In Lebanon and to a certain extent Syria, politics would be organised through sects, and the period left a legacy of ethno-sectarian polarisation and aspirations for territorial autonomy. As in British India, people were asked about sectarian affiliation on census ballots, and the numerical strength of a community influenced its share in government. Groups that under the Ottomans had been classified as Muslims were encouraged to identify as Ismailis, Alawites, Druze, Shia, and Sunni (in India, newly formed sects such as Ahmadis and 'Wahhabis' petitioned for inclusion in the censuses). Where these identities were still ambiguous, censuses, formation of personal status law courts, clerical representation of each community, and territorial autonomy would do away with that. The mandates spurred a further differentiation between Muslims.

The separate institutionalisation, juridically and at times politically, of Muslim communities strengthened confessional boundaries between them at a time when urbanisation and migration brought people into closer contact. Christians and Jews had under the Ottomans, and especially during the Tanzimat, been organised separately. But the institutionalisation of non-Sunni Muslims as separate communities was unprecedented. Many denounced these divisions in response. Sunni and Shii revivalisms would in theory embrace pan-Islam, even if they in practice lead to more differentiation. Nationalism in its pan-Arab and national form, too, claimed to be an antidote to sectarian division. But the 'question of minorities' that arose in the era of European intervention, would remain a permanent feature of these societies and a discourse that could be invoked and instrumentalised but also downplayed at different moments.[165] As the mandates came to an end, nationalists were suspicious about identity divisions, lest they be exploited again by foreign powers. The post-independence state's nationalism could have empowering effects, including for members of 'minorities' and lead to strong emotional attachments to the nation but could similarly lead to discrimination and exclusion of those that did not fit that ideal.

IO

The Muslim Response

Rashid Rida was born in 1865 near Tripoli, that Mediterranean port city, which had Shii rulers during the Shii Century, but then assumed a staunchly Sunni identity and prospered under Mamluk and Ottoman rule, only to be overshadowed by Latakia and Beirut from the nineteenth century onwards. Rida, the Sunni cleric and man of letters discussed earlier for his role in Faisal's short-lived Arab Kingdom in Damascus, epitomises perhaps better than anyone else how Muslim intellectuals responded to the rapid changes of the early twentieth century. He started out as a reformer in the late Ottoman Empire, then moved to British-ruled Egypt, then became an advocate of Arab nationalism and Islamic revivalism. Rida, like many Tripolitans, felt closer to the largely Sunni cities of the Syrian interior than to the Alawite, Ismaili, and Twelver Shii settlements that separated them from Tripoli. And as noted, it were those Syrian cities where a growing sense of togetherness was expressing itself in Syrian and Arab nationalism. Rida initially studied with a Naqshbandi master, and in 1897 moved to Cairo to work with Muhammad Abduh, the Egyptian reformer, who from 1899 acted as chief judge of British-controlled Egypt. The group around Abduh had a good relationship with leading British officials and it was British rule that allowed them to publish freely, yet they would ultimately seek to unite Muslims against Empire. A year after arriving in Cairo, in 1898, Rida founded the influential journal *al-Manar, The Lighthouse*.[1] In its pages, Rida would discuss the tremendous political changes the Islamic world underwent in the first decades of the twentieth century, and in the process become the main proponent of Islamic modernism—the intellectual heir of both Abduh and his close companion, Jamal al-Din al-Afghani, discussed earlier for his role in pan-Islam.

Confronted with growing European political, economic, and cultural influence, Muslim intellectuals sought to appropriate some of the things that seemed promising in Europe, including, at times, representative government and national solidarity. Most agreed that the history of Islam and the Arabs had to be reinterpreted and that Islam should be reformed, though they disagreed over how this should be done. An emphasis on the idea of one Arab nation was, as noted, one approach. Another was to rethink Islam altogether.[2] 'Islamic modernists' shared with the proponents of Islamic revivalism in India and the Arabian Peninsula discussed before the idea that by going back to the sources and to the period of the *Salaf*, the Companions of the Prophet, Islam could reinvent itself and learn to deal with the challenges of European Empire and modern science. The nineteenth-century *Salafi* reformists, as they are known, saw some aspects of the European model as worthy of emulation. On the other hand, the trend epitomised by the Wahhabis was inward-looking, directed at doctrine and ritual practice of Muslims. Somewhat confusingly, these two trends were both subsumed under the term *Salafiyya*, which would later gain widespread traction to describe mainly the Sunni fundamentalist groups that were influenced by the Wahhabis rather than for 'liberal' Muslim reformers.

The reformist trend of the *Salafiyya*, centred in Cairo and personified by Abduh and al-Afghani, sought to unite Muslims through pan-Islam, which could only function, of course, if doctrinal difference wasn't an impediment to political unity. The revival of Islam, and a return to its early and divisive period, thus contained the seeds for an ecumenical, pan-Islamic branch of the *Salafiyya*, that has been termed its 'left-wing' and a more fundamentalist, and anti-Shii, 'right-wing'.[3]

Rida oscillated between the two, starting out as the heir to the Islamic modernist project, then eventually coming to symbolise the *Salafiyya's* right-wing turn. He likewise embraced Arab nationalism, and epitomised a new-found Sunni Arab consciousness. Rida became disenchanted with the state-sponsored Sunnism and Sufism of the late Ottoman period, and critical of Egyptian Sufis that venerated the *Ahl al-Bayt*, a legacy of a more ecumenical past.[4] Rida initially tried to convince the Young Turks to open a modernist religious education institution in 1909, but when he failed this contributed to his disillusionment with the Ottoman state.[5] Instead, he established a more modest education institution in Cairo for aspiring clerics that was financed by Indian Muslims. In 1912, Rida travelled to India, where *al-Manar* was widely read by Muslim elites, to lecture and meet with the Indian Sunni Revivalists and reformists discussed above.[6] Alienated by both the Ottoman state and growing Turkish nationalism, he supported the

Arab Revolt and the Hashemite cause (and recruited one of the sons of Sharif Hussein, Abdullah, into an Arab nationalist organisation). However, after their failure in Syria, he became disillusioned with the Hashemites and their dependence on Britain.

As noted, this period was so exceptionally transformative because it constituted a shift from the last of the multi-ethnic and multi-religious Muslim-led Empires, to nation states. The latter now became the dominant form of political organisation around the world, symbolised by the Wilsonian 'spring time' of Nations, the formation of the League of Nations, and the establishment of many new nation states out of larger entities, and the emergence of former colonies into political independence. These changes reshaped not only borders but every aspect of people's lives. People now found themselves in new borders, and had to define themselves vis-à-vis a new state. And they embraced new ideologies. Some were pan-identities, such as pan-Islam and pan-Arabism, others were tied to a specific national territory, and others still were Leftist or liberal. The question of how and by whom society should be governed lay at the heart of these debates. These were made even more relevant by the abolishing of the Caliphate in 1924.

As we have seen throughout, the Caliphate had long remained, at least nominally, the spiritual authority of Sunni Muslims, and the Ottoman Caliphate had been widely accepted. Even Shia had, despite some doctrinal reservations, accommodated that reality, and even defended it. After Russian troops had entered Iran and several Ottoman provinces, in December 1910, for example, a fatwa by leading Shii clerics in Iraq, in agreement with Sunni clerics of Baghdad, called for Jihad to defend Ottoman and Iranian territories (Rida published it in *al-Manar* and hailed it as a milestone of Sunni–Shia cooperation). Shii and Sunni clerics signed a fatwa for Jihad against the Italian occupation of Libya (then still an Ottoman province) in October 1911.[7] In India, Sunna and Shia joined forces to condemn Italy over the Libya attack and Russia over the invasion of Iran as well as the bombing of the shrine in Mashhad in 1912.[8] And as noted when British troops landed in southern Iraq in late 1914, the clerics reiterated their call for Jihad, and thousands of Shii volunteers took up arms against the British.[9]

Nevertheless, as also noted, after the Ottomans participated on the losing side in the First World War, the Allies reduced the Ottoman Empire to a fraction of its former might in the Treaty of Sèvres in 1920. An armed struggle, led by the new Turkish leader, Mustafa Kemal, led the Allies to concede more territory to Turkey in the treaty of Lausanne in 1923. Kemal became the foundational figure of the modern Turkish state and known as Atatürk, Father of Turks. To prevent a reaction from the Ottoman ancien régime, his faction, the so-called Kemalists, abolished the office of the Sultan in 1922, the Caliphate in 1924, Islam as state religion in 1928, and replaced the Arabic alphabet with the Latin.

Some saw these secularising reforms as a model to be followed in their own societies. Others, like Rida, were alarmed. Faced with British domination, many Indian Muslims, including Shia, who recast the Caliphate as a sort of Imamate-Caliphate, from the late nineteenth century onwards had put their hopes in the Ottoman Caliph, which, unlike the defeated Mughals, was still nominally independent and a symbol of Muslim power.[10] Indian Shii elites, who had seen their influence wane after the demise of princely states like Awadh, hoped that pan-Islam could help them regain some of their standing.[11] In late 1923, the Nizari Ismaili leader, the Aga Khan, and the Twelver Shii jurist Syed Ameer Ali, wrote a public letter to the Turkish Prime Minister, urging Turkey to retain the Caliphate. It was in turn cited by the Kemalists as a reason to abolish the Caliphate, arguing that it had become a vehicle for foreign interference (though the decision had mainly to do with the fear that the Sultan may invoke his position as Caliph to attempt a restoration).[12] A letter by an Ismaili and a Twelver Shii from India in support of the Caliphate was thus used as a pretext by secularising, but nominally Sunni, Turkish politicians, to abolish the Sunni Ottoman Caliphate.[13] In this period, a secular-religious divide was often more important than the Sunni–Shia one.

This rekindled the question as to whether Muslims needed a Caliphate. If so, then, who should be Caliph, and where should he be based? If not, what would replace it? Rida, deeply shocked by the Kemalist reforms, took centre stage in this debate.[14] As noted, in the early 1920s, Rida still embraced constitutionalism and democracy, and criticised the Mandates in the emerging language of international law. But the brutality of colonial rule, the shattering of Arab nationalist dreams in Syria, and the creation of Palestine and Lebanon, the Christian-dominated state in which his hometown, Tripoli, was now located, as states favouring non-Muslim religious groups, were traumatic and contributed to a perception that Arab Sunnis were being side-lined. Tripoli was precisely such a case where the newly drawn borders diminished the importance of cities other than the capital, in this case Beirut, where the new state institutions were chiefly located. Rida would now argue that the Caliphate was a necessity for Muslims, and turn towards what he saw as the fundamentals of Islam, and a political movement on the Arabian Peninsula.[15]

The Al Saud and allied tribal forces from Najd and Wahhabi clerics had been pushed out of the Arabian Peninsula by successive Ottoman-Egyptian military campaigns in the nineteenth century. At the start of the twentieth century, however, from their base in Kuwait, where the Al Saud lived in exile as guests of the Emirs of Kuwait, the Al Sabah, they embarked on a conquest of the Arabian Peninsula, starting with Najd. As part of its push to extend its alliances amongst Arab leaders, Britain had established contacts with their leader Abdulaziz Al Saud—referred to as Ibn Saud. On the eve of war, in 1913, Britain acquiesced to Ibn Saud's conquest of the Eastern Arabian Peninsula from the Ottomans.[16]

Ibn Saud's forces faced little resistance as they took the oasis of al-Ahsa, home to a mixed Sunni–Shia population, and the Shii port town of Qatif, in 1913. Faced with overwhelming military might, local notables decided that it was wiser to accommodate. Shii notables claimed that they received Ibn Saud's assurances that their safety and freedom to worship in private would be ensured in return for peaceful submission. Those who vowed resistance were forced either to emigrate, including a Shii cleric who had previously called for Jihad against the Italians in Libya, or, if they retained links to the Ottomans, as some Shii notables did, face punishment and confiscation of their wealth.[17] Wahhabi clerics were appointed to indoctrinate the locals, and rule according to Wahhabi jurisprudence. The situation for Shia in the area was dire, as the Wahhabis saw them as non-Muslims and not equal to Sunnis before the law and suppressed Shii religious practices and destroyed houses of worship.[18] Al-Ahsa and Qatif, old centres of Shiism and fertile agricultural regions, came under Saudi control.

Ibn Saud then set his sights on the Hijaz. Despite their war-time alliance with the Hashemites, British officials saw their rival Ibn Saud as a rising force, and paid him a stipend.[19] After the war, Sharif Hussein had sought to turn the Hijaz into the centre of Arab politics, and founded an independent state. He even tried to be recognised as Caliph (something Rida denounced) and organised pan-Arab and pan-Islamic conferences to bolster his legitimacy and assert Hashemite supremacy over the Saudis. But the Hijaz was increasingly coming under Egyptian influence, and the military edge on the Peninsula was shifting in favour of Ibn Saud.[20]

Although Britain put Hashemites on the throne in Iraq and Jordan, in the Hijaz, it now openly supported Ibn Saud, who in 1924/5 entered Mecca and Medina. Many Hijazi families came to terms with the new reality, but some Sufi and non-Hanbali opponents of the Wahhabis went into exile, as Sufism was repressed and Hanbali-Wahhabism became state doctrine.[21] Upon entering Medina, the Saudi-Wahhabi forces destroyed historical sites deemed un-Islamic by Wahhabi clerics, including the tombs over the graves of the Shii Imams in the al-Baqia cemetery.[22] Selected by the Prophet himself, located next to his mosque, it was the first exclusively Muslim cemetery, where many of his earliest Companions are buried.[23] As noted, mausolea had been erected over key graves, especially over those of the *Ahl al-Bayt*. In the nineteenth century, the Wahhabis had already destroyed many of the tombs, which the Ottomans, true to their confessionally ambiguous policy, subsequently restored, and which many Sunnis likewise visited.[24] Muslims around the world were outraged by the renewed destruction.[25] Ibn Saud organised an international conference during the Hajj in 1926 in order to debate the future of the holy sites, and be accepted as de facto leader of the Hijaz, but was only partly successful in swaying global Muslim opinion.[26]

Developments in the Hijaz were followed closely in India. Leading Sunni and Shii voices of the Khilafat movement called for an international investigation and the rebuilding of the sites under joint Sunni–Shia supervision. When an Indian delegation to the Hijaz conference in 1926 investigated who was responsible for their destruction, it was expelled. But some Sunni Revivalists in the Khilafat movement endorsed Ibn Saud, splitting the movement that only a few years earlier had still united Indian Muslims in support of the Ottoman Caliphate. Indian supporters of the Wahhabis, mostly Sunni Revivalists, adopted the latter's criticism of shrine visitation to legitimise the destruction, while those with a less anti-Shii attitude, including the Farangi Mahall clerics in Lucknow, endorsed Sharif Hussein.[27]

As Hashemites and Saudis vied for international support, Rida came to the Wahhabis' defence. He was by now probably the most important figure of Islamic modernism, and *al-Manar,* with a readership from Indonesia to Brazil, carried tremendous weight over Arab and wider Muslim public opinion. Rida had long looked for an Arab leader to back, and felt there was a notable absence of Sunni religio-political leadership. He wanted the Caliphate to be held by independent Arab leaders of Qurayshi (the tribe of the Prophet) descent.[28] Rida's defence of the Caliphate was welcomed by the Khilafat movement, which had previously accused him of undermining the Ottoman Caliphate by promoting Arab nationalism.[29] In his 1922/3 treatise on the Caliphate, Rida pointed out that the Ottomans had not been of Qurayshi descent (as noted, Ottoman clerics had long glossed over this fact). As also noted, he had had high hopes for the Hashemites, and, according to Rida, had they not undermined their position by association with Britain, they would have fulfilled that requirement. A famous fictionalised text about a secret Muslim society in Mecca working to establish a Hashemite Caliphate had even been serialised in *al-Manar* in 1902–3. Ironically, the notion that their Qurayshi origins would make them good Caliphs had driven British officials and Islamic unionists such as al-Afghani since the late nineteenth century to support them.[30] Because at the time of publication in 1922/3 the Hashemites were still in control of the Hijaz, Rida even advocated re-establishing the Caliphate in Ankara, or in an intermediary region between Turkish and Arabic spheres of influence, such as Mosul.[31] As Ibn Saud was not of Qurayshi origin, Rida even briefly advocated that the Zaydi Imam Yahya of Yemen be considered a candidate. Rida held favourable views of pro-Sunni Zaydi scholars like al-Shawkani and Ibn al-Amir, and Rida published and reviewed reformist Zaydi works, paving the way for their integration into the Salafi canon.[32]

Eventually, however, Rida embraced Ibn Saud and the Wahhabis, who had long been frowned upon by the Ottomans, the British, and urban Arab elites. Rida wrote a book legitimising the Wahhabi takeover of the Hijaz, and many articles specifically defending the Wahhabis against Shii attacks (and would do so until his death in 1935 on the way back from a meeting with Ibn Saud in the Hijaz).[33] Rida's embrace of the Wahhabis was influenced by Salafi supporters of Ibn Saud, including Shaykh Muhammad Hamid al-Fiqqi, founder of the Jamaat Ansar al-Sunna al-Muhammadiyya in Egypt, and Muhammad Hussain Nasif, a Hijazi merchant.[34] Al-Fiqqi's group was, together with Indian Salafis, amongst the earliest supporters of Ibn Saud, and a crucial node in Salafism's global spread. Shortly after the conquest of the Hijaz in 1925, al-Fiqqi came to Mecca to support Ibn Saud, who appointed him as teacher in the Great Mosque of Mecca and head of the government printing house.[35] The Nasifs, originally from Egypt, had become one of Jeddah's wealthiest families, and Muhammad Hussain a Wahhabi even before Ibn Saud's conquest.[36] Nasif brought organisational talent, financial muscle, and the ear of Ibn Saud to the Salafi movement. Rida stayed at Nasif's house in Jeddah, which contained a large library, and the two maintained an active correspondence. Nasif paid for the printing of Salafi classics, including books by Ibn al-Qayyim, Ibn Taymiyya, and Ibn Abd al-Wahhab, and financed the publication of older anti-Shii polemics and commissioned and edited new ones.[37]

Many of these were printed at the Salafiyya Press in Cairo, run by two Syrian émigrés with close ties to Rida, one of whom, Muhibb al-Din al-Khatib (1886–1969), was, as we will shortly see, another noteworthy critic of Shiism. Up until the nineteenth century, printed books on Islamic topics, were rare in the Ottoman Empire. Religious debates were confined to scholars with access to manuscripts and polemics were rarely available to the wider population, who, in any case, was largely illiterate. Printing presses had been allowed for non-Muslims, and printing in Ottoman Turkish was allowed from 1727, but excluded works of Hadith, Quranic exegesis, or jurisprudence, and permission to print the Quran in the Ottoman Empire was only granted in 1874.[38] The arrival of mass printing of religious books and editing of Islamic 'classics', often in areas under colonial control such as Egypt or India, from the nineteenth century onwards was therefore trans-formative. The example of Ibn Taymiyya, noted earlier for his role in the Mamluk campaigns in the Kisrawan, as an anti-Shii polemicist, and as an inspiration for Ibn Abd al-Wahhab, is telling. Marginal for centuries, the publication of his treatises, fatwas and letters in the nineteenth and early twentieth century turned him into a mainstream figure.[39] Rida, as many other Salafis, was drawn to Ibn Taymiyya and Ibn al-Qayyim, and their pro-nounced anti-Shiism. Their reception signalled an embrace of scripturalism and an emphasis on the study of Hadith, something Hanbalis had long advocated, and which, in turn, increased hostility towards Shiism.[40] Diatribes against Shiism were a way for Salafis to assert their position in the crowded religious field of the late Ottoman period.

The Alusis, a prominent Sunni clerical family in Baghdad, epitomise this process. Originally Shafii, the family is said to have become Hanafi to facili-tate relations with the Ottoman state and in the mid-nineteenth century Abu al-Thana' al-Alusi became Mufti of Baghdad.[41] He wrote *The Iraqi Answers to the Questions from Lahore,* a response to questions from Sunnis in Lahore as to who exactly was a Companion of the Prophet and therefore infallible. The Lahoris argued that the circle should be narrowed, and that, for example, Muawiya, who had fought against Ali, should not be counted as such, and could therefore be criticised (a stance that smoothed relations with Shia on the Indian subcontinent). al-Alusi refused, however, arguing, paradigmatically for the *Salafiyya*, that anyone who had met the Prophet once, including Muawiya, was a Companion and beyond reproach, refuting the Shii and moderate Sunni view on the Companions.[42]

Abu al-Thana' al-Alusi, wrote another book on the Imamate that followed the anti-Shii polemic *Gift for Twelver Shia* by Shah Abd al-Aziz, which as noted had proven so influential in India.[43] Even before Rida, the al-Alusis symbolised Sunni Revivalism's global connections. Abu al-Thana's son, Nu'man al-Alusi, continued his father's work, and published a book in defence of Ibn Taymiyya in 1881, based on a biography in the possession of Siddiq Hasan Khan of Bhopal, one of the first Salafi books to appear in print.[44]

A growing number of clerics started to identify with Ibn Taymiyya, including in his native Syria. But he was still a controversial figure in the nineteenth-century Ottoman Empire, not least because the Wahhabis, which the official Ottoman clergy of course despised as rebels, embraced him.[45] The al-Alusis, with their Shafii and then Hanafi background, and their position in the Ottoman system, gave the Salafi-Wahhabis, and Ibn Taymiyya, additional legitimacy in mainstream Muslim circles.[46] Later Salafis would reject the rigidity of the system of the four Sunni schools of jurisprudence altogether, and vow, despite their intellectual debt to Hanbalism, to devise independent rulings that crossed their boundaries.[47] Al-Alusi argued that Ibn Taymiyya had done precisely that and was thus exemplary.[48] Another member of the family, Mahmud Shukri al-Alusi, expanded ties with Islamic revivalists in India, especially with Siddiq Hasan Khan, and published an abridged version of his grandfather's anti-Shii treatise based on the *Gift for Twelver Shia*. It was first printed in India in 1884/5 and dedicated to the Ottoman Sultan Abdulhamid, and later reissued in 1922/3 by the Salafiyya Press in Cairo. The treatise was in turn widely refuted by Shia, who accused al-Alusi of ignorance and unfair representation.[49]

European Orientalists picked up on these debates. They corresponded with Salafi leaders, amplifying their message and propagating the view that they constituted a new and authentic form of Sunni Islam. Mahmud Shukri al-Alusi, for example, corresponded with Louis Massignon, the prominent French Orientalist we have come to know as the one advocating a French pro-Sunni policy, and his work was praised at Orientalist congresses. Al-Alusi became so well-known that Gertrude Bell, the Arabist and key architect of the British Mandate in Iraq, thought he or another member of his family would be a good senior religious official in mandatory Iraq.

While this did not happen, the very notion that British officials considered an anti-Shii polemicist as the highest religious official in a majority Shii state gives pause.[50]

Orientalists also 'discovered' Ibn Taymiyya based on these books. Henri Laoust, who headed the French Institute in Damascus during the latter part of the French Mandate, wrote extensively about 'schisms' in Islam based on close readings of Sunni heresiography, and edited and translated Ibn Taymiyya's works, as well as Rida's treatise on the Caliphate.[51] Simultaneously, in Syria under the French Mandate, as noted Ibn Taymiyya's fatwas against the Nusayris were invoked as proof that Alawites and Sunnis could not get along, and why Alawites should therefore have their own state.

Syrian and Iraqi Salafis, and Sunni Revivalists in India, agreed with Sunni Sufis like the Naqshbandis, on opposition to Shiism. But they were also rivals. Rida, and many Indian Sunni Revivalists, came from a Naqshbandi background. The al-Alusis, and the Sunni establishment of Baghdad, on the other hand, were at odds with the Naqshbandis. The rivalry was in part about patronage by the late Ottoman state, which reinforced its support for Hanafism and Sunni-minded Sufism just as the *Salafiyya* was rising in prominence.[52]

After the official Ottoman religious institutions declined and were then abolished by the Kemalists, and state-backed Sufi orders banned, Salafis, with their tight-knit networks, and global connections, became powerful players on the post-Ottoman, Sunni Arab religious scene.[53] In Syria and Iraq, Salafis were boosted by the conquests of the Wahhabis, who, as noted, needed support in the old Arab cities and in India to establish their legitimacy. While there was competition between Sunni-minded Sufi orders such as the Naqshbandis, the Salafis, and early Arab nationalists, they all agreed that the golden era of Islam was to be found in the early Sunni Caliphates, and that Shiism was its antithesis. In places like Baghdad and Damascus, Sunni religious elites embraced the Arab nationalists' glorification of the Arab past and of the Sunni Caliphal dynasties, of Umayyads and Abbasids, propagating a Sunni view of early Islamic history.[54]

This Salafi–Arab nationalist synthesis was epitomised by the circle around the Damascene cleric and senior Ottoman education official Tahir al-Jaza'iri.[55] al-Jaza'iri's students would become influential in all walks of life. One of them was Muhammad Kurd Ali, minister of education in Syria between 1920 and 1922 and subsequently founder and president of the Arab

Academy of Damascus, a post he held for thirty years. The Arab Academy, founded on the orders of Faisal in 1919 on the model of the Académie Française, and crucially important in shaping standardised views on Arabic language and history, became a platform for Salafi-inspired Arab nationalism. Kurd Ali was a defender of the Umayyads, who, with their capital at Damascus and their role in the spread of Islam, seemed to him an ideal reference point. But this embrace of the Umayyads, and criticism of Shiism, would lead to tensions with the few Shii members of the Academy such as Muhsin al-Amin.[56]

Muhibb al-Din al-Khatib, the co-founder of the Salafiyya Press and Bookstore in Cairo and collaborator of Rida and Nasif, was another of al-Jaza'iri's students. In the First World War, he supported the Arab Revolt and worked for the British government. A supporter of the Hashemites, and together with Rida and Faisal a member of an Arab nationalist secret society, after the conquest of the Hijaz by Ibn Saud he, like Rida, endorsed the Saudi-Wahhabi movement, symbolising the Salafi-Arab nationalist synthesis.[57] Al-Khatib thought that the Companions of the Prophet had lived in harmony with each other, and that histories of disagreements and strife were the result of evil machinations of non-Arab enemies of Islam. Right-wing Salafis such as al-Khatib praised the establishment of dynastic rule under the Umayyads, and monarchs such as Ibn Saud if they broadly supported Sunni Islamic and Arab causes.[58] On both counts, conflict with Shiism was inevitable.

Print entrepreneurs like al-Khatib or Rida popularised older religious debates, brought semi-forgotten sectarian polemics back to the fore, and facilitated interactions between the Arab world, India, and beyond. Initially financed by Indian patrons, Salafi publishing houses and institutions increasingly found patrons in the Gulf. Qatar's ruling family, the Al Thani, hailed from the Banu Tamim, the same tribe as Ibn Abd al-Wahhab, and the Gulf Emirate also embraced the Wahhabi tradition. They financed the publications of Salafi classics, and, once revenues from oil and gas skyrocketed in the second part of the twentieth century, became major funders of Sunnism, and, later, Islamist movements.[59]

The most important support of all would come from the Saudis. The establishment of a Salafi-Wahhabi state in the heart of the Arabian Peninsula, with substantial revenues from the pilgrimage, and later oil, changed Sunnism forever. By the end of the 1920s, the Al Saud ruled over a vast territory, incorporating their homeland in central Najd, the fertile Eastern part of the peninsula, the religiously symbolic Hijaz in the West, and large areas in the north and south, where they were only checked by the Zaydi Imams. After these conquests, Ibn Saud faced the question as to what to do with the Ikhwan, who had been his main military force, and who were committed to implement Wahhabi teachings. In a show of force, in 1927, Ikhwan leaders and Wahhabi clerics demanded that Ibn Saud adhere more strictly to Wahhabi norms, also demanding that he convert, or expel, all Shia under his rule.[60] Ibn Saud feared that a too-rigorous implementation of these demands would destabilise the country, and would allow the Ikhwan to establish themselves as alternative power brokers. He moved to repress recalcitrant Ikhwan leaders, and sedentarise them.[61]

To do this, and to support his state-building project, Ibn Saud needed the support of the clergy, which he integrated into the nascent state apparatus.[62] The Al Saud repressed memories of tribal conflict, including their own violence towards dissident tribes and territories, by publicly adhering to Wahhabism.[63] The notion of the ideal Saudi as a loyal Sunni tribesman was doubly exclusionary for the Shia of al-Ahsa and Qatif, who were largely not tribally organised, and moreover represented a wide swath. Some were sedentary, others were peasants in the oases; they were pearl divers, or traders and urban notables. While the most extreme Wahhabi demands were only implemented briefly, Shii public rituals, books, and religious schools remained forbidden, and Shia were marginalised in state employment and public life. Any resistance was crushed.[64] A small Shii community in Medina, and a community of Ismailis in the southern province of Najran, on the border with Yemen, also came under Saudi rule. Unlike Shia in the East, both were part of important tribes, and especially the Ismailis more accepted than Twelver Shia in the Saudi system, so long as they were willing to de-emphasise their sectarian identity.[65] By the end of the 1930s, the identity of the Saudi state would become closely associated with a specific kind of Hanbali-Wahhabi Sunnism, one that marginalised Shia, Sufis, and Shafii, Maliki and Hanafi Sunnis in the Hijaz and al-Ahsa.[66] It was symbolised by the moving of the state's capital from Jeddah in the Hijaz to Riyadh, a small town not far from the old desert fortress of the Al Saud, Diriyya, in the Saudi-Wahhabi heartland, now the centre of the Kingdom of Saudi Arabia.

That general Sunni Arab resurgence deeply affected Iraq in the late 1920s and early 1930s. Protégés of the above-mentioned Sunni Arab nationalist al-Husri published books glorifying the Umayyads and criticising Ali, questioning the Shia's Arab credentials. This outraged Shii clerics and parts of the

Iraqi public sphere.[67] Shii delegations petitioned King Faisal to fire the authors, which he did in one case, although Arab nationalists such as al-Husri defended them. As Shia protested against these books, Sunnis organised counter-demonstrations.[68] This contributed to Shii suspicions of Sunni Arab nationalists, and entrenched anti-Shia feelings amongst the latter.

Some Iraqi Shia (and Jews) embraced Arab nationalism.[69] Others felt that it favoured a vision of the past in which they were at best marginalised and at worst cast as the Other.[70] In 1928, the vice president of the above-mentioned Arab Academy of Damascus, for example, argued that Shia had to understand that for Arab nationalists the Umayyad era was a source of pride. Shii Arab nationalists should find a middle ground between their support for the Arab cause—and the Umayyads—and their confession, which condemned the Umayyads, in effect asking Shia to accept the Sunni Arab view of the early Caliphates.[71]

Ostracised by Sunni Arab nationalists, some Arab Shia sought to make Arab nationalism their own. Others turned towards Communism or Shii revivalism. To prove their authenticity, Shii authors sought to write Shia into the history of Arabism, and into the history of Islam more broadly, emphasising the Arab roots of key Shii clerics, and the chain of scholarship and transmission that linked them to the early Islamic period. At the forefront of this project were Najaf-trained Arab Shii reformist clerics such as the ubiquitous Muhsin al-Amin, who criticised Kurd Ali for his defence of the Umayyads and his attacks on the Shia.[72] Al-Amin spearheaded a wider Shii intellectual revival, symbolised by his encyclopaedia *Notables of the Shia*, on the history of Shiism especially in the Arab world and Iran, which assembled Shii sources and writings by Shii authors.[73] These clerics cooperated with lay intellectuals, the *effendiyya*, that were to play key roles in civil society, in the emerging print industry, and in politics.

The growing Shii printing industry in Iran, Lebanon, Iraq, and India published Shii classics, including anti-Sunni polemics.[74] Many of these were assertions of Shii identity, but sometimes omitted anti-Sunni material from important Shii works for the sake of inner-Islamic harmony.[75] The destruction of the shrines of the *Ahl al-Bayt* in Medina in 1925 gave disparate Shii communities a sense of common purpose. Print media spread the news that the holy sites were under attack. A book on Shii holy sites by an Iraqi cleric documenting the destruction, with before-and-after pictures, underwent different printings, including one in Bombay, financed by Indian Shia.[76] Shii communities on the Indian subcontinent marked the day in January 1926 that the tombs were levelled as an annual day of mourning on which crowds decry the crimes of the Wahhabis against the Imams.[77]

Shii intellectuals responded forcefully to Wahhabism, including in the journal *al-Irfan* (Knowledge).[78] Published in Sidon, present-day Lebanon, starting in 1909, the periodical initially benefited from the political opening in the late Ottoman period after the promulgation of the constitution and the new press law under the 'Young Turks'.[79] Under the French Mandate, it became the leading voice of an emerging Shii identity politics, fostered a Shii transnational public sphere, and connected Arab Shii communities closer to each other.[80] *Al-Irfan* became the Shii counterpart to Rida's *al-Manar*. Both published pan-Islamic and pan-Arab appeals, and simultaneously became conduits of Sunni- and Shii-centric reformisms.[81] They were part of a general Muslim Arab public sphere, in which many themes were shared, especially modernist concerns, but in which Sunnis and Shia also developed their own discourses and outlets.[82] When in 1900 *al-Manar* accused Shii scholars in Najaf of converting Sunnis, Mushin al-Amin and other Shia responded, including in *al-Irfan*, defending key Shii principles from Sunni attacks, and blaming the rise of Wahhabism for Sunni–Shia tensions.[83] By the 1920s, Rida's embrace of Wahhabism and open attacks on Shiism enraged al-Amin, and so the two clashed on the pages of *al-Manar* and *al-Irfan*, respectively, and published competing books that invoked arguments of earlier polemics but linked them to current affairs.[84] Rida, who could set aside religious difference to facilitate political alliances, became more assertive towards Christianity and Shiism.[85] He never accepted Shiism as a valid school of jurisprudence equal to the Sunni schools, and his debates with Shii scholars in *al-Manar*, attuned many readers that were not familiar with the intricacies of Sunni–Shia debates with the Sunni fundamentalist position.[86]

Shii clerics in Lebanon had hoped that pan-Islam would resolve disputes between Muslims and their plight under imperial rule, and their specific predicament as a marginal community in a Lebanese state dominated by Christians and Sunnis.[87] To this end, and to prove their modernism, they and other reformist Shii scholars were willing to tone down aspects of Shiism deemed offensive by Sunnis, including flagellations during Muharram, some aspects of shrine visitation, or the Shii call to prayer and temporary marriage. Some argued that one could choose between the four Sunni schools of jurisprudence and the Twelver Shii one to devise rulings. But many of these practices, including the Shii call to prayer, had become so popular that these clerics faced resistance from Shii purists, who felt these reforms were endangering the very essence of Shiism.[88]

Shii and Sunni leaders held joint congresses to strengthen Muslim unity in the 1920s and 1930s.[89] During a congress in Jerusalem in 1931 to highlight Muslim solidarity in the face of Zionism, Sunni participants suggested that the Iraqi Shii cleric Muhammad Hussain Kashif al-Ghita, whom we have got to know for his anti-colonial stance, lead the Friday prayer in the al-Aqsa mosque. This was significant, for by praying behind a Shii prayer leader, the Sunnis accepted his authority, and Shia as Muslims.[90] Kashif al-Ghita had been a key Shii advocate of pan-Islam and Arab nationalism.[91] He had previously engaged in a debate with the Syrian Salafi Jamal al-Din al-Qasimi. Written in a more respectful tone than other polemics, it started when al-Qasimi reacted to a manuscript sent to him by a Yemeni cleric residing in Singapore who had likewise argued that the cursing of Muawiya was lawful. Al-Qasimi denied this in *al-Manar*, and while he had previously used Shii and Khariji sources, he now took a Sunni fundamentalist stance. Kashif al-Ghita in turn replied in *al-Irfan*.[92] The 1931 congress was widely praised, and even Rida, who attended, initially voiced his support for Sunni–Shia rapprochement. But other Salafis condemned it, and tensions rose during some of the Congress' committee meetings. Eventually, Rida came away from the conference stressing the limits of Sunni–Shia rapprochement.[93] Both he and Kashif al-Ghita re-emerged as forceful defenders of Sunnism and Shiism, respectively. Shortly after the conference, Kashif al-Ghita published a book outlining the doctrines of Shiism aimed at a Sunni audience, a book he had written after receiving complaints from Iraqi students in Cairo, who were allegedly told by clerics at al-Azhar that Shiism stood outside of Islam. Meant as a forceful doctrinal defence of Shiism, but one that still occurred in the context of dialogue with Sunnis, it had the opposite effect on Rida, who wrote a negative review, undermining the common ground found in Jerusalem. Kashif al-Ghita also rebuked the Wahhabi fatwas against the Shia.[94]

This was the context in which Hasan al-Banna, the founder of the Muslim Brotherhood, the probably most famous, and oldest, of the Sunni Islamist movements, came of age. He was influenced by the modernism and pan-Islamism of al-Afghani and Abduh and the *Salafiyya's* right-wing, personified by Rida and al-Khatib. When al-Banna moved to Cairo in 1923, at age seventeen, the latter were in ascendance, and he frequented the house of

Rida, and became close to al-Khatib, whose journal and press would publish al-Banna's first pamphlet and the Brothers' first magazine.[95] In 1927, al-Banna moved to Ismailia, a city on the Suez Canal, and started preaching and organising a grass-roots social movement that focused on social welfare, education, and reshaping Muslim society and religious practice. This was the starting point of the Society of the Muslim Brothers, which gained ground in the 1930s, when admiring coverage in Islamic magazines raised its profile.[96] Unlike the Salafi intellectuals, who had sought to influence elite opinion, al-Banna sought to organise the masses.

Al-Banna and his followers saw divisions amongst Muslims, even between the Sunnis schools of law, as weakness. They saw themselves as a pan-Islamic movement and hoped that through a return to the Quran and the Sunna, Muslims could overcome their differences.[97] For the Egyptian Brothers, unlike for Rida and al-Khatib, Shiism was not a primary concern. Nonetheless, they saw themselves as building on Rida's work. After Rida's death in 1935, al-Banna was proud to revive *al-Manar*.[98] Anti-Shiism became more pronounced once, by the 1940s, the Muslim Brotherhood spread beyond Egypt, gaining followers in places like Syria, Lebanon, Bahrain (and later Iraq), with mixed Sunni–Shia populations, and once it moved closer to Saudi Arabia.[99]

Like Rida, al-Khatib, and other Islamic revivalists, al-Banna saw in Ibn Saud an independent Arab-Islamic ruler worthy of support, and a potential source of patronage. By the mid-1930s, the Brothers were urging Egyptians to go on Hajj as part of a more Islamic lifestyle. Al-Banna and a Brotherhood delegation visited the Hijaz and met with Saudi officials, who were keen to increase the number of pilgrims. The Brotherhood started to enlist wealthy Hijazis and the Saudi King as subscribers to its publications.[100] These connections were facilitated by Nasif and the Egyptian Salafis who had started working for Ibn Saud—the same people that had already brought Rida closer to the Wahhabis.[101] Saudi Arabia would support the Brotherhood abroad and allow Brothers to settle in the Kingdom on the condition that they would not organise politically there. The endorsement by pan-Islamists of the Saudi State signified an acknowledgement that the nation state would, at least for the time being, become the dominant form of political organisation. While advocating in principle the necessity of the Caliphate, Rida, too supported the Saudi state as coming closest to the ideal of an Islamic state. The idea of the Islamic state slowly but surely became the ideal type of political organisation, first amongst Sunni Islamists, and later amongst Shii ones.[102] The tension between that aspiration to uniting Muslims, and the realities of the nation state, and Sunni–Shia division, was to remain.

Sensing that no agreement was possible with Salafis, reformist Shii clerics instead strengthened relations with al-Azhar, the Islamic University in Cairo that had as noted been founded under the Fatimids, and which was now the most significant institution of Sunni learning in the Arab world and yet a place where Salafi influence was still limited.[103] When the future Shah of Iran, Mohammad Reza Pahlavi, whose father had in 1925 overthrown the last Qajar ruler in a coup, married the sister of King Farouq of Egypt in 1939, he visited al-Azhar.[104] This facilitated rapprochement initiatives, especially one spearheaded by Mohammad Taqi Qommi (d. 1990), an Iranian cleric who had accompanied the Shah on his visit. Qommi was spurred into action by an incident during the Mecca pilgrimage in 1943, when an Iranian Shii pilgrim was arrested by the Saudis and subsequently beheaded. This led to a crisis between Saudi Arabia and Iran, and an Iranian boycott of the Hajj. Iranian and other Shii pilgrims had been harassed and charged extra fees when the Wahhabis first established control over the Hijaz, and then again since 1925. Regulating the Hajj and organising it according to proper, read Sunni Hanbali-Wahhabi norms, served to assert the Saudi state's authority and identity.[105] In 1947 Qommi founded the *Centre for Rapprochement* (*Dar al-Taqrib*) in Cairo, which featured major Sunni figures, including moderate Salafis.[106] Even Hasan al-Banna participated in its early meetings.[107] The Centre organised conferences with Sunni and Shii clerics from across the Islamic world, and issued regular publications.[108] The most respected Shii cleric at the time, Ayatollah Burujirdi of Qom, quietly supported its activities, as did Najaf-trained reformist Shii clerics.[109] Instead of referring to sects (*ta'ifa*) when talking about Sunnism and Shiism, it argued that one should refer to schools of jurisprudence (*madhhab*). This meant an upgrading of Shiism (and Zaydism) to the status of the other Sunni legal schools, a move that was accepted by the Sunni participants in the endeavour (though rejected by its Sunni detractors), and an approach this book has adopted throughout as well.[110]

Its most noteworthy legacy was a 1959 fatwa by al-Azhar's rector, Mahmoud Shaltut, accepting Shiism as a valid school of Islam. The fatwa stated that 'in Muslim law it is as valid to worship according to the Jafari Doctrine known as the Ithna-Ashariyya as it is according to any Sunni school. Therefore, it is necessary for Muslims to know this fact and to rid themselves

of the unwarranted fanaticism in favour of certain sects.'[111] Shaltut proclaimed
that the four Sunni schools of jurisprudence and the Twelver Shii and Zaydi
schools would be studied without prejudice, and that a Muslim could decide
to follow any one of them, and switch between them. He even encouraged
Azhar students and scholars to consult all those schools and to adopt the
reasoning of the Shia schools when they proved more convincing on a
given topic (though to what extent this was implemented is not known).[112]
While al-Azhar, for example, did not go as far as allowing the establishment
of a Shii chair at the university, this was ground-breaking.[113]

To facilitate smooth relations, the Centre chose to ignore the most
contentious aspects of Sunni–Shia relations.[114] While the finances of the
Centre were never publicised, Egypt and Iran likely supported it (which
was in turn criticised by Salafis).[115] Scholars and lay authors affiliated with
the Centre visited each other, and wrote books advocating Sunni–Shia
rapprochement. But this antagonised hardliners on both sides.[116] While
Shii purists didn't approve of the concessions of Shii participants, Sunni
Revivalists denounced the project. Initially, the Centre had sought to include
Wahhabi scholars.[117] But they boycotted the Centre's activities contributing to the frustration of Shii intellectuals with the rise of Salafi-Wahhabism.
The Lebanese Shii cleric Muhammad Jawad Mughniyya, for example, who
had been a key participant, published books that detailed encounters with
Sunnis in Egypt and accounts of disputations with Wahhabi clerics and
Saudi officials during a visit to the Hijaz, and became a leading Shii critic
of the Wahhabiyya.[118]

Al-Khatib, who edited the official journal of al-Azhar, and represented
the conservative faction in the institution, on the other hand, outrightly
denounced the project. To that effect he published a highly offensive and
influential anti-Shii treatise in Jeddah in 1961 that was financed by
Muhammad Nasif, who wrote an accompanying note likewise denouncing
rapprochement, and subsequent editions were financed by a former Qatari
ruler and by the Mufti of Saudi Arabia, and it was widely translated, including into Turkish and Urdu. He rehashed old accusations, such as that the
Shia prefer pilgrimage to Najaf and Karbala, where al-Khatib claimed the
Imams were not even buried, to Mecca, or that Shia believed in the falsification
of the Quran, an accusation that reemerged forcefully in anti-Shii polemics.[119]

On a political level, the rapprochement initiative may have been an
attempt to bolster Egypt's standing amongst Arab Shia.[120] But when Egypt
and Iran increasingly emerged as leaders of competing regional Cold War

blocs, leading to a complete rupture of relations in 1960, the project lost its momentum.[121]

Ecumenical efforts would eventually fail not just due to political circumstances. There was a limit as to how much doctrinal rapprochement could take place without one side or the other losing its sense of identity. While pan-Islam had sought to unite Muslims in the face of Empire, a return to the 'golden age' of Arabs and Islam, under the Rashidun Caliphs, set the *Salafiyya* on a collision course with Shiism.[122] The more conciliatory Salafis became marginalised by those who argued that the early period was to be emulated. The Islamic revival aimed at purifying and unifying Muslims, and many came to see themselves for the first time as part of one interconnected 'Islamic world'.[123] Yet, simultaneously, many started to see themselves more consciously as Sunni or Shii, and increasingly had to come to terms with new boundaries drawn up in the inter-war period, and a new ideology: nationalism.

The decline of the Centre for Rapprochement coincided with the rise of the Salafis as influential players in the Sunni public sphere, the increased role of pro-Western monarchies, and the founding of new pan-Islamic organisations in Saudi Arabia such as the *Muslim World League* (1962) and the *Organisation of Islamic Cooperation* (OIC) (1969)—organisations that largely excluded the Shia. Crown Prince Faisal bin Abdulaziz, a rival to Nasser, who had come to power in a coup overthrowing the monarchy in 1952, sought to position Saudi Arabia at the centre of the Muslim world, legitimised by Salafi-Wahhabism and funded by growing oil revenues. Faisal was appointed Crown Prince after the death of Ibn Saud in 1953, and King in 1964.[124]

Faisal had his power base amongst the clergy (his mother was a descendant of Ibn Abd al-Wahhab, whose family had remained Saudi Arabia's most important clerical family). Faisal empowered the clerics, and positioned Saudi Arabia as the leader of the conservative Arab camp, turned political Sunnism into a rival to Nasser's Arab nationalism, and allied himself with the US.[125] The new institutions headquartered in and to a large extent funded by Saudi Arabia, became powerful bodies, and spread a Salafi-inspired interpretation of Sunnism around the world.[126] Nasser, on the other hand, cracked down increasingly on the Muslim Brothers, leading even more to move to Saudi Arabia and other Gulf States, where they entered the religious and educational fields, and staffed those new institutions. While the brothers and the local Wahhabi clerics maintained their differences, for the time being they made common cause, primarily against Communism and secularism, and then against Shiism. While the Saudis agreed with Pahlavi Iran on a pro-Western and anti-Communist stance, and a common enmity to Nasser, the Iranians saw the Arabs of the Peninsula as backward junior partners in Gulf and wider Cold War politics. Meanwhile, the Saudis retained their anti-Shii and anti-Iranian prejudices, and resented the Shah's grandstanding.

Saudi rivals in the region embraced Socialist-leaning Arab nationalism, and accused the Saudis of being reactionary, subservient to imperial interests, and of using religion to undermine them. To the Saudis this was absurd. They saw themselves as the original Arabs, and the Arabs as the chosen people of Islam. In time, even the Saudis would adopt some Arab nationalist rhetoric. And Sunni Arab nationalists, such as the leaders of the Iraqi Baath party, would agree with the Saudis on an anti-Iranian and anti-Shii outlook. Islamism, Arabism, and the various nationalisms that emerged in this period, were fluid ideologies that new actors could embrace and mould to their liking.

Both pan-Islam and pan-Arabism remained popular aspirations but failed to realise their ambitions of establishing larger unifying political entities. The consolidation of Lebanon as a separate state and increasing Zionist immigration to Palestine and the eventual declaration of the State of Israel in 1948 shattered hopes of uniting Greater Syria, which Arab nationalists from the region had seen as a short-term goal. At the same time pan-Islamists could not agree on a way forward, or on one leadership, after the end of the Caliphate, and Muslims had to define their position vis-à-vis new nation states, at a time when state identity was being negotiated. Because sectarian identity often played a role in state identity, earlier memories of sectarian strife resurfaced.

Apart from pan-Islam, Sunni and Shii revivalisms, and pan-nationalisms, especially after the end of World War II, nationalism seemed to offer an antidote to class and identity divisions, leading countries out of imperial tutelage and into political independence.[127] Many territorial nationalisms were ostensibly 'secular' and anti-sectarian, or tried to downplay sectarian identity so as to deflect attention from the ruling elite's identity. Others were tied to a specific sectarian identity (as in the Saudi case), or the memory of a pre-modern empire that had legitimised itself in sectarian terms (such as Turkey, Iran, and Afghanistan). This was akin to developments in Europe, for example in England, Ireland, Greece, the Balkans, Russia, Italy, Spain, or Portugal, where confessional identity and nationalism were often intertwined.[128] As noted, some saw religious identity as the equivalent of ethnicity, and claimed the right to a certain territory and national self-determination on this basis. Zionism, which its founders saw as the Jewish equivalent of European ethnic nationalism, uniting all Jews regardless of their geographical background, and Maronite Christian Lebanese nationalism, were such examples (as were the anti-Ottoman Christian nationalisms in the Balkans and in Greece).

Arab nationalism had sought to unite Arabs, Christians, Jews, and Muslims. But recurring debates about the early history of Arabs and Islam, and about dynasties such as the Umayyads, and Jewish and Christian nationalist projects undermined the anti-sectarian aspect of Arab nationalism, tying it more closely to a Sunni Arab view of history. This vision increasingly clashed with that of non-Sunni Muslims. In countries that were not clear successor states of a dynasty, or where the population was confessionally mixed, such as Lebanon, Syria, Iraq, Yemen, Bahrain, and Kuwait competing nationalisms incorporated different sectarian identities. Sunna and Shia in Iraq, for example, both came to see themselves as authentically Iraqi and developed distinctive views of what proper Iraqi nationalism was.

On the Indian subcontinent, the categories of Muslim and Hindu, fashioned under British rule, became the foundations for religious nationalism. They were used to stake political claims, and in 1947 became invoked as cause for Partition, the separate creation of India and Pakistan. In Pakistan, religious nationalism became the very foundation of the post-colonial order. After Partition, millions of Hindus and Muslims (and others) had to move from one territory to the other. But what exactly constituted Muslim (and Hindu) identity was debated and its meaning profoundly transformed by Empire, and Sunnis, Shia and Ismailis also started to see themselves as part of larger, global confessional communities apart from their belonging to an overarching Muslim community.

Confessional identity thus played a key role in the transition from pre-modern empires to centralised nation states. This was so in territories where that process occurred under direct European control, in places where the Ottomans set it in motion, as well as in territories where European influence was limited, such as in Saudi Arabia, the Yemeni Highlands, Afghanistan, and Iran. In all these cases, people had to define themselves vis-à-vis a new nation state. The non-Sunni Muslims that were not Twelver Shia, became the object of missionaries and nationalist anxiety. In Turkey, the secularising policies that so enraged the Khilafatists and Rida, initially allowed these communities to become more accepted. Especially in border regions, some were both ethnically and religiously different from the dominant nationalist identity.

A nascent Iranian nationalism, and an Arab nationalism that defined itself against Iran, complicated the situation of Arab Shia, and Shia elsewhere, such as in Afghanistan. As noted, the Qajars had already embraced an Iranian nationalism that appropriated Shiism.[129] They, for example, further tried to link Shiism to Iran by propagating the notion already widespread in Iran that Hussain had married Shahrbanu, the daughter of the last Sassanid Shah, Yazdegerd III (632–651) (they also invented genealogies linking themselves to them and created a national flag that included a lion, an ancient Iranian symbol, holding Ali's sword, the *Dhu l-Faqar*, that ubiquitous Ahl al-Baytist symbol).[130] In the late nineteenth and early twentieth century, a sense of racial superiority, based on the presumed Aryan origins of the Iranian nation, in part defined in relation to Arabs, became widespread amongst the intelligentsia. Ultimately, the sort of royalist Shiism of the Qajars and the pan-Islamic constitutionalist project of the Constitutional Revolution of 1906–11 both failed and were replaced by an Iranian nationalism that sought inspiration in Iran's pre-Islamic past and in a strong, modernising state, a project that, after 1925, became embodied in the Pahlavi dynasty—until 1979, that is.[131] Given that Arabs had brought Islam to Iran, the position of Islam in Iranian nationalism was complicated. Arabic had had a profound influence on Persian, and many older Iranian words had been replaced by Arabic ones, especially religious vocabulary. Reza Shah Pahlavi, the army officer who came to power in 1921 after a coup against the last Qajar ruler, Ahmad Shah, who then formally abdicated in 1925, and Mohammad Reza Shah, who replaced his father in 1941, all tried to encourage an allegedly more authentic form of Persian by replacing Arabic words. This was part of the Pahlavis' attempt to portray themselves as successors to ancient Iranian empires, and was influenced by Atatürk's switch from Arabic to Latin script and advocacy for the use of old Turkish words, or new ones, as opposed to Ottoman and Arabic ones. In the 1930s, Reza Shah also insisted on the use of *Iran*, meaning 'land of the Aryans', in international affairs, instead of Persia, a term long used by European powers.[132]

While ethnic nationalists strove to regain a sense of racial purity, their attempts, more than anything, highlighted that language reflected interaction.[133] The border regions between Iran and the newly-constituted

'Arab World' were frontier zones characterised by transnational networks of pilgrimage, trade, and migration that had left their mark in language, culture and religious practice.[134] But demands of loyalty and allegiance by competing modernising states now hardened boundaries that had long been fluid. We had seen how that process started when Ottomans and Qajars delineated their border more clearly in the second half of the nineteenth century. This now intensified. All this was not couched in explicitly sectarian terms, but an increasingly powerful and nationalist Iran heightened suspicions of Shii and Sunni Persian-speaking communities in neighbouring states, including in Iraq and Gulf States such as Kuwait and Bahrain, who were stigmatised by local Arab nationalists. It problematised the role of ethnic minorities in Iran such as Kurds and Azeris in the North, Arabs near the border with Iraq and on Iran's Persian Gulf coast, the Baluch in Baluchistan, on the border with Pakistan, and Sunnis near the border with Afghanistan, a situation that was exacerbated if ethnic minority status overlapped with Sunni sectarian identity, as it often did.

On the one hand, in contrast to Safavids and Qajars, for whom Shiism was central to legitimisation, it played less of a role under the Pahlavis, who embraced the pre-Islamic period as Golden Age of Persian identity.[135] State-funded research propagated a Sufi tradition as a sort of apolitical national heritage, and a bulwark against the growing mobilisation of the Left and the activist clergy, a notion that was further popularised by French Orientalists.[136] The state also supported Sufi orders, including those that had been repressed by the Safavids as potential rivals.[137] In the first years of his reign, Reza Shah faced clerical backlash to his secularising authoritarianism, to restrictions on public Shii rituals, and to his attempts to modernise the clergy's education. The clerics were especially unhappy with conscription and the secularisation and codification of the legal system. It was the first time Shii law was codified for use by a modern Muslim-ruled state (outside of the British Empire, that is), following developments in Sunni states, and which was influenced in its ambition, scope and organisation by earlier Ottoman legal codes. By extending the realms over which the state, and its lay jurists and not the clergy could adjudicate, it undermined the latter's authority.[138] But then, and especially under Mohammad Reza Shah from 1941 onwards, the state found a working arrangement with Shii clerics, and endorsed them on issues of common concern. The state backed the clerics against those they deemed heretics (such as Bahais), in return for acquiescence in the deposition of nationalist Prime Minister Muhammad Mossadeq in 1953 and the restoration of Muhammad Reza Shah to power, or the repression of Communism, which had become a major political force by mid-century.[139] Under Muhammad Reza Shah, the state built mosques and supported religious education, both Shii and Sunni, sponsored Muharram processions, portrayed Shii passion plays as a sort of Iranian folklore, and facilitated and regulated pilgrimage to Shii shrines and the Hijaz.[140] It also acted on occasion as defender of Shia abroad and helped expand Shii shrines in Syria, for example, to facilitate Iranian pilgrimage.[141]

Like their predecessors, the Pahlavis maintained relations with the clergy in Najaf and Karbala, but the focus of their patronage for Shiism was on Qom and Mashhad. Qom's position was bolstered when the Shii religious hierarchy, increasingly more centralised, moved there from Najaf after the death of the Iraq-based Grand Ayatollah Abu al-Hasan Isfahani in 1946. The Qom-based Hussain Burujirdi, who as noted supported the rapprochement with al-Azhar, emerged as the sole Grand Ayatollah, accepted by most Shia around the world as spiritual authority.[142] Burujirdi and the Shah's relationship rested on an assumption that Burujirdi would remain aloof from politics, and that, in return, the Shah would not interfere with the expansion of the seminary and its networks. That tied global Shiism more closely to Qom. Some of Burujirdi's pupils tried, unsuccessfully, to push him into open opposition to the Shah. One of them, Ruhollah Khomeini, would take on that role himself after Burujirdi's death in 1961, as we will see in the next chapter.[143]

As noted, the Shah, and Ayatollah Burujirdi quietly supported rapprochement with al-Azhar in Cairo. But Iran's emergence as a regional power, alongside Cold War tensions, meant that Arab-Iranian relations were unsteady. Iran's growing relationship with Israel was an affront for many Arab states, above all Nasserist Egypt.[144] And Nasser's anti-colonial message resonated in the Gulf and the Arabian Peninsula, where Britain's aggression in the Suez War of 1956, reminded many of their own plight, and where anti-Iranian feelings ran high. That Nasser had married the daughter of an Iranian merchant did not stop him and the Shah from becoming rivals.[145]

Iran saw itself as hegemon of the Gulf and regarded Nasser's goal of uniting Arabs under his leadership, and expanding influence in the Gulf and Iraq, with suspicion.[146] Egyptian media like the popular radio station *Voice of the Arabs*, emphasised the Arabness of the Gulf States and denounced Iranian immigration into what Nasser called the 'Arabian Gulf' as opposed to the 'Persian Gulf' (a naming dispute that continues to upset Arab-Iranian relations). Egyptian media referred to the province of Khuzistan in Iran, where many ethnic Arabs live, as 'Arabistan', enraging Iranian nationalists.[147] The Shah, in turn, reasserted Iran's claim to sovereignty over Bahrain (a claim dating back to the Safavid period), leading to tensions with Britain, Bahrain's patron and quasi-colonial power, and Gulf rulers. Arab Nationalists replied that Bahrain was an integral part of the Arab Nation, implying its Sunni nature, and portraying Shii populations as alien. When Britain withdrew militarily from the Gulf in 1971, however, the Shah accepted Bahrain's independence and renounced Iranian claims, but in turn occupied islands that had hitherto formed part of the Trucial States, the newly formed United Arab Emirates, and soured relations with the latter.[148]

While the rhetoric Nasser and the Shah used against each other generally did not contain religious references (and they had previously sponsored ecumenical movements), many of the themes of Arab-Iranian animosity would later, after 1979, be 'upgraded' with more explicitly sectarian references, which would make them even more explosive. And while the Shah was on good terms with pro-Western Arab countries such as Saudi Arabia, strong mutual suspicions remained there, too.

How complicated reality was show the diverging trajectories of the two main incarnations of Baathism, in Syria and Iraq, Baathism being another main variant of Arab nationalism. While in principle anti-sectarian, both factions became dominated by members of specific sectarian groups, who entered the army under the Mandates, and then recruited members of their family, tribe, village, and sect. In Syria, as noted, Arab nationalism initially expressed the resentments of Sunni Arabs against the French Mandate, and special representation for 'minorities'. Alawites and Druze, often poor and rural, alongside Sunnis, by the middle of the twentieth century, migrated to Syria's towns, where they embraced Arab nationalism as an expression of the interests of poor peasants and an emerging middle class. Many joined the army, and in Syria, and across the region, army officers from humble backgrounds now rose to power benefitting from the reluctance of the nobility to enlist their sons. In Iraq, Libya, Egypt, and Yemen, the army overthrew monarchies, and officers from non-elite backgrounds assumed power. In post-independence Syria, the army intervened in politics numerous times, until in 1963, officers affiliated with the Baath Party putsched. Alawites had by then risen through the ranks of the party, and the heavy recruitment of Alawites (as well as Druze, Ismailis, Tscherkesses, and others) into the armed forces under the French Mandate made itself felt.

Arab nationalism was now transformed from an ideology largely expressing Sunni Arab interests into one legitimising power held by non-Sunni religious groups.[149]

The Baath party was not anti-religious per se. The founders of the Baath party, many of whom were Christian, had, for example, long emphasised that Islam was a key part of Arab history.[150] Baathists from an Alawite background like Zaki al-Arsuzi, whom we have gotten to know for his role in Alexandretta, did not describe themselves as Alawites, yet substituted Sunni symbolism in Arab nationalism with symbols more familiar to Alawites and other non-Sunnis.[151] Officers from non-Sunni backgrounds now rose to prominence, but did not yet act as a group, and purged each other. From 1963 to 1970, the two Alawite officers Saleh Jadid and Hafez al-Assad competed for power, and in the process accused each other of using 'sectarianism' to bolster their relative faction. But the result of these struggles for power was that officers from minority groups asserted their control of the party and the state.[152] In 1970 al-Assad asserted his supremacy and purged Jadid and his allies. Despite internal rivalries, this symbolised the rise of Alawites from a peripheral peasant community to the highest echelons of the state. Al-Assad and others had undermined a short-lived union between Syria and Nasserist Egypt, which, rather than a union of equals, many Syrian Baathists saw as Egyptians asserting their power. Baath land reforms, ostensibly socialist in nature, favoured peasants in the countryside, many of whom were Sunni, and many of whom were Alawite and Druze, and hurt the traditional land-owning bourgeoisies of the Syrian towns like Hama and Aleppo, which were predominantly Sunni. At the same time al-Assad toned down some of the more Leftist policies of his predecessors, and appeased the Sunni bourgeoisie of Damascus and the official Sunni clergy. The regime would not have been able to consolidate itself without cross-sectarian support but a sense of relative socio-economic and political decline amongst other Sunni elites fuelled support for the Muslim Brotherhood, founded in 1945 by Syrian students in Egypt.[153] Unlike its Egyptian mother organisation, however, the Syrian branch was influenced by Damascene Salafis, and the Salafi-Arabist synthesis described above, invoked Ibn Taymiyya, and embarked on a collision course with Alawism and Shiism.[154] It endorsed the Sunni view of history, and saw itself as representing Arab Sunnis.[155] Its founder, Mustafa al-Siba'i, opposed Sunni–Shia rapprochement.[156] After Syrian independence in 1946 the Brotherhood won seats in Parliament but faced repression in the 1950s.[157]

The Baath Party's ever-tightening grip on the levers of power drove the Brothers underground. After the Baath coup in 1963, Sunni landed elites and the Brotherhood supported an uprising in Hama in 1964, and its crushing became an early indication of the Baath's brutality (Hama became the scene of another Brotherhood-led rising in 1982 that met with fierce repression). The Brotherhood was now cast as an internal enemy, and Hafez al-Assad used its spectre to secure the loyalty of Alawites and other non-Sunnis. The suppression, in turn, radicalised and sectarianised the Brotherhood.[158] Within a generation, Arab nationalism in Syria had undergone tremendous shifts—from being a movement largely associated with Arab Sunnis, to one more associated with Arab non-Sunnis. Opposition to it assumed the language of Sunni Islamism, with its increasingly global connections. Fleeing Syrian Brothers would join their colleagues from Egypt in the Gulf States, bringing with them memories of a struggle against a regime associated with a branch of Shiism. Syrian Brothers would in turn play a leading role in sectarianising not just their branch, but the wider Brotherhood, contributing, as they did, to the foundation and consolidation of Brotherhood branches in the Gulf States.[159]

Despite their common origin, the Baath Party in Syria and the one in Iraq would become fierce rivals. In Iraq, a group of officers had overthrown the Hashemite monarchy in 1958 (and killed the royal family). Initially, a three-men council made up of a Kurd, a Sunni, and a Shii was to rule jointly. But a year later, General Abd al-Karim Qassim, who was from a mixed Sunni-Shia background, assumed more direct power in alliance with the Communist Party. He relaxed some restrictions on Shia in the military, but other reforms put him on a collision course with the Shii clergy, who resented his unified Code of Personal Status, which undermined them and gave women more rights (some of their concerns were heeded). Iraqi law had largely been a continuation of codified Ottoman (Sunni) law, with which Shii clerics had long had issues.[160] In 1963, Baathist officers in turn overthrew Qassim. The Iraqi Baath was initially a diverse party, characterised by Sunni–Shia pan-Arab 'youth' cooperation. While the officers in the party were overwhelmingly Sunni Arab, many of its early leaders and members were Shia.[161] But the Shii role gradually diminished, and the Sunni one increased. Out of fifty-three members of the party's governing body between November 1963 to 1970, only 5.7 per cent were Shii Arabs, with Sunni Arabs accounting for 84.9 per cent (Kurds were also underrepresented). Shii Baathists had backed a losing side in a party crisis, and were policed more harshly for digressions than Sunnis after the coup and ascension of the Arif brothers to the presidency in 1963. Their rule heightened sectarian tensions and turned the Baath into a predominantly Arab Sunni party. Sunni officers constituted the core of the police and the Departments of Interior and Security. When their kin was arrested, they were treated more lightly than Shia, who often lacked connections.[162]

Men from Tikrit in Northern Iraq, such as Ahmad Hasan al-Bakr and Saddam Hussein, who had been key in the party's military branch, now rose in prominence, and in 1968 fully asserted their power (al-Bakr became President, and his cousin, Saddam, Vice-President).[163] For Tikritis, recruitment into the army offered one of the few ways to make a living. Once the army was in power, Tikritis were well positioned.[164] Consequently, the Iraqi Baath became associated with one group of Arab Sunnis, although it retained a diverse membership, and Shia assumed senior functions in the state.[165]

Secular political movements facilitated cross-sectarian cooperation, and most political parties had diverse memberships. But the repressive political environment led many to rely on family members and close friends, people they could fully trust, and these were often of the same sect. A certain village, city or region might be over-represented in a given movement (such as Alawites in the Syrian Baath Party and Tikritis in the Iraqi one, or Shia in Arab Communist Parties).[166] Regimes preferred certain groups over others, and so opposition movements that emerged among disenfranchised groups were themselves more successful at recruiting within certain sections of society. This explains why a party emerging from one ideological origin could develop so differently in two neighbouring countries with different ethno-sectarian makeups.

The Iraqi Baath evoked a Golden Age of Arabs and Islam under the Baghdad-based Abbasids, a link that made the predominance of Sunni Arabs seem 'natural', and emphasised the anti-Iranian element of Arab nationalism. While not explicitly anti-Shii, that connection was implied, as the Shii shrine cities and the clerics retained links to Iran, and propagated a Sunni view of history through the educational system. At the same time, however, giving the demographic weight of Shia and Kurds, the Baath tried to avoid outrightly provoking them, de-emphasising the most contentious historical disputes, and focusing on historical figures revered by both (such as Ali and Hussain).[167] The Shii masses, in turn, focused on rituals and processions, which, despite frequent bans by the government, would grow in size, especially mourning ceremonies during Muharram, and the Arbain pilgrimage to Karbala, in which people walk to the city from all over Iraq, re-enacting their own version of the Iraqi national story, one in which Shiism took centre stage.[168]

The Shii poor that migrated in masses to the cities, initially lacked political representation. They found it in a movement that promised inclusion regardless of religion or ethnicity: Communism.[169] Scores of Shia in Iraq, Lebanon, and the Gulf joined Communist and other Leftist Parties (and of course many more in Iran, Azerbaijan, Afghanistan, Pakistan, Yemen and beyond). The Shii role in Communist movements even led to the coinage of a term in Arabic, *Shi'i-Shuyu'i*, playing on the similarity between the terms 'Shii' and 'communist'. Because Qassim had been allied with the Communists, and because it saw them as a rival, and an obstacle in its goal of unifying the Arab world, the Baath swiftly moved against Communists (despite allying itself with the Soviet Union) after 1963.[170] Communism's promise of radical social, economic, and political change proved appealing across the spectrum. In Iraq, several Sunni Arabs were in the upper echelons of the Communist Party, far fewer in the lower levels, where Arab Shia and Kurds predominated, but that trend was gradually reversed.[171] Communism challenged traditional pillars of Shii society, appealing even to scions of major clerical families. In turn, fearing for their prominence in their own societies, Shii clerics allied with the Iranian and Iraqi states to combat Communism (something on which they agreed with Sunni clerics, and that was one more factor driving the pan-Islamic clerical dialogues of the mid-twentieth century). When senior Iraqi Shii clerics issued fatwas declaring support of Communism illegal, this undermined support for it amongst Shia around the world.

These anti-Communist clerical networks became the nucleus for the first Shii Islamist party.[172] Founded in the 1950s to fight secularism, the Dawa (Call) Party was influenced by Sunni Islamists like the Muslim Brotherhood and Hizb al-Tahrir (Liberation Party), which had been founded in 1953 with the goal of re-establishing the Caliphate. A primarily Sunni party, Hizb al-Tahrir had some Shii members from Lebanon and Iraq. In the 1960s and 1970s one of them would become the head of the Dawa Party, and he and his wing sought to emphasise pan-Islam, downplay its Shii identity and welcome Sunnis into the ranks. But Shii clerics in Najaf and Karbala, who had been foundational in the Party, disagreed. While they appreciated the importance of pan-Islam, they wanted Dawa to represent Iraq's Shia, integrating their ideology and views of history, and clerics to play a major role.[173]

Like the Shii clergy, the Iraqi branch of the Muslim Brotherhood felt threatened by Communism, and the secularising aspects of the Baath. As noted, some brothers sought to work with Shia, and influenced early Shii Islamists, but like their Syrian counterpart, many other Iraqi Brothers saw Shiism as a threat.[174] The Baath, who saw in it a challenger for the loyalties of Arab Sunnis, repressed the Brotherhood, alongside the nascent Shii organisations, and the Communists, turning Iraq more and more into a totalitarian one-party state.[175]

In Lebanon, Communists and Arab nationalists mobilised Shia with promises to upend the sectarian political system set up under the French Mandate, which placed Maronites and some Sunnis on top. Lebanese Communists such as Mahdi Amil would pen some of the most incisive critiques of the politics of sectarianism, which had made collective action across sectarian lines, and along class lines, difficult, and formulate demands that anti-sectarian actors in later periods would invoke. They advocated, for example, civil marriage courts across all sects to weaken clerical control.[176] Shia working in the Saudi oil fields cooperated with Sunnis in a labour movement. A range of left-wing underground parties emerged that had links with Leftists in Bahrain, Kuwait, and Iraq. Here, too, crackdowns hit Shii Leftists especially hard.[177] In neighbouring Bahrain, just a short boat ride from the Eastern Province, Communists had been prominent since the 1950s, and fared well in parliamentary elections in the 1970s. When the parliament was abolished in 1975, they were driven underground or into exile. A Leftist Arab nationalist group with a significant Shii membership was also targeted. The Bahraini regime saw Shii clerics and nascent Shii Islamist movements as a useful counterweight to Leftists in the Shii community. Playing up sectarian divisions served to limit the appeal of Leftist movements, as well as of Sunni–Shia unity.[178] In Soviet Azerbaijan, with its nominally Sunni and Shii population, ties to the shrine cities were cut in 1928. As part of their general crackdown on religion, the Soviets banned Ashura and other Shii processions, something secularising Shii intellectuals had tried since the late nineteenth century, and suppressed Shii scholarship and institutions. The Soviets also upended Tsarist Russian practice of institutionalising Sunnism and Shiism separately, and established a unified Islamic representative body for Sunnis and Shia (though at others reinstated separate representation). There are indications that the Bolsheviks used Sunni–Shia division in their general crackdown on religion, in response to which, Sunni and Shii religious elites cooperated.[179] Socialism, and a stronger focus on Turkic ethnic identity, replaced religious attachments.

In Turkey itself, the notion of ethnic identity as the primary marker of identity, initially proved transformative for non-Sunni Muslims. The two main groups of relevance for my purposes are the Alawites of the coast—whom I've discussed earlier—and the pro-Alid groups of Anatolia, the former Qizilbash, who started to be called *Alevi*.[180] While some contest any notion of continuity between the Qizilbash of the Safavid era and modern Alevis, the most plausible story of Alevi origins is that they are connected to and descendants of Qizilbash who refused to fully embrace either Ottoman Sunnism or Twelver Shiism.[181] The Islamic element of their identity was moderated once they were embraced by Turkish nationalists, who by the early twentieth century argued that Alawites and Alevis preserved pre-Islamic rituals of the 'original' Turks. As noted, Alawites of Cilicia and Alexandretta, for example, that were incorporated into Turkey were portrayed as Hittites, the ancient group of Indo-Europeans thought to have established dominion over what is now Anatolia. While their mother tongue was primarily Arabic, they now had to use Turkish, de-emphasised difference from Sunnis and decorated their shrines with Turkish flags and pictures of Atatürk.[182]

Alevis had embraced the Ottoman constitutional reforms of 1908 that had promised equality regardless of religious or ethnic origin. The dislocations of the First World War, and the mass murder of Armenians from around 1915 until 1923, however, were a terrifying reminder of the potential repercussions for populations portrayed as disloyal and religiously and ethnically alien to the national body politic. Of the roughly two million Armenians in the Ottoman Empire, mostly in Anatolia, around one million had perished by 1918, with hundreds of thousands more displaced and forced into exile by 1923 (Turkey disputes these figures, and the term genocide to describe the events).[183] This frightened non-Sunni Muslims and Kurds, especially Kurdish-speaking Alevi populations, who constitute about a third of Alevis (though it is at times a form of Kurdish unintelligible to other Kurdish speakers and they use Turkish as a ritualistic language).[184]

For ethnically and religiously diverse populations in the Ottoman-Iranian frontier zones, the establishment of new, harder borders and the emergence of Turkish, Iranian, and Syrian Arab and Iraqi Arab nationalisms, had dramatic consequences. Like the other ethnic denominators that gained traction at this time, 'Kurd' denoted highly diverse communities, divided by clan, tribal, local and religious loyalties, and dialect. Kurdish nationalists sought but failed to achieve independence at the post-First World War conferences redrawing the borders of the Middle East.[185] And so Kurds became citizens of Turkey, Iran, Syria, and Iraq (and Azerbaijan), but were often portrayed as alien to these nations.

In general, most Kurds are Shafii Sunnis, and, as noted, Sufi orders, especially the Naqshbandis, were prominent amongst them. Moreover, pro-Alid movements such as the Ahl-e Haqq developed amongst Kurds in the confessionally ambiguous milieus of the fourteenth and fifteenth centuries, and the Safavid-Qizilbash period in Iran in the sixteenth century. But due to a lack of written sources and constant refashioning, their origin and confessional identity remains contested.[186] They embraced some elements of Shiism, but at times went beyond its confines to deify Ali. Sunnis and Shia oscillated between trying to bring them closer to their respective side, and condemning them as heretics. While some nationalists, such as in Turkey, briefly embraced them in the hope that their religion and customs might provide a link to a pre-Islamic past, many ethnic nationalists and Islam-centred activists viewed them with suspicion.

In Northern Iraq, pro-Alid groups identified neither as Sunni nor as Shii and spoke dialects of Kurdish, doubly at odds with the Arab Sunni-led state.[187] In their Arabist vein, Syrian and Iraqi Arab nationalists looked down on Kurds (although they forged alliances with Kurdish elites). Amongst Kurds in what would become Iran, pro-Alid groups were also prominent. But most Iranian Kurds are Sunnis, and were seen as alien to Iranian nationalism and Shiism. And the pro-Alid groups would also have to defend themselves against accusations of heterodoxy from Twelver Shii clerics, and would in turn emphasise similarities with Shiism.[188]

In Turkey, where of course most Kurds lived, some Kemalists argued that because of their difference from the wider Kurdish population and their Alevi faith, Alevi Kurds were Turks who had lost their way.[189] Many Alevis indeed embraced the policies of the Turkish state and revered Atatürk.[190] Socially, however, a gap remained. At the outset of the Turkish Republic in the 1920s, most Alevis lived in villages somewhat separate from Sunni villages. Once mass migration to the cities set in, which it did in Turkey and throughout the region, a certain social segregation persisted (although here, too, Alevi participation in secular political movements led to much interaction).[191]

In turn, one of the earliest and most prominent revolts against the secularising and the ethnic Turkish policies of the Kemalists, in 1925, was led by a Kurdish Naqshbandi, Shaykh Saad. Some Kurdish Alevis even supported the Kemalists in their harsh treatment of these Sunni Kurds, with whom they had long-standing feuds.[192] Naqshbandis had played an important role in the Turkish War of Liberation alongside the Kemalists. But once the state adopted secularism, it, and other Sufi orders, became the backbone of resistance to it, and were in turn suppressed, from the Sunni-leaning Naqshbandis to the Shii-leaning Bektashis, who as noted had already been weakened a century earlier.[193] All Sufi orders were banned, their lodges, monasteries and guesthouses confiscated or turned into museums.[194] Sufis went underground, or into exile. A branch of the Bektashi order moved their headquarters to Albania, a former Ottoman province, where the order had been strengthened by a semi-autonomous governor, Ali Pasha, in the late eighteenth/early nineteenth century.[195] Bektashis in turn played a key role in Albanian nationalism—despite the fact that Bektashis only constituted a fraction of Albanian Muslims. They were repressed alongside other religious groups under the Communist regime in the 1950s.[196]

In communities outside of Turkey, and a semi-underground manner in Turkey, Sufis reinvented themselves. The Shaykh Saad Revolt was invoked by Kurdish nationalists as an early instance of resistance to the Turkish state, and by Turkish Islamists, as resistance to its secularising policies. And some of the orders, especially the Naqshbandis, reorganised after the closure of their lodges around mosques and business networks. They re-emerged from the mid-twentieth century onwards, as the position of Islam in Turkey was renegotiated. By then, the notion of a Turkish-Islamic synthesis, according to which nationalism rested on a combination of pre-Islamic values and an Islamic legacy, gained traction.[197] Turkish intellectuals no longer portrayed the Ottoman Empire as the antithesis of the modern state, as the Kemalists had, but as a model: tolerant of difference but forceful in its defence of religion and nation.[198] Turkish historians started to analyse Ottoman history through the binaries of orthodoxy (official Ottoman Sunnism) and heterodoxy (Alevis/Qizilbash), and Turkish Islamists sought to link themselves to the former and position against the latter.[199] Turkish Sunni Revivalists sought to counter the secularism at the heart of the Turkish state, with which Alevis were closely identified. They often invoked Islamic unity, but also saw Shiism as misguided and Alevis as not properly Muslim.[200] Embracing a free-market ideology, and a turn towards a more Islamic society, Naqshbandi networks were key in the creation of an Islamic bourgeoisie that rivalled the old urban Kemalist elites, and provided the organisational background for successive Islamist socio-political movements. They also helped open markets in the Gulf countries for Turkish exports, fostering new Turkish-Gulf ties in which an adherence to Sunni norms was key.[201]

Alevis had gained positions in the state, but the promises of equality that early Turkish nationalism had made to them, had been difficult to fulfil. The state elites had remained largely Sunni, as had the religious establishment. Turkey's Sunni *ulama*, who had been marginalised by the Kemalists but still retained much authority over religious policy, refused to recognise Alevism as a separate branch of Islam, or give its places of worship, the Cemevis, formal recognition or state funding.[202] Now, in the struggle between Islamists and Kemalist state elites, Alevis, who were associated with the latter, became the new Others. As secular Turkish nationalism gave way to a Turkish-Sunni synthesis, and successive military regimes allied with Sunni Revivalists, not least to stave off challenges by the Left, the position of Alevis, in particular Kurdish ones, was reproblematised.[203] This, in turn, led Alevis to organise themselves as they were perceived to be—a distinct group.

In the 1960s, new migrants to the cities in Turkey (and Germany) had set up the first Alevi associations, and a first party representing Alevis (its first symbol was a lion, widely thought to represent Ali). This led to Sunni back-lash, which spurred Alevi politicisation, and by the 1980s led to a stronger assertion of Alevi identity in the public sphere.[204] Some would adhere more strongly to Hajji Bektash and the teachings of the Bektashi order, trying to revive the former headquarter of the order, while others, especially migrants outside of Turkey, claimed that Alevism was not Shii, and instead a separate religion outside of Islam altogether.[205]

Like Kurds, and Arab Shia, Alevis embraced the promises of equality of the Left, and two key Leftist movements became associated with Alevis and Kurds, respectively. Harsh repression against the Left in the context of Turkey's emergence as a key NATO member then targeted Alevis and Kurds disproportionately.[206]

Turkey's secularising state-building project thus left a complex legacy. Sectarian difference, born out of a period of confessional ambiguity, a mixture of local tradition and Islamic practice, and sectarianised rivalries between the Ottomans and the Safavids and Qajars, gained new meanings in the age of nationalism. After initially promising equality, nationalist aspirations were undermined by disputes about religious orthodoxy that polarised society.[207]

It's now clear how closely developments in Turkey, like the abolishing of the Caliphate, affected populations in Turkey, and were followed by Muslims outside of Turkey. In India, the Khilafat movement had galvanised Muslims from diverse backgrounds. Leaders of this initially pan-Islamic movement in support of the Caliphate eventually helped establish a separate state for the subcontinent's Muslims. Key to the idea of a homeland for the subcontinent's Muslims was the notion that the Muslim faith above all else could bind people together. But because of the diversity of South Asian Islam and the nature of Sunni Revivalism, the question what kind of Islam should be at the core of national identity soon emerged. Earlier memories of sectarian rivalries, of competing dynasties and Sunni and Shii revivalisms, would prove divisive. Many of the Muslim nationalist elites and intellectuals were Twelver Shii or Ismaili, including the founders and financiers of the Muslim League, and the most significant early political leaders of Pakistan. While they de-emphasised their sectarian identity in favour of pan-Islam, this Shii participation is noteworthy.[208] The founding figures of Muslim nationalism, including Muhammad Iqbal, advocated Islamic unity.[209]

However, the growth of Muslim nationalism in the 1930s and 1940s, coincided, as noted, with more antagonistic and globally connected Sunni and Shii identities. The conflicts in the Hijaz drew in Indian Sunnis and Shia on competing sides. And as Sunni clerics of the Deobandi school started to become more prominent in the Muslim League—the main nationalist movement—some Shia started to criticise the idea of a separate homeland for Muslims, arguing that it would become hostile territory for Shia. The leaders of the Pakistan movement were unwilling to give assurances to Shii communal leaders as to the future status of Shiism for fear of undermining Muslim unity. Soon enough, some of the new Shii political organisations accused Pakistan of being a 'Sunnistan'. While the nationalist historiography of Pakistan sought to downplay Sunni–Shia division, there were disagreements of what the 'Land of the Pure' (Pakistan) should look like, and what kind of Muslims should or should not be included in the new polity.[210] This was reminiscent of the Khilafat Movement, which some Shia had supported and others opposed, and in which some Sunni Revivalists criticised the Shii role. A few leading Shii clerics, and some of the old Shii elites, had refused to take part in a movement supporting the Caliphate, pointing to the difference between Caliphate and Imamate, a distinction that proponents of pan-Islam had of course been seeking to blur.[211] Pakistan was founded in 1947, following Indian independence and partition. Initially, there were few limits to Shii advancement. Shii businessmen became key in shipping, banking, and aviation. In the period between its founding and 1977, three heads of state, as well as president Zulfikar Ali Bhutto, came from a Shii background.

Recruitment into government ministries did not favour specific sectarian groups, and Shia were well represented in the army.[212]

The founder of Pakistan, Mohammed Ali Jinnah, had an Ismaili Khoja background and may have converted to Twelver Shiism. As a statesman, however, he responded to questions about sect with his own: 'Was Muhammad the Prophet a Shia or a Sunni?'[213] Anti-sectarian in life, after his death in 1948, Jinnah's background became a matter of public concern— not due to doctrinal debates but because of his funeral (and the issue of which rite was to be observed) and a court case to resolve inheritance disputes about his estate. Jinnah's sister opined that he had been a Twelver Shii, which would entitle her to more of his inheritance than had he been Ismaili (who were exempt from Sharia laws) or Sunni. It proved difficult for the court to establish to which school of jurisprudence Jinnah had pertained, because he, in the spirit of ecumenism and as the country's founding figure, had not publicly stated his adherence to a particular school. The process dragged on for decades. In 1976, almost thirty years after Jinnah had died, the court ruled according to Shii law. In 1984, a subsequent judgement, however, ruled according to Sunni law, in favour of male agnates.[214] The whole drawn-out process epitomised a shift away from Pakistan's ecumenical foundational idea towards more sect-centric identities.[215] Given these differences in inheritance law, and the chance this afforded to make claims about someone's sectarian identity, the Jinnah case was only the most prominent of many such cases in India and Pakistan.[216]

Sunni traditionalists initially singled out Ahmadis, whose ritual practice differed little from that of Sunni Muslims, but who attributed quasi-prophetic status to their nineteenth century founder, for retribution.[217] Sunni polemicists, such as Ihsan Ilahi Zahir, denounced them as non-Muslims and 'agents of Imperialism'.[218] In 1974, Sunni religious organisations pushed the state to declare them non-Muslims and they were frequently targeted. Some of those at the forefront of anti-Ahmadi activities, such as Zahir, then turned their attention to Shia (and Hindus and Christians), as we'll see in the next chapter.[219]

Tensions between Pakistan and India problematised the situation of Muslims who remained in India and whom Indian nationalists now portrayed as potentially disloyal. It drew Pakistan, which became the second most populous Islamic country in the world—and with a large number of Shia Muslims—closer to the Middle East. Shia in Pakistan, though they had been foundational in the new political and economic system, were transformed into a 'minority'. In India, they became a minority of a minority, at odds with both a Sunni Revivalism and a Hindu nationalism that differentiated little between Muslims. After some landowners and Sayyids left for Pakistan, and sources of patronage dried up, Shii institutions and Muharram rituals in places such as Lucknow and Hyderabad declined. Expropriations of estates held by those whose relatives left for Pakistan further undermined family wealth and Muslim communal organisations.[220] In short, Shii Muslims in both India and Pakistan faced challenges when trying to inscribe themselves into post-independence imaginings of the nation.

The two states would embrace competing visions of the past. Some Mughals, such as Akbar, could be accepted as ecumenical figures in India. Nonetheless Hindu nationalists would define themselves against the Mughals, accusing them of subduing Hindus. They especially railed against Aurangzib, the last of the independent Mughal Emperors, who instead became an icon for Sunni Islamists in Pakistan. That he had treated Shia and Ismailis harshly, did not endear him to the subcontinent's Shia, and made his embrace by Sunni Islamists doubly problematic. In Pakistan, however, the era of the Indian Muslim dynasties was embraced as a golden age. Shia in India, on the other hand, developed a nostalgia for a past under Shii dynasties, and put their efforts into the vigorous observation of their rituals, and the strengthening of wider Shii causes, especially as democratic India offered new prospects for religious media and proselytisation.[221]

The heritage of the Muslim Empires also shaped nationalisms in Turkey and Iran. As noted, early twentieth century 'modernising' leaders initially side-lined the old imperial dynasties and instead promoted secularism and a focus on ancient Turkish and Persian history. This de-emphasis of the Islamic past initially gave religious minorities unprecedented opportunities to participate in public life. Yet, as the twentieth century progressed, political movements came to power that more closely associated themselves with the legacies of the Islamic empires that had shaped the territory and history of their countries.

In the collective memory of Turkish and Iranian Islamists, the respective empires offered positive examples precisely because they had adopted confessional identity (in the Ottoman case, as the spiritual and political centre of Sunnism, of course, and in the Iranian case the conversion to Shiism and the turning of Iran into the centre of Shiism).[222] This in turn made the position of non-dominant religious and ethnic groups more precarious. In many other new nation states, too, memories of pre-modern empires or local rulers, and the legacy of sectarian identity at the heart of some of them, were imported into the nationalist foundational myth, linking the two periods.

In Bahrain and Kuwait, national narratives were Sunni-centric, and Gulf Shia started to long for a different ancient homeland, the 'Lands of Bahrain', that they claimed had prospered under Shii rule.[223] In Saudi Arabia, the alliance between Ibn Saud and Muhammad Ibn Abd al-Wahhab became crucial in the national myth, cementing the relationship between Wahhabism and state identity. In Afghanistan, as noted, aspects of the modern state were established in the context of anti-Shii violence. In countries that were not clear successor states of a dynasty, or where the population was confessionally heterogeneous, competing visions of the nation developed, incorporating different sectarian identities, and linking themselves back to dynasties of the respective sect.

In yet other states, such as Egypt, where the Ismaili Fatimids had been foundational but where Shiism later played no role, their memory became secularised, and their confessional identity de-emphasised. In Morocco, where an Alid dynasty was important in the Islamisation of the country (and the royal family retains the name Alaouite), or in Jordan, where the successors to the Hashemites, descendants of the Prophet and with a confessionally ambiguous heritage, survived, this history was largely erased from collective memory. Although both dynasties, which placed themselves at the centre of their national narratives, embraced the legitimacy that descent from the Prophet offered them, they became known as 'Sunni' monarchies.

In Yemen, where Zaydi Imams had ruled for a millennium, the Imams, who Rida had in the 1920s still hailed as traditional, independent Arab leaders, on the one hand portrayed themselves as pan-Islamic leaders, and on the other hand embraced a stronger Zaydi identity.[224] After the disintegration of the Ottoman Empire, the Zaydi Imam Yahya, had expanded his influence into largely Shafii formerly Ottoman held-regions in the South, while Britain spread its influence from its base at Aden into surrounding regions.[225] Both Britain's and the Imam's armed forces were made up of Shafii and Zaydi soldiers, although the Imam's was much larger, and Zaydis occupied the highest echelons.[226] The Imam's government claimed that the British were trying to further Zaydi–Shafii hostility in order to weaken it.[227]

But new political movements critical of Empire, and the Imamate, gained ground. The Imamate managed to survive a coup in 1948, but increasingly, the Imams came to be seen as remnants of a feudal and 'backward' order. Eventually, a group of republicans inspired by Nasser overthrew the Imamate in 1962, leading to an internationalised civil war. Nasser sent troops in support of the republicans to undermine the remaining royals of the Arabian Peninsula. Saudi Arabia, on the other hand, backed the deposed Imam and his supporters, even though the latter were Zaydis, because they feared the republicans even more.[228] After the republicans had won and the Zaydi political and religious elite lost their institutional support, the Imam was blamed for instrumentalising sect-based identity, and for having discriminated against Shafii Sunnis. The revolution's first proclamation called for a 'correct Islamic Sharia, after its death had been caused by tyrannical and wicked rulers', and the 'elimination of hatreds and envies, and divisions of descent and of confession (*madhhab*)'.[229]

The new republic sought to create a unified Islam to overcome sectarian affiliation, in part through a new legislative code, drawn up by Shafii and Zaydi scholars.[230] Implicitly, however, official Islam was based more on Sunnism than Zaydism, and owed much to al-Shawkani, the eighteenth-century scholar and Salafi icon. His arguments allowed republicans to undermine traditional Zaydism and still claim historical continuity.[231] Many republicans were nominally Zaydi, but as they were from non-elite and anti-Imamate families, they doubted the loyalties of the old elites.[232] The old elite families became the anti-thesis of the republic, and were defamed in public.[233] But Zaydism was not entirely suppressed, and some royalists eventually became integrated into the state.[234] The republic's Sunnitising religious policies facilitated a rapprochement with Saudi Arabia, as both saw the Marxist-Leninist state that emerged in Yemen's South, the People's Democratic Republic of Yemen, as a threat. Millions of Yemenis went to Saudi Arabia to work, Yemeni clerics attended Saudi Universities, and Saudi Arabia shaped North Yemeni politics through direct aid, cash handouts to tribes and political factions, control over remittances from Yemeni workers, and the funding of religious institutes.[235] In time, and to differentiate itself from its Marxist neighbour, the religious element in the republic's identity became more important. With the South establishing the Arab world's only Marxist state, and the North overthrowing a Zaydi Imamate and establishing a Republic that invoked Islam as formulated by al-Shawkani, and thus with a Sunni orientation, as official religion, religion and politics was also profoundly transformed in Yemen.

In neighbouring Oman, the Al Bu Said dynasty established dynastic rule with British help, upending a tradition of rotating and partly elected Sultans. Here, too, the rudimental state that revolved around the Sultan, and the

Ibadi religious tradition, was increasingly at odds with Arab nationalism and republicanism. A Leftist movement had Ibadi members, and even some amongst the small Shii community, but was strongest in the largely Sunni Southern parts of the country, in Dhofar, where it led an insurgency with help from Arab internationalists and neighbouring Marxist South Yemen. Eventually, with military support from Britain and Iran, Sultan Qaboos overthrew his father, defeated the rebels, and asserted his position. The Sultanate became closely associated with Ibadism as legitimising confession, which was presented as a moderate branch of Islam, an alternative to Marxism or Sunni Islamism, which made some inroads into Sunni communities, and political Shiism.

To sum it up, even though many nationalisms started as anti-sectarian projects, religious identity often became key, either explicitly or implicitly. Those in the dominant group saw confessional identity as overlapping with national identity. Pan-identities, such as pan-Arabism and pan-Islam, further contended that apart from national loyalties there were more important supra-national loyalties (and some saw the very creation of national borders as anathema to their aspirations).[236]

Sectarian collective identities could themselves become mass identities akin to nationalism, uniting co-sectarians across geographical boundaries, spurred by the recognition, measurement, and institutionalisation of this difference by the modern state, and new forms of communication and organisation.[237] Sect-centric political movements, led by clerics that sought to counter the secularising impetus of nationalism and socialism, would imagine Sunnis and Shia as distinct transnational communities. In Lebanon, reformulated confessional and national identities developed alongside each other.[238] Nationalist Arab leaders would pay lip-service to pan-Arabism, while focusing on national politics.

Arab nationalism was an ideology that because of its enormous reach became very diverse. On a most basic level, it became the expression of most Arabs, and since most Arabs are Sunnis, it was natural that there was some Sunni symbolism inherent in it. Even Shii Arab nationalists had to concede that the early Sunni Caliphates that they could not agree with on a religious level, spread Islam and the Arab language, and founded important dynasties and cities. Hence Arabism had a powerful emotional appeal for Arab Christians, Druze, Shia, Alawites, Zaydis, and others. The foundational figures of the Arab renaissance had been Christian, a Druze leader would become one of Arab nationalism's most important advocates, and one of the longest-lasting incarnations of Arab nationalism, the Syrian Baath, eventually became dominated by Shii-influenced Arab Muslims. Under the French and British mandates, Arab nationalism had a Sunni bent. But that content of its ideology, and makeup of the movement, changed. Arab nationalism became a discursive field in which different actors could compete, invoke similar language and organise in the same parties. While some, such as Sati al-Husri, argued that Shiism and Arabism were binary opposites, Arab Shii intellectuals like al-Amin argued that Shiism *was* Arabism, for the Imams had been Arabs, as had been their earliest followers, the original Shia. That this happened in the context of rapprochement initiatives led to more interaction between religious elites, and correspondingly to doctrinal debates.

Pan-Islam likewise remained a powerful idea, but failed to unite Muslims in one state, and, despite the efforts of Rida and others, did not manage to re-establish a central religious authority after the end of the Caliphate. That those seeking such a central authority, and a return to the fundamentals of the faith, put their hopes in Ibn Saud and the Wahhabi movement, was to have the profoundest of consequences once Saudi Arabia became a central US Cold War ally, and oil revenues started to flow. Salafism would influence most Sunni Islamist movements of the later twentieth century. That Sunni religious authority shifted from Istanbul and Cairo towards the Arabian Peninsula, and towards a Salafi understanding of Sunnism, further undermined the prospects of rapprochement between Sunnism and Shiism.

Because these struggles occurred at the seats of the early Caliphates, the places of the early splits, with a sacred topography (Hijaz, Iraq, Syria, and Palestine) these debates were also followed by Arabs and Muslims in places further away. And as elsewhere, the age of nationalism had its own pitfalls. By the 1970s, the Arab States had twice been defeated on the battlefield by Israel, and Arab nationalism lost much of its appeal. Many states failed to live up to people's expectations and their own promises, and became authoritarian and repressive. And economically, Arab States (and many non-Arab Muslim ones) increasingly depended on oil revenue from the Gulf region, which allowed Gulf rulers to extend their influence in the Arab and Islamic world, and propagate their anti-Shii views of Arabism and Islam (and, in the case of Iran, Iranian nationalism in which Shiism played first a minor, and, after 1979, a major role).

Faced with authoritarian rulers that legitimised themselves through secular nationalism, Political Islam emerged as an alternative language of politics as we will see in Part IV.[239] The question of legitimate leadership, which had long been debated, would preoccupy the Islamist movements that gained in strength just as secular ones lost ground. As noted, Sunni and Shii Islamists shared many goals and influenced each other, and the ideal of Muslim unity was advocated by most. However, a greater focus on Islam as the core of political identity, lead to more attention as to what kind of Islam one espoused, and could turn pan-Islamists into sect-centric activists. On the Sunni scene, the late Rashid Rida, and then the Muslim Brothers and King Faisal of Saudi Arabia, epitomised that turn away from Arab nationalism towards a new Sunni internationalism that largely excluded the Shia.

On the Shii scene, several charismatic figures started to advocate a wider Shii revival, and claimed both political and spiritual authority. That the followers of two of them called them Imam, different of course from the early Shii Imams, but with a special charisma nonetheless, was indicative of a wider shift in Shiism towards a more assertive role of the clergy. In the Islamic calendar, a century was slowly coming to an end. Some thought the end of times was near, and the end of the fourteenth century after the emigration of the Prophet from Mecca to Medina, proved profoundly transformative, in the world of Islam and beyond. In the Christian lunar calendar, the year 1400 since the emigration of the Prophet fell on the year 1979.

PART IV

Revolution and
Rivalry, 1979–

In 1979, a Shii cleric, Ayatollah Khomeini, established the first modern Islamic state in the country with the largest number of Shii Muslims in the world and vowed to export its revolution. Ever since, Sunni–Shia relations have been affected by the fallout from the revolution, and the regional and global response to it.

The revolution had pan-Islamic ambitions, and many Sunnis, especially Islamists, initially supported it. But its stark Shii symbolism, and the rise of anti-Shiism, led to much polarisation. Sunni and Shii Islamists may have influenced each other, but they would also fight each other. Iran embraced a specific form of Shiism as state ideology and in foreign policy. In consequence, Sunni-led states, too, adopted a more Sunni identity. States perceived Shii communities in Sunni-ruled states such as Iraq, Saudi Arabia, Bahrain, Kuwait, and Pakistan, and Sunnis in Iran, as potential avenues for influence, or as fifth-columnists, depending on their sectarian identity.

Because of Iran's location—between the Arab and Turkish-speaking worlds and the Muslims of Central and South Asia, and dominating the oil-rich Persian Gulf—the revolution affected all these regions and connected them in novel ways. And given Iran's previous centrality in American Cold War strategy, the revolution upset that strategy. US support shifted away from Iran, and towards Saudi Arabia, which increasingly portrayed itself as the centre of the Sunni worlds. As the Islamic Republic tried to export its revolution and establish new alliances, its Sunni enemies, besides Saudi Arabia especially Iraq and Egypt, alongside the US, tried to contain and overthrow it, primarily through the Iran–Iraq war, which dragged on for eight years between 1980 and 1988. The civil war in Afghanistan, where Sunni militants supported by Sunni states and the US fought against Soviet troops, who had arrived in 1979, also served to strengthen ties between the US and Sunni internationalism, and to keep Iran at bay. Sunni–Shia relations had become tied to American foreign policy and wider international relations.

After a period of detente in the 1990s, and amidst a sense of omnipotence, 9/11 led the Americans to try and reshape key countries in which Sunnis and Shia lived side by side. In 2002, a NATO coalition led by the US invaded Afghanistan and overthrew the Sunni Islamist Taliban. In 2003, the US and the UK invaded Iraq, and installed a Shii-led government, the first in a millennium. This turned Iraq from a player in regional conflicts (and a staunch enemy of Iran) into an arena in which regional and international powers fought out their rivalries.

The interventions set up ethnic and sectarian categories as bases of the political system (in Iraq by institutionalising Lebanon-style ethno-sectarian power-sharing, and in Afghanistan by placing much importance on ethnic difference, and institutionalising Shiism separately).[1] They overthrew sworn enemies of Iran, thereby strengthening Iran's relative position (and increasing its Sunni rivals' fears). As a long-term sponsor of the Shii opposition in Iraq, Iran thrived. As it has over the centuries, as we've seen throughout this book, sectarianism became a tool of foreign policy and alliance-formation—and a way for ruling elites to maintain their power by playing on fears of civil strife.

This intensified after 2011, when the Arab uprisings—the so-called Arab Spring, which originated in North Africa—initially anti-sectarian and challenging authoritarianism, led to further polarisation, and in Syria, Yemen and Libya descended into civil war. Two major alliances of political Sunnism, one led by Saudi Arabia and the UAE, and the other by Turkey, Qatar, and the Muslim Brotherhood vied for regional supremacy, and clashed with the Iran-led alliance of political Shiism. The rivalry between the Sunni coalitions could be as severe as tensions with the Iran-led one. It is too simplistic to characterise the alliances formed by Iran and its adversaries as Sunni or Shii, given that both contained members of the relative other sect. But the rivalry's sectarian angle proved especially explosive. Thousands died in targeted sectarian killings, and hundreds of thousands in the various conflicts in Iraq, Syria, and Yemen. Millions have been displaced and subjected to starvation. As state authority in countries with combined Sunni–Shia populations weakened (or was destroyed, as in Iraq), this toxic mix turned

Sunni and Shii against each other. Old sectarian polemics were invoked to justify ethno-sectarian cleansing. They reached a mass audience, first in print, on cassette tapes, and radio, then on satellite TV, and social media. As fighting escalated in Iraq and Syria, where the split between Sunna and Shia, between Caliph and Imam, had originated, it seemed to many as if contemporary struggles were a re-enactment of earlier ones, though with Shia now in a much stronger position, leading some to re-envision the Caliphate as an ideal type of Sunni authority.

11

The Religion of Martyrdom

Ayatollah Ruhollah Khomeini was born in 1902, in the village of Khomein into a family of religious scholars. His forefathers had emigrated from Iran to Awadh in India in the eighteenth century, when its rulers patronised Shiism. A distant relative of his wrote the *Abaqat al-Anwar* in the second half of the nineteenth century, the influential Indian Shii refutation of the anti-Shii polemic *The Gift* by Shah Abd al-Aziz. In the 1830s, his grandfather went on pilgrimage to Najaf, and thereafter settled in Khomein in Iran, where his family bought land.[2] Bolstered by social and economic capital, Khomeini followed the path of an aspiring cleric, studying first with local grandees, and then in 1922 moving to Qom.[3] In the Shii seminary system, only senior clerics can teach the most advanced classes, and students spend years attending them. In Qom, Khomeini studied with Ayatollah Burujirdi, then widely seen as the spiritual leader of the world's Shia. Khomeini became his disciple, and tried to push Burujirdi, who was on good terms with the Shah, into a more oppositional role. But Burujirdi argued that the clergy should guide the masses, rather than get involved in politics. Only after his death in 1961 did some of his former disciples, such as Khomeini, confront the Shah head on. Their politics differed, but the connection to Burujirdi facilitated Khomeini's rise.[4]

In 1963, the Shah, Mohammad Reza Pahlavi, declared the start of a top-down modernisation and reorganisation of the country, known as the 'White Revolution', rubber-stamped by a toothless referendum. But much of the Shii clergy resented the Shah's secularising authoritarianism. On 3 June 1963, during a speech in Qom, on Ashura, Khomeini compared the Shah to Yazid, the Umayyad Caliph who had ordered the killing of Hussain. Tens of thousands chanted anti-government slogans in front of the Shah's palace in Tehran. Furious, the Shah ordered Khomeini's arrest, sparking further protests. The security forces killed hundreds, and the Shah's regime

exiled Khomeini to Turkey. A year later, Khomeini settled in Najaf in Iraq.[5]
With dozens of colleges and thousands of students from around the world,
and a constant flow of pilgrims, Najaf was, next to Qom, the key intellectual
centre of the Shii world.[6] It was a good place for Khomeini to stay in touch
with his followers, who smuggled writings and sermons into Iran after
returning from pilgrimage. Some clerics in Najaf had already formed the
nucleus of the Dawa party, the first Arab Shii Islamist party, to fight against
secularism, and ensure clerical influence. Khomeini maintained cordial relations with these clerics, but they did not openly endorse his anti-Shah
activism. They focused on Iraq, and some even maintained relations with
the Shah. And the most senior clerics in the city, Ayatollah Muhsin al-
Hakim, who had succeeded Burujirdi, and Abu al-Qasim al-Khu'i, who
would succeed al-Hakim after his death in 1970, disagreed profoundly with
Khomeini's approach. They were personally critical of the authoritarian
rulers of Iran and Iraq, but were wary of mobilising openly against them, for
fear of repression, and, under pressure by the Iraqi state, did not want to
antagonise the Shah, who even though a secularising autocrat was still at
times patronising Shiism in the tradition of earlier (and later) Iranian rulers.
These clerical grandees saw Khomeini as inferior in terms of religious hierarchy, and as a challenge.[7]

In the old city of Najaf, in the winding alleys around the shrine of Ali, so
central to Shiism, Khomeini would write and meet with students in a house
that today houses a small museum (funded by Iran). Here he delivered lectures on Islamic government (*Hokumat-i Islami*) in January and February
1970, in which he argued that the ideal political system was an Islamic state
ruled by a senior Shii cleric.[8] While Khomeini had long advocated similar
positions, his blueprint for an Islamic state now went further. He had read
Sunni Islamists from Egypt and Pakistan, whose arguments he appropriated,
and complemented with the Shii tradition and the precedents of clerics in
government under the Safavids, Qajars, and Indian Shii dynasties, and in the
Iranian Constitutional Revolution of 1906. As discussed above, this was
facilitated by the rise of rationalist Usuli Shiism, which allowed senior clerics
to come to new judgments through interpretation of the sources, vis-à-vis
more scripturalist Akhbarism.[9] Arab Shii clerics had founded clergy-led
political movements, especially in Iraq and Lebanon, since the late 1950s.
Still, Khomeini's vision of a modern Islamic State led by a Supreme Leader,
the so-called 'Guardianship of the Jurisprudent' (*velayat-e faqih/wilayat al-
faqih*) was ground-breaking.[10] His teachings increasingly reached Iran,

both in print and by means of cassette tapes, a new medium that made it easy to reproduce sermons, giving clerics the opportunity to reach much larger audiences.[11]

Khomeini's role as a figurehead of anti-government sentiment in Iran was reinforced in 1977, when his son, Mostafa, died under suspicious circumstances in Najaf. Rumours that the Shah's intelligence service had assassinated him, sparked protests in Qom and other cities, again meeting with fierce repression.[12] Shocked by the extent of popular anger, the Shah tried to defuse tensions through a limited political opening. That, however, broke the barrier of fear, and allowed the opposition to organise publicly. When in January 1978 a government-approved article attacked Khomeini and the clergy, the masses chanted his name and raised his image. After security forces shot several protesters, the activist clergy urged people to mourn them after forty days, a traditional mourning period. More were killed, and four forty-day mourning periods for the martyrs fallen in the previous demonstration set the Revolution in motion in the first half of 1978.[13] Desperate, the Shah asked Iraq to expel Khomeini. For fear of alienating the Shah, countries in the region refused to host him, and so he went to Paris. Far from marginalising the cleric, which was the Shah's hope, Khomeini emerged as the leader of the revolution in front of the global press.

In Iran, more and more people joined the protests. The regime's repression increased public anger. Strikes in the oil industry drained the state's revenues, and Leftist guerrillas undermined the government's control. Millions of Iranians took to the streets to protest against the Shah, first in forty-day intervals inspired by religious mourning periods, and then, invoking the original tragedy of Karbala, in a massive mobilisation during the first ten days of Muharram, which fell on 1–10 December 1978. Protesters equated the Shah with the Umayyad Caliph Yazid, responsible for Hussain's death, and mourned the slain Imam. Initially, Leftists and Islamists joined forces. Eventually, the faction backing Ayatollah Khomeini, increasingly referred to as *Imam*, emerged as the most powerful. The masses called upon a new Imam to emerge.[14] On 16 January 1979, the Shah fled the country. Two weeks later, on 1 February, Khomeini arrived in Tehran.[15] Iranian newspaper headlines read: 'The Shah went', and then, 'the Imam arrived'.[16]

The final days of the revolution epitomised the linking of contemporary struggles to distant ones, and the potential of Shiism to mobilise the masses. The saying *Every day is Ashura and every land is Karbala*, attributed to Imam al-Sadiq and long invoked by Khomeini and another galvanising figure, Ali Shariati, became omnipresent across Iran.[17] Shariati died in 1977 and his supporters attributed his death to the Shah, giving the revolution greater impetus. Shariati had studied Sociology in Paris, fusing Marxism and his own reading of Shii history into a powerful revolutionary ideology.[18] Throughout the 1960s and 1970s, he criticised the kind of status quo thinking that legitimised Shii dynasties, differentiating it from original Shiism, which had striven for social justice, martyrdom, resistance to injustice, and revolutionary action. According to Shariati, the *Religion of Mourning* should again become the *Religion of Martyrdom*. Original Shiism for him was activist, not unlike that espoused by Khomeini and the Islamists.[19] Shariati's books not only popularised this view of Shiism in accessible language, they spread these ideas around the Islamic world. Sunni audiences from Morocco to Indonesia to South Africa, and Iran's own Sunni minorities, found his message appealing, and appropriated his ideas for their own struggles (that he was a lay intellectual, and not a cleric, helped the diffusion of his ideas beyond Shii circles).[20] Other ideologues of the revolution, such as Murtaza Mutahhari, though self-consciously Shii, advocated Sunni–Shia unity and emphasised the contributions of Iranian Sunnis and Shia to Islamic history, thus fusing Iranian nationalism and Islamism.[21] During the revolution, their pictures were carried alongside those of Khomeini, and they increasingly outnumbered those of Leftists, and nationalists.

In a referendum on 30 and 31 March 1979, the Islamic Republic, as outlined in Khomeini's Najaf lectures, was adopted as official system of government, and Khomeini became its supreme leader (many non-Khomeinists boycotted the referendum, arguing that a simple yes or no question on the ballot on a little-understood new system of government did not do justice to the ambitions of the revolution). Soon the newly established Guardians of the Revolution would move against enemies, real and perceived, of Khomeini's line and decimate the networks of Leftists, Nationalists, and other Islamists.[22] A Shii cleric established the first modern Islamic state in the country with the largest number of Shii Muslims in the world and vowed to export its revolution.

In Lebanon, where the seeds of Iran's revolution had been partly sown, Shii clerics and politicians also adopted a more activist and revolutionary form of Shiism. Iranian Marxists and Islamists had trained in Lebanon with Palestinian Leftists, and Lebanese Shii militants, facilitated by Lebanon's comparatively open political system, its weak state, free press, militant movements, and large Shii community.[23] The influx of Palestinians after the wars against Israel in 1948 and 1967, and the PLO's expulsion from Jordan in 1970 and 1971, created a revolutionary atmosphere that contributed to the Lebanese Civil War in 1975. Initially, the war was largely waged between Christians and Sunni Muslims. Many Lebanese Christians saw Palestinians primarily as armed Muslims, paying little attention to the differences between Sunna and Shia.[24] Lebanese Sunnis, on the other hand, especially those on the Left, felt that the Maronite-dominated state's attempt to expel the Palestinian militants were unjustified, and many solidarized themselves with them.[25] As we've seen, Lebanon's political system had been set up under the French Mandate based on the representation of religious communities. Political positions were largely divided between Christians and Sunnis, with lesser roles played by Shia and Druze. Over the course of the twentieth century, the Maronites, who in the census of 1932 made up about 30 per cent of the Lebanese population and were the largest sect, saw their relative percentage as part of the population replaced by Muslims, especially Shia (who in 1932 stood at 22 per cent, with Sunnis at 20 per cent). This demographic shift challenged a system in which state positions were by constitutional law allocated proportionally to particular sects. It did so even more because everyone was aware of the shifting dynamics, but refused to carry out a new census.[26]

In the first decades after independence in 1943, the growing population in the largely Shii areas in the South and the Bekaa remained neglected, and so many Shia joined Leftist parties.[27] Musa al-Sadr, a scion of the prominent al-Sadr clerical family in Iraq and Iran, had come to Lebanon in 1960 to lead the Shia community in Southern Lebanon. He pushed for more Shii political representation, and founded schools and the Higher Shii Council. Maronite leaders, and the Lebanese deep state, would eventually support that initiative because, by the 1960s, they had come to see Arab nationalism inspired by Gamal Abdel Nasser amongst Lebanese Sunnis as a threat they sought to counter-balance.[28] Like Khomeini, he exemplified the new politically activist Shii clergy.

Musa al-Sadr and other Shii communal leaders argued that Shia had no choice but to positively identify with 'their' sect.[29] He found allies in the Lebanese Shia migrant communities in West Africa, the Americas, Europe, and Australia, whose remittances transformed Lebanese Shii society, leading to the formation of a Shii bourgeoisie. Resented by the old elites, they supported Musa al-Sadr's sect-focused mobilisation, and allied with poor Shia, who had been migrating en masse to Beirut's south. Shia from different parts of the country now started to see themselves as one Shii community.[30] Sadr found support in neighbouring Syria, where the Alawite Hafez al-Assad had eliminated rivals in the Baath party, and become president in 1971.

Supporting the emergent Shii revolutionary networks opened new opportunities for Syria. The Syrian constitution of 1973 sought to limit the role of Sharia in jurisprudence, but at the same time, in a concession to the country's Arab Sunni majority, required the president to be an Arab Muslim. Syria's strongman al-Assad and other Alawites thus had to be accepted as Muslims.[31] Over the preceding decades, the alignment of Alawites with Twelver Shiism deepened. Twelver Shia founded associations, built mosques and religious schools and distributed Shii books in Alawite areas, and Alawite clerics published books on their doctrine that differed little from Twelver Shiism.[32] Alawites had often described themselves as Shia, and pro-regime Sunni scholars, such as the Mufti of Damascus, recognised this, though many senior Shia (and Sunni) clerics did not. But al-Assad found two activist Shia clerics from prominent scholarly families that were willing to do so. One of them was Musa al-Sadr, who recognised Alawites as Shia Muslims in 1973, and then received Syrian backing.[33] The other was Hasan al-Shirazi, who was himself trying to mobilise Lebanon's Shia, and after recognising Alawites as Shia developed close relations with al-Assad.[34] His prominent Iraqi Shia clerical family was heading another Shia Islamist trend (one of his forefathers had led the Tobacco rebellion in the late nineteenth century), but alongside other Shii activists had come under attack by the Iraqi regime in the early 1970s. Originally from Karbala, members of the Shirazi trend fled to Lebanon, Syria, and Kuwait (from where they mobilised Shia communities in Bahrain and Saudi Arabia). Al-Assad, locked in a bitter rivalry with the Baath in Iraq, was keen to support an Iraqi opposition figure such as al-Shirazi (the Iraqis in turn supported the Syrian Muslim Brotherhood), and in 1975 allowed al-Shirazi to establish the first Shia seminary in Sayyida Zaynab.[35]

Sayyida Zaynab, the suburb of Damascus that grew around the Zaynab shrine, attained newfound importance, and simultaneously, Shariati and others portrayed Zaynab, Fatima, and Khadija, as archetypal female figures of early Islam, and role models for revolutionary Islamist women.[36] Shariati himself, who died in 1977, was interred near Zaynab's shrine. The millions of Iranians, and other Shia, that would visit the shrine in coming decades, would pay their respects to him.[37] The Shirazis gradually expanded their presence in the suburb, and turned it into a haven for Shii students, activists, and revolutionaries. In the 1970s, the Shah had already paid for the renewal of some Shii shrines in Syria, including Sayyida Zaynab. But these projects expanded after 1979, when the Islamic Republic funded the refurbishment and expansion of the Sayyida Zaynab shrine, turning it into a symbol of its alliance with Syria, and of growing Shii influence.[38] Together with Zaynab, Fatima served as an inspiration to Muslim, especially Shii women (although Fatima and insignia such as the iconic hand of Fatima are common in many other Muslim contexts, such as in North Africa, as is Zaynab, not least in Cairo).[39]

The Iranian revolution was based upon these networks. While pilgrims to Iraq smuggled Khomeini's sermons back to his followers in Iran, Iranian revolutionaries in Lebanon mingled with militants from Musa al-Sadr's Amal movement, Palestinian factions, Shirazis, and others. The perhaps most famous of the Iranians in Lebanon was Mustafa Chamran, an exiled militant in the Freedom Movement, a network to which Ali Shariati had also belonged. In 1971 he went to Lebanon, where he became a founding member of Amal, and worked with Palestinians to train Iranians, before becoming first defence minister of revolutionary Iran.[40] Apart from links with Lebanese Shia, the ties these Iranians established with Palestinians would be crucial. Khomeini himself had long been vocal in his support for Palestine, and saw the Palestine question as an avenue towards closer relations with Sunni Arabs.[41]

Khomeini's main foes were of course the Shah's and other secularising regimes. The Shah was nominally Shii, but that did not stop Khomeini from comparing him, just as his followers did, with Yazid, the Umayyad who had Hussain killed. Khomeini had long lamented the lack of Islamic unity, and in the vein of the Islamic modernists blamed internal division for Muslims' political and economic stagnation.[42] He called for Sunni–Shia unity and allowed Shia to pray behind a Sunni Imam.[43] Iran established an ecumenical society that organised annual conferences on pan-Islam and unity between the sects, using the same name as the society that had been active in the 1950s (*Taqrib/Rapprochement*). The society published a journal and books to foster rapprochement, which involved trying to bridge the gap with those Sunnis willing to accept Shiism as part of Islam, and denouncing those who would not, especially Salafi-Wahhabis, as an anomaly amongst Sunnis.[44] The idea was to place revolutionary Iran at the heart of the global *Umma*, the community of Muslims, an idea that enraged especially the Saudis and other Sunni rulers, who worked to undermine that attempt.[45] Sunnism was respected, and those Sunnis willing to work with Tehran on its terms embraced. Anti-Sunni aspects of the Shii tradition, including of Shii theological works, were de-emphasised, or no longer published, and the most anti-Sunni rituals banned or toned down.[46]

But Shiism reigned supreme. Khomeini, now the probably most powerful Shii cleric in history, had spent his whole life in the Shii seminaries, and mounted a strong doctrinal and political defence of Shiism. He detested Wahhabi-Salafism, and the rulers of Saudi Arabia, and denied them Islamic legitimacy. From his earliest writings up until his testament, which was published after his death and to which Khomeini's followers still refer, he declared that fighting Wahhabism and the Al Saud, which he called the arch enemies of Islam, and removing their control of the Holy Places of Islam, was a duty for Muslims.[47] Throughout the 1970s, Khomeini attacked Saudi Arabia, and when the revolution gained momentum, demonstrators carried his picture during the Hajj and in the Saudi Eastern Province.[48] This struggle between political Shiism and a version of political Sunnism led by Saudi Arabia intensified Sunni–Shia conflict.

The reformulation of Shiism towards a religion of protest and mass mobilisation had involved activist clerics and lay intellectuals from across the Shii worlds, and an appropriation of ideas from Marxism and Sunni Islamism. What it changed once and for all was the idea that the Shii experience, born out of centuries of oppression, grieving for the Imams, and periodic dissimulation, was one of marginality, fit not for political rule but only for lamentation, and quiet survival. Instead, Shii history was reinterpreted, places, names, and tragedies given new meaning, and formed the basis of an activist Shii ideology. That under Khomeini it became state ideology in Iran affected Shia everywhere. The final resting grounds of the Imams in Iran, Iraq, and Saudi Arabia, the shrines in Sayyida Zaynab outside of Damascus, and countless other, smaller ones, associated with the *Ahl al-Bayt*, became part of a religious topography invoked on a continuous basis by the highest officials of the Iranian state, and by activist Shii clerics around the world. This rekindled debates about the early disputes, older polemics, and the shrines themselves. It was not as if Shia had forgotten these episodes, but with Khomeini taking over Iran, they were reactivated in Shii collective memory.[49] They served to remind Shia that the Al Saud had destroyed the tombs over the graves of the Imams in Medina, and were repressing Saudi Shia, and that the Iraqi Baath did the same to Iraqi Shia, policed Najaf and Karbala, and rallied troops against Iran. And, they, instead, emphasised the importance of shrines in Iran, Mashhad, and Qom, as well as Sayyida Zaynab in Damascus, which was soon expanded at the expense of Iran. The original Sunni–Shia split, the lives of the Imams and the *Ahl al-Bayt*, and the first competing dynasties, had all centred on the Arabian Peninsula, Iraq, Syria, and Iran (and to a lesser extent Egypt and Afghanistan). As the struggle between Iran and its adversaries was largely fought out in this geographical space, the two sides instrumentalised the many ancient sites and mythical locations in diametrically opposed ways.

Iran tried to be accepted by Sunnis, but relied heavily on Shii symbolism. If martyrdom had already played a role during the revolution, and amongst activist Shii movements outside of Iran, that aspect of self-sacrifice, and the iconography of activist Shiism, soon became propaganda tools in a major war effort, and influenced global Shiism.[50] While Imam Khomeini would rule Iran for the next decade, Musa al-Sadr vanished under mysterious circumstances on a visit to Libya shortly after the Iranian revolution. He may have been trying to mediate between different Iranian factions and parts of the Shah's regime: a major affront to Khomeini, who had little tolerance for clerical rivals. It is likely that he was killed by Muammar Ghaddafi, possibly on orders of the pro-Khomeini trend in Iran. To his supporters in Lebanon, who remember him as Imam Musa al-Sadr, this added to his semi-divine qualities. Many drew analogies to the disappearance of the twelfth Imam, and, as his death was never confirmed, hoped he would return.[51] His disappearance at the height of the Lebanese Civil War opened the Lebanese Shii scene to a new, pro-Iran, force.

Expectations of the millennium, and of the return of the Mahdi, the Messiah, were also ripe amongst Sunnis. The oil boom of the 1970s that brought consumerism, wider access to education, urbanisation, and exposure to new ideas, meant that Saudi society started looking too secular to many conservatives. In 1975 King Faisal was assassinated by a relative who resented his policies. His successor Khalid was seen as weak, and Sunni and Shii Islamists vowed to overthrow the old order. In November 1979, at the start of Muharram 1400, Kalashnikov-wielding Sunni rebels proclaiming the start of a new dawn and the return of the Mahdi took over the holiest site of Islam, the Grand Mosque in Mecca. In the East, Shii Islamists of the Shirazi movement carried pictures of Khomeini, called for Islamic Revolution, and seized control of Qatif, a town near the world's largest oil-fields. That domestic challenge, coupled with calls for the export of the revolution from across the waters of the Gulf, shook the Saudi ruling family, and their American allies, to their core. Their response was to shape the future of Islam, and the world.

12

Export and Containment
of Revolution

On 17 February 1979, shortly after Khomeini's triumphal return to Iran and the collapse of the Shah's government, Palestine Liberation Organization (PLO) leader Yasser Arafat and a Fatah delegation embraced Khomeini in Qom and praised the revolution as a 'major victory for Muslims as well as a day of victory for Palestine'. Two days later, the Israeli embassy in Tehran was handed over to the PLO. Iran-Israel trade stopped, and Iran-Israel relations, which had been strong since the 1960s, took a U-turn.[1] One of Israel's allies became its fiercest opponent. Israel's military superiority, especially in 1973, had undermined Arab nationalism and pan-Arab solidarity. In a blow to the Palestinians, Egyptian president Anwar Sadat was the first Arab leader to sign a peace treaty with Israel on 26 March 1979. So Arafat saw revolutionary Iran as a new patron, and hoped the revolution could force Arab states to renew their support. The new PLO ambassador to Iran argued that Arab-Iranian conflict is what Zionism and the enemies of Iran and the Arabs want, and that the Palestinian revolution would work to prevent that.[2] Given their extensive networks and popularity amongst Sunni Arabs and the global Left, the PLO's embrace of the revolution was symbolically important.

Given that Egypt had been the Shah's first stop on his way to exile in January 1979, and Sadat refused to recognise the new government, Egypt and Iran were immediately at loggerheads.[3] In March 1980, Sadat granted the Shah permanent asylum, and when the Shah died shortly afterwards, Sadat ordered a state funeral, and he was interred in the al-Rifai Mosque in Cairo, next to former Egyptian Kings, a site to which Pahlavi loyalists would flock.[4] Sadat's signing of the peace treaty with Israel increased animosity with Iran, and spurred Islamist opposition. He was assassinated on 6 October 1981 by Sunni militants inspired by the Iranian revolution. When Iran named a major Tehran street after the assassin, tense relations between the two countries were set in stone.[5]

Iran was soon at odds with pro-Western Sunni Arab autocrats, though on a popular level the story was different. The revolution's appeal to Leftist Palestinians and Sunni Islamists problematises descriptions of the revolution as 'Shii'. The discourse of the revolution owed much to the global radicalism of the 1970s, to Third Worldism and the Iranian Left (even though the Islamists soon purged the Left).[6] Its impact was strong amongst Shia, but also appealed to Sunnis. Sunni political elites in turn feared the revolution. Because the Shah had been such an important Cold Warrior, his overthrow sent shockwaves through the international system. From the end of World War II until 1979, the Cold War had pitted Arab nationalist regimes allied with the Soviet Union against pro-Western monarchies. The Shah had convinced Richard Nixon that only he could contain Communism as Britain withdrew from the Gulf in the early 1970s. Hence, Nixon's Middle East policy was built on two pillars, Israel and Iran, with Saudi Arabia as junior partner.[7] After 1979, US support shifted away from Iran, and towards Saudi Arabia. As the Islamic Republic tried to export its revolution and establish new alliances, its Sunni enemies such as Iraq, Saudi Arabia, and Egypt, and, now, the US, formed an anti-Iran bloc. This led to a long-term containment strategy against the only country ruled by Shii clerics, tying Sunni–Shia relations to global power struggles and American foreign policy.

For many Iranians, the spectre of 1953, when the CIA and MI6 orchestrated a coup against a nationalist mass movement, and re-installed the Shah, loomed large. The activities of foreign embassies were thus a concern. And there were some in the American government, who toyed with the idea of a coup, although officials on the ground dismissed that idea as impossible given the pull of the Iranian masses. Eventually, the army declared its neutrality, and allowed a government appointed by Khomeini to take over power, and dismantle the old regime.[8] The US tried to maintain relations with the new government, seeing the ascent of Shii clerics as a lesser evil compared with Communism (although Shiism, which had previously been seen as quietist and anti-Communist, was now recast as inherently revolutionary).[9] In that vein, the Americans were initially reluctant to let the Shah enter the US (hence his stay in Egypt). But in October 1979, the Shah, severely ill with cancer, flew to the US for medical treatment. Feelings in Iran boiled over. On 4 November 1979, protesters broke into the US embassy, seizing the compound and taking hostages. The 400 students involved in the operation wore wristbands designating them as 'Muslim Students following the Imam's Line', indicating that they were followers of Khomeini, who they referred to as Imam.[10] Many hostages remained in Iranian hands for 444 days, an episode that had a traumatic impact on Americans and ruptured US–Iran relations.[11] Washington's strategy would from now on oscillate between containment and regime change in Iran.

The Islamic Republic established a 'normal' foreign service, and the interim government in charge from February to November 1979 sought to continue diplomatic relations with neighbouring countries. Yet many revolutionaries sought to export the revolution. Iran's foreign policy became characterised by that duality.[12] In coming years, diplomatic facilities of Iraq, Saudi Arabia, Kuwait, and Bahrain would be attacked. Initially, neither Iraq nor Saudi Arabia was openly hostile. Iraq had disliked the Shah, who had supported a Kurdish insurgency in the North together with the Americans. The Saudi King sent Khomeini a congratulatory telegram after his installation, advocating cooperation in the spirit of 'Islamic solidarity'. While much of the Kuwaiti press had turned critical of Iran by mid-1979,[13] the Kuwaiti FM visited Iran with several Shii ministers, and found kind words for the revolution.[14]

But as 1979 progressed, Iran provoked Iraq and Saudi Arabia, who were shaken by uprisings at home, and became convinced that war was the only solution. In Iraq, Shii Islamists had organised for years, and demonstrators had chanted anti-Baath slogans in Karbala and Najaf during Muharram 1977. Muhammad Baqir al-Sadr, co-founder of the Dawa party and cousin of Musa al-Sadr, became the figurehead of dissent. Al-Sadr was a towering figure with a dedicated following, whose substantial works on philosophy and Islamic economics were widely read by Sunnis as well, and who, like Khomeini, sported the black turban indicating descent from the Prophet.[15] In early 1979, al-Sadr called upon his followers to take to the streets. He similarly called on Sunnis to abandon the regime, and emphasised Sunni–Shia harmony.[16] In response, the regime placed him under house arrest, which led to more protests. From July 1979 onwards, al-Dawa and the Shirazis urged their followers to overthrow the regime by any means. Iraqi Shia set up training camps in Iran, and took over the Arabic-language service of Iranian radio and television to spread anti-Baath and anti-Gulf propaganda. They organised attacks on senior Iraqi regime figures, and beginning in 1980 hostilities between Iraq and Iran escalated. Muhammad Baqir al-Sadr now openly endorsed Khomeini and called for revolution, which led the Baathists to execute him, together with his sister, on 9 April 1980. This became a symbol of the regime's repression of the activist Shii clergy, and hardened the positions of those in exile or underground, and added to the historical pedigree of the Sadr family. Saddam—increasingly paranoid about Iran's impact on Iraqi Shia—decided to attack Iran. He found a receptive ear in the Gulf States, where Sunni leaders, too, were horrified by the turn of events.[17]

That neither the Shah's vast military and security apparatus, nor his alliance with the US, saved him, raised fears amongst the Gulf monarchs that they could face a similar fate. The Saudi monarchy was challenged by two simultaneous rebellions. In the East of the country, a new political movement amongst the Shia had planned protests on the first day of Muharram 1400, or 20 November 1979. This rising was symbolic of how Shii communities outside of Iran were affected by the revolution. Here, Shia had long been discriminated against, and the Wahhabi clergy considered them apostates. Feelings of neglect were made more acute by proximity to the oil fields of ARAMCO, which had once been America's largest private foreign venture, although the Saudi state had been buying back its shares since 1973, and the sense that little of the oil wealth benefitted locals. In recent years, they had been mobilised by the Shirazi movement, which had indoctrinated young Saudis during study courses in Kuwait. One of them was a teenager, Hasan al-Saffar, who would later become the figurehead of Saudi Shia. These young activists challenged the Shii elite families, who had found a modus vivendi with the government and opposed Islamism. The relationship between the notable families and the revolutionaries was symptomatic of what was happening in other Shii communities, where the new brand of activist Shiism challenged the landed elites and established clerics. In Saudi Arabia, as elsewhere, the Shii Islamist movements were also rebelling against the old elites.[18] In other places such as India, which did not feel threatened in the same way by Iran, some of the old Shii elites embraced the revolution, but even here new organisations challenged these elites as representative of a royalist Shiism that activist Shia vowed to overcome.[19]

Shii rituals were officially banned in Saudi Arabia, but, emboldened by the revolution a year earlier during Muharram, young activists decided to hold them openly. This was a clear defiance of the Saudi state. In addition, the ties to Iran and the revolution could be direct. A senior Iraqi Shirazi cleric, Murtada al-Qazwini, who had fled Saddam's persecution in the early

1970s, had come to preach in the Gulf during Muharram for years. In 1979, however, he went first on Hajj before going to Qatif. There he met Ali Khamenei, a close associate of Khomeini, and the one who would succeed him as Supreme Leader of Iran. Khamenei urged him to defend the Iranian Revolution in Qatif. In Qatif, al-Qazwini found people supportive of the revolution, but after the first day of Muharram the government said that he should lower his language. Yet, the youth wanted the opposite. He, al-Saffar and others gave fiery sermons at night, after which people would go out in the streets and chant political slogans. Saudi police arrested al-Qazwini on 8 Muharram, and expelled him to Kuwait. There, he heard the news that dozens of his followers had been killed and hundreds wounded in Qatif's old town when Saudi security forces employed helicopter gunships to quash the rebellion. The Saudi state demolished the old town, and turned its centre into a car park, complete with a Sunni mosque, embodying the victory of the state over the Shii rising.[20]

On the other side of the country, in the Hijaz, the birthplace of Islam, another group of rebels chose 20 November 1979 as a new dawn. Several hundred well-armed men took over the Grand Mosque in Mecca by force, killed the guards and took pilgrims hostage.[21] Initially described as an Iran-inspired movement because one of them claimed to be the Mahdi that would bring about the day of judgment, these were in fact Sunni militants with ties to senior Wahhabi clerics that were reacting against the country's alleged deviation from Islam. They held out for weeks, but as their former mentors distanced themselves from them, their rebellion was quashed with the help of French special forces.

These two risings shook the Saudi monarchy profoundly. Hundreds were murdered in Islam's holiest place. Protecting them was the state's responsibility towards global Islam, and the Al Saud had failed. That foreign troops had to be called in was doubly humiliating: it showed that the vast expenditures on security had not born fruit, and because non-Muslims are not supposed to enter Mecca and its Grand Mosque, caused further outrage. Meanwhile in the East, thousands had taken over control of a key city near the world's largest oil fields. The movement that claimed responsibility for the rising, and soon came to be based in Iran with the young cleric al-Saffar as its leader, called itself Organisation for the Islamic Revolution in the Arabian Peninsula. The spectre of Iran's revolution was haunting neighbouring Sunni Arab leaders, for whom the threat was both internal and external.[22]

In response, the Saudi Arabian government started giving greater power to Wahhabi clerics and increasing funding for religious causes. This served to deflect Wahhabi criticism of royal lifestyles and policies, as exemplified by the Mecca rising, and to undermine the appeal of revolutionary Iran by spreading the anti-Shiism inherent in Wahhabism. By relying more on the Wahhabi clergy, Saudi policies themselves became even more anti-Shii. To that point the Saudi rulers had never followed through on the most extreme Wahhabi demands—a complete suppression of Shia in Medina and the Eastern Province—and had allowed Shia to come on pilgrimages if they did not perform Shii rituals or demonstrate in public.[23] This was about to be challenged.

For his part, as he had for years, Khomeini delivered fiery sermons coinciding with the Hajj. In 1981 he appointed Mohammad Mousavi Khoeiniha, a hard-line revolutionary and mentor of the students who had seized the US embassy in Tehran, as leader of Iranian pilgrims. This was an obvious provocation. In 1982, Khoeiniha chose the al-Baqia cemetery in Medina for a series of demonstrations. After they had destroyed the tombs and mausolea of the *Ahl al-Bayt* in 1925, the Saudi government forbade Shia visitations. This became more of an issue after 1979 when Iran and Shia movements invoked the cemetery to denounce Saudi Arabia and Wahhabism.[24] As the burial ground of both Caliphs and Imams, it symbolised the struggle over the right interpretation of Islam, with Wahhabis banning grave visitation and building of shrines, and Shia honouring the legacy of the Imams. Predictably, the Saudis did not take lightly the arrival of thousands of Iranians, carrying images of Khomeini, to the birthplace of Islam. They briefly arrested Khoeiniha and many others.[25] Tensions eased slightly over the coming years (Khoeiniha was replaced, and the Foreign Ministers of both countries paid each other a visit).[26] Then in 1987 clashes between Iranian pilgrims and Saudi police and a stampede claimed hundreds of lives. Khomeini and the Iranian and wider Shii public were furious (that a relative of his had been killed did not help).[27] Iran called for the Hajj to be placed under international Islamic oversight, questioning Saudi competence as guardians of the two holy places (the Saudi King had a year prior adopted the formal title 'Custodian of the Two Holy Places').[28] And Iran organised attacks on Saudi diplomats and oil facilities in the Eastern Province through a group of Saudi dissidents. Harsh repression against Saudi Shia, and a disruption of diplomatic relations, followed.[29]

Apart from Saudi Arabia, other Gulf States with substantial Shia communities—Kuwait and Bahrain—worried about the revolution. In Kuwait, Shia, who had had good relations with the ruling family, became radicalized by the Shirazis and Dawa from neighbouring Iraq in the 1970s. Young Shia from Saudi Arabia, Bahrain and elsewhere would spend their holidays in Kuwait, attending religious courses and indoctrination sessions. These networks were crucial in 1979 during the uprising in Qatif, and in Bahrain, where Shii protests shook the Al Khalifa ruling family. The subsequent crackdown on Shii political organisations drove many underground and into exile, including the Iraqi Shirazi cleric Hadi al-Mudarrisi, who had lived in Bahrain for years. Bahraini Shia, most of whom felt they were not reaping the spoils of Bahrain's transformation into a regional banking hub, and had long been mobilised by Leftist movements, were increasingly mobilised by Iraqi Shii Islamist networks, and by followers of Khomeini himself. In Bahrain, the situation was made even more explosive by the fact that some Shia were of Iranian origin.[30]

Hundreds of Bahrainis and Saudis joined the Shirazi leadership in Iran. They believed that a revolution was most likely to succeed in Bahrain, with a disenfranchised and politicised Shia majority (despite the presence of an American naval base, and a British-led security service). A force of a hundred young men, armed and trained by the Iranian government, arrived by boat and plane in early 1981. Their mission was to take over ministries and the media, as well as assassinate senior Al Khalifa figures. A faction of the IRGC was supposed to provide aid with speed boats, and al-Mudarrisi would arrive in Bahrain shortly afterward to head up a new clergy-led government allied to Iran.

It was wishful thinking. When they arrived at Bahrain airport via the UAE, many of the young men were wearing military boots from their training camps in Iran. This aroused suspicions, and after they were arrested the plot quickly unravelled. Those who were not immediately apprehended boarded ships to Iran. Some were arrested just as the last ship was leaving the island. In the end, some seventy-three individuals, including some Saudis, were put on trial and jailed.[31] Iranian support for Bahraini Shia was sensitive because Bahrain had been a part of Iran during the Safavid period, and Iran had maintained a claim to Bahrain until 1971. While the Islamic Republic did not officially reassert that claim, Iranian officials at times called for the reintegration of Bahrain into Iran, enraging Gulf rulers and Arab nationalists. The coup attempt poisoned relations between Iran and its Gulf neighbours, and was invoked to justify repression against Gulf Shia. It gave Gulf Arab leaders, who founded the Gulf Cooperation Council (GCC) in Bahrain in May 1981, a few months after the coup attempt, a sense of urgency and common purpose.

Kuwait, where Shii merchants were well integrated into the elite, and Shii institutions like those of the Shirazis had been allowed to operate freely, also suffered from sectarian tensions. Parliamentary elections in 1981 were gerrymandered to undermine both Leftist and Arab nationalist opposition, and in turn brought Sunni and Shii Islamists to parliament, as a result of which public life in Kuwait, like in Saudi Arabia, became charged. The rivalries in the region were discussed in the relatively free Kuwaiti press and on the floor of parliament. As Kuwait started supporting Saddam's war against Iran, Shii militants allied with Dawa and Iran attacked the Kuwaiti state, hijacked airliners, and even tried to assassinate the Emir. This meant that, here too, repression against Shia intensified. Shii political movements that previously had been seen as a useful counterweight to Sunni Islamists and Arab Nationalists, were now closely monitored.[32] Sixteen members of a group of Kuwaiti Shia found guilty of smuggling explosives during the Hajj in 1989 were beheaded in Saudi Arabia.[33] The Shii communities in the other three Gulf States—Oman, Qatar, and the UAE—were much smaller, better integrated, and less prone to the call of the revolutionary message. It helped that their governments took a more accommodating stance towards Iran than Saudi Arabia.[34]

Even politicians from countries with a limited or no Shii presence, such as Jordan, Egypt, and Morocco, emulated their Gulf counterparts by invoking the Shia 'threat'. Egypt supported Iraq in the Iran-Iraq war, and clamped down on all Shia activity in Egypt, becoming deeply suspicious of Shia and Iranian proselytising, a fear fuelled ironically by the growing Sunni Islamist movement in Egypt that had been partly inspired by Iran's revolution.[35] This further alienated Arab Shia, and harsh repression drove many into exile. Iran supported older Shii networks like the Shirazis and Dawa, and set up new ones that followed Khomeini directly and were tied to the so-called Revolutionary Guards established during the revolution (the most famous of these Hizbullah, or Party of God, movements was the one in Lebanon, about more below).[36]

As noted, Shia Islamists had long engaged with the ideas of Sunni Islamists. Ali Khamenei, who succeeded Ayatollah Khomeini as Supreme Leader, translated the works of Sayyid Qutb, as we've seen the chief ideologue of the

Egyptian Muslim Brotherhood, the oldest of the Sunni Islamist movements, into Persian. The Muslim Brotherhood had a strong influence on Shii Islamists, and in turn initially embraced the revolution.[37] Muslim Brotherhood leaders from Tunisia, Lebanon, Syria, Sudan, and beyond saw the Islamic Republic as a model, covered the revolution widely in their publications, and often praised Khomeini, without seeing the latter's Shii identity as a problem. They also visited Iran soon after the toppling of the Shah.[38] The Egyptian Muslim Brotherhood and other Egyptian Islamists were initially enthusiastic not least because the Revolution had overthrown a close ally of Sadat (they even criticised the Egyptian media campaign against Iran of trying to divide Sunni and Shia). They hailed the revolution as clergy-led, Islamic, anti-imperialist and pro-Palestinian, and engaged with Khomeini's writings. Some hoped nationalism and confessional tendencies would be replaced by unity between Sunnis and Shia, perhaps even in one state. The Muslim Brotherhood's international organisation called upon all Islamic groups to support Iran, 'the only Islamic system in the world'.[39] More Salafi-inspired, and pro-Saudi Islamists, however, published anti-Khomeini pamphlets early on.[40]

Iran initially saw the Muslim Brotherhood as a main ally. Leaders of Hizb al-Tahrir, the Sunni Islamist movement advocating a global Caliphate, which as noted had previously cooperated with the Shii Dawa Party, met Khomeini in early 1979 to find common ground for a Caliphate. They were apparently willing to accept Khomeini as head of state—in other words, as Shii Caliph. Hizb al-Tahrir only changed its position when the Iranians started drafting a new constitution in the second half of 1979 (it was adopted by referendum on 2 and 3 December 1979). The constitution stipulated the centrality of Twelver Shiism (though it granted recognition to the four Sunni schools of jurisprudence, especially in areas where there is a Sunni majority).[41] This was a middle-ground between Shii-centric and ecumenical positions. Shiism was given preference, but Sunnism, too, was officially recognised.[42] Khomeini and other senior clerics had ensured that centrality of Shiism, and that the senior clergy would have wide-ranging powers over the legislative process, and decision-making.[43]

This, together with the brutality and symbolism of the Iran–Iraq war, contributed to the alienation of Sunnis from the revolution, which came to be seen in more Shii terms.[44] In January 1982, Shaykh Umar al-Tilmisani, the general guide of the Muslim Brotherhood in Egypt, stated that Shia and Sunni Islam were fundamentally different.[45] He had tried to mediate the release of the American hostages in Iran, and end the Iran Iraq war, but had failed on both counts. When Iran refused ceasefire offers in 1982, and pushed back militarily, it was no longer seen as victim, which gave some Muslim Brothers pause.[46] Iraq and Saudi Arabia sponsored anti-Shii publications and may have influenced Sunni religious figures in Egypt and elsewhere to adopt an anti-Shia stance.[47]

Still, the flirtation with the revolution led some Egyptians to reconsider Egypt's Shii history. One Sunni militant of al-Jihad, for example, Salih al-Wardani, later converted to Shiism, and wrote *The Shia in Egypt from Imam Ali to Imam Khomeini* in which he attacked Saladin for ending the Fatimid Caliphate, drawing the ire of Sunni commentators.[48] Such publications were provocative as Egyptians had long tried to de-confessionalise the history of the Fatimids.

Some Egyptian Sunnis, and Sunnis from elsewhere, converted to Shiism under the influence of the Islamic revolution. Their numbers were limited in number but because some of them became outspoken advocates of Shiism, and public figures, this lead to accusations Iran was trying to convert Sunnis, and sectarian tensions.[49] The number of Shia in Egypt is small, making up perhaps 1 or 2 per cent of the population or between one and two million, and yet debates about Shiism are intertwined with the fact that Egypt was once ruled by a Shii dynasty. We have seen how the old city of Cairo, one of the great cities of Islamic history, was built by the Ismaili Shia Fatimids (who ruled Egypt from 969 until 1171). Elsewhere in Africa, for example in Senegal, new converts to Shiism also linked their recent conversions to North Africa's Shii history.[50] Shiism in West Africa was boosted by Lebanese Shii migrants who arrived throughout the twentieth century, and prospered. Some of them now cooperated with Iranian embassies in Africa to proselytise. Saudi and Iranian-funded institutes started to compete in trying to convert people from the prevalent Sufism to their respective versions of Sunnism and Shiism.[51] In Nigeria, for example, Shii literature spread rapidly after the revolution of 1979, and converts would found a Shii Islamic Movement. This led to a Sunni counter-reaction, and the publication of anti-Shii literature, and, eventually, to violence.[52] Saudi-funded Salafi-Wahhabi networks also expanded their proselytisation efforts.[53]

In Southeast Asia, too, the Iranian revolution had an impact. *Ahl al-Baytism* and Shii themes abounded in literature and popular practice, including in some Sufi movements that became prominent in Indonesia and Malaysia by the nineteenth century, and highly syncretistic versions of Ashura, but few people would have self-identified, or been seen by outsiders, as Shii (or even as Sunni, for in the absence of openly Shii Muslims most just self-identified as Muslims). Sectarian constructions only gained pace after 1979. Admirers of Khomeini and Ali Shariati led some Indonesians to openly embrace Shiism, and some went to study in Qom. Sunni Islamists with connections to Saudi Arabia in turn became anti-Shii. Anti-Shii polemics appeared alongside books praising the Iranian revolution. The proselytisation of Shii movements, and an anti-Shii campaign by Sunni Islamists constructed the very categories of Sunni and Shii.[54] In turn, and under influence of Saudi Arabia, Malaysia issued a wholescale ban on Shiism (meaning that practising Shii rituals can lead to a prison sentence), and anti-Shii persecution would intensify over coming decades.[55] The visual repertoire, and activist reinterpretation of Shiism, and the emergence of pro-Iranian clerics as communal leaders, meant that the revolution had a strong impact on Indian Shiism, too.[56]

In Syria, the Muslim Brothers had long used sectarian language to denounce Alawites and the regime (a chief ideologue, Said Hawwa, invoked Ibn Taymiyya's fatwa that had declared 'Nusayris' apostates). According to that logic, the regime was dominated by minorities with questionable Islamic credentials, and Sunni Islamists the representative of the majority of (Sunni) Syrians. The regime, on the other hand, tried to either downplay sectarian difference of its key constituents or portray Alawites as a part of Islam. The opposition, from the mid-1970s onwards, tried to conflate Alawites with the regime, and held much of the Alawite community responsible for state repression. Delegitimising the Alawites' Islamic credentials became a way to undermine the legitimacy of the regime.[57] After the crackdown on the Hama uprising in 1964, parts of the Muslim Brotherhood had become radicalised amid internal power shifts. Hama-based radicals wanted to continue armed struggle, and following the constitutional crisis of 1973, when Hafez al-Assad limited the role of Sharia in jurisprudence and asked Shia and Sunni scholars to confirm that Alawites are Muslim, started assassinating Alawites affiliated with the regime. This reached a climax in 1979 in a massacre at Aleppo of eighty-three Alawite cadet officers. The regime responded by tightening its grip, purging Sunnis from the army and the Baath party, and empowering Alawites. Units used to crack down on Sunnis would now be led by Alawite officers.[58]

By 1979, the Syrian Brotherhood was thus engaged in what it saw as a sectarian war against a quasi-Shii regime, and had adopted strong sectarian rhetoric (although mainly against Alawites, and not yet against Shiism in general). The Syrian brothers initially endorsed the overthrow of the Shah and appealed to Khomeini for help (a Syrian brotherhood delegation including Hawwa visited Iran in May 1979 and met with Khomeini, who allegedly promised to talk to Hafez al-Assad about the situation in Syria).[59] Some Iranians wanted to support the Syrian Muslim Brotherhood.[60] But Syria was also the first Arab state to recognise the revolutionary regime in Tehran in February 1979 and the two states formed an enduring alliance that was based on a common disdain for the pro-Western alliance in the region, an enmity towards Iraq, and similar interests in Lebanon, forming a new axis from Lebanon via Damascus to Tehran in which Shii symbolism started to play a role.[61] After initially hoping that Iran would support them, the Syrian Brothers came to see Iran as an enemy, and criticised it for allying with what they described as an Alawite regime.[62] They instead accepted support from Iraq. In 1980, they led another uprising in Hama, stylising themselves as defenders of Sunnis against an Alawite regime. A new political programme appealed to the 'wise men' of the Alawite community. 'Nine or ten percent of the population', the appeal reads, 'cannot dominate the majority in Syria.' The appeal ended with the hope that Alawites would shake off the 'guardianship' of the al-Assad clan and 'prevent the tragedy from reaching its sad end'.[63]

The regime crushed the uprising in 1982 with utmost brutality, killing tens of thousands and destroying large parts of one of Syria's most historic cities. The Brothers who survived largely fled the country, to Lebanon, Europe or the Gulf States. The regime won militarily, but the opposition in exile would continue to frame grievances in sectarian terms. These events entrenched the sectarian discourse and feelings amongst much of the opposition, and tied Alawites ever more closely to the regime.[64] Iran's muted response further alienated the Brotherhood from Iran. Khomeini may have told Hafez al-Assad that his crackdown had gone too far, but he did not alter the strategic relationship with Syria, though an ostensibly secular regime was slaughtering Islamists.[65]

The Syrian Brothers in the Gulf, for example, who had long been influenced by Salafism and the Naqshbandiyya, moved closer to Wahhabi-Salafism, and turned hostile towards all Shia. One of them was Muhammad Surur, a former Syrian Brother who had moved first to Saudi Arabia and then to Kuwait, and had become a Salafi leader in his own right.[66] To limit the impact of the revolution on the Kuwaiti Brothers, he published an anti-Iranian polemic, *The Time of the Magian has Come*, in 1981 under a pen name. Its title referred to Iran's pre-Islamic Zoroastrian past, implying that Iranians, and Shia in general, were non-Muslims. He warned of the dangers to Arabs and Sunnism, claiming that Iran sought to re-establish the ancient Persian Empire.[67] He rehashed anti-Persian and anti-Shia narratives and argued that Gulf Shia would act as bridgeheads for Shia-Iranian infiltration. He was specific in detail, listing names and addresses of Shia businesses and places of worship in Kuwait, and claiming that Shia controlled parts of the economy and subverted Sunni society, and criticised Sunni Arab governments that tolerated Shiism. The book was republished numerous times, and widely distributed by Saudi clerics.[68]

Because he became a sort of godfather of Salafism and Syrian Islamism, his anti-Shii narratives carried special weight. Later polemics also linked doctrinal and political anti-Shiism, denouncing Shia as fifth columnists for Iran. A prominent Saudi cleric published a similar book denouncing Shia in Saudi Arabia entitled *The Situation of the Rejectionists in the Lands of Monotheism*, one of many such books published since 1979.[69] Saudi-funded organisations and mosques distributed them for free in Arabic, Persian, English, Urdu, Malay, Turkish, and other languages.[70] The older polemics, too, were republished and became widely available.[71]

Hawwa, the Syrian Brother who had visited Khomeini in 1979, published an anti-Shia polemic in 1987 entitled *Khomeinism: Deviations from Faith, Deviations from Political Positions*. He started the book by arguing that love of the *Ahl al-Bayt* was a part of Sunnism, but that the Shii exaggerators had through that love found a way to spread their doctrines. As historical evidence of Shii treachery, he referred amongst others to the Shii cleric Nasir al-Din al-Tusi (1201–74), whom he blames for having convinced the Mongol Khan Hulegu to abolish the Abbasid Caliphate, as well as to the Abbasid Wazir Ibn al-Alqami, whom he accuses of having assisted the Mongols in taking over Baghdad in 1258. He criticised not only the revolution and Shiism but the treatment of Sunnis in Iran.[72] This was a sore point. Officially, Iran emphasised that it recognised Sunnism, and pointed to Saudi Arabia, which long did not even recognise the other three Sunni schools apart from Hanbalism, out of which Wahhabism had emerged, let alone Shiism.[73] But since the conversion of the bulk of the population to Shiism in the Safavid period, Sunnism was a potential source of opposition. Sunnis were mainly located in border regions, and Sunni identity often overlapped with non-Persian ethnic and linguistic identity (as we've seen, the Safavids were overthrown by Sunni Afghans).

Iran's Kurds had initially participated in the revolution, and sought to emphasise a common Muslim identity, but a major uprising against the new regime broke out in March 1979. The revolutionaries showed little mercy. Mustafa Chamran, who had been so crucial in the revolutionary networks between Lebanon and Iran, and had cooperated with Sunni Palestinians, now—as defence minister—oversaw the brutal crackdown of Kurds. By redefining the ideology of the state, the revolution recast the relationship between ethnic and religious minorities and the state. Some Kurds were Shii, or adherents of pro-Alid movements, and these had less problems with the new clergy-led state, and participated in the political process. But most were Sunni, and while theirs was an ethno-nationalist cause, Sunni religious leaders became increasingly central in resistance to the new state, which resulted in a stronger identification of Kurds with Sunnism, which they claimed was repressed alongside their Kurdish identity.[74]

Similar processes were under way amongst Sunni Baluchs and Arabs, Sunni Persian-speakers on the Gulf coast, and Sunni Turkmen. The Baluch, located on the border with Afghanistan and Pakistan, with their own language and close ties to Baluch across both borders, were almost exclusively Sunni, and had long been influenced by the brand of Sunni Revivalism that originated in the nineteenth century in the Indian seminary of Deoband. Successive Iranian governments had encouraged the settlement of Iranian Shia to dilute their ethno-sectarian specificity (like in the case of other minorities). Deobandis, as noted, were doctrinally assertive towards Shiism, but both the Pahlavi state and the Islamic Republic reached agreements with Baluch Deobandi clerics. And just as Shia in Saudi Arabia, Bahrain, Kuwait, and elsewhere, including Iraq, now started to mobilise as Shia, rather than as part of Leftist, nationalist or regionalist organisations, so did new groups emerge that claimed to represent 'the Sunnis' in Iran, and that spread their narrative first in print and later online. As noted, Sunnism was officially recognised in the Iranian constitution, though clearly in inferior terms to Shiism, and Sunnis were effectively barred from high office. And ethno-sectarian opposition groups linking themselves to global anti-Shii rhetoric would also emerge here.[75]

In Iran as elsewhere, minorities with ties across borders could be susceptible to foreign influence. Some sections of marginalised communities might be convinced to take up arms, although that was played up to legitimise repression, or intervention. Iraq used the Arab minority in Iran as a pretext for war. The Baath regime claimed that Iran sought to destroy Arab identity in Ahwaz, a territory in Iran that is home to large numbers of ethnic Arabs (and had at times been called 'Arabistan'). As part of the Baath regime's ethno-sectarian conspiracy theories, it argued that the same was happening in the Gulf region, in places like Bahrain and Kuwait. But many Arabs in Iran, especially those in Ahwaz, were Shii not Sunni, and while some were wary of the new regime, others had participated in the revolution and would attain high office in the new state.[76]

In September 1980, Iraq, poorer and smaller than Iran, with a third of its population yet a more modern army, invaded Iran, initially in Khorramshahr and Abadan. Saddam Hussein feared that the revolution might be exported to Iraq and embolden Iraqi Shia. He hoped that his invasion would embolden Arabs to rise up and support the Iraqi army. As the Iranian army had been purged of pro-Shah loyalists, especially in the officer corps and the army's more technical ranks, Saddam sensed a historic opportunity. Given that the Shah had been a bitter rival, post-revolutionary Iran seemed easier to tackle.[77] Saddam hoped to force Iran into concessions over the southern border, along the Shatt al-Arab. The old Ottoman–Safavid frontier had been demarcated earlier, and a 1975 agreement between Saddam and the Shah was meant to solve any points of dispute, but Iraq kept reasserting wider territorial claims. Saddam thought his army would make quick gains by wiping out Iran's air force and conquering frontier regions such as Ahwaz, and he could then negotiate from a position of strength.

Instead, he started the longest conventional war of the twentieth century, one that claimed hundreds of thousands of lives. Some Arabs in Iran rose, but most didn't, just as most Iraqi Shia stayed loyal to the Iraqi state despite Iran's attempts to incite them. Saddam felt emboldened because the Gulf States, the Soviet Union, the US and European countries backed him and, over the coming years, would transfer a massive amount of weaponry to Iraq.[78] The US assisted Iraq economically and militarily.[79] Gulf support, too, was crucial. From 1981 to 1988, Saudi Arabia paid Iraq $60 billion, allowed the transit of weapons to Iraq, and sought to break the Chinese supply of arms to Iran.[80]

As the Iraqi officer corps was largely Arab Sunni and the infantry Arab Shii, the latter bore the brunt of casualties. Nonetheless, not many soldiers defected (those that did formed the core of Iraqi Shii militias based in Iran), meaning that the Iran–Iraq war was to a large extent fought between Iraqi and Iranian Shii soldiers.[81] The Iraqi regime linked the war to a battle in 637, which the Arabs won over the Persians and then spread Islam further in Iran. As this battle had taken place *before* the Sunni–Shia split, it was an attempt to rally Iraqi Shia for the war effort.[82] Saddam called the war against Iran a racial war against the Persian '*Majus*', invoking the Arab-Persian dichotomy. This was reinforced by the emphasis on an Arab tribalism that included Sunni and Shii Arabs. The regime was careful not to openly allow directly anti-Shii rhetoric, but Sunni biases in the party's ideology and its religious policies persisted. Politicised Shii clerics and those of Persian origin were portrayed as potentially disloyal and subject to surveillance and repression. Others were cultivated as clients and forced to support the war. Shia that distanced themselves from religiosity and stayed true to the Baath party could advance.[83] The regime even refurbished the shrines in Karbala and Najaf, established a toothless National Assembly, appointed Shia as speakers of parliament and even, briefly, as PM, and named missiles directed at Iranian cities 'Ali' and 'Hussain'.[84] It encouraged public adherence to Islamic norms, and Saddam started portraying himself as a pious Muslim, while tightly controlling Shii processions.[85]

Iran, in contrast, portrayed the war as an attack on Islam itself, invoked the Karbala paradigm and the Imams, and decried Saddam as a Muawiya and Yazid—an enemy of the *Ahl al-Bayt*.[86] Given that the Iraqi army was much better equipped, and provided with cutting-edge military hardware, Iran had to rely on young men marching up to the front lines. Tens of thousands died in the trenches. Shii martyrology promised young Iranians (and a few Shii volunteers from outside Iran) rewards in the afterlife. Using martyrdom as a major part of an effort to induce Shia to fight for a Shii cause in a foreign land would set precedents for later wars, and lead to the formation of the Revolutionary Guards (IRGC) alongside the regular army. These Guards became an increasingly important factor in domestic and foreign policy, and the Iranian economy, and one closely associated with revolutionary Shii ideology.[87]

Iraq and Iran also competed over support for Palestine. Khomeini framed it in Islamic terms (the Arabic name for Jerusalem, al-Quds, was invoked during an annual solidarity event, International Quds Day, and became the name of the Guards' international branch tasked with supporting like-minded movements—the Quds Force). Iraq emphasised the Arab dimension.[88] In 1980, Iran helped found a new movement in Palestine, Islamic Jihad, and would later also emerge as the main foreign patron of Hamas, which emerged in 1987 out of the Palestinian branch of the Muslim

Brotherhood. One of Islamic Jihad's co-founders, Fathi al-Shiqaqi (d. 1995), wrote a glowing tribute to Khomeini, and praised the revolution as Islamic resistance to Western imperialism, in the spirit of pan-Islam and ecumenism. He advocated armed struggle, and placed Iran at the centre of a renewed Islamic push for the liberation of Palestine.[89] When the PLO chose relations with Iraq and the Gulf States over ties with Iran, Iran expanded its support for other Palestinian groups.[90]

In Lebanon, too, Iran tried to not only empower Shia but establish relations with Sunnis. The ties that had facilitated the revolution now served its export to a country in civil war. Iran's Revolutionary Guards trained Shia cadres and in 1982 set up what was to become Lebanon's most powerful militia and political force: the Party of God (Hizbullah).[91] That same year, Israel invaded Lebanon, and occupied its south. Israel had long sought allies on the borders of the Arab world, like the Shah's Iran, and amongst 'minorities' in the region, such as Maronite Christians in Lebanon.[92] Christian elites and Israel saw the Palestinian armed movement, which had attacked Israeli forces from Lebanon, as an existential threat. Israel's intervention was supposed to weaken the Palestinians and to prevent Christian militias, who were faring badly, from losing the war.[93] As the south of Lebanon that Israel was to occupy until 2000—for eighteen years—was majority Shia, Israel became a new factor in Shii politics. Some Shia initially welcomed the Israelis, hoping that their presence would end the fighting and drive out Palestinian militias, which had at times clashed with local Shia, who had suffered from Israeli reprisals for Palestinian attacks. Israel created the South Lebanon Army, made up of Christians and Shia and probably hoped that the anti-Palestinian militant feeling amongst Shia near the border would favour its presence.[94] But sentiments soon shifted, and by pushing Palestinian armed groups out of South Lebanon and West Beirut, Israel inadvertently gave Shii Islamist movements the space to take over.[95] Initially, the Amal movement profited from this power vacuum. But with its charismatic leader Musa al-Sadr vanished, it was increasingly challenged by Hizbullah, an amalgam of different networks inspired by the Iranian revolution, some of whom had been rivals of Amal. Hizbullah now positioned itself as the vanguard in the fight against Israel. And as it became clear that the Israelis were going to stay in the South, resistance grew.[96] Hizbullah benefitted from a general Islamic turn in society, and from the support of new Shii religious schools that trained the party's clerical cadres. The party also soon set about establishing social service provision with the help of Iran.[97] Saddam Hussein's war on Iran, and the Israeli invasion of Lebanon, both instigated by American allies, cemented the alliance between Syria and Iran, which vowed to resist the US and Israel (the 1983 bombing of US Marine barracks in Beirut, 241 American and fifty-eight French military personnel, six civilians, and two attackers, likely carried out by a pro-Iranian Shii group led to the US withdrawal from Lebanon).[98] By 1984, Amal, since Sadr's disappearance led by the lawyer Nabih Berri, which had been trying to take a middle ground in the civil war, and perhaps negotiate a settlement with President Gemayel, had broken fully with the latter, and expanded its hold over West Beirut. It also signified the military and political ascent of Lebanese Shia largely at the expense of Sunnis of Beirut.[99]

Syria and Iran initially had different Shii clients in Lebanon, Amal, and Hizbullah, who at times clashed during the civil war. But both wanted to empower Lebanese Shia and anti-Western forces, keep Gulf influence limited, and push Israel out of South Lebanon, and relations between Syria and Hizbullah eventually improved.[100]

Tripoli, Lebanon's second-largest city, was a case in point. The city's integration into Lebanon had relegated this northern port town to peripheral status, cutting it off from its economic hinterland in Syria, and the political aspirations of its inhabitants often embraced causes larger than Lebanon, such as Arab nationalism, and Sunni Islamism. Tripoli also had an Alawite community with connections to the Alawite heartlands further up the coast, and to the Baath regime in Damascus. In the 1970s, more Alawites settled in Tripoli and mobilised politically to gain recognition in Lebanon as a separate religious community (Musa al-Sadr's acknowledgement of Alawites as Shia Muslims helped that cause, and served to earn him the goodwill of Lebanon's Alawites). Simultaneously, the PLO expanded its presence around Tripoli's large Palestinian refugee camp. The Syrian regime, however, feared that Tripoli could provide a base for the Syrian opposition, some of whom had fled to the city after the crackdown on Hama. In 1983, a major confrontation between them—with the Palestinians on one side, and the Syrian army on the other—led the Syrian regime and Lebanese Shia to see Palestinians less as Leftist internationalists and more as armed Sunnis. Over the coming years, Amal besieged Palestinian camps in other parts of Lebanon. This so-called 'war of the camps' started to be framed in a Shia-Sunni vein. It was the sad climax of tensions between Amal and the Palestinian armed groups that dated back to Israeli reprisals on Southern Lebanese Shia in response to Palestinian attacks on Israeli forces there. Yet some Sunnis embraced the Iranian revolution. In the wake of the Israeli invasion of 1982, a Sunni Imam formed the Islamic Unification Movement in Tripoli inspired by Iran. Parts of the Lebanese Brotherhood, and a clerical body made up of Sunni and Shia, similarly embraced the revolution, and called for Sunni–Shia unity.[101]

Other young Sunnis from the city, both Lebanese and Palestinians, enrolled in the Islamic University of Medina, where they became influenced by Wahhabism.[102] Upon their return to Lebanon they spread Salafism with funding from Saudi Arabia and Qatar, adding a doctrinally anti-Shii and anti-Alawite dimension to Lebanese Sunnism.[103] They argued that a conspiracy between Shiism and the West was undermining Sunnism.[104] They were influenced by Syrian Salafis like Surur, who had written the important anti-Shii and anti-Iranian polemic *Magians*. He attacked Lebanese Shia movements and deplored the fate of 'Sunnis in Lebanon' and became a godfather of Lebanese and Syrian Salafism.[105] Leadership of the Shii community was contested, too. Amal and then Hizbullah came to dominate it. The Communist Party, which had historically mobilised many Shia but declined in influence, allied itself with Hizbullah in the resistance against Israel. Hizbullah saw itself as the representative of the Shii community. It was open about its alliance with Iran, invited more Iranian intervention, was loyal to Imam Khomeini (and later Khamenei) as its spiritual leader, and Iran as the centre of Islamic revolutionary action. Nonetheless, it retained a strong pan-Islamic rhetoric, and allied itself with Sunni Islamists like Tripoli's Islamic Unification Movement, and with Palestinians, and its resistance discourse was influenced by the Lebanese Left. Its 1985 open letter, for example, denounced Sunni–Shia discord and called it a colonial fabrication and tool. Some Sunnis were willing to work with Hizbullah, and overlook its Shii-centricity. Others weren't (ideological and doctrinal tensions would emerge especially with Salafi-Jihadis and could complicate relations with Palestinian organisations).[106]

Symbolic of the difficulty of Sunnis organising as a community akin to Christians, Druze, and Shia in countries where they are a numeric minority, Sunni leadership in Lebanon and foreign patronage of the community was more fragmented and diverse.[107] Saudi Arabia increasingly became the key patron, replacing Egypt and Syria in that role, relying less on religious figures than on sectarian entrepreneurs.[108] For example, Rafiq Hariri, the son of a fruit-picker from Sidon, had gone to work in Saudi Arabia during the oil-bonanza of the 1970s. He built real estate projects for the Saudi ruling family and got involved in diplomacy. By the second half of the 1980s, Hariri was *the* Saudi man in Lebanon, and facilitated peace talks.[109] Through intermarriage with the Sunni bourgeoisie of Beirut, the Al Saud had personal interests and investments in Lebanon.

In sum, by the 1980s, both Saudi Arabia and Iran, which had played marginal roles in Lebanon before the civil war, were heavily backing Sunnis and Shia, respectively. By the end of the decade, and after fourteen years of war, all sides were exhausted, and agreed to compromise. The Ta'if agreement, signed on 22 October 1989 in the Saudi Arabian resort town of the same name, altered the pre-war political pact, and transferred power away from Maronite Christians towards Sunni and Shia Muslims. It shifted power away from the Lebanese president, who remained a Christian, to the Council of Ministers headed by a Sunni prime minister, and to the Shii speaker of parliament.[110] The agreement was a victory for Saudi Arabia and its client Hariri. But it also accommodated Syrian interests. Although the text called for the gradual withdrawal of Syrian troops, they were allowed to stay temporarily, and it generally allowed for much Syrian economic and political influence (Israel continued its occupation of the South for another decade).[111] The agreement also called for the disarmament of Lebanese militias. And while most handed in their weapons, the by now strongest militia, Hizbullah didn't, a move supported by Iran and Syria. These contradictions were glossed over for now, only to erupt later.[112]

Iran gained significant influence in Lebanon, to which it was now connected via a land bridge through its ally Syria, turning the Syria-Iran axis into a major force in the Eastern Mediterranean. However, the war with Iraq bogged down Iran to the West and the export of the revolution to the Gulf States failed. Moreover, the struggle over Afghanistan limited Iran's influence to the East.

In 1978, the Communist Party overthrew the monarchy in Kabul. Backed by the Soviet Union, the party started widespread social and economic reforms. In a departure from Sunni and Pashtu-dominated monarchical Afghanistan, the Communists reached out to Shia. For the first time in Afghanistan's history, a Shii Hazara became prime minister, the Hazara's history of oppression was openly discussed, and the Communist regime was willing to make wide-ranging concessions to appease Hazara and try to win over Iran-based Hazara Islamist movements.[113] The few Ismaili Afghans, too, were hopeful that their discrimination would come to an end.[114] But traditionally minded Islamist and Maoist Shia, like many Sunnis, especially in rural areas, opposed the Communists, and joined the resistance that quickly sprung up. US President Carter authorised covert aid to the rebels as the Soviet Union deployed troops. American, Saudi, and Pakistani intelligence delivered arms and money to the rebels, the Mujahedin.[115]

The Hazara region was largely outside of government or Russian control for much of the 1980s, leading to greater self-determination, but also to a Hazara civil war between pro-Iranian Islamists and traditionalists. Many fled to Iran as Afghan Shii clerics in Qom espoused the Iranian revolution. Islamist Hazara eventually defeated other Hazara forces, and formed numerous parties in the 1980s, some with the help of Iran, which tried to expand its influence amongst the Afghan resistance. This culminated in 1989 with the formation of an Hazara umbrella party, the Hezb-e Wahdat.[116]

Shia and Sunnis resistance forces cooperated to a certain degree. Still, the Mujahedin's Sunni sponsors sought to limit the role of these Shii parties and did not want Iran gaining influence outside of Shii circles. The Saudis and Pakistanis ensured that rebel factions not aligned to them, including Afghan Shii militias, were not represented in subsequent Mujahedin governments and not involved in discussions about a future state. The Saudis were especially adamant, and successful, at keeping Shii parties out.[117] While some Mujahedin were inspired by Sunni Islamism, and others of a local Afghan Sunni tradition rooted in Sufi orders like the Naqshbandiyya, fighting Communists, not Shia, was their primary motivation. Even Arab fighters and financiers, such as Usama bin Laden or Abdullah Azzam, the ideologue and mastermind of the Jihad, initially sought to establish a working relationship with local Shia. Both had become politicised in the Muslim Brotherhood with its ecumenical ambition. Azzam had admired the Iranian revolution, which contributed to his expulsion from Jordan and move to Afghanistan. Their first camp in Afghanistan was in Hazara territory, where local Shia would train alongside the nucleus of al-Qaeda. Some Arabs became enthralled by Shii religious songs, and appropriated them. Others rejected them as an innovation (they would stay an important feature of Jihadi cultural propaganda). One support network was made up of Salafis with strong backing from the Gulf and Saudi Arabia. When this network, which Saudi clerics deemed ideologically 'safe' for young volunteers, gained in strength, anti-Shiism became more prominent, and Shia were expelled. By the late 1980s, and then the early 1990s, Bin Laden and other al-Qaeda leaders had turned more anti-Shii.[118] Support to the Mujahedin was organised through Pakistan, whose politics became intimately tied to the Afghan Jihad, and the Middle East.

Three figures epitomise this turn in Pakistan: General Zia ul-Haqq, who implemented a top-down Sunnification of the country; Ihsan Ilahi Zahir, the Sunni polemicist and anti-Shii activist with links to Saudi Arabia; and Arif al-Husaini, the figurehead of a Shii revivalist movement inspired by Iran. The second-most-populous Islamic country with a large number of Shia came under pressure by the late 1970s. On 5 July 1977, General Zia ul-Haqq, Chief of the Army Staff, overthrew the government of Zulfikar Ali Bhutto in a bloodless coup (the Bhuttos themselves were partly Shia).[119] Allied to a Sunni Islamist movement, Zia ul-Haqq implemented a Sunni interpretation of the Sharia and drew Pakistan closer to Saudi Arabia, and the other Gulf States.

By the late 1970s, the remittances that the millions of Pakistanis who started working in the Gulf States were sending home, had become vital for the Pakistani economy, and they returned with altered religious practices, and a heightened sense of sectarian difference.[120] Saudi Arabia financed parts of Pakistan's military budget, gave it the seed money for the country's largest charitable fund, and delivered oil on deferred payment. Together with official Pakistan's fear of revolutionary Shiism, Saudi Arabia's support for the Afghan Jihad, which flowed through Pakistan, explains why Pakistan allied itself with Saudi Arabia. Pakistan's intelligence service took the lead in supporting the Mujahedin, although unlike Saudi Arabia it had less of a problem also funding Shii and pan-Islamic Sunni groups (and maintained relations with Iran).[121] Pakistan thought that a Sunni Islamist regime in Afghanistan would ally with Pakistan and serve as a bulwark against Iran and India, and would no longer encourage autonomy movements in the Afghan–Pakistan border region.[122] Pakistani society underwent mass mobilisation and militarisation not only for the Afghan Jihad but against India in disputed Jammu and Kashmir. Here, Sunni Islamists were likewise key (and at times clashed with Kashmir's old Shii community).

Major Sunni Islamists, such as Abu al-A'la Mawdudi, were initially thrilled by the Iranian revolution.[123] But the Sunni mass movements that gained in prominence in the 1980s, such as the Defenders of the Sahaba SSP (Sepah-e Sahaba), were staunchly anti-Shia. It may in fact have been the very appeal of the Islamic revolution, and Shii Islamism, to Sunnis that eventually turned the Sunni Islamists against the Shia.[124] Matching the Shii eulogising of the Imams, they elevated the early Companions (*Sahaba*) of the Prophet to towering figures beyond reproach and called for a law criminalising the Shii cursing of the Companions (and of Aisha).[125] When the Deobandi seminaries of Pakistan and India issued a fatwa declaring Shia non-Muslims, this seemed to legitimise violence against them.[126] The government strengthened Sunni *madrasas,* especially in regions bordering Iran and Afghanistan, in an attempt to mobilise pupils for the Jihad, and block Iranian influence.[127] Poor public schooling, widespread poverty and population growth meant that for many the *madrasa* was one of the few ways to escape a life of destitution. Most *madrasas* catered only to Sunnis, but Shii movements sponsored by Iran established their own *madrasas,* promoting activist Shiism over more traditional Sufi-inspired Shiism.[128]

Zia ul-Haqq's Sunni Islamist authoritarianism alienated Pakistan's Shia, and made them more susceptible to the revolutionary message from Iran. Initially, a Shii scholar was appointed to a clerical council overseeing Zia ul-Haqq's religious policies, but resigned after the government enforced Sunni jurisprudence.[129] When the state tried to impose a religious tax in 1980, Shia protested, arguing that they were already paying a tax to their clerics. Defying martial law, they staged mass protests, and forced the state to concede.[130] In 1979, Shii leaders formed a nation-wide Shii communal organisation, the Movement for the Conservation of Jafari Law.[131] It demanded that Shia be able to resort to Shii jurisprudence, and that Shii clerics be represented in government.[132] Sunni state elites saw this as a threat to national security, while Sunni Islamists criticised any concession to Shia.[133] In 1983, when a traditionalist cleric who had led the Shii community for years died, an activist cleric and follower of Khomeini, Arif al-Husaini, became the group's new leader. He transformed it into a major political party with the aim of turning Pakistan into an Islamic state with significant Shii input.[134] In response to attacks by Sunni militants, Shia developed their own militant movements. Both were able to recruit amongst the millions of *madrasa* graduates, whose sense of sectarian difference had been sharpened by their education in sect-specific *madrasas.*

As discussed earlier, the Naqshbandi, Barelvi, and Deobandi tradition of Sunni Revivalism on the Indian subcontinent was anti-Shii. But it had often found a modus vivendi with Shiism, and had not attempted its wholescale eradication. The connection between this tradition and a more Arabian-focused and Salafi-influenced Sunnism, however, provided for a toxic mix, which led to even more negative views of Shiism, and laid the ideological groundwork for sectarian violence.[135]

Ihsan Ilahi Zahir did much to combine these two traditions of anti-Shiism. Zahir, too, had studied at the Islamic University of Medina in the 1960s and then started to become involved in Pakistani politics, and publish polemics against Ahmadis and Bahais, and Shia. *The Sunnis and the Shia*, originally published in Arabic, reiterates old anti-Shia stereotypes and racist prejudices, and another book rehashed the idea, widely discredited, that Shia believe the Quran was falsified. After 1979 his books were reprinted, translated and distributed across South and Southeast Asia.[136] Like Arab anti-Shii polemicists, Zahir rejected Shiism on political and doctrinal grounds. He saw Pakistan as a Sunni state in which Shia advances had to be stopped. Zahir founded and became secretary general of a Wahhabi movement, Jam'iyyat Ahl al-Hadith, and rallied against Shia. Likely in retaliation for his anti-Shii polemics, a car bomb wounded him in March 1987. He was flown to Saudi Arabia, where he died. At his funeral, Ibn Baz, the later Grand Mufti of Saudi Arabia, praised him as a great scholar for his work on the Shia, and Salafi groups eulogized him as a martyr.[137] The Saudi state honoured him by burying him in the al-Baqia graveyard.[138] Possibly in retaliation, Sunni militants assassinated the Shii leader al-Husaini a year later.

Thousands more fell victim to sectarian violence.[139] The city of Jhang in central Punjab, where the Defenders of the Sahaba movement had been founded in 1985, saw the worst violence. Here, as elsewhere in South Asia, many feudal families were Shia, and an emergent middle class, many of them made up from people who moved to Pakistan at partition, embraced Sunni Islamism, in part to protest against the local Shii elite. The main Shii movement also started to be active in Jhang. Younger clerics, who had been educated in Iran, opened *madrasas* with Iranian support and attracted large crowds to their sermons. These clerics were rivals of the Shia gentry, but despite that rivalry and the fact that the elites had little control over the clerics, Sunnis started to blame the latter for the new Shia assertiveness.[140] In other areas, conflict was driven by older feuds between Sunni and Shia tribes.[141]

General Zia ul-Haqq, too, died a violent death in 1988 (conspiracy theories have long circled around the mysterious plane crash in which he died). After a decade under his rule, Pakistan was a transformed country. His authoritarian rule had militarised the country, made Pakistan a cornerstone of the new Sunni Internationalism, and deepened the Sunni–Shia divide, a far cry from the ecumenical foundational ideal of Pakistan.[142] Pakistan's involvement in the Afghan Jihad, and its closer alliance to Saudi Arabia, had contributed to this.

Much less known than the Saudis' support for Islamists in the Afghan war, was their attempt to counter Marxist South Yemen, as well as regain influence in North Yemen by sponsoring Salafism. Muqbil al-Wadi, the most influential Yemeni Salafi, was born in late 1920s or early 1930s North Yemen into a Zaydi family. Like many other Yemenis, he worked in Saudi Arabia. Back in Yemen, his low tribal status excluded him from the religious hierarchy. In comparison, Saudi Sunnism seemed more egalitarian. In the 1960s, he, too, studied Hadith at the Islamic University of Medina and became close to the group that stormed the Grand Mosque at Mecca in 1979. This led to his expulsion, but back in North Yemen he received funding from Saudi organisations and clerics for Salafi educational centres.[143]

Al-Wadi argued that the foundational texts of Zaydism were of questionable authorship, a charge that the Sunnitising Zaydi reformists of the eighteenth century had already invoked. But he took their criticism further, and denounced Zaydism wholeheartedly.[144] He published a polemic against the alleged doctrinal flaws and historical crimes of the 'rejectionists', of Khomeini and the Iranian Revolution, and even linked Shiism to Judaism.[145] That he was himself of a Zaydi background, gave his call special resonance. This Sunni turn occurred under the watchful eye of Ali Abdullah Saleh, who had assumed the presidency in 1978, and would dominate North Yemen for decades. Himself, too, of a nominally Zaydi background, his close association with Iraq, and opening towards Saudi Arabia, made him part of the anti-Iran alliance.[146] Yemeni veterans of the Afghan Jihad were integrated into Saleh's patronage networks.[147] While they did not see Zaydism as primary enemy, these battle-hardened militants eventually clashed with Zaydi revivalists.[148] Salafis, for example, went to Zaydi mosques and emphasised previously little-noted minor differences in prayer.[149] Ibn Baz, the godfather of Saudi Salafism and patron of al-Wadi, who had praised Zahir at his funeral in 1987, was crucial in exacerbating sectarian tensions in Yemen. Already as early as 1975, Ibn Baz had issued a fatwa prohibiting prayer behind a Zaydi imam, implying that Zaydis were not proper Muslims.[150] Since his fatwa expanded this prohibition to all Shia, it led to backlash not just from Zaydis but also Alawites, and other Shia.[151]

Salafi attacks, the marginalisation of Zaydi elites in the Yemeni republic, and the rise of activist Shiism prompted a Zaydi response. In 1979, the Zaydi scholar Badr al-Din al-Huthi refuted Ibn Baz's fatwa, reiterating that Zaydis can pray behind Sunnis and vice versa, and attacked Wahhabism.[152] The al-Huthi family emerged as figureheads of Zaydi revivalism.[153] Badr al-Din's son, Hussain, founded a political movement—nicknamed the Huthis—to empower Zaydis. He and other Zaydis visited Iran, and were impressed by its anti-imperialism. They agreed that clerics and descendants of the Prophet (like Khomeini and the Huthis) should lead the community. Most Zaydis who studied in Iran did not embrace Twelver Shiism, or Khomeini's Guardianship of the Jurisprudent. Some, however, adopted an earlier, more marginal trend within Zaydism, the Jarudiyya, that was doctrinally opposed to Sunnism, and closer to Twelver Shiism, facilitating relations with Iran.[154] Hussain al-Huthi criticised pro-Sunni Zaydis, and advocated a return to Quran and Zaydi Hadith.[155] He blamed core concepts of Sunnism for the colonial subjugation of the Islamic world (while praising the stance of Iran and Lebanese Hizbullah).[156] To counter Wahhabism, and revitalise Zaydism, Zaydi revivalist clerics founded a political party in 1990. The party, Hizb al-Haqq, stated that it did not seek the restoration of the Zaydi Imamate, though its detractors claim otherwise.[157] They restarted Shii rituals and public commemorations, opened Zaydi revivalist *madrasas,* established a religious curriculum, printed books, and set up charities.[158] In the first half of the 1990s, Yemen was preoccupied by a civil war between the North and the South. But once the war was over, and Saleh's and the North's supremacy over the South consolidated, the sectarianisation set in motion in the late 1970s would lead to serious conflict amongst Northerners.

The Iranian revolution transformed Shiism, Sunnism, and Sunni–Shia relations. That most global powers supported Sunni autocrats and Islamists against the world's central Shii country had the most profound impact on Sunni–Shia relations. Opposition to the revolution took many forms. On the one hand, Sunni Arab nationalists like Iraq's Saddam Hussein, who highlighted the racial superiority of Arabs over Persians, led the fight against Iran. On the other hand, global Salafi networks and the anti-Shia ideologues and movements in South Asia, who combined Wahhabi and Deobandi anti-Shiism, and were funded by Saudi Arabia, attacked Shiism on the religious level, and militarily and politically across the many fronts that opened across the Islamic world. These struggles occurred at a time when Gulf States saw their oil and gas revenues multiply, and Saudi Arabia acquired the means to export Wahhabi-Salafism. That many Sunni Islamists moved to the Gulf States, where they worked in the religious, educational, media, and financial sectors, contributed to their turn away from Iran. Gulf donors became vital for the Islamic charities and banks that formed the financial backbone of these movements, and even small states like Qatar and Kuwait acquired the means to become significant patrons. Iran's oil revenues, even if smaller than those of the Sunni-led Gulf Arab States, allowed the revolution to entrench itself, expand a welfare system, and fund the export of the revolution and the propagation of Shiism. And Iraq's oil revenues had paid for much of its army's arsenal (and once the Iran–Iraq war was underway, oil money from the Gulf States kept Iraq going).

The history of Sunni–Shia relations since 1979 is a history of the Iranian revolution and reactions towards it—of export versus containment. The rivalry between Iran and Sunni-led countries, and the shift of many Sunni Islamic movements from a pan-Islamic vision to an anti-Shii stance, turned the Sunni–Shia divide into a key feature of Middle Eastern politics. This had different outcomes in different places, as local factors shaped how local elites perceived Iran and to what extent this antagonism became violent or not. Throughout the 1980s, as Iran exported its revolution and the Saudis their Salafi-Wahhabism as anti-Shiism, the latter became influential, in some cases the dominant interpretation of Islam even in countries where it hitherto had been marginal, such as in Africa, and South and Southeast Asia. Within a few decades, these societies, too, became affected by the Sunni–Shia divide and after the end of the Cold War, subject to outside powers that again sought to reshape the Middle East—by adopting, once again, a sectarian lens.

13

Regime Change

The end of the Cold War coincided with major transformations in the Middle East and the wider Islamic world. Iran and Iraq ended their eight-year war, the warring parties and their backers ended the Lebanese Civil War, and Khomeini's death and the election of the reformist Akbar Hashemi Rafsanjani as Iranian president meant that relations between Iran and the world turned a page. These were not the only changes that came within an astonishing short period of time. The withdrawal of Soviet troops from Afghanistan, completed in 1989, precipitated the fall of the Communist government there in 1992, and the end of the Afghan Jihad (although followed by a vicious civil war). Most importantly, the disintegration of the Soviet Union, culminating in its dissolution in late 1991, removed a protective shield from its allies in the region, such as Iraq and Communist Afghanistan, and left the US as the world's sole hegemon.[1]

The period from 1990/1 until around 2010 was an age of American hegemony. Military interventions in the Middle East symbolised American power but also highlighted its limits, and would not have happened during the Cold War, when the US and the Soviet Union rarely invaded a country outright with the attempt of regime change, for fear of provoking nuclear war, and instead focused on proxy warfare and influencing the domestic politics of other states to their advantage.[2] These interventions would have profound consequences for Sunnis and Shia.

It became crucial how Americans viewed the Islamic world, and more specifically Sunnism and Shiism. The latter was much less known and sustained American interest only emerged with the Iranian Revolution, after which Shiism was depicted as inherently revolutionary. Shii distrust of temporal power was now turned into an explanation for why Shia would inevitably rebel. In foreign reporting on the Lebanese civil war, for example, Shia featured often as 'terrorists'.[3] Middle East experts and historians gave this narrative scholarly backing.[4] The hostage affair and his fatwa against Salman Rushdie for the book *Satanic Verses*, published in 1989, turned Ayatollah Khomeini into a hate figure in 1980s America. At the same time, it was also a global moment in which Sunni and Shii Muslims united around the figure of the Prophet.[5]

In contrast, Sunni monarchs were generally presented as enlightened modernisers, and Sunni militants in Afghanistan as 'freedom fighters'. Ronald Reagan even welcomed a Mujahedin delegation to the Oval Office and dedicated the launch of a Space Shuttle to the people of Afghanistan.[6] Views in Europe tended to be more nuanced. French Philosopher Michel Foucault, who travelled to Iran to report on the revolution, epitomised an initial fascination with the transformation in Iran.[7] But in the 1980s, the image of Iran became a threatening one in Europe, too, as the US and European powers jointly tried to isolate Iran.[8]

At the start of the 1990s, however, Iran and Arab Shii movements reshaped their image, and reached out to regional foes, including Saudi Arabia. Saddam's fortunes, on the other hand, declined. His war with Iran had been a disaster. The borders remained unchanged, the country was broke and in ruins, and hundreds of thousands had died. Indebted to the Gulf States who had bankrolled him out of fear of Iran, Saddam invaded Kuwait in 1990. Iraqi nationalists had long claimed Kuwait as part of Iraq, and Saddam hoped Kuwait's oil would solve his financial woes. The United States now worried that Saddam had become uncontrollable and might follow through on threats to also seize the Saudi oil fields, and intervened to push Iraqi forces out of Kuwait. America's first major post-Cold War intervention was a rapid military victory. When the Americans negotiated the surrender of Iraqi forces, the latter argued that they needed their helicopters to retreat as the Americans had blown up all the bridges. Iraq was denied an air force but kept its helicopters.

As news of the Iraqi defeat spread, uprisings erupted amongst Kurds in the North, and Shia in the South. Parts of the local population rebelled and were soon joined by elements of the underground Shii opposition, and defecting Shii soldiers, amidst signals that the US Army might move into Iraq, or stop the regime from cracking down, and encouragement from American politicians, including President Bush, for Iraqis to rebel. The rebels took over major towns such as Najaf, Karbala, and Basra. But Saddam's republican guards and special forces returning from Kuwait restored Baath Party rule, causing massive destruction and thousands of casualties. They even shelled the Shii shrines to which some rebels had taken refuge and used the attack helicopters to crush the uprising from the air.[9] While the US established a no-fly zone in the North of the country, effectively preventing the Kurds from a similar fate, the South was left to its own devices, and the US did not intervene. The Americans feared a Shia takeover, and the loss of Iraq as buffer against Iran, and instead imposed heavy sanctions that crippled the economy and impoverished Iraqis but left the regime hanging on. President George H. W. Bush and his entourage were personally deeply unhappy of 'not having finished the job', and when his son, George W. Bush, took the decision to invade Iraq a decade later, that feeling of not having protected Iraq's Shia from slaughter, and not having removed a dictator Bush senior called 'Hitler', lingered on. Still, this episode deepened mistrust between Iraqis and Americans.[10]

The Baath Party's mouthpiece blamed the Iraqi people's disunity, 'Shii fanaticism' and Iran for the rising. That it openly discussed previously taboo sectarian categories meant that the issue had become too pressing and dangerous to ignore.[11] By blaming the uprising directly on deviant Shii elements and Iran, the regime sought to reassure Sunnis and give Shii party members a line they could adhere to.[12] Many Shia perceived the state's response as anti-Shii, however, and became alienated, and the uprising had frightened Arab Sunnis. Still, Shii officers were involved in the crackdown, as were Shii tribes, and in the aftermath of 1991, the regime enforced a ban on sectarian hate speech, including against Shia, for fear that heightened Sunni–Shia tensions could undermine it. This also meant a more thorough policing of Wahhabi networks. The regime had seen Wahhabis as useful allies in the 1980s, but after Iraq's falling out with their Saudi patrons in the Gulf War, perceived them as a threat and as fostering Sunni–Shia division.[13] Saddam even portrayed himself as a descendant of Ali, and therefore of the *Ahl al-Bayt.*[14]

In 1993, the regime started a so-called 'faith campaign' to strengthen public adherence to religious norms and depict the state as more religious (the slogan 'God is Greatest' was added to the Iraqi flag). This was a continuation of the invoking of Islam and Arabism during the Iran–Iraq war, and the Gulf War of 1990/1.[15] It promoted a form of Sunnism moulded to support the state and not be susceptible to Saudi influence. Forms of political Islam that could have formed a challenge, such as the Muslim Brotherhood or Shii Islamists, remained on the outside. In charge of this campaign was Saddam's closest advisor, Izzat al-Duri, a senior member of the Naqshbandi Sufi order, popular, as noted, in Iraq's North.[16] The 'faith campaign', established new ties between Baathists, Salafis, and Naqshbandis. Despite major ideological differences, these groups had one common denominator: anti-Shiism (as noted, the Naqshbandiyya was the most anti-Shii of Sufi orders, and had played a major anti-Shii role elsewhere). Yet the campaign was marked by an implicit Sunni Arab supremacism, expressed through a mix of Arab Nationalism and Salafism, rather than open anti-Shiism, which remained forbidden.[17] While the campaign allowed for more religious expressions, its decidedly Salafi and Naqshbandi nature was not lost on Shia, who spent more energy on their religious activities, too. In the decade preceding the invasion of 2003 sectarian identity in Iraq therefore became more relevant politically.[18]

The opposition to Saddam, which could now operate from Northern Iraq, likewise adopted a more openly sectarian discourse and organised accordingly. At a conference there in 1992, it advocated a roadmap for a future Iraq based on power-sharing amongst ethno-sectarian parties.[19] Following passage of the 1998 Iraq Liberation Act, the US provided direct support to Iraqi opposition groups, including Shii organisations with bases in Iran, such as the Supreme Council for the Islamic Revolution in Iraq. The latter and other Iraqi Shii organisations reformulated their ideology to receive US support. Opposition groups in exile, especially in London, invoked oppression of Kurds and Shia to make the case for intervention, which resounded in Washington.[20] The communal claims of Shii parties and human rights groups were amplified by American scholars and policy makers.[21]

By turning Iraq into an international pariah, the Gulf Crisis of 1990/1 improved the relative standing of its rivals Iran and Syria. Syria, which had been relatively isolated in regional affairs, emerged as a partner for the Gulf States, including Saudi Arabia, which allowed, for example, a stabilisation of Lebanon in the 1990s.[22] In their opposition to the Iraqi regime, Iran, Syria, and Saudi Arabia found common ground. The Shii opposition movements based in Iran (and Syria) tempered their discourse, moving away from revolution and armed struggle and towards human rights, democracy, and Shii identity politics. Shia were portrayed as separate 'communities' that simultaneously played important, in some cases foundational, roles in their respective nations. Shii historians wrote communal histories[23] and opposition activists tried to achieve political settlements and separate juridical recognition for Shia. Many argued that these goals were best achieved through gradual change.[24] In 1993, the Saudi Shii opposition made a deal with Saudi Crown Prince Abdullah, and their leader, Hasan al-Saffar, and those that left the country after the 1979 uprising in the Eastern Province, returned home.[25] Though engaged in another uprising throughout the 1990s, the Bahraini Shii opposition also emphasised human rights and democratic reforms; by the end of that decade, it was coming to terms with a new Emir, who proclaimed himself King and promised political reforms, and, in the early 2000s, reinstated a parliament.[26] Pakistani Shii parties helped elect Pakistan's first female prime minister, Benazir Bhutto, herself from a mixed Sunni–Shia background, in 1988 and again in 1993 (although Pakistani intelligence would at the same time play a key role in founding and supporting the Sunni Islamist Afghan Taliban).[27]

Sunni–Shia relations in places like Iraq and Bahrain were tense throughout the 1990s, and threatened to get even worse. And Pakistan was a harbinger of things to come, with Sunni militants stepping up their attacks on Shii targets throughout the 1990s, and Shii movements retaliating increasingly. But the regional and international environment was not yet as heavily sectarianised, and different arenas not as connected as in the years after 1979—or after 2003.

The Gulf Crisis led to a rift between Saudi Arabia and Sunni Islamists. Usama bin Laden offered to defend Saudi territory against Saddam's army, but when the Saudis invited in the American Army instead, lost all faith in the Saudi state. Muslim Brothers in the Kingdom, too, mobilised more publicly and criticised the monarchy, leading to a fracture in the alliance between Saudi Arabia and the Brotherhood that had been so crucial in preceding decades.[28]

In Iran, Rafsanjani, and then his successor, the reformist Sayyid Mohammad Khatami (1997–2005), tentatively opened to the West, and to former foes. Relations between Iran and Saudi Arabia reached a high point in the mid-1990s not seen since 1979, with mutual visits by their respective leaders, and the exchange of pleasantries. After a massive car bomb killed American personnel at a US Army barracks in al-Khobar in Eastern Saudi Arabia in 1996, the Americans concluded that it had been carried out by a Saudi Shii opposition movement bent on continuing the revolutionary approach with the help of Iran and Lebanese Hizbullah. This led to a crackdown amongst Saudi Shia, but Saudi Arabia was reluctant to blame Iran directly, for fear the Americans could use it as a pretext of war against Iran, and instead signed a security agreement with Iran that forbade support for opposition in the relative other country. Oman, which positioned itself as a mediator between Sunni-led Gulf States and Iran, facilitated the rapprochement.[29] Such periods of respite in the Saudi-Iran rivalry had a calming effect on Sunni–Shia relations.

The massive military and political interventions that followed the attacks of 9/11, however, set in motion processes that repolarised Saudi-Iranian and wider Sunni-Shia relations. That fifteen of the nineteen 9/11 hijackers were Saudis, and were directed by Usama bin Laden, whose family formed part of the Saudi elite, puzzled many. Sunnis not Shia were now portrayed as potentially 'radical' Muslims, susceptible to the ideology of al-Qaeda.[30] The 'Neocons' around George W. Bush argued that the region's authoritarianism was in part to blame, and military interventions were supposed to usher in a 'New Middle East' of pro-Western democracies (that would make peace with Israel).[31]

Bin Laden and al-Qaeda had its bases in Afghanistan, where they were tolerated by the Taliban. When the US asked the Taliban to expel al-Qaeda, they refused. That refusal, and the conflation of al-Qaeda and the Taliban in the minds of NATO officials, contributed to the decision to not just carry out air strikes, as the US initially did, but launch a ground invasion and full-scale military occupation of the country, one that was to last for twenty years.[32] The Taliban were one of the Sunni Islamist rebel factions that had emerged out of the Afghan War, and had side-lined other factions in a civil war after the Soviet withdrawal. When the Taliban officially took over power in 1996 and declared an Islamic Emirate, only Pakistan, Saudi Arabia, and the United Arab Emirates recognised it (Pakistan had played a key role in their race to power). The Taliban were heirs to the Sunni Revivalist tradition on the Indian subcontinent, of a Hanafism linked to the Deobandi school. They were anti-Shii, though not as uncompromisingly as some of the Salafi-Wahhabi groups in Afghanistan (Deobandis at times considered Shia to be Muslims, with the respective protections afforded to them, something beyond the pale for Wahhabis). And they had had significant ideological differences with al-Qaeda when it came to Shiism, and other issues.[33]

The Taliban's backers in the Gulf and Pakistani intelligence had hoped its anti-Shiism would foreclose any cooperation with Iran. After the fall of the Afghan Communist government in 1992, the Shii Hazara party, Hezb-e Wahdat, emerged as a powerful military force, controlling large parts of Kabul and other areas. Faced with a successful Taliban campaign, some Hazara politicians negotiated with the Taliban, while others vowed to resist. The Taliban's stance oscillated between pragmatism to solidify their military conquests (such as by the acceptance of Shii defectors into their ranks), and the occasional assertion that Shia are heretics.[34] After the Taliban took Herat and Kabul in 1996, Mazar-i-Sharif, the Afghan city home to an Ali shrine and a Hazara stronghold, and then under Hezb-e Wahdat control, became the scene of intense fighting. In 1997, when the Taliban moved into the town, Hezb-e Wahdat fighters killed hundreds of them. Partly in response, the Taliban massacred several thousand Shia Hazara there in 1998, including women and children. When they assassinated several Iranian diplomats a year later, Iran almost invaded. Despite the violence, some Afghan Shii Islamists hoped to play a part in the Taliban's Islamic Emirate, but the latter were not interested in sharing power with a group they had defeated militarily, and despised doctrinally and ethnically.[35]

Meanwhile, in Pakistan, the end of the Afghan Jihad had seen a dramatic rise of Sunni–Shia violence, with Sunni militants, often returnees from Afghanistan, attacking Shia. These veterans, who had lost their sense of purpose, started to see the fight against Shia at home as a continuation of the Jihad. In fact, in the 1990s tit-for-tat assassinations of communal leaders and ordinary citizens and bombings of civilians became commonplace. Sunni militants started this campaign, but the Shii movements, which in the preceding decade had focused on Shii rights and juridical recognition, swiftly established military wings, and retaliated.[36]

Sunni–Shia violence contributed to a breakdown of public order that in turn paved the way for the 1999 coup in which General Pervez Musharraf overthrew Benazir Bhutto. Presenting himself as a secularist hardliner, Musharraf initially tried not to ally too closely with Sunni Islamists, and after 9/11 cooperated in the US war on terror. This caused much popular resentment, however, as did the fall of the Taliban in Afghanistan, with their historic ties to Pakistani *madrasas*, fellow Islamists, and the intelligence services. Throughout the 2000s, Pakistan saw even more Sunni–Shia violence, which had local causes, but where tensions increased due to the American interventions and sectarian violence in Afghanistan and Iraq. Suicide bombings of Shii mosques and mourning houses, and Shii Ashura processions, became common, and Shii militants retaliated. The Sunni extremist movements detested Musharraf, and tried to assassinate him. Tensions between the state and Sunni extremists escalated, as did Sunni–Shia violence.[37] After the overthrow of the Taliban in Afghanistan, their local allies founded the strongly anti-Shii Taliban Movement in Pakistan. Under US pressure, Musharraf broke with the Taliban. That the details of Pakistan's support for

Sunni militants remain murky is most famously illustrated by the fact that Bin Laden would move there from Afghanistan.

At the start of the Allied campaign against the Taliban in 2001, Iran, no friend of the Taliban, given that they had killed Shii Hazara and Iranian diplomats, provided limited support to the US near the border with Afghanistan. In November, Secretary of State Colin Powell shook hands with the Iranian foreign minister, Kamal Kharrazi, at the UN headquarters in New York.[38] Many Hazara, who had suffered heavily from the war, and often had to find refuge abroad, hoped that the intervention could improve their lot. At a December 2001 conference held in Bonn under UN auspices to plan a post-invasion political future for Afghanistan, Hazara demands for political representation and a separate Shii personal status law were granted. Hazara were strongly represented in the transitional government, and Twelver Shiism recognised independently of Sunnism, a concession no previous Afghan government had ever made.

Imperial knowledge production that dated back to the British invasions of Afghanistan in the nineteenth century, and that saw tribal and ethno-sectarian division as a key feature of Afghan society and politics, shaped NATO's 'nation-building'.[39] While not officially based on ethnic power-sharing, Afghan politics became characterised by a contest between ethnic groups. The Hazara started to function more as one such ethnic group, rather than being represented by Shii Islamist or Leftist movements, as in the past.[40] The Taliban's repression of women and Hazara was used as moral argument to justify the intervention. The ascent of the Hazara then contributed to a sense that the intervention was empowering Shia and undermining Sunnis (and Pashtus), a narrative the Taliban and other groups furthered.[41] When the Aga Khan and other donors refurbished sites associated with Afghanistan's ecumenical and Shii legacy, this raised the visibility not just of Hazara but also of Ismailis and Qizilbash.[42]

The US swiftly followed up with regime change plans in other countries. As noted, when it came to Iraq, they moved along ethno-sectarian lines and had long been in the making. During George W. Bush's State of the Union address on 29 January 2002, he accused Iraq, Iran, and North Korea of constituting an 'Axis of Evil', combining references to the Second World War axis with Bush's religiously informed notion of a fight between good and evil. A few months later, then-Undersecretary of State John Bolton (later one of Donald Trump's National Security Advisers) added Syria, Libya, and Cuba to the list.[43] For Bush to throw in regional arch-enemies Iran and

Iraq into one category was confounding to many, and was seen as a major affront by the Iranians, who had just started considering a reset of relations with the US in the wake of 9/11 and provided assistance in the campaign against the Taliban.[44] To add Syria, Iraq's other arch-enemy (let alone Libya, North Korea, and Cuba) to the mix, and threaten punishment for a terrorist attack committed by Saudis, Emiratis, Lebanese, and Egyptians was even more so. Little wonder that Saddam thought the Americans were bluffing. He was wrong. A secret US–UK agreement—between Bush's and Tony Blair's government—to invade was sealed in 2002. Botched intelligence suggesting Saddam had a chemical weapons programme that could be used to attack Britain, and that Saddam had links to al-Qaeda, were used to legitimise the intervention. These allegations turned out to be false but despite mass protests against the war swayed enough public opinion in both countries to enable the war.[45]

The invasion of Iraq began on 19 March 2003. Coalition troops defeated the Iraqi army in a month and took Baghdad. Weakened by sanctions and made up of demoralised soldiers who did not want to die for a brutal dictator, the Iraqi army largely surrendered in the face of overwhelming force. But even as President Bush declared 'Mission Accomplished', America's, and the region's, woes were just beginning. The invasion of a country at the heart of the Sunni–Shia split that had long been crucial to regional politics was fateful. It brought to power a Shii-led government, and paved the way for civil war. From a player in regional conflicts (and a staunch enemy of Iran), Iraq became an arena for proxy war between regional rivals, as did Afghanistan. And both interventions strengthened Iran's relative position.

Saddam and other leading Baathists, such as Izzat al-Duri, had long been paranoid about a coup or an intervention and established a system of safe houses, and decentralised networks. They immediately went into hiding, and played the sectarian card, invoking Iraq's symbolism in the Sunni Arab collective memory. In a message from 28 April 2003 broadcast on pan-Arab satellite TV stations, Saddam referred to the alleged treachery of the Shii Vizier al-Alqami against the Abbasid Caliph during the Mongol conquest, implying that, once again, Shia were betraying a Sunni leader: 'Just as Hulegu entered Baghdad, so did the criminal Bush enter Baghdad, with the help of Alqami—indeed, even more than one Alqami.'[46] The analogy resonated with Sunnis across the region, and was spread on a new medium that did much to rally Arabs against coalition forces in Iraq (and against the Shia cooperating with it): satellite TV. *Al-Jazeera* was the most famous of these channels, and from its broadcasts, video clips were uploaded to the internet. The Arabist ideology and criticism of the intervention that was prevalent on *al-Jazeera* did lead to a new Arab Public Sphere that was, in theory, inclusive of both Sunni and Shii views. But the violence in Iraq, and editorial decisions, led to a division of that Arab public sphere into more consciously Shii and Sunni ones.[47] Sunni-owned media now focused on Iraq, highlighting Sunni suffering, encouraging support from 'Sunni brothers' elsewhere. Reporting on the Iraq war became constitutive of a Sunni public sphere, one that now defined itself against a more self-conscious Shii public sphere.

Post-invasion Iraq quickly became a hub for new TV channels, including Shii ones, a process facilitated by the Coalition Provisional Authority's (CPA) permissive media policy. Media outlets advocating attacks on US forces were closed, but those furthering sectarian polarisation but not directly attacking the CPA and foreign troops were not. The National TV channel and other state-associated media started to highlight the crimes of the Baath regime, and as the state became more closely associated with Shii Islamists, its media became imbued with Shii symbolism (such as the call to prayer).[48] Sunni TV stations and websites, in contrast, tended to focus on the insurgency, and some republished and translated old anti-Shia polemics. Some websites and discussion forums, such as '*In Defence of the Sunna*,' specialised in tracking news of Shia communities and clerics around the world, and 'revealing' their allegedly outrageous practices and statements.[49] This contributed to feelings that the Shia were taking over Iraq, and becoming more assertive elsewhere, too, and linked these current political developments to earlier political and doctrinal disputes.

One of the CPA's first acts was the dissolution of the Iraqi Army, followed by a de-Baathification campaign. Scores of men who may not have had strong loyalties for the regime and now found themselves without a job and under scrutiny joined the insurgency. That many were battle-hardened soldiers or had experience with surveillance, clandestine networks, and weapons, explained its potency. The alliance of Baathists, Salafis, and Naqshbandis that had been part of the regime's faith campaigns, helped. These Iraqi networks partnered with Sunni Jihadi organisations, especially with a group led by a Jordanian, Abu Musab al-Zarqawi. Al-Zarqawi had initially tried to join the Jihad in Afghanistan but arrived just as it drew to a close, and failed to impress al-Qaeda's leadership there. In 2002, he went to Northern Iraq and formed his own militant group. He saw Iraq as a new battleground that could appeal to Sunni recruits and donors from abroad. The Americans had tried to use his presence there to claim that Saddam had links to al-Qaeda to justify the invasion. But the Iraqi state had no control over the North, which was under an American-enforced no-fly zone, and tried to keep him out of the rest of Iraq. After the invasion, however, al-Zarqawi managed to move into the Arab Sunni heartlands, and from there helped organise the insurgency, now in alliance with former Baathists.[50]

Al-Zarqawi was more anti-Shii than most Iraqis, who, despite disagreements, lived side by side with Shia. He popularised the Salafi idea that Muslims who did not follow 'correct' ideology or practice could be excommunicated (takfir) and applied this to the Shia. He argued that the insurgency had to resist the CPA and the new state they were building, and by implication the Shia that were cooperating with the US. In a famous message legitimising his anti-Shii stance, al-Zarqawi announced that 'the Grandchildren of Ibn al-Alqami' had returned and had to be fought.[51] Many Sunnis indeed saw their worst nightmares come true, as the CPA appointed an Iraqi Governing Council largely made up of ethno-sectarian parties, in which Kurds and Arab Shia held key positions.[52]

Ahmad Chalabi, a Shii, had been instrumental in the Iraqi opposition and the planning of the intervention, and had received US funding for his opposition alliance. He and other exiles, who were well-connected in the region and in the UK and the US, but lacked popularity at home, became members of the Iraqi Governing Council in 2003.[53] He had extensive knowledge of the workings of the Lebanese sectarian power-sharing system, which had plunged Lebanon into a fifteen-year civil war.[54] Despite its obvious shortcomings, the post-2003 Iraqi system bore resemblance to it. The Iraqi civil law of 1959, which had been administered by civil judges, and over time incorporated elements of Sunni and Shii jurisprudence was abrogated, and replaced by separate personal status law courts for Sunnis and Shia (and Christians).[55] Separate sections of the Ministry of Endowments (Awqaf), were instituted, as well, and the Shii shrines, along with their large endowments, put under the administration of the Shii section. Unlike in Lebanon, the constitution of 2005/6 did not specify ethno-sectarian quotas, or federalism. But Shii deputies, many from Islamist parties, played a dominant role in a constitution-drafting process that proved divisive. And de facto, the position of Prime Minister was reserved for an Arab Shii, that of President for a Kurd, and that of Vice-President and Speaker of Parliament for an Arab Sunni. And as in Lebanon, a class of politicians realised that sectarian power sharing was a way to sustain them in office (despite much infighting between members of the same ethno–sectarian group).[56]

Feeling that the invasion had empowered Shii Islamists, many Sunnis, urged on by insurgent groups and political parties, boycotted the first parliamentary elections in January 2005. The Shii clerical leadership did the opposite, and pressed Shia to participate, leading to Sunni marginalisation in the first elected government (in the Sunni Anbar governorate, the heartland of the insurgency, turnout was 2 per cent, in contrast to 58 per cent across the country). An alliance of Shii Islamist parties with significant clerical representation led by the Supreme Council for Islamic Revolution in Iraq, the former opposition group whose leadership had been based in Iran, won half the seats. The parties that sat on the Governing Council and won the 2005 elections dominated Iraqi politics in subsequent years. They divided different parts of the state amongst them, as its cadres moved into the Baathists' mansions.[57]

Despite Iraq's social sectarianism and history as battle-ground for rivalries between Sunni and Shii powers (the Ottomans and the Safavids, for example), the level of sectarian polarisation, and the organisation of the political system along sectarian lines, was new.[58] Some even advocated the creation of a federal system in which not only the Kurdish North but also the largely Shii South and largely Sunni territories like Anbar would receive autonomy. These voices remained marginal, however, except amongst the Kurds, and Arab Sunnis and Shia instead competed for control of state institutions.[59]

The Sunni Jihadi insurgency increasingly targeted not only the state and the occupying forces but Shii clerics, holy sites, politicians, and even civilians. One of the first prominent attacks was a massive car bomb near the Ali shrine in Najaf in August 2003 that killed the leader of the Supreme Council for Islamic Revolution in Iraq, Muhammad Baqir al-Hakim. al-Hakim had returned from exile to try to unite the Shii masses and mobilise the clerical seminary at Najaf. In a speech from the gates of the Ali shrine just weeks before his assassination he seemingly advocated a clergy-led government to the cheers of thousands of supporters, a scene in some ways reminiscent of Khomeini's return to Iran in 1979. As descendants of one of the leading Grand Ayatollahs of the twentieth century, the al-Hakim family held much pedigree, and would remain involved in politics. But his assassination empowered opposing clans. The killing of the son of another Grand Ayatollah, al-Khu'i, in Najaf the same year likewise limited the role of the al-Khu'i family, who had been crucial in organising the Iraqi opposition in exile and in strengthening pan-Shii identities. The weakening of these two main Shii scholarly and political families contributed to the rise of a scion of another major family of Iraqi Shiism to renewed prominence: Muqtada al-Sadr (whose followers are thought to have been behind al-Khu'i's killing).[60]

Meanwhile, in the North, al-Zarqawi, whose group is blamed for the bombing that killed al-Hakim (though no one claimed responsibility), targeted Shia directly. The leadership of al-Qaeda, which was under pressure in Afghanistan following the NATO invasion there, supported the insurgency, but tried to rein in al-Zarqawi, whose views they considered extreme. Zarqawi's position on Shia was spelled out in a January 2004 letter to Usama Bin Ladin:

> These are a people who added to their infidelity and augmented their atheism with political cunning and a feverish effort to seize upon the crisis of governance and the balance of power in the state, whose features they are trying to draw and whose new lines they are trying to establish through their political banners and organizations in cooperation with their hidden allies the Americans.[61]

Al-Qaeda's leadership was not convinced, though accepted when al-Zarqawi pledged allegiance and founded al-Qaeda in Iraq.

For Zarqawi, all Shia were legitimate targets, and he sent Sunni Jihadis on suicide missions against both coalition troops and Shia. Practised en masse by Iran during the war with Iraq, and then by Lebanese Hizbullah, suicide missions had only recently become adopted by Sunni Jihadis, another example of how Sunni and Shii Islamism influenced each other.[62] Now, they were being used against Shii civilians. However, al-Qaeda's leaders disapproved of this large-scale targeting of Shii civilians and mosques. In 2005, the deputy leader of al-Qaeda, Ayman al-Zawahiri, an Egyptian who would succeed Bin Laden after his death in 2011, wrote to al-Zarqawi, urging him to reconsider.[63] Zawahiri did not oppose al-Zarqawi's excommunication of the Shia, but he disagreed with the targeting of Shia civilians. Zawahiri excused lay Shia for their ignorance and said they do not deserve to die for their beliefs (Shia leaders, on the other hand, who spread Shii beliefs, he saw as fair targets).[64] With their background in the Muslim Brotherhood, Zawahiri and Bin Laden had been inspired by the Iranian revolution, and did not see the benefit of Sunni–Shia civil war. They first wanted to target the 'far enemy', the Americans, and while they saw Shia as misguided, regarded Muslim divisions as a distraction from larger political goals. In addition, some members of al-Qaeda were under house arrest or in prison in Iran, and before its affiliate in Iraq started doing so, al-Qaeda never attacked Shii targets, or Iran.[65]

It was a Salafi trend within al-Qaeda, of which al-Zarqawi became the figurehead, that advocated anti-Shii action.[66] Because al-Zarqawi spearheaded operations in Iraq, a new focus for international Jihadis, his views carried weight. Even when an influential Jordanian Salafi whom al-Zarqawi regarded as a mentor and who was himself strongly anti-Shii criticised the attacks on Shia civilians for undermining the Sunni Jihad and Sunni Islamism more broadly, al-Zarqawi remained steadfast and argued that by voting for Shii politicians and thereby accepting the US-led new political order, ordinary Shia had waved any protections they may have had. By the time of his assassination in 2006, al-Zarqawi had set in motion a deadly spiral of Sunni–Shia violence, added an anti-Shii element to the anti-occupation Sunni insurgency, and had set a precedent by excommunicating and killing Shii civilians. The most extreme form of anti-Shiism was imported to Iraq by an outsider, someone seen as too radical even by the al-Qaeda leadership.[67]

Saudi Arabia and other Sunni-led states had bankrolled Saddam Hussein in the 1980s, but distrusted him after the invasion of Kuwait. Still, they regarded what they saw as a Shia takeover of Iraq as an even worse nightmare (the Saudis had counselled the US not to invade). The American government advocated minor political reforms and in the wake of the rise of Iraqi Shia Western media paid more attention to the situation of Shia in Saudi Arabia and other Gulf States. This heightened Gulf rulers' anxieties. They could not believe that their long-standing allies in Washington would, as it were, hand Iraq to Shii Islamists allied with Iran. Many assume that the Saudis supported the Sunni insurgency. At the very least, many in Saudi Arabia, other Gulf States and Jordan turned a blind eye when their nationals went to Iraq to fight against the 'Crusaders' and the 'rejectionists', or raised funds for the Jihad and spread anti-Shii rhetoric. Some Gulf media portrayed the insurgency as an uprising against an occupation army. Quite a few of the suicide bombers who targeted Shia in Iraq were likewise foreigners.[68]

Those Iraqis who had become influenced by Sunni Islamism under the Baath's religious turn, and were traumatised by the changes of 2003, adopted a virulent anti-Shiism. The Sunni insurgency was a cross-ideological alliance of Jihadis, disaffected Sunni tribesmen, and former Baathists, some with roots in the Naqshbandi order. In principle, the Salafi-Jihadis and the Naqshbandi Sufis had little in common, were it not for a disdain for the occupation, and for Shiism. They started to portray themselves as the military force of 'Sunnis' against attacks by Shii militias and the Shii-dominated state.[69] The support from the Gulf, and from Iraqi Baathists who had found refuge in Jordan, was key. Saddam Hussein had had good relations with Jordan, and despite having almost no indigenous Shia population, Jordan was wary of Iranian support for Palestinian Islamists (Iran had by now become Hamas' most important international ally). Indeed, it was King Abdullah of Jordan who coined the term 'Shia crescent' describing the new Shii assertiveness across the region since 2003, and an axis of 'Shii' powers in Iran, Iraq, Syria, and Lebanon, highlighting a new Sunni paranoia about Shiism (notwithstanding the fact that Palestinian Hamas is a Sunni movement).[70] The notion that Sunnis were under threat by Shiism and Iran was propagated widely, and gained traction even amongst Arab Sunnis in countries without a politically relevant Shii community.[71] It would, however, be wrong to simply describe the insurgency as only 'Sunni'. Some Shia immediately vowed resistance to the CPA, too, and organised militarily to counter attacks on Shii targets by Jihadi groups. Iran had supported Iraqi Shia parties and militias since 1979 (some had fought during the Iran–Iraq war, in the 1991 Intifada, and had carried out smaller attacks against the regime). These Shii militias moved across the border into Iraq a few days into the invasion.

Over the coming years, Iran helped set up more Shii militias. The armed groups tied to one man immediately stood out: Muqtada al-Sadr, heir to the Sadr family's historical pedigree (his uncle was Muhammad Baqir al-Sadr, the cleric executed by Saddam in 1980, and his cousin Musa al-Sadr, the 'vanished Imam' who had mobilised Lebanese Shia, while his father the cleric Muhammad Sadiq al-Sadr galvanised Iraqi Shia with his sermons in the difficult 1990s, which led to his assassination in 1999 most likely at the hands of the regime). Youthful and not associated with the exiled politicians who cooperated with the coalition, Muqtada al-Sadr filled the power vacuum in the Shii slums of Baghdad and the South after the invasion. Unlike the political exiles, he had remained in Iraq through the difficult last years of the Baath, when the country was reeling under sanctions imposed after the invasion of Kuwait, and now quickly called for the invading armies to leave the country. Early on, he sought to bring about a Sunni–Shia national coalition to end the occupation. But his militia, the Mahdi Army, named after the twelfth Imam, which moved to protect Shii areas under his control, became notorious for killing former Baathists, coalition forces, and Sunni militants and civilians. Over the coming years, he would oscillate between allegiance to Iran, and assertion of independence.[72]

While Iran immediately expanded its influence—many of Iraq's new politicians had been exiled in Iran—the most senior clergy in Najaf took a middle ground. Ayatollah Sayyid Ali al-Sistani was the successor of al-Khu'i, who himself had succeeded al-Hakim and Burujirdi, and represented the traditional clerical leadership that had not agreed with Khomeini's notion that clerics rule in an Islamic state. Despite his Iranian origin, al-Sistani had an ambiguous relationship with Iran, and over the coming years would emerge as a key defender of Iraqi national unity and independence, and, as someone who tried to limit sectarian bloodshed, intervening in politics at key moments in the country's history.[73] Under his leadership, the shrines in Najaf and Karbala were refurbished and significantly expanded, and started to host millions of pilgrims and thousands of students from around the world. The old Shii centres of Iraq emerged as rivals to Iran amongst global Shia, with much of that expansion paid for by the religious taxes that al-Sistani received from wealthy Shia around the world, including from the Gulf, South Asia, and the West.[74] Shia from all over the world, including Ismailis and Shii-leaning Sufi orders, travelled to Najaf and Karbala.[75] These shrine cities became the focal point of massive processions during Muharram and during Arbain, suppressed under the Baath, during which millions march on foot to Karbala from across Iraq and Iran.[76] With his symbolic, financial, and political power fast expanding, al-Sistani became the most powerful person in post-invasion Iraq and intervened at key moments in the country's history. al-Sadr and al-Sistani stood at opposite ends of the Shii political spectrum, cooperating only if the very survival of the Shii community was at stake.

That two of Iraq's most powerful people were based in Najaf highlighted a power shift towards the shrine cities, and the importance Shii clerics attained in the country, even if formal politics would be left to party cadres. The Mahdi Army and al-Qaeda in Iraq (AQI) both fought against the coalition forces, causing heavy casualties. Increasingly styling themselves as armed wings of Shia and Sunnis, respectively, they also targeted leaders, civilians, and holy sites of the relative other sect. Al-Zarqawi and his group sought to push Shii militias to overreact. In February 2006, Sunni militants bombed the al-Askari shrine in Samarra, where Shia believe the tenth and eleventh Imam are buried. Images of the collapsed golden dome over their graves went around the world, enraging Shii public opinion.[77] Two months later, suicide bombers blew themselves up in a key Shii mosque in Baghdad.[78] Suicide bomber videos, undergirded with martial music, a specific media product of the Iraq war, went viral on dedicated satellite channels, and on the internet, vastly increasing their impact in Iraq and beyond.

The targeting of some of the holiest sites of Shiism led to a full-blown sectarian civil war from 2006 to 2007. People were stopped at checkpoints, their identity cards checked, and if their names or places of birth indicated they were of the other sect, they could be killed. Mosques, shrines, or other holy places were fired upon, blown up, or taken over completely, and clerics killed. Much of the violence came from Shii militias against Sunni targets. The damage to social cohesion was tremendous.[79] When Nuri al-Maliki from the Shii Islamist Dawa Party became Prime Minister in 2006, state institutions were further purged of Sunnis, and Shii commanders appointed to the army. Shii militias controlled much of the capital and the south, and increased their grip over key parts of the state. This further alienated Sunnis, who defined themselves stronger as 'Sunnis' and developed sect-centric organisations. Shii infighting was severe, but at the height of the civil war they could set aside their differences to fight what they saw as the 'Sunni threat'.[80] People left mixed neighbourhoods, which now became more homogeneously inhabited by one sect or the other (the flight of many Christians since 2003 further eroded that diversity). Across the South, including in Basra, for example, remaining Sunni inhabitants and quarters came under pressure, and the South thus more exclusively Shii. Internal displacement was especially difficult for the many mixed Sunni–Shia families, who had to decide whether to move to a predominantly Sunni or a predominantly Shii area.[81] When Saddam Hussein was executed on 30 December 2006—one of his executioners was filmed shouting that this was in revenge for the execution of Muhammad Baqir al-Sadr in 1980—Sunni militants and former Baathists renewed their efforts. Some Naqshbandis formed a so-called Naqshbandi Army with ties to al-Duri in early 2007.[82] Sectarian hate-speech sky-rocketed, with wide ramifications across the region. Shii militias and radical clerics also embraced openly anti-Sunni rhetoric, invoking terms such as *Wahhabi*, *Takfiri*, or *Nasibi* to denigrate Sunnis.[83]

The scale of sectarian bloodshed in Iraq was such that it led to polarisation in territories far away, but also spurred ecumenical efforts (though cynics argued that the mediators were not necessarily 'honest brokers'). In 2004 and 2005, Jordan, which had positioned itself against the ascent of Shii Islamism across the region, organised conferences leading to the so-called 'Amman Message', in which Twelver Shiism and Zaydism were recognised as valid schools of Jurisprudence alongside the four Sunni schools.[84]

Saudi Arabia hosted a meeting of Sunni and Shia leaders in Mecca in 2006, which culminated in a document recognising the validity of Sunnism and Shiism and emphasising that no houses of worship should be targeted. A big step for the Saudis, its impact was limited, as al-Qaeda no longer recognised the religious authority of Saudi state-aligned clerics.[85] In Southeast Asia, too, the conflict in Iraq led to a renewed push to calm sectarian tensions.[86] Yusuf al-Qaradawi, the spiritual leader of the Muslim Brotherhood, organised a conference on Sunni–Shia relations in Doha in 2007. Originally from Egypt, he had settled in Qatar in the 1960s and saw his profile rise by airtime on *al-Jazeera*. He claimed to take a middle ground on Shiism, seeing Shia as innovators but not infidels, as Salafis do.[87] At the conference, he outlined three conditions for rapprochement: That Shia stop cursing the Companions, stop proselytising in Sunni countries, and that Iran play a positive role in Iraq. Given that he had previously supported the Jihad in Iraq, and even legitimised suicide bombings there, al-Qaradawi's was a welcome move, although his tone remained accusatory.[88] The security situation in Iraq improved somewhat after 2007, partly through the growth of tribal Sunni resistance to Sunni Jihadis, who were also increasingly seen as a threat by Saudi Arabia, Turkey, and Qatar, who all styled themselves as patrons of 'Sunnis' in Iraq, although their Iraqi allies were frequently at each other's throats. That intense sectarian polarisation and unity could coincide is highlighted by the very different developments in Iraq and Lebanon in 2006. In Iraq, as noted, this was the height of the civil war.

But in Lebanon, the war between Israel and Hizbullah in 2006, when Israel destroyed large parts of the Southern suburbs of Beirut, led to Sunni–Shia solidarity, and even al-Qaradawi voiced support for Hizbullah and criticised Saudi Salafi clerics, who denounced support of Hizbullah because it was Shii.[89] This highlighted how even though regional alliances and public spheres had started fragmenting along sectarian lines, there were still other processes at work that enabled a more pan-Arab, pan-Islamic stance.

In Lebanon, the influence of Iran and the Gulf States had increased after the peace accord of 1990 brokered in Saudi Arabia, as had the relative influence of Muslims in the political system. Lebanon became a major outlet for Gulf capital, and while some of the Lebanese expatriates in the Gulf that acted as interlocutors were Shia, most were Sunni or Christian, and they channelled funds to their preferred projects and parties. Rafiq Hariri was the most successful of them all. He used Gulf capital to rebuild central Beirut—devastated by war—and side-line Sunni notables and Islamists as leaders of 'Sunnis' in Lebanon, and allied with the Sunni Mufti.[90]

Hariri became prime minister in 1992, and re-established Beirut as a glitzy Mediterranean Jet-Set destination. His embrace of neoliberalism perpetuated the weak state and lack of services, and meant that people had to resort to clientelism and service-provision of sectarian parties. The state institutions that did exist suffered from sectarian quotas and appointments and neoliberal reconstruction strengthened a political economy organised along sectarian lines with an oligarchy on top.[91] Syria accepted Hariri and his neoliberal project, as long as Syrian elites profited, too, and the thaw in relations in the 1990s between Saudi Arabia, Syria, and Iran facilitated this.[92] But as that reconstruction turned Hariri into a prominent international figure, and a very wealthy man, he tried to align Lebanon closer to France and the Gulf, and away from Syria and Iran. In Syria, Hafez al-Assad's son Bashar, who was being groomed as a successor to his father, and given the Lebanese file to prove himself, increasingly saw him as a problem. Bashar and his entourage suspected Hariri of trying to weaken the regime in Damascus in alliance with his Saudi and Western friends.[93] The removal of Hariri as prime minister in 1998 foreshadowed his downfall.

When Israel withdrew from South Lebanon in 2000, many Lebanese, especially those on the Left, saw Hizbullah as defender of Lebanese territory. Hizbullah was the only major militia that did not give up the bulk of its weapons after the end of the civil war, officially to continue the fight against Israel. Calls for it to hand them in now that Israel had left increased, but in vain. Instead, the party strengthened its position militarily, politically, and economically.[94] That same year, Hafez al-Assad, who had shaped Syrian and regional politics for decades, died. As his son Bashar assumed power, an opening of civil space in Syria was termed the 'Damascus Spring'. But the regime was nervous that it could not control a political opening, and that long-suppressed opposition, especially Sunni Islamists, could re-emerge.[95] That fear increased as President Bush included Syria in his 'Axis of Evil' and of course overthrew the Baath regime in neighbouring Iraq. In September 2004, French- and US-backed UN Security Council resolution 1559 called on Syria, whose army had been stationed in Lebanon since the civil war, to withdraw and for the disarming of Hizbullah. Syria and Hizbullah perceived Hariri and his allies as the driving force behind the resolution. In February 2005, a massive explosion blew up Hariri's motorcade on Beirut's beachfront, killing him and several others. Many blamed Syria and Hizbullah for the assassination.[96]

Lebanese protesters, mostly young and from all walks of life, denounced the Syrian presence, Hizbullah's grip on the country, and the sectarian political system per se.[97] Termed the 'Cedar Revolution', the protests, together with international pressure, led Syria to withdraw, though Hizbullah still did not disarm.[98] The removal of the political leader of the Sunni community led to infighting amongst Sunnis over his succession (Rafiq's son Saad would eventually win out, though his Sunni rivals would limit his power). In July 2006, the Israeli army vowed to punish Hizbullah after the latter had kidnapped Israeli soldiers near the border. Despite massive bombings of Hizbullah positions in the South of the country and in Southern Beirut, however, the Israelis failed to crush Hizbullah.

Hizbullah claimed victory, though many of its strongholds were destroyed. Iranian funds were vital to rebuilding these areas, strengthening ties between their residents, the party and Iran (although the Gulf States and critics of Iran sought to limit that involvement, and raised their own funds). The 2006 war with Israel gave Hizbullah a strong argument to retain its weapons: to continue the resistance both against Israel and to defend Lebanese territory. During and after the war, Hizbullah became popular even amongst non-Shii and non-Islamist Lebanese, and across the Arab world. Indeed, it may have been that popularity amongst many Sunni Arabs, which translated into support from Muslim Brotherhood leaders like al-Qaradawi, that spurred pro-American Sunni regimes, especially Saudi Arabia, Jordan, and Egypt, to further a sectarian narrative to undermine Hizbullah's popularity and gain favours in the US by playing up fears of a 'Shia crescent' (at the time of the war, only a few Saudi clerics argued Hizbullah should not be supported because it was Shii). But it also deepened the rivalry in Lebanon between a Sunni and Shii-led political camp, and regionally between largely Sunni and Shii states and non-state actors. Saudi Arabia and Iran emerged as leaders at opposite ends of the spectrum.[99] Salafis and anti-Iranian states like Egypt, Jordan, and Morocco increased their propaganda against Shiism, played up the alleged Shiitisation of Palestine and Syria, and portrayed Hizbullah as an extension of Iran to undermine its popularity amongst Sunni Arabs.[100] Sunni Islamists in Morocco and Algeria invoked the threat of conversions to Shiism, which led Morocco to temporarily cut diplomatic relations with Iran.[101] This coincided with Hamas' electoral victory in Gaza. Its enemies, from Leftists to Salafis to Israel, now accused Iran of Shiitising Palestine and Hamas of being a Shii-Iranian movement.[102]

As Hizbullah's standing grew, and its enemies' relative position weakened, domestic tensions reached a climax. When Saad Hariri and some of the Christian and Druze elites tried to challenge Hizbullah outright, and blamed it for the killing of Rafiq Hariri and other critics of Syria and Hizbullah, Hizbullah, in 2008, deployed gunmen across Beirut and surrounded Hariri's residence. Beirutis were reminded of the dark days of the civil war. The Saudi ambassador fled on his yacht.[103] The regional agreement on Lebanon that had stabilised it in the 1990s and early 2000s faltered, as Iran and Hizbullah asserted their dominance and Gulf influence waned. Tensions abated somewhat after the May 2008 Doha accords brokered by Qatar, which paved the way for the election of a new president (and symbolised the rise of Qatar as another resourceful player on the Sunni political scene, one that did not shy away from reaching out to pro-Iran movements).[104]

However, by 2008 Hizbullah had asserted itself as the strongest force in Lebanese politics. Apart from military supremacy, its superiority was facilitated by disunity amongst Christians and Sunnis, and its tightening grip on the Shii community (its erstwhile rival, Musa al-Sadr's Amal, became a junior partner in Shii politics, and mostly allied with it). Indeed, Shii critics of the party, which increased as Hizbullah became more dominant and authoritarian, were treated harshly. With the assassination of Hariri in 2005, and the political crises of subsequent years that culminated in Hizbullah's quasi-coup of 2008, the Sunni-Shia conflict in its regional political dimension—hitherto more of an afterthought in Lebanese politics—became its key dividing line.[105] Inner-Lebanese Sunni–Shia dialogue initiatives failed to halt this polarisation.[106] Christians were left a choice of allying with one side or the other, and the Sunni 'community' became more fragmented, as Saad Hariri was challenged by other players, including by Salafis, some of whom took an uncompromising stance towards Hizbullah and the Lebanese state, and played on Sunni feelings of marginalisation to undermine him and mobilise support.[107] As Syria and Iran feared they might be the next target of US-led regime change, and their interests in Lebanon converged, they strengthened their alliance, and formalised ties with non-state actors in the region, apart from Hizbullah, especially with Hamas and Islamic Jihad in Palestine, and later the Huthis in Yemen and Iraqi Shii militias. In a twist on the Axis of Evil, this alliance became known as the Axis of Resistance.[108]

In the 1980s, the Syria-Iran alliance was based on Realpolitik. Over time, however, it attained a growing religio-cultural dimension, in which anti–imperialism, resistance to Israel and the United States, and a disdain for Saudi-sponsored Salafism and a common Shii link gained in importance. This was exemplified by Sayyida Zaynab, the Damascus suburb that its tiny Shii community had started to develop under the French Mandate, and that was expanded by the Shirazis and Iran since the 1970s. Iraqi Shia fleeing Baathist repression and then post-2003 violence boosted the suburb's population, and up to one million pilgrims visited every year. The pilgrims would fill the main street leading to the mosque and then proceed inside to pray near the tomb of Zaynab in the centre of the mosque. Syria was one of the only countries to which Iranians could travel without a visa, and they would stay on in the hotels near the Zaynab shrine, built by Shii investors from Iran and Kuwait. They could pay with Iranian currency; their notes with the iconic picture of Khomeini bundled in the hands of the street vendors. Shii clerics, students and activists from around the Shii world would have late-night discussions in the religious schools and bookshops surrounding the shrine.[109] It resembled the Shii shrines in Iran and those in Iraq, which were also expanding after 2003. These fast-expanding shrines in Iran, Iraq and Syria together fostered stronger connections between the world's Shia, and tied them more closely to the territory on which the *Ahl al-Bayt* lived and died. That stronger Shii presence accelerated a development noted earlier—of Alawites moving religiously closer to Twelver Shiism. Alawite clerics and intellectuals responded more forcefully to criticism of their religious beliefs, and outlined their history, and doctrine, and placed it within the sphere of Islam and Shiism.[110]

Apart from Sayyida Zaynab, numerous Shii shrines were built across the country since the late 1970s, and previously disputed or 'undiscovered' shrines reappropriated as Shii ones. Most visible perhaps, because in the immediate vicinity of the Umayyad mosque in central Damascus, was the Iran-funded expansion of the shrine of Sayyida Ruqayya. It added a distinctly Shii element to the old city of Damascus, and drew many Iranian and other Shii pilgrims.[111] In the mid-2000s a large Shii shrine commemorating those fallen in the battle of Siffin, the original battle between Ali and Muawiya, was built in Raqqa, a predominantly Sunni city in the Euphrates region. The Persian Shii architectural style of the mausoleums, and the Shii pilgrims, alienated locals.[112]

After Hizbullah's victory in the 2006 war, enemies of the Assad regime amplified fears of Iranian influence and Shia proselytising in Syria. In 2006, the American embassy in Damascus advocated drawing attention to this in cooperation with Sunni countries like Saudi Arabia and Egypt and Syrian

Sunni religious leaders.[113] Syrian opposition groups portrayed Shii education and pilgrimage in Sayyida Zaynab, and the commemoration of Karbala in the Umayyad Mosque, as proof that the Assad regime was teaming up with Iran and the region's Shia in order to dominate or convert Sunni Syrians.[114] Iran had indeed expanded its footprint in recent years not just near the shrines, but through cultural centers and other Shii institutions.[115] Still, vast differences remained between the ideology of the Arab Socialist Baath Party ruling Syria and the Islamic Republic of Iran, and some of the Shii movements operating in Syria, like the Shirazis, had long fallen out with Iran. Claims of large-scale conversion were overblown.[116] And for all their rapprochement towards Twelver Shiism, Alawites also retained a distinct identity.[117]

And once the Syrian government realised that its policy of supporting a greater visibility of Shiism in Syria led to resentment, a plan to establish a new set of shrines leading to a Shii pilgrimage route from Karbala to Damascus was shelved.[118] In addition, ever since the massive violence inflicted on the city of Hama and its residents after the uprising of 1982, a state-sponsored Sunnism sought to deflate those challenges and broaden the definition of publicly acceptable displays of religiosity. This public embrace of Islamic norms shifted the regime's avowed secularism towards a religious nationalism in which Sunnis, too, were allowed to practise religiosity in public, especially through Syria's Sufi orders, including the Naqshbandiyya, without this constituting a challenge to the state.

The regime's policy was long associated with the Grand Mufti of Syria from 1964 to 2004, Ahmad Kuftaru. A Kurd and a Naqshbandi, he helped the state to build up support amongst Sunnis and Kurds, from which opposition could potentially emerge, and counter Salafis and Muslim Brothers in the Sunni religious field (and some clerical Sunni elites), and secular Kurdish nationalist ones in the Kurdish field. Kuftaru established a Naqshbandi sub-order, the Kuftariyya, which became popular amongst Kurds and which he expanded into a transnational movement with state patronage. Institutions associated with this official Sunni Islam also cooperated with Shii and Iranian-financed programmes, although this remained at a superficial level and did not involve a thorough reconsideration of the Naqshbandiyya's anti-Shii heritage.[119] It supported Syrian Sufi rituals that showed a respect and love for the *Ahl al-Bayt*, and a lamentation for the death of Hussain during Ashura, practices that are close to Shii ones.[120] The entrusting of official Sunni Islam into the hands of largely Kurdish Sufis further marginalised and alienated Syrian Arab clerics that linked themselves to Syria's Salafi heritage.

Throughout the 2000s, the Assad regime engaged in 'authoritarian upgrading', embraced some aspects of a market economy and re-established ties with former foes.[121] But there were cracks in the facade of public obedience,[122] and the decade laid the conditions for the mass rising in the 2010s. A widespread drought pushed many to abandon their lands, especially in Eastern Syria, and move to the cities.[123] The most affected were Sunnis, who started to articulate their resentment in sectarian terms (i.e. with Sunni farmers arguing that the regime was looking after Alawite farmers but not after them).[124] In addition, as Bashar tightened his grip on power and brought in new constituencies, he retired many of the 'old guard', which weakened the Baath party and undermined its cohesion. By embracing a slow neoliberal opening, he introduced contradictions in Syria's political economy. The regime claimed it was working for a 'social market economy', but empowered a new class of crony capitalists, often Alawite (and Sunni) businessmen close to the Assads. A famous example was the introduction of mobile phones, with a duopoly held by Syriatel, a company controlled by Alawite oligarch Rami Makhlouf, and another company controlled by the First Lady's Bassma al-Assad's Sunni family.[125] This exacerbated resentment of the regime, and the Alawite oligarchs became an easy target for opposition propaganda. Internationally, the UN inquiry into the Hariri assassination, which increasingly pointed at Hizbullah and Syria, threatened to derail Syria's opening to the world. Despite its military withdrawal then, it was imperative that it maintain influence in Lebanon, and, where possible, prevent cooperation with the inquiry. An even closer alliance with Hizbullah was the result.

While all these conflicts, Afghanistan, Iraq, Lebanon, Syria, had local causes and dynamics, a sectarianised public sphere, an assertive Iran, and Sunni rulers who were highly sensitive to any sign of Shii mobilisation and sought to counter this, connected them.

No place epitomises this better than Yemen. I have noted that the spreading of Salafism across Yemen with Saudi funding, and the emergence of Zaydi revivalism inspired by the Iranian revolution throughout the 1980s, resulted in increased sectarian tensions. President Ali Abdullah Saleh long managed to play competing forces against each other, presenting himself as an ally of the Saudis in return for patronage. After Yemeni unification in 1990, a political opening allowed a Zaydi revivalist party to gain a few seats in the Yemeni parliament and mobilise Zaydis as Zaydis. Its founder,

Hussain al-Huthi, had been elected to parliament in 1993, and was initially not on bad terms with the government.[126] Al-Huthi established a youth movement to counter Salafism, and adopted anti-American rhetoric in the context of the government's close cooperation with the United States. On a discursive level, the movement was influenced by Iran's revolutionary and anti-imperialist rhetoric, but relations with Iran were limited (when Hussain al-Huthi's term in parliament ended in 1997, for example, he opted to study in Sudan and not in Iran (he returned in 2000)).[127] The Americans worried especially about a local al-Qaeda affiliate, whose Saudi branch had increasingly attacked the Saudi state in the 2000s. After it was repressed in Saudi Arabia, the remaining Saudi Jihadis moved to Yemen, where they merged in 2009 with the local branch to create al-Qaeda in the Arabian Peninsula (AQAP), and carved out territorial enclaves. After the anti-Shii turn of al-Qaeda's affiliate in Iraq, AQAP, which had hitherto not focused much on Zaydis, started to refer to them as enemies. From safe havens in remote parts of Yemen, AQAP organised attacks on the US and Saudi Arabia, which urged the Yemeni state to move against them.[128] Saleh agreed, and presented himself as an ally in the 'war on terror', but used his so-called 'anti-terror' campaign against political enemies, including the Huthis.

Given his cooperation with the US after 9/11, the Huthis' strong anti-Americanism (their main slogan invokes 'Death to America') was an embarrassment to Saleh. The regime sensed that it, too, was vulnerable after the overthrow of the Baath Party in Iraq, which had been a close ally, and worried about the rising fortunes of Arab Shia.[129] Given the long history of Zaydi Sayyid rule, Saleh saw al-Huthi, a Sayyid from an old Zaydi family, as a threat. On 18 June 2004, the governor of Saada tried but failed to arrest al-Huthi. His followers resisted, and after ten weeks of fighting that exposed the frailty of the government's security apparatus, a US-trained 'Counter Terrorism' force killed Hussain al-Huthi in a cave on 10 September 2004.[130] His younger brother, Abd al-Malik, born around 1980, emerged as new figurehead of the movement, which started to call itself *Ansar Allah* ('Partisans of Allah').[131] Over the next six years, Saleh waged six successive campaigns against the Huthis, partly in alliance with Salafi-influenced tribes.[132]

The government and regional actors, such as Saudi Arabia, which intervened directly from 2009 onwards, framed the Huthis as a sectarian movement, ignoring the socio-economic and political grievances of a marginalised province such as Saada that drove much of local support, and the complicated political history of Yemen that undermined analyses of its politics along a Zaydi–versus–Shafii line.[133] Saudi actions against and denigration of the Huthis intensified. The Saudi Grand Mufti, Abd al-Aziz Al Shaykh, and other clerics lent religious legitimacy to Saudi soldiers bombing the Huthis.[134] The Yemeni government, Saudi Arabia, and local Salafis invoked alleged connections between the Huthis and Iran/Hizbullah to legitimise the fight and gain support.[135] The American government knew that this was largely a fiction, but supported its allies nonetheless. US government cables stated in 2009 that the only visible sign of Iranian activity in Yemen was positive media portrayal of the Huthis in order to counter Saudi-sponsored outlets that criticised them[136] and that the relationship with Hizbullah was virtually non-existent.[137] The US ambassador in Yemen wrote: 'We can think of few ways to more effectively encourage Iranian meddling in the Huthi rebellion than to have all of Yemen's Sunni neighbors line up to finance and outfit Ali Abdullah Saleh's self-described "Operation Scorched Earth".'[138] The convergence between the Saudi and Yemeni regimes, the Saudi religious establishment, and Saudi and Yemeni Salafis in their stance on the Huthis, led to the conflict being framed in sectarian terms.[139] Slowly but surely, Yemen became connected to the other conflicts in the region.

Saudi Arabia (and other Gulf States like the UAE), already anxious about an Iraq that they felt had turned over to the Shii side, now were confronted with a Shii movement that was outright hostile to them on Saudi Arabia's southern border. In their view, all of this was connected. In addition, Gulf Shii political movements, many of them remnants of the revolutionary Islamist parties founded in the 1970s and 1980s, also felt emboldened by the ascent of Iraqi Shia, making matters worse in the minds of decision-makers.[140]

In Bahrain, Shii Islamist parties had won almost half the seats in the reconstituted parliament of the 2000s, and were pushing the limits of how far the Al Khalifa ruling family was willing to reform. Many hoped that the Crown Prince could one day take over and push ahead with reforms, but more hawkish members of the family and the wider regime saw any advantage gained by Shii parties as a threat. Parts of the Shii community, too, were becoming disillusioned with a political process inevitably rigged against them.[141] And parts of the Bahraini Sunni establishment, reinforced by Sunni officials and security personnel from Baathist Iraq, Sudan, and Pakistan who came to work in Bahrain, saw local events as closely related to the regional Shii resurgence. These Sunnis devised their own plan to deal with it: in reaction to Shii electoral gains in Bahrain (and Iraq) in the early 2000s, they naturalised tens of thousands of Sunnis from the Middle East and Pakistan to dilute the influence Shia could reach through the ballot box in Bahrain. When one of the officials in charge of the plan, a British-Sudanese, defected, and published details of the scheme, they were shocking even to critics of the Bahraini regime. Here was nothing less than a full-blown attempt to turn the Shii majority into a minority by bringing in people loyal to the ruling family due to patronage and sectarian affinity.[142] This provided ample ammunition to those parts of the opposition that saw the reform process as a sham, and had returned to exile or mobilised outside of formal politics, and undermined the standing of those participating in the political process.

Shia in Eastern Saudi Arabia—just across the causeway—had seen their visibility increase after 9/11. As the US exerted pressure on its allies to reform, Shia were elected to largely powerless municipal bodies, submitted petitions detailing the Shia's historic grievances, and were included in what was touted a 'National Dialogue'. Online portals covered news of the community, and Shii clerics were shown in the national press, for the first time ever. The ascent of Iraqi Shia had a strong appeal amongst the most marginalised of Shii groups in the Gulf. But these reforms were cosmetic, and undermined by serious sectarian incidents, stemming in part from conflict in neighbouring Iraq, and by the publication of anti-Shii fatwas, sermons, and publications by Saudi scholars. Institutionally, little changed, and here, too, some former opposition activists started pushing the boundaries of what the Saudi ruling family deemed acceptable.[143]

On Iraq's southern border, Kuwait was likewise affected by the invasion of Iraq in 2003, though perhaps not in the ways one would imagine. After the expulsion of Iraqi troops from Kuwait in 1991 by an American-led coalition, the ruling family reached a new social contract with all sectors of Kuwaiti society, and agreed to reopen parliament. The Shia, who had proven their loyalty during the Iraqi invasion, were now transformed from potentially troublesome threats to the Kuwaiti system, with its open media landscape and parliament, as they had been seen throughout the 1980s, into possible allies—both of the opposition and of the ruling family. Throughout the 1990s and the early 2000s, Shii Islamists joined Arab nationalist, Leftist and Sunni Islamist politicians in a push towards a constitutional monarchy with an empowered parliament. Immediately after the invasion of Iraq in 2003, however, parts of the ruling family, who felt increasingly challenged, sensed an opportunity to divide the opposition, and win over the Shia as a loyalist voting bloc.

The Kuwaiti state thus reacted to the invasion of Iraq and the rise of Iraqi Shia not by repression, but by empowering and co-opting Shii merchants and Islamists. A long-standing Shii demand of stronger separate judicial representation through personal status law courts was granted, as were more permits for mosques, and Shii-owned TV stations and newspapers. Public Shii processions were allowed, and Kuwaiti Shia flocked to the shrine cities in Iraq that had been off limits for so long due to bad relations with Iraq and political instability. Kuwait became a media hub for Shii media from across the region, and many of the regional rivalries were in part fought out in the press here. A major turnaround in Sunni–Shia relations came in December 2008, when Kuwaiti Shii Islamist politicians from a pro-Iranian trend mourned the Israelis' assassination a few days earlier in Damascus of Imad Mughniyah, architect of Hizbullah's military and revolutionary networks across the region, and a key figure in the 'Axis of Resistance'. This open partisanship for a major pro-Iranian military leader, one who was blamed for attacks in Kuwait in the 1980s, led to the expulsion of the Shii parliamentarians from a cross-sectarian opposition bloc, and was invoked by those Sunnis who had long suspected Shii loyalties. Rather than crack down on the pro-Iranian Shii party, however, as many Muslim Brothers, Salafis, and others demanded, parts of the regime protected the Shia, and allied with them.

Competing contenders for the throne now intermittently supported Shia or anti-Shii forces to differentiate themselves from their rivals, and to gain influence. This occasionally inflamed tensions that looked to outsiders as 'Sunni–Shia' strife, but was actually a struggle for power between contenders to the throne from the Al Sabah family. The U-turn in Shia-ruling family relations contributed to cries of foul play by the Sunni opposition, driven in part by Muslim Brothers and Salafis, who saw the preferential treatment of Kuwaiti Shia politicians as one more example of Shii ascent in the region. While leading to closer relations between parts of the regime and Shii Islamists, the Mughniyah case fostered Sunni–Shia distrust, and showed how developments across the region were connected, but could play out very differently depending on local circumstances.[144]

Videos of a speech by a controversial Kuwaiti Shia cleric, Yasir al-Habib, further polarised Sunni–Shia relations. Originally affiliated with the Shirazi movement, al-Habib was expelled from Kuwait in 2004 and lost his citizenship because, according to a legal ruling, he 'offended Sunnis'. The Shirazi movement had long been assertive about Shii beliefs and rituals, refusing to tone them down for the sake of harmony with Sunnis. Al-Habib took this to the extremes. He voiced openly some of the most contentious issues in the doctrinal debates between Sunnis and Shia, and cursed the Companions of the Prophet, especially His wives Aisha and Hafsa. In 2010 a sermon al-Habib delivered denouncing Aisha led to a major political crisis in Kuwait; he then doubled down with a book on Aisha's alleged crimes against the Prophet and Islam. In exile in the UK, al-Habib set up a TV channel and websites, attacking Shia who advocated accommodation with Sunnis. This made him a hated figure for many Shia and all Sunnis.[145] While most mainstream Shii clerics and parties, and Iran's Supreme Leader, denounced al-Habib's position, even calling it 'British Shiism', new media allowed a previously marginal cleric in exile to fan the flames from a distance.[146] It was just one example of how new media reshaped and reproblematised Sunni–Shia relations.

Online dissemination turned local into global events. In late February 2009, a group of young Saudi Shia boys left the concrete pathways that lead around and across the cemetery of al-Baqia in Medina. These pathways were created so that visitors could look at the tombs of the Imams without approaching them or reciting prayers, which is contrary to Wahhabi norms and forbidden.[147] The boys ran towards what are said to be the burial grounds of the Imams, touching them and grabbing some of the soil. The religious police chased the boys away, and in ensuing clashes between security forces, Shii pilgrims, and local Sunnis, several were injured. On social media, the official version of events that was advanced asserted that the pilgrims had 'trampled upon' the graves of the Prophet's wives and Companions. They claimed that this alleged offence, and the pilgrims' other 'Zoroastrian rituals' and insults to the Prophet's Companions, had led security forces to disperse them and then provoked local Sunni worshippers into clashing with the Shii pilgrims. As triumphal music plays, the videographers brag that a 'lion-hearted' local youth stabbed 'one of those who rejects true Islam' and joke that only the 'merciful' presence of security forces protected the 'grandchildren of Khosraw', a reference to them being Persian, from further harm.

The Shii pilgrims' version of events was quite different and incited protests in the Eastern Province, from where the pilgrims came.[148] Defying a government ban, a local cleric named Nimr al-Nimr led the protests in Awamiya, a poor Shii village surrounded by date farms, where Nimr was born in 1959 into a family with a long history of resistance to the state. Nimr's grandfather had led an armed revolt in 1929 against Saudi tax collectors and Wahhabi missionaries. Nimr had become radicalized in the late

1970s by the Shirazis, and after the uprising of 1979, Nimr, too, had gone into exile first to Iran and then to Syria. Contrary to his erstwhile colleagues in the Saudi Shirazi movement, who had reached a deal with the Saudi state, and became elected to local councils and engaged with the ruling family, Nimr remained a vocal critic.[149] In sermons he delivered after the clashes in Medina, he declared that Shia might one day secede if they could not realise their political demands in Saudi Arabia. To avoid punishment for these comments, Nimr went into hiding, but his reaction was a harbinger of things to come, and he became a hate figure on Sunni websites.[150]

The Saudis and other Sunni leaders became so paranoid about Shii ascendance that they even feared that the husband of assassinated former President Benazir Bhutto, who had won elections in Pakistan, after General Musharraf's reign ended in 2008, could make common cause with Iran and Shii-ruled Iraq because of his Shii background. The Saudis in turn supported his political enemies, including later Prime Minister Nawaz Sharif.[151]

Images and videos of the Medina clashes, of Saddam's execution, of bombings in Iraq, of the collapsed golden dome of the Askari shrine, and countless other incidents strengthened the conviction among many Sunnis that Shia were overstepping their mark, and that they needed to mobilise as Sunnis to counter that.[152] They also galvanised senses of Shii victimhood and assertion. As the American-led interventions reshaped the region, and Iraq became the focus of a sectarianised rivalry between Saudi Arabia and Iran, mixed Sunni–Shia societies were affected, each in its own way. In general, however, the interventions broadened and deepened the global Sunni–Shia divide. Although the 2000s witnessed efforts to overcome divisions, the decade saw tremendous sectarian violence and polarisation. The different conflicts in Iraq and Afghanistan, as well as Lebanon and Yemen, and in the Gulf and Palestine, all had local dynamics, but they were increasingly connected to each other. When Arabs took to the streets from late 2010 onwards they became connected in novel ways.

14

The Arab Uprisings

The Arab uprisings that started in late 2010 in Tunisia and rapidly spread across the Arab world to the streets and squares of Tunis, Cairo, Sanaa, Manama, Qatif, Damascus, and Kuwait City, and later, in 2019, Baghdad and Beirut, carried the hopes of a generation for justice, dignity, freedom, economic opportunities, and less sectarian division. On the Pearl Roundabout outside of Bahrain's capital Manama—the busiest traffic area in the country—most protesters were Shia, some others were Sunnis, and one of the slogans I heard often when I walked around that square in the early days of the uprising in late February 2011 was *la sunniyya, la shiiyya, wahda wahda watani-yya* (Not Sunni, not Shii, National Unity).[1]

At that point, Syria was still quiet, and many thought it would remain an outlier, as Syrians feared the violence the regime deployed in the past, and that protests could lead to sectarian conflict. By March and April 2011, however, protesters would take to the streets and chant non-sectarian slogans, initially in peripheral areas like Deraa. The regime reacted with a heavy hand, which, rather than stifling dissent as it had done for decades, in the context of the Arab Spring led to a country-wide rising. Protests spread to the outskirts of Damascus, and central towns like Homs and Hama with a long history of dissent, amongst other areas. While most were Sunnis, other Syrians also joined the protests.[2] By the end of 2011 protesters across Syria would take to the streets.

It was the same in Yemen. On Sanaa's so-called *Change Square*, Zaydis and Shafiis came together to debate Yemen's future. And in all other Arab countries, even in those that later descended into conflict, protesters vowed to unite regardless of religious, regional, or ethnic identity, directing their anger against repressive states and not a certain religious group.

Despite all this, by the end of the 2010s, the region had experienced extreme ethno-sectarian violence. How could it be that when so many denounced sectarian division, that division could contribute to the deaths of tens of thousands of lives and ruin those of millions?[3] An answer can be found in how regimes in heterogeneous societies were formed in previous decades, which I have discussed above, and how they now responded to the protests: In Syria, Bahrain, Yemen, Turkey, Kuwait, Saudi Arabia, Lebanon, Iraq (and Iran), state elites divided their populations to prevent cross-sectarian opposition movements. Middle East political scientists coined a term to describe this process: *sectarianisation*. By linking domestic political issues to regional rivalries, and portraying protesters from the relative other sect as directed by regional enemies, these elites ensured support by core groups and regional allies. They fostered a zero-sum, us-versus-them mentality, in which those belonging to the religious group of the elite were tied more closely to the regime. That regional enemies then scaled up their efforts to support protest movements turned this into a self-fulfilling prophecy. Any foreign support, however marginal, was exaggerated, protests repressed and uprisings militarised, and foreign patrons were pulled in by local actors. In some contexts, there was truth to some claims of foreign support. But in the end, perceptions mattered more than facts.[4]

In addition, while most Arab States experienced protests or calls for reform after 2011, some regimes fell, and others lost control over parts of their territory. Still others, including the wealthy Arab Gulf States, above all Saudi Arabia, the UAE, and Qatar, alongside non-Arab powers such as Iran, Israel, and Turkey strengthened their position in the region. The uprisings further weakened an Arab state system that had been in disarray since the 2003 Iraq war and deepened rivalries between states that weathered the storm.[5] Two major alliances of political Sunnism, one led by Saudi Arabia and the other by Turkey, vied for supremacy. Saudi Arabia turned from a major supporter of political Islam, and the Muslim Brotherhood, to the leader of the anti-Muslim Brotherhood camp, alongside the UAE, but still wanted to be seen as defender of Sunnis, supporting insurgencies in Iraq and Syria, and intervening militarily in Bahrain and in Yemen. The Brotherhood in turn found resourceful and well-organised supporters in Turkey and Qatar. Mistrust between Saudi Arabia and the Muslim Brotherhood had deepened since Brothers in the Kingdom criticised the monarchy after the American intervention of Kuwait in 1991. When the Saudi Brothers openly endorsed democratic transitions in Egypt, Tunisia, and elsewhere, and the Saudi royal family hosted the deposed Tunisian dictator Ben Ali and ensured that the overthrown

Egyptian dictator Mubarak could live out his days by the Red Sea, the rupture was complete.[6]

The third alliance was the so-called *Axis of Resistance* of Iran, Syria, and pro-Iran movements, mainly Shii, though also including Sunni ones such as Palestinian groups Hamas and Islamic Jihad.[7] When protests started in Syria in late 2011, Syria became, much like Iraq in the 2000s, the focus of region-alised rivalries, and given Syria's constitutive role in the Axis of Resistance, put that alliance in jeopardy.[8] The Axis saw itself primarily as responding to United States' attempts to reshape the region, though the US and Europe had adopted contradictory policies. On the one hand, they welcomed calls for democracy and transition from authoritarianism, above all in Tunisia and Egypt. On the other, however, they had backed the authoritarian regimes, looked the other way when Saudi Arabia sent its troops to Bahrain in March 2011, and maintained strong ties to the Gulf States as well as to the Muslim Brotherhood/Turkey axis. And, to the horror of the Gulf States and Israel, President Obama signed a nuclear agreement with Iran in 2015. NATO also intervened militarily in Libya and eventually in Syria, and elsewhere—but the US and European powers lacked a clear political line and failed to substantially support those transitions that were under way.[9] President Obama, a critic of the Iraq war of 2003, was wary of committing US troops for another major war.

That relative reluctance to shape the post-2011 Middle East, and the contradictions inherent in Western foreign policy, allowed for regional rivalries to escalate, Russia to re-emerge as a major power, and China to expand—especially its economic influence. The age of American unipolarity, which had symbolically started with the 1991 intervention in Kuwait, was waning, and the era of proxy warfare, and the connection of local and regional con-flicts with international rivalries was back.[10] The intense sectarian polarisa-tion of the preceding decade, and the nature of regional alliances, meant that these conflicts were also played out along sectarian lines. This became most evident in Syria, a conflict that became as relevant for Sunni–Shia relations as Iraq had been in the preceding decade. And like Iraq, Syria's past as the seat of the Umayyad Caliphate, the location of *Ahl al-Bayt* shrines, and Shii dynasties during the 'Shii Century', and of the ensuing Sunni reassertion, provided an ample historical repertoire to symbolically link current strug-gles to past ones in contrasting ways. As relations between the Muslim Brotherhood, Qatar, and Turkey, on the one hand, and Saudi Arabia and the UAE on the other, deteriorated, it seemed as if the pro-Muslim Brotherhood coalition, which had been empowered by its early successes in the Arab Spring, might grow closer to Iran. The anxieties of the pro-Saudi axis grew when the Muslim Brother Mohammad Morsi came to power in Egypt in 2012 and re-established diplomatic relations with Iran. Given the antagonism between the two countries since the revolution of 1979, when President Sadat hosted the deposed Shah, this was a major step. Morsi was the first Egyptian president to visit Iran since then. He went because Tehran was hosting a meeting of the Non-Aligned Movement, of which Egypt had been a founding member, and only flew to Tehran after having visited Saudi Arabia first. Nonetheless the anti-Muslim Brotherhood coalition was appalled. It did not matter that during his visit Morsi praised the Syrian uprising in Tehran, which angered his hosts so much that the Iranian state broadcaster replaced Syria with Bahrain in a dubbing of Morsi's speech. It also did not matter that Morsi and other Muslim Brotherhood leaders made anti-Shii remarks, that violence against Egypt's small Shii community increased, or that during his time in office al-Azhar issued a fatwa arguing that the Jafari school of jurisprudence was not valid and should not be followed, and thereby contradicting al-Azhar's famous ecumenical 1959 fatwa recognising Shiism.[11] Despite all this Saudi Arabia and its Salafi allies in Egypt feared that the 2011 revolution had given Shia in Egypt, previously controlled even more tightly, room to proselytise, and that Iran could strengthen ties with al-Azhar. Salafi and Gulf-based TV channels and social media accounts played up the threat of Shii rituals and prayers in some of Cairo's mosques, especially in the Sayyida Zaynab mosque.[12] Fears of the rise of the Muslim Brotherhood to power in the most populous Arab state were coupled with fears of a rapprochement with Iran and a possible alliance of the two axes, one rivalling the Saudi and UAE-backed monarchical-militaristic one. This led the latter to back a former Egyptian military attaché in Riyadh, Abdel-Fattah al-Sisi, in a coup against Morsi in summer 2013, that had significant support amongst non-Islamist Egyptians.[13]

As protests in Saudi Arabia's Eastern Province and Bahrain gained pace in February and March 2011, long-held fears amongst Gulf elites of Shii empowerment were reinforced. Dissatisfaction with the slow reform process in Bahrain, and with the state's repressive tactics, had led to protests and an online campaign there. Emboldened by events in Tunisia and Egypt, thousands took to the streets on 14 February 2011, urged on by a coalition of Leftists and Shii Islamists. Mass protests called for major political reforms, and some for abolishing the monarchy. These reforms would have empowered all Bahrainis, but given the island's demographic profile—despite the mass naturalisation of Sunnis there was still a slight Shii majority—it would have given Shii politicians more say. But after a month of protests, and with the help of the Saudi army, the state opted for repression instead of dialogue, killing dozens and driving much of the opposition into exile, underground, or jail.[14] Protests had already occurred in the Eastern Province after the above-mentioned events in Medina in 2009. Nimr al-Nimr, the figurehead of these protests, who had gone into hiding to avoid arrest, now re-emerged. He believed that a revolution in Bahrain would change the situation in the Eastern Province and urged youth to protest in support of Bahrain and against the Saudi ruling family.

The Saudi authorities likewise saw the two movements as interlinked, so they sent their armed forces to Bahrain in mid-March 2011 to quell protests. In the Eastern Province, a protest campaign challenged the Saudi state throughout 2011 and 2012. The movement tried to ally with Sunnis, but repression, and fear of being associated with a Shii movement, meant those efforts were unsuccessful (mass protests in other parts of Saudi Arabia largely failed to materialise). The Saudi state, built up militarily for decades by Western powers, proved a fierce and resilient opponent. The movement was repressed, and dozens shot or executed. Nimr, too, was arrested in 2012, and given the death sentence.[15] To contain these protests and legitimise repression, Gulf regimes portrayed them as a Shia/Iranian conspiracy (cartoons in Saudi newspapers literally depicted a hand reaching across the Gulf from Iran to direct Saudi Shii protesters). This served to rally Sunnis in Saudi Arabia and in the other Gulf States around the respective ruling families. In Bahrain and elsewhere, invoking sectarian division was a way to legitimise repression, prevent broad-based opposition and ensure loyalty amongst a core segment of the population.[16] A Saudi Sunni human rights activist, for example, who tried to document anti-Shii repression, and advocated Sunni–Shia unity, was shot by his own son, a veteran of the Jihad in Iraq in the 2000s.[17]

In 2012, a protest movement led by youth groups, the Muslim Brotherhood, and Salafis challenged the Kuwaiti ruling family's authoritarian tendencies. Shii Islamists, meanwhile, backed the monarchy. Local political context and ruling bargains, and sectarian dynamics, affected the positions of local branches regarding transnational movements: In Kuwait, for example, Muslim Brothers and Salafis supported protests, while in Bahrain they denounced them. Shii Islamists, on the other hand, condemned protesters in Kuwait yet backed them in Bahrain.[18] But taken together, protests in the Gulf heightened its rulers' anxieties that the Arab uprisings might empower Shia and the Muslim Brotherhood. This shaped their stance on the Arab uprisings, and on Syria, where an uprising was gaining pace in late 2011.

Initially, the slogans of the Syrian revolution were non-sectarian, and nationalist, directed against a regime whose brutality, repressiveness, and all-pervasive intelligence services had long been infamous. Most protesters were Sunnis, though that should not come as a surprise since most Syrians are as well. Some Alawites, for example, embraced the protest movement early on, and there have long been prominent Alawite opponents of the regime.[19]

But the regime swiftly moved to demonise protesters as part of a regional conspiracy and bent on creating sectarian strife, by pitting members of different sectarian communities against one another. Bashar al-Assad's first major televised speech in the People's Assembly since the start of protests, on 30 March 2011, already used this discourse to denounce protests.[20] With this speech, and the violence unleashed from April onwards, it became clear that the regime was not willing to accommodate, would stop at nothing to remain in power, and would stoke the fears of Alawites, Druze, Ismailis, and Christians of a genocide in case the Assad regime should fall. How complicated things would become was immediately on display in cities that had both a large Alawite community, but also saw mass protests, such as Latakia and Tartus, and in the central Syrian city of Homs. Some Alawites joined Sunnis in early protests. Alawite dissidents were vilified by loyalist Alawites and targeted directly, and from early in the protests, the regime, and loyalist armed gangs, organised false flag operations to prevent cross-sectarian solidarity. Protesters condemned sectarianism but also voiced support for Gulf-based sectarian preachers. Homs became known as the *Capital of the Revolution*, and for parts of 2011 and 2012 was out of regime control. In Homs, conflict between Alawites and Sunnis emerged early on. Once the regime cracked down, it used the Alawite neighbourhoods established over recent decades as Alawites had moved to the city from nearby villages and mountainous areas as bastions of support and encircled and bombed Sunni ones. The brutal siege of Baba Amr in Homs would eventually be successful, and restore regime control over a vital city, but one largely destroyed and emptied of much of its Sunni inhabitants.[21]

The sectarianisation of the conflict had an important spatial dimension because of deliberate Baath Party policies. In Damascus, too, Alawites, who had moved to the city after the takeover of Hafez al-Assad, settled in specific neighbourhoods filled with vast concrete apartment blocks. Many of its residents came to work in the security forces, and their physical separation reinforced a sense of difference. Officers in the army could also buy property in an army neighbourhood termed 'Assad's Suburb', further tying their loyalty to each other and to the regime, and separating them from the rest of society. The officers, often from a humble background, not only Alawite but also Sunni, depended on this patronage. As the rebels started to encircle the capital, basing themselves in the popular quarters around Damascus, these neighbourhoods, and those perceived to be Alawite (or Christian) ones, became bastions of regime support. It were the connections of the residents of these neighbourhoods to the apparatus of coercion and other elements of the state that ensured their loyalty, while the marginalisation of lower-class neighbourhoods made many of their residents, often Sunni, join the uprising.[22] The regime, now under severe stress, organised people's militias in loyalist neighbourhoods into the National Defense Forces (NDF), and informal militias termed the 'ghosts' (*shabiha*). The establishment of similar protection units in rebel neighbourhoods pushed the conflict towards civil war. As the regime used extreme violence on protesters, many officers refused to obey orders, and defected, to join the Free Syrian Army. By default, these were more likely ones whose families and friends had few ties to the regime, or whose hometowns had joined the uprising. These defectors were primarily Sunni, which gave the militarised opposition a Sunni character, and increased the relative share of non-Sunnis in the army (although a substantial amount of Sunni soldiers and officers did not defect, owing to their dependence on state patronage, and the repression meted out at potential defectors and their families). The establishment and strengthening of elite units, made up of Alawites, and their use in suppression of protests and in attacks on pro-uprising areas further sectarianised repression, as did the employment of NDF units, often made up of Alawites but also of Druze, Christians, and Twelver Shia (and some Sunnis) away from their original neighbourhoods or villages.[23] They, and the Syrian army, are accused of massacres of Sunni civilians.[24]

That protesters increasingly used religious rhetoric in protests and organised through mosques in some ways reflected Bashar al-Assad's own utilisation of Islamic discourses in the 2000s, in developments reminiscent of the faith campaigns in neighbouring Iraq in the 1990s. Islamic terms of reference were initially seen as not very provocative, since the state itself had used them for years, and mosques, which were one of the few spaces where people could gather, served to facilitate protests and bring various segments of

Sunni society together.[25] Gradually, however, the Islamic networks adopted a more self-consciously Sunni discourse to denounce the regime. Oppositional actors based in the Gulf and Gulf-based satellite TV channels played a crucial role here. And the civilian phase of the uprising gave way to a militarised conflict dominated by Islamist groups.

Who started the sectarianisation process in Syria remains highly contested. Supporters of the opposition, and many Western analysts, would say that from the outset the Syrian regime heightened sectarian tensions to present itself as 'defender of the minorities'. They claim that the regime deliberately targeted protests across the country, and then freed from prison Sunni Jihadis who had previously fought the Americans in Iraq. Once released, many of them took up arms, and both strategies served to militarise the uprising, which then justified its violent repression. According to this narrative, the regime described all protesters as terrorists, and was never serious in engaging in any kind of accommodation or reform.[26] Pro-regime narratives contest this, and point towards the sectarian inclinations of much of the opposition, to its early militarisation and foreign support, and to the emergence of anti-Alawite and anti-Christian slogans at protests. This has led to two almost completely different perceptions of the Syrian civil war.[27]

The sectarian discourse of parts of the opposition may have resonated with some Sunnis. Assassinations of Alawite security officers, and attacks on Alawite villages, as well as the anti-Alawite tone of the opposition, on the other hand, rekindled memories of past violence against Alawites and old Alawite fears of annihilation at the hands of the Sunni majority were the regime to fall.[28] That fear explains why most Alawites remained loyal, which allowed the regime to survive. The extreme violence by the regime's security forces was a function of that mentality.[29]

Much of the Syrian opposition had long portrayed the regime as sectarian and spread that narrative to rally Sunnis (as early as the late 1970s and early 1980s it argued that a 'minority' was ruling over a 'majority'). The political utilisation of a minority/majority discourse harkened back to the French Mandate, when French officials openly sided with *minorités*, and the Arab Nationalist opposition claimed to represent the majority. The opposition and its backers, namely Turkey, Qatar, and Saudi Arabia, and the US, France, and the UK, now sought to exploit the numerical superiority of Sunnis in Syria. They supported the rebels with a concerted media campaign, with funding and diplomatic support, and, eventually, with military aid (the precise timing and nature of military aid is still disputed, though by 2012 and 2013, it was extensive). Their support for the opposition, and that of Russia, Iran, and Shii militias for the regime, further militarised the uprising, prolonging and deepening the civil war, and entrenching its sectarian dimension, as regional backers were more openly sectarian than either the regime or the opposition had been before 2011.[30] But rebel groups and foreign sponsors were soon at loggerheads, in part over the question which group to back in the war (where many thought the Muslim Brotherhood, with its long history of opposition to the Assad regime, would stand to profit, although it eventually lost out to other Sunni Islamist rebels).[31]

Saudi Arabia was a main backer of the opposition. A revival of long-standing anti-Shii rhetoric accompanied its military intervention in Bahrain, the crackdown on Shii protesters at home, and its support for the Syrian rebels, which served to portray it as defender of Sunnis against an axis of political Shiism. Supporting the Syrian uprising was something that many Saudis could agree on. Saudi clerics and elites supported the uprising in Syria with sectarian arguments, framing support in terms of help for Sunnis against an 'Alawite' or 'rejectionist' regime.[32] It supported the broad-based Syrian opposition coalition and the Free Syrian Army, and at the same time tried to contain Islamists who might be critical of Saudi Arabia such as the Muslim Brothers and al-Qaeda. But it also supported Islamists sympathetic to Saudi Arabia, whose outlook was no less radical or sectarian. In an important suburb of Damascus, it supported the Salafi Army of Islam, founded by Zahran Alloush, the son of a Syrian Salafi cleric who had lived in Saudi Arabia for decades.[33] Zahran Alloush had become radicalised seeing the US invade Iraq and Shii forces gain power there, and was imprisoned in Syria for supporting the Iraqi insurgency. He was one of those released from prison in the first months of the uprising. Alloush was extremely anti-Shii, and his idea was to build a sort of Islamic state with Damascus as its capital, restoring the glory of the Umayyad Caliphate.[34]

Even the 'moderate' rebels, and parts of Syria's intelligentsia, invoked sectarian terms to denounce the regime. Burhan Ghalioun, for example, a professor of sociology at the Sorbonne, and in 2011 the first president of the opposition's umbrella organisation, the Syrian National Council, had long decried the Syrian regime as sectarian and had published extensively about the 'problem of minorities' in Syria. He now supported the Free Syrian Army and called for foreign intervention.[35] Sadiq Jalal al-Azm, a famous Syrian Philosopher, too, had argued that the solution for the crisis would have to involve the fall of 'Political Alawism'.[36] Ghalioun was succeeded as head of the Syrian National Council by Moaz al-Khatib, a previous Imam at the Umayyad mosque, who advocated sectarian coexistence. Still, with his ideological links to the Muslim Brotherhood—with of course its long history of using sectarian language against the regime—and with his clerical Sunni background, he may have amplified fears among non-Sunnis. But he was a well-known and relatively moderate figure, and when he resigned in 2013 the opposition lost a figurehead and became divided further, and even more influenced by Qatar and Saudi Arabia.[37] The Muslim Brotherhood cooperated with different political forces, and non-Sunni dissidents, in the Council, to facilitate support from Europe and the United States. But the Council's support in Syria, and the Free Syrian Army's military successes remained limited, and so Salafis, with their strong anti-Shiism, gained in strength. These had a well-delineated and strict ideology, committed fighters, sustained sources of funding and weapons, and soon, a string of highly motivated volunteers from abroad. By 2013 then, the conflict had become internationalised and sectarianised, with sectarian Islamists the strongest force fighting the regime.[38]

Intra-opposition competition, amongst different Salafi networks, the Muslim Brotherhood, and other factions, intensified as they competed for attention and foreign funds, and sought to represent themselves as successful militarily and ideologically committed. Supporters in Turkey and the Gulf appreciated their anti-Shii outlook. Qatar, which emerged as a small but resource-rich rival to Saudi Arabia for the leadership of political Sunnism, and became allied with Turkey, backed sectarian Islamists from the outset.[39] Kuwaiti Salafi charities became conduits for donations to the Syrian opposition, including extreme sectarian forces. For Kuwaiti Sunnis, supporting anti-Shii movements in Syria was part of a wider struggle against political Shiism.[40] Kuwaiti Shii MPs and businessmen, on the other hand, supported the Assad regime, and one, with family ties to the Alawite oligarchy around Bashar al-Assad, became an outright advocate of the regime, and was eventually expelled from Kuwait and had his citizenship revoked.[41] Bahraini Salafi MPs likewise supported militant groups in Syria, travelled to Syria, and invoked strong anti-Shii language as a reason for their support.[42] And some Bahrainis and many more Saudis would travel to Syria to fight against what they saw as a 'rejectionist' regime.

The anti-Shiism of the Gulf now became connected to Sunni grievances in Syria, as the older generation of Salafis and Muslim Brothers with connections to the Gulf, including Muhammad Surur—the aforementioned anti-Shii and anti-Iranian ideologue—became figureheads of the Syrian opposition. Surur helped found the Turkey- and Qatar-backed Syrian Islamic Council and contributed to the sectarian outlook of the opposition.[43] Syrian opposition clerics founded openly sectarian TV stations based in Saudi Arabia. The most prominent of them, Adnan al-Arour, notoriously proposed that Alawites should be put through the meat grinder. These outlets constantly described the regime and its backers as sectarian, and the war as a sectarian conflict of Sunnis against the rest. Al-Arour's network even added a Persian service to highlight the plight of Sunnis in Iran, displaying both its ambition and sustained sources of funding.[44] Such discourse resonated with the extreme end of the militant Syrian opposition, and with some Sunnis in the Gulf, but heightened the anxieties of non-Sunnis.

Sunni militant networks in Iraq sensed an opportunity. After the assassination of al-Zarqawi in 2006, AQI merged with other Sunni Islamist militant groups to form the Islamic State of Iraq (ISI). After the 2007 'surge' of US-led coalition troops and Sunni tribes, its reach decreased, but it continued a low-level insurgency against the coalition, and maintained al-Zarqawi's strong anti-Shiism. In 2010, Abu Bakr al-Baghdadi took up leadership of the organisation.[45] The group's heartland was the northern border region with Syria, which had been a major recruiting and transit point. When the Syrian uprising started, here is where the ISI had contacts and extensive networks. The Syrian regime had long co-opted Sunni tribes in this area. But the region remained fundamentally marginalised, and the symbiosis between the Syrian state and the tribes broke down in 2011. Tribal groups now provided the backbone of opposition movements, and when protests met with fierce state violence that humiliated tribesmen, some took up arms against the state.[46] It was here, in Deir al-Zur, that Abu Muhammad al-Julani founded the Jabhat al-Nusra li-Ahl al-Sham ('Support Front for the People of the Levant') in January 2012 on behalf of the ISI, and adopted strong sectarian rhetoric.[47]

Military aid to Syrian rebels flowed through Turkey, Jordan, and Northern Lebanon. Turkey under the Justice and Development Party (AKP) emerged as a rival to Saudi Arabia for the leadership of political Sunnism. The AKP, founded in 2001 with Recep Tayyip Erdogan at its head and influenced by the Muslim Brotherhood, had won in the 2002 Turkish elections, initially adopting a 'neo-Ottoman' and 'zero-problems-with-neighbours' foreign policy. It tried to re-establish Turkish influence in the former provinces of the Ottoman Empire and maintain good relations with Iran, Syria, and the

Kurdish Regional Government in Iraq. It also promised to reach out to Alevis, while also trying to bring them closer to Turkish Sunnism.[48] Erdogan, like many other figures associated with Turkish Sunni Islamism, was a disciple of the Naqshbandi-Khalidi order, with its strong doctrinal defence of Sunnism vis-à-vis Shiism and Alevism, and a linking to the more assertive political Sunnism dating back to the Ottoman period (rather than to the more confessionally ambiguous parts of Ottoman history, which, as noted, had been so prominent a feature). By the 2010s then, Turkey's zero-problems-with-neighbours policy, which had involved a rapprochement with Syria, gave way to a policy of supporting Sunni Islamists and attempting regime change in Syria.

Turkey also tried to expand its influence amongst Turkic populations outside of Turkey, some of whom, like in Azerbaijan, were Shii. After the disintegration of the Soviet Union, Sunni and Shii missionaries, often from Turkey or Iran, flocked to Central Asia and the Caucasus, vying for influence amongst an ecumenically minded population that under Soviet rule had been cut off from developments in the rest of the Muslim world. Salafi Sunnis singled out Shia, who themselves were trying to reorganise. Azerbaijan's difficult relationship with Iran, and pan-Turkic ethnic identity that favoured Turkey, meant that post-Soviet Azeri elites saw Turkish Sunni religious networks as less of a threat than Iranian ones. They were thus successful despite much of Azerbaijan's population's nominal Shiism. The confessional ambiguity that Communist rule had fostered gave way to a gradual polarisation.[49]

And the Turkish government engaged in sectarianisation at home especially after the so-called Gezi protests in 2013, which the government portrayed as Alevi-led and then heavily policed Alevi neighbourhoods. That most Alevis and also Alawites near the Syrian border opposed Turkey's backing of Sunni Islamists in Syria, heightened sectarian tensions.[50] Throughout the 2010s, Turkey would become the most significant backer of Sunni Islamists in Syria, and the conduit for international Jihadis, and place of refuge for millions of Syrians. For Turkey and President Erdogan, support for the Syrian rebels became a national priority, and rebel-held areas near the border survived largely due to Turkish support and military coordination.[51]

On the other side of Syria, Jordan acted as conduit for US-backed opposition groups and the site of a major CIA-run and Saudi-funded rebel training programme that began in earnest in 2013, and a place to which many defectors fled. Saudi support was organised by Prince Bandar, head of Saudi intelligence and former ambassador to the US. A frequent visitor to Middle

Eastern and Western capitals, he handed out funds and weapons to Syrian opposition groups. But the US-trained force produced only limited results, and the Saudis increasingly backed other groups.[52] Support also flowed through Lebanon, especially Tripoli. Many Sunnis there had memories of repression by the Syrian regime, and ties to those backing the uprising. Members of the Lebanese parliament, business leaders, and officials affiliated with Hariri, in conjunction with Prince Bandar, organised that supply line (although in another example of how sectarian identity did not have to dictate political alignments, the MP heading that supply line was a Shii).[53] In a reverse process from that of 1975–90, when regional powers had fought out their differences in Lebanon, Lebanese factions now did so in Syria. The influx of over a million Syrian refugees, many of them Sunnis, and the emergence of sectarian actors on the Sunni scene in Syria, led to a further rapprochement between Shii and Christian political forces in Lebanon amidst stronger Sunni–Shia polarisation.[54]

In 2012 and the first half of 2013, the rebels, now fully armed and with international support, made quick headway, and conquered much of the border region with Turkey, Iraq, Israel, and Jordan, and Syria's second-largest city, Aleppo. The very survival of the Assad regime was in doubt. The Saudis and other backers of the opposition had hoped that the United States would send in its own military, or carry out airstrikes against the regime. President Obama said in 2012 that use of chemical weapons would prompt US military intervention. But when the regime used them, Obama did not follow through. Instead, he expanded support for the rebels, and allowed Saudi Arabia to provide guided missiles to the opposition.[55] Obama did not want to repeat the mistakes of the past. He was aware that an intervention in Syria could quickly spiral out of control, and possibly lead to war with Syria's allies Iran and Russia. That was a risk he considered not worth taking, and it allowed the regime and its allies to regroup.

With many Sunnis hoping for the overthrow of Assad, many non-Sunnis worried what would happen to them if he fell. With half the country under opposition control, and the capital itself under siege, the regime called upon its allies. Russia's support was a continuation of Cold War ties (Russia's Mediterranean naval base is in Syria), and its military and diplomatic support proved crucial in ensuring the Syrian regime's survival. Russia established close ties with the Axis of Resistance but when the opportunity arose also worked with the Gulf States and Turkey, and maintained close ties with

Israel. Still, the re-emergence of Russia as a major player symbolised the end of an era of American hegemony after the end of the Cold War.

The second major layer of support for the regime came from Iran and Shii militias. As noted, the Syrian opposition had for years invoked Sayyida Zaynab to decry the allegedly pro-Shii tendencies of the Assad regime. Now it indeed became the main symbol that Shii forces invoked. When Sayyida Zaynab started to be threatened by rebels in 2012, Shia fighters from Syria, Lebanon, Iraq, and beyond formed the Abu al-Fadl al-Abbas brigades, named after a son of Ali and half-brother of Zaynab, Abbas, who was killed in the Battle of Karbala in 680 AD alongside his half-brother Hussain at the hands of the Umayyad Caliph Yazid's army.[56] Sending a brigade named after this heroic Shii figure to Damascus, the former seat of the Umayyad Caliphate, connected current struggles to Islam's foundational period. Many of the Iraqi fighters were members of militias notorious for their role in the Iraqi civil war and in the fight against coalition troops.[57] Several Sunni rebel groups similarly adopted names from Syria's past, including those tied to the Umayyad dynasty or to figures of the twelfth century 'Sunni Revival', such as Nur al-Din Zangi, in Aleppo.[58]

In early April 2013, fearing the fall of Damascus, Hizbullah deployed its troops along the Lebanese border with Syria to secure one of its strongholds, the Bekaa valley, reduce the flow of weapons to Syrian rebel groups, stabilise its own supply lines from Iran, and inside Syria to prevent the fall of the regime. Officially, however, Hizbullah claimed to be defending the Sayyida Zaynab shrine.[59] This intensified Sunni–Shia tensions in Lebanon, where many Sunnis, especially Salafis, already mistrustful of Hizbullah for years, saw this as ultimate betrayal and proof of its sectarian agenda.[60] In response, two Sunni suicide bombers targeted Beirut's Shii-inhabited southern suburbs and the Iranian embassy.[61] Apart from Iraqis and Lebanese, those who flocked to Syria to defend the regime were primarily Afghan, and to a lesser extent, Pakistani Shia. Many Afghan Shia had fled to Iran, where tens of thousands were recruited to fight in Syria (they faced the choice between staying illegally in Iran, risking deportation, or fighting). Many were promised a residence permit and housing in Iran after the end of their deployment (and there were rumours that some were given housing in Syria). After a short training programme, these Afghan fighters were flown to Syria and deployed in Sayyida Zaynab, Damascus, and Aleppo.[62] Named *Fatimiyyun* after Fatima, the daughter of the Prophet, wife of Ali and mother of the subsequent Shii Imams, these fighters linked Afghanistan directly to the conflicts of the Arab world. All fallen foreign Shii fighters were described as 'martyrs in the defense of the holy shrines of Sayyida Zaynab', and their funerals were publicised widely across Iran.[63] The Pakistani Shia went to fight in Syria under the label *Zaynabiyyun*—'defenders of Zaynab'. Trained by Iranian Special Forces, they were driven by a sense that Shii shrines were under attack, and told to believe this was a region-wide struggle between Shii groups on the one hand, and 'Takfiris', 'Wahhabis', terrorists, and Western stooges on the other, linking conflicts in their home countries with Syria.[64]

The architect of this regional alliance was a man who had long remained in the shadows but increasingly became a household name—first in Iran, then beyond: Qassem Soleimani, the commander of the Islamic Revolutionary Guard Corps' (IRGC) Quds Force, tasked with supporting like-minded movements abroad. For Soleimani, who had tirelessly built the connections with pro-Iran militias and political movements, and the Syrian state, the security of Tehran was defended in Syria, and the regime had to survive.[65] Working with foreign Shii fighters ensured that Iranian casualties in Syria (and later in Iraq) remained limited. And those Shia fighters that did die were heralded as following in the footsteps of the hundreds of thousands of Iranians and several thousand foreign Shia who perished on the Iranian side during the Iran–Iraq war.[66]

Sayyida Zaynab was strategically important in more ways than one. The shrine lies between the airport and Damascus' city centre, and by holding on to it—with the help of foreign Shii militias—the Assad regime prevented the rebels from encircling the capital, which might have precipitated the regime's fall. Rebel forces nonetheless remained close to the suburb, however, and would attack Sayyida Zaynab and other Shii shrines over the coming years. In May 2013, rebels destroyed a shrine outside Damascus and exhumed the body of Hujr Ibn Adi, a historical figure revered by Shia.[67] The Shii militias, in turn, participated in operations with the Syrian Army in other areas, where they are accused of taking part in massacres of Sunnis.[68] By putting so much emphasis on Shii symbolism, they reinforced the notion that this was a religious war. Sunni views of Hizbullah, which had been largely positive in the aftermath of the 2006 war with Israel, and of Iran, deteriorated drastically.[69] In response to Hizbullah's deployment, al-Qaradawi, who had advocated Sunni–Shia unity and previously supported Hizbullah, called on all able Muslim men to go fight in Syria against the regime. He called Hizbullah, the 'Party of God', *Hizb al-Shaytan*, the 'Party of the Devil', and said protests in Bahrain were not worthy of support because they were Shia-led.[70] Internationalists from all ideological backgrounds—Shia Jihadis on one side, Sunni Jihadis on the other; Leftists on the side of the Kurds; even Russian mercenaries on the side of the regime—flocked to Syria.

The influx of Shia and Sunni Jihadis reinforced the sectarianisation of the uprising. The Shii foreign fighters were using sectarian imagery and symbolism, claiming for example to defend the shrine of Sayyida Zaynab, and Sunni Islamists in turn became even more anti-Shii. As noted, al-Qaeda had primarily fought the far enemy, i.e. Western powers, and above all the US. After the 2003 invasion of Iraq, however, its offshoots declared war simultaneously on the far and the near enemy, i.e. Western powers and what they saw as heretics within Islam, above all Shia. They fuelled Sunni resentment at Shii elites' monopolisation of the Iraqi state, and a sense that Shia were on the rise. In Sunni provinces of Iraq, a protest movement embracing the language and tactics of the region-wide Arab uprisings, mobilised people, and voiced Sunni grievances, throughout 2013. It invoked Syria and the idea of a regional Sunni struggle (on social media it was even referred to as a 'Sunni Spring'). Protests were repressed, and the uprising in Iraq became increasingly militant.[71] When Syrian regime control waned in the border areas between Syria and Iraq, a cross-border movement claiming to defend Sunnis emerged. From 2013 onwards, that movement, now operating in both Iraq and Syria, started to refer to itself as the Islamic State in Iraq and the Levant (actually the Lands of Greater Syria, *al-Dawla al-Islamiyya fil-ʿIraq wa-l-Sham*), abbreviated ISIS or ISIL. Major Sunni-majority cities fell quickly. On 10 June 2014, ISIS took control of Iraq's second-largest city, Mosul, and soon conquered Tikrit, Saddam Hussein's birthplace, and other areas, including Iraq's main oil refinery, and large areas in Syria. Abu Bakr al-Baghdadi took to the pulpit in Mosul's main mosque on 4 July 2014, and declared himself Caliph of a new-founded Caliphate with Mosul as its capital. Its rapid military success was the result not only of the seriousness of its fighters and the disarray of the Iraqi government forces but also of foreign support, and an alliance with former Baathists and tribesmen. Its take-over of Mosul, for example, was facilitated by an alliance with the Naqshbandi Army headed by al-Duri, the former Baathist leader, who vowed to return dignity to Sunnis.[72]

The movement then renamed itself simply Islamic State (IS).[73] As we've seen Rashid Rida, the early-twentieth-century Salafi-Arab nationalist cleric, stunned by Ataturk 's abolishing of the Ottoman Caliphate in the 1920s, had advocated re-establishing the Caliphate in Mosul, sufficiently far from the main capitals and imperial strongholds to allow the project to succeed. Rida had been prescient. State authority, as well as the reach of regional powers and the US, which still had troops in Iraq, was indeed limited in the frontier zone between Syria and Iraq. Unlike AQ, which had operated through dispersed networks, seldom held territory, and had been based far from the Arab heartlands, IS controlled large swaths of territory in Iraq and Syria where it could implement its ideology, build a state, and organise external operations.[74] IS vowed to kill, convert or expel Muslims of other persuasions and non-Muslim groups, such as Alawites, Shia, Yazidis, and Christians, portraying itself as the Sunni vanguard in an epic struggle with Shiism. It immediately carried out purges and massacres of non-Sunni groups under its control. When it took territory where significant Shii shrines or mosques were located, it blew them up, as happened to a Shii shrine complex in Raqqa in 2015. The shrine for the Companions of Ali in the battle of Siffin had been built just a decade earlier, and had symbolised the Syria–Iran alliance, and the growing visibility of Shiism in Syria, much to the chagrin of locals.[75] IS also killed and enslaved Yazidis and Turkmen Twelver Shia.[76] It even denounced AQ, which had generally avoided the targeting of Shii civilians and mosques, as too lenient on the Shia and Middle Eastern regimes.[77]

IS appropriated Salafi-Wahhabi anti-Shii narratives and took them to their logical, genocidal, conclusion. To legitimise large-scale attacks on Shia civilians, IS used arguments by al-Zarqawi and Saudi clerics, especially bin Jibrin, who argued that Shia masses could be excommunicated. A young Bahraini cleric from a family with ties to Bahrain's ruling family, Turki al-Binali, had studied with bin Jibrin in Saudi Arabia, and adopted his point of view. Al-Binali had travelled across the region in the years before 2014 to recruit and establish support networks. After 2014, he became IS's 'Grand Mufti', authoring its key texts under pseudonyms and providing guidance on religious and legal matters. Al-Binali's hatred of the Shia reflected the intellectual and political milieux of Saudi Arabia and Bahrain, but he applied it in Iraq and Syria.[78] The significant number of Saudis and other Gulf nationals in IS probably played a role in IS's decision to attack Shia in the Gulf. Between 2014 and 2016, IS carried out bombings and shootings in several Shia mosques and mourning houses in Eastern Saudi Arabia and Kuwait. Together with an attack on an Ismaili mosque in Najran, attacks on Saudi security forces, and attacks on Zaydis in Yemen, this was the start of a campaign to bring down the Saudi ruling family and 'cleanse' the Arabian

Peninsula from 'rejectionists'.[79] IS carried out more attacks on Shii targets as far away as Bangladesh.[80]

IS's overall aim was to start a sectarian civil war in the Gulf like in Iraq in 2006/7, pushing Gulf Shia to take up arms against Sunni neighbours and the state. Many Saudi Shia indeed felt let down by the state and feared more attacks.[81] Community leaders and senior clerics established protection committees to protect mosques.[82] But in Kuwait and Saudi Arabia, the attacks did not lead to militancy, as communities were still reeling from the heavy repression meted out against protesters at the start of the Arab Spring. It instead led to soul-searching, and to a public embrace of Shia by the state. Many Sunnis in Saudi Arabia, Qatar, and other Gulf States had been sympathetic to IS, seeing it as a Sunni vanguard against the Assad regime, Iran, and Shiism as a whole. But the attacks in the Gulf States shifted perspectives.[83] Together with its attacks in Europe, such as the ones in Paris, Nice, or Brussels, IS's over-reach led to its downfall. Nearly every government and most major political and military movements in the region, worked together to bring about its demise.

In Iraq itself, after Mosul, IS tried to move south and take over Baghdad. It came close enough to the capital to establish checkpoints and hideouts on its outskirts. The fall of the Iraqi capital, the ancient seat of the Abbasid Caliphate, would have been of incalculable symbolic and strategic value to the movement.[84] IS also wanted to conquer Najaf and Karbala, and destroy their shrines, just as the Wahhabis had done in 1802. Within the span of a few weeks IS had taken control of a third of Iraqi territory, and was expanding in Syria, too. On 12 June 2014, IS carried out a massacre of over 1,000 Shii cadets at Camp Speicher near Tikrit in Northern Iraq (Sunnis were let off unharmed). In response, Grand Ayatollah Ali al-Sistani on 13 June 2014 called on all able men to join the newly established Popular Mobilization Forces (PMF) to fight IS.[85] His fatwa was nationalist, and did not exclusively refer to Shia. However, given that many Iraqi Shia viewed him as their spiritual guide the fatwa had a much wider resonance amongst Shia. Tens of thousands of Iraqi Shia responded to it, as did some Sunnis and Christians.[86] The official discourse of the PMF was inclusive, emphasizing the threat IS posed to all Iraqis. The highest Sunni religious authority in Iraq also issued a fatwa against IS to undermine the propaganda from IS—and some Gulf media channels— that al-Sistani's fatwa was calling for a war against Sunnis.[87]

Despite attempts to not portray the fight against IS as a Shii versus Sunni one, but rather an Iraqi effort to defeat a 'terrorist' insurgency, sectarian discourse accompanied the campaign and the PMF incorporated Shii militias with a history of violence against Sunnis. Many Iraqi Shia fighters in Syria returned home to fight IS, highlighting how interconnected conflicts in the two countries had become (in Syria, they were replaced by Lebanese Hizbullah fighters, and Russians).[88] Many joined out of a sense of religious and nationalist duty and because they wanted to protect Najaf and Karbala.[89] And different militias and fighters had their own ideas of what the fight was about, and what slogans were appropriate. Shii imagery was widespread. Shii militias fighting against IS in Ramadi, for example, dubbed their campaign *Labbaik Ya Hussain* ('At your service, O *Hussain*'), in retaliation for an IS attack on a Shii mosque in Qatif in 2015 on the birthday of Imam Hussain. As noted, Sunnis likewise hold Hussain in high regard, but the sectarian symbolism was not lost on anyone, and after widespread outrage, the name of the campaign was changed to *Labbaik Ya Iraq*.[90] On social media, Shia used terms such as 'Wahhabi', 'Salafi', and 'Daeshi' (the Arabic acronym for IS based on its Arabic name) in a derogatory way to describe Sunni Muslims in general.[91] Speaking at an Ashura festival, the leader of one of the most powerful Shii militias said 'the liberation of Mosul will be a revenge for the killing of Imam Hussain and preparation for a state of divine justice'.[92] This, and videos of atrocities allegedly committed by Shia soldiers, were then picked up on Sunni TV channels and social media accounts to denounce the sectarian nature of the campaign, which prompted senior Saudi clerics to call on the 'People of the Sunna' to support Sunnis in Mosul against the Shia.[93]

It took nearly two years to amass enough manpower on the ground, and international support, to drive IS out of Iraqi towns. In 2016 and 2017, the international coalition to defeat IS, a coalition that was led by the US, fought alongside Iran, the Shii militias, and the PMF, with the latter doing much of the fighting on the ground with Kurdish forces. Sunnis also fought against IS, which was, after all, a divisive actor amongst Sunnis. The heavy reliance on Shii militias in the defeat of IS, however, and the subsequent large-scale destruction of Mosul and the slow reconstruction efforts, did little to alleviate the same Sunni resentment that had led to the rise of IS in the first place. For Iran and Shii militias, defeating IS allowed them to re-establish an overland route connecting Tehran with Damascus and Lebanon.[94]

Much of the struggle between IS and Shii actors (and the anti-IS coalition) was fought out online, where people spread sectarian (and at times anti-sectarian) narratives, graphic videos of massacres or inflammatory speeches.

Given high social media usage in the rich Gulf countries, Gulf-based accounts exerted an outsized influence in Arab-language social media (as had Gulf-funded TV channels a decade earlier). This spread Gulf-specific sectarian attitudes more widely. Prominent Gulf-based Sunni clerics used social media to disseminate anti-Shiism in the context of the wars in Syria, Iraq, and then Yemen. Some even used automated accounts. The more violent these conflicts became, the more divided debates across the Arab world became as well.[95] TV channels, websites and social media accounts across the Shii world, on the other hand, highlighted the threat of IS. The anti-IS campaign led to a stronger Shii public sphere that operated separately from and in competition with a Sunni public sphere. This strengthened transnational ties and a global Shii identity.[96]

Sunni and Shii Jihadi networks further connected the Middle East, Central and South Asia, and the West. In Afghanistan, the local branch of IS targeted Hazara in a way the Taliban never had. IS suicide bombers blew themselves up during a Hazara protest against government neglect in July 2016, killing dozens and wounding hundreds.[97] In early October 2016, IS militants killed dozens more Hazara on the eve of Ashura at a popular shrine in Kabul and northern Balkh province.[98] The Taliban now portrayed themselves as more moderate towards the Shia than their Sunni rivals from IS. The Taliban also reached out to Iran (while simultaneously negotiating with the US for an American troop withdrawal). Once foreign troops started to withdraw, and the Taliban took over the country in the summer of 2021, they were careful not to be seen as too anti-Shii. While there were reports of Taliban violence against Hazara, in fact, they now even had a few Shii members, and allowed and even attended Muharram processions in Kabul just days after their takeover. IS, on the other hand, conducted suicide bombings against Shii targets, in part to undermine the Taliban.[99] In Pakistan, returnees from Syria strengthened Shii militant networks just as Sunni Islamists attacked Shii mosques and processions.[100] This even included attacks on Ismailis, who had seldom been attacked before. As Ismailis were increasingly organising as one global community, Sunni militants also started seeing them as such. In Pakistan and Syria Sunni Islamists justified attacks on Ismailis with their alleged heretic beliefs, and the fact that they maintained relations with the Syrian regime.[101] And just as returning Sunni Jihadis had transformed their societies after the Afghan Jihad in the 1980s, so would Shii Jihadis bring back memories of sectarian violence and contribute to a hardening of sectarian identities at home.[102] In Northern India, occasional outbursts of violence and protests, and intensifying polemics, undermined Sunni–Shia relations in places such as Lucknow, and contributed to a further organisational differentiation.[103] In response, many called for Muslim unity, and organised co-sectarian communal prayers and other initiatives, especially in the face of a more assertive Hindu nationalism that did not differentiate much between Muslim confessions.[104] And when the Hindu nationalist government in India abolished the special administrative status of Kashmir in 2019, Sunni and Shii Muslims across South Asia, and countries such as Iran and Pakistan, came together to denounce that act.[105] In Nigeria, Sunni Jihadi movements like Boko Haram, whose founder had become influenced by Wahhabi Salafism as a student in Saudi Arabia (Boko Haram would later also claim allegiance to IS), took up arms against the state and the Islamic Movement of Nigeria, founded by a convert to Shiism with links to Iran.[106] The Nigerian Army fought against both, and on one occasion, in 2015, killed dozens of Shia, and shot and arrested the leader of the Shii movement, which was banned.[107] In China, some Sunni Uyghurs started to claim that they faced a threat not only from Han Communism but from Shiism as well, and that close Sino–Iranian relations allowed Iran to proselytise in Xinjiang, which in turn led to renewed Saudi proselytisation.[108] In the Balkans, Salafis, who had gained in prominence after support for Sunnis in the 1990s civil war, turned their attention towards the Bektashis.[109]

Finally, Sunni–Shia tensions also rose in the West. At times, a common Muslim link and the sense of being a religious minority could lead to togetherness, and the toning down of difference (symbolised by the use of common spaces, and the permission to pray in mosques of other schools, for example).[110] In the US and the UK, where many Muslims hail from mixed Sunni–Shia countries, an institutional differentiation contributed to new pan-identities—such as between Twelver Shia and Ismailis from South Asia and the Middle East (and amongst Sunnis from different regions).[111] But deteriorating Sunni–Shia relations in their countries of origin exacerbated tensions in the diaspora, especially when Syrians, Iraqis, Afghans, Pakistanis, Bahrainis, and Yemenis arrived in the 2000s and 2010s.[112] That Salafism spread in the diaspora and amongst new converts also meant that anti-Shiism reached new audiences, and was disseminated in European languages.[113]

Meanwhile, in Syria, where the civil war was increasingly connected with events in Iraq, the tables started to turn on the battlefield. Shia fighters were crucial not only in holding Sayyida Zaynab and Damascus but in reconquering Aleppo in late September 2016. A leader of Iraqi militia Kata'ib Hezbollah told his fighters in a village outside of Aleppo: 'We are facing monsters, the grandsons of Yazid and Muawiya, and the grandsons of those who carried out the Karbala massacres – and today they want to repeat them.'[114] Suleimani himself would visit troops on the frontlines. The taking of Aleppo in 2012 had been, as we've seen, a turning point, giving the opposition control over much of Syria's second largest city. But in late 2016, the Syrian army, under Russian air support, and with Shii militias on the frontlines, retook the city. This ended the military prospects of the opposition. Infighting, including between IS and other rebel forces, contributed to this.[115] As the regime re-gained the upper hand, it carried out ethno-sectarian cleansing in central and coastal areas, which Assad termed 'useful Syria'. The regime killed or forced into exile many pro-opposition Syrians, who tended to be Sunni, and in their place settled pro-regime populations, including, allegedly, foreign Shia fighters.[116] With Sunnis killed or driven out, the small Twelver Shia community in Syria became more visible and institutionalised, and its proportion of the population increased.[117] In ideological terms, the regime presented Bashar al-Assad as a heroic saviour of the nation, and emphasised a sort of religious nationalism to give Sunnis a line they could adhere to if they wanted to remain loyal to the regime. The Sunni clerics dependent on state patronage, like the Mufti and the Minister of Awqaf, stayed pro-regime, while others backed the uprisings, though a large group of clerics tried to stay neutral.[118] The opposition, under pressure by regime forces and by IS, which attacked just about every group hostile to it, even its former allies in Jabhat al-Nusra, was increasingly desperate. They started to rely even more heavily on support from Turkey and held on to a small enclave around Idlib near the Turkish border, under de facto protection by the Turkish army.

The Sunni coalition had failed to overthrow the Assad regime, and the Axis of Resistance emerged strengthened from the fight against Sunni militants in Syria and Iraq. In Iraq itself, the PMF emerged as major political actors, with its leaders trying to translate their battlefield victory into electoral (and personal) gains. Ordinary volunteers in the PMF, who may not even have received a salary, felt left out after their sacrifices. This contributed to a general sense of alienation from the political elite in Iraq, one that was to translate into widespread anti-government protests two years later, and led to infighting amongst different Shii actors.[119]

Iraq and Syria had become thoroughly interconnected, and devastated. One other country was to also suffer tremendously due to foreign intervention and the framing of local struggles in sectarian terms. This was Yemen. In March 2011, mainly young Yemenis organised rallies and sit-ins across the country. Established political actors, including former regime figures and Muslim Brothers, quickly capitalised on the movement.[120] With mass protests continuing throughout 2011, the Gulf States, worried about instability, tried to broker a negotiated solution. Their fears were heightened as the young revolutionaries were calling for full-scale democracy, and the Huthis and Southern secessionists were also mobilising.[121] According to a transition plan devised by Saleh's inner circle in coordination with the Gulf States, and then sanctioned by the UN, Saleh was to step down. He and his family, who had enriched themselves, were given immunity from prosecution. And the role of young revolutionaries, Huthis and Southern secessionists, was to remain limited.[122] The transition, limited though it was, failed. With key actors underrepresented, national dialogue and a transitional government were unstable, and competing political forces jockeyed for control amidst the fallouts of the Arab uprisings. In 2013, clashes between the Huthis and Salafis were portrayed as sectarian, drew condemnation from regional Salafi networks and led to the arrival of a number of foreign fighters bent on fighting the Huthis.[123] And in 2014, in a spectacular U-turn, Saleh, sidelined through the transition, made common cause with the Huthis, and facilitated their move into the capital, Sanaa.[124] The Gulf States, especially Saudi Arabia, felt betrayed by Saleh, and feared being encircled by pro-Iran forces.[125] The interim government, headed by President Hadi, who was forced to flee, turned towards the Gulf States for help. In response, in early 2015, the Saudis and their regional and international allies started a military intervention officially to support the internationally recognised transition government. Unofficially, and in the media, it was partly justified in religious terms, with claims that this was part of a Jihad against the 'rejectionist' Huthis and their Iranian backers.[126] The Saudis even argued they had to intervene because the Huthis were seeking to re-establish the Zaydi Imamate.[127] The spokesman of the Saudi-led military coalition stated outright that it could not 'let Yemen be ruled by a minority'.[128]

As we've seen, although sympathetic to the Iranian revolution, the Huthis were a local organisation, with a history, ideology, and sectarian identity distinct from Twelver Shiism. But in the wake of the wars against them, Iran, Arab Shii movements, and some Shii clerics started to see the Huthis as worthy of support, not least for its anti–Saudi and anti–American stance. They started providing media, financial, diplomatic, and limited military support.[129] The Huthi's TV channel, for example, broadcast from Hizbullah-controlled south Beirut. Allegations about military assistance from Hizbullah abounded, as the Huthis were included in the propaganda of the Axis of Resistance. Highlighting the association of the Huthis with Shiism and Iran was a way for pro-Saudi and pro-UAE media to delegitimise them.[130] When the US Navy intercepted Iranian ships delivering arms to the Huthis, this was much publicised.[131]

The anti-Saleh coalition took much of the south of the country, but the Huthi forces remained in control of the Zaydi heartland around Saada and Sanaa, launched attacks inside Saudi territory and pushed back on other fronts. Militarily, the intervention faced difficulties from the start. The Saudi and Emirati armies suffered casualties early on, then largely attacked from the air, and relied on Yemeni soldiers and foreign mercenaries. The two coalition armies that were supposed to do much of the fighting, the Egyptian and Pakistani, refused to send ground troops. The Egyptian army declined to get engaged in a similar quagmire like in the 1960s, when Nasser had sent troops to Yemen and tens of thousands died; Pakistan refused because the intervention was unpopular at home, especially amongst Pakistani Shia because it was portrayed as an anti-Shii intervention (and because of rumours that the Gulf States had asked only for Pakistani Sunni soldiers, which would have had devastating consequences for the cohesion of the Pakistani army).[132] And so local proxies and mercenaries, including from Sudan, did much of the fighting, and the coalition relied on airstrikes and a sea blockade that was devastating for the whole population.

The Yemen war, which the UN has termed the largest humanitarian crisis in the world, pushing millions into hunger,[133] was closely associated with King Salman and with Muhammad bin Salman, Saudi Crown Prince and Defence Minister, who came to power after the death of King Abdullah in January 2015. For Muhammad bin Salman, the intervention in Yemen offered a way to portray himself as countering Iranian 'expansionism'. But the prolonged war instead turned him into a controversial figure internationally, and the Saudi problems in Yemen, and the Huthis' steadfastness, proved a PR victory for Iran and the Axis of Resistance. In January 2016, Saudi Arabia executed Nimr al-Nimr, the Shii cleric leading the uprising in 2011/12, who had been in prison for years. Last-ditch efforts to prevent his execution failed. The execution involved amputation, bleeding to death, and then the displaying of his limb on a stick. The grisly nature of it made al-Nimr a household name and martyr across the Shii public sphere.[134] Pro-Saudi pundits portrayed al-Nimr as a pro-Iranian 'terrorist' to legitimise his execution alongside al-Qaeda militants, who had been jailed for taking part in the Jihadi insurgency from 2003 to 2006 in Saudi Arabia.[135] Their execution was intended as a show of force towards Sunni Jihadis, who had attacked the Kingdom in recent years, and it deepened the rift between Saudi Arabia and militant Salafi-Jihadis. In response, IS called for the execution of Saudi scholars who had approved the sentencing, claiming that they, unlike IS, do not truly follow the example of Ibn Abd al-Wahhab.[136] Despite Saudi Arabia's long-standing anti-Shiism, IS attacked the Saudi state for not following through on Wahhabi demands for the full-scale conversion or expulsion of Shia, and that Saudi Shia are allowed to practise their rituals.[137] The Saudis faced an unlikely charge: that of not being anti-Shii enough.

That nuance of intra-Sunni competition was lost on many in the Shii public sphere, however, just as nuances of disagreements amongst Shii actors were lost on Sunnis (or deliberately glossed over).[138] Al-Nimr's execution sent shockwaves through the regional system, inflaming conflicts between the pro-Saudi and the pro-Iran axis and Shii protesters across the world denounced it.[139] Shii militias in Iraq invoked his name in their fight against IS. But the harshest reaction came from Iran. Iranian protesters set fire to and ransacked the grounds of the Saudi Embassy in Tehran and the Saudi Consulate in Mashhad. Iran denounced the execution, and unofficially renamed the street in front of the Saudi embassy Nimr al-Nimr Street.[140] A stampede during the Hajj in 2015, in which hundreds of Iranian pilgrims had lost their lives, had already worsened Saudi–Iranian relations.[141] The execution of al-Nimr and the storming of the Saudi embassy in Tehran and the attack on the consulate in Mashhad now led to a break in diplomatic relations between Saudi Arabia, Bahrain, and Iran.

Yet while al-Nimr's connection to Iran was invoked to legitimise his execution, his relationship with Iran was complicated. He remained a follower of the Shirazi trend, which by the mid-1980s had fallen out so completely with the Iranian government that most Shirazis had to leave Iran, and the founding leader of the movement and his successor had to live under house arrest in Iran.[142] Over time, Iranian leaders claimed the Shirazis were paid by Western intelligence to sow Sunni–Shia division (while most of the Shirazis' TV channels are based in Iraq and Kuwait, some are based in the UK and the US).[143] Iranian media even blamed the attacks on Saudi diplomatic missions that followed al-Nimr's execution on Shirazis in Iran.[144] And al-Nimr had called for the overthrow of Bashar al-Assad, despite having lived in exile in Damascus. Following his execution, as huge posters of al-Nimr were put up on the streets and squares of Southern Beirut, across Iran, parts of Iraq, and other parts of the Shii world, few remembered that al-Nimr was not, in fact, an Iranian 'proxy', just as the relationship between Sunni states and Sunni Jihadis was more complicated than often assumed. Many brushed over contestations within political Shiism and political Sunnism to fit events into simple categories of 'Sunni' vs 'Shii'.[145] Still, the whole affair led to the most serious Saudi–Iran tensions since the 1980s.

When Saudi Arabia banned Iranian pilgrims from the Hajj in the fall of 2016, Khamenei and Friday prayer leaders across Iran denounced Saudi Arabia.[146] In response, Saudi Arabia's highest-ranking cleric, Grand Mufti Abd al-Aziz Al Shaykh, said that Iranians were 'not Muslims'.[147] The Iranian foreign minister Jawad Zarif, blamed Saudi Arabia and Wahhabism for the Middle East's ills.[148] Iran propagated the notion that IS was the continuation of the early Wahhabi movement and supported by Saudi Arabia (as noted, IS claimed to be the real successor to the Wahhabi movement, but IS attacks in Saudi Arabia undermined the latter idea).[149] The Saudi Foreign Minister, in turn, accused Iran of exporting extremism. Saudi Arabia supported Iranian dissidents, gave them airtime on Gulf-owned media channels and financed their media activities.[150] Saudi Arabia was even said to have bankrolled a state-of-the-art Iranian opposition TV station based in London.[151] Iran blamed several attacks by Sunni movements in Iran on its regional enemies. These included attacks by separatist Islamist movements from the country's Sunni minorities, especially Baluch, which were accompanied with anti-Shii rhetoric that linked them to the regional Sunni–Shia conflict.[152] Iran in turn supported the Bahraini and Saudi Shii opposition in exile. Small Shii militant movements with openly sectarian rhetoric targeted the Sunni-staffed Bahraini security forces.[153] The conflict also played out further afield. In 2020, Denmark charged an Iranian intelligence officer with planning a failed assassination attempt of the exiled leader of an Arab separatist group in Iran, and charged several members of that group with spying for Saudi Arabia.[154] And the US accused Iran of trying to assassinate the Saudi ambassador to the US, Adil al-Jubayr.[155] Iran also continued to proselytise through its embassies and cultural missions, in which it was supported by the Shii shrines in Iraq, who expanded their global reach. This led to some conversions, but heightened long-standing Sunni anxiety about such activities.[156]

The Gulf States also feared that the nuclear agreement with Iran, finalised on 14 July 2015 with the blessing of US President Obama, would allow the US and Iran to reshape the region without them. Gulf leaders criticised President Obama for reaching out to Iran and failing to intervene more decisively in Syria.[157] They were thus overjoyed by the election of Donald Trump in January 2017. Breaking with tradition, President Trump, keen to undo every aspect of his predecessor' legacy, including the nuclear agreement with Iran, took his first foreign trip to Saudi Arabia, where he affirmed the US's alliance with Saudi Arabia and denounced Iran: 'For decades', he announced, 'Iran has fueled the fires of sectarian conflict and terror.' 'Until the Iranian regime is willing to be a partner for peace', he continued, 'all nations of conscience must work together to isolate Iran, deny it funding for terrorism, and pray for the day when the Iranian people have the just and righteous government they deserve'.[158] This was nothing short of calling for regime change. The heads of state gathered by the Saudis for Trump's benefit were all Sunnis, their presence intended to reaffirm Saudi Arabia as leader of the Sunni world.[159] Shii-led countries in the region such as Iran, Iraq, and Syria were not invited. When the Qatari News Agency carried a story in which the Emir criticised the summit for this reason, saying that Iran was a major Islamic country that should not be excluded, he was attacked in Gulf media. Just hours later, the statement was retracted and blamed on hackers and 'fake news'. Nonetheless, the UAE and Saudi Arabia treated the announcements as real, and condemned Qatar.[160] The row quickly escalated, as Saudi Arabia demanded Qatar expel Muslim Brotherhood leaders and cut ties with Iran.

The rift between the two major alliances of political Sunnism led the Qatar–Turkey axis of political Sunnism to temporarily ally with Iran. After Saudi Arabia, the UAE, and Bahrain closed their airspace to Qatari aircraft, they had no other option but to fly via Iranian airspace. Similarly, when Saudi Arabia closed its border to Qatar, food imports had to come in by sea, with Iran the nearest supplier, and Turkey another major one.[161] The Iranians were pleased to see this Sunni infighting.[162] Qatar's ties with Iran and Turkey improved.[163] Some argued that the crisis started because Qatar had paid a large ransom for the release of members of its ruling family kidnapped in Iraq to an Iraqi Shii militia, and that the deal involved a population swap in Syria between Sunni and Shia villages. Critics of Qatar portrayed this as Qatari funding for Iraqi Shii militias.[164] This was a stretch. Qatar had funded anti-Shii publications and movements for decades. Yet, despite being doctrinally Wahhabi and thus anti-Shii, Qatar had long found a modus vivendi with Shiism and Iran (Qatar's small Shii community is well-integrated).[165]

The war of words between Saudi Arabia and Iran escalated further. Muhammad bin Salman announced that they were not 'not waiting until there becomes a battle in Saudi Arabia, so we will work so that it becomes a battle for them in Iran'.[166] These threats came a day before the first attack claimed by IS in Iran, when five attackers, four of whom were Sunni Kurds from Iran, attacked the Parliament and the shrine of Imam Khomeini, core symbols of the Islamic Republic. In its first Persian-language video in March 2017, IS vowed to 'conquer Iran and restore it to the Sunni Muslim nation as it was before'.[167] Iran, now under direct attack, dug in its heels, and blamed Saudi Arabia.[168]

Trump's visit gave Saudi Arabia cover for crushing the remnants of a Shii uprising that had started in 2011 in Awamiya, al-Nimr's hometown, and had become militarised. Saudi soldiers, invoking anti-Shii language, moved into the town, destroyed much of it, and killed dozens.[169] Similarly, a Bahraini court issued a sentence in a long-delayed trial against the most prominent Shii cleric on the island, and spiritual leader of the largest opposition party. As Trump left the Arabian Peninsula for Israel, troops moved into the cleric's village and attacked the crowds that had gathered around his house to protect him, killing five. He was eventually expelled and moved to Iran.[170]

Trump backed the Saudis on Yemen, too, even if things there did not work out as planned. In December 2017, Saleh attempted another U-turn, and called upon his followers to rebel against the Huthis to bring Yemen back in to the Arab and Gulf orbit and expel Iranian influence. This was immediately supported by the UAE–Saudi coalition with the Emirati Foreign Minister tweeting that the uprising was part of an effort to protect the Arabian Peninsula from Iran.[171] Gulf media had long called them 'Iranian Huthi militias', while emphasising the Arabness of the coalition, in another attempt at de-Arabising Arab Shia (which in this case was particularly absurd, as the Huthis and their supporters claim descent from the ancient Arab tribes of the Arabian Peninsula, and the Prophet Muhammad).[172] Saleh forces took large areas of Sanaa on 2 December, aided by coalition airstrikes against Huthi positions. The next day, however, the Huthis made gains in Sanaa, took over strategic locations of pro-Saleh forces, and found and killed Saleh himself.[173] When Huthi soldiers paraded Saleh's body on the back of a pick-up truck to shouts of 'Praise be to God!' and 'Hussain has been avenged!', here referring to Hussain al-Huthi, the group's founder that as noted government forces had killed in 2004, their enemies saw this as a sign of sectarian motivations, reminiscent of the slogans shouted during the hanging of Saddam Hussein, Saleh's former ally. Things were more complicated, however, as Saleh, too, was a Zaydi from the North. Nonetheless, to their detractors it was yet more evidence linking the Huthis to the 'Shia Crescent'.[174] The Huthis became the dominant power in North Yemen, and retained control despite further coalition offensives. As few countries were willing to deal with them, relations with Iran became more important.

The Trump presidency also strengthened ties between some Gulf States and Israel. The two sides had cooperated secretly for years, especially against Iran. As a veteran Israeli Diplomat put it in 2012, 'Israeli interests appear to be aligned with the Sunnis in this struggle.'[175] Israeli academics published widely about the alleged hostility between Iran and Sunni Arabs. Iran's support for Sunni Palestinian organisations belied these simplistic notions, even if the fallout from the Syrian conflict caused a temporary rupture. Hamas moved its headquarters from Damascus to Doha in the mid-2010s after its Sunni backers pressured Hamas to disassociate itself from a regime that was killing Syrian (and Palestinian) Sunnis. By the late 2010s, however, Hamas re-established ties with the Axis of Resistance because of the continuing isolation of Gaza and the rapprochement between some Gulf States and Israel.[176] And the anti-Iran security alliance between Israel and the Gulf States was made public in 2020, and led to formal recognition of Israel by Bahrain, the UAE and Oman. For Bahrain, the location of the conference for the Abraham Accords, this was a way to rehabilitate its image after its crackdown on Shii dissent.[177]

In 2019, protesters took to the streets in Iraq, Lebanon, Sudan, and Algeria, in what some called the second wave of the Arab Spring. In Iraq and Lebanon, the protests were directed against a sectarian political system, and the corruption and disfunction of sectarian elites (with the most powerful ones being Shii parties aligned to Iran).[178] Protesters came from all walks of life and all religious groups. Influential Lebanese Shia had long criticised Hizbullah's support for the Assad regime, and called for a disassociation from the war. One of them, stated that 'Sayyida Zaynab does not want bloodshed in the name of defending her shrine, but rather unity and shunning sedition.'[179] In Iraq, dissatisfaction with the influence of Iran, and the policies of pro-Iranian politicians and militias was likewise on the rise, especially after the campaign against IS.[180] Even in Iran, reformists criticised Iran's support

for the Assad regime and argued that it increased Sunni-Shia tensions.[181]
But criticising the Shii political parties so central to the Axis of Resistance
could be dangerous. In Iraq, repression was especially fierce. Security forces
and masked gunmen not only shot at protesters indiscriminately, they also
assassinated protest leaders, critical journalists, and activists, leading to
hundreds of casualties. In Lebanon, Luqman Slim, a prominent Shii critic
of Hizbullah, who lived in Hizbullah-controlled territory, was likewise
assassinated.[182]

As Iran and its allies sought to extend their control over Shii communities,
for some the Axis of Resistance became one of repression. That intensified
as Saudi Arabia tried to establish relations with Arab Shia critical of Iran.
Saudi Arabia re-engaged with Iraq to check Iranian influence and invited
Iraqi Shii leaders—even Muqtada al-Sadr, and reached out to senior clerics
in Najaf. For the leaders of the rival axes could embrace players of the relative
other sect if it served their interests. By the end of the decade, under the
leadership of Muhammad bin Salman, the Saudis toned down their anti-
Shii religious rhetoric, and even empowered some Shia at home as part of a
wider shift away from political Islam, though not their anti–Iran attitude.
Much political contestation took place within Sunnism and Shiism.[183]

The US invasions of Afghanistan and Iraq had set in motion processes
that were exacerbated during the Arab Spring, as regimes and identity
entrepreneurs found in the sectarianisation tool book a way to maintain
power and further their interests. The 2010s were a decade of high hopes
and deep disappointments. Even if by the end of the decade, the Sunni–Shia
fault-line had ceased to be the dominant one in Iraq and Lebanon, as protesters denounced sectarian elites, it was especially tragic that a decade that
started with anti-sectarian slogans saw such shocking violence and polarisation. And foreign intervention could always inflame things again.

On 3 January 2020, the United States assassinated Iranian general Qassem
Soleimani, commander of the Revolutionary Guards' Quds Force and the
architect of the Axis of Resistance, and Abu Mahdi al-Muhandis, the leader
of an Iraqi militia and deputy commander of the PMF, both key figures in
the suppression of Iraqi protests, at Baghdad airport.[184] The Trump administration argued this was a cumulative retaliation for alleged attacks by Iran
or pro-Iranian Shii militias in Iraq on the Saudi oil industry, and on military
bases used by American forces in Iraq, and the near-breach of the US embassy.
This shook the region. In Iraq, it temporarily united competing political forces
against the US, and undermined anti-government protests.[185] In a display of

Iraqi–Iranian solidarity replete with Shii symbolism, mourners carried the bodies of both men in coffins around the shrines of the Imams in Iraq and Iran. The attacks empowered hardliners in Iran (Ebrahim Raisi, a conservative cleric, was elected President in 2021) and the Shii public sphere was up in arms. In the end it didn't lead to all-out war but US–Iran relations hit rock bottom.

In 2020, a novel virus spread rapidly around the region. Some accused visitors to Shii shrines in Iraq and Iran of being the region's first 'super-spreaders'. In the Gulf, Shii pilgrims to these sites had to report to a new hotline, and were isolated en masse.[186] Even something as non-discriminatory as a respiratory virus had become sectarianized. It was a sad end to a decade that had started with such optimism.

1. Illustration from the Ta'rikh-i Alfi manuscript depicting the historical destruction of the Tomb of Hussain at Karbala on the orders of Caliph al-Mutawakkil, India, c. 1590–1595.
Source: British Museum.

2. Scholars in the Library of the 'House of Wisdom' in Baghdad, from *Maqamat al-Hariri* by Yahya al-Wasiti, Baghdad, 1237.

Source: French National Library.

3. Hulagu Khan Destroys the Fort at Alamut, from *Chinghiz-nama* manuscript by Basawan, 1596.

Source: Virginia Museum of Fine Arts.

4. Conquest of Baghdad by the Mongols 1258, from *Jami' al-tawarikh* by Rashid Al-Din Hamadani, Tabriz, first quarter of fourteenth century.

Source: Staatsbibliothek zu Berlin.

5. Conversion of Ghazan to Islam, from *Jami' al-tawarikh* by Rashid Al-Din Hamadani, Tabriz, first quarter of fourteenth century.

Source: Le Royaume Arménien de Cilicie by Claude Mutafian.

6. The declaration of Shiism as the state religion of Iran by Shah Ismail—Safavid dynasty, by unknown artist, Safavid Era.

Source: *Safavid Iran: Rebirth of a Persian Empire* by Andrew Newman.

7. Portrait of Shah Ismail I of Persia (1487–1524), by Cristofano dell'Altissimo, sixteenth century.

Source: Uffizi Gallery.

8. Battle of Chaldiran, by Agha (Mohammed) Sadeq, Isfahan, c. 1801.

Source: Chehel Sotoun palace, photograph by Stefan Auth.

9. Portrait of Ottoman Sultan Suleiman I the Magnificent, by unknown Venetian artist (possibly, Tiziano Vecellio), Venice, c. 1530s.
Source: Kunsthistorisches Museum Vienna.

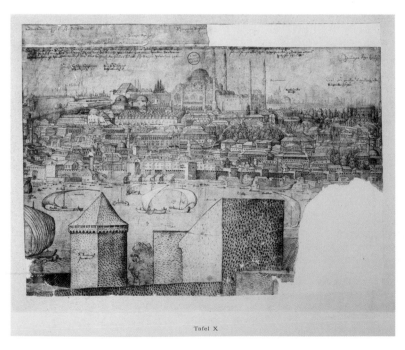

10. Part of the panoramic view of Istanbul: Kasimpasa shipyard is visible on the right, by Melchior Lorck, Istanbul, 1559.
Source: The Gennadius Library—The American School of Classical Studies at Athens.

11. Suleimaniye Mosque, by Bruno Peroussse, Istanbul.
Source: Alamy.

12. Jannat al-Baqia before demolition, by unknown photographer, Medina,
c. 1910s.
Source: Al-Nabi Museum.

13. Lucknow—Bara Imambara, by unknown photographer, Lucknow, c. 1920.
Source: Mary Evans / Grenville Collins Postcard Collection.

14. Imambara, Fort of Rampur, by unknown photographer, Uttar Pradesh, c. 1911.
Source: The British Library, Oriental and India Office Collection.

15. Darul Uloom Deoband, by Jonathan O'Rourke, Uttar Pradesh, 2009.
Source: Wikimedia Commons.

16. Postcard of entrance to Najaf shrine with clerics and officials, by Eldorado, Baghdad, c. 1920–30.

Source: The British Museum.

17. View of the mosque of Imam Hussain, from *Sketches between Persian Gulf and Black Sea* by Robert H. Clive, Karbala, 1852.
Source: The British Museum.

18. Dawlat Hall, by Kamal-ol-molk, Tehran, 1892.
Source: Wikimedia Commons.

19. Faisal party at Versailles Conference. Left to right: Rustum Haidar, Nuri as-Said, Prince Faisal (front), Captain Pisani (rear), T. E. Lawrence, Faisal's slave (name unknown), Captain Hassan Khadri, by an unknown photographer, Versailles, 1919.
Source: Wikimedia Commons.

20. Graffiti Wall with Ayatollah Khomeini and Ali Shariati, by unknown photographer, 1981, Iran, University of Chicago Middle Eastern Posters Collection.

21. Every Day is Ashura and Every Soil is Karbala, by an unknown artist, c. 1981.
Source: University of Chicago Middle Eastern Posters Collection.

22. Stamp issued by the Islamic Republic of Iran commemorating the uprising in Iraq and its crackdown in 1991, 'The Catastrophe of Iraq Baʿthi Regime Invasion of the Holy Shrines', by Islamic Republic of Iran, c. 1991.
Source: Shutterstock.

Conclusion
Every Place is Karbala

As *The Caliph and the Imam* has shown, Sunnism and Shiism have a long and complex history. Periods of convergence could give way to intense polarisation. As I have argued throughout, seeing Sunnism and Shiism as hermetically sealed binaries perpetually at odds with each other is wrong. This is true in religious terms as much as in social and political ones. The further back one goes in time, the more the definitions of what was Sunni and what was Shii become hazy and during the beginnings of Islam these categories did not exist in the way we understand them now. It took centuries before these terms became the self-description of distinct groups with a cohesive identity and they make sense only in juxtaposition to each other and to strands that would fall outside of them. It was, for example, initially far from clear that Sunnism would become Islam's majority trend, or 'Sunnism' and 'Shiism' its main branches. They only developed gradually, as other branches and movements were integrated into the two consensuses, were marginalised, or died out. Eventually, Shiism was left as Sunnism's only major challenger and the one against which Sunnism came to define itself. And although it was a minority contender, it also claimed leadership of Islam. It is that closeness in origin and long and intimate relationship and competition over leadership and meaning of Islam, and over key sites, that explains the emotionality that often accompanied relations between Sunnis and Shia.

The split originated with a political question, of whether the *Caliph* or the *Imam* should lead Muslims after the Prophet Muhammad's death. On a basic level, Shia thought that the Imams not only were related to the Prophet by blood but also were the Prophet's legitimate and chosen successors, who had special charisma and knowledge. Their commandments were law. Shia saw the Family of the Prophet as akin to Islam's ruling family, as stripped of their rightful role, and themselves as the chosen ones amongst Muslims. Sunnis instead thought that the Caliphs were the Prophet's legitimate successors and that his Companions transmitted his message most authoritatively. The Caliphs then side-lined the Imams for fear they could constitute a political challenge.

This political disagreement was soon accompanied by social, spiritual, and legal differences. Clerics wrote down doctrinal and historical positions that in principle became hard to reconcile (even if they were often over-looked in lived reality). Their entangled history, and the fact that in many times and places the line between the two was blurred, and that there were some who wanted to unite the two, problematises notions of perpetual strife. Many defied these categories on a social level and on the level of popular religiosity—Sufis, for example, and ordinary Muslims, who did not spend their time penning or reading polemics or jurisprudential texts, and who instead held the Family of the Prophet in high regard. As noted, Karbala and other sites associated with them were not only anchors of competing memory cultures but also spaces of coexistence and a shared religious heritage.

Still, the Sunni–Shia split is Islam's foundational conflict, and one that has been exceptionally powerful emotionally, stimulating intellectually, and explosive politically. As I have shown throughout, that paradox, the tension between Islamic unity and ambiguity, and particularity and polarisation, can only be explained through a global approach that incorporates long time-frames. Earlier periods shaped later ones and Sunnism and Shiism consti-tuted each other across a vast geographical space. Facing repression in one region, adherents of one branch could migrate to a different region, where rulers were more supportive, and re-emerge with a vengeance at a later stage.

Relations became most contentious when doctrinal debates were coupled with socio-economic changes and political rivalries, and when tied to spe-cific sites of memory. Muslims united politically across confessional lines, especially when threatened by outside powers, and could downplay doctri-nal divisions. But these doctrinal and historical disagreements were never fully overcome, and hence easy to rekindle.

Muslim rulers of the early and middle periods often embraced one side or the other with vigour. Sunni and Shii clerics tried to sway rulers by penning polemics and works of political theory. In general, however, rulers did not wage a prolonged campaign against the relative other branch, or enforced mass conversion, or legitimised inter-state war with reference to sectarian identity. The lives of many Muslims were confessionally ambiguous, and clerics struggled to have their normative worldview widely accepted.

As I've shown, a shift occurred around 1500, symbolised by the Safavids' conversion of much of Iran's population to Shiism, and the rise of the Ottomans and Indian Muslim and Central Asian dynasties. A period in which rulers were reluctant to police the beliefs of their populations gave way to an age of confessionalisation, when sectarian identity became more relevant in the everyday, and states expended more resources to shape and investigate their subjects' beliefs. Sufi orders like the Safavids adopted a more sect-centric identity, and turned Shiism into the national religion of Iran and Iran into the centre of the Shii worlds. Challenged by the Safavids and European powers that likewise increasingly stylised themselves as Protestants or Catholics, the Ottomans, in turn, claimed to be the new Sunni Caliphs. Their rivalry sectarianised frontier zones and all sides invoked sectarian identity in state-building and foreign affairs. And yet even their policies were more nuanced than is commonly believed. Once they made peace, as they repeatedly did, doctrinal concerns could be disregarded. Neither side wholeheartedly suppressed the relative other branch of Islam in its domains. The Ottomans never formally recognised Shiism but ruled over large Shii populations, and patronised Sufi orders with Shii leanings, and shrines under their control, such as in Iraq.

And though many Sunnis in Safavid Iran converted or had to flee, others could retain their faith, and attain high office. The Safavids even helped the Sunni Mughals to ascend to power in North India. Faced with a largely non-Muslim population, Muslims on the Indian subcontinent often disregarded sectarian divisions. Connections between the Middle East, Central Asia, and the Indian subcontinent intensified just as sectarian identity became tied closer to specific territories (and problematised in frontier regions) and was used to delineate realms. Some Indian Muslim dynasties, and Mughal successor states, embraced Shiism to differentiate themselves from the Mughals. Still, despite all their invocation of sectarian identity, lived reality under early modern Muslim Empires was still relatively tolerant and ambiguous outside of core areas and beyond sectarianised crises.

From the eighteenth century onwards, however, this would change. Empire and Muslim reactions to it, and the emergence of the modern state, transformed the meaning of religious identity forever. As European overseas trading companies expanded their grip over the economies of Muslim-inhabited territories, they also expanded political influence and control.

To counter the waning authority of Muslim rulers and resist European Empires, some advocated Islamic unity. Others looked to the early period of Islam for inspiration. This rekindled divisive issues and undermined the modus vivendi that had been found under the multi-confessional Muslim Empires. Sunni Revivalists singled out the Shia with their opposing view of the early period as objects of their puritan zeal. The Wahhabis' attacks on Shiism's core sites of memory, Najaf and Karbala, intensified a Shii revival that was already under way. These processes internal to Islam were intensified by and interacted with wider structural changes such as the print revolution and more intrusive forms of imperial rule, and faster connections and communications across the Islamic world and with imperial capitals.

The modern state, which in the Islamic world often came in the form of the colonial state, would enact sweeping transformations from the nineteenth century onwards. It reshaped the meaning of sectarian identity, both in territories directly ruled by a colonial power, like on the Indian subcontinent, and where Muslim rulers retained control. The British in India, for example, created separate written legal codes for Sunnis and Shia and sectarian identity was reinforced in interactions with the state. European Orientalists recognised and imposed boundaries between Sunnism and Shiism based on the translations and editions of old doctrinal and legal texts that bore little resemblance to lived reality. They also based much of their understanding of Shiism on Sunni heresiography. Communal identity entrepreneurs furthered that sectarian vision to claim leadership of 'their' 'community'. And Sunni Revivalists, and a reinvigorated Shii movement, also policed doctrinal boundaries between the two branches more strongly and disseminated doctrinal and polemical texts. Printing facilitated Muslim reformism and unity, while also reinforcing divisions, as long-forgotten polemics became widely available, sometimes edited jointly by Orientalists and Muslim scholars, and divisive events in the Middle East became topics splitting the global Islamic public sphere that had just been constituting itself. Taken together, these processes strengthened Sunnism and Shiism as mutually exclusive categories of belonging. Divisions were intensified when European Empires intervened in favour of certain ethno-religious groups, and when the British and French invoked a sectarian vision to dismantle the Ottoman Empire after World War I and establish Iraq, Syria, and Lebanon.

Reacting against that colonial past, with its strong invocation of sectarian difference, Nationalism and Leftist ideologies were outspokenly anti-sectarian. Yet, especially in frontier zones, which became hard borders, those who did not conform to nationalist ideals were turned into 'minorities'. Their fear was that they would become second-class citizens. Who was an Arab, a Turk, an Iranian, an Afghan or an Indian Muslim, and what role, if any, did religion play in that identity? Which periods should constitute the 'golden age' to which these nationalisms should relate? Answers to these questions could shift over time but rekindled debates about sectarian identity.

Post-colonial states became often tied to a specific sectarian identity. Some single-party regimes officially embraced Arab nationalism but instrumentalised sectarian loyalties and fears of minority groups, all the while sectarian categories became a taboo. Other Arab nationalisms became associated with the aspirations of Arab Sunnis. Leftist movements promised to overcome divisions yet were often more successful in recruiting amongst non-dominant groups (with a remarkable success amongst Shia, where Shii Leftists evoked Hussain's revolt against injustice as an example). When Leftists were repressed, the repression disproportionately targeted outgroups. This led to polarities: the (mis-) perception that the modern state was 'owned' by certain ethno-sectarian groups while others were rebelling against it, which was exacerbated when religion overlapped with class, regional, urban-rural, tribal, neighbourhood, or other identities.

Still, sectarian identity was less explicitly invoked, and lost in social relevance, especially in the rapidly expanding cities, where people from different backgrounds went to school, studied, worked, traded, and mobilised together, and, occasionally, intermarried. And it did not play a major role in inter-state relations (in the 1950s and 1960s, for example, al-Azhar hosted attempts to unite Sunnism and Shiism with the blessing of Nasser and the Shah). When the Shah embraced Iranian nationalism and turned Iran into a major regional power, it raised suspicions amongst Iran's Sunni neighbours. However, these were expressed in nationalist rather than in sectarian terms.

The Iranian Revolution of 1979 then added sectarian overtones to fears of Iranian power, and linked Sunni–Shia to international relations. '*Every place is Karbala*', went one of the slogans of the 1979 revolution that sought to inspire Iranians to revolt against injustice just as Hussain did, and that was then invoked to export the revolution. Hussain was of course revered by Sunnis and Shia alike. But he was clearly more important for Shia, and while the Iranian revolution was welcomed by many Sunnis at the time, not least by Sunni Islamists, and Palestinians, its Shii symbolism was impossible to ignore. That Shia established the first modern clergy-led Islamic state, a long-term aspiration of Sunni Islamists, inspired the latter, and upset Sunni autocrats and puritans. Revolutionary Iran challenged Sunni autocrats as leaders of the Islamic world, and by supporting Palestinians, won popular good will amongst Arab Sunnis, even if it made Sunni Arab elites even more wary of Iran.

Because the revolution politicised Shia (and some Sunnis) in Sunni-ruled states, those states fought against Iran and pushed Sunni Islamists to take anti-Shii positions and funded the publication and translation of old anti-Shii polemics, often from the Hanbali–Wahhabi tradition. The regional system became polarised between pro- and anti-Iran axes. Some Sunnis allied with Iran, and some Shia suspected Iran's intentions but generally, Iran's revolution and the reaction to it deepened the Sunni–Shia divide in unprecedented ways. Just as Iran used oil and gas revenues to sponsor activist Twelver Shiism around the world, so did Saudi Arabia and smaller Gulf States like Qatar, with their even larger revenues, sponsor Sunni Islamism, often in its Salafi–Wahhabi variant, to undermine Shiism. The revolution's anti-Americanism, which soon became a two-way street, exacerbated inter-state tensions not least because most American allies in the region were Sunni. This tied Sunni–Shia relations to inter-state rivalries in ways not seen since the Ottoman–Safavid rivalry.

The American-led interventions following 9/11 exacerbated these tensions. The interventions in Afghanistan and Iraq deposed Sunni rulers, sworn enemies of Iran, and turned ethno-sectarian divisions into the basis of politics. Fights over sites of memory rekindled adversarial communal memories. Iran backed the Shii Islamists the US had empowered in Iraq, while Arab Sunnis and their regional allies largely boycotted them. This led to Sunni marginalisation, civil war, and the expansion of Iranian influence.

Syria was about to witness similar dynamics. The commemorations of Karbala that I had experienced in Damascus in the 2000s, for example, were increasingly decried by the Syrian opposition and their backers in the Gulf States and the West. It made Sunni Syrians feel that the state was teaming up with Iran and Shii movements.[1] Even if that alliance was largely political and included Sunni forces, these feelings were real, and contributed to polarisation. But simplistic explanations were especially wrong when it came to Syria's horrific war, which many started to falsely describe as a war of religion rooted in 'conflicts that date back millennia'.[2] Instead, the war was the result of the activation of communal memory in the context of civil war, regional polarisation, foreign intervention and the institutionalisation of sectarian identity in the modern state. It became so explosive because a regime had long used sectarian loyalties to strengthen its grip on society, and because the opposition, and its backers, in the region and beyond, instrumentalised the grievances of Arab Sunnis by fostering sectarian narratives, and because facing military defeat, the regime asked its Shii allies (and, not to forget, its Russian ones), for help. Amidst the fallouts of the wars in Iraq and Syria, and a sense of Sunni victimhood, and a century after its abolition by (Sunni) Turkish nationalists, Sunni Jihadis rekindled the idea of the Caliphate. Its support amongst Sunnis in the region rested not least on its claim to finally counter what many perceived as Shii-led regimes in Syria, Iraq, and Iran. In some of the worst episodes of sectarian polarisation ever, Sunnis joined IS to fight against Shia, and Iraqi Shia took up arms in a counter-Jihad against IS following a fatwa by Shiism's most revered cleric.

The post-1979 polarisation was thus driven by inter-state rivalry and was exacerbated through civil wars near the original sites of memory of Sunnism and Shiism and through foreign intervention on the side of co-religionists. It provided a language of politics and legitimisation which, though most potent near the contested sites of memory, resonated far and beyond in an increasingly sectarianised global Muslim public sphere, affecting even Muslims that knew little of the difference between Sunnism and Shiism, or where confessional ambiguity was the norm.[3] Countries in Southeast Asia, and Africa, where Shiism was almost non-existent before a series of conversions inspired by the Iranian revolution, underwent sectarian polarisation. Shii converts were often outspoken, and Sunnis here adopted even stronger anti-Shii views than in countries where despite sporadic conflict there was a history of coexistence.[4] In migratory contexts and amongst converts in the West, sectarian attitudes likewise hardened.

The Sunni–Shia divide became globalised just as it was being invoked to fight over the very places where it originated. The degree of violence was so shocking that religious and political leaders tried to foster reconciliation. The Karbala conference was one such example (even if apart from Islamic unity it had also other political agendas, such as solidifying the shrines' position in Iraqi and regional politics, marginalising competing Shii forces, and highlighting that the religious taxes the shrines receive are spent on something useful). But the polarisation of preceding decades was hard to undo. As anti-government protesters in Iraq and Lebanon after 2019 were to find out, once sectarian identity was entrenched in the institutions of the modern state, and tied to international alliances, it was hard to 'desectarianise'.

As I've tried to show throughout, Sunnism and Shiism shaped each other across time and space. While the two sides were not always at each other's throats, the divide was not invented out of thin air either—not in 1501, 1918, 1979, or 2003. Now, as before, it galvanised people's emotions most when doctrinal debates were related to socio-economic struggles, political rivalries and fights over contested sites of memory. That most Muslims lament Hussain's death at Karbala does not gloss over the fact that Islam's main divide has been hard to overcome and easy to invoke.

Endnotes

PROLOGUE

1. Google Books Ngram Viewer for terms 'Sunni' and 'Shii' since 1800. https://books.google.com/ngrams/graph?content=Sunni&year_start=1800&year_end=2000&corpus=15&smoothing=3&share=&direct_url=t1%3B%2CSunni%3B%2Cco.

2. Sahar Bazzaz, 'The Discursive Mapping of Sectarianism in Iraq: The "Sunni Triangle" in the Pages of the New York Times', in: Sahar Bazzaz, Yota Batsaki, and Dimiter Angelov (eds), *Imperial Geographies in Byzantine and Ottoman Space* (Washington, DC: Center for Hellenic Studies, 2013), 245–61.

3. Reidar Visser, 'The Western Imposition of Sectarianism on Iraqi Politics', *Arab Studies Journal* 15/6, 2/1 (2007/8), 83–99; Visser, 'The Sectarian Master Narrative in Iraqi Historiography: New Challenges since 2003', in: Jordi Tejel, Peter Sluglett, Riccardo Bocco, and Hamit Bozarslan (eds), *Writing the Modern History of Iraq: Historiographical and Political Challenges* (Hackensack: World Scientific, 2012), 47–59; Tareq Y. Ismael and Jacqueline S. Ismael, 'Entrenching Sectarianism: How Chilcot Sees Iraq', *International Journal of Contemporary Iraqi Studies* 11, 1–2 (2017), 23–46. Sectarianism became a term that described complex processes, events, and interactions in dozens of countries, simplifying violence, political conflict, and doctrinal polemics that could have been more accurately described differently. Elizabeth Shakman Hurd, 'Politics of Sectarianism: Rethinking Religion and Politics in the Middle East', *Middle East Law and Governance* 7 (2015), 61–75. Some started to speak of a 'sectarian substructure that runs beneath Middle East politics', which could explain much of what was happening. Nasr, *The Shia Revival*, 26. See also Lisa Blaydes, *State of Repression: Iraq under Saddam Hussein* (Princeton: Princeton University Press, 2018), 313–23.

4. Valerie J. Hoffman, 'Devotion to the Prophet and His Family in Egyptian Sufism', *International Journal of Middle East Studies* 24, 4 (1992), 615–37; Anna Madoeuf, 'Mulids of Cairo: Sufi Guilds, Popular Celebrations, and the "Roller-Coaster Landscape" of the Resignified City', in: Diane Singerman and Paul Amar (eds), *Cairo Cosmopolitan: Politics, Culture, and Urban Space in the New Globalized Middle East* (Cairo: American University in Cairo Press, 2006), 465–87; Salwa Samir, 'Egypt Celebrates Prophet's Birthday with Sufi Music Stars', *al-Monitor*, 19 October 2021; Paula Sanders, *Ritual, Politics, and the City in Fatimid Cairo* (Albany: SUNY Press, 1994); Samuli Schielke, 'Policing Ambiguity: Muslim Saints-Day

Festivals and the Moral Geography of Public Space in Egypt', *American Ethnologist* 35, 4 (2008), 539—52.

5. Personal observations, Albania, 2019. See also Nathalie Clayer, 'The Pilgrimage to Mount Tomor in Albania: A Changing Sacred Place in a Changing Society', in: Tsypylma Darieva, Thede Kahl, and Svetoslava Toncheva (eds), *Sakralität und Mobilität im Kaukasus und in Südosteuropa* (Vienna: Verlag der Österreichischen Akademie der Wissenschaften, 2017), 125—42. For Abbas, see J. Calmard, "ABBĀS B. 'ALĪ B. ABŪ ṬĀLEB', *EIr*.

6. See, for example, Matthew Pierce, *Twelve Infallible Men: The Imams and the Making of Shi'ism* (Cambridge, MA: Harvard University Press, 2016). This has long preoccupied sociologists and historians. The French sociologist Maurice Halbwachs argued in 1941 that cultural and religious groups possess a 'collect-ive memory' linked to specific sites and that those who visit them activate that historic memory. Halbwachs' last and most influential book, containing his more theoretical writings on collective memory, remained fragmentary because of his death in the Buchenwald concentration camp in 1945. The 1941 study has not been translated into English (although a German translation was published in the 2000s) and is relatively little-known outside of Francophone academia. See Maurice Halbwachs, *On Collective Memory* (Chicago: University of Chicago Press, 1992), and Halbwachs, *La topographie légendaire des Évangiles en Terre Sainte: Étude de memoire collective* (Paris: Presses Universitaires de France, 1941). For an introduction to his work, see Dietmar J. Wetzel, *Maurice Halbwachs* (Konstanz: UVK, 2009). One such battle ground is Palestine as the birthplace of the Abrahamic religions, something that Maurice Halbwachs already described in the period before the establishment of the State of Israel. Jewish, Christian, and Muslim religious nationalisms instrumentalised links to a distant past and the remnants of the past and used them to mobilise constituencies and denounce competing claims. Sean F. McMahon, *The Discourse of Palestinian–Israeli Relations: Persistent Analytics and Practices* (New York: Routledge, 2010). Based on Halbwachs' work, scholars have distinguished 'communicative' and 'cultural' 'collective memory'. The former refers to events that a person has personally experienced, or that immediate ancestors have passed along. Cultural memory, on the other hand, refers to the founding myths of a com-munity in a distant past. No one in that community knows anyone who has experienced these events personally. They only become relevant through texts, oral narratives, re-enactments, or the visitation of physical places. Jan Assmann introduced this distinction in his analysis of ancient Egypt. Jan Assmann, *Das kulturelle Gedächtnis: Schrift, Erinnerung und politische Identität in frühen Hochkulturen* (Munich: C. H. Beck, 1997). For an English account, see Jan Assmann, 'Communicative and Cultural Memory', in: Astrid Erll and Ansgar Nünning (eds), *Cultural Memory Studies: An International and Interdisciplinary Handbook* (Berlin: De Gruyter, 2008), 109—18. For sites of memory, see Pierre Nora and Lawrence D. Kritzman (eds), *Realms of Memory: The Construction of the French Past*, 3 Vols (New York: Columbia University Press, 1996—8). For an engagement

with Nora's work in the context of the commemoration of Ashura in Lebanon, see Natacha Yazbeck, 'The Karbalization of Lebanon: Karbala as Lieu de Mémoire in Hezbollah's Ashura Narrative', *Memory Studies* 11, 4 (2018), 469–82.

7. For a literature review that emphasises the 'Sunni bias' in Sufi studies, see now Denis Hermann and Mathieu Terrier, 'Introduction: New Perspectives on Imami Shi'i–Sufi Relations in the Modern and Pre-Modern Periods', in: Denis Hermann and Mathieu Terrier (eds), *Shi'i Islam and Sufism: Classical Views and Modern Perspectives* (London: I.B. Tauris/Institute of Ismaili Studies, 2020), 1–24.

8. See Babak Rahimi, *Theater State and the Formation of Early Modern Public Sphere in Iran: Studies on Safavid Muharram Rituals, 1590–1641 CE* (Leiden: Brill, 2011), ch. 4, 204n19, as well as Yitzhak Nakash, 'An Attempt to Trace the Origin of the Rituals of 'Āshūrā'', *Die Welt des Islams* 33, 2 (1993), 161–81.

9. For the 'architecture of coexistence', see Stephennie Mulder, *The Shrines of the 'Alids in Medieval Syria: Sunnis, Shi'is and the Architecture of Coexistence* (Edinburgh: Edinburgh University Press, 2014), and Julia Gonnella, *Islamische Heiligenverehrung im urbanen Kontext am Beispiel von Aleppo (Syrien)* (Berlin: Klaus Schwarz, 1995), 141ff. See also Antoine Borrut, 'Remembering Karbalā': The Construction of an Early Islamic Site of Memory', *Jerusalem Studies in Arabic and Islam* 42 (2015), 249–82.

10. For the term Confessional Ambiguity, see Ulrich Haarmann, 'Staat und Religion in Transoxanien im frühen 16. Jahrhundert', *Zeitschrift der Deutschen Morgenländischen Gesellschaft* 124, 2 (1974), 332–69, 350; John E. Woods, *The Aqquyunlu: Clan, Confederation, Empire*, 2nd ed. (Salt Lake City: University of Utah Press, 1999), 3–10, term on page 4; A. Bausani, 'Religion under the Mongols', in: J. A. Boyle (ed.), *The Cambridge History of Iran*, Vol. 5 (Cambridge: Cambridge University Press, 1968), 538–49; Judith Pfeiffer, 'Confessional Ambiguity vs. Confessional Polarization: Politics and the Negotiation of Religious Boundaries in the Ilkhanate', in: Judith Pfeiffer (ed.), *Politics, Patronage and the Transmission of Knowledge in 13th–15th Century Tabriz* (Leiden: Brill, 2014), 129–68. For the application of the concept in a different context, see Andreas Pietsch and Barbara Stollberg-Rilinger (eds), *Konfessionelle Ambiguität: Uneindeutigkeit und Verstellung als religiöse Praxis in der Frühen Neuzeit* (Gütersloh: Gütersloher Verlagshaus, 2013). For an example, see this ethnography of the important Sunni Sufi shrine of Abd al-Qadir al-Gilani in Baghdad, which is visited by Shia and Sunnis alike: Noorah al-Gailani, *The Shrine of 'Abd al-Qādir al-Jīlānī in Baghdad & the Shrine of 'Abd al-'Azīz al-Jīlānī in 'Aqra: Mapping the Multiple Orientations of Two Qādirī Sufi Shrines in Iraq* (PhD, University of Glasgow, 2016).

11. See, for example, Mahmoud Ayoub, *Redemptive Suffering in Islam: A Study of the Devotional Aspects of 'Ashura' in Twelver Shiism* (The Hague: Mouton, 1978); Toby Howarth, *The Twelver Shi'a as a Muslim Minority in India: Pulpit of Tears* (London: Routledge, 2005); David Pinault, *The Shiites: Ritual and Popular Piety in a Muslim Community* (New York: St Martin's, 1992); Pinault, *Horse of Karbala: Muslim Devotional Life in India* (New York: Palgrave Macmillan, 2001). There is a vast

literature on the history of Muharram rituals and the ritual practices in different Shii (and some Sunni) communities around the world. For a useful overview, see Karen Ruffle, 'Muharram', *OBi*; Rahimi, *Theater State*, 31–50. In the era of mass migration, starting in the nineteenth century, they also took place amongst migrant communities and new converts across Europe (with a famous one in London's Hyde Park), the Americas, Australia, the Caribbean, and beyond. Yafa Shanneik, 'Remembering Karbala in the Diaspora: Religious Rituals among Iraqi Shii Women in Ireland', *Religion* 45, 1 (2015), 89–102; Paul Tabar, 'Ashura in Sydney: A Transformation of a Religious Ceremony in the Context of a Migrant Society', *Journal of Intercultural Studies* 23, 3 (2002), 285–305; Frank J. Korom, *Hosay Trinidad: Muharram Performances in an Indo-Caribbean Diaspora* (Philadelphia: University of Pennsylvania Press, 2003).

12. Werner Ende, 'The Flagellations of Muharram and the Shi'ite 'Ulama', *Der Islam* 55, 1 (1978), 19–36. See also Sabrina Mervin, 'Ashura: Some Remarks on Ritual Practices in Different Shiite Communities (Lebanon and Syria)', in: Alessandro Monsutti, Silvia Naef, and Farian Sabahi (eds), *The Other Shiites: From the Mediterranean to Central Asia* (Bern: Peter Lang, 2008), 137–47; Marion Holmes Katz, *The Birth of the Prophet Muhammad: Devotional Piety in Sunni Islam* (Abingdon: Routledge, 2007), 148f., 158.

13. While the Prophet himself is said to have used *taqiyya* to avert danger, it was mainly practised by Shia after Hussain and his followers had been massacred at Karbala. The fifth Shii Imam, Muhammad al-Baqir (677–733), made it a key feature. For Shia living under what they considered unjust and illegitimate governments, *taqiyya* allowed interactions with the surrounding world without being corrupted by it or taking responsibility for it. Some Shii clerics even allowed Shii jurists to judge according to Sunni law if doing otherwise would put them in danger. But there were also Shii scholars who argued that it should only be used if a Shii faced real danger because of his beliefs. When Shii beliefs did not lead to persecution, as under Shii rule, it should not be used. Longstanding and well-known Shii communities were hardly able to simply hide their identity through *taqiyya*. For more, see Tamima Bayhom-Daou, *Shaykh Mufid* (Oxford: Oneworld, 2005), 124; Maria Dakake, 'Hiding in Plain Sight: The Practical and Doctrinal Significance of Secrecy in Shi'ite Islam', *Journal of the American Academy of Religion* 74, 2 (2006), 324–55; Asaf A. A. Fyzee, *A Shi'ite Creed: A Translation of Risālatu l-Iʿtiqādāt of Muḥammad b. ʿAlī ibn Bābawayhi al-Qummī, Known as Shaykh Ṣadūq* (Bombay: Oxford University Press, 1942), 110; Ignaz Goldziher, 'Das Prinzip der 'taḳijja' im Islam', *Zeitschrift der Deutschen Morgenländischen Gesellschaft* 60, 1 (1906), 213–26; Etan Kohlberg, 'Some Imāmī-shīʿī Views on Taqiyya', *Journal of the American Oriental Society* 95, 3 (1975), 395–402; Stefan Winter, *A History of the ʿAlawis: From Medieval Aleppo to the Turkish Republic* (Princeton: Princeton University Press, 2016), 5f.

14. For Shii senses of superiority, see Maria Dakake, *The Charismatic Community: Shi'ite Identity in Early Islam* (Albany: SUNY Press, 2007), 10f.; Josef van Ess, *Theologie und Gesellschaft im 2. und 3. Jahrhundert Hidschra: Eine Geschichte des*

religiösen Denkens im frühen Islam, Vol. 1 (Berlin: De Gruyter, 1991), 276f. This can be seen in the Shii creeds.

15. Good examples are some of the polemics discussed later in the book, especially those of the post-1979 period discussed in Part IV. Other, older examples exist as well, such as the Ibn Saba conspiracy theory discussed below. More recent conspiracy theories hold that European powers such as Britain and Russia created sectarian movements to divide the Ottoman and Iranian empires and Muslims in general. One such story, published for the first time in the late nineteenth century in Turkish and subsequently reprinted in different languages, claims that the Wahhabi doctrines were given to Ibn Abd al-Wahhab by a British spy, Mr Hempher, to divide Muslims and undermine the Ottoman Empire. The book, purporting to be Mr Hempher's personal account, shares some similarities with the *Protocols of the Elders of Zion*. It has remained influential amongst some Shia and anti-Wahhabi actors.

    Another conspiracy theory, the *Confessions of Dolgoruki*, purport to be the political confessions of Dimitri Ivanovich Dolgorukov, the Russian Minister in Iran from 1845 to 1854, who had allegedly come to Iran to study Islam and then went to the shrine cities in Iraq, where he persuaded a young seminary student to launch the Babi movement and return to Iran. He then allegedly returned to Iran as the Russian Minister and gave orders to his agent to establish Bahaism in order to undermine the unity of Iran and Muslims in general and serve Russian interests. It was first published in 1930s Iran. See Mina Yazdani, 'The Confessions of Dologoruki: The Crisis of Identity and the Creation of a Master Narrative', in: Abbas Amanat and Farzin Vejdani (eds), *Iran Facing Others: Identity Boundaries in a Historical Perspective* (London: Palgrave, 2012), 243–64; Yazdani, 'The Confessions of Dolgoruki: Fiction and Masternarrative in Twentieth-Century Iran', *Iranian Studies* 44, 1 (2011), 25–47.

16. The idea of salience is prevalent in the literature on ethnic conflict and was elaborated in the context of contemporary Sunni–Shia relations by Fanar Haddad, *Sectarianism in Iraq: Antagonistic Visions of Unity* (London: Hurst, 2011).

17. For a useful overview, see Morten Valbjørn, 'Beyond the Beyond(s): On the (Many) Third Way(s) beyond Primordialism and Instrumentalism in the Study of Sectarianism', *Nations and Nationalism* 26, 1 (2020), 91–107; Fanar Haddad, *Understanding 'Sectarianism': Sunni-Shi'a Relations in the Modern Arab World* (London: Hurst, 2020), 49–80. For a review of Arabic and English works on sectarianism, see Khalil Osman, *Sectarianism in Iraq: The Making of State and Nation since 1920* (Abingdon: Routledge, 2015), 8–16.

18. For a similar position, see Jürgen Osterhammel, *Die Verwandlung der Welt: Eine Geschichte des 19. Jahrhunderts* (Munich: C. H. Beck, 2011), 15. Some of the most important primary sources I read in Arabic and Persian and cited directly. Others, if available, I cited in translations for the benefit of the non-specialist reader, and, although the notes are extensive, there was much that had to be left out due to space and time considerations. I could not read works in Turkish, Urdu, and some other languages that are of relevance, but have made wide use

of secondary literatures employing these sources. The interested reader may consult the references in the notes for further leads. Entries of the *Encyclopaedia of Islam* and *Encyclopaedia Iranica* contain especially extensive bibliographical references for further reading.

Accounts that mention earlier periods while emphasising the importance of the modern period are to be found in: Lesley Hazelton, *After the Prophet: The Epic Story of the Shia-Sunni Split in Islam* (New York: Doubleday, 2009); John McHugo, *A Concise History of Sunnis and Shi'is* (London: Saqi, 2017). These readable introductions do not, however, have the ambition to engage thoroughly with the vast literature that exists on the topic. Laurence Louër's *Sunnis and Shi'a: A Political History* (Princeton: Princeton University Press, 2020) takes a more holistic angle, yet with a focus on the twentieth century. Fanar Haddad's book focuses, as the title suggests, on the modern Arab world. Haddad, *Understanding 'Sectarianism'*. Maréchal and Zemni's edited volume likewise focuses on the modern period. Brigitte Maréchal and Sami Zemni (eds), *The Dynamics of Sunni-Shia Relationships: Doctrine, Transnationalism, Intellectuals and the Media* (London: Hurst, 2013).

19. This approach is inspired by the work of the French Annales school and global and world history. The former was paradigmatically outlined in the Journal *Annales: Économies, Sociétés, Civilisations* and, for example, in the work of Fernand Braudel on the Mediterranean. Fernand Braudel, 'La longue durée', *Annales* 13, 4 (1958), 725–53; Braudel, *The Mediterranean and the Mediterranean World in the Age of Philip II*, 2 Vols (New York: Harper & Row, 1973); Braudel, *Memory and the Mediterranean* (New York: Knopf, 2001); Braudel, *The Mediterranean in the Ancient World* (London: Allen Lane, 2001). For a collection of key texts, see Claudia Honegger (ed.), *M. Bloch, F. Braudel, L. Febvre u. a.: Schrift und Materie der Geschichte: Vorschläge zur systematischen Aneignung historischer Prozesse* (Frankfurt am Main: Suhrkamp, 1977). I would also like to acknowledge the work of Christopher Bayly, and the discussions of the Cambridge World History Seminar at Cambridge, which I was fortunate enough to attend in the early 2010s. Christopher A. Bayly, *The Birth of the Modern World, 1780–1914: Global Connections and Comparisons* (Oxford: Blackwell, 2004). For a recent defence of the general approach, see Richard Drayton and David Motadel, 'Discussion: The Futures of Global History', *Journal of Global History* 13, 1 (2018), 1–21. For a recent application to the Middle East, see Cyrus Schayegh, *The Middle East and the Making of the Modern World* (Cambridge, MA: Harvard University Press, 2017). For the moyenne durée argument with regards to Sunni–Shia relations, see Martin Thomas Riexinger, 'Gammelt had eller nutidskonflikter? Et moyenne durée-perspektiv på aktuelle sekteriske konflikter', *TIFO: Tidsskrift for Islamforskning (Islamic Studies Journal)* 13, 1 (2019), 87–111.

20. In that sense, it is inspired by Marshall G. S. Hodgson, *The Venture of Islam*, 3 Vols (Chicago: University of Chicago Press, 1974–7). His work is, amongst many other qualities, significant for taking Shiism seriously and writing it into wider Islamic history. While seeing Sunnism and Shiism as separate categories and the

clerics of the two sides as trying to further their relative positions, the book also details their interactions. Edmund Burke, 'Islamic History as World History: Marshall Hodgson, "The Venture of Islam"', *International Journal of Middle East Studies* 10, 2 (1979), 241–64, 254f.; Edmund Burke and Robert J. Mankin, 'The Ventures of Marshall G. S. Hodgson', in: Edmund Burke and Robert J. Mankin (eds), *Islam and World History: The Ventures of Marshall Hodgson* (Chicago: University of Chicago Press, 2018), 1–15, 1. See also Francis Robinson, 'Global History from an Islamic Angle', in: James Belich, John Darwin, Margret Frenz, and Chris Wickham (eds), *The Prospect of Global History* (Oxford: Oxford University Press, 2016), 127–45.

21. Here I am following Maurer, who developed these ideas (and the term 'confessional cultures') in the European context: Michael Maurer, *Konfessionskulturen: Die Europäer als Protestanten und Katholiken* (Paderborn: Ferdinand Schöningh, 2019).

22. In general, see Etan Kohlberg, 'Western Studies of Shiʿa Islam', in: Martin Kramer (ed.), *Shīʿism, Resistance, and Revolution* (Boulder, CO: Westview Press, 1987), 31–44. Al-Shahrastani's *Kitab al-Milal wa-l-Nihal* was translated into English and German in the mid-nineteenth century. See Edward E. Salisbury, 'Translation of Two Unpublished Arabic Documents, Relating to the Doctrines of the Ismâ'ilis and Other Bâṭinian Sects, with an Introduction and Notes', *Journal of the American Oriental Society* 2 (1851), 257–324; Abu al-Fath Ibn ʿAbd al-Karim al-Shahrastani, *Religionspartheien und Philosophen-Schulen*, trans. by Theodor Haarbrücker, 2 Vols (Halle: Schwetschke, 1850–1); David Thomas, 'Kitāb al-milal wa-l-niḥal', *CMR*. Al-Shahrastani, generally known as a Shafii and an Ashari, may have in fact had sympathies for the Ismailiyya. Wilferd Madelung, 'Aš-Šahrastānīs Streitschrift gegen Avicenna und ihre Widerlegung durch Naṣīr ad-Dīn aṭ-Ṭūsī', in: Albert Dietrich (ed.), *Akten des VII. Kongresses für Arabistik und Islamwissenschaft Göttingen, 1974* (Göttingen: Vandenhoeck & Ruprecht, 1976), 250–9, 250f., 258. Abu Mansur al-Baghdadi's (d. 1037) *Al-Farq Bayn al-Firaq* was edited by an Egyptian scholar, Muhammad Badr, printed in 1910, and then published in an English translation in 1919 as *Moslem Schisms and Sects*. Abu Mansur ʿAbd al-Kahir ibn Tahir al-Baghdadi, *Moslem Schisms and Sects (Al-Fark Bain al-Firak), Being the History of the Various Philosophic Systems Developed in Islam, Part I*, trans. by Kate Chambers Seelye (New York: Columbia University Press, 1919). See the review by D. S. Margoliouth in *Journal of the Royal Asiatic Society of Great Britain & Ireland* 53, 2 (1921), 294; Henri Laoust, 'La classification des sectes dans le Farq d'al-Baghdadi', *Revue des études islamiques* 29 (1961), 19–59. Ibn Hazm's *Kitab al-Milal*, infamous for its polemics against Jews, Christians, and Asian religions, also includes diatribes against Shiism, and those sections were translated and commented on in 1908 as Israel Friedlaender, 'The Heterodoxies of the Shiites in the Presentation of Ibn Hazm', *Journal of the American Oriental Society* 29 (1908), 1–183. For more on Ibn Hazm, see Camilla Adang, Maribel Fierro, and Sabine Schmidtke (eds), *Ibn Ḥazm of Cordoba: The Life and Works of a Controversial Thinker* (Leiden: Brill, 2013). In the words of

twentieth-century Indian Ismaili lawyer, scholar, and diplomat Asaf Fyzee, who sought to counter the trend of relying on Sunni heresiographers: 'All of these are devout Sunnis, convinced of the pernicious errors of the *rawafid*, the Shia. With such an attitude, it is impossible for them to be just or fair to the Shiite point of view. One may as well expect a sober account of the Church of England from a Catholic priest. The result is that the earlier orientalists believed that Shiism was a pernicious corruption of Islam, concocted mainly, if not solely, for political reasons.' Fyzee, *A Shi'ite Creed*, 3.

23. The Lebanese Shii leader Musa al-Sadr attended, though he never sent in a paper for the edited volume. The proceedings are published as: Centre de Recherches d'Histoire des Religions Strasbourg (ed.), *Le shî'isme imâmite: Colloque de Strasbourg (6–9 mai 1968)* (Paris: Presses Universitaires de France, 1970). For a bibliography of writings on Shiism, see Andrew J. Newman, 'Shi'i Islam', *Oxford Bibliographies Online*, and, for the German angle, Stefanie Brinkmann, 'Ein Mangel an Quellen oder fehlendes Interesse? Zum späten Einstieg der deutschen Schia-Forschung', *Orient* 50, 4 (2009), 25–43. For early counter-points, see Seyyed Hossein Nasr, Hamid Dabashi, and Seyyed Vali Reza Nasr (eds), *Shi'ism: Doctrines, Thought, and Spirituality* (Albany: SUNY Press, 1988); Seyyed Hossein Nasr, Hamid Dabashi, and Seyyed Vali Reza Nasr, *Expectation of the Millennium: Shi'ism in History* (Albany: SUNY Press, 1989).

24. During a research trip to Najaf in Iraq in 2018, a Shii cleric who had just returned from a visit to Rome as part of an ongoing Shii-Catholic dialogue welcomed me to what he called the 'Shii Vatican'. Sitting in a Shii clerical insti-tution and pointing at the golden dome of the shrine of Ali outside his office windows, he continued, 'we have a lot to learn from the Vatican'. Interviews with Shii clerics, Najaf, Iraq, 2018. For more on the dialogue particularly between Iranian Shii clerics and Catholic clerics, see Sasan Tavassoli, *Christian Encounters with Iran: Engaging Muslim Thinkers after the Revolution* (London: I. B. Tauris, 2011); Anthony O'Mahony, Timothy Wright, and Mohammad Ali Shomali (eds), *A Catholic-Shi'a Dialogue: Ethics in Today's Society* (Bishop's Stortford: Melisende, 2008); James A. Bill and John Alden Williams, *Roman Catholics and Shi'i Muslims: Prayer, Passion, and Politics* (Chapel Hill, NC: University of North Carolina Press, 2002); Christoph Marcinkowski, *Shi'ite Identities: Community and Culture in Changing Social Contexts* (Münster: LIT, 2010), 225–32.

25. Robert Langer and Udo Simon, 'The Dynamics of Orthodoxy and Heterodoxy: Dealing with Divergence in Muslim Discourses and Islamic Studies', *Die Welt des Islams* 48, 3/4 (2008), 273–88; Riza Yildirim, 'Sunni Orthodox vs Shi'ite Heterodox? A Reappraisal of Islamic Piety in Medieval Anatolia', in: A. C. S. Peacock, Bruno De Nicola, and Sara Nur Yıldız (eds), *Islam and Christianity in Medieval Anatolia* (Burlington: Ashgate, 2015), 287–307. For an especially influential view, that of Max Weber, which was also applied to Islam, see Michael Cook, 'Max Weber und islamische Sekten', in: Wolfgang Schluchter (ed.), *Max Webers Sicht des Islams: Interpretation und Kritik* (Frankfurt am Main: Suhrkamp, 1987), 334–41; Max Weber, 'Kirchen und Sekten', in: Dirk Kaesler (ed.),

Schriften 1894–1922 (Stuttgart: Alfred Kröner, 2002), 227–42, 234–6. That Shii communities were indeed often located at the relative periphery, or at least a bit remote from the big urban centres and political capitals, allowed for this Church-sect/centre-periphery view to persist well into the twentieth century. This perception is also present in the otherwise outstanding comparative historical sociology of sects in Islam by the Lebanese anthropologist Fuad Khuri. He also makes a distinction between sects and religious minorities. Fuad I. Khuri, *Imams and Emirs: State, Religion and Sects in Islam* (London: Saqi, 1990), 22. See also A. Kevin Reinhart, 'On Sunni Sectarianism', in: Yasir Suleiman (ed.), *Living Islamic History: Studies in Honour of Professor Carole Hillenbrand* (Edinburgh: Edinburgh University Press, 2010), 209–25.

26. *Ta'ifa*, as a noun, does not need to be something bad. A founding figure of Shiism, Shaykh al-Tusi, for example, is referred to as Shaykh al-Ta'ifa with pride. I thank Hasan al-Qarawee for this point. In the Ottoman Empire, for example, *ta'ifa* was sometimes used as the equivalent of 'guild', as a term describing members of a professional body in an urban setting, seemingly without religious connotations. Such *ta'ifas* as guilds seem to have made their appearance in Syria in the second half of the sixteenth century. The *ta'ifa* was hierarchically organised (with a Shaykh al-Ta'ifa at the top interacting with the state), representing the interests of a particular profession. Some *ta'ifas* were restricted to members of a specific religious community while others were not, and this could vary over time. In court records, non-Muslim members of the *ta'ifas* are distinguished from Muslims, but no reference is made to the sectarian affiliation of Muslims. Abdul-Karim Rafeq, 'Craft Organizations and Religious Communities in Ottoman Syria', in: *Convegno sul tema: La Shī'a nell'Impero Ottomano (Roma, 15 aprile 1991)* (Rome: Accademia Nazionale dei Lincei, 1993), 25–56, 27–35. For terminology, see Mark Farha, 'Searching for Sectarianism in the Arab Spring: Colonial Conspiracy or Indigenous Instinct?', *The Muslim World* 106, 1 (2016), 8–61. Haddad has argued that the terms 'sectarian' and 'sectarianism' have been so misused that they should no longer be used at all. Fanar Haddad, '"Sectarianism" and Its Discontents in the Study of the Middle East', *Middle East Journal* 71, 3 (2017), 363–82; Haddad, *Understanding 'Sectarianism'*, 15–47. For a recent reconsideration, see Azmi Bishara, *Sectarianism without Sects* (London: Hurst, 2021).

27. Rainer Brunner, 'Sunnis and Shiites in Modern Islam: Politics, Rapprochement and the Role of Al-Azhar', in: Brigitte Maréchal and Sami Zemni (eds), *The Dynamics of Sunni–Shia Relationships: Doctrine, Transnationalism, Intellectuals and the Media* (London: Hurst, 2013), 25–38, 26. See also Patricia Crone, *Medieval Islamic Political Thought* (Edinburgh: Edinburgh University Press, 2004); Tamima Bayhom-Daou, *The Imami Shii Conception of the Knowledge of Imam and the Sources of Religious Doctrine in the Formative Period: From Hisham b. al-Hakam (d. 179 A.H.) to Kulini (d. 329 A.H.)* (PhD, University of London, 1996); Bayhom-Daou, 'The Imam's Knowledge and the Quran According to al-Faḍl b. Shādhān al-Nīsābūrī (d. 260 A.H./874 A.D.)', *Bulletin of the School of Oriental and African*

Studies 64, 2 (2001), 188–207. These two positions are paradigmatically spelled out in Sunni and Shii creeds. For a Sunni example, see the creed by Abu Hafs al-Nasafi (d. 1142), which was edited and translated in the nineteenth century: Abu Hafs an-Nasafi, *Pillar of the Creed of the Sunnites: Being a Brief Exposition of their Principal Tenets* (London: James Madden & Co., 1843). See also W. Montgomery Watt, *Islamic Creeds: A Selection* (Edinburgh: Edinburgh University Press, 1994). For a Shii creed, see Hasan b. Yusuf 'al-Allama' al-Hilli, *Al-Bâbu 'l-Ḥâdî 'Ashar: A Treatise on the Principles of Shi'ite Theology*, trans. by William McElwee Miller (London: Royal Asiatic Society, 1928), 98; Duncan B. MacDonald, *Development of Muslim Theology, Jurisprudence, and Constitutional Theory* (London: Routledge, 1903), 314. See also Asma Afsaruddin, *Excellence and Precedence: Medieval Islamic Discourse on Legitimate Leadership* (Leiden. Brill, 2002), 3. For an account of when the differentiation between Imamate and Caliphate occurred, see Jihad Taki Sadiq al-Hassani, *The Question of Imama, Political and Religious Authority, in Twelver Shi'ite Thought* (PhD, University of Manchester, 1979), 94–106, who argues that it occurred before Jafar al-Sadiq. Still a good introduction to political theory of Sunnism and Shiism is Ann K. S. Lambton, *State and Government in Medieval Islam: An Introduction to the Study of Islamic Political Theory: The Jurists* (Oxford: Oxford University Press, 1981). For Sunni and Shii views on the afterlife, see Christian Lange, *Paradise and Hell in Islamic Traditions* (Cambridge: Cambridge University Press, 2016), chs 5 and 6 and passim.

28. Michael M. J. Fischer, *Iran: From Religious Dispute to Revolution* (Cambridge, MA: Harvard University Press, 1980), 204ff.; Stephan Rosiny, *Islamismus bei den Schiiten im Libanon: Religion im Übergang von Tradition zur Moderne* (Berlin: Das Arabische Buch, 1996), 249f.

CHAPTER 1

1. There are many later biographies of Muhammad. F. Buhl et al.,'Muḥammad', *EI2*.

2. Ibn Ishaq, *Das Leben des Propheten*, trans. by Gernot Rotter (Kandern: Spohr, 1999), 49ff.; Ishaq, *Al-Sira al-Nabawiyya li-Ibn Hisham* (Beirut: Mu'assasat al-Ma'arif, 2005), 125ff.

3. al-Tabari, *The History of al-Tabari*, Vol. 6, *Muhammad at Mecca*, trans. by Montgomery Watt and M. V. McDonald (Albany: SUNY Press, 1988), 80–7.

4. W. Montgomery Watt,'Abū Bakr', *EI2*; Khalil Athamina,'Abū Bakr', *EI3*.

5. That source criticism, not always welcomed by Muslim scholars, was epitomised by the work of Patricia Crone (and the early Michael Cook). In the words of two of those sceptics,'what purport to be accounts of religious events in the seventh century are utilisable only for the study of religious ideas in the eighth'. Patricia Crone and Michael Cook, *Hagarism: The Making of the Islamic World* (Cambridge: Cambridge University Press, 1977), 3. This book acknowledges the influence of the source criticism of John Wansbrough.

See John Wansbrough, *The Sectarian Milieu: Content and Composition of Islamic Salvation History* (Oxford: Oxford University Press, 1978), and Wansbrough, *Quranic Studies: Sources and Methods of Scriptural Interpretation* (Oxford: Oxford University Press, 1977). Patricia Crone continued to publish source-critical books on early Islam. See also Chase F. Robinson, *Islamic Historiography* (Cambridge: Cambridge University Press, 2003); Hugh Kennedy, *The Prophet and the Age of the Caliphates: The Islamic Near East from the 6th to the 11th Century*, 2nd ed. (Harlow: Pearson, 2004), 346–57; Angelika Neuwirth, *Der Koran als Text der Spätantike* (Frankfurt am Main: Verlag der Weltreligionen, 2010).

6. Najam Haider, *Shiʿi Islam: An Introduction* (Cambridge: Cambridge University Press, 2014), 219.

7. Gudrun Krämer, *Geschichte des Islam* (Munich: C. H. Beck, 2005), 9f., 17. See, for example, Najam Haider, *The Origins of the Shīʿa: Identity, Ritual, and Sacred Space in Eighth-Century Kūfa* (Cambridge: Cambridge University Press, 2014), ch. 2; Haider, *The Rebel and the Imam in Early Islam: Explorations in Muslim Historiography* (Cambridge: Cambridge University Press, 2019), ch. 1; Wilferd Madelung, 'Introduction: History and Historiography', in: Farhad Daftary and Gurdofarid Miskinzoda (eds), *The Study of Shiʿi Islam: History, Theology and Law* (London: I. B. Tauris, 2014), 3–16.

8. See L. Veccia Vaglieri, "ʿAlī b. Abī Ṭālib', *EI2*; Robert M. Gleave, "ʿAlī b. Abī Ṭālib', *EI3*.

9. Asma Afsaruddin, 'The Epistemology of Excellence: Sunni-Shiʿi Dialectics on Legitimate Leadership', in: Gudrun Krämer and Sabine Schmidtke (eds), *Speaking for Islam: Religious Authorities in Muslim Societies* (Leiden: Brill, 2006), 49–69, 55ff.

10. Shii authors disagree about the exact powers of Ali and to what extent he had knowledge of the unseen and other supernatural powers. Afsaruddin, 'Epistemology', 59–66. As Sunnis emphasised the virtue of the Rashidun Caliphs, Shia emphasised that Alids, the descendants of Ali, had a right to rule based on kinship and their alleged excellence. Afsaruddin has identified such arguments about precedence and excellence particularly in the first century of Islam. Afsaruddin, *Excellence and Precedence*, 6. Her book looks at al-Jahiz's (d. 868–9) *Kitab al-Uthmaniyya* and a Shii refutation composed in the thirteenth century by Ibn Tawus (d. 1274/5). For a discussion of these two authors on the question of whether Ali or Abu Bakr was the first Muslim, see her chapter 1. In his advocacy of Ali, Ibn Tawus claims that Ali had reached puberty when he accepted Islam. Ibid., 57. While lineage was a crucial argument, the knowledge and excellence of Ali and his descendants also became important in pro-Alid narratives after the disappearance, also called occultation, of the twelfth Imam in 874. Ibid., ch. 3; Etan Kohlberg, 'Imam and Community in the Pre-Ghayba Period', in: Said Amir Arjomand (ed.), *Authority and Political Culture in Shiʿism* (Albany: SUNY Press, 1988), 25–53.

11. Krämer, *Geschichte*, 17–21.
12. Wilferd Madelung, *The Succession to Muḥammad: A Study of the Early Caliphate* (Cambridge: Cambridge University Press, 1997), 41.
13. Ibid., 44f.
14. Ibid., 54f.
15. For more on Abu Bakr, see W. Montgomery Watt, 'Abū Bakr', *EI2*; Khalil Athamina, 'Abū Bakr', *EI3*.
16. This was an allegation made in some of the Shii literature, and it was picked up relatively early in Orientalist scholarship: Henri Lammens, 'Le "triumvirat" Aboû Bakr, 'Omar et Aboû 'Obaida', *Mélanges de la Faculté orientale de l'Université St. Joseph de Beyrouth* 4 (1910), 113–44.
17. Henri Laoust, *Les schismes dans l'Islam: Introduction à une étude de la religion musulmane* (Paris: Payot, 1965), 3; Madelung, *Succession*, 360–3. For the Sunni response as formulated by al-Ashari, quoting a Hadith of the Prophet saying that he would not leave any inheritance, see Daniel Gimaret, *La doctrine d'al-Ash'ari* (Paris: Editions du CERF, 1990), 562f. See also Henri Laoust, *Essai sur les doctrines sociales et politiques de Taki-d-Din Ahmad b. Taimiya, canoniste hanbalite, né à Harrān en 661/1262, mort à Damas en 728/1328* (Cairo: Institut Français d'Archéologie Orientale, 1939), 209. Depending on their relations with the Alids, various Abbasid Caliphs either reinstated them as owners of Fadak or dispossessed them again. It is an important topic in Shii writings, including in the modern period. Khomeini, for example, discussed it in *Hokumat-i Islami*, and Muhammad Baqir al-Sadr wrote his first book on Fadak in 1955, altering the more traditional Shii view of Fatima as an activist heroine resisting injustice. Harry Munt, 'Fadak', *EI3*; Rachel Kantz Feder, 'Fatima's Revolutionary Image in Fadak fi al-Ta'rikh (1955): The Inception of Muhammad Baqir al-Sadr's Activism', *British Journal of Middle Eastern Studies* 41, 1 (2014), 79–96; 'Izz al-Dīn ibn al-Athīr, *The Chronicle of Ibn al-Athīr for the Crusading Period from al-Kāmil fī'l-Ta'rīkh*, trans. by D. S. Richards, 3 Vols, Vol. 3 (Aldershot: Ashgate, 2008), 249.
18. Madelung, *Succession*, 50.
19. Ibid., 55.
20. Ibn Taymiyya blames his murder on a conspiracy by what he saw as the enemies of Islam (Jews, foreigners, and Shia). Laoust, *Essai*, 212.
21. Madelung, *Succession*, 62–8.
22. Ibid., 68–72.
23. Laoust, *Essai*, 212f.
24. Madelung, *Succession*, 78f.
25. Ibid., 81–140; van Ess, *Theologie*, Vol. 1, 151f.
26. Madelung, *Succession*, 108–13.
27. Ibid., 113–40.
28. Martin Hinds, 'The Murder of the Caliph 'Uthmān', *International Journal of Middle East Studies* 3, 4 (1972), 450–69.
29. Madelung, *Succession*, 141–50.

30. Erling L. Petersen, "Ali and Mu'awiyah: The Rise of the Umayyad Caliphate, 656–661', *Acta Orientalia* 23 (1959), 157–96, 157–60.

31. The so-called 'Uthmaniyya' continued to advocate the three-Caliphs thesis, but did not survive past the tenth century. Patricia Crone, "U<u>th</u>māniyya', *EI2*; Afsaruddin, *Excellence and Precedence*.

32. Madelung, *Succession*, 151–5. Shia also obviously do not recognise those Caliphs deemed Rashidun by Sunnis, but instead see Ali as the Prophet's legitimate successor.

33. This was even though the Arab aristocracy of Kufa had tended to support a rival trend and the Shii supporters in Kufa were largely members of the lower and middle classes. Van Ess, *Theologie*, Vol. 1, 395.

34. al-Tabari, *The History of al-Tabari*, Vol. 17, *The First Civil War*, trans. by G. R. Hawting (Albany: SUNY Press, 1997); Julius Wellhausen, *Das arabische Reich und sein Sturz* (Berlin: Georg Reimer, 1902), 47–71. For an analysis of al-Tabari's position on Ali and his conflict with Muawiya, see Erling L. Petersen, *Ali and Muawiya in Early Arabic Tradition* (Aarhus: Odense University Press, 1974), 149–58.

35. Hinds, 'Murder', 454; Madelung, *Succession*, 147.

36. Al-Tabari, *The History of al-Tabari*, Vol. 16, *The Community Divided*, trans. by Adrian Brockett (Albany: SUNY Press, 1997). For Aisha's involvement in the first civil war in light of later Sunni and Shii reinterpretations, see Denise A. Spellberg, *Politics, Gender, and the Islamic Past: The Legacy of 'A'isha bint Abi Bakr* (New York: Columbia University Press, 1994), 101–49. See also Madelung, *Succession*, 158–78.

37. Madelung, *Succession*, 179. He also allowed Marwan, one of his fiercest opponents, to leave unharmed and join Muawiya in Syria. Ibid., 181.

38. Petersen, *Ali and Muawiya*, 10.

39. Al-Tabari, *History*, Vol. 17, 78.

40. Ibid., esp. translator's foreword (xi–xiii).

41. M. Lecker, 'Ṣiffīn', *EI2*; Martin Hinds, 'The Ṣiffīn Arbitration Agreement', *Journal of Semitic Studies* 17 (1972), 93–113.

42. For more, see John C. Wilkinson, *Ibâdism: Origins and Early Development in Oman* (Oxford: Oxford University Press, 2010); Ersilia Francesca (ed.), *Ibadi Theology: Rereading Sources and Scholarly Works* (Hildesheim: Georg Olms, 2015); Julius Wellhausen, *Die religiös-politischen Oppositionsparteien im alten Islam* (Berlin: Weidmannsche Buchhandlung, 1901), 1–55. Parts of the Ibadi historical narrative have been challenged by recent scholarship: Valerie J. Hoffman, 'Ibāḍism: History, Doctrines, and Recent Scholarship', *Religion Compass* 9 (2015), 297–307.

43. Hannah-Lena Hagemann, *History and Memory: Khārijism in Early Islamic Historiography* (PhD, University of Edinburgh, 2014); Petersen, *Ali and Muawiya*. Their portrayal has for much of Islamic history and in Orientalist scholarship until the second half of the twentieth century been largely based on heresiographies. An early attempt to bypass the heresiographical literature and go back to their own sources was made in Laura Veccia Vaglieri, 'Il conflitto 'Ali-Mu'awiya

e la secessione kharigita riesaminati alla luce di fonti ibadite', *Annali dell'Istituto Universitario Orientale di Napoli* NS 4 (1952), 1–94.

44. Mohammad Ali Amir-Moezzi and Christian Jambet, *What is Shi'i Islam? An Introduction* (Abindgon, OX: Routledge, 2018), 56; Ignaz Goldziher, *Beiträge zur Literaturgeschichte der Śī'â und der sunnitischen Polemik* (Vienna: Karl Gerold's Sohn, 1874), 55–60; Nebil A. Husayn, *Opposing the Imam: The Legacy of the Nawasib in Islamic Literature* (Cambridge: Cambridge University Press, 2021).

45. Rose Aslan, *From Body to Shrine: The Construction of Sacred Space at the Grave of 'Ali ibn Abi Talib in Najaf* (PhD, University of North Carolina, 2014), 41, 112–84. Al-Khatib al-Baghdadi (d. 1071), for one, claimed that the tomb in Najaf contained the body of Mughira Ibn Shu'ba, a known enemy of the Alids who was expelled from government service for adultery. This theory was picked up by anti-Shii figures such as Ibn Taymiyya (d. 1328) and his student Ibn Kathir (d. 1373). Ironically, both were Hanbali clerics, although Ibn Shu'ba was also infamous for his anti-Hanbali activities. Ibid., 136, 146. Al-Khatib al-Baghdadi's life itself was the subject of some controversy. At one point, he was expelled from Damascus (whose rulers at the time were Shii). Later biographers gave different reasons for this, which ranged from him allegedly having illicit relations with a handsome boy to his expulsion being explained with his having taken offence at the Shii version of the *call to prayer* including *hayya ala khayr al-'amal*, which angered the ruler. Many later writers explained this episode through a Sunni/Shii lens, choosing to omit the story about the boy. Douglas implies that perhaps some writers who were positively inclined towards him chose to leave out an embarrassing detail of his life, which might or might not have been true, and replace it with an easier and more acceptable explanation, the sectarian one. But this episode also shows the difficulty of trusting the at times diametrically opposed sources and reading too much into incidents of 'sectarianism' in earlier periods that might have more mundane causes. Fedwa Malti Douglas, 'Controversy and Its Effects in the Biographical Tradition of al-Khaṭīb al-Baghdādī', *Studia Islamica* 46 (1977), 115–31. Another tradition claims that the Shii Hamdanids transferred the tomb to the *Madrasa* al-Firdaws in Aleppo. Gonnella thinks this was a nineteenth-century invention of tradition. Gonnella, *Islamische Heiligenverehrung*, 141, 182f.

46. Maria E. Subtelny, *Timurids in Transition: Turko-Persian Politics and Acculturation in Medieval Iran* (Leiden: Brill, 2007), 210f.; Xavier de Planhol, 'MAZĀR-E ŠARIF', *EIr*.

47. Yasser Tabbaa and Sabrina Mervin, *Najaf, the Gate of Wisdom: History, Heritage and Significance of the Holy City of the Shi'a* (Paris: UNESCO, 2014), 22; E. Honigmann and C. E. Bosworth, 'al-Nadjaf', *EI2*; Aslan, *From Body to Shrine*, 130.

48. Aslan, *From Body to Shrine*, 150ff.; James A. Bellamy, 'Sources of Ibn Abī 'l-Dunyā's Kitāb Maqtal Amīr al-Mu'minīn 'Alī', *Journal of the American Oriental Society* 104, 1 (1984), 3–19.

49. Aslan, *From Body to Shrine*, 119. The Shii point of view was systematised by Ibn Tawus. Ibid., 144.

50. For a short genealogy, see Farhad Daftary, "Alids', *EI3*; B. Lewis, "Alids', *EI2*.

51. As stated by Ibn Babawayh: 'He who denies infallibility to them in any matter appertaining to their status is ignorant of them, and such a one is a kafir (unbeliever).' Fyzee, *A Shiʿite Creed*, 100. Despite being infallible, the Imams, however, could not overrule the Quran or the Tradition (Sunna) of the Prophet or the preceding Imams. In the Shii view, their knowledge was identical with that of the Prophet and the preceding Imams, and thus, logically, they would not counteract the Sunna that had preceded them. Wilferd Madelung, 'Authority in Twelver Shiism in the Absence of the Imam', in: G. Makdisi, D. Sourdel, and J. Sourdel-Thomine (eds), *La notion d'autorité au moyen âge* (Paris: Presses Universitaires de France, 1982), 163–73.

52. Most at the very least argued that the two first ones, Abu Bakr and Umar, were especially worthy, the so-called *Taqdim al-Shaykhayn* (pre-eminence of the two Shaykhs), with some disagreement as to whether Uthman or Ali were more so. For Ibn Taymiyya in *Minhaj al-Sunna*, there is no question that Abu Bakr was the best possible successor. Henri Laoust, *Comment définir le sunnisme et le chiisme* (Paris: Librairie orientaliste Paul Geuthner, 1979), 11; Laoust, *Essai*, 205, 207–10. See also Afsaruddin, *Excellence and Precedence*, 16ff.; Nebil A. Husayn, 'The Rehabilitation of ʿAli in Sunni Hadith and Historiography', *Journal of the Royal Asiatic Society* 29, 4 (2019), 565–83; van Ess, *Theologie*, Vol. 1, 233ff., 308–12. Ibadis, on the other hand, embrace the Caliphates of Abu Bakr and Umar and the first halves of the Caliphates of Uthman and Ali respectively, after which they reject almost all Sunni Caliphs or Shii Imams and recognise their own leaders. Valerie J. Hoffman, *The Essentials of Ibadi Islam* (New York: Syracuse University Press, 2012), 7–10, 17.

53. Madelung, *Succession*, 150f.; E. Kohlberg, "ALI B. ABI TALEB ii. ʿAli as seen by the Community', *EIr*; Reza Shah-Kazemi, *Justice and Remembrance: Introducing the Spirituality of Imam ʿAli* (London: I. B. Tauris/Institute of Ismaili Studies, 2006); Hassan Abbas, *The Prophet's Heir: The Life of ʿAli ibn Abi Talib* (New Haven: Yale University Press, 2021); Mohammad Ali Amir-Moezzi, *Ali, le secret bien gardé: Figures du premier Maître en spiritualité shiʿite* (Paris: CNRS Editions, 2020).

54. Jane Hathaway, *A Tale of Two Factions: Myth, Memory, and Identity in Ottoman Egypt and Yemen* (Albany: SUNY Press, 2003), 167f.

55. Francesca Bellino, 'Dhū l-Faqār', *EI3*; David G. Alexander, 'Dhū'l-Faqār and the Legacy of the Prophet, Mirāth Rasūl Allāh', *Gladius* 19, 1 (1999), 157–87; Hathaway, *A Tale of Two Factions*; Jean Calmard, 'DU'L-FAQĀR', *EIr*. Twelver Shii tradition maintains that it remained in the line of Ali until the disappearance of the twelfth Imam in 873. The Abbasids, having initially risen to power on the claim of association with the *Ahl al-Bayt*, claimed to have possessed and used it in battle. According to some accounts, the Fatimids may have then wrested it from them and used it to legitimise their Ismaili counter-Caliphate. Hathaway, *A Tale of Two Factions*, 169f. In later years, one of two major political factions in Ottoman Egypt in the seventeenth and eighteenth centuries was named the Faqari faction, and there is some speculation as to whether it may

have taken the name of the famous sword on the Ottoman banners. Interestingly, the factions were formed in part during the Ottoman intervention in Yemen in the early seventeenth century. See, in general, ibid., 185, 190. One thus finds Fatimids, Ottomans, Mughals, Ahmad Shah Durrani of Afghanistan, Mahmut Pasha Bushatli of Albania, and even the Pahlavi dynasty using the sword on their flags and standards. Even Saddam Hussein used it during the Iran–Iraq War to try to mobilise Iraqi Shia for the war effort. I owe knowledge of this latter point to a conversation with Hasan al-Qarawee. See, for example, D. Gershon Lewental, '"Saddam's Qadisiyyah": Religion and History in the Service of State Ideology in Ba'thi Iraq', *Middle Eastern Studies* 50, 6 (2014), 891–910.

56. Syed Husain Mohammad Jafri, *The Origins and Early Development of Shi'a Islam* (London: Longman, 1979), 1–23; Wilferd Madelung, 'Shi'ism in the Age of the Rightly-Guided Caliphs', in: Sabine Schmidtke (ed.), *Studies in Medieval Shi'ism* (Aldershot: Ashgate, 2012), 9–18, 17f.

57. As outlined by Ibn Taymiyya in *Minhaj al-Sunna*. Laoust, *Essai*, 213.

58. See in general Husayn, *Opposing the Imam*.

59. Madelung, *Succession*, 1f.; M. G. S. Hodgson, "Abd Allāh b. Saba", *EI2*; Sean Anthony, *The Caliph and the Heretic: Ibn Saba' and the Origins of Shī'ism* (Leiden: Brill, 2012), ch. 4.

60. The argument had also been made, however, that this was a later reversal or reinterpretation of the earlier notion of the Caliphs as both political and religious leaders. The Umayyad Caliphs, for example, would call themselves *Khalifat Allah*, the successors of God, and not just *Khalifat Rasul Allah* (successor of the Prophet of God). Crone and Hinds thus argue that 'the early caliphate was conceived along the lines familiar from Shi'ite Islam'. They would go on to argue that *Khalifa* meant deputy of God from the start, not 'only' successor to the Prophet. Patricia Crone and Martin Hinds, *God's Caliph: Religious Authority in the First Centuries of Islam* (Cambridge: Cambridge University Press, 1986), 1–6.

61. M. Hinds, 'Mu'āwiya I', *EI2*.

62. According to Veccia Vaglieri, those are originally called the *Ahl al-Sunna wa-l-Jamaa*. Laura Veccia Vaglieri, 'Sulla origine della denominazione Sunniti', in: *Studi Orientalistici in onore di Giorgio Levi della Vida*, Vol. 2 (Rome: Istituto per l'Oriente, 1956), 573–85.

63. Madelung, *Succession*, 133, 311–33; Madelung, 'ḤASAN B. 'ALI B. ABI ṬĀLEB', *EIr*.

64. Wellhausen, *Oppositionsparteien*, 61–8. This largely follows al-Tabari, *The History of al-Tabari*, Vol. 19, *The Caliphate of Yazid b. Mu'awiyah A.D. 680–3/A.H. 60–64*, trans. by I. K. A. Howard (Albany: SUNY Press, 1990). For an elaboration of the different narratives, see Haider, *Shi'i Islam*, 66–81. Several famous classical Shii books narrate the tragedy, and countless more have been published over the centuries. One of the most important is the one by Abu Mikhnaf, which is available in translation: Abū-Miḥnaf, *Der Tod des Ḥusein ben 'Alī und die Rache: Ein historischer Roman aus dem Arabischen* (Göttingen: Dieterich, 1883), and in English. See also Ursula Sezgin, *Abū Miḥnaf: Ein Beitrag zur Historiographie der umaiyadischen Zeit* (Leiden: Brill, 1971).

65. The publication of al-Tabari's history in a Leiden edition in the late nineteenth century spurred great interest amongst European Orientalists, and many of the earlier European accounts of early Islam are largely based on him. See, for example, Julius Wellhausen, *Das arabische Reich und sein Sturz* (Berlin: Georg Reimer, 1902).

66. Gerald R. Hawting, *The First Dynasty of Islam: The Umayyad Caliphate AD 661–750*, 2nd ed. (London: Routledge, 2000), 125f.

67. Even the early Hanbalis, including Ahmad Ibn Hanbal, criticised the Umayyads while recognising their legitimacy. In fact, pro-Umayyad accounts primarily survived amongst Hanbalis after the Abbasids asserted their view of history. Werner Ende, *Arabische Nation und islamische Geschichte: Die Umayyaden im Urteil arabischer Autoren des 20. Jahrhunderts* (Beirut/Wiesbaden: Orient-Institut/Franz Steiner, 1977), 22–6; Erling L. Petersen, 'Studies on the Historiography of the 'Ali-Mu'awiya Conflict', *Acta Orientalia* 27 (1963), 83–118, 104–10, 118. See also Khaled Keshk, *The Historian's Mu'awiya: The Depiction of Mu'awiya in the Early Islamic Sources* (Saarbrücken: VDM Verlag Dr. Müller, 2008); Keshk, 'How to Frame History', *Arabica* 56, 4/5 (2009), 381–99.

68. Haider, *The Rebel and the Imam*, 22, 26f., 132–6, and passim.

69. Wellhausen, *Oppositionsparteien*, 71ff.

70. For a detailed account of the Mukhtar rebellion, see ibid., 77–89; G. R. Hawting, 'al-Mukhtār b. Abī 'Ubayd', *EI2*.

71. Apart from the idea of the Mahdi, he also emphasised the inner meaning of texts (*batin*). Haider, *The Rebel and the Imam*, ch. 2; Adel S. al-Abdul Jader, 'The Origin of Key Shi'ite Thought Patterns in Islamic History', in: Yasir Suleiman (ed.), *Living Islamic History: Studies in Honour of Professor Carole Hillenbrand* (Edinburgh: Edinburgh University Press, 2010), 1–13; Wellhausen, *Oppositionsparteien*, 74f. See also Jan-Olaf Blichfeldt, *Early Mahdism: Politics and Religion in the Formative Period of Islam* (Leiden: Brill, 1985).

72. Patricia Crone, 'Mawālī and the Prophet's Family: An Early Shī'ite View', in: Monique Bernards and John Abdallah Nawas (eds), *Patronate and Patronage in Early and Classical Islam* (Leiden: Brill, 2005), 167–94, 183f. Crone cites Twelver Shii, Ismaili, and Zaydi scholars, arguing that the Zaydis came round to this later.

73. Martin Hinds, 'Kufan Political Alignments and their Background in the Mid-Seventh Century A.D.', *International Journal of Middle East Studies* 2, 4 (1971), 346–67, 347ff.

74. William F. Tucker, *Mahdis and Millenarians: Shi'ite Extremists in Early Muslim Iraq* (Cambridge: Cambridge University Press, 2008).

75. Wilferd Madelung, 'Zayd b. 'Alī b. al-Husayn', *EI2*; Wellhausen, *Oppositionsparteien*, 96ff.; Haider, *Shi'i Islam*, 85–90. See also W. Montgomery Watt, 'Shi'ism under the Umayyads', *Journal of the Royal Asiatic Society* 92, 3–4 (1960), 158–72. There is a shrine in his name in Iraq, not far from Kufa, and one in Karak, Jordan, where some believe his head was buried. See Jordan Tourism Board, 'Kerak', https://international.visitjordan.com/Wheretogo/Kerak.aspx.

76. One major branch followed Zayd immediately, while a second one first followed Muhammad al-Baqir and then joined the followers of Zayd and not

al-Baqir's son Jafar. This group was led by a traditionist of Muhammad al-Baqir and named the Jarudiyya after him. It was marked by a strong rejection of the first Caliphs. Wilferd Madelung, *Der Imam al-Qāsim ibn Ibrāhīm und die Glaubenslehre der Zaiditen* (Berlin: Walter de Gruyter, 1965), 44–8; Madelung, 'Zaydiyya', *EI2*. Non-Zaydi Shia see Muhammad al-Baqir as a crucial figure who systematised Shiism. Arzina R. Lalani, *Early Shīʿī Thought: The Teachings of Imam Muḥammad al-Bāqir* (London: I. B. Tauris/Institute of Ismaili Studies, 2000).

77. There are contradictory positions attributed to Zayd on this point. Rudolf Strothmann, 'Das Problem der literarischen Persönlichkeit Zaid b. ʿAli', *Der Islam* 13 (1923), 1–52, 12f.; Maher Jarrar, 'Some Aspects of Imami Influence on Early Zaydite Theology', in: Rainer Brunner, Monika Gronke, Jens P. Laut, and Ulrich Rebstock (eds), *Islamstudien ohne Ende: Festschrift für Werner Ende* (Würzburg: Deutsche Morgenländische Gesellschaft/Ergon, 2002), 201–23. Early Zaydi dogma became more critical of the first three Caliphs. Madelung, *Der Imam*, 45. And some Zaydi scholars made a distinction between Abu Bakr, Umar, both of whom they accepted as legitimate rulers even though there would have been a more suitable one (Ali), and Uthman (in particular the six last years of his reign). Ibid., 63. This was a point on which different branches of the Zaydiyya disagreed. Robert B. Serjeant, 'The Zaydis', in: A. J. Arberry (ed.), *Religion in the Middle East: Three Religions in Concord and Conflict*, Vol. 2 (Cambridge: Cambridge University Press, 1969), 285–301, 288f.

78. Rudolf Strothmann, *Das Staatsrecht der Zaiditen* (Strasbourg: Karl J. Trübner, 1912), 28.

79. Etan Kohlberg, 'Some Zaydi Views on the Companions of the Prophet', *Bulletin of the School of Oriental and African Studies* 39, 1 (1976), 91–8, 97; Gabriele vom Bruck, 'How the Past Casts its Shadows: Struggles for Ascendancy in Northern Yemen in the Post-Salih Era', in: Gabriele vom Bruck and Charles Tripp (eds), *Precarious Belongings: Being Shiʿi in Non-Shiʿi Worlds* (London: Centre for Academic Shia Studies, 2017), 257–332, n61. Al-Qasim Ibn Ibrahim wrote the treatise *Risalat al-Radd ala al-Rafida (Treatise on the Renunciation of the Rejectionists)*, in which he refutes the Imamate doctrine of the Twelver Shia. A second book of similar title and topic has been attributed to him but is likely of later origin. Madelung, *Der Imam*, 98f., 145f. See also van Ess, *Theologie*, Vol. 1, 239, 252–72.

80. Serjeant, 'The Zaydis', 285. See also Friedlaender, 'Heterodoxies'. Ibn Taymiyya, for example, in his classification of Shii sects, sees the Zaydis as the least bad of the Shia. Henri Laoust, 'Remarques sur les Expéditions du Kasrawan sous les Premiers Mamluks', *Bulletin du Musée de Beyrouth* 4 (1940), 93–115, 108; Laoust, *Essai*, 96.

81. Kohlberg has argued that some Twelver Shia also adopted it as a self-description. Etan Kohlberg, 'The Term 'Rāfida' in Imāmī Shīʿī Usage', *Journal of the American Oriental Society* 99, 4 (1979), 677–9; Kohlberg, 'Some Zaydi Views'.

82. Strothmann, *Staatsrecht*, 42f. Although there were Zaydi clerics that advised others to stay away from power, and important works of Zaydi *fiqh* were written by scholars and Imams that had little military or political prowess. I thank Gabriele vom Bruck for clarifying this point.

83. For a detailed, if dated, elaboration on this, see Strothmann, *Staatsrecht*.
84. In the early tenth century, they recognised Fatimid authority. They eventually lost their power amidst struggles between the Fatimids and the Umayyads. Chafik T. Benchekroun, 'Idrīsids', *EI3*. Another subsect of Shiism had adherents in the Sus area of Morocco from the mid-ninth century. Wilferd Madelung, 'Some Notes on Non-Ismā'īlī Shiism in the Maghrib', *Studia Islamica* 44 (1976), 87–97. See also Biancamaria Scarcia Amoretti, 'Shi'a Devotion to the Ahl al-Bayt in Historical Perspective', in: Chiara Formichi and R. Michael Feener (eds), *Shi'ism in Southeast Asia: 'Alid Piety and Sectarian Constructions* (London: Hurst, 2015), 17–29, 19.
85. This example is used in Roy P. Mottahedeh, *Loyalty and Leadership in an Early Islamic Society* (Princeton: Princeton University Press, 1980), 7. See also Moojan Momen, *An Introduction to Shi'i Islam: The History and Doctrines of Twelver Shi'ism* (New Haven: Yale University Press, 1985), 16; Abdulaziz Abdulhussein Sachedina, *Islamic Messianism: The Idea of the Mahdi in Twelver Shi'ism* (Albany: SUNY Press, 1981), 102f.
86. G. H. A. Juynboll and D. W. Brown, 'Sunna', *EI2*; Joseph Schacht, *The Origins of Muhammadan Jurisprudence* (Oxford: Clarendon Press, 1953).
87. Veccia Vaglieri, 'Sulla origine'. See also A. J. Wensinck, 'Sunna', *EI*; L. Gardet and J. Berque, 'Djamā'a', *EI2*. Marshall Hodgson therefore argued that a better way would be to use Jamai-Sunni to denote those who were willing to be part of the broad consensus of Muslims and accept some core beliefs and notions about history. He ends up using it 'only in the minimal sense, as contrasted to Shi'i'. Marshall G. S. Hodgson, *The Venture of Islam*, Vol. 1 (Chicago: University of Chicago Press, 1974), 276–9.
88. Daphna Ephrat, *A Learned Society in a Period of Transition: The Sunni 'Ulama' of Eleventh-Century Baghdad* (Albany: SUNY Press, 2000); Scott C. Lucas, *Constructive Critics, Hadīth Literature, and the Articulation of Sunnī Islam* (Leiden: Brill, 2004); Christopher Melchert, *The Formation of the Sunni Schools of Law, 9th–10th Centuries CE* (Leiden: Brill, 1997); G. Burak, 'Madhhab', *EIL*. See also Harald Motzki, *The Origins of Islamic Jurisprudence: Meccan Fiqh before the Classical Schools* (Leiden: Brill, 2002).
89. They are the collections of al-Bukhari (d. 870), Muslim (d. 815), Ibn Majah (d. 886), Abu Daud (d. 889), al-Tirmidhi (d. 892), and al-Nasai (d. 889). S. H. Nasr and M. Mutahhari, 'The Religious Sciences', in: R. N. Frye (ed.), *The Cambridge History of Iran*, Vol. 4 (Cambridge: Cambridge University Press, 1975), 464–80; Jonathan Brown, *The Canonization of al-Bukhārī and Muslim: The Formation and Function of the Sunnī Hadīth Canon* (Leiden: Brill, 2007).
90. Michael Dann, *Contested Boundaries: The Reception of Shī'ite Narrators in the Sunnī Hadith Tradition* (PhD, Princeton University, 2015).
91. Christine D. Baker, *Medieval Islamic Sectarianism* (Bradford: Arc Medieval Press, 2019), esp. ch. 1.
92. Mottahedeh, *Loyalty*, 7–24; Spellberg, *Politics*, 5; Wilferd Madelung, 'Early Sunni Doctrine Concerning Faith as Reflected in the "Kitāb al-Imān" of Abū 'Ubayd

al-Qāsim b. Sallām (d. 224/839)', *Studia Islamica* 32 (1970), 233–54; G. H. A. Juynboll and D. W. Brown, 'Sunna', *EI2*. Some have, for example, argued that Sunna and Shia agreed on key points of ritual practice, and on what they categorically rejected, until at least the ninth century. Christopher Melchert, 'Renunciation (Zuhd) in the Early Shi'i Tradition', in: Farhad Daftary and Gurdofarid Miskinzoda (eds), *The Study of Shi'i Islam: History, Theology and Law* (London: I. B. Tauris, 2014), 271–94.

93. For a detailed account of this process, see van Ess, *Theologie*, Vol. 1, 233ff., 308–12.

94. Ali had also given his daughter Umm Kulthum to Umar in marriage, and Jafar al-Sadiq was a descendant of Abu Bakr through his mother. Van Ess, *Theologie*, Vol. 1, 310.

95. Wilferd Madelung, 'The Shiite and Kharijite Contribution to Pre-Ash'arite Kalam', in: Parviz Morewedge (ed.), *Islamic Philosophical Theology* (Albany: SUNY Press, 1979), 120–39; Meir M. Bar Asher, *Scripture and Exegesis in Early Imāmī Shiism* (Leiden: Brill, 1999), 10ff.

96. His school was completed by his disciples Abu Yusuf (d. 798) and al-Shaybani (d. 805), the latter of whom was a *Qadi* (an Islamic jurist) in Raqqa under the Caliph Harun al-Rashid. Laoust, *Comment définir*, 6f.; W. Heffening and J. Schacht, 'Ḥanafiyya', *EI2*; van Ess, *Theologie*, Vol. 1, 183–219.

97. N. Cottart, 'Mālikiyya', *EI2*.

98. Al-Shafii himself was accused by critics of supporting a rebellion by the Hasanid Yahya bin Abdallah, and thus of some Shii sympathies in a political sense. E. Chaumont, 'al-Shāfiʿī', *EI2*. For a recent account of his impact, see Ahmed El Shamsy, *The Canonization of Islamic Law: A Social and Intellectual History* (Cambridge: Cambridge University Press, 2015).

99. E. Chaumont, 'al-Shāfiʿiyya', *EI2*.

100. Laoust, *Comment définir*, 7f.

101. Guido Steinberg, 'Jihadi-Salafism and the Shi'is: Remarks about the Intellectual Roots of Anti-Shi'ism', in: Roel Meijer (ed.), *Global Salafism: Islam's New Religious Movement* (London: Hurst, 2009), 107–25, 112f.; David Commins, *Islam in Saudi Arabia* (London: I. B. Tauris, 2015), 15–18. For more on the Hanbali school, see Henri Laoust, 'Le Hanbalisme sous le califat de Bagdad', *Revue des études islamiques* 27 (1959), 67–128; Livnat Holtzman, 'Aḥmad b. Ḥanbal', *EI3*. See also, in general, Robert Gleave, *Islam and Literalism: Literal Meaning and Interpretation in Islamic Legal Theory* (Edinburgh: Edinburgh University Press, 2012).

102. See, for example, Muhammad ibn Abd al-Wahhab, *Al-Radd 'ala al-Rafida*, quoted in: Steinberg, 'Jihadi-Salafism', 113. The book is a refutation of various aspects of belief and ritual practice of the Shia. It has seen numerous reprints in many locations around the world. The copy I consulted was printed in Sanaa, Yemen, in the 2000s. Muhammad ibn Abd al-Wahhab, *Al-Radd 'ala al-Rafida* (Sanaa: Dar al-Athar, 2006).

103. Madelung, *Der Imam*, 223–8; Christopher Melchert, *Ahmad ibn Hanbal* (Oxford: Oneworld, 2006), 93–8. Ibn Taymiyya lauds him for this and incorporates this point as a key anchor of the Sunna. Laoust, *Essai*, 238.

104. Madelung, *Succession*, 18–27. In general, see Etan Kohlberg, *The Attitude of the Imāmī-Shīʿīs to the Companions of the Prophet* (PhD, Oxford University, 1972).

105. Spellberg, *Politics*, 1–11, 32f. For Aisha as a transmitter of Hadith, see ibid., 51–8.

106. Ibid., 35f. Some Shii polemicists went as far as countering the Sunni designations of her as the 'vindicated' with a particularly incendiary remark, something that was taken up in the early twenty-first century by a controversial Kuwaiti Shii author based in the UK, Yasir al-Habib, who rehashed a polemical debate in which some Shii authors had claimed that Aisha and Hafsa had poisoned the Prophet. Etan Kohlberg, 'Shīʿī Views of the Death of the Prophet Muḥammad', in: Rotraud Hansberger, M. Afifi al-Haytham, and Charles Burnett (eds), *Medieval Arabic Thought: Essays in Honour of Fritz Zimmermann* (London: Warburg Institute, 2012), 77–86.

107. Spellberg analyses the defences of Aisha by Ibn Batta (d. 387/977), Nizam al-Mulk, Ibn Taymiyya, and in the form of a famous poem by al-Andalusi. Spellberg, *Politics*, 11, 30, 84–95, 174–8. The Ottomans included this point in peace treaties with the Safavids, as will be outlined later.

108. They also claimed that not Aisha but Umm Salama, who allegedly supported the position of the *Ahl al-Bayt*, was the Prophet's favourite wife. Interview with a teacher in the Shii seminary (*hawza*) of Najaf, Najaf, Iraq, 2018; Spellberg, *Politics*, 151ff.; Barnaby Rogerson, *The Heirs of the Prophet Muhammad: Islam's First Century and the Origins of the Sunni-Shia Schism* (New York: Overlook, 2007); Mary F. Thurlkill, *Chosen among Women: Mary and Fatima in Medieval Christianity and Shiʿite Islam* (Notre Dame, IN: University of Notre Dame Press, 2008). For Umm Salama's support for Ali, see Madelung, *Succession*, 148, 165.

109. Spellberg, *Politics*, 177. That one of the most famous Iranian poets was Umar Khayyam is owed to the fact that Iran was a largely Sunni country in the eleventh and twelfth centuries, when he lived. To complicate matters further, however, Ali had a son named Umar, as did a brother of Zayd bin Ali and Muhammad al-Baqir. Van Ess, *Theologie*, Vol. 1, 310. For nuances amongst Indian Sunnis, see Claudia Preckel, *Islamische Bildungsnetzwerke und Gelehrtenkultur im Indien des 19. Jahrhunderts: Muhammad Ṣiddīq Ḥasan Khān (st. 1890) und die Entstehung der Ahl-e Ḥadīth-Bewegung in Bhopal* (PhD, Ruhr University Bochum, 2005), 469f.; Muhammad Khalid Masid, 'Fatwa Advice on Proper Muslim Names', in: Barbara D. Metcalf (ed.), *Islam in South Asia in Practice* (Princeton: Princeton University Press, 2009), 339–51. For a comparison of the use of Ali and Mehmed (Muhammad) in the Ottoman Empire and Turkey, see Hülya Canbakal, 'An Exercise in Denominational Geography in Search of Ottoman Alevis', *Turkish Studies* 6, 2 (2005), 253–71. Given their affinity for the *Ahl al-Bayt*, Shia names include Abd al-Rasul (Slave of the Prophet), Abd al-Nabi (Slave of the Prophet), Abd Ali (Slave of Ali), or Abd al-Mahdi (Slave of the Messiah).

110. van Ess, *Theologie*, Vol. 1, 70f.

111. Ibid., 3–10. For more on the Abbasids, see Bernard Lewis, "Abbāsids', *EI2*.

112. Jonathan Berkey, *The Formation of Islam: Religion and Society in the Near East, 600–1800* (Cambridge: Cambridge University Press, 2003), 103f.

113. This was, for example, the case for the rebellion of Abdallah bin Muawiya, who briefly managed to establish a Hashemite state. Teresa Bernheimer, 'The Revolt of 'Abdallāh b. Mu'āwiya, AH 127–130: A Reconsideration through the Coinage', *Bulletin of the School of Oriental and African Studies* 69, 3 (2006), 381–93; Antoine Borrut, "Abdallāh b. Mu'āwiya', *EI3*.

114. Wilferd Madelung, 'The Hashimiyyat of al-Kumayt and Hashimi Shi'ism', *Studia Islamica* 70 (1989), 5–26; Marshall G. S. Hodgson, 'How did the Early Shi'a Become Sectarian?', *Journal of the American Oriental Society* 75, 1 (1955), 1–13.

115. W. W. Rajkowski, *Early Shi'ism in Iraq* (PhD, University of London, 1955); Jafri, *Origins*.

116. Hugh Kennedy, *The Early Abbasid Caliphate: A Political History* (London: Routledge, 2015); Andrew Marsham, *Rituals of Islamic Monarchy: Accession and Succession in the First Muslim Empire* (Edinburgh: Edinburgh University Press, 2009), 186f.

117. Crone, 'Mawālī'; Crone, *From Arabian Tribes to Islamic Empire: Army, State and Society in the Near East c.600–850* (Aldershot: Ashgate, 2008), 178f.; van Ess, *Theologie*, Vol. 3, 28ff.

118. van Ess, *Theologie*, Vol. 3, 17ff.

119. Berkey, *Formation of Islam*, 104.

120. Muhammad Qasim Zaman, *Religion and Politics under the Early 'Abbasids: The Emergence of the Proto-Sunnī Elite* (Leiden: Brill, 1997), 33–48; Moshe Sharon, *Black Banners from the East: The Establishment of the Abbasid State: Incubation of a Revolt* (Jerusalem: Magnes Press, 1983). See also Michael Cooperson, *Classical Arabic Biography: The Heirs of the Prophets in the Age of al-Ma'mūn* (Cambridge: Cambridge University Press, 2000), 70–106.

121. Muawiya Ibn Abu Sufyan (d. 680) is criticised for being the first Muslim ruler to claim the title of King and instituting hereditary monarchy. But Sunnis tame their criticism of Muawiya because he was a Companion of the Prophet, whom they see as infallible. Ende, *Arabische Nation*, 14ff.; Petersen, *Ali and Muawiya*, 124; Ende, 'Studies', 110, 114. For the development of Abbasid and Shii historiography of the first *fitna*, see Petersen, *Ali and Muawiya*, 71–108, esp. 71ff., 113f., 121–4, 178f., and Ende, 'Studies'.

122. This belief is even included in Shii creeds. See Fyzee, *A Shi'ite Creed*, 102f.

123. For a related development amongst Christians in the Near East, see Christian C. Sahner, *Christian Martyrs under Islam: Religious Violence and the Making of the Muslim World* (Princeton: Princeton University Press, 2018), 185–93, 250f.

124. F. Omar, 'Hārūn al-Rashīd', *EI2*; E. Kohlberg, 'Mūsā al-Kāzim', *EI2*; van Ess, *Theologie*, Vol. 3, 93ff. See also A. Azfar Moin, 'Partisan Dreams and Prophetic Visions: Shi'i Critique in al-Masudi's History of the Abbasids', *Journal of the American Oriental Society* 127, 4 (2007), 415–28, 422ff.

125. This is not satisfactorily explained in the literature. Aslan, *From Body to Shrine*, 164–76.

126. Subsequent Caliphs largely no longer attempted to set unified religious policies. Christopher Melchert, 'Religious Policies of the Caliphs from al-Mutawakkil to al-Muqtadir, A H 232-295/A D 847–908', *Islamic Law and Society* 3, 3 (1996), 316–42.

127. Bayhom-Daou argues that this was not the case, and a passage in which al-Mamun refers to this may have been a later addition by Ibn Tawus. Tamima Bayhom-Daou, 'Al-Ma'mūn's Alleged Apocalyptic Beliefs: A Reconsideration of the Evidence', *Bulletin of the School of Oriental and African Studies* 71, 1 (2008), 1–24.

128. This is, for example, the view of Shaykh al-Mufid. Bayhom-Daou, *Shaykh Mufid*, 47. See also Wilferd Madelung, "ALĪ AL-REŻĀ', *EIr*.

129. By the fourteenth century, however, a Sunni traveller, Ibn Battuta, would report that Shia (whom he called *rafidis*) were visiting the grave of al-Rida, while at the same time cursing the grave of Harun al-Rashid. May Farhat, 'Shi'i Piety and Dynastic Legitimacy: Mashhad under the Early Safavid Shahs', *Iranian Studies* 47, 2 (2014), 201–16, 202f.

130. Mohammad Ali Amir-Moezzi, 'Šahrbānu', *EIr*; Amir-Moezzi, 'Shahrbānū, princesse sassanide et épouse de l'imam Ḥusayn: De l'Iran préislamique à l'Islam shiite', *Comptes rendus des séances de l'Académie des Inscriptions et Belles-Lettres* 146, 1 (2002), 255–85; Mary Boyce, 'Bībī Shahrbānū and the Lady of Pārs', *Bulletin of the School of Oriental and African Studies* 30, 1 (1967), 30–44; Boyce, 'Bībī Shahrbānū', *EIr*.

131. Tahera Qutbuddin, 'Ibn Abī l-Ḥadīd', *EI3*; W. Madelung, "ABD-AL-ḤAMĪD B. ABU'L-ḤADĪD', *EIr*. While its enemies did adopt some methodologies of the Mu'tazila, this generally did not extend to the views of the early period. Suffice it to say that, in subsequent centuries, when Sunni–Shia polarisation increased, the Hadith-focused scholars, especially from the Hanbali school, and some of the later Abbasid Caliphs were also reacting against what they saw as the 'threat' of the Mu'tazila, and not 'just' against the Shia. Bayhom-Daou, *Shaykh Mufid*, 84–91. The relationship between Shiism and the Mu'tazila itself is, however, also complicated and, as Madelung argues, has sometimes been overstated, because the two also disagreed on fundamental points of doctrine, and several figures associated with the Mu'tazila were harsh critics of Shiism. Wilferd Madelung, 'Imamism and Mu'atazilite Theology', in: Centre de Recherches d'Histoire des Religions Strasbourg (ed.), *Le shî'isme imâmite: Colloque de Strasbourg (6–9 mai 1968)* (Paris: Presses Universitaires de France, 1970), 13–30, 13; Hussein Ali Abdulsater, *Shi'i Doctrine, Mu'tazili Theology: Al-Sharif al-Murtada and Imami Discourse* (Edinburgh: Edinburgh University Press, 2017).

132. Shia were less outspoken than the non-Mu'tazili Sunnis in their denunciation of the concept, adopting a middle position. Richard C. Martin, 'Createdness of the Qur'ān', *EQur*; George Makdisi, *Ibn 'Aqil et la résurgence de l'Islam traditionaliste au XIe siècle, Ve siècle del'Hégire* (Damascus: Institut Français de Damas, 1963), 326; H. S. Nyberg, 'al-Mu'tazila', *EI*; Walter M. Patton, *Ahmed Ibn*

Hanbal and the Mihna: A Biography of the Imam Including an Account of the Mohammedan Inquisition Called the Mihna, 218–34 AH (Leiden: Brill, 1897), 54; John Abdallah Nawas, Al-Ma'mun, the Inquisition, and the Quest for Caliphal Authority (Atlanta, GA: Lockwood Press, 2015); Wilferd Madelung, 'The Origins of the Controversy Concerning the Creation of the Qur'an', in: J. M. Barral (ed.), Orientalia Hispanica: Sive studia F. M. Pareja octogenaria dicata (Leiden: Brill, 1974), 504–25; Josef van Ess, 'Ibn Kullāb und die Miḥna', Oriens 18/9 (1965/6), 97–142; Rasul Ja'fariyan, Ukdhubat tahrif al-Qur'an bayn al-Shi'a wa-l-Sunna (Tehran: Mu'awaniyyat al-'Alaqat al-Duwaliyya fi Munazzama al-I'lam al-Islami, 1985).

133. There is a debate in the literature as to whether there was a more gradual introduction of Mu'tazili dogmas and concepts from the late ninth century into Twelver Shii thinking, i.e. before al-Mufid. See Bayhom-Daou, Shaykh Mufid, 83; Paul Sander, Zwischen Charisma und Ratio: Entwicklungen in der frühen imāmitischen Theologie (Berlin: Klaus Schwarz, 1994); Hassan Ansari and Sabine Schmidtke, Studies in Medieval Islamic Intellectual Traditions (Atlanta: Lockwood Press, 2017), 293–309. See also al-Hilli, Al-Bābu 'l-Ḥādî 'Ashar, 92–7.

134. He would, for example, also excuse Aisha from any wrongdoing. Gimaret, La doctrine, 559–66. He also wrote a Sunni creed that clearly included acceptance of the Rashidun Caliphs as the basis of faith. See the translation of a short creed by al-Ashari in Duncan B. MacDonald, Development of Muslim Theology, Jurisprudence, and Constitutional Theory \ (London: Routledge, 1903), 297.

135. Ssekamanya Siraje Abdallah, 'Ibn Taymiyyah on the Hadith of the 73 Sects', Jurnal Akidah & Pemikiran Islam 7, 1 (2006), 35–62, 40; Frank Griffel, Apostasie und Toleranz im Islam: Die Entwicklung zu al-Ġazālīs Urteil gegen die Philosophie und die Reaktionen der Philosophen (Leiden: Brill, 2000), 127, 132; Laoust, Comment définir, 4; Laoust, 'La classification des sectes dans l'hérésiographie ash'arite', in: George Makdisi (ed.), Arabic and Islamic Studies in Honor of Hamilton A. R. Gibb (Leiden: Brill, 1965), 377–86; Makdisi, 'L'hérésiographie musulmane sous les Abbassides', Cahiers de civilisation médiévale 10, 38 (1967), 157–78. Al-Ashari's Maqalat al-Islamiyyin was taken up by al-Baghdadi in his al-Farq bayn al-Firaq. Several scholars from the Shafii-Ashari tradition later elaborated on these texts, including al-Shahrastani in his al-Milal wa-l-Nihal. Many other scholars were influenced by the genre, even if they did not explicitly write firaq texts that resembled the structures named above, in other words the listing of seventy-three sects. Farouk Mitha, Al-Ghazali and the Ismailis: A Debate on Reason and Authority in Medieval Islam (London: I. B. Tauris/ Institute of Ismaili Studies, 2001), 35ff. See also Josef van Ess, Der Eine und das Andere: Beobachtungen an islamischen häresiographischen Texten, 2 Vols (Berlin: De Gruyter, 2011); Ignaz Goldziher, Beiträge zur Literaturgeschichte der Šî'â und der sunnitischen Polemik (Vienna: Karl Gerold's Sohn, 1874).

136. The term was coined by Marshall Hodgson, who in response termed the next period the 'Sunni Revival' or 'Sunni internationalism'. Hodgson, Venture, Vol. 2, esp. 36–9. Louis Massignon had already described it as the 'Ismaili century'.

Louis Massignon, 'Mutanabi devant le siècle ismaélien de l'Islam', in: *Al Mutanabbî: Recueil publié à l'occasion de son millénaire* (Beirut: Institut Français de Damas, 1936), 1–17.

137. For one such example, see Wadad al-Qadi, 'Abu Hayyan al-Tawhidi: A Sunni Voice in the Shi'i Century', in: Farhad Daftary and Josef W. Meri (eds), *Culture and Memory in Medieval Islam: Essays in Honour of Wilferd Madelung* (London: I. B. Tauris/Institute of Ismaili Studies, 2003), 128–59.

138. For a concise account, see M. S. Khan, 'The Early History of Zaydi Shi'ism in Daylaman and Gilan', *Zeitschrift der Deutschen Morgenländischen Gesellschaft* 125 (1975), 301–14. See also W. Madelung, 'The Minor Dynasties of Northern Iran', in: R. N. Frye (ed.), *The Cambridge History of Iran*, Vol. 4 (Cambridge: Cambridge University Press, 1975), 198–249.

139. Serjeant, 'The Zaydis', 290. See also Madelung, *Der Imam*, 154–222.

140. This was contentious, for some Shii Imams were still alive and the dogmas were still being formulated. Strothmann, *Staatsrecht*, 11–25, 48, and in particular Madelung, *Der Imam*. For more on his life, see Madelung, *Der Imam*, 86–96. For edited and translated examples of his writings, see Qasim b. Ibrahim al-Rassi, *Anthropomorphism and Interpretation of the Qur'ān in the Theology of al-Qāsim ibn Ibrāhīm: Kitāb al-Mustarshid*, trans./ed. by Binyamin Abrahamov (Leiden: Brill, 1996).

141. H. S. Nyberg, 'al-Mu'tazila', *EI*; Madelung, *Der Imam*, 2–85; D. Gimaret, 'Mu'tazila', *EI2*; Ansari and Schmidtke, *Studies in Medieval Islamic Intellectual Traditions*, 99. This is a growing field of study that is vitalised by the discovery, editing, and digitisation of Zaydi manuscripts. See, for example, Jan Thiele, *Theologie in der jemenitischen Zaydiyya: Die naturphilosophischen Überlegungen des al-Ḥasan ar-Raṣṣāṣ* (Leiden: Brill, 2013); Thiele, *Kausalität in der mu'tazilitischen Kosmologie: Das Kitab al-Mu'aththirāt wa-miftaḥ al-muşkilāt des Zayditen al-Ḥasan ar-Raṣṣāṣ (st. 584/1188)* (Leiden: Brill, 2011).

142. The two branches were generally known as the Qasimis (followers of Qasim) and Nasiris (followers of al-Utrush). Madelung, *Der Imam*, 4. See also Rudolf Strothmann, 'Die Literatur der Zaiditen', *Islam* 2 (1911), 49–78, 63.

143. For classical accounts of his role in the establishment of the Imamate, see Cornelis van Arendonk, *Les débuts de l'imamat zaidite au Yémen*, trans. by Jacques Ryckmans (Leiden: Brill, 1960), the original of which is *De Opkomst van het Zaidietische Imamaat in Yemen* (Leiden: Brill, 1919).

144. Rudolf Strothmann, 'Die Literatur der Zaiditen', *Islam* 1 (1910), 354–68, 361. See also Ansari and Schmidtke, *Studies in Medieval Islamic Intellectual Traditions*, 141–57, 231–45.

145. Wilferd Madelung, *Arabic Texts Concerning the History of the Zaydī Imāms of Tabaristān, Daylamān and Gīlān* (Beirut/Wiesbaden: Orient-Institut der Deutschen Morgenländischen Gesellschaft/Franz Steiner, 1987), 11–14.

146. Bernard Haykel, *Revival and Reform in Islam: The Legacy of Muhammad al-Shawkani* (Cambridge: Cambridge University Press, 2003), 5f.; Paul Dresch, *A History of Modern Yemen* (Cambridge: Cambridge University Press, 2000), 15.

See also Madelung, *Der Imam*, 144, who emphasises the importance of knowledge and wisdom in al-Qasim's Imamate theory.

147. Both in Yemen and during the period when there were Zaydi states outside of Yemen (between the Imams in Yemen and those in Iran and North Africa). Strothmann, *Staatsrecht*, 90–101.

148. Several epistles attributed to him were later suspected by twentieth-century European scholars to have been forgeries by later followers of the Jarudiyya branch of the Zaydiyya, though they remain part of the Zaydi canon. See Strothmann, 'Das Problem'; Madelung, *Der Imam*, 53f.

149. Madelung, *Der Imam*, 45f. For Zaydi critiques of Sunni Hadith, see Rudolf Strothmann, 'Die Literatur der Zaiditen', *Islam* 2 (1911), 49–78, 73. For anti-Zaydi polemics by a key Shii cleric, see Bayhom-Daou, *Shaykh Mufid*, 48–51.

150. Scrjeant, 'The Zaydis', 290–7; Paul Dresch, *Tribes, Government, and History in Yemen* (Oxford: Clarendon, 1989), 14of., 158–67; Robert B. Serjeant, 'The Interplay between Tribal Affinities and Religious (Zaydı) Authority in Yemen', *al-Abhath* 30 (1982), 11–50; Gianni Albergoni and Genviève Bédoucha, 'Hiérarchie, médiation, et tribalisme en Arabie du Sud: La hijra yéménite', *L'Homme* 31, 118 (1991), 7–36; Wilferd Madelung, 'The Origins of the Yemenite Hijra', in: Alan Jones (ed.), *Arabicus Felix, Luminosus Brittanicus: Essays in Honour of A. F. L. Beeston on his Eightieth Birthday* (Reading: Ithaca, 1991), 25–44; Gerd-R. Puin, 'The Yemeni Hijrah Concept of Tribal Protection', in: Tarif Khalidi (ed.), *Land Tenure and Social Transformation in the Middle East* (Beirut: American University of Beirut Press, 1984), 483–94. We should beware, however, of using generalising sociological categories such as sect and tribe, even if colonial officials used them in their correspondence. These categories have meant different things to different people at different times, have often proven fluid, and have failed to adequately represent the situation in complex locales such as Yemen. Isa Blumi, *Rethinking the Late Ottoman Empire: A Comparative Social and Political History of Albania and Yemen, 1878–1918* (Istanbul: Isis Press, 2003), 44f., 80.

151. Sachedina, *Islamic Messianism*, 14–17; Afsaruddin, *Excellence and Precedence*, 197; Krämer, *Geschichte*, 116; M. G. S. Hodgson, 'Dja'far al-Ṣādiḳ', *EI2*; Hodgson, *Venture*, Vol. 1, 370–6. Ibn Taymiyya disputes, however, that Abu Hanifa studied with al-Sadiq. Ahmad Ibn Taymiyya, *Minhaj al-Sunna al-Nabawiyya fi Naqd Kalam al-Shi'a wa-l-Qadariyya* (The Way of the Prophetic Sunna in the Criticism of the Words of the Shia and the Qadiriyya), 4 Vols (Cairo: Bulaq, 1903–5), Vol. 4, 143. There are also Sunni works that seek to fashion Jafar al-Sadiq as a good Sunni scholar and as non-responsible for later Shii 'deviations'. Some Shii works, on the other hand, relate denigrating accounts by Jafar al-Sadiq about Abu Hanifa (they are less negative about Malik bin Anas). Robert Gleave, 'JA'FAR AL-ṢĀDEQ ii. Teachings', *EIr*.

152. The details of the succession disputes are considerably more complicated than outlined here. Farhad Daftary, *The Ismailis: Their History and Doctrines*, 2nd ed.

(Cambridge: Cambridge University Press, 2007), 87–98, esp. 90ff. on Ismail ibn Jafar. They had to invoke a concept in Shii theology that allowed a divine ruling to be changed based on new factual circumstances (*bada*). This concept has at times been used by critics of Shiism to point to inconsistencies within Shiism, who argued it was inconsistent with the omnipotence of God. Shia have sometimes responded that Sunnis know a similar concept, abrogation (*naskh*), which can be used to solve 'apparent inconsistencies within and between the Qur'ān and the *sunna*'. Andrew Rippin, 'Abrogation', *EI3*. See also Haider, *Shi'i Islam*, 91f.; W. Madelung, 'BADĀ'', *EIr*; Mohammad Ali Amir-Moezzi, 'Badā'', *EI3*.

153. H. Kennedy, 'al-Mutawakkil 'Alā 'llāh', *EI2*.

154. First developed by the Hamdanid Nasir al-Dawla in 333/944–945, it was expanded by the Buyids, then by Arslan al-Basasiri, and then in 606/1209–10 by the 'ecumenical' Abbasid Caliph al-Nasir. The Qajar ruler Nasir al-Din Shah (1848–96) ordered in 1868–9 that the whole complex be rebuilt, and a golden dome was added in 1905. Teresa Bernheimer, "Alī l-Hādī', *EI3*; A. Northedge, 'Sāmarrā'', *EI2*; Haider, *Shi'i Islam*, 94ff.

155. For an overview, see Robert Gleave, 'Recent Research into the History of Early Shi'ism', *History Compass* 7 (2009), 1593–605. Amidst a large literature, see especially Afsaruddin, *Excellence and Precedence*, 1; Mohammad Ali Amir-Moezzi, *The Divine Guide in Early Shi'ism: The Sources of Esotericism in Islam,* trans. by David Streight (New York: State University of New York Press, 1994); Hassan Ansari, *L'imamat et l'Occultation selon l'imamisme: Etude bibliographique et histoire des textes* (Leiden: Brill, 2017); Seyyed Hossein Modarressi, *Crisis and Consolidation in the Formative Period of Shi'ite Islam: Abū Ja'far ibn Qiba al-Rāzī and his Contribution to Imāmite Shi'ite Thought* (Princeton: Darwin Press, 1993); Andrew J. Newman, *The Formative Period of Twelver Shī'ism: Ḥadīth as Discourse between Qum and Baghdad* (Abingdon: Routledge, 2000); Sachedina, *Islamic Messianism*, 30–5; M. Hinds, 'Miḥna', *EI2*; Verena Klemm, 'Die vier Sufarā' des Zwölften Imām: Zur formativen Periode der Zwölferšī'a', *Die Welt des Orients* 15 (1984), 126–43; Said Amir Arjomand, 'ĠAYBA', *EIr*; Arjomand, 'The Crisis of the Imamate and the Institution of Occultation in Twelver Shiism: A Sociohistorical Perspective', *International Journal of Middle East Studies* 28, 4 (1996), 491–515; Sachedina, *Islamic Messianism*, 4–9; Etan Kohlberg, 'From Imāmiyya to Ithnā-'Ashariyya', *Bulletin of the School of Oriental and African Studies* 39, 3 (1976), 521–34; Haider, *Shi'i Islam*, 1; Brannon Wheeler, 'The Ancient Authority of the Imam and Mahdi in Imami Shi'i Scholarship', in: *Community, State, History and Changes: Festschrift for Ridwan al-Sayyid on his Sixtieth Birthday* (Beirut: al-Shabaka al-'Arabiyya li-l-Abhath wa-l-Nashr, 2011), 137–74. For the Ghulat in general, see Mushegh Asatryan, *Controversies in Formative Shi'i Islam: The Ghulat Muslims and their Beliefs* (London: I.B. Tauris, 2017); Heinz Halm, *Die islamische Gnosis: Die extreme Schia und die 'Alawiten* (Zurich: Artemis, 1982); M. G. S. Hodgson, 'Ghulāt', *EI2*. For a revisionist

account on the 'ambassadors' and early network of the Imam's agents, see now also Edmund Hayes, *Agents of the Hidden Imam: Forging Twelver Shi'ism, 850–950 CE* (Cambridge: Cambridge University Press, 2022).

156. Gregor Voss, *'Alawīya oder Nusairīya?': Schiitische Machtelite und sunnitische Opposition in der Syrischen Arabischen Republik: Untersuchung zu einer islamisch-politischen Streitfrage* (PhD, University of Hamburg, 1987); Matti Moosa, *Extremist Shiites: The Ghulat Sects* (Syracuse: Syracuse University Press, 1987), 255–66.

157. Mohamed El-Moctar, *The Crusades' Impact on Sunni-Shi'a Relations* (PhD, Texas Tech University, 2011), 132.

158. Massignon, 'Mutanabi'.

159. Winter, *History*, 12–21.

160. Ibid., 23ff., 32f.

161. Haider, *Shi'i Islam*, 95. The most famous example may be Hasan al-Sabbah, who stemmed from a Twelver Shii family in Qom and would become the leader of the Ismailis at Alamut. Ibid., 131.

162. A subgenre of Shii heresiography by Twelver Shia became directed against other Shia. It was in the twentieth century also integrated into the Orientalist canon. The most famous example of this genre was probably written by al-Nawbakhti and first edited and published by the German Orientalist Hellmut Ritter in Istanbul in 1931. Abi Muhammad al-Hasan ibn Musa al-Nawbakhti, *Kitāb Firaq al-Shī'a* (The Sects of the Shia) (Istanbul: Maṭba'at al-Dawlah/ Deutsche Morgenländische Gesellschaft, 1931). See also al-Nawbakhti, *Les sectes shiites*, annot. by M. Javad Mashkour (Tehran: n.p., 1980); Wilferd Madelung, 'Bemerkungen zur imamitischen Firaq-Literatur', *Der Islam* 43 (1967), 37–52. For an example of an Ismaili heresiography that also includes the Shia, see Wilferd Madelung and Paul E. Walker, *An Ismaili Heresiography: The 'Bāb al-Shayṭān' from Abū Tammāms' Kitāb al-Shajara* (Leiden: Brill, 1998).

163. Strothmann, *Staatsrecht*, 102. Zaydis reject the notion of *taqiyya*, of concealing one's beliefs in the face of danger, and instead emphasise the need to enforce the Quranic verse to 'command the right and forbid the wrong'. Serjeant, 'The Zaydis'. For a detailed account of the duty to 'command the right and forbid the wrong' in Zaydism (and comparisons with other schools of jurisprudence), see Michael Cook, *Commanding Right and Forbidding Wrong in Islamic Thought* (Cambridge: Cambridge University Press, 2000), 227–51. From the seventeenth century on, and then in particular with al-Shawkani, traditionally Sunni argumentations on the topic replaced Zaydi argumentations. Ibid., 247–51. The concept of Jihad is also significant in Zaydism. Strothmann, 'Literatur', 367f.; Hans Kruse, 'Takfīr und Ǧihād bei den Zaiditen des Jemen', *Die Welt des Islams* 23/4 (1984), 424–57. Other differences include the Zaydi rejection of temporary marriage, of the *khums* tax, and of inheritance and some aspects of ritual practice. Strothmann, 'Das Problem', 48f.; Madelung, *Der Imam*, 134ff., 147f.; Rudolf Strothmann, *Kultus der Zaiditen* (Strasbourg: Karl J. Trübner, 1912), 21–46. For a positive account of Zayd bin Ali's rising by a famous twentieth-century Twelver Shii scholar, see al-Sayyid Muhsin

al-Amin, *Al-Shahid Zayd ibn ʿAli wa-l-Zaydiyya* (Beirut: Dar al-Murtada, 2003). See also this book published in Qom, Iran, looking at the Zaydiyya and its relations with both Twelver Shia and Sunnis: Sami al-Ghariri, *Al-Zaydiyya: Bayn al-Imamiyya wa Ahl al-Sunna* (Qom: Dar al-Kitab al-Islami, 2006), esp. 587–93, listing the differences between the three. There is an interesting book by Yahya bin al-Hussein al-Huthi, *Sublime Answers to the Iraqi's Questions (Al-Jawāb ar-Rāqi ʿala al-Masāʾil al-Irāqi)*, available at https://www.scribd.com/document/36214491/الراقي-الجواب, which outlines the differences between Twelvers and Zaydis in detail. Zaydis also do not recognise, for example, the idea that a child could be an Imam, that Imams are infallible, or the idea that the twelfth Imam would return as the Mahdi. This refers to the fact that, upon the death of the eighth Imam, Ali al-Rida, his son Muhammad al-Jawad was only three or four years old and, when he died, his son was also still a child (Ali al-Hadi). Ali al-Hadi was the Shii Imam at the time when al-Qasim wrote his treatises against the Shia. See Strothmann, *Staatsrecht*, 49ff., 63. For more on the early doctrinal history of the Zaydis, see Madelung, *Der Imam*; Strothmann, *Kultus*. Those criticisms of Twelver Shiism have been reaffirmed by some members of the Huthi family, such as Hussain al-Huthi. See Ibrahim Zabad, *Middle Eastern Minorities: The Impact of the Arab Spring* (Abingdon: Routledge, 2017), 193. For the occultation, see Maher Jarrar, ʿAl-Manṣūrbi-Llāh's Controversy with Twelver Šiʿites Concerning the Occultation of the Imam in his Kitāb al-ʿIqd al-tamīn', *Arabica* 59, 3–4 (2012), 319–31. See also Wilferd Madelung, ʿImama', *EI*.

164. Some authors have thus argued that Sunni and Shii schools of jurisprudence influenced each other in a dialectical process, especially the Shafii and Twelver Shii schools. Devin J. Stewart, *Islamic Legal Orthodoxy: Twelver Shiite Responses to the Sunni Legal System* (Salt Lake City: University of Utah Press, 1998), 1f., 209–39. Others say Stewart's sources cannot prove this closeness between the Shafii and Shii schools. See, for example, the review by Sabine Schmidtke in *Iranian Studies* 37, 1 (2004), 123–6. Al-Jamil has emphasised that Shii scholars studied with Sunni scholars from all the schools, not just with Shafiis, and that claims about the close affiliation between the Shii and Shafii schools are premature. Tariq al-Jamil, *Cooperation and Contestation in Medieval Baghdad (656/1258–786/1384): Relationships between Shīʿī and Sunnī Scholars in the Madīnat al-Salām* (PhD, Princeton University, 2004), 93. For an early elaboration of the importance of Jafar al-Sadiq in the codification of Shiism, see Marshall G. S. Hodgson, ʿHow Did the Early Shiʿa Become Sectarian?', *Journal of the American Oriental Society* 75, 1 (1955), 1–13.

165. Wilferd Madelung, "Abd Allah b. ʿAbbas and Shiʿite Law', in: U. Vermeulen and J. M. F. van Reeth (eds), *Law, Christianity and Modernism in Islamic Society: Proceedings of the Eighteenth Congress of the Union Européenne des Arabisants et Islamisants Held at the Katholieke Universiteit Leuven* (Leuven: Peeters, 1998), 13–26, 22f.; Edmund Hayes, ʿAlms and the Man: Fiscal Sectarianism in the Legal Statements of the Shiʿi Imams', *Journal of Arabic and Islamic Studies* 17 (2017), 280–98. For the Shii point of view, see Sayyid Muhammad Rizvi,

'Zakat in Shi'a Fiqh', *Al-Islam.org*, https://www.al-islam.org/articles/zakat-shia-fiqh-sayyid-muhammad-rizvi. Shia were also discouraged from taking up office under an illegitimate ruler. In practice, however, Shii officials and jurists justified their engagement with the powers of the day by arguing that such a position might help the wider Shii community or enforce good and prevent evil. Madelung has argued that the extent to which Shii jurists saw governments in the absence of the Imam as illegitimate has been overstated. Wilferd Madelung, 'A Treatise of the Sharīf al-Murtaḍā on the Legality of Working for the Government (Mas'ala Fī 'l-'Amal Ma'a 'l-Sulṭān)', *Bulletin of the School of Oriental and African Studies* 43, 1 (1980), 18–31; Madelung, 'Authority in Twelver Shiism', 170f.

166. Abdulaziz Abdulhussein Sachedina, *The Just Ruler (al-Sultān al-'Ādil) in Shī'ite Islam: The Comprehensive Authority of the Jurist in Imamite Jurisprudence* (Oxford: Oxford University Press, 1988); Etan Kohlberg, 'From Imāmiyya to Ithnā-'Ashariyya', *Bulletin of the School of Oriental and African Studies* 39, 3 (1976), 521–34.

167. William Harris, *Lebanon: A History, 600–2011* (Oxford: Oxford University Press, 2012), 43. For the standard account, see Daftary, *The Ismailis*. For a contemporary source, see Wilferd Madelung and Paul E. Walker (eds), *The Advent of the Fatimids: A Contemporary Shi'i Witness: An Edition and English Translation of Ibn al-Haytham's Kitab al-Munazarat* (London: I. B. Tauris/ Institute of Ismaili Studies, 2000).

168. Daftary, *The Ismailis*, 95ff.

169. The first position disappeared with time, however, in particular after the end of the Qarmatian polities, and all surviving Ismaili groups locate the Imam amongst what they see as Muhammad bin Ismail's descendants. Haider, *Shi'i Islam*, 124; Krämer, *Geschichte*, 117–27.

170. Daftary, *The Ismailis*, 98–116; S. M. Stern, 'The Early Ismā'īlī Missionaries in North-West Persia and in Khurāsān and Transoxania', *Bulletin of the School of Oriental and African Studies* 23, 1 (1960), 56–90; Stern, 'Ismā'īlī Propaganda and Fatimid Rule in Sind', *Islamic Culture* 23/4 (1949), 289–307. In general, see Heinz Halm, *Kosmologie und Heilslehre der frühen Ismā'īlīya: Eine Studie zur islamischen Gnosis* (Wiesbaden: Franz Steiner, 1978); Halm, *Das Reich des Mahdi: Der Aufstieg der Fatimiden 875–973* (Munich: C. H. Beck, 1991) (Engl. Transl.: *The Empire of the Mahdi: The Rise of the Fatimids* (Leiden: Brill, 1996).

171. Haider, *Shi'i Islam*, 127ff.; Heinz Halm, *The Fatimids and their Traditions of Learning* (London: I. B. Tauris, 2001), 3–16.

172. Paul E. Walker, 'The Responsibilities of Political Office in a Shi'i Caliphate and the Delineation of Public Duties under the Fatimids', in: Asma Afsaruddin (ed.), *Islam, the State, and Political Authority: Medieval Issues and Modern Concerns* (New York: Palgrave Macmillan, 2011), 93–110.

173. Juan R. I. Cole, 'Rival Empires of Trade and Imami Shiism in Eastern Arabia, 1300–1800', *International Journal of Middle East Studies* 19, 2 (1987), 177–203, 178; Daftary, *The Ismailis*, 109f.; Michael Jan de Goeje, *Mémoire sur les Carmathes du Bahraïn et les Fatimides* (Leiden: Brill, 1886).

174. But we know little about the exact religious dimension of their rule from their own sources. Nasir Khusraw (d. 1088), for example, who visited the region, reports divisions between the rulers of al-Ahsa and Qatif (and states that the normal obligations for Muslims were not enforced or practised in al-Ahsa). Nāṣir-i Khusraw, *Naser-e Khosraw's Book of Travels (Safarnāma)*, trans. by W. M. Thackston, Jr. (Albany, NY: Bibliotheca Persica, 1986), 86–90.

175. C. E. Bosworth, 'Sanawbari's Elegy on the Pilgrims Slain in the Carmathian Attack on Mecca (317/930): A Literary-Historical Study', *Arabica* 19, 3 (1972), 222–39.

176. Toby Matthiesen, 'Shiʿi Historians in a Wahhabi State: Identity Entrepreneurs and the Politics of Local Historiography in Saudi Arabia', *International Journal of Middle East Studies* 47, 1 (2015), 25–45.

177. Stefan Heidemann, 'Numismatics', in: Chase F. Robinson (ed.), *The New Cambridge History of Islam*, Vol. 1 (Cambridge: Cambridge University Press, 2010), 648–63, 662.

178. Mottahedeh, *Loyalty*, 24.

179. Heinz Halm, *Kalifen und Assassinen: Ägpyten und der Vordere Orient zur Zeit der ersten Kreuzzüge 1074–1171* (Munich: C. H. Beck, 2014), 28–37.

180. The previous site of the head in Palestine also retained significance as a local pilgrimage site, though other places also claim to be the final resting ground of his head. Krämer, *Geschichte*, 124; N. J. G. Kaptein, *Muhammad's Birthday Festival: Early History in the Central Muslim Lands and Development in the Muslim West until the 10th/16th Century* (Leiden: Brill, 1993), 27. Most scholars agree that Hussain's body is buried in Karbala, and, apart from the dispute about Ali's final resting ground, the debate about the location of Hussain's head is the only other serious debate about the location of an Imam's final burial place. Aslan, *From Body to Shrine*, 177. See also Institute of Ismaili Studies, 'The Cenotaph of Imam Husayn', 28 February 2018, https://iis.ac.uk/content/sarcophagus-cenotaph-imam-husayn. For Palestine, where the shrine for Hussain was rebuilt in the nineteenth century but blown up by Israel in the 1950s, see Andrew Petersen, *Bones of Contention: Muslim Shrines in Palestine* (Basingstoke: Palgrave Macmillan, 2018), 108ff., 125f.; Daniel de Smet, 'La translation du "ra's al-Husayn" au Caire fatimide', in: Urbain Vermeulen and J. van Steenbergen (eds), *Egypt and Syria in the Fatimid, Ayyubid and Mamluk Eras* (Leuven: Peeters, 1995), 29–44; Yaron Friedman, *The Shīʿis in Palestine: From the Medieval Golden Age until the Present* (Leiden: Brill, 2020). Ibn Taymiyya, as part of his push against Shiism and the worship of shrines, issued a fatwa stating that both the mausoleum in Askalon and the subsequent one in Cairo were inventions and that the head of Hussain never rested in either place. For a translation, see Friedman, *The Shīʿis*, 156–70.

181. Goldziher, *Beiträge*, 20, citing al-Maqrizi. See also Bayard Dodge, 'The Fatimid Legal Code', *The Muslim World* 50, 1 (1960), 30–8.

182. Sumaiya A. Hamdani, *Between Revolution and State: The Path to Fatimid Statehood: Qadi al-Nuʿman and the Construction of Fatimid Legitimacy* (London:

I. B. Tauris, 2006); Wilferd Madelung, 'The Sources of Ismāʿīlī Law', *Journal of Near Eastern Studies* 35, 1 (1976), 29–40; Ismail K. Poonawala, 'The Evolution of al-Qadi al-Nuʿman's Theory of Ismaili Jurisprudence as Reflected in the Chronology of his Works on Jurisprudence', in: Farhad Daftary and Gurdofarid Miskinzoda (eds), *The Study of Shiʿi Islam: History, Theology and Law* (London: I. B. Tauris, 2014), 295–351; Agostino Cilardo, *The Early History of Ismaili Jurisprudence: Law under the Fatimids* (London: I. B. Tauris/Institute of Ismaili Studies, 2012). Some Twelver Shia later argued that the *Qadi* al-Numan was in fact a Twelver Shii and not an Ismaili practising *taqiyya*. He did not, however, include Hadith by those Imams not recognised by Ismailis but recognised by Twelver Shia. Farhad Daftary, *Ismaili History and Intellectual Traditions* (Abingdon: Routledge, 2018), 162–9.

183. Dodge, 'The Fatimid Legal Code'.
184. Kaptein, *Muhammad's Birthday Festival*, 20–9.
185. In the words of al-Maqrizi, the Shia 'felt strengthened by al-Muʾizz's presence in Egypt'. Shainool Jiwa, *Towards a Shiʿi Mediterranean Empire: Fatimid Egypt and the Founding of Cairo* (London: I. B. Tauris, 2009), 115. Though the extent of their impact on Islamic funerary architecture is disputed. Christopher S. Taylor, 'Reevaluating the Shiʿi Role in the Development of Monumental Islamic Funerary Architecture: The Case of Egypt', *Muqarnas* 9 (1992), 1–10. See also Taylor, *In the Vicinity of the Righteous: Ziyāra and the Veneration of Muslim Saints in Late Medieval Egypt* (Leiden: Brill, 1999).
186. Haider, *Shiʿi Islam*, 130; Yaacov Lev, *State and Society in Fatimid Egypt* (Leiden: Brill, 1991), 133–52; Haider, 'The Fāṭimid Imposition of Ismāʾilism on Egypt (358–386/969–996)', *Zeitschrift der Deutschen Morgenländischen Gesellschaft* 138, 2 (1988), 313–25; Gary La Viere Leiser, *The Restoration of Sunnism in Egypt: Madrasas and Mudarrisun 495–647/1101–1249* (PhD, University of Pennsylvania, 1976), 89–109.
187. Daftary, *The Ismailis*, 186–91; Marshall G. S. Hodgson, 'Al-Darazî and Ḥamza in the Origin of the Druze Religion', *Journal of the American Oriental Society* 82, 1 (1962), 5–20. See also Kais M. Firro, *A History of the Druzes* (Leiden: Brill, 1992).
188. Harris, *Lebanon*, 18, 46f., 67.
189. Daftary, *The Ismailis*, 181ff.; El-Moctar, *The Crusades' Impact*, 125; Wilferd Madelung, 'The Religious Policy of the Fatimids toward their Sunni Subjects in the Maghrib', in: Marianne Barrucand (ed.), *L'Egypte Fatimide: Son art et son histoire* (Paris: Presses de l'Université de Paris-Sorbonne, 1999), 97–104; Ballandalus, 'Sectarianism and Violence in 11th-c. North Africa: The Anti-Ismaili Massacre of 1016', 31 July 2016, https://ballandalus.wordpress.com/2016/07/31/sectarianism-and-violence-in-11th-c-north-africa-the-anti-ismaili-massacre-of-1016/. For the assertion of Malikism as the dominant religious school over both Kharijism and Ismailism in North Africa, see Mansour Hasan Mansour, *The Spread and the Domination of the Maliki School of Law in North and West Africa, Eighth-Fourteenth Century* (PhD, University of Illinois Chicago, 1981), esp. 95–159.

190. Yaacov Lev, *Saladin in Egypt* (Leiden: Brill, 1999), 118f.; Lev, *State and Society*, 138; Adel Allouche, 'The Establishment of Four Chief Judgeships in Fāṭimid Egypt', *Journal of the American Oriental Society* 105, 2 (1985), 317–20.

191. Lev, *Saladin*, 79.

192. The minister sought the advice of clerics on the matter, receiving an answer from a Sunni scholar and from a Twelver Shii one, who argued that the Fatimids were not Imams. This thus reflects the early Twelver Shii opposition to the Ismaili split, although the Twelver Shii cleric wanted nothing to do with the plan of deposing the Caliph, which in any case failed after it was uncovered. Halm, *Kalifen und Assassinen*, 195.

193. Berkey, *The Formation of Islam*, 192.

194. Ibid.

195. Lev, *Saladin*, 4f. This has been thoroughly documented in Kaptein, *Muhammad's Birthday Festival*, 28–34. Lasting legacies of the Ismaili period can, for example, be found in the Egyptian built environment and popular culture and in negative depictions of Aisha and Umar in the Egyptian vernacular. Devin J. Stewart, 'Popular Shiism in Medieval Egypt: Vestiges of Islamic Sectarian Polemics in Egyptian Arabic', *Studia Islamica* 84 (1996), 35–66, 41–5. See also Sanders, *Ritual, Politics, and the City*.

196. Ibn Taymiyya explained that neither mourning nor celebration on the day of Ashura was appropriate, and that those who celebrate are anti-Shii zealots who are pushing it too far in their hatred of Hussain and the Prophet's family. The only practice he endorsed on Ashura was fasting, because the Prophet had fasted on that day. Marion Holmes Katz, *The Birth of the Prophet Muhammad: Devotional Piety in Sunni Islam* (Abingdon: Routledge, 2007), 113–6, 157f. Another example are celebrations of the nights of mid-Shaban, which seem to have been practised in both Sunni and Shii contexts. While initially opposed by the Hanbalis of Baghdad, by the twelfth century a Hanbali rural community performed these rituals. Katz, *The Birth*, 157f.; Daniella Talmon-Heller, 'The Shaykh and the Community: Popular Hanbalite Islam in 12th–13th Century Jabal Nablus and Jabal Qasyūn', *Studia Islamica* 79 (1994), 103–20, 116.

197. Initially an employee in the Saljuq administration, Khusraw set out on his journey as part of a pilgrimage to Mecca and embraced Ismailism. It is possible that the policies of the Saljuqs influenced his decision to embark on his journey. Khusraw, *Nāser-e Khosraw's Book*.

198. Wilferd Madelung, 'al-Ukhaydir', *EI2*. 'The emirs there are Alids of old, and no one has ever been able to wrest the region from their control, since, in the first place there is not, nor has there been, a conquering sultan or king anywhere near, and, in the second, those Alids possess such might that they can mount three to four hundred horsemen. They are of the Zaydi sect, and when they stand in prayer they say, "Mohammad and Ali are the best of mankind," and, "Come to the best deed!" [the Shii call to prayer].' Khusraw, *Nāser-e Khosraw's Book*, 86.

199. Momen, *An Introduction to Shi'i Islam*, 90f.

200. For an overview, see Hugh Kennedy, *Caliphate: The History of an Idea* (New York: Basic Books, 2016). See also Mona Hassan, *Longing for the Lost Caliphate: A Transregional History* (Princeton: Princeton University Press, 2017).

201. They also allowed, and at times supported, philosophical discussions and scholarship. Joel L. Kraemer, *Humanism in the Renaissance of Islam: The Cultural Revival during the Buyid Age*, 2nd ed. (Leiden: Brill, 1992).

202. Bayhom-Daou, *Shaykh Mufid*, 28; Cl. Cahen, 'Buwayhids or Būyids', *EI2*.

203. Joseph Schacht, *An Introduction to Islamic Law* (Oxford: Oxford University Press, 1964), 16. Given the disagreement about how to arrive at certain rulings (i.e. the sources of jurisprudence), the similarity of the majority of rulings amongst Sunna and Shia is remarkable. Wilferd Madelung, 'Shi'i Attitudes toward Women as Reflected in "fiqh"', in: Afaf Lutfi al-Sayyid-Marsot (ed.), *Society and the Sexes in Medieval Islam* (Malibu, CA: Undena, 1979), 69–79, 70f. It is difficult to find systematic and clear juxtapositions of the different positions. One attempt is Harald Löschner, *Die dogmatischen Grundlagen des Šī'itischen Rechts: Eine Untersuchung zur modernen imāmitischen Rechtsquellenlehre* (Cologne: Carl Heymanns, 1971).

204. G. H. A. Juynboll and D. W. Brown, 'Sunna', *EI2*; Schacht, *The Origins*, 11–20; Strothmann, *Kultus*, 17.

205. Ibn Babuya (or Babawayh) al-Qummi (d. 991), Shaykh al-Mufid (d. 1022/3), Shaykh al-Tusi (d. 1067), and Abu Ali al-Fadl bin al-Hasan al-Tabrisi affirmed the authenticity of the Quran, thereby establishing a new, fragile Shii consensus. Mohammad Ali Amir-Moezzi, 'Al-Shaykh al-Mufid (m. 413/1022) et la question de la falsification du Coran', *Rivista Degli Studi Orientali* 87, 1 (2014), 155–76; Amir-Moezzi, *The Silent Qur'an and the Speaking Qur'an: Scriptural Sources of Islam between History and Fervor* (New York: Columbia University Press, 2016); Rainer Brunner, *Die Schia und die Koranfälschung* (Würzburg: Ergon, 2001), 5f., 70–117; Brunner, 'La question de la falsification du Coran dans l'exégèse chiite duodécimaine', *Arabica* 52, 1 (2005), 1–42; J. Eliash, 'The Šī'ite Qur'ān: A Reconsideration of Goldziher's Interpretation', *Arabica* 16 (1969), 15–24; Seyfeddin Kara, *In Search of Alī ibn Abī Tālib's Codex: History and Traditions of the Earliest Copy of the Qur'ān* (Berlin: Gerlach Press, 2018); Etan Kohlberg, 'Some Notes on the Imamite Attitude to the Quran', in: S. M. Stern, Albert Habib Hourani, and Vivian Brown (eds), *Islamic Philosophy and the Classical Tradition* (Columbia: University of South Carolina Press, 1972), 209–24; Seyyed Hossein Modarressi, 'Early Debates on the Integrity of the Qur'ān: A Brief Survey', *Studia Islamica* 77 (1993), 5–39; van Ess, *Theologie*, Vol. 1, 282; Etan Kohlberg and Mohammad Ali Amir-Moezzi (ed. and trans.), *Revelation and Falsification: The Kitāb al-Qirā'āt of Aḥmad b. Muḥammad al-Sayyārī* (Leiden: Brill, 2009), 24–30, and passim. Some Shii Iranian authors accuse Western Orientalists of appropriating some of this and unfairly portraying and sensationalising Shii views. Hasan Rezaee Haftador and Fatemeh Sarvi, 'Criticism of Ethan Kohlberg's View on the

Distortion of the Quran', *Iranian Journal for the Quranic Sciences & Tradition* 46, 1 (2013), 73–87 (in Persian).

206. The Akhbari school of Shiism, which was a literalist school denouncing the use of *ijtihad*, was particularly keen to base its interpretation on the Hadith, in particular the Hadith of the Imams, and thus the falsification of the Quran debate resurfaced during this time. When the Akhbari school slowly lost ground, however, this did not mean that its points of view on this issue disappeared with it, and it seems Usulis were influenced by Akhbaris on this point. Brunner, *Die Schia*, 12–69.

207. Madelung, *Succession*, 6–18.

208. For 33:33 and 42:23 in Arabic text and English translation, see https://quran. com/33/33–43 and https://quran.com/42/23–33?translations=20, respectively. Translations are contested, however.

209. Interestingly, al-Tabari tends to relate more traditions supporting the former interpretation than the latter one, while al-Thalabi tends to support the latter. Al-Tabari's rendering of the traditions of the other verse that has been disputed between Sunna and Shia, 42:23, is more anti-Shii. Al-Thalabi, on the other hand, includes more traditions that interpret this verse as ordering Muslims to respect and love those close to the Prophet, in some interpretations his family. Walid A. Saleh, *The Formation of the Classical Tafsīr Tradition: The Qur'ān Commentary of al-Thaʿlabī (d. 427/1035)* (Leiden: Brill, 2004), 178–88. According to Wilferd Madelung, 'the Quran thus accorded the *ahl al-bayt* of Muhammad an elevated position above the rest of the faithful, similar to the position of the families of the earlier prophets'. Madelung, *Succession*, 16. See also I. K. A. Howard, 'AHL-E BAYT', *EIr*; I. Goldziher, C. van Arendonk, and A. S. Tritton, 'Ahl al-Bayt', *EI2*.

210. Saleh, *Formation*, 178–88.

211. Mustafa Shah (ed.), *Tafsir: Interpreting the Qur'an*, Vol. 1 (Abingdon: Routledge, 2013), 41–4. For Shii *tafsir*, see Meir M. Bar-Asher, 'Introduction', in: Farhad Daftary and Gurdofarid Miskinzoda (eds), *The Study of Shiʿi Islam: History, Theology and Law* (London: I. B. Tauris, 2014), 78–94; Bar-Asher, 'Exegesis ii. In Shiʿism', *EIr*; Bar-Asher, *Scripture and Exegesis in Early Imāmī Shiism* (Leiden: Brill, 1999); Andrew Rippin, 'What Defines a (Pre-Modern) Shiʿi Tafsīr? Notes towards the History of the Genre of Tafsīr in Islam, in the Light of the Study of the Shiʿi Contribution', in: Farhad Daftary and Gurdofarid Miskinzoda (eds), *The Study of Shiʿi Islam: History, Theology and Law* (London: I. B. Tauris, 2014), 95–112; Tehseen Thaver, *Ambiguity, Hermeneutics, and the Formation of Shiʿi Identity in al-Sharif al-Radi's (d. 1015 CE) Qur'an Commentary* (PhD, University of North Carolina at Chapel Hill, 2013); Robert G. Morrison, *Islam and Science: The Intellectual Career of Nizam al-Din al-Nisaburi* (New York: Routledge, 2007).

212. See, for example, Afsaruddin, *Excellence and Precedence*, 197f.

213. For a list of works on this topic, see Kumail Rajani, 'Hadith: Shiʿi', *OBi*; Etan Kohlberg, 'Introduction: Shiʿi Hadith', in: Farhad Daftary and Gurdofarid

Miskinzoda (eds), *The Study of Shiʿi Islam: History, Theology and Law* (London: I. B. Tauris, 2014), 165–79. For the position of Ali in Shii Hadith scholarship, see Joseph Eliash, *ʿAli b. Abi Talib in Ithna-ʿAshari Shii Belief* (PhD, University of London, 1966), 97–114. See also al-Hilli, *Al-Bâbu 'l-Ḥâdî ʿAshar*, 64–8.

214. They are the collections by al-Kulayni (d. 940), Ibn Babuya (d. 991), and Abu Jafar al-Tusi (d. 1067/8). The reports by the Imams were also sometimes called *akhbar*, as opposed to the Hadith of the Prophet. See Robert Gleave, 'Between Ḥadīth and Fiqh: The "Canonical" Imāmī Collections of Akhbār', *Islamic Law and Society* 8, 3 (2001), 350–82; A. Kazemi-Moussavi, 'HADITH ii. IN SHIʿISM', *EIr*; Elisheva Machlis, *Shiʿi Sectarianism in the Middle East: Modernisation and the Quest for Islamic Universalism* (London: I. B. Tauris, 2014), 127. These were later complemented by Hadith collections and commentaries by Muhsin al-Fayd al-Kashani, Muhammad al-Hurr al-Amili, Muhammad Baqir al-Majlisi, and Hussain al-Nuri. Seyyed Hossein Modarressi, *An Introduction to Shīʿī Law: A Bibliographical Study* (London: Ithaca Press, 1984), 4ff.; Jonathan A. C. Brown, *Hadith: Muhammad's Legacy in the Medieval and Modern World*, 2nd ed. (Oxford: Oneworld, 2017).

215. Madelung, 'Authority in Twelver Shiism', 168f.; Modarressi, *An Introduction to Shīʿī Law*, 32–9; Bayhom-Daou, *Shaykh Mufid*, 91–4. For more on debates within Twelver Shiism at the time, see Andrew J. Newman, '"Minority Reports": Twelver Shiʿi Disputation and Authority in the Buyid Period', in: Farhad Daftary and Gurdofarid Miskinzoda (eds), *The Study of Shiʿi Islam: History, Theology and Law* (London: I. B. Tauris, 2014), 433–52.

216. Moktar Djebli, 'Nahḏj al-Balāgẖa', *EI2*; Machlis, *Shiʿi Sectarianism*, 128; Hans-Jürgen Kornrumpf, 'Untersuchungen zum Bild ʿAlīs und des frühen Islams bei den Schiiten (nach dem Nahǧ al-Balāǧa des Šarīf ar-Raḍī)', *Der Islam* 45, 1 (1969), 2–63, and *Der Islam* 45, 2 (1969), 261–98. See this book by a Sunni Maliki author on the 'Imams', using both Sunni and Shii sources. It was frequently republished by Shii publishing houses. Ibn Sabbagh al-Maliki, *Al-Fusul al-Muhimma fi Maʿrifat al-A'imma* (Cairo: Dar al-Hadith, 2001). Ibn Taymiyya posed questions about the authenticity of the *Nahj al-Balagha* in his *Minhaj al-Sunna*. Laoust, *Essai*, 108.

217. Shii scholars complain that, while Sunnis generally hold the *Ahl al-Bayt* in high esteem, this is not sufficiently reflected in Sunni Hadith collections. See, for example, Nowrouz Amini and Sayyed Rezā Moʾaddab, 'Attitude of al-Tabari, Ibn Kathir, and Thaʿalibi towards Commentatorial Hadiths of Ahl al-Bayt', *Iranian Journal for the Quranic Sciences & Tradition* 46, 1 (2013), 21–50 (in Persian).

218. Goldziher, *Beiträge*, 12–16; Goldziher, *Muhammedanische Studien*, Vol. 2 (Halle: Max Niemeyer, 1890), esp. 88–152.

219. Muhammad Baqir al-Sadr, *Principles of Islamic Jurisprudence: According to Shiʿi Law* (London: Islamic College for Advanced Studies Press, 2003), 32. The book is an exposition of Shii jurisprudence by a major modern Shii scholar, translated into English. Another such example is Jafar Sobhani, *Doctrines of Shiʿi*

Islam: A Compendium of Imami Beliefs and Practices, trans. by Reza Shah-Kazemi (London: I. B. Tauris/Institute of Ismaili Studies, 2001).

220. Modarressi, *An Introduction to Shīʿī Law*, 7ff.; Stewart, *Islamic Legal Orthodoxy*, 17f.

221. Modarressi, *An Introduction to Shīʿī Law*, 40–4.

222. Sachedina, *Islamic Messianism*, 37; Modarressi, *An Introduction to Shīʿī Law*, 44; Mohammad Ali Amir-Moezzi, 'al-Ṭūsī', *EI2*. See also al-Shaykh al-Ta'ifa al-Imam Abu Jafar Muhammad b. al-Hasan al-Tusi, *Kitab al-Khilaf*, Vols 1 and 2 (Qom: Mu'assasat al-Nashr al-Islami, 1407/1987). Of the six volumes, I only accessed the first two.

223. Al-Sadr quotes from the introduction to al-Tusi's *al-Mabsut*. Al-Sadr, *Principles of Islamic Jurisprudence*, 34.

224. The topic would thus be of relevance in Sunni–Shia polemics, such as in the al-Hilli-Ibn Taymiyya one. On the other hand, in the intra-Sunni debate, Ibn Taymiyya tried to revert to Quran and Sunna as key sources of jurisprudence and downplay the importance of *ijmaʿ* that had become dominant by his time. Laoust, *Essai*, 239–42; Josef van Ess, 'Sunniten und Schiiten: Staat, Recht und Kultus', in: Hinrich Biesterfeldt (ed.), *Kleine Schriften by Josef van Ess* (Leiden: Brill, 2018), 556–69, 562. For a detailed account, see Amjad Hussain Shah, *The Concept of Ijmāʿ in Imāmī Shīʿī Uṣūl al-Fiqh* (PhD, University of Edinburgh, 1999). In the Shii view, consensus is only valid if the Imam and all scholars agree, which was only sometimes the case when the Imams were still alive and is impossible to verify, so that it is hardly ever used in practice. Comments by Abbas Kadhim, Oxford, 16 February 2019. See Madelung, 'Authority in Twelver Shiism', 168.

225. Stewart, *Islamic Legal Orthodoxy*, 15; Modarressi, *An Introduction to Shīʿī Law*, 2ff., 29ff. For a discussion of the importance of reason in Shii jurisprudence, see Abu l-Fadl Izzati, *An Introduction to Shiʿi Islamic Law and Jurisprudence with an Emphasis on the Authority of Human Reason as a Source of Law According to Shiʿi and Persian Law* (Tehran/Lahore: University of Tehran/Ashraf Press, 1974). For a general account of the historical genesis of the sources of jurisprudence amongst the Shia, see Robert Brunschvig, 'Les usul al-fiqh imamites a leur stade ancien (Xe et XIe siècles)', in: Centre de Recherches d'Histoire des Religions Strasbourg (ed.), *Le shiʿisme imâmite: Colloque de Strasbourg (6–9 mai 1968)* (Paris: Presses Universitaires de France, 1970), 201–13. For a comparison between Sunni and Shii jurisprudence by a prominent Shii cleric, see al-ʿAllama al-Sayyid Murtada al-ʿAskari, *Maʿalim al-Madrasatayn*, Vol. 2 (Tehran: Mu'assasat al-Baʿatha, 1405/1985).

226. Modarressi, *An Introduction to Shīʿī Law*, 2ff. We should bear in mind that this overview refers to the now dominant Usuli school of Shii law, not the Akhbari one. The latter only recognises the Quran and the Sunna (tradition) and is against the use of other sources of jurisprudence, in particular reason (*aql*) and *ijtihad*. The conflict between these two Shii schools was won by the Usulis in the eighteenth century.

227. Shia did not use the term *ijtihad* until the twelfth century because it related to an earlier controversy amongst Shia. Madelung, 'Authority in Twelver Shiism', 169; Modarressi, *An Introduction to Shīʿi Law*, 29f.; Izzati, *An Introduction*, 88–98. Stewart argues that Sunni and Shii positions on *ijtihad* are very similar. Stewart, *Islamic Legal Orthodoxy*, 226–9. For a detailed discussion with extensive bibliographical references, see Aron Zysow, 'EJTEHĀD in Shiʿism', *EIr*.

228. See, for example, Wael B. Hallaq, 'Was the Gate of Ijtihad Closed?', *International Journal of Middle East Studies* 16, 1 (1984), 3–41; Ahmed Fekry Ibrahim, *Pragmatism in Islamic Law: A Social and Intellectual History* (Syracuse, New York: Syracuse University Press, 2015), 10–18 and passim.

229. These are questions raised in Shahab Ahmed, *What is Islam? The Importance of Being Islamic* (Princeton: Princeton University Press, 2015), esp. 115–29. See also Ahmed, *Before Orthodoxy: The Satanic Verses in Early Islam* (Cambridge, MA: Harvard University Press, 2017). For a reconsideration of the related notion of the relationship between the 'secular' and Islam, see Rushain Abbasi, 'Did Premodern Muslims Distinguish the Religious and Secular? The Dīn–Dunyā Binary in Medieval Islamic Thought', *Journal of Islamic Studies* 31, 2 (2020), 185–225.

230. James Grehan, *Twilight of the Saints: Everyday Religion in Ottoman Syria and Palestine* (New York: Oxford University Press, 2014), 13.

231. A key difference between Shia and Sunna involves the number of prayer sessions. Muslims should say five prayers a day. For Sunni Muslims, it is one of the five pillars of Islam (the others are pronouncing the Shahada, fasting during Ramadan, Zakat, and Hajj). Shii Muslims have a slightly different understanding of the pillars of Islam and see the prayer as one of the practices that a Muslim should perform as part of the Ancillaries of the Faith. While Shii Muslims also say five prayers a day, they twice combine two prayers a day, which means that they do three separate prayer sessions. Most observant Sunnis are only allowed to combine the prayers under special circumstances. Shia must thus only go to the mosque three times a day. Sunnis are generally only allowed to do this when on Hajj. Though some Shii scholars argued that, particularly in the modern period, praying five times a day was an inconvenience for some people, who as a result were no longer praying at all. Islamic scholars should therefore find a solution that is realistic, which resulted in rulings about praying 'only' on three occasions during the day. Machlis, *Shiʿi Sectarianism*, 142f. The rhythm and times of prayers thus became a marker of difference, even though the content of prayers is similar. There is also a debate over how loudly the prayer should be said. Allegedly, Ali said the Fatiha, which opens every prayer, loudly, something many Shia have adopted, while Sunnis generally whisper it. Goldziher, *Beiträge*, 15f. For the views of al-Sistani on this point, see his official website: Official Website of the Office of His Eminence al-Sayyid Ali al-Husseini al-Sistani, 'Obligatory Acts Relating to

Namaz: Standing (qiyām)', https://www.sistani.org/english/book/48/2221/. Another debate revolves around washing one's feet before prayer. There are some differences between the schools, especially between Shia and Hanafis, which stem from the fact that they regard different Hadith as authentic on this point. In practice, this means that Shia do not consider the washing of the whole foot as necessary. And some Sunnis argue that, if circumstances make the washing difficult (such as travelling), this can be replaced by merely cleaning the shoes, something Shia do not accept because they reject the saying of the Prophet upon which this is based. Goldziher, *Beiträge*, 87f.; Schacht, *The Origins*, 263f. See also Madelung, "Abd Allah b. 'Abbas', 14f., 19ff.; Madelung, 'Shi'i Attitudes', 69; A. J. Wensinck, *The Muslim Creed: Its Genesis and Historical Development* (Cambridge: Cambridge University Press, 1932), 129, 158f., 187, 192. Sunnis, Kharijis, and Zaydis demand that the feet are washed during the ablution (*wudu*), while Twelver Shia accept the cleaning of the feet without water. Some Sunnis at times allow the cleaning of footwork (*mash ala al-khuffayn*), i.e. the cleaning of one's shoes with one's hand while travelling without washing them 'properly', something Twelver Shia, Kharijis, and Zaydis categorically reject. Strothmann, *Kultus*, 21–46, esp. 26; Madelung, *Der Imam*, 128f. Strothmann's account is full of sarcastic comments on the inner-Islamic debates. Ch. Pellat, 'al-Mash 'Alā 'l-Khuffayn', *EI2*.

232. Funeral prayers also vary slightly between Sunna and Shia, as do funeral rites. Shia and Shafiis generally think that tombs should be flat, not slightly elevated like those of other Sunnis. Sunnis read four *takbir* (Allahu Akbar) at a funeral prayer, while Shia recite five and add a eulogy on the Prophet's family and a Surah (113). Zaydis agree with Twelver Shia on this point. Strothmann, *Kultus*, 58–65.

233. There is always the danger of giving the impression that differences outweigh similarities because they mirror the contents of the polemics themselves, and of the *ikhtilaf* literature and its appropriation in Orientalist literature, and this literature specifically focuses on the differences rather than the commonalities. Overviews can be found in Rainer Brunner, *Islamic Ecumenism in the 20th Century: The Azhar and Shiism between Rapprochement and Restraint* (Leiden: Brill, 2004), 14ff., in Momen, *An Introduction to Shi'i Islam*, and in some of the polemical literature from either a Sunni or a Shii point of view. See also the notes on the Shii creed in al-Hilli, *Al-Bâbu 'l-Hâdî 'Ashar*, 92–101.

234. Temporary marriage (*muta'a*) is permissible in Shia Islam, even for a relationship that lasts only for a few hours or days, and is a common theme of anti-Shii polemics. Hailed by some as giving legal status and protection to children born outside of marriage and to couples engaged in extra-marital sexual relationships, Sunni polemicists see it as legitimising prostitution and adultery. Probably a pre-Islamic arrangement allowed during the time of the Prophet

and amongst the earliest Muslims, it was then banned by the Caliph Umar. Some have speculated that it is allowed in Shiism precisely because Umar banned it. Schacht, *The Origins*, 266f. Ali, following Umar's ruling, actually upheld the ban, and it is interesting to note that Twelver Shii law thus goes against Ali's ruling on the matter. According to some sources, the Prophet also briefly banned it, but it seems to have been practised under Abu Bakr and the early part of Umar's Caliphate. As Madelung has shown, Abdallah bin Abbas, the Prophet's and Ali's paternal cousin, on the other hand, defended temporary marriage, and Shii law may have followed him on this and some other matters. Madelung, "Abd Allah b. 'Abbas', 13–25. For a Shii defence engaging with some anti-Shii polemics on the matter, see Muhammad al-Hussayn Al Kashif al-Ghita, *Asl al-Shi'a wa Usuliha*, 7th ed. (Najaf: al-Matba'a al-Haydariyya, 1950), 144–55; Al Kashif al-Ghita, *Le Shi'isme: Origins et principes* (Beirut: Albouraq, 2007), 168–88. For detailed discussions, see D. von Denffer, 'Mut'a: Ehe oder Prostitution? Beitrag zur Untersuchung einer Institution des šī'itischen Islam', *Zeitschrift der Deutschen Morgenländischen Gesellschaft* 128 (1978), 299–325; Werner Ende, 'Ehe auf Zeit (mut'a) in der innerislamischen Diskussion der Gegenwart', *Die Welt des Islams* 20 (1980), 1–43; Shahla Haeri, *Law of Desire: Temporary Marriage in Shi'i Iran* (Syracuse, NY: Syracuse University Press, 1989); W. Heffening, 'Mut'a', *EI2*; Abd al-Latif Abd al-Rahman al-Hasan, *The Khulāṣat al-Ījāz of Shaykh al-Mufīd, Together with an Introductory Study of the Man and his Writings* (PhD, Manchester University, 1974); Syed Ameer Ali, *Mahommedan Law: Compiled from Authorities in the Original Arabic*, Vol. 2 (Calcutta and Simla: Thacker, Spink & Co., 1929), 320. Ali differentiates between the Akhbari and Usuli standpoint. Ibn Taymiyya argued that it was banned by the Prophet. Laoust, *Essai*, 211. Umar also banned the combination of Umrah and Hajj. This was called *muta'a al-hajj*. See Arthur Gribetz, *Strange Bedfellows: Mut'at al-nisā' and mut'at al-hajj: A Study Based on Sunnī and Shī'ī Sources of tafsīr, ḥadīth and fiqh* (Berlin: Klaus Schwarz, 1994); Laoust, *Essai*, 212.

235. Under Shii law, women can marry when they have reached adulthood, even against the wish of their male guardian, and no witnesses need to be present for the marriage to be legal under Shii law (unlike under Sunni law). Regarding divorce, however, the situation is the reverse, with Shia insisting on witnesses to be present for the dissolution of the marriage. Malikis apparently also do not insist on witnesses, while Hanafis do. Izzati, *An Introduction*, 139–44; Ali, *Mahommedan Law*, 269–327, esp. 286f., 295, 303, 309. For a disposition of the legitimacy of children according to the different schools of jurisprudence, see Ali, *Mahommedan Law*, 190–234. On divorce, Twelver Shii law forbids the so-called *talaq al-bid'a*, which is considered morally wrong but is still accepted in Sunni law. The question is whether a man can divorce his wife by uttering a triple repudiation at one time or three times over three months for the divorce to be valid. It has been claimed that the latter practice, which nowadays is the

Twelver Shii one, had been practised at the time of Muhammad and Abu Bakr, but that *talaq al-bidʿa* at a single time was recognised by Umar. Madelung, "Abd Allah b. ʿAbbas', 16f. For more, see some of the notes on marriage above and Izzati, *An Introduction*, 145–50. As for slavery, there are diverging opinions on the fate of a slave concubine who has born children to the slave owner, a so-called *umm al-walad*, upon the death of the slave owner. Umar ruled that she would be freed upon the death of the owner, while Ali seems to have reversed this ruling, stating that she would only be freed if she had also been explicitly manumitted by the owner before his death. Subsequent Shii Imams and jurists adopted this position, which seems to have corresponded with pre-Islamic tradition and practice up until Umar's ruling. Madelung, "Abd Allah b. ʿAbbas', 17ff.; Schacht, *The Origins*, 265; Madelung, 'Umm al-Walad', *EI2*; Marion H.Katz, 'Concubinage, in Islamic law', *EI3*.

236. Sabrina Mervin, 'On Sunnite-Shiite Doctrinal and Contemporary Geopolitical Tensions', in: Brigitte Maréchal and Sami Zemni (eds), *The Dynamics of Sunni–Shia Relationships: Doctrine, Transnationalism, Intellectuals and the Media* (London: Hurst, 2013), 11–24, 15; Madelung, 'Shiʿi Attitudes', 71, 74f. For the views of Zaydis and Ismailis on the subject, see ibid., 77ff. In an ecumenical context, however, a Shii cleric such as Kashif al-Ghita could, in an overview of Shii doctrine, downplay the difference amongst Shia and Sunna regarding inheritance. Al Kashif al-Ghita, *Asl al-Shiʿa*, 170–3. See also Al-Ghita, *Le Shiʿisme*, 197ff., which contains information on al-Ghita's *taqrib* efforts. It was written in part to clarify Shiism in the context of the *taqrib* efforts and to repudiate the anti-Shii views of Egyptian authors such as Ahmad Amin. It is discussed in Frank Bagley, 'The Azhar and Shiʿism', *The Muslim World* 50, 2 (1960), 122–9, 127f., and Brunner, *Islamic Ecumenism*. One author claims that in the mid-twentieth century Tunisia and Pakistan, when codifying their personal status laws, modified their law in accordance with Shii law and doctrine. Izzati, *An Introduction*, 126–38, esp. 136, 158–61. For a detailed exposition of the differences of Sunni and Shii law regarding inheritance produced to administer law in the British Raj, see Ali, *Mahommedan Law*, 19–147, esp. 101ff.; Standish Grove Grady, *A Manual of the Mahommedan Law of Inheritance and Contract, Comprising the Doctrines of the Soonee and Sheea Schools, and Based upon the Text of Sir W. H. Macnaghten's Principles and Precedents, Together with the Decisions of the Privy Council and High Courts of the Presidencies in India* (London: W. H. Allen, 1869), 146–57. See also Chibli Mallat, *Introduction to Middle Eastern Law* (Oxford: Oxford University Press, 2007), 37ff.

237. John J. Donohue, *The Buwayhid Dynasty in Iraq 334H./945 to 403H./1012: Shaping Institutions for the Future* (Leiden: Brill, 2003), 263; Tilman Nagel, 'Buyids', *EIr*. In what way Shii clerics thought their rule was legitimate in the absence of an Imam is also not entirely clear. Sachedina, *Islamic Messianism*, 8f. The Abbasids, the descendants of Hashim, and the Talibids, the descendants of the Prophet,

had by that time become organised with a representative as a liaison with the government. The Buyids appointed Zaydis and Twelver Shia to these positions and as Friday prayer leaders. The Talibid syndicate thus became another rallying point for the Shia. Donohue, *Buwayhid Dynasty*, 303–14, 352.

238. Mottahedeh, *Loyalty*, 28, 38.

239. Donohue, *Buwayhid Dynasty*, 72–6; Donohue, "Aḍud al-Dawla', *EI3*. Buyid relations with the Byzantines may have been shaped by a fear that Sunnis would be especially enthusiastic for holy war against Byzantium and perhaps undermine their position. Bayhom-Daou, *Shaykh Mufid*, 26f.; Nagel, 'Buyids'.

240. This structure burned down in the fourteenth century. Aslan, *From Body to Shrine*, 10f.; E. Honigmann and C. E. Bosworth, 'al-Naḏjaf', *EI2*.

241. Bayhom-Daou, *Shaykh Mufid*, 133; Aslan, *From Body to Shrine*, 194–206.

242. Teresa Bernheimer, 'Shared Sanctity: Some Notes on Ahl al-Bayt Shrines in the Early Ṭālibid Genealogies', *Studia Islamica* 108, 1 (2013), 1–15; Ahmed T. Karamustafa, *Sufism: The Formative Period* (Edinburgh: Edinburgh University Press, 2007), 130f.; Stephennie Mulder, 'Abdülhamid and the 'Alids: Ottoman Patronage of "Shi'i" Shrines in the Cemetery of Bāb al-Ṣaghīr in Damascus', *Studia Islamica* 108, 1 (2013), 16–47, 17f.; Taylor, *In the Vicinity of the Righteous*.

243. Teresa Bernheimer, *The 'Alids: The First Family of Islam, 750–1200* (Edinburgh: Edinburgh University Press, 2013); Aslan, *From Body to Shrine*, 33f.; Kazuo Morimoto (ed.), *Sayyids and Sharifs in Muslim Societies: The Living Links to the Prophet* (Abingdon: Routledge, 2012); Biancamaria Scarcia Amoretti and Laura Bottini (eds), *The Role of the Sadat/Asraf in Muslim History and Civilization* (Naples: Istituto per l'Oriente C. A. Nallino, 1999); Nebil A. Husayn, 'Aḥkām Concerning the Ahl al-Bayt', *Islamic Law and Society* 27, 3 (2020), 145–84.

244. L. Massignon et al., 'Taṣawwuf', *EI*; E. Geoffroy et al., 'Ṭarīḳa', *EI2*.

245. J. Spencer Trimingham, *The Sufi Orders in Islam* (Oxford: Oxford University Press, 1971), 134; Oliver Scharbrodt, 'The Qutb as Special Representative of the Hidden Imam: The Conflation of Shii and Sufi Vilayat in the Ni'matullahi Order', in: D. Hermann and S. Mervin (eds), *Courants et dynamique chiites à l'époque moderne (XVIIIe–XXe siècles)* (Beirut: Orient Institute Beirut, 2010), 33–49; Shayesteh Ghofrani, *Comparative Analysis of Wilāya in the Formative Period of Shi'ism and Sufism* (PhD, University of Exeter, 2014). See also Hodgson, *Venture*, Vol. 2, 227–30; Kamil M. al-Shaibi, *Sufism and Shi'ism* (Surbiton: LAAM, 1991), 59–65; Arthur F. Buehler, 'Overlapping Currents in Early Islam: The Sufi Shaykh and Shī'î Imam', *Journal of the History of Sufism* 3 (2001), 1–20. For Shia, see Dakake, *The Charismatic Community*, 7; Aslan, *From Body to Shrine*, 110; Liyakat Takim, *The Heirs of the Prophet: Charisma and Religious Authority in Shi'ite Islam* (Albany: SUNY Press, 2006).

246. Louis Massignon, *The Passion of al-Hallāj: Mystic and Martyr of Islam*, trans. by Herbert Mason, Vol. 1 (Princeton: Princeton University Press, 1982), 248f.,

295–337. According to Massignon, '[t]he political atmosphere of the proceedings brought against Hallaj before Sunnite courts is saturated, as we shall see, with the sectarian mentality and terminology of Shi'ite secretaries in the various ministries'. Ibid., 305. In later centuries, however, the Shii verdict was far from unanimous, and some particularly anti-Sunni and Sufi-inclined Shii scholars sought to rehabilitate and defend al-Hallaj. Massignon, *Passion*, Vol. 2, 16ff., 193f. But key figures such as al-Mufid and Ibn Babuya systematised the mainstream Shii criticism of al-Hallaj. Massignon, *Passion*, Vol. 3, 236. For background, see Alexander D. Knysh, *Islamic Mysticism: A Short History* (Leiden: Brill, 2000), 68–82. For a criticism of Massignon's argument, see Sean W. Anthony, 'NAWBAKHTI FAMILY', *EIr*.

247. Ondřej Beránek and Pavel Ťupek, *The Temptation of Graves in Salafi Islam: Iconoclasm, Destruction and Idolatry* (Edinburgh: Edinburgh University Press, 2018). This is in part related to burial practices themselves. In principle, Sunni jurists agreed that writing on a tombstone was not allowed, as it was not practised by the Prophet. Shia (Zaydis, Ismailis, and Twelver) took a different approach and argued that, while this was not the practice of the Prophet, it was adopted by the seventh Imam Musa al-Kazim (d. 799), and therefore permissible. Shia tombstones could thus include the name of the deceased. Despite the formal Sunni ban on this practice, the writing of the profession of faith on tombstones became common practice in many Sunni Muslim societies, illustrating a discrepancy between law and lived reality. But others, such as traditionalist Hanbalis, took this ban seriously. Leor Halevi, *Muhammad's Grave: Death Rites and the Making of Islamic Society* (New York: Columbia University Press, 2007), 38–41. On other aspects of funerary practice, however, it is not easy to generalise about 'Sunni' and 'Shii' positions. Rather, different Sunni schools side with Shii ones on particular aspects, though not on others. Ibid., 308–35. For Hanbalism and Sufism, see George Makdisi, 'The Hanbali School and Sufism', *Humaniora Islamica* 2 (1974), 61–72; Christopher Melchert, 'The Ḥanābila and the Early Sufis', *Arabica* 48, 3 (2001), 352–67.

248. See L. Veccia Vaglieri, 'Ghadīr Khumm', *EI2*; Mohammad Ali Amir-Moezzi, 'Ghadīr Khumm', *EI3*; Brunner, *Islamic Ecumenism*, 8f., 13.

249. Such as Bukhari and Ahmad Ibn Hanbal's collection of Hadith. Dodge, 'The Fatimid Legal Code', 33; Massignon, *Passion*, Vol. 1, 301; Goldziher, *Beiträge*, 60f.; Goldziher, *Muhammedanische Studien*, Vol. 2, 115ff.; Melchert, *Ahmad ibn Hanbal*, 94; Momen, *An Introduction to Shi'i Islam*, 15.

250. Simha Sabari, *Mouvements populaires à Bagdad à l'époque 'Abbasside* (Paris: Libraire d'Amérique et d'Orient, 1981), 106–12. In 389/998, a visit to the tomb of Musab bin al-Zubayr was organised on 18 Muharram for Sunnis to rival the Shii visitation of the tomb of Hussain. Makdisi, *Ibn 'Aqil et la résurgence*, 312–16, 326. This did not always lead to conflict, and there is an account from 1109, for example, that relates that the Sunni procession to the tomb of Musab

bin al-Zubayr had even passed through the Shii al-Karkh quarter without any problems. Ibn al-Athir, *Chronicle*, Vol. 1, 143f.

251. Henri Laoust, 'al-Barbahārī', *EI2*; Christopher Melchert, 'al-Barbahārī', *EI3*; Sabari, *Mouvements*, 14, 101–20. For more, see Nassima Neggaz, 'Al-Karkh: The Development of an Imāmī-Shīʿī Stronghold in Early Abbasid and Būyid Baghdad (132-447/750-1055)', *Studia Islamica* 114, 3 (2020), 265–315.

252. El-Moctar, *The Crusades' Impact*, 118.

253. His ideas would influence the Caliph al-Qadir in the early eleventh century, who sought to overturn the Shii policies of the Buyids. H. Laoust, 'Ibn Baṭṭa, ʿUbayd Allāh b. Muḥammad Abū ʿAbd Allāh al-ʿUkbari', *EI2*. See also Laoust, *La profession de foi d'Ibn Baṭṭa* (Damascus: Institut Français de Damas, 1958).

254. Jon Hoover, 'Creed', *EI3*. See Fyzee, *A Shīʿite Creed*.

255. Sachedina, *Islamic Messianism*, 19; Fyzee, *A Shīʿite Creed*, 26, 65; W. Montgomery Watt, "Akīda', *EI2*. The Shii creeds also spelled out that a believer had to accept the historical narrative surrounding every succession from the Prophet to Ali and the twelfth Imam (thus excluding non-Twelver Shia). Al-Hilli, *Al-Bâbu 'l-Ḥâdî ʿAshar*, 69–81.

256. Bayhom-Daou, *Shaykh Mufid*, 18–21; Martin J. McDermott, *The Theology of al-Shaikh al-Mufīd (d. 413/1022)* (Beirut: Dar el-Machreq, 1978), 17–22.

257. The Arabic historiography speaks of these groups as factions, using the term *ta'ifa* (the word describing sect in Arabic today). And while they were often associated with a school of law, that did not have to be the case, indicating a more sociological meaning of the term rather than a purely religious one. Mottahedeh, *Loyalty*, 159f.; ʿIzz al-Din ibn al-Athir, *The Annals of the Saljuq Turks: Selections from al-Kāmil fi'l-Ta'rīkh of ʿIzz al-Dīn Ibn al-Athīr*, trans. by D. S. Richards (London: Routledge, 2002), 75–81. Ibn al-Athir also reports, for example, that, upon the death in 1173 of an Amir with Shii sympathies, Yazdan, Shia mourned him while Sunnis cheered, which led to a battle between the two groups with several casualties. Al-Athir, *Chronicle*, Vol. 2, 215.

258. Donohue, *The Buwayhid Dynasty*, 352; Sabari, *Mouvements*, 108.

259. Mottahedeh, *Loyalty*, 25.

CHAPTER 2

1. The term was coined by Hodgson. Hodgson, *Venture*, Vol. 2, 255–92. See also Ira M. Lapidus, *A History of Islamic Societies*, 2nd ed. (Cambridge: Cambridge University Press, 2002), 142; Mottahedeh, *Loyalty*, 35.

2. On the religious level, there was still plenty of infighting amongst Sunnis, and one could also speak of a traditionalist Sunni Revival against rationalist trends, which included the Muʿtazila and, to a certain extent, Shiism. Makdisi argues that the 'Sunni Revival' started with al-Qadir and not, as had previously been assumed, with the Saljuqs. George Makdisi, 'Sunni Revival', in: D. S. Richards (ed.), *Islamic Civilisation 950–1150* (Oxford: Cassirer, 1973), 155–68, 157.

3. El-Moctar, *The Crusades' Impact*, 3f.

4. Harris, *Lebanon*, 55ff.

5. Maher Y. Abu-Munshar, 'Fāṭimids, Crusaders and the Fall of Islamic Jerusalem: Foes or Allies?', *Al-Masāq* 22, 1 (2010), 45–56.

6. They may initially have had some links to the Qarmatians, but then switched allegiance to the Fatimids. Daftary, *The Ismailis*, 166f. Another local dynasty, the Sumras, would later adopt Fatimid Ismailism, rebel against the Ghaznavids, and rule in Thatta for almost three centuries. Ibid. As one of the poets he patronised lamented after his death: 'Alas and alack, that the Carmathian heretics should now be rejoicing, for they will now find security from being showered with stones and the gallows! Alas and alack, that the Byzantine Emperor should now be free of the burdensome necessity of having to erect towers and walls! Alas and alack, that the Brahmans of the whole of India should now be able to (re)construct a place for their idols afresh in the spring!' C. E. Bosworth, 'Farrukhī's Elegy on Maḥmūd of Ghazna', *Iran* 29 (1991), 43–9, 45.

7. C. E. Bosworth, 'MAḤMUD B. SEBÜKTEGIN', *EIr*; Makdisi, *Ibn 'Aqil et la résurgence*, 287.

8. Ruth Stellhorn Mackensen, 'Moslem Libraries and Sectarian Propaganda', *American Journal of Semitic Languages and Literatures* 51, 2 (1935), 83–113. A later Saljuq Sultan, Barkiyaruq, for example, executed hundreds of Ismailis in 1101 and had Ismaili books such as the *Treatises of the Brethren of Purity* burned in Baghdad. Makdisi, *Ibn 'Aqil et la résurgence*, 287; Ibn al-Athir, *Chronicle*, Vol. 1, 40–7.

9. Klaus Hachmeier, 'Bahā' al-Dawla', *EI3*. For background, see Heribert Busse, *Chalif und Großkönig: Die Buyiden im Irak (945–1055)* (Beirut/Wiesbaden: Franz Steiner, 1969); Donohue, *The Buwayhid Dynasty*, 277–87.

10. Berkey, *The Formation of Islam*, 195f.; Donohue, *The Buwayhid Dynasty*, 283, 287.

11. Bayhom-Daou, *Shaykh Mufid*, 24f.; Lapidus, *A History*, 141; Sabari, *Mouvements*, 110. See also Makdisi, *Ibn 'Aqil et la résurgence*, 315f.; Makdisi, *Ibn 'Aqil: Religion and Culture in Classical Islam* (Edinburgh: Edinburgh University Press, 1997), 3–16. For a very positive description of al-Qadir's time, 'who, taking his responsibility as leader seriously, was able [...] to break the Shi'ite annexation of the Abbasid state and to lay the groundwork for a theological and moral restoration of Sunnite Islam', see Massignon, *Passion*, Vol. 2, 135f. See, in general, Udjang Tholib, *The Reign of the Caliph al-Qādir Billāh (381/991–422/1031)* (PhD, McGill University, 2002), esp. 241–50 and passim.

12. See, for example, Henri Laoust, 'Les agitations religieuses à Baghdad aux IVe et Ve siècles de l'Hégire', in: D. S. Richards (ed.), *Islamic Civilization 950–1150* (Oxford: Cassirer, 1973), 169–86.

13. Sabari, *Mouvements*, 111, 120.

14. Ibn al-Athir, *Chronicle*, Vol. 3, 249.

15. A. C. S. Peacock, *Early Seljūq History: A New Interpretation* (London: Routledge, 2010), 101–4.

16. Nishapur was ruled by the Samanids and later the Ghaznavids while experiencing a short takeover by the Ismailis. Saleh, *The Formation*, 26ff.; Richard Bulliet, *The Patricians of Nishapur: A Study in Medieval Islamic Social History* (Cambridge, MA: Harvard University Press, 1972); Bulliet, 'The Political-Religious History

of Nishapur in the Eleventh Century', in: D. S. Richards (ed.), *Islamic Civilisation 950–1150* (Oxford: Cassirer, 1973), 71–91; Lapidus, *A History*, 136f.; Sohaira Siddiqui, *Law and Politics under the Abbasids: An Intellectual Portrait of al-Juwayni* (Cambridge: Cambridge University Press, 2019).

17. Interestingly, the decree issued at al-Qadir's request was signed by a number of Alids. Daftary, *The Ismailis*, 100f.

18. Al-Suyuti, *Tarikh al-Khulafa* (*History of the Caliphs*), quoted in: Stewart, 'Popular Shiism', 40; E. Geoffroy, 'al-Suyūṭī', *EI2*.

19. Jalal al-Din al-Suyuti, *History of the Caliphs*, trans. by Major H. S. Jarrett (Calcutta: Asiatic Society, 1881), 548; Jiwa, *Towards a Shiʿi Mediterranean Empire*, 41. About the Qarmatians, he has this to say: 'In the third century occurred the irruption of the Carmathians, and that will suffice.' Al-Suyuti, *History of the Caliphs*, 550. Correspondingly, he wrote denigratingly about Shiism and its prominence under the Fatimids. El-Moctar, *The Crusades' Impact*, 106.

20. El-Moctar, *The Crusades' Impact*, 109f. Despite negative references about Shiism, Ibn Khaldun includes Shii dynasties in his historical sociology. Ibn Khaldun, *The Muqaddimah: An Introduction to History*, trans. by Franz Rosenthal (Princeton: Princeton University Press, 2015).

21. He even criticises Saladin for ending their reign. Al-Maqrizi differentiates between the Fatimids and the Druze and Hasan al-Sabbah to deflate doctrinal criticism to the latter. El-Moctar, *The Crusades' Impact*, 203; Paul E. Walker, 'Al-Maqrizi and the Fatimids', *Mamluk Studies* 7, 2 (2003), 83–97. Despite being a Shafii Sunni writing under the Mamluks, he accepted the Fatimids as legitimate successors of the Prophet and saw some Fatimids as role models, for they had made his homeland, Egypt, the centre of a substantial Mediterranean empire. Some have also explained this by saying that he may have been a descendant of the Fatimids. Jiwa, *Towards a Shiʿi Mediterranean Empire*, 28f. But in the political context in which he wrote, his relation to the Fatimids was more a charge levied at him by his opponents, and one that could have been dangerous for him. Ibid., 40–4. In other works, al-Maqrizi showed affection for the *Ahl al-Bayt*. He also went beyond the narrow definition of who belongs to the *Ahl al-Bayt* that the Shia had adopted. Jiwa argues that this was a feature of the confessional ambiguity that characterised the fourteenth century after the fall of the Abbasid Caliphate. Ibid., 34. See also Luke Yarbrough, 'Medieval Sunni Historians on Fatimid Policy and Non-Muslim Influence', *Journal of Medieval History* 45, 3 (2019), 331–46.

22. El-Moctar, *The Crusades' Impact*, 11; El-Moctar, 'Defensive Jihad: Islamization of the Turks and Turkification of Islam', *İnönü University International Journal of Social Sciences* 6, 1 (2017), 1–21.

23. Berkey, *The Formation of Islam*, 181.

24. Ibn al-Athir, *The Annals of the Saljuq Turks*, 89.

25. Daftary, *The Ismailis*, 195–8; Nagel, 'Buyids'.

26. Berkey, *The Formation of Islam*, 189; C. E. Bosworth, 'Ṭoghrïl (I) Beg', *EI2*; George Makdisi, 'Les rapports entre Calife et Sultan à l'époque Saljuqide',

International Journal of Middle East Studies 6, 2 (1975), 228–36; Eric J. Hanne, *Putting the Caliph in his Place: Power, Authority and the Late Abbasid Caliphate* (Madison, WI: Farleigh Dickinson University Press, 2007).

27. Daphna Ephrat, 'The Seljuqs and the Public Sphere in the Period of Sunni Revivalism: The View from Baghdad', in: Christian Lange and Songül Mecit (eds), *The Seljuqs: Politics, Society and Culture* (Edinburgh: Edinburgh University Press, 2011), 139–56; Sabari, *Mouvements*, 119. See also Robert Gleave, 'Shiʻi Jurisprudence during the Seljuq Period: Rebellion and Public Order in an Illegitimate State', in: Christian Lange and Songül Mecit (eds), *The Seljuqs: Politics, Society and Culture* (Edinburgh: Edinburgh University Press, 2011), 205–27. Graffiti was a tool of expression from the earliest days of Islam, including for expressions of faith. Frédéric Imbert, 'L'Islam des pierres: L'expression de la foi dans les graffiti arabes des premiers siècles', *Revue des mondes musulmans et de la Méditerranée* 129 (2011), 57–78. There is some evidence that the Shii al-Karkh quarter did not fight against the Saljuq army and was thus not as devastated by the initial conquest as other quarters. Peacock, *Early Seljūq History*, 120.

28. Abdel Rahman Azzam, 'Sources of the Sunni Revival: Nizam u-Mulk & the Nizamiyya: An 11th Century Response to Sectarianism', *The Muslim World* 106, 1 (2016), 97–108; Lapidus, *A History*, 135f., 142; Makdisi, 'Les rapports entre Calife', 234f.

29. Whether *madrasas* changed the nature of Sunni education qualitatively has been debated. Michael Chamberlain, *Knowledge and Social Practice in Medieval Damascus, 1190–1350* (Cambridge: Cambridge University Press, 1994), 52, 70, 82. Makdisi has argued that who established the *madrasas*, and for what purpose, did not matter particularly. Some of the earlier descriptions of the 'Sunni Revival' have been revised. Makdisi, 'Sunni Revival'; Peacock, *Early Seljūq History*, 105–8. But there has been some opposition to Makdisi's arguments. Lev, *Saladin*, 130ff. See also Leiser, *The Restoration of Sunnism*, 427–31. For a reassessment of the Saljuq period, the argument that they established an ideological state apparatus, and their self-legitimisation against the Ismailis, see also Omid Safi, *The Politics of Knowledge in Premodern Islam: Negotiating Ideology and Religious Inquiry* (Chapel Hill: University of North Carolina Press, 2006), 93ff. and passim.

30. Al-Ghazali's *Kitab al-Mustazhiri* accused Ismailis of believing that the internal meaning of the word of God was not contained in its outer meaning, that there was a deeper spiritual essence, and that the Fatimid Imams were quasi-divine. Mitha, *Al-Ghazali*.

31. He thought that, because of possible *taqiyya*, a 'heretical' conviction was enough to be convicted of apostasy, even if it was not outwardly professed. He made a distinction between ordinary Ismailis, who could be spared if they repented, and missionaries and clerics, who should be killed even if they did not repeat their convictions in court. Berkey, *The Formation of Islam*, 194; Frank Griffel, 'Toleration and Exclusion: Al-Shāfiʻī and al-Ghazālī on the Treatment of Apostates', *Bulletin of the School of Oriental and African Studies* 64, 3 (2001), 339–54. Other key scholars such as Ibn Aqil also penned treatises against Ismailis

and issued fatwas legitimising their execution. His refutation of the Ismailis is not preserved. Makdisi, *Ibn 'Aqil: Religion and Culture*, 141.

32. He is also a complex figure and was an early Sufi, so he should not be reduced to his anti-Ismaili polemic. W. Montgomery Watt, 'al-G̲h̲azālī', *EI2*. It is telling that such a prominent and prolific figure would focus on Ismailis, and that he remains highly revered for it. Take, for example, this eulogy in a contemporary Egyptian newspaper: 'From the ubiquitous nature of ancient Greek philosophy to the rising tide of political Shi'ism, Imam al-Ghazali did not leave a stone unturned in his effort to bring back serious Islamic scholarship in the face of heterodox threats.' *Egypt Today*, 'Imam al-Ghazali and the Revival of Islamic Scholarship', 8 June 2017.

33. Massimo Campanini, 'In Defence of Sunnism: Al-Ghazālī and the Seljuqs', in: Christian Lange and Songül Mecit (eds), *The Seljuqs: Politics, Society and Culture* (Edinburgh: Edinburgh University Press, 2011), 228–39; Marshall G. S. Hodgson, *The Secret Order of Assassins: The Struggle of the Early Nizārī Ismāʿīlīs against the Islamic World* (Philadelphia: University of Pennsylvania Press, 1955).

34. M. G. S. Hodgson, 'The Ismāʿīlī State', in: J. A. Boyle (ed.), *The Cambridge History of Iran*, Vol. 5 (Cambridge: Cambridge University Press, 1968), 422–82. The so-called Mustaili Tayyibi branch of Ismailism would continue with a separate line of Imams and Daʿis and become particularly important in India, Yemen, and Najran. Daftary, *The Ismailis*, 238–300.

35. El-Moctar, *The Crusades' Impact*, 13, 117, 127; Hodgson, *Venture*, Vol. 2, 183–8, 283; Krämer, *Geschichte*, 112.

36. Daftary, *The Ismailis*, 9; El-Moctar, *The Crusades' Impact*, 88. There seem to be some manuscripts of his book that use the term 'Shia', while others refer to 'Seveners', which would only mean Ismailis. It is now thought that the latter is the originally intended meaning. Nizam al-Mulk, *The Book of Government or Rules for Kings: The Siyar al-Muluk or Siyasat-Nama of Nizam al-Mulk*, trans. by Hubert Darke (London: Routledge and Kegan Paul, 1978), xixf. He devotes a whole chapter, entitled 'On the risings of the Qarmatis and Batinis and their evil doctrines (may Allah curse them)', to condemning Ismailis and especially condemns the Qarmatians of Bahrain and al-Ahsa. Ibid., 227–31.

37. Al-Mulk, *The Book of Government*, 65f., 159ff. In another, rather bizarre story, he relates the danger of being falsely accused of being a '*rafidi*', as a foreign ambassador once did after he spotted the Wazir playing with a ring on his right hand, a ring he had just won in a game of chess. He uses this as an example to be vigilant in the conduct with foreign ambassadors, but shows how grave a threat such an accusation could be at the time. Ibid., 96ff.

38. Ibid., 164. For other instances of distinction, see ibid., 211.

39. Spellberg, *Politics*, 86.

40. See Etan Kohlberg, "Ali b. Musa ibn Tawus and his Polemic against Sunnism', in: Bernard Lewis and Friedrich Niewöhner (eds), *Religionsgespräche im Mittelalter* (Wiesbaden: Harrassowitz, 1992), 325–50, 348f. But others continued to lambast Aisha in anti-Sunni books. Ibid., 349.

41. Berkey, *The Formation of Islam*, 191; H. Bowen and C. E. Bosworth, 'Niẓām al-Mulk', *EI2*.

42. Peacock, *Early Seljūq History*, 119; Jean Calmard, 'Le chiisme imamite en Iran à l'époque seldjoukide d'après le Kitab al-Naqd', *Le monde Iranien et l'Islam: Sociétés et cultures* 1 (1971), 43–66.

43. Peacock, *Early Seljūq History*, 120f. Raymond of Aguilers, however, wrote that the Turks offered the Fatimids that they would embrace the cause of Ali if they joined them in an attack against the Crusaders: 'Si venire cum ipsis contra nos in praelium, colerent Alim, quem ipse colit qui est de genere Mahumet.' ('The Turks indeed, as it was explained to us, wished to make a deal with him [the Fāṭimid Vizier] that if he should march with his men against us in battle, they would revere Ali, who he [the Vizier] reverences, who is from the family of Mohammed.') Raimond d'Aguilers, *Le 'Liber' de Raymond d'Aguilers*, ed. by J. H. Hill and L. L. Hill (Paris: P. Geuthner, 1969), 110, cited after: Rainer Christoph Schwinges, *Kreuzzugsideologie und Toleranz: Studien zu Wilhelm von Tyrus* (Stuttgart: Anton Hiersemann, 1977), 111; Nicholas Morton, 'The Saljuq Turks' Conversion to Islam: The Crusading Sources', *Al-Masāq* 27, 2 (2015), 109–18, 114f.

44. A. Bausani, 'Religion in the Saljuq Period', in: J. A. Boyle (ed.), *The Cambridge History of Iran*, Vol. 5 (Cambridge: Cambridge University Press, 1968), 283–302.

45. This episode is related in Ibn al-Athir, *Chronicle*, Vol. 2, 109f.; Wilferd Madelung, 'ĀL-E BĀVAND', *EIr*; C. E. Bosworth and S. Blair, 'Astarābād', *EIr*. And while the Wazir Amid al-Mulk al-Kunduri had convinced Sultan Tughril Beg to order the cursing of Shia in Khorasan, this practice was reversed when Nizam al-Mulk came to power. It seems that this was part of an anti-Shafii movement, and many religious scholars in Khorasan disliked this policy and went into exile. Ibn al-Athir, *The Annals of the Saljuq Turks*, 148, 257.

49. Peacock, *Early Seljūq History*, 121f.

47. Saleh, *The Formation*, 218f.; Kohlberg, "Ali b. Musa ibn Tawus'. For another early example of a Shii scholar using Sunni sources, see Matthew Pierce, 'Ibn Shahrashub and Shi'a Rhetorical Strategies in the 6th/12th Century', *Journal of Shi'a Islamic Studies* 5, 4 (2012), 441–54.

48. Mohammad Heidari-Abkenar, *Die ideologische und politische Konfrontation Schia-Sunna am Beispiel der Stadt Rey des 10.-12. Jh. n. Chr.* (PhD, University of Cologne, 1992), 49–63.

49. Twelver Shia made common cause with Sunnis in the persecution of Ismailis, however, while both sides were more conciliatory towards Zaydism. Heidari-Abkenar, *Die ideologische und politische Konfrontation*, 64ff.

50. Ibid., 74–105.

51. Wilferd Madelung, "ABD-AL-JALĪL RĀZĪ', *EIr*; Mohammad-Dja'far Mahdjoub, 'The Evolution of Popular Eulogy of the Imams among the Shi'a', in: Said Amir Arjomand (ed.), *Authority and Political Culture in Shi'ism* (Albany: SUNY Press, 1988), 54–79, 55–60; 'Abd al-Jalil ibn Abi al-Hasan Qazvini, *Kitab al-Naqd ma'ruf beh ba'd mathalib al-Nawasib fi Naqd 'ba'd fada'ih al-Rawwafid'* (Tehran: n.p., 1952); Sayyed Mohammad Hossein Manzoor al-Adjdad, 'The Naqīb of Ray

Alids and His Support of Scientists', *Iranian Studies* 41, 4 (2008), 529–35. See also Calmard, 'Le chiisme imamite en Iran'; Heidari-Abkenar, *Die ideologische und politische Konfrontation*, 106–90, 202.

52. David Durand-Guédy, 'MALEKŠĀH', *EIr*; H. Bowen and C. E. Bosworth, 'Niẓām al-Mulk', *EI2*.

53. Berkey, *The Formation of Islam*, 204.

54. Ismailis chose the Shafii school of jurisprudence when they became Sunni, and, while this outward shift of sectarian loyalty facilitated their political alliances and survival, later Ismaili sources claimed that this was dissimulation. Daftary, *The Ismailis*, 375ff.; Haider, *Shiʿi Islam*, 135ff.

55. Angelika Hartmann, 'al-Nāṣir Li-Dīn Allāh', *EI2*. See also Teresa Bernheimer, "Alī l-Hādī', *EI3*; A. Northedge, 'Sāmarrā", *EI2*.

56. Hartmann, 'al-Nāṣir Li-Dīn Allāh'. Over time, and in particular in the fifteenth and sixteenth centuries, a stronger Shii tendency characterised some of the *futuwwa*. Riza Yildirim, 'Shīʿitisation of the Futuwwa Tradition in the Fifteenth Century', *British Journal of Middle Eastern Studies* 40, 1 (2013), 53–70.

57. Sabari, *Mouvements*, 90.

58. Some medieval Muslim observers such as al-Suyuti argued that the new Caliph was more like a Shii Imam than a Sunni Caliph. Berkey, *The Formation of Islam*, 182, 185. For more, see Angelika Hartmann, *An-Nasir li-Din Allah: Politik, Religion, Kultur in der späten Abbasidenzeit* (Berlin: De Gruyter, 1975).

59. His book is available in French and English. Gonnella, *Islamische Heiligenverehrung*, 126ff., 141ff.; Daniella Talmon-Heller, *Islamic Piety in Medieval Syria: Mosques, Cemeteries and Sermons under the Zangids and Ayyubids (1146–1260)* (Leiden: Brill, 2007), 197; ʿAli ibn Abi Bakr al-Harawi, *A Lonely Wayfarer's Guide to Pilgrimage: ʿAlī ibn Abī Bakr al-Harawī's Kitāb al-Ishārāt ilā Maʿrifat al-Ziyārāt*, trans. by Josef W. Meri (Princeton: Darwin Press, 2004).

60. The alleged son, Muhassin bin al-Hussain, was said to have been born after Hussain's women and children in his entourage had been deported from Karbala to Damascus, but was then said to have died at an early age, perhaps as a way to countenance the fact that he was not a central part of the Shii tradition. M. Canard, 'Ḥamdānids', *EI2*; Archnet, 'Mashhad al-Muhassin', https://www.archnet.org/sites/1810; Terry Allen, *Ayyubid Architecture* (Occidental, CA: Solipsist Press, 1999).

61. Talmon-Heller, *Islamic Piety*, 196f.

62. In the late twentieth century, the al-Hussain mausoleum was the only one whose upkeep was financed by members of the small Shii communities in the villages outside of Aleppo, and that was particularly visited by Shia. Gonnella, *Islamische Heiligenverehrung*, 127n197, 195ff. In the middle ages, a number of other mausoleums were established for members of the *Ahl al-Bayt* that people had seen in dreams, but they later disappeared. Ibid., 127f.; J. Sauvaget, 'Deux sanctuaires chiites d'Alep', *Syria* 9, 4 (1928), 320–7; Archnet, 'Mashhad al-Husayn', https://www.archnet.org/sites/1811; Allen, *Ayyubid Architecture*.

63. Some authors argued that this shrine was expanded after some Shia had become resentful of the Sunni appropriation of the shrine of Muhassin bin al-Hussain. Talmon-Heller, *Islamic Piety*, 196f.

64. For an overview of the scholarship, see Robert Riggs, 'Shi'i Shrine Cities', *OBi*; J. W. Meri et al., 'Ziyāra', *EI2*; Richard J. McGregor, 'Grave Visitation/Worship', *EI3*; Yasser Tabbaa, 'Review of "The Shrines of the 'Alids in Medieval Syria" by Stephennie Mulder', *Shii Studies Review* 1, 1–2 (2017), 265–71. See also Josef Meri, *The Cult of Saints among Muslims and Jews in Medieval Syria* (Oxford: Oxford University Press, 2002); Yasser Tabbaa, *The Transformation of Islamic Art during the Sunni Revival* (Seattle: University of Washington Press, 2001).

65. Upon their conquest of Aleppo, the Saljuqs thus not only continued to expand *Ahl al-Bayt* shrines but founded new ones, including one for the Hebrew prophet Abraham, in order to counter-balance the shrines associated with Shiism. Oleg Grabar, 'The Earliest Islamic Commemorative Structures, Notes and Documents', in: *Jerusalem: Constructing the Study of Islamic Art*, Vol. 4 (Aldershot: Ashgate, 2005), 65–110, 90, 102ff., first published in *Ars Orientalis* 6 (1966), 7–46.

66. Berkey, *The Formation of Islam*, 182; Peacock, *Early Seljūq History*, 128–52.

67. Robert Irwin has pointed out that, in his book, one does not find any reference to the notion of Jihad, which Irwin explains with Munqidh's Shii background and the illegitimacy of Jihad in Shiism in the absence of the Imam or a legitimate ruler. Robert Irwin, 'Der Islam und die Kreuzzüge 1096–1699', in: Jonathan Riley-Smith (ed.), *Illustrierte Geschichte der Kreuzzüge* (Frankfurt am Main: Campus, 1999), 251–98, 269f. The book exists in numerous translations into European languages, for example: Usamahibn Munqidh, *An Arab-Syrian Gentleman and Warrior in the Period of the Crusades: Memoirs of Usāmah ibn Munqidh (Kitāb al-I'tibār)*, trans. by Philip K. Hitti (New York: Columbia University Press, 1929); Munqidh, *Usâma ibn Munqidh: Ein Leben im Kampf gegen Kreuzritterheere*, trans. by Gernot Rotter (Lenningen: Edition Erdmann, 2004).

68. Winter, *A History of the 'Alawis*, 32; Harris, *Lebanon*, 49.

69. Khusraw, *Nāser-e Khosraw's Book*, 13.

70. El-Moctar, *The Crusades' Impact*, 147–61; F. Buhl, C. E. Bosworth, and M. Lavergne, 'Ṭarābulus (or Aṭrābulus) al-Shām', *EI2*; Alex Mallett, "'Ammār, Banū (Syria)', *EI3*; Kevin James Lewis, *The Counts of Tripoli and Lebanon in the Twelfth Century: Sons of Saint-Gilles* (London: Routledge, 2017), 30ff.; 'Ali al-Ibrahim al-Tarabulsi, *Al-Tashayyu' fi Tarablus wa Bilad al-Sham: Adwa' 'ala Dawlat Bani 'Ammar* (Beirut: Dar al-Saqi, 2007).

71. M. Canard, 'Ḥamdānids', *EI2*.

72. J. Sauvaget, 'Ḥalab', *EI2*.

73. Kamal Eddin ibn al-Adim, *Zubdat al-Halab fi Ta'rikh Halab*, 3 Vols, Vol. 2 (Damascus: Institut Français de Damas, 1954), 188f., quoted in: Salah Zaimeche, 'Aleppo', *Muslim Heritage*, 9 July 2008, https://muslimheritage.com/aleppo/#_edn131; Irwin, 'Der Islam und die Kreuzzüge', 260; Berkey, *The Formation of Islam*, 191. For an example of his positive depiction, see Amin Maalouf, *Der*

Heilige Krieg der Barbaren: Die Kreuzzüge aus der Sicht der Araber (Munich: DTV, 2004), 110 and passim. For the English translation, see Maalouf, *The Crusades through Arab Eyes* (London: Saqi, 2006).

74. Ross Burns, *Aleppo: A History* (Abingdon: Routledge, 2017), 122.

75. Berkey, *The Formation of Islam*, 191; El-Moctar, *The Crusades' Impact*, 170f.; Nikita Elisséeff, *Nūr ad-Dīn: Un grand prince musulman de Syrie au temps des Croisades (511–569 H./118–1174)*, 3 Vols (Damascus: Institut Français de Damas, 1967), Vol. 2, 340f., 428ff., 488, Vol. 3, 750–79, 901–35; Irwin, 'Der Islam und die Kreuzzüge', 265; Henri Michel Khaÿat, 'The Šī'ite Rebellions in Aleppo in the 6th A. H./12th A. D. Century', *Rivista degli Studi Orientali* 46, 3/4 (1971), 167–95; Sauvaget, 'Ḥalab'; Talmon-Heller, *Islamic Piety*, 197. See also Anne-Marie Eddé, 'Sunnites et Chiites à Alep sous le règne d'al-Salih lsma'il (569–77/1174–81): Entre conflits et réconciliations', in: Carole Hillenbrand (ed.), *Syria in Crusader Times: Conflict and Co-Existence* (Edinburgh: Edinburgh University Press, 2019), 197–210; Carole Hillenbrand, 'The Shi'is of Aleppo in the Zengid Period: Some Unexploited Textual and Epigraphic Evidence', in: H. Biesterfeldt and V. Klemm (eds), *Difference and Dynamism in Islam: Festschrift for Heinz Halm on his 70th Birthday* (Würzburg: Ergon, 2012), 163–79; Marco Salati, 'Shiism in Ottoman Syria: A Document from the Qadi-Court of Aleppo (963/1555 A.D.)', *Eurasian Studies* 1, 1 (2002), 77–84; Salati, 'Shiite Survival in Ottoman Aleppo: The Endowment Deed of Ahmad and Baha' al-Din al-Zuhrawi (1066/1656) (Aleppo Court Records, Vol. 3, pp. 788–790)', *Eurasian Studies* 14, 1 (2016), 205–30.

76. El-Moctar, *The Crusades' Impact*, 176–9. Talai Ibn Ruzzik was a Twelver Shii (or possibly an Alawite), who endowed a large *waqf* in support of the Ashraf. Lev, *Saladin*, 12.

77. Schwinges, *Kreuzzugsideologie*, 256.

78. When discussing the situation at the time of the First Crusade and the conquest of Jerusalem, he states: 'There existed at this time a persistent strife between the Egyptians and the Persians, induced by bitter rivalry over the supremacy. The fact that these nations held diametrically opposed doctrines contributed largely to the feeling of hatred between them. Even at the present day, this difference of religious views is the subject of such controversy between the two nations that they hold no communication, for each looks upon the other as sacrilegious. This feeling is carried so far that they wish to be different even in name. Hence, those who follow the tenets of the East are called in their own tongue Sunnites, while those who prefer the tradition of Egypt, which apparently inclines more toward our own faith, are known as Shiites.' William of Tyre, *A History of Deeds Done beyond the Sea*, 2 Vols (New York: Columbia University Press, 1943), Vol. 1, 65f. With the Abbasids, on the other hand, the Crusaders had more indirect contact, and thus limited knowledge. Still, William described the Abbasids as having greater spiritual and worldly authority than the Fatimids. Schwinges, *Kreuzzugsideologie*, 112ff. For the problem of dating the time of writing of his *Historia*, and the fact that parts seem to have been written while the Fatimids were still in power, thus before 1171, and parts after, as he himself

asserts in the text, see Benjamin Z. Kedar, 'Some New Light on the Composition Process of William of Tyre's Historia', in: Susan B. Edgington and Helen J. Nicholson (eds), *Deeds Done beyond the Sea: Essays on William of Tyre, Cyprus and the Military Orders Presented to Peter Edbury* (Aldershot: Ashgate, 2014), 3–11, 3ff.

79. His account is, according to his own statements, based on old history books but also on oral sources, perhaps Shia living under Christian rule. It stresses the centrality of Ali and ascribes to the Shia a belief that Ali is a Prophet, and that the archangel Gabriel had made a mistake by revealing the revelation to Muhammad, when it had in fact been meant for Ali. Schwinges, *Kreuzzugsideologie*, 110; William of Tyre, *A History of Deeds*, Vol. 1, 65f., and Vol. 2, 323ff. Jacques de Vitry also wrote about the schism in Islam. See also Christiane M. Thomsen, *Burchards Bericht über den Orient: Reiseerfahrungen eines staufischen Gesandten im Reich Saladins 1175/1176* (Berlin: De Gruyter, 2018), 294f. In the report of Burchard, however, the split is not mentioned. A Dominican missionary, Riccoldo da Monte di Croce, who apparently met some Shia in Iraq, thought they were less evil (*minus mali*) than Sunnis (likely because by that time they no longer posed a political challenge to Christendom). Kohlberg, 'Western Studies', 31f.

80. 'Moreover, the caliph of Egypt, the most powerful of all infidel potentates because of his riches and military forces, had sent his envoys to our leaders. The reason for this embassy was as follows. For many years, a deep and inveterate enmity had existed between the Orientals and the Egyptians, arising out of differences in their religious beliefs and their opposite dogmas. This hatred has persisted without interruption to the present day. Thus these two kingdoms, often at war with each other, were in constant rivalry, each striving to extend its own boundaries and to reduce the limits of the other [...]. At different periods, according as the prowess, now of the former and now of the latter, gained the upper hand, each kingdom, with the success of its arms, expanded its territory. The result was that whatever increased the domains of one kingdom decreased that of the other. [...] The Egyptian monarch regarded with suspicion any increase of the Persians or Turks. Accordingly the news that Qilij Arslan had lost Nicaea, where his army was reported to have been badly treated, and also that the Christians had laid siege to Antioch pleased him greatly. He regarded the losses of the Turks as a gain for himself and their troubles as affording peace and safety for himself and his subjects. Fearing, therefore, that weariness of the long-continued siege might cause our people to fail, he sent envoys, members of his own household staff, to beg the leaders to continue the siege. The deputies were commissioned to assure the Christians that the sultan would aid them with military support and resources.' William of Tyre, *A History of Deeds*, Vol. 1, 223f., also quoted in: El-Moctar, *The Crusades' Impact*, 186f.

81. William of Tyre, *A History of Deeds*, Vol. 1, 394; El-Moctar, *The Crusades' Impact*, 14.

82. Meriem Pages, *The Image of the Assassins in Medieval European Texts* (PhD, University of Massachusetts Amherst, 2007).

83. Eventually, Ismailis were ascribed strange beliefs that involved the idea of a paradise garden into which intoxicated assassins were initiated by the 'Wise Man of the Mountain' before being sent on their missions. Many of those stories were fabrications of Crusader times or later European imaginations of the Orient. Tellingly, even the Sunni polemicists that heavily criticised the Ismailis did not refer to them as *hashishi* in a literal sense. The literal interpretation of (perpetual) hashish smokers seems to have been a European invention, a sign of the limited knowledge medieval European scholars had of Islam, and of how easily the appropriation of Sunni polemics could lead to misunderstandings. Daftary, *The Ismailis*, 7–22; Bernard Lewis, 'Ḥaṣhīṣhiyya', *EI2*; Farhad Daftary, 'Assassins', *EI3*. Crusader historians also wrote about the Druze, an offshoot of Ismailism based in the Lebanese mountains, portraying them as fierce mountain warriors with rather strange beliefs (though they were apparently unaware of the split that had occurred between the Druze and other Ismailis). Harris quotes Benjamin of Tudela and William of Tyre, the latter conflating the Druze with the Ismaili assassins. Harris, *Lebanon*, 59. Even later, scholars who were aware of these fabrications, such as Bernard Lewis, would describe them as a 'radical sect' and as inventors of 'terrorism'. Bernard Lewis, *The Assassins: A Radical Sect in Islam* (London: Weidenfeld & Nicolson, 1967). Lewis' generally problematic and biased views of Islam thus extend to Shiism, which he describes as a disruptive force against the political status quo. Bernard Lewis, 'The Shi'a in Islamic History', in: Martin Kramer (ed.), *Shi'ism, Resistance, and Revolution* (Boulder, CO: Westview Press, 1987), 21–30. See also Heinz Halm, *Die Assassinen: Geschichte eines islamischen Geheimbundes* (Munich: C. H. Beck, 2017), 72ff.; Farhad Daftary, 'The "Order of the Assassins": J. von Hammer and the Orientalist Misrepresentations of the Nizari Ismailis', *Iranian Studies* 39, 1 (2006), 71–81.

84. Halm, *Kalifen und Assassinen*, 282–8; Irwin, 'Der Islam und die Kreuzzüge', 267; Lev, *Saladin*, 85, 125. Scholars still debate whether or not this was really a key aspect of a Sunni Revival against Shiism. Stephennie Mulder has argued that the expansion of the al-Shafii complex may have had more to do with rivalries within Sunnism, between Asharis and Hanbalis, rather than with a Sunni effort to supplant Shiism. She points to the fact that al-Shafii's mausoleum had already existed and been a site of visitation, including for Shia, before the advent of the Ayyubids. Stephennie Mulder, 'The Mausoleum of Imam al-Shafi'i', *Muqarnas* 23 (2006), 15–46, 19f. See also Leiser, *The Restoration of Sunnism*, 187–267.

85. D. Fairchild Ruggles, *Tree of Pearls: The Extraordinary Architectural Patronage of the 13th-Century Egyptian Slave-Queen Shajar al-Durr* (Oxford: Oxford University Press, 2020), 39, 51. New tombs also continued to be built and patronised by the Sunni Ayyubids and Mamluks. Ibid., 89.

86. Ibid., 55.

87. Lev, *Saladin*, 136f.

88. See also Taylor, *In the Vicinity of the Righteous*, 7–167.

89. Irwin, 'Der Islam und die Kreuzzüge', 267–74. See also Carole Hillenbrand, *The Crusades: Islamic Perspectives* (Edinburgh: Edinburgh University Press, 1999); Eric

Böhme, *Die Außenbeziehungen des Königreiches Jerusalem im 12. Jahrhundert* (Berlin: De Gruyter, 2019), 51–266.

90. El-Moctar, *The Crusades' Impact*, 172f.
91. Berkey, *The Formation of Islam*, 181.
92. Such as in the account of the historian Ibn Tulun (d. 1546). See Harris, *Lebanon*, 85.
93. Taef El-Azhari, *Zengi and the Muslim Response to the Crusades: The Politics of Jihad* (London: Routledge, 2016); H. A. R. Gibb, 'Notes on the Arabic Materials for the History of the Early Crusades', *Bulletin of the School of Oriental and African Studies* 7, 4 (1935), 739–54, 743.
94. Daftary, *The Ismailis*, 367ff.
95. Schwinges, *Kreuzzugsideologie*, 270f., 280f.
96. Daftary, *The Ismailis*, 369f.; Nasseh Ahmad Mirza, *Syrian Ismailism: The Ever Living Line of the Imamate, AD 1100–1260* (Richmond: Curzon, 1997), 38f.; Winter, *A History of the 'Alawis*, 36. For an account of one assassination attempt, see Ibn al-Athir, *Chronicle*, Vol. 2, 243.
97. Majed Halawi, *A Lebanon Defied: Musa al-Sadr and the Shi'a Community* (Boulder, CO: Westview Press, 1992), 29; Harris, *Lebanon*, 35, 50.
98. Khusraw, *Nāser-e Khosraw's Book*, 16.
99. One of these, for example, was Tibnin castle. Harris, *Lebanon*, 50, 60.
100. Nasir Khusraw relates a Shii presence in Tiberias. Khusraw, *Nāser-e Khosraw's Book*, 19; Friedman, *The Shī'īs in Palestine*.
101. Harris, *Lebanon*, 62, quoting Ibn al-Qalanisi, although in another section he seems to refer to soldiers from Jabal Amil reinforcing Muslim troops. See also Antonia Durrer, *Die Kreuzfahrerherrschaften des 12. und 13. Jahrhunderts zwischen Integration und Segregation: Zeitgenössische und moderne Stimmen im Vergleich* (Ostfildern: Jan Thorbecke, 2016), 41–5.
102. Guy Le Strange, *Palestine under the Moslems: A Description of Syria and the Holy Land from AD 650 to 1500* (London: Alexander P. Watt, 1890), 545; Harris, *Lebanon*, 63, quoting Ibn Jubayr. Ibn Jubayr's account, in turn, is denounced in modern Shii historiography as inaccurate and naive. No Muslim community wants to be seen as having aided the Crusaders. Ibid.
103. Mohamed El-Moctar, 'Saladin in Sunni and Shi'a Memories', in: Nicholas Paul and Suzanne Yeager (eds), *Remembering the Crusades: Myth, Image, and Identity* (Baltimore: Johns Hopkins University Press, 2012), 197–214, 198f.
104. Christopher Tyerman, *The World of the Crusades: An Illustrated History* (New Haven: Yale University Press, 2019); Christopher H. MacEvitt, *The Crusades and the Christian World of the East: Rough Tolerance* (Philadelphia: University of Pennsylvania Press, 2008).
105. Harris, *Lebanon*, 63f.
106. Sabrina Mervin, '"Āmil, Jabal', *EI3*; Mervin, *Un réformisme chiite: Ulémas et lettrés du Ǧabal Āmil (actuel Liban-Sud) de la fin de l'Empire ottoman à l'indépendance du Liban* (Paris: Karthala, 2000), 19–22; Harris, *Lebanon*, 18.
107. Harris, *Lebanon*, 64.

108. While little is known of their situation under the Franks, there are reports of conversions to Christianity. Winter, *A History of the 'Alawis*, 36f.
109. Ibid., 37–42.
110. See, for example, Abdel Rahman Azzam, *Saladin: The Triumph of the Sunni Revival* (Cambridge: Islamic Texts Society, 2014). The Arabic translation of his book makes an even stronger point, termed '*Ihiya' al-Madhhab al-Sunni*'. I thank Mark Farha for this point. While most Sunni and Shii authors saw Saladin as a heroic figure (Ismailis disagreed), accounts of his role in later periods would start to diverge sharply. Ibn Abi Tayy', an Aleppan Shii biographer and contemporary of Saladin, for example, painted a positive image of Saladin and denounced the Ismailis as well as Nur al-Din Zangi, because the latter had suppressed Shiism in Aleppo. Claude Cahen, 'Une chronique chiite au temps des Croisades', *Comptes rendus des séances de l'Académie des Inscriptions et Belles-Lettres* 79, 3 (1935), 258–69; Lev, *Saladin*, 41ff.; Anne-Marie Eddé, 'Ibn Abī Ṭayyi'', *EI3*. Abu Shama, a prominent Sunni historian, on the other hand, emphasised the Sunni credentials of Nur al-Din and Saladin, praising Nur al-Din for 'humiliating the Shia of Aleppo and suppressing their rituals, and strengthening the Sunnis'. Abu Shama, *Kitab al-Rawdatayn fi Akhbari al-Dawlatayn*, cited after: El-Moctar, 'Saladin', 202. This emphasis on Saladin's sectarian identity would later be cemented by Sunni hardliners such as Ibn Taymiyya and his disciples. In this vein, modern Sunni historians, and many Salafis, see the defeat of the Fatimids as one of Saladin's main achievements, thereby adopting a sectarian reading of events. El-Moctar, 'Saladin', 203. Persian chronicles from Mongol times, which were composed before the Safavids converted much of Iran to Shiism and were thus largely written by Sunni authors, likewise emphasise his role in the deposition of the Ismaili Fatimid dynasty. Daniel Beben, 'Remembering Saladin: The Crusades and the Politics of Heresy in Persian Historiography', *Journal of the Royal Asiatic Society* 28, 2 (2018), 231–53. These diverging sectarian memory cultures are also intertwined with modern nationalist memories. Saladin would in the twentieth century become a key figure of Arab nationalism, even though he was of Kurdish origin. At the same time, Kurdish identity entrepreneurs would claim him as a Kurdish leader. In the late twentieth and early twenty-first century, he was portrayed in popular TV dramas as a pan-Arab and pan-Islamic leader. In a series produced in Syria, his fight against the Fatimids was downplayed, and he was even invoked by the leader of Lebanese Hizbullah, Hasan Nasrallah, in the context of the 2006 war with Israel. Omar Sayfo, 'From Kurdish Sultan to Pan-Arab Champion and Muslim Hero: The Evolution of the Saladin Myth in Popular Arab Culture', *Journal of Popular Culture* 50 (2017), 65–85. Starting in 1979, Shii authors, on the other hand, started to criticise Saladin, focusing instead on the role of the Fatimids and the pro-Shii Caliph al-Nasir in Baghdad at the time of Saladin. An example is Salih al-Wardani. El-Moctar, 'Saladin', 204ff. In addition, modern Syrian Ismaili historians try to portray

the Ismailis in Syria as having been allies of Saladin. Ibid., 207. See also Elisséeff, *Nūr ad-Dīn*, Vol. 1, 2f.

111. Winter, *A History of the 'Alawis*, 42; Berkey, *The Formation of Islam*, 189f.; Afsaruddin, *Excellence and Precedence*, 12ff.

112. Reinhart, 'On Sunni Sectarianism', 210.

CHAPTER 3

1. See also references in note 10 of the Prologue. Ulrich Haarmann, 'Staat und Religion in Transoxanien im frühen 16. Jahrhundert', *Zeitschrift der Deutschen Morgenländischen Gesellschaft* 124, 2 (1974), 332–69, 350; John E. Woods, *The Aqquyunlu: Clan, Confederation, Empire*, 2nd ed. (Salt Lake City: University of Utah Press, 1999), 3–10, term on page 4. See also A. Bausani, 'Religion under the Mongols', in: J. A. Boyle (ed.), *The Cambridge History of Iran*, Vol. 5 (Cambridge: Cambridge University Press, 1968), 538–49; Stefan Winter, *The Shiites of Lebanon under Ottoman Rule, 1516–1788* (Cambridge: Cambridge University Press, 2010), 9; Judith Pfeiffer, 'Confessional Ambiguity vs. Confessional Polarization: Politics and the Negotiation of Religious Boundaries in the Ilkhanate', in: Judith Pfeiffer (ed.), *Politics, Patronage and the Transmission of Knowledge in 13th–15th Century Tabriz* (Leiden: Brill, 2014), 129–68. Michel M. Mazzaoui, *The Origins of the Safawids: Shiism, Sufism, and the Ghulat* (Wiesbaden: Franz Steiner/Freiburger Islamstudien, 1972), 22–40, tends to emphasise Sunni–Shia coexistence in this period, while also discussing the polemics of Ibn Taymiyya against Shiism. This contrast is not satisfactorily explained in his account. See the critical review by Ann E. Mayer in *Iranian Studies* 8, 4 (1975), 268–77.

2. Momen, *An Introduction to Shi'i Islam*, 91f. For this period in general, see also Jean Calmard, 'Le chiisme imamite sous les Ilkhans', in: Denise Aigle (ed.), *L'Iran face à la domination mongole* (Tehran: Institut Français de Recherche en Iran, 1997), 261–92.

3. Al-Jamil, *Cooperation and Contestation*, 35.

4. Berkey, *The Formation of Islam*, 182.

5. Reuven Amitai, *Holy War and Rapprochement: Studies in the Relations between the Mamluk Sultanate and the Mongol Ilkhanate (1260–1335)* (Turnhout: Brepols, 2013), 95; David Ayalon, 'Studies on the Transfer of the 'Abbāsid Caliphate from Baġdād to Cairo', *Arabica* 7, 1 (1960), 41–59; Jonathan P. Berkey, 'Mamluk Religious Policy', *Mamluk Studies Review* 13, 2 (2009), 6–22, 11f.; Hassan, *Longing for the Lost Caliphate*, 66–97.

6. This policy led to some resistance by the Shafii *ulama*. D. P. Little, 'Religion under the Mamluks', *The Muslim World* 73 (1983), 165–81, 169f., 173f.; Jorgen S. Nielsen, 'Sultan al-Zāhir Baybars and the Appointment of Four Chief Qādīs, 663/1265', *Studia Islamica* 60 (1984), 167–76; Yossef Rapoport, 'Legal Diversity in the Age of Taqlīd: The Four Chief Qādīs under the Mamluks', *Islamic Law and Society* 10, 2 (2003), 210–28; Rebecca Hernandez,

The Legal Thought of Jalāl al-Dīn al-Suyūṭī: Authority and Legacy (Oxford: Oxford University Press, 2017), 56ff. For Baybars and the Ismailis, see Laoust, *Essai*, 59; Berkey, 'Mamluk Religious Policy', 9ff.

7. Amitai, *Holy War and Rapprochement*, 95; Mustafa Banister, *The Abbasid Caliphate of Cairo (1261–1517): History and Tradition in the Mamluk Court* (PhD, University of Toronto, 2015), 79. See also Anne F. Broadbridge, *Kingship and Ideology in the Islamic and Mongol Worlds* (Cambridge: Cambridge University Press, 2008).

8. Little, 'Religion under the Mamluks', 168; Reuven Amitai, *Mongols and Mamluks: The Mamluk-Ilkhanid War, 1260–1281* (Cambridge: Cambridge University Press, 1995), 2; Amitai, *Holy War and Rapprochement*, ch. 2. For conversion to Islam under the Mamluks, see also Donald P. Little, 'Coptic Conversion to Islam under the Baḥrī Mamlūks, 692–755/1293–1354', *Bulletin of the School of Oriental and African Studies* 39, 3 (1976), 552–69.

9. Peter Jackson, 'The Mongols and the Faith of the Conquered', in: Reuven Amitai and Michal Biran (eds), *Mongols, Turks, and Others: Eurasian Nomads and the Sedentary World* (Leiden: Brill, 2005), 245–90, esp. 253–62; Jackson, *The Mongols and the West, 1221–1410* (Harlow: Pearson/Longman, 2005).

10. Charles Melville, 'Pādshāh-i Islām: The Conversion of Sultan Maḥmūd Ghāzān Khān', *Pembroke Papers* 1 (1990), 159–77. Although it took a while for the Mamluks to accept that the Mongols were indeed serious about their conversion. Reuven Amitai, 'Ghazan, Islam and Mongol Tradition: A View from the Mamlūk Sultanate', *Bulletin of the School of Oriental and African Studies* 59, 1 (1996), 1–10. See also Amitai, 'GĀZĀN KHAN, MAḤMŪD', *EIr.* For earlier conversion to Islam and a discussion of the role of Sufi orders, some with Shii leanings, in this, see Judith Pfeiffer, 'Reflections on a "Double Rapprochement": Conversion to Islam among the Mongol Elite during the Early Ilkhanate', in: Linda Komaroff (ed.), *Beyond the Legacy of Genghis Khan* (Leiden: Brill, 2006), 369–89.

11. Morimoto has detailed the story of an Iraqi Shii genealogist specialising in the history of the *Ahl al-Bayt* at the court of Özbek Khan. Ibn Battuta describes meeting him, but does not mention his sectarian identity, which is rare for Ibn Battuta. There were also merchants from Karbala, most likely Shii, in Golden Horde territory, in particular in the Qipchaq Steppe. Kazuo Morimoto, 'Sayyid Ibn ʿAbd al-Ḥamīd: An Iraqi Shiʿi Genealogist at the Court of Özbek Khan', *Journal of the Economic and Social History of the Orient* 59 (2016), 661–94, 677–81. See also Devin DeWeese, *Islamization and Native Religion in the Golden Horde: Baba Tükles and Conversion to Islam in Historical and Epic Tradition* (University Park: Penn State University Press, 1994).

12. Sabine Schmidtke, *The Theology of al-ʿAllama al-Ḥilli (d. 726/1325)* (Berlin: Klaus Schwarz, 1991), 24–8.

13. Judith Pfeiffer, 'Twelver Shiʿism as State Religion in Mongol Iran: An Abortive Attempt, Recorded and Remembered', *Pera-Blätter* 11 (1999), 3–38, 4.

14. Schmidtke, *The Theology*, 24–8.

15. Harris, *Lebanon*, 67.

16. This follows the account by Ibn Kathir as rendered in Laoust, 'Remarques', 99. See also Donald Presgrave Little, *An Introduction to Mamluk Historiography: An*

Analysis of Arabic Annalistic and Biographical Sources for the Reign of al-Malik an-Nāṣir Muḥammad ibn Qalā'ūn (Wiesbaden: Franz Steiner, 1970), 71ff. Ibn Taymiyya referred in more detail to the cooperation between the people of Kisrawan and the Franks of Cyprus in order to legitimise action against them. Ibid., 110n2.

17. Harris, *Lebanon*, 70; Laoust, 'Remarques', 101f.

18. The sources are far from clear on this, however. This is based on Ibn Kathir. Laoust, 'Remarques', 102f.

19. Laoust, *Essai*, 7–39.

20. Ibid., 117–23; Reuven Amitai, 'The Mongol Occupation of Damascus in 1300: A Study of Mamluk Loyalties', in: Michael Winter and Amalia Levanoni (eds), *The Mamluks in Egyptian and Syrian Politics and Society* (Leiden: Brill, 2004), 21–41.

21. Denise Aigle, *The Mongol Empire between Myth and Reality: Studies in Anthropological History* (Leiden: Brill, 2014), 283–305; Aigle, 'The Mongol Invasions of Bilād al-Shām by Ghāzān Khān and Ibn Taymīyah's Three "Anti-Mongol" Fatwas', *Mamluk Studies Review* 11, 2 (2007), 89–120; Amitai, *Holy War and Rapprochement*, 71–80.

22. Teresa Fitzherbert, 'Religious Diversity under Ilkhanid Rule c. 1300 as Reflected in the Freer Bal'amī', in: Linda Komaroff (ed.), *Beyond the Legacy of Genghis Khan* (Leiden: Brill, 2006), 390–406, 396f.

23. Ahmad Beydoun, *Identité confessionnelle et temps social chez les historiens libanais contemporains* (Beirut: Université Libanaise, 1984), 78ff.

24. Winter, *The Shiites of Lebanon*, 62f., and esp. Beydoun, *Identité confessionnelle*, 77–160. Salibi also emphasises the Maronite presence and role in the fight against the Mamluks. Kamal S. Salibi, 'The Maronites of Lebanon under Frankish and Mamluk Rule (1099–1516)', *Arabica* 4, 3 (1957), 288–303.

25. Ibn Kathir, who has related Ibn Taymiyya's involvement in the affair, declares them to be rejectionists (*rafida*). Laoust, 'Remarques', 109.

26. Abu al-Fida, *Kitab al-Mukhtasar*, quoted in: Harris, *Lebanon*, 71.

27. Harris, *Lebanon*, 72.

28. According to Ibn Kathir, Ibn Taymiyya went to Kisrawan and managed to bring the inhabitants under the laws of Islam, after which he returned victorious. Laoust, 'Remarques', 103; Stefan Winter, 'Shams al-Dīn Muḥammad ibn Makkī "al-Shahīd al-Awwal" (d. 1384) and the Shi'ah of Syria', *Mamluk Studies Review* 3 (1999), 149–82, 153f.

29. Winter, *A History of the 'Alawis*, 52, 56–9.

30. Ibn Taymiyya, *Risala fi Radd ala al-Nusayriyya*, quoted in: Mazzaoui, *The Origins of the Safawids*, 35. He also claims that the Nusayris (Alawites) collaborated with the Crusaders. The exact dating of the fatwa is disputed. Laoust dates it to the last years of his life, not around the 1305 Kisrawan campaign. Laoust, 'Remarques', 108; Tariq al-Jamil, 'Ibn Taymiyya and Ibn al-Mutahhar al-Hilli: Shi'i Polemics and the Struggle for Religious Authority in Medieval Islam', in: Yossef Rapoport and Shahab Ahmed (eds), *Ibn Taymiyya and his Times* (Oxford: Oxford University Press, 2010), 229–46, 234; Yaron Friedman, 'Ibn Taymiyya's Fatāwā against the Nuṣayrī-'Alawī Sect', *Der Islam* 82, 2 (2005), 349–63; Yvette Talhamy, 'The Fatwas and the Nusayri/Alawis of Syria', *Middle Eastern Studies* 46, 2 (2010),

175–94. It received scholarly attention from the nineteenth century onwards. Stanislas Guyard, 'Le Fetwa d'Ibn Taymiyah sur les Noṣairis', *Journal Asiatique* 18 (1871), 158–98; Edward E. Salisbury, 'Translation of Two Unpublished Arabic Documents, Relating to the Doctrines of the Ismâ'ilis and Other Bâṭinian Sects, with an Introduction and Notes', *Journal of the American Oriental Society* 2 (1851), 257–324. Ibn Taymiyya might have encountered Nusayris and talked to them about their beliefs. Laoust, *Essai*, 37.

31. Winter, *A History of the 'Alawis*, 60; Winter, 'Shams al-Dīn', 154. For more detail, see also Little, *An Introduction to Mamluk Historiography*, 10, 45. Lammens thinks, partly based on Ibn Taymiyya's writings and those of Arab chroniclers, that the campaigns were waged against "heretics", especially Nusayris (Alawites). Henri Lammens, 'Les Nosairis dans le Liban', *Revue de l'Orient Chrétien* 7 (1902), 452–77. For a largely political explanation, see Laoust, 'Remarques', 109–15. See also Harris, *Lebanon*, 68.

32. Laoust, 'Remarques', 111.

33. Winter, *A History of the 'Alawis*, 52.

34. Ibid., 59; Winter, 'Shams al-Dīn', 151; Kamal S. Salibi, 'The Buḥturids of the Garb: Mediaeval Lords of Beirut and of Southern Lebanon', *Arabica* 8, 1 (1961), 74–97, 91f.

35. Winter, *A History of the 'Alawis*, 60.

36. Ibid., 53f.; Winter, 'Shams al-Dīn', 154; Charles Melville, '"Sometimes by the Sword, Sometimes by the Dagger": The Role of the Ismailis in Mamluk–Mongol Relations in the 8th/14th Century', in: Farhad Daftary (ed.), *Mediaeval Isma'ili History and Thought* (Cambridge: Cambridge University Press, 1996), 247–63.

37. Berkey, 'Mamluk Religious Policy', 8f.

38. Laoust, 'Remarques', 112.

39. Ibid., 114.

40. He even invokes that, in combatting the rejectionists, the Sultan would follow the example not only of the Prophet but also of Ali, who had fought the Haruriyya (Kharijis). Laoust, *Essai*, 124f.; Laoust, 'Remarques', 112; Winter, 'Shams al-Dīn', 152. Ibn Taymiyya's letter was little known in Lebanon until 1978, when it was published in the journal *al-Fikr al-Islami*, edited by the Sunni Dar al-Ifta. This in turn drew the ire of Musa al-Sadr, head of the Higher Shii Council. Beydoun, *Identité confessionnelle*, 83, 107f. The editor of the text seems to identify quite closely with Ibn Taymiyya, adopting the term '*rawafid*' and denouncing the Maronite-Shii 'separatist plan' that had allegedly been implemented in Kisrawan. Ibid., 111f. In subsequent issues, Dar al-Ifta's director general apologised for the affair and published a response by the Shii historian M. Ali Makki on the request of the vice president of the Higher Shii Council, Muhammad Mahdi Shams al-Din. Given that Lebanon was three years into a civil war, this was sensitive, and Makki emphasised that many Shia had also been killed for standing with the (Sunni) Palestinians in South Lebanon. Ibid., 113.

41. He also denounced the high office attained by Christians under the Fatimids. Laoust, *Essai*, 265ff. Ibn Taymiyya also issued a fatwa against the Fatimids. See

ibid., 37n3; Yahya M. Michot, 'Ibn Taymiyya's Critique of Shī'ī Imāmology: Translation of Three Sections of his Minhaj al-Sunna', *The Muslim World* 104, 1–2 (2014), 109–49, 122f. He seems to largely rely on polemical literature against the Fatimids and finds them more dangerous than Nusayris (Alawites). Laoust, *Essai*, 97. In the now infamous 'Mardin fatwa', Ibn Taymiyya also blames the *rafidis* (in this case meaning Fatimids) for giving Christians too much power.

42. Laoust, *Essai*, 95.

43. Wesley Williams, 'Aspects of the Creed of Imam Ahmad ibn Hanbal: A Study of Anthropomorphism in Early Islamic Discourse', *International Journal of Middle East Studies* 34, 3 (2002), 441–63.

44. Livnat Holtzman, 'Accused of Anthropomorphism: Ibn Taymiyya's Miḥan as Reflected in Ibn Qayyim al-Jawziyya's al-Kāfiya al-Shāfiya', *The Muslim World* 106 (2016), 561–87; Laoust, *Essai*, 125–36; Eduard Strauss, 'L'inquisition dans l'état mamlouk', *Rivista degli Studi Orientali* 25 (1950), 11–26, 14ff. See now also Carl Sharif El-Tobgui, *Ibn Taymiyya on Reason and Revelation: A Study of Dar' ta'āruḍ al-'aql wa-l-naql* (Leiden: Brill, 2020). For the complicated relationship of Ibn Taymiyya with Sufism, see George Makdisi, 'Ibn Taymīya: A Ṣūfī of the Qādiriyya Order', *American Journal of Arabic Studies* 1 (1974), 118–29; Thomas Michael, 'Ibn Taymiyya's Sharḥ on the Futūḥ al-Ghayb of 'Abd al-Qādir al-Jīlānī', *Hamdard Islamicus* 4, 2 (1981), 3–12; Th. Emil Homerin, 'Ibn Taymiyya's al-Ṣūfīyah wa-al-Fuqarā'', *Arabica* 32 (1985), 219–44; Ovamir Anjum, 'Sufism Without Mysticism? Ibn Qayyim al-Ǧawziyyah's Objectives in Madāriǧ al-Sālikīn', in: Caterina Bori and Livnat Holtzman (eds), *A Scholar in the Shadow: Essays in the Legal and Theological Thought of Ibn al-Qayyim al-Jawziyya* (Rome: Herder, 2010), 161–88.

45. Donald Presgrave Little, 'The Historical and Historiographical Significance of the Detention of Ibn Taymiyya', *International Journal of Middle East Studies* 4, 3 (1973), 311–27; Little, 'Did Ibn Taymiyya Have a Screw Loose?', *Studia Islamica* 41 (1975), 93–111; Chamberlain, *Knowledge and Social Practice*, 170.

46. Chamberlain, *Knowledge and Social Practice*, 169f.

47. Ibid., 167–75.

48. Strauss, 'L'inquisition'. Eduard Strauss would later change his name to Eliyahu Ashtor. For a good reply, see Chamberlain, *Knowledge and Social Practice*, 168f.

49. The rebellion in Jabala in 1318 started in the context of a survey of the province of Tripoli that would have had financial and doctrinal consequences for Alawites and was suppressed by the Mamluks. Sunni historians, often religious scholars, underlined the religious nature of the revolt, decrying the rebels as heretics and invoking Ibn Taymiyya's fatwa. Winter, *A History of the 'Alawis*, 61–8, 71; Urbain Vermeulen, 'Some Remarks on a Rescript of an-Nāṣir Muḥammad b. Qalā'ūn on the Abolition of Taxes and the Nuṣayris (Mamlaka of Tripoli, 717/1317)', *Orientalia Lovaniensia Periodica* 1 (1970), 195–201.

50. Urbain Vermeulen, 'The Rescript against the Shī'ites and Rāfiḍites of Beirut, Ṣaidā and District (764 A.H./1363 A.D.)', *Orientalia Lovaniensia Periodica* 4 (1973), 169–75, 174; Strauss, 'L'inquisition', 13f.; Laoust, *Les schismes dans l'Islam*, 259.

51. It was confined to the coastal areas of Beirut and Sidon (Sayda). Vermeulen, 'The Rescript against the Shīʿites'.

52. Stewart, *Islamic Legal Orthodoxy*, 82f.; Albert Hourani, 'From Jabal ʿAmil to Persia', in: H. E. Chehabi, *Distant Relations: Iran and Lebanon in the Last 500 Years* (London: I. B. Tauris, 2006), 51–61, 54; Rula Abisaab, 'History and Self-Image: The ʿAmili Ulema in Syria and Iran (Fourteenth to Sixteenth Centuries)', in: H. E. Chehabi, *Distant Relations: Iran and Lebanon in the Last 500 Years* (London: I. B. Tauris, 2006), 62–95, 68ff.; Muhsin al-Amin, *Mustadrakat Aʿyan al-Shiʿa: Haqqaqahu wa Akhrajahu Hasan al-Amin* (Amelioration of Outstanding Men of the Shia: Checked and Published by Hasan al-Amin), 11 Vols (Beirut: Dar al-Taʿarruf li-l-Matbuʿat, 1986), Vol. 10, 59–64.

53. Harris, *Lebanon*, 83f.; Winter, 'Shams al-Dīn', 155. See also Berkey, 'Mamluk Religious Policy'.

54. Anne F. Broadbridge, 'Apostasy Trials in Eighth/Fourteenth Century Egypt and Syria: A Case Study', in: J. Pfeiffer and S. A. Quinn (eds), *History and Historiography of Post-Mongol Central Asia and the Middle East: Studies in Honor of John E. Woods* (Wiesbaden: Harrassowitz, 2006), 363–82; Rapoport, 'Legal Diversity', 223–6.

55. Winter, *A History of the ʿAlawis*, 72f.

56. Chamberlain, *Knowledge and Social Practice*, 86.

57. One Ashraf family retained this post into the modern period. Louis Pouzet, *Damas au VIIe/XIIIe siècle: Vie et structures religieuses d'une métropole islamique* (Beirut: Dar el-Machreq, 1988), 200, 245–62; Winter, 'Shams al-Dīn', 154.

58. A. Havemann, 'Naḳīb al-Ashrāf', EI2; Kazuo Morimoto, 'The Formation and Development of the Science of Talibid Genealogies in the 10th & 11th Century Middle East', *Oriente Moderno* 18, 2 (1999), 541–70; Winter, *The Shiites of Lebanon*, 28f.; Pouzet, *Damas*, 246ff., 253; Marco Salati, *Ascesa e caduta di una famiglia di Ašrāf sciiti di Aleppo: I Zuhrāwī o Zuhrāzāda, 1600–1750* (Rome: Istituto per l'Oriente C. A. Nallino, 1992).

59. Pouzet, *Damas*, 26f., 255.

60. Ibid., 249.

61. Harris, *Lebanon*, 83.

62. Yitzhak Nakash, *Reaching for Power: The Shiʿa in the Modern Arab World* (Princeton: Princeton University Press, 2006), 30.

63. Harris, *Lebanon*, 84.

64. Ibid., 68.

65. Ibid., 80.

66. Daftary, *The Ismailis*, 388ff. See also ibid., 397ff.

67. See this in-depth study of the Mongol invasion and its post-2003 uses: Nassima Neggaz, *The Falls of Baghdad in 1258 and 2003: A Study in Sunnī-Shīʿī Clashing Memories* (PhD, Georgetown University, 2013). See also Neggaz, 'Sectarianization and Memory in the Post-Saddam Middle East: The ʿAlāqima', *British Journal of Middle Eastern Studies* 49, 1 (2022), 159–76; Stefan Heidemann, *Das Aleppiner Kalifat (A.D. 1261): Vom Ende des Kalifates in Bagdad über Aleppo zu den*

Restaurationen in Kairo (Leiden: Brill, 1994), 61f.; J. A. Boyle, 'Ibn al-Alḳamī', *EI2*; Hassan, *Longing for the Lost Caliphate*, 8f.

68. George Lane, *Early Mongol Rule in Thirteenth-Century Iran: A Persian Renaissance* (London: RoutledgeCurzon, 2003), 220f.; Reuven Amitai, 'Hülegü and his Wise Men: Topos or Reality?', in: Judith Pfeiffer (ed.), *Politics, Patronage and the Transmission of Knowledge in 13th–15th Century Tabriz* (Leiden: Brill, 2013), 13–34, 20; al-Jamil, *Cooperation and Contestation*, 31–4. For his own account of the fall of Baghdad, see G. M. Wickens, 'Nasir ad-Din Tusi on the Fall of Baghdad: A Further Study', *Journal of Semitic Studies* 7, 1 (1962), 23–35.

69. H. Daiber and F. J. Ragep, 'al-Ṭūsī, Naṣīr al-Dīn', *EI2*; Wilferd Madelung, 'Nasir al-Din Tusi's Ethics: Between Philosophy, Shiʿism and Sufism' (London: Institute of Ismaili Studies, 2011); Farhad Daftary, 'Naṣir al-Dīn al-Ṭūsī and the Ismailis of the Alamūt Period', in: N. Pourjavady and Z. Vesel (eds), *Naṣir al-Dīn Ṭūsī: Philosophe et savant du XIIIe siècle* (Tehran: Institut Français de Recherche en Iran, 2000), 59–67; Hamid Dabashi, 'Philosopher/Vizier Khwāja Naṣir al-Dīn al-Ṭūsī and the Ismaʿilis', in: Farhad Daftary (ed.), *Mediaeval Ismaʿili History and Thought* (Cambridge: Cambridge University Press, 1996), 231–45; George E. Lane, 'ṬUSI, NAṢIR-AL-DIN i. Biography', *EIr*; Lane, *Early Mongol Rule*, 214, 221ff. See also the passages in the *Habib al-Siyar*, which paint a different picture of al-Tusi's relationship with the Ismailis, and with Ibn al-Alqami. Khwandamir, 'Genghis Khan's Progeny who Ruled Autonomously and Independently in Iran', in: *Classical Writings of the Medieval Islamic World: Persian Histories of the Mongol Dynasties*, trans. by Wheeler M. Thackston, Vol. 2 (London: I. B. Tauris, 2012), 53–139.

70. S. J. Badakhchani, 'Introduction', in: S. J. Badakhchani (ed.), *Shiʿi Interpretations of Islam: Three Treatises on Islamic Theology and Eschatology* (London: I. B. Tauris/Institute of Ismaili Studies, 2010), 1–21, 6f. For the latter, see George Saliba, 'Horoscopes and Planetary Theory: Ilkhanid Patronage of Astronomers', in: Linda Komaroff (ed.), *Beyond the Legacy of Genghis Khan* (Leiden: Brill, 2006), 357–68.

71. Madelung, 'Aš-Šahrastānīs Streitschrift', 259.

72. Hassan, *Longing for the Lost Caliphate*, 20–65.

73. Heidemann, *Das Aleppiner Kalifat*, 62ff.; al-Jamil, *Cooperation and Contestation*, 46. Hulegu is even said to have stated: 'What can be expected of a person who is unfaithful to his benefactor?' Quoted in: Khwandamir, 'Genghis Khan's Progeny', 54.

74. While some pre-modern Shii authors endorsed the view that al-Tusi had played a decisive role in the attack on Baghdad, after the Iranian Revolution, Shii authors would defend al-Tusi and argue that his story was an anti-Shii conspiracy theory. Rudolf Strothmann, *Die Zwölfer-Schīʿa: Zwei religionsgeschichtliche Charakterbilder aus der Mongolenzeit* (Leipzig: Otto Harrassowitz, 1926), 32; Heidemann, *Das Aleppiner Kalifat*, 5n8, 64. For an analysis of the different theories and accounts of his death, see Nassima Neggaz, 'The Many Deaths of the Last ʿAbbāsid Caliph al-Mustaʿṣim bi-llāh (d. 1258)', *Journal of the Royal Asiatic Society* 30, 4 (2020), 585–612. For a Shii refutation of both accusations against

al-Tusi and al-Alqami, see Rasul Jaʿfariyan, 'The Alleged Role of Khawajah Nasir al-Din al-Tusi in the Fall of Baghdad', *Al-Islam.org*, https://www.al-islam.org/al-tawhid/vol8-n2/alleged-role-khawajah-nasir-al-din-al-tusi-fall-baghdad/alleged-role-khawajah; Jaʿfariyan, 'Die vorgebliche Rolle von Hwâǧa Nasîr ad-Dîn at-Tûsî bei dem Fall von Bagdad', *Spektrum Iran* 3 (1990), 30–53. See also Abdulhadi Hairi, *Naṣīr al-Dīn Ṭūsī: His Supposed Political Role in the Mongol Invasion of Baghdad* (MA, McGill University, 1968).

75. Al-Jamil, *Cooperation and Contestation*, 32; Hend Gilli-Elewy, 'Al-awādi al-ǧāmia: A Contemporary Account of the Mongol Conquest of Baghdad, 656/1258', *Arabica* 58, 5 (2001), 353–71, 368; Judith Pfeiffer, '"Faces Like Shields Covered with Leather": Keturah's Sons in the Post-Mongol Islamicate Eschatological Traditions', in: İlker Evrim Binbaş and Nurten Kılıç-Schubel (eds), *Horizons of the World: Festschrift for İsenbike Togan* (Istanbul: İthaki, 2011), 556–94.

76. Etan Kohlberg, *A Medieval Muslim Scholar at Work: Ibn Tawus and his Library* (Leiden: Brill, 1992), 10–13; Amitai, 'Hülegü', 20f.; al-Jamil, *Cooperation and Contestation*, 69f.

77. Heidemann, *Das Aleppiner Kalifat*, 66. And Ibn al-Alqami's library, one of the largest libraries in Baghdad and probably the largest Shii library in the city, was destroyed, alongside many others, during the Mongol invasion. The Mongol invasion was thus particularly devastating for Shii manuscripts, as they were held in comparatively fewer locations, while Sunni literature was partly preserved in territory outside of Mongol control. Kohlberg, *A Medieval Muslim Scholar*, 80.

78. Heidemann, *Das Aleppiner Kalifat*, 65ff.

79. Al-Jamil, *Cooperation and Contestation*, 28, 44.

80. He was then accused of having staffed the judiciary with Shafii scholars at the expense of others. Ibn Kathir linked his admiration for Ibn Arabi to a Sufi-Shii mix of 'transgressions'. Pouzet, *Damas*, 250; Alexander D. Knysh, *Ibn ʿArabi in the Later Islamic Tradition: The Making of a Polemical Image in Medieval Islam* (Albany: SUNY Press, 1999), 31f.

81. William Chittick, 'Ibn ʿArabî', *EPhil*.

82. Pouzet, *Damas*, 295.

83. Kohlberg, "Ali b. Musa ibn Tawus', 325f.; Kohlberg, *A Medieval Muslim Scholar*. In a text written for his sons, he relates a debate between himself and a Sunni cleric from the Mustansiriyya *madrasa*, in which the four Sunni schools were taught. Ibn Tawus agreed to take part in a disputation in which both sides were only allowed to use the Quran and traditions seen as trustworthy by both sides. By relying on Hadith from the Sunni Hadith collections of Bukhari and Muslim, according to his own account, Ibn Tawus managed to leave the Sunni cleric speechless. When the Sunni cleric mentioned pro-Sunni traditions on the early Companions from the same transmitters, Ibn Tawus reminded him that those were not accepted by the Shia and thus not allowed in their disputation. Hearing this, the cleric allegedly repented. Ibn Tawus, *Kashf al-Mahajja*, quoted in: Kohlberg, "Ali b. Musa ibn Tawus', 333. Ibn Tawus seems to have

authored another anti-Sunni book under a pen name to avoid problems with the Abbasid authorities. The book gives the impression that its author is a Christian or Jew inquiring about Islam, who becomes convinced of the Shii position. The more the fictive author learns about Islam, the more his intuition leads him to accept that it is better to follow a member of the Prophet's family rather than a founding father of the four Sunni schools of jurisprudence, who lived after the Prophet's death. For him, numerical strength does not imply truth, and being in the minority does not imply that Shia are wrong. The author then seeks out Shii scholars who convince him of the rightfulness of Shiism by using Sunni traditions. In the same book, he relates further conversations with Hanbali clerics, other Sunnis, and a Zaydi. Abd al-Mahmud b. Dawud, *Al-Tara'if fi Ma'rifat Madhahib al-Tawa'if*, discussed in: Kohlberg, "Ali b. Musa ibn Tawus', 335–43.

84. This has long been thought to have been the work primarily of al-Hilli, but Afsaruddin has shown the influence of Ibn Tawus. Afsaruddin, *Excellence and Precedence*, 202–6. Their focus on Hadith was a forerunner of the Akhbari school. For more on Ibn Tawus, see Kohlberg, *A Medieval Muslim Scholar*; Kohlberg, "Ali b. Musa ibn Tawus', 349.

85. Interestingly, he himself spoke fondly of his Sunni teachers. Al-Jamil, *Cooperation and Contestation*, 83f., 96ff.

86. Goldziher, *Beiträge*, 33–9. For an English translation, see al-Hilli, *Al-Bâbu'l-Ḥâdî 'Ashar*.

87. Muhammad Khudabanda is the name Uljaytu adopted when he became a Muslim (it is a Persian version of Abdallah, 'servant of God'). Probably not coincidentally, Muhammad Abdallah is the name that the Mahdi is supposed to carry upon his return. Pfeiffer, 'Twelver Shi'ism', 3n3, 25n101. See also Pfeiffer, 'Reflections'; Schmidtke, *The Theology*, 31; Schmidtke, 'ḤELLI, ḤASAN B. YUSOF B. MOṬAHHAR', *EIr*.

88. The accounts are contradictory and often leave out some of the elements. Other elements are a dream. One account states that the Shii Amir Taramtaz compared the Shia to Uljaytu with the leading Mongol tribe, while comparing the Sunni schools of jurisprudence to the subordinate tribes. Another account, related in al-Majlisi's *Bihar al-Anwar*, has al-Hilli making this point. Pfeiffer, 'Twelver Shi'ism', 7–13, 29. For his travels, see Charles Melville, 'The Itineraries of Sultan Öljeitü, 1304–16', *Iran* 28 (1990), 55–70. See also Anne F. Broadbridge, *Mamluk Ideological and Diplomatic Relations with Mongol and Turkic Rulers of the Near East and Central Asia (658–807/1260–1405)* (PhD, University of Chicago, 2001), 113ff.

89. An 'official' history of his reign states that Ghazan Khan was visited by the Prophet, Ali, Hasan, and Hussain in a dream, and that the Prophet made Ghazan Khan embrace the three, which became key to his success. Peter Jackson, *The Mongols and the Islamic World: From Conquest to Conversion* (New Haven: Yale University Press, 2017), 335, 362, 372; al-Jamil, *Cooperation and Contestation*, 116, 120f.; Momen, *An Introduction to Shi'i Islam*, 92; Arnold Nöldeke, *Das Heiligtum*

al-Husains zu Kerbelâ (PhD, University of Erlangen, 1909), 39f.; Hamid Algar, "Atabāt', *EI2*.

90. Broadbridge, *Mamluk Ideological and Diplomatic Relations*, 116.

91. Schmidtke, *The Theology*, 52, 95; Henri Laoust, 'La critique du Sunnisme dans la doctrine d'al-Hilli', *Revue des études islamiques* 34 (1966), 35–60; Laoust, 'Les fondaments de l'Imamat dans le Minhaj d'al-Hilli', *Revue des études islamiques* 46 (1978), 3–55. I consulted Hasan b. Yusuf 'al-Allama' al-Hilli, *Sharh Minhaj al-Karama fi Ma'rifat al-Imama*, ed. by S. Ali al-Milani (Qom: Dar al-Hijra, 1997).

92. Laoust, *Essai*, 37. I consulted the following editions, one published in Cairo in the early twentieth century and another published in Saudi Arabia: Ibn Taymiyya, *Minhaj al-Sunna al-Nabawiyya fi Naqd Kalam al-Shi'a wa-l-Qadariyya* (The Way of the Prophetic Sunna in the Criticism of the Words of the Shia and the Qadiriyya), 4 Vols (Cairo: Bulaq, 1903–5), and 9 Vols (Riyadh: Imam Mohammad Ibn Saud Islamic University, 1991–). There is no agreement on the exact dating of the manuscript. Sometime between 1313 and 1321 is likely. Jon Hoover, *Ibn Taymiyya's Theodicy of Perpetual Optimism* (Leiden: Brill, 2007), 10f. Laoust states that it was written in 1317, after Ibn Taymiyya agitated against Humayda, Amir of Mecca, who had formed an alliance with Uljaytu and seemed favourable to the Shia in the city. H. Laoust, 'Ibn Taymiyya', *EI2*; al-Jamil, 'Ibn Taymiyya', 235.

93. Laoust, *Essai*, 97.

94. Michot, 'Ibn Taymiyya's Critique', 113.

95. Ibid., 132f.; al-Jamil, 'Ibn Taymiyya', 236–40; Laoust, *Essai*, 179–83, 187.

96. Al-Jamil, 'Ibn Taymiyya', 229ff., 241.

97. Shia often extend that argument to the Imams, who are considered infallible, and some (such as al-Razi) seem to extend that argument saying that someone who was once an unbeliever could never become an Imam, thus proving the illegitimacy of the Caliphates of Abu Bakr and Umar ipso facto (as Ali was young when he converted, this would not apply to him). Al-Hilli argues that the Prophets are infallible from the moment they are born. Ibn Taymiyya argues that the Prophet became infallible from the moment that God started the revelation to him. Laoust, *Essai*, 187–92, quoting al-Razi, *Muhassal*. See also Roy Vilozny, 'Some Remarks on Ibn Taymiyya's Acquaintance with Imāmī Shī'ism in Light of his Minhāj al-Sunna al-Nabawiyya', *Der Islam* 97, 2 (2020), 456–75. For al-Dhahabi's refutation of Shiism, see Hassan, *Longing for the Lost Caliphate*, 115–18.

98. Laoust goes as far as saying that there is a period before and after *Minhaj al-Sunna* in Ibn Taymiyya's life, and that in later works he takes up ideas already alluded to in *Minhaj al-Sunna* to develop them further. He seems to be saying that Ibn Taymiyya appropriated some ideas of the political sociology of the ideal Islamic state as outlined by al-Hilli to explain them from a Sunni perspective, such as the idea of the Imamate. Laoust, *Essai*, 98ff. Laoust even states that 'sa pensée a été profondément pénétrée du Shi'isme orthodoxe plus élaboré de l'école d'at-Tusi et d'al-Hilli', and that his political sociology and ideal of community and state

constitute 'une manière de "Karmatisme sunnite"'. Ibid., 109. See also ibid., 187–92. He notes that a supporter of Ibn Taymiyya who wrote a poem when the latter was released from prison in Cairo was repeatedly accused of Shii tendencies for composing poems against Abu Bakr. Ibid., 136n1. There is some similarity in Ibn Taymiyya's and Shii positions on divorce oaths. Yossef Rapoport, 'Ibn Taymiyya on Divorce Oaths', in: Michael Winter and Amalia Levanoni (eds), *The Mamluks in Egyptian and Syrian Politics and Society* (Leiden: Brill, 2004), 191–217, 202f. See also Hoover, *Ibn Taymiyya's Theodicy*.

99. Laoust, *Essai*, 215–18; Husayn, *Opposing the Imam*, 112–60; Michot, 'Ibn Taymiyya's Critique', 137. For a translation, see Ibn Taymiyya, *Majmūʿ al-Fatāwa* 3: 411, translated in: Ballandalus, 'Ibn Taymiyya (d. 1328) on the Martyrdom of Imam Husayn (d. 680)', 12 November 2013, https://ballandalus.wordpress.com/2013/11/12/ibn-taymiyya-d-1328-on-the-martyrdom-of-imam-husayn-d-680.

100. Here, a particular controversy surrounds the transmission of the Hadith, the question of the name of the Mahdi, and his lineage. Michot, 'Ibn Taymiyya's Critique', 121f. See W. Madelung, 'al-Mahdi', *EI2*.

101. For an attempt to refute Ibn Taymiyya's criticism based on Sunni sources, see Mahdi Akbarnezhad, 'Criticism of Ibn Taymiyya's View Concerning Imam Mahdi (P.b.u.h.)', *Iranian Journal for the Quranic Sciences & Tradition* 42, 1 (2009), 25–42 (in Persian).

102. Michot, 'Ibn Taymiyya's Critique', 129. A bit later, he states: 'The Shīʿīs do not follow the example of an imām possessing knowledge and asceticism without the people of the Sunna also following his example as well as the example of groups of others who share with him this knowledge and asceticism, or, rather, are more knowledgeable than him and more ascetic.' Ibid., 136.

103. Ibid., 127–31, 134.

104. Ibid., 135f.

105. Laoust, *Essai*, 220f.

106. Ibn Taymiyya understood the prophetic Hadith, 'Don't embark on travelling but to my Mosque (of Madina), al-Haram Mosque (of Makka) and al-Aqsa Mosque (of Jerusalem)', literally, stating that any visitation to a mosque other than these as an act of ritual is forbidden. Basheer M. Nafi, 'Salafism Revived: Nuʿmān al-Alūsī and the Trial of Two Aḥmads', *Die Welt des Islams* 49, 1 (2009), 49–97, 84; Taylor, *In the Vicinity of the Righteous*, 168–94.

107. He published extensively on the subject. See the passages quoted in Niels Henrik Olesen, *Culte des saints et pèlerinages chez Ibn Taymiyya (661/1263–728/1328)* (Paris: Paul Geuthner, 1991), 33f.

108. Ibn Taymiyya, *The Madinan Way: The Soundness of the Basic Premises of the School of the People of Madina* (Norwich: Bookwork, 2000), 21; al-Jamil, 'Ibn Taymiyya', 234.

109. Little, 'Religion under the Mamluks', 170.

110. Werner Ende, 'The Nakhawila, a Shiʿite Community in Medina: Past and Present', *Die Welt des Islams* 37, 3 (1997), 264–348; Richard Mortel, 'The Ḥusaynid Amirate of Madīna during the Mamlūk Period', *Studia Islamica* 80

(1994), 97–123; Mortel, 'Zaydi Shi'ism and the Ḥasanid Sharīfs of Mecca', *International Journal of Middle East Studies* 19, 4 (1987), 455–72.

111. Laoust, *Essai*, 145–50. That the Mongols, once they had come to terms with the Mamluks in 1323, asked for Ibn Taymiyya's detention played no role in this, but is nonetheless interesting. Charles Melville, 'The Year of the Elephant: Mamluk-Mongol Rivalry in the Hejaz in the Reign of Abu Saʿid (1317–1335)', *Studia Iranica* 21, 2 (1992), 197–214, 206. For the Sunni defence of shrine visitation, including the tomb of the Prophet in Medina, see Taylor, *In the Vicinity of the Righteous*, 195–218.

112. Saleh, *The Formation*, 220.

113. A substantial section of *Minhaj al-Sunna* is dedicated to undermining al-Thalabi. Ibn Taymiyya also criticised Sunni scholars who continued his work or used him, such as al-Wahidi, and his criticism entered several important manuals of Quranic sciences, including those by al-Suyuti and al-Dhahabi, dealing a long-lasting blow to the position of al-Thalabi. Saleh, *The Formation*, 40, 218–22.

114. For the relationship between the two and in particular Ibn al-Qayyim, whose influence has been neglected in Western scholarship, and the way they have been appropriated especially by Salafi movements around the world, see Birgit Krawietz and Georges Tamer (eds), *Islamic Theology, Philosophy and Law: Debating Ibn Taymiyya and Ibn Qayyim al-Jawziyya* (Berlin: De Gruyter, 2013); Caterina Bori and Livnat Holtzman (eds), *A Scholar in the Shadow: Essays in the Legal and Theological Thought of Ibn al-Qayyim al-Jawziyya* (Rome: Herder, 2010).

115. H. Laoust, 'Ibn Kathir', *EI2*; Aslan, *From Body to Shrine*, 146; Younus Y. Mirza, 'Ibn Kathīr, ʿImād al-Dīn', *EI3*.

116. This is his *Kitab al-Bidaya wa-l-Nihaya*, which is also a key source on the Mamluk expeditions in the Kisrawan and on Ibn Taymiyya. Aaron Hagler, 'Sapping the Narrative: Ibn Kathir's Account of the Shūrā of ʿUthman in Kitab al-Bidaya wa-l-Nihaya', *International Journal of Middle East Studies* 47, 2 (2015), 303–21. Ibn Taymiyya had already mentioned some of these points in *Minhaj al-Sunna*, where he denounced Muawiya's rebellion against Ali but claimed that, after Ali's death, Muawiya's Caliphate was legitimate, and that even Hasan had submitted to it. Laoust, *Essai*, 219f. See also Laoust, 'Ibn Kathir historien', *Arabica* 2 (1955), 42–88. The *Kitab al-Bidaya wa-l-Nihaya* was first printed in Cairo in the 1930s in 14 volumes and later translated into many languages such as Urdu, Malay, and, interestingly, English by a Saudi-based publisher. See Australian Islamic Library, 'Al-Badaya wan Nahaya: Tareekh Ibn e Kathir (History of Islam by Ibn e Kathir)', https://www.australianislamiclibrary.org/al-bidaya-wan-nahaya.html.

117. There is some evidence that the 'rediscovery' thesis of Ibn Taymiyya is more nuanced and less fitting than previously thought. Caterina Bori, 'Ibn Taymiyya (14th to 17th Century): Transregional Spaces of Reading and Reception', *The Muslim World* 108 (2018), 87–123. In Yemen, Ibn al-Wazir (d. 840/1436), a

Sunni scholar born into a Zaydi family, engaged with Ibn Taymiyya. Ibid., 102–12. For the classic thesis of Ibn Taymiyya's reappropriation by the *Salafiyya*, see Laoust, *Essai*, 506–40; Daniel Lav, *Radical Islam and the Revival of Medieval Theology* (Cambridge: Cambridge University Press, 2012).

118. The sixteenth-century Ottoman fatwas against Shiism and Qizilbash discussed later bear some resemblance to his arguments but do not cite him, although some do reference earlier rulings on the Shia, including by Ahmad Ibn Hanbal. An anonymous anti-Safavid polemic, *Risale der Redd-i Revafiz*, does refer to him. Winter, *A History of the 'Alawis*, 60f.; Winter, *The Shiites of Lebanon*, 21. Ibn Taymiyya's fatwa against the Druze, however, seems to have been used by the Damascene Hanbali al-Muhibbi (d. 1111/1699). Bori, 'Ibn Taymiyya', 114. The fifteenth century also saw a number of polemics, and Shah Abd al-Aziz's *Tuhfat* follows Ibn Taymiyya's arguments to a certain extent, but does not mention him explicitly as a source. Indeed, Ibn Taymiyya's reception in South Asia may have been limited by his strong Hanbali inclinations and his criticism of Sufism and the Imamate. Saiyid Athar Abbas Rizvi, *Shah 'Abd al-'Aziz: Puritanism, Sectarian Polemics and Jihad* (Canberra: Marifat, 1982), 251–60.

119. It is today a key example of Ilkhanid architecture in Iran. The only other remaining tomb next to the Sultan's is the grave of a certain Baraq Baba, a Sufi Shaykh who in non-Ilkhanid sources is said to have believed that Ali was a divine reincarnation, and that he had also reappeared in Uljaytu. Hamid Algar, 'BARĀQ BĀBĀ', *EIr*; Pfeiffer, 'Twelver Shi'ism', 21–4.

120. Sheila S. Blair, 'The Epigraphic Program of the Tomb of Uljaytu at Sultaniyya: Meaning in Mongol Architecture', *Islamic Art* 2 (1987), 43–96; British Library, 'Sultan Uljaytu's Qur'an', https://www.bl.uk/collection-items/sultan-uljaytu-quran.

121. Pfeiffer, 'Twelver Shi'ism', 19f.

122. See ibid., 28. But patronage of Alid shrines actually expanded in Iran in the Mongol period, as evidenced for example by tile production for Alid shrines. Oliver Watson, 'Pottery under the Mongols', in: Linda Komaroff (ed.), *Beyond the Legacy of Genghis Khan* (Leiden: Brill, 2006), 325–45, 331.

123. Ibn Battuta suggests that Sunni resistance played a role in this. Pfeiffer, 'Twelver Shi'ism', 14–18. See also Pfeiffer, 'Conversion Versions: Sultan Öljeytü's Conversion to Shi'ism (709/1309) in Muslim Narrative Sources', *Mongolian Studies* 22 (1999), 35–67. Abu Said ascended the throne when he was twelve years old, and his early reign was thus shaped by the regency of Amir Chupan Sulduz, with whom many of his policies in this period, including the rapprochement with the Mamluks, are associated. Charles Melville, 'ČOBĀN', *EIr*.

124. Some chroniclers even argued that Uljaytu would have given the expedition orders to exhume the bodies of Abu Bakr and Umar, who are buried next to the Prophet Muhammad in Medina, if the campaign had been successful. Axes and shovels for that purpose were allegedly captured from the force. This probably says more about how this episode, and Uljaytu's dangling with Shiism, was perceived. Melville, 'The Year of the Elephant', 199ff. The episode

had an aftermath in that, in 1318, the *khutba* was read in Mecca in honour of Abu Said, after which the Mamluks sent an expeditionary force, re-established control over the Hijaz, and killed Humaida, the Abu Qatada heir supported by the Mongols. Ibid., 202f. The Mongols also tried to extend their influence through sponsoring the Iraqi pilgrimage caravan to Mecca. Ibid., 203–11.

125. Reuven Amitai, 'The Resolution of the Mongol-Mamluk War', in: Reuven Amitai and Michal Biran (eds), *Mongols, Turks, and Others: Eurasian Nomads and the Sedentary World* (Leiden: Brill, 2005), 359–90, 378; Broadbridge, *Mamluk Ideological and Diplomatic Relations*, 125ff.; Melville, 'The Year of the Elephant'. For more general background on this complicated and mutually influential relationship, including the Mamluk alliance with the Golden Horde Mongols, see David Ayalon, 'The Great Yāsa of Chingiz Khān: A Re-Examination (Part C1)', *Studia Islamica* 36 (1972), 113–58, esp. 140f.

126. Ibn Khaldun, quoted in: F. E. Peters (ed.), *Judaism, Christianity, and Islam: The Classical Texts and their Interpretation*, Vol. 3 (Princeton: Princeton University Press, 1990), 259f. See also Seyyed Hossein Nasr, 'Shi'ism and Sufism: Their Relationship in Essence and in History', *Religious Studies* 6, 3 (1970), 229–42, 230. Following Ibn Khaldun, Ali al-Wardi also emphasised the closeness of Sufism and Shiism. Ali al-Wardi, *Soziologie des Nomadentums: Studie über die iraqische Gesellschaft* (Neuwied: Luchterhand, 1972), 267. For the early history of Sufism and its relationship with Sunnism and Shiism in Iran, see S. H. Nasr, 'SŪFISM', in: R. N. Frye (ed.), *The Cambridge History of Iran*, Vol. 4 (Cambridge: Cambridge University Press, 1975), 442–63; Wilferd Madelung, *Religious Trends in Early Islamic Iran* (Albany: SUNY Press, 1988); I. P. Petrushevsky, *Islam in Iran*, trans. by Hubert Evans (Albany: SUNY Press, 1985). For a selection of articles on the early and middle periods, see the first two volumes of Leonard Lewisohn (ed.), *The Heritage of Sufism*, 3 Vols (Oxford: Oneworld, 1999).

127. Al-Shaibi, *Sufism and Shi'ism*. See also al-Shaibi, *Studies in the Interaction of Sufism and Shiism to the Rise of the Safawids* (PhD, University of Cambridge, 1961), accessed in the library of the Institute of Ismaili Studies, London; Trimingham, *The Sufi Orders*.

128. Knysh, *Ibn 'Arabi*, 54, 192f., 300n27; Berkey, *The Formation of Islam*, 158. For background on the general phenomenon, see Ahmed T. Karamustafa, *God's Unruly Friends: Dervish Groups in the Islamic Middle Period 1200–1550* (Salt Lake City: University of Utah Press, 1994).

129. Even Naqshbandis, who trace their spiritual lineage through Abu Bakr, reserve a special place for Ali. Robert M. Gleave, "Alī b. Abī Tālib', *EI3*; Etan Kohlberg, "ALĪ B. ABĪ TĀLEB ii. 'Alī as seen by the Community', *EIr*; Asma Afsaruddin and Seyyed Hossein Nasr, "Alī', *EBr*; Hamid Algar, 'Naqshbandis and Safavids: A Contribution to the Religious History of Iran and Her Neighbours', in: Michel M. Mazzaoui (ed.), *Safavid Iran & Her Neighbors* (Salt Lake City: University of Utah Press, 2003), 7–48, 27f.; al-Shaibi, *Sufism and Shi'ism*, 57f.

130. Gleave, "Alī b. Abī Tālib'; Algar, 'Naqshbandis and Safavids', 27–31. Shah Wali Allah, the famous Indian Naqshbandi, argues that he asked the question of the

preference of the Caliphs to the Prophet Muhammad in a dream. He further states that he himself loves Ali more than Abu Bakr and Umar, but that the Prophet confirmed to him that the latter two were superior to Ali. Saiyid Athar Abbas Rizvi, *Shāh Walī-Allāh and His Times: A Study of Eighteenth Century Islam, Politics, and Society in India* (Canberra: Marifat, 1980), 217, 249f. See also Trimingham, *The Sufi Orders*, 136.

131. Hodgson, *Venture*, Vol. 2, 446–53; Momen, *An Introduction to Shi'i Islam*, 94–7. For Alid loyalty, see also Mulder, *The Shrines of the 'Alids*.

132. Maria E. Subtelny, 'Tamerlane and his Descendants: From Paladins to Patrons', in: D. Morgan and A. Reid (eds), *The New Cambridge History of Islam*, Vol. 3 (Cambridge: Cambridge University Press, 2010), 169–200, 169f.

133. Denis Hermann, 'Aspectos de ia penetración del shiismo en Irán durante los periodos ilkhâní y timurí: El éxito político de los movimientos sarbedâr, mar'ashi y musha'sha'yân', *Estudios de Asia y Africa* 39, 3 (2004), 673–709.

134. Some members of the dynasty were, however, buried in Najaf. Some showed a preference for names such as Ali, Hasan, and Hussain, while others were named after the Sunni Caliphs. Only a few of their coins invoke the Twelve Imams like the one struck by Hasan Buzurg at Amol in 741/1340. The quote is found in Patrick Wing, *The Jalayirids: Dynastic State Formation in the Mongol Middle East* (Edinburgh: Edinburgh University Press, 2016), 139f. For more, see Peter Jackson, 'JALAYERIDS', *EIr*; J. M. Smith, 'Djalāyir, Djalāyirid', *EI2*; H. R. Roemer, 'The Jalayirids, Muzaffarids and Sarbardārs', in: P. Jackson and L. Lockhart (eds), *The Cambridge History of Iran*, Vol. 6 (Cambridge: Cambridge University Press, 1986), 1–40, 9.

135. These are Malik Pir Ali's campaigns against Nishapur. Before 759/1357–8, they minted coins bearing the names of the Rashidun Caliphs, thereafter they were replaced by the phrase 'Ali is the friend of God' and the names of the Twelve Shii Imams, indicating that, until then, they had been 'officially' Sunni and were now 'officially' Shii, even though this may have meant little for their subjects. Several scholars and a Sufi dervish organisation played a considerable role in this, which led to problems with local Sunnis. John Masson Smith, *The History of the Sarbadar Dynasty 1336–1381 AD and its Sources* (The Hague: Mouton, 1970), 31, 55–60, 77; Biancamaria Scarcia Amoretti, 'Religion in the Timurid and Safavid Periods', in: Peter Jackson and Lawrence Lockhart (eds), *The Cambridge History of Iran*, Vol. 6 (Cambridge: Cambridge University Press, 1986), 610–55, 612ff.; Shivan Mahendrarajah, 'The Sarbadars of Sabzavar: Re-Examining their 'Shi'a' Roots and Alleged Goal to "Destroy Khurasanian Sunnism"', *Journal of Shi'a Islamic Studies* 5, 4 (2012), 379–402; Roemer, 'The Jalayirids', 17f., 25, 28, 39.

136. Momen, *An Introduction to Shi'i Islam*, 93; Roemer, 'The Jalayirids', 38f.; J. Calmard, 'Mar'ashis', *EI2*.

137. Yukako Goto, 'Kār Kiyā dynasty', *EI3*.

138. Subtelny, *Timurids in Transition*, 196.

139. C. E. Bosworth, 'ĀL-E AFRĀSĪĀB (1)', *EIr*; Beatrice Forbes Manz, *The Rise and Rule of Tamerlane* (Cambridge: Cambridge University Press, 1989), 17.

Calmard speculates that their special position as Sayyids may have saved them from annihilation, as opposed to the Sarbadars of Sabzavar, who were not Sayyids. He also argues that some of Timur's military elites, who were Sunni, were particularly set against attacking the Marashis. Calmard, 'Mar'ashis'. See also Subtelny, *Timurids in Transition*, 11ff.; Subtelny, 'Tamerlane', 170ff.

140. Vasilii Vladimirovitch Barthold, *Four Studies on the History of Central Asia*, Vol. 2 (Leiden: Brill, 1963), 23; H. R. Roemer, 'Timur in Iran', in: P. Jackson and L. Lockhart (eds), *The Cambridge History of Iran*, Vol. 6 (Cambridge: Cambridge University Press, 1986), 42–97, 89f.; Jean Aubin, *Matériaux pour la biographie de Shāh Ni'matullāh Walī Kermānī* (Tehran: Institut Franco-Iranien, 1956). For an Alid genealogical chart that links Shah Rukh back to Ali, see Kazuo Morimoto, 'An Enigmatic Genealogical Chart of the Timurids: A Testimony to the Dynasty's Claim to Yasavi-'Alid Legitimacy?', *Oriens* 44, 1–2 (2016), 145–78. For encounters related in Safavid chronicles about Timur and leaders of the early Safavid order, see Ayşe Baltacıoğlu-Brammer, 'The Emergence of the Safavids as a Mystical Order and their Subsequent Rise to Power in the Fourteenth and Fifteenth Centuries', in: Rudi Matthee (ed.), *The Safavid World* (London: Routledge, 2021); S. Quinn, 'Iran under Safavid Rule', in: D. Morgan and A. Reid (eds), *The New Cambridge History of Islam*, Vol. 3 (Cambridge: Cambridge University Press, 2010), 201–38, 204f. Timur is reported to have killed Ismailis on several occasions, in particular in Anjudan. Daftary, *The Ismailis*, 418.

141. Subtelny, 'Tamerlane', 172f.

142. The *madrasas* focused on Shafii and Hanafi *fiqh*. Maria E. Subtelny and Anas B. Khalidov, 'The Curriculum of Islamic Higher Learning in Timurid Iran in the Light of the Sunni Revival under Shāh-Rukh', *Journal of the American Oriental Society* 115, 2 (1995), 210–36; Maria E. Subtelny, *Timurids in Transition: Turko-Persian Politics and Acculturation in Medieval Iran* (Leiden: Brill, 2007), 25ff.

143. Subtelny, 'Tamerlane', 182.

144. Beatrice F. Manz, 'Shāh Rukh', *EI2*; Manz, 'Tīmūr Lang', *EI2*; Manz, *Power, Politics and Religion in Timurid Iran* (Cambridge: Cambridge University Press, 2007), 208–44, esp. 208ff.; Amoretti, 'Religion', 615f. Amoretti has argued that 'an "officially" Shi'i dynasty could hardly have been more obsequious' towards the *Ahl al-Bayt*. Amoretti, 'Religion', 616.

145. S. de Laugier de Beaureceuil, "ABDALLĀH ANṢĀRĪ', *EIr*; Knysh, *Islamic Mysticism*, 135–40. Farhadi points out that, while his books continued to be printed in Iran, in the Wahhabi/Hanbali domains his legacy was little known. A. G. Ravan Farhadi, *Abdullah Ansari of Herat: An Early Sufi Master* (Abingdon: Routledge, 2013), 13.

146. Subtelny, *Timurids in Transition*, 200–5; Subtelny, 'The Cult of Abdullah Ansari under the Timurids', in: Alma Giese and J. Christoph Bürgel (eds), *Gott ist schön und Er liebt die Schönheit: Festschrift für Annemarie Schimmel zum 7. April 1992 dargebracht von Schülern, Freunden und Kollegen* (Bern: Peter Lang, 1994), 377–406.

147. McChesney has suggested 'Ahl al-Baytism' as more appropriate a term to explain reverence and pilgrimage to shrines, festivities, and memorabilia associated with the *Ahl al-Bayt* than rigid categories such as Sunnism or Shiism imposed anachronistically on earlier periods. R. D. McChesney, *Waqf in Central Asia: Four Hundred Years in the History of a Muslim Shrine, 1480–1889* (Princeton: Princeton University Press, 1991), 33f., 268f. For the story of the discovery of the shrine in 885/1480–1, see the translation of a passage in *Habib al-Siyar* in Khwandamir, 'The History of the Reign of Sultan Husayn Mirza', in: *Classical Writings of the Medieval Islamic World: Persian Histories of the Mongol Dynasties*, trans. by Wheeler M. Thackston, Vol. 2 (London: I. B. Tauris, 2012), 403–520, also in: Wheeler M. Thackston (comp./trans.), *A Century of Princes: Sources on Timurid History and Art* (Cambridge, MA: Agha Khan Program for Islamic Architecture, 1989), 213ff. See also H. R. Roemer, 'The Successors of Timūr', in: P. Jackson and L. Lockhart (eds), *The Cambridge History of Iran*, Vol. 6 (Cambridge: Cambridge University Press, 1986), 98–146, 135–8; Philip Bockholt, *Weltgeschichtsschreibung zwischen Schia und Sunna: Ḫvāndamīrs Ḥabīb as-Siyar im Handschriftenzeitalter* (Leiden: Brill, 2021).

148. Subtelny, *Timurids in Transition*, 208. Non-Islamic festivals were, until the rise of the Taliban at least, still practised near the shrine. But it seems that the majority of Sunni Afghans think that this is indeed the burial place of Ali. See Jonathan Leonard Lee, *The New Year's Festivals and the Shrine of Ali ibn Abi Talib Sy Mazar-i-Sharif, Afghanistan* (PhD, University of Leeds, 1999); Xavier de Planhol, 'MAZĀR-E ŠARIF', *EIr*.

149. McChesney, *Waqf*, 33f., 268f.; Subtelny, *Timurids in Transition*, 212ff., 219f.

150. Farhat, 'Shi'i Piety', 204.

151. Charles Melville, 'The Itineraries of Shahrukh b. Timur (1405–47)', in: David Durand-Guédy (ed.), *Turko-Mongol Rulers, Cities and City Life* (Leiden: Brill, 2013), 285–315, 291ff.

152. Shah Rukh himself is not recorded as having ordered any major constructions at the shrine, as he focused more on the Ansari shrine in Herat. The major building works are associated with his wife, Gawhar Shad, and their son, Baysunghur. Subtelny, *Timurids in Transition*, 206. Sultan Abu Said went to Mashhad and other shrines in 872/1468 before a campaign against the White Sheep. Farhat, 'Shi'i Piety', 202f.; Beatrice F. Manz, 'GOWHAR-ŠĀD ĀĠĀ', *EIr*. For more, see May Farhat, *Islamic Piety and Dynastic Legitimacy: The Case of the Shrine of 'Alī b. Mūsā al-Ridā in Mashhad (10th–17th Century)* (PhD, Harvard University, 2002).

153. Colin P. Mitchell, 'Two Tales of One City: Herat under the Early Modern Empires of the Timurids and Safavids', in: Eric Nelson and Jonathan Wright (eds), *Layered Landscapes: Early Modern Religious Space across Faiths and Cultures* (Abingdon: Routledge, 2017), 207–22. Subtelny makes the argument about the connection between the expansion of the shrines and agro-management. Subtelny, *Timurids in Transition*, 206.

154. Binbaş points out that even Shah Rukh minted Shii coins in Sari, Northern Iran, likely because the population was Shii. İlker Evrim Binbaş, 'The Jalayirid Hidden King and the Unbelief of Shāh Mohammad Qara Qoyunlu', *Journal of Persianate Studies* 12, 2 (2020), 206–36, 227f.

155. Woods, *The Aqquyunlu*, 4.

156. A descendant of Jahan Shah, Sultan Quli became the founder of the Qutb Shahi dynasty in Golkonda, which would become one of the Shii ruling dynasties in the Deccan. H. R. Roemer, 'The Türkmen Dynasties', in: P. Jackson and L. Lockhart (eds), *The Cambridge History of Iran*, Vol. 6 (Cambridge: Cambridge University Press, 1986), 147–88, 166ff.; V. Minorsky, 'Jihān-Shāh Qara-Qoyunlu and his Poetry (Turkmenica, 9)', *Bulletin of the School of Oriental and African Studies* 16, 2 (1954), 271–97; Momen, *An Introduction to Shiʻi Islam*, 98f.

157. Woods, *The Aqquyunlu*, 83. One should thus beware of contrasting these two dynasties, which competed for control of Iraq, Iran, Central Asia, Anatolia, and Afghanistan, too strongly with the Safavids and ascribing to them clearly defined confessional boundaries. R. Quiring-Zoche, 'Aq Qoyunlū', *EIr*; Roemer, 'The Türkmen Dynasties', 184; Roemer, 'The Successors of Tīmūr', 136.

158. Sümer downplays any association between this dynasty and Shiism. F. Sümer, 'Ḳarā-Ḳoyunlu', *EI2*. For the counter-argument, see S. M. Shahmoradi, M. Moradian, and A. Montazerolghaem, 'The Religion of the Kara Koyunlu Dynasty: An Analysis', *Asian Culture and History* 5, 2 (2013), 95–103. For a recent assessment, see Binbaş, 'The Jalayirid Hidden King', 209–12, 222–9.

159. Hamid Algar, 'ASTARĀBĀDĪ, FAŻLALLĀH', *EIr*; Orkhan Mir-Kasimov, *Words of Power: Ḥurūfī Teachings between Shiʻism and Sufism: The Original Ḥurūfī Doctrine of Faḍl Allāh Astarābādī* (London: I. B. Tauris/Institute of Ismaili Studies, 2015), 16.

160. Trimingham, *The Sufi Orders*, 101f.

161. İlker Evrim Binbaş, *Intellectual Networks in Timurid Iran: Sharaf al-Dīn ʻAlī Yazdī and the Islamicate Republic of Letters* (Cambridge: Cambridge University Press, 2016). For more on the relationship between Sufism and Shiism in the Timurid period, see al-Shaibi, *Sufism and Shiʻism*, 164–291. For the order's chain of transmitters (going back to Ali) as found on its official website, see Nimatullahi Sufi Order, 'Masters of the Path', https://www.nimatullahi.org/our-order/history/masters-of-the-path.

162. Hamid Algar, 'Niʻmat-Allāhiyya', *EI2*; Knysh, *Islamic Mysticism*, 239ff.

163. Saiyid Athar Abbas Rizvi, *A Socio-Intellectual History of the Isnā ʾAsharī Shīʾīs in India*, Vol. 1 (Canberra: Marifat, 1986), 160f.

164. Marijan Molé, 'Les Kubrawiya entre sunnisme et shiisme aux huitième et neuvième siècles de l'hégire', *Revue des études islamiques* 29 (1961), 61–142; Knysh, *Islamic Mysticism*, 234–9. For a bibliography, see T. Jack Rowe, 'Kubraviyya', *EI3*. But see the caveats in DeWeese, who has shown that the later Shii turn of the Nurbakhshiyya should not be taken as evidence for the

proto-Shii nature of earlier figures associated with the Kubrawiyya and generally argues that the Kubrawiyya should not be seen as Shii in a doctrinal sense.
Devin DeWeese, 'The Eclipse of the Kubravīyah in Central Asia', *Iranian
Studies* 21, 1/2 (1988), 45–83, esp. 55f., 61. Similar arguments are made by Algar,
who argues that 'the heightened reverence for the Twelve Imams that ultimately led certain Kobrawis to the profession of Shi'ism was alien to Kobrā,
who was indubitably a Sunnite, despite later attempts to appropriate him for
Shi'ism'. Hamid Algar, 'KOBRAWIYA ii. THE ORDER', *EIr*. See also Algar,
'Kubrā', *EI2*.

165. Hamid Algar, 'Nūrbakhshiyya', *EI2*; Shahzad Bashir, *Messianic Hopes and
Mystical Visions: The Nūrbakhshīya between Medieval and Modern Islam* (Columbia,
SC: University of South Carolina Press, 2003). The anecdote is related in
J. Biddulph, *Tribes of the Hindoo Koosh* (Calcutta: Office of the Superintendent
of Government, 1880), 118–25, as quoted by Algar. See also Rizvi, *A Socio-
Intellectual History*, Vol. 1, 162–6.

166. P. Luft, 'Musha'sha'', *EI2*.

167. Daftary, *The Ismailis*, 410–42; Shafique N. Virani, *The Ismailis in the Middle Ages:
A History of Survival, a Search for Salvation* (Oxford: Oxford University Press, 2007),
48f., 112ff.; Hodgson, *Venture*, Vol. 2, 220; Hodgson, 'The Ismā'īlī State', 425.

168. Hodgson, *Venture*, Vol. 2, 494–500. See also Farida Stickel, *Zwischen Chiliasmus
und Staatsräson: Religiöser Wandel unter den Safaviden* (Berlin: De Gruyter,
2019), 21–81.

169. Ahab Bdaiwi, 'Some Remarks on the Confessional Identity of the Philosophers
of Shiraz: Ṣadr al-Dīn al-Dashtakī (d. 903/1498) and his Students Mullā Shams
al-Dīn al-Khafrī (942/1535) and Najm al-Dīn Maḥmūd al-Nayrīzī (948/1541)',
Ishraq 5 (2014), 61–85; Adam Jacobs, *Sunni and Shii Perceptions, Boundaries and
Affiliations in Late Timurid and Early Safawid Persia: An Examination of Historical
and Quasi-Historical Narratives* (PhD, University of London, 1999); Ismail Lala,
*Knowing God: Ibn 'Arabī and 'Abd al-Razzāq al-Qāshānī's Metaphysics of the
Divine* (Leiden: Brill, 2019), 22ff.

170. Al-Jamil, *Cooperation and Contestation*, 93f.; Robert G. Morrison, *Islam and Science:
The Intellectual Career of Nizam al-Din al-Nisaburi* (New York: Routledge, 2007).

171. Al-Jamil, *Cooperation and Contestation*, 64.

172. Ibid., 74–8.

173. While al-Tabari was an adherent of the Sunni Shafii school of jurisprudence
founded by Imam al-Shafii, and in his defence of the 'rightly-guided' Caliphs
was certainly anti-Shii, because of this and other fairly positive statements
about Ali he was accused of being pro-Shii by adherents of Ahmad Ibn Hanbal
(780–855, d. in Baghdad), after whom another Sunni school of jurisprudence
with a strong anti-Shii bent, the Hanbali school, is named, and with whom he
had come into conflict. Al-Tabari portrayed Ali positively and virtuously,
though in the same manner as he defended the virtues of all the Rashidun
Caliphs. C. E. Bosworth, 'al-Ṭabarī', *EI2*; Petersen, *Ali and Muawiya*, 156f. The
historian and geographer al-Masudi, for example, is claimed by many Shii

authors as a Shii, yet not dismissed as a Shii by all Sunnis, most of whom 'just' see him as an adherent of the Mu'tazila. Charles Pellat, 'Mas'ūdī et l'Imāmisme', in: Centre de Recherches d'Histoire des Religions Strasbourg (ed.), *Le shî'isme imâmite: Colloque de Strasbourg (6–9 mai 1968)* (Paris: Presses Universitaires de France, 1970), 69–80; Pellat, 'al-Mas'ūdī', *EI2*; Moin, 'Partisan Dreams'. The philosopher Ibn Sina (Avicenna) is claimed by Ismailis, Twelver Shia, and Sunnis. Malik Merchant, 'A Brief Discussion on Avicenna's Madhab', *Simerg*, 28 April 2011 (updated 9 June 2014), https://simerg.com/literary-readings/a-brief-discussion-on-avicennas-madhab/.

174. Ibn Abi al-Hadid also wrote a collection of poetry on Ali's virtues and prominent role at the side of the Prophet, likewise presented to Ibn al-Alqami. While Sunni critics accused him of being Shii, he did not explicitly state this in his work, and it is difficult to classify him as either Sunni or Shii. Ibn Abi al-Hadid came from a Shafii family and described himself as a Mu'tazili, advancing the view, prominent amongst the Baghdadi Mu'tazila, that Ali was the most excellent of the Companions of the Prophet, but without supporting the Shii claim that the Prophet had designated Ali as his successor, and defending the legitimacy of the first three Rashidun Caliphs. Trying to sum up the ways in which Muslim authors have described him subsequently, Veccia Vaglieri writes that he was 'Mu'tazilī for the *uṣūl*, but S̲h̲āfi'i for the *furū'* (thus decidedly Sunnī in this field), but objective in his attitude to the *Ahl al-Bayt* [*q.v.*] and explicit in his affirmation of the rights of 'Alī (therefore S̲h̲ī'ī); or else it has been suggested that, at first a Mu'tazilī, he later became a S̲h̲ī'ī; it has also been said that he was between the S̲h̲ī'ī and the Sunnī parties (*bayn al-farīḳayn*), since he was inspired by a sense of equity (*inṣāf*)', before concluding that 'it may, however, now be taken as certain that he was not an Imāmī'. L. Veccia Vaglieri, 'Ibn Abi 'l-Ḥadīd', *EI2*. See also Tahera Qutbuddin, 'Ibn Abī l-Ḥadīd', *EI3*; Wilferd Madelung, "ABD-AL-ḤAMĪD B. ABU'L-ḤADĪD', *EIr*. In the book, Ibn Abi al-Hadid also discusses the Mongol invasions, but without emphasising the confessional dimension. In an account of the 643/1245 Mongol attempt to take Baghdad, Ibn al-Alqami is praised for advising the Muslim army on how to defend the city. Moktar Djebli, *Les invasions mongoles en Orient vécues par un savant médiéval arabe Ibn Abi l-Hadid al-Mada'ini (1190–1258), extrait du Sharh Nahj al-Balagha* (Paris: L'Harmattan, 1995), 67f.

175. Mohammad Ahmad Masad, *The Medieval Islamic Apocalyptic Tradition: Divination, Prophecy and the End of Time in the 13th Century Eastern Mediterranean* (PhD, Washington University, 2008).

176. Jacobs, *Sunni and Shii Perceptions*, 50–80; Maria E. Subtelny, 'Ḥusayn Vā'iẓ Kāshifī', *EI3*; Abbas Amanat, 'Meadow of the Martyrs: Kāshifī's Persianization of the Shi'i Martyrdom Narrative in Late Tīmūrid Herat', in: Farhad Daftary and Josef W. Meri (eds), *Culture and Memory in Medieval Islam: Essays in Honour of Wilferd Madelung* (London: I. B. Tauris/Institute of Ismaili Studies, 2003), 250–75.

177. Saiyid Athar Abbas Rizvi, *A History of Sufism in India*, Vol. 2 (New Delhi: Munshiram Manoharlal, 1983), 174–81; Hamid Algar, 'Naḳs̲h̲band', *EI2*; Knysh,

Islamic Mysticism, 218–21. There are serious disagreements and debates surrounding the early history of the Naqshbandiyya and their relationship with the Yasawiyya, another Central Asian Sufi order that has received much less attention. Devin DeWeese, 'The Mashā'ikh-i Turk and the Khojagān: Rethinking the Links between the Yasavī and Naqshbandī Sufi Traditions', *Journal of Islamic Studies* 7, 2 (1996), 180–207; DeWeese, 'Succession Protocols and the Early Khwajagani Schism in the Maslak al-'Ārifīn', *Journal of Islamic Studies* 22, 1 (2011), 1–35.

178. There were thus originally two Alid lines and one Bakri one. Over time, the Bakri line became more important, perhaps to differentiate the Naqshbandiyya from more Alid Sufi orders. This process is still debated in the scholarship, with disagreements between Algar and Le Gall in particular. Itzchak Weismann, *The Naqshbandiyya: Orthodoxy and Activism in a Worldwide Sufi Tradition* (London: Routledge, 2007), 22ff.; Hamid Algar, 'The Naqshbandī Order: A Preliminary Survey of its History and Significance', *Studia Islamica* 44 (1976), 123–52, 128ff.; Dina Le Gall, *A Culture of Sufism: Naqshbandīs in the Ottoman World, 1450–1700* (Albany: SUNY Press, 2013), 127–35. That said, they claim to have the double golden chain, spiritually through Abu Bakr but then also through Jafar al-Sadiq, and thus directly through the Prophet. They claim Jafar al-Sadiq as a spiritual forefather but think the Shia have misrepresented him. The two ways of relating to the Prophet, one through a link to one of his closest Companions, Abu Bakr, and the other through blood by virtue of the *Ahl al-Bayt*, together constitute the golden chain. Jürgen Paul, *Die politische und soziale Bedeutung der Naqšbandiyya in Mittelasien im 15. Jahrhundert* (Berlin: De Gruyter, 1991), 29. For a contemporary list, see Naqshbandi Sufi Way, 'The Chain', https://naqshbandi.org/the-golden-chain/the-chain, and Ghaffari, 'Golden Chain', http://maktabah.org/blog/?page_id=1402. For Jafar al-Sadiq and Sufism, see Hamid Algar, 'JA'FAR AL-ṢĀDEQ iii. And Sufism', *EIr*.

179. These were, amongst others, the Halvatis, Nimatullahis, and Safavids, all of whom shared certain Shii affinities that would become clearer in the sixteenth century. R. M. Savory, 'A 15th-Century Ṣafavid Propagandist at Harāt', in: D. Sinor (ed.), *The American Oriental Society, Middle West Branch Semi-Centennial Volume* (Bloomington: Indiana University Press, 1969), 189–97. Abd al-Rahman Jami excludes particularly the Nimatullahis and the Nurbakhshis from a major hagiographical compendium, the *Nafahat al-Uns min Hadarat al-Quds*, probably because of their Shii tendencies. Hamid Algar, *Jami* (Oxford: Oxford University Press, 2013), 105f.

180. On his way to the Hajj in Mecca, Jami visited Karbala, where he composed poems exalting the Imams, but on the same trip engaged in fierce polemics with Shii scholars in Baghdad. After being accused of attacks on Shiism in his writings, a sort of trial was organised in a Baghdad *madrasa* in the presence of the Hanafi and Shafii *Qadis* as well as Khalil Beg, the White Sheep governor of the city. Passages from his work were read out and he was absolved from his accusations. He then went to Najaf, where he penned a poem that revered Ali

but included diatribes against Shiism. Algar, *Jami*, 50–4; Algar, 'Naqshbandis and Safavids', 27–31. For a modern take on this, see Talib Ghaffari, 'The Twelve Imams and the Naqshbandi Saints', *Ghaffari*, 20 August 2013, http://maktabah. org/blog/?p=307. Algar uses the argument that Naqshbandis themselves put great emphasis on the admiration of the *Ahl al-Bayt* without, however, adopting the Shii argument politically, to criticise the notion that Sufi orders like the Kubrawiyya paved the way for the emergence of Safavid Shiism. Algar, 'Naqshbandis and Safavids', 32; Algar, 'Some Observations on Religion in Safavid Persia', *Iranian Studies* 7, 1–2 (1974), 287–93. See also Algar, 'Jāmi ii. And Sufism', *EIr*. There are also indications that Jami may have been influential at the White Sheep court in Tabriz. Chad G. Lingwood, *Politics, Poetry and Sufism in Medieval Iran: New Perspectives on Jāmī's Salāmānva Absāl* (Leiden: Brill, 2013), esp. ch. 3. Though in his review of the book, Algar disagrees and thinks the evidence is slim. Hamid Algar, 'Review of "Politics, Poetry and Sufism in Medieval Iran: New Perspectives on Jāmī's Salāmānva Absāl" by Chad G. Lingwood', *Journal of Islamic Studies* 27, 1 (2016), 54–65.

181. Maria E. Subtelny, 'Sulṭān Ḥusayn Bāyqarā', *EI3*; Subtelny, *Timurids in Transition*, 61f.; Amoretti, 'Religion', 612; Algar, *Jami*, 41f. Khwandamir relates: 'Since the Victorious Khaqan always held in great reverence the house of the Prophet and never thought of anything except veneration of that pure family, when he acceded to the throne of Khurasan he decided that the *khutba* and coinage would be adorned by the names of the Immaculate Imams. However, a group of Hanafite fanatics who held great power in Herat at that time hastened to the throne and spoke in preference of the Sunnis, and Sultan Hussain decided not to change the *khutba*. Since the time was not ripe to override that group's request, the *khutba* was read on the Id al–Fitr as before.' Khwandamir, 'The History', 413. Roemer argues that this episode should not be taken at face value, because it contradicts his support to the Ali shrine and to the Nurbakhshis. H. R. Roemer, 'ḤOSAYN BĀYQARĀ', *EIr*. But his rule may have still facilitated Shii tendencies. Hamideh Shahidi, 'Religious Politics of Sultan Husain Bayqara (A Case Study: The Impact on Shi'ism)', *Historical Studies of Islam* 8, 29 (2016), 61–82 (in Persian).

182. Algar, *Jami*, 58f., 119f.

183. His tomb in Herat was in turn desecrated during the Safavid conquest of 1510 but this did not prevent a senior Safavid prince and governor of Mashhad, Sultan Ibrahim bin Bahram Mirza (d. 985/1577), to commission an illustrated copy of Jami's key work, *Haft Awrang*. Christine Nölle-Karimi, 'Herat art and architecture', *EI3*; Algar, *Jami*, 126ff.; Marianna S. Simpson, 'EBRĀHĪM MĪRZĀ', *EIr*; Simpson, *Sultan Ibrahim Mirza's Haft Awrang: A Princely Manuscript from Sixteenth-Century Iran* (New Haven: Yale University Press, 1997).

184. Saiyid Athar Abbas Rizvi, *Muslim Revivalist Movements in Northern India in the Sixteenth and Seventeenth Centuries* (Agra: Agra University, 1965), 176–91.

185. Weismann, *The Naqshbandiyya*, 49–67. This would contribute to the relative decline of the Kubrawiyya vis-à-vis the Naqshbandiyya in the Central Asian

context, where the pro-Ali stance of the Kubrawiyya as opposed to the pro-Abu Bakr stance of the Naqshbandiyya may have been seen as suspicious. DeWeese, 'The Eclipse', 81f.

CHAPTER 4

1. For a discussion of this in the context of the Venetian 'Empire', see Noel Malcolm, *Agents of Empire: Knights, Corsairs, Jesuits and Spies in the Sixteenth-Century Mediterranean World* (New York: Oxford University Press, 2015), 19f. See also Karen Barkey, *Empire of Difference: The Ottomans in Comparative Perspective* (Cambridge: Cambridge University Press, 2008), 3–27.

2. The term 'Gunpowder Empires' was coined by McNeill and Hodgson. See William H. McNeill, *The Age of Gunpowder Empires, 1450–1800* (Washington, DC: American Historical Association, 1989), title; Hodgson, *Venture*, Vol. 3, title and esp. pages 16ff. Hodgson used the term as a title to the third volume of his seminal work *The Venture of Islam*. This work, including the periodisation of Islamic history with a major rupture at the start of the sixteenth century and the chapter on the Safavids, is still influential. For an assessment particularly of the third volume, see Christopher A. Bayly, 'Hodgson, Islam, and World History in the Modern Age', in: E. Burke III and R. J. Mankin (eds), *Islam and World History: The Ventures of Marshall Hodgson* (Chicago: University of Chicago Press, 2018), 38–54. For recent comparative overviews of these empires, see Stephen J. Dale, *The Muslim Empires of the Ottomans, Safavids, and Mughals* (Cambridge: Cambridge University Press, 2010); Douglas E. Streusand, *Islamic Gunpowder Empires: Ottomans, Safavids, and Mughals* (Boulder, CO: Westview Press, 2011). For a slightly different take on the term, see Giancarlo Casale, 'The Islamic Empires of the Early Modern World', in: J. Bentley, S. Subrahmanyam, and M. Wiesner-Hanks (eds), *The Cambridge World History*, Vol. 6 (Cambridge: Cambridge University Press, 2015), 323–44. Matthee has argued that in the Safavid case gunpowder, especially in the latter part of their reign, played a subordinate role. Rudi Matthee, 'Unwalled Cities and Restless Nomads: Firearms and Artillery in Safavid Iran', in: Charles Melville (ed.), *Safavid Persia: The History and Politics of an Islamic Society* (London: I. B. Tauris, 1996), 389–416. See also Michael Axworthy, 'The Army of Nader Shah', *Iranian Studies* 40, 5 (2007), 635–46, 635f.

3. Matthee, in his discussion of Safavid Iran, invokes the notion of the 'territorialisation of faith', building on Benedict Anderson, *Imagined Communities: Reflections on the Origin and Spread of Nationalism* (London: Verso, 1991), esp. ch. 1; Rudi Matthee, 'Was Safavid Iran an Empire?', *Journal of the Economic and Social History of the Orient* 53, 1/2 (2010), 233–65, 242f.

4. The main periods of war were 1514, 1532–55, 1578–90, and 1623–39, ended by the peace agreements of Amasya (1555), Istanbul (Constantinople) (1590), and Kasr-i Shirin (Zuhab) (1639). See Ayşe Baltacıoğlu-Brammer, 'The Formation of Kızılbaş Communities in Anatolia and Ottoman Responses, 1450s–1630s',

International Journal of Turkish Studies 20, 1/2 (2014), 21–47, 23. For an annotated bibliography of Ottoman–Safavid relations, see Rudi Matthee, 'Safavid Dynasty', *EIr.*

5. Matthew Melvin-Koushki, 'Early Modern Islamicate Empire: New Forms of Religiopolitical Legitimacy', in: Armando Salvatore, Roberto Tottoli, and Babak Rahimi (eds), *The Wiley-Blackwell History of Islam* (Hoboken: Wiley-Blackwell, 2018), 353–75.

6. While his name may have originally been a Turkic name spelled slightly differently, and none of his close contemporary family (including his father, grandfather, uncles, brothers, sons, etc.) had overtly Sunni names such as Uthman or Umar, eventually, his name became spelled in Arabic script like the name of the third Caliph, Uthman, whom the Sunnis see as 'rightly-guided' and the Shia reject. While the origin of his name may thus not have had Sunni connotations, his name and that of the dynasty would later develop Muslim and Sunni connotations. I thank Ayşe Baltacıoğlu-Brammer for clarifying this. Cemal Kafadar, *Between Two Worlds: The Construction of the Ottoman State* (Berkeley: University of California Press, 1996), 124f.

7. For classic narrative accounts of the early period, see Halil İnalcik, 'The Emergence of the Ottomans', in: P. M. Holt, Ann K. S. Lambton, and Bernard Lewis (eds), *The Cambridge History of Islam*, Vol. 1A (Cambridge: Cambridge University Press, 1977), 263–92; Kafadar, *Between Two Worlds*.

8. For the religious climate in which the early Ottomans emerged, see Irène Mélikoff, 'L'origine sociale des premiers Ottomans', in: Elizabeth Zachariadou (ed.), *The Ottoman Emirate (1300–1389)* (Rethymno: Crete University Press, 1993), 135–44; Ahmet Yasar Ocak, 'Les milieux soufis dans les territoires du Beylicat Ottoman et le probleme des "Abdalan-i Rum" (1300–1389)', in: Elizabeth Zachariadou (ed.), *The Ottoman Emirate (1300–1389)* (Rethymno: Crete University Press, 1993), 145–58.

9. Kafadar, *Between Two Worlds*, 67f.; Yildirim, 'Sunni Orthodox vs Shi'ite Heterodox?'. For an early elaboration, see Claude Cahen, 'Le problème du shī'isme dans l'Asie mineure turque préottomane', in: Centre de Recherches d'Histoire des Religions Strasbourg (ed.), *Le shī'isme imâmite: Colloque de Strasbourg (6–9 mai 1968)* (Paris: Presses Universitaires de France, 1970), 115–29; H. R. Roemer, 'The Safavid Period', in: P. Jackson and L. Lockhart (eds), *The Cambridge History of Iran*, Vol. 6 (Cambridge: Cambridge University Press, 1986), 189–350, 191–8.

10. Baltacıoğlu-Brammer, 'The Emergence of the Safavids'. For a comprehensive annotated bibliography on the Safavids, see Andrew J. Newman, 'Safavids', *OBi.* For a discussion of 'Safavid Studies' and the ways in which post-1979 approaches differ from older accounts, see Andrew J. Newman, *Safavid Iran: Rebirth of a Persian Empire* (London: I. B. Tauris, 2006).

11. Dimitris Kastritsis, *The Sons of Bayezid: Empire Building and Representation in the Ottoman Civil War of 1402–13* (Leiden: Brill, 2007).

12. Riza Yildirim, *Turkomans between Two Empires: The Origins of the Qizilbash Identity in Anatolia, 1447–1514* (PhD, Bilkent University, 2008).

13. This support began in the fifteenth century and may have continued until as late as 1604. The payment could be halted at times of tension, however. Baltacıoğlu-Brammer, 'The Formation of Kızılbaş Communities', 25, 32, 34.

14. Ibid., 34f.

15. It was not just used for Ottoman subjects who sympathised with the Safavids, but also variously for Safavid soldiers, spies, and missionaries, as well as for the Safavid state and its leaders. As a result, historians that did not pay close enough attention to nuance and context have at times read too much into Ottoman uses of the term. While initially worn by many Safavid supporters, the head-dress would later become confined to the Safavid elite. The term remains in use in Turkish to negatively designate Shia, supporters of the Safavids and Iran, and Alevis, which further complicates the matter. Walter Posch, *Osmanisch-safavidische Beziehungen (1545–1550): Der Fall Alḳâs Mîrzâ* (Wien: Österreichische Akademie der Wissenschaften, 2013), 159–267; Ayşe Baltacıoğlu-Brammer, 'One Word, Many Implications: The Term "Kızılbaş" in the Early Modern Ottoman Context', in: Vefa Erginbaş (ed.), *Ottoman Sunnism: New Perspectives* (Edinburgh: Edinburgh University Press, 2019), 47–70; Baltacıoğlu-Brammer, 'The Formation of Kızılbaş Communities', 27.

16. This is from his *Divan*, cited after: Baltacıoğlu-Brammer, 'The Formation of Kızılbaş Communities', 28. For more, see V. Minorsky, 'The Poetry of Shāh Ismāʿīl I', *Bulletin of the School of Oriental and African Studies* 10, 4 (1942), 1006–29; Amelia Gallagher, 'Shah Ismaʿil's Poetry in the Silsilat al-Nasab-i Safawiyya', *Iranian Studies* 44, 6 (2011), 895–911.

17. Max Scherberger, 'The Confrontation between Sunni and Shiʿi Empires: Ottoman-Safavid Relations between the Fourteenth and the Seventeenth Century', in: Ofra Bengio and Meir Litvak (eds), *The Sunna and Shiʿa in History: Division and Ecumenism in the Muslim Middle East* (New York: Palgrave Macmillan, 2011), 51–67, 53; Josef Matuz, 'Vom Übertritt osmanischer Soldaten zu den Safawiden', in: Ulrich Haarmann and Peter Bachmann (eds), *Die islamische Welt zwischen Mittelalter und Neuzeit: Festschrift für Hans Robert Roemer zum 65. Geburtstag* (Beirut/Wiesbaden: Orient-Institut/Steiner, 1979), 402–15.

18. Ayşe Baltacıoğlu-Brammer, '"Those Heretics Gathering Secretly...": Qizilbash Rituals and Practices in the Ottoman Empire according to Early Modern Sources', *Journal of the Ottoman and Turkish Studies Association* 6, 1 (2019), 39–60, 43–55.

19. Baltacıoğlu-Brammer, 'Neither Victim nor Accomplice: The Kızılbaş as Borderland Actors in the Early Modern Ottoman Realm', in: Tijana Krstić and Derin Terzioğlu (eds), *Historicizing Sunni Islam in the Ottoman Empire, c. 1450-c. 1750* (Leiden: Brill, 2021), 423–50.

20. See H. Erdem Cipa, *The Making of Selim: Succession, Legitimacy, and Memory in the Early Modern Ottoman World* (Bloomington: Indiana University Press, 2017).

21. The extent of this influx of Arab Shii clerics to Iran may have been overstated in the literature. This is the argument made in Andrew J. Newman, 'The Myth of the Clerical Migration to Safavid Iran: Arab Shiite Opposition to ʿAli al-Karaki and Safawid Shiism', *Die Welt des Islams* 33 (1993), 66–112. For other

accounts, see Rula Jurdi Abisaab, *Converting Persia: Religion and Power in the Safavid Empire*, 2nd ed. (London: I. B. Tauris, 2015), 12f.; Abisaab, 'The Ulama of Jabal 'Āmil in Safavid Iran, 1501–1736: Marginality, Migration and Social Change', *Iranian Studies* 27, 1–4 (1994), 103–22; Abisaab, 'History and Self-Image: The 'Amili Ulema in Syria and Iran (Fourteenth to Sixteenth Centuries)', in: H. E. Chehabi, *Distant Relations: Iran and Lebanon in the Last 500 Years* (London: I. B. Tauris, 2006), 62–95; Devin J. Stewart, 'Notes on the Migration of 'Āmilī Scholars to Safavid Iran', *Journal of Near Eastern Studies* 55, 2 (1996), 81–103; Hourani, 'From Jabal 'Amil to Persia', 56ff.

22. Rula Abisaab, 'KARAKI', *EIr*.

23. Abisaab, *Converting Persia*, 27. While it had been a practice popular amongst some Shia, though practised mostly in private for fear of Sunni retribution and under Shii dynasties such as the Fatimids, it attained wider significance under the Safavids. The practice, which initially meant disassociation, can either encompass 'just' Abu Bakr, Umar, and Uthman, or can also include other anti-Shii Companions, including the women Aisha, Hafsa, Hind, and Umm al-Hakam. For background, see Etan Kohlberg, 'Barā'a in Shī'ī Doctrine', *Jerusalem Studies in Arabic and Islam* 7 (1986), 139–75; Kohlberg, 'Some Imami Shi'i Views on the Sahaba', in: Etan Kohlberg (ed.), *Belief and Law in Imami Shi'ism* (Aldershot: Variorum, 1991), 143–75; J. Calmard, 'Tabarru'', *EI2*.

24. See J. Eliash, 'On the Genesis and Development of the Twelver-Shii Three-Tenet Shahadah', *Der Islam* 47 (1971), 265–72; I. K. A. Howard, 'The Development of the Adhan and Iqama of the Salat in Early Islam', *Journal of Semitic Studies* 26 (1981), 219–28, esp. 228; Liyakat A. Takim, 'From Bid'a to Sunna: The Wilāya of 'Alī in the Shī'ī Adhān', *Journal of the American Oriental Society* 120, 2 (2000), 166–77.

25. The importance of these anti-Sunni enforcers may in turn have been inflated in anti-Safavid polemics, but they seem to have existed at least in some form or another in the sixteenth century. Rosemary Stanfield-Johnson, 'The Tabarra'iyan and the Early Safavids', *Iranian Studies* 37, 1 (2004), 47–71; Michele Membrè, *Mission to the Lord Sophy of Persia (1539–1542)*, trans. by A. H. Morton (London: School of Oriental and African Studies, 1993), 52.

26. Shah Tahmasp-i Safavi, *Majmu'a-yi Asnad wa Mukhatibat Tarikhi*, ed. by A. H. Nava'i (Tehran: n.p., 1358–63h), 215, quoted in: Stanfield-Johnson, 'The Tabarra'iyan', 51. See also Calmard, 'Tabarru''.

27. Abisaab, *Converting Persia*, xv; Calmard, 'Tabarru''; Hamid Enayat, *Modern Islamic Political Thought: The Response of the Shi'i and Sunni Muslims to the Twentieth Century*, 2nd ed. (London: I. B. Tauris, 2005), 33; Rosemary Stanfield-Johnson, 'Sunni Survival in Safavid Iran: Anti-Sunni Activities during the Reign of Tahmasp I', *Iranian Studies* 27, 1/4 (1994), 123–33, 127n23. There was also a shrine in Kashan, where some believed Abu Lulua, the slave who murdered Umar, was buried. It was expanded in the Safavid period, and there were apparently some annual re-enactments of the killings of Umar. Sayyid Ali, 'Is Abu Lulu Buried in Kashan?', *Iqra Online*, 12 November 2018, https://www.iqraonline.net/is-abu-lulu-buried-in-kashan/; Ch. Pellat, 'ABŪ LO'LO'A', *EIr*; Stanfield-Johnson, 'Sunni Survival', 127f.

28. Amoretti, 'Religion', 617f.; Elke Eberhard, *Osmanische Polemik gegen die Safawiden im 16. Jahrhundert nach arabischen Handschriften* (Freiburg: Klaus Schwarz, 1970), 108ff.; Hodgson, *Venture*, Vol. 3, 30; E. G. Browne, *A Literary History of Persia*, Vol. 4 (Cambridge: Cambridge University Press, 1928), 52–63; Abisaab, *Converting Persia*, 26; Stanfield-Johnson, 'Sunni Survival', 131. See also Jean Aubin, 'Les sunnites du Larestán et la chute des Safavides', *Revue des études islamiques* 33 (1965), 151–71; Denis Hermann, 'La instauración del shiismo como religión de Estado en Irán bajo los safávidas: Del shiismo qizilbāsh al shiismo imamita', *Estudios de Asia y África* 41, 3 (2006), 439–72, 448–53; Jean Aubin, 'Etudes safavides: I. Šāh Ismāʿīl et les notables de l'Iraq persan', *Journal of the Economic and Social History of the Orient* 2, 1 (1959), 37–81. For Shiism in Iran before the Safavids, see Rasul Jaʿfariyan, *Tarikh-i Tashayyuʿ dar Iran: Az Aghaz ta Qarn-i Dahum-i Hijri*, 2 Vols (Qom: Ansariyan, 1375/1996–7).

29. Hamid Algar, 'Niʿmat-Allāhiyya', *EI2*; Algar, 'IRAN ix. RELIGIONS IN IRAN (2) Islam in Iran (2.3) Shiʿism in Iran since the Safavids', *EIr*; Nile Green, *Sufism: A Global History* (Chichester: Wiley-Blackwell, 2012), 161; Said Amir Arjomand, *The Shadow of God and the Hidden Imam: Religion, Political Order, and Societal Change in Shiʿite Iran from the Beginning to 1890* (Chicago: University of Chicago Press, 1984), 109–21; Knysh, *Islamic Mysticism*, 221–5. The polemics surrounding the *Abu Muslimnama*, the tales of heroism of Abu Muslim (d. 755), who had played a key role in overthrowing the Umayyads and the rise of the Abbasids, and which were popular amongst the Qizilbash, can be seen in this vein. Anti-Sufi polemics took aim at this. Andrew J. Newman, 'The Limits of "Orthodoxy"? Notes on the Anti-Abū Muslim Polemic of Early 11th/17th-Century Iran', in: Denis Hermann and Mathieu Terrier (eds), *Shiʿi Islam and Sufism: Classical Views and Modern Perspectives* (London: I. B. Tauris/Institute of Ismaili Studies, 2019), 65–119; Kathryn Babayan, 'The Safavid Synthesis: From Qizilbash Islam to Imamite Shiʿism', *Iranian Studies* 27, 1/4 (1994), 135–61, 144ff. Babayan also shows that Naqshbandi Shaykhs could live and maintain a *tekke* in Tabriz up until the seventeenth century. Ibid., 150n52. See also Le Gall, *A Culture of Sufism*, 23–33. Shii clerics of the Safavid period would occasionally pen anti-Sufi polemics and sentence Sufis to death. Trimingham, *The Sufi Orders*, 243; Andrew J. Newman, 'Sufism and Anti-Sufism in Safavid Iran: The Authorship of the "Hadiqat al-Shiʿa" Revisited', *Iran* 37 (1999), 95–108; Sajjad H. Rizvi, 'Sayyid Niʿmat Allāh al-Jazāʾirī and his Anthologies: Anti-Sufism, Shiʿism and Jokes in the Safavid World', *Die Welt des Islams* 50 (2010), 224–42; Rizvi, 'A Sufi Theology Fit for a Shīʿī King: The Gawhar-i Murād of ʿAbd al-Razzāq Lāhījī (d. 1072/1661-2)', in: A. Shihadeh (ed.), *Sufism and Theology* (Edinburgh: Edinburgh University Press, 2007), 83–98; Rasul Jaʿfariyan, *Din va Siyasat dar Dawrah-yi Safavi* (Qom: Ansariyan, 1370/1991–2), 221–95. See also Nasrollah Pourjavady, 'Opposition to Sufism in Twelver Shiism', in: F. de Jong and B. Radtke (eds), *Islamic Mysticism Contested: Thirteen Centuries of Controversies and Polemics* (Leiden: Brill, 1999), 614–23.

30. Richard Gramlich, 'Pol und Scheich im heutigen Derwischtum der Schia', in: Centre de Recherches d'Histoire des Religions Strasbourg (ed.), *Le shiʿisme*

imâmite: Colloque de Strasbourg (6–9 mai 1968) (Paris: Presses Universitaires de France, 1970), 175–82.

31. Gramlich, *Die schiitischen Derwischorden Persiens*, Vol. 3 (Wiesbaden: Deutsche Morgenländische Gesellschaft/Franz Steiner, 1981), 15ff., 20, 23, 30–4, and many other examples across the volume.

32. Hamid Algar, 'DAHABĪYA', *EIr*; Gramlich, *Die schiitischen Derwischorden*, Vol. 3, 42–5.

33. Though there were also people with Naqshbandi ties who entered the government service of the Safavids, such as Mir Siraj al-Din Abd al-Vahab Hamadani in Tabriz. Hamid Algar and K. A. Nizami, 'Nakshbandiyya', *EI2*; Algar, 'Naqshbandis and Safavids', 7–48; Knysh, *Islamic Mysticism*, 225–34; Weismann, *The Naqshbandiyya*, 46.

34. Algar, 'Naqshbandis and Safavids', 27; Le Gall, *A Culture of Sufism*; Bakhtiyar Babajanov, 'La naqshbandiyya sous les premiers Sheybanides', *Cahiers d'Asie centrale* 3/4 (1997), 69–90. The Mughals employed Naqshbandis as ambassadors to the Turkish dynasties of Transoxiana, who played their role in their common rivalry with the Safavids. Weismann, *The Naqshbandiyya*, 51.

35. Zackery Heern, *The Emergence of Modern Shi'ism: Islamic Reform in Iraq and Iran* (London: Oneworld, 2015), 43.

36. Though there were other Shii clerics who opposed this view. Andrew J. Newman, 'Fayd al-Kashani and the Rejection of the Clergy/State Alliance: Friday Prayer as Politics in the Safavid Period', in: Linda Walbridge (ed.), *The Most Learned of the Shi'a: The Institution of the Marja' Taqlid* (Oxford: Oxford University Press, 2001), 34–52; Newman, 'The Vezir and the Mulla: A Late Safavid Period Debate on Friday Prayer', *Eurasian Studies* 5, 1–2 (2006), 237–70; Abisaab, *Converting Persia*, 20ff.; Devin J. Stewart, 'Polemics and Patronage in Safavid Iran: The Debate on Friday Prayer during the Reign of Shah Tahmasb', *Bulletin of the School of Oriental and African Studies* 72, 3 (2009), 425–57.

37. In the thirteenth century, a Shii scholar already legitimised participation in defensive Jihad, i.e. against a foreign invader, in the absence of the twelfth Imam. Etan Kohlberg, 'The Development of the Imāmī Shī'ī Doctrine of Jihād', *Zeitschrift der Deutschen Morgenländischen Gesellschaft* 126, 1 (1976), 64–86.

38. See also the section on the Qajars. Robert Gleave, 'Jihad and Religious Legitimacy in the Early Qajar State', in: Robert Gleave (ed.), *Religion and Society in Qajar Iran* (London: Routledge, 2004), 41–70; Ann K. S. Lambton, 'A Nineteenth Century View of Jihād', *Studia Islamica* 32 (1970), 181–92. When Ali al-Karaki, the highest religious official in the Safavid state, received a village in Iraq after the Safavid conquest to support his livelihood, some Shii clerics in Najaf considered this outrageous and started a polemical debate with al-Karaki, arguing that the state had no right to collect land taxes in the absence of the Hidden Imam. This became known as the al-Karaki vs. al-Qatifi polemic. Abisaab, *Converting Persia*, 22f.; Wilferd Madelung, 'Shi'ite Discussions on the Legality of the Kharaj', in: Rudolf Peters (ed.), *Proceedings of the Ninth Congress of the Union Européenne des Arabisants et Islamisants* (Leiden: Brill, 1981), 193–202.

39. Ja'fariyan, *Din va Siyasat.*

40. Laurence Lockhart, *The Fall of the Safavi Dynasty and the Afghan Occupation of Persia* (Cambridge: Cambridge University Press, 1958), 70–9. Many such polemics were written by Shii scholars employed by the Safavids, for example Hussain bin Abd al-Samad's account of a debate with a Sunni from Aleppo, whom he managed to convince of the validity of Ali's Imamate after using Shafii arguments to delegitimise Abu Hanifa's traditions against Ali. Abisaab, *Converting Persia*, 33ff. One al-Majlisi scholar wrote a treatise criticising Abu Bakr's appointment as the first Caliph after the Prophet's death. He combined this with a denunciation of *ijtihad* from an Akhbari perspective. Robert Gleave, 'Muhammad Taqi al-Majlisi and Safavid Shi'ism: Akhbarism and Anti-Sunni Polemic during the Reigns of Shah 'Abbas the Great and Shah Safi', *Iran* 55, 1 (2017), 24–34.

41. Al-Majlisi did not manage to finish many volumes of the collection. It would eventually be published in 110 volumes. Pampus, *Die theologische Enzyklopädie*, 142–7; Etan Kohlberg, 'BEḤĀR AL-ANWĀR', *EIr.* While seen as a towering and incredibly influential figure by later Shii clerics, he has been described critically in foreign scholarship and travelogues, in part because of his role in the persecution of Sunnis and other non-Shia in the late Safavid period. Rainer Brunner, 'MAJLESI, Moḥammad-Bāqer', *EIr.* See also Colin Turner, *Islam without Allah? The Rise of Religious Externalism in Safavid Iran* (Richmond: Curzon, 2000).

42. Abisaab, *Converting Persia*, 28; Pampus, *Die theologische Enzyklopädie*, 38, 116–34.

43. See, for example, Nile Green (ed.), *The Persianate World: The Frontiers of a Eurasian Lingua Franca* (Berkeley: University of California Press, 1997); Bert G. Fragner, *Die Persophonie: Regionalität, Identität und Sprachkontakt in der Geschichte Asiens* (Berlin: Das Arabische Buch, 1999).

44. Ahmed, *What is Islam?*, 76–80; Francis Robinson, 'Ottomans-Safavids-Mughals: Shared Knowledge and Connective Systems', *Journal of Islamic Studies* 8, 2 (1997), 151–84.

45. Selim Güngörürler, *Diplomacy and Political Relations between the Ottoman Empire and Safavid Iran, 1639–1722* (PhD, Georgetown University, 2016), 80f.; Willem Floor and Hasan Javadi, 'The Role of Azerbaijani Turkish in Safavid Iran', *Iranian Studies* 46, 4 (2013), 569–81; John Perry, 'The Historical Role of Turkish in Relation to Persian of Iran', *Iran & the Caucasus* 5 (2001), 193–200.

46. R. D. McChesney, 'The Central Asian Hajj-Pilgrimage in the Time of the Early Modern Empires', in: Michel M. Mazzaoui (ed.), *Safavid Iran & Her Neighbors* (Salt Lake City, UT: University of Utah Press, 2003), 129–56; McChesney, '"Barrier of Heterodoxy"? Rethinking the Ties between Iran and Central Asia in the 17th Century', in: Charles Melville (ed.), *Safavid Persia: The History and Politics of an Islamic Society* (London: I. B. Tauris, 1996), 231–67. See also Hodgson, *Venture*, Vol. 3, 33; Firuza Melville, 'Hilali and Mir 'Ali: Sunnis among the Shi'is, or Shi'is among the Sunnis between the Shaybanids, Safavids and the Mughals', *Iran* 59, 2 (2021), 245–62.

47. Priscilla Soucek, 'BEHZĀD, KAMĀL-AL-DĪN', *EIr*; Hodgson, *Venture*, Vol. 3, 40; Chad Kia, *Art, Allegory and the Rise of Shi'ism in Iran, 1487–1565* (Edinburgh: Edinburgh University Press, 2019).

48. In the early eighteenth century, the Ottoman ambassador, Ahmet Durii Efendi, who visited in 1720, claimed that a third of the Safavid population was still Sunni. Matthee, 'Was Safavid Iran an Empire?', 253; Rudi Matthee, 'Blinded by Power: The Rise and Fall of Fath 'Alī Khān Dāghestānī, Grand Vizier under Shāh Solṭān Ḥoseyn Ṣafavī (1127/1715–1133/1720)', *Studia Iranica* 33 (2004), 179–219; Matthee, 'Administrative Stability and Change in Late-17th-Century Iran: The Case of Shaykh Ali Khan Zanganah (1669–89)', *International Journal of Middle East Studies* 26, 1 (1994), 77–98.

49. Rizvi, 'Sayyid Ni'mat Allāh al-Jazā'irī', 227, 239f.

50. The earliest record of the Safavid ceremonies is from Tabriz on 19 May 1540 by Michele Membrè, a Venetian diplomat (before the Safavid capital moved to Isfahan). Membrè, *Mission*, 43, cited in: Rahimi, *Theater State*, 219.

51. Jean Calmard, 'Shi'i Rituals and Power II: The Consolidation of Safavid Shi'ism: Folklore and Popular Religion', in: Charles Melville (ed.), *Safavid Persia: The History and Politics of an Islamic Society* (London: I. B. Tauris, 1996), 139–90; Calmard, 'Muharram Ceremonies'.

52. William Morris inspected the carpet for the museum, commenting on its beauty. The English firm that bought the carpets, however, chopped up one of the two to add to the first one and make it seemingly more complete. Victoria and Albert Museum, 'The Ardabil Carpet', https://www.vam.ac.uk/articles/the-ardabil-carpet. For the shrine in the context of the Safavids' shifting sectarian identity, see Kishwar Rizvi, *The Safavid Dynastic Shrine: Architecture, Religion and Power in Early Modern Iran* (London: I. B. Tauris, 2011).

53. For an in-depth discussion, see Kazuo Morimoto, 'The Earliest 'Alid Genealogy for the Safavids: New Evidence for the Pre-dynastic Claim to Sayyid Status', *Iranian Studies* 43, 4 (2010), 447–69.

54. Babayan, 'The Safavid Synthesis'.

55. Winter, *The Shiites of Lebanon*, 12.

56. Colin H. Imber, *Ebu's-Su'ud: The Islamic Legal Tradition* (Stanford: Stanford University Press, 1997), 74; Imber, 'The Ottoman Dynastic Myth', *Turcica* 19 (1987), 7–27; Tijana Krstić, *Contested Conversions to Islam: Narratives of Religious Change in the Early Modern Ottoman Empire* (Stanford: Stanford University Press, 2011), 82; Markus Dressler, 'Inventing Orthodoxy: Competing Claims for Authority and Legitimacy in the Ottoman-Safavid Conflict', in: Hakan T. Karateke and Maurus Reinkowski (eds), *Legitimizing the Order: The Ottoman Rhetoric of State Power* (Leiden: Brill, 2005), 151–73, 164; Kaya Şahin, *Empire and Power in the Reign of Süleyman: Narrating the Sixteenth-Century Ottoman World* (Cambridge: Cambridge University Press, 2013), 67f., 190–3. Even in correspondence with the Habsburgs, Ottoman officials would at times refer to leadership of Sunni Islam and the names of the Sunni Caliphs. Ibid., 226.

57. Krstić, *Contested Conversions*, 97.

58. Guy Burak, *The Second Formation of Islamic Law: The Hanafi School in the Early Modern Ottoman Empire* (Cambridge: Cambridge University Press, 2015).

59. Abdurrahman Atçıl, *Scholars and Sultans in the Early Modern Ottoman Empire* (Cambridge: Cambridge University Press, 2016).

60. Rainer Brunner, 'SHI'ITE DOCTRINE ii. Hierarchy in the Imamiyya', *EIr*; Said Amir Arjomand, 'The Clerical Estate and the Emergence of a Shi'ite Hierocracy in Safavid Iran: A Study in Historical Sociology', *Journal of the Economic and Social History of the Orient* 28, 2 (1985), 169–219; Willem Floor, 'The ṣadr or Head of the Safavid Religious Administration, Judiciary and Endowments and Other Members of the Religious Institution', *Zeitschrift der Deutschen Morgenländischen Gesellschaft* 150 (2000), 461–500.

61. Winter has borrowed the term 'sharp delineation' of confessions (*mezhep farkı keskinleştirme*) from a book by Turkish journalist Taha Akyol. Winter, *The Shiites of Lebanon*, 12. See also Derin Terzioglu, 'How to Conceptualize Ottoman Sunnitization: A Historiographical Discussion', *Turcica* 44 (2012–3), 301–38; Tijana Krstić, 'From Shahāda to 'Aqīda: Conversion to Islam, Catechisation and Sunnitisation in Sixteenth-Century Ottoman Rumeli', in: A. C. S. Peacock (ed.), *Islamisation: Comparative Perspectives from History* (Edinburgh: Edinburgh University Press, 2017), 296–314, 297. For more on the growth of a bureaucratic tradition in the sixteenth century, see Şahin, *Empire and Power*, 243–52; Barkey, *Empire of Difference*, 107f.

62. Kemalpashazade also differed from Sarigürz in that he recognised the right of apostate unbelievers to repent, which would have allowed prisoners of war, for example, to be spared if they gave up their previous beliefs (Sarigürz stated that they should have no such right). Abdurrahman Atçıl, 'The Safavid Threat and Juristic Authority in the Ottoman Empire during the 16th Century', *International Journal of Middle East Studies* 49, 2 (2017), 295–314, 303f. For an in-depth analysis of the different fatwas issued by prominent Ottoman clerics against the Safavids and the Qizilbash in this period, see Eberhard, *Osmanische Polemik*, 45–229. For a German translation and Arabic text, see 'Fatwa Concerning the Disbelief of the Sect of the Kizilbash (1581)', in: Eberhard, *Osmanische Polemik*, 220–9. For the text of Kemalpashazade's fatwa, see Kemalpashazade (Ahmad ibn Suleiman ibn Kamal), 'Fatwa/Epistle Concerning the Qizilbash (1513/1514)', in: Adel Allouche, *The Origins and Development of the Ottoman-Safavid Conflict, 906–966/1500–1555* (Berlin: Klaus Schwarz, 1983), 170–3. See also, more generally, Devin J. Stewart, 'The Historical Roles of Jihād in Sunnī-Shī'ī Relations', *Journal of the Middle East and Africa* 12, 2 (2021), 127–56.

63. Dressler, 'Inventing Orthodoxy', 171.

64. Translation of Sarigürz's fatwa, quoted in: Scherberger, 'The Confrontation', 54f., original in Selahattin Tansel, *Yavuz Sultan Selim* (Ankara: Milli Eğitim Basimevi, 1969), 35.

65. For example, the polemics by Qasim al-Nahjuwani, Hussain bin Abdallah al-Shirwani, and Mirza Makhdum Sharifi. Eberhard, *Osmanische Polemik*, 53–61.

Their polemics took issue with the cursing of the Companions and emphasised the good nature of the first three Caliphs (and Aisha). Ibid., 68f., 104–8.

66. The list of accusations against the Safavids is long: standing above the Sharia, lawlessness, allowing their followers to worship the Safavid leaders, sexual libertarianism, drinking wine, laxity in performing prayers, belittling or criticism of the Quran, an alleged attempt by the Qizilbash to change the direction of prayer from Mecca to Ardabil and to elevate the status of the pilgrimage to Mashhad to that of the Hajj to Mecca. They would also use terms such as *rafida*, *zandaqa*, *mubah*, *batini*, *mulhid*, all the way to *mushrik* and *kafir*. Eberhard, *Osmanische Polemik*, 84–128. At another point, Eberhard states, however, that the term '*kafir*' is usually reserved in Ottoman chronicles for Christians, with whom the Ottomans were at war in Europe, and does not usually designate the Qizilbash. Ibid., 113.

67. Ibid., 114f.; Osman G. Özgüdenli, 'Ottoman-Persian Relations i. Under Sultan Selim I and Shah Esmāʿil I', *EIr*. Mirroring the portrayal of Safavids by the Ottomans, the Ottoman image in Safavid chronicles was not flattering. The Sultans that ruled before the conflict with the Safavids erupted were portrayed more positively for their valour in fighting against Christian powers. Sultans who fought against the Safavids, on the other hand, were portrayed critically, though in fact the Sunni–Shia aspect is seldom mentioned in Safavid chronicles. Tilmann Trausch, *Abbildung und Anpassung: Das Türkenbild in safawidischen Chroniken des 16. Jahrhunderts* (Berlin: Klaus Schwarz, 2008), 41, 119–27. The Safavid leaders may have also seen the Ottomans as heretics, although this trait was not elaborated on as much as on the Ottoman side. Dressler, 'Inventing Orthodoxy', 157.

68. Özgüdenli, 'Ottoman–Persian Relations'.

69. Riza Yildirim, 'The Safavid-Qizilbash Ecumene and the Formation of the Qizilbash-Alevi Community in the Ottoman Empire, c. 1500–c. 1700', *Iranian Studies* 52, 3–4 (2019), 449–83, 472.

70. İnalcik, 'The Emergence'; Banister, *The Abbasid Caliphate*.

71. Allouche, *The Origins*, 66, 149; Jean-Louis Bacqué-Grammont, *Les Ottomans, les Safavides et leurs voisins: Contribution à l'histoire des relations internationales dans l'Orient islamique de 1514 à 1524* (Istanbul: Nederlands Historisch-Archeologisch Instituut te Istanbul, 1987), 187–224. Eberhard, on the other hand, emphasises the religious and ideological dimension of the rivalries of the period. Eberhard, *Osmanische Polemik*.

72. Eberhard, *Osmanische Polemik*, 159; Michael Winter, 'Egypt and Syria in the Sixteenth Century', in: Stephan Conermann and Gül Şen (eds), *The Mamluk–Ottoman Transition: Continuity and Change in Egypt and Bilād al-Shām in the Sixteenth Century* (Göttingen: Vandenhoeck & Ruprecht, 2016), 33–56, 36f.

73. Allouche, *The Origins*, 15–20.

74. Winter, 'Egypt and Syria', 46–53.

75. Jane Hathaway, 'The Forgotten Province: A Prelude to the Ottoman Era in Yemen', in: David J. Wasserstein and Ami Ayalon (eds), *Mamluks and Ottomans:*

Studies in Honour of Michael Winter (London: Routledge, 2006), 195–205; Jon E. Mandaville, 'The Ottoman Province of al-Hasā in the Sixteenth and Seventeenth Centuries', *Journal of the American Oriental Society* 90, 3 (1970), 486–513, 496–9; Mehmet Mehdi Ilhan, 'The Katif District (Liva) during the First Few Years of Ottoman Rule: A Study of the 1551 Ottoman Cadastral Survey', *Belleten (Türk Tarih Kurumu)* 51, 200 (1987), 780–98.

76. Caroline Finkel, *Osman's Dream: The Story of the Ottoman Empire, 1300–1923* (London: John Murray, 2006), 110f.

77. Imber, *Ebu's-Su'ud*, 98–106.

78. Dressler, 'Inventing Orthodoxy', 163.

79. Hüseyin Yılmaz, *Caliphate Redefined: The Mystical Turn in Ottoman Political Thought* (Princeton: Princeton University Press, 2018).

80. Suraiya Faroqhi, *Pilgrims and Sultans: The Hajj under the Ottomans*, 2nd ed. (London: I. B. Tauris, 2014), 127–39; F. E. Peters, *The Hajj: The Muslim Pilgrimage to Mecca and the Holy Places* (Princeton: Princeton University Press, 1994), 175–80.

81. McChesney, 'The Central Asian Hajj-Pilgrimage'.

82. Ende, 'The Nakhawila'; al-Shaykh Salih al-Jad'an, *Ayatallah al-Shaykh Muhammad 'Ali al-'Amri: Sira wa 'Ita'* (n.p.: n.p., 2011); Yousif al-Khoei, 'The Marja and the Survival of a Community: The Shia of Medina', in: Linda Walbridge (ed.), *The Most Learned of the Shi'a: The Institution of the Marja' Taqlid* (Oxford: Oxford University Press, 2001), 247–50, 249f.; Hasan bin Marzuq Rija' al-Sharimi al-Nakhli, *Al-Nakhawila (al-Nakhliyyun) fi al-Madina al-Munawwara: Al-Takwin al-Ijtima'i wa-l-Thaqafi* (Beirut: Mu'assasat al-Intishar al-'Arabi, 2012); Richard Francis Burton, *Personal Narrative of a Pilgrimage to al-Madinah and Meccah*, 2 Vols (London: Tylston and Edwards, 1893), Vol. 2, 1ff. See also Marco Salati, 'Toleration, Persecution and Local Realities: Observations on the Shiism in the Holy Places and the Bilâd al-Shâm (16th–17th Centuries)', in: *Convegno sul tema: La Shī'a nell'Impero Ottomano (Roma, 15 aprile 1991)* (Rome: Accademia Nazionale dei Lincei, 1993), 121–48; Salati, 'A Shiite in Mecca: The Strange Case of Mecca-Born Syrian and Persian Sayyid Muhammad Haydar (d. 1139/1727)', in: Rainer Brunner and Werner Ende (eds), *The Twelver Shia in Modern Times: Religious Culture & Political History* (Leiden: Brill, 2001), 3–24.

83. This was Shihab al-Din Ibn Hajar al-Haytami (d. 1567). Goldziher, *Beiträge*, 17ff.; C. van Arendonk and J. Schacht, 'Ibn Ḥadjar al-Haytamī', *EI2*. Many more Sunni–Shia polemics were written in the context of the Ottoman-Safavid rivalry. Several polemics were written in the fifteenth century, but many more in the sixteenth century. Rizvi, *Shah 'Abd al-'Azīz*, 251–6.

84. Imber, *Ebu's-Su'ud*, x.

85. This is related in a fascinating micro-study of a provincial court in 1540–1. Peirce relates, for example, the case of Haciye Sabah, who was charged first with violating codes on gender mixing during a religious education group she ran at her house and then with heresy for propagating Qizilbash teachings. Leslie P. Peirce, *Morality Tales: Law and Gender in the Ottoman Court of Aintab* (Berkeley: University of California Press, 2003), 35f., 251–75. See also Fariba

Zarinebaf, 'Qizilbash "Heresy" and Rebellion in Ottoman Anatolia during the Sixteenth Century', *Anatolia Moderna* 7 (1997), 1–15, 11f.; Baltacıoğlu-Brammer, '"Those Heretics Gathering Secretly..."', 55–9. For witch trials in early modern Europe, see, as an example of a vast body of literature, Claudia Honegger (ed.), *Die Hexen der Neuzeit: Studien zur Sozialgeschichte eines kulturellen Deutungsmusters* (Frankfurt am Main: Suhrkamp, 1978).

86. Colin H. Imber, 'The Persecution of the Ottoman Shi'ites according to the Mühimme Defterleri, 1565–1585', *Der Islam* 56 (1979), 245–73; H. Sohrweide, 'Der Sieg der Safaviden in Persien und seine Rückwirkungen auf die Schiiten Anatoliens im 16. Jahrhundert', *Der Islam* 41 (1965), 95–223; Krisztina Kehl-Bodrogi, *Kizilbas / Aleviten: Untersuchungen über eine esoterische Glaubensgemeinschaft in Anatolien* (Berlin: Klaus Schwarz, 1988), 29–35. For a map of the geographical distribution of Qizilbash denunciations across Anatolia, see Suraiya Faroqhi, *Der Bektaschi-Orden in Anatolien (vom späten fünfzehnten Jahrhundert bis 1826)* (Vienna: Institut für Orientalistik der Universität Wien, 1981), 38–42 and appendix. These studies are largely based on Ottoman imperial decrees (*mühimme defterleri*), something that has been criticised in more recent scholarship.

87. Krstić, *Contested Conversions*, 107. For the Catholic inquisition, see Francisco Bethencourt, *The Inquisition: A Global History, 1478–1834* (Cambridge: Cambridge University Press, 2009).

88. Şahin, *Empire and Power*, 139–45; Gülru Necipoğlu, *The Age of Sinan: Architectural Culture in the Ottoman Empire* (London: Reaktion, 2010).

89. This process was reinforced in the 1540s through an armistice between the Ottomans and King Ferdinand of Hungary and Bohemia. Jean-Louis Bacqué-Grammont, 'Les Ottomans et les Safavides dans la première moitié du XVIe siècle', in: *Convegno sul tema: La Shī'a nell'Impero Ottomano (Roma, 15 aprile 1991)* (Rome: Accademia Nazionale dei Lincei, 1993), 7–24.

90. Allouche, *The Origins*, 136–40.

91. Ali al-Wardi, *Understanding Iraq: Society, Culture, and Personality*, trans. by Fuad Baali (Lewiston, NY: Lampeter/Edwin Mellen Press, 2008), 39f.; Rudi Matthee, 'IRAQ iv. RELATIONS IN THE SAFAVID PERIOD', *EIr*; al-Wardi, *Soziologie des Nomadentums*, 158f. Writing in the mid-twentieth century, the Iraqi historian Ali al-Wardi argued that in no other Muslim country was the split between Sunnis and Shia more severe, long-lasting, and consequential than in Iraq. Ibid., 262. A significant part of his study on Iraqi society was dedicated to sectarian (and tribal) rivalries. Ali al-Wardi, *Dirasa fi Tabi'a al-Mujtam'a al-'Iraqi* (Baghdad: Matba'a al-'Ani, 1965). In Persian, it was referred to as *'Iraq-i 'Arab* as opposed to *'Iraq-i 'Ajam*. Iraq is thus used here somewhat anachronistically.

92. Rudi Matthee, 'The Safavid-Ottoman Frontier: Iraq-i Arab as Seen by the Safavids', *International Journal of Turkish Studies* 9, 1–2 (2003), 157–73.

93. Hanna Batatu, *The Old Social Classes and the Revolutionary Movements of Iraq: A Study of Iraq's Old Landed and Commercial Classes and of its Communists, Ba'thists, and Free Officers* (Princeton: Princeton University Press, 1978), 18f.; Burak, *The Second Formation*, 1ff.; Şahin, *Empire and Power*, 98–102; A. Duri, 'Baghdad', *EI2*.

The tomb of Abd al-Qadir al-Gilani of the popular Qadiriyya Sufi order fared similarly. Peirce, *Morality Tales*, 281; Scherberger, 'The Confrontation', 58f. The destruction of these tombs and those of prominent Sunnis in Iran is decried in anti-Safavid polemics. Eberhard, *Osmanische Polemik*, 110f. See also https://abu-hanefa.blogspot.com/ and the sources presented on this website, which seeks to promote the Sunni cause in Iran (and tries to outline historical crimes committed by Shii powers, such as the Safavids): https://sonsofsunnah.com/2016/08/03/the-graveworshipping-shiite-safavids-defiled-abu-hanifahs-grave (accessed 14 February 2022).

94. Vefa Erginbaş, 'Problematizing Ottoman Sunnism: Appropriation of Islamic History and Ahl al-Baytism in Ottoman Literary and Historical Writing in the Sixteenth Century', *Journal of the Economic and Social History of the Orient* 60, 5 (2017), 614–46, 619ff.; Meir Litvak, 'Kazemayn', *EIr*; Winter, *The Shiites of Lebanon*, 26f.

95. Though that stipend was apparently never paid out. Fuzuli had initially written a poem praising one of the last White Sheep rulers, then lauded the Safavids and eventually the Ottomans, and also wrote an ode to the Shii ruler of the Indian state of Ahmadnagar. He became known as one of the finest poets writing in Azerbaijani Turkish. *Encyclopædia Iranica*, 'FOŻŪLĪ, MOḤAMMAD', *EIr*; Baltacıoğlu-Brammer, 'The Formation of Kızılbaş Communities', 33. For the general atmosphere in Baghdad at the time, see Melis Taner, *Caught in a Whirlwind: A Cultural History of Ottoman Baghdad as Reflected in Its Illustrated Manuscripts* (Brill: Leiden, 2019).

96. Barkey, *Empire of Difference*, 91f.

97. C. Fleischer, 'ALQĀS MĪRZA', *EIr*; Posch, *Osmanisch-safavidische Beziehungen*; Şahin, *Empire and Power*, 120f. Other such dissidents, would, in exile, occasionally convert to the relative other confession. On one occasion, in 1582, the Safavid ambassador was invited to a festivity because a ceasefire had just been signed. During the event, however, news reached the party that the Safavids had breached the ceasefire. The Safavid ambassador was reprimanded and public conversions, some of them fake, and a theatre humiliating the Safavids, including by 'actors' wearing the Qizilbash headdress on their rears, were immediately staged. This was the Imperial Circumcision Festival of 1582. Derin Terzioğlu, 'The Imperial Circumcision Festival of 1582: An Interpretation', *Muqarnas* 12 (1995), 84–100, 86. At the 1578 festival, a Safavid governor's chief steward had converted in front of the Imperial Council, as is reported by Stefan Gerlach. Krstić, *Contested Conversions*, 108, 200.

98. Baltacıoğlu-Brammer, 'The Formation of Kızılbaş Communities', 43f.; Riza Yildirim, 'An Ottoman Prince Wearing a Qizilbash Tāj: The Enigmatic Career of Sultan Murad and Qizilbash Affairs in Ottoman Domestic Politics, 1510–1513', *Turcica* 43 (2011), 91–119.

99. Fariba Zarinebaf, 'Rebels and Renegades on the Ottoman–Iranian Frontier', in: Abbas Amanat and Farzin Vejdani (eds), *Iran Facing Others: Identity Boundaries in a Historical Perspective* (London: Palgrave, 2012), 79–97, 80–7.

100. Cornell H. Fleischer, *Bureaucrat and Intellectual in the Ottoman Empire: The Historian Mustafa Ali (1541–1600)* (Princeton: Princeton University Press, 1986), 78; Şahin, *Empire and Power*, 146ff.

101. Baltacıoğlu-Brammer, 'The Formation of Kızılbaş Communities', 26f.

102. Zarinebaf, 'Rebels and Renegades', 90f.

103. He also wrote one of the most famous and earliest histories of the Kurds, the *Šarafnāma*. Erika Glassen, 'BEDLĪSĪ, ŠARAF-AL-DĪN KHAN', *EIr*; Metin Atmaca, 'Bidlisī, Sharaf Din', *EI3* (forthcoming). I thank Metin Atmaca for sharing a draft of this entry with me.

104. He also argued that, because of the diversity of opinion on the matter of repentance, it was up to the Sultan to decide what to do with captured Qizilbash. He did not consider the Qizilbash and the Safavids to be Shia but a group outside of Islam. He also refuted the Safavids' claim that they were descendants of the Prophet Muhammad. Atçıl, 'The Safavid Threat', 306–9. These fatwas also regulated war booty: Abu s-Suud argued that Qizilbash women and children should not be enslaved, implying that he did not see the Safavids as, in Imber's words, 'straightforward infidels'. Imber, *Ebu's-Su'ud*, 85–99.

105. Adel Allouche, 'Amasya, Treaty of', *EI3*; Scherberger, 'The Confrontation', 60; Algar, 'Caliphs and the Caliphate'. There are interesting parallels but also major differences with the Peace of Augsburg signed in the same year. See Şahin, *Empire and Power*, 131–6, 211ff.

106. Rudi Matthee, 'The Ottoman–Safavid War of 986–998/1578–90: Motives and Causes', *International Journal of Turkish Studies* 20, 1–2 (2014), 1–20.

107. Fleischer, *Bureaucrat*, 77f.

108. Eberhard, *Osmanische Polemik*; Scherberger, 'The Confrontation', 61; Spellberg, *Politics*, 88.

109. Matthee, 'Was Safavid Iran an Empire?', 256.

110. Bacqué-Grammont, 'Les Ottomans et les Safavides', 20f.; Özgüdenli, 'Ottoman–Persian Relations'.

111. Hodgson, *Venture*, Vol. 2, 266f.

112. Bertold Spuler, 'CENTRAL ASIA v. In the Mongol and Timurid Periods', *EIr*.

113. Yuri Bregel, 'ABU'L-KHAYRIDS', *EIr*. Khunji also refers to him as both Caliph and Imam in his *Bukharan Guestbook*. Ursula Ott, *Transoxanien und Turkestan zu Beginn des 16. Jahrhunderts: Das Mihmān-nāma-yi Buḫārā des Fadlallāh b. Rūzbihān Ḫungī* (Freiburg im Breisgau: Klaus Schwarz, 1974), 311.

114. Martin B. Dickson, *Shah Tahmasb and the Uzbeks (The Duel for Khurasan with 'Ubayd Khan, 930–946/1524–1540)* (PhD, Princeton University, 1958).

115. His history of the White Sheep dynasty has been partly translated: Fazl Allah ibn Ruzbahan, *Persia in A.D. 1478–1490, Turkmenica 12*, trans. by Vladimir Minorsky and John E. Woods (London: Royal Asiatic Society, 1992).

116. Amoretti points out that Khunji fled Tabriz for Kashan even though Kashan was known as a centre of Shiism even before the Safavid takeover. Amoretti, 'Religion', 619. This work, in turn, was refuted by Nurullah Shustari in Lahore

in 1014/1605–6. Goldziher, *Beiträge*, 50–77; U. Haarmann, 'Khundjī', *EI2*; Amoretti, 'Staat und Religion in Transoxanien', 347f.

117. He was keen to emphasise that, despite all the devotion shown to the *Ahl al-Bayt* and to Imam Rida on this visit, the group never deviated from the straight path of the Sunna and the Community. He argued that those love the *Ahl al-Bayt* the most who also love the Companions of the Prophet and the Rashidun Caliphs. Khunji said he recited a Hadith about Imam Rida's visit to the Abbasid Caliph Mamun, who wanted to appoint him as his successor, a crucial moment in which Sunnis and Shia could have become united. In contrast to earlier arguments about his confessional ambiguity, he seems to have been quite aware of a dividing line between Sunnism and Shiism and sought to re-enforce that. Ott, *Transoxanien und Turkestan*, 304–12, esp. 312. He also laid out under what circumstances the visitation of shrines was permissible and accompanied Muhammad Shaybani Khan on a visitation of the shrine of Ahmad Yasawi in Turkestan (Yasi) in 914/1509. Subtelny, *Timurids in Transition*, 193f.; Ott, *Transoxanien und Turkestan*, 254–60, 304. Subsequent Uzbek rulers also performed the pilgrimage to Mashhad. Farhat, 'Shi'i Piety', 202f. For more, see Farhat, *Islamic Piety*. The endowment of the shrine was also expanded, and its administrators started playing important roles in the management of agricultural lands in the surrounding areas. Farhat, 'Shi'i Piety', 203f.

118. Haarmann argues that the objective of the *Bukharan Guestbook*, compiled by Khunji in 1508/9, was to drive Shaybani Khan to attack the Safavids and replace their Shii heresy with the Sunna in Iran. He unsuccessfully urged Shaybani Khan to attack the Safavids before the Kazakhs. Haarmann, 'Khundjī'; Ott, *Transoxanien und Turkestan*, 32; Ali Anooshahr, *Turkestan and the Rise of Eurasian Empires: A Study of Politics and Invented Traditions* (Oxford: Oxford University Press, 2018), 84–113, esp. 94f.

119. Khunji differentiates between the Safavid rulers, their Qizilbash supporters, and the rest of the population under their rule. In 1514, he took a more differentiated view on this matter than in his anti-Shii polemic of 1503 and his earlier calls to Jihad against the Safavids. Haarmann, 'Staat und Religion in Transoxanien', 360f. For an analysis of his views on Shiism, see Jacobs, *Sunni and Shii Perceptions*, 81–103. See also Matthew Melvin-Koushki, 'Khunjī Iṣfahānī, Fażl Allāh b. Rūzbihān (1455–1521): Sulūk al-Mulūk' (forthcoming, published on Academia); Lambton, *State and Government*, 178–200.

120. For Khunji's visit to Mamluk Egypt in the late fifteenth century and his representation of the Mamluks and the Caliphate, see Ulrich Haarmann, 'Yeomanly Arrogance and Righteous Rule: Fażl Allāh b. Rūzbihān Khunjī and the Mamluks of Egypt', in: K. Eslami (ed.), *Iran and Iranian Studies: Essays in Honor of Iraj Afshar* (Princeton: Zagros, 1998), 109–24; Banister, *The Abbasid Caliphate*, 376–9.

121. Yuri Bregel, 'ABU'L-KHAYRIDS', *EIr*; Robert D. McChesney, 'CENTRAL ASIA vi. In the 16th–18th Centuries', *EIr*; McChesney, 'Islamic Culture and the Chinggisid Restoration: Central Asia in the Sixteenth and Seventeenth

Centuries', in: D. Morgan and A. Reid (eds), *The New Cambridge History of Islam*, Vol. 3 (Cambridge: Cambridge University Press, 2010), 239–65.

122. Farhat, 'Shi'i Piety', 204–9.
123. Haarmann, 'Staat und Religion in Transoxanien', 333–9.
124. Bregel, 'ABU'L-KHAYRIDS'.
125. Dickson, *Shah Tahmasb*; McChesney, *Waqf*, 60. He then conquered Herat in 1535, killing Shia and Qizilbash, for which he was denounced in Safavid chronicles. Trausch, *Abbildung und Anpassung*, 137–44.
126. Colin P. Mitchell, *The Practice of Politics in Safavid Iran: Power, Religion and Rhetoric* (London: I. B. Tauris, 2009), 73–9. Safavid chronicles portrayed the struggle with the Uzbeks in part in religious terms. Trausch, *Abbildung und Anpassung*, 144.
127. Biancamaria Scarcia Amoretti, 'Una polemica religiosa tra "ulamâ" di Mashad e "ulamâ" uzbechi nell anno 977/1588–1589', *Annali dell'Istituto orientale di Napoli* 14 (1964), 647–71, esp. 653; Amoretti, 'Religion', 648f.; Rizvi, *Shah 'Abd al-'Aziz*, 253. This polemic thus went further than many Ottoman polemics, which were primarily directed at the Qizilbash and Safavids, in that it explicitly focused on Shii doctrine, not the Qizilbash's actions. Eberhard, *Osmanische Polemik*, 137.
128. Ahmad Sirhindi (b. 971/1564) wrote his famous anti-Shii polemic *Radd-i Rawafiz* in response to the Shii letter to the Uzbeks. Rizvi, *A Socio-Intellectual History*, Vol. 1, 241–5.
129. Trausch, *Abbildung und Anpassung*, 136f. Despite the polemics, after the Uzbek conquest of Mashhad in 1589, the leading Tuqay-Timurid clansman, who was an ally of Abdullah Khan Uzbek, married the Shii daughter of an official at the shrine of Imam Rida and descendant of the eighth Imam to symbolise the union of Genghisid and Shii genealogies and solidify control over the city in a 'Sunni–Shia' political marriage. The descendants were given the title 'Hussaini', which, as McChesney has argued, did not have to carry a Shii connotation at the time. McChesney, *Waqf*, 74.
130. Rizvi, *A Socio-Intellectual History*, Vol. 1, 207.
131. The term 'confessionalisation' was coined by German historians of the reformation and subsequent religio-political conflicts in Europe. For the original German debate, see Wolfgang Reinhard, 'Zwang zur Konfessionalisierung? Prolegomena zu einer Theorie des konfessionellen Zeitalters', *Zeitschrift für historische Forschung* 10, 3 (1983), 257–77; Heinz Schilling, 'Confessionalization: Historical and Scholarly Perspectives of a Comparative and Interdisciplinary Paradigm', in: John M. Headley, Hans J. Hillerbrand, and Anthony J. Papalas (eds), *Confessionalization in Europe, 1555–1700: Essays in Honor and Memory of Bodo Nischan* (Aldershot: Ashgate, 2004), 21–35. For applications of the term 'confessionalisation' to the Ottoman Empire, see the work of Tijana Krstić and Derin Terzioğlu: Krstić, *Contested Conversions*, 12–16; Krstić, 'Illuminated by the Light of Islam and the Glory of the Ottoman Sultanate: Narratives of Conversion to Islam in the Age of Confessionalization', *Comparative Studies in*

Society and History 51, 1 (2009), 35–63. See also Guy Burak, 'Faith, Law and Empire in the Ottoman "Age of Confessionalization" (Fifteenth to Seventeenth Centuries): The Case of "Renewal of Faith"', *Mediterranean Historical Review* 28, 1 (2013), 1–23; Yasir Yılmaz, 'Confessionalization or a Quest for Order? A Comparative Look at Religion and State in the Seventeenth-Century Ottoman, Russian, and Habsburg Empires', in: Vefa Erginbaş (ed.), *Ottoman Sunnism: New Perspectives* (Edinburgh: Edinburgh University Press, 2019), 90–120.

132. The appropriation of the term 'confessionalisation' in the Middle Eastern context should not, however, lead one to overstate the importance of overarching religious identities at the expense of other, more localised developments, or to equate the Protestant-Catholic split with the Sunni–Shia one. Christopher Markiewicz, 'Europeanist Trends and Islamicate Trajectories in Early Modern Ottoman History', *Past & Present* 239, 1 (2018), 265–81. Differences between developments in Christian Europe and the Ottoman Empire include periodisation, especially the fact that the confessions, while now imbued with new vigour, had existed for centuries, the role of mass education, and the situation of adherents of the relative other confession in adversarial territory. Şahin, *Empire and Power*, 208ff.; Riza Yildirim, 'The Rise of the "Religion and State" Order: Re-Confessionalisation of State and Society in the Early Modern Ottoman Empire', in: Vefa Erginbaş (ed.), *Ottoman Sunnism: New Perspectives* (Edinburgh: Edinburgh University Press, 2019), 12–46. For an early critical assessment, see Hodgson, *Venture*, Vol. 3, 33f.

133. In Dante's early fourteenth-century opus *La divina commedia*, not only is the Prophet Muhammad hacked to death as a schismatic, but so is Ali. Dante, *La divina commedia*, Inf. XXVIII, vv. 32–36, https://dante.princeton.edu/pdp. For a discussion of where Dante might have got knowledge of Ali from, see Stefano Resconi, 'Dante e gli Sciiti: L'Alì di "Inf.", XXVIII, alla luce delle possibili fonti', *Rivista di Studi Danteschi* 2 (2016), 365–88.

134. See, for example, Ahmad Gunny, *Images of Islam in Eighteenth-Century Writings* (London: Grey Seal, 1996), 190. In a book on the Ottoman Empire, the English diplomat Sir Paul Rycaut (1629–1700) discusses Shiism under 'sects and heresies'. He relates similar anti-Shii arguments and thus misrepresents Shiism quite starkly: 'The Shii are the Sect spoken of before, opposed by the Subjects of the whole [...] Empire, as the most heretical of any of the rest, in regard they prefer Ali before Mahomet in the prophetical Office, and restrain the prophetick gift to the natural line derived from Ali, and that none is worthy of the Title of a Prophet, who is guilty of sin, though of the lower nature; some of which Professors called Alnosairi [...] affirm that God appeared in the form of Ali, and with his tongue proclaimed the most hidden Mysteries of Religion; and some have proceeded yet farther, to attribute to their Prophets divine honours, asserting them to be elevated above degree and stare of the creatures: these expect the return of their Prophet Ali in the Clouds, and have placed that belief as an Article of their Faith, from whence may seem to be grounded that mistake amongst our vulgar, that the Turks believe Mahomet shall again

return into the world.' Paul Rycaut, *The History of the Present State of the Ottoman Empire: Containing the Maxims of the Turkish Polity, the Most Material Points of the Mahometan Religion, Their Sects and Heresies, Their Convents and Religious Votaries: Their Military Discipline, with an Exact Computation of Their Forces Both by Sea and Land: Illustrated with Divers Pieces of Sculpture Representing the Variety of Habits amongst the Turks: In Three Books* (London: John Starkey and Henry Brome, 1668), 127. A seventeenth-century history by the first Laudian Professor of Arabic at Oxford University, Edward Pococke, who had previously been chaplain in Aleppo, contained a section on Islamic sects based on such heresiographical literature. Kohlberg, 'Western Studies', 33f. See also Gunny, *Images of Islam*, 63.

135. The imperial Tercüman, Ali Bey, explained to him the difference between Sunni and Shii from a decidedly Sunni point of view. Krstić, *Contested Conversions*, 107f. Gerlach's successor as chaplain, Salomon Schweigger (1551–1622), explained renewed Ottoman–Safavid hostilities in 1578 with long-standing hatred between the two empires. Matthee, 'The Ottoman–Safavid War', 4.

136. This story is related in the *Imperial Festival Book* by Intizami of Foca, cited after: Krstić, *Contested Conversions*, 108. According to Krstić, '[t]he Habsburg ambassador therefore recognized the Ottoman vision of a hierarchy of "orthodoxies"'. Ibid. A separate tribune thus had to be constructed, although Terzioğlu notes that the story does not make much sense because the Safavid envoy sat with other Muslim rulers, including the Crimean Khan as well as the Polish ambassador. Terzioğlu, 'The Imperial Circumcision Festival', 85.

137. Allouche, *The Origins*, 130ff.; Mitchell, *The Practice of Politics*, 90f. For more, see Kenneth M. Setton, *The Papacy and the Levant (1204–1571)*, Vols 3 and 4 (Philadelphia: American Philosophical Society, 1976–84); Mario Casari, 'Italy ii. DIPLOMATIC AND COMMERCIAL RELATIONS', *EIr*; H. R. Roemer, 'Die Safawiden: Ein orientalischer Bundesgenosse des Abendlandes im Türkenkampf', *Saeculum* 4 (1953), 27–44; Giorgio Rota, *Under Two Lions: On the Knowledge of Persia in the Republic of Venice (ca. 1450–1797)* (Vienna: Verlag der Österreichischen Akademie der Wissenschaften, 2009); Niels Steensgaard, *The Asian Trade Revolution: The East India Companies and the Decline of the Caravan Trade* (Chicago: University of Chicago Press, 1975); Barbara von Palombini, *Bündniswerben abendländischer Mächte um Persien 1453–1600* (Wiesbaden: Franz Steiner, 1968); Bacqué-Grammont, *Les Ottomans*, 128–45; Rudi Matthee, 'Anti-Ottoman Concerns and Caucasian Interests: Diplomatic Relations between Iran and Russia, 1587–1639', in: Michel M. Mazzaoui (ed.), *Safavid Iran & Her Neighbors* (Salt Lake City: University of Utah Press, 2003), 101–28.

138. The earliest recorded instance of using the word Sunni in Portuguese sources is 1529, while the word Shii is first used in 1553 (although some Shii beliefs are described earlier). Luis Filipe F. R. Thomaz, 'Iranian Diaspora and the Deccan Sultanates in India: A Study of Sixteenth Century Portuguese Sources', *Studies in History* 30, 1 (2014), 1–42, 1–5. See also Joao Teles e Cunha, 'The Eye of the Beholder: The Creation of a Portuguese Discourse on Safavid Iran', in: Rudi

Matthee and Jorge Flores (eds), *Portugal, the Persian Gulf and Safavid Persia* (Leuven: Peeters, 2011), 11–50.

139. Giancarlo Casale, 'Imperial Smackdown: The Portuguese between Imamate and Caliphate in the Persian Gulf', in: Rudi Matthee and Jorge Flores (eds), *Portugal, the Persian Gulf, and Safavid Persia* (Leuven: Peeters, 2011), 177–90.

140. See the note by Philip III in Jorge Flores, *Unwanted Neighbours: The Mughals, the Portuguese, and their Frontier Zones* (Oxford: Oxford University Press, 2018), 60–5. Though Ibrahim II of Bijapur wrote a letter to Shah Abbas in 1612/13 presenting the Deccan as a part of the Safavid Empire and claiming that the *khutba* was being read in honour of the Safavid Shah, despite Bijapur being nominally Sunni at that time. Ibid., 65; Joao Teles e Cunha, 'PORTUGAL i. RELATIONS WITH PERSIA IN THE EARLY MODERN AGE (1500–1750)', *EIr*.

141. Kohlberg, 'Western Studies', 33; Rahimi, *Theater State*, 218f.; Margaret Meserve, 'The Sophy: News of Shah Ismail Safavi in Renaissance Europe', *Journal of Early Modern History* 18 (2014), 579–608; Chloë Houston, '"Thou Glorious Kingdome, Thou Chiefe of Empires": Persia in Early Seventeenth-Century Travel Literature', *Studies in Travel Writing* 13, 2 (2009), 141–52; Gunny, *Images of Islam*, 9–36.

142. Rudi Matthee argues that Minadoi's book contains the first substantial European account of the Sunni–Shia split. Rudi Matthee, 'Introduction', in: Giovanni-Tommaso Minadoi, *The War between the Turks and the Persians: Conflict and Religion in the Safavid and Ottoman Worlds* (London: I. B. Tauris, 2019), vii–xiv.

143. J. T. P. de Bruijn, 'Iranian Studies in the Netherlands', *Iranian Studies* 20, 2/4 (1987), 161–77; Willem Floor, 'DUTCH-PERSIAN RELATIONS', *EIr*.

144. The Portuguese Augustinians led the first such mission to Safavid Iran. John M. Flannery, *The Mission of the Portuguese Augustinians to Persia and Beyond (1602–1747)* (Leiden: Brill, 2013); Leonard Harrow, 'Notes on Catholic-Shi'i Relations during the Safavid Period', *Journal of Eastern Christian Studies* 63, 1–2 (2011), 99–121. See also Christian Windler, *Missionare in Persien: Kulturelle Diversität und Normenkonkurrenz im globalen Katholizismus (17.-18. Jahrhundert)* (Cologne: Böhlau, 2018).

145. Susan Mokhberi, *The Persian Mirror: Reflections of the Safavid Empire in Early Modern France* (Oxford: Oxford University Press, 2019), 8–26; Francis Richard, 'Catholicisme et Islam chiite au "grand siècle": Autour de quelques documents concernant les Missions catholiquesen Perse au XVIIème siècle', *Euntes Docete* 33, 3 (1980), 339–403; Ina Baghdiantz McCabe, *Orientalism in Early Modern France: Eurasian Trade, Exoticism, and the Ancien Régime* (New York: Berg, 2008); Chloë Houston, 'Turning Persia: The Prospect of Conversion in Safavid Iran', in: Lieke Stelling, Harald Hendrix, and Todd Richardson (eds), *The Turn of the Soul: Representations of Religious Conversion in Early Modern Art and Literature* (Leiden: Brill, 2012), 85–107; Harrow, 'Notes on Catholic-Shi'i Relations'.

146. Don Juan of Persia (formerly Oruj Beg Bayat), *Relaciones de Don Juan de Persia*, trans. as *Don Juan of Persia: A Shi'ah Catholic, 1560–1604* (London: Routledge, 1926), e.g. 104–11. For more on Spain and Iran, see E. García, J. Cutillas, and

R. Matthee (eds), *The Spanish Monarchy and Safavid Persia in the Early Modern Period: Politics, War and Religion* (Valencia: Albatros, 2016).

147. From there, they established global trade networks. Edmund M. Herzig, *The Armenian Merchants of New Julfa, Isfahan: A Study in Pre-Modern Asian Trade* (PhD, University of Oxford, 1991); Sebouh D. Aslanian, *From the Indian Ocean to the Mediterranean: The Global Trade Networks of Armenian Merchants from New Julfa* (Berkeley: University of California Press, 2010).

148. Gunny himself is critical of the Shii point of view, quoting the Capuchin friar Gabriel de Chinon, who spent two years in Isfahan from 1640 on. Gunny, *Images of Islam*, 25ff.

149. This was Adriaan Reland, *De Religione Mohammedica Libri Duo* (Utrecht: Willem Broedelet, 1717). For more, see de Bruijn, 'Iranian Studies', 170; Gunny, *Images of Islam*, 54–7.

150. For example, the Protestant Jean Chardin's *Voyages en Perse*. Gunny, *Images of Islam*, 27.

151. Ros Ballaster, *Fabulous Orients: Fictions of the East in England 1662–1785* (New York: Oxford University Press, 2005), 78; Thomas Kaiser, 'The Evil Empire? The Debate on Turkish Despotism in Eighteenth-Century French Political Culture', *Journal of Modern History* 72, 1 (2000), 6–34; Joan-Pau Rubiés, 'Oriental Despotism and European Orientalism: Botero to Montesquieu', *Journal of Early Modern History* 9, 1–2 (2005), 109–80.

152. Gunny, *Images of Islam*, 107–24.

153. Maria Baramova, 'Non-Splendid Isolation: The Ottoman Empire and the Thirty Years' War', in: Olaf Asbach and Peter Schröder (eds), *The Ashgate Research Companion to the Thirty Years' War* (Farnham: Ashgate, 2014), 115–24.

154. Abisaab, *Converting Persia*, 41ff. See also Mitchell, *The Practice of Politics*, 148–58; Arjomand, *The Shadow of God*, 120; Stanfield-Johnson, 'Sunni Survival', 128.

155. Kioumars Ghereghlou, 'A Safavid Bureaucrat in the Ottoman World: Mirza Makhdum Sharifi Shirazi and the Quest for Upward Mobility in the İlmiye Hierarchy', *Osmanlı Araştırmaları/Journal of Ottoman Studies* 53 (2019), 153–94; Ghereghlou, 'MAKDUM ŠARIFI ŠIRĀZI', *EIr*; Ghereghlou, 'ESMĀʿIL II', *EIr*; Rosemary Stanfield-Johnson, *Mirza Makhdum Sharifi: A 16th-Century Sunni Ṣadr at the Safavid Court* (PhD, New York University, 1992); Shohreh Gholsorkhi, 'Ismail II and Mirza Makhdum Sharifi: An Interlude in Safavid History', *International Journal of Middle East Studies* 26, 3 (1994), 477–88. Sharifi claimed that he had previously been obliged by the anti-Sunni enforcers mentioned above to curse the Companions from the pulpit of his mosque, which he did for fear of his life.

156. This was Nurullah Shustari (d. 1610/11), who claimed that Sharifi's *al-Nawaqid fi Radd al-Rawafid* was such a weak text that he wrote his response in seventeen days. Stanfield-Johnson, 'Sunni Survival', 123–33; Eberhard, *Osmanische Polemik*, 53–61; Sajjad H. Rizvi, 'Shīʿi Polemics at the Mughal Court: The Case of Qāżi Nūrullāh Shūshtarī', *Studies in People's History* 4, 1 (2017), 53–67, 58; Jaʿfariyan, *Tarikh-i Tashayyuʿ dar Iran*, Vol. 2, 799–818.

157. For an attempt to bring to life the mystical worlds that gave rise to the Qizilbash and their beliefs as well as the struggles in the sixteenth century to drive them away from power, see Kathryn Babayan, *Mystics, Monarchs, and Messiahs: Cultural Landscapes of Early Modern Iran* (Cambridge, MA: Harvard University Press, 2002); Babayan, 'The Safavid Synthesis'. See also Posch, *Osmanisch-safavidische Beziehungen*, 171–9; Stickel, *Zwischen Chiliasmus und Staatsräson*, 129–240.

158. This is called *al-niyaba al-amma*. Norman Calder, *The Structure of Authority in Imami Shi'i Jurisprudence* (PhD, University of London, 1980).

159. But Safavid rulers continued to need their support. I would like to thank Baltacıoğlu-Brammer for clarifying this point to me. Baltacıoğlu-Brammer, 'The Formation of Kızılbaş Communities', 25.

160. Dressler, 'Inventing Orthodoxy', 171f.

161. Babayan, 'The Safavid Synthesis', 137; Quinn, 'Iran under Safavid Rule', 221–4. For a readable account of his reign, see Sholeh Quinn, *Shah 'Abbas: The King Who Refashioned Iran* (London: Oneworld, 2015).

162. Heern, *The Emergence of Modern Shi'ism*, 44; Charles Melville, 'New Light on Shah 'Abbas and the Construction of Isfahan', *Muqarnas* 33, 1 (2016), 155–76; Sussan Babaie and Robert Haug, 'Isfahan x. Monuments (3) Mosques', *EIr*; Sussan Babaie, *Isfahan and its Palaces: Statecraft, Shi'ism and the Architecture of Conviviality in Early Modern Iran* (Edinburgh: Edinburgh University Press, 2008); Bernard O'Kane, 'DOMES', *EIr*.

163. The city became the centre of a group of scholars and a body of work that synthesised philosophy, esoteric Shiism, and mysticism. Sajjad H. Rizvi, 'ISFAHAN SCHOOL OF PHILOSOPHY', *EIr*; Hodgson, *Venture*, Vol. 3, 41–6; Maryam Moazzen, *Formation of a Religious Landscape: Shi'i Higher Learning in Safavid Iran* (Leiden: Brill, 2018).

164. Called '*al-masuma*', 'the sinless', Fatima is the subject of poems and her shrine a site of pilgrimage. Andreas Drechsler, *Geschichte der Stadt Qom im Mittelalter (650–1350)* (Berlin: Klaus Schwarz, 1999); Zohreh Sadeghi, *Fatima von Qum: Ein Beispiel für die Verehrung heiliger Frauen im Volksglauben der Zwölfer-Schia* (Berlin: Klaus Schwarz, 1996).

165. For a general discussion of this, see Barkey, *Empire of Difference*.

166. After the conquest of Cyprus in 1571, the Ottomans resettled landless peasants and Qizilbash there. Suraiya Faroqhi, *Geschichte des Osmanischen Reiches* (Munich: C. H. Beck, 2006), 37; Zarinebaf, 'Qizilbash "Heresy"', 10. Others were expelled to Bulgaria. Frederick de Jong, 'Problems Concerning the Origins of the Qizilbash in Bulgaria: Remnants of the Safaviyya?', in: *Convegno sul tema: La Shī'a nell'Impero Ottomano (Roma, 15 aprile 1991)* (Rome: Accademia Nazionale dei Lincei, 1993), 203–24.

167. In the sixteenth and seventeenth centuries, the number of Sayyids recognised by the Ottoman state thus increased in areas with a strong Qizilbash presence. Hülya Canbakal, 'The Ottoman State and Descendants of the Prophet in Anatolia and the Balkans (c. 1500–1700)', *Journal of the Economic and Social*

History of the Orient 52, 3 (2009), 542–78, 560f. See also Canbakal, 'An Exercise in Denominational Geography in Search of Ottoman Alevis', *Turkish Studies* 6, 2 (2005), 253–71.

168. For the relationship between these Sufis and the Ottoman state, see Derin Terzioğlu, 'Sunna-Minded Sufi Preachers in Service of the Ottoman State: The Nasīhatnāme of Hasan Addressed to Murad IV', *Archivum Ottomanicum* 27 (2010), 243–59; Terzioğlu, 'Sufis in the Age of State-Building and Confessionalization', in: Christine Woodhead (ed.), *The Ottoman World* (London: Routledge, 2012), 86–99.

169. Le Gall, *A Culture of Sufism*, 129–33. Le Gall seeks to revisit the thesis that the Naqshbandis were staunchly Sunni and anti-Shii and aided the Ottomans in their struggle against the Safavids. Ibid., 137–56.

170. This was the case of the Halvetis. Curry argues that, rather than signifying the influence of Shiism on Sufism, this exemplifies the fact that the *Ahl al-Bayt* could be important in both. John Curry, *The Transformation of Muslim Mystical Thought in the Ottoman Empire: The Rise of the Halveti Order, 1350–1650* (Edinburgh: Edinburgh University Press, 2010), 25.

171. Followers of a sub-branch of the order emphasised a Shii part of their identity when dealing with the Qizilbash and the new Safavid rulers, but were nonetheless suppressed. These followers then initially chose Mamluk Egypt over the Ottoman realms as a place of exile, perhaps for fear of repression by the Ottomans of this Shii-leaning order. In later periods, they invented tensions with the Qizilbash in their hagiography to facilitate good relations with the Ottomans. Ibrahim Gulshani, the leader of that branch, seems to have safeguarded money of the defeated White Sheep dynasty upon the Safavids' conquest of Tabriz and was thus attacked and tortured. Hagiographers of the order emphasised that this was due to religious rather than economic or political reasons. Side Emre, *Ibrahim-i Gulshani and the Khalwati-Gulshani Order: Power Brokers in Ottoman Egypt* (Leiden: Brill, 2017), 58ff., 169f. After the rise of the Safavids, the inclusion of the Imams and of teachers that also taught the founders of the Safavid order was seen as a problem and increased the propagation of alternative spiritual lineages. Curry, *The Transformation*, 25, 33, 40, 45, 256; Emre, *Ibrahim-i Gulshani*, 68ff. The Halvetis thus reasserted their doctrinal position as Sunni and cooperated with the state. Nathalie Clayer, *Mystiques, état et société: Les Halvetis dans l'aire balkanique de la fin du XVe siècle à nos jours* (Leiden: Brill, 1994), 63–142 and passim; Curry, *The Transformation*, 255f., 293f. They at times excluded some Shii Imams from their spiritual lineages in the sixteenth century. Le Gall, *A Culture of Sufism*, 132.

172. Irène Mélikoff, *Hadji Bektach: Un mythe et ses avatars: Genèse et évolution du soufisme populaire en Turquie* (Leiden: Brill, 1998), 51–103. Mélikoff's thesis that the Bektashis and Alevis are a form of 'chamanisme islamisé' has been frequently criticised and somewhat toned down by her as well.

173. Atçıl, 'The Safavid Threat', 306; Winter, *The Shiites of Lebanon*, 10f.; Suraiya Faroqhi, 'Conflict, Accommodation and Long-Term Survival: The Bektashi

Order and the Ottoman State', in: Alexandre Popovic and Gilles Veinstein (eds), *Bektachiyya: Études sur l'ordre mystique des Bektachis et les groupes relevant de Hadji Bektach* (Istanbul: Isis Publications, 1995), 171–84; Faroqhi, *Der Bektaschi-Orden*, 38–43; Barkey, *Empire of Difference*, 164–9; Zeynep Yürekli, *Architecture and Hagiography in the Ottoman Empire: The Politics of Bektashi Shrines in the Classical Age* (Abingdon: Routledge, 2012).

174. See the translation of a discharge paper of a Janissary soldier from 1822. John Kingsley Birge, *The Bektashi Order of Dervishes* (London: Luzac Oriental, 1994, 1937), 74f. For more examples of the Shiitising nature of the Bektashi order, see ibid., 132, 139–48, 169f., 185–98, 213. And the poetry of Shah Ismail Safavi continued to be relevant in the rituals and beliefs of the order. Amelia Gallagher, *The Fallible Master of Perfection: Shah Ismail in the Alevi-Bektashi Tradition* (PhD, McGill University, 2004); Hamid Algar, 'BEKTĀŠĪYA', *EIr*.

175. Depictions of the sword are also to be found on Janissary and Bektashi tomb-stones, and wooden replicas may have been used in processions. Hathaway, *A Tale of Two Factions*, 170. In the Ottoman tradition, it is primarily found as a stand-alone symbol and not in the hand of a warrior. Some have argued that portrayals of the sword have almost human features. Ibid., 172; Zdzislaw Zygulski, *Ottoman Art in the Service of the Empire* (New York: NYU Press, 1992), 46–50. Given that until the seventeenth century many Janissaries were prison-ers of war or Christian boys from the Balkans and Anatolia, the association with a popular sword served as a way of linking sword legends such as those of Arthur to the *Dhu l-Faqar*, thereby facilitating these recruits' integration into the Janissary corps. For one such account by a Serbian soldier who became a Janissary in the mid-fifteenth century, see Hathaway, *A Tale of Two Factions*, 175f. See also Hathaway, 'The Forgotten Icon: The Sword Zülfikâr in its Ottoman Incarnation', *Turkish Studies Association Journal* 27, 1–2 (2003), 1–14.

176. Hathaway, *A Tale of Two Factions*, 175.

177. A similar process occurred with the Hand of Fatima, another symbol popular across the Islamic world with strong Alid symbolism that was Sunnified in the Ottoman Empire. Zeynep Yürekli, 'The Sword Dhū'l-Faqār and the Ottomans', in: Fahmida Suleman (ed.), *People of the Prophet's House: Artistic and Ritual Expressions of Shiʿi Islam* (London: Azimuth Editions/Institute of Ismaili Studies, 2015), 163–72, 164.

178. Erginbas, 'Problematizing Ottoman Sunnism'.

179. Dressler, 'Inventing Orthodoxy', 160f.; Cornell H. Fleischer, 'The Lawgiver as Messiah: The Making of the Imperial Image in the Reign of Süleymân', in: Gilles Veinstein (ed.), *Soliman le magnifique et son temps* (Paris: La Documentation française, 1992), 159–77.

180. This is the Shii-influenced biography of the Prophet Muhammad *Siyer-i Nebi* with a Turkish text by Mustafa Darir (written in 790/1388), illustrated at the request of Sultan Murad III (r. 1574/5–95) and completed around 1004/1595. Spellberg, *Politics*, 179–90; Vefa Erginbaş, 'Reappraising Ottoman Religiosity in the Last Decades of the Sixteenth Century: Mustafa Darir's Siret and its Alid

Content', in:Vefa Erginbaş (ed.), *Ottoman Sunnism: New Perspectives* (Edinburgh: Edinburgh University Press, 2019), 71–89, 83. It was commissioned by Murad III, who restarted war with the Safavids. Curry speculates that, rather than a contradiction, this could have been a way to show pro-Alid parts of the population that they were recognised in the realm and heighten the spirits of the Janissaries and the Bektashis at a time of renewed hostilities with the Habsburgs after 1593. John Curry, 'Some Reflections on the Fluidity of Orthodoxy and Heterodoxy in an Ottoman Sunni Context', in:Vefa Erginbaş (ed.), *Ottoman Sunnism: New Perspectives* (Edinburgh: Edinburgh University Press, 2019), 193–210, 201.

181. Hathaway, *A Tale of Two Factions*, 107, to whom I also owe knowledge of this passage from Lane. Lane describes in detail the Ashura celebrations in Cairo in the first half of the nineteenth century. He also describes a celebration of the birthday of Hussain (*Mawlid al-Hasanayn*, in honour of Hussain and his brother Hasan), which was performed at the mosque of Hussain, where Hussain's head is said to be buried. Edward William Lane, *An Account of the Manners and Customs of the Modern Egyptians* (London: J. M. Dent, 1923), 433–9, 462–70.

182. A decree ordering the ban of Ashura in Mosul in 1574 is translated in Zarinebaf, 'Qizilbash "Heresy"', 15.

183. Eberhard, *Osmanische Polemik*, 155–8.

184. Ibid., 160ff.

185. Winter, *The Shiites of Lebanon*, 16f.

186. See, for example, the fatwa by Abu s-Suud. Eberhard, *Osmanische Polemik*, 74, 84, 128–37, 166. For *takfir*, see ibid., 155.

187. Ibid., 103, 131. For a reassessment, see Atçıl, 'The Safavid Threat'.

188. Rycaut, *The History of the Present State*, 120ff.; J. H. Mordtmann, 'Sunnitisch-schiitische Polemik im 17. Jahrhundert', *Mitteilungen des Seminars für orientalische Sprachen an der Friedrich-Wilhelms-Universität zu Berlin* 29 (1926), 112–29, 119f.

189. Şahin, *Empire and Power*, 129f., 210f.

190. Derin Terzioğlu, 'Where 'Ilm-i Ḥāl Meets Catechism: Islamic Manuals of Religious Instruction in the Ottoman Empire in the Age of Confessionalization', *Past & Present* 220, 1 (2013), 79–114, 109. Interestingly, some authors of these manuals advocated precisely a more thorough involvement of the state and a regular state-led examination of righteous beliefs at the neighbourhood level. Ibid., 99f.

191. Ismail Safa Üstün, *Heresy and Legitimacy in the Ottoman Empire in the Sixteenth Century* (PhD, University of Manchester, 2009).

192. It is also unclear to what extent these prohibitions were implemented or enforced before the nineteenth century, but they probably limited such intermarriage. Karen M. Kern, *Imperial Citizen: Marriage and Citizenship in the Ottoman Frontier Provinces of Iraq* (Syracuse: Syracuse University Press, 2011), 43–9. In the second half of the eighteenth century, al-Muradi, a Hanafi Mufti in Damascus, issued a treatise invalidating marriage between Sunnis and Shia. Ibid., 51. In Medina, intermarriage between the Nakhawila, a local Twelver

Shii group, and local Sunnis was at times prohibited. Ibid., 43, 52; Ende, 'The Nakhawila', 293, 302.

193. Winter, *The Shiites of Lebanon*, 8, 18ff. When a Shii preacher became too popular in Homs, for example, the local Sunni religious authorities intervened with the Ottoman authorities, who expelled him from the town but allowed him to settle in Baalbek, where he apparently continued to convert Sunnis to Shiism. Grehan, *Twilight of the Saints*, 59.

194. Winter, *The Shiites of Lebanon*, 5; Winter, 'The Kizilbaş of Syria and Ottoman Shiism', in: Christine Woodhead (ed.), *The Ottoman World* (London: Routledge, 2011), 171–83, 172; Sa'dun Hammada, *Tarikh al-Shi'a fi Lubnan*, 2 Vols, 2nd ed. (Beirut: Dar al-Khayyal, 2013), esp. Vol. 1.

195. Hamza al-Hasan, *Al-Shi'a fi al-Mamlaka al-'Arabiyya al-Su'udiyya*, 2 Vols (Beirut: Mu'assasat al-Baqi' li-Ihya' al-Turath, 1993), Vol. 1, 18; Nakash, *Reaching for Power*, 21f.

196. While many scholars were Usulis, there was also a strong presence of Akhbaris and a strong Shii Sufi and philosophical tradition. 'Ali al-Biladi al-Bahrani, *Anwar al-Badrayn fi Tarajim 'Ulama' al-Qatif wa-l-Ahsa' wa-l-Bahrayn* (Beirut: Dar al-Murtada, 1991), 227f., 318–21; Cole, 'Rival Empires', 178–82; Sabine Schmidtke, *Theologie, Philosophie und Mystik im zwölferschiitischen Islam des 9./15. Jahrhunderts: Die Gedankenwelten des Ibn Abi Gumhur al-Ahsai* (Leiden: Brill, 2000).

197. The presence of Twelver Shiism and the four Sunni schools of law made al-Ahsa a regional centre of religious learning. Abdallah al-Salih al-'Uthaymin, *Tarikh al-Mamlaka al-'Arabiyya al-Su'udiyya*, 9th ed., 2 Vols, Vol. 1 (Riyadh: Obeikan, 1998), 34.

198. W. Caskel, "Abd al-Ḳays', *EI2*; Muhammad Sa'id al-Muslim, *Sahil al-Dhahab al-Aswad: Dirasa Tarikhiyya Insaniyya li-Mintaqat al-Khalij al-'Arabi*, 2nd ed. (Beirut: Manshurat Dar Maktabat al-Haya, 1962); Muhammad al-'Abd al-Qadir al-Ansari al-Ahsa'i, *Tuhfat al-Mustafid bi-Tarikh al-Ahsa' fi al-Qadim wa-l-Jadid*, 2 Vols, Vol. 1 (Riyadh: Matabi' al-Riyyad, 1960), 4–45; Muhammad Mahmud Khalil, *Tarikh al-Khalij wa Sharq al-Jazira al-'Arabiyya al-Musamma Iqlim Bilad al-Bahrayn fi Zill Hukm al-Duwaylat al-'Arabiyya 469–963 A.H./1076–1555* (Cairo: Maktaba Madbuli, 2006).

199. Rudi Matthee, 'Between Arabs, Turks and Iranians: The Town of Basra, 1600–1700', *Bulletin of the School of Oriental and African Studies* 69, 1 (2006), 53–78; 'Ali bin Ibrahim al-Darura, *Tarikh al-Ihtilal al-Burtughali li-l-Qatif 1521–1572* (Abu Dhabi: Majma' al-Thaqafi, 2001); Abdul Aziz M. Awad, 'The Gulf in the Seventeenth Century', *Bulletin (British Society for Middle Eastern Studies)* 12, 2 (1985), 123–34; Werner Caskel, 'Eine "unbekannte" Dynastie in Arabien', *Oriens* 2, 1 (1949), 66–71; Cole, 'Rival Empires', 182f.

200. G. Rentz, 'al-Qatif', *EI2*; Jon E. Mandaville, 'The Ottoman Province of al-Hasā in the Sixteenth and Seventeenth Centuries', *Journal of the American Oriental Society* 90, 3 (1970), 486–513, 496–9. See also Mehmet Mehdi Ilhan, 'The Katif District (Liva) during the First Few Years of Ottoman Rule: A Study of the 1551 Ottoman Cadastral Survey', *Belleten (Türk Tarih Kurumu)*

51, 200 (1987), 780–98; Salih Özbaran, 'Ottomans and the India Trade in the Sixteenth Century: Some New Data and Reconsiderations', *Oriente Moderno* 25, 86 (2006), 173–9, 174ff.

201. Devin J. Stewart, 'An Episode in the 'Amili Migration to Safavid Iran: Husayn b. 'Abd al-Samad al-'Amili's Travel Account', *Iranian Studies* 39, 4 (2006), 481–508.

202. He is known in Shii historiography as the 'Second Martyr'. See al-Amin, *Mustadrakat A'yan al-Shi'a*, Vol. 7, 143–58. See also Devin J. Stewart, 'The Ottoman Execution of Zayn al-Dīn al-'Āmilī', *Die Welt des Islams* 48, 3/4 (2008), 289–347; Marco Salati, 'Ricerche sullo sciismo nell'Impero ottomano: Il viaggio di Zayn al-Din al-Shahid al-Thani a Istanbul al tempo di Solimano il Magnifico (952/1545)', *Oriente Moderno* 9 (1990), 81–92; Winter, *The Shiites of Lebanon*, 20–4; Richard Blackburn, *Journey to the Sublime Porte: The Arabic Memoir of a Sharifian Agent's Diplomatic Mission to the Ottoman Imperial Court in the Era of Suleyman the Magnificent: The Relevant Text from Quṭb al-Dīn al-Nahrawālī's al-Fawā'id al-Sanīyah fī al-Riḥlah al-Madanīyah wa al-Rūmīyah* (Beirut: Orient-Institut/Würzburg: Ergon, 2005), 208ff.; Hourani, 'From Jabal 'Amil to Persia', 55; Abisaab, 'History and Self-Image', 71ff.

203. Interview with a senior Lebanese Shii cleric, Beirut, 2018.

204. Grehan, *Twilight of the Saints*, 33, 47f.

205. Stefan Winter, 'The Alawis in the Ottoman Period', in: Michael Kerr and Craig Larkin (eds), *The Alawis of Syria: War, Faith and Politics in the Levant* (London: Hurst, 2015), 49–62, 54–7.

206. Sabrina Mervin, *Un réformisme chiite: Ulémas et lettrés du Ǧabal Āmil (actuel Liban-Sud) de la fin de l'Empire ottoman à l'indépendance du Liban* (Paris: Karthala, 2000), 24f.; Maurus Reinkowski, *Ottoman 'Multiculturalism'? The Example of the Confessional System in Lebanon* (Beirut: Orient-Institut der Deutschen Morgenländischen Gesellschaft, 1999), 13.

207. Grehan, *Twilight of the Saints*, 35ff., 215–26.

208. Winter, 'The 'Alawis', 50–4; Winter, *A History of the 'Alawis*, 71.

209. M. O. H. Ursinus, 'Millet', *EI2*. It has been a heavily contested and much debated concept. Benjamin Braude, 'Foundation Myths of the Millet System', in: Benjamin Braude and Bernard Lewis (eds), *Christians and Jews in the Ottoman Empire: The Functioning of a Plural Society* (New York: Holmes & Meier, 1982), 69–88. For a broader deconstruction of the millet-to-confessionalism theory, see Maurus Reinkowski, *Die Dinge der Ordnung: Eine vergleichende Untersuchung über die osmanische Reformpolitik im 19. Jahrhundert* (Berlin: De Gruyter, 2005), 17ff., 197.

210. In Aleppo, a Shii notable was even responsible for collecting taxes from Christians. Marco Salati, 'Tre documenti sull'uso della ǧizyah nella Aleppo ottomana del XVII secolo', *Oriente Moderno* 94, 1 (2014), 176–85. For more, see Salati, *Ascesa e caduta di una famiglia di Ašrāf sciiti di Aleppo: I Zuhrāwī o Zuhrāzāda, 1600–1750* (Rome: Istituto per l'Oriente C. A. Nallino, 1992).

211. Farhat, 'Shi'i Piety'; Mitchell, 'Two Tales of One City'.

212. He also frequently visited Ardabil, the ancestral seat of the Safavid dynasty. Charles Melville, 'Shah 'Abbas and the Pilgrimage to Mashhad', in: Charles Melville (ed.), *Safavid Persia: The History and Politics of an Islamic Society* (London: I. B. Tauris, 1996), 191–229. For more on the history of the shrine, see Amoretti, 'Una polemica', 647–53; Farhat, 'Shi'i Piety'.

213. Babayan, 'The Safavid Synthesis', 157.

214. Flores, *Unwanted Neighbours*, 57–60; Flores, 'Solving Rubik's Cube: Hormuz and the Geopolitical Challenges of West Asia, c. 1592–1622', in: Rudi Matthee and Jorge Flores (eds), *Portugal, the Persian Gulf and Safavid Persia* (Leuven: Peeters, 2011), 191–215.

215. Cole, 'Rival Empires', 186–94; X. de Planhol and J. A. Kechichian, 'BAHRAIN', *EIr*; Fereydoun Adamiyat, *Bahrein Islands: A Legal and Diplomatic Study of the British-Iranian Controversy* (New York: F. A. Praeger, 1955).

216. Scherberger, 'The Confrontation', 64.

217. Interestingly, the Safavid envoys to the Ottoman Empire were almost exclusively from the Qizilbash nobility in this period, which is not reported as a problem in Ottoman sources. Güngörürler, *Diplomacy and Political Relations*, 78.

218. Ibid., 250ff.

219. Sine Arcak, *Gifts in Motion: Ottoman-Safavid Cultural Exchange, 1501–1618* (PhD, University of Minnesota, 2012).

220. Matthee, 'The Safavid-Ottoman Frontier', 171f. This and the corpse traffic for burial near the shrines became also officially discussed in Ottoman–Safavid diplomatic correspondence. Güngörürler, *Diplomacy and Political Relations*, 282f., 380ff.; Güngörürler, 'Ottoman Archival Documents on the Shrines of Karbala, Najaf, and the Hejaz (1660s–1720s): Endowment Wars, the Spoils System, and Iranian Pilgrims', *Journal of the Economic and Social History of the Orient* 64 (2021), 897–1032.

221. Rudi Matthee, 'Safavid Iran and the "Turkish Question" or How to Avoid a War on Multiple Fronts', *Iranian Studies* 52, 3–4 (2019), 513–42.

222. Dressler, 'Inventing Orthodoxy', 173; Ayfer Karakaya-Stump, *Subjects of the Sultan, Disciples of the Shah: Formation and Transformation of the Kizilbash/Alevi Communities in Ottoman Anatolia* (PhD, Harvard University, 2008); Kafadar, *Between Two Worlds*, 66f., 137f.; Yildirim, 'The Safavid-Qizilbash Ecumene'.

223. Ayfer Karakaya-Stump, 'The Forgotten Dervishes: The Bektashi Convents in Iraq and Their Kizilbash Clients', *International Journal of Turkish Studies* 16, 1/2 (2011), 1–24, 20–4.

224. Allouche, *The Origins*, 65.

225. Rudi Matthee, 'Anti-Ottoman Politics and Transit Rights: The Seventeenth-Century Trade in Silk between Safavid Iran and Muscovy', *Cahiers du Monde Russe* 35, 4 (1994), 739–61; Suraiya Faroqhi, 'Trade between the Ottomans and Safavids: The Acem Tüccari and Others', in: Willem Floor and Edmund Herzig (eds), *Iran and the World in the Safavid Age* (London: I. B. Tauris, 2012), 237–52.

226. Trausch, *Abbildung und Anpassung*, 153ff.

227. Matthee, 'Was Safavid Iran an Empire?', 258f.; Quinn, 'Iran under Safavid Rule', 237; Roemer, 'The Safavid Period', 312ff. For a detailed analysis of this process, see Rudi Matthee, *Persia in Crisis: Safavid Decline and the Fall of Isfahan* (London: I. B. Tauris, 2012). For the Sunni–Shia dimension, see ibid., 173ff.

228. Muriel Atkin, *Russia and Iran, 1780–1828* (Minneapolis: University of Minnesota Press, 1980), 4; Richard Tapper, *Frontier Nomads of Iran: A Political and Social History of the Shahsevan* (Cambridge: Cambridge University Press, 1997), 95ff.; Clemens P. Sidorko, '"Kampf den ketzerischen Qizilbash!": Die Revolte des Haggi Da'ud (1718–1728)', in: Raoul Motika and Michael Ursinus (eds), *Caucasia between the Ottoman Empire and Iran, 1555–1914* (Wiesbaden: Reichert, 2000), 133–45; 'Abbas Qoli Aqa Bakikhanov, *The Heavenly Rose-Garden: A History of Shirvan and Daghestan*, trans./annot. by Willem Floor and Hasan Javadi (Washington, DC: Mage, 2009), 113.

229. Ernest Tucker, 'Ottoman–Persian Relations ii. Afsharid and Zand Periods', *EIr*.

230. He thus authorised the killing of male heretics and the enslavement of women and children, who had to convert to Islam. Robert W. Olson, *The Siege of Mosul and Ottoman–Persian Relations, 1718–1743* (Bloomington: Indiana University Press, 1975), 44. See also Lockhart, *The Fall of the Safavi Dynasty*, 251f.

231. Fariba Zarinebaf, 'Azerbaijan between Two Empires: A Contested Borderland in the Early Modern Period (Sixteenth-Eighteenth Centuries)', *Iranian Studies* 52, 3–4 (2019), 299–337, 328–32. On Isfahan, see Friar Alexander of Malabar, 'The Story of the Sack of Ispahan by the Afghans in 1722', *Journal of the Royal Central Asian Society* 23, 4 (1936), 643–53.

232. Babaie, *Isfahan*, 269; Hamid Algar, 'Shi'ism and Iran in the Eighteenth Century', in: Thomas Naff and Roger Owen (eds), *Studies in Eighteenth Century Islamic History* (Carbondale: Southern Illinois University Press, 1977), 288–302, 290; Judas Thaddaeus Krusiński, *The History of the Revolution of Persia: Taken from the Memoirs of Father Krusinski* (Dublin: S. Powell, 1729), 116–26. But Krusiński characterises Mahmud's early rule in Isfahan and takeover from the Safavids as surprisingly just. See ibid., 254–60.

233. Rahimi, *Theater State*.

234. Hodgson, *Venture*, Vol. 3, 38. For a similar argument, invoking the term 'confessional cultures' in Europe, see Maurer, *Konfessionskulturen*.

235. This argument has recently been made by several scholars, including Baltacıoğlu-Brammer, 'The Formation of Kızılbaş Communities', and Dressler, 'Inventing Orthodoxy'.

236. Allouche, *The Origins*, 4f., 8–15, 65f., 149.

237. Zarinebaf, 'Rebels and Renegades', 80; Zarinebaf, 'Azerbaijan'.

238. Abbas Amanat, *Iran: A Modern History* (New Haven: Yale University Press, 2017), ch. 1–3.

239. Hodgson, *Venture*, Vol. 3, 24.

CHAPTER 5

1. A. Wink, 'The Early Expansion of Islam in India', in: D. Morgan and A. Reid (eds), *The New Cambridge History of Islam*, Vol. 3 (Cambridge: Cambridge University Press, 2010), 78–99, esp. 94f.

2. André Wink, 'III. "Al-Hind" India and Indonesia in the Islamic World-Economy, c. 700–1800 A.D.', *Itinerario* 12, 1 (1988), 33–72; Wink, *Al-Hind: The Making of the Indo-Islamic World: Early Medieval India and the Expansion of Islam 7th–11th Centuries* (Leiden: Brill, 1991).

3. I am grateful to Irfan Habib for this point, which he made in comments on a paper I gave at Aligarh Muslim University in 2019. See also his earlier assessment of Mughal India's political economy. Irfan Habib, *The Agrarian System of Mughal India 1556–1707*, 3rd ed. (New Delhi: Oxford University Press, 2013).

4. For a general history of Sufism in India, see Rizvi, *A History of Sufism in India*.

5. Hasan Ali Khan, *Constructing Islam on the Indus: The Material History of the Suhrawardi Sufi Order, 1200–1500 AD* (Cambridge: Cambridge University Press, 2016). Other Sufi orders in Northern India also had proto-Shii leanings, in the sense that they emphasised the importance of Ali and Hussain. Juan R. I. Cole, *Roots of North Indian Shi'ism in Iran and Iraq: Religion and State in Awadh, 1722–1859* (Berkeley: University of California Press, 1988), 89f.

6. Ansar Zahid Khan, 'Ismailism in Multan and Sind', *Journal of the Pakistan Historical Society* 23 (1975), 36–57.

7. Richard M. Eaton, *India in the Persianate Age, 1000–1765* (Berkeley: University of California Press, 2019), 41. The Ghurids were initially followers of an off-shoot of Hanafi Sunnism, known as the Karramiyya, a sect that was soon bitterly attacked and considered heretic by other Hanafi Sunnis. Aron Zysow, 'KARRĀMIYA', *EIr*.

8. Eaton, *India in the Persianate Age*, 47–53. For a general account, see P. Jackson, 'Muslim India: The Delhi Sultanate', in: D. Morgan and A. Reid (eds), *The New Cambridge History of Islam*, Vol. 3 (Cambridge: Cambridge University Press, 2010), 100–27.

9. Eaton, *India in the Persianate Age*, 73–6. Apart from Sufis of the Chishti and the Suhrawardi orders, the wandering dervishes of the Qalandari movement likewise eulogised Ali and the *Ahl al-Bayt*. Rizvi, *A Socio-Intellectual History*, Vol. 1, 152. For the Chishtiyya and Shiism, see Syed Akbar Hyder, *Reliving Karbala: Martyrdom in South Asian Memory* (Oxford: Oxford University Press, 2006), 105; Rizvi, *Shāh Walī-Allāh*, 376; Syed Ali Nadeem Rezavi, 'The Shia Muslims', in: J. S. Grewal (ed.), *Religious Movements and Institutions in Medieval India* (New Delhi: Oxford University Press, 2006), 280–95, 285. For general studies of the Chishtiyya, see, amongst others, Carl W. Ernst and Bruce B. Lawrence, *Sufi Martyrs of Love: The Chishti Order in South Asia and Beyond* (New York: Palgrave Macmillan, 2002).

10. Rizvi, *A Socio-Intellectual History*, Vol. 1, 155ff.

11. Francis Robinson, 'Global History from an Islamic Angle', in: James Belich, John Darwin, Margret Frenz, and Chris Wickham (eds), *The Prospect of Global History* (Oxford: Oxford University Press, 2016), 127–45, 129.

12. See, for example, Ibn Battuta, *The Travels of Ibn Battuta, AD 1325–1354*, Vol. 4, trans./ed. by H. A. R. Gibb and C. F. Beckingham (London: Hakluyt Society, 1994), 817, i.e. his account of a Shii merchant community from Iraq in Kawlam (Quilon). Although on other occasions, such as when a Shii Sayyid working at the court of Uzbek Khan introduces him to the Khan, he does not mention the former's sectarian identity. Morimoto, 'Sayyid Ibn 'Abd al-Ḥamīd', 680; Syed Ali Nadeem Rezavi, 'The State, Shia's and Shi'ism in Medieval India', *Studies in People's History* 4, 1 (2017), 32–45, 33.

13. Rizvi, *A Socio-Intellectual History*, Vol. 1, 149f.

14. Ibid., 157f. For examples of anti-Shii publications and actions during his reign, see Rezavi, 'The State, Shia's and Shi'ism', 33f.

15. Rizvi, *A Socio-Intellectual History*, Vol. 1, 158f.

16. Zahir ud-Din Muhammad Babur, *The Baburnama: Memoirs of Babur, Prince and Emperor*, trans./ed. by Wheeler M. Thackston (New York: Modern Library, 2002), 8f., 22.

17. The coalition of Uzbeks was of a different ethnicity than Timur's Chagatai section of Turco-Mongols, of whom the Mughals were a part. Babur described himself in his autobiography as the inheritor of the Timurid religio-political legacy critical of Shiism. In his portrayal of Hussain Bayqara, for example, he emphasised that the latter was thinking of including the Twelve Imams in the prayer, but was discouraged from doing so. In this and other passages of the *Baburnama*, he emphasises the importance of sticking to Sunni orthodoxy. Stephen F. Dale, *Babur: Timurid Prince and Mughal Emperor, 1483–1530* (Cambridge: Cambridge University Press, 2018), 71ff., 78, 96ff.; A. Azfar Moin, 'Peering through the Cracks in the Baburnama: The Textured Lives of Mughal Sovereigns', *Indian Economic & Social History Review* 49, 4 (2012), 493–526, 501–4.

18. Eaton, *India in the Persianate Age*, 200; Roemer, 'The Successors of Tīmūr', 126f.

19. Dale, *Babur*, 96ff.; Rizvi, *A Socio-Intellectual History*, Vol. 1, 189ff. For Babur, the Uzbeks, and the Safavids, see Haarmann, 'Staat und Religion in Transoxanien', 333–9. For a general narrative of the period, see I. H. Qureshi, 'India under the Mughals', in: P. M. Holt, Ann K. S. Lambton, and Bernard Lewis (eds), *The Cambridge History of Islam*, Vol. 2A (Cambridge: Cambridge University Press, 1977), 35–63.

20. Eaton, *India in the Persianate Age*, 205; Rizvi, *A History of Sufism in India*, Vol. 2, 180f. See in general also Richard Foltz, 'The Central Asian Naqshbandī Connections of the Mughal Emperors', *Journal of Islamic Studies* 7, 2 (1996), 229–39.

21. N. C. Mehta, 'An Unpublished Testament of Babur', *The Twentieth Century* (1936), 339–44, 340, quoted in: Anthony Black, *The History of Islamic Political Thought: From the Prophet to the Present* (New York: Routledge, 2001), 239. Another translation is: 'Overlook the dissensions of the Shias and the Sunnis,

else the weakness of Islam is manifest.' Quoted in: Rajendra Prasad, *India Divided* (New Delhi: Penguin, 2010), 51.

22. S. Dale, 'India under Mughal Rule', in: D. Morgan and A. Reid (eds), *The New Cambridge History of Islam*, Vol. 3 (Cambridge: Cambridge University Press, 2010), 266–314, 267.

23. Muzaffar Alam, 'Trade, State Policy and Regional Change: Aspects of Mughal-Uzbek Commercial Relations, c. 1550–1750', *Journal of the Economic and Social History of the Orient* 37, 3 (1994), 202–27; Stephen F. Dale, *Indian Merchants and Eurasian Trade, 1600–1750* (Cambridge: Cambridge University Press, 1994).

24. Humayun also visited the Imam Rida shrine at Mashhad. Eaton, *India in the Persianate Age*, 212f.; Rizvi, *A Socio-Intellectual History*, Vol. 1, 192–9; Quinn, 'Iran under Safavid Rule', 211f.; Saiyid Athar Abbas Rizvi, *Religious and Intellectual History of Muslims in Akbar's Reign: With Special Reference to Abu'l Fazl (1556–1605)* (New Delhi: Munshiram Manoharlal, 1975), 51; Eskandar Beg Monshi, *History of Shah 'Abbās the Great (Tārīkh-e 'Ālamārā-ye 'Abbāsī)*, trans. by Roger M. Savory, Vol. 1 (Boulder, CO: Westview Press, 1978), 164f.

25. Rizvi, *A Socio-Intellectual History*, Vol. 1, 197ff. See also Afzal Husain, 'Liberty and Restraint: A Study of Shiaism in the Mugial Nobility', *Proceedings of the Indian History Congress* 42 (1981), 275–88; Husain, 'Accommodation and Integration: Shi'as in the Mughal Nobility', *Proceedings of the Indian History Congress* 69 (2008), 211–24.

26. Sri Ram Sharma, *The Religious Policy of the Mughal Emperors* (Bombay: H. Milford/Oxford University Press, 1940), 16.

27. Ibid., 10, 18; Douglas E. Streusand, 'Bayrām Khān', *EI3*. Bairam Khan also served as a liaison between Shah Tahmasp and Humayun when the latter was in Iran and sought the Shah's help. N. H. Ansari, 'BAYRAM KHAN', *EIr*. Bairam Khan's wife, on the other hand, was the daughter of a Naqshbandi Shaykh who had married one of Babur's daughters. After Bairam Khan's death, she became one of Akbar's wives. Bairam Khan himself has at times been described as a disciple of an Iranian Naqshbandi. Stephen F. Dale, 'The Legacy of the Timurids', *Journal of the Royal Asiatic Society* 8, 1 (1998), 43–58, 49. Rizvi says that the evidence for Bairam Khan's Shiism is inconclusive and that he did not openly advertise Shii beliefs. Rizvi, *A Socio-Intellectual History*, Vol. 1, 199–205.

28. C. Collin Davies, 'Akbar', *EI2*; Douglas E. Streusand, 'Akbar', *EI3*. Subsequent Mughal rulers further expanded that shrine. Eaton, *India in the Persianate Age*, 234; P. M. Currie, *The Shrine and Cult of Mu'īn al-Dīn Chishtī of Ajmer* (Oxford: Oxford University Press, 1989).

29. See Syed Ali Nadeem Rezavi (ed.), *Fathpur Sikri Revisited* (New Delhi: Oxford University Press, 2013).

30. Rizvi, *A Socio-Intellectual History*, Vol. 1, 213–9; Rizvi, *Religious and Intellectual History*, 107–31, esp. 124f.; Syed Ali Nadeem Rezavi, 'Religious Disputations and Imperial Ideology: The Purpose and Location of Akbar's Ibadatkhana', *Studies in History* 24, 2 (2008), 195–209, 201f.

31. Eaton, *India in the Persianate Age*, 235.

32. Tadd Fernée, *Enlightenment and Violence: Modernity and Nation-Making* (New Delhi: Sage, 2014), ch. 1.

33. Rizvi, *Religious and Intellectual History*. For a new translation, see Abu'l Fazl, *The History of Akbar*, ed./trans. by Wheeler M. Thackston, 8 Vols (Cambridge, MA: Harvard University Press, 2015–22).

34. André Wink, *Akbar* (Oxford: Oneworld, 2009), 104. He claimed to be a greater leader than Saladin because he managed to unite Sunna and Shia and have Hindus play an important military role. Black, *The History of Islamic Political Thought*, 244.

35. Rizvi, *A Socio-Intellectual History*, Vol. 1, 218f.

36. Rizvi, 'Shī'i Polemics', 55; Rizvi, *A Socio-Intellectual History*, Vol. 1, 199–203. Undermining notions of a harmonious religious life under the Mughals, some chronicles frequently employ strong anti-Shii references, describing Shiism as a threat to the imperial polity. This can be seen in 'Abdul Qadir al-Badauni, *Muntakhab al-Tawarikh*, 3 Vols (Calcutta: Asiatic Society, 1898–1925), for example Vol. 2, 318, 327, 365, 376. For more, see Rizvi, *A Socio-Intellectual History*, Vol. 1, 4f., 235; Jamal Malik, *Islamische Gelehrtenkultur in Nordindien: Entwicklungsgeschichte und Tendenzen am Beispiel von Lucknow* (Leiden: Brill, 1997), 90, 93.

37. This refers to Mir Abdul Latif. Quoted in the *Akbarnama* of Abu'l Fazl in: Rizvi, *A Socio-Intellectual History*, Vol. 1, 206; Rizvi, *Religious and Intellectual History*, 52f. See also Reyaz Ahmad Khan, 'Naqib Khan: Secretary to Emperors Akbar and Jahangir', *Proceedings of the Indian History Congress* 74 (2013), 240–4.

38. Hodgson, *Venture*, Vol. 3, 83; Rizvi, 'Shī'i Polemics', 58. There are also some prominent examples of Persian migrants to India sponsoring religious building projects in Iran, such as the case of the Masjed-e Hakim in Isfahan, which was built in 1067–73/1656–63 and commissioned by Hakim Muhammad Dawud, a Jew who had converted to Shiism and initially served the Safavids and then joined Shah Jahan's court, where he became wealthy. Sussan Babaie with Robert Haug, 'Isfahan x. Monuments (3) Mosques', *EIr*.

39. Rizvi, *A Socio-Intellectual History*, Vol. 1, 207.

40. Lisa Balabanlilar, *Imperial Identity in the Mughal Empire: Memory and Dynastic Politics in Early Modern South and Central Asia* (London: I. B. Tauris, 2012).

41. Nile Green, *Indian Sufism since the Seventeenth Century: Saints, Books and Empires in the Muslim Deccan* (London: Routledge, 2006), 29.

42. Muzaffar Alam, 'The Pursuit of Persian: Language in Mughal Politics', *Modern Asian Studies* 32, 2 (1998), 317–49, 319f.

43. Eaton, *India in the Persianate Age*, 225f. In particular the *Akhlaq-i Nasiri* (*Nasirean Ethics*), which may have come to India with Babur by way of Timurid Central Asia and its more ecumenical tradition. Muzaffar Alam, *The Languages of Political Islam: India 1200–1800* (London: Hurst, 2004), 50ff.

44. Rizvi, 'Shī'i Polemics', 57f.

45. Rizvi, *A Socio-Intellectual History*, Vol. 1, 208f.

46. Rizvi, *Religious and Intellectual History*, 53.

47. For other examples, see Rezavi, 'The State, Shia's and Shi'ism', 38ff.

48. Subsequently, despite the split with the Sunni Bohras and political repression, the Ismaili Shii Bohras, called Tayyibi Bohras, became more important in terms of numbers and finance than the Ismailis in Yemen, who were suffering in the sixteenth century from the Ottoman invasion of Yemen and at the hands of anti-Ismaili Zaydi Imams. A further split occurred in the Tayyibi Bohra community, with one leadership permanently based in India and henceforth called Daudis, while another branch continued to follow the Da'is in Yemen and became known as Suleimanis. Daftary, *The Ismailis*, 276–81; Jonah Blank, *Mullahs on the Mainframe: Islam and Modernity among the Daudi Bohras* (Chicago: University of Chicago Press, 2001), 36–41.

49. Daftary, *The Ismailis*, 280f.; Samira Sheikh, 'Aurangzeb as Seen from Gujarat: Shi'i and Millenarian Challenges to Mughal Sovereignty', *Journal of the Royal Asiatic Society* 28, 3 (2018), 557–81, 574; M. A. E. Dockrat, *Between Orthodoxy and Mysticism: The Life and Works of Shaikh Muhammad ibn Tahir al-Fattani (914/1508–986/1578)* (PhD, University of South Africa, 2002), esp. 65–9.

50. Rizvi, 'Shī'i Polemics', 55. For more on him, see Rizvi, *A Socio-Intellectual History*, Vol. 1, 342–87. Badauni, no friend of the Shia, writes of him: 'Although he is by religion a Shia he is distinguished for his impartiality, justice, virtue, modesty, piety, continence, and such qualities as are possessed by noble men, and is well known for his learning, clemency, quickness of understanding, singleness of heart, clearness of perception, and acumen.' Badauni then recalls a story in which Shustari adopted the Shii point of view in a discussion over a Hadith on the succession to the Prophet. Al-Badauni, *Muntakhab al-Tawarikh*, Vol. 3, 193ff. Abu'l Fazl also refers to him as a Shii, albeit initially practising *taqiyya*: 'He came from Shustar and was introduced to Akbar by Hakím Abul Fath. He was a Shia, but practised taqiyya among Sunnis, and was even well acquainted with the law of Abu Hanifa. When Shaikh Mu'in, Qazi of Lahore, retired, he was appointed his successor, and gave every satisfaction. After Jahangir's accession, he was recalled. Once he offended the emperor by a hasty word, and was executed.' Abu'l Fazl, *The Aín-i Akbari*, Vol. 1, trans. by H. Blochmann (Calcutta: Asiatic Society, 1873), 545.

51. In a letter to a high religious official in Safavid Iran, he wrote: 'Through divine grace and blessings, I obtained a lofty position and the honour of the companionship of the emperor [whose] patronage and favours increase daily. In these circumstances, I came to the conclusion that in India, taqiya was a great calamity. [...] Reinforced by the kindness and the bounty of the Sultan, I threw away the scarf of taqiya from my shoulders and, taking with me an army of arguments, I plunged myself into Jihad against the Sunni "'ulama" of this country.' Quoted in: Rizvi, 'Shī'i Polemics', 56. For more, see Wayne R. Husted, *Shahid-i Salis Qazi Nurullah Shushtari: An Historical Figure in Shi'ite Piety* (PhD, University of Wisconsin-Madison, 1992).

52. Rizvi, 'Shī'i Polemics', 58f.; Rizvi, *A Socio-Intellectual History*, Vol. 1, 370–6; Ja'fariyan, *Tarikh-i Tashayyu' dar Iran*, Vol. 2, 807–13.

53. Goldziher, *Beiträge*, 50–77.

54. Alam, *The Languages of Political Islam*, 68f.

55. Nurullah Ibn Abdallah Shushtari, *Kitab-i Mustatab-i Majalis al-Muminin*, 2 Vols (Tehran: Kitabfurush-i Islamiyya, 1998/99). See also Rizvi, 'Shī'i Polemics', 56; Rizvi, *A Socio-Intellectual History*, Vol. 1, 351–7, 365–8.

56. A. S. Bazmee Ansari, 'D̲j̲ahāngīr', *EI2*; Rizvi, 'Shī'i Polemics', 64–7. See also Rizvi, *Muslim Revivalist Movements*, 314–23. For records of Jahangir's conversations on the matter, see Reyaz Ahmad Khan, 'Jahangir on Shias and Sunnis in Majalis-i Jahangiri', *Proceedings of the Indian History Congress* 72 (2011), 302–7; Shireen Moosvi, 'The Conversations of Jahangir 1608-11: Table Talk on Religion', *Proceedings of the Indian History Congress* 68 (2007), 326–31.

57. Eaton, *India in the Persianate Age*, 247–50. For more on Persian officials at his court, see Corinne Lefèvre, *Pouvoir impérial et élites dans l'Inde moghole de Jahāngīr (1605–1627)* (Paris: Les Indes Savantes, 2017), 201–21.

58. 'Followers of various religions and a place in the broad scope of his peerless empire—unlike other countries of the world, like Iran, where there is room for only Shiites, and Rum, Turan, and Hindustan, where there is room for only Sunnis. Just as all groups and the practitioners of all religions have a place within the spacious circle of God's mercy, in accordance with the dictum that a shadow must follow its source, in my father's realm, which ended at the salty sea, there was room for practitioners of various sects and beliefs, both true and imperfect, and strife and altercation were not allowed. Sunni and Shiite worshiped in one mosque, and Frank and Jew in one congregation.' Jahangir, *The Jahangirnama: Memoirs of Jahangir, Emperor of India*, trans. by Wheeler M. Thackston (New York: Oxford University Press, 1999), 40. See also Rezavi, 'The State, Shia's and Shi'ism', 41. Otherwise, his memoirs contain almost no mention of Shiism, only mentioning that in Kashmir a large section of the military are Imami Shia. Sajida S. Alvi, 'Religion and State during the Reign of Mughal Emperor Jahăngǐr (1605–27): Nonjuristical Perspectives', *Studia Islamica* 69 (1989), 95–119, 112; Alvi, *Perspectives on Mughal India: Rulers, Historians, 'Ulamā and Sufis* (Oxford: Oxford University Press, 2012), 219–31. The book on the art of government is Muhammad Baqir, *Advice on the Art of Governance: Mau'iẓah-i Jahāngīrī of Muḥammad Bāqir Najm-i S̲ānī: An Indo-Islamic Mirror for Princes*, trans. by Sajida S. Alvi (Albany: SUNY Press, 1989), 11ff., 31. However, there was little specifically Shii about this book. Ibid., 113n88.

59. Rezavi, 'The State, Shia's and Shi'ism', 42; Rizvi, 'Shī'i Polemics', 64; Rizvi, *A History of Sufism in India*, Vol. 2, 372; Rizvi, *Muslim Revivalist Movements*, 286–302. According to Sirhindi's biographers, it was Shii influence at court that got him arrested (a view Jahangir himself refuted in his autobiography, however). Weismann, *The Naqshbandiyya*, 56.

60. *Maktubat-i Imam Rabbani*, Vol. 1 (Lucknow: Nawal Kishore, n.d.), letter 54, cited after: Irfan M. Habib, 'The Political Role of Shaikh Ahmad Sirhindi and Shah Waliullah', *Proceedings of the Indian History Congress* 23 (1960), 209–23, 211.

61. Rizvi, *A History of Sufism in India*, Vol. 2, 198–223; Rizvi, *Muslim Revivalist Movements*, 207f., 226, 238f.; Annemarie Schimmel, *Mystical Dimensions of Islam* (Chapel Hill, NC: University of North Carolina Press, 1975), 367.

62. Alvi, 'Religion and State', 111f.; Ellison Banks Findly, *Nur Jahan: Empress of Mughal India* (Oxford: Oxford University Press, 1993), 209ff.; Habib, 'The Political Role', 213, 221n34.

63. For the general notion, see Monica Corrado, *Mit Tradition in die Zukunft: Der taǧdīd-Diskurs in der Azhar und ihrem Umfeld* (Würzburg: Ergon, 2011); John Obert Voll, 'Renewal and Reform in Islamic History: Tajdid and Islah', in: John L. Esposito (ed.), *Voices of Resurgent Islam* (New York: Oxford University Press, 1983), 32–47.

64. Rizvi, *Muslim Revivalist Movements*, 202–60. For Sirhindi, see Yohanan Friedmann, *Shaykh Ahmad Sirhindi: An Outline of his Thought and a Study of his Image in the Eyes of Posterity* (Montreal: McGill University, 1971). For an attempt to put Sirhindi's writings in the sociological and historical context of his time, see Arthur F. Buehler, 'Ahmad Sirhindī: A 21st-Century Update', *Der Islam* 86, 1 (2011), 122–41. See also Warren Edward Fusfeld, *The Shaping of Sufi Leadership in Delhi: The Naqshbandiyya Mujaddidiyya, 1750 to 1920* (PhD, University of Pennsylvania, 1981).

65. Muzaffar Alam, 'The Mughals, the Sufi Shaikhs and the Formation of the Akbari Dispensation', *Modern Asian Studies* 43, 1 (2009), 135–74, 157–63; Lefèvre, *Pouvoir impérial*, 295–312.

66. See Arthur F. Buehler, 'The Naqshbandiyya in Tīmūrid India: The Central Asian Legacy', *Journal of Islamic Studies* 7, 2 (1996), 208–28, 219ff.

67. Dale, 'The Legacy of the Timurids', 43–51.

68. I thank Professor Syed Ali Nadeem Rezavi from Aligarh Muslim University in India for this point. Rezavi, 'The State, Shia's and Shi'ism', 42; Rizvi, *Shāh Walī-Allāh*, 190–5; Afzal Husain, 'Accommodation and Integration: Shi'as in the Mughal Nobility', *Proceedings of the Indian History Congress* 69 (2008), 211–24, 222. Francisco Pelsaert mentions Muharram processions in Agra in the 1620s. Francisco Pelsaert, *Jahangir's India: The 'Remonstrantie' of Francisco Pelsaert* (Cambridge: Heffer, 1925). The practice of walking on hot coals carrying *alams* during Muharram is reported by Monserrate, who however thinks that the martyrs of Karbala were killed by Christians. Antonio Monserrate, *The Commentary of Father Monserrate, S. J., on his Journey to the Court of Akbar*, trans. by John S. Hoyland (London: H. Milford/Oxford University Press, 1922), 22. I owe knowledge of this reference to Rezavi, 'The Shia Muslims', 290. The *Dabistan-i Madhahib*, an encyclopaedic work in Persian anonymously produced in seventeenth-century India, which purports to record the different religious groups prevalent at the time, discusses Twelver Shiism and Ismailism, and gives a sense of how religious debates may have played out. It also contains a Surah on Ali that was allegedly purged from the Quran. A. Azfar Moin, 'Dabistān-i madhāhib', *EI3*; David Shea and Anthony Troyer (trans.), *The Dabistán or School of Manners*, 2 Vols (Paris: Oriental Translation Fund, 1843), Vol. 2, 322–36; Rezavi, 'The State, Shia's and Shi'ism', 42; Fath-Allāh Mojtabāī, 'DABESTĀN-E MADĀHEB', *EIr*.

69. Rizvi, *Religious and Intellectual History*, 54f.

70. Rizvi, *A Socio-Intellectual History*, Vol. 1, 166–9.

71. Their rule would lead to the expansion and consolidation of several *khanqahs*. Ibid., 166–86. See also John Norman Hollister, *The Shi'a of India* (London:

Luzac & Co., 1953), 141–50; Annemarie Schimmel, *Islam in the Indian Subcontinent* (Leiden: Brill, 1980), 46f.

72. Rizvi, *A History of Sufism in India*,Vol. 1, 298f.,Vol. 2, 184.

73. In his own historical work, Mirza Haidar boasts of his resoluteness against Shia and Sufis and represses the Shafii school in favour of the Hanafi one. Rizvi, *A Socio-Intellectual History*,Vol. 1, 170–5. See also Darakhshan Abdullah, *Religious Policy of the Sultans of Kashmir (1320–1586 A.D.)* (PhD, University of Kashmir, 1991), 130–49.

74. Rizvi, *A Socio-Intellectual History*,Vol. 1, 176ff.

75. Ibid., 185.

76. Ibid., 178–83. See also Rezavi, 'The State, Shia's and Shi'ism', 36; Abdullah, *Religious Policy*, 150–60.

77. Juan Cole, 'CONVERSION iii.To Imami Shi'ism in India', *EIr*.The sectarian identity of those defectors is not entirely clear. He apparently even gave Shii defectors land grants, a practice that continued until Aurangzib's reign: 'All these men were not of use to the Mogul, since the Moguls are of a different sect, and do not follow Ali as do the Persians, they were sent to the province of Kashmir, where they lived upon their allowances comfortably and without care.' Niccolao Manucci, *Storia do Mogor or Mogul India, 1653–1708*, trans. by William Irvine,Vol. 2 (London: John Murray, 1907), 16; Cole, *Roots*, 25.

78. Rizvi, *A Socio-Intellectual History*,Vol. 1, 184, 364f.

79. Ibid., 185f.; Andreas Rieck, 'The Nurbakhshis of Baltistan: Crisis and Revival of a Five Centuries Old Community', *Die Welt des Islams* 35, 2 (1995), 159–88.

80. The tomb of Sultan Ahmad, for example, contains strong Shii symbolism, but, like the rest of the Nimatullahi order in the fifteenth century, the Bahmani rulers had not publicly proclaimed their Shiism. But the Nimatullahi influence on the Bahmanis facilitated the spread of Shii ideas. Rizvi, *A Socio-Intellectual History*, Vol. 1, 247–56; Rizvi, *A History of Sufism in India*, Vol. 2, 55ff. See also Wolseley Haig, 'The Religion of Ahmad Shah Bahmani', *Journal of the Royal Asiatic Society* 1 (1924), 73–80; Cole, 'CONVERSION'; Muhammad Suleman Siddiqi, 'Sufi–State Relationship under the Bahmanids (A.D. 1348–1538)', *Rivista degli Studi Orientali* 64, 1/2 (1990), 71–96. In the Shii period of the Adil Shahis, on the other hand, the influence of Sufism and the influx of foreign Sufis waned, a development that Eaton explains with Shii hostility towards Sufism born out of the Safavid experience. Richard M. Eaton, *The Sufis of Bijapur, 1300–1700: Social Rules of Sufis in Medieval India* (Princeton: Princeton University Press, 1978), 62–7.

81. The Adil Shahi dynasty only adopted the title 'Shah' in 1536, but for the sake of consistency they are referred to as Adil Shahis here. M. A. Nayeem, *External Relations of the Bijapur Kingdom, 1489–1686 A.D.: A Study in Diplomatic History* (Hyderabad: Bright, 1974), 55.

82. Nayeem, *External Relations*, 33, 48, 54ff., 78f., 115.

83. Ibid., 21f.

84. Eaton, *India in the Persianate Age*, 152.

85. Nayeem, *External Relations*, 49–59. See also Colin Paul Mitchell, 'Sister Shi'a States? Safavid Iran and the Deccan in the 16th Century', *Deccan Studies* 2, 2 (2004), 44–72; Matthee, 'Was Safavid Iran an Empire?', 254f.

86. Eaton, *India in the Persianate Age*, 164; Thomaz, 'Iranian Diaspora', 15.

87. Nayeem, *External Relations*, 60f.

88. Ibid., 56f.; Eaton, *The Sufis of Bijapur*, 67f. Strong Shii references can be found on the coins, in the built environment, and on the *farmans* of at times even the Sunni rulers of Bijapur. Nayeem, *External Relations*, 68. Several Shii clerics also moved to the Deccan in this period. M. Z. A. Shakeb, *Relations of Golkonda with Iran: Diplomacy, Ideas, and Commerce, 1518–1687* (Delhi: Primus, 2017), 115–51.

89. Rizvi, *A Socio-Intellectual History*, Vol. 1, 262–81. For general histories of the Deccan Sultanates, see Muhammad Firishta, *Ferishta's History of Dekkan, from the First Mahummedan Conquests*, trans./ed. by Jonathan Scott, 2 Vols (Cambridge: Cambridge University Press, 2013); J. D. B. Gribble, *History of the Deccan* (New Delhi: Rupa, 2002); Richard M. Eaton, 'INDIA vi. Political and Cultural Relations (13th–18th centuries)', *EIr*; Shakeb, *Relations of Golkonda with Iran*; Deborah S. Hutton, "Ādil Shāhīs', *EI3*; Christopher D. Bahl, *Histories of Circulation: Sharing Arabic Manuscripts across the Western Indian Ocean, 1400–1700* (PhD, University of London, 2018); Hollister, *The Shi'a of India*, 101–25.

90. Thomaz, 'Iranian Diaspora', 9–22; Eaton, *The Sufis of Bijapur*, 42f.

91. Thomaz, 'Iranian Diaspora', 22. Interestingly, a Portuguese wrote in 1608 that, unlike his predecessors, being a Sunni was a factor that would undermine Ibrahim Adil Shah's rule. Flores, *Unwanted Neighbours*, 169. Moreover, Iran's relations with the Deccan Sultanates are even referred to in the post-1979 era. See this book, which emphasises the role that Iranian migrants played in promoting religious harmony and was published 'on the occasion of the historic visit of H. E. Akber Hashemi Rafsanjani, Honourable President of Islamic Republic of Iran to India': Sadiq Naqavi, *The Iran–Deccan Relations* (Hyderabad: Bab-ul-Ilm Society, 1994).

92. Nayeem, *External Relations*, 61–5; Muzaffar Alam and Sanjay Subrahmanyam, *Writing the Mughal World: Studies on Culture and Politics* (New York: Columbia University Press, 2011), 178f.

93. Nayeem, *External Relations*, 73f. Several Sufis migrated to Bijapur in this 'Sunni' period. Eaton, *The Sufis of Bijapur*, 70–5.

94. Nayeem, *External Relations*, 77–117.

95. Roy S. Fischel, 'Niẓām Shāhīs', *EI3*; Fischel, 'Aḥmadnagar', *EI3*; Rizvi, *A Socio-Intellectual History*, Vol. 1, 281–92; Farhad Daftary, 'Husayni, Shah Tahir b. Radi al-Din (d. 956 AH/1549 CE)', *Institute of Ismaili Studies*, https://iis.ac.uk/encyclopaedia-articles/husayni-shah-tahir-b-radi-al-din-d-956-ah-1549-ce; Daftary, *The Ismailis*, 452–5; Anooshahr, *Turkestan*, 161f.; Pushkar Sohoni, 'Patterns of Faith: Mosque Typologies and Sectarian Affiliation in the Kingdom of Ahmadnagar', in: David J. Roxburgh (ed.), *Envisioning Islamic Art and Architecture: Essays in Honor of Renata Holod* (Leiden: Brill, 2014), 109–26; Sohoni,

The Architecture of a Deccan Sultanate: Courtly Practice and Royal Authority in Late Medieval India (London: I. B. Tauris, 2018), 133–64.

96. Andreas Rieck, *The Shias of Pakistan: An Assertive and Beleaguered Minority* (London: Hurst, 2015), 1f.; Rizvi, *A Socio-Intellectual History*, Vol. 1, 292–341.

97. See, amongst many other sources, M. A. Nayeem, *The Heritage of the Qutb Shahis of Golconda and Hyderabad* (Hyderabad: Hyderabad Publishers, 2006), 10–16; Rizvi, *A Socio-Intellectual History*, Vol. 1, 305f. For the limits of that narrative, see J. Burton-Page, 'Ḥaydarābād', *EI2*; Richard M. Eaton and Phillip B. Wagoner, *Power, Memory, Architecture: Contested Sites on India's Deccan Plateau, 1300–1600* (New Delhi: Oxford University Press, 2014), 203–38, esp. 223f.

98. I visited three sites that were said to contain a footprint of the Prophet Muhammad, a hand of Ali, and a part of the shackles of the fourth Imam, Ali bin Hussain 'Zayn al-Abidin', respectively.

99. For a selection of articles on these connections, see Keelan Overton (ed.), *Iran and the Deccan: Persianate Art, Culture, and Talent in Circulation, 1400–1700* (Bloomington: Indiana University Press, 2020).

100. Scott A. Kugle, *When Sun Meets Moon: Gender, Eros, and Ecstasy in Urdu Poetry* (Chapel Hill: University of North Carolina Press, 2016), 120–40. For the development of poetry in Awadh, see Cole, *Roots*, 97f. For other examples, see Denis Hermann, 'Shiism, Sufism and Sacred Space in the Deccan: Counter-Narratives of Saintly Identity in the Cult of Shah Nur', in: Alessandro Monsutti, Silvia Naef, and Farian Sabahi (eds), *The Other Shiites: From the Mediterranean to Central Asia* (Bern: Peter Lang, 2008), 195–218.

101. Baqir, *Advice on the Art of Governance*, 111. But Aurangzib, during the 1687 siege of the Qutb Shahi fort, kept Shia who were in his service, including one of his most senior generals, from the frontlines. Jadunath Sarkar, *History of Aurangzib: Based on Original Sources*, Vol. 3 (Calcutta: M. C. Sarkar, 1921), 366. On the other hand, when a Muslim from Bukhara who entered Mughal service around that time asked the Emperor to deny Persian advancement in the Empire on the grounds that they were Shia, the Emperor refused. Audrey Truschke, *Aurangzeb: The Life and Legacy of India's Most Controversial King* (Palo Alto: Stanford University Press, 2017), 58.

102. Sarkar, *History of Aurangzib*, Vol. 1, 236. For the Mughal-Safavid rivalry over Afghanistan, see Eaton, *India in the Persianate Age*, 292–6. For relations between Shah Abbas II and Aurangzib, see Sarkar, *History of Aurangzib*, Vol. 3, 105–13.

103. When Aurangzib replaced his *Qadi*, Shaikh al-Islam, his successor counselled the same, an advice the Emperor ignored. Sheikh, 'Aurangzeb', 576; Sarkar, *History of Aurangzib*, Vol. 4, 366f. Shaikh al-Islam was the son of the Sunni Bohra cleric that had endorsed Aurangzib's coup against his own father and spurred him to suppress the Shia of Gujarat. Sarkar, *History of Aurangzib*, Vol. 3, 73f.

104. Howarth, *The Twelver Shiʿa*, 12, 20f.

105. Green, *Indian Sufism*, 50.

106. Hodgson, *Venture*, Vol. 3, 93; Alan Guenther, 'Hanafi Fiqh in Mughal India: The Fatāwá-i ʿĀlamgīrī', in: Richard M. Eaton (ed.), *India's Islamic Traditions, 711–1750* (New Delhi: Oxford University Press, 2003), 207–30.

107. Sarkar remarks here in a rather dismissive tone that '[t]he theory that the Sultan of Turkey is the spiritual head of the Muslim world is a fiction of the late nineteenth century, which we owe to the Indian pilgrims to Mecca'. Sarkar, *History of Aurangzib*, Vol. 3, 117f.

108. Debates about his legacy continue, and some of the stark characterisations of earlier periods may have to be revisited. For a recent account, see Truschke, *Aurangzeb*.

109. Aurangzib thus persecuted the Daudi Ismaili Bohras both when he was governor of Gujarat and later as Emperor. He even supervised a kind of re-education programme for Bohras by which they were taught Sunni doctrine by Sunni functionaries, who also took over custodianship of their mosques. In this period, Daudi Ismaili Bohras survived by practising *taqiyya* again. Daftary, *The Ismailis*, 283f.; Eaton, *India in the Persianate Age*, 335f.; Sheikh, 'Aurangzeb'; Sarkar, *History of Aurangzib*, Vol. 3, 100.

110. Sheikh, 'Aurangzeb', 570. For more and possible Shii dimensions of Dara Shukuh's thought, see Craig Davis, *Dara Shukuh and Aurangzib: Issues of Religion and Politics and their Impact on Indo-Muslim Society* (PhD, Indiana University, 2002), esp. 78–83.

111. Richard M. Eaton, *The Rise of Islam and the Bengal Frontier, 1204–1760* (Berkeley: University of California Press, 1993), 168; Richard M. Eaton, N. H. Ansari, and S. H. Qasemi, 'BENGAL', *EIr*.

112. For example prayers for the Imams. Eaton, *The Rise of Islam*, 268. In Jahangirabad, later named Dhaka, today the capital of Bangladesh, some of the Mughal-appointed governors and officials were of Persian Shii origin, and some Shii clerics also settled there in the seventeenth and eighteenth centuries. After the EIC had taken control of the region, some of the local risings against it also had Shii overtones. Rizvi, *A Socio-Intellectual History*, Vol. 2, 127. See also Schimmel, *Islam*, 47–50. The Nawabs continued to patronise Muharram ceremonies and Hussainid shrines until the nineteenth century. Banglapedia, 'Alimullah, Khwaja', http://en.banglapedia.org/index.php?title=Alimullah,_Khwaja; Banglapedia, 'Husaini Dalan', http://en.banglapedia.org/index.php?title=Husaini_Dalan. After the death of the last Nawab, Ghazi al-Din Haydar, in 1843, Shii influence waned. A merchant originally of Kashmiri origin, Khwaja Alimullah, took over the patronage of a shrine in honour of Hussain and the expenses of the annual Muharram celebrations. Sharif Uddin Ahmed, *Dacca: A Study in Urban History and Development* (London: Routledge, 2018), 14f. Apart from Shia, Urdu-speaking Bihari Sunni Muslims organise Muharram ceremonies in Dhaka. There are some marked differences between the two Sunni and Shii versions of the ceremonies, however. See Claire Alexander, Joya Chatterji, and Annu Jalais, *The Bengal Diaspora: Rethinking Muslim Migration* (London: Routledge, 2016), ch. 6.

113. Abhishek Kaicker, *Unquiet City: Making and Unmaking Politics in Mughal Delhi, 1707–39* (PhD, Columbia University, 2014), 389–416, esp. 399ff.
114. Eaton, *India in the Persianate Age*, 341–5; Schimmel, *Islam*, 50f.
115. Nizamat Imambara in Murshidabad, which was rebuilt in 1847, is 680 feet long. P. J. Marshall, *Bengal: The British Bridgehead: Eastern India 1740–1828* (Cambridge: Cambridge University Press, 1988), 31, 69; Humayun Mirza, *From Plassey to Pakistan: The Family History of Iskander Mirza, the First President of Pakistan* (Lahore: Ferozsons, 2000), 21–122, 396–73; Rizvi, *A Socio-Intellectual History*, Vol. 2, 46ff.; Jadunath Sarkar, 'Bengal under Murshid Quli Khan', in: Jadunath Sarkar (ed.), *The History of Bengal*, Vol. 2 (Dhaka: BRPC, 1943), 397–421, 419. See also Richard M. Eaton, N. H. Ansari, and S. H. Qasemi, 'BENGAL', *EIr*.
116. Rizvi, *A Socio-Intellectual History*, Vol. 2, 48. In 1806 and subsequent years, an Iranian cleric, Abu-l-Fath Hasani Hussaini, visited Murshidabad and organised a Shii congregational prayer in a mosque nominally under Sunni control. He read the *khutba* in honour of the Qajar Shah at the time, Fath Ali Shah, to which some Sunnis strongly objected and complained to the EIC governor general. Hussaini also claims to have engaged in Sunni–Shia disputations and, in Madras, to have issued a fatwa to a Shii prohibiting service with the EIC. Ibid., 126f.
117. For this period, see Muzaffar Alam, *The Crisis of Empire in Mughal North India: Awadh and the Punjab, 1707–48* (New Delhi: Oxford University Press, 1986); Barbara N. Ramusack, *The Indian Princes and their States* (Cambridge: Cambridge University Press, 2004), 24ff.; Eaton, *India in the Persianate Age*, 346–50.
118. The Shii ruler was Nawab Nizam Ali Khan Asaf Jah II (r. 1175/1761–1218/1803), the second Nizam, who reinstituted Shii practices abolished under his predecessor and built Ashurkhanas. Patronage of Shiism declined again under the third and fourth Nizam, until they changed again under the fifth Nizam, Afzal al-Dawla (r. 1857–69), who had a Shii prime minister, Sir Salar Jung I, who patronised Shiism and brought Shii administrators and clerics to Hyderabad. Rizvi, *A Socio-Intellectual History*, Vol. 1, 341. See also Barbara D. Metcalf, *Islamic Revival in British India: Deoband, 1860–1900* (Princeton: Princeton University Press, 1982), 41; Umar Khalidi, 'The Shi'ites of the Deccan: An Introduction', *Rivista degli Studi Orientali* 64, 1/2 (1990), 5–16, 7f. See also other articles in that special issue of *Rivista degli Studi Orientali* entitled 'Glances on Shi'ite Deccan Culture'; Howarth, *The Twelver Shi'a*, esp. 20–5; Karen G. Ruffle, *Gender, Sainthood, and Everyday Practice in South Asian Shi'ism* (Chapel Hill: University of North Carolina Press, 2011).
119. Khalidi, 'The Shi'ites of the Deccan', 8ff.
120. See in general Hollister, *The Shi'a of India*, 151–63.
121. Malik, *Islamische Gelehrtenkultur*, 52–62. Asaf al-Dawla also gave direct aid to the Hindu reformer Jagjivan Das of Kotwa, founder of the Satnami sect. Christopher A. Bayly, 'The Pre-History of "Communalism"? Religious Conflict in India, 1700–1860', *Modern Asian Studies* 19, 2 (1985), 177–203, 182f. This was a result of a process that intensified in the seventeenth and eighteenth centuries,

whereby more Muslims became landowners (*zamindars*), facilitated by their position as judges and officials in the Mughal polity, which came at the expense of Hindus and contributed to tensions with the latter. Ibid., 189–93. Because most of their subjects were Hindu, the rulers of Mahmudabad, who were governing a township in the Awadhi countryside and had become Shii through marriage, were given the title of Raja (a title for a ruler ruling over many Hindu subjects) by the Mughals. Interview with Suleiman, the Raja of Mahmudabad, Mahmudabad, 2019. For Hindu–Shia relations in Awadh, see Cole, *Roots*, 224–9.

122. Ashirbadi Lal Srivastava, *The First Two Nawabs of Awadh*, 2nd ed. (Agra: Shiva Lal Agarwala, 1954), 59–73; Cole, *Roots*, 41. A report of a conversation between Nadir Shah and Burhan al-Mulk after his capture refers to Burhan al-Mulk's Persian origin with a surprising reference to Shiism from Nadir Shah, who was known for his pan-Islamic policy: 'You are a Persian (like us) and yet without any regard for our common faith (Shiaism), you were the first to come to fight us.' Srivastava, *The First Two Nawabs*, 65.

123. Cole, *Roots*, 45; Srivastava, *The First Two Nawabs*, 89–98, 152, 225, 227, 243.

124. William Dalrymple, *The Anarchy: The East India Company, Corporate Violence, and the Pillage of an Empire* (London: Bloomsbury, 2019), 196–203.

125. P. Basu, *The Relations between Oudh and the East India Company from 1785 to 1801* (PhD, University of London, 1938); Cole, *Roots*, 252ff.

126. Richard B. Barnett, *North India between Empires: Awadh, the Mughals, and the British, 1720–1801* (Berkeley: University of California Press, 1980).

127. The coronation ceremony took place on 9 October 1819, which was the day of Ghadir Khumm, where Shia believe Ali was designated by the Prophet as his successor. It thus had Shii connotations and may have been a way to symbolise the righteousness of the Shii Awadhi rulers and the illegitimacy of the 'Sunni' Mughals. Before the actual coronation, the whole party, made up of Awadhi nobility and EIC officials, went to the replica of the Abbas shrine outside of Lucknow. In subsequent years, EIC residents, wary that they, not the Shii *mujtahids*, should be seen as bestowing legitimacy on the King, assumed the role of giving the crown to the ruler, who put it on his own head. Michael H. Fisher, 'The Imperial Coronation of 1819: Awadh, the British and the Mughals', *Modern Asian Studies* 19, 2 (1985), 239–77, 261ff.; Cole, *Roots*, 174–7.

128. After sealing marriage alliances with Shii families at the Mughal court and some of the local Shii notables of the Awadhi townships, they forced a Mughal prince residing in Lucknow to give a daughter in marriage to an Awadhi ruler, symbolising their equality if not superiority to the Mughals. Michael H. Fisher, 'Political Marriage Alliances at the Shi'i Court of Awadh', *Comparative Studies in Society and History* 25, 4 (1983), 593–616.

129. Fisher, 'The Imperial Coronation', 267f.

130. Hussein Keshani, 'Imāmbāra', *EI3*.

131. William Howard Russell, *My Diary in India, in the Year 1858–9* (Cambridge: Cambridge University Press, 2011), 257; Cole, *Roots*, 94.

132. In general, the Usuli clerics supported the holding of Friday prayers, while the Akhbaris of India opposed it. It was eventually ironically an alliance of Usuli clerics and local Sufis, with a background in the Sunni Chishtiyya order but now embracing Imami Shiism, that convinced the rulers to start the practice in 1786. Initially started in Lucknow, Friday prayers were then also held in Faizabad, Nasirabad, Deoghata, Amroha, Patna, and elsewhere, often in newly built Friday prayer mosques. Cole, *Roots*, 127–37.

133. To facilitate possible conversions by Hindus, the egalitarian character of Islam was emphasised (as opposed to caste-based Hinduism), Hindu elements were incorporated into the processions, and songs lamenting Karbala were sung in patterns adopted from Hindu music. Dalits ('untouchables') participated in the rituals as drummers, and it was not uncommon for them to convert to escape their caste in Hinduism. There are many records of Shia and Sunni Muslims as well as Hindus participating in the processions. Hollister, *The Shi'a of India*, 175–80. See also Keith Guy Hjortshoj, 'Shi'i Identity and the Significance of Muharram in Lucknow, India', in: Martin Kramer (ed.), *Shi'ism, Resistance, and Revolution* (Boulder, CO: Westview Press, 1987), 289–309. This is a process that is ongoing. Personal observations during fieldwork in Lucknow, India, during Muharram 2019, and interviews with Ali Khan Mahmudabad and participants of Muharram, Mahmudabad, 2019.

134. For Muharram and popular Shiism in Awadh under the Nawabs, see Cole, *Roots*, 92–119. For clashes during Muharram, especially in the 1820s, see ibid., 240–3. The Shii clerics, rulers, and administrators also took a different stance from Sunnis on the Ayodhya mosque issue, which emerged in 1855 in Ayodhya, a suburb of Faizabad, and thus under Awadhi control. Ibid., 244–9.

135. Sajjad H. Rizvi, 'Faith Deployed for a New Shi'i Polity in India', in: Justin Jones and Ali Usman Qasmi (eds), *The Shi'a in Modern South Asia: Religion, History and Politics* (Cambridge: Cambridge University Press, 2015), 12–35, 16ff., 35; Rizvi, *A Socio-Intellectual History*, Vol. 2, 128–39; Juan R. Cole, *Sacred Space and Holy War: The Politics, Culture and History of Shi'ite Islam* (London: I. B. Tauris, 2002), 74–7; Cole, *Roots*, 21, 134f., 152–69.

136. Cole, *Roots*, 178–83, 189–204.

137. Malik, *Islamische Gelehrtenkultur*, 86–95, 493; Sharif Husain Qasemi, 'FATḤ-ALLĀH ŠĪRĀZĪ, SAYYED MĪR', *EIr*. Badauni claims that Akbar knew he was a Shii, although he was taken aback at how openly Shirazi practised his Shiism. Al-Badauni, *Muntakhab al-Tawarikh*, Vol. 2, 325.

138. Asad Q. Ahmed, 'Dars-i Niẓāmī', *EI3*; Francis Robinson, *The 'Ulama of Farangi Mahall and Islamic Culture in South Asia* (New Delhi: Permanent Black, 2001), 41–68.

139. Interview with a descendant of the Farangi Mahall family, Lucknow, 2019; Robinson, *The 'Ulama of Farangi Mahall*, 223; Cole, *Roots*, 61ff., 128ff.; Metcalf, *Islamic Revival*, 29–34.

140. By clerics from the Naqshbandiyya and the Ahl-i Hadith. Robinson, *The 'Ulama of Farangi Mahall*, 27–30; Malik, *Islamische Gelehrtenkultur*, 168–86.

141. Interestingly, when one Nawab previously tried to install a Shii judiciary, the Usuli clerics were not interested but rather content to have the Sunni Farangi Mahall clerics occupy these delicate positions. This at times inevitably brought conflict with the rulers, and/or accusations of subservience to state power. Cole, *Roots*, 139ff., 209–13; Malik, *Islamische Gelehrtenkultur*, 162–8.

142. The Shahi Madrasa was founded in 1843 in Lucknow (but closed again upon British annexation). Cole, *Roots*, 204–9; Syed Najmul Raza Rizvi, 'Shi'a Madaris of Awadh: Historical Development and Present Situation', in: Jan-Peter Hartung and Helmut Reifeld (eds), *Islamic Education, Diversity and National Identity: Dīnī Madāris in India Post 9/11* (New Delhi: Sage, 2006), 104–31, 107–12; Justin Jones, *Shi'a Islam in Colonial India: Religion, Community and Sectarianism* (Cambridge: Cambridge University Press, 2012), 55.

143. The most famous case is that of Bahr al-Ulum. Francis Robinson, *Jamal Mian: The Life of Maulana Jamaluddin Abdul Wahab of Farangi Mahall, 1919–2012* (Karachi: Oxford University Press, 2017), 18–22. See also Malik, *Islamische Gelehrtenkultur*, 129–86, esp. 155, 160–8; Muhammad Ahmad Munir and Brian Wright, 'Fatwās of 'Abd al-Ḥayy of Farangī Maḥall and Their Role in the Formation of Sunnī Identity in British India', *Journal of Islamic Thought and Civilization* 11, 2 (2021), 20–43.

144. Christopher A. Bayly, *Rulers, Townsmen and Bazaars: North Indian Society in the Age of British Expansion, 1770–1870* (Cambridge: Cambridge University Press, 1983), 132–5.

145. Cole, *Roots*, 229–33; Jones, *Shi'a Islam*, 10ff. In Amroha, for example, home to an important Shii Sayyid community, Shiism was strengthened at the expense of the Chishtiyya and the Naqshbandi-Mujaddidiya. Malik, *Islamische Gelehrtenkultur*, 58–61; Justin Jones, 'The Local Experiences of Reformist Islam in a "Muslim" Town in Colonial India: The Case of Amroha', *Modern Asian Studies* 43, 4 (2009), 871–908. Another example are the Nawabs of Rampur, who converted to Shiism in the mid-nineteenth century. Metcalf, *Islamic Revival*, 41; Bayly, 'The Pre-History of "Communalism"?', 185f.

146. Cole, *Roots*, 72–84.

147. Ibid.

148. Conversion was a drawn-out process and could involve families splitting along sectarian lines, including over inheritance disputes. The family of the later Rajas of Mahmudabad had become Shii through marriage. A Sunni man had married a Shii wife, and their son eventually adopted Shiism (but another branch of the family initially remained Sunni). They had originally traced their lineage back to the Prophet through Abu Bakr, giving them some prestige amongst local Sunnis. Interview with Suleiman, the Raja of Mahmudabad, Mahmudabad, September 2019. See also Muhammad Amir Ahmad Khan, 'Local Nodes of a Transnational Network', in: Justin Jones and Ali Usman

Qasmi (eds), *The Shi'a in Modern South Asia: Religion, History and Politics* (Cambridge: Cambridge University Press, 2015), 57–79; Cole, *Roots*, 103f.

149. Tahir Kamran and Amir Khan Shahid, 'Shari'a, Shi'as and Chishtiya Revivalism: Contextualising the Growth of Sectarianism in the Tradition of the Sialvi Saints of the Punjab', *Journal of the Royal Asiatic Society* 24, 3 (2014), 477–92.

150. Rizvi, *A History of Sufism in India*, Vol. 2, 252–9; Rizvi, *Shāh Walī-Allāh*, 207, 214f.; Marcia Hermansen, ''Abd al-Raḥīm Dihlawī', *EI3*; Hermansen, 'DEHLAVĪ, ŠĀH WALĪ-ALLĀH QOṬB-AL-DĪN AḤMAD ABU'L-FAYYĀẒ', *EIr*.

151. J. O. Voll, 'Hadith Scholars and Tarīqahs: An Ulama Group in the 18th Century Haramayn and their Impact in the Islamic World', *Journal of Asian and African Studies* 15, 3 (1980), 264–73.

152. The original argument is made by J. O. Voll, 'Muḥammad Ḥayyā al-Sindī and Muḥammad ibn 'Abd al-Wahhab: An Analysis of an Intellectual Group in Eighteenth-Century Madīna', *Bulletin of the School of Oriental and African Studies* 38, 1 (1975), 32–9. See also Charles Allen, 'The Hidden Roots of Wahhabism in British India', *World Policy Journal* 22, 2 (2005), 87–93; Basheer M. Nafi, 'A Teacher of Ibn 'Abd al-Wahhāb: Muḥammad Ḥayāt al-Sindī and the Revival of Asḥāb al-Ḥadīth's Methodology', *Islamic Law and Society* 13, 2 (2006), 208–41; J. O. Voll, ''Abdallah ibn Salim al-Basri and 18th Century Hadith Scholarship', *Die Welt des Islams* 42, 3 (2002), 356–72.

153. For the 'Wahhabi' threat in India, see Preckel, *Islamische Bildungsnetzwerke*, 503–19; Julia Stephens, 'The Phantom Wahhabi: Liberalism and the Muslim Fanatic in Mid-Victorian India', *Modern Asian Studies* 47, 1 (2013), 22–52.

154. Rieck, *The Shias of Pakistan*, 15f.; Rizvi, *A History of Sufism in India*, Vol. 2, 376ff.; Rizvi, *Shāh Walī-Allāh*, 221, 227, 229, 249–56, 269–73, 315f., 396f.; Metcalf, *Islamic Revival*, 40ff. Another Naqshbandi, on the other hand, Shaykh Sulayman Qunduzi (d. 1877), wrote a compendium on the *Ahl al-Bayt* that is frequently cited and reprinted by Shii publishing houses. Algar, 'Naqshbandis and Safavids', 47. It has been argued that Shah Wali Allah managed a rapprochement between Naqshbandis and Chishtis in India. Moin Ahmad Nizami, *Reform and Renewal in South Asian Islam: The Chishti-Sabris in 18th–19th Century North India* (New Delhi: Oxford University Press, 2017), 98ff.

155. Rizvi, *Shāh Walī-Allāh*, 296ff.

156. Jos J. L. Gommans, *The Rise of the Indo-Afghan Empire, c. 1710–1780* (Leiden: Brill, 1994), 127, 142.

157. But for him, and for others, Shii tendencies could be used by their enemies to accuse them of disloyalty. In this case, it was a Sunni minister, Abdul Ahad Khan, who, jealous of Najaf Khan, sought to convince Shah Alam that Najaf Khan was trying to build an alliance with the Shii rulers of Awadh to replace the Mughals. Dalrymple, *The Anarchy*, 282. Najaf Khan was responsible for renaming Ramgarh to Aligarh, in honour of Ali, after his conquest of the place. Ibid., 281; Rizvi, *Shah 'Abd al-'Aziz*, 22–9.

158. This was the famous Naqshbandi poet from Delhi, Mirza Mazhar Jan-i Janan, who was widely seen as a staunch advocate of the Sunna and even termed *sunnitarash*, 'sunniciser'. On the other hand, he had written that it was permissible

for a Hanafi to convert to Shiism and vice versa if that conversion stemmed from religious conviction. Rizvi, *Shāh Walī-Allāh*, 328f., 340f.; Weismann, *The Naqshbandiyya*, 65ff. He also tried to limit rivalry with the Shia over the *Sahaba* (Companions of the Prophet). Itzchak Weismann, 'Jān-i Jānān, Maẓhar', *EI3*.

159. For that general argument and some examples, see Abhishek Kaicker, *The King and the People: Sovereignty and Popular Politics in Mughal Delhi* (Oxford: Oxford University Press, 2020), esp. 231–52, for the example of Bahadur Shah's proclamations cited above. Kaicker argues that resisting a change of the prayer was an expression of people power vis-à-vis the sovereign rather than an assertion of sectarian identity. For another example, Qadi Thana' Allah Panipati, who published several anti-Shii polemics, see Alvi, *Perspectives on Mughal India*, 184f.

160. Gommans, *The Rise of the Indo-Afghan Empire*, 168f.

161. Metcalf, *Islamic Revival*, 264–347. See also Martin Riexinger, *Sana'ullah Amritsari (1868–1948) und die Ahl-i-Hadis im Punjab unter britischer Herrschaft* (Würzburg: Ergon, 2004). For their stance on Shiism, see Metcalf, *Islamic Revival*, 273, 284, 291f.

162. Metcalf, *Islamic Revival*, 58ff.; Cole, *Roots*, 233–9.

163. Rizvi, *Shah 'Abd al-'Aziz*, 98ff. Like his father, he included dreams, in his case an encounter in a dream with Ali, to bolster his argument and undermine the Shia. Ibid., 164ff.

164. Ibid., 245–355; Rieck, *The Shias of Pakistan*, 15.

165. Another argument that Rizvi sees as being in line with Naqshbandi refutations of Shiism is the *Tuhfat*'s insistence that the *Ahl al-Bayt* have nothing to do with Shiism and are instead part of the Sunni tradition. Rizvi, 'Faith Deployed', 30–3; Algar, 'Naqshbandis and Safavids', 32, 47.

166. Because of the generally more controversial nature of Uthman's rule, there is less emphasis on his example. Rizvi, *Shāh Walī-Allāh*, 75f.; Rizvi, *Shah 'Abd al-'Aziz*, 199–204; Metcalf, *Islamic Revival*, 48. Shah Wali Allah may have seen the period of the early Caliphs as a continuation of the prophetic mission, implying that what they did should serve as an example for later Muslims. He reiterates the argument of Ibn Taymiyya, though without quoting him, on the relationship between legitimacy and political power, arguing that Sunnis in some way established their legitimacy by ruling, and Ali's and the Shii Imams' inability to rule effectively or establish political power undermines their claim. On this point, see Muhammad Qasim Zaman, 'Political Power, Religious Authority, and the Caliphate in Eighteenth-Century Indian Islamic Thought', *Journal of the Royal Asiatic Society* 30, 2 (2020), 313–40. Indian Islamic modernists such as Shibli Numani (d. 1914) from the circle around Sayyid Ahmad Khan (d. 1898) likewise wrote an influential book about Umar. See Shibli Nu'mani, *Al-Farooq: The Life of Omar the Great* (Lahore: Muhammad Ashraf, 1939).'

167. Rizvi, *Muslim Revivalist Movements*, 135–75.

168. Claudia Preckel, 'Ahl-i Ḥadīth', *EI3*.

169. For more, see Riexinger, *Sana'ullah Amritsari*. And so Shia, Shii-influenced Sufis, philosophers, and adherents of the Mu'tazila all found themselves at the receiving end of the purifying ambitions of Sunni Revivalists. Rizvi, *Shāh Walī-Allāh*, 280, 287.

CHAPTER 6

1. Homa Katouzian, *The Persians: Ancient, Medieval, and Modern Iran* (London: Yale University Press, 2009), 133; Tucker, 'Ottoman-Persian Relations'; Stanford J. Shaw, 'Iranian Relations with the Ottoman Empire in the Eighteenth and Nineteenth Centuries', in: P. Avery, G. Hambly, and C. Melville (eds), *The Cambridge History of Iran*, Vol. 7 (Cambridge: Cambridge University Press, 1991), 295–313, 296ff.

2. Roemer, 'The Safavid Period', 327; Tucker, 'Ottoman-Persian Relations'; D. Balland, 'AŠRAF ḠILZAY', *EIr*; Gommans, *The Rise of the Indo-Afghan Empire*, 46.

3. Zarinebaf, 'Rebels and Renegades', 91.

4. Ibid., 92.

5. Michael Axworthy, *The Sword of Persia: Nader Shah, from Tribal Warrior to Conquering Tyrant* (London: I. B. Tauris, 2006), 50. For fuller accounts, see Lockhart, *The Fall of the Safavi Dynasty*; Willem Floor, *The Afghan Occupation of Safavid Persia, 1721–1729* (Paris: Association pour l'Avancement des Études Iraniennes, 1998).

6. Juan R. I. Cole, 'Shi'i Clerics in Iraq and Iran, 1722–1780: The Akhbari–Usuli Conflict Reconsidered', *Iranian Studies* 18, 1 (1985), 3–34; Cole, *Roots*, 29.

7. Given the dislocations after the fall of Isfahan, historiography of Iran has long contrasted the Safavid period with an eighteenth century characterised by decline and chaos, a stark periodisation that is increasingly being rethought. Algar, 'Shi'ism and Iran'; Andrew Newman, 'Of Mullas, Manuscripts, and Migration: Aspects of Twelver Shi'i Community Life in the 18th Century', in: Michael Axworthy (ed.), *Crisis, Collapse, Militarism and Civil War: The History and Historiography of 18th Century Iran* (Oxford: Oxford University Press, 2018), 105–24; Rudi Matthee, 'Nader Shah in Iranian Historiography: Warlord or National Hero?', *Institute for Advanced Study*, 2018, https://www.ias.edu/ideas/2018/matthee-nader-shah.

8. Carsten Niebuhr, *Travels through Arabia and Other Countries in the East*, 2 Vols, Vol. 2 (Edinburgh: R. Morison & Son, 1792), 158.

9. Olson, *The Siege of Mosul*, 93. See also Laurence Lockhart, *Nadir Shah: A Critical Study Based Mainly upon Contemporary Sources* (London: Luzac, 1938), 21, 27, 59f., 278ff.; Momen, *An Introduction to Shi'i Islam*, 124ff.

10. This is the argument of Ernest Tucker, 'Nadir Shah and the Ja'fari Madhhab Reconsidered', *Iranian Studies* 27, 1/4 (1994), 163–79. See also Katouzian, *The Persians*, 134f.; Lockhart, *Nadir Shah*, 96–104; Algar, 'Shi'ism and Iran', 291–9.

11. Cited after: Tucker, 'Nadir Shah', 168. See also Peter Avery, 'Nadir Shah and the Afsharid Legacy', in: P. Avery, G. Hambly, and C. Melville (eds), *The Cambridge History of Iran*, Vol. 7 (Cambridge: Cambridge University Press, 1991), 1–62, 35f.

12. Lockhart, *Nadir Shah*, 101; Tucker, 'NĀDER SHAH', *EIr*.

13. Lockhart, *Nadir Shah*, 105f. In a letter to the Shah, the Sultan explained why he could not recognise the Jafari school. Ibid., 121. See also Olson, *The Siege of Mosul*, 99–104.

14. Tucker, 'Nadir Shah'. He thus did show interest in religious matters. During his campaign against Dagestan, for example, Nadir Shah attended a disputation

between Sunni and Shii clerics in Qazvin. The clerics debated a Surah of the Quran (48:29), and the Sunni party seems to have eventually won the disputation. Ignaz Goldziher, *Muhammedanische Studien*, Vol. 2 (Halle: Max Niemeyer, 1890), 113f.

15. Sussan Babaie, 'Nader Shah, the Delhi Loot, and the 18th-Century Exotics of Empire', in: Michael Axworthy (ed.), *Crisis, Collapse, Militarism and Civil War: The History and Historiography of 18th Century Iran* (Oxford: Oxford University Press, 2018), 215–34, 225f.; Sheila S. Blair, 'An Amulet from Afsharid Iran', *Journal of the Walters Art Museum* 59 (2001), 85–102, 89f.

16. Tucker, 'Nadir Shah', 171.

17. Heern, *The Emergence of Modern Shi'ism*, 49ff.; Ernest Tucker, *Nadir Shah's Quest for Legitimacy in Post-Safavid Iran* (Gainesville: University Press of Florida, 2006); Lockhart, *Nadir Shah*, 232ff.; M. Sait Özervarlı, 'Between Tension and Rapprochement: Sunni-Shi'ite Relations in the Pre-Modern Ottoman Period, with a Focus on the Eighteenth Century', *Historical Research* 90, 249 (2017), 526–42.

18. Lockhart, *Nadir Shah*, 232f.

19. Abdullah ibn Husain al-Suwaydi, 'Mu'tamar al-Najaf (The Najaf Conference)', https://ar.wikisource.org/wiki/%D9%85%D8%A4%D8%AA%D9%85%D8%B1_%D8%A7%D9%84%D9%86%D8%AC%D9%81 (accessed 26 December 2021); Brunner, *Islamic Ecumenism*, 28ff.; Tucker, 'Nadir Shah', 171f.

20. Cited after: Tucker, 'Nadir Shah', 174.

21. Lockhart, *Nadir Shah*, 255; Tucker, 'Nadir Shah', 175. See this collection of letters between Nadir Shah and the Ottoman Sultan, including on the religious questions. The collection also includes the letters between the clerics of the two sides, which were written in Arabic (as opposed to the diplomatic correspondence which was in Ottoman Turkish and Persian, respectively). I. Mahmud-Nadir Şah Mektuplaşmaları, *3 Numaralı Nâme-i Hümâyûn Defteri* (Istanbul: Osmanli Arşivi Daire Başkanlığı Yayınları, 2014) (available on https://www.devletarsivleri.gov.tr/). See the review by Metin Atmaca in the *Journal of the Ottoman and Turkish Studies Association* 2, 2 (2015), 424–6.

22. Michael Axworthy, 'The Awkwardness of Nader Shah: History, Military History, and Eighteenth-Century Iran', in: Michael Axworthy (ed.), *Crisis, Collapse, Militarism and Civil War: The History and Historiography of 18th Century Iran* (Oxford: Oxford University Press, 2018), 43–60, 52; John Gordon Lorimer, *Gazetteer of the Persian Gulf, 'Omān, and Central Arabia*, Vol. 1 (Farnsborough: Gregg, 1970), 83f.

23. Axworthy, 'The Army of Nader Shah', 643.

24. Niebuhr, *Travels through Arabia*, Vol. 2, 158. He was apparently so worried about sectarian divisions amongst his army and subjects that, when during the plundering of Delhi in 1739 some of his soldiers performed a song lamenting the death of Hussain, Nadir Shah had them executed, for he did not want his soldiers to display Shii leanings. Lockhart, *Nadir Shah*, 151.

25. Axworthy, *The Sword of Persia*; Sanjay Subrahmanyam, 'Un Grand Dérangement: Dreaming an Indo-Persian Empire in South Asia, 1740–1800', *Journal of Early Modern History* 4, 3–4 (2000), 337–78.

26. John Perry, 'ZAND DYNASTY', *EIr*; Perry, 'KARIM KHAN ZAND', *EIr*. Upon the conquest of Basra in 1776, for example, by Sadeq Khan, coins were struck in the name of the ruler Karim Khan Zand with references honouring the Shii Imams, and Shii mosques refurbished. John R. Perry, *Karim Khan Zand: A History of Iran, 1747–1779* (Chicago: University of Chicago Press, 1979), 192. The twelve districts of Shiraz, for example, were believed to be presided over by each of the Twelve Imams, who were commemorated on a weekly basis. Hamid Algar, *Religion and the State in Iran, 1785–1906: The Role of the Ulama in the Qajar Period* (Berkeley: University of California Press, 1969), 32f.; Perry, *Karim Khan Zand*, 117–26.

27. Amanat, *Iran*, 152–8. For Arab tribes along the Iranian coast, see Shahnaz Nadjmabadi, 'The Arab Presence on the Iranian Coast of the Persian Gulf', in: Lawrence G. Potter (ed.), *The Persian Gulf in History* (New York: Palgrave Macmillan, 2009), 129–45. See also Willem Floor, *The Persian Gulf: The Rise of the Gulf Arabs: The Politics of Trade on the Persian Littoral, 1747–1792* (Washington, DC: Mage, 2007); Michael Crawford, 'Religion and Religious Movements in the Gulf, 1700–1971', in: John Peterson (ed.), *The Emergence of the Gulf States: Studies in Modern History* (London: Bloomsbury, 2016), 43–84.

28. Algar, *Religion and the State in Iran*, 41f.; Amanat, *Iran*, 158–70.

29. For a concise account of his life, which I used as a basis for my description, see Commins, *Islam in Saudi Arabia*, 12–36. See also Commins, *The Wahhabi Mission and Saudi Arabia* (London: I. B. Tauris, 2006). For background on him, see H. Laoust, 'Ibn 'Abd al-Wahhāb', *EI2*; Michael Crawford, *Ibn 'Abd al-Wahhab* (London: Oneworld, 2014); 'Abdallah al-Salih al-'Uthaymin, *Muhammad ibn 'Abd al-Wahhab: The Man and his Works* (London: I. B. Tauris, 2009); Alexei Vassiliev, *The History of Saudi Arabia* (London: Saqi, 2000), 64–82. More fanciful descriptions of his journeys, which have him spending time in Iran, are likely wrong. Vassiliev, *The History of Saudi Arabia*, 65f. It is difficult to reconstruct the exact details of his journey and there are widely differing accounts, but most sources agree that he spent a considerable amount of time in Basra. Michael Cook, 'On the Origins of Wahhābism', *Journal of the Royal Asiatic Society* 2, 2 (1992), 191–202; Steinberg, 'Jihadi-Salafism', 112f.; Ibn Bishr, *'Unwan al-Majd fi Tarikh Najd*, Vol. 1 (Riyadh: Maktaba al-Riyyad al-Haditha, n.d., likely facsimile from the 1980s), 7ff.

30. For the translation of an epistle outlining the basis of the Wahhabi worldview, see Michael Cook, 'Written and Oral Aspects of an Early Wahhābī Epistle', *Bulletin of the School of Oriental and African Studies* 78, 1 (2015), 161–78.

31. Esther Peskes and Werner Ende, 'Wahhābiyya', *EI2*.

32. At times, the term was also used by supporters, including by Rashid Rida in his book *al-Wahhabiyyun wa-l-Hijaz*, discussed later.

33. Wahhabism was generally critical of Sufism, yet there were links between the two, as some key Sufi orders were established in nineteenth-century Arabia. The famous Sufi master Ahmad bin Idris lived in Arabia, where he died in 1837. In precisely that year, his pupil Muhammad bin Ali al-Sanusi established his own order in Mecca. George Rentz, 'The Wahhabis', in: A. J. Arberry (ed.),

Religion in the Middle East: Three Religions in Concord and Conflict, Vol. 2 (Cambridge: Cambridge University Press, 1969), 270–84.

34. Steinberg, 'Jihadi-Salafism', 112f.; Commins, *Islam in Saudi Arabia,* 15–18.

35. Muhammad ibn Abd al-Wahhab, *Al-Radd 'ala al-Rafida,* quoted in: Steinberg, 'Jihadi-Salafism', 113. The book is a refutation of various aspects of belief and ritual practice of the Shia. It has seen numerous reprints in many locations around the world. The copy I consulted was printed in Sanaa, Yemen, in the 2000s. In it, he quoted Allama al-Hilli and Nasir al-Din al-Tusi to make clear that he targeted key Shii clerics. Apart from the rejection of the first three Caliphs and the practice of *taqiyya,* he took issue with the Shii position towards the Prophet's Companions, with its implication for the Hadith. Guido Steinberg, 'The Wahhabiyya and Shi'ism, from 1744/45 to 2008', in: Ofra Bengio and Meir Litvak (eds), *The Sunna and Shi'a in History: Division and Ecumenism in the Muslim Middle East* (New York: Palgrave Macmillan, 2011), 163–82. For a discussion of Ibn Taymiyya's view on the Companions, see Laoust, *Essai,* 205–25.

36. Such as the effort of Nadir Shah. Crawford, 'Religion and Religious Movements', 53.

37. Apart from Ibn Taymiyya, Ibn Abd al-Wahhab often refered to Ibn al-Qayyim. In his condemnation of the veneration of tombs, he also cites Abu al-Wafa Ibn Aqil (d. 513/1119). Ibn Abd al-Wahhab's critics pointed out that he was selective in his appropriation of sources from the Hanbali tradition and did not make much use of earlier Hanbalis, or later ones, but instead focused on Ibn Taymiyya and Ibn al-Qayyim. Cook, 'On the Origins of Wahhābism'; Cole Michael Bunzel, *Manifest Enmity: The Origins, Development, and Persistence of Classical Wahhābism (1153–1351/1741–1932)* (PhD, Princeton University, 2018), 208–20.

38. John S. Habib, 'Wahhabi Origins of the Contemporary Saudi State', in: Mohammed Ayoob and Hasan Kosebalaban (eds), *Religion and Politics in Saudi Arabia: Wahhabism and the State* (London: Lynne Rienner, 2008), 57–73. The classical chronicles detailing the rise of the Wahhabis are Ibn Bishr and Ibn Ghannam. Ibn Bishr, *'Unwan al-Majd.* For a general narrative account, see Commins, *The Wahhabi Mission,* 10–30; Madawi al-Rasheed, *A History of Saudi Arabia* (Cambridge: Cambridge University Press, 2002), 14–23. For conditions in Najd that gave rise to the movement, see Uwaidah M. al-Juhany, *Najd before the Salafi Reform Movement: Social, Political and Religious Conditions during the Three Centuries Preceding the Rise of the Saudi State* (Reading: Ithaca, 2002); Michael Cook, 'The Historians of Pre-Wahhābī Najd', *Studia Islamica* 76 (1992), 163–76. For a thorough and somewhat revisionist account by a contemporary Saudi scholar, see Khalid al-Dakhil, *Al-Wahhabiyya: Bayn al-Shirk wa Tasaddu'a al-Qabila* (Beirut: al-Shabaka al-'Arabiyya li-l-Abhath wa-l-Nashr, 2013).

39. For a critique of that notion, see al-Rasheed, *A History of Saudi Arabia,* 188–217.

40. For the Rashidis, see Madawi al-Rasheed, *Politics in an Arabian Oasis: The Rashidi Tribal Dynasty* (London: I. B. Tauris, 1991). For the Bani Khalid, see 'Abd al-Karim bin 'Abdallah al-Munif al-Wahbi, *Banu Khalid wa 'Alaqatuhum bi-Najd, 1669–1794* (n.p.: Dar Thaqif li-l-Nashr wa-l-Ta'lif, 1989); al-Shaykh

Ahmad al-ʿAmari al-Nasiri, *Qabilat Bani Khalid fi al-Tarikh* (Beirut: Dar al-Rafidayn li-l-Tibaʿa wa-l-Nashr wa-l-Tawziʿ, 2009).

41. A famous anti-Wahhabi polemic is by the Hijazi Ahmad b. Zayni b. Ahmad Dahlan, *Al-Durar al-Saniyya fi l-Radd ʿala-l-Wahhabiyya* (Cairo: n.p., 1299h/1882). See Esther Peskes, *Muhammad b. ʿAbdalwahhab (1703–92) im Widerstreit: Untersuchungen zur Rekonstruktion der Frühgeschichte der Wahhābīya* (Beirut: Franz Steiner, 1993), 54–8, 125–52; Peskes, 'Dahlān, Ahmad b. Zaynī', *EI3*; Samer Traboulsi, 'An Early Refutation of Muhammad ibn ʿAbd al-Wahhāb's Reformist Views', *Die Welt des Islams* 42, 3 (2002), 373–415. For Eastern Arabia, see Muhammad A. al-Zekri, *The Religious Encounter between Sufis and Salafis of East Arabia: Issue of Identity* (PhD, University of Exeter, 2004). For a list of anti-Wahhabi epistles, see Bunzel, *Manifest Enmity*, 33–95, 320–9. Given the Wahhabis' attacks on the Ottomans' legitimacy and territory, they were seen negatively in Ottoman Iraq (although, as we will see, there were also a few that supported them). Dina Rizk Khoury, 'Who is a True Muslim? Exclusion and Inclusion among Polemicists of Reform in Nineteenth-Century Baghdad', in: Virginia H. Aksan and Daniel Goffman (eds), *The Early Modern Ottomans: Remapping the Empire* (Cambridge: Cambridge University Press, 2007), 256–74. For Shii anti-Wahhabi texts, see Ende, *Arabische Nation*, 116.

42. Niebuhr, *Travels through Arabia*, passim. For the general religious atmosphere of the eighteenth century in the region, see Crawford, 'Religion and Religious Movements'.

43. Giovanni Bonacina, *The Wahhabis Seen through European Eyes (1772–1830): Deists and Puritans of Islam* (Leiden: Brill, 2015), 6–9.

44. Steinberg, 'The Wahhabiyya and Shiʿism'.

45. Vassiliev, *The History of Saudi Arabia*, 83–91.

46. Some early European and many Shii sources give horrific details of the events. But even the account in the semi-official pro-Wahhabi chronicle of Ibn Bishr is chilling and speaks of 2000 deaths. Ibn Bishr, *ʿUnwan al-Majd*, Vol. 1, 121f. For a translation, see Ballandalus, 'The Wahhabi Sack of Karbala (1802 AD)', 2 August 2014, https://ballandalus.wordpress.com/2014/08/02/the-wahhabi-sack-of-karbala-1802-a-d/. This might have been not only an act of religious fanaticism but an act of revenge for an attack on Wahhabi traders by a Shii tribe from Iraq. The attack had previously at times been dated wrongly to 1801, but it took place in 1802. Johannes Reissner, 'Kerbela 1802: Ein Werkstattbericht zum "islamischen Fundamentalismus", als es ihn noch nicht gab', *Die Welt des Islams* 28, 1/4 (1988), 431–44; Vassiliev, *The History of Saudi Arabia*, 96ff.

47. Aslan, *From Body to Shrine*, 13; Yitzhak Nakash, *The Shiʿis of Iraq*, 2nd ed. (Princeton: Princeton University Press, 2003), 13.

48. Vassiliev, *The History of Saudi Arabia*, 102.

49. In 2019, a book market between the two major shrines in Karbala, covering some of the ground on which the original tragedy of Karbala was supposed to have taken place, sold large oil paintings depicting the Wahhabi raids as a reminder for pilgrims. Personal observation.

50. Vassiliev, *The History of Saudi Arabia*, 98–105; Commins, *The Wahhabi Mission*, 30–9; al-Hasan, *Al-Shiʿa*, Vol. 1, 110f.; H. St John Philby, *Saʿudi Arabia* (London: Benn, 1955), 197; R. Bayly Winder, *Saudi Arabia in the Nineteenth Century* (London: Macmillan, 1965), 151f.; William Gifford Palgrave, *Personal Narrative of a Year's Journey through Central and Eastern Arabia* (London: Macmillan, 1868), 349–78; Abdul-Wahab S. Babeair, *Ottoman Penetration of the Eastern Region of the Arabian Peninsula, 1814–1841* (PhD, Indiana University, 1985), 70–4, 90–4, 121ff.; George Forster Sadleir and Patrick Ryan, *Diary of a Journey across Arabia from el-Khatif in the Persian Gulf, to Yambo in the Red Sea, during the Year 1819* (Bombay: Education Society's Press, 1866), 26–32; P. J. L. Frankl and K. Jopp, 'Lieutenant Jopp's Report on a Visit to Hufuf, 1257/1841', *New Arabian Studies* 1 (1993), 215–27; Lorimer, *Gazetteer of the Persian Gulf*, Vol. 1, 947–99; Maryam bint Khalaf al-ʿUtaybi, *Al-Ahsaʾ wa-l-Qatif fi ʿAhd al-Dawla al-Suʿudiyya al-Thaniyya (1245–1288 AH)* (Beirut: Jadawel, 2012); al-ʿUthaymin, *Tarikh al-Mamlaka al-ʿArabiyya al-Suʿudiyya*, Vol. 1, 117–23. For the 1818 execution, see Michael Crawford and William Henry Dyke Facey, "Abd Allāh al-Saʿūd and Muḥammad ʿAlī Pasha: The Theatre of Victory, the Prophet's Treasures, and the Visiting Whig, Cairo 1818', *Journal of Arabian Studies* 7, 1 (2017), 44–62.

51. For a good overview, see Zackery Heern, 'One Thousand Years of Islamic Education in Najaf: Myth and History of the Shiʿi Ḥawza', *Iranian Studies* 50, 3 (2017), 415–38.

52. Khalil Osman, *Sectarianism in Iraq: The Making of State and Nation since 1920* (Abingdon: Routledge, 2015), 65f.

53. Batatu, *The Old Social Classes*, 41; Ibrahim al-Haidari, *Zur Soziologie des schiitischen Chiliasmus* (Freiburg im Breisgau: Klaus Schwarz, 1975), 25f., 100–9; Meir Litvak, 'IRAQ x. SHIʿITES OF IRAQ', *EIr*; Nakash, *The Shiʿis of Iraq*, 27–45; al-Wardi, *Understanding Iraq*, 74; al-Wardi, *Soziologie des Nomadentums*, 258–62, 274–80. For the Mamluks, see Tom Nieuwenhuis, *Politics and Society in Early Modern Iraq: Mamluk Pashas, Tribal Shayks and Local Rule between 1802 and 1831* (The Hague: M. Nijhoff, 1982). In the post-2003 period, this became very visible through the many tribally sponsored *hussainiyyas* or rest houses along the way to Karbala for the Arbain pilgrimage, which would be named after the tribe or subsection of a tribe or family that had paid for it. Personal observations, Iraq, 2018 and 2019. In 1831, Ali Rida, who may have been a member of the Bektashi order, became governor of Baghdad. He also patronised poets praising the *Ahl al-Bayt*. At the same time, however, he also supported Abu al-Thanaʾ al-Alusi, who would pen important anti-Shii treatises. Ali al-Wardi, *Lamahat Ijtimaʿiyya min Tarikh al-ʿIraq al-Hadith*, Vol. 2 (Baghdad: Matbaʿat al-Irshad, 1971), 106–11; Alev Masarwa, *Bildung, Macht, Kultur: Das Feld des Gelehrten Abū t-Tanāʾ al-Ālūsī (1802–1854) im spätosmanischen Bagdad* (Würzburg: Ergon, 2011), 162–5, 176–84. His Shii leanings did not, however, mean that he was welcomed by all Shia in the shrine cities. In fact, he failed to assert his autonomy over Karbala, which was more or less autonomously governed by various clans at the time. He did not break a major revolt in the city, and it fell

to his successor to use overwhelming force against the city. Masarwa, *Bildung, Macht, Kultur*, 201–5; Juan R. I. Cole and Moojan Momen, 'Mafia, Mob and Shiism in Iraq: The Rebellion of Ottoman Karbala 1824–1843', *Past & Present* 112, 1 (1986), 112–43.

54. Hala M. Fattah, *The Politics of Regional Trade in Iraq, Arabia, and the Gulf, 1745–1900* (Albany: SUNY Press, 1997).

55. Mohammad al-Habib, *The Formation of the Shi'a Communities in Kuwait: Migration, Settlement and Contribution between 1880 and 1938* (PhD, University of London, 2017).

56. Cole, 'Rival Empires', 183–94.

57. At times, rulers of Arab tribal descent based in Bushire on the Iranian side of the Gulf also retained sovereignty over Bahrain. The precise nature of the arrangement is not entirely clear. Sectarian identity could at this point occasionally be shifted to suit political aims. According to Niebuhr, Shaykh 'Naser was a Sunnite; but, in hopes of being appointed Admiral of the Persian fleet, he became a Shiite, and married a Persian lady. These two steps have proved very injurious to him and his family. He is odious to his subjects and neighbours; and his children are no longer counted among the Arabian nobility.' Niebuhr, *Travels through Arabia*, Vol. 2, 165; Cole, 'Rival Empires', 194–8; John R. Perry, 'The Zand Dynasty', in: P. Avery, G. Hambly, and C. Melville (eds), *The Cambridge History of Iran*, Vol. 7 (Cambridge: Cambridge University Press, 1991), 63–103, 87.

58. Nelida Fuccaro, *Histories of City and State in the Persian Gulf: Manama since 1800* (Cambridge: Cambridge University Press, 2009), 16–29; Lorimer, *Gazetteer of the Persian Gulf*, Vol. 1, 836–96 and passim. Biographies of clerics have become important reference points for the history of Shiism in the Bahrain region. Yusuf bin Ahmad al-Bahrani, *Lu'lu'at al-Bahrayn fi al-Ijazat wa Tarajim Rijal al-Hadith* (Najaf: Matba'a al-'Uthman, 1966); Marco Salati, 'La Lu'lu'a al-Bahrayn fî l-ijâza li-qurratay al-'ayn di Shaykh Yûsuf b. Ahmad al-Bahrânî (1107–1186/1695–1772): Per lo studio della shî'a di Bahrayn', *Annali di Ca' Foscari* 28, 3 (1989), 111–45. See also Muhammad 'Ali bin Ahmad bin 'Abbas al-Tajir al-Bahrani, *Muntazzam al-Durrayn fi Tarajim 'Ulama' wa Udaba' al-Ahsa' wa-l-Qatif wa-l-Bahrayn*, 3 Vols (Qom/Beirut: Mu'assasa Tayyiba li-Ihya' al-Turath, 2009); Hashim Muhammad al-Shakhs, *A'lam Hajar min al-Madiyyin wa-l-Mu'asirin*, 4 Vols (Beirut: Mu'assasat Umm al-Qura li-l-Tahqiq wa-l-Nashr, 1996–2006).

59. Muhammad 'Ali al-Hirz, *Ahsa'iyyun Muhajirun* (Beirut: Dar al-Mahajja al-Bayda', 2010).

60. Cole, 'Rival Empires', 197.

61. For the Akhbari-Usuli dispute, see Robert Gleave, *Inevitable Doubt: Two Theories of Shi'i Jurisprudence* (Leiden: Brill, 2000). The positions of Akhbaris and Usulis towards Sunnism are complex. Stewart argues that Akhbaris accused Usulis of incorporating Sunni principles and engaged in anti-Sunni polemics. Stewart, *Islamic Legal Orthodoxy*, 201; Stewart, 'The Genesis of the Akhbārī Revival', in: Michel M. Mazzaoui (ed.), *Safavid Iran & Her Neighbors* (Salt Lake City: University of Utah Press, 2003), 169–93. On the other hand, Momen argues

that Akhbarism was moving closer to Sunnism in the sense that, by rejecting some of the principles of jurisprudence and theology that had previously defined Shiism, some of which had come from the Mu'tazila, and by giving the Imams a position akin to the Sunni founding fathers of the schools of jurisprudence, there was a certain resemblance between Akhbarism and Sunnism. He also points out that the height of Akhbari influence coincides with Nadir Shah's ecumenical proposal. Momen, *An Introduction to Shi'i Islam*, 117f., 222–5.

62. Toby Matthiesen, 'Mysticism, Migration and Clerical Networks: Ahmad al-Ahsa'i and the Shaykhis of al-Ahsa, Kuwait and Basra', *Journal of Muslim Minority Affairs* 34, 4 (2014), 386–409; Muhammad 'Ali al-Hirz, 'Malamih min al-Haya al-'Ilmiyya fi 'Asr al-Shaykh al-Ahsa'i (1210-1241 A.H.)', *al-Waha* 50 (2008), 62–78.

63. Denis M. MacEoin, *From Shaykhism to Babism: A Study in Charismatic Renewal in Shi'i Islam* (PhD, University of Cambridge, 1979), 75–81; Moojan Momen, 'The Trial of Mulla 'Ali Bastami: A Combined Sunni-Shi'i Fatwa against the Bab', *Iran* 20 (1982), 113–43.

64. This is forcefully argued in Heern, *The Emergence of Modern Shi'ism*, ch. 4 and 5.

65. Juan R. I. Cole, '"Indian Money" and the Shi'i Shrine Cities of Iraq, 1786–1850', *Middle Eastern Studies* 22, 4 (1986), 461–80; Nakash, *The Shi'is of Iraq*, 19f., 29ff.

66. Archival sources on the Oudh Bequest in the archives of the India Office in London are extensive. See, for example, The National Archives, 'Oudh Bequest', DO189/376, http://discovery.nationalarchives.gov.uk/details/r/C1194146. See Cole, '"Indian Money"'; Cole, *Sacred Space and Holy War*, 80f.; Meir Litvak, 'Money, Religion, and Politics: The Oudh Bequest in Najaf and Karbala', 1850–1903', *International Journal of Middle East Studies* 33, 1 (2001), 1–21; Litvak, 'A Failed Manipulation: The British, the Oudh Bequest and the Shi'i 'Ulama' of Najaf and Karbala', *British Journal of Middle Eastern Studies* 27, 1 (2000), 68–89.

67. Meir Litvak, 'IRAQ x. SHI'ITES OF IRAQ', *EIr.*

68. Nakash argues that this led to a sort of state formation that was only aborted by British rule and the crushing of the 1920 revolt. Nakash, *The Shi'is of Iraq*, 4f.

69. By 1919, Shia would constitute 53 per cent of the population and, by 1932, 56 per cent. Ibid., 25.

70. Ibid., 22; Cole and Momen, 'Mafia, Mob and Shiism'.

71. Batatu, *The Old Social Classes*, 37; al-Wardi, *Soziologie des Nomadentums*, 270.

72. Nakash, *The Shi'is of Iraq*, 24f.

73. Gökhan Çetinsaya, *Ottoman Administration of Iraq, 1890–1908* (London: Routledge, 2006), 102.

74. As seems to have happened in 1894. Kern, *Imperial Citizen*, 87.

75. Interviews with Shii clerics from various countries, over the period from 2008 to 2019; Meir Litvak, *Shi'i Scholars of Nineteenth-Century Iraq: The 'Ulama' of Najaf and Karbala* (Cambridge: Cambridge University Press, 1998); Litvak, 'The Finances of the Ulama Communities of Najaf and Karbala, 1796–1904', *Die Welt des Islams* 40, 1 (2000), 41–66; Robert Gleave, 'Khums', *EI2.*

76. Lawrence J. Baack, *Undying Curiosity: Carsten Niebuhr and the Royal Danish Expedition to Arabia (1761–1767)* (Stuttgart: Franz Steiner, 2014), 245. That number

increased to 7558 by 1912/3. Abdullah Fahad al-Nafeesi, *The Role of the Shīʿah in the Political Development of Modern Iraq (1914–1921)* (PhD, University of Cambridge, 1971), 120–4.

77. Algar, *Religion and the State in Iran*, 45–9. In a departure from previous practice, he also minted coins with the Shah's name and now that of the Imam's, and termed Tehran Dar al-Khilafa, seat of the Caliphate, perhaps indicating a differentiation and separate authority from both the Ottoman Caliphate and the Shii clergy. Abbas Amanat, 'FATḤ-ʿALĪ SHAH QĀJĀR', *EIr*.

78. Though they were at times banned from them in the second half of the nineteenth century. Jean Calmard, 'Muharram Ceremonies and Diplomacy: A Preliminary Study', in: Edmund Bosworth and Carole Hillenbrand (eds), *Qajar Iran: Political, Social and Cultural Change, 1800–1925* (Edinburgh: Edinburgh University Press, 1983), 213–28. See also Ehsan Yarshater, 'The Qajar Era in the Mirror of Time', *Iranian Studies* 34, 1/4 (2001), 187–94, 187f.

79. Fath Ali Shah allegedly stated that 'our rulership is on behalf [...] of the *mujtahids* of the Age'. Quoted in: Said Amir Arjomand, 'Political Ethic and Public Law in the Early Qajar Period', in: Robert Gleave (ed.), *Religion and Society in Qajar Iran* (London: Routledge, 2004), 21–40, 21.

80. Robert Gleave, 'Jihad and Religious Legitimacy in the Early Qajar State', in: Robert Gleave (ed.), *Religion and Society in Qajar Iran* (London: Routledge, 2004), 41–70; Lambton, 'A Nineteenth Century View of Jihād'; Abdul-Hadi Hairi, 'The Legitimacy of the Early Qajar Rule as Viewed by the Shiʿi Religious Leaders', *Middle Eastern Studies* 24, 3 (1988), 271–86; Said Amir Arjomand, 'The Shiʿite Hierocracy and the State in Pre-Modern Iran: 1785–1890', *European Journal of Sociology* 22, 1 (1981), 40–78; Momen, *An Introduction to Shiʿi Islam*, 191–6.

81. Until it was curtailed as part of Rida Shah's secularisation policies. It was only re-established as a practice after World War II. Machlis, *Shiʿi Sectarianism*, 144–51.

82. Willem Floor, *The Persian Gulf: Bandar Abbas: The Natural Trade Gateway of Southeast Iran* (Washington, DC: Mage, 2011), 20f.; Floor, *The Persian Gulf: The Rise and Fall of Bandar-e Lengeh: The Distribution Center for the Arabian Coast, 1750–1930* (Washington, DC: Mage, 2010), 10f.

83. Afshin Marashi, *Nationalizing Iran: Culture, Power, and the State, 1870–1940* (Seattle: University of Washington Press, 2008), 35–48; Abbas Amanat, *Pivot of the Universe: Nasir al-Din Shah Qajar and the Iranian Monarchy, 1831–1896* (Berkeley: University of California Press, 1997), 435.

84. Amanat, *Pivot of the Universe*, 434. This foreshadowed his famous travelogues of his European trips. See David Motadel, 'Qajar Shahs in Imperial Germany', *Past & Present* 213, 1 (2011), 191–235. See also Zeinab Azarbadegan, 'Imagined Geographies, Re-Invented Histories: Ottoman Iraq as Part of Iran', *Journal of the Ottoman and Turkish Studies Association* 5, 1 (2018), 115–41.

85. Maria Vittoria Fontana, *Iconografia dell'Ahl al-Bayt: Immagini di arte persiana del XII al XX secolo* (Naples: Istituto Universitario Orientale, 1994).

86. Fuchsia Hart, 'Pictorial Narration of the Battle of Karbala in Qajar Iran: A Combined Art Historical and Anthropological Approach', *Iran Namag* 1, 4

(2017), 4–22. This visual culture of Shiism would remain prominent and be used even more widely by the Islamic Republic. Ingvild Flaskerud, *Visualizing Belief and Piety in Iranian Shi'ism* (London: Continuum, 2010).

87. Markus Ritter, *Moscheen und Madrasabauten in Iran 1785–1848: Architektur zwischen Rückgriff und Neuerung* (Leiden: Brill, 2005).

88. Such as Majlisi's Shii compendium *Bihar al-Anwar*. From the nineteenth century onwards, facsimiles and editions of single volumes were published in India and Iran, and a full printed edition was published under the Qajars in the late nineteenth century. This edition was dedicated to Nasir al-Din Shah and his son Muzaffar al-Din. Together with later, more complete and annotated editions of the twentieth century, it was integral in popularising the book, and it would eventually be published in 110 volumes. Pampus, *Die theologische Enzyklopädie*, 142–7.

89. Peter J. Chelkowski (ed.), *Ta'ziyeh: Ritual and Drama in Iran* (New York: NYU Press, 1979); al-Haidari, *Zur Soziologie des schiitischen Chiliasmus*.

90. Although a group of Babis tried to assassinate Nasir al-Din Shah in 1852. Moojan Momen, 'Millennialism and Violence: The Attempted Assassination of Nasir al-Din Shah of Iran by the Babis in 1852', *Nova Religio* 12, 1 (2008), 57–82. The Kermani branch of the Shaykhiyya was founded by Hajj Muhammad Karim Khan Kermani (1846–1906), a Qajar prince. For more on the Kermani branch, see Denis Hermann, *Aspects de l'histoire sociale et doctrinale de l'ecole shaikhi au cours de la periode Qajar (1843–1911)* (PhD, École Pratique des Hautes Études, 2007); Denis Hermann and Omid Rezai, 'Le rôle du VAQF dans la formation de la communauté Shaykhi Kermani à l'époque Qājār (1259–1324/1843–1906)', *Studia Iranica* 36, 1 (2007), 87–131; Armin Eschraghi, 'Promised One (maw'ūd) or Imaginary One (mawhūm)? Some Notes on Twelver Shī'ī Mahdī Doctrine and its Discussion in Writings of Bahā'Allāh', in: Orkhan Mir-Kasimov (ed.), *Unity in Diversity: Mysticism, Messianism and the Construction of Religious Authority in Islam* (Leiden: Brill, 2013), 111–35.

91. Matthijs van den Bos, *Mystic Regimes: Sufism and the State in Iran, from the Late Qajar Era to the Islamic Republic* (Leiden: Brill, 2002); Hossein Kamaly, *God and Man in Tehran: Contending Visions of the Divine from the Qajars to the Islamic Republic* (New York: Columbia University Press, 2018), 145–75.

92. In general on this, see Mangol Bayat, *Mysticism and Dissent: Socioreligious Thought in Qajar Iran* (Syracuse: Syracuse University Press, 1982); Abbas Amanat, *Resurrection and Renewal: The Making of the Babi Movement in Iran, 1844–1850* (Ithaca: Cornell University Press, 1989); Peter Smith, *The Babi and Baha'i Religions: From Messianic Shi'ism to a World Religion* (Cambridge: Cambridge University Press, 1987).

93. Ann K. S. Lambton, 'A Reconsideration of the Position of the Marja' al-Taqlīd and the Religious Institution', *Studia Islamica* 20 (1964), 115–35. While in the early twentieth century many Shii communities still produced their own senior clerics, by the mid-twentieth century, most Shia around the world would follow (taqlid) one of the senior clerics in the shrine cities.

94. Willem Floor, 'The Economic Role of the Ulama in Qajar Persia', in: Linda Walbridge (ed.), *The Most Learned of the Shi'a: The Institution of the Marja' Taqlid*

(Oxford: Oxford University Press, 2001), 53–81; Floor, *Guilds, Merchants, and Ulama in Nineteenth-Century Iran* (Washington, DC: Mage, 2009), 69–98.

95. Martin van Bruinessen, 'The Naqshbandi Order in Seventeenth-Century Kurdistan', in: Marc Gaborieau, Alexandre Popovic, and Thierry Zarcone (eds), *Naqshbandis: Cheminements et situation actuelle d'un ordre mystique musulman* (Paris: Éditions Isis, 1990), 337–60.

96. Butrus Abu-Manneh, 'Sheikh Murād al-Bukhārī and the Expansion of the Naqshbandī-Mujaddidī Order in Istanbul', *Die Welt des Islams* 53, 1 (2013), 1–25.

97. Metin Atmaca, 'Contesting the Politics of Sectarianism: Naqshbandi-Khalidi Sufis on the Ottoman-Iranian Frontier and their Relations with Shi'a and Non-Muslims', paper presented at the *ACRPS Winter School on Communitarianism, Sectarianism, and the State*, Doha Institute, Qatar, 4–14 January 2020; Knysh, *Islamic Mysticism*, 224; Sean Foley, 'The Naqshbandiyya-Khalidiyya, Islamic Sainthood, and Religion in Modern Times', *Journal of World History* 19, 4 (2008), 521–45; Foley, 'Temporal and Spiritual Power in Nineteenth-Century Ottoman Politics: Shaykh Khalid, Gürcü Necib Pasha and the Naqshbandiyya-Khalidiyya', *Türkiyat Araştırmaları* 9 (2008), 227–44; Albert Hourani, 'Sufism and Modern Islam: Mawlana Khalid and the Naqshbandi Order', in: Albert Hourani (ed.), *The Emergence of the Modern Middle East* (London: Macmillan, 1981), 75–89; Butrus Abu-Manneh, 'The Naqshbandiyya-Mujaddidiyya in the Ottoman Lands in the Early 19th Century', *Die Welt des Islams* 22, 1/4 (1982), 1–36, 15f.; Şerif Mardin, *Religion and Social Change in Modern Turkey: The Case of Bediüzzaman Said Nursi* (Albany: SUNY Press, 1989), 54–60.

98. When one leader of the Khalidiyya, Ismail al-Shirvani (1783–1848), tried to proselytise in his largely Shii home region of Shirvan (today's Azerbaijan) in the nineteenth century, he abandoned the anti-Shii elements of the order in favour of Muslim unity. Weismann, *The Naqshbandiyya*, 105ff. This was also the position of Shah Abu al-Khayr, who was based in Delhi and Quetta and advocated Islamic unity in the face of colonialism in the early twentieth century. Ibid., 116.

99. Weismann, *The Naqshbandiyya*, 95f.; Weismann, *Taste of Modernity: Sufism and Salafiyya in Late Ottoman Damascus* (Leiden: Brill, 2001); Weismann, 'The Naqshbandiyya-Khalidiyya and the Salafi Challenge in Iraq', *Journal of the History of Sufism* 4 (2004), 229–40; Butrus Abu-Manneh, 'Salafiyya and the Rise of the Khālidiyya in Baghdad in the Early Nineteenth Century', *Die Welt des Islams* 43, 3 (2003), 349–72.

100. Wilkinson, *Ibâdism*. See also Khuri, *Imams and Emirs*.

101. At least in theory, the Imams were supposed to be *mujtahids*, i.e. capable of *ijtihad*, of deducting independent judgment from the sources of jurisprudence. Strothmann, *Staatsrecht*, 67–71. Zaydi clerics had thus tried to emphasise the role of *ijtihad* in deducing Zaydi law. Al-Shawkani forcefully made the case that the so-called 'door of *ijtihad*' should not be closed, something that later scholars of the early *Salafiyya*, such as Rashid Rida, took up. Brinkley Messick, *The Calligraphic State: Textual Domination and History in a Muslim Society* (Berkeley: University of California Press, 1993), 42f., 56.

102. Dresch, *Tribes*, 167–73. For a list of Imams, see Strothmann, *Staatsrecht*, 106–9.

103. Madelung, *Der Imam*, 124–30; Strothmann, *Staatsrecht*, 67–71. In Shafii schools in Ibb, on the other hand, the manual (*waraqat*) by the early Shafii jurist al-Juwayni (d. 1086) was taught. It focuses on the *usul al-fiqh*, with four sources: Quran, Sunna, *qiyas*, and *ijma'*. Messick, *The Calligraphic State*, 44f.

104. Haykel quotes Zaydi scholars using and discussing Sunni Hadith collections, such as al-Bukhari and Muslim. Haykel, *Revival and Reform*, 9.

105. A Zaydi cleric can, for example, use sources from any of the other valid schools to rule on a particular matter. Gabriele vom Bruck, 'Regimes of Piety Revisited: Zaydī Political Moralities in Republican Yemen', *Die Welt des Islams* 50 (2010), 185–223, 186; Serjeant, 'The Zaydis', 301. This is epitomised, for example, by the scholars of the al-Kibsi family. Ahmad bin Zayd al-Kibsi (d.1854), for example, was taught by al-Shawkani and studied the Sunni Hadith collection of al-Bukhari, but also taught one of the future Zaydi Imams. Gabriele vom Bruck, 'al-Kibsī family', *EI3*. I thank Gabriele vom Bruck for this reference.

106. Messick, *The Calligraphic State*, 19ff.

107. For Shafii stances on religious practices that are similar to Shii interpretations, such as in burial (both argue that a grave should be flat) and the loud recitation of the prayer, see Goldziher, *Beiträge*, 85f. There are differences, however. Twelver Shia advocate putting two green palm leaves into the grave, which Zaydis forbid. Strothmann, *Kultus*, 65. There are also differences between Zaydis and Shafiis when it comes to the prayer recitation at a funeral. Ibid., 64. Zaydis also do not accept 'sinners' to lead prayers and may refuse them to be buried according to the faith. Sunnis generally follow al-Ashari, who stated that, even though a pious prayer leader is better than a non-pious one, the latter will also do. Ibid., 73.

108. See Messick, *The Calligraphic State*, 39; Wilferd Madelung, 'Imāma', *EI2*; D. Sourdel et al., 'Khalīfa', *EI2*. For doctrinal developments in the Middle Ages, see Hassan Ansari, Sabine Schmidtke, and Jan Thiele, 'Zaydī Theology in Yemen', in: Sabine Schmidtke (ed.), *The Oxford Handbook of Islamic Theology* (Oxford: Oxford University Press, 2016), 473–93.

109. One important local Zaydi shrine, for example, is the one of the founding father of the Zaydiyya in Yemen, Imam al-Hadi, in the main mosque of Saada, which is named after him. Strothmann, *Kultus*, 69f.

110. For example, Imam al-Mu'ayyid bi'llah Yahya bin Hamza (r. 1329–49). The Ayyubids occupied Southern Arabia in 1174. Daftary, *Ismaili History*, 41f.

111. Vassiliev, *The History of Saudi Arabia*, 109f.

112. Floor, *The Persian Gulf: The Rise of the Gulf Arabs*.

113. Crawford, 'Religion and Religious Movements', 61f., 70; Patricia Risso, *Oman and Muscat: An Early Modern History* (London: Croom Helm, 1986); Lorimer, *Gazetteer of the Persian Gulf*, Vol. 1, 397–491.

114. Vassiliev, *The History of Saudi Arabia*, 106–9. The Sultans sponsored Ibadism in Zanzibar, but also respected and institutionalised Sunnism. For a thorough account, including problems that emerged because of conversions, see

Valerie J. Hoffman, 'Ibadi Muslim Scholars and the Confrontation with Sunni Islam in Nineteenth- and Early Twentieth-Century Zanzibar', *Bulletin of the Royal Institute for Inter-Faith Studies* 7, 1 (2005), 91−118.

115. Hussein Ghubash, *Oman: The Islamic Democratic Tradition* (London: Routledge, 2006).

116. Hathaway, *A Tale of Two Factions*, 84f. The Ismailis in Najran had generally acceptable relations with the Zaydi Imams, but were at times mistreated by the Zaydi Imams, which is why the Ismailis sided with the Ottomans in the latter's 1569−71 campaign against the Zaydi Imam. Qutb al-Din al-Nahrawali al-Makki, *Lightning over Yemen: A History of the Ottoman Campaign 1569−71*, trans. by Clive Smith (London: I. B. Tauris, 2002), 9, 72−5. There is a longstanding rivalry between the Zaydi Imams and the Ismailis of the Yam tribe in Najran. Serjeant, 'The Zaydis', 293. When the Zaydis conquered Ismaili communities in Haraz, Ismailis were forced to abandon some of their practices and were sent Zaydi Imams to instruct them in the 'proper' religion. Ibid., 297.

117. Daftary, *The Ismailis*, 276−81; Wilferd Madelung, 'Makramids', *EI2*.

118. Thomas Kuehn, *Empire, Islam, and Politics of Difference: Ottoman Rule in Yemen, 1849−1919* (Leiden: Brill, 2011), 58f., 73, 81. See also al-Makki, *Lightning over Yemen*, 3.

119. 'A number of Zaydi were slain, hastened to the fire by the angel of hell; and two of the Sultan's troops met their death, delivered by Ridwan to Paradise. [...] With shining sabre, drawn sword and swift horse, the people of the Sunnah swarmed over the apostates who were absolutely broken. They were swept to the ground and across their minds flashed their fall into hell-fire on Judgment Day. The people of the Sunnah set upon their faces and shoulders, blunting their swords thereon. [...] When afternoon came the Sunni people gained victory and the heretics were defeated in death and capture, with destruction and subjection in their train. [...] Countless Zaydi were slaughtered while few of religion's loyal were martyred.' Al-Makki, *Lightning over Yemen*, 75f., 81, 124, 157.

120. Ibid., 42. For more on the book, see Alessandro Gori, ''Al-barq al-Yamānī fī l-fath al-'Uthmānī', *CMR2*. It also claims that al-Mutahhar, in departure of previous practice, introduced the line '*hayya 'ala khayr al-'amal*' ('hurry towards the best of deeds') in the call to prayer and began to curse the first three Caliphs. Hathaway, *A Tale of Two Factions*, 85.

121. The Ottomans also encouraged visitation of the shrine. Several Ottoman officials were also buried there, increasing the importance of the link between the tomb and the Ottoman government. Nancy Um, *The Merchant Houses of Mocha: Trade and Architecture in an Indian Ocean Port* (Seattle: University of Washington Press, 2009), 104, 113ff. During the second Ottoman occupation in 1893, an Ottoman official asked for funds to renovate the tombs of three saints from Tihama and adjacent mosques to strengthen the loyalty and morale of Shafiis in that area, in the context of a rebellion in the North. Kuehn, *Empire*, 174f. Other Sufi shrines were expanded, for example in Taiz and Yafrus.

Barbara Finster, 'An Outline of the History of Islamic Religious Architecture in Yemen', *Muqarnas* 9 (1992), 124–47, 142f. For a description of the Imam's mausoleums in Saada, see ibid., 140f.

122. Dresch, *Tribes*, 198ff.

123. See Dresch, *A History of Modern Yemen*, 11–18.

124. Messick, *The Calligraphic State*, 41f.

125. The Shafii Mufti of Ibb, Abd al-Rahman al-Haddad, for example, who had been allied with the Ottomans and had defended the town of Ibb against Zaydi attacks, wrote a versification of the Sharia interpretations of the Zaydi Imam Yahya after Ibb had come under the control of the Imam. Ibid., 48.

126. Messick quotes a circular of Imam al-Mahdi al-Abbas (b. 1719) that all judges of his realm had to apply the Zaydi Sharia. He also notes a certain marginalisation of Ibb in biographical dictionaries and other histories after it came under the control of the Zaydi Imams. Ibid., 40f., 271. After the Ottoman period, the Imams again appointed largely Zaydi jurists to Ibb from 1919 until 1962. It should be noted, however, that it was common administrative practice in Yemen to send jurists to serve away from their home regions (while Zaydis could be sent everywhere, Shafiis could only be sent elsewhere in Lower Yemen, i.e. to other majority Shafii regions). Ibid., 192f. See also Uzi Rabi, *Yemen: Revolution, Civil War and Unification* (London: I. B. Tauris, 2015), 6; Robert W. Stookey, *Yemen: The Politics of the Yemen Arab Republic* (Boulder, CO: Westview Press, 1978), 172f.

127. According to one scholar, it is these political considerations that are key in relations between the two sects: 'Minor ritual variations, such as that in the adhan or call to prayer, are naturally of far less moment than questions of taxation.' Serjeant, 'The Zaydis', 285.

128. For more on Aden's role, see Roxani Eleni Margariti, *Aden and the Indian Ocean Trade: 150 Years in the Life of a Medieval Arabian Port* (Chapel Hill: University of North Carolina Press, 2007).

129. Haykel, *Revival and Reform*, 16; Dresch, *Tribes*, 200.

130. Small amounts of East African coffee were also re-exported through Mocha, further bolstering the identification of coffee with 'Mocca'. Um, *The Merchant Houses*, 3ff., 24–8, 35, 48–95. With commercial success came higher visibility for religious minorities, and the era witnessed pogroms and the controversial, if ultimately not enforced, decision to expel Jews from Yemen. The influence of more puritanical Sunni ideas may have played a role in this. While Zaydi jurists were strict in their enforcement of discriminatory laws against Jews, it was the Sunni-oriented scholars who, going back to the Prophet Muhammad's final commands, concluded that Jews should not reside on the Arabian Peninsula. See Haykel, *Revival and Reform*, 118–21; Um, *The Merchant Houses*, 167f. Hathaway has argued that it may have been precisely Yemen's complicated multi-confessional make up of Zaydis, Ismailis, and Shafiis that did not allow for a messianic Jewish movement to upset that balance. Jane Hathaway, 'The

Mawzaʿ Exile at the Juncture of Zaydi and Ottoman Messianism', *Association for Jewish Studies Review* 29, 1 (2005), 111–28. In the mid-eighteenth century, a Banyan temple was destroyed in Mocha by Imam al-Mahdi Abbas under the influence of Ibn al-Amir, the pro-Sunni jurist. Um, *The Merchant Houses*, 169f.

131. Haykel, *Revival and Reform*, 11, 41ff.; vom Bruck, 'Regimes of Piety Revisited', 186. Al-Amir and al-Shawkani would enter the Salafi canon and become included in the curriculum of the Islamic University of Medina. Al-Albani, for example, edited a treatise of Ibn al-Amir to refute Ibn Taymiyya on the question of whether hell is eternal or not (Ibn al-Amir thought it was, Ibn Taymiyya might have thought it was not). Alexander Thurston, *Salafism in Nigeria: Islam, Preaching, and Politics* (Cambridge: Cambridge University Press, 2016), 47f. Ibn al-Amir wrote a book on *tawhid* that is still being printed and translated globally. See al-Imam al-Amir Muhammad ibn Ismaʿil al-Sanaʿani, *The Purification of Tawhid from the Filth of Deviation* (Birmingham: Dar as-Sunnah, 2009).

132. For Ibn al-Amir, see Dresch, *Tribes*, 213; Bernard Haykel, 'al-Amīr, Muḥammad b. Ismāʿīl', *EI3*. See also Haykel, *Revival and Reform*, passim, e.g. 22; Haykel, 'Al-Shawkâni and the Jurisprudential Unity of Yemen', *Revue des mondes musulmans et de la Méditerranée* 67 (1993), 53–65.

133. Haykel, *Revival and Reform*, 83–6. Despite these changes on the doctrinal level, the Qasimi Imamate did, however, retain Ali's double-bladed sword *Dhu l-Faqar* on their banner on red ground. Sir Robert Lambert Playfair, *History of Arabia Felix or Yemen from the Commencement of the Christian Era to the Present Time: Including an Account of the British Settlement of Aden* (Bombay: Education Society's Press, 1859), 29. I owe this reference to Kuehn, *Empire*, 39.

134. Haykel, *Revival and Reform*, 14, 128f. Ibn al-Amir initially welcomed the teachings and actions of Ibn Abd al-Wahhab, but then changed his mind and attacked the latter. Cook, 'On the Origins of Wahhābism', 201.

135. Haykel, *Revival and Reform*, 127–38.

136. After the overthrow of the Imamate, the Yemeni republic and its religious establishment also adopted this view. Ibid., 139f. For a more thorough discussion of this, including of the transformation of al-Shawkani's own thinking on this issue and on the position of Ali, see ibid., 139–64.

137. For more on the riots of 1796 and 1802 and the refutations by Zaydi scholars, see Haykel, *Revival and Reform*, 165–89. Interestingly, the 1802 riots seem to have started after al-Shawkani was teaching al-Bukhari's *Sahih* in Sanaa's Great Mosque, in response to which a Zaydi minister urged Sayyid Yahya bin Muhammad al-Huthi to teach a pro-Alid Zaydi work. Al-Huthi read the book in the Saladin mosque but then wanted to read it in the Great Mosque from which he was barred, after which his supporters started rioting.

138. It has long been a contested issue amongst Zaydis and between Zaydis and Twelver Shia. Kohlberg, 'The Term "Rāfida"'; Kohlberg, 'Some Zaydi Views'.

139. For a short account, see Dresch, *Tribes*, 212ff.

140. Um, *The Merchant Houses*, 6f.

141. For an account of the different Imams in the late eighteenth and nineteenth centuries, see Husayn b. 'Abdullah al-'Amri, *The Yemen in the 18th and 19th Centuries: A Political and Intellectual History* (London: Ithaca, 1985).

142. Kuehn terms it 'based on the institutionalization and reproduction of perceived difference'. Kuehn, *Empire*, 16f.

143. In 1882, Muhammad al-Huthi 'declared himself Imam at Barat and took the name al-Mahdi. He persisted in the claim until his death in 1901, but he was quite overshadowed by the Imams al-Hādī Sharaf al-Dīn (1879–90) and al-Manṣūr Muḥammad (1890–1904)'. Dresch, *Tribes*, 219–24, quote on page 219.

144. Kuehn, *Empire*, 18f., 179.

145. For the same argument in the Indian context, see Bayly, 'The Pre-History of "Communalism"?'.

CHAPTER 7

1. Hodgson, *Venture*, Vol. 3, 176–248. Bayly describes the transformation of these empires into modern nation-states by way of colonialism. Bayly, *The Birth of the Modern World*, 29–36, 89–92, and passim. See also Rudi Matthee, 'The Decline of Safavid Iran in Comparative Perspective', *Journal of Persianate Studies* 8, 2 (2015), 276–308; Rohan D'Souza, 'Crisis before the Fall: Some Speculations on the Decline of the Ottomans, Safavids and Mughals', *Social Scientist* 30, 9/10 (2002), 3–30.

2. The figure of a hundred million is an estimation. For an overview, see Francis Robinson, 'The British Empire and the Muslim World', in: R. Louis and J. Brown (eds), *The Oxford History of the British Empire*, Vol. 4 (Oxford: Oxford University Press, 1999), 398–420. For the figures on the Saudis, see Vassiliev, *The History of Saudi Arabia*, 111.

3. Christina Phelps Harris, 'The Persian Gulf Submarine Telegraph of 1864', *Geographical Journal* 135, 2 (1969), 169–90; Roland Wenzlhuemer, *Connecting the Nineteenth-Century World: The Telegraph and Globalization* (Cambridge: Cambridge University Press, 2013).

4. Bayly, *The Birth of the Modern World*, 247–83. Amongst the vast literature emphasising the profoundly transformative nature of the modern state, and the ways in which it was different from earlier forms of political organisation, see James C. Scott, *Seeing Like a State: How Certain Schemes to Improve the Human Condition have Failed* (New Haven: Yale University Press, 1998); Michael Mann, *The Sources of Social Power: The Rise of Classes and Nation-States, 1760–1914* (Cambridge: Cambridge University Press, 1993). In classical social theory, Max Weber's theorisation of the workings of the modern state, in particular the bureaucracy, has been especially influential and shaped much later enquiry. See, for example, Max Weber, 'Politik als Beruf (1919)', in: Dirk Kaesler (ed.), *Schriften 1894–1922* (Stuttgart: Alfred Kröner, 2002), 512–56, 513ff.

5. Christopher A. Bayly, *Empire and Information: Intelligence Gathering and Social Communication in India, 1780–1870* (Cambridge: Cambridge University Press, 1996). One such compendium was Lorimer's *Gazetteer*, which included much discussion of Sunni–Shia relations in the Gulf and focused on ethno-sectarian difference. Nelida Fuccaro, 'Knowledge at the Service of the British Empire: The Gazetteer of the Persian Gulf, Oman and Central Arabia', in: Inga Brandell, Marie Carlson, and Önver A. Cetrez (eds), *Borders and the Changing Boundaries of Knowledge* (Istanbul: Swedish Research Institute in Istanbul, 2015), 17–34; Omar al-Shehabi, *Contested Modernity: Sectarianism, Nationalism, and Colonialism in Bahrain* (London: Oneworld, 2019), 1, 13–25, and passim.

6. Edward Said's critique of the connection between knowledge and power in Oriental Studies is still powerful. See Edward W. Said, *Orientalism* (New York: Pantheon Books, 1978). He was of course not the first to voice such criticisms. For example, one of the first Shii English-language publications, the Lucknow-based *Muslim Review*, decried the anti-Shii bias of a lot of Orientalist scholarship. The journal carried a book review section in which such themes were often discussed. See, for example, S. M. A. Imam, 'The Orientalists', *The Muslim Review* 39, 4/5 (1952), 91–4, and 6/7 (1952), 130–2, who takes aim at Philip K. Hitti, *History of the Arabs* (London: Macmillan, 1937).

7. This whole idea has so thoroughly been problematised both by the rise of new religious movements in the 'West' as well as by arguments such as those of Bruno Latour. Bruno Latour, *We have Never been Modern* (Cambridge, MA: Harvard University Press, 1993).

8. Saba Mahmood, *Religious Difference in a Secular Age: A Minority Report* (Princeton: Princeton University Press, 2015). See also Talal Asad, *Formations of the Secular: Christianity, Islam, Modernity* (Stanford: Stanford University Press, 2003).

9. Bayly, *The Birth of the Modern World*, 325–65.

10. For example Krusiński, *The History of the Revolution of Persia*, viif., 2ff.

11. Jürgen Osterhammel, *Die Entzauberung Asiens: Europa und die asiatischen Reiche im 18. Jahrhundert* (Munich: C. H. Beck, 1998). It was translated as Osterhammel, *Unfabling the East: The Enlightenment's Encounter with Asia* (Princeton: Princeton University Press, 2018).

12. It was the only such eighteenth-century expedition to emanate from Scandinavia or Germany. Osterhammel refers to Niebuhr in his book on eighteenth-century European writings on Asia as an example of a relatively objective observer. Osterhammel, *Die Entzauberung Asiens*, passim, e.g. 81ff. Niebuhr at times referred to how Denmark could exploit business opportunities on his travels. There is a tendency particularly in Nordic scholarship to downplay this imperial context. Baack, *Undying Curiosity*, 246, 355, 380f., 390. See also Stephan Conermann, 'Carsten Niebuhr und das orientalistische Potential des Aufklärungsdiskurses—oder: Ist das Sammeln von Daten unverdächtig?', in: J. Wiesehöfer and S. Conermann (eds), *Carsten Niebuhr (1733–1815) und seine Zeit: Beiträge eines interdisziplinären Symposiums vom 7.-10. Oktober 1999 in Eutin* (Stuttgart: Franz Steiner, 2002), 403–32. For a collection of his writings on Islam, see Michel-Pierre Detalle and Renaud Detalle, 'L'Islam vu par Carsten

Niebuhr, voyageur en Orient (1761–1767)', *Revue de l'histoire des religions* 225, 4 (2008), 487–543. See also Thorkild Hansen, *Arabia Felix: The Danish Expedition of 1761–1767* (London: Collins, 1964).

13. Niebuhr relates: 'The Turks and Persians have been almost constantly at war; and their respective Princes have generally contrived to represent to their subjects disputes which originated from their ambition, as prompted by religious considerations. This is the reason for the violent hatred with which the Shiites and Sunnites are animated against one another. [...] In Persia, no Sunnite mosque is allowed, and the Turks tolerate the Shiites in the exercise of no other part of their worship, except their pilgrimage to their Prophet's tomb in the vicinity of Bagdad; and for this permission they pay very dear to the Ottoman Porte. In Yemen, the Sunnites and Zeidites live happily together; for the latter, who are the more tolerant of the two, are the predominant sect.' Niebuhr, *Travels through Arabia*, Vol. 2, 208.

14. For examples, see Ballaster, *Fabulous Orients*, 78; Mokhberi, *The Persian Mirror*, ch. 1; Gunny, *Images of Islam*, 35. For a critique of this analogy, see Strothmann, *Kultus*, 5f., 71–6; Strothmann, *Staatsrecht*, 62. Wellhausen juxtaposes the Shia with 'catholic Islam', which for him is Sunni Islam. Wellhausen, *Die religiös-politischen Oppositionsparteien*, 89. Schacht sees Sunni Islam as orthodox Islam in both his books. Schacht, *The Origins*. Even the *Encyclopaedia of Islam*, the monumental standard reference work in Islamic Studies, simply defines the 'Ahl al-Sunna' as '"Sunnites", i.e. the orthodox Muslims'. This entry is just a brief definition, does not have an author, and is linked to the entry on 'Sunna' by Juynboll and Brown. See 'Ahl al-Sunna', *EI2*.

15. Ballaster, *Fabulous Orients*, 149, 171.

16. Gunny, *Images of Islam*, 54; Suzanne L. Marchand, *German Orientalism in the Age of Empire: Religion, Race, and Scholarship* (Cambridge: Cambridge University Press, 2010), 25.

17. J. L. Burckhardt, *Notes on the Bedouins and Wahábys* (1830), quoted in: Bonacina, *The Wahhabis*, 108. See also ibid., 6–9.

18. Yildirim, 'Sunni Orthodox vs Shi'ite Heterodox?'.

19. Tariq al-Jamil, 'Sectarianism, Pre-Modern Islamic History, and the Bequest of Orientalism', *Maydan*, 23 October 2016, https://www.themaydan.com/2016/10/sectarianism-pre-modern-islamic-history-and-the-bequest-of-orientalism.

20. Madelung, *The Succession to Muḥammad*, 4ff. Madelung, on the other hand, argues that the sources indicate the designation of Ali as successor.

21. For example in the debate about the location of the tomb of Ali, in which some European scholars adopted the Sunni sources' scepticism as to whether he was actually buried in Najaf, as the Shia believe. Aslan claims to have discerned such a bias. After Ali's death, the legend goes, his body was buried in secret by his family members and closest associates, out of fear that his enemies, the Umayyads and Kharijis, could exhume and desecrate it. Aslan claims that the authors of the 'al-Nadjaf' entry in the *Encyclopaedia of Islam 2*, Honigmann and Bosworth, implicitly gave Sunni sources such as Ibn Battuta more weight and adopted the scepticism regarding the actual location of Ali's

tomb when they wrote that '[p]erhaps, then, the sanctuary of al-Nadjaf is not the real burial-place but a tomb held in reverence in the pre-Islamic period, especially as the graves of Adam and Noah were also shown there'. Aslan, *From Body to Shrine*, 41. See also E. Honigmann and C. E. Bosworth, 'al-Nadjaf', *EI2*.

22. During his only trip to the Middle East, he visited Damascus in 1873, where he found an important and controversial Shii manuscript (by Shustari, the Shii *Qadi* working under the Mughals who led a Shii assertion and was then put to death) in the library of a prominent Sunni. But the owner would only give him the manuscript on the condition that he not reveal that he had found it in his collection, for fear of reprisals. This was *Ihqaq al-Haqq wa Izhaq al-Batil* by Shustari. The Damascus library was the al-Sibai library. Kohlberg, 'Western Studies', 39.

23. He called Shiism a 'sektiererische Bewegung' and a 'Nährboden für Absurditäten [...], geeignet, die Gotteslehre des Islam völlig zu zersetzen und aufzulösen'. Ignaz Goldziher, *Vorlesungen über den Islam*, 1st ed. (Heidelberg: Carl Winter, 1910), 208, 220, cited after: Rainer Brunner, 'Die Schia', in: Rainer Brunner (ed.), *Islam: Einheit und Vielfalt einer Weltreligion* (Stuttgart: W. Kohlhammer, 2016), 310–37, 310. He denounced Shiism as unorthodox, especially in the early centuries of Islam, with his language being at times truly denigrating: 'So wie sie keine feste Organisation hat, so hat sie auch keine feste dogmatische Stellung; ihre Lehrsätze ranken sich wild und frei, an dem Lehrinhalt des orthodoxen Islam empor. Selbst gutgesinnte, regierungs- und religionstreue fromme Männer sind von den 'alidischen Liebhabereien der ältern Shi'a durchdrungen.' Also: 'Als wirkliche Sekten innerhalb des Islam können nur jene Gruppen betrachtet werden, deren Anhänger in Grundfragen, die für die Gesamtheit des Islams richtunggebende Bedeutung haben, sich von der Sunna, von der geschichtlich sanktionierten Gestaltung des Islams trennen und in ebensolchen Grundfragen sich dem Idschma' widersetzen.' Goldziher, *Muhammedanische Studien*, Vol. 2, 110. Goldziher held similarly derogatory views of Ismailis. In the introduction to his translation of al-Ghazali's anti-Ismaili heresiographical polemic *Kitab al-Mustazhiri*, Goldziher denounced the Ismailis' 'confessional nihilism', which 'must have seemed the most serious threat to the Muslim faithful'. Goldziher, *Streitschrift des Gazali gegen die Batinijja-Sekte* (Leiden: Brill, 1916), 22–5, who here seems to identify with the author rather than with the subject of the polemic he translated: 'Der konfessionelle Nihilismus, der die Grundlagen des Islams zersetzende Allegorismus, den die Emissäre dem Volke ebenso wie den Gebildeten stufenweise eingaben, musste den Vertretern der islamischen Glaubenstreue als die gefährlichste Bedrohung der Religion erscheinen.' Ibid., 23. Goldziher partially recognised this problem in the introduction to his volume on Sunni polemics towards the Shia, but nonetheless based much of his analysis of Shiism on these sources. Goldziher, *Beiträge*.

24. The Shia are thus dealt with in his chapter on 'Das Sektenwesen'. Ignaz Goldziher, *Vorlesungen über den Islam*, 2nd ed. (Heidelberg: Carl Winter, 1925), 189.

25. Ignaz Goldziher, *Die Richtungen der islamischen Koranauslegung: An der Universität Upsala gehaltene Olaus-Petri-Vorlesungen* (Leiden: Brill, 1920), 263–309, esp. 270ff.

He further says: 'Dies sind Ansätze zu einer bald üppig in die Halme schies-senden schiitischen Parteiexegese. Es ist auf keinem Gebiete der tendentiösen Koranauslegung in so unersättlicher Weise und mit solch übertreibenden Resultaten gearbeitet worden als eben in diesem Kreise.' Ibid., 269f.

26. Goldziher, *Die Richtungen*, 309. Nödelke's German original is an 'elendes Gewebe von Lügen und Dümmheiten'. Theodor Nöldeke, *Geschichte des Qorâns* (Göttingen: Dieterichsche Buchhandlung, 1860), xxix.

27. Nöldeke, *Geschichte*, xxix.

28. Eberhard, *Osmanische Polemik*, 85. It is even the title of a book published as late as 1987: Moosa, *Extremist Shiites*.

29. David Pinault, *The Shiites: Ritual and Popular Piety in a Muslim Community* (New York: St Martin's, 1992), 63–76. An interesting example is the account of a British woman who had married into a Shii family in Lucknow, capital of the Shii state of Awadh: B. Meer Hassan Ali, *Observations on the Mussulmauns of India: Descriptive of their Manners, Customs, Habits, and Religious Opinions, Made during a Twelve Years' Residence in their Immediate Society*, 2 Vols (London: Parbury, Allen & Co., 1832). See also Rianne Siebenga, 'Picturing Muharram: Images of a Colonial Spectacle, 1870–1915', *South Asia: Journal of South Asian Studies* 36, 4 (2013), 626–43.

30. Theodor Nöldeke, 'Zur Ausbreitung des Schiitismus', *Der Islam* 13, 1–2 (1923), 70–81. Wellhausen, for example, also refutes the strongly anti-Iranian views of Reinhart Dozy. Wellhausen, *Die religiös-politischen Oppositionsparteien*, 90.

31. Kohlberg, 'Western Studies', 35. Another extreme example was the Austrian Orientalist and diplomat Alfred von Kremer, who wrote a whole book explor-ing the 'foreign' influence on Arabs and Islam. He took issue with the alleged diffusion of the strong Arab national character and base of the Islamic move-ment through non-Arab elements, especially Persians, and saw Shiism as emer-ging out of this amalgam. Alfred von Kremer, *Culturgeschichtliche Streifzüge auf dem Gebiete des Islams* (Leipzig: F. A. Brockhaus, 1873), 12f. Upon his return from the 'Orient', he tried to apply racial theory to the Austro-Hungarian Empire and wrote a book against the 'Slavisation' of the Empire, in which he advocated social engineering in the Balkans. Alfred von Kremer, *Die Nationalitätsidee und der Staat* (Vienna: Carl Ronegen, 1885). Wellhausen empha-sises that, after Mukhtar's defeat, a group of Mawali 'knüpfte Verbindungen mit Churasan an, wo die iranische Volkskraft ihren eigentlichen Sitz hatte, und entfachte dort den Sturm, der die arabische Herrschaft hinweg fegte'. Wellhausen, *Die religiös-politischen Oppositionsparteien*, 89, 94.

32. Wortabet, a missionary in Aleppo, dedicated a chapter to the 'religion of the Metawileh', using a derogatory term for Shia. John Wortabet, *Researches into the Religions of Syria: Or Sketches, Historical and Doctrinal, of its Religious Sects, Drawn from Original Sources* (London: James Nisbet, 1860), 261, 282–5.

33. For an elaboration of different theories of origin, see Sayed A. Mousavi, *The Hazaras of Afghanistan: An Historical, Cultural, Economic and Political Study* (Richmond: Curzon, 1998), 19–43, 73; Hassan Poladi, *The Hazāras* (Lahore:

Mughal, 1989), 1–29. For the ascription of specific racial features, see, for example, N. L. St Pierre Bunbury, *A Brief History of the Hazara Pioneers (Indian Army): 1904 to 1933* (n.p./n.d., possibly London: 1949), 5–9; Hazara.net, 'The Hazara Pioneers (1904)', 2012, https://www.hazara.net/2012/11/the-hazara-pioneers-1904/.

34. Tomoko Masuzawa, *The Invention of World Religions: Or, How European Universalism was Preserved in the Language of Pluralism* (Chicago: University of Chicago Press, 2005), 202.

35. Rudolf Strothmann, 'Die Literatur der Zaiditen', *Islam* 1 (1910), 354–68, 356f.; Jarrar, 'Some Aspects of Imami Influence'; Daniel Peterson, 'Zaydiyya', *OBi*; Sabine Schmidtke, 'The History of Zaydī Studies: An Introduction', *Arabica* 59, 3–4 (2012), 185–99; Thiele, *Theologie*, 1–11. Many of these sources are still in manuscript form, although large-scale digitalisation projects are under way that will shed new light on the history of the Zaydiyya. Sabine Schmidtke and Jan Thiele, *Preserving Yemen's Cultural Heritage: The Yemen Manuscript Digitization Project* (Sanaa: Botschaft der Bundesrepublik Deutschland/Deutsches Archäologisches Institut, 2011).

36. Abdulrahman al-Salimi, 'Ibadi Studies and Orientalism', in: Angeliki Ziaka (ed.), *On Ibadism* (Hildesheim: Georg Olms, 2013), 23–34.

37. This was a translation of Jafar ibn al-Hasan al-Hilli al-Muhaqqiq al-Awwal by the 'consul de France à Tébriz'. Amédée Querry, *Droit musulman: Recueil de lois concernant les musulmans schyites*, 2 Vols (Paris: Imprimerie nationale, 1871/2).

38. 'Abd al-Jabar Naji, *Al-Tashayi' wa-l-Istishraq: 'Ard Naqdi Muqarin li-Dirasat al-Mustashriqin 'an al-'Aqida al-Shi'iyya wa A'imatiha* (Beirut: al-Jamal, 2011).

39. Thomas R. Trautmann, *Aryans and British India* (Berkeley: University of California Press, 1997). At times, Sufism was ascribed a Persianness as opposed to the Arabness of Islam. Masuzawa, *The Invention of World Religions*, 202.

40. This can be seen in the extensive reporting from Bahrain in the nineteenth and first half of the twentieth century in the India Office Records, much of which is digitised and word-searchable here: Qatar National Library, 'Qatar Digital Library', https://qdl.qa/en. See also Marc Owen Jones, *Political Repression in Bahrain* (Cambridge: Cambridge University Press, 2020), 1–4.

41. Bayly, *The Birth of the Modern World*, 351–7; Eileen M. Kane, *Russian Hajj: Empire and the Pilgrimage to Mecca* (Ithaca: Cornell University Press, 2015); John Slight, *The British Empire and the Hajj: 1865–1956* (Cambridge, MA: Harvard University Press, 2015); Eric Tagliacozzo, 'The Dutch Empire and the Hajj', in: David Motadel (ed.), *Islam and the European Empires* (Oxford: Oxford University Press, 2014), 73–89; Rasul Ja'fariyan, *Chahardah Safarnamah-i Hajj-i Qajar-i Digar* (Tehran: Ilm, 2013).

42. Barbara N. Ramusack, *The Indian Princes and Their States* (Cambridge: Cambridge University Press, 2004).

43. Jones, *Shi'a Islam*, 12; E. I. Brodkin, 'The Struggle for Succession: Rebels and Loyalists in the Indian Mutiny of 1857', *Modern Asian Studies* 6, 3 (1972), 277–90.

44. Michael H. Fisher, 'British Expansion in North India: The Role of the Resident in Awadh', *Indian Economic & Social History Review* 18, 1 (1981), 69–82.

45. There are several biographies of Wajid Ali Shah. For the most recent and read-able one, see Rosie Llewellyn-Jones, *The Last King in India: Wajid Ali Shah, 1822–1887* (London: Hurst, 2014).

46. Fisher, 'The Imperial Coronation', 276f. For Awadh–British relations in this period, see John Pemble, *The Raj, the Indian Mutiny, and the Kingdom of Oudh, 1801–1859* (New Delhi: Oxford University Press, 1979).

47. Cole, *Roots*, 272–81. For more on Maulavi Ahmadullah Shah, see Saiyid Zaheer Husain Jafri, *Awadh from Mughal to Colonial Rule: Studies in the Anatomy of a Transformation* (New Delhi: Gyan, 2016), 211–24, esp. 216.

48. Bayly, *Rulers, Townsmen and Bazaars*, 361.

49. There is a vast literature on this subject. For one account, see Roshan Taqui, *Lucknow 1857: The Two Wars at Lucknow: The Dusk of an Era* (Lucknow: New Royal Book, 2019).

50. Cole, *Roots*, 270f., 281; Jones, *Shi'a Islam*, 1ff.

51. On the grounds of the British Residency in Lucknow, for example, which the rulers built for the British, they also included an Imambara and a mosque. On his re-coronation as King on behalf of the British Resident in 1839, Muhammad Ali Shah sent fifty-one covered trays of food to the Queen Mother 'in the name of prayer for Hazrat Ali'. Rosie Llewellyn-Jones, *Engaging Scoundrels: True Tales of Old Lucknow* (New Delhi: Oxford University Press, 2000), 5. A Tyrolean scholar, Aloys Sprenger, was tasked by the Government of India with cata-loguing the library of the Shii ruler of Awadh at Lucknow in 1847, at a time when he was still nominally independent. Sprenger eventually stayed in India for years, published the catalogue, and edited several books, including Shii ones, and a key bibliography of Shii writings with the help of Indian Shii scholars. This was Shaykh al-Ta'ifa al-Imam Abu Jafar Muhammad b. al-Hasan al-Tusi, *Fihrist Kutub al-Shī'a*, ed. by Aloys Sprenger (Calcutta: 1848), and Aloys Sprenger (comp.), *A Catalogue of the Arabic, Persian and Hindustany Manuscripts: Of the Libraries of the King of Oudh*, Vol. 1 (Calcutta: 1854; reprint Osnabrück: 1979). A work of colonial ethnography written by an Indian Shii Muslim in the service of the British included Muharram descriptions. Jaffur Shurreef and G. A. Herklots, *Qanoon-e-Islam: Or, the Customs of the Moosulmans of India, Comprising a Full and Exact Account of their Various Rites and Ceremonies, from the Moment of Birth till the Hour of Death* (London: Parbury, Allen & Co., 1832).

52. There is extensive Ottoman critical reporting about relations between the Shii *mujtahids* and Britain. See, for example, Çetinsaya, *Ottoman Administration*, 113, 199. Initiated by the British ambassador to Tehran, Sir Arthur Hardinge, British officials extended contacts with the shrine cities. He was open about using the bequest to influence the clerics and disburse funds in a way that it would not become 'a hot-bed of sedition against its own founders and friends'. Ibid., 120; Arthur Henry Hardinge, *A Diplomatist in the East* (London: J. Cape, 1928), 319–24, quote on page 324. Hardinge was keenly aware of Ottoman attempts to use pan-Islam and to establish an alliance with Shiism and Iran against European colonial powers. Hardinge, *A Diplomatist in the East*, 273f.

53. For a recent reassessment, see Ajay Verghese, *The Colonial Origins of Ethnic Violence in India* (Stanford: Stanford University Press, 2016).

54. See, for example, Ayesha Jalal, *The Sole Spokesman: Jinnah, the Muslim League, and the Demand for Pakistan* (Cambridge: Cambridge University Press, 1985).

55. For an early elaboration, see Vinayak Damodar Savarkar, *Essentials of Hindutva* (n.p.: n.p., 1923).

56. Rieck, *The Shias of Pakistan*, 9. Just after independence and partition, the journal published by the Shii *madrasa* in Lucknow hoped that 'the conditions which 90 years of British rule in this country, with its basic principle of non-intervention and religious toleration had made us accustomed to' would continue in independent India. Editor's Table, *The Muslim Review* 35, 1 (1948), 1.

57. Sandria B. Freitag, *Collective Action and Community: Public Arenas and the Emergence of Communalism in North India* (Berkeley: University of California Press, 1989).

58. The seminaries that trained preachers in these disputations also started to publish widely and send missionaries across India and other parts of the British Empire. Rieck, *The Shias of Pakistan*, 12; Jones, *Shi'a Islam*, 89ff. For that general idea, see Metcalf, *Islamic Revival*, 198–234.

59. Abdul Halim Sharar, *Lucknow: The Last Phase of an Oriental Culture* (New Delhi: Oxford University Press, 1994), 86, 95.

60. This was Maqbool Ahmad. Jones, *Shi'a Islam*, 86f. On the Sunni side, Abd ul-Shakoor became the most famous anti-Shii polemicist. Ibid., 89.

61. Naval Kishore Press, run by a Hindu, was one of the most important publishers. It was based in Lucknow but had strong connections to Deobandi *ulama*. It also published crucial early translations into Urdu of key Islamic texts. Ulrike Stark, *An Empire of Books: The Naval Kishore Press and the Diffusion of the Printed Word in Colonial India* (Ranikhet: Permanent Black, 2007), 285–91.

62. These included biographies of the Imams, life stories of early Muslims and other members of the *Ahl al-Bayt*, and quite a few focused on personal piety and the 'proper' conduct of the ideal Muslim woman. These were printed by specific Shii printing presses established in Lucknow from the 1870s. Jones, *Shi'a Islam*, 58–72. The popularisation of texts and their printing undermined the position of the *ulama*. For the general impact of print, see Francis Robinson, 'Technology and Religious Change: Islam and the Impact of Print', *Modern Asian Studies* 27, 1 (1993), 229–51.

63. Interviews with teachers and students at Dar al-Ulum Deoband, India, 2019. For example the Urdu translation completed in 1307 and published by Mustafai Press in Lucknow in 1311. I found several copies of the Urdu translation in the library of the Madrasat al-Wazain and the Mahmudabad Library. For the early Deobandi positions on Shiism, see Metcalf, *Islamic Revival*, 149–53. There are some variations on this point, however, and at times Deobandis and the Dar al-Ulum have cooperated with Shia in political campaigns. An analysis of the fatwas produced on Shiism shows that they take what they themselves consider a 'middle ground': 'All the Shias are not kafir. Only the Shias are kafir who believe in the following: that Hazrat Gebriel (the angle [sic]) mistakenly put

revelation to Prophet Muhammad (Sallallahu Alaihi Wasallam) instead of Hazrat Ali; who believe that Hazrat Ali (Razi Allahu anhu) was a god; who blame on Hazrat Ayshah (Razi Allahu anha) of adultery; who believe corruption in the Holy Quran and who deny the companionship (Suhbat) of Hazrat Abu Bakr Siddique (Razi Allahu anhu) (Fatawa Shami, 4/135). But the Shias who believe only that Hazrat Ali was better (Afzal) than other companions and do not have other Shiite beliefs then they will not be considered as kafir.' (Fatwa: 108/L) Especially harsh judgments are reserved for Bohras and Ismailis. They are listed here: https://darulifta-deoband.com/home/qa/false-sects/3; e.g. https://darulifta-deoband.com/home/en/deviant-sects/1566; https://darulifta-deoband.com/home/en/false-sects/127.

64. Rizvi, 'Faith Deployed', 14, 33; Rizvi, *Shah 'Abd al-'Aziz*, 356–470; Metcalf, *Islamic Revival*, 211f.

65. It was the *'Abaqat al-Anwar fi Imamat A'imat al-Athar*, completed by his son. See 'A.-N. Monzavi, "Abaqāt al-Anwār', *EIr*; Al-Islam.org, 'Hadith al-Thaqalayn', https://www.al-islam.org/es/hadith-al-thaqalayn; Khan, 'Local Nodes', 62; Jones, *Shi'a Islam*, 53f. See also Ali al-Hussayni al-Milani (ed.), *Khalasa 'Abaqat al-Anwar fi Imamat A'imat al-Athar*, 6 Vols (Tehran: Mu'assassat al-Ba'atha, 1404h); interviews with Suleiman, the Raja of Mahmudabad, and Shii clerics, Mahmudabad and Lucknow, 2019.

66. Jones argues that these polemical works constitute a departure in the systematisation of Sunnism and Shiism. Jones, *Shi'a Islam*, 52–6.

67. Ali Khan Mahmudabad, *Poetry of Belonging: Muslim Imaginings of India 1850–1950* (New Delhi: Oxford University Press, 2020).

68. Jones, *Shi'a Islam*, 78ff.

69. Ibid., 94f.

70. The report on the census in Awadh in 1869 does refer to Sunnis and Shia as distinct categories, but states: 'I regret that the census papers afford no information as to the relative numbers of the two great Muhammadan sects, the Shi'as and Sunis. The latter are known to be by far the most numerous, but the Shi'a religion is the more fashionable, and more richly endowed in this province; and the ex-royal family and the greater part of the higher classes among the Muhammadan community belong to it.' J. Charles Williams, *The Report on the Census of Oudh*, Vol. 1 (Lucknow: Oudh Government Press, 1869), 76. The report then also briefly mentions 'Wahhabis' and the Bohras and 'Sadiqiyyas'. Ibid., 76f. The census also asked Muslims to identify with castes, which led to much confusion, as acknowledged by the census commissioner. Ibid., 86. See also Jones, *Shi'a Islam*, 7; Cole, *Roots*, 69–89.

71. India Census Commissioner, *Report on the Census of British India, Taken on the 17th February 1881*, Vol. 1 (London: Eyre & Spottiswoode, 1883), 26.

72. In the 1891 census, the columns of religion and caste/race were separately recorded. Jervoise A. Baines, *General Report on the Census of India, 1891* (London: Eyre & Spottiswoode, 1893), 186. For an overview of census questions since 1872, see Office of the Registrar General & Census Commissioner, India,

'Questions', https://censusindia.gov.in/Data_Products/Library/Indian_perceptive_link/Census_Questionaires_link/questions.htm. The 1881, 1891, and 1931 censuses ask specifically about sect, whereas the others do not. Hollister states that, in 1911 and 1921, Sunnis and Shia were counted separately in most provinces, generalising a practice that had been adopted in some provinces before, but that this was discontinued in 1931 and 1941. Hollister, *The Shi'a of India*, 181. The 1921 census was seemingly the last to differentiate Sunnis and Shia in the provinces that would become Pakistan, and no census was ever taken in Pakistan asking for sectarian identity. This increased the relevance of the 1921 census for later claims by communal organisations from both sides and meant that the number of Shia in Pakistan would henceforth be a constant source of debate. Rieck, *The Shias of Pakistan*, 13. This report also includes the curious comment that 'Sunni and Shiah fight shoulder to shoulder, leaving their own sectarian differences to be settled after the disposal of the common enemy'. Ibid., 169. In another example of using Sunni and Shii as distinct categories, the author favourably compares Indian Islam to Arabian Islam, arguing that 'in the former the "mild spirit of antiquity," as we have seen above, mitigated the asperity of sectarian hostility, so that Shiah and Sunni joined issue in doctrinal discussion without recourse to arms'. Ibid., 168.

73. For caste and the Raj more generally, see Susan Bayly, *Caste, Society and Politics in India from the Eighteenth Century to the Modern Age* (Cambridge: Cambridge University Press, 1999); Nicholas B. Dirks, *Castes of Mind: Colonialism and the Making of Modern India* (Princeton: Princeton University Press, 2001); Ram B. Bhagat, 'Census and Caste Enumeration: British Legacy and Contemporary Practice in India', *Genus* 62, 2 (2006), 119–34. For the general debate about counting 'minorities' and 'majorities' in a globalised world, see Arjun Appadurai, *Fear of Small Numbers: An Essay on the Geography of Anger* (Durham: Duke University Press, 2006), 47–86, 118, and passim.

74. The 1881 census had added the category of 'Wahabi' under sect, and 9,296 declared themselves as such. The census administrators were particularly worried that so few declared themselves as 'Wahabi', for they sought to get a better idea of the strength of this 'sect' that was seen as hostile to British government. India Census Commissioner, *Report on the Census of British India*, 26ff. These were, however, not the Wahhabis of the Arabian Peninsula, and the Indian group to which this was meant to apply eventually embraced a different name, Ahl-i Hadith: 'Certain members of the sect in the North-Western Provinces petitioned that the use of the name was not recognized by them and that they should be described as Ahli—Hadis or the people of the traditions.' D. C. Baillie, *Census of India, 1891*, Vol. 16 (Allahabad: North-Western Provinces and Oudh Government Press, 1894), 178.

75. Cole, *Roots*, 70ff.; Fisher, 'Political Marriage Alliances', 609; Hollister, *The Shi'a of India*, 181. The number of 'Shia' was comparatively small, especially in Awadh with its long history of Shii rule. R. Burn, *Census of India, 1901*, Vol. 16 (Allahabad: North-Western Provinces and Oudh Government Press, 1902), 79f.

76. Baillie, *Census of India, 1891,* Vol. 16, 177. I owe knowledge of this passage to Cole, *Roots,* 86 (the volume in Cole seems to be wrong; it is not 26 but 16). The census takers were aware of this 'problem' and the fact that they were imposing rigid boundaries on communities, as can be seen, for example, in their discussion of the difficulty of identifying groups that did not fall neatly into some of the categories in 1881. Baillie, *Census of India, 1891,* Vol. 16, 17ff.

77. Burn, *Census of India, 1901,* Vol. 16, 96.

78. In the 1901 census in the North-Western Provinces and Awadh, 6,430,766 were Sunnis and 183,208 Shias, while only 8,969 'were unable to state what their sect was, and 36443 more who were also ignorant of their sect, returned the name of a Muhammadan saint'. Burn, *Census of India, 1901,* Vol. 16, 96. In Bombay, however, only a quarter of Muslims filled in a sectarian affiliation. R. E. Enthoven, *Census of India, 1901,* Vol. 9 (Bombay: Government Central Press, 1902), 69. For figures of Sunnis and Shia, see ibid., 78.

79. Mushirul Hasan, 'Traditional Rites and Contested Meanings: Sectarian Strife in Colonial Lucknow', *Economic and Political Weekly* 31, 9 (1996), 543–50, 546.

80. Shriram Maheshwari, *The Census Administration under the Raj and After* (New Delhi: Concept, 1996), 111.

81. The Ahmadis feature in the 1901 census: 'The founder of this sect, Mirza Ghulam Ahmad, Chief of Qadian, has made special efforts to secure the complete return of his followers at this Census. He claims to be a Messiah, and has described the particular tenets of his sect in a document received at an early stage of the Census operations.' Enthoven, *Census of India, 1901,* Vol. 9, 69. The Ismailis are mentioned in the analysis of the census of Bombay, but there seems to be some confusion as to their identity, and the writer seems to assume that everyone who ticked 'Shiah' is part of the Ismaili community (though the author then also refers to the Aga Khan Khoja Ithna Ashari split). Ibid. The Khojas are also listed as a caste. Ibid., 106. A senior Shii *mujtahid* from Lahore, S. Ali al-Hairi, wrote a treatise on 'Census and Shiah Sect under the Benign British Government'. Hollister, *The Shi'a of India,* 40. Al-Hairi was the president of the AISC in 1914. Rieck, *The Shias of Pakistan,* 27. The AISC seems to even have toyed with the idea of establishing a Shia Directory and conducting a Shia census, though neither was ever realised. Ibid., 29.

82. Malik, *Islamische Gelehrtenkultur,* 322. See also Saiyid Naqi Husain Jafri, 'A Modernist View of Madrasa Education in Late Mughal India', in: Jan-Peter Hartung and Helmut Reifeld (eds), *Islamic Education, Diversity and National Identity: Dīnī Madāris in India Post 9/11* (New Delhi: Sage, 2006), 39–55.

83. David Lelyveld, *Aligarh's First Generation: Muslim Solidarity in British India* (Princeton: Princeton University Press, 1978), 123f.; Metcalf, *Islamic Revival,* 329f., 342f. See, for example, an account of Gertrude Bell's visit to Aligarh University: 'The College prides itself upon making no distinction between Shiah and Sunni. There are only 60 Shiahs—Lucknow is the great Shiah country. The prayers are however separate, there being a Shiah Maulvi though in the same mosque. The old Sunni used to teach the younger boys their earliest

education in Islam, but he became so polemical that they had to stop him and they no longer undertake any part of the religious training. Many of the masters do not know which of them is which.' Gertrude Bell Archive, 'Diaries: 29/1/1903', http://www.gerty.ncl.ac.uk/diary_details.php?diary_id=293. Much of the scholarship has emphasised the ecumenical nature of Aligarh, while Justin Jones has shown that soon a significant part of the Shii clergy and some of the old Shii elite turned away from Aligarh, eventually also forcing Aligarh's remaining Shii donors to stop their support and support more Shii educational institutions instead. Jones, *Shiʿa Islam*, 153–65. The founder of Aligarh, Sir Sayyid Ahmad Khan, had been particularly interested in the intellectual tradition of Shah Wali Allah and Shah Abd al-Aziz and had himself written a short treatise denouncing the mistakes of the Shia. Lelyveld, *Aligarh's First Generation*, 72. When he was criticised for his project by conservative Muslim circles and sought clerical endorsement, on the other hand, the founders of Deoband replied that they did not want to be involved with Aligarh because the latter included Shias. Ibid., 134. Initially, there were plans to have separate Sunni and Shii mosques on campus, Sunni and Shii Arabic teachers were hired, and there were separate religious teaching committees and 'deans' for Sunnis and Shia. Ibid., 157, 186, 200, 276.

84. Rizvi, *Shāh Walī-Allāh*, 379–92; Malik, *Islamische Gelehrtenkultur*, 187–248; Muhammad Qasim Zaman, 'Tradition and Authority in Deobandi Madrasas of South Asia', in: Robert W. Hefner and Muhammad Qasim Zaman (eds), *Schooling Islam: The Culture and Politics of Modern Muslim Education* (Princeton: Princeton University Press, 2007), 61–86; Sana Haroon, *Frontier of Faith: Islam in the Indo-Afghan Borderland* (New York: Columbia University Press, 2007), 33–124; Brannon D. Ingram, *Revival from Below: The Deoband Movement and Global Islam* (Oakland: University of California Press, 2018), 37, 56–64, 103, 106, and passim. For the institution's official history, see its website: Darul Uloom Deoband, 'Darul Uloom Deoband', http://www.darululoom-deoband.com/english.

85. Ẓafarul-Islām Khān, 'Nadwat al-ʿUlamā'', *EI2*; Malik, *Islamische Gelehrtenkultur*, 251–4, 270f., 279f., 489; Metcalf, *Islamic Revival*, 342; Jones, *Shiʿa Islam*, 55f. A report from 1901 still states that 'another object advocated by its adherents is a more friendly spirit between members of different sects and it specially aims at keeping Sunnis and Shia on good terms, according to some authorities even attempting to obliterate all sectarian differences, though this has been denied'. Burn, *Census of India, 1901*, Vol. 16, 89. Plans for the establishment of a Dar al-Ifta, a Fatwa Institute, associated with the Nadwat al-Ulama, further contributed to the exclusion of Shiism from the institution (though it did strive to represent different Sunni schools). Malik, *Islamische Gelehrtenkultur*, 423. See also Jan-Peter Hartung, 'The Nadwat al-ʿUlama': Chief Patron of Madrasa Education in India and a Turntable to the Arab World', in: Jan-Peter Hartung and Helmut Reifeld (eds), *Islamic Education, Diversity and National Identity: Dīnī Madāris in India Post 9/11* (New Delhi: Sage, 2006), 135–57.

86. At the same time, he wrote poetry adoring the *Ahl al-Bayt*. Metcalf, *Islamic Revival*, 307f.; Usha Sanyal, *Ahmad Riza Khan Barelwi: In the Path of the Prophet* (Oxford: Oneworld, 2005), 76, 78, 96f., 108. See also Ahmad Raza Khan, *Majmūʿa-yi Risāʾil-i Radd-i Ravāfiẓ: Radd al-Rafaẓa: Al-Adillat al-Tāʿina: Risala-yi Tāʿziyadari / Tasnif Imam Aḥmad Raza Qadiri Barelvi* (Lahore: Markazi Majlis-i Riza, 1986).

87. Eaton, *The Rise of Islam*, 282; Muin-ud-din Ahmad Khan, *History of the Faraʾidi Movement in Bengal, 1818–1906* (Karachi: Pakistan Historical Society, 1965), xxxiii, liv, lxii, lxxxvff., and passim.

88. His father, Aulad Hasan, especially was against *taqiyya*. Preckel, *Islamische Bildungsnetzwerke*, 143f.

89. Siddiq Hasan Khan banned their Muharram processions. Saeedullah, *The Life and Works of Muhammad Siddiq Hasan Khan, Nawab of Bhopal: 1248–1307/1832–1890* (Lahore: Ashraf, 1973), 65, 139; Preckel, *Islamische Bildungsnetzwerke*, 425f. Under previous Nawabs, some Shia had been patronised by the rulers and maintained close links to the Chishtiyya. Ibid., 74f. Khan took anti-Shii positions in numerous of his writings. Ibid., 375–80.

90. When the question arose as to whether al-Shawkani was a Zaydi, his defenders in India emphasised that the Zaydiyya was close to Sunnism. Preckel, *Islamische Bildungsnetzwerke*, 121f. For more on the reception of al-Shawkani, see Johanna Pink, 'Where does Modernity Begin? Muhammad al-Shawkani and the Tradition of Tafsīr', in: Johanna Pink and Andreas Görke (eds), *Tafsir and Intellectual History: Exploring the Boundaries of a Genre* (Oxford: Oxford University Press/Institute of Ismaili Studies, 2014), 323–60.

91. Preckel, *Islamische Bildungsnetzwerke*, 217–28; Guido Steinberg, *Religion und Staat in Saudi-Arabien: Die wahhabitischen Gelehrten 1902–1953* (Würzburg: Ergon, 2002), 91, 117.

92. Such as the Iraqi al-Alusi family, who encouraged the Ottomans to counter Shii proselytisation in nineteenth-century Iraq. They came across his books in Cairo. Nafi, 'Salafism Revived', 57; Seema Alavi, *Muslim Cosmopolitanism in the Age of Empire* (Cambridge, MA: Harvard University Press, 2015), 276–330.

93. Rizvi, 'Shiʿa Madaris of Awadh', 112–15; Jones, *Shiʿa Islam*, 32–9.

94. It propagated general Islamic principles, and specifically Shii ones. Jones, *Shiʿa Islam*, 39f., 65f., 188; Rizvi, 'Shiʿa Madaris of Awadh', 115f.; Khan, 'Local Nodes'.

95. Malik, *Islamische Gelehrtenkultur*, 270; Jones, *Shiʿa Islam*, 160–5.

96. Jones, *Shiʿa Islam*, 40f.

97. Pro-British Shii leaders emphasised, for example, that Shia did not believe in the concept of Jihad in the absence of the Imam. Jones, *Shiʿa Islam*, 165–72, 184.

98. Faisal Devji, *Muslim Zion: Pakistan as a Political Idea* (London: Hurst, 2013), 67.

99. It replaced an association that had been founded by the senior Shii clerics of Lucknow in 1901, but tensions between the AISC and the senior clerics would characterise intra-Shii politics in the coming decades. Hollister, *The Shiʿa of India*, 181, 187f.; Simon Wolfgang Fuchs, *In a Pure Muslim Land: Shiʿism between Pakistan and the Middle East* (Chapel Hill: University of North Carolina Press, 2019), 16–52; Jones, *Shiʿa Islam*, 117ff., 156–64.

100. Jones, *Shi'a Islam*, 120–3.
101. For example in Hyderabad, Lucknow, Hooghly, Bihar, and Dhaka. Claire Alexander, Joya Chatterji, and Annu Jalais, *The Bengal Diaspora: Rethinking Muslim Migration* (London: Routledge, 2015), ch. 6.
102. Hyder, *Reliving Karbala*, 84f. See also, in general, Jamal Malik, *Islam in South Asia: A Short History* (Leiden: Brill, 2008), 111–7.
103. Burn, *Census of India, 1901*, Vol. 16, 96.
104. Francis Robinson, 'The Emergence of Lucknow as a Major Political Centre, 1899–1923', in: Violette Graff (ed.), *Lucknow: Memories of a City* (New Delhi: Oxford University Press, 1999), 196–212.
105. Peter Reeves, 'Lucknow Politics: 1920–47', in: Violette Graff (ed.), *Lucknow: Memories of a City* (New Delhi: Oxford University Press, 1999), 213–26, 224.
106. Jones, *Shi'a Islam*, 114; Veena Talwar Oldenburg, *The Making of Colonial Lucknow, 1856–1877* (Princeton: Princeton University Press, 1984), 112f.
107. This was the 'Piggot Committee'. Rieck, *The Shias of Pakistan*, 20; Jones, *Shi'a Islam*, 100–4. For an in-depth study of the ecumenical and divisive legacy of Muharram in Lucknow, see Keith Hjortshoj, *Kerbala in Context: A Study of Muharram in Lucknow, India* (PhD, Cornell University, 1977), 214–47.
108. Jones, *Shi'a Islam*, 105–12. See also Sharar, *Lucknow*, 151.
109. This has been studied in depth: Imtiaz Ahmad, 'The Shia-Sunni Dispute in Lucknow, 1905–1980', in: Milton Israel and Narendra K. Wagle (eds), *Islamic Society and Culture: Essays in Honour of Professor Aziz Ahmad* (New Delhi: Manohar, 1983), 335–50; Freitag, *Collective Action and Community*; Hollister, *The Shi'a of India*, 188ff.; Jones, *Shi'a Islam*, 186–221; Fuchs, *In a Pure Muslim Land*, 22–5; Shereen Ilahi, 'Sectarian Violence and the British Raj: The Muharram Riots of Lucknow', *India Review* 6, 3 (2007), 184–208; Nandini Gooptu, *The Politics of the Urban Poor in Early Twentieth-Century India* (Cambridge: Cambridge University Press, 2001), 301ff.; Hasan, 'Traditional Rites'.
110. This was Nawab Sayyid Raza Ali Khan, who was installed as Rampur's ruler in August 1930 by the governor of the United Provinces, Sir Malcolm Hailey. Lance Brennan, 'A Case of Attempted Segmental Modernization: Rampur State, 1930–1939', *Comparative Studies in Society and History* 23, 3 (1981), 350–81, 354, 361ff., 372.
111. Fuchs, *In a Pure Muslim Land*, 33.
112. Haroon, *Frontier of Faith*, 149–53, 158.
113. Rizvi, *A Socio-Intellectual History*, Vol. 1, 1–6, 158. Two competing English-language editions were, for example, published in 1860s India of Abdul Qadir Badauni's *Muntakhab al-Tawarikh*, which contained strong anti-Shii references. Ulrike Stark, *An Empire of Books: The Naval Kishore Press and the Diffusion of the Printed Word in Colonial India* (Ranikhet: Permanent Black, 2007), 302.
114. Rubin argues that, rather than dividing the Ottoman court system into secular and religious spheres, the Nizamiyya and Sharia courts were actually 'entwined components of a single judicial system, converging in some aspects and departing in others', leading to what he calls 'legal pluralism'. Avi Rubin,

Ottoman Nizamiye Courts: Law and Modernity (New York: Palgrave Macmillan, 2011), 15, ch. 2.

115. There are reports of the Ottoman government in nineteenth-century Jabal Amil appointing Shii judges, and of Ottoman administrators tolerating similar Shii judges in al-Ahsa and Qatif. Mervin, *Un réformisme chiite*, 91f.; Wortabet, *Researches into the Religions of Syria*, 281f.; al-Amin, *Mustadrakat Aʿyan al-Shiʿa*, Vol. 8, 298f.; Steinberg, *Religion und Staat*, 474–7; ʿAbdallah ibn Nasir al-Subayʿi, *Al-Qadaʾ wa-l-Awqaf fi al-Ahsaʾ wa-l-Qatif wa Qatar Athnaʾ al-Hukm al-ʿUthmani al-Thani 1871–1913* (Judiciary and Religious Endowments in al-Ahsa, Qatif, and Qatar during the Second Period of Ottoman Rule 1871–1913) (Riyadh: Matabiʿ al-Jumʿa al-Iliktruniyya, 1999), 38ff., 77, 85; Muhammad ʿAli al-Hirz, ʿAl-Qadaʾ al-Jaʿfari fi al-Ahsaʾ, *al-Waha* 20 (2001), 19–38, 23.

116. Some of the differences related both to the territories under colonial control and to the legal traditions in the colonising countries (i.e. common law in Britain). In the Dutch East Indies, a mix of Sunni Shafii law and 'customary' law was applied. William R. Roff, 'Customary Law, Islamic Law, and Colonial Authority: Three Contrasting Case Studies and their Aftermath', *Islamic Studies* 49, 4 (2010), 455–62.

117. This is a vast and expanding field of inquiry. For an overview of the literature, see Nandini Chatterjee, 'Reflections on Religious Difference and Permissive Inclusion in Mughal Law', *Journal of Law and Religion* 29, 3 (2014), 396–415. See also Eaton, *India in the Persianate Age*, 336f.; Mouez Khalfoui, 'Together but Separate: How Muslim Scholars Conceived of Religious Plurality in South Asia in the Seventeenth Century', *Bulletin of the School of Oriental and African Studies* 74, 1 (2011), 87–96. For a micro-study, see Nandini Chatterjee, *Negotiating Mughal Law: A Family of Landlords across Three Indian Empires* (Cambridge: Cambridge University Press, 2020). For an older account, see Wahed Husain, *Administration of Justice during the Muslim Rule in India: With a History of the Origin of the Islamic Legal Institutions* (Calcutta: University of Calcutta, 1934). Basheer Ahmad argues that there was no difference between the administration of justice in the Shii-led states and the rest of the Mughal Empire or other Sunni-led dynasties. Muhammad Basheer Ahmad, *The Administration of Justice in Medieval India: A Study in Outline of the Judicial System under the Sultans and the Badshahs of Delhi Based Mainly upon Cases Decided by Medieval Courts in India between 1206–1750 A. D.* (Allahabad: Aligarh Historical Research Institute, 1941), 96.

118. '[A]s the judgments in the Baqiat and the Collections which relate to North and South India respectively show, there was no difference between the Sunni and the Shiah systems of the administration of justice.' Ahmad, *The Administration of Justice*, 96.

119. It is reported that, in Bijapur in the early sixteenth century, the Hanafi, Shafii, and Jafari schools of jurisprudence coexisted, but it is not clear what that meant for the judiciary. Hollister, *The Shiʿa of India*, 113.

120. Muhammad Khalid Masud, 'Anglo-Muhammadan law', *EI3*. Julia Stephens has argued that, because the EIC actually did apply aspects of Islamic law much more broadly until the mid-nineteenth century, the late-eighteenth-century narrative of the origin of 'personal law' in India is problematic. Julia Stephens, *Governing Islam: Law, Empire, and Secularism in Modern South Asia* (Cambridge: Cambridge University Press, 2018), 29ff.

121. W. H. Macnaghten, *Principles and Precedents of Moohummudan Law: Being a Compilation of Primary Rules Relative to the Doctrine of Inheritance (Including the Tenets of the Schia Sectaries), Contracts and Miscellaneous Subjects* (Calcutta: Church Mission Press, 1825). See also Grady, *A Manual of the Mahommedan Law*.

122. Gregory C. Kozlowski, *Muslim Endowments and Society in British India* (Cambridge: Cambridge University Press, 1985), 118. Anderson quotes 'Rajah Deedar Hossain v. Ranee Zuhoornussa (1841) 2 MIA 441' as the first case making the distinction. Michael Anderson, 'Islamic Law and the Colonial Encounter in British India', in: David Arnold and Peter Robb (eds), *Institutions and Ideologies: A SOAS South Asia Reader* (Richmond: Curzon, 1993), 165–85. But there is also a case from 1822 that revisits an earlier inheritance case of 1820, which was ruled according to Sunni doctrine, but in 1822 the Shii doctrine of the parties was taken into account and the case settled accordingly. Grady, *A Manual of the Mahommedan Law*, 148.

123. The introduction to the 1825 compendium, written by W. H. Macnaghten, an influential British Orientalist and official, who would later play a key role in the Anglo-Afghan war, states this paradox clearly: 'This Code has hitherto had no weight in India, and even at Lucknow, the seat of heterodox majesty itself, the tenets of the Soonees are adhered to. I have however given a compendium of their law of inheritance, extracted from the "Shuraya ool Islam", a work of the highest authority among them. This I was induced to do, as no account has ever been rendered, to my knowledge, of the doctrine of the sect in question, on the law of inheritance; and as I have reason to believe that our Courts of justice have passed decisions avowedly in conformity to its principles. Considering the universal toleration that prevails throughout the British dominions of India, it is perhaps but equitable, that the Law should be administered to the sectaries in question, agreeably to their own notions of jurisprudence, especially in matters affecting the succession to property, in which cases both parties are of course always of the same persuasion.' Macnaghten, *Principles and Precedents*, xii.

124. Sayyid Dildar Ali, the senior Shii cleric in Awadh, even commended the British for allowing Muslim, including Shii, law to be practised in territory under their control and thus differentiated this territory from territory under the control of unbelievers against whom Muslims must wage war (for example Punjab under the Sikhs). Cole, *Roots*, 255. Taking employment in the service of the British became more widespread amongst Shia, facilitated by a ruling by a Lucknow-based senior *mujtahid* that justified it in the 1830s. Ibid., 258.

125. Muhammad Quli Kinturi (1773–1844), after training with Dildar Ali in Lucknow, entered the service of the British government of Delhi in the Pargana of Meerut in 1806, rose in ranks, and, upon retiring in 1841, was essential in establishing the Shii court system in Awadh after writing a work advocating a Shii judicial system dedicated to Amjad Ali Shah. In Delhi he mainly dealt with property and criminal cases and apparently ruled according to Shii jurisprudence. Cole, *Roots*, 139ff., 209–13, 257f. And suits between Sunnis, or between Sunnis and Hindus, continued to be judged according to Sunni law. Neil B. E. Baillie, *A Digest of Moohummudan Law on the Subjects to which it is Usually Applied by British Courts of Justice in India* (London: Smith, Elder & Co., 1865), xi.

126. Thereafter, however, Shii law was only applied to marriage and inheritance 'where the parties [were] Sheeahs'. Baillie, *A Digest of Moohummudan Law on the Subjects to which it is Usually Applied*, xii. Baillie's introduction then gives an overview of major differences between Shia and Hanafis in these fields for the English reader, and for British judges. Ibid., xiv–xxvii.

127. A first volume by John Baillie (started by William Jones), *A Digest of Mohummudan Law: According to the Tenets of the Twelve Imams (by a Native Jurist) Extended, so as to Comprize the Whole of the Imameea Code of Jurisprudence* (Calcutta: Honourable Company's Press, 1805), and a second volume on Shii law by Neil B. E. Baillie, *A Digest of Moohummudan Law on the Subjects to which it is Usually Applied by British Courts of Justice in India* (London: Smith, Elder & Co., 1865). John Baillie had been commissioned in 1798 by officials in Calcutta to continue a project started by the Orientalist William Jones, who had started to translate Shii law texts on inheritance and contracts. The latter volume includes only what by then had become known as personal law, to which the application of Islamic law had by then become confined. It was the first separate manual on Shii law published in British India and, given that seventy years had passed between its commissioning and its final publication, cannot have been the most pressing undertaking. Stephens, *Governing Islam*, 22f. See also Kohlberg, 'Western Studies', 36.

128. Grady, *A Manual of the Mahommedan Law*, xxxiii. It is not entirely clear when this distinction was first made, and the earliest British legal manuals contradict themselves on this. Ibid., xxxvi. For a further elaboration on the differences between Sunni and Shii law, see ibid., xxxvii–lii.

129. Muhammad Khalid Masud, 'Anglo-Muhammadan law', *EI3*; Scott Alan Kugle, 'Framed, Blamed and Renamed: The Recasting of Islamic Jurisprudence in Colonial South Asia', *Modern Asian Studies* 35, 2 (2001), 257–313.

130. Ali, *Mahommedan Law*. For the importance of the schools of jurisprudence, see ibid., 24. The book's original title when it was first published in 1880 makes even more explicit reference to this: Ameer Ali, *The Personal Law of the Mahommedans (According to All the Schools) Together with a Comparative Sketch of the Law of Inheritance among the Sunnis and the Shias* (London: W. H. Allen, 1880).

131. It was applied in British colonies such as the Sudan, Nigeria, Palestine, and East Africa, although with variations taking into account Maliki or Shafii legal doctrines predominant in those countries. Masud, 'Anglo-Muhammadan law'.

132. Kozlowski, *Muslim Endowments*, 118f.

133. In this way, the Shii Imambara in Hooghly became Hooghly College, a training institution for EIC civil servants. Kugle, 'Framed, Blamed and Renamed', 293f.

134. David S. Powers, 'Orientalism, Colonialism, and Legal History: The Attack on Muslim Family Endowments in Algeria and India', *Comparative Studies in Society and History* 31, 3 (1989), 535–71, 554–7.

135. Jones, *Shiʿa Islam*, 78.

136. Ibid., 125–38; Oldenburg, *The Making of Colonial Lucknow*, 191–9. For a study of the impact of the transition from Nawabi to British rule on a Sufi *khanqah* in Awadh, including on the *awqaf* that supported it, see Jafri, *Awadh*, esp. 125–62, 277–305.

137. Some of the Indian Shii clerics involved in the disbursing of the funds argued that it could be a pro-British, Shii counterweight to the pan-Islamism supported by the Ottoman Sultan. Jones, *Shiʿa Islam*, 134–7.

138. Cited in: Elisa Giunchi, 'The Reinvention of Sharīʿa under the British Raj: In Search of Authenticity and Certainty', *Journal of Asian Studies* 69, 4 (2010), 1119–42, 1134.

139. Farhad Daftary, 'Religious Identity, Dissimulation and Assimilation: The Ismaili Experience', in: Yasir Suleiman (ed.), *Living Islamic History: Studies in Honour of Professor Carole Hillenbrand* (Edinburgh: Edinburgh University Press, 2010), 47–61. Another group of Ismailis, the Guptis, at times claimed to be Hindus. Shafique N. Virani, 'Taqiyya and Identity in a South Asian Community', *Journal of Asian Studies* 70, 1 (2011), 99–139.

140. There were even subsequent debates about whether major figures in the community were Sunni or Shii, such as in the case of Pir Mashayakh (d. 1697). Daftary, *The Ismailis*, 444–51.

141. For the interplay between the colonial state and Indians in the construction of a Hindu identity, see Brian K. Pennington, *Was Hinduism Invented? Britons, Indians, and the Colonial Construction of Religion* (Oxford: Oxford University Press, 2005).

142. See, for example, W. F. P. Napier, *The Conquest of Scinde: With Some Introductory Passages in the Life of Major-General Sir Charles James Napier* (Cambridge: Cambridge University Press, 2012), 25–61.

143. Hamid Algar, 'The Revolt of Agha Khan Mahallati and the Transference of the Ismaili Imamate to India', *Studia Islamica* 29 (1969), 55–81, 75–80; Teena Purohit, *The Aga Khan Case: Religion and Identity in Colonial India* (Cambridge, MA: Harvard University Press, 2012), 18–22; Hamid Algar, 'ĀQĀ KHAN', *EIr*. Once the Aga Khan reached Sindh, Richard Burton was appointed as a kind of liaison officer between the EIC and him. Edward Rice, *Captain Sir Richard Francis Burton: The Secret Agent Who Made the Pilgrimage to Mecca, Discovered the Kama Sutra, and Brought the Arabian Nights to the West* (New York: Scribner, 1990), 89–102.

144. Daftary, *The Ismailis*, 463–76; Haider, *Shiʻi Islam*, 141, 182–9.
145. I thank Adrian Ruprecht for pointing me towards some of this literature. Nile Green, *Bombay Islam: The Religious Economy of the West Indian Ocean, 1840–1915* (Cambridge: Cambridge University Press, 2011), 171–4; Purohit, *The Aga Khan Case*; Daftary, *The Ismailis*, 474ff.; Michel Boivin, 'The Ismaʻili-Isna ʻAshari Divide among the Khojas: Exploring Forgotten Judicial Data from Karachi', *Journal of the Royal Asiatic Society* 24, 3 (2014), 381–96.
146. Faisal Devji, 'The Idea of Ismailism', *Critical Muslim* 10 (2014), 51–62; Soumen Mukherjee, *Ismailism and Islam in Modern South Asia: Community and Identity in the Age of Religious Internationals* (Cambridge: Cambridge University Press, 2017); Mukherjee, 'Universalising Aspirations: Community and Social Service in the Ismaʻili Imagination in Twentieth-Century South Asia and East Africa', *Journal of the Royal Asiatic Society* 24, 3 (2014), 435–53. The Institute of Ismaili Studies, established in London in 1977, is devoted to the systematic editing and publication of Ismaili texts and studies about Ismaili history.
147. Grady, *A Manual of the Mahommedan Law*, 8. For an analysis of this, leading up to the Aga Khan case, see Amrita Shodhan, 'Legal Formulation of the Question of Community: Defining the Khoja Collective', *Indian Social Science Review* 1, 1 (1999), 137–51.
148. Suleimani Bohras, for example, became prominent in law. Kozlowski, *Muslim Endowments*, 116f.; Daftary, *The Ismailis*, 300; Blank, *Mullahs on the Mainframe*, 42. A. A. A. Fyzee (1899–1981) is a case in point. A member of the Suleimani Ismaili Bohra community, he studied law in India, then Arabic and Persian at Cambridge, and became an advocate in the Bombay High Court and prominent author and Principal and Professor of Jurisprudence at Government Law College, Mumbai, from 1938 to 1947. After partition, he served as India's first ambassador to Egypt (1949–51). Farhad Daftary, 'Professor Asaf A. A. Fyzee (1899–1981)', *Arabica* 31, 3 (1984), 327–30. See Asaf Ali Asghar Fyzee, *Outlines of Muhammadan Law* (New Delhi: Oxford University Press, 1974). See also, for example, his works on Ismaili law: Fyzee, *The Ismaili Law of Wills* (London: Oxford University Press, 1933); Qadi al-Nuʻman, *Daʻaʼim al-Islam*, ed. by A. A. A. Fyzee, 2 Vols (Cairo: Dar al-Maʻarif, 1951/60). And on Twelver Shiism: Fyzee, *A Shiʻite Creed*. For a similar process amongst the Parsis, who from the 1860s on entered the law profession and through litigation against each other established a set of personal status law precedents that boosted their prominence in the legal field, see Mitra Sharafi, *Law and Identity in Colonial South Asia: Parsi Legal Culture, 1772–1947* (New York: Cambridge University Press, 2014). As a community originally from Iran, Parsis would be aware of sectarian difference in Islam.
149. S. T. Lokhandwalla, 'Islamic Law and Ismaili Communities (Khojas and Bohras)', *Indian Economic & Social History Review* 4, 2 (1967), 155–76.
150. Seema Alavi, 'Slaves, Arms, and Political Careering in Nineteenth-Century Oman', in: Eric Tagliacozzo, Helen F. Siu, and Peter C. Perdue (eds), *Asia Inside Out: Itinerant People* (Cambridge, MA: Harvard University Press, 2019),

179–200, 182ff. There is a large literature on this. On Zanzibar, for example, see Judy Aldrick, *The Sultan's Spymaster: Peera Dewjee of Zanzibar* (Naivasha: Old Africa Books, 2015).

151. For the Khojas, see Khoja (Pirhai) Shia Isna Asheri Jamaat, 'Our History: Origin of Khoja Community', https://kpsiaj.org/our-history. *The Muslim Review*, the English-language publication of the Madrasat al-Waizin in Lucknow, founded in 1911 by Maharaja Sir Mohammad Ali Mohammad Khan Bahadur, was in later years co-financed by members of the Khoja Ithna Ashari community, such as Haji Dawood Nasser Saheb, who is described as a 'leading Shia millionaire'. *The Muslim Review* 42 (1950), back cover. For Bohras, see Blank, *Mullahs on the Mainframe*; Kartikeya, 'Mumbai Bohras Breathe New Life into Iraq Shrine', *Times of India*, 21 March 2010. See also this in-depth study of the Bohra of Madagascar and their connections to other Bohra communities and Iraq. Denis Gay, *Les Bohra de Madagascar: Religion, commerce et échanges transnationaux dans la construction de l'identité ethnique* (Zurich: LIT, 2009), 117–44.

152. For the example of the Khoja World Islamic Network, see Shireen Mirza, 'Travelling Leaders and Connecting Print Cultures: Two Conceptions of Twelver Shi'i Reformism in the Indian Ocean', *Journal of the Royal Asiatic Society* 24, 3 (2014), 455–75.

153. In the context of colonial Zanzibar, for example, differences again crystallised themselves over inheritance and marriage with non-Khojas. The Aga Khan also issued regulations limiting interactions of his followers with Twelver Shii Khojas. The latter and the Sunni Khojas practised exogamy and at times temporary marriage, while Ismaili Khojas tried to practise endogamy. Iqbal Akhtar, 'Negotiating the Racial Boundaries of Khōjā Caste Membership in Late Nineteenth-Century Colonial Zanzibar (1878–1899)', *Journal of Africana Religions* 2, 3 (2014), 297–316. See also Richa Nagar, 'Religion, Race, and the Debate over Mut'a in Dar es Salaam', *Feminist Studies* 26, 3 (2000), 661–90; Ludovic Gandelot, 'Islam Shia Ithna Asheri et migrations: Chez les Khojas, 1860–1925', in: Michel Boivin (ed.), *Les Ismaéliens d'Asie du sud: Gestion des héritages et productions identitaires* (Paris: L'Harmattan, 2007), 199–219; Hardinge, *A Diplomatist in the East*, 99f.; Crawford, 'Religion and Religious Movements'.

154. Ingram, *Revival from Below*, 164f.

155. James Onley, 'Transnational Merchants in the Nineteenth-Century Gulf: The Case of the Safar Family', in: Madawi al-Rasheed (ed.), *Transnational Connections and the Arab Gulf* (London: Routledge, 2005), 59–89; Onley, *The Arabian Frontier of the British Raj: Merchants, Rulers, and the British in the Nineteenth-Century Gulf* (Oxford: Oxford University Press, 2007), 136–88.

156. Staci Strobl, *Sectarian Order in Bahrain: The Social and Colonial Origins of Criminal Justice* (Lanham: Lexington Books, 2018), 94ff.

157. Nelida Fuccaro, 'Mapping the Transnational Community: Persians and the Space of the City in Bahrain, c. 1869–1937', in: Madawi al-Rasheed (ed.), *Transnational Connections and the Arab Gulf* (London: Routledge, 2005), 39–58.

158. Conor Meleady, '"Far from the Orthodox Road": Conceptualizing the Shi'a in the Nineteenth-Century Official Mind', in: Justin Quinn Olmstead (ed.), *Britain in the Islamic World: Imperial and Post-Imperial Connections* (Basingstoke: Palgrave Macmillan, 2019), 57–85.

159. Senzil K. Nawid, *Religious Response to Social Change in Afghanistan, 1919–29: King Aman-Allah and the Afghan Ulama* (Costa Mesa: Mazda, 1999), 6ff.

160. Solaiman M. Fazel, *Ethnohistory of the Qizilbash in Kabul: Migration, State, and a Shi'a Minority* (PhD, Indiana University, 2017); Gommans, *The Rise of the Indo-Afghan Empire*, 49–59.

161. Nazif M. Shahrani, 'State Building and Social Fragmentation in Afghanistan: A Historical Perspective', in: Ali Banuazizi and Myron Weiner (eds), *The State, Religion, and Ethnic Politics: Pakistan, Iran, and Afghanistan* (Syracuse, NY: Syracuse University Press, 1986), 23–74, 33f.; Ben D. Hopkins, *The Making of Modern Afghanistan* (Basingstoke: Palgrave Macmillan, 2008), 90–105. For later examples of accusations against Qizilbash, see Fayz Muhammad Katib Hazara, *The History of Afghanistan: Fayż Muḥammad Kātib Hazārah's Sirāj al-Tawārīkh*, 3 Vols (Leiden: Brill, 2013), Vol. 3, Part 1, 299 (529); Part 2, 573f. (673f.), 945f. (870); Part 3, 1285f. (1041).

162. Christine Noelle-Karimi, *State and Tribe in Nineteenth-Century Afghanistan: The Reign of Amir Dost Muhammad Khan (1826–1863)* (London: Curzon, 1997), 1f., 4, 12f., 25–30.

163. Niamatullah Ibrahimi, *The Hazaras and the Afghan State: Rebellion, Exclusion and the Struggle for Recognition* (London: Hurst, 2017), 28–34.

164. Martin J. Bayly, *Taming the Imperial Imagination: Colonial Knowledge, International Relations, and the Anglo-Afghan Encounter, 1808–1878* (Cambridge: Cambridge University Press, 2016), 160f.; Amin H. Tarzi, 'DŌST MOḤAMMAD KHAN', *EIr*; Hopkins, *The Making of Modern Afghanistan*, 105ff.

165. Noelle-Karimi, *State and Tribe*, 50–5. Noelle-Karimi engages with Yapp, who emphasises regional, ethnic, and Sunni–Shia difference in his analysis of the rising, which he does not want to call a nationalist rising. M. E. Yapp, 'The Revolutions of 1841–2 in Afghanistan', *Bulletin of the School of Oriental and African Studies* 27, 2 (1964), 333–81, 380 and passim.

166. Ibrahimi, *The Hazaras*, 57–64; Hopkins, *The Making of Modern Afghanistan*, ch. 2 and 3.

167. For an assessment of different theories, see Alessandro Monsutti, *War and Migration: Social Networks and Economic Strategies of the Hazaras of Afghanistan* (London: Routledge, 2005), 60ff.; Mousavi, *The Hazaras*, 73ff.; Poladi, *The Hazāras*, 121–6 and passim. See also Naysan Adlparvar, *'When Glass Breaks, It Becomes Sharper': De-Constructing Ethnicity in the Bamyan Valley, Afghanistan* (PhD, University of Sussex, 2015). For a bibliography, see Arash Khazeni, Alessandro Monsutti, and Charles M. Kieffer, 'HAZĀRA', *EIr*; Hazara Encyclopaedia Foundation, *Hazara Encyclopaedia*, Vol. 1 (Kabul: Hazara Encyclopaedia Foundation, 2019).

168. Noelle-Karimi, *State and Tribe*, 32.

169. Hazara, *The History of Afghanistan*, Vol. 3, Part 1, 91f. (424).

170. Ibid., Vol. 3, Part 2, 557 (665). See also ibid., Vol. 3, Part 2, 1631 (1221); Ibrahimi, *The Hazaras*, 67ff.

171. Hazara, *The History of Afghanistan*, Vol. 3, Part 2, 946f. (871).

172. Ibid., Vol. 3, Part 2, 600f. (689). See also ibid., Vol. 3, Part 2, 856 (826).

173. Hollister, *The Shi'a of India*, 183; Mousavi, *The Hazaras*, 142–53; Poladi, *The Hazāras*, 182–256, 261–9; Muhammad Yusuf Riyazi Harawi, *'Ayn al-Waqayi': Tarikh-i Afghanistan dar Salha-yi 1207–1324*, ed. by Muhammad Asif Fikrat (Tehran: Bunyad-i Mawqufat-i Duktur Mahumd Afshar Yazdi, 1990), 206–28; Bunbury, *A Brief History of the Hazara Pioneers*; Hazara, *The History of Afghanistan*, Vol. 3, Part 2, 979–91 (888–94); Part 3, 1178 (988f.), 1183 (991). Another group of Afghan Shii Qizilbash left Afghanistan to India in the context of the First Anglo-Afghan War, and its leader was awarded villages by the British for his loyalty. He and his descendants became major patrons of Shiism in Lahore. Nile Green, 'Introduction: Afghanistan's Islam: A History and its Scholarship', in: Nile Green (ed.), *Afghanistan's Islam: From Conversion to the Taliban* (Oakland, CA: University of California Press, 2017), 1–37, 18f.

174. Ibrahimi, *The Hazaras*, 74–85; M. Hasan Kakar, *The Pacification of the Hazaras of Afghanistan* (New York: Afghanistan Council/Asia Society, 1973); Mousavi, *The Hazaras*, 111–38. See also Lillias A. Hamilton, *Die Tochter des Wesirs: Eine Erzählung aus dem Hazara-Krieg (Afghanistan, 1887–1893)* (Bubendorf: Bibliotheca Afghanica, 2000); M. Hasan Kakar, *Government and Society in Afghanistan: The Reign of Amir Abd al-Rahman Khan* (Austin: University of Texas Press, 1979), 147–61; Green, 'Introduction', 15; Amin Tarzi, 'Islam, Shari'a, and State Building under 'Abd al-Rahman Khan', in: Nile Green (ed.), *Afghanistan's Islam: From Conversion to the Taliban* (Oakland, CA: University of California Press, 2017), 129–44, 137; Hazara, *The History of Afghanistan*, Vol. 3, Part 3, 1332f. (1065f.), 1429f. (1115f.), 1537f. (1172f.), 1626 (1218); Ali Karimi, 'The Bazaar, the State, and the Struggle for Public Opinion in Nineteenth-Century Afghanistan', *Journal of the Royal Asiatic Society* 30, 4 (2020), 613–33, 618f.

175. Nawid, *Religious Response*, 10f.

176. This was, for example, the case in Bamian. Canfield found that it was almost impossible to leave and convert from one group to the other, but also that ethnic and sectarian identity did not always overlap. Robert L. Canfield, *Faction and Conversion in a Plural Society: Religious Alignments in the Hindu Kush* (Ann Arbor: University of Michigan, 1973).

177. Hazara, *The History of Afghanistan*, Vol. 3, Part 3, 1273f. (1035f.).

178. Shah Mahmoud Hanifi, *Connecting Histories in Afghanistan: Market Relations and State Formation on a Colonial Frontier* (Stanford: Stanford University Press, 2011), 8.

179. R. D. McChesney and A. H. Tarzi, 'FAYŻ MOḤAMMAD KĀTEB', *EIr*; Robert D. McChesney, '"The Bottomless Inkwell": The Life and Perilous Times of Fayz Muhammad 'Katib' Hazara', in: Nile Green (ed.), *Afghan History*

through Afghan Eyes (London: Hurst, 2015), 97–129, 103, 127f.; McChesney, *Kabul under Siege: Fayz Muhammad's Account of the 1929 Uprising* (Princeton: Markus Wiener, 1999), 15–22; Hazara, *The History of Afghanistan*.

180. Nawid, *Religious Response*.

181. Fayz Muhammad, who witnessed the events in Kabul, tried to persuade Hazara to find an agreement with Amir Habib Allah, even if his interregnum was short-lived. McChesney, *Kabul under Siege*, 2f., 32, 119ff., 154f., 244–71.

182. Green, 'Introduction', 17; Mousavi, *The Hazaras*, 155–71.

183. Faridullah Bezhan, 'Nationalism, not Islam: The 'Awaken Youth' Party and Pashtun Nationalism', in: Nile Green (ed.), *Afghanistan's Islam: From Conversion to the Taliban* (Oakland, CA: University of California Press, 2017), 163–85, 165, 173.

184. Christine Noelle-Karimi, *The Pearl in its Midst: Herat and the Mapping of Khurasan (15th–19th Centuries)* (Vienna: Verlag der Österreichischen Akademie der Wissenschaften, 2014), 11, 59f., 143–203; Green, 'Introduction'; Nawid, *Religious Response*, 18. In the Khanate of Khiva, Russian Christians and Persian Shia were at times enslaved. Ben D. Hopkins, 'Race, Sex and Slavery: "Forced Labour" in Central Asia and Afghanistan in the Early 19th Century', *Modern Asian Studies* 42, 4 (2008), 629–71, 641–6.

185. For example, around the uprising of Qazi Muhammad in 1832. Eva-Maria Auch, *Muslim, Untertan, Bürger: Identitätswandel in gesellschaftlichen Transformationsprozessen der muslimischen Ostprovinzen Südkaukasiens (Ende 18.-Anfang 20. Jh.): Ein Beitrag zur vergleichenden Nationalismusforschung* (Wiesbaden: Reichert, 2004), 277–91; Ilia Brondz and Tahmina Aslanova, 'Sunni-Shia Issue in Azerbaijan', *Voice of the Publisher* 5, 1 (2019), 1–11; Bayram Balci and Altay Goyushov, 'Changing Islam in Post-Soviet Azerbaijan and its Weighting on the Sunnite–Shiite Cleavage', in: Brigitte Maréchal and Sami Zemni (eds), *The Dynamics of Sunni–Shia Relationships: Doctrine, Transnationalism, Intellectuals and the Media* (London: Hurst, 2013), 193–213, 195ff. In an interesting twist, a 1850 *Exposition of the Principles of Muslim Jurisprudence* by Nikolai Tornau relied to a significant extent on Shii law; other studies by Mirza Alexander Kazem-Bek, who was a scion of a Shii notable family who converted to Christianity under the influence of Scottish missionaries, and then became an important scholar and state consultant, tried to ensure application of Hanafi law amongst Russian Muslims. Robert D. Crews, *For Prophet and Tsar: Islam and Empire in Russia and Central Asia* (Cambridge, MA: Harvard University Press, 2006), 176–91. For examples of the description of Shia as more rebellious than Sunnis, see Firouzeh Mostashari, *On the Religious Frontier: Tsarist Russia and Islam in the Caucasus* (London: I. B. Tauris, 2017), 10. For more examples of the separate organisation of Sunnism and Shiism, see ibid., 88f. For efforts trying to limit the influence of clerics from Iran and ties to the shrine cities in Iraq amongst Shia Muslims in Russia, see ibid., 115f.

CHAPTER 8

1. For classic accounts of the transformation of the Ottoman Empire, see Stanford J. Shaw, *History of the Ottoman Empire and Modern Turkey: Reform, Revolution, and Republic: The Rise of Modern Turkey, 1808–1975* (Cambridge: Cambridge University Press, 1977); Shaw, *Between Old and New: The Ottoman Empire under Sultan Selim III, 1789–1807* (Cambridge, MA: Harvard University Press, 1971); R. H. Davison, 'Tanẓīmāt', *EI2*. For revisionist accounts, see Ali Yaycioglu, *Partners of the Empire: The Crisis of the Ottoman Order in the Age of Revolutions* (Stanford: Stanford University Press, 2017); Marinos Sariyannis, *A History of Ottoman Political Thought up to the Early Nineteenth Century* (Leiden: Brill, 2018); Virginia H. Aksan, *Ottoman Wars, 1700–1870: An Empire Besieged* (Harlow: Pearson, 2007); M. Fatih Çalışır, 'Decline of a "Myth": Perspectives on the Ottoman "Decline"', *The History School* 9 (2011), 37–60; M. Şükrü Hanioğlu, *A Brief History of the Late Ottoman Empire* (Princeton: Princeton University Press, 2008), esp. 45, 53f., 58ff., and passim. I have also benefitted from Alexander Schölch, 'Der arabische Osten im neunzehnten Jahrhundert: 1800–1914', in: Ulrich Haarmann, *Geschichte der arabischen Welt*, 4th ed. (Munich: C. H. Beck, 2001), 365–431.

2. Birge, *The Bektashi Order*, 74ff.; Winter, *The Shiites of Lebanon*, 12; Faroqhi, *Der Bektaschi-Orden*, 107–27; Hathaway, *A Tale of Two Factions*, ch. 11. In the next century, Bektashis thus had to survive and organise in secret, until the ban on all Sufi orders in 1925 dealt another blow to them. Ibid., 78–86. See also Ceren Lord, *Religious Politics in Turkey: From the Birth of the Republic to the AKP* (Cambridge: Cambridge University Press, 2018), 132. Though these texts could also be changed over time, with 'orthodox' Twelver Shia less targeted than other Shii groups. Benjamin Weineck, 'Fabricating the Great Mass: Heresy and Legitimate Plurality in Harputlu İshak Efendi's Polemics against the Bektaşi Order', in: Vefa Erginbaş (ed.), *Ottoman Sunnism: New Perspectives* (Edinburgh: Edinburgh University Press, 2019), 146–65; Ilber Ortayli, 'The Policy of the Sublime Porte towards Naqshbandis and Other Tariqas during the Tanzimat', in: Elisabeth Özdalga (ed.), *Naqshbandis in Western and Central Asia: Change and Continuity* (Istanbul: Swedish Research Institute, 1999), 67–72.

3. Yvette Talhamy, 'Conscription among the Nusayris ('Alawis) in the Nineteenth Century', *British Journal of Middle Eastern Studies* 38, 1 (2011), 23–40; Talhamy, 'The Nusayri and Druze Minorities in Syria in the Nineteenth Century: The Revolt against the Egyptian Occupation as a Case Study', *Middle Eastern Studies* 48, 6 (2012), 973–95; Dick Douwes, 'Reorganizing Violence: Traditional Recruitment Patterns and Resistance against Conscription in Ottoman Syria', in: Erik J. Zürcher (ed.), *Arming the State: Military Conscription in the Middle East and Central Asia, 1775–1925* (London: I. B. Tauris, 1999), 111–27, 123–6.

4. The wealth of material Heyberger has discovered in the archives of the Sacra Congregatio de Propaganda Fide allows the reconstruction of a sustained engagement in the seventeenth and eighteenth centuries. Bernard Heyberger, 'Peuples "sans loi, sans foi, ni prêtre": Druzes et nusayrîs de Syrie découverts par

les missionnaires catholiques (XVIIe–XVIIIe siècles)', in: Bernard Heyberger and Rémy Madinier (eds), *L'Islam des marges: Mission chrétienne et espaces périphériques du monde musulman, XVI–XXe siècles* (Paris: IISMM/Karthala, 2011), 45–80.

5. This was Fakhr al-Din ibn Maʻn.T. J. Gorton, *Renaissance Emir: A Druze Warlord at the Court of the Medici* (Northampton, MA: Interlink, 2014); Hafez Chehab, 'Reconstructing the Medici Portrait of Fakhr al-Din al-Maʻani', *Muqarnas* 11 (1994), 117–24. For background on the Maʻn family, which were important local tax lords for the Ottoman state in the sixteenth and early seventeenth century, see Massoud Daher, 'The Lebanese Leadership at the Beginning of the Ottoman Period: A Case Study of the Maʻn Family', in: Peter Sluglett and Stefan Weber (eds), *Syria and Bilad al-Sham under Ottoman Rule: Essays in Honour of Abdul Karim Rafeq* (Leiden: Brill, 2010), 323–45.

6. Birgit Schäbler, *Aufstände im Drusenbergland: Ethnizität und Integration einer ländlichen Gesellschaft Syriens vom Osmanischen Reich bis zur staatlichen Unabhängigkeit, 1850–1949* (Gotha: Perthes, 1996). See also Max L. Gross, *Ottoman Rule in the Province of Damascus, 1860–1909* (PhD, Georgetown University, 1979); Moshe Maʻoz, *Ottoman Reform in Syria and Palestine, 1840–1861: The Impact of the Tanzimat on Politics and Society* (Oxford: Clarendon Press, 1968), 123–8.

7. Shrine visitation, popular ceremonies, and interaction with locally important Shaykhs took centre stage in their daily socio-religious life. Jacques Weulersse, *Le pays des Alaouites*, Vol. 1 (Tours: Arrault & Co., 1940), 245–65.

8. Sabrina Mervin, 'L'"entité alaouite", une création française', in: Pierre-Jean Luizard (ed.), *Le choc colonial et l'Islam: Les politiques religieuses des puissances colonials en terres d'Islam* (Paris: La Découverte, 2006), 343–58, 346, 349; France Archives, 'Lattaquié (Vice-Consulat)', 348PO/1/1–15, https://francearchives. fr/findingaid/7b77e891b769e0aa5d7150fe7cfbc7a224d57990. See this article by the vice consul of France in Latakia: M. Félix Dupont, 'Mémoire sur les mœurs et les cérémonies religieuses des Nesserié, connus en Europe sous le nom d'Ausari', *Journal Asiatique* 5 (1824), 129–39. (There was also a consulate in the South, in Sidon, which produced similar information on the Shia of Sidon and Jabal Amil.) The chapters on the eighteenth and nineteenth centuries of Winter's *A History of the 'Alawis* are in significant parts based on French consular correspondence. Before the establishment of the consulate, French officials in Tripoli covered the area and, from the 1720s onwards, reported on the rise of Latakia's port. Winter, *A History of the 'Alawis*, 138.

9. In addition, tribal divisions between them became more entrenched. Dick Douwes, *The Ottomans in Syria: A History of Justice and Oppression* (London: I. B. Tauris, 2000), 142f.; Weulersse, *Le pays des Alaouites*, Vol. 1, 111f.; Winter, *A History of the 'Alawis*, 74–160. For the notion of the politics of notables, see Albert Hourani, 'Ottoman Reform and the Politics of Notables', in: William R. Polk and Richard L. Chambers (eds), *Beginnings of Modernization in the Middle East: The Nineteenth Century* (Chicago: University of Chicago Press, 1968), 41–68.

10. Winter, *A History of the 'Alawis*, 161–217.

11. Weulersse, *Le pays des Alaouites*, Vol. 1, 114f.; Winter, *A History of the 'Alawis*, 181–92, esp. 190; Winter, 'La revolte alaouite de 1834 contre l'occupation egyptienne: Perceptions alaouites et lecture ottomane', *Oriente Moderno* 79, 3 (1999), 60–71. For Muhammad Ali and his army, see Khaled Fahmy, *All the Pasha's Men: Mehmed Ali, his Army and the Making of Modern Egypt* (Cairo: American University in Cairo Press, 2002). See also Ma'oz, *Ottoman Reform*, 13f., 109ff.

12. Nasseh Ahmad Mirza, *Syrian Ismailism: The Ever Living Line of the Imamate, AD 1100–1260* (Richmond: Curzon, 1997).

13. Dick Douwes, 'Modern History of the Nizari Ismailis of Syria', in: Farhad Daftary (ed.), *A Modern History of the Ismailis: Continuity and Change in a Muslim Community* (London: I. B. Tauris, 2011), 19–44, 21–4; Douwes, *The Ottomans in Syria*, 116, 169f.; Weulersse, *Le pays des Alaouites*, Vol. 1, 341. See also Dick Douwes, 'Migration, Faith and Community: Extra-Local Linkages in Coastal Syria', in: Peter Sluglett and Stefan Weber (eds), *Syria and Bilad al-Sham under Ottoman Rule: Essays in Honour of Abdul Karim Rafeq* (Leiden: Brill, 2010), 483–95.

14. Amaan Merali, 'Legitimising Authority: A Muslim Minority under Ottoman Rule', in: Amyn B. Sajoo (ed.), *The Shari'a: History, Ethics and Law* (London: I. B. Tauris, 2018), 153–71. See also Norman N. Lewis, *Nomads and Settlers in Syria and Jordan, 1800–1980* (Cambridge: Cambridge University Press, 1987); Alain Nimier, *Les Alaouites* (Paris: Asfar, 1987).

15. Frederick F. Anscombe, *State, Faith, and Nation in Ottoman and Post-Ottoman Lands* (Cambridge: Cambridge University Press, 2014).

16. For background, see Bruce Masters, *Christians and Jews in the Ottoman Arab World: The Roots of Sectarianism* (Cambridge: Cambridge University Press, 2001).

17. Rafeq, 'Craft Organizations and Religious Communities', 48–52. See also Rafeq, 'Craft Organization, Work Ethics, and the Strains of Change in Ottoman Syria', *Journal of the American Oriental Society* 111, 3 (1991), 495–511; Rafeq, 'New Light on the 1860 Riots in Ottoman Damascus', *Die Welt des Islams* 28, 1/4 (1988), 412–30; Ussama Samir Makdisi, *The Culture of Sectarianism: Community, History, and Violence in Nineteenth-Century Ottoman Lebanon* (Berkeley, CA: University of California Press, 2000), 10f.; Makdisi, 'Diminished Sovereignty and the Impossibility of "Civil War" in the Modern Middle East', *American Historical Review* 120, 5 (2015), 1739–52; Ma'oz, *Ottoman Reform*, 200–5; Eugene L. Rogan, 'Sectarianism and Social Conflict in Damascus: The 1860 Events Reconsidered', *Arabica* 51, 4 (2004), 493–511; Leila Tarazi Fawaz, *An Occasion for War: Civil Conflict in Lebanon and Damascus in 1860* (London: Centre for Lebanese Studies/I. B. Tauris, 1994); Fawwaz Traboulsi, *A History of Modern Lebanon* (London: Pluto, 2007), 33–40.

18. Feroz Ahmad, 'Ottoman Perceptions of the Capitulations 1800–1914', *Journal of Islamic Studies* 11, 1 (2000), 1–20.

19. Maurits H. van den Boogert, *The Capitulations and the Ottoman Legal System: Qadis, Consuls and Beratls in the 18th Century* (Leiden: Brill, 2005).

20. William I. Shorrock, *French Imperialism in the Middle East: The Failure of Policy in Syria and Lebanon, 1900–1914* (Madison: University of Wisconsin Press, 1976). For the general economic history of this period, see Roger Owen, *The Middle*

East in the World Economy, 1800–1914 (London: I. B. Tauris, 1993). For the Levant and France, see Philip S. Khoury, *Syria and the French Mandate: The Politics of Arab Nationalism, 1920–1945* (Princeton: Princeton University Press, 1987), 30–40 and references cited therein; Michel Seurat, 'Le rôle de Lyon dans l'installation du mandat français en Syrie: Intérêts économiques et culturels, luttes d'opinion (1915–1925)', *Bulletin d'études orientales* 31 (1979), 129–65; Jean-David Mizrahi, 'La France et sa politique de mandat en Syrie et au Liban (1920–1939)', in: Nadine Méouchy (ed.), *France, Syrie et Liban 1918–1946: Les ambiguïtés et les dynamiques de la relation mandataire* (Damascus: Presses de l'Ifpo, 2002), 35–71; Jacques Thobie, *Les intérêts économiques, financiers et politiques français dans la partie asïatique de l'empire Ottoman de 1895 à 1914*, 3 Vols (PhD, University of Lille, 1973). Particularly important were Article 32 of the Treaty of Paris (1856) and Article 8 of the Treaty of Berlin (1878).

21. Dalrymple, *The Anarchy*, 332f., 343; Juan R. I. Cole, *Napoleon's Egypt: Invading the Middle East* (New York: Palgrave Macmillan, 2007).

22. Greek independence had problematised the situation of Greek Orthodox in the Ottoman Empire. Ma'oz, *Ottoman Reform*, 200–20.

23. See now Jonathan Parry, *Promised Lands: The British and the Ottoman Middle East* (Princeton: Princeton University Press, 2022), 206–77, and passim.

24. See especially the report of French military attaché in Istanbul Capitaine Louis de Torcy's tour of Syria in 1880 and French Consul Flesch's correspondence in 1880 and 1881. This policy backfired, however, as the Ottomans were either following the French or intercepting their correspondence, and, after de Torcy's second tour a year later, which coincided with the French occupation of Tunisia, he was put under arrest in Suwayda, and the Ottomans subsequently carried out an investigation about the people the French had been in touch with, especially amongst the Alawites, and reprimanded them. Flesch was also eventually recalled. But the general notion of supporting Christians, Druze, and Alawites, and relying on their support, to be implemented during the mandate was already formulated in this correspondence. Schäbler, *Aufstände*, 170f., 193f.; Gross, *Ottoman Rule*, 347–53.

25. Shakeeb Salih, 'The British-Druze Connection and the Druze Rising of 1896 in the Hawran', *Middle Eastern Studies* 13, 2 (1977), 251–7; Parry, *Promised Lands*, 232–9.

26. Parry, *Promised Lands*, 373–402.

27. Editors of Encyclopaedia Britannica, 'Levant', *EBr*; Max Weiss, 'Mosaic, Melting Pot, Pressure Cooker: The Religious, the Secular, and the Sectarian in Modern Syrian Social Thought', in: Jens Hanssen and Max Weiss (eds), *Arabic Thought against the Authoritarian Age: Towards an Intellectual History of the Present* (Cambridge: Cambridge University Press, 2018), 181–202, 184f.

28. Eugene L. Rogan, *The Arabs: A History* (London: Allen Lane, 2009), 89–98; Ussama Samir Makdisi, *Artillery of Heaven: American Missionaries and the Failed Conversion of the Middle East* (Ithaca: Cornell University Press, 2008), 160ff.; Schäbler, *Aufstände*, 168ff.

29. Bayly, *The Birth of the Modern World*, ch. 9.
30. Hans-Lukas Kieser, *Der verpasste Friede: Mission, Ethnie und Staat in den Ostprovinzen der Türkei, 1839–1923* (Zurich: Chronos, 2000), 79–85; Reinkowski, *Die Dinge der Ordnung*, 273; Eugene L. Rogan, *Frontiers of the State in the Late Ottoman Empire: Transjordan, 1850–1921* (Cambridge: Cambridge University Press, 1999), 124, 140, 159; Makdisi, *Artillery of Heaven*. The influx eventually led to conversions to Protestantism and the recognition of Protestants in the Ottoman Empire (in 1835, American missionaries pointed out that 'a native Protestant sect is not yet acknowledged, nor even known to the government of Turkey'). Abdul Latif Tibawi, *American Interests in Syria, 1800–1901: A Study of Educational, Literary and Religious Work* (Oxford: Clarendon Press, 1966), 77. A separate Protestant millet was organised in 1847 and recognised by the Ottoman state in 1850 and would soon come under British protection. Hans-Lukas Kieser, 'Muslim Heterodoxy and Protestant Utopia: The Interactions between Alevis and Missionaries in Ottoman Anatolia', *Die Welt des Islams* 41, 1 (2001), 89–111, 93. See also Bruce Masters, 'The Establishment of the Melkite Catholic Millet in 1848 and the Politics of Identity in Tanzimat Syria', in: Peter Sluglett and Stefan Weber (eds), *Syria and Bilad al-Sham under Ottoman Rule: Essays in Honour of Abdul Karim Rafeq* (Leiden: Brill, 2010), 455–73.
31. Osterhammel, *Die Verwandlung der Welt*, 1261–8.
32. For Alevis (Qizilbash) in Anatolia, whose 'discovery' by American missionaries proceeded in the 1850s, see Kieser, *Der verpasste Friede*, 69–78, 99f., 167–70; Kieser, 'Muslim Heterodoxy'; Selim Deringil, *The Well-Protected Domains: Ideology and the Legitimation of Power in the Ottoman Empire* (London: I. B. Tauris, 1998), 112–34. For relations between Alevis and Armenians, which were seen with suspicion by Ottoman officials, and in particular Turkish nationalist ideologies, see Kieser, *Der verpasste Friede*, 85. For Yazidis, see ibid., 69n88; Selçuk Akşin Somel, *The Modernization of Public Education in the Ottoman Empire, 1839–1908: Islamization, Autocracy, and Discipline* (Leiden: Brill, 2001), 230ff. Though there were also missionaries who believed that possibilities amongst Yazidis were limited. Christine Allison, '"Unbelievable Slowness of Mind": Yezidi Studies, from Nineteenth to Twenty-First Century', *Journal of Kurdish Studies* 6 (2008), 1–23, 6–9. Two serious attempts were made at conversion of Druze, in 1835 and 1841, but failed. It seems Druze were trying to find a way to avoid conscription into the Egyptian army by converting to Christianity and receiving foreign protection, but Muhammad Ali and the Egyptian authorities reminded them that as Muslims they were bound by Islamic law on the question of apostasy and asked the local authorities to prevent Druze conversions, which in any case were negligible. Druze then reappeared in missionary annals by the 1870s and 1880s. Tibawi, *American Interests*, 77f., 92ff., 239f. For missionaries amongst the Ahl-e Haqq and other Kurdish communities, see Florence Hellot, 'Tentatives missionnaires auprès des musulmans de Perse et dans les montagnes kurdes (sur les marges de l'Empire ottoman et de la Perse, avant la Première Guerre mondiale)', in: Bernard Heyberger and Rémy Madinier (eds),

L'Islam des marges: Mission chrétienne et espaces périphériques du monde musulman, XVI–XXe siècles (Paris: IISMM/Karthala, 2011), 145–205; Mojan Membrado, 'L'impact des missionnaires chrétiens du début du XXe siècle sur l'étude d'une communauté initiatique kurde: Les "Fidèles de Vérité" (Ahl-e Haqq)', in: Bernard Heyberger and Rémy Madinier (eds), *L'Islam des marges: Mission chrétienne et espaces périphériques du monde musulman, XVI–XXe siècles* (Paris: IISMM/Karthala, 2011), 207–29. For Alawites, see Winter, *A History of the 'Alawis*, 204.

33. Grehan, *Twilight of the Saints*, 33f.; Necati Alkan, 'Fighting for the Nusayrī Soul: State, Protestant Missionaries and the 'Alawīs in the Late Ottoman Empire', *Die Welt des Islams* 52, 1 (2012), 23–50; Yvette Talhamy, 'American Protestant Missionary Activity among the Nusayris (Alawis) in Syria in the Nineteenth Century', *Middle Eastern Studies* 47, 2 (2011), 215–36; Leon Goldsmith, '"God Wanted Diversity": Alawite Pluralist Ideals and their Integration into Syrian Society 1832–1973', *British Journal of Middle Eastern Studies* 40, 4 (2013), 392–409; Samuel Lyde, *The Ansyreeh and Ismaeleeh: A Visit to the Secret Sects of Northern Syria, with a View to the Establishment of Schools* (London: Hurst and Blackett, 1853). Initially very dismissive of Alawite beliefs, the English missionary Lyde then wrote a more substantial work on Alawite history and doctrine. See Samuel Lyde, *The Asian Mystery: Illustrated in the History, Religion, and Present State of the Ansaireeh or Nusairis of Syria* (London: Longman, Green & Co., 1860). For the manuscript it was based on, see Bella Tendler Krieger, 'The Rediscovery of Samuel Lyde's Lost Nuṣayrī Kitāb al-Mashyakha (Manual for Shaykhs)', *Journal of the Royal Asiatic Society* 24, 1 (2014), 1–16. For an account of an American missionary, see Henry Harris Jessup, *Fifty-Three Years in Syria*, 2 Vols (New York: Fleming H. Revell, 1910), esp. Vol. 1, 255–64. In general, see now Necati Alkan, *Non-Sunni Muslims in the Late Ottoman Empire: State and Missionary Perceptions of the Alawis* (London: I.B. Tauris, 2022). And for the Anglican and general British role, see Parry, *Promised Lands*, 206–48, and passim.

34. The French vice consul in Tripoli, Isidore Blanche, published a detailed study of Alawite leader Ismail Khayr Bey shortly after the latter's death in 1858. Blanche claims to have intervened with the Ottomans on behalf of Ismail, who emerged as a sort of renegade leader, but managed to unite different key families and was eventually de facto recognised by the Ottoman state after proclaiming his loyalty to the Porte. Charles-Isidore Blanche, 'Études sur la Syrie: L'ansarié Kaïr-Beik', *Revue européenne* 2, 12 (1860), 384–402, 582–601. For the latter, see also Yvette Talhamy, 'The Nusayri Leader Isma'il Khayr Bey and the Ottomans (1854-58)', *Middle Eastern Studies* 44, 6 (2008), 895–908. The French then, however, corresponded with a rival Alawite religious Shaykh to undermine Ismail, a message that was intercepted by the Ottomans, who shared it with the British, in a development demonstrating the increasingly interconnected nature of local, regional, and global politics. Winter, *A History of the 'Alawis*, 197.

35. The interpreter of the Prussian consulate in Beirut, Joseph Catafago, himself a Syrian Christian, published some early accounts. J. Catafago, 'Die drei

Messen der Nossairier', *Zeitschrift der Deutschen Morgenländischen Gesellschaft* 2, 3 (1848), 388–94. Catafago apparently sent the Arabic original of an Alawite catechism to the Prussian king, for which he was honoured with a golden watch. N.a.,'Aus einem Briefe von Dr. Schultz, Kön. Preussischem Consul in Jerusalem', *Zeitschrift der Deutschen Morgenländischen Gesellschaft* 1, 3/4 (1847), 352f. Some, such as Lammens, argued that they were originally Christians who had adopted elements of Shiism in order to assimilate into Muslim society. In a meeting with Nusairi leaders, who allegedly lamented a lack of foreign protection, Lammens even suggested that, if they were to convert to Christianity, France could act as their protector (though the Alawites did not do so). Mervin, 'L'"entité alaouite"', 348.

36. Winter, *A History of the 'Alawis*, 205–8.

37. Mervin, 'L'"entité alaouite"', 345f. Apart from the article cited above, his writings are: Henri Lammens, 'Voyage au pays des Nosairis', *Revue de l'Orient chrétien* 4, 1 (1899), 572–90; Lammens, 'Les Nosairis furent-ils chrétiens? A propos d'un livre récent', *Revue de l'Orient chrétien* 6 (1901), 33–50; Lammens, 'Voyage au pays des Nosairis', *Revue de l'Orient chrétien* 5 (1900), 99–117, 303–18, 423–44. See also René Dussaud, *Histoire et religion des Nosairîs* (Paris: É. Bouillon, 1900). For Ibn Taymiyya's fatwa, see Stanislas Guyard, 'Le Fetwa d'Ibn Taymiyah sur les Noṣairis', *Journal Asiatique* 18 (1871), 158–98. For other studies, see Edward E. Salisbury, 'Notice of الاذنى افندى سليمان تأليف النصرية الديانة اسرار كشف فى السليمانية الباكورة كتاب: The Book of Sulaimân's First Ripe Fruit, Disclosing the Mysteries of the Nusairian Religion', *Journal of the American Oriental Society* 8 (1866), 227–308.

38. They were released after the rise of the Young Turks in 1908. Dick Douwes and Norman N. Lewis, 'The Trials of Syrian Ismailis in the First Decade of the 20th Century', *International Journal of Middle East Studies* 21, 2 (1989), 215–32; Amaan Merali, 'Fear and Violence in Late Ottoman Syria: The Isma'ilis and the School of Agriculture', *Diyâr* 1, 1 (2020), 58–83.

39. Carol Hakim, *The Origins of the Lebanese National Idea, 1840–1920* (Berkeley: University of California Press, 2013), 10, 52, 65–98; Makdisi, *The Culture of Sectarianism*, xi, 2, 85; Max Weiss, *In the Shadow of Sectarianism: Law, Shi'ism, and the Making of Modern Lebanon* (Cambridge, MA: Harvard University Press, 2010), 11f.; Reinkowski, *Ottoman 'Multiculturalism'?*; Reinkowski, *Die Dinge der Ordnung*, 269–73; Fawaz, *An Occasion for War*, 25–30 and passim.

40. Makdisi, *The Culture of Sectarianism*, 171–4. See also Mark Farha, *Lebanon: The Rise and Fall of a Secular State under Siege* (Cambridge: Cambridge University Press, 2019); Caesar E. Farah, *The Politics of Interventionism in Ottoman Lebanon, 1830–1861* (London: I. B. Tauris, 2000); Traboulsi, *A History of Modern Lebanon*, 43ff.

41. Hakim, *The Origins*, 10; Makdisi, *The Culture of Sectarianism*, 81f.; Kamal S. Salibi, *Maronite Historians of Medieval Lebanon* (New York: AMS Press, 1959). For a similar development amongst the Shia of Eastern Arabia, see Matthiesen, 'Shi'i Historians'.

42. Makdisi, *The Culture of Sectarianism*, 163; Ussama Samir Makdisi, *Age of Coexistence: The Ecumenical Frame and the Making of the Modern Arab World*

(Oakland: University of California Press, 2019), 64–74; Butrus al-Bustani, *The Clarion of Syria: A Patriot's Call against the Civil War of 1860*, trans. by Jens Hanssen and Hicham Safieddine (Oakland: University of California Press, 2019); Albert Hourani, *Arabic Thought in the Liberal Age, 1798–1939*, 2nd ed. (Cambridge: Cambridge University Press, 1983), 101.

43. Hourani, *Arabic Thought*, esp. 95–102, 245–59, and passim; Maʿoz, *Ottoman Reform*, 241–8; Traboulsi, *A History of Modern Lebanon*, 63–8. A classic account is George Antonius, *The Arab Awakening: The Story of the Arab National Movement* (London: Hamish Hamilton, 1938).

44. Michael Provence, 'Ottoman Modernity, Colonialism, and Insurgency in the Interwar Arab East', *International Journal of Middle East Studies* 43, 2 (2011), 205–25; Traboulsi, *A History of Modern Lebanon*, 68–71.

45. See, for example, Selim Deringil, 'The Invention of Tradition as Public Image in the Late Ottoman Empire, 1808 to 1908', *Comparative Studies in Society and History* 35, 1 (1993), 3–29, 12–21; Deringil, *The Well-Protected Domains*, 40ff.; Carter Findley, 'The Tanzimat II', in: R. Kasaba (ed.), *The Cambridge History of Turkey*, Vol. 4 (Cambridge: Cambridge University Press, 2008), 9–37.

46. The state massively expanded the school system, sponsored the teaching of Islam in newly-built schools, and sent around travelling Sunni clerics. Benjamin C. Fortna, *Imperial Classroom: Islam, the State, and Education in the Late Ottoman Empire* (Oxford: Oxford University Press, 2002), esp. 87–129. Although history textbooks used in those schools for example write approvingly of the violence unleashed by the Ottomans against the Qizilbash of Anatolia during the struggle with the Safavids. Somel, *The Modernization*, 197. See also Necati Alkan, 'The Ottoman Policy of "Correction of Belief(s)"', in: Vefa Erginbaş (ed.), *Ottoman Sunnism: New Perspectives* (Edinburgh: Edinburgh University Press, 2019), 166–92; Winter, *A History of the ʿAlawis*, 220–8.

47. From the 1880s onwards, more Sunni instructors were appointed to regions such as Sivas, and schools were built to that effect. Deringil, *The Well-Protected Domains*, 82f.; Somel, *The Modernization*, 220ff. See also Janina Karolewski, 'What is Heterodox about Alevism? The Development of Anti-Alevi Discrimination and Resentment', *Die Welt des Islams* 48, 3/4 (2008), 434–56.

48. For the policy of conversion to Hanafi Sunnism of the Yazidi Kurds in the 1890s in particular, see Deringil, *The Well-Protected Domains*, 68–75; Nelida Fuccaro, 'Ethnicity, State Formation, and Conscription in Postcolonial Iraq: The Case of the Yazidi Kurds of Jabal Sinjar', *International Journal of Middle East Studies* 29, 4 (1997), 559–80, 567ff.; Edip Gölbaşı, 'Turning the "Heretics" into Loyal Muslim Subjects: Imperial Anxieties, the Politics of Religious Conversion, and the Yezidis in the Hamidian Era', *The Muslim World* 103, 1 (2013), 3–23; John S. Guest, *Survival among the Kurds: A History of the Yezidis* (London: Kegan Paul, 1993), 124–45.

49. The state built schools and mosques for Alawites that embraced Sunnism, roads to connect the Alawite hinterland, and established local councils. Ilber Ortayli, 'Les Groupes Hétérodoxes et l'Administration Ottomane', in: Krisztina

Kehl-Bodrogi, Barbara Kellner-Heinkele, and Anke Otter-Beaujean (eds), *Syncretistic Religious Communities in the Near East: Collected Papers of the International Symposium 'Alevism in Turkey and Comparable Syncretistic Religious Communities in the Near East in the Past and Present', Berlin, 14–17 April 1995* (Leiden: Brill, 1997), 205–11, esp. 209f.; Winter, *A History of the 'Alawis*, 179, 199–217.

50. Deringil, 'The Invention of Tradition', 15f.; Winter, *A History of the 'Alawis*, 218–38; Deringil, *The Well-Protected Domains*, 83f.; Somel, *The Modernization*, 158. Interestingly, the Ottoman government banned several ethnographic and religious studies dealing with Alawite difference, including the books by the missionary Samuel Lyde. Winter, *A History of the 'Alawis*, 232. Some of the mosque and school building efforts may have come at the request of Alawite notables, who resented the lack of schools in their areas. Pierre Bazantay, *Les états du Levant sous mandat français: La pénétration de l'enseignement dans le sandjak autonome d'Alexandrette* (Beirut: Imprimerie catholique, 1935), 33ff., 39f.

51. For a narrative history of the Ottoman presence, see Caesar E. Farah, *The Sultan's Yemen: Nineteenth-Century Challenges to Ottoman Rule* (London: I. B. Tauris, 2002).

52. Kuehn, *Empire*, 6–12, 37. See also Mostafa Minawi, *The Ottoman Scramble for Africa: Empire and Diplomacy in the Sahara and the Hijaz* (Stanford: Stanford University Press, 2016).

53. For this general story, see Frederick F. Anscombe, *The Ottoman Gulf: The Creation of Kuwait, Saudi Arabia, and Qatar* (New York: Columbia University Press, 1997). In twentieth-century historical writings of Shia from al-Ahsa and Qatif, Ottoman rule in the late nineteenth/early twentieth century is portrayed favourably, especially in comparison with the experiences under the various Saudi/Wahhabi polities. Matthiesen, 'Shi'i Historians'. For al-Ahsa, see also Nelida Fuccaro, 'Between Imara, Empire and Oil: Saudis in the Frontier Society of the Persian Gulf', in: Madawi al-Rasheed (ed.), *Kingdom without Borders: Saudi Political, Religious and Media Frontiers* (London: Hurst, 2008), 39–64.

54. Al-Habib, *The Formation*.

55. The Ottomans themselves applied a sectarian vision to far-flung territories with inhabitants of different ethnicities and confessions, not unlike the European Orientalists and officials discussed above. For the general notion, see Ussama Makdisi, 'Ottoman Orientalism', *American Historical Review* 107, 3 (2002), 768–96.

56. The book is Ahmed Rashid's two-volume *Tarih-i Yemen we Sana'*, published in 1875. The author, of course, also argued that the Zaydi Imams had no spiritual authority and had made up their lineage to the Prophet. He defended Ottoman claims on Yemen with the argument that, when the Ottomans won against the Mamluks in 1517, they became legal heirs to their possessions, including in Arabia. Cited in: Kuehn, *Empire*, 55, 64, 70f. Unlike earlier Ottoman authors, who had described the sixteenth-century conquest as a victory of the righteous Ottoman Sultan over the heretical Zaydis, he did not decry Zaydism as heresy. Rather, he reframed these earlier anti-Shii discourses in the context of imperial modernity, advocating the rule of the civilised centre over the backward periphery. Kuehn, *Empire*, 71.

57. Ibid., 73f.
58. Ibid., 176. A later report advocated establishing a *madrasa* for teaching Shafii and Hanafi jurisprudence to counter Zaydism. Farah, *The Sultan's Yemen*, 253.
59. Instead, they opted for an alliance with the merchants and *ulama* of Sanaa. Kuehn, *Empire*, 35. The Ottomans had since the mid-nineteenth century had such an alliance with the Emir of Asir, Muhammad bin Aid, who retained considerable autonomy and power on the Arabian Peninsula, but later rebelled and was eventually defeated by the Ottomans. Ibid., 37, 95.
60. Vincent Steven Wilhite, *Guerilla War, Counterinsurgency, and State Formation in Ottoman Yemen* (PhD, Ohio State University, 2003).
61. Kuehn, *Empire*, 24, 129, 151ff., 161; Messick, *The Calligraphic State*, 50ff. Alcohol consumption by Ottoman officials and their apparently relatively lax morals, and the permission to sell alcohol, were cited by the Imams as a key reason for the pronouncement of *takfir* against the Ottomans and a key trope in Zaydi anti-Ottoman propaganda. Alcohol was eventually banned by the Ottomans, who also forced their officials to adopt 'local dress'. Ibid., 192f. Declaring Jihad allowed the Imam to regularly collect the *zakat* tax, which the Ottomans saw as a partial explanation for the revolt. Ibid., 177.
62. In the Yemeni case, this mainly elevated the status of Jews, although one of the conditions set by the Imam for the 1911 agreement with the Ottomans was that Yemeni Jews would revert to being classified as *dhimmis*. Kuehn, *Empire*, 106. According to the Mejelle, the *hudud* punishments were no longer enforced.
63. Kuehn, *Empire*, 108–13.
64. Ibid., 130. Another Ottoman author, Abdülgani Seni, argued in 1910 that, to undermine the power of the Imam and the rebels, the government should establish Sharia courts that would operate according to the Shafii and Zaydi schools and organise tribesmen into a local militia. Ibid., 233.
65. Dresch, *A History of Modern Yemen*, 3–6.
66. Ibid., 5f. For more, see John Baldry, 'Imam Yahya and the Yamani Uprising of 1904–1907', *Abr-Nahrain* 18 (1978–9), 33–73.
67. Kuehn, *Empire*, 198. In December 1905, Memduh Pasha, minister of the interior and chair of an interdepartmental commission on Yemen, advocated guaranteeing Zaydis some form of autonomy in most matters if they replaced the current Imam with another leader, who would receive the official title 'head of the Zaydi community' and thus accept the supremacy of the Ottoman Sultan. Ibid., 227f.
68. Kuehn, *Empire*, 172–80, 229f.
69. The quotes stem from a report by Sayyid Fadl Pasha al-Alawi, one of the Sultan's advisors on Arabian affairs, of the early 1890s. Kuehn, *Empire*, 228, 230. For more on the former, see S. Tufan Buzpinar, 'Abdulhamid II and Sayyid Fadl Pasha of Hadramawt: An Arab Dignitary's Ambitions (1876–1900)', *Osmanlı Araştırmaları / Journal of Ottoman Studies* 13 (1993), 227–39.
70. Kuehn, *Empire*, 231. Some Shafii scholars, however, also disapproved of some of these practices. See Messick, *The Calligraphic State*, 49f. There was intermarriage between Ottoman officials and Shafiis and, when Ibb was besieged by Imam

Yahya's forces in 1904, locals remained loyal to the Ottomans. Ibid., 50. One Ottoman author, Hasan Kadri, claimed in a book on Yemen that sectarianism was not a key reason for the uprising, because how could this explain opposition amongst Shafiis such as the uprising of Muhammad Ali al-Idrisi, a descendant of the Sufi teacher Ahmad bin Idris, in Asir in 1906/7, who also framed his rebellion as a fight to safeguard the Sharia. Kuehn, *Empire*, 233. For Zaydi attitudes towards Sufism, see Serjeant, 'The Zaydis', 294f., 297; Messick, *The Calligraphic State*, 50, 276n40; Wilferd Madelung, 'Zaydī Attitudes to Sufism', in: F. de Jong and B. Radtke (eds), *Islamic Mysticism Contested: Thirteen Centuries of Controversies and Polemics* (Leiden: Brill, 1999), 124–44; Muhammad Ali Aziz, *Religion and Mysticism in Early Islam: Theology and Sufism in Yemen* (London: I. B. Tauris, 2011), ch. 8.

71. Kuehn, *Empire*, 234.
72. According to Kuehn, it established 'a sectarian order unprecedented in the history of Yemen'. Kuehn, *Empire*, 19. For a detailed discussion, see ibid., 201–45. It coincided with a military build-up and despatch of naval units to cut weapons supplies from the Horn of Africa and the start of construction on a railway linking Hudaydah and Sanaa, in part to facilitate Ottoman military movements to the highlands (the project was soon aborted, however). Ibid., 238f. At the same time, the Imam was threatened by the Idrisi Emirate of Asir, as al-Idrisi had conquered some areas the Imam claimed and was supported by some Zaydi tribes after the Imam's agreement with the Ottomans. Blumi, *Rethinking the Late Ottoman Empire*, 54. See also Stookey, *Yemen*, 164.
73. In those areas the Imam could appoint judges who would deal with cases involving people of those areas according to the Zaydi school of jurisprudence (while the Ottoman government would be responsible for cases involving Hanafi Sunnis from outside the area, i.e. Turks). Mixed courts made up of Zaydi and Hanafi judges would be created for cases involving Zaydis and members of other Muslim sects from outside the areas. Though, in theory, the government retained some important checks on his authority over the judiciary. Kuehn, *Empire*, 241f. For a summary of the agreement, see Farah, *The Sultan's Yemen*. Within a demarcated territory, he could thus exercise 'judicial authority over the entire indigenous population according to the Zaydi version of the shari'a but remained ultimately answerable to the imperial government in Istanbul'. Kuehn, *Empire*, 19. Earlier, there had already been suggestions that he should also be allowed to apply the Sharia to Shafiis living in 'his' realm, which would have incorporated him into the Ottoman polity in a non-sectarian way as Amir. These negotiations in 1906 and 1907 failed, however. Ibid., 231f. While this does seem to resemble the millet system instituted elsewhere, it is different, for the Zaydi Imam was also given juridical authority over non-Zaydis in 'his' areas. Ibid., 245. For the argument that the Imam's powers were in fact limited according to this agreement, see M. Şükrü Hanioğlu, 'Contract or Treaty? The Da'an Agreement of 1911 and the Limits on Imam Yahya's Authority', *Journal of Arabian Studies* 8, 1 (2018), 25–46.

74. In the following years, the Imam even used Ottoman troops against his enemies, in particular the Idrisis of Asir, and remained fairly loyal to the Empire throughout the First World War. Kuehn, *Empire*, 242f.; Blumi, *Rethinking the Late Ottoman Empire*, 57–81.

75. Yahya retained *Qadi* Hussain al-Amri, who had also been recognised by the Ottomans in Sanaa as Shaykh al-Islam. Al-Amri, who had been a teacher to Imam Yahya, had mediated the truce and previously been the Ottomans' supervisor of *waqf* and was now appointed president of the appeal court. Dresch, *A History of Modern Yemen*, 7f. See also Harold F. Jacob, *Kings of Arabia: The Rise and Set of the Turkish Sovranty in the Arabian Peninsula* (London: Mills & Boon, 1923), 123f.

76. Amanat, *Iran*, 194–200; Gleave, 'Jihad and Religious Legitimacy'; Lambton, 'A Nineteenth Century View of Jihād'.

77. Sabri Ateş, *Ottoman-Iranian Borderlands: Making a Boundary, 1843–1914* (Cambridge: Cambridge University Press, 2015), 12f., 42–57. See also Graham Williamson, 'The Turko-Persian War of 1821–1823: Winning the War but Losing the Peace', in: Roxane Farmanfarmaian (ed.), *War and Peace in Qajar Persia: Implications Past and Present* (London: Routledge, 2008), 88–109.

78. See Fahaad J. M. M. Alenezi, *Usuli Shi'ism and State Approaches to Islamic Unity: The Ecumenical Movement in Post-Safavid Iran* (PhD, Durham University, 2009), ch. 4; H. Busse, "ABBĀS MĪRZĀ QAJAR', *EIr*.

79. Ateş, *Ottoman-Iranian Borderlands*, 131.

80. Amanat, *Iran*, 210–4; Stephanie Cronin, 'ARMY v. Qajar Period', *EIr*.

81. Mostashari, *On the Religious Frontier*; Bayram Balci, 'Between Sunnism and Shiism: Islam in Post-Soviet Azerbaijan', *Central Asian Survey* 23, 2 (2004), 205–17, 206f.; Volker Adam, 'Why Do They Cry? Criticisms of Muḥarram Celebrations in Tsarist and Socialist Azerbaijan', in: Rainer Brunner and Werner Ende (eds), *The Twelver Shia in Modern Times: Religious Culture & Political History* (Leiden: Brill, 2001), 114–34; Balci and Goyushov, 'Changing Islam in Post-Soviet Azerbaijan', 196ff.; Volker Adam, 'Auf der Suche nach Turan: Panislamismus und Panturkismus in der aserbaidschanischen Vorkriegspresse', in: Raoul Motika and Michael Ursinus (eds), *Caucasia between the Ottoman Empire and Iran, 1555–1914* (Wiesbaden: Reichert, 2000), 189–205, 198ff.; Brondz and Aslanova, 'Sunni-Shia Issue'.

82. Ateş, *Ottoman-Iranian Borderlands*, 173–83. The Ottoman envoy to the border commission even appeared in mosques emphasising the Sunni–Shii divide and the position of the Ottoman Sultan as Caliph over Sunni Muslims. Ibid., 174. The Iranians on the other hand sought to win over the Shii Turkic Karapapak to their side. Ibid., 179. For the 1905–1911 attempts to occupy the Iranian Kurdish territories, see ibid., 229–83. A detailed map of the border regions, where the border was for the first time delineated, was presented in 1869. Richard Schofield, 'Narrowing the Frontier: Mid-Nineteenth Century Efforts to Delimit and Map the Perso-Ottoman Border', in: Roxane Farmanfarmaian (ed.), *War and Peace in Qajar Persia: Implications Past and Present* (London: Routledge, 2008), 149–73. The situation of tribes and communities along the

frontier was put in question, as in the case of the Babans. See Ateş, *Ottoman-Iranian Borderlands*, 42–9; Metin Atmaca, *Politics of Alliance and Rivalry on the Ottoman-Iranian Frontier: The Babans (1500–1851)* (PhD, University of Freiburg, 2013); Atmaca, 'Negotiating Political Power in the Early Modern Middle East: Kurdish Emirates between the Ottoman Empire and Iranian Dynasties (Sixteenth to Nineteenth Centuries)', in: Hamit Bozarslan, Cengiz Gunes, and Veli Yadirgi (eds), *The Cambridge History of the Kurds* (Cambridge: Cambridge University Press, 2021), 45–72. See also Parry, *Promised Lands*, 299–304.

83. Stephanie Cronin, 'Building a New Army: Military Reform in Qajar Iran', in: Roxane Farmanfarmaian (ed.), *War and Peace in Qajar Persia: Implications Past and Present* (London: Routledge, 2008), 47–87.

84. Ervand Abrahamian, *A History of Modern Iran* (Cambridge: Cambridge University Press, 2008), 8–12.

85. Heern, *The Emergence of Modern Shi'ism*, 68f.; Selim Deringil, 'The Struggle against Shi'ism in Hamidian Iraq: A Study in Ottoman Counter-Propaganda', *Die Welt des Islams* 30 (1990), 45–62; Gökhan Cetinsaya, 'The Ottoman View of the Shiite Community of Iraq in the Late Nineteenth Century', in: Alessandro Monsutti, Silvia Naef, and Farian Sabahi (eds), *The Other Shiites: From the Mediterranean to Central Asia* (New York: Peter Lang, 2008), 19–40. Apparently, Abdulhamid at one point even considered forcibly converting the Shii subjects of his realm but was dissuaded from this. Azmi Özcan, *Pan-Islamism: Indian Muslims, the Ottomans and Britain (1877–1924)* (Leiden: Brill, 1997), 55. In general, see also Pierre-Jean Luizard, *La formation de l'Irak contemporain: Le rôle politique des ulémas chiites à la fin de la domination ottomane et au moment de la construction de l'État irakien* (Paris: CNRS Editions, 2002), 186–214.

86. Çetinsaya, *Ottoman Administration*, 105f., 124f.; Kern, *Imperial Citizen*, 65–88. More reports on the 'Shii problem' were drawn up by Ottoman officials in 1907 and 1908, proposing a sustained effort to strengthen Sunnism institutionally, but little to none of it was implemented. Çetinsaya, *Ottoman Administration*, 122–6. Here, one can also detect an entangled history of confessionalism and imperial learning. In a late nineteenth-century report on countering the Shii threat, an Ottoman official argued that the Ottomans should follow the example of American missionaries, who were educating Armenians in their schools to later send them to become missionaries amongst the Armenians. The same should be done with Shii students from across Iraq, who should be educated at al-Azhar and won over to Sunnism to then go back and preach amongst their communities. That latter idea was not implemented, however, because of Ottoman fears that this could increase the position of Egypt as a rival centre of Sunni authority to the Ottoman Caliphate. A school was instead established in Istanbul, though it had only very few students and was short-lived. Ibid., 107.

87. Çetinsaya, *Ottoman Administration*, 108; Hala Fattah, 'Islamic Universalism and the Construction of Regional Identity in Turn-of-the-Century Basra: Sheikh Ibrahim al-Haidari's Book Revisited', in: Leila Tarazi Fawaz and C. A. Bayly (eds), *Modernity and Culture: From the Mediterranean to the Indian Ocean*

(New York: Columbia University Press, 2002), 112–29, esp. 119–25. Despite this connection to the Ottoman state, he then became the head of the clandestine Arab nationalist al-Ahd Society in 1914, which was largely made up of former Arab officers in the Ottoman army that supported the Arab Revolt and Faisal (and organised anti-British actions after 1918). Weismann, *The Naqshbandiyya*, 95f.; Weismann, 'The Naqshbandiyya-Khalidiyya and the Salafi Challenge in Iraq', *Journal of the History of Sufism* 4 (2004), 229–40; Abu-Manneh, 'Salafiyya'; Pierre-Jean Luizard, 'Les confréries soufies en Irak arabe aux dix-neuvième et vingtième siècles face au chiisme duodécimain et au wahhabisme', in: F. de Jong and B. Radtke (eds), *Islamic Mysticism Contested: Thirteen Centuries of Controversies and Polemics* (Leiden: Brill, 1999), 283–309; Thomas Eich, 'Abū l-Hudā, the Rifā'iya and Shiism in Ḥamīdian Iraq', *Der Islam* 80, 1 (2003), 142–52.

88. Hakan Yavuz, 'The Matrix of Modern Turkish Islamic Movements: The Naqshbandī Sufi Order', in: Elisabeth Özdalga (ed.), *Naqshbandis in Western and Central Asia: Change and Continuity* (Istanbul: Swedish Research Institute, 1999), 129–46, 131–5; Mardin, *Religion and Social Change*, 48ff.; Butrus Abu-Manneh, 'Shaykh Ahmad Ziya al-Din al-Gümüshhanevi and the Ziyai-Khalidi Suborder', in: F. de Jong (ed.), *Shī'a Islam, Sects and Sufism: Historical Dimensions, Religious Practice and Methodological Considerations* (Utrecht: M. Th. Houtsma, 1992), 105–17.

89. Sayyid families were organised separately as Sunni and Shii Sayyids, with the number of Shii Sayyids being much higher than that of the Sunni ones. The Ottomans appointed syndics for the Ashraf in traditional strongholds of Alid presence such as Karbala, Najaf, and Kazimiyya. Batatu, *The Old Social Classes*, 153–210.

90. Çetinsaya, *Ottoman Administration*, 101f.; Kern, *Imperial Citizen*, 70ff.

91. Kern, *Imperial Citizen*, 78–81.

92. Çetinsaya, *Ottoman Administration*, 101f.

93. Jacob M. Landau, *The Politics of Pan-Islam: Ideology and Organization* (Oxford: Clarendon Press, 1990), 13–21.

94. Nikki R. Keddie, *Sayyid Jamāl ad-Dīn 'al-Afghānī': A Political Biography* (Berkeley: University of California Press, 1972), 2; Hourani, *Arabic Thought*, 108.

95. Hazara, *The History of Afghanistan*, Vol. 3, Part 1, 211–5 (484–7).

96. Özcan, *Pan-Islamism*, 55–60; Juan R. I. Cole, 'Shaikh al-Ra'is and Sultan Abdülhamid II: The Iranian Dimension of Pan-Islam', in: Israel Gershoni, Hakan Erdem, and Ursula Wokoeck (eds), *Histories of the Modern Middle East: New Directions* (Boulder, CO: Lynne Rienner, 2002), 167–85.

97. Çetinsaya, *Ottoman Administration*, 112.

98. Cited after: Cole, 'Shaikh al-Ra'is', 173.

99. This was the view of al-Afghani and of Shaykh al-Ra'is, who had outlined his ideas in a booklet entitled *Ittihad al-Islam* (*Unity of Islam*), which he wrote in Bombay, where he was staying as a guest of the Ismaili leader, the Aga Khan, and finished in Muscat in 1894. Cole, 'Shaikh al-Ra'is', 178; Keddie, *Sayyid Jamāl ad-Dīn 'al-Afghānī'*, 396; Landau, *The Politics of Pan-Islam*, 32; Mehrdad Kia, 'Pan-Islamism in Late Nineteenth-Century Iran', *Middle Eastern Studies* 32, 1 (1996), 30–52, 45–8.

100. This was the view of Talibov Tabrizi and, again, Shaykh al-Ra'is. Kia, 'Pan-Islamism', 35, 46.

101. Quoted in: Çetinsaya, *Ottoman Administration*, 103f. See also Kieser, *Der verpasste Friede*, 70.

102. Ahmet Şeyhun, *Islamist Thinkers in the Late Ottoman Empire and Early Turkish Republic* (Leiden: Brill, 2014), 80ff., 129, and passim.

103. Indeed, Britain did try to influence politics in the shrine cities through the disbursing of funds from the bequest, while also seeking to use the *mujtahids* as a lever of influence in Iranian politics. Çetinsaya, *Ottoman Administration*, 100, 105, 113, 121, 199.

104. According to the memoirs of a contemporary observer: 'When the Sayyed's group was formed, he spoke to it as follows: Today the religion of Islam is like a ship whose captain is Mohammad, peace be with him, and all Moslems are passengers of this holy ship, and this unhappy ship is caught in a storm and threatened with sinking, and unbelievers and freethinkers from every side have pierced this ship. What is the duty of the passengers of such a ship, threatened with sinking, and its inhabitants close to perdition? Should they first try to preserve and save this ship from the storm and from sinking, or instead bring the ship and each other to the verge of ruin through discord, personal motives, and petty disagreements? All with one voice answered that preserving the territory of Islam and this holy ship was the religious duty of every Muslim. [...] Then the Sayyed asked all to write to every acquaintance and friend in Iran and the shrines of Iraq, in general, and in particular to the Shiite ulama in India, Iran and Arab lands, Balkh, and Turkestan, about the kindness and benevolence of the great Islamic Sultan toward all Moslems of whatever opinion and group they might be. If the Shii ulama united in this Islamic unity the Sultan would give every one of them, according to his rank, special favor and a monthly salary, and would order Ottoman officials to observe the same good conduct toward Iranians in Mecca and Medina as toward their own people, and in recognition of this great action of the Shii ulama and the state of Iran he would bestow on them the holy cities of Iraq. [The society agreed] and about 400 letters were written in all directions, and a report of this society was given to the Ottoman Sultan. [...] After six months about 200 petitions from the Arab and Iranian Shii ulama with some gifts and antiques were sent the Sultan through Sayyed Jamal ed Din. [He translated the petitions into Turkish and took them to the Sultan.] The Ottoman Caliph was so happy to see these letters that he embraced the late Sayyed and kissed his face and said to him: since some are such fanatical Sunnites and will find a pretext to accuse me of Shiism, it is better that we turn over the accomplishment of this holy goal to the Prime Minister and the High Gate. We will have the Sheikh of Islam collaborate with us confidentially. He accepted the royal will in this matter and an imperial command went to the High Gate. I was delegated to go to the holy cities of Iraq to investigate the mentality and affairs of the ulama and give a report to the High Gate.' *Biography of Mirza Aqa Khan Kirmani by Afzal al-Mulk Kirmani,*

quoted in: Nikki R. Keddie, 'Religion and Irreligion in Early Iranian Nationalism', *Comparative Studies in Society and History* 4, 3 (1962), 265–95, appendix. See also Çetinsaya, *Ottoman Administration*, 114f.

105. Mulder, 'Abdülhamid and the 'Alids'; Anja Pistor-Hatam, 'Pilger, Pest und Cholera: Die Wallfahrt zu den Heiligen Stätten im Irak als gesundheitspolitisches Problem im 19. Jahrhundert', *Die Welt des Islams* 31, 2 (1991), 228–45. They also granted Iranian consuls special rights to legal assistance for Iranian subjects. Nakash, *The Shi'is of Iraq*, 17f.

106. Kern, *Imperial Citizen*, 73ff.; Mervin, *Un réformisme chiite*, 240–9. For descriptions in the Iranian press published in Cairo of Ashura commemorations of Iranian and Arab Shia as well as joint commemorations with the Bektashis in the Mukattam Hills, see Anja W. M. Luesink, 'The Iranian Community in Cairo at the Turn of the Century', in: Th. Zarcone and F. Zarinebaf (eds), *Les Iraniens d'Istanbul* (Paris: Institut Français de Recherches en Iran/Institut Français d'Études Anatoliennes, 1993), 193–200, 197. In the late Ottoman period, for example, the Ottoman government paid for a festivity on the 10th of Muharram at the Hussain shrine in Aleppo, which Ottoman officials used to attend. Gonnella, *Islamische Heiligenverehrung*, 196.

107. Anja Pistor-Hatam, "Āšūrā in Istanbul: Religiöse Feierlichkeiten als Ausdruck persisch-schiitischen Selbstverständnisses am Ende des 19. Jahrhunderts', *Die Welt des Islams* 38, 1 (1998), 95–119; Hamid Algar, 'Participation by Iranian Diplomats in the Masonic Lodges of Istanbul', in: Th. Zarcone and F. Zarinebaf (eds), *Les Iraniens d'Istanbul* (Paris: Institut Français de Recherches en Iran/ Institut Français d'Études Anatoliennes, 1993), 33–44, 36. There are detailed descriptions of ceremonies from 1881 to 1926. Before the 1860s, they were likely only held in private and more or less in secret. Erika Glassen, 'Muharram-Ceremonies ('Azâdârî) in Istanbul at the End of the XIXth and the Beginning of the XXth Century', in: Th. Zarcone and F. Zarinebaf (eds), *Les Iraniens d'Istanbul* (Paris: Institut Français de Recherches en Iran/Institut Français d'Études Anatoliennes, 1993), 113–29.

108. Thierry Zarcone, 'La situation du Chi'isme à Istanbul à la fin du XIXe et au début du XXe siècle', in: Th. Zarcone and F. Zarinebaf (eds), *Les Iraniens d'Istanbul* (Paris: Institut Français de Recherches en Iran/Institut Français d'Études Anatoliennes, 1993), 97–111.

109. Algar, 'Caliphs and the Caliphate'; Algar, *Religion and the State in Iran*, 231; Çetinsaya, *Ottoman Administration*, 118; Ende, *Arabische Nation*, 113f.; Landau, *The Politics of Pan-Islam*, 205; Elie Kedourie, 'The Iraqi Shi'is and their Fate', in: Martin Kramer (ed.), *Shi'ism, Resistance, and Revolution* (Boulder, CO: Westview Press, 1987), 135–57, 142; Kia, 'Pan-Islamism', 48.

110. When in the 1880s the Iranian ambassador in Istanbul asked permission for Nasir al-Din Shah to repair the shrine in Najaf, the Ottoman government first replied that it would pay for the repair itself, but then granted the permission in keeping with tradition for the sake of Sunni–Shii harmony and to please the Shah. Çetinsaya, *Ottoman Administration*, 102f. In February 1890, Abdulhamid

ordered the repair of the Hussain shrine in Karbala at considerable expense. Ibid., 105.

111. Sabri Ateş, 'Bones of Contention: Corpse Traffic and Ottoman-Iranian Rivalry in Nineteenth-Century Iraq', *Comparative Studies of South Asia, Africa and the Middle East* 30, 3 (2010), 512–32; Birsen Bulmuş, *Plague, Quarantines and Geopolitics in the Ottoman Empire* (Edinburgh: Edinburgh University Press, 2012), 153–9; F. G. Clemow, 'The Shiah Pilgrimage and the Sanitary Defences of Mesopotamia and the Turco-Persian Frontier', *The Lancet* 188, 4853 (1916), 441–3; Pistor-Hatam, 'Pilger, Pest und Cholera'. This also led to a debate amongst Shii clerics about the corpse traffic in the early twentieth century. Werner Ende, 'Eine schiitische Kontroverse über Naql al-Ğanā'iz', *Zeitschrift der Deutschen Morgenländischen Gesellschaft* 4 (1980), 217–18. The corpse traffic declined once the twentieth-century Iraqi and Iranian nation states developed in antagonism towards each other, and only re-emerged after 2003. Nakash, *The Shi'is of Iraq*, 184–201, esp. 200f. On my visit to Najaf in 2018, I would frequently encounter groups of (male) mourners carrying a coffin on their shoulders to shouts of Allahu Akbar around the shrine of Ali. After blessing the coffin by walking into the shrine, they would then carry it back to the cemetery, where it would be buried. A similar practice occurs at the two shrines in Karbala, with coffins being carried through the Hussain and Abbas shrine before burial nearby.

112. This longstanding policy that existed in theory was formalised in two laws in 1822 and 1874. The first edict urged religious officials to be particularly vigilant that Ottoman Sunni women would not marry Iranian men and vowed to punish officials that would not take this matter seriously. Kern, *Imperial Citizen*, 27, 53f., 60, 155f. In 1892, it was established that the ban also applied to Iranian Sunnis seeking to marry Ottoman women. Ibid., 111. Importantly, the ban only applied to Ottoman women marrying Iranian men, while Ottoman men seeking to marry Shii women were still allowed to, even if these were Iranian. Ibid., 112. But the ban was enacted for political, not purely sectarian reasons. And when legal advisors to the Ottoman government advocated for the abolition of the law in 1920, they argued that Sunni–Shia marriage was legal according to Islamic law. Ibid., 142. See also ibid., 89–113; Ateş, *Ottoman-Iranian Borderlands*, 192f., 197f.

113. One of the pan-Islamists was a Qajar prince and scholar, Abu al-Hasan Mirza 'Shaykh al-Ra'is' Qajar, who wrote up a list of actions the Ottomans should perform, including a stop to incitement against Iran and Shiism and a further improvement of conditions in the shrine cities and a refurbishment of the shrines. Cole, 'Shaikh al-Ra'is', 170f.

114. Mansoor Moaddel, 'Shi'i Political Discourse and Class Mobilization in the Tobacco Movement of 1890–1892', *Sociological Forum* 7, 3 (1992), 447–68.

115. Çetinsaya, *Ottoman Administration*, 110f.

116. Cole, 'Shaikh al-Ra'is', 172–5.

117. Keddie, *Sayyid Jamāl ad-Dīn 'al-Afghānī'*, 380ff.

118. Cole, 'Shaikh al-Ra'is', 182ff.; Kia, 'Pan-Islamism', 33f.

119. Çetinsaya, *Ottoman Administration*, 116; Keddie, *Sayyid Jamāl ad-Dīn 'al-Afghānī'*, 380ff.

120. Abdul-Hadi Hairi, *Shī'ism and Constitutionalism in Iran: A Study of the Role Played by the Persian Residents of Iraq in Iranian Politics* (Leiden: Brill, 1977); Hairi, 'Why did the 'Ulamā Participate in the Persian Constitutional Revolution of 1905–1909?', *Die Welt des Islams* 17, 1/4 (1976–7), 127–54; Vanessa Martin, *Islam and Modernism: The Iranian Revolution of 1906* (London: Tauris, 1989); Ervand Abrahamian, 'The Crowd in the Persian Revolution', *Iranian Studies* 2, 4 (1969), 128–50; Abrahamian, 'The Causes of the Constitutional Revolution in Iran', *International Journal of Middle East Studies* 10, 3 (1979), 381–414; Abbas Amanat, 'CONSTITUTIONAL REVOLUTION i. Intellectual background', *EIr*, Janet Afary, *The Iranian Constitutional Revolution: Grassroots Democracy, Social Democracy, and the Origins of Feminism* (New York: Columbia University Press, 1996). See Ali M. Ansari (ed.), *Iran's Constitutional Revolution of 1906: Narratives of the Enlightenment* (London: Gingko Library, 2016). See also M. J. Sheikh-ol-Islami, 'AḤMAD SHAH QĀJĀR', *EIr*.

121. Çetinsaya, *Ottoman Administration*, 119f. Comparatively little is known about Russian ties with the shrine cities, but the Russian Empire had also been corresponding with and sending gifts to the clerics in the shrine cities, so that they would maintain a quietising effect on the Shii population in Daghestan. Çetinsaya, 'The Caliph and Mujtahids: Ottoman Policy towards the Shiite Community of Iraq in the Late Nineteenth Century', *Middle Eastern Studies* 41, 4 (2005), 561–74, 563.

122. Luizard, *La formation de l'Irak contemporain*, 217–41, 292–304; Rainer Brunner and Werner Ende, 'Preface', in: Rainer Brunner and Werner Ende (eds), *The Twelver Shia in Modern Times: Religious Culture & Political History* (Leiden: Brill, 2001), ix–xx, xiii.

123. For the notion of sect-centricity, see Haddad, *Understanding 'Sectarianism'*.

124. Weiss, *In the Shadow of Sectarianism*, 11, 17ff.

125. Werner Ende, 'Iraq in World War I: The Turks, the Germans, and the Shi'ite Mujtahids' Call for Jihad', in: Rudolph Peters (ed.), *Proceedings of the Ninth Congress of the Union Européenne des Arabisants et Islamisants: Amsterdam, 1st to 7th Septembre 1978* (Leiden: Brill, 1981), 57–71; Tilman Lüdke, *Jihad Made in Germany: Ottoman and German Propaganda and Intelligence Operations in the First World War* (Münster: LIT, 2005); Nasrollah Salehi, 'Les fatwas des ulémas persans de Najaf et Kerbala', in: Oliver Bast (ed.), *La Perse et la grande guerre* (Tehran: Institut Français de Recherche en Iran, 2002), 157–76; Erik-Jan Zürcher, *Jihad and Islam in World War I: Studies on the Ottoman Jihad on the Centenary of Snouck Hurgronje's 'Holy War Made in Germany'* (Leiden: Leiden University Press, 2016). In the Second World War, as part of its general policy towards Muslims and Islam, Nazi Germany also acknowledged and reproduced sectarian division. The SS trained Muslim clerics to accompany Muslim troops fighting on Nazi Germany's side. Initially, Sunni Turkestanis and Shii

Azerbaijanis were taught together. On the advice of the German Orientalist Bertold Spuler, who was teaching at the Islam Institute at the University of Göttingen, Sunni and Shia were taught separately after ethnic and confessional tensions had emerged during previous courses. In 1945, at the instigation of Alimjan Idris, Sunnis and Shia were taught jointly again at the SS Mullah school in Dresden, with strong anti-sectarian discourse. The SS was obviously interested in overcoming the sectarian divide to strengthen the unity of its Muslim troops. Titus Lenk, 'Die SS-Mullah-Schule und die Arbeitsgemeinschaft Turkestan in Dresden', *Zukunft braucht Erinnerung*, 12 November 2006, http://www.zukunft-braucht-erinnerung.de/die-ss-mullah-schule-und-die-arbeitsgemeinschaft-turkestan-in-dresden/; Peter Heine, 'Die Imam-Kurse der deutschen Wehrmacht im Jahre 1944', in: Gerhard Höpp (ed.), *Fremde Erfahrungen: Asiaten und Afrikaner in Deutschland, Österreich und in der Schweiz bis 1945* (Berlin: Das Arabische Buch, 1996), 229–38, 234. The German embassy in Iran also specifically targeted propaganda at Iranians incorporating Shii elements, especially expectations of the Mahdi. Apparently, some Iranians thought that Adolf Hitler was the Mahdi. David Motadel, *Islam and Nazi Germany's War* (Cambridge, MA: Harvard University Press, 2014), 104ff., 109f., 273, 280, 463f.

126. Jones, *Shi'a Islam*, 176; Naeem M. Qureshi, *Pan-Islam in British Indian Politics: A Study of the Khilafat Movement, 1918–1924* (Leiden: Brill, 1999), 73ff. This, in turn, may have contributed to allegedly German-inspired attempts to assassinate the Aga Khan in Switzerland in 1917. Y. D. Prasad, 'The Aga Khan as a British Imperial Agent during World War I', *Proceedings of the Indian History Congress* 39, 2 (1978), 946–53, 949. Press reports in Indonesia, for example, that sought to undermine his position pointed out that he was Shii and not Sunni like most Muslims, that he wore a British suit, and that he generally enjoyed a flamboyant life in Europe, which is why true Muslims should not take his opinions seriously. Cornelis van Dijk, *The Netherlands Indies and the Great War, 1914–1918* (Leiden: Brill, 2007), 308.

127. They also published anti-Ottoman petitions by Shia from Najaf and Karbala. Gertrude L. Bell, *Review of the Civil Administration of Mesopotamia* (London: HM Stationery Office, 1920), 19, 30. After the war, the Government Press at Basra would publish 'illustrated supplements dealing with pilgrimages to the holy towns and an illustrated book of the Shrines of the Iraq'. Ibid., 116.

128. However, Henry McMahon, the British High Commissioner in Egypt, argued this would only apply in purely Arab territories, implying that being an Arab was equivalent to being an Arab Muslim and excluding what would later become Lebanon, i.e. territories with large Christian populations. N.a., *Correspondence between Sir Henry McMahon, G.C.M.G., G.C.V.O., K.C.I.E., C.S.I., His Majesty's High Commissioner at Cairo, and the Sherif Hussein of Mecca, July 1915–March 1916* (London: HM Stationery Office, 1939); Makdisi, *Age of Coexistence*, 114.

CHAPTER 9

1. Eric J. Hobsbawm, *Nations and Nationalism since 1780: Programme, Myth, Reality*, 2nd ed. (Cambridge: Cambridge University Press, 1992), 131.

2. Susan Pedersen, *The Guardians: The League of Nations and the Crisis of Empire* (Oxford: Oxford University Press, 2015).

3. It is interesting to note that the report distinguishes between 'Kizilbash' and Sunni Kurds and uses that as an argument of why an independent Kurdistan may be difficult to realise: 'The Kurds claim a very large area, on the basis of their distribution, but since they are greatly mixed with Armenians, Turks, and others, and divided among themselves into Kizilbash, Shiite and Sunnites it seems best to limit them to the natural geographical area which lies between the proposed Armenia on the north and Mesopotamia on the south, with the divide between the Euphrates and the Tigris as the western boundary, and the Persian frontier as the eastern boundary. A measure of autonomy can be allowed them under close mandatory rule, with the object of preparing them for ultimate independence or for federation with neighboring areas in a larger self-governing union. It is possible to shift most of the comparatively small numbers of both Turks and Armenians out of this area by voluntary exchange of population and thus obtain a province containing about a million and a half people, nearly all Kurds. Full security must needs [*sic*] be provided for the Syrian, Chaldean and Nestorian Christians who dwell in the area. This plan would probably provide for all of the Sunnite Kurds in Turkey, and the Kizilbash group lies almost wholly to the west. The area contemplated looks more to the south than the west and lies wholly about the upper waters of the Tigris and its tributaries. It would seem better, therefore, unless the population itself strongly prefers the other plan. to [*sic*] place it under the control of the power which cares for Mesopotamia, than to connect it with Armenia across the mountains at the north, or with Anatolia with which it would have only narrow contact at the west.' The World War I Document Archive, 'The King-Crane Commission Report, August 28, 1919', https://wwi. lib.byu.edu/index.php/The_King-Crane_Report. For background, see, amongst a vast literature, Ussama Samir Makdisi, *Faith Misplaced: The Broken Promise of U.S.–Arab Relations, 1820–2001* (New York: PublicAffairs, 2010), 137–46.

4. Rida was not a member of the constitution-drafting committee, but Thompson argues that, as president of the Congress, he must have approved of it. Elizabeth F. Thompson, 'Rashid Rida and the 1920 Syrian-Arab Constitution: How the French Mandate Undermined Islamic Liberalism', in: Cyrus Schayegh and Andrew Arsan (eds), *The Routledge Handbook of the History of the Middle East Mandates* (London: Routledge, 2015), 244–57. For the role of the Arab nationalist secret society al-Fatat, of which Rida was a member, see Eliezer Tauber, *The Formation of Modern Syria and Iraq* (London: Cass, 1995), 16–48. Rida had also become a member of the Syrian Union Party in 1918 and had to defend his decision to prioritise one part of the Arab homeland over others, which he did

by arguing that it was the only way to achieve cooperation of Muslims and Christians for the independence of Syria. Ibid., 150ff. See also Tauber, 'Rashid Rida and Faysal's Kingdom in Syria', *The Muslim World* 85, 3–4 (1995), 235–45; Tauber, 'Rashid Rida's Political Attitudes during World War I', *The Muslim World* 85, 1-2 (1995), 107–21; Tauber, 'Rashid Rida as Pan-Arabist before World War I', *The Muslim World* 79, 2 (1989), 102–12; Winter, *A History of the 'Alawis*, 248. Rida and other Arab nationalists had initially also embraced the 1908 Ottoman constitution, but then became disillusioned with the CUP's turn towards a more Turkish ethno-nationalism and authoritarianism. Anne-Laure Dupont, 'The Ottoman Revolution of 1908 as Seen by al-Hilâl and al-Manâr: The Triumph and Diversification of the Reformist Spirit', in: Christoph Schumann (ed.), *Liberal Thought in the Eastern Mediterranean: Late 19th Century until the 1960s* (Leiden: Brill, 2008), 123–46.

5. James L. Gelvin, *Divided Loyalties: Nationalism and Mass Politics in Syria at the Close of Empire* (Berkeley: University of California Press, 1998); Malcolm B. Russell, *The First Modern Arab State: Syria under Faysal, 1918–1920* (Minneapolis: Bibliotheca Islamica, 1985); Schayegh, *The Middle East*.

6. Khoury, *Syria and the French Mandate*, 41.

7. Edmund Burke, 'A Comparative View of French Native Policy in Morocco and Syria, 1912–1925', *Middle Eastern Studies* 9, 2 (1973), 175–86; Burke, *The Ethnographic State: France and the Invention of Moroccan Islam* (Oakland, CA: University of California Press, 2014); Julia Clancy-Smith, 'Islam and the French Empire in North Africa', in: David Motadel (ed.), *Islam and the European Empires* (Oxford: Oxford University Press, 2014), 90–111.

8. If he focused on Shiism, he did so by looking at the movements on its fringes, those he termed 'extremist', and outsider figures that died as martyrs. Christian Krokus, *The Theology of Louis Massignon: Islam, Christ, and the Church* (Washington, DC: Catholic University of America Press, 2017), 108; Pierre Rocalve, *Louis Massignon et l'Islam* (Damascus: Institut Français de Damas, 1993), 67–84. Massignon did teach courses on Shiism at the Collège de France from 1930 onwards, however. Ibid., 83f. An account of 'extremist' Shii bureaucrats working in the Sunni Abbasids' administration in early-tenth-century Baghdad, whom he blames for the indictment and eventual execution of the Sufi al-Hallaj, is telling: 'More enterprising, because they were externally Muslims; more cunning and more cynical, because, deep down, they considered the Abbasid state, which they were serving, as illegitimate, and all of the canonical acts concluded under the flag of its usurpation as invalid: which kept their consciences from being troubled over all of the embezzlements and deceptions they carried out in the exercise of their official duties. By accepting positions in the Abbasid administration they were able to work more effectively for the success of the Shi'ite conspiracy, and that alone was uppermost in their minds. It was an application of the Shi'ite principle of taqiya or dissimulation, which became all the more strictly applied as their Shi'ism became more extremist in nature (as happened, in fact, in the case of all of the kuttab).' Massignon, *The Passion of al-Hallāj*, Vol. 1, 305. See also

ibid., 389–92. This tendency was somewhat broken through the work of his student Henry Corbin, who wrote key works on religion in Iran, in particular Shiism and Sufism, and the interactions between the two. Henry Corbin, *En Islam Iranien: Aspects spirituels et philiosophiques*, 4 Vols (Paris: Gallimard, 1971). But even Corbin would eventually criticise Massignon for his tendency to side with the Sunni tradition, while others criticised Massignon's focus on marginal figures in Islamic history. Rocalve, *Louis Massignon*, 67f. He also published cricially about Alawites/Nusayris. Louis Massignon, 'Nuṣairī', *EI*, and numerous other *EI* entries.

9. Gérard D. Khoury, 'Robert de Caix et Louis Massignon', in: Peter Sluglett and Nadine Méouchy (eds), *The British and French Mandates in Comparative Perspectives* (Leiden: Brill, 2004), 165–83, esp. 169–74. See also Gérard D. Khoury, *Une tutelle coloniale: Le mandat français en Syrie et au Liban: Écrits politiques de Robert de Caix* (Paris: Belin, 2006), e.g. 15ff. For an analysis of *L'Asie française* in the context of Syria and the way it started to frame the 'minority' question there, see Benjamin T. White, *The Emergence of Minorities in the Middle East: The Politics of Community in French Mandate Syria* (Edinburgh: Edinburgh University Press, 2011), 134–43. For French disdain for Arab nationalism, see Khoury, *Syria and the French Mandate*, 53f.

10. Meir Zamir, 'Faisal and the Lebanese Question, 1918–20', *Middle Eastern Studies* 27, 3 (1991), 404–26; Makdisi, *Faith Misplaced*, 148f.

11. For good introductory essays, literature reviews, and overviews, see Cyrus Schayegh and Andrew Arsan, 'Introduction', in: Cyrus Schayegh and Andrew Arsan (eds), *The Routledge Handbook of the History of the Middle East Mandates* (London: Routledge, 2015), 1–23. For succinct introductions, see, amongst many others, Michael Provence, *The Last Ottoman Generation and the Making of the Modern Middle East* (Cambridge: Cambridge University Press, 2017); David K. Fieldhouse, *Western Imperialism in the Middle East, 1914–1958* (Oxford: Oxford University Press, 2006); Stephen H. Longrigg, *Syria and Lebanon under French Mandate* (London: Oxford University Press, 1958).

12. Had this experiment in Arab self-rule and constitutional monarchy been allowed to proceed, the modern history of the Middle East may have played out very differently indeed. Elizabeth F. Thompson, *How the West Stole Democracy from the Arabs: The Syrian Arab Congress and the Destruction of its Historic Liberal-Islamic Alliance* (London: Grove Press, 2020).

13. Pedersen, *The Guardians*, 80ff. For more on the role of Syrian émigrés and efforts to publicise French atrocities at the League of Nations and other fora, see Reem Bailony, *Transnational Rebellion: The Syrian Revolt of 1925–1927* (PhD, University of California, 2015); Friedhelm Hoffmann, *Die syro-palästinensische Delegation am Völkerbund und Šakīb Arslān in Genf 1921–1936/46* (Zurich: LIT, 2010); William L. Cleveland, *Islam against the West: Shakib Arslan and the Campaign for Islamic Nationalism* (Austin: University of Texas Press, 1985).

14. Pedersen, *The Guardians*, 95–103; Ussama Samir Makdisi, 'The Problem of Sectarianism in the Middle East in an Age of Western Hegemony', in: Nader

Hashemi and Danny Postel (eds), *Sectarianization: Mapping the New Politics of the Middle East* (London: Hurst, 2017), 23–34, 33; Makdisi, *Age of Coexistence.*

15. It may have given similar assurances to the *mujtahids*. This summary states that the safety of the Shii shrine cities was also addressed in conversations with Gulf Chiefs. Qatar National Library, 'Papers on British Policy and the Arab Movement [153v] (310/380)', Mss Eur F112/277, https://www.qdl.qa/archive/81055/vdc_100079857499.0x00006f. In general, see Kristian Coates Ulrichsen, 'The British Occupation of Mesopotamia, 1914–1922', *Journal of Strategic Studies* 30, 2 (2007), 349–77.

16. It was the view of Sir Percy Cox. Peter Sluglett, *Britain in Iraq: Contriving King and Country*, 2nd ed. (London: I. B. Tauris, 2007), 221. Initially, Hamid Khan, a cousin of the Aga Khan, an Ismaili, represented British interests in Najaf, and a Christian Arab at Kufa. Arnold T. Wilson, *Loyalties: Mesopotamia, 1914–1917* (London: Oxford University Press, 1930), 268f.

17. He continued: 'The deep-rooted cleavage between the two great branches of the Islamic faith was a factor of profound importance in all political discussions and made extreme caution necessary in introducing the constitutional experiments advocated from Syria, where the tradition of Sunni predominance was unquestioned.' Wilson, *Loyalties*, 236f. This paragraph in his book is accompanied by a population estimate of 1919 detailing the population figures for Sunni, Shia, Jewish, Christian, and other religions.

18. Gertrude Bell Archive, 'Diaries: 29/1/1903', http://www.gerty.ncl.ac.uk/diary_details.php?diary_id=293; Gertrude Bell Archive, 'Letters: 16 December 1902: From Gertrude Bell to her Stepmother, Dame Florence Bell', http://www.gerty.ncl.ac.uk/letter_details.php?letter_id=1343; Gertrude Bell Archive, 'Letters: 7 December 1919: From Gertrude Bell to her Father, Sir Hugh Bell', http://www.gerty.ncl.ac.uk/letter_details.php?letter_id=363.

19. Bell, *Review*, 14f. It was initially difficult to establish Shii judges in Najaf and Karbala because they were seen as undermining the *mujtahids*, who were not keen to see their powers transferred to state authority. Ibid., 98. The main Sharia courts continued from Ottoman times were only dealing with personal status law matters amongst Sunnis, 'while the jurisdiction formerly possessed by the Sunni Shar'ah Courts over Shi'ahs, Jews, or Christians was transferred to the civil Courts of First Instance, and is exercised in accordance with the personal law of those concerned, or any custom applicable to them. The courts were authorised to refer this type of case respectively to a Shi'ah religious priest or to the Christian or Jewish religious authorities.' Ibid., 95.

20. One hour a week was set aside for religious teaching, with Sunni teachers recommended by the Awqaf committee tasked by default to teach this, 'while the Christian, Jewish, and Shi'ah communities were invited to send teachers to give instruction to the boys of their respective creeds at the appointed time. But no definitive syllabus had been drawn up and practice varied in different schools. [...] In each school a religious teacher was appointed who belonged to the community of the majority. The minority are exempt and are allowed facilities

to obtain instruction in their own faith where these exist. The Department, however, does not undertake to place religious teachers of the minority on the establishment unless its numbers reach a certain proportion of the total attendance. [...] The religious syllabus, adopted in those Government schools in which the majority of boys are Mohammedan, was dawn [sic] up as far as possible to meet the views of both Sunnis and Shi'ahs; but in response to a special request from certain of the Shi'ah centres, a religious syllabus based on purely Shi'ah lines has recently been introduced into a few schools such as Karbala and Najaf, where the pupils are entirely composed of Shi'ahs.' Bell, *Review*, 103f. The first years of British administration also saw an expansion of 'denominational schools' and increasing funding to Christian, Jewish, Sunni, and Shii schools. Ibid., 104. In the Training College in Baghdad, 'Sunnis, Shi'ahs and Christians work, play and live together in a spirit of camaraderie and good fellowship, which a few years ago would have been thought impossible.' Ibid., 105. Shii officials in the Ministry of Education tended to be quite fervently nationalist. Magnus T. Bernhardsson, 'Gertrude Bell and the Antiquities Law of Iraq', in: Paul Collins and Charles Tripp (eds), *Gertrude Bell and Iraq: A Life and Legacy* (Oxford: Oxford University Press, 2017), 241–55, 251.

21. The new administration was petitioned to raise the level of salaries in Shii mosques and shrines to the level paid to Sunni religious functionaries, a request that was refused based on the argument that salary levels inherited from Ottoman times were to be kept intact. Bell, *Review*, 10, 102. The administration also had to regulate and monitor the corpse traffic, largely continuing Ottoman public health practices. Ibid., 114.

22. Toby Dodge, *Inventing Iraq: The Failure of Nation-Building and a History Denied* (London: Hurst, 2003), 5–41. See also Priya Satia, 'Developing Iraq: Britain, India and the Redemption of Empire and Technology in the First World War', *Past & Present* 197, 1 (2007), 211–55; Rosie Llewellyn-Jones, 'The British Raj and the British Mandate in Iraq', *Asian Affairs* 46, 2 (2015), 270–9.

23. In a letter of January 1918, Gertrude Bell, who would become Oriental Secretary in Iraq, could still write that '[i]t's the Shias of the saiyid class who know that they would have the least to gain by the return of the Turks: The alienation of the Shias has been a great asset to us and has meant for instance that we have never had any serious religious feeling to contend with in Karbala and Najaf.' 'Letter from Gertrude Bell to Sir Valentine Chirol, January 1918', in: Elizabeth Burgoyne, *Gertrude Bell: From her Personal Papers, 1914–1926*, Vol. 1 (London: Ernest Benn, 1961), 76, quoted in: Peter Sluglett, 'The British, the Sunnis and the Shi'is: Social Hierarchies of Interaction under the British Mandate', *International Journal of Contemporary Iraqi Studies* 4, 3 (2010), 257–73, 263f. See now also Juan Cole, 'British Policy toward the Iraqi Shiites during World War I', *Journal of Contemporary Iraq & the Arab World* 15, 3 (2021), 285–304.

24. See, for example, the account in Bell, *Review*, 2ff. See also Luizard, *La formation de l'Irak contemporain*, 319–44.

25. Charles Tripp, *A History of Iraq* (Cambridge: Cambridge University Press, 2000), 32f.; Sluglett, *Britain in Iraq*, 220.
26. Nakash, *The Shīʿis of Iraq*, 67; Sluglett, 'The British'; Tripp, *A History of Iraq*, 33f.
27. Al-Nafeesi, *The Role of the Shīʿah*, 79–98; Luizard, *La formation de l'Irak contemporain*, 351–64. Rumours in Afghan and Indian newspapers that British forces had bombed the shrine of Ali in Najaf and killed senior clerics, including Mirza Muhammad Taqi al-Shirazi, led to protests in Lucknow and the formation of an organisation to protect the shrine cities. Jones, *Shīʿa Islam*, 180ff.
28. Al-Nafeesi, *The Role of the Shīʿah*, 98–104.
29. Dodge, *Inventing Iraq*, 68f.
30. He also advocated a kingdom ruled by a descendant of the Sharifs of Mecca. Abbas Kadhim, *Reclaiming Iraq: The 1920 Revolution and the Founding of the Modern State* (Austin: University of Texas Press, 2012). When I attended a conference organised by the shrines in Karbala in 2019, a book on his role was published to coincide with the conference and the centenary of the revolt: 'Ala' al-Safi, *Al-Shaykh Muhammad Taqi al-Shirazi al-Ha'iri wa Dawrihi al-Siyyasi min 'am 1918–1920* (Karbala: Dar al-Kafil, 2019). Gertrude Bell, on the other hand, was cheerful on the news in August 1920 of the death of al-Shirazi, the senior cleric that had endorsed the uprising. Gertrude Bell Archive, 'Letters: 23 August 1920: From Gertrude Bell to her Father, Sir Hugh Bell', http://www.gerty.ncl.ac.uk/letter_details.php?letter_id=411. In another letter, she refers to a 'mourning gathering for the Premier Mujtahid, the Shaikh al Shariʿah, who has done the only good thing he ever did, namely died.' Gertrude Bell Archive, 'Letters: 25 December 1920: Gertrude Bell to her Father, Sir Hugh Bell', http://www.gerty.ncl.ac.uk/letter_details.php?letter_id=445.
31. Batatu, *The Old Social Classes*, 123, 173, 294–7; Tripp, *A History of Iraq*, 40–5, 71; Luizard, *La formation de l'Irak contemporain*, 385–422.
32. Cited after: Nakash, *The Shīʿis of Iraq*, 70. Apart from being a famous poet, al-Ubaydi became the Sunni Mufti of Mosul, a highly symbolic and important position in the Sunni scene of Iraq. He adopted numerous nationalist, unifying, and anti-imperialist stances. See, for example, Mohammad Waleed Abid Saleh, 'Of Arab Issues in the Letters of al-Mufti Muhammad Habib al-Obeidi to International Bodies and Western Leaders', *Al Malweah for Archaeological and Historical Studies* 7, 20 (2020), 133–62.
33. See, for example, Bell, *Review*, 140; Tripp, *A History of Iraq*, 41.
34. Sluglett, 'The British'. Bell put it as follows: 'The Sunnis all go about protesting that the revolt was solely due to those rogues of Shiʿahs. To a certain extent they are right, but only because the Sunnis have no influence with the tribes, whereas the Shiʿah divines have.' Gertrude Bell Archive, 'Letters: 12 September 1920: Gertrude Bell to her Father, Sir Hugh Bell', http://gertrudebell.ncl.ac.uk/letter_details.php?letter_id=418.
35. Tripp, *A History of Iraq*, 31–9.
36. Though they could not have run the country without the cooperation of the largely Shii landowners in the South. Sluglett, 'The British', 258f.

37. Gertrude Bell Archive, 'Letters: 3 October 1920: Gertrude Bell to her Father, Sir Hugh Bell', http://www.gerty.ncl.ac.uk/letter_details.php?letter_id=425. At the end of the same letter, this is contrasted with the pure Arab traits of the Sunni Najdis at a coffee shop of the Uqayl in Baghdad: 'I do like them so much. They are to me an endless romance.' Ibid. While we should not personalise history too much, and there has been a focus on Bell in accounts of the British mandate in Iraq, this is in part warranted by both the role she played in the establishment of modern Iraq and because of the wealth of written material she has left us with. Paul Collins and Charles Tripp, 'Introduction', in: Paul Collins and Charles Tripp (eds), *Gertrude Bell and Iraq: A Life and Legacy* (Oxford: Oxford University Press, 2017), 1–21, 16. Bell saw the overrepresentation of Sunnis in politics and economy under the Ottomans as inevitable, emphasising the 'finer features and superior education' of Sunnis. Bell, *Review*, 27. See also her positive portrayal of Faisal and that of Ibn Saud during a visit to Basra in 1916. Qatar National Library, '"A Ruler of the Desert" [108r] (3/8)', IOR/L/PS/18/B248, https://www.qdl.qa/archive/81055/vdc_100032846136.0x000004.

38. Dodge, *Inventing Iraq*, 67f. There might have been a gender element to the antipathy Bell felt towards the *mujtahids*, for most *mujtahids* refused to see her, but the influence of the anti-British rising was a more decisive factor. Gertrude Bell Archive, 'Letters: 4 January 1920: Gertrude Bell to her Father, Sir Hugh Bell', http://www.gerty.ncl.ac.uk/letter_details.php?letter_id=368. She got to meet a cleric of the al-Sadr family in March 1920, and, while she appreciated being received by a senior Shii cleric after all, her account is denigrating towards the *mujtahid* class. Gertrude Bell Archive, 'Letters: 14 March 1920: Gertrude Bell to her Stepmother, Dame Florence Bell', http://www.gerty.ncl.ac.uk/letter_details.php?letter_id=384. Comparing the Shii *mujtahids* to 'alien popes', Bell made an analogy to British views of the Catholic Church in Rome as hindering the development of the modern British state. In a letter to her father, Sir Hugh Bell, she wrote that the 'position of the mujtahids is you know one which will always be a difficulty. It's as though you had a number of alien Popes permanently settled at Canterbury and issuing edicts which take precedence of the law of the land.' She noted that the Turks 'were always at loggerheads with them' and the 'Govt of the future will find itself in the same case'. Gertrude Bell Archive, 'Letters: 23 August 1920: Gertrude Bell to her Father, Sir Hugh Bell', http://www.gerty.ncl.ac.uk/letter_details.php?letter_id=411; Dodge, *Inventing Iraq*, 197n19. 'Najaf and Karbala, more particularly Najaf, have from all time been the centres of religious fanaticism of a Persian type, centres also of hostility to existing authority, and will continue to be so whatever government obtains in the rest of the "Iraq".' Bell, *Review*, 28. Bell invokes here the role of the *mujtahids* in the famous Tobacco Revolt of 1891/2. The Oudh Bequest is invoked only briefly and without much consequence, when she states: 'Our connection with the Najaf-Karbala mujtahids had begun long before the war. Since 1849 the Indian Government had been in relations with both towns in connection with the Oudh bequest.' Ibid. For the 'Persianness' of Shii beliefs, and the clergy,

see also Bell, *Review*, 27 and 40, for example. For an earlier argument by the former British ambassador to Tehran about the authority of the clergy, see Hardinge, *A Diplomatist in the East*, 307–10.

39. Tripp, *A History of Iraq*, 45. See, for example: 'The Naqib loathes the superstition of the Shi'ahs and to hear the King, in his more expansive moments, on the Shi'ah divines – well, it's a privilege. My Sunni guests, all of them really free-thinkers, were equally outspoken, and I can't help hoping that in this matter of the Bahai house the mujtahids – damnation to all of them – may find that they have embarked on a pretty tough proposition.' Gertrude Bell Archive, 'Letters: 26 February 1922: Gertrude Bell to her Father, Sir Hugh Bell', http://www.gerty.ncl.ac.uk/letter_details.php?letter_id=541.

40. Batatu, *The Old Social Classes*, 44f. See also Peter Sluglett and Marion Farouk-Sluglett, 'Some Reflections on the Sunni/Shi'i Question in Iraq', *Bulletin (British Society for Middle Eastern Studies)* 5, 2 (1978), 78–87.

41. Phebe Marr, *The Modern History of Iraq* (Boulder, CO: Westview Press, 1985), 40ff.

42. 'High Commissioner of Iraq to Secretary of State for the Colonies', 23 September 1921, F0371/6347, National Archives, Kew, quoted in: Saad B. Eskander, 'Gertrude Bell and the Formation of the Iraqi State: The Kurdish Dimension', in: Paul Collins and Charles Tripp (eds), *Gertrude Bell and Iraq: A Life and Legacy* (Oxford: Oxford University Press, 2017), 215–38, 233. For further discussion of these points, see ibid., esp. 229–34. While some Sunni Kurdish tribes had embraced the pan-Islamic project of Sultan Abdulhamid and initially found ways of arranging themselves with the new Iraqi state, groups such as the Yazidi Kurds were equally alienated by the late Ottoman and early Hashemite state-building projects, reinforcing a sense of communal identity. Nelida Fuccaro, 'Communalism and the State in Iraq: The Yazidi Kurds, c. 1869–1940', *Middle Eastern Studies* 35, 2 (1999), 1–26.

43. Sluglett, 'The British', 264–8. The Sunni leader in Baghdad, the *naqib*, got along well with Sir Percy Cox and extended to him a level of support that surprised even Gertrude Bell. Bell, *Review*, 32. The Shii *mujtahids* also issued a fatwa prohibiting participation in elections to the Constituent Assembly in 1923. Osman, *Sectarianism in Iraq*, 70f.

44. Sluglett, 'The British', 270f.; Osman, *Sectarianism in Iraq*, 172. The exception were Shii officials appointed in the shrine cities. Tripp, *A History of Iraq*, 45. This was ironic, in part because the British sought to differentiate the new state as much as possible from the in their view backward and tyrannical Ottoman period, which they perceived in starkly Orientalist terms. Dodge, *Inventing Iraq*, 43–61. See, for example, this nonchalant assessment by Bell of a new cabinet in 1921: 'The two new men are Naji Suwaidi (Justice) perhaps one of the ablest of the younger generation, and a Shi'ah who takes Education in place of another Shi'ah– I don't think there's much to choose between him and his predecessor but capable Shi'ahs grow on very few bushes.' Gertrude Bell Archive, 'Letters: 11 September 1921: Gertrude Bell to her Father, Sir Hugh Bell', http://www.gerty.ncl.ac.uk/letter_details.php?letter_id=505. A Sunni notable was made

mayor of Baghdad, while the largely Shii Karkh quarter of Baghdad received a Shii *mudir*. Bell, *Review*, 132.

45. Nakash, *The Shi'is of Iraq*, 114ff.

46. Britain established the Levies, an army contingent recruited solely from Assyrian Christians, further communalising the politics of repression, which eventually led to violent backlash against the Assyrians in 1933. Marr, *The Modern History*, 37ff.; David Omissi, 'Britain, the Assyrians and the Iraq Levies, 1919–1932', *Journal of Imperial and Commonwealth History* 17, 3 (1989), 301–22. Assyrians were in turn subject to an attack by the nascent Iraqi army in 1933. Sami Zubaida, 'Contested Nations: Iraq and the Assyrians', *Nations and Nationalism* 6, 3 (2000), 363–82.

47. However, when both Shia and Sunni notables of Iraq then proposed the idea that Faisal should be declared Caliph at a time when the Ottoman Caliphate was being officially abolished, she was not amused. Gertrude Bell Archive, 'Letters: 12 March 1924: Gertrude Bell to her Father, Sir Hugh Bell', http://www.gerty.ncl.ac.uk/letter_details.php?letter_id=693. Bell even drew up a rather odd historical analogy on the occasion of the Muharram processions between Faisal's arrival to Iraq and Hussain's martyrdom at Karbala. Gertrude Bell Archive, 'Letters: 11 September 1921: Gertrude Bell to her Father, Sir Hugh Bell', www.gerty.ncl.ac.uk/letter_details.php?letter_id=505. See also Myriam Yakoubi, 'Gertrude Bell's Perception of Faisal I of Iraq and the Anglo-Arab Romance', in: Paul Collins and Charles Tripp (eds), *Gertrude Bell and Iraq: A Life and Legacy* (Oxford: Oxford University Press, 2017), 187–213, esp. 199ff.; Stuart Erskine, *King Faisal of Iraq: An Authorised and Authentic Study* (London: Hutchinson, 1933), 136. Sharif Hussein of Mecca may have planted that idea amongst British officials that the Hashemites were close to the Shia and would thus also be accepted by Shia in Iraq. This was likely a political move on the part of Hussein, one that British officials adopted and turned to their own advantage. Lawrence even described Hussein as a crypto-Shia. Jeffery A. Rudd, *Abdallah bin al-Husayn: The Making of an Arab Political Leader, 1908–1921* (PhD, University of London, 1993), 170–91.

48. Faisal's brother Abdallah was at one point considered a possible king by some in Iraq, including senior Sunnis and Shia, because of his lineage. Nakash, *The Shi'is of Iraq*, 68. When Hussain was briefly proclaimed Caliph, *al-Qibla* published *bayahs* from all over Iraq, including Najaf and Karbala and thus by Shia. Joshua Teitelbaum, *The Rise and Fall of the Hashemite Kingdom of Arabia* (London: Hurst, 2001), 245. Hussain himself, however, wrote in 1915 in correspondence with the British that on the question of the choice of the Caliph he did not feel the need to take into consideration the opinion of the Shia, 'who lack the necessary qualifications and every other right (to decide the question of the chosen Caliph of Islam)'. Qatar National Library, 'Papers on British Policy and the Arab Movement [10r] (21/380)', Mss Eur F112/277, https://www.qdl.qa/archive/81055/vdc_100079857498.0x000016; Rudd, *Abdallah bin al-Husayn*, 170–91. On 11 January 1919, a petition by Sunnis and Shia of Baghdad called

for the three Ottoman provinces to be united under the leadership of a Muslim Arab King, one of the sons of Sharif Hussein. Tauber, *The Formation*, 279.

49. Batatu, *The Old Social Classes*, 26.

50. Abu Khaldun Sati al-Husri, *Mudhakkirati fi al-Iraq*, Vol. 1 (Beirut: Dar al-Tali'a, 1967), 87f., quoted in: Sami Zubaida, 'The Fragments Imagine the Nation: The Case of Iraq', *International Journal of Middle East Studies* 34, 2 (2002), 205–15, 213; Elie Podeh, *The Politics of National Celebrations in the Arab Middle East* (Cambridge: Cambridge University Press, 2011), 121.

51. Nakash, *The Shi'is of Iraq*, 76–9; Luizard, *La formation de l'Irak contemporain*, 440–8. For a thorough analysis of Hashemite–Saudi relations and their impact on Iraq, see al-Wardi, *Lamahat Ijtima'iyya*.

52. Gertrude Bell Archive, 'Letters: 12 April 1922: Gertrude Bell to her Stepmother, Dame Florence Bell', http://www.gerty.ncl.ac.uk/letter_details.php?letter_id=550. Some Sunni clerics, such as the pro-Wahhabi Mahmud Shukri al-Alusi, were against retaliation. Nakash, *The Shi'is of Iraq*, 79.

53. 'I've just come in from having tea with the King, and a heart to heart talk about the line he is going to take with the mujtahids. I've been encouraging him to stand up to them boldly. He and his Govt have made all the concessions they honourably can and there's nothing now but to fight it out. There are even chances that the mujtahids won't dare to face the music if the King calls the tune with sufficient decision, but no hope that he'll win them over by further concessions, short of turning down the treaty which he can't and won't contemplate.' Gertrude Bell Archive, 'Letters: 16 December 1922: Gertrude Bell to her Father, Sir Hugh Bell', http://www.gerty.ncl.ac.uk/letter_details.php?letter_id=601.

54. Tripp, *A History of Iraq*, 47f. The one major exception was Rustum Haidar, a Shii from the Bekaa valley, who had been an early Arab nationalist and Faisal's secretary at the Paris Peace Conference. He became minister of finance and of works in several early cabinets and was sent as ambassador to Iran to negotiate the first Iraqi–Iranian agreement. But his foreign and Shii identity was at times used by his opponents to denigrate him, and he was eventually assassinated in 1940. Edmund A. Ghareeb and Beth Dougherty, *Historical Dictionary of Iraq* (Oxford: Scarecrow Press, 2004), 92; Rustum Haydar, *Mudhakkirat Rustum Haydar: Haqqaqaha wa Kataba laha Muqaddima 'an Sirat Rustum Haydar wa Maqtalihi Najda Fathi Safwa* (Beirut: al-Dar al-'Arabiyya li-l-Mawsu'at, 1988).

55. Rogan, *The Arabs*, 234ff.; Muhammad Mahdi Kubba, *Mudhakkirat fi Samim al-Ahdath, 1918–1958* (Beirut: Dar al-Tali'a, 1965), 22–9. I thank Eugene Rogan for pointing me towards Kubba's memoirs. See also Gertrude Bell Archive, 'Letters: 12 April 1923: Gertrude Bell to her Father, Sir Hugh Bell', http://www.gerty. ncl.ac.uk/letter_details.php?letter_id=621.

56. The fatwa was supported by other senior clerics, such as al-Naini and al-Isfahani. Tripp, *A History of Iraq*, 55f.; Luizard, *La formation de l'Irak contemporain*, 458–88. Faisal then wrongly claimed that he was not involved in the decision and kept in touch with the exiled clerics, who argued that they would come back and rescind the ban on participation in elections if Faisal 'overturn[ed] Muhsin

Sa'dun's Cabinet, put in a Shi'ah ministry with a Shi'ah premier, recall[ed] the Mujtahids and reject[ed] the treaty'. Gertrude Bell Archive, 'Letters: 18 September 1923: Gertrude Bell to her Father, Sir Hugh Bell', http://www. gerty.ncl.ac.uk/letter_details.php?letter_id=639; Gertrude Bell Archive, 'Letters: 29 November 1923: Gertrude Bell to her Father, Sir Hugh Bell', http://www. gerty.ncl.ac.uk/letter_details.php?letter_id=660. See also Abbas Kelidar, 'The Shii Imami Community and Politics in the Arab East', *Middle Eastern Studies* 19, 1 (1983), 3–16, 9; Marr, *The Modern History*, 43–6; Nakash, *The Shi'is of Iraq*, 79–85. Faisal's government also arrested Shii missionaries in the North, thus trying to prevent the spread of Shiism. Nakash, *The Shi'is of Iraq*, 88.

57. For the issue of nationality, see Kelidar, 'The Shii Imami Community', 10, 13. For biographies of al-Khalisi, see Muhammad ibn Muhammad Mahdi al-Khalisi, *La vie de l'ayatollah Mahdî al-Khâlisî* (Paris: La Martinière, 2005); Pierre-Jean Luizard, 'Shaykh Muhammad al-Khalisi (1890–1963) and his Political Role in Iraq and Iran in the 1910s/20s', in: Rainer Brunner and Werner Ende (eds), *The Twelver Shia in Modern Times: Religious Culture & Political History* (Leiden: Brill, 2001), 223–35.

58. Especially Muhammad Hussain Kashif al-Ghita (d. 1954) and Muhammad Ali Bahr al-Ulum (d. 1936). Nakash, *The Shi'is of Iraq*, 85f.

59. Ibid., 100–8.

60. In December 1957, Najaf had some 24 colleges and a scholarly population of 1954, of whom 896 were from Iran, 326 from Iraq, 324 from Pakistan, 270 from Tibet, 71 from India, Pakistan, and Kashmir, 47 from Syria and Lebanon, and 20 from Hasa, Qatif, and Bahrain. Fadil Jamali, 'Theological Colleges of Najaf', *The Muslim World* 50, 1 (1960), 15–22, 15. Others cite quite different, higher numbers, which might result from the fluidity of the definition of a student at Najaf.

61. Nakash, *The Shi'is of Iraq*, 164–73, 238–62; Sabrina Mervin, 'The Clerics of Jabal 'Amil and the Reform of Religious Teaching in Najaf since the Beginning of the 20th Century', in: Rainer Brunner and Werner Ende (eds), *The Twelver Shia in Modern Times: Religious Culture & Political History* (Leiden: Brill, 2001), 79–86; al-Husri, *Mudhakkirati*; Kelidar, 'The Shii Imami Community'; Osman, *Sectarianism in Iraq*, 172–86. The Shii *mujtahid* Hibat al-Din al-Shahristani was nominated as minister of education in September 1921. Nakash, *The Shi'is of Iraq*, 107.

62. In one such instance, al-Husri attempted to block the appointment of Muhammad Mahdi al-Jawahiri, who was from a prominent Najafi family, to a teaching position in a Kadhimiya school, on the grounds that the latter had Iranian citizenship. Osman, *Sectarianism in Iraq*, 175. See also the references in the previous note and William L. Cleveland, *The Making of an Arab Nationalist: Ottomanism and Arabism in the Life and Thought of Sati' al-Husri* (Princeton: Princeton University Press, 1971).

63. Ende, *Arabische Nation*, 134f.

64. Roy P. Mottahedeh, 'The Shu'ûbîyah Controversy and the Social History of Early Islamic Iran', *International Journal of Middle East Studies* 7, 2 (1976), 161–82;

Osman, *Sectarianism in Iraq*, 205. See also *al-Ahram*, 'History, Iran and the Arabs', 22–8 March 2007.

65. This is the case, for example, in the writings of Yusuf al-Dijwi and Abdallah al-Qasimi in a long refutation of Shiism. Brunner, *Die Schia*, 76f. Abdallah al-Qasimi then still wrote from a Wahhabi perspective, but would soon become a famous atheist and critic of Islam.

66. Nakash, *The Shi'is of Iraq*, 157–62. See, in general, Adeed Dawisha, *Arab Nationalism in the Twentieth Century: From Triumph to Despair* (Princeton: Princeton University Press, 2003).

67. Batatu, *The Old Social Classes*, 26.

68. Ali A. Allawi, *Faisal I of Iraq* (New Haven: Yale University Press, 2014), 537f.; Osman, *Sectarianism in Iraq*, 71.

69. For more on Faisal, see this overwhelmingly positive biography by the Shii politician Ali Allawi, who held cabinet positions after the overthrow of Saddam Hussein in 2003. Allawi, *Faisal*.

70. By 1927, the *mujtahids* withdrew their ban on Shii employment in the state. For this about-turn and Shii attempts to encourage more direct British administration, see Nakash, *The Shi'is of Iraq*, 116ff.

71. Ibid., 120–5.

72. Batatu, *The Old Social Classes*, 47–50. For an analysis of cabinets according to sectarian and ethnic affiliation, see Osman, *Sectarianism in Iraq*, 118ff.; Ayad al-Qazzaz, 'Power Elite in Iraq, 1920-1958: A Study of the Cabinet', *The Muslim World* 61, 4 (1971), 267–83. There were only two times, in 1934 and in the 1950s, when Shia almost reached parity in high government office. Tripp, *A History of Iraq*, 56f.; Nakash, *The Shi'is of Iraq*, 88–96ff. See, for example, the memoirs of this senior Shii politician, who also worked as an Iraqi diplomat in Iran: 'Abd al-Karim al-Uzri, *Tarikh fi Dhikrayat: Al-'Iraq 1930–1958* (Beirut: n.p., 1982).

73. Nakash, *The Shi'is of Iraq*, 125–32.

74. Peter Sluglett, 'The Mandates: Some Reflections on the Nature of the British Presence in Iraq (1914–1932) and the French Presence in Syria (1918–1946)', in: Peter Sluglett and Nadine Méouchy (eds), *The British and French Mandates in Comparative Perspectives* (Leiden: Brill, 2004), 103–27, 121–4.

75. White, *The Emergence*.

76. Sluglett, 'The Mandates', 112ff.; Hakim, *The Origins*, 37–44.

77. Khoury, *Syria and the French Mandate*, 57–60. The State of Greater Lebanon was declared as an *état* in 1920, became the Lebanese Republic (*république libanaise*) in 1926, and finally Lebanon in its present-day form after independence in 1943. The French left three years later, in 1946. The Territory of the Alawites (*territoire des Alaouites*) existed from 1920 to 1922, when it was transformed into the Alawite State (*état des Alaouites*). In 1936/7, it was incorporated into the Syrian Republic. The State of Jabal Druze suffered a similar fate. First named the State of Souaida from its inception in 1921, it was renamed in 1927 and finally incorporated into Syria in the same year as the Alawite State, 1936. Syria itself started out under French rule from 1922 on as the Syrian Federation, a

conglomerate of the State of Damascus, the State of Aleppo, and the Alawite State, but was renamed the State of Syria (*état de Syrie*) two years later, in 1924, when the Alawite State seceded from the federation. In 1930, it was then declared the Syrian Republic with a new constitution. As in Lebanon, the French withdrew in 1946, shortly after formal Syrian independence in 1944/5. The Sanjak of Alexandretta, on the other hand, was annexed to the State of Aleppo in 1923 and, in 1925, to the newly formed State of Syria, only to be granted autonomy in 1937 with formal links to both France and Turkey. In 1938, it was proclaimed the Hatay State (*état du Hatay*) under both French and Turkish military supervision and was finally incorporated into modern-day Turkey as its Hatay Province a year later, in 1939.

78. White, *The Emergence*, 43–61, esp. 53. For the Kurds, see Jordi Tejel Gorgas, *Le mouvement kurde de Turquie en exil: Continuités et discontinuités du nationalisme kurde sous le mandat français en Syrie et au Liban (1925–1946)* (Bern: Peter Lang, 2007), 58–63.

79. Jens Hanssen, *Fin de Siècle Beirut: The Making of an Ottoman Provincial Capital* (Oxford: Clarendon Press, 2005); Raghid K. el-Solh, 'Lebanese Arab Nationalists and Consociational Democracy during the French Mandate Period', in: Christoph Schumann (ed.), *Liberal Thought in the Eastern Mediterranean: Late 19th Century until the 1960s* (Leiden: Brill, 2008), 217–36, e.g. 226; Traboulsi, *A History of Modern Lebanon*, 52–72.

80. See Najla Wadih Atiyah, *The Attitude of the Lebanese Sunnis towards the State of Lebanon* (PhD, University of London, 1973).

81. Simon Jackson, '"What is Syria Worth?": The Huvelin Mission, Economic Expertise and the French Project in the Eastern Mediterranean, 1918–1922', *Monde(s)* 2, 4 (2013), 83–103. Henri Lammens, a Belgian Flemish Catholic and Jesuit who lived in *fin-de-siècle* Beirut and wrote about Islam, stated in 1902 that the Shia were 'hated by all, Christians and Muslims', implying that they were not 'normal' Muslims. He described them as impoverished and powerless: 'A l'heure actuelle – on peut le dire – leur importance est nulle' ('At the present moment, we can conclude that they have no importance whatsoever'). He referred to religious groups as different '*nationalités*' or '*peuples*'. Lammens, 'Les Nosairis', 452, 475.

82. Nakash, *Reaching for Power*, 30f.; Rula Jurdi Abisaab and Malek Hassan Abisaab, *The Shi'ites of Lebanon: Modernism, Communism, and Hizbullah's Islamists* (Syracuse: Syracuse University Press, 2014), 5–26.

83. When the Ottomans tried to draft Shii clerics into the army (Sunni clerics had an official certificate exempting them from military service, one that Shii clerics lacked because there were no officially recognised Shii theological seminaries), ad hoc arrangements would be found to exempt them, stopping short of officially recognising Shiism. Mervin, *Un réformisme chiite*, 392f.

84. 'With few exceptions the Moslems were for American or British assistance according to the "Damascus Program"; the Druses were for an English Mandate, the Maronites and all varieties of Catholics were for France. But the Greek Orthodox were divided, instead of standing for a British Mandate as usually in

Palestine and Damascus. The Ismailians were mostly for France, and the Nusairiyeh were divided. [...] The Druses ask emphatically to be left out of the Lebanon in case it be given to France, But [*sic*] outside the Lebanon proper, in the areas which it is proposed to include in the "Greater Lebanon," such as Tyre, Sidon, "Hollow Syria," and Tripoli, a distinct majority of the people is probably averse to French rule. This includes practically all the Sunnite Moslems, most of the Shiites, a part of the Greek Orthodox Christians, and the small group of Protestants. Most of these ask earnestly for America, with Britain as second choice; the balance for Britain with America as second choice.' The World War I Document Archive, 'The King-Crane Commission Report'. See also Bailony, *Transnational Rebellion*, 122f.

85. Leyla Dakhli, *Une génération d'intellectuels arabes: Syrie et Liban, 1908–1940* (Paris: Karthala/IISMM, 2009), 193ff.

86. Mervin, *Un réformisme chiite*, 43–9, 393ff.; Nakash, *Reaching for Power*, 100–3; Tamara Chalabi, *The Shi'is of Jabal 'Amil and the New Lebanon: Community and Nation-State, 1918–1943* (New York: Palgrave Macmillan, 2006), 76–82; Hakim, *The Origins*, 250ff.; Max Weiss, 'Institutionalizing Sectarianism: The Lebanese Ja'fari Court and Shi'i Society under the French Mandate', *Islamic Law and Society* 15, 3 (2008), 371–407.

87. Mervin, *Un réformisme chiite*, 394–8. Indeed, in countries such as modern-day Saudi Arabia, for example, where Shii personal status law courts operated in a grey area, clerics and activists have often seen personal status law courts in Lebanon and Bahrain as a model to be emulated. I have heard this repeatedly from Shii clerics during my fieldwork in Saudi Arabia.

88. Weiss, *In the Shadow of Sectarianism*.

89. Max Weiss, 'Practicing Sectarianism in Mandate Lebanon: Shi'i Cemeteries, Religious Patrimony, and the Everyday Politics of Difference', *Journal of Social History* 43, 3 (2010), 707–33.

90. Halawi, *A Lebanon Defied*, 77.

91. See the argument of prominent Syrian journalist Najib al-Rayyis, quoted in: White, *The Emergence*, 57, 65n57.

92. Weiss, *In the Shadow of Sectarianism*, 23f.

93. Mervin, *Un réformisme chiite*, 36f.

94. Linda Sayed, 'Education and Reconfiguring Lebanese Shi'i Muslims into the Nation-State during the French Mandate, 1920–43', *Die Welt des Islams* 59, 3–4 (2019), 282–312; Mervin, *Un réformisme chiite*, 161ff., 177ff.; Traboulsi, *A History of Modern Lebanon*, 60f. Clergy-run Shii education institutions strengthened ties with other Arab Shia and Iran. Mervin, *Un réformisme chiite*, 130–41.

95. Andrew Arsan, *Interlopers of Empire: The Lebanese Diaspora in Colonial French West Africa* (London: Hurst, 2014); Albert Hourani and Nadim Shehadi (eds), *The Lebanese in the World: A Century of Emigration* (London: I. B. Tauris, 1992).

96. Sayed, 'Education', 301. For the Jafari schools in Tyre and Baalbek, see Mervin, *Un réformisme chiite*, 186–91.

97. Sayed, 'Education', 301f. For the later twentieth century, see Catherine Le Thomas, *Les écoles chiites au Liban: Construction communautaire et mobilisation politique* (Paris: Karthala, 2012).

98. This is the argument of Max Weiss. See also Kais Firro, *Metamorphosis of the Nation (al-Umma): The Rise of Arabism and Minorities in Syria and Lebanon, 1850–1940* (Brighton: Sussex Academic Press, 2009); Firro, 'Ethnicizing the Shi'is in Mandatory Lebanon', *Middle Eastern Studies* 42, 5 (2006), 741–59; Firro, 'The Shi'is in Lebanon: Between Communal 'Asabiyya and Arab Nationalism, 1908–21', *Middle Eastern Studies* 42, 4 (2006), 535–50; Firro, *Inventing Lebanon: Nationalism and the State under the Mandate* (London: I. B. Tauris, 2003).

99. Michael Johnson, *Class and Client in Beirut: The Sunni Muslim Community and the Lebanese State, 1840–1985* (London: Ithaca, 1986).

100. WIPO, 'Constitution of Lebanon', https://www.wipo.int/edocs/lexdocs/laws/en/lb/lb018en.

101. Mervin, *Un réformisme chiite*, 26f.

102. Nakash, *Reaching for Power*, 103–8.

103. Weiss, *In the Shadow of Sectarianism*, 12.

104. Melanie S. Tanielian, *The Charity of War: Famine, Humanitarian Aid, and World War I in the Middle East* (Stanford: Stanford University Press, 2018).

105. Amongst a vast literature, see especially Michael Provence, *The Great Syrian Revolt and the Rise of Arab Nationalism* (Austin: University of Texas Press, 2005).

106. Daniel Neep, *Occupying Syria under the French Mandate: Insurgency, Space and State Formation* (Cambridge: Cambridge University Press, 2012).

107. Martin C. Thomas, 'French Intelligence-Gathering in the Syrian Mandate, 1920–40', *Middle Eastern Studies* 38, 1 (2002), 1–32.

108. Though some defected in the latter part of the mandate. N. E. Bou-Nacklie, 'Les Troupes Spéciales: Religious and Ethnic Recruitment, 1916–46', *International Journal of Middle East Studies* 25, 4 (1993), 645–60; Neep, *Occupying Syria*, 110ff. For an example in Latakia in 1933, see P. P. T. W. van Caldenborgh, *Savage Human Beasts or the Purest Arabs? The Incorporation of the Alawi Community into the Syrian State during the French Mandate Period (1918–1946)* (PhD, Radboud University, 2005), 95–9.

109. After independence, the government then doubted Alawites because of their service in the colonial troops and appointed Sunnis in areas inhabited by Alawites, fuelling more resentment. Raphaël Lefèvre, *Ashes of Hama: The Muslim Brotherhood in Syria* (London: Hurst, 2013), 65–9; Hanna Batatu, 'Some Observations on the Social Roots of Syria's Ruling, Military Group and the Causes for its Dominance', *Middle East Journal* 35, 3 (1981), 331–44; Alasdair Drysdale, 'Ethnicity in the Syrian Officer Corps: A Conceptualization', *Civilisations* 29, 3–4 (1979), 359–74.

110. Douwes, 'Modern History', 33; van Caldenborgh, *Savage Human Beasts*, 58–70; Winter, *A History of the 'Alawis*, 244–56; Douwes, *The Ottomans*; Mervin, 'L'"entité alaouite"'; Weulersse, *Le pays des Alaouites*, Vol. 1, 118; Khoury, *Syria and the French Mandate*, 99–102. The rebellion may have gained further impetus

by French attempts to give discounted land to their collaborators. Gelvin, *Divided Loyalties*, 124. See also Russell, *The First Modern Arab State*, 84f., 166f. There was some cooperation between Salih al-Ali and Ibrahim Hananu, another major rebel leader. Watenpaugh, *Being Modern*, 177ff. In response, the Alawites were also cast as a warrior race. Neep, *Occupying Syria*, 35, 46. In 1922, al-Ali surrendered to French authorities and was pardoned, and would in Syrian nationalism be portrayed as a major anti-imperial rebel leader. Ismailis were perceived as pro-French, even if that was not necessarily an accurate depiction of events. Douwes, 'Modern History', 34.

111. In 1921 already, the French re-attached certain largely Sunni areas to the Territoire des Alaouites, primarily for economic reasons. Weulersse, *Le pays des Alaouites*, Vol. 1, 48–73, 119ff.; Mervin, 'L'"entité alaouite"'; Mervin, *Un réformisme chiite*, 322; van Caldenborgh, *Savage Human Beasts*, 70–82. Initially, in 1920, the entity was called Territoire des Alaouites. Its upgrading to L'État des Alaouites might have happened due to an administrative error, after it was declared as such in the High Commissioner's decree of 28 June 1922. While sounding more official, this État des Alaouites was integrated in the Fédération des États de Syria, together with the states of Damascus and Aleppo, but that attempt at integration was abolished in 1924, after which the territory was administered autonomously as L'État indépendant des Alaouites. As a concession to Arab nationalists, when the French wanted to de-emphasise its confessionalist nature, they termed it, less controversially, Gouvernement de Lattaquié in 1930, and then L'État des Alaouites again when they sought to re-emphasise it. In 1936, the Syrian government assumed sovereignty over the Gouvernement de Lattaquié, symbolised by the appointment of a new governor from Damascus and the change from the flag of the Alawite State to the Syrian flag. White, *The Emergence*, 11, 16f.; Winter, *A History of the 'Alawis*, 257; Weulersse, *Le pays des Alaouites*, Vol. 1, 121f. That even social scientists with a deep engagement with the region were completely bound by a sectarian vision of the region is symbolised by this quote from Weulersse: '[L]a masse alaouite ne se montra pas à la hauteur de l'occasion historique qui lui était offerte: numériquement majoritaire, elle restait politiquement minoritaire. Comment donc faire vivre un État organisé par et pour l'émancipation d'une communauté religieuse, si elle-ci demeurait socialement et économiquement inférieure aux minorités étrangères établies dans le pays et si elle apparaissait incapable par ailleurs de se dégager de son archaïsme pour s'affirmer sur un plan moderne?' Weulersse, *Le pays des Alaouites*, Vol. 1, 120.

112. The French initially urged Ismailis to draw up their own communal law, but the small Ismaili community had no religious authorities capable of this. Ismaili leaders urged the French to detach the largely Ismaili-inhabited area of Salamiyah from Hama and recognise it as a separate Sanjak with its own small Ismaili cavalry in 1926 and a similar one in 1939, but to no avail. They started, however, to be counted separately in French registries and were allowed to administer their own *waqfs* and have their Imams officiate at weddings and

regulate matters of succession. White, *The Emergence*, 51, 89, 145, 182. Ismailis of Salamiyah would do fairly well economically under the French Mandate, as the area was very fertile and would receive substantial attention from the state. Norman N. Lewis, 'The Isma'ilis of Syria Today', *Journal of the Royal Central Asian Society* 39, 1 (1952), 69–77.

113. Winter, *A History of the 'Alawis*, 238–44.

114. Muhammad Amin Ghalib Tawil, *Tarikh al-'Alawiyyin* (Latakia: Matba'at al-Taraqqi, 1924); Joshua M. Landis, *Nationalism and the Politics of Za'ama: The Collapse of Republican Syria, 1945–1949* (PhD, Princeton University, 1997), 105. See also Abdallah Naaman, *Les Alawites: Histoire mouvementée d'une communauté mystérieuse* (Paris: Éditions Érick Bonnier, 2017).

115. See, for example, Pierre May, *L'Alaouite: Ses croyances, ses moeurs, les Cheikhs, les lois de la tribu et les chefs* (Beirut: Imprimerie catholique, 1931); Weulersse, *Le pays des Alaouites*. For a discussion of these writings, which used sociological categories to emphasise the notion of a distinct and cohesive Alawite community, see Max Weiss, 'Community, Sect, Nation: Colonial and Social Scientific Discourses on the Alawis in Syria during the Mandate and Early Independence Periods', in: Michael Kerr and Craig Larkin (eds), *The Alawis of Syria: War, Faith and Politics in the Levant* (Oxford: Oxford University Press, 2015), 63–75. For conversions, see Chantal Verdeil, 'Une "révolution sociale dans la montagne": La conversion des Alaouites par les jésuites dans les années 1930', in: Bernard Heyberger and Rémy Madinier (eds), *L'Islam des marges: Mission chrétienne et espaces périphériques du monde musulman, XVI–XXe siècles* (Paris: IISMM/Karthala, 2011), 81–105.

116. Colonel Nieger, 'Choix de documents sur le territoire des Alaouites (Pays des Noseiris)', *Revue du Monde Musulman* 49 (1922), 1–69.

117. Paul Jacquot, *L'État des Alaouites: Terre d'art, de souvenirs, et de mystère* (Beirut: Imprimerie catholique, 1929). For tourism under the French Mandate as a form of cultural imperialism, see Idir Ouahes, *Syria and Lebanon under the French Mandate: Cultural Imperialism and the Workings of Empire* (London: I. B. Tauris, 2018), ch. 2.

118. Ouahes, *Syria and Lebanon*, 164f. The French also expanded education, some of it in French, in the Alawite State, as they did in other parts of the mandate. Another focus was agricultural instruction. Ibid., 94–100. See also Jennifer M. Dueck, *The Claims of Culture at Empire's End: Syria and Lebanon under French Rule* (Oxford: Oxford University Press, 2010).

119. Sabrina Mervin, 'Quelques jalons pour une histoire du rapprochement (taqrîb) des alaouites vers le chiisme', in: Rainer Brunner, Monika Gronke, Jens P. Laut, and Ulrich Rebstock (eds), *Islamstudien ohne Ende: Festschrift für Werner Ende* (Würzburg: Deutsche Morgenländische Gesellschaft/Ergon, 2002), 281–8, 282f.; Mervin, *Un réformisme chiite*, 321f.

120. Mervin, *Un réformisme chiite*, 161–77; Werner Ende, 'al-Amīn, Muḥsin', *EI3*.

121. Al-Amin, *Mustadrakat A'yan al-Shī'a*, Vol. 10, 370. It was a conflict over the control of *awqaf* amongst members of the Shii community that in 1931 drew

in the colonial authorities and the Shii officials in charge of *awqaf* in Lebanon and led to debates on the possible institutionalisation of a Shii community at the League of Nations, including by Robert de Caix. Eventually, the Jafari court in Lebanon at times had some responsibility for the affairs of Shia in Syria, including over *awqaf*. See Mervin, *Un réformisme chiite*, 398–402; Weiss, *In the Shadow of Sectarianism*, 138. Sabrina Mervin has translated Muhsin al-Amin's autobiography: Muhsin al-Amin, *Autobiographie d'un clerc chiite du Ğabal ʿĀmil: Tiré de: Les notables chiites (Aʿyān al-šīʿa)*, trans. by Sabrina Mervin (Damascus: Presses de l'Ifpo, 1998).

122. Mervin, *Un réformisme chiite*, 248–53. For a similar, simultaneous debate in Najaf, see Nakash, *The Shīʿis of Iraq*, 154–7.

123. Jones, *Shīʿa Islam*, 32–72, esp. 49; Chalabi, *The Shīʿis of Jabal ʿAmil*, 140; Nikki R. Keddie, *Religion and Rebellion in Iran: The Tobacco Protest of 1891–1892* (London: Cass, 1966); Luizard, *La formation de l'Irak contemporain*, 242–83.

124. Mervin, *Un réformisme chiite*, 325f.; Mervin, 'Quelques jalons', 283ff. See also Nadine Méouchy, 'La réforme des juridictions religieuses en Syrie et au Liban (1921–1939): Raisons de la puissance mandataire et raisons des communautés', in: Pierre-Jean Luizard (ed.), *Le choc colonial et l'Islam: Les politiques religieuses des puissances colonials en terres d'Islam* (Paris: La Découverte, 2006), 359–82; Winter, *A History of the ʿAlawis*, 241ff.

125. The fatwa to that effect was published in Rio de Janeiro, where many Syrians, including many Alawites, had emigrated to and established associations and publications, signifying the increasingly global dimensions of these debates and the importance of diaspora communities intervening in political developments in their places of origin. Paulo Boneschi, 'Une fatwà du Grand Muftī de Jérusalem Muḥammad ʾAmīn al-Ḥusaynī sur les ʿAlawītes', *Revue de l'histoire des religions* 122 (1940), 42–54; Boneschi, 'Une fatwà du Grand Muftī de Jérusalem Muḥammad ʾAmīn al-Ḥusaynī sur les ʿAlawītes (Deuxième article)', *Revue de l'histoire des religions* 122 (1940), 134–52. See also Voss, *"ʿAlawīya oder Nusairīya?"*, 87–100. For more on Alawites in South America, including on rapprochement with Shiism, see Silvia Montenegro, "Alawi Muslims in Argentina: Religious and Political Identity in the Diaspora', *Contemporary Islam* 12 (2018), 23–38.

126. Kais M. Firro, 'The Attitude of the Druzes and ʿAlawis vis-à-vis Islam and Nationalism in Syria and Lebanon', in: Krisztina Kehl-Bodrogi, Barbara Kellner-Heinkele, and Anke Otter-Beaujean (eds), *Syncretistic Religious Communities in the Near East: Collected Papers of the International Symposium 'Alevism in Turkey and Comparable Syncretistic Religious Communities in the Near East in the Past and Present', Berlin, 14–17 April 1995* (Leiden: Brill, 1997), 87–99; Khoury, *Syria and the French Mandate*, 465f.; V. V., 'Libano e Siria', *Oriente Moderno* 16, 5 (1936), 260–8, 267f.

127. Khoury, *Syria and the French Mandate*, 520–5; Weiss, 'Community, Sect, Nation', 67; Gitta Yaffe-Schatzmann, 'Alawi Separatists and Unionists: The Events of 25 February 1936', *Middle Eastern Studies* 31, 1 (1995), 28–38. The *conseil représentatif* consisted of sixteen members: nine Alawites, three Sunnis, two

Orthodox Christians, one Ismaili, and one representative of other Christian groups (Maronites, Armenians, and Greek Catholics). Weulersse, *Le pays des Alaouites*, Vol. 1, 121. For the administrative history of the Alawite State, see the *Journal officiel de l'Etat des Alaouites*, published in Latakia from 1925 to 1929 and available at https://gallica.bnf.fr/ark:/12148/bpt6k9776349k/f1.item. Inter-Alawite tribal disputes and political dynamics also intermittently gave rise to messianic movements such as that of the Alawite Shaykh Suleiman al-Murshid, who was establishing himself as a power broker in the Alawite region and tried to be too close neither to the French authorities nor to the nationalists (he was hanged a year after independence by the nationalist government in Damascus). While he clashed with the mandatory authorities but then supported Alawite autonomy under the French, in 1936, he supported the nationalists in parliamentary elections. Gitta Yaffe and Uriel Dann, 'Suleiman al-Murshid: Beginnings of an Alawi Leader', *Middle Eastern Studies* 29, 4 (1993), 624–40; Patrick Franke, *Göttliche Karriere eines syrischen Hirten: Sulaimān Muršid (1907–1946) und die Anfänge der Muršidiyya* (Berlin: Klaus Schwarz, 1994); Weulersse, *Le pays des Alaouites*, Vol. 1, 334–7; van Caldenborgh, *Savage Human Beasts*, 83–94, 104–12. See also Stefan Winter, 'The Asad Petition of 1936: Bashar's Grandfather Was Pro-Unionist', *Syria Comment*, 14 June 2016.

128. Mervin, *Un réformisme chiite*, 327.
129. During World War II, Britain sent E. E. Evans-Pritchard, who later became Professor of Social Anthropology at Oxford, as a political liaison officer to Latakia, where he was meant to establish relations with Alawite leaders in order to carry out sabotage operations in the event of a German invasion (which had then been a possibility). Instead, he sought to intervene against Alawite leader Sulaiman al-Murshid and the local Free French officials, because he accused the former of brutality and the latter of complacency, and was eventually accused even by the British Foreign Office of trying to set up Sunnis against Alawites and overstepping the boundaries of his role. He also wrote a general report on the Alawite region. See Itamar Rabinovich and Gitta Yaffe, 'An Anthropologist as a Political Officer: Evans-Pritchard, the French and the Alawis', in: Haim Shamir (ed.), *France and Germany in an Age of Crisis, 1900–1960: Studies in Memory of Charles Bloch* (Leiden: Brill, 1990), 177–89; Patrick Seale, *Asad of Syria: The Struggle for the Middle East* (Berkeley: University of California Press, 1988/95), 13, 497; van Caldenborgh, *Savage Human Beasts*, 170–8.
130. Winter, *A History of the 'Alawis*, 262f. For more, in particular on the incorporation of Alawites into a Turkish mythical version of history, see Gisela Procházka-Eisl and Stephan Procházka, *The Plain of Saints and Prophets: The Nusayri-Alawi Community of Cilicia (Southern Turkey) and its Sacred Places* (Wiesbaden: Harrassowitz, 2010), esp. 67–80.
131. Khoury, *Syria and the French Mandate*, 494–514. Turkish propaganda, on the other hand, accused France of placing large numbers of Alawites in the administration. Ibid., 499. The King-Crane Commission simply stated: 'The Arabs

(who are mainly Turkish-speaking, but are chiefly Nusairiyeh or Alouites) ask for union with Syria under a French mandate.' The World War I Document Archive, 'The King-Crane Commission Report'. The French sectarian vision of the population in the Sanjak becomes evident in French publications, both official and semi-official, of the time, such as Bazantay, *Les états*, e.g. 102–35.

132. Sarah D. Shields, *Fezzes in the River: Identity Politics and European Diplomacy in the Middle East on the Eve of World War II* (New York: Oxford University Press, 2011), esp. 203, 279; Winter, *A History of the 'Alawis*, 265ff. That the rise of Alawites to power in Syria would problematise the situation of Alawites in Turkey, however assimilated, was perhaps inevitable. Aghiad Ghanem, *Les Alaouites de Turquie dans les relations turco-syriennes: Une diplomatie de résilience* (Paris: L'Harmattan, 2017).

133. Keith D. Watenpaugh, '"Creating Phantoms": Zaki al-Arsuzi, the Alexandretta Crisis, and the Formation of Modern Arab Nationalism in Syria', *International Journal of Middle East Studies* 28, 3 (1996), 363–89; Dalal Arsuzi-Elamir, *Arabischer Nationalismus in Syrien: Zakī al-Arsūzī und die arabisch-nationale Bewegung an der Peripherie Alexandretta/Antakya, 1930–1938* (Münster: LIT, 2003).

134. Schäbler, *Aufstände*, 186–94.

135. Ibid., 194–203.

136. Ibid., 207–14.

137. Itamar Rabinovich, 'The Compact Minorities and the Syrian State, 1918–45', *Journal of Contemporary History* 14, 4 (1979), 693–712, 697. For the compact minorities, see Albert Hourani, *Minorities in the Arab World* (London: Oxford University Press, 1947), esp. 96f. See also Neep, *Occupying Syria*, 48.

138. Al-Atrash had been in touch with Damascene nationalists since the events of 1910. Some Druze also became involved with Amir Abdullah bin Hussein in Transjordan, who was keeping Arab nationalist sentiment alive, in particular when it went against French interests. Neep, *Occupying Syria*, 67–77; Provence, *The Great Syrian Revolt*; Schäbler, *Aufstände*, 221–59; Lenka Bokova, 'Le traité du 4 mars 1921 et la formation de l'État du Djebel druze sous le Mandat français', *Revue des mondes musulmans et de la Méditerranée* 48–9 (1988), 213–22; Bokova, 'Les Druzes dans la révolution syrienne de 1925 a 1927', *Guerres mondiales et conflits contemporains* 153 (1989), 91–104.

139. Michael Provence, 'French Mandate Counterinsurgency and the Repression of the Great Syrian Revolt', in: Cyrus Schayegh and Andrew Arsan (eds), *The Routledge Handbook of the History of the Middle East Mandates* (London: Routledge, 2015), 136–51. The widespread support of the revolt across classes and regions was indeed remarkable, although the Alawite territory remained remarkably quiet. Khoury, *Syria and the French Mandate*, 206.

140. Firro, 'The Attitude of the Druzes', 94ff.

141. It also invoked the slogan 'Religion is for God and the Fatherland for all' (*al-din li-llah wa-l-watan li-l-jamia*), which had been the rallying cry of the Arab Revolt and King Faisal. Schäbler, *Aufstände*, 255; Lenka Bokova, 'La Révolution française dans le discours de l'insurrection syrienne contre le mandat français (1925–1927)', *Revue des mondes musulmans et de la Méditerranée* 52–3 (1989), 207–17.

142. Ibn Saud did not seem to have a problem with the Druze's religious identity, although he was suspicious of them for their Hashemite links. Schäbler, *Aufstände*, 258f.

143. Khoury, *Syria and the French Mandate*, 515–9; Cyril Roussel, *Les Druzes de Syrie: Territoire et mobilité* (Beirut: Presses de l'Ifpo, 2011), 49–61. In 1941, Abd al-Ghaffar al-Atrash, a Druze, became defence minister in the government of Hasan al-Hakim, and Munir al-Abbas, an Alawite, minister of post and telecoms, although there were no Druze or Alawites in the 1943 cabinet. Schäbler, *Aufstände*, 280f. Politically, a separate administrative entity was established for the Jabal Druze in 1921, entitled L'État du Djebel Druze. In 1930, it received a *statut organique*, was in 1936, now called Territoire, integrated into the Syrian state, separated from it in 1939, and reintegrated in 1942. Ibid., 221.

144. Neep, *Occupying Syria*, 47f.

145. There are some examples from late Ottoman times that Druze were able to settle their own affairs, precedents that were submitted in French translations to the French authorities to petition for further Druze autonomy in terms of personal status law. White, *The Emergence*, 179f. For background on Ottoman–Druze relations, see Abdul-Rahim Abu-Husayn, *The View from Istanbul: Ottoman Lebanon and the Druze Emirate* (London: I. B. Tauris, 2003).

146. For an interesting case involving a Druze family, see White, *The Emergence*, 179f.

147. Schäbler, *Aufstände*, 273–9.

148. Close identification with France could be dangerous. Some Christian villages were attacked during the Great Revolt, which was invoked by the French authorities to denounce the alleged fanaticism and sectarianism of the rebels. The French also fortified the Christian quarter of Damascus and tied the fate of Christians to their own. Neep, *Occupying Syria*, 79, 151.

149. Khoury, *Syria and the French Mandate*, e.g. 6–13, 245–84; Keith D. Watenpaugh, *Being Modern in the Middle East: Revolution, Nationalism, Colonialism, and the Arab Middle Class* (Princeton: Princeton University Press, 2006), 218ff., 227f., ch. 9, and passim. For the earlier period, see Philip S. Khoury, *Urban Notables and Arab Nationalism: The Politics of Damascus, 1860–1920* (Cambridge: Cambridge University Press, 1983).

150. For the international outcry over France's suppression of the Syrian Revolt, see Pedersen, *The Guardians*, 142–68. Ultimately, however, France managed to assuage its critics at the League of Nations and the Mandates Commission.

151. White, *The Emergence*, 131–61; Khoury, *Syria and the French Mandate*, 465. For discussions on Alawite and Druze (and other) separateness and autonomy in the Syrian press, see Ouahes, *Syria and Lebanon*, 146ff.

152. V., 'Libano e Siria', 260; n.a., 'Il nuovo Statuto delle Comunità religiose nei paesi sotto Mandato francese', *Oriente Moderno* 16, 6 (1936), 302–5.

153. White, *The Emergence*, 181–4.

154. For a detailed account of this, see ibid., 162–208.

155. Mervin, *Un réformisme chiite*, 400. He was adamant that Muslims should be seen as one group, and not as subdivided into different sects. Al-Amin, *Mustadrakat A'yan al-Shi'a*, Vol. 10, 370.

156. Khoury, *Syria and the French Mandate*, 21f.
157. Schäbler, *Aufstände*, 281–4.
158. Michel Seurat, *Syrie: L'état de barbarie* (Paris: Presses Universitaires de France, 2012), 198ff.
159. Druze were also recognised as a separate community in Lebanon with their own personal status law, as well as in Israel. Unlike in Lebanon, however, in Syria, the Druze personal status law is part of the general civil law, something that apparently has to do with the Druze role in the nationalist movement and the push not to have too much judicial difference from the rest of Syria's Muslims. Esther van Eijk, *Family Law in Syria: Patriarchy, Pluralism and Personal Status Codes* (London: I. B. Tauris, 2016), 5f.; Schäbler, *Aufstände*, 282f.
160. And it was the Hanafi school that was predominant as a source of reference for the personal status law for Muslims. SLJ, 'A Comprehensive Insight into Syrian Family Law', *Syrian Law Journal*, 3 October 2019, http://www.syria.law/index.php/comprehensive-insight-syrian-family-law.
161. An Alawite leader, Suleiman al-Murshid, was executed, and Druze efforts at autonomy and/or integration into Transjordan, ruled by Amir Abdullah bin Hussein and supported by his British officials, were repressed. In 1947, the Druze elites were themselves challenged by a new popular movement aimed at curbing their privileges and furthering integration with the rest of Syria. Schäbler, *Aufstände*, 284–94.
162. Another party that proved attractive to non-Sunnis was the Syrian Social Nationalist Party, which was secular and rejected pan-Arabism in favour of Syrian nationalism. Khoury, *Syria and the French Mandate*, 525.
163. Schäbler, *Aufstände*, 294–7.
164. For a good introductory account on this topic, see James L. Gelvin, *The Modern Middle East: A History*, 4th ed. (New York: Oxford University Press, 2016).
165. For an early, yet representative overview, see this book, prepared during the final stages of World War II by a later major historian of the Middle East and published by Chatham House: Hourani, *Minorities*. That the notion remained one of concern for Syrian intellectuals is epitomised by publications such as Burhan Ghaliun, *Al-Ma'sala al-Ta'ifiyya wa Mushkila al-Aqalliyyat* (The Sectarian Question and the Problem of Minorities) (Beirut: Dar al-Tali'a, 1979). See also Valentina Zecca, 'The Ṭā'ifiyyah or Sectarianism in Syria: Theoretical Considerations and Historical Overview', *Oriente Moderno* 98, 1 (2018), 33–51.

CHAPTER 10

1. W. Ende, 'Rashīd Riḍā', *EI2*.
2. For the classic account of this period, see Hourani, *Arabic Thought*.
3. The idea of the left and right wing of the *Salafiyya* was elaborated by Werner Ende. See Ende, *Arabische Nation*, 91ff., and passim.
4. Albert Hourani, 'Rashid Rida and the Sufi Orders: A Footnote to Laoust', *Bulletin d'études orientales* 29 (1977), 231–41, 238f.; Elizabeth Sirriyeh, 'Rashid Rida's Autobiography of the Syrian Years, 1865–1897', *Arabic & Middle Eastern Literature*

3, 2 (2000), 179–94; Weismann, *The Naqshbandiyya*, 144; Umar Ryad, 'A Printed Muslim "Lighthouse" in Cairo: Al-Manār's Early Years, Religious Aspiration and Reception (1898–1903)', *Arabica* 56, 1 (2009), 27–60, 33, 39, 45. Though influenced by Abduh on this point, Rida's criticism of Sufi practices would also take a much more serious form than Abduh's. Oliver Scharbrodt, 'The Salafiyya and Sufism: Muḥammad 'Abduh and his Risālat al-Wāridāt (Treatise on Mystical Inspirations)', *Bulletin of the School of Oriental and African Studies* 70, 1 (2007), 89–115.

5. For Rida in Istanbul, see Ilham Khuri-Makdisi, 'Ottoman Arabs in Istanbul, 1860–1914: Perceptions of Empire, Experiences of the Metropole through the Writings of Aḥmad Fāris al-Shidyāq, Muḥammad Rashīd Riḍā, and Jirjī Zaydān', in: Sahar Bazzaz, Yota Batsaki, and Dimiter Angelov (eds), *Imperial Geographies in Byzantine and Ottoman Space* (Washington, DC: Center for Hellenic Studies, 2013), 254–97.

6. He visited the Nadwat al-Ulama in Lucknow and met influential Ahl-i Hadith clerics. Claudia Preckel, 'Screening Siddiq Hasan Khan's (1832–1890) Library: The Use of Hanbali Literature in 19th-Century Bhopal', in: Birgit Krawietz, Georges Tamer, and Alina Kokoschka (eds), *Islamic Theology, Philosophy and Law: Debating Ibn Taymiyya and Ibn Qayyim al-Jawziyya* (Berlin: De Gruyter, 2013), 162–219, 216f.

7. Landau, *The Politics of Pan-Islam*, 135; Luizard, *La formation de l'Irak contemporain*, 284–91; Nakash, *The Shi'is of Iraq*, 57–61.

8. Mahmudabad, *Poetry of Belonging*, 217–19; Qureshi, *Pan-Islam*, 56.

9. Al-Nafeesi, *The Role of the Shī'ah*, 134–7; Nakash, *The Shi'is of Iraq*, 60.

10. Because some of the key proponents of the Khilafat Movement were Twelver Shii and Ismaili, most scholarship on the issue has emphasised this Sunni–Shia cooperation. Gail Minault, *The Khilafat Movement: Religious Symbolism and Political Mobilization in India* (New York: Columbia University Press, 1982), 73–6, 82, 94, 97, 129f., 194, 203; Özcan, *Pan-Islamism*, 66; Qureshi, *Pan-Islam*, 34, 277. In 1917, the Shii Raja of Mahmudabad emphasised the question of the Caliphate and warned European diplomats not to toy with it: 'It is a question which has got its seat in the very fibre of the faith of a vast majority of the Mahomedans of the world, no less than of India.' N.a., *Speech by the Hon'ble Raja Sir Mohammad Ali Mohammad Khan, Khan Bahadur, of Mahmudabad, President of the All-India Moslem League, 30 December 1917, Calcutta* (Calcutta: Statesman Press, n.d.), 12. The fusion of Imamate and Caliphate can be seen in the work of Syed Ameer Ali, who wrote positively about the Caliphate. For an example, see Syed Ameer Ali, *A Short History of the Saracens: Being a Concise Account of the Rise and Decline of the Saracenic Power and of the Economic, Social and Intellectual Development of the Arab Nation from the Earliest Times to the Destruction of Bagdad, and the Expulsion of the Moors from Spain* (London: Macmillan, 1921); Ali, *Mahommedan Law*, 4. See also Jones, *Shi'a Islam*, 174; Christopher A. Bayly, *Recovering Liberties: Indian Thought in the Age of Liberalism and Empire* (Cambridge: Cambridge University Press, 2012), 234ff.; Adrian P. Ruprecht, *De-Centering Humanitarianism: The Red Cross and India, c. 1877–1939* (PhD, University of Cambridge, 2017), 201.

11. Some of the movement's earliest and most famous proponents had a Shii background, such as Muhammad and Shaukat Ali of Rampur, who came from a mixed Sunni–Shia background. Jones, *Shi'a Islam*, 172f.

12. Devji, *Muslim Zion*, 82.

13. Even still, the Turkish politicians did not miss out on the opportunity to condemn the two as 'heretics', denying them the right to speak on behalf of Sunnis. The sharp rebuttal of their letter by Turkey led to a split between them and the wider Khilafat Movement in Turkey, which at least initially backed Turkey. Qureshi, *Pan-Islam*, 368ff.

14. Muhammad Rashid Rida, *Maqalat al-Shaykh Rashid Rida al-Siyyasiyya*, 5 Vols (Beirut: Dar Ibn Arabi, 1994), Vol. 3, 1480–511, cf. *al-Manar* 25 (1924), 273–92. This went hand in hand with a wider critique of imperialism, 'the West', and secularism, which in the region became spearheaded by figures such as Ataturk. Emad Eldin Shahin, *Through Muslim Eyes: Muhammad Rashid Rida and the West* (Herndon, VA: International Institute of Islamic Thought, 1994).

15. Philip S. Khoury, 'Factionalism among Syrian Nationalists during the French Mandate', *International Journal of Middle East Studies* 13, 4 (1981), 441–69, 450ff.; Thompson, 'Rashid Rida', 245f. It has been argued that it makes sense to divide Rida's career into two periods: before and after 1918 (end of World War I), or before and after 1924 (end of the Caliphate, start of the Saudi conquest of the Hijaz). Simon A. Wood, *Christian Criticisms, Islamic Proofs: Rashid Rida's Modernist Defence of Islam* (Oxford: Oneworld, 2006), 49, and the rest of ch. 4. For a revisionist account that argues that Rida's thought was much more characterised by continuities, see Leor Halevi, *Modern Things on Trial: Islam's Global and Material Reformation in the Age of Rida, 1865–1935* (New York: Columbia University Press, 2019), 20f.

16. Jacob Goldberg, 'The 1913 Saudi Occupation of Hasa Reconsidered', *Middle Eastern Studies* 18, 1 (1982), 21–9; Goldberg, 'The Origins of British-Saudi Relations: The 1915 Anglo-Saudi Treaty Revisited', *The Historical Journal* 28, 3 (1985), 693–703; Steven B. Wagner, *British Intelligence and Policy in the Palestine Mandate, 1919–1939* (PhD, University of Oxford, 2014), 329–66.

17. This was the case, for example, of the Bin Jumaa family. Toby Matthiesen, *The Other Saudis: Shiism, Dissent and Sectarianism* (Cambridge: Cambridge University Press, 2015), 45–54; Fu'ad al-Ahmad, *Al-Shaykh Hasan 'Ali al-Badr al-Qatifi* (Beirut: Mu'assasat al-Baqi' li-Ihya' al-Turath, 1991).

18. Steinberg, *Religion und Staat*, 471–509; al-Hasan, *Al-Shi'a*; Jacob Goldberg, 'The Shi'i Minority in Saudi Arabia', in: Juan R. I. Cole and Nikki R. Keddie (eds), *Shi'ism and Social Protest* (New Haven: Yale University Press, 1986), 230–46, 231f.

19. Geoffrey Hamm, *British Intelligence and Turkish Arabia: Strategy, Diplomacy, and Empire, 1898–1918* (PhD, University of Toronto, 2012), 205–64; Jacob Goldberg, 'Captain Shakespear and Ibn Saud: A Balanced Reappraisal', *Middle Eastern Studies* 22, 1 (1986), 74–88; Gary Troeller, 'Ibn Sa'ud and Sharif Husain: A Comparison in Importance in the Early Years of the First World War', *The Historical Journal* 14, 3 (1971), 627–33; Teitelbaum, *The Rise and Fall*, 99–104.

20. Dorl Boberg, *Ägypten, Nagd und der Higaz: Eine Untersuchung zum religiös-politischen Verhältnis zwischen Ägypten und den Wahhabiten, 1923–1936, anhand von in Kairo veröffentlichten pro- und antiwahhabitischen Streitschriften und Presseberichten* (Bern: Peter Lang, 1991), 52–68; Werner Ende, 'Schiitische Tendenzen bei sunnitischen Sayyids aus Ḥaḍramaut: Muḥammad b. 'Aqīl al-'Alawī (1863–1931)', *Der Islam* 50, 1 (2009), 82–97. See also Joshua Teitelbaum, 'Hashemites, Egyptians and Saudis: The Tripartite Struggle for the Pilgrimage in the Shadow of Ottoman Defeat', *Middle Eastern Studies* 56, 1 (2020), 36–47. For these wider topics, see Malik R. Dahlan, *The Hijaz: The First Islamic State* (London: Hurst, 2018), esp. 99–153; Reinhard Schulze, *Islamischer Internationalismus im 20. Jahrhundert: Untersuchungen zur Geschichte der Islamischen Weltliga* (Leiden: Brill, 1990), 70–3.

21. Of these, one of the most prominent was Ahmad bin Zayni Dahlan (d. 1886), the Shafii Mufti of Mecca, whose anti-Wahhabi publications had gained him fame across the Islamic world. For these, he was in turn attacked by pro-Wahhabi voices from near and far, including from scholars associated with the quasi-Salafi state of Bhopal under Siddiq Hasan Khan. Preckel, 'Screening Siddiq Hasan Khan's (1832–1890) Library', 216. Descendants of the Dahlan scholarly family, for example, became the Muftis of Singapore after 1925. Esther Peskes, 'Daḥlān, Aḥmad b. Zaynī', *EI3*. See also Mark J. R. Sedgwick, 'Saudi Sufis: Compromise in the Hijaz, 1925–40', *Die Welt des Islams* 37, 3 (1997), 349–68.

22. After a Wahhabi scholar issued a religious judgment declaring these structures un-Islamic, Ibn Saud ordered their destruction. Ali Bahramian and Rahim Gholami, 'al-Baqī'', *EIs*.

23. The graveyard includes the tombs of the famous jurist Malik bin Anas (d. 179/795), Muhammad's uncle Abbas (d. c. 32/653), the ancestor of the Abbasid dynasty, the Caliph Uthman, and the four Shii Imams Hasan bin Ali (d. 49/669–670), Ali Zayn al-Abidin, Muhammad al-Baqir (d. c. 117/735), and Jafar al-Sadiq (d. 148/765). In addition, there are the graves of nine of the Prophet's wives (including Aisha and Hafsa) and at least three of his daughters. At the same time, countless pilgrims, clerics, and others were buried at the site, which turned it into a pilgrimage site for followers of a Sufi Shaykh or charismatic figure. Werner Ende, 'Baqī' al-Gharqad', *EI3*. See also Ende, 'Steine des Anstoßes: Das Mausoleum der Ahl al-Bayt in Medina', in: H. Biesterfeldt and V. Klemm (eds), *Differenz und Dynamik im Islam: Festschrift für Heinz Halm zum 70. Geburtstag* (Würzburg: Ergon, 2012), 181–200.

24. Richard Burton, for example, visits the site with a group of Sunni pilgrims. In an interesting episode of the British 'recognition' and exacerbation of sectarian difference, Burton, in disguise as an Afghan Muslim, throws in some anti-Shii remarks to keep up his disguise. On his visit to the Hijaz and the al-Baqia, he mistakes the 'decaying place of those miserable schismatics the Nakhawilah for al-Bakia, the glorious cemetery of the Saints. Hamid corrected my blunder with tartness, to which I replied as tartly, that in our country—Afghanistan—we burned the body of every heretic upon whom we could lay our hands. This

truly Islamitic custom was heard with general applause.' Nakhawilah is the name of the local Shii community. Having thus established his 'Sunni' identity, he and his group praise the martyrs of al-Baqia, and he is led by his guide to visit the mausoleum over the Caliph Uthman's grave, the mausoleum for the Imams, and other sites. Burton, *Personal Narrative*, Vol. 2, 31–44, quote on page 31. For the Ottoman restoration of the sites in the Hijaz, see François Georgeon, *Abdülhamid II: Le sultan calife (1876–1909)* (Paris: Fayard, 2003), 202–7.

25. In Indonesia, for example, a Hijaz committee petitioned Ibn Saud to protect the tomb of the Prophet and allow visitors of all the four Sunni schools of law, as fear spread that the Wahhabis would prioritise Hanbali visitors. Robert Bianchi, *Guests of God: Pilgrimage and Politics in the Islamic World* (Oxford: Oxford University Press, 2004), 209; Halifa Haqqi and Ida Mujtahidah, 'International Political Analysis on the Second Committee of Hejaz', in: M. F. Mujahidin et al. (eds), *Proceeding: International Conference on Middle East and South East Asia (ICoMS) 2016* (Surakarta: Sebelas Maret University, 2016), 134–45. The question of the Caliphate in the context of the dissolution of the Ottoman Empire led to a mobilisation amongst Indonesian Muslims. Martin van Bruinessen, 'Muslims of the Dutch East Indies and the Caliphate Question', *Studia Islamika* 2, 3 (1995), 115–40.

26. Schulze, *Islamischer Internationalismus*, 74. For the Saudi view, see Saeed M. Badeeb, *Saudi-Iranian Relations, 1932–1982* (London: Centre for Arab and Iranian Studies, 1993), 79–82.

27. Boberg, *Ägypten*, 21–34, 178–99; Schulze, *Islamischer Internationalismus*, 85; Martin Kramer, *Islam Assembled: The Advent of the Muslim Congresses* (New York: Columbia University Press, 1986), 106–22; Robinson, *The 'Ulama of Farangi Mahall*, 145–76. Although a decade later, some Indian Shia could see Ibn Saud in a more positive light because of his stance on Palestine. Mahmudabad, *Poetry of Belonging*, 220–3.

28. Henri Laoust, *Le califat dans la doctrine de Rašīd Riḍā: Traduction annotée d'al-Ḫilāfa au al-imāma al-ʿuẓmā (Le califat ou l'Imāma suprême)* (Beirut: n.p., 1938).

29. John Willis, 'Debating the Caliphate: Islam and Nation in the Work of Rashid Rida and Abul Kalam Azad', *International History Review* 32, 4 (2010), 711–32.

30. This was Abd al-Rahman al-Kawakibi's (c. 1849–1902) *Umma al-Qura*. Al-Kawakibi was another important figure who combined early pan-Arab nationalism and Islamic revivalism. Teitelbaum, *The Rise and Fall*, 42–6; Itzchak Weismann, 'al-Kawākibī, 'Abd al-Raḥmān', *EI3*. While Rida published al-Kawakibi's writings, they were not in agreement on every point. See Bassam Tibi, *Vom Gottesreich zum Nationalstaat: Islam und panarabischer Nationalismus* (Frankfurt: Suhrkamp, 1987), 79, 160ff. For a thorough engagement with Rida's ideas on the Caliphate, see Mahmoud Haddad, 'Arab Religious Nationalism in the Colonial Era: Rereading Rashīd Riḍā's Ideas on the Caliphate', *Journal of the American Oriental Society* 117, 2 (1997), 253–77. During World War I, Rida had even briefly supported the notion of a Sharifian Caliphate, but after the war,

now loathing the Hashemites, ruled them out as possible candidates. Teitelbaum, *The Rise and Fall*, 51, 237.

31. Haddad, 'Arab Religious Nationalism in the Colonial Era', 275; Willis, 'Debating the Caliphate'.

32. In his treatise on the necessity of the Caliphate, Rida argued for example that even Zaydis (and Ibadis) are in favour of the Caliphate. Laoust, *Le califat*, 178, 268f. For more, see Haykel, *Revival and Reform*, 206–10.

33. Muhammad Rashid Rida, *Al-Wahhabiyyun wa-l-Hijaz* (Cairo: Matbaʿat al-Manar, 1344/1925). His book is noteworthy in part for the use of the term 'Wahhabi' by a supporter of the movement rather than one of its critics. For more on Rida's defence of Wahhabism, see Henri Lauzière, *The Making of Salafism: Islamic Reform in the Twentieth Century* (New York: Columbia University Press, 2015), ch. 2; Brunner, *Die Schia*, 74; Commins, *The Wahhabi Mission*, 136–40; Schulze, *Islamischer Internationalismus*, 79ff. For some of his articles on the Hashemite-Saudi rivalry, see Rida, *Maqalat*, Vol. 4, 1516–25, cf. *al-Manar* 25 (1924), 390–400. Ibn Saud's standing in the wider Arab world, in particular in Syria, was boosted by his employment of Syrian nationalists as personal advisors. Fuad Hamza, a Lebanese Druze, was shaping Saudi foreign affairs, and Yusuf al-Yasin, a Sunni from Latakia, was Ibn Saud's private secretary. Khoury, *Syria and the French Mandate*, 339; Laila Parsons, *The Commander: Fawzi al-Qawuqji and the Fight for Arab Independence 1914–1948* (London: Saqi, 2017). Another important defender of the Wahhabiyya was Abdallah al-Qasimi, who published his *Wahhabi Revolution* in Cairo in 1936, arguing that the movement on the Arabian Peninsula was a wider intellectual movement to liberate Islam from its deviations. Jürgen Wasella, *Vom Fundamentalisten zum Atheisten: Die Dissidentenkarriere des Abdallah al-Qasimi (1907–1996)* (Stuttgart: Klett, 1997), 62.

34. Later Salafis sought to claim Rida for their movement, arguing that he was a true Salafi. Bernard Haykel, 'On the Nature of Salafi Thought and Action', in: Roel Meijer (ed.), *Global Salafism: Islam's New Religious Movement* (London: Hurst, 2009), 33–57, 46f.

35. Chanfi Ahmed, *West African ʿUlamāʾ and Salafism in Mecca and Medina: Jawāb al-Ifrīqī, the Response of the African* (Leiden: Brill, 2015), 86–9.

36. They built the largest and most impressive house in Jeddah that served as a kind of social salon, which is why prominent pilgrims arriving by boat would often stop there, and some were invited to stay at the house. Umar Nasif (1822–1908) expanded the family fortunes in trade and real estate and acted as a representative of the Sharif of Mecca and sometimes the Ottoman governor of the Hijaz. When King Abdulaziz entered Jeddah after the Sharif left, he stayed at that house. Nasif also maintained relations with the Imams of Yemen. For more on Nasif, see Ulrike Freitag, 'Scholarly Exchange and Trade: Muhammad Husayn Nasif and his Letters to Christiaan Snouck Hurgronje', in: Michael Kemper and Ralf Elger (eds), *The Piety of Learning: Islamic Studies in Honor of Stefan Reichmuth* (Leiden: Brill, 2017), 292–300; Teitelbaum, *The Rise and Fall*, 27f. See

also Qatar National Library, 'Coll 6/40 "Hejaz-Nejd. Changes in Government Appointments." [73r] (146/150)', IOR/L/PS/12/2107, https://www.qdl.qa/archive/81055/vdc_100036353061.0x000093; Qatar National Library, '"File 61/11 VI (D 102) Hejaz-Nejd Miscellaneous" [191r] (408/522)', IOR/R/15/1/569, https://www.qdl.qa/archive/81055/vdc_100023576506.0x000009. At the same time, a British source quotes him as having preferred Sharif Hussein's rule to that of Ibn Saud, despite Nasif's Wahhabi inclinations. Qatar National Library, 'File 2182/1913 Pt 9 "Arabia Policy towards Bin Saud" [36v] (70/406)', IOR/L/PS/10/390/1, https://www.qdl.qa/archive/81055/vdc_100036528094.0x00004e.

37. He had books printed across the Islamic world, and, as late as 1965, the Kuwaiti Ministry of Awqaf asked for his advice on choosing what works to edit from the Islamic tradition. Among the books are the famous *Kitab al-Tawhid* of Ibn Abd al-Wahhab and a defence of Ibn Taymiyya by Ibn Nasir al-Din, as well as newer books by Muhammad bin Salih al-Uthaymin and Muhibb al-Din al-Khatib. Freitag, 'Scholarly Exchange', 299. Among the anti-Shii books were ones by al-Alusi and al-Dhahabi. Brunner, *Islamic Ecumenism*, 322. He seems to have urged Abdallah al-Qasimi to write his massive anti-Shii polemic *Al-Sira' bayn al-Islam wa-l-Wathaniyya* (The Conflict between Islam and Paganism) in two volumes of more than 1,600 pages as a reply to Muhsin al-Amin. See also Wasella, *Vom Fundamentalisten zum Atheisten*, 65f.

38. Napoleon brought a printing press to Egypt, and by the 1820s Egyptian schools used printed textbooks. Slowly, this changed religious education, but a ban on printed books partly persisted at al-Azhar and the schools under the Zaydi Imam's control in Yemen, amongst other places. Messick, *The Calligraphic State*, 115f. See also Juan R. I. Cole, 'Printing and Urban Islam in the Mediterranean World, 1890–1920', in: Leila Tarazi Fawaz and C. A. Bayly (eds), *Modernity and Culture: From the Mediterranean to the Indian Ocean* (New York: Columbia University Press, 2002), 344–64.

39. A list of Ibn Taymiyya's books organised by printing dates states that the earliest work was printed in 1310/1893. Laoust, *Essai*, 634–9. The first printing of *Minhaj al-Sunna* was in Cairo in 1903. The 1991 Riyadh edition, which includes an extensive index and commentary, was printed on the orders of Prince Abdullah bin Abdulaziz on the occasion of the opening of a Saudi University. It was published by the education ministry in conjunction with Imam Muhammad Ibn Saud Islamic University. See Ibn Taymiyya, *Minhaj al-Sunna al-Nabawiyya fi Naqd Kalam al-Shi'a wa-l-Qadariyya* (The Way of the Prophetic Sunna in the Criticism of the Words of the Shia and the Qadiriyya), 4 Vols (Cairo: Bulaq, 1903–5), and 9 Vols (Riyadh: Imam Mohammad Ibn Saud Islamic University, 1991–). Different editions are listed here: The University of Chicago Library, 'Mamluk Bibliography Online', http://mamluk.lib.uchicago.edu/mamluk-primary.php?caller=3&start=1&op=AND&searchauthor0=&searchauthor1=&searchauthor2=&searchtitle0=&searchtitle1=&searchtitle2=&searchsubject=Heresiography&limit=50&searchlanguage. A now infamous

mistake occurred in the printing of the Mardin fatwa, in which the word 'treated' was replaced with 'killed', as discussed below in note 51. It was also translated into Urdu, with an open-source version available at https://archive. org/details/MukhtasirMinhajAlSunnahByAllamaIbnTaimiya.

40. See Ende, *Arabische Nation*, 61f.; Steinberg, 'Jihadi-Salafism', 117.

41. Abu al-Thana' al-Alusi was appointed Hanafi Mufti of Baghdad from 1835 to 1847. Basheer M. Nafi, 'Abu al-Thana' al-Alusi: An Alim, Ottoman Mufti, and Exegete of the Qur'an', *International Journal of Middle East Studies* 34, 3 (2002), 465–94.

42. The group from Lahore responded with a poem rebutting these ideas, which in turn would be refuted by al-Alusi's grandson, Mahmud Shukri (1857–1924). Masarwa, *Bildung, Macht, Kultur*, 53ff.

43. Ibid., 67. An interesting nuance here is that Abu al-Thana' al-Alusi had contact with some early proponents of a heterodox movement within Shiism at the time, the Shaykhiyya and Babiyya, and granted asylum in his house to a woman accused of such tendencies in 1847. He also knew Kazim al-Rashti, one of the most important leaders of the Shaykhiyya. But he was then also crucial in the joint fatwa and trial against a disciple of the Bab. Ibid., 219–37.

44. The book was prefaced with correspondence between Khan and al-Alusi. Nafi, 'Salafism Revived'; Masarwa, *Bildung, Macht, Kultur*, 89–93; David Commins, *Islamic Reform: Politics and Social Change in Late Ottoman Syria* (Oxford: Oxford University Press, 1990), 25.

45. Nafi, 'Salafism Revived', 50f.; Commins, *The Wahhabi Mission*, 132f.

46. Nafi, 'Salafism Revived', 64; Commins, *Islamic Reform*, 24ff., 32; Itzchak Weismann, 'Genealogies of Fundamentalism: Salafi Discourse in Nineteenth-Century Baghdad', *British Journal of Middle Eastern Studies* 36, 2 (2009), 267–80.

47. A key point of difference, not least with the Ottoman authorities, lay in their rejection of the schools of jurisprudence. Nafi, 'Salafism Revived', 87–90. See also Commins, *Islamic Reform*; Namira Nahouza, *Wahhabism and the Rise of the New Salafists: Theology, Power and Sunni Islam* (London: I. B. Tauris, 2018). See al-Uthaymeen's treatise on the subject: Shaikh Muhammad ibn Uthaimeen, 'The Methodology of the Salaf Concerning Ijtihad and Taqlid' (published on salafipublications.com), http://www.salafipublications.com/sps/sp.cfm?subsecI D=MNJ06&articleID=MNJ060001&articlePages=1. This perspective already somewhat exists in Ibn Taymiyya. Laoust, *Essai*, 226–30. In the twentieth century, the neo-*Salafiyya* argued that those who claimed to be Salafis, such as the Wahhabis, were actually following the Hanbali School and were therefore Salafis in creed but not in law. This was the position of Nasir al-Din al-Albani, who highlighted and denounced this tension inherent in Wahhabism, something the Saudi religious establishment, trained in the Hanbali school of jurisprudence, did not approve of. Stéphane Lacroix, 'Between Revolution and Apoliticism: Nasir al-Din al-Albani and his Impact on the Shaping of Contemporary Salafism', in: Roel Meijer (ed.), *Global Salafism: Islam's New Religious Movement* (London: Hurst, 2009), 58–80, 60f., 68.

48. Nafi, 'Salafism Revived', 86. This was even though many Salafis, like the Alusis, were members of a Sufi *tariqa*. Interestingly, one point of contention between his adherents and his critics was that Ibn Taymiyya criticised both Umar and Ali, two Companions and Caliphs, for some of their actions. Some of his critics argued that, in doing so, he was departing from the established point of view of the Sunna, which saw the Companions as infallible. Al-Alusi's book is written as a response to critiques of Ibn Taymiyya by al-Haythami. Ibid., 70, 74.

49. Mahmud Shukri al-Alusi's book is widely known as *Mukhtasar al-Tuhfa* (*The Concise Gift*). The below book, published in Saudi Arabia, includes a study of al-Alusi and his family's role, as well as a reproduction of another anti-Shii manuscript. Mahmud Shukri al-Alusi, *Sabb al-'Adhab 'ala man Sabba al-Ashab*, ed. by 'Abdallah al-Bukhari (Riyadh: Adua' al-Salaf, 1997). For his anti-Shii stance, see ibid., 88–94 and passim. One of many Shii refutations is Amir Muhammad Qazwini, *Al-Islam wa-l-Alusi* (Kuwait: Dar al-Tali'a, 1977). For more on him, see Hala Fattah, '"Wahhabi" Influences, Salafi Responses: Shaikh Mahmud Shukri and the Iraqi Salafi Movement, 1745–1930', *Journal of Islamic Studies* 14, 2 (2003), 127–48. Shortly after his death, in 1924, Rashid Rida and the Salafiyya Press published his private papers, which contained a strong articulation of Salafi ideas and defence of Wahhabism. This was his *Tarikh Najd* (*History of Najd*). Commins, *The Wahhabi Mission*, 134–40.

50. Masarwa, *Bildung, Macht, Kultur*, 84–7; Masarwa, 'Der Irak: Identitätskonzepte im Wandel', in: Rüdiger Robert, Daniela Schlicht, and Shazia Saleem (eds), *Kollektive Identitäten im Nahen und Mittleren Osten: Studien zum Verhältnis von Staat und Religion* (Münster: Waxmann, 2010), 335–58.

51. This later gained him recognition in Saudi Arabia, and he acted as an intermediary between France and the Kingdom. Laoust was a serious scholar, however, who defies easy classifications and read Shii authors such as al-Hilli and al-Mufid. Charles Pellat, 'Notice sur la vie et les travaux de Henri Laoust, membre de l'Académie [note biographique]', *Comptes rendus des séances de l'Académie des Inscriptions et Belles-Lettres* 130, 3 (1986), 502–18. For background, see Renaud Avez, *L'Institut français de Damas au Palais Azem (1922–1946): À travers les archives* (Damascus: Institut Français de Damas, 1993), 94–106; Leyla Dakhli, 'L'expertise en terrain colonial: Les orientalistes et le mandat français en Syrie et au Liban', *Matériaux pour l'histoire de notre temps* 3, 99 (2010), 20–7. Yahya Michot, a Belgian academic and convert to Islam, has carried on the project to rehabilitate Ibn Taymiyya and translate his writings. His translations have at times stirred considerable controversy because he chose to translate, and thus make publicly available in Western languages, Ibn Taymiyya's texts legitimising violence against Christians and Shia. Under the pseudonym Nasreddin Lebatelier, Michot published in Beirut the translation of Ibn Taymiyya's fatwa about Christian monks in the context of the killing of monks in Algeria. It caused a scandal in Christian circles. While Michot denied having supported the killing and in the book seems to endorse the consensus of Muslim scholars against the killing of monks, the story was further complicated by the discovery that, by working

with the printed text of Ibn Taymiyya's fatwa collection, a major mistake had entered the twentieth-century appropriation of this fatwa and Michot's translation. Instead of the passage 'unbelievers must be treated as they deserve to be treated', which is found in several manuscripts, the printed fatwa collection contained 'unbelievers must be killed', and that was the text used by many Jihadist groups, including al-Qaeda, as well as by Michot in his translation. A whole conference was eventually organised in Mardin to discuss and popularise a new, more tolerant reading of the Mardin fatwa. Michot eventually accepted the mistake, although he claimed that the change of this one word would not have a profound impact. Yahya M. Michot, 'Ibn Taymiyya's "New Mardin Fatwa": Is Genetically Modified Islam (GMI) Carcinogenic?', *The Muslim World* 101, 2 (2011), 130–81; Hassan Hassan, 'A Religious Basis for Violence Misreads Original Principles', *The National*, 9 April 2012; David Thomas and Alexander Mallett (eds), *Christian-Muslim Relations: A Bibliographical History*, Vol. 4 (Leiden: Brill, 2012), 863ff.; Sarah Albrecht, *Dār al-Islām Revisited: Territoriality in Contemporary Islamic Legal Discourse on Muslims in the West* (Leiden: Brill, 2018), 180f. Self-identifying as a Sunni Muslim, he is coming at this from a different angle than Laoust, the Christian Orientalist, but is likewise clearly sympathetic towards Ibn Taymiyya's refutation of Shiism. Michot, 'Ibn Taymiyya's Critique', e.g. 115. In a chronology he composed in a book that seeks to rehabilitate Ibn Taymiyya's image in the wake of 9/11, his entry for June 704 AD reads: 'Expedition of Ibn Taymiyya and a group of his disciples against the Rafidis of Kasrawan, to alert them to the risks they court by persisting in their heresy and to impose on them the Law of Islam.' Yahya M. Michot, *Muslims under Non-Muslim Rule* (Oxford: Interface, 2006), 156.

52. Weismann, *The Naqshbandiyya*, 119.
53. Nafi, 'Salafism Revived', 96.
54. Ende, *Arabische Nation*, 63.
55. J. H. Escovitz, '"He was the Muḥammad 'Abduh of Syria": A Study of Ṭāhir al-Jazā'irī and his Influence', *International Journal of Middle East Studies* 18 (1986), 293–310; Rainer Hermann, *Kulturkrise und konservative Erneuerung: Muḥammad Kurd 'Alī (1876–1953) und das geistige Leben in Damaskus zu Beginn des 20. Jahrhunderts* (Frankfurt am Main: Peter Lang, 1990), 26–34. For an in-depth account of this period and the influence of neo-Hanbali and Wahhabi/Salafi ideas in Syria, see Commins, *Islamic Reform*; P. Shinar and W. Ende, 'Salafiyya', *EI2*.
56. Brunner, *Islamic Ecumenism*, 159ff.; Ende, *Arabische Nation*, 64–75; Hermann, *Kulturkrise*, 246–51. For the academy, see J. D. J. Waardenburg, M. A. Jazayery, J. M. Landau, 'Madjma' 'Ilmī', *EI2*; Shaadi Khoury, *Instituting Renaissance: The Early Work of the Arab Academy of Science in Damascus, 1919–1930* (PhD, George Washington University, 2016).
57. He also worked for the British in Yemen in 1907/8. W. Ende, 'Muḥibb al-Dīn al-Khaṭīb', *EI2*; Ende, *Arabische Nation*, 91–110; Hermann, *Kulturkrise*, 99–112. For more on him, see Nimrod Hurvitz, 'Muhibb al-Din al-Khatib's Semitic

Wave Theory and Pan-Arabism', *Middle Eastern Studies* 29, 1 (1993), 118–34; Catherine Mayeur-Jaouen, 'Les débuts d'une revue néo-salafiste: Muḥibb al-Dîn al-Khaṭîb et al-Fatḥ de 1926 à 1928', *Revue des mondes musulmans et de la Méditerranée* 95–8 (2002), 227–55; Teitelbaum, *The Rise and Fall*, 106, 192f. See also William L. Cleveland, 'The Role of Islam as Political Ideology in the First World War', in: Edward Ingram (ed.), *National and International Politics in the Middle East* (London: Frank Cass, 1986), 84–101. For the Salafiyya Bookstore, see Henri Lauzière, 'The Construction of Salafiyya: Reconsidering Salafism from the Perspective of Conceptual History', *International Journal of Middle East Studies* 42, 3 (2010), 369–89.

58. Ende, *Arabische Nation*, 92f. This was and is another important source of debate amongst Islamic scholars. Particularly figures of the Muslim Brotherhood, such as Muhammad al-Ghazali, denounced monarchy as a system of government alien to Islam, and one that was institutionalised through Muawiya's pledging of allegiance to his son (Yazid). This is a thesis that, while not dominant, recently resurfaced in accounts seeking to explain the weakness of Islamic political rule. Muhammad al-Ghazali published an article with that argument in 1952, shortly after the revolution in Egypt, denouncing a book on Umayyad history edited by Muhibb al-Din al-Khatib. Ende, *Arabische Nation*, 99ff.

59. Reem Ahmad M. al-Sada, *The Introduction of Shaykh ʿAbd al-Wahhāb's Doctrine in Qatar: Religion and Politics in the Writings of Shaykh Qāsim al-Thānī (1827–1913)* (MA, Hamad Bin Khalifa University, 2019).

60. A fatwa by Wahhabi clerics of 1927, which calls for the application of Wahhabi teachings in the Hijaz, gives a sense of the Wahhabi clerics' views of Shii Muslims. While this policy was probably only briefly applied in 1927, it gives an idea of the maximalist demands of the Wahhabi clerics and their backers: 'As to the Shiʿites (al-rafida), we have told the Imam that our religious ruling is that they must be obliged to become true Muslims, and should not be allowed to perform the rites of their misguided religion publicly. It is incumbent on the Imam to order his governor in Hasa to summon the Shiʿites to Shaykh Ibn Bishr [i.e. the Wahhabi judge of the oasis], before whom they should swear to follow the religion of God and His Prophet, to cease all prayer to the saintly members of the Prophet's house or others, to cease their heretical innovations such as the commemoration rites performed on the anniversaries of the deaths of members of the House of the Prophet and all other such rites of their misguided creed, and that they should cease to visit their so-called sacred cities Karbala and Najaf. They must also be forced to attend the five prayers in the Mosques, along with the rest of the congregation. Sunni Imams, muezzins and religious policemen should be appointed to instruct them. They must also force them to study Ibn Abd al-Wahhab's Three Principles. Any places specially erected for the practice of their rites must be destroyed, and these practices forbidden in mosques and anywhere else. Any Shiʿites who refuse to keep to these rules must be exiled from Muslim territory. With regard to the Shiʿites of

Qatif, the Imam should compel Shaykh Ibn Bishr to go and see personally that all the above-mentioned requirements are carried out. We have advised the Imam to send missionaries and teachers to certain districts and villages which have only recently come under the rule of the Muslims, and to order his governors and other officials to bring these people back to Islam and forbid sinful behaviour. As to the Shi'ites of Iraq who have infiltrated and become mingled with the desert people under Muslim rule, we have advised the Imam to forbid them entry into Muslim pastures or other territory.' Guido Steinberg, 'Wahhabi 'Ulama and the State in Saudi Arabia, 1927', in: Camron Michael Amin, Benjamin C. Fortna, and Elizabeth Brown Frierson (eds), *The Modern Middle East: A Sourcebook for History* (Oxford: Oxford University Press, 2006), 57–61.

61. Steinberg, *Religion und Staat*, 432–70. For background on the Ikhwan, see John S. Habib, *Ibn Sa'ud's Warriors of Islam: The Ikhwan of Najd and their Role in the Creation of the Sa'udi Kingdom, 1910–1930* (Leiden: Brill, 1978).

62. Reinhard Schulze, *Geschichte der islamischen Welt: Von 1900 bis zur Gegenwart* (Munich: C. H. Beck, 2016), 97f.

63. For the repression of dissident narratives, see Rosie Bsheer, *Archive Wars: The Politics of History in Saudi Arabia* (Palo Alto, CA: Stanford University Press, 2020); Nadav Samin, *Of Sand or Soil: Genealogy and Tribal Belonging in Saudi Arabia* (Princeton, NJ: Princeton University Press, 2016).

64. Matthiesen, *The Other Saudis*; Fouad N. Ibrahim, *The Shi'is of Saudi Arabia* (London: Saqi, 2006).

65. Called the Makarima, these Ismailis had for a long time followed their own line of Imams and were related to the branch of Ismailis with their base in Yemen and India.

66. While the state did not completely repress them, those marginalised religious traditions were only accepted in private. Sedgwick, 'Saudi Sufis'; n.a., *Al-Tasawwuf fi al-Su'udiyya wa-l-Khalij* (Sufism in Saudi Arabia and the Gulf) (Dubai: Markaz al-Misbar li-l-Dirasat wa-l-Buhuth, 2011). It was not until 2009 that non-Wahhabi scholars were appointed to the highest clerical body in the country, the Council of the Committee of Senior Ulama, though Shia remained excluded from it. Matthiesen, *The Other Saudis*, 2. For the Nakhawila, see al-Nakhli, *Al-Nakhawila*.

67. Batatu, *The Old Social Classes*, 398f.

68. The affair was also notable insofar as the defenders of al-Nusuli were using liberal and nationalist arguments while avoiding religious language, and Shii students may have demonstrated in support of al-Nusuli. The first publication is Anis al-Nusuli's *The Umayyad State in Syria* (1927), and the second is Abdul Razaq al-Hassan's *Arabism in the Balance* (1933), which argued that 'Shiism was no more than a means to vitiate Arab supremacy in the name of religion' and questioned the Arab origins of the Shii tribes of Iraq. Kelidar, 'The Shii Imami Community', 13. For an in-depth account of Anis al-Nusuli's view of the Umayyads and the whole affair, see Ende, *Arabische Nation*, 132–45. For al-Hassan's book, see ibid.,

146f. See also Tripp, *A History of Iraq*, 62f.; N. Masalha, 'Faisal's Pan-Arabism, 1921–33', *Middle Eastern Studies* 27, 4 (1991), 679–93, 690f.; Nakash, *The Shiʿis of Iraq*, 111ff.

69. Orit Bashkin, *The Other Iraq: Pluralism and Culture in Hashemite Iraq* (Stanford: Stanford University Press, 2008).

70. Eric Davis, *Memories of State: Politics, History, and Collective Identity in Modern Iraq* (Berkeley: University of California Press, 2005).

71. He argued this in an article in *al-Irfan*. Abd al-Qadir al-Maghribi, *al-Irfan* 15 (1928), 1159f., cited after: Ende, *Arabische Nation*, 122f. See also ibid., 125ff.

72. This criticism was voiced in articles by Shii authors in the journal *al-Irfan*. See Ende, *Arabische Nation*, 120–4.

73. Al-Amin, *Mustadrakat Aʿyan al-Shiʿa*; Machlis, *Shiʿi Sectarianism*, 80f. For efforts to revitalise 'Shii heritage' by Shii historians from the Saudi Eastern Province, see Matthiesen, 'Shiʿi Historians'.

74. For example al-Hilli's *Minhaj al-Karama*, published in 1294/1877. Saleh, *The Formation*, 220n58.

75. See, for example, the Najaf edition of al-Qummi's Quran commentary, discussed in Bar-Asher, *Scripture and Exegesis*, 39–45.

76. For the Bombay print, see 'Abd al-Rida Al Kashif al-Ghita, *Al-Anwar al-Hussayniyya wa-l-Shaʾaʾir al-Islamiyya* (Bombay: Hur Printing, 1346h).

77. Personal observations, Lucknow, 2019. For background on the impact of the destruction of al-Baqia on Indian Shia, and the role the issue played in community mobilisation over subsequent years, see Fuchs, *In a Pure Muslim Land*, 12, 48–9.

78. Mervin, *Un réformisme chiite*, 288–301.

79. Ibid., 150–9; Silvia Naef, 'Aufklärung in einem schiitischen Umfeld: Die libanesische Zeitschrift al-ʿIrfān', *Die Welt des Islams* 36, 3 (1996), 365–78; Tarif Khalidi, 'Shaykh Ahmad ʿArif az-Zain and al-ʿIrfān', in: Marwan R. Buheiry (ed.), *Intellectual Life in the Arab East, 1890–1939* (Beirut: American University of Beirut, 1981), 110–24.

80. Already its cover page made clear in its subtitle that it was a monthly journal that specifically concerned itself with the affairs of the Shia. See, for example, *al-Irfan* (1909), available at https://digitale-sammlungen.ulb.uni-bonn.de/ulbbnioa/periodical/pageview/3373269.

81. Mervin, *Un réformisme chiite*, 285–90.

82. Orit Bashkin, 'The Iraqi Afghanis and ʿAbduhs: Debate over Reform among Shiʿite and Sunni ʿUlamaʾ in Interwar Iraq', in: Meir Hatina (ed.), *Guardians of Faith in Modern Times: ʿUlamaʾ in the Middle East* (Leiden: Brill, 2008), 141–69.

83. For a reply of al-Amin to Rida, see Muhsin al-Hussayni al-ʿAmili, *Al-Husun al-Maniʿa fi Radd ma Awradahu Sahib al-Manar fi Haqq al-Shiʿa* (Damascus: Matbaʿa al-Islah, 1327/1909). See also Mervin, 'On Sunnite-Shiite Doctrinal and Contemporary Geopolitical Tensions', 18; Mervin, *Un réformisme chiite*, 290–301. That said, Rida seems to have suggested that the conversion of Iraqi tribesmen

to Shiism was not that bad, primarily since he considered them barely Muslim beforehand because of their limited knowledge of Islam. See a 1908 article in *al-Manar*, quoted in: Nakash, *The Shi'is of Iraq*, 44. Rida was also critical of Bahaism. Juan R. I. Cole, 'Rashid Rida on the Bahá'í Faith: A Utilitarian Theory of the Spread of Religions', *Arab Studies Quarterly* 5, 3 (1983), 276–91.

84. Rida's articles on Shiism and Sunni–Shia unity, which illustrate his shifting, but always Sunni-centric, stance on the issue, were collected in a booklet. See Muhammad Rashid Rida, *Al-Sunna wa-l-Shi'a aw al-Wahhabiyya wa-l-Rafida: Haqa'iq Diniyya Ta'rihiyya Ijtima'iyya Islahiyyya*, 2nd ed. (Cairo: Dar al-Manar, 1947). See also W. Ende, 'Rashīd Riḍā', *EI2*; Mervin, *Un réformisme chiite*, 290–301; Boberg, *Ägypten*, 200–32; Brunner, *Islamic Ecumenism*, 92. For a collection of the correspondence, see Ja'far al-Subhani (ed.), *Hiwarat 'Ilmiyya bayna al-'Alamayn al-Sayyid Muhsin al-Amin al-'Amili wa-l-Sayyid Muhammad Rashid Rida* (Qom: Mu'assasat al-Imam al-Sadiq, 2017).

85. He published doctrinal refutations of Christianity and criticised mandatory powers, but at times also welcomed cooperation with European powers and favoured local Christian-Muslim cooperation in Syria. Wood, *Christian Criticisms*; Umar Ryad, 'Islamic Reformism and Great Britain: Rashid Rida's Image as Reflected in the Journal al-Manār in Cairo', *Islam and Christian-Muslim Relations* 21, 3 (2010), 263–85.

86. Brunner, *Islamic Ecumenism*, 39ff.

87. Mervin, *Un réformisme chiite*, 275–85.

88. Ende, 'The Flagellations of Muharram'; Mervin, *Un réformisme chiite*, 229–74. Those Shii clerics, such as Muhammad Ibn Muhammad Mahdi al-Khalisi (1890–1963), who were willing to make the most serious concessions in toning down Shii religious practices deemed provocative by Sunnis to facilitate rapprochement were also criticised by other Shii clerics, who argued that there was a limit as to how far Shia were willing to accommodate to secure Sunni acceptance. Al-Khalisi, who advocated abolishing the Shii call to prayer, was attacked harshly by senior Shii clerics in the mid-1950s, and by Sunni polemicists, and hence marginalised. Machlis, *Shi'i Sectarianism*, 123,137; Werner Ende, 'Success and Failure of a Shiite Modernist: Muhammad ibn Muhammad Mahdi al-Khalisi (1890–1963)', in: Alessandro Monsutti, Silvia Naef, and Farian Sabahi (eds), *The Other Shiites: From the Mediterranean to Central Asia* (Bern: Peter Lang, 2008), 231–44. See, for example, Muhammad Jawad Mughniyya's comparative studies of the five schools: Muhammad Jawad Mughniyya, *Al-Fiqh 'ala al-Madhahib al-Khamsa: Al-Ja'fari, al-Hanafi, al-Maliki, al-Shafi'i, al-Hanbali*, 6th ed. (Beirut: Dar al-'Ilm li-l-Mallayyin, 1979).

89. The Syrian Abd al-Rahman al-Kawakibi played a key role in this. Shii scholars were eventually even invited to the Caliphate Conference organised by al-Azhar in 1926, but ultimately did not attend, and the congress failed to reach a consensus on a new Caliph due to intra-Sunni differences. Diplomatic and personal manoeuvrings meant that an invitation came relatively late, owing to initiatives of the Egyptian ambassador to Iran, and led Reza Shah to decline on

behalf of Iran's Shii clerics, who he argued had not had sufficient time to study the issue of the Caliphate. Brunner, *Islamic Ecumenism*, 87f.; Kramer, *Islam Assembled*, 91ff. The central organising committee of the conference was not particularly interested in Shii participants. Eventually, an Iranian merchant sent from the Iranian consulate attended. Schulze, *Islamischer Internationalismus*, 78.

90. Kramer, *Islam Assembled*, 132f.

91. Elisheva Machlis, 'A Shi'a Debate on Arabism: The Emergence of a Multiple Communal Membership', *British Journal of Middle Eastern Studies* 40, 2 (2013), 95–114.

92. Commins, *Islamic Reform*, 69, 84ff. Commins argues that his more polite tone, especially in comparison to al-Alusi, showed the difference between the Syrian and Iraqi *Salafiyya* when it came to Shiism (as Shiism was not such a significant force in Syria as it was in Iraq). Ibid., 88.

93. Werner Ende, 'Sunniten und Schiiten im 20. Jahrhundert', *Saeculum* 36 (1985), 187–200; Uri M. Kupferschmidt, 'The General Muslim Congress of 1931 in Jerusalem', *Asian and African Studies* 12 (1978), 123–57, 134, 148; Basheer M. Nafi, 'The General Islamic Congress of Jerusalem Reconsidered', *The Muslim World* 86, 3-4 (1996), 243–72, 262ff. Apparently, Kashif al-Ghita complained about intrigants who had sought to prevent Iraqi Shii clerics from participating in the meeting. And a subsequent speech by Rida brought to the fore the differing views regarding the schools of jurisprudence, especially Shiism. Ende, *Arabische Nation*, 117; Brunner, *Islamic Ecumenism*, 88–98. The conference was important, however, in placing the issue of Palestine and anti-Zionism at the heart of both Sunni and Shii pan-Islamic imaginations. Nicholas E. Roberts, 'Making Jerusalem the Centre of the Muslim World: Pan-Islam and the World Islamic Congress of 1931', *Contemporary Levant* 4, 1 (2019), 52–63.

94. Al Kashif al-Ghita, *Asl al-Shi'a*, 48f., and passim; Brunner, *Islamic Ecumenism*, 99–102; Muhammad al-Hussayn Al Kashif al-Ghita, *Naqd Fatawa al-Wahhabiyya* (Qom: Mu'assasat Al al-Bayt li-Ihya' al-Turath, 1416/1995). For other assertions of Shiism around this time, see, for example, Muhammad Mahdi al-Kazimi al-Qazwini, *Kitab Minhaj al-Shari'a fi al-Radd 'ala Ibn Taymiyya*, 2 Vols (Najaf: al-Matba'a al-'Alawiyya, 1929–30).

95. In al-Khatib's journal *al-Fath*. Brynjar Lia, *The Society of the Muslim Brothers in Egypt: The Rise of an Islamic Mass Movement, 1928–1942* (Reading: Ithaca, 1998), 27–32, 123.

96. Ibid., 32–43, esp. 42. See also Richard P. Mitchell, *The Society of the Muslim Brothers* (Oxford: Oxford University Press, 1993).

97. Tariq Ramadan, *Aux sources du renouveau musulman: D'al-Afghani à Hassan al-Banna, un siècle de réformisme islamique* (Paris: Bayard/Centurion, 1998), 249–61; Ishaq Musa Husayni, *The Moslem Brethren: The Greatest of Modern Islamic Movements* (Beirut: Khayat, 1956), 86; Gudrun Krämer, *Hasan al-Banna* (Oxford: Oneworld, 2010). Al-Banna would be close to members of the Rapprochement

Society in the late 1940s and even participate in some of its meetings. Brunner, *Islamic Ecumenism*, 180ff.

98. Lia, *The Society of the Muslim Brothers*, 56f. As a result of criticism of the monarchy, the Ministry of Interior temporarily banned *al-Manar* and the Muslim Brotherhood's newspaper *al-Nadhir* in 1939 (*al-Manar* was allowed to resume publication months later, though with restrictions, but was then permanently banned in 1940). Ibid., 220f., 260.

99. For the early spread of the movement, see Lia, *The Society of the Muslim Brothers*, 154ff. The early Syrian Muslim Brotherhood, however, officially denounced sectarian division. Husayni, *The Moslem Brethren*, 77. In Iraq, the movement faced difficulties obtaining a licence to operate. Some Shia apparently joined the movement in Iraq, but the Shii presence hindered the spread of the movement. Ibid., 84f.

100. Its religious production for a while became closer to Hanbalism. Hasan al-Banna's father, Shaykh Ahmad al-Banna, had authorised a new multi-volume classification of the traditions of Ibn Hanbal. The initial volumes were printed by the Society of Muslim Brothers publishing house and in large parts financed by subscriptions from Saudi Arabia, including a hundred sets of the multi-volume work published by the King. Lia, *The Society of the Muslim Brothers*, 140–4.

101. But Ibn Saud did not allow the Brotherhood to officially set up a party structure in his domains. By the late 1930s, the relationship was already becoming frayed. Lia, *The Society of the Muslim Brothers*, 143; Husayni, *The Moslem Brethren*, 83f.

102. Enayat, *Modern Islamic Political Thought*, 69–83; Constance Arminjon Hachem, *Une brève histoire de la pensée politique en Islam contemporain* (Geneva: Labor et Fides, 2017), 79–127.

103. Young Shii clerics had started to see this reform and modernisation of al-Azhar positively and compare it favourably with the institutions of Shii learning in Iraq and Iran. Shii scholars thus started to respect al-Azhar and see it as a Sunni counterpart of their seats of higher learning, in particular Najaf. Brunner, *Islamic Ecumenism*, 47ff. This was symbolised by one of the most famous books ever published on Sunni–Shia dialogue, *al-Murajaat*. It purports to be a dialogue between a Shii scholar from Jabal Amil and the rector of al-Azhar in Cairo that had allegedly taken place during a visit of the former to Cairo in 1911/12. While it is largely the work of the Shii scholar, and its authenticity disputed by Sunni critics, it was widely republished since its first appearance in 1936 and has often been invoked by Shia. It showed a Shii interest to be taken seriously at al-Azhar. It was also translated and, after the revolution in Iran, used by the Islamic Republic in ecumenical propaganda efforts. Ibid., 51–81; Mervin, *Un réformisme chiite*, 304–10. See this English translation that was published in 1983: Sayyid Abd al-Husain Sharaf al-Din, *The Right Path* (Blanco: Zahra/Peermohammed Ebrahim Trust, 1983). Another English version was published in Lebanon in 1994. See Sharaf al-Din, *Al-Muraja'at: A Shi'i-Sunni Dialogue* (Beirut: Imam Husayn Islamic Foundation, 1994),

available at http://alhassanain.org/english/?com=book&id=635. For Shii scholars and al-Azhar in the 1930s, see Brunner, *Islamic Ecumenism*, 103–18; al-Uzri, *Tarikh fi Dhikrayat*, 63.

104. The marriage was dissolved in 1948. Brunner, *Islamic Ecumenism*, 119; E. R., 'EGITTO', *Oriente Moderno* 19, 4 (1939), 226–30, 227f.

105. Brunner, *Islamic Ecumenism*, 124–30; Badeeb, *Saudi-Iranian Relations*, 50f., 84f.; Peters, *The Hajj*, 172–80; John M. Willis, 'Governing the Living and the Dead: Mecca and the Emergence of the Saudi Biopolitical State', *American Historical Review* 122, 2 (2017), 346–70.

106. It was first called the Society for Taqrib, then Dar al-Taqrib (Centre for Rapprochement). Brunner, *Islamic Ecumenism*, 131ff.

107. Until al-Banna's assassination in 1949, that is. Brunner, *Islamic Ecumenism*, 180–5.

108. Its journal *Risalat al-Islam* started in 1949 and was published for twenty-three years. Brunner, *Islamic Ecumenism*, 143–52. For its associated scholarly network and conferences, see ibid., 153–207.

109. Though Burujirdi's involvement and support was never officially mentioned so as not to heighten Sunni fears that this was a Shii-led organisation. Brunner, *Islamic Ecumenism*, 187–207. They were primarily Iraqi and Lebanese, though a Saudi Shii cleric was also involved. Ali al-Khunaizi, a senior Shii cleric from Qatif in Saudi Arabia, wrote a book on Islamic unity. 'Ali Abu al-Hasan ibn Hasan bin Mahdi al-Khunayzi, *Al-Da'wa al-Islamiyya ila Wahdat Ahl al-Sunna wa-l-Imamiyya*, 2 Vols (Beirut: Dar al-Fikr, 1956).

110. Brunner, *Islamic Ecumenism*, 170. Some Zaydi authors also wrote in the Society's publications. See ibid., 187.

111. Mahmoud Shaltut, 'The Official Councel (Fatwa) Given by His Eminence on the Validity of Worshipping According to the Doctrine of the Imamite Shi'â', in: *Two Historical Documents* (Cairo: Dar al-Taqreeb, 1963), 14–16. For a collection of articles published by the Dar al-Taqrib, and somewhat a history of the movement, see Muhammad Muhammad al-Madani (ed.), *Da'wa al-Taqrib min Khilal Risala al-Islam* (Cairo: Dar al-Taqrib, 1966); Mahmoud Shaltut, 'The Introduction of the Story of Taqreeb', in: *Two Historical Documents* (Cairo: Dar al-Taqreeb, 1963), 3–13; Brunner, *Islamic Ecumenism*, 165ff.

112. At the same time, however, he denounced some Shii groups as having gone too far, but stated that these were also denounced by Twelver Shia. He claimed that one of the reasons for the need for Islamic unity was imperialism: 'Imperialism is rooted in the principle of divide and rule, and has exploited the differences of madhhab in order to give effect to this principle.' He also stated: 'In their creed ('aqida) and jurisprudence (shari'a) there is no greater difference between them and the Sunni madhhabs than there is between the Sunni madhhabs themselves.' Interview with Mahmoud Shaltut in *Majallat al-Azhar* (1959), quoted in: Bagley, 'The Azhar and Shi'ism', 123f.

113. Brunner, *Islamic Ecumenism*, 301.

114. Ibid., 208.

115. Ibid., 140.

116. This was the case with Muhammad Abu Zahra and Ahmad Amin. Ibid., 169–79.

117. Ibid., 157f. This was spurred by diplomatic niceties such as a meeting between King Saud and Ayatollah Burujirdi during a state visit of the Saudi King to Iran in 1955. Ibid.; Badeeb, *Saudi–Iranian Relations*, 52, 87.

118. Karl-Heinrich Göbel, *Moderne schiitische Politik und Staatsidee nach Taufiq al-Fukaiki, Muhammad Gawad Mugniya, Ruhulläh Humaini (Khomeyni)* (Opladen: Leske, 1984), 89–94. The book against the Wahhabiyya was Muhammad Jawad Mughniyya, *Hadhihi hiya al-Wahhabiyya* (Tehran: Munazzamat al-'Ilam al-Islami, 1987). See Brunner, *Islamic Ecumenism*, 202ff. For him, see also Chibli Mallat, *Aspects of Shi'i Thought from the South of Lebanon: Al-'Irfan, Muhammad Jawad Mughniyya, Muhammad Mahdi Shamseddin, Muhammad Husain Fadlallah* (Oxford: Centre for Lebanese Studies, 1988).

119. Muhibb al-Din al-Khatib, *Al-Khutut al-'Arida*, 3rd ed. (Qatar: n.p., 1386/1966). This edition was printed at the insistence of the former Qatari Emir, Shaykh Ali bin Abdallah bin Qasim al-Thani. See, for example, also the Turkish translation: Muhibb al-Din al-Khatib, *Şiilik (Imamiyye-Isnaaşeriyye) dini esaslarının görünen çizgileri* (n.p., n.d.). See also Brunner, *Die Schia*, 70–117, esp. 71, 331f.; Ende, *Arabische Nation*, 119; Christoph Marcinkowski, *Shi'ite Identities: Community and Culture in Changing Social Contexts* (Münster: LIT, 2010), 49–65.

120. Already in 1938, Egypt's minister in Iraq advocated a rapprochement between Sunni and Shia led by al-Azhar to strengthen Egypt's influence amongst Shia in Iraq, Yemen, Iran, Afghanistan, and India. Kramer, *Islam Assembled*, 102.

121. Nader Entessar, 'The Lion and the Sphinx: Iranian–Egyptian Relations in Perspective', in: Hooshang Amirahmadi and Nader Entessar (eds), *Iran and the Arab World* (Basingstoke: Macmillan, 1993), 161–79, 161–4; Kamyar Abdi, 'The Name Game: The Persian Gulf, Archaeologists, and the Politics of Arab-Iranian Relations', in: Philip L. Kohl, Mara Kozelsky, and Nachman Ben-Yehuda (eds), *Selective Remembrances: Archaeology in the Construction, Commemoration, and Consecration of National Pasts* (Chicago: University of Chicago Press, 2007), 206–43.

122. Gustave E. von Grunebaum, *Modern Islam: The Search for Cultural Identity* (Berkeley: University of California Press, 1962), 73–96, esp. 86–90.

123. Cemil Aydin, *The Idea of the Muslim World: A Global Intellectual History* (Cambridge, MA: Harvard University Press, 2017).

124. Sarah Yisraeli, *The Remaking of Saudi Arabia: The Struggle between King Saud and Crown Prince Faysal, 1953–1962* (Tel Aviv: Moshe Dayan Center for Middle Eastern and African Studies, 1997).

125. This period was the Arab version of the Cold War, with conservative monarchies led by Saudi Arabia and backed by the United States on the one side and revolutionary military regimes with the support of the Soviet Union on the other. Malcolm Kerr, *The Arab Cold War: Gamal 'Abd al-Nasir and his Rivals, 1958–1970*, 3rd ed. (London: Oxford University Press, 1971); Jesse Ferris, *Nasser's Gamble: How Intervention in Yemen Caused the Six-Day War and the Decline of Egyptian Power* (Princeton: Princeton University Press, 2013).

126. Schulze, *Islamischer Internationalismus*.

127. For the wider developments in the colonial world, see Amitav Acharya and Barry Buzan, *The Making of Global International Relations: Origins and Evolution of IR at its Centenary* (Cambridge: Cambridge University Press, 2019), 1–32.

128. Amongst a vast literature, see Siniša Malešević, 'Nationalisms and the Orthodox Worlds', *Nations and Nationalism* 26, 3 (2020), 544–52; Shane Nagle, 'Confessional Identity as National Boundary in National Historical Narratives: Ireland and Germany Compared', *Studies in Ethnicity and Nationalism* 13, 1 (2013), 38–56; Anthony W. Marx, *Faith in Nation: Exclusionary Origins of Nationalism* (Oxford: Oxford University Press, 2003); Bayly, *The Birth of the Modern World*, 361ff. See also Anthony D. Smith, *Chosen Peoples: Sacred Sources of National Identity* (Oxford: Oxford University Press, 2003).

129. Marashi, *Nationalizing Iran*, 35–48.

130. Abrahamian, *A History of Modern Iran*, 16–20.

131. Marashi, *Nationalizing Iran*, 85.

132. It had long been claimed that this was inspired by the Nazi Party's Aryan myth, or by closeness to Germany, but decisive evidence for this is lacking. The Iranian embassy in Berlin played a role in this change of name, however. Reza Zia-Ebrahimi, 'Self-Orientalization and Dislocation: The Uses and Abuses of the "Aryan" Discourse in Iran', *Iranian Studies* 44, 4 (2011), 445–72; Zia-Ebrahimi, '"Arab Invasion" and Decline, or the Import of European Racial Thought by Iranian Nationalists', *Ethnic and Racial Studies* 37, 6 (2014), 1043–61; Zia-Ebrahimi, *The Emergence of Iranian Nationalism: Race and the Politics of Dislocation* (New York: Columbia University Press, 2016); David Motadel, 'Iran and the Aryan Myth', in: Ali M. Ansari (ed.), *Perceptions of Iran: History, Myths and Nationalism from Medieval Persia to the Islamic Republic* (London: I. B. Tauris, 2014), 119–45, 132–5. Turkish-Iranian relations also improved markedly in this period, symbolised, for example, by the permission of limited Shii publishing in Turkey. Johann Strauss, 'Sii ne demekdir? Ein türkisches Traktat über die Schia aus dem Jahre 1925', in: Rainer Brunner, Monika Gronke, Jens P. Laut, and Ulrich Rebstock (eds), *Islamstudien ohne Ende: Festschrift für Werner Ende* (Würzburg: Deutsche Morgenländische Gesellschaft/Ergon, 2002), 471–84.

133. After the Iranian Revolution, it became more common again to use Arabic terms, especially when it came to religious matters. The Turkish Islamists, too, by using more religious language, employed more Arabic words in their discourse.

134. H. E. Chehabi, 'Iran and Iraq: Intersocietal Linkages and Secular Nationalisms', in: Abbas Amanat and Farzin Vejdani (eds), *Iran Facing Others: Identity Boundaries in a Historical Perspective* (London: Palgrave, 2012), 193–218.

135. Bagley, 'The Azhar and Shi'ism', 126.

136. For example Henry Corbyn. Kamaly, *God and Man*, 168ff.

137. After 1979, the association of some Sufi orders with the Pahlavi regime led to their partial suppression (although, in other ways, even the leaders of the Islamic Republic invoked Sufi themes). For that complicated relationship, see van den Bos, *Mystic Regimes*; Kamaly, *God and Man*, 145–75. The Pahlavis even

supported a Sunni Naqshbandi on the border between Iran and Iraq. This was Uthman Siraj al-Din, who after 1958 left Biyara in Iraq and established himself in Duru on the Iranian side to unite the Naqshbandis in Iran. After the 1979 revolution, he fought against the new government, but was quickly defeated and withdrew to Iraq (the Naqshbandiyya retains some presence amongst Iranian Kurds, especially in Mahabad and Talish). Knysh, *Islamic Mysticism*, 224f. See also Farhad Shakely, 'The Naqshbandi Shaikhs of Hawraman and the Heritage of Khalidiyya-Mujaddidiyya in Kurdistan', *International Journal of Kurdish Studies* 19, 1–2 (2005), 119–35.

138. Stephanie Cronin, 'Conscription and Popular Resistance in Iran, 1925–1941', in: Erik J. Zürcher (ed.), *Arming the State: Military Conscription in the Middle East and Central Asia, 1775–1925* (London: I. B. Tauris, 1999), 145–68, 151–60; Constance Arminjon Hachem, *Les droits de l'homme dans l'Islam shi'ite: Confluences et lignes de partage* (Paris: Les Éditions du Cerf, 2017), 46–50; Mallat, *Introduction*, 256.

139. Shahrough Akhavi, *Religion and Politics in Contemporary Iran: Clergy–State Relations in the Pahlavi Period* (Albany: SUNY Press, 1980), passim, but esp. 76–90; Nakash, *The Shi'is of Iraq*, 87; Mohammad Mesbahi, 'Dynamic Quietism and the Consolidation of the ḥawza 'ilmīyya of Qum during the Pahlavi Era', *British Journal of Middle Eastern Studies* (online, 2021); Majid Yazdi, 'Patterns of Clerical Political Behavior in Postwar Iran, 1941–53', *Middle Eastern Studies* 26, 3 (1990), 281–307.

140. Stéphane A. Dudoignon, *The Baluch, Sunnism and the State in Iran: From Tribal to Global* (London: Hurst, 2017), 111f.; Dudoignon, 'Zahedan vs. Qom? L'émergence du Baloutchistan d'Iran comme foyer de droit hanafite, sous la monarchie Pahlavi', in: Denise Aigle, Isabelle Charleux, Vincent Goossaert, and Roberte N. Hamayon (eds), *Miscellanea Asiatica: Mélanges en l'honneur de Françoise Aubin* (Sankt Augustin: Institute Monumenta Serica, 2010), 271–315; Nakash, *The Shi'is of Iraq*, 158. See Fischer, *Iran*, 133f.

141. Nadia von Maltzahn, *The Syria–Iran Axis: Cultural Diplomacy and International Relations in the Middle East* (London: I. B. Tauris, 2013), 187–91.

142. Imam Reza Network, 'Ayatullah al-Uzma Sayyid Abul Hasan Isfahani', 3 March 2016, https://web.archive.org/web/20160303201123/http://www.imamreza.net/eng/imamreza.php?id=6951; Nakash, *The Shi'is of Iraq*, 258.

143. The Shah, for example, visited the Ayatollah in hospital and in the seminary at Qom. Hamid Algar, 'BORŪJERDĪ, ḤOSAYN ṬABĀṬABĀ'Ī', *EIr*.

144. Shaltut even wrote to the Shah, criticising Iran's ties to Israel and suggesting that Iran would be rewarded with better relations with Egypt and Iraq were the Shah to continue pushing rapprochement efforts with Sunni Islam and severe those with Israel. And even as some of the Shii clergy started to distance themselves from the Shah in the 1960s, Qommi maintained a relationship with the Shah, perhaps to save the chances of his endeavour. Akhavi, *Religion and Politics*, 99, 103.

145. Mohamed al-Araby, 'Identity Politics, Egypt and the Shia', *al-Ahram*, 25 April 2013.

146. Arshin Adib-Moghaddam, *The International Politics of the Persian Gulf: A Cultural Genealogy* (London: Routledge, 2006).

147. Svat Soucek, 'Arabistan or Khuzistan', *Iranian Studies* 17, 2–3 (1984), 195–213.

148. Masoumeh Rad Goudarzi and Sediqeh Nazarpour, 'The Separation of Bahrain from Iran', in: Mansoureh Ebrahimi, Masoumeh Rad Goudarzi, and Kamaruzaman Yusoff (eds), *The Dynamics of Iranian Borders: Issues of Contention* (Cham: Springer, 2019), 95–114; J. B. Kelly, 'The Persian Claim to Bahrain', *International Affairs* 33, 1 (1957), 51–70; Majid Khadduri, 'Iran's Claim to the Sovereignty of Bahrayn', *American Journal of International Law* 45, 4 (1951), 631–47; Rouhollah K. Ramazani, 'The Settlement of the Bahrain Dispute', *Indian Journal of International Law* 12, 1 (1972), 1–14.

149. Nikolaos van Dam, *The Struggle for Power in Syria: Politics and Society under Asad and the Ba'th Party*, 4th ed. (London: I. B. Tauris, 2011); Batatu, 'Some Observations'; Alasdair Drysdale, 'The Syrian Political Elite, 1966–1976: A Spatial and Social Analysis', *Middle Eastern Studies* 17, 1 (1981), 3–30; Seale, *Asad of Syria*, 60–85; Raymond Hinnebusch, 'Syria's Alawis and the Ba'ath Party', in: Michael Kerr and Craig Larkin (eds), *The Alawis of Syria: War, Faith and Politics in the Levant* (Oxford: Oxford University Press, 2015), 107–24, 109–13; Fabrice Balanche, '"Go to Damascus, my Son": Alawi Demographic Shifts under Ba'ath Party Rule', in: Michael Kerr and Craig Larkin (eds), *The Alawis of Syria: War, Faith and Politics in the Levant* (Oxford: Oxford University Press, 2015), 79–106, 81–92.

150. Van Dam, *The Struggle for Power in Syria: Politics*, 17. For the original debate between Islamic authorities and the early Arab nationalists, see Enayat, *Modern Islamic Political Thought*, 111–20.

151. In the official Syrian Baath publications, this was not acknowledged, of course, and Arabic works published in Syria never mentioned the fact that al-Arsuzi was of an Alawite background. Watenpaugh, '"Creating Phantoms"'. According to Landis, 'to become part of the Arab nation, the Alawites had to reinvent it'. Landis, *Nationalism*, 105. See also Rahaf Aldoughli, 'Revisiting Ideological Borrowings in Syrian Nationalist Narratives: Sati al-Husri, Michel 'Aflaq and Zaki al-Arsuzi', *Syria Studies* 8, 1 (2016), 7–39.

152. How complicated the interplay between sectarian identity and political alliances was shows this struggle for power between different factions in the military. In his rivalry with Jadid, and with Muhammad Umran, both were in fact accused by al-Assad of using sectarian identity and of trying to counter Sunnis, although all three were Alawites. The utilisation of accusations of sectarianism by different factions probably heightened the fears amongst Syrians of the relationship between sectarian affiliation and political allegiance and conspiratorial networks. Hans Günter Lobmeyer, *Opposition und Widerstand in Syrien* (Hamburg: Deutsches Orient-Institut, 1995), 106–9; Seurat, *Syrie*, 166ff., 171; Hinnebusch, 'Syria's Alawis', 112f.

153. Joseph Bahout, *Les entrepreneurs syriens: Économie, affaires et politique* (Beirut: Presses de l'Ifpo, 1994); Thomas Pierret, *Religion and State in Syria: The Sunni*

Ulama from Coup to Revolution (Cambridge: Cambridge University Press, 2013); Robert W. Olson, *The Ba'th and Syria, 1947 to 1982: The Evolution of Ideology, Party, and State, from the French Mandate to the Era of Hafiz al-Asad* (Princeton, NJ: Kingston Press, 1982), 51–8; Bassam Haddad, *Business Networks in Syria: The Political Economy of Authoritarian Resilience* (Stanford: Stanford University Press, 2011), 54–60; Volker Perthes, *Staat und Gesellschaft in Syrien, 1970–1989* (Hamburg: Deutsches Orient-Institut, 1990), 184f.; Hinnebusch, 'Syria's Alawis', 114–17.

154. Lefèvre, *Ashes of Hama*, 23–7.

155. In the 1950s, a founding figure argued that sectarian societies had existed within the larger Syrian society for a long time and had contributed to 'sectarian social formation'. As a way out, he called for the Arabisation of non-Arab people and fusing Islamic sects in the 'melting pot of general Islam', in essence promoting the Arab and (Sunni) view of Syrian society and national identity. This was Muhammad al-Mubarak. Cited after: Weiss, 'Mosaic, Melting Pot, Pressure Cooker', 193.

156. Werner Ende, 'Sunni Polemical Writings on the Shi'a and the Iranian Revolution', in: David Menashri (ed.), *The Iranian Revolution and the Muslim World* (Boulder, CO: Westview Press, 1990), 219–32, 223. He was also critical of Sufism and became famous for advocating a sort of Islamic socialism, broadening the appeal of the movement. Arnaud Lenfant, 'L'évolution du salafisme en Syrie au XXe siècle', in: Bernard Rougier (ed.), *Qu'est-ce que le salafisme?* (Paris: Presses Universitaires de France, 2008), 161–78.

157. Johannes Reissner, *Ideologie und Politik der Muslimbrüder Syriens: Von den Wahlen 1947 bis zum Verbot unter Adīb aš-Šišaklī 1952* (Freiburg: K. Schwarz, 1980).

158. Fabrice Balanche, *La région alaouite et le pouvoir syrien* (Paris: Karthala, 2006); Balanche, 'Les Alaouites: Une secte au pouvoir', *Outre-Terre* 2, 14 (2006), 73–96; Eyal Zisser, 'The Alawis, Lords of Syria: From Ethnic Minority to Ruling Sect', in: Ofra Bengio and Gabriel Ben-Dor (eds), *Minorities and the State in the Arab World* (Boulder, CO: Lynne Rienner, 1999), 129–45. Though the rise of military and political leaders from an Alawite and Druze background also sidelined traditional elite families in the Alawite and Druze communities. Firro, 'The Attitude of the Druzes', 98f.; Olson, *The Ba'th and Syria*, 77ff.; Seurat, *Syrie*, 20ff., 40.

159. See, for example, Courtney Jean Freer, *Rentier Islamism: The Influence of the Muslim Brotherhood in Gulf Monarchies* (New York: Oxford University Press, 2018), 47ff.

160. The multi-volume Shii commentary on the Majalla by Kashif al-Ghita, for example. Chibli Mallat, 'Shi'ism and Sunnism in Iraq: Revisiting the Codes', *Arab Law Quarterly* 8, 2 (1993), 141–59; Arminjon Hachem, *Les droits de l'homme*, 50ff.; Mallat, *Introduction*, 257f. For an in-depth study, see now Sara Pursley, *Familiar Futures: Time, Selfhood, and Sovereignty in Iraq* (Stanford: Stanford University Press, 2019).

161. Batatu, *The Old Social Classes*, 1017; Adeed Dawisha, *Iraq: A Political History* (Princeton: Princeton University Press, 2013), 144.

162. Batatu, *The Old Social Classes*, 1078f.; Osman, *Sectarianism in Iraq*, 77ff.

163. Batatu, *The Old Social Classes*, 1079–88, 1132.

164. This process was facilitated by Mawlud Mukhlis, an ally of Faisal I and vice-president of the Iraqi Senate, who had family connections to and land holdings in Tikrit. Batatu, *The Old Social Classes*, 1088f.

165. Sunnis were, for example, more often awarded 'friends of the President' status. Blaydes, *State of Repression*, 164, 180–95.

166. Batatu, *The Old Social Classes*.

167. One figure who was largely taken out of the curriculum was Abu Hurayra, a Companion of the Prophet held in high esteem amongst Sunnis but despised by Shia. Osman, *Sectarianism in Iraq*, 183. See also Davis, *Memories of State*, 7.

168. Al-Haidari, *Zur Soziologie des schiitischen Chiliasmus*, 56–69; Faleh A. Jabar, *The Shi'ite Movement in Iraq* (London: Saqi, 2003), 185–98.

169. Batatu, *The Old Social Classes*, ch. 4.

170. Osman, *Sectarianism in Iraq*, 74–7.

171. Jews and Assyrian Christians also played an important role. Batatu, *The Old Social Classes*, 422f., 649f., 998. For more on the Iraqi Communist Party, including the Shii role in it, see Dawisha, *Iraq*, 171ff.; Johan Franzén, *Red Star over Iraq: Iraqi Communism before Saddam* (London: Hurst, 2011); Tareq Y. Ismael, *The Rise and Fall of the Communist Party of Iraq* (Cambridge: Cambridge University Press, 2008).

172. Nakash, *The Shi'is of Iraq*, 132–6; Ahmed Khalid al-Rawi, 'The Campaign of Truth Program: US Propaganda in Iraq during the Early 1950s', in: Philip E. Muehlenbeck (ed.), *Religion and the Cold War: A Global Perspective* (Nashville: Vanderbilt University Press, 2012), 113–38; Fouad Jabir Kadhem, *The Sacred and the Secular: The 'Ulama of Najaf in Iraqi Politics between 1950 and 1980* (PhD, University of Exeter, 2012).

173. Keiko Sakai, 'Modernity and Tradition in the Islamic Movements in Iraq: Continuity and Discontinuity in the Role of the Ulama', *Arab Studies Quarterly* 23, 1 (2001), 37–53, 39–44; Salah al-Khurasan, *Hizb al-Da'wa al-Islamiyya: Haqa'iq wa Watha'iq: Fusul min Tajriba al-Haraka al-Islamiyya fi al-'Iraq Khilala 40 'Aman* (Damascus: al-Mu'assasa al-'Arabiyya li-l-Dirasat wa-l-Buhuth al-Istiratijiyya, 1999), 39ff., 66f., and passim. See also Ferhad Ibrahim, *Konfessionalismus und Politik in der arabischen Welt: Die Schiiten im Irak* (Münster: LIT, 1997).

174. There were incidents when Shii members were refused. Ende, 'Success', 237.

175. Muhanad Seloom, 'An Unhappy Return: What the Iraqi Islamic Party Gave up to Gain Power', *Carnegie Middle East Center*, 19 November 2018, https://carnegie-mec.org/2018/11/19/unhappy-return-what-iraqi-islamic-party-gave-up-to-gain-power-pub-77747.

176. Abisaab and Abisaab, *The Shi'ites of Lebanon*, 65; Mahdi Amil, *Madkhal ila Naqd al-Fikr al-Ta'ifi: Al-Qadiyya al-Filastiniyya fi Idiyulujiyyat al-Burjwaziyya al-Lubnaniyya* (Beirut: Dar al-Farabi, 1989); Amil, *Fi al-Dawla al-Ta'ifiyya* (Beirut: Dar al-Farabi, 2003, first published 1986); Samer Frangie, 'Theorizing from the Periphery: The Intellectual Project of Mahdi 'Amil', *International Journal of*

Middle East Studies 44, 3 (2012), 465–82; Hideaki Hayakawa, 'What does Antisectarianism Oppose? Lebanese Communists' Debates on Sectarianism, 1975–1981', *British Journal of Middle Eastern Studies* (published online, 1 September 2021).

177. Toby Matthiesen, 'The Cold War and the Communist Party of Saudi Arabia, 1975–1991', *Journal of Cold War Studies* 22, 3 (2020), 32–62; Matthiesen, 'Migration, Minorities, and Radical Networks: Labour Movements and Opposition Groups in Saudi Arabia, 1950–1975', *International Review of Social History* 59, 3 (2014), 473–504.

178. Staci Strobl, 'From Colonial Policing to Community Policing in Bahrain: The Historical Persistence of Sectarianism', *International Journal of Comparative and Applied Criminal Justice* 35, 1 (2011), 19–37; Strobl, *Sectarian Order in Bahrain: The Social and Colonial Origins of Criminal Justice* (Lanham: Lexington, 2018); Marc Owen Jones, *Political Repression in Bahrain* (Cambridge: Cambridge University Press, 2020); 'Abd al-Nabi al-'Akri, *Al-Tanzimat al-Yasariyya fi al-Jazira wa-l-Khalij al-'Arabi* (Beirut: Dar al-Kunuz al-Adabiyya, 2003); al-Shehabi, *Contested Modernity*.

179. Raoul Motika, 'Islam in Post-Soviet Azerbaijan', *Archives de sciences sociales des religions* 46, 115 (2001), 111–24; Brondz and Aslanova, 'Sunni-Shia Issue'; Adam, 'Why Do They Cry?'; Balci, 'Between Sunnism and Shiism', 206f.; Balci and Goyushov, 'Changing Islam in Post-Soviet Azerbaijan', 198ff. At the height of World War II, however, under pressure by German forces pushing eastwards, separate Sunni and Shii spiritual directorates were established in 1943/4, with the Shii one based in Baku. Motadel, *Islam and Nazi Germany's War*, 175.

180. There is some confusion about the relationship between the two groups and their origin, in part spurred by their similar name. Alawites were previously called Nusayris, and we have gotten to know them as a sub-branch of Shiism concentrated predominantly along the Syrian coast (and as important in the Syrian Baath party).

181. See earlier mentions of Qizilbash for full references. For a discussion of the link between the Qizilbash and modern Alevis, see Ayfer Karakaya-Stump, 'The Vefa'iyye, the Bektashiyye and Genealogies of "Heterodox" Islam in Anatolia: Rethinking the Köprülü Paradigm', *Turcica* 44 (2012–3), 279–300; Karakaya-Stump, *Subjects of the Sultan, Disciples of the Shah: Formation and Transformation of the Kizilbash/Alevi Communities in Ottoman Anatolia* (PhD, Harvard University, 2008); Kafadar, *Between Two Worlds*, 66f., 137f.; Yildirim, 'The Safavid-Qizilbash Ecumene'. These communities, for example, retained texts that showed strong Shii and Sufi influences from the Safavid period, even though their ritual practices diverged from those proscribed by the texts. Anke Otter-Beaujean, 'Stellenwert der Buyruk-Handschriften im Alevitum', in: Krisztina Kehl-Bodrogi, Barbara Kellner-Heinkele, and Anke Otter-Beaujean (eds), *Syncretistic Religious Communities in the Near East: Collected Papers of the International Symposium 'Alevism in Turkey and Comparable Syncretistic Religious Communities in the Near East in the Past and Present', Berlin, 14–17 April 1995*

(Leiden: Brill, 1997), 213–26; Ayfer Karakaya-Stump, 'Documents and "Buyruk" Manuscripts in the Private Archives of Alevi Dede Families: An Overview', *British Journal of Middle Eastern Studies* 37, 3 (2010), 273–86.

182. Soner Cagaptay, *Islam, Secularism and Nationalism in Modern Turkey: Who is a Turk?* (London: Routledge, 2006), 116–21; Procházka-Eisl and Procházka, *The Plain of Saints and Prophets*, 172f. These Alawites also increasingly downplayed difference in ritual practice and largely participated in the Sunni Muslim ritual calendar celebrated in their surroundings, except for Eid al-Ghadir. Ibid., 93–108. They also held the *Ahl al-Bayt* in high regard. Ibid., 87–90.

183. For the debate on whether the mass killing of the Armenians should be called a genocide, see, amongst others, Rouben Paul Adalian, 'Armenian Genocide (1915–1923)', Armenian National Institute, https://www.armenian-genocide.org/genocide.html.

184. Martin van Bruinessen, 'Between Dersim and Dâlahû: Reflections on Kurdish Alevism and the Ahl-i Haqq Religion', in: Shahrokh Raei (ed.), *Islamic Alternatives: Non-Mainstream Religion in Persianate Societies* (Wiesbaden: Harrassowitz, 2017), 65–93; van Bruinessen, '"Aslını inkar eden haramzadedir!": The Debate on the Ethnic Identity of the Kurdish Alevis', in: Krisztina Kehl-Bodrogi, Barbara Kellner-Heinkele, and Anke Otter-Beaujean (eds), *Syncretistic Religious Communities in the Near East: Collected Papers of the International Symposium 'Alevism in Turkey and Comparable Syncretistic Religious Communities in the Near East in the Past and Present', Berlin, 14–17 April 1995* (Leiden: Brill, 1997), 1–23; Kieser, *Der verpasste Friede*, 382–408; David Shankland, *The Alevis in Turkey: The Emergence of a Secular Islamic Tradition* (London: RoutledgeCurzon, 2003), 18f. See also the special issue of *Kurdish Studies* 8, 1 (2020) on Alevi Kurds.

185. See, amongst others, Metin Atmaca, 'The Road to Sèvres: Kurdish Elites' Quest for Self-Determination after World War I', *International Journal of Conflict and Violence* 16 (2022), forthcoming.

186. Irène Mélikoff, *Hadji Bektach: Un mythe et ses avatars: Genèse et évolution du soufisme populaire en Turquie* (Leiden: Brill, 1998), 179–97.

187. The Shabaks, who lived in what would become part of Iraq, may also have origins in the Qizilbash milieus. Martin van Bruinessen, 'A Kızılbash Community in Iraqi Kurdistan: The Shabak', *Les annales de l'autre Islam* 5 (1998), 185–96. On the Fayli Kurds, see van Bruinessen, 'Faylis, Kurds and Lurs: Ambiguity on the Frontier of Iran and Iraq: An Overview of the Literature', Conference Paper, 12 April 2018; Michiel Leezenberg, 'Between Assimilation and Deportation: The Shabak and the Kakais in Northern Iraq', in: Krisztina Kehl-Bodrogi, Barbara Kellner-Heinkele, and Anke Otter-Beaujean (eds), *Syncretistic Religious Communities in the Near East: Collected Papers of the International Symposium 'Alevism in Turkey and Comparable Syncretistic Religious Communities in the Near East in the Past and Present', Berlin, 14–17 April 1995* (Leiden: Brill, 1997), 155–74.

188. Nur Ali (b. 1896), for example, was an Ahl-e Haqq leader who studied in Qom and sought to downplay the differences between the Ahl-e Haqq and Twelver Shiism. He was the founder of a reformist faction amongst the Ahl-e Haqq,

which were generally accepted by the Shii clergy, including after 1979, while the other part of the community was not. See Ziba Mir-Hosseini, 'Breaking the Seal: The New Face of the Ahl-e Haqq', in: Krisztina Kehl-Bodrogi, Barbara Kellner-Heinkele, and Anke Otter-Beaujean (eds), *Syncretistic Religious Communities in the Near East: Collected Papers of the International Symposium 'Alevism in Turkey and Comparable Syncretistic Religious Communities in the Near East in the Past and Present', Berlin, 14–17 April 1995* (Leiden: Brill, 1997), 175–94, 185–93; Mir-Hosseini, 'Inner Truth and Outer History: The Two Worlds of the Ahl-i Haqq of Kurdistan', *International Journal of Middle East Studies* 26, 2 (1994), 267–85; Mir-Hosseini, 'Redefining the Truth: Ahl-i Haqq and the Islamic Republic of Iran', *British Journal of Middle Eastern Studies* 21, 2 (1994), 211–28.

189. This was particularly the case of Zaza-speaking Alevi Kurds in Dersim. Cagaptay, *Islam*, 109.

190. Markus Dressler, *Die civil religion der Türkei: Kemalistische und alevitische Atatürk-Rezeption im Vergleich* (Würzburg: Ergon, 1999); Dressler, *Die alevitische Religion: Traditionslinien und Neubestimmungen* (Würzburg: Ergon, 2002), 170.

191. Shankland, *The Alevis in Turkey*.

192. Van Bruinessen, '"Aslını inkar eden haramzadedir!"', 13; David McDowall, *A Modern History of the Kurds* (London: I. B. Tauris, 2007), 194–202.

193. Hakan Yavuz, *Islamic Political Identity in Turkey* (Oxford: Oxford University Press, 2003), 139f.; Yavuz, 'The Matrix of Modern Turkish Islamic Movements'.

194. Dressler, *Die alevitische Religion*, 133f.; Martin van Bruinessen, 'Vom Osmanismus zum Separatismus: Religiöse und ethnische Hintergründe der Rebellion des Scheich Said', in: Jochen Blaschke and Martin van Bruinessen (eds), *Islam und Politik in der Türkei* (Berlin: Edition Parabolis, 1989), 109–65. For the Bektashis, see Cem Kara, *Grenzen überschreitende Derwische: Kulturbeziehungen des Bektaschi-Ordens 1826–1925* (Göttingen: Vandenhoeck & Ruprecht, 2019).

195. Birge, *The Bektashi Order*, 72f.

196. Most famous are the Frasheri brothers, whose literary output has clear Shii overtones and who are still revered in Albania, for example in the Albanian National Museum in Tirana. See H. T. Norris, *Popular Sufism in Eastern Europe: Sufi Brotherhoods and the Dialogue with Christianity and 'Heterodoxy'* (London: Routledge, 2006); Birge, *The Bektashi Order*; Nathalie Clayer, 'The Bektashi Institutions in Southeastern Europe: Alternative Muslim Official Structures and their Limits', *Die Welt des Islams* 52, 2 (2012), 183–203. In general, see now Robert Elsie, *The Albanian Bektashi: History and Culture of a Dervish Order in the Balkans* (London: I. B. Tauris, 2019).

197. Dressler, *Die alevitische Religion*, 127–70; Yavuz, *Islamic Political Identity*, 140f.

198. Şahin, *Empire and Power*, 244f. See also Gökhan Çetinsaya, 'Rethinking Nationalism and Islam: Some Preliminary Notes on the Roots of "Turkish-Islamic Synthesis" in Modern Turkish Political Thought', *The Muslim World* 89, 3–4 (1999), 350–76, 368–76; Baki Tezcan, 'Lost in Historiography: An Essay on the Reasons for the Absence of a History of Limited Government in the Early Modern Ottoman Empire', *Middle Eastern Studies* 45, 3 (2009), 477–505, 488–95.

199. Yildirim, 'Sunni Orthodox vs Shi'ite Heterodox?'; Markus Dressler, *Writing Religion: The Making of Turkish Alevi Islam* (Oxford: Oxford University Press, 2013); Dressler, 'Inventing Orthodoxy', 173; Ayfer Karakaya-Stump, 'The Vefa'iyye, the Bektashiyye and Genealogies of "Heterodox" Islam in Anatolia: Rethinking the Köprülü Paradigm', *Turcica* 44 (2012–3), 279–300. For translations, see Devin DeWeese, 'Foreword', in: Mehmed Fuad Köprülü, *Early Mystics in Turkish Literature*, ed./trans. by Gary Leiser and Robert Dankoff (London: Routledge, 2006); Mehmed Fuad Köprülü, *Islam in Anatolia after the Turkish Invasion: Prolegomena*, ed./trans. by Gary Leiser (Salt Lake City: University of Utah Press, 1993). An upsurge in writings about, and re-editing of, Ottoman archival sources on the Qizilbash, the Bektashis, or other 'unorthodox' groups that were published since the late twentieth century implied those connections. Stefan Winter, 'The Kizilbaş of Syria and Ottoman Shiism', in: Christine Woodhead (ed.), *The Ottoman World* (London: Routledge, 2011), 171–83, 171.

200. Dressler, *Die alevitische Religion*, 154–70; Mardin, *Religion and Social Change*, 100f.

201. Sencer Ayata, 'Patronage, Party, and State: The Politicization of Islam in Turkey', *Middle East Journal* 50, 1 (1996), 40–56, 44f.; Svante E. Cornell and M. K. Kaya, 'Political Islam in Turkey and the Naqshbandi-Khalidi Order', *Current Trends in Islamist Ideology* 19 (2015), 39–62; Omer F. Erturk, 'The Myth of Turkish Islam: The Influence of Naqshbandi-Gümüşhanevi Thought in Turkish Islamic Orthodoxy', *British Journal of Middle Eastern Studies* 49, 2 (2022), 223–47; Yavuz, *Islamic Political Identity*, 133–50; Yavuz, *Secularism and Muslim Democracy in Turkey* (Cambridge: Cambridge University Press, 2009), 40, 50ff., 122ff., 178–80, 186; Simon A. Waldman and Emre Caliskan, *The New Turkey and its Discontents* (London: Hurst, 2016), 49–82; Banu Eligür, *The Mobilization of Political Islam in Turkey* (Cambridge: Cambridge University Press, 2010), 55ff.

202. Ceren Lord, 'Between Islam and the Nation: Nation-Building, the Ulama and Alevi Identity in Turkey', *Nations and Nationalism* 23, 1 (2017), 48–67.

203. Hans-Lukas Kieser, 'The Anatolian Alevis' Ambivalent Encounter with Modernity in Late Ottoman and Early Republican Turkey', in: Alessandro Monsutti, Silvia Naef, and Farian Sabahi (eds), *The Other Shiites: From the Mediterranean to Central Asia* (Bern: Peter Lang, 2008), 41–57, 57; Ioannis N. Grigoriadis, *Instilling Religion in Greek and Turkish Nationalism: A 'Sacred Synthesis'* (Basingstoke: Palgrave Macmillan, 2012), 50–90.

204. Martin van Bruinessen, 'Kurds, Turks and the Alevi Revival in Turkey', *Middle East Report* 200 (1996), 7–10; Yavuz, *Islamic Political Identity*, 65–70; Karin Vorhoff, '"Let's Reclaim our History and Culture!": Imagining Alevi Community in Contemporary Turkey', *Die Welt des Islams* 38, 2 (1998), 220–52.

205. David Shankland, 'Are the Alevis Shi'ite?', in: Lloyd Ridgeon (ed.), *Shi'i Islam and Identity: Religion, Politics and Change in the Global Muslim Community* (London: I. B. Tauris, 2012), 210–28.

206. The DHKP-C, a Marxist-Leninist militant movement, had recruited heavily amongst Alevis. Some of its ideology, including the symbolism around the

martyrdom of its prisoners, who have engaged in hunger strikes to protest prison conditions that have led to their death, have clear Shii overtones. Ariane Bonzon, 'Behind Bars: Resisting the Turkish State', *Le Monde diplomatique*, October 2021.

207. Dressler, 'Inventing Orthodoxy', 173.

208. Devji, *Muslim Zion*; Rieck, *The Shias of Pakistan*, xi; Justin Jones, '"The Pakistan that is Going to be Sunnistan": Indian Shi'i Responses to the Pakistan Movement', in: Ali Usman Qasmi and Megan Eaton Robb (eds), *Muslims against the Muslim League: Critiques of the Idea of Pakistan* (Cambridge: Cambridge University Press, 2017), 350–80, 354f. See, for example, n.a., *Presidential Address Delivered by Raja Mohammad Amir Ahmad Khan of Mahmudabad at the Bombay Presidency Muslim League Conference, Hubli, May 24–25, 1940* (Lucknow: Lucknow Publishing House, n.d.).

209. This included a possible confederation of Islamic states, of which, he thought, Iran would also be supportive. Landau, *The Politics of Pan-Islam*, 226f. Iqbal's doctoral dissertation showed a certain Ismaili influence, although he later downplayed that influence. Muhammad Iqbal, *The Development of Metaphysics in Persia: A Contribution to the History of Muslim Philosophy* (Lahore: Bazm-i-Iqbal, 1959). I owe this point to Faisal Devji, 'The Problem of Muslim Universality', in: Edmund Burke and Robert J. Mankin (eds), *Islam and World History: The Ventures of Marshall Hodgson* (Chicago: University of Chicago Press, 2018), 145–64. The role of Shia in the Muslim League has been compared with that of Christians in Arab nationalism, itself a movement that was supposed to overcome religious and sectarian difference. Devji, *Muslim Zion*, 67.

210. Fuchs, *In a Pure Muslim Land*, 17, 38–47; Jones, '"The Pakistan that is Going to be Sunnistan"'.

211. Three senior *mujtahids* issued a joint fatwa in 1920 arguing that 'Shia should keep strictly aloof from the proposals published by the Khilafat committees'. Jones, *Shi'a Islam*, 172–83, quote on page 178. For other Sunni–Shia fissures in the movement, see Qureshi, *Pan-Islam*, 114, 169, 276.

212. Afak Haydar, 'The Politicization of the Shias and the Development of the Tehrik-e-Nifaz-e-Fiqh-e-Jafaria in Pakistan', in: Charles H. Kennedy (ed.), *Pakistan: 1992* (Boulder, CO: Westview Press, 1993), 75–93, 77.

213. Cited after: Khaled Ahmed, *Sectarian War: Pakistan's Sunni-Shia Violence and its Links to the Middle East* (Oxford: Oxford University Press, 2011), 7. For more on him, see Jalal, *The Sole Spokesman*.

214. For an account of the court proceedings between 1968 and 1984, see Devji, *Muslim Zion*, 215–22.

215. Ibid., 221.

216. The Jinnah case was not the first or last in Pakistan during which the sectarian affiliation of a deceased person was debated to determine inheritance, but it was certainly the most prominent and consequential. Lucy Carroll, 'Application of the Islamic Law of Succession: Was the Propositus a Sunnī or a Shī'ī?', *Islamic Law and Society* 2, 1 (1995), 24–42. The descendants of the Nawabs of

Rampur, a Shii princely state in Northern India, also fought out a bitter inheritance dispute after Indian independence, in which one side argued that Shii law should be used to divide the inheritance. *India Legal*, 'Rampur Dispute: The Great Indian Property Row', 10 August 2019, https://www.indialegallive. com/legal-eye/rampur-dispute-the-great-indian-property-row/.

217. For background on the history of the Ahmadis, see Adil Hussain Khan, *From Sufism to Ahmadiyya: A Muslim Minority Movement in South Asia* (Bloomington: Indiana University Press, 2015).

218. Linking Ahmadis to the legacy of British imperialism, he claimed that 'in the four corners of the world there was no power which could confront them except Islam. For this reason, it became inevitable for the imperialistic power to try to disintegrate the forces of Islam, not through direct attack, but by raising, within Islam, false sects which, bearing the name of Islam, might really pull down its principles and its fundamental bases. These sects were to be extended all possible financial aid, so that they should work on the imperialists' account and spy on the Muslims.' His book was also translated into English: Ehsan Elahi Zaheer, *Qadiyaniat: An Analytical Survey* (Lahore: Idara Tarjuman al-Sunnah, 1972), 17. He wrote a similar treatise on the Bahai movement. I consulted the Arabic version. Ehsan Elahi Zaheer, *Al-Babiyya: 'Ard wa Naqd* (Lahore: Idara Tarjuman al-Sunnah, 1981).

219. For Devji, there is a clear logic that follows from the denunciation of the Ahmadis by figures such as Muhammad Iqbal to the persecution of other groups. For Iqbal's anti-Ahmadi thought, see Devji, *Muslim Zion*, 152–61.

220. Jones, *Shi'a Islam*, 222. In Hyderabad, the last large Muslim state that had remained semi-independent, many of the old Shii elites fled after the integration of Hyderabad into the new Indian state, and the old town, which had been largely Muslim and Shii, fell into disrepair, while the ownership of a number of *waqfs* that had supported Ashurkhanas and Muharram ceremonies became contested. Shireen Mirza, 'Waqf and Urban Space: Production of Minority Identity in Hyderabad's Old City', in: Jyotirmaya Tripathy and Sudarsan Padmanabhan (eds), *Becoming Minority: How Discourses and Policies Produce Minorities in Europe and India* (Los Angeles: Sage, 2014), 293–313. A famous case of expropriation relates to the Mahmudabad estate, which the Indian state confiscated after the Raja of Mahmudabad, a major financier of the Muslim League, took Pakistani citizenship, even though the rest of his family remained in India. Amy Kazmin, 'India, Pakistan and One Man's Battle to Recover his Ancestral Home', *Financial Times*, 9 June 2017.

221. In 1948, the English-language journal of the Shii *madrasa* in Lucknow, for example, hoped that 'the conditions which 90 years of British rule in this country, with its basic principle of non-intervention and religious toleration had made us accustomed to', would continue in independent India. Editor's Table, *The Muslim Review* 35, 1 (1948), 1. A few years later, it argued that this religious freedom existed, and that it was able to send preachers across Northern India and to East Africa and Burma. See Khan, 'Local Nodes'.

222. Şahin, *Empire and Power*, 205ff.
223. Laurence Louër, *Transnational Shia Politics: Religious and Political Networks in the Gulf* (London: Hurst, 2008), 12–30.
224. Markus Wachowski, *Sāda in Ṣanaʿāʾ: Zur Fremd- und Eigenwahrnehmung der Prophetennachkommen in der Republik Jemen* (Berlin: Klaus Schwarz, 2004), 139; Stookey, *Yemen*, 180ff.
225. Dresch, *A History of Modern Yemen*, 9.
226. Jacob, *Kings of Arabia*, 101, 273f.; Rabi, *Yemen*, 22.
227. 'It is the Christians who say there is a difference between Zaidis and Shafiʿis. But they are ignorant in these matters because they even say that the Shafiʿis do not want to be ruled by the Zaidis. Now, who could believe this?' I owe this quote to Messick, *The Calligraphic State*, 53, 278, who has it from Gerald J. Obermeyer, 'Al-Iman and al-Imam: Ideology and State in Yemen', in: Marwan R. Buheiry (ed.), *Intellectual Life in the Arab East, 1890–1939* (Beirut: American University of Beirut, 1981), 178–92, and Ettore Rossi, 'La Stampa nel Yemen', *Oriente Moderno* 18, 10 (1938), 568–80, 569. When the governor of Ibb under both the Ottomans and the Imam, Ismail Basalama, was asked about the issue of Zaydi rule over a Shafii district, he likewise replied that it was no problem, and that 'everything you have heard in the way of foreign propaganda is nothing but lies and slander against Yemen and its people'. Messick, *The Calligraphic State*, 52.
228. Ferris, *Nasser's Gamble*.
229. Quoted in: Messick, *The Calligraphic State*, 53.
230. The commission started work in 1975, and one of its aims was to overcome *madhhab* particularities, while it also resorted to the other *madhhabs* to inform certain rulings. Messick, *The Calligraphic State*, 68ff.; vom Bruck, 'Regimes of Piety Revisited', 187.
231. Haykel, *Revival and Reform*, 193, 218f. For an account of Zaydi–Shafii relations, see John E. Peterson, *Yemen: The Search for a Modern State* (Baltimore: Johns Hopkins University Press, 1982).
232. Ayman Hamidi, 'Inscriptions of Violence in Northern Yemen: Haunting Histories, Unstable Moral Spaces', *Middle Eastern Studies* 45, 2 (2009), 165–87, 166. See also Gabriele vom Bruck, 'Disputing Descent-Based Authority in the Idiom of Religion: The Case of the Republic of Yemen', *Die Welt des Islams* 38, 2 (1998), 149–91.
233. For an in-depth study of the Sada and their ways of remembering the past and coping with their situation since 1962, see Gabriele vom Bruck, *Islam, Memory, and Morality in Yemen: Ruling Families in Transition* (New York: Palgrave Macmillan, 2005). See also Wachowski, *Sāda in Ṣanaʿāʾ*.
234. Specific calls to prayer in Zaydi mosques were allowed, and the Mufti of the republic was usually of Zaydi origin. Laurent Bonnefoy, *Salafism in Yemen: Transnationalism and Religious Identity* (London: Hurst, 2011), 266. The Zaydi call to prayer differs marginally from the call to prayer of the Shafiis. They have, for example, only a twofold *takbir* at the start of the call to prayer (not a

fourfold one like the Shafiis) and add *hayy ala khayr al-amal* (onwards towards the best of works). See Strothmann, *Kultus*, 47–54, esp. 54. There are also debates amongst Zaydis on this point: Strothmann, 'Das Problem', 32f., and it seems that al-Qasim initially favoured the Sunni call to prayer and was not in favour of adding *ala khayr al-amal*, which was edited out in later Zaydi tradition. Madelung, *Der Imam*, 133f. The actual prayer also differs marginally, and different aspects are close to Imamis, Shafiis, and Malikis, but rather different from Hanafis. In sum, it is difficult to position Zaydis easily on the Shii-Sunni spectrum regarding prayer. Strothmann, *Kultus*, 55–8.

235. Bernard Haykel, 'Rebellion, Migration or Consultative Democracy? The Zaydis and their Detractors in Yemen', in: R. Leveau, F. Mermier, and U. Steinbach (eds), *Le Yémen contemporain* (Paris: Karthala, 1999), 193–201; vom Bruck, *Islam*, 239; F. Gregory Gause, *Saudi-Yemeni Relations: Domestic Structures and Foreign Influence* (New York: Columbia University Press, 1990). At the same time, Yemenis and academics allege that Saudi Arabia followed a policy of coordinated instability, with the aim of preventing the central government from collapsing but also from becoming too strong. Saudi Arabia was alleged to have paid stipends to most important tribal leaders and politicians, often backing various opposing forces—sometimes the southern secessionists, sometimes others—in the process. Bonnefoy, *Salafism in Yemen*, 5ff.

236. Enayat, *Modern Islamic Political Thought*. Some of the activist Shii clerics, such as Murtaza Mutahhari, denounced nationalism as a modern ideology bent on dividing Muslims. Ibid., 120–5.

237. See, in general, Sally N. Cummings and Raymond Hinnebusch (eds), *Sovereignty after Empire: Comparing the Middle East and Central Asia* (Edinburgh: Edinburgh University Press, 2011).

238. Weiss, *In the Shadow of Sectarianism*, 19.

239. That this was not always the case shows Gerges in his double history of Arab nationalism and Sunni Islamism in Egypt. Fawaz A. Gerges, *Making the Arab World: Nasser, Qutb, and the Clash that Shaped the Middle East* (Princeton, NJ: Princeton University Press, 2018).

CHAPTER 11

1. Toby Dodge, 'Intervention and Dreams of Exogenous Statebuilding: The Application of Liberal Peacebuilding in Afghanistan and Iraq', *Review of International Studies* 39, 5 (2013), 1189–212.

2. Baqer Moin, *Khomeini: Life of the Ayatollah* (London: I. B. Tauris, 1999), 7ff. Moin's biography is the standard account. For more, see Katajun Amirpur, *Khomeini: Der Revolutionär des Islams* (Munich: C. H. Beck, 2021); Arshin Adib-Moghaddam, *A Critical Introduction to Khomeini* (Cambridge: Cambridge University Press, 2014).

3. Hamid Algar, 'KHOMEINI', *EIr*.

4. Vanessa Martin, *Creating an Islamic State: Khomeini and the Making of a New Iran* (London: I. B. Tauris, 2000), 53–64.

5. Moin, *Khomeini*, 92–106; Algar, 'KHOMEINI'.

6. See references in note 60 on page 613 and note 139 on page 643, as well as related literature throughout the book.

7. Elvire Corboz, *Guardians of Shi'ism: Sacred Authority and Transnational Family Networks* (Edinburgh: Edinburgh University Press, 2015); Elvire Corboz, 'Khomeini in Najaf: The Religious and Political Leadership of an Exiled Ayatollah', *Die Welt des Islams* 55, 2 (2015), 221–48.

8. There is an English translation: Sayyid Ruhullah Musawi Khomeini, *Islamic Government: Governance of the Jurist*, trans. by Hamid Algar (Institute for the Compilation and Publication of the Works of Imam Khomeini, n.d.), https://www.al-islam.org/islamic-government-governance-jurist-sayyid-ruhullah-musawi-khomeini.

9. Martin, *Creating an Islamic State*, 116ff.; Mateo Mohammad Farzaneh, *The Iranian Constitutional Revolution and the Clerical Leadership of Khurasani* (Syracuse: Syracuse University Press, 2015). See also Eskandar Sadeghi-Boroujerdi, *Revolution and its Discontents: Political Thought and Reform in Iran* (Cambridge: Cambridge University Press, 2019), 59–135.

10. Hamid Enayat, 'Iran: Khumayni's Concept of the "Guardianship of the Jurisconsult"', in: James P. Piscatori (ed.), *Islam in the Political Process* (Cambridge: Cambridge University Press, 1983), 160–80. See also Constance Arminjon Hachem, *Chiisme et État: Les clercs à l'épreuve de la modernité* (Paris: CNRS Editions, 2013).

11. Annabelle Sreberny-Mohammadi and Ali Mohammadi, *Small Media, Big Revolution: Communication, Culture, and the Iranian Revolution* (Minneapolis: University of Minnesota Press, 1994). See also Charles Hirschkind, *The Ethical Soundscape: Cassette Sermons and Islamic Counterpublics* (New York: Columbia University Press, 2006).

12. Michael Axworthy, *Revolutionary Iran: A History of the Islamic Republic* (London: Allen Lane, 2013), 101f.

13. Ibid., 104–8.

14. Fischer, *Iran*; Theda Skocpol, 'Rentier State and Shi'a Islam in the Iranian Revolution', *Theory and Society* 11, 3 (1982), 265–83. See also Hamid Dabashi, *Shi'ism: A Religion of Protest* (Cambridge, MA: Belknap Press, 2011).

15. Paul Lewis, 'On Khomeini's Flight: The Morning Prayers on Newspaper Mats', *New York Times*, 2 February 1979. Amongst the vast literature on the revolution, see sources cited in this chapter as well as Charles Kurzman, *The Unthinkable Revolution in Iran* (Cambridge, MA: Harvard University Press, 2004); Mehran Kamrava, *Revolution in Iran: The Roots of Turmoil* (London: Routledge, 1990).

16. Axworthy, *Revolutionary Iran*, 1.

17. There is debate, however, as to whether it is authentic according to Shii Hadith or not. See WikiShia, 'Every Day is Ashura and Every Land is Karbala',

7 December 2020, https://en.wikishia.net/view/Every_Day_Is_Ashura_and_ Every_Land_Is_Karbala.

18. Ali Rahnema, *An Islamic Utopian: A Political Biography of Ali Shariati* (London: I. B. Tauris, 1998).

19. Ali Shariati, 'Red Shi'ism (the Religion of Martyrdom) vs. Black Shi'ism (the Religion of Mourning)', *Iran Chamber*, http://www.iranchamber.com/ personalities/ashariati/works/red_black_shiism.php.

20. *Shafaqna English*, 'Indonesian Students are under the Influence of Ali Shariati's Thoughts', 22 June 2019. In response to the enthusiasm with which some South African Muslims embraced the revolutionary and pan-Islamic message from Iran after 1979, some Deobandi-influenced scholars invoked anti-Shiism to undermine these ties and criticise the revolution and Iran. Ingram, *Revival from Below*, 184. In South Africa, this had a domestic political angle as well given the Shah's close ties with the Apartheid Regime. Houchang E. Chehabi, 'South Africa and Iran in the Apartheid Era', *Journal of Southern African Studies* 42, 4 (2016), 687–709.

21. Hamid Dabashi, *Theology of Discontent: The Ideological Foundation of the Islamic Revolution in Iran*, 2nd ed. (London: Routledge, 2017), 163, 166, 180f., 196; Mahmood T. Davari, *The Political Thought of Ayatollah Murtaza Mutahhari: An Iranian Theoretician of the Islamic State* (London: Routledge, 2005).

22. Amongst a very large literature on the revolution, see Said Amir Arjomand, *The Turban for the Crown: The Islamic Revolution in Iran* (New York: Oxford University Press, 1988). For the struggles at the heart of the new state, see Siavush Randjbar-Daemi, *The Quest for Authority in Iran: A History of the Presidency from Revolution to Rouhani* (London: I. B. Tauris, 2017). For the Tudeh and the revolution, see, amongst others, Jeremy Friedman, 'The Enemy of my Enemy: The Soviet Union, East Germany, and the Iranian Tudeh Party's Support for Ayatollah Khomeini', *Journal of Cold War Studies* 20, 2 (2018), 3–37.

23. H. E. Chehabi, 'The Anti-Shah Opposition and Lebanon', in: H. E. Chehabi, *Distant Relations: Iran and Lebanon in the Last 500 Years* (London: I. B. Tauris, 2006), 180–98. See also Roschanack Shaery-Eisenlohr, *Shi'ite Lebanon: Transnational Religion and the Making of National Identities* (New York: Columbia University Press, 2008).

24. Interview with a former fighter of the Lebanese Forces, Beirut, 2018.

25. Johnson, *Class and Client*, 174–87.

26. Nakash, *Reaching for Power*, 100. See also Rania Maktabi, 'The Lebanese Census of 1932 Revisited: Who are the Lebanese?', *British Journal of Middle Eastern Studies* 26, 2 (1999), 219–41; Halawi, *A Lebanon Defied*, 77; Monika Pohl-Schöberlein, *Die schiitische Gemeinschaft des Südlibanon (Ğabal ʿĀmil) innerhalb des libanesischen konfessionellen Systems* (Berlin: Klaus Schwarz, 1986). For background on the Lebanese confessional system, see Mayssoun Zein al-Din, *Religion als politischer Faktor? Eine Untersuchung am Beispiel der Frage des politischen Konfessionalismus in Libanon* (Baden-Baden: Nomos, 2010).

27. The Communist Party and the Socialist Action Party (although one should not forget that the Communist Party retains a formal alliance with Hizbullah, which is the reason for why their project is called the 'resistance' and not the Islamic resistance). Abisaab and Abisaab, *The Shi'ites of Lebanon*; Halawi, *A Lebanon Defied*, 62.

28. Nakash, *Reaching for Power*, 109–16. See also H. E. Chehabi and Majid Tafreshi, 'Musa Sadr and Iran', in: H. E. Chehabi, *Distant Relations: Iran and Lebanon in the Last 500 Years* (London: I. B. Tauris, 2006), 137–61; Augustus R. Norton, *Amal and the Shi'a: Struggle for the Soul of Lebanon* (Austin: University of Texas Press, 1987), 39ff., and passim. For more on this, see Rodger Shanahan, *The Shi'a of Lebanon: Clans, Parties and Clerics* (London: I. B. Tauris, 2005), 165; Johnson, *Class and Client*, 149.

29. Weiss, *In the Shadow of Sectarianism*, 2f. Simultaneously, Shii intellectuals challenged dominant historical narratives of Lebanon in which Shia featured little. Halawi, *A Lebanon Defied*, 25.

30. Ibid., 68, 74f.; Johnson, *Class and Client*, 170–4. For background, see Max Weiss, '"Don't Throw Yourself Away to the Dark Continent": Shi'i Migration to West Africa and the Hierarchies of Exclusion in Lebanese Culture', *Studies in Ethnicity and Nationalism* 7, 1 (2007), 46–63. On donations to Tyre, see Machlis, *Shi'i Sectarianism*, 228n16. For the story of Christian Lebanese migrants, see Arsan, *Interlopers of Empire*.

31. Rahaf Aldoughli, 'Interrogating the Constructions of Masculinist Protection and Militarism in the Syrian Constitution of 1973', *Journal of Middle East Women's Studies* 15, 1 (2019), 48–74.

32. Lebanese clerics such as Muhammad Jawad Mughniyya, Yusuf al-Faqih, and Habib al-Ibrahim sought to proselytise amongst Alawites and bring them closer to Twelver Shiism, in part supported by the Grand Ayatollah at the time, Muhsin al-Hakim. In 1952, a delegation of Alawite Shaykhs was received by the then Mufti of Syria, Muhammad Shukri al-Ustuwani, who also accepted their 'Jafari' credentials and allowed them to establish a committee that would organise examinations for future clerics in Latakia. See Mervin, 'Quelques jalons', esp. 287; Mervin, 'Des nosayris aux ja'farites: Le processus de "chiitisation" des alaouites', in: Baudouin Dupret (ed.), *La Syrie au present: Reflets d'une société* (Paris: Sindbad, 2007), 359–64; Mervin, 'L'"entité alaouite"'. But see also Alkan, *Non-Sunni Muslims in the Late Ottoman Empire*, 33.

33. He was first given support for his movement of the downtrodden and then its armed wing, Amal. Fouad Ajami, *The Vanished Imam: Musa al-Sadr and the Shia of Lebanon* (Ithaca: Cornell University Press, 1986), 174; Yaron Friedman, 'Musa al-Sadr and the Missing Fatwa concerning the 'Alawi Religion', *British Journal of Middle Eastern Studies* (online, 2022).

34. Martin Kramer, 'Syria's Alawis and Shi'ism', in: Martin Kramer (ed.), *Shi'ism, Resistance, and Revolution* (Boulder, CO: Westview Press, 1987), 237–54, 247ff.; Talhamy, 'The Fatwas'.

35. In general for the Shirazis, see Louër, *Transnational Shia Politics*, 120–8 and passim. For Iraqi support to the Syrian Brotherhood, see Brynjar Lia, 'The Islamist Uprising in Syria, 1976–82: The History and Legacy of a Failed Revolt', *British Journal of Middle Eastern Studies* 43, 4 (2016), 541–59, 549.

36. Machlis, *Shi'i Sectarianism*, 161; Stephan Rosiny, '"The Tragedy of Fāṭima al-Zahrā"' in the Debate of Two Shiite Theologians in Lebanon', in: Rainer Brunner and Werner Ende (eds), *The Twelver Shia in Modern Times: Religious Culture & Political History* (Leiden: Brill, 2001), 207–19; Kantz Feder, 'Fatima's Revolutionary Image'. For an example, see Ali Shariati, *Fatima is Fatima*, trans. by Laleh Bakhtiar (Tehran: Shariati Foundation, 1981). See also Rawand Osman, *Female Personalities in the Qur'an and Sunna: Examining the Major Sources of Imami Shi'i Islam* (Abingdon: Routledge, 2015).

37. Von Maltzahn, *The Syria–Iran Axis*, 25f. Shariati wanted to be buried in Iran, but given the difficulty of transporting his body back to Iran at a time of heightened repression, he was buried in Sayyida Zaynab. Zeinab Safari, 'Ehsan-e Shariati: Mikhwahim Vaziat-e Pedaram Ejra Shavad', *Tarikh-e Irani*, 24 June 2014, http://tarikhirani.ir (accessed 31 December 2021). I thank Mohammad Ataie for this reference.

38. For more, see Sabrina Mervin, 'Sayyida Zaynab, banlieue de Damas ou nouvelle ville sainte chiite?', *Cahiers d'études sur la Méditerranée orientale et le monde turco-iranien* 22, 1 (1996), 149–62.

39. Zayn Kassam and Bridget Blomfield, 'Remembering Fatima and Zaynab: Gender in Perspective', in: Farhad Daftary, Amyn B. Sajoo, and Shainool Jiwa (eds), *The Shi'i World: Pathways in Tradition and Modernity* (London: I. B. Tauris, 2015), 211–28. See also Kamran Scot Aghaie, *The Martyrs of Karbala: Shi'i Symbols and Rituals in Modern Iran* (Seattle: University of Washington Press, 2004), 113–30. An Egyptian Sunni female writer, Bint al-Shati (pseudonym), wrote several works on the women around the Prophet, including Zaynab. Ruth Roded, 'Bint al-Shati's Wives of the Prophet: Feminist or Feminine?', *British Journal of Middle Eastern Studies* 33, 1 (2006), 51–66.

40. He even organised the despatch of units of Amal militants to Tehran on the final days of the revolution. Mohammad Ataie, 'Revolutionary Iran's 1979 Endeavor in Lebanon', *Middle East Policy* 20, 2 (2013), 137–57. For the Freedom Movement, see Houchang Chehabi, *Iranian Politics and Religious Modernism: The Liberation Movement of Iran under the Shah and Khomeini* (London: Tauris, 1990); Kim Ghattas, *Black Wave: Saudi Arabia, Iran, and the Forty-Year Rivalry that Unravelled Culture, Religion, and Collective Memory in the Middle East* (New York: Henry Holt, 2020).

41. In general, see Shaery-Eisenlohr, *Shi'ite Lebanon*, 119–57.

42. Martin, *Creating an Islamic State*, 115.

43. See, for example, Khomeini's speech on the occasion of the Hajj in 1980: Ruhollah Khomeini, *Islam and Revolution: Writings and Declarations of Imam Khomeini*, trans. by Hamid Algar (Berkeley: Mizan Press, 1981), 301f.; Landau, *The Politics of Pan-Islam*, 258ff. Khomeini's fatwa allowing Shia to pray behind a Sunni Imam specifically referred to Iranian Shia travelling in Europe, or to Shia

living in predominantly Sunni areas of Iran. Machlis, *Shiʻi Sectarianism*, 151; Hamid Algar, 'EMĀM-E JOMʻA', *EIr*.

44. See the coverage of the Taqrib conference, including videos of the sessions since the 1990s, on http://www.taghrib.org. See, for example, Kamyar Sadaqat Thamar Hussayni, *Shiʻahshinasi-i Ahl-i Sunnat va Chalishha-yi Fararuy-i An dar Dawran-i pas az Inqilab-i Islami-i Iran* (Tehran: World Forum for the Proximity of Islamic Schools of Thought, 2012). See the back issues of *Risalat al-Islam* and *Risalat al-Taqrib*: http://taqrib.ir/ar/magazine/categories. See also Wilfried Buchta, *Die iranische Schia und die islamische Einheit 1979–1996* (Hamburg: Deutsches Orient-Institut, 1997). Iran also established a university and a journal for the study of Islamic denominations. See https://urd.ac.ir/fa; https://mazaheb.urd.ac.ir.

45. James P. Piscatori and Amin Saikal, *Islam beyond Borders: The Umma in World Politics* (Cambridge: Cambridge University Press, 2019), esp. ch. 2 and 3.

46. Apparently, the anti-Sunni parts of Majlisi's *Bihar al-Anwar* were initially not published. Rainer Brunner, 'MAJLESI, Moḥammad-Bāqer', *EIr*. Following criticism by earlier modernist Shii clerics, they criticised flagellations during Muharram, arguing that they portrayed Shiism in a negative light. Ende, 'The Flagellations of Muharram'; Mervin, 'Ashura'. Ayatollah Khamenei and the Lebanese cleric Muhammad Hussain Fadlallah were against it. Other Shii clerics allow or even encourage it because it is a grassroots Shii practice popular amongst their followers. See, for example, Khamenei's official website: Khameini.ir, 'Tatbir is a Wrongful and Fabricated Tradition: Imam Khamenei', 7 October 2016, http://english.khamenei.ir/news/4209/Tatbir-is-a-wrongful-and-fabricated-tradition-Imam-Khamenei. On top of this, a dedicated pro-Khamenei website, http://tatbir.org, collects the testimonies of a wide range of senior Shii clerics discouraging the practice. Ali al-Sistani seems to allow it, and the Shirazis encourage it, although http://tatbir.org quotes al-Sistani as saying that some of the aspects of the rituals that are difficult to understand for outsiders should be avoided. See also Simon Wolfgang Fuchs, 'Third Wave Shiʻism: Sayyid 'Arif Husain al-Husaini and the Islamic Revolution in Pakistan', *Journal of the Royal Asiatic Society* 24, 3 (2014), 493–510, 502f.; Raihan Ismail, *Saudi Clerics and Shiʻa Islam* (New York: Oxford University Press, 2016), 92f.; Oliver Scharbrodt, 'Contesting Ritual Practices in Twelver Shiism: Modernism, Sectarianism and the Politics of Self-Flagellation (taṭbīr)', *British Journal of Middle Eastern Studies* (online, 2022).

47. *Middle East Contemporary Survey* (1988), 189f., 689–92; Moin, *Khomeini*, 305.

48. Martin, *Creating an Islamic State*, 72; Martin Kramer, *Arab Awakening and Islamic Revival: The Politics of Ideas in the Middle East* (New Brunswick, NJ: Transaction, 1996), 166f. Iranians thus put on display a politicised form of pilgrimage as advocated by Shariati and Khomeini. Ali Shariati, *Hajj* (Bedford, OH: Free Islamic Literature, 1977).

49. This here served similar functions as myths and symbols in nationalism. See, for example, Anthony D. Smith, *Ethno-Symbolism and Nationalism: A Cultural Approach* (London: Routledge, 2009). This should not, however, imply that I

subscribe to the notion of cultural continuity throughout the ages of well-defined and closed cultural communities. Alexander Maxwell, 'Primordialism for Scholars Who Ought to Know Better: Anthony D. Smith's Critique of Modernization Theory', *Nationalities Papers* 48, 5 (2020), 826–42.

50. See, for example, Kinda Chaib, 'Hezbollah Seen through its Images: The Representation of the Martyr', in: Sabrina Mervin (ed.), *The Shi'a Worlds and Iran* (London: Saqi, 2010), 115–35; Rola el-Husseini, 'Resistance, Jihad, and Martyrdom in Contemporary Lebanese Shi'a Discourse', *Middle East Journal* 62, 3 (2008), 399–414; Assaf Moghadam, 'Mayhem, Myths, and Martyrdom: The Shi'a Conception of Jihad', *Terrorism and Political Violence* 19, 1 (2007), 125–43; Sami Zubaida, 'Sectarian Violence as Jihad', in: Elisabeth Kendall and Ewan Stein (eds), *Twenty-First Century Jihad: Law, Society and Military Action* (London: I. B. Tauris, 2015), 141–8. But Sunnis, too, would eventually adopt martyrdom as a major tool of war, influenced at least implicitly by Iranian-style activist Shiism. See, for example, the appropriation of Mukhtar by the Islamic Republic of Iran and activist Shii movements as an early example of Shii military and political activity and martyrdom for the sake of Hussain and the cause of the people of the *Ahl al-Bayt*. The *Mukhtarname* produced by Iranian TV emphasises Iranian/Arab (Ajam/Arab) unity in the fight for the cause of Ali and his descendants. The TV series was initially produced by IRIB and shown on Iranian TV, but later also shown on other Shii TV channels such as the Shirazi Ahlulbayt TV.

51. The circumstances of his disappearance are still murky, but he may have been killed by Ghaddafi to forestall a negotiation between Sadr and a part of the Shah's regime. Rick Gladstone, 'The Shah of Iran, the Islamic Revolution and the Mystery of the Missing Imam', *New York Times*, 14 January 2016; Andrew Scott Cooper, *The Fall of Heaven: The Pahlavis and the Final Days of Imperial Iran* (New York: Henry Holt, 2016).

CHAPTER 12

1. 'Abu Mayzar Interviewed', Paris, *al-Mustaqbal*, 9 June 1979, *Foreign Broadcast Information Service, Middle East & North Africa* (hereafter *FBIS*).

2. Quoted in: Chris P. Ioannides, 'The PLO and the Islamic Revolution in Iran', in: Augustus R. Norton and Martin H. Greenberg (eds), *The International Relations of the Palestine Liberation Organization* (Carbondale: Southern Illinois University Press, 1989), 74–108, 81.

3. Edward Cody, 'Shah Arrives in Cairo', *Washington Post*, 25 March 1980.

4. When the Shah died in July 1980, Sadat ordered a full state funeral, even though no other acting heads of state were willing to attend (Nixon and the deposed King Constantine of Greece were the only former heads of state in attendance). The Shah was buried in a tomb in Egypt, which became a shrine visited by Pahlavi loyalists ever since. Edward Cody, 'Shah Entombed after State Funeral',

Washington Post, 30 July 1980. See the scenes at the shrine in Cairo in the 2008 documentary *The Queen and I* on Farah Diba Pahlavi.

5. Iran changed the name in 2004 to please Egypt. *Irish Times*, 'Tehran Renames Street to Improve Egypt Ties', 6 January 2004. For background on this issue, see Nael Shama, *Egyptian Foreign Policy from Mubarak to Morsi: Against the National Interest* (London: Routledge, 2014), 133f. For an account of Egypt–Iran relations, see ibid., 114–52.

6. For background on the Iranian Left, see, amongst a growing literature, Stephanie Cronin (ed.), *Reformers and Revolutionaries in Modern Iran: New Perspectives on the Iranian Left* (London: Routledge, 2004); Maziar Behrooz, *Rebels with a Cause: The Failure of the Left in Iran* (London: I. B. Tauris, 1999); Peyman Vahabzadeh, *A Guerrilla Odyssey: Modernization, Secularism, Democracy, and the Fadai Period of National Liberation in Iran, 1971–1979* (Syracuse: Syracuse University Press, 2010); Siavush Randjbar-Daemi, 'The Tudeh Party of Iran and the Peasant Question, 1941–53', *Middle Eastern Studies* 56, 6 (2020), 969–87; Stephanie Cronin, 'The Left in Iran: Illusion and Disillusion', *Middle Eastern Studies* 36, 3 (2000), 231–43; Yassamine Mather and David Mather, 'The Islamic Republic and the Iranian Left', *Critique: Journal of Socialist Theory* 30, 1 (2002), 179–91.

7. Roham Alvandi, *Nixon, Kissinger, and the Shah: The United States and Iran in the Cold War* (New York: Oxford University Press, 2014).

8. Ray Takeyh, *The Last Shah: America, Iran, and the Fall of the Pahlavi Dynasty* (New Haven: Yale University Press, 2021).

9. Mattin Biglari, '"Captive to the Demonology of the Iranian Mobs": U.S. Foreign Policy and Perceptions of Shi'a Islam during the Iranian Revolution, 1978–79', *Diplomatic History* 40, 4 (2016), 579–605; Mohammad Ayatollahi Tabaar, *Religious Statecraft: The Politics of Islam in Iran* (New York: Columbia University Press, 2018), 75–80, 111–46.

10. 'Followers of the Imam's Line' was later going to become the name of a whole range of loyalist groups, revolutionary guards, and pro-Iranian movements amongst Shia outside of Iran.

11. The political leadership of Iran long maintained that it had not approved of the operation. Mohsen M. Milani and EIr, 'HOSTAGE CRISIS', *EIr*. For a vivid account, see Seyed Hossein Mousavian and Shahir Shahidsaless, *Iran and the United States: An Insider's View of the Failed Past and the Road to Peace* (New York: Bloomsbury, 2014); Muhammad Sahimi, 'The Power behind the Scene: Khoeiniha', *PBS Frontline*, 30 October 2009.

12. Rouhollah K. Ramazani, *Revolutionary Iran: Challenge and Response in the Middle East* (Baltimore: Johns Hopkins University Press, 1986). For the general debate on revolution and foreign policy, see Stephen M. Walt, *Revolution and War* (Ithaca: Cornell University Press, 1996); Fred Halliday, *Revolution and World Politics: The Rise and Fall of the Sixth Great Power* (Basingstoke: Macmillan, 1999); Halliday, *Revolution and Foreign Policy: The Case of South Yemen, 1967–1987* (Cambridge: Cambridge University Press, 1990).

13. So much so that the Iranian chargé d'affaires complained to the Kuwaiti Foreign Ministry about negative press coverage of Iran, media support to the unrest in Khuzestan, and the use of the word 'Arabistan' to describe the area. Iraqi–Iranian and Kuwaiti–Iranian Relations, United States Embassy. Kuwait. Confidential, Cable. 11 June 1979: 2 pp. DNSA collection: Iran Revolution; Arab-Iranian Relations United States Embassy. Kuwait. Secret, Cable. 18 June 1979: 4 pp. DNSA collection: Iran Revolution.

14. The US embassy thought that this visit was supposed to 'serve Kuwait's larger interest by showing support for a stable, non-leftist Iran'. It also concludes that 'the existing government in Iran is far preferable to any leftist alternative, in Kuwaiti eyes'. Kuwaiti Foreign Minister's Visit to Iran [Includes Perceptions on Gulf Security] United States Embassy. Kuwait. Confidential, Cable. 24 July 1979: 6 pp. DNSA collection: Iran Revolution.

15. Although especially his earlier historical writings, such as on Fadak, were clearly Shii. Chibli Mallat, *The Renewal of Islamic Law: Muhammad Baqer as-Sadr, Najaf, and the Shi'i International* (Cambridge: Cambridge University Press, 1993), 9, 124; Kantz Feder, 'Fatima's Revolutionary Image'. For a translation of his work on Islamic economics, see Andreas Rieck, *Unsere Wirtschaft: Eine gekürzte kommentierte Übersetzung des Buches Iqtisaduna von Muhammad Baqir as-Sadr* (Berlin: Klaus Schwarz, 1984).

16. The message, which invoked past Sunni–Shia cooperation in support of the Ottoman Empire during World War I, read as follows:'The despotic regime and its followers try to suggest to our noble Sunni sons that it is a matter of Shia and Sunni, so as to separate Sunni from the real struggle against the common enemy. I want to say to you, O sons of 'Ali and Hussain and sons of Abu Bakr and 'Omar! The fight is not between Shia and Sunni rule. 'Ali unsheathed his sword in defense of the Sunni rule represented by the Guided Caliphs, which was based on Islam and justice, as he fought during the wars waged against the apostates [in the aftermath of the death of the Prophet] under the standard of the first caliph Abu Bakr. All of us should fight for the banner of Islam to be hoisted high and to march under the banner, no matter what the color of the proponent. The Sunni rule that bore the flag of Islam elicited the fatawa of the Shia clergy, half a century ago, of the necessity to wage Jihad for it. Hundreds of thousands of Shia marched out and sacrificed their lives unselfishly to safeguard the standard of Islam and to protect the Sunni rule that was based on Islam. This present de facto rule is not Sunni rule, even though the dominant group is historically related to Sunnism.' Quoted by: Mohsen Araki, 'A Short Biography of Martyr Ayatullah al-Sadr', in: Muhammad Baqir al-Sadr, *Principles of Islamic Jurisprudence: According to Shi'i Law* (London: Islamic College for Advanced Studies Press, 2003), 16. See also Amatzia Baram, 'Religious Extremism and Ecumenical Tendencies in Modern Iraqi Shi'ism', in: Meir Litvak and Ofra Bengio (eds), *The Sunna and Shi'a in History: Division and Ecumenism in the Muslim Middle East* (Basingstoke: Palgrave Macmillan, 2011), 105–23, 111; Chibli Mallat, 'Religious Militancy in Contemporary Iraq: Muhammad Baqer

as-Sadr and the Sunni-Shia Paradigm', *Third World Quarterly* 10, 2 (1988), 699–729; Jabar, *The Shiʿite Movement*, 225–34.

17. F. Gregory Gause, 'Revolution and Threat Perception: Iran and the Middle East', *International Politics* 52, 5 (2015), 637–45, 641. See also David E. Long, 'The Impact of the Iranian Revolution on the Arabian Peninsula and the Gulf States', in: John L. Esposito (ed.), *The Iranian Revolution: Its Global Impact* (Miami: Florida International University Press, 1990), 100–15; Christin Marschall, *Iran's Persian Gulf Policy: From Khomeini to Khatami* (London: RoutledgeCurzon, 2003), 26–45; Rouhollah K. Ramazani, 'Shiʿism in the Persian Gulf', in: Juan R. I. Cole and Nikki R. Keddie (eds), *Shiʿism and Social Protest* (New Haven: Yale University Press, 1986), 30–54; Ramazani, 'Iran's Export of the Revolution: Politics, Ends, and Means', in: John L. Esposito (ed.), *The Iranian Revolution: Its Global Impact* (Miami: Florida International University Press, 1990), 40–62; Ramazani, *Revolutionary Iran*.

18. Matthiesen, *The Other Saudis*, 101–12; Toby C. Jones, 'Rebellion on the Saudi Periphery: Modernity, Marginalization, and the Shiʿa Uprising of 1979', *International Journal of Middle East Studies* 38, 2 (2006), 213–33; Ibrahim, *The Shiʿis of Saudi Arabia*, 117–22.

19. In Hyderabad, for example, new organisations emerged that sought to shape Muharram in a more political direction and away from the control of old Shii elites. Mirza, 'Travelling Leaders', 469–72.

20. Interview with Murtada al-Qazwini in Karbala, Iraq, 2018; interview with Hasan al-Saffar, Qatif, Saudi Arabia, 2008.

21. Thomas Hegghammer and Stéphane Lacroix, 'Rejectionist Islamism in Saudi Arabia: The Story of Juhayman al-ʿUtaybi Revisited', *International Journal of Middle East Studies* 39, 1 (2007), 103–22; Yaroslav Trofimov, *The Siege of Mecca: The Forgotten Uprising* (London: Allen Lane, 2007).

22. F. Gregory Gause, *The International Relations of the Persian Gulf* (Cambridge: Cambridge University Press, 2010), 45–87.

23. Werner Ende, 'Zwischen Annäherung und Konflikt: Schiiten und Sunniten in Geschichte und Gegenwart', in: John D. Patillo-Hess (ed.), *Islam: Dialog und Kontroverse* (Vienna: Löcker, 2007), 73–84. Anti-Shiism became something that all actors of the Sunni Saudi religious field could agree on. Stéphane Lacroix, *Awakening Islam: The Politics of Religious Dissent in Contemporary Saudi Arabia* (Cambridge, MA: Harvard University Press, 2011), 124.

24. Saudi Shia published books on the topic, created an al-Baqia Foundation, and named one of their journals *al-Baqia*. Matthiesen, *The Other Saudis*, 129f.

25. *UPI*, 'Iranian Pilgrims Arrested at Mecca', 24 September 1982.

26. In May 1985, Foreign Minister Saud al-Faisal visited Tehran, and at the end of the year Iranian Foreign Minister Ali Akbar Velayati made a return visit to Riyadh. Henner Fürtig, *Iran's Rivalry with Saudi Arabia between the Gulf Wars* (Reading: Ithaca, 2002), 47. The new pilgrimage representative was Mehdi Karroubi, who would later become the reformist presidential candidate in the 2009 Iranian elections that were officially won by Mahmud Ahmedinejad.

27. For background on the Hajj events of 1987, see Martin Kramer, 'Islam's Enduring Feud', *Middle East Contemporary Survey* 11 (1987), 153–79.

28. James P. Piscatori, 'Managing God's Guests: The Pilgrimage, Saudi Arabia and the Politics of Legitimacy', in: Paul Dresch and James P. Piscatori (eds), *Monarchies and Nations: Globalisation and Identity in the Arab States of the Gulf* (London: I. B. Tauris, 2005), 222–45. For the Saudi view, see Saud al-Sarhan, 'The Saudis as Managers of the Hajj', in: Eric Tagliacozzo and Shawkat M. Toorawa (eds), *The Hajj: Pilgrimage in Islam* (New York: Cambridge University Press, 2016), 196–212.

29. Toby Matthiesen, 'Hizbullah al-Hijaz: A History of the Most Radical Saudi Shi'a Opposition Group', *Middle East Journal* 64, 2 (2010), 179–97.

30. In general, see Joseph Kostiner, 'Shi'i Unrest in the Gulf', in: Martin Kramer (ed.), *Shi'ism, Resistance, and Revolution* (Boulder, CO: Westview Press, 1987), 173–86; Louër, *Transnational Shia Politics*, 155–76. See also 'Abbas Mirza al-Mirshid and 'Abd al-Hadi al-Khawaja', *Al-Tanzimat wa-l-Jama'iyyat al-Siyyasiyya fi al-Bahrayn* (Bahrain: Faradis lil-Nashr wa-l-Tawzi', 2008); Falah 'Abdallah al-Mudayris, *Al-Harakat wa-l-Jama'at al-Siyyasiyya fi al-Bahrayn 1937–2002* (Beirut: Dar al-Kunuz al-Adabiyya, 2004). For background on Bahrain, see Fuad I. Khuri, *Tribe and State in Bahrain: The Transformation of Social and Political Authority in an Arab State* (Chicago: University of Chicago Press, 1980); Emile A. Nakhleh, *Bahrain: Political Development in a Modernizing Society* (Lanham: Lexington Books, 1976); Muhammad G. Rumaihi, *Bahrain: Social and Political Change since the First World War* (London: Bowker/Centre for Middle Eastern and Islamic Studies of the University of Durham, 1976).

31. Interview with a Bahraini dissident involved in the 1981 Bahrain coup attempt, 2015. For background, see Hasan Tariq Alhasan, 'The Role of Iran in the Failed Coup of 1981: The IFLB in Bahrain', *Middle East Journal* 65, 4 (2011), 603–17; Rashid Hammada, '*Asifa Fawq Miyah al-Khalij: Qissa Awwal Inqilab 'Askari fi al-Bahrayn 1981* (London: al-Safa li-l-Nashr wa-l-Tawzi', 1990); John Vinocur, '1981 Plot in Bahrain Linked to Iranians', *New York Times*, 25 July 1982.

32. 'Abd al-Muhsin Yusuf Jamal, *Lamahat min Tarikh al-Shi'a fi al-Kuwayt: Al-Fitra min Nasha'at al-Kuwayt ila al-Istiqlal* (Kuwait: Dar al-Naba' lil-Nashr, 2005); Louër, *Transnational Shia Politics*, 46–57, 167–76; Falah 'Abdallah al-Mudayris, *Al-Haraka al-Shi'iyya fi al-Kuwayt* (Kuwait: Dar al-Qurtas, 1999); Lori Plotkin Boghardt, *Kuwait amid War, Peace and Revolution: 1979–1991 and New Challenges* (Basingstoke: Palgrave Macmillan, 2006); Falah Abdullah al-Mdaires, *Islamic Extremism in Kuwait: From the Muslim Brotherhood to al-Qaeda and Other Islamist Political Groups* (Abingdon: Routledge, 2010); Rivka Azoulay, 'The Politics of Shi'i Merchants in Kuwait', in: Steffen Hertog, Giacomo Luciani, and Marc Valeri (eds), *Business Politics in the Middle East* (London: Hurst, 2013), 67–99; Mary Ann Tétreault, *Stories of Democracy: Politics and Society in Contemporary Kuwait* (New York: Columbia University Press, 2000).

33. Youssef M. Ibrahim, 'Saudi Arabia Beheads 16 Kuwaitis Linked to Pro-Iranian Terrorism', *New York Times*, 22 September 1989.

34. Louër, *Transnational Shia Politics*, 9f., 118ff., 146ff.; Michael Stephens, 'Ashura in Qatar', *openDemocracy*, 26 November 2012, https://www.opendemocracy.net/en/ashura-in-qatar/; interviews with Omani Shia, Muscat, Oman, February 2013.

35. Asef Bayat and Bahman Baktiari, 'Revolutionary Iran and Egypt: Exporting Inspirations and Anxieties', in: Nikki R. Keddie and Rudolph P. Matthee (eds), *Iran and the Surrounding World: Interactions in Culture and Cultural Politics* (Seattle: University of Washington Press, 2002), 305–26; Alam Saleh and Hendrik Kraetzschmar, 'Politicized Identities, Securitized Politics: Sunni-Shi'a Politics in Egypt', *Middle East Journal* 69, 4 (2015), 545–62.

36. See, for example, Naim Qassem, *Hizbullah: The Story from Within* (London: Saqi, 2005).

37. Ataie, 'Revolutionary Iran's 1979 Endeavor'; Siarhei Bohdan, '"They were Going Together with the Ikhwan": The Influence of Muslim Brotherhood Thinkers on Shi'i Islamists during the Cold War', *Middle East Journal* 74, 2 (2020), 243–62; John L. Esposito (ed.), *The Iranian Revolution: Its Global Impact* (Miami: Florida International University Press, 1990); Shadi Hamid, 'The Lesser Threat: How the Muslim Brotherhood Views Shias and Shiism', *Mediterranean Politics* 26 (2021), 511–17; David Menashri (ed.), *The Iranian Revolution and the Muslim World* (Boulder, CO: Westview Press, 1990); Olivier Roy, 'The Impact of the Iranian Revolution on the Middle East', in: Sabrina Mervin (ed.), *The Shi'a Worlds and Iran* (London: Saqi, 2010), 29–44. Shia Islamist movements, for example the Shirazis, made their recruits read the classics of Sunni political Islam, in particular the writings of Hasan al-Banna, Sayyid Qutb, and Abu al-A'la Mawdudi. Fu'ad Ibrahim, *Al-Faqih wa-l-Dawla: Tatawwur al-Fikr al-Siyyasi al-Shi'i* (Beirut: Dar al-Kunuz al-Adabiyya, 1998), 357–69; Ibrahim, *The Shi'is of Saudi Arabia*, 73–104; Louër, *Transnational Shia Politics*, 124; 'Adil Ra'uf, *Al-'Amal al-Islami fi al-'Iraq bayn al-Marji'iyya wa-l-Hizbiyya: Qira'a Naqdiyya li-Masirat Nisf Qarn (1950–2000)* (Damascus: al-Markaz al-'Iraqi li-l-I'lam wa-l-Dirasat, 2000), 265–81.

38. Nicolas Dot-Pouillard, 'Iran and the Muslim Brotherhood: The Best of Enemies?', *Middle East Eye*, 4 July 2016; Anne M. Wolf, *Political Islam in Tunisia: The History of Ennahda* (London: Hurst, 2017), 48–51; Rory McCarthy, *Inside Tunisia's al-Nahda: Between Politics and Preaching* (Cambridge: Cambridge University Press, 2018), 37, 42f., 51; 'Remarks by Muslim Brotherhood Representative Reported', *Tehran Domestic Service*, 16 February 1980, *FBIS*; Mohammad Ataie, Raphaël Lefèvre, and Toby Matthiesen, 'How Iran's 1979 Revolution Affected Sunni Islamists in the Middle East', *LSE Middle East Centre Blog*, 26 April 2021, https://blogs.lse.ac.uk/mec/2021/04/26/how-irans-1979-revolution-affected-sunni-islamists-in-the-middle-east.

39. Walid M. Abdelnasser, 'Islamic Organizations in Egypt and the Iranian Revolution of 1979: The Experience of the First Few Years', *Arab Studies Quarterly* 19, 2 (1997), 25–39; 'Interview with Muhammad Abd al-Rahman Khalifa, Spokesman for the International Organisation of the Muslim Brotherhood, in Amman', *Le Monde*, 26 February 1980, *FBIS*; 'Muslim Brotherhood

Assails U.S. Praises Revolution', *Pars*, 15 July 1980, *FBIS*; al–Tilmisani in *al-Dawa* 34 (1979), quoted in: Johannes J. G. Jansen, 'Echoes of the Iranian Revolution in the Writings of Egyptian Muslims', in: David Menashri (ed.), *The Iranian Revolution and the Muslim World* (Boulder, CO: Westview Press, 1990), 207–18, 207; Jansen, 'Echoes of the Iranian Revolution', 208ff.; Emmanuel Sivan, 'Sunni Radicalism in the Middle East and the Iranian Revolution', *International Journal of Middle East Studies* 21, 1 (1989), 1–30.

40. The Salafi movement and the Society of Muslims (Jamat al-Muslimin) opposed the revolution early on. Abdelnasser, 'Islamic Organizations'. A pamphlet written at the time in response to an interview with Khomeini in an Arab journal, where he called for Sunni–Shia unity, is a vicious diatribe against him: Muhammad Mal-Allah, *Mawqif al-Khumayni min Ahl al-Sunna* (Cairo: al-Muslim Publishing House, 1982).

41. Hizb al-Tahrir also criticised the constitution of Iran because it applied to one country, thereby accepting the notion of the nation state (something Hizb al-Tahrir opposes, as it stands in confrontation with the idea of the Caliphate that the party wants to establish). The party criticises, for example, that Iran chose a distinct national flag and that Persian and not Arabic, the language of the Quran, became the national language. Amongst many other points, the party also criticises that in an exceptional case the leader (*rahbar*), who in its view is supposed to be the Caliph, can be replaced. Fritz Steppat, 'Islamisch-fundamentalistische Kritik an der Staatskonzeption der Islamischen Revolution in Iran', in: Hans Roemer and Albrecht Noth (eds), *Studien zur Geschichte und Kultur des Vorderen Orients: Festschrift für Bertold Spuler zum siebzigsten Geburtstag* (Leiden: Brill, 1981), 443–52, esp. 446 and 452; Ende, 'Sunni Polemical Writings', 228. Still, the idea that Hizb al-Tahrir was willing to accept a Shii Caliph to further its goal is remarkable. This was reasserted by one of the party's US representatives. *CBN*, 'Would Muslims Accept Iran as the Leader of a New Caliphate?', 26 October 2011. Hizb al-Tahrir seeks to overcome divisions between Muslims. Mahan Abedin, 'Inside Hizb ut-Tahrir: An Interview with Jalaluddin Patel, Leader of Hizb ut-Tahrir in the UK', *Jamestown Foundation*, 11 August 2004, https://jamestown.org/program/inside-hizb-ut-tahrir-an-interview-with-jalaluddin-patel-leader-of-hizb-ut-tahrir-in-the-uk/. See also Rasmus Christian Elling, *Minorities in Iran: Nationalism and Ethnicity after Khomeini* (New York: Palgrave Macmillan, 2013), 50ff.

42. While the 1906 Iranian constitution had still called Shiism the true school of jurisprudence, this term was removed here. The official recognition of the Sunni schools of jurisprudence was also new. H. E. Chehabi, 'The Islamic Republic of Iran and the Muslim World', in: *Iranian Influences in Oecumenic Cultural Exchanges* (Seoul: Korean Association of Central Asian Studies, 2013), 77–84, 78.

43. Siavush Randjbar-Daemi, 'Building the Islamic State: The Draft Constitution of 1979 Reconsidered', *Iranian Studies* 46, 4 (2013), 641–63; Said Saffari, 'The Legitimation of the Clergy's Right to Rule in the Iranian Constitution of 1979',

British Journal of Middle Eastern Studies 20, 1 (1993), 64–82. For the constitution, see http://www.servat.unibe.ch/icl/ir00000_.html.

44. Roy, 'The Impact of the Iranian Revolution', 31.

45. Rudi Matthee, 'The Egyptian Opposition on the Iranian Revolution', in: Juan R. I. Cole and Nikki R. Keddie (eds), *Shi'ism and Social Protest* (New Haven: Yale University Press, 1986), 247–74.

46. Abdelnasser, 'Islamic Organizations', in part quoting the memoirs of Umar al-Tilmisani. For more on al-Tilmisani, see Jeffry R. Halverson, *Theology and Creed in Sunni Islam: The Muslim Brotherhood, Ash'arism, and Political Sunnism* (New York: Palgrave Macmillan, 2010). Al-Tilmisani's successor as general guide, Muhammad Hamid Abu al-Nasr, also denounced the war. See Barry M. Rubin, *Islamic Fundamentalism in Egyptian Politics* (London: Macmillan, 1990), 118f. It is interesting that Rubin, unlike Abdelnasser, is dismissive of the prospect that the Iranian Revolution was, or could be, a model for Egyptian Islamists, mainly referring to allegedly unbridgeable gaps between Iranians and Arabs as well as between Sunnis and Shia. See ibid., 115–18.

47. Salih al-Wardani, *Al-Haraka al-Islamiyya fi Misr: Ru'iya Waqi'iyya li-Rihlat al-Sab'inat* (Cairo: al-Bidaya, 1986), 197–203; al-Wardani, *Misr wa Iran: Sira' al-Amn wa-l-Siyyasa* (Cairo: Maktaba Nakhrush, 1995), 47–50, 99–114.

48. This was Salih al-Wardani, *Al-Shi'a fi Misr: Min al-Imam 'Ali hatta al-Imam al-Khumayni* (Cairo: Maktabat Madbuli al-Saghir, 1993). See also el-Moctar, 'Saladin', 204; Stéphane Valter, *Norm and Dissidence: Egyptian Shi'a between Security Approaches and Geopolitical Stakes* (Doha: Center for International and Regional Studies, 2019), 17f.

49. The most famous was probably Salih al-Wardani, who wrote an account of his conversion that provoked many Sunnis: Salih al-Wardani, *Al-Khud'a: Rihlati min al-Sunna ila al-Shi'a* (Cairo: al-Hadaf, 2001). He also called for Sunni–Shia rapprochement, but other books of his are strong critiques of Sunni Islamism, both in Egypt and according to the Wahhabi tradition and of the clerics sponsored by the Saudi state, or by the state in general. Al-Wardani, *'Aqa'id al-Sunna wa 'Aqa'id al-Shi'a: Al-Taqarub wa-l-Taba'ud* (Beirut: al-Ghadir, 1999); al-Wardani, *Azmat al-Haraka al-Islamiyya al-Mu'asira: Min al-Hanabila ila Taliban* (Cairo: al-Hadaf, 2002); al-Wardani, *Ahl al-Sunna: Sha'b Allah al-Mukhtar wa Dirasa fi Fasad 'Aqa'id Ahl al-Sunna* (Cairo: Kanuta, 1997). In general, see Rainer Brunner, '"Then I was Guided": Some Remarks on Inner-Islamic Conversions in the 20th and 21st Centuries', *Orient* 50, 4 (2009), 6–15. Egypt at times also arrested people accused of planning armed acts on behalf of Iran and trying to propagate Shiism. Rubin, *Islamic Fundamentalism*, 156. See, for example, 'Iranian-Backed "Terrorist" Group "Uncovered"', *al-Safir*, 11 July 1987, *FBIS*; 'More Details on Underground Group Uncovered', *Cairo MENA*, 15 June 1988, *FBIS*.

50. Mara A. Leichtman, 'Shi'i Islamic Cosmopolitanism and the Transformation of Religious Authority in Senegal', *Contemporary Islam* 8, 3 (2014), 261–83.

51. Leichtman, *Shi'i Cosmopolitanisms in Africa: Lebanese Migration and Religious Conversion in Senegal* (Bloomington: Indiana University Press, 2015); Tim Cocks

and Bozorgmehr Sharafedin, 'In Senegal, Iran and Saudi Arabia Vie for Religious Influence', *Reuters*, 12 May 2017.

52. Kabiru Haruna Isa, 'Sunni Literary Responses to the Spread of Shia Ideology in Northern Nigeria', *Studies in African Languages and Cultures* 52 (2018), 113–30.

53. Andrea Brigaglia, 'A Contribution to the History of the Wahhabi Da'wa in West Africa: The Career and the Murder of Shaykh Ja'far Mahmoud Adam (Daura, ca. 1961/1962-Kano 2007)', *Islamic Africa* 3, 1 (2012), 1–23; Krithika Varagur, *The Call: Inside the Global Saudi Religious Project* (New York: Columbia Global Reports, 2020).

54. Chiara Formichi and R. Michael Feener (eds), *Shi'ism in Southeast Asia: 'Alid Piety and Sectarian Constructions* (London: Hurst, 2015); Siti Sarah Muwahidah, 'For the Love of Ahl al-Bayt: Transcending Sunni-Shi'i Sectarian Allegiance', *Journal of Shi'a Islamic Studies* 9, 3 (2016), 327-58; M. Ismail Marchinkowski, 'Southeast Asia ii. Shi'ites in', *EIr*; Syed Farid Alatas, 'The Ṭariqat al-'Alawiyyah and the Emergence of the Shi'i School in Indonesia and Malaysia', *Oriente Moderno* 18, 2 (1999), 322–39; Martin van Bruinessen, 'Najmuddin al-Kubra, Jumadil Kubra and Jamaluddin al-Akbar: Traces of Kubrawiyya Influence in Early Indonesian Islam', *Bijdragen tot de Taal-, Land- en Volkenkunde* 150, 2 (1994), 305–29; Christoph Marcinkowski, 'Aspects of Shi'ism in Contemporary Southeast Asia', *The Muslim World* 98, 1 (2008), 36–71; Zulkifli, 'Qom Alumni in Indonesia: Their Role in the Shi'i Community', in: Masooda Bano and Keiko Sakurai (eds), *Shaping Global Islamic Discourses: The Role of al-Azhar, al-Medina and al-Mustafa* (Edinburgh: Edinburgh University Press, 2015), 117-41; Arnold Yasin Mol, Majid Daneshgar, and Faisal Ahmad Shah, 'Ashura in the Malay-Indonesian World: The Ten Days of Muharram in Sumatra as Depicted by Nineteenth-Century Dutch Scholars', *Journal of Shi'a Islamic Studies* 8, 4 (2015), 491–505; Margaret Kartomi, 'Tabut: A Shia Ritual Transplanted from India to Sumatra', in: David P. Chandler and Merle C. Ricklefs (eds), *Nineteenth and Twentieth Century Indonesia: Essays in Honour of Professor J. D. Legge* (Clayton: Monash University, 1986), 141–62; R. Michael Feener and Chiara Formichi, 'Debating "Shi'ism" in the History of Muslim Southeast Asia', in: Chiara Formichi and R. Michael Feener (eds), *Shi'ism in Southeast Asia: 'Alid Piety and Sectarian Constructions* (London: Hurst, 2015), 3–16; Majid Daneshgar, 'The Study of Persian Shi'ism in the Malay-Indonesian World: A Review of Literature from the Nineteenth Century Onwards', *Journal of Shi'a Islamic Studies* 7, 2 (2014), 191–229; Chiara Formichi, 'Violence, Sectarianism, and the Politics of Religion: Articulations of Anti-Shi'a Discourses in Indonesia', *Indonesia* 98 (2014), 1–27; Formichi, 'Shaping Shi'a Identities in Contemporary Indonesia between Local Tradition and Foreign Orthodoxy', *Die Welt des Islams* 54 (2014), 212–36; Formichi, 'From Fluid Identities to Sectarian Labels: A Historical Investigation of Indonesia's Shi'i Communities', *Al-Jami'ah: Journal of Islamic Studies* 52, 1 (2014), 101–26; Zulkifli, *The Struggle of the Shi'is in Indonesia* (Canberra: ANU Press, 2013); Krithika Varagur, 'Iran-Funded Center a Lifeline for Jakarta's Marginalized Shia Minority', *Voice of America*, 4 October 2017;

Navhat Nuraniyah, *The Anti-Shi'a Movement in Indonesia* (Jakarta: Institute for Policy Analysis of Conflict, 2016); Human Rights Watch, 'Indonesia: Ensure Safe Return Home of Evicted Shia Villagers: Government Capitulation to Militants Sets Dangerous Precedent', 30 June 2013.

55. Mohd Faizal Musa, 'The Malaysian Shi'a: A Preliminary Study of their History, Oppression, and Denied Rights', *Journal of Shi'a Islamic Studies* 6, 4 (2013), 411–63; Rodger Shanahan, 'Malaysia and its Shi'a "Problem"', *Middle East Institute*, 25 July 2014. See, for example, Maulana Muhammad 'Asri Yusoff, *Syiah Rafidhah: Di Antara Kecuaian 'Ulama' dan Kebingungan Ummah* (n.p.: DarulKautsar.net, n.d.); Syed Farid Alatas, 'Salafism and the Persecution of Shi'ites in Malaysia', *Middle East Institute*, 30 July 2014; Mohd Fauzi bin Abu-Hussin and Asmady Idris, 'Malaysia Navigates the Sectarian Dimension of the Saudi-Iran Rivalry', *Middle East Institute*, 8 August 2017.

56. Radhika Gupta, 'Experiments with Khomeini's Revolution in Kargil: Contemporary Shi'a Networks between India and West Asia', *Modern Asian Studies* 48, 2 (2014), 370–98.

57. Umar F. Abd-Allah, *The Islamic Struggle in Syria* (Berkeley: Mizan Press, 1983); Hans Günter Lobmeyer, *Islamismus und sozialer Konflikt in Syrien* (Berlin: Das Arabische Buch, 1990), 45–51; Lobmeyer, *Opposition und Widerstand*, 364–76; Itzchak Weismann, 'Sa'id Hawwa and Islamic Revivalism in Ba'thist Syria', *Studia Islamica* 85 (1997), 131–54; van Dam, *The Struggle for Power in Syria: Politics*; Raphaël Lefèvre, 'The Syrian Muslim Brotherhood's Alawi Conundrum', in: Michael Kerr and Craig Larkin (eds), *The Alawis of Syria: War, Faith and Politics in the Levant* (Oxford: Oxford University Press, 2015), 125–37; Voss, '*'Alawīya oder Nusairīya?*', 6–86 and passim.

58. Lefèvre, *Ashes of Hama*, 73ff. For an account of the radicalisation of the group, see ibid., 81–107. See also Lobmeyer, *Opposition und Widerstand*, 190–213, 259–336.

59. Sa'id Hawwa, *Hadhihi Tajribati wa Hadhihi Shahadati* (Cairo: Maktabat Wahba, 1987), 137; Meir Hatina, 'Debating the "Awakening Shi'a": Sunni Perceptions of the Iranian Revolution', in: Meir Litvak and Ofra Bengio (eds), *The Sunna and Shi'a in History: Division and Ecumenism in the Muslim Middle East* (Basingstoke: Palgrave Macmillan, 2011), 203–21, 211.

60. Arab Shii circles in post-revolutionary Iran, for example, published a short-lived magazine criticising the Assad regime and cautiously supporting the Syrian Muslim Brotherhood to maintain good relations with the Muslim Brotherhood. The magazine was stopped after a few issues, however. Interview with an Arab Shii dissident based in Iran in 1980, London, 2017.

61. For more on the Syria–Iran alliance, see Jubin M. Goodarzi, *Syria and Iran: Diplomatic Alliance and Power Politics in the Middle East* (London: I. B. Tauris, 2006); von Maltzahn, *The Syria–Iran Axis*; Anoushiravan Ehteshami and Raymond A. Hinnebusch, *Syria and Iran: Middle Powers in a Penetrated Regional System* (London: Routledge, 1997); Seale, *Asad of Syria*, 351–65; Hussein J. Agha and Ahmad S. Khalidi, *Syria and Iran: Rivalry and Cooperation* (London: Pinter/Chatham House, 1995).

62. See, for example, Walid al-Aʻzam, *Al-Khumayniyya: Warithat al-Harakat al-Haqida wa-l-Afkar al-Fasida* (Amman: Dar ʻAmmar, 1988), and the denouncing of the 'Nusayri-Khomeinist' alliance on pages 72–84. The Amman-based Dar ʻAmmar became a major publisher of anti-Iranian and anti-Shii pamphlets, publishing dozens such books throughout the 1980s. For another example, see Muhammad al-Bindari, *Al-Tashayyuʻ bayna Mafhum al-Aʼimma wa-l-Mafhum al-Farisi* (Amman: Dar ʻAmmar, 1988).

63. Command of the Islamic Revolution in Syria, *Bayan al-Thawra al-Islamiyya fi Suriya wa Manhajuha* (Declaration and Programme of the Islamic Revolution in Syria) (Damascus: n.p., 1980), 10ff., cited after: Hanna Batatu, 'Syria's Muslim Brethren', *Middle East Report* 110 (1982), 12–20/34/36. See also Seurat, *Syrie*, 124–9, 134ff.

64. Lefèvre, *Ashes of Hama*, 137–79; Seurat, *Syrie*, 61–74. For the memory culture around 1982, see Salwa Ismail, *The Rule of Violence: Subjectivity, Memory and Government in Syria* (Cambridge: Cambridge University Press, 2018), 131–58. For more on the Brotherhood, see Dara Conduit, *The Muslim Brotherhood in Syria* (New York: Cambridge University Press, 2019).

65. That letter was published in 2012, at the height of the Syrian Civil War, by Khomeini's website, seemingly to deflect blame for the war from Iran. Imam-Khomeini.ir, 'Imam's Confidential Letter to Hafiz al-Assad', 24 July 2012, http://en.imam-khomeini.ir/en/news/3739/News/Imam%E2%80%99s_Confidential_Letter_to_Hafiz_al-Assad; Yvette Talhamy, 'The Syrian Muslim Brothers and the Syrian–Iranian Relationship', *Middle East Journal* 63, 4 (2009), 561–80.

66. Lefèvre, *Ashes of Hama*, 86, 96.

67. Ende, 'Sunni Polemical Writings', 225. During fieldwork trips to the Gulf States, the book was recommended to me by Sunnis as a thorough study of the Shia communities and the danger they allegedly pose to the GCC.

68. Bernard Haykel, 'Al-Qaʼida and Shiism', in: Assaf Moghadam and Brian Fishman (eds), *Fault Lines in Global Jihad: Organizational, Strategic, and Ideological Fissures* (London: Routledge, 2011), 184–202, 188. In the mid-1970s, he was expelled from Saudi Arabia to Kuwait because his activities were considered subversive. For Surur's impact on Saudi Arabia and the Sururis, see Lacroix, *Awakening Islam*. While Surur was influential in Saudi Arabia, and his narrative on Iran fit in with that of official circles in the country, he was disliked by those officials for his political activism in the Gulf countries and criticism of Saudi Arabia. For a record of a conversation between US and Saudi intelligence officials on the Sururiyya, see US Diplomatic Cable Released by Wikileaks: From Embassy Riyadh to Department of the Treasury, *Saudi Ministry of the Interior on Terrorist Financing Issues*, 25 March 2009, 09RIYADH460, https://wikileaks.org/plusd/cables/09RIYADH460_a.html. In this conversation, Saudi intelligence claimed that Saudi Arabia expelled him in the 1970s and that they had tried to get Kuwait to stop Surur's activities while he was there. He left to the UK in the mid-1980s. Surur claims that he was one of the few to see

the real nature of Iran and Shiism, but that in the meantime what had been hidden, i.e. the distortion of the Shia 'religion' and Iran's 'ethnic enmity towards the Arabs', had become obvious. Muhammad Surur Zayn al-'Abidin, *Wa Ja'a Dawr al-Majus: Al-Ab'ad al-Tarikhiyya wa-l-'Aqa'idiyya wa-l-Siyyasiyya li-l-Thawra al-Iraniyya*, 10th ed. (n.p.: n.p., 2008), 6, available on www.surour.net.

69. Nasir ibn Sulayman al-'Umar, *Waqi' al-Rafida fi Bilad al-Tawhid*, available on http://ar.islamway.net/book/3165. For more on Saudi clerics' views towards Shia Islam, see Ismail, *Saudi Clerics*. For a good overview, in particular of books printed in Cairo, see Ende, 'Sunni Polemical Writings'.

70. Osman mentions the Muslim Students Association on US campuses and mosques affiliated with the Islamic Society of North America (ISNA). Osman, *Sectarianism in Iraq*, 55n63. He also includes a number of titles of the publications involved, for example an anti-Shii publication by the US branch of the World Assembly of Muslim Youth published in 1995, in which the notion that the Prophet designated Ali as his successor, this 'cornerstone of the Shia faith', is accused of being 'false and baseless': Saeed Ismaeel, *The Difference between the Shee'ah and the Muslims* (US Office, World Assembly of Muslim Youth, 1995), 30.

71. These included, for example, Abdallah al-Qasimi's *The Conflict between Islam and Paganism*. Wasella, *Vom Fundamentalisten zum Atheisten*, 67. While many books focused on Twelver Shiism, old anti-Alawite tracts were also republished. A 1980 book published in Cairo, for example, includes texts written on the Alawites from the early heresiographical literature to Ibn Taymiyya and European Orientalists and presents them as a branch of Shiism, but with a clearly negative connotation. Abdallah al-Hussayni (ed.), *Al-Judhur al-Tarikhiyya li-l-Nusayriyya al-'Alawiyya* (Cairo: Dar al-I'tisam, 1980). For more, see Voss, *'Alawiya oder Nusairiya?'*.

72. The book was published in Amman, where Hawwa had lived in exile since 1978 up until his death in 1989. Sa'id Hawwa, *Al-Khumayniyya: Shudhudh fi al-'Aqa'id wa Shudhudh fi al-Mawaqif* (Amman: Dar 'Ammar, 1987), 5f., 44f. See also Muhammad Surur Zayn al-'Abidin, *Ahwal Ahl al-Sunna fi Iran* (n.p.: n.p., 2006, first published in 1990), available on https://www.surour.net. It is discussed in Hatina, 'Debating the "Awakening Shi'a"', 211—14, and Steinberg, 'Jihadi-Salafism', 119f.

73. For such an argumentation, see Shahbaz Mohseni, 'Der sunnitische Islam im Iran', *Spektrum Iran* 30, 3 (2017), 71—82. Saudi Arabia for a long time only recognised the Hanbali school, expanding that to include the other Sunni schools in the 2000s, but not Shiism.

74. McDowall, *A Modern History*, 261—74, 278; Patricia J. Higgins, 'Minority—State Relations in Contemporary Iran', in: Ali Banuazizi and Myron Weiner (eds), *The State, Religion, and Ethnic Politics: Pakistan, Iran, and Afghanistan* (Syracuse: Syracuse University Press, 1986), 167—97, 186f. See also Elling, *Minorities in Iran*; Ziba Mir-Hosseini, 'Redefining the Truth: Ahl-i Haqq and the Islamic Republic of Iran', *British Journal of Middle Eastern Studies* 21, 2 (1994), 211—28; Allan Hassaniyan, *Kurdish Politics in Iran: Crossborder Interactions and Mobilisation since*

1947 (Cambridge: Cambridge University Press, 2021); Abbas Vali, *Kurds and the State in Iran: The Making of Kurdish Identity* (London: I. B. Tauris, 2014). The religious element of the Kurd-Islamic Republic conflict should not be overemphasised, however. Martin van Bruinessen, 'Nationalismus und religiöser Konflikt: Der kurdische Widerstand im Iran', in: Kurt Greussing (ed.), *Religion und Politik im Iran* (Frankfurt am Main: Syndikat, 1981), 372–409.

75. Dudoignon, *The Baluch, Sunnism and the State*; Dudoignon, 'Sunnites and Shiites in Iran since 1979: Confrontations, Exchanges, Convergences', in: Brigitte Maréchal and Sami Zemni (eds), *The Dynamics of Sunni–Shia Relationships: Doctrine, Transnationalism, Intellectuals and the Media* (London: Hurst, 2013), 141–61. See, for example, the Association of Sunnis in Iran, which was active in publishing a newsletter and maintaining a website in the 1990s and 2000s: https://web.archive.org/web/19990508043125/http://www.isl.org.uk/. For another website, see http://sunnionline.us. In general, see Farian Sabahi, 'Iran, Iranian Media and Sunnite Islam', in: Brigitte Maréchal and Sami Zemni (eds), *The Dynamics of Sunni-Shia Relationships: Doctrine, Transnationalism, Intellectuals and the Media* (London: Hurst, 2013), 163–77.

76. Majid S. Moslem, *Frieden im Islam: Die Instrumentalisierung des Islam im irakisch-iranischen Krieg* (Berlin: Klaus Schwarz, 2005), 191f.

77. For accounts of Iraqi leadership meetings discussing whether to invade Iran, including an assessment of an uprising in Khuzestan, see Amatzia Baram, *Saddam Husayn and Islam, 1968–2003: Ba'thi Iraq from Secularism to Faith* (Washington, DC: Woodrow Wilson Center Press, 2014), 145–56. Interestingly, in 1979, the decision was made not to invade, in part because Saddam and others sensed Khomeini's popularity in the Arab world and amongst Iraqi Shia, but in 1980 the Iraqi leadership changed its position.

78. Mohiaddin Mesbahi, 'The USSR and the Iran-Iraq War: From Brezhnev to Gorbachev', in: Farhang Rajaee (ed.), *The Iran-Iraq War: The Politics of Aggression* (Gainesville: University Press of Florida, 1993), 69–102.

79. Shane Harris and Matthew M. Aid, 'Exclusive: CIA Files Prove America Helped Saddam as He Gassed Iran', *Foreign Policy*, 26 August 2013. US economic support continued until Iraq's invasion of Kuwait. In what became known as the Iran-Contra affair (1985–7), the US briefly delivered arms to Iran, albeit in much smaller quantities than those supplied to Iraq (France also sold arms to both sides). See the files in the Digital National Security Archive, 'Iraqgate: Saddam Hussein, U.S. Policy and the Prelude to the Persian Gulf War, 1980–1994', https://proquest.libguides.com/dnsa/iraqgate.

80. The Kingdom also agreed to produce and sell oil from a neutral zone between Iraq and Saudi Arabia on Iraq's behalf (roughly 300,000 barrels per day) to compensate for Iraq's loss in revenue. Pierre Razoux, *The Iran–Iraq War* (Cambridge, MA: Harvard University Press, 2015), 103. See also Williamson Murray and Kevin M. Woods, *The Iran–Iraq War: A Military and Strategic History* (Cambridge: Cambridge University Press, 2014). Saudi Arabia also wanted ballistic missiles, which the US was refusing to sell to the Kingdom. In July 1985, Prince Bandar

travelled to China. Officially, he was there to persuade the Chinese to stop arming Iran and instead ship the weapons to Iraq. Saudi Arabia would compensate China with $1 billion, even though at that point it did not maintain diplomatic relations with China. Rachel Bronson, *Thicker than Oil: America's Uneasy Partnership with Saudi Arabia* (Oxford: Oxford University Press, 2006), 188ff.

81. Davis, *Memories of State*, 188–92; Ibrahim al-Marashi and Sammy Salama, *Iraq's Armed Forces: An Analytical History* (Abingdon: Routledge, 2008), 151f.

82. Davis, *Memories of State*, 191–9.

83. In general and for relations between the Baath party and Shiism in the 1980s, see Adib-Moghaddam, *International Politics*; Blaydes, *State of Repression*, 237–65; Davis, *Memories of State*, 184–8, 273f.; Samuel Helfont, *Compulsion in Religion: Saddam Hussein, Islam, and the Roots of Insurgencies in Iraq* (New York: Oxford University Press, 2018), 52–68; Abbas Kadhim, *The Hawza under Siege: A Study in the Ba'th Party Archive* (Boston: Boston University Institute for Iraqi Studies, 2013); Moslem, *Frieden im Islam*, 147.

84. Davis, *Memories of State*, 181f., 190f.; Haddad, *Understanding 'Sectarianism'*, 72; Associated Press, 'Saddam's Ally, Former Iraqi Baath Party Leader and Prime Minister, Dies', *International Herald Tribune*, 16 March 2007; Dina Rizk Khoury, *Iraq in Wartime: Soldiering, Martyrdom, and Remembrance* (Cambridge: Cambridge University Press, 2013), 58–66; Shahram Chubin and Charles Tripp, *Iran and Iraq at War* (London: I. B. Tauris, 1988).

85. There is a controversy amongst scholars of Iraq as to whether Saddam himself was becoming more pious or whether he just instrumentalised Islam. The first view is represented by Baram, the second by Sassoon. See Baram, *Saddam Husayn*, and Joseph Sassoon, *Saddam Hussein's Ba'th Party: Inside an Authoritarian Regime* (Cambridge: Cambridge University Press, 2011). For more on relations between the state and the Shia in the 1970s, see Baram, *Saddam Husayn*, 81–138; Osman, *Sectarianism in Iraq*, 124; Jabar, *The Shi'ite Movement*, 201–15. For Saddam's religious turn, see Baram, *Saddam Husayn*, 73–80.

86. Moslem, *Frieden im Islam*, 129–47.

87. Afshon Ostovar, *Vanguard of the Imam: Religion, Politics, and Iran's Revolutionary Guards* (New York: Oxford University Press, 2016), 62–140.

88. Ibid., 146.

89. He subsequently published several articles on the topic in the early 1980s. Ziad Abu-Amr, *Islamic Fundamentalism in the West Bank and Gaza: Muslim Brotherhood and Islamic Jihad* (Bloomington: Indiana University Press, 1994), 101; Wissam Alhaj, Nicolas Dot-Pouillard, and Eugénie Rébillard, *De la théologie à la libération? Histoire du Jihad islamique palestinien* (Paris: La Découverte, 2014); Elie Rekhess, 'The Iranian Impact on the Islamic Jihad Movement in the Gaza Strip', in: David Menashri (ed.), *The Iranian Revolution and the Muslim World* (Boulder, CO: Westview Press, 1990), 189–206; Erik Skare, *A History of Palestinian Islamic Jihad: Faith, Awareness, and Revolution in the Middle East* (Cambridge: Cambridge University Press, 2021), 129–39; Hatina, 'Debating the "Awakening Shi'a"', 204–11.

90. Ioannides, 'The PLO', 82; Jean-François Legrain, 'The Shiite Peril in Palestine: Between Phobias and Propaganda', in: Brigitte Maréchal and Sami Zemni (eds), *The Dynamics of Sunni-Shia Relationships: Doctrine, Transnationalism, Intellectuals and the Media* (London: Hurst, 2013), 41–60, 57ff. Initially, a new (but largely unfounded) fear gained ground in the Gulf, Israel, and the US that Palestinian émigrés and Gulf Shia could cooperate to overthrow the Gulf monarchies and export the revolution. For an example of this kind of argument, see John K. Cooley, 'Iran, the Palestinians, and the Gulf', *Foreign Affairs* 57, 5 (1979), 1017–34.

91. Ostovar, *Vanguard of the Imam*, 112–17.

92. For the alliance of the periphery, see Avi Shlaim, *The Iron Wall: Israel and the Arab World*, 2nd ed. (London: Penguin, 2014), 198–231. For an elaboration of the concept, see Yossi Alpher, *Periphery: Israel's Search for Middle East Allies* (Lanham: Rowman & Littlefield, 2015); Avi Shlaim, 'Israel, the Great Powers, and the Middle East Crisis of 1958', *Journal of Imperial and Commonwealth History* 27, 2 (1999), 177–92. See also Nakash, *Reaching for Power*, 112f.

93. Kirsten E. Schulze, *Israel's Covert Diplomacy in Lebanon* (Basingstoke: Macmillan, 1998).

94. Only when Hizbullah stepped up attacks on Israel and the SLA did Shia in the SLA slowly break away. After the Israeli withdrawal in 2000, around 500 Shia from the SLA moved to Israel, in particular the officer corps, for fear of reprisals in Lebanon. Khalid Sindawi, 'Are There any Shi'ite Muslims in Israel?', *Journal of Holy Land and Palestine Studies* 7, 2 (2008), 183–99, 192f. In 1948, Israel took over seven largely Shii-inhabited villages near the border with Lebanon, whose inhabitants either were killed or fled to Lebanon. The Israeli Department of Minorities initially negotiated with village elders for their surrender and integration into Israel, and some Israeli officials thought that Sunni–Shia difference could facilitate that. However, this policy was not pursued and the population was expelled. Ibid., 187; Asher Kaufman, 'Between Palestine and Lebanon: Seven Shi'i Villages as a Case Study of Boundaries, Identities, and Conflict', *Middle East Journal* 60, 4 (2006), 685–706; Nicholas Blanford, *Warriors of God: Inside Hezbollah's Thirty-Year Struggle against Israel* (New York: Random House, 2011).

95. Clinton Bailey, 'Lebanon's Shi'is after the 1982 War', in: Martin Kramer (ed.), *Shi'ism, Resistance, and Revolution* (Boulder, CO: Westview Press, 1987), 219–36. For failed Israeli attempts to co-opt Amal, see Norton, *Amal and the Shi'a*, 109f. See also Clinton Bailey, 'How Israel Misread Lebanon, Failed Ron Arad and Helped Hezbollah Rise to Power', *Haaretz*, 28 November 2016.

96. Aurélie Daher, *Hezbollah: Mobilisation and Power* (London: Hurst, 2019), 17–59; Mallat, *Aspects of Shi'i Thought from the South of Lebanon*; Amal Saad-Ghorayeb, *Hizbu'llah: Politics and Religion* (London: Pluto, 2002), 112–33.

97. Rula Jurdi Abisaab, 'The Cleric as Organic Intellectual: Revolutionary Shi'ism in the Lebanese Hawzas', in: H. E. Chehabi, *Distant Relations: Iran and Lebanon in the Last 500 Years* (London: I. B. Tauris, 2006), 231–58; Judith Harik, 'Hizballah's Public and Social Services and Iran', in: H. E. Chehabi, *Distant Relations: Iran and Lebanon in the Last 500 Years* (London: I. B. Tauris, 2006), 259–86.

98. Goodarzi, *Syria and Iran*, 3, 7ff.

99. Johnson, *Class and Client*, 208—14.

100. Na'im Qasim, *Hizbullah: Al-Manhaj, al-Tajruba, al-Mustaqbal*, 4th ed. (Beirut: Dar al-Hadi, 2008), 355—60.

101. Interview with Talal Atrisi, Beirut, 2019; Michael Humphrey, 'Ḥarakāt al-Tawḥīd al-Islāmī', *EIW*; Humphrey, *Islam, Sect and State: The Lebanese Case* (Oxford: Centre for Lebanese Studies, 1989); Hassan Awada, 'Le Liban et le flux islamiste', *Social Compass* 35, 4 (1988), 645—73; Bernard Rougier, *The Sunni Tragedy in the Middle East: Northern Lebanon from al-Qaeda to ISIS* (Princeton: Princeton University Press, 2015), 1—13; Raphaël Lefèvre, *Jihad in the City: Militant Islam and Contentious Politics in Tripoli* (Cambridge: Cambridge University Press, 2021); Lefèvre, *The Roots of Crisis in Northern Lebanon* (Washington, DC: Carnegie Endowment for International Peace, 2014); Ataie, 'Revolutionary Iran's 1979 Endeavor'; Agha and Khalidi, *Syria and Iran*, 21—5; Norton, *Amal and the Shi'a*, 59—70; Seurat, *Syrie*, 235—84; Mohammad Ataie, 'Exporting the Iranian Revolution: Ecumenical Clerics in Lebanon', *International Journal of Middle East Studies* 53, 4 (2021), 672—90.

102. Michael Farquhar, *Circuits of Faith: Migration, Education, and the Wahhabi Mission* (Stanford: Stanford University Press, 2017).

103. See Zoltan Pall, *Lebanese Salafis between the Gulf and Europe: Development, Fractionalization and Transnational Networks of Salafism in Lebanon* (Amsterdam: Amsterdam University Press, 2013); Rougier, *The Sunni Tragedy*, 13—7, 63f. This would lay the nucleus for what later would emerge as Fatah al-Islam, a group that would lead a Jihadi uprising in the Nahr al-Bared camp in 2007. Ibid., 124—70. A second Salafi movement, less bent on political work and rather focusing on preaching and proselytising (*dawa*), called 'Scientific (*ilmi*) Salafism', rivalled the activist networks and was financed by a Kuwaiti Salafi charity. Zoltan Pall, *Kuwaiti Salafism and its Growing Influence in the Levant* (Washington, DC: Carnegie Endowment for International Peace, 2014); Pall, 'Between Ideology and International Politics: The Dynamics and Transformation of a Transnational Islamic Charity', in: Philip Fountain, Robin Bush, and R. Michael Feener (eds), *Religion and the Politics of Development* (Basingstoke: Palgrave Macmillan, 2015), 177—200. Lebanese Salafi émigrés also played a key role in organising the global protests against the cartoons of the Prophet Muhammad published in a Danish daily, *Jyllands-Posten*, in late 2005. The protests saw significant Sunni—Shia cooperation and a joint fatwa. One of the key organisers, however, lost his job at the mosque in Denmark later that year, after he denounced Hizbullah and the Shia as infidels and targets for a Jihad, bringing him into conflict with others at the mosque at the height of Hizbullah's popularity amongst Arabs and Muslims because of its performance in the 2006 war with Israel. Jytte Klausen, *The Cartoons that Shook the World* (New Haven: Yale University Press, 2009), 94. See also Ana Maria Luca, *Sectarian Conflict and Sunni Islamic Radicalization in Tripoli, Lebanon* (MA, Lebanese American University, 2015).

104. One Salafi Shaykh from Tripoli, Zakariyya al-Masri, who had studied at the Imam Muhammad Ibn Saud Islamic University in Riyadh in the 1980s, published numerous pamphlets denouncing Shiism and Hizbullah. Rougier, *The Sunni Tragedy*, 72ff.

105. He published, for example, books on the Shia in Lebanon and the Amal movement, on the assassination of Hariri, in which he denounces Iran's role in Lebanon, and on Sunnis in Iran, whom he seeks to support with his writings. For a list of his books, see his website: http://www.surour.net/index.php?group=viewg&gid=9. In general, see also Raihan Ismail, *Rethinking Salafism: The Transnational Networks of Salafi 'Ulama in Egypt, Kuwait, and Saudi Arabia* (New York: Oxford University Press, 2021), 63–103.

106. Martin Kramer, 'Redeeming Jerusalem: The Pan-Islamic Premise of Hizballah', in: David Menashri (ed.), *The Iranian Revolution and the Muslim World* (Boulder, CO: Westview Press, 1990), 105–30; Saad-Ghorayeb, *Hizbu'llah*, 69–76; Luke Wilkinson, 'Troubled Beginnings: The First Decade of Hizbullah's Interaction with Pan-Islamic Ideas', *MENAF*, 13 March 2020; Joseph Alagha, *Hizbullah's Identity Construction* (Amsterdam: Amsterdam University Press, 2011), 173f.; Alagha, *Hizbullah's Documents: From the 1985 Open Letter to the 2009 Manifesto* (Amsterdam: Amsterdam University Press, 2011), 53. See also Bashir Saade, *Hizbullah and the Politics of Remembrance: Writing the Lebanese Nation* (Cambridge: Cambridge University Press, 2016); Qasim, *Hizbullah*, 42–5, 307–15, 333–7, and passim; Joseph Alagha, *The Shifts in Hizbullah's Ideology: Religious Ideology, Political Ideology and Political Program* (Amsterdam: Amsterdam University Press, 2006); Daher, *Hezbollah*, 33; Joseph Alagha, 'Ideological Tensions between Hizbullah and Jihadi Salafism: Mutual Perceptions and Mutual Fears', in: Brigitte Maréchal and Sami Zemni (eds), *The Dynamics of Sunni-Shia Relationships: Doctrine, Transnationalism, Intellectuals and the Media* (London: Hurst, 2013), 61–82; Laleh Khalili, '"Standing with my Brother": Hizbullah, Palestinians, and the Limits of Solidarity', *Comparative Studies in Society and History* 49, 2 (2007), 276–303, 297f.; Robert G. Rabil, *Salafism in Lebanon: From Apoliticism to Transnational Jihadism* (Washington, DC: Georgetown University Press, 2014), esp. 126ff., 153–89.

107. In general, see Louër, *Sunnis and Shi'a*, 176–93, 196.

108. This also related to foreign involvement in the selection of candidates for the (Sunni) Grand Muftis of the republic. Alexander D. M. Henley, *Religious Authority and Sectarianism in Lebanon* (Washington, DC: Carnegie Endowment for International Peace, 2016).

109. Hannes Baumann, *Citizen Hariri: Lebanon's Neoliberal Reconstruction* (London: Hurst, 2016), 17–56. See also Kamal Dib, 'Predator Neoliberalism: Lebanon on the Brink of Disaster', *Contemporary Arab Affairs* 13, 1 (2020), 3–22.

110. Joseph Bahout, 'The Unraveling of Taif: The Limits of Sect-Based Power-Sharing in Lebanon', in: Frederic Wehrey (ed.), *Beyond Sunni and Shia: The Roots of Sectarianism in a Changing Middle East* (Oxford: Oxford University Press, 2018), 135–56, 142ff.; Bassel F. Salloukh, 'The Architecture of Sectarianization in

Lebanon', in: Nader Hashemi and Danny Postel (eds), *Sectarianization: Mapping the New Politics of the Middle East* (London: Hurst, 2017), 215–34, 220ff.

111. This allowed the Syrian regime to reward allies politically and economically, as the post-war reconstruction of Lebanon gained pace. See Reinoud Leenders, *Spoils of Truce: Corruption and State-Building in Postwar Lebanon* (Ithaca: Cornell University Press, 2012).

112. Alan Cowell, 'Syria and Iran Agree Militias Can Remain in Parts of Lebanon', *New York Times*, 30 April 1991; 'The Taif Agreement', https://www.un.int/ lebanon/sites/www.un.int/files/Lebanon/the_taif_agreement_english_ version_.pdf (accessed 1 January 2022).

113. Zalmay Khalilzad, 'The Iranian Revolution and the Afghan Resistance', in: Martin Kramer (ed.), *Shiʿism, Resistance, and Revolution* (Boulder, CO: Westview Press, 1987), 257–73, 270; Mousavi, *The Hazaras*, 175–9. For a discussion of the disputed sectarian identity of this PM, Kisthmand, see M. Hasan Kakar, *Afghanistan: The Soviet Invasion and the Afghan Response, 1979–1982* (Berkeley: University of California Press, 1995), 180ff., 310f.

114. Ismaili elites became integrated into the PDPA government. Hafizullah Emadi, 'The End of Taqiyya: Reaffirming the Religious Identity of Ismailis in Shughnan, Badakhshan: Political Implications for Afghanistan', *Middle Eastern Studies* 34, 3 (1998), 103–20.

115. Olivier Roy, *Islam and Resistance in Afghanistan* (Cambridge: Cambridge University Press, 1986); Steve Coll, *Ghost Wars: The Secret History of the CIA, Afghanistan and Bin Laden, from the Soviet Invasion to September 10, 2001* (New York: Penguin, 2004).

116. Monsutti, *War and Migration*, 68f., 94; Roy, *Islam and Resistance*, 50–3, 139–48; Khalilzad, 'The Iranian Revolution', 261; Mousavi, *The Hazaras*, 179–98; Ibrahimi, *The Hazaras*, 117–75; Alessandro Monsutti, 'Islamism among the Shi'a of Afghanistan: From Social Revolution to Identity-Building', in: Sabrina Mervin (ed.), *The Shi'a Worlds and Iran* (London: Saqi, 2010), 45–62; David B. Edwards, 'The Evolution of Shi'i Political Dissent in Afghanistan', in: Juan R. I. Cole and Nikki R. Keddie (eds), *Shiʿism and Social Protest* (New Haven: Yale University Press, 1986), 201–29; Hafizullah Emadi, 'Exporting Iran's Revolution: The Radicalization of the Shiite Movement in Afghanistan', *Middle Eastern Studies* 31, 1 (1995), 1–12; Kakar, *Afghanistan*, 94f., 118.

117. Roy, *Islam and Resistance*, 212; Ibrahimi, *The Hazaras*, 186; Barnett R. Rubin, *The Search for Peace in Afghanistan: From Buffer State to Failed State* (New Haven: Yale University Press, 1995), 105; Kakar, *Afghanistan*, 266f.; Alex Vatanka, *Iran and Pakistan: Security, Diplomacy and American Influence* (London: I. B. Tauris, 2015), 202f., 206; Peter Tomsen, *The Wars of Afghanistan: Messianic Terrorism, Tribal Conflicts, and the Failures of Great Powers* (New York: PublicAffairs, 2011). Rubin alleges that Saudi intelligence spent $25 million a week while the discussions in Peshawar were going on, and that each delegate received $25,000 to keep the Shia out. See also Benazir Bhutto, *Daughter of Destiny: An Autobiography* (London: Simon & Schuster, 1989), 399. Iran, in turn, in 1991

sought to bring about a rapprochement of Shii Hazara and Sunni Tajiks, focusing on common Persian linguistic bonds and downplaying sectarian difference. Vatanka, *Iran and Pakistan*, 203.

118. Thomas Hegghammer, *The Caravan: Abdallah Azzam and the Rise of Global Jihad* (Cambridge: Cambridge University Press, 2020), 99–102, 291, 337, 344f., 593n17; Lawrence Wright, *The Looming Tower: Al-Qaeda's Road to 9/11* (London: Allen Lane, 2006), 317. See also Anne Stenersen, *Al-Qaida in Afghanistan* (Cambridge: Cambridge University Press, 2017); Faisal Devji, *Landscapes of the Jihad: Militancy, Morality, Modernity* (London: Hurst, 2005), 51–4.

119. Immigration and Refugee Board of Canada, 'Pakistan: Whether Benazir Bhutto is a Shia; whether her Father, Z. A. Bhutto, was a Shia; and whether her Husband, Asif Ali Zardari is a Shia', 25 March 2002.

120. See, for example, Jonathan S. Addleton, *Undermining the Centre: The Gulf Migration and Pakistan* (Karachi: Oxford University Press, 1992), 158. For the general argument of Saudi Arabia using its importance as a migration destination, see Helene Thiollet, 'Migration as Diplomacy: Labor Migrants, Refugees, and Arab Regional Politics in the Oil-Rich Countries', *International Labor and Working-Class History* 79 (2011), 103–21.

121. There was apparently one Shia party, the Harakat-i Islami, which received help from Pakistan and was based in Islamabad, but this was mainly because, unlike the other Shia parties, it had a bad relationship with Iran. Gilles Dorronsoro, 'Pakistan's Afghan Policy', in: Soofia Mumtaz, Jean-Luc Racine, and Imran Anwar Ali (eds), *Pakistan: The Contours of State and Society* (Oxford: Oxford University Press, 2002), 251–65, 263. Some groups received support from both Iran and Pakistan. Pakistan's policy thus diverged from that of Saudi Arabia in that it also supported non-Wahhabi and non-Salafi groups that had a pan-Islamic angle and accepted Iranian support, such as Hekmatyar's group. See also Vatanka, *Iran and Pakistan*, 171–94, esp. 186.

122. Dorronsoro, 'Pakistan's Afghan Policy'. For Pakistan was fearful of subversion from Afghanistan, which never recognised the border between the two countries (the Durand Line). Afghan governments supported autonomy movements in the border region, the North-West Frontier Province of Pakistan (Afghanistan was the only country not to vote in favour of Pakistan's entry into the UN in 1947). Olivier Roy, 'The Taliban: A Strategic Tool for Pakistan', in: Christophe Jaffrelot (ed.), *Pakistan: Nationalism without a Nation?* (New Delhi: Manohar, 2002), 149–59.

123. He would die in September 1979, and so we have no way of knowing how he would have seen later developments. Mawdudi had previously been critical of Shiism; Khomeini, on the other hand, criticised the Jamaat-i Islami for its gradualist, peaceful approach to Islamic revolution. Seyyed Vali Reza Nasr, *Mawdudi and the Making of Islamic Revivalism* (Oxford: Oxford University Press, 1996), 165; Nasr, *The Shia Revival: How Conflicts within Islam will Shape the Future* (New York: Norton, 2006), 138; Jan-Peter Hartung, *A System of Life: Mawdudi and the Ideologisation of Islam* (New York: Oxford University Press, 2014), 67.

124. Devji, *Landscapes of the Jihad*, 54–60.

125.   Roy, 'The Impact of the Iranian Revolution', 32; Simon Wolfgang Fuchs, 'The Long Shadow of the State: The Iranian Revolution, Saudi Influence, and the Shifting Arguments of Anti-Shi'i Sectarianism in Pakistan', in: Laurence Louër and Christophe Jaffrelot (eds), *Pan-Islamic Connections: Transnational Networks between South Asia and the Gulf* (London: Hurst, 2017), 217–32. See also Seyyed Vali Reza Nasr, 'The Rise of Sunni Militancy in Pakistan: The Changing Role of Islamism and the Ulama in Society and Politics', *Modern Asian Studies* 34, 1 (2000), 139–80.

126.   The anti-Shia fatwas came in response to a request by Manzur Numani, an Indian Deobandi scholar with links to the Saudi-funded Muslim World League, who had already written a book against Iran and Khomeini. Ahmed, *Sectarian War*, xiiif. The Jamiyat al-Ulum al-Islamiyya, a Deobandi *madrasa* in Karachi founded in 1955 by Muhammad Yusuf Banuri (d. 1977), played a key role in anti-Shii activism. Zaman, 'Tradition and Authority', 72f.

127.   Seyyed Vali Reza Nasr, 'Islam, the State and the Rise of Sectarian Militancy in Pakistan', in: Christophe Jaffrelot (ed.), *Pakistan: Nationalism without a Nation?* (New Delhi: Manohar, 2002), 85–114, 90.

128.   In a later phase, from the 1990s onwards, Iran also set up a network of *madrasas* for female students across Pakistan, some of whom are tied to the Jamiyat al-Zahra, the main university for female students in Qom. Thousands of female students have graduated from these *madrasas*. Mariam Abou-Zahab, 'Between Pakistan and Qom: Shi'a Women's Madrasas and New Transnational Networks', in: Sabrina Mervin (ed.), *The Shi'a Worlds and Iran* (London: Saqi, 2010), 303–20. For more on female religious authority in Shia Islam, with a focus on Iran, see Mirjam Künkler and Roja Fazaeli, 'The Life of Two Mujtahidahs: Female Religious Authority in Twentieth-Century Iran', in: Masooda Bano and Hilary E. Kalmbach (eds), *Women, Leadership, and Mosques: Changes in Contemporary Islamic Authority* (Leiden: Brill, 2012), 127–60.

129.   Haydar, 'The Politicization of the Shias', 78f.

130.   Ahmed, *Sectarian War*, 30.

131.   Roy, 'The Impact of the Iranian Revolution', 32.

132.   For a list of the group's demands, see Haydar, 'The Politicization of the Shias', 79, 84, 87–90.

133.   Nasr, 'Islam, the State and the Rise', 89.

134.   For an account of the history of the group, see Haydar, 'The Politicization of the Shias', 79–86; Maleeha Lodhi, 'Pakistan's Shia Movement: An Interview with Arif Hussaini', *Third World Quarterly* 10, 2 (1988), 806–17. See also an affiliated website: http://www.tnfj.org.uk.

135.   Mariam Abou-Zahab, 'Sectarianism as Substitute Identity: Sunnis and Shias in Central and South Punjab', in: Soofia Mumtaz, Jean-Luc Racine, and Imran Anwar Ali (eds), *Pakistan: The Contours of State and Society* (Oxford: Oxford University Press, 2002), 77–95, 77, 93n51.

136.   Ehsan Elahi Zaheer, *Al-Shi'a wa-l-Sunna* (Lahore: Idara Tarjuman al-Sunnah, 1975). This book, which describes Shiism as a Jewish invention, argues that Shia practise widespread dissimulation, criticises the position of the Imams in

Shiism, and saw numerous reprints in Cairo, Jordan, and Lahore. The above edition features as a price indication that it should be sold for '5 Saudi riyals or the equivalent', indicating that it was aimed at the Saudi market. See also Fuchs, *In a Pure Muslim Land*, 152–85; Marcinkowski, *Shi'ite Identities*, 80; Haykel, 'Al-Qa'ida and Shiism', 191; Khalid Zafarullah Daudi, 'Ihsan Ilâhî Zahîr', *Islâm Ansiklopedisi*, https://islamansiklopedisi.org.tr/ihsan-ilahi-zahir; Simon Wolfgang Fuchs, 'Faded Networks: The Overestimated Saudi Legacy of Anti-Shi'i Sectarianism in Pakistan', *Global Discourse* 9, 4 (2019), 703–15; Mariam Abou-Zahab, 'Salafism in Pakistan: The Ahl-e Hadith Movement', in: Roel Meijer (ed.), *Global Salafism: Islam's New Religious Movement* (London: Hurst, 2009), 126–42, 131. For a list of his books held in libraries across the world, which indicates translations published in Malaysia, Indonesia, and beyond, see https://www.worldcat.org/search?qt=worldcat_org_all&q=+++ +++++Z%CC%A3ahi%CC%84r%2C+Ih%CC%A3sa%CC%84n+Ila%CC %84hi%CC%84.

137. Salafi-dawah.com, 'Shaykh Ehsan Elahi Zaheer was a Mujahid!', http://www. salafi-dawah.com/shaykh-ehsan-elahi-zaheer-was-a-mujahid.html.

138. Ende, 'Sunni Polemical Writings', 226.

139. For a journalistic account with a list of attacks during that period, see Musa Khan Jalalzai, *The Sunni–Shia Conflict in Pakistan* (Lahore: Book Traders, 1998).

140. Mariam Abou-Zahab, 'The Sunni–Shia Conflict in Jhang (Pakistan)', in: Imtiaz Ahmed and Helmut Reifeld (eds), *Lived Islam in South Asia: Adaptation, Accommodation and Conflict* (New Delhi: Social Science, 2004), 135–48, 136; Abou-Zahab, 'Sectarianism', 87; Nasr, 'Islam, the State and the Rise', 95ff.

141. Mariam Abou-Zahab, '"It's Just a Sunni–Shia Thing": Sectarianism and Talibanism in the FATA (Federally Administered Tribal Areas) of Pakistan', in: Brigitte Maréchal and Sami Zemni (eds), *The Dynamics of Sunni–Shia Relationships: Doctrine, Transnationalism, Intellectuals and the Media* (London: Hurst, 2013), 179–92. See also Haroon, *Frontier of Faith*.

142. Nasr, 'Islam, the State and the Rise', 86; Rieck, *The Shias of Pakistan*, 231–8.

143. Laurent Bonnefoy, 'Biography: Muqbil ibn Hadi al-Wadi'i: Founder of Salafism in Yemen', in: Roel Meijer (ed.), *Global Salafism: Islam's New Religious Movement* (London: Hurst, 2009), 431–2. Despite some ambiguity in their relationship with the Saudi and Yemeni states, Salafis in Yemen were seen as pro-Saudi. Bonnefoy, 'How Transnational is Salafism in Yemen?', in: Roel Meijer (ed.), *Global Salafism: Islam's New Religious Movement* (London: Hurst, 2009), 321–41, 323, 327, 333f., 336.

144. Vom Bruck, 'Regimes of Piety Revisited', 187–91. For a fatwa by Muqbil on marriage with Zaydis, see http://www.muqbel.net/fatwa.php?fatwa_id=2400. For more of his statements on the Zaydis, see http://www.muqbel.net/search. php?keyword=%D8%A7%D9%84%D8%B2%D9%8A%D8%AF%D9%8A%D 8%A9&searchIn=0&search=%D8%A8%D8%AD%D8%AB. For the issue of *taqrib*, see http://www.muqbel.net/fatwa.php?fatwa_id=4666.

145. Abi ʿAbd al-Rahman Muqbil ibn Hadi al-Wadiʿi, *Al-Ilhad al-Khumayni fi Ard al-Haramayn*, 2nd ed. (Sanaa: Dar al-Athar, 2000). It is discussed in Ismail, *Saudi Clerics*, 149f., and Meir Litvak, '"More Harmful than the Jews": Anti-Shiʿi Polemics in Modern Radical Sunni Discourse', in: Mohammad Ali Amir-Moezzi, Meir M. Bar-Asher, and Simon Hopkins (eds), *Le shīʿisme imāmite quarante ans après: Hommage à Etan Kohlberg* (Turnhout: Brepols, 2009), 293–314, 303.

146. Hamidi, 'Inscriptions of Violence', 170.

147. After the fall of Marxist South Yemen in 1990, some of them participated as allies of the North Yemeni government in a brief civil war between the North and the South in 1994. Gregory D. Johnsen, *The Last Refuge: Yemen, al-Qaeda, and the Battle for Arabia* (London: Oneworld, 2013), ch. 1 deals with Yemenis in Afghanistan, ch. 2 deals with the use of the Mujahedin in South Yemen after 1990.

148. Barak Barfi, 'AQAP's Soft Power Strategy in Yemen', *CTC Sentinel* 3, 11–12 (2010), 1–5.

149. Zaydis pray with their arms extended, Sunnis fold their arms. Bonnefoy, *Salafism in Yemen*, 266.

150. He justified it by saying that a Muslim could not pray behind those who were known to practise *ghuluw* (exaggeration) in their relationship with the Prophets. The fatwa came in response to a question he had received from a Saudi Education Commission in Yemen. He acknowledged that there was some uncertainty surrounding the question of whether the majority of Zaydi scholars were really practising *ghuluw* and were therefore to be associated with *shirk*. Some Yemeni students at the Islamic University in Medina had spoken to him in this regard, but until there was a clear statement by Zaydi scholars rectifying their positions, he had to forbid praying behind them. See the fatwas and sayings of Ibn Baz on his website, previously available at https://www.binbaz.org.sa/article/71 and https://www.binbaz.org.sa/article/325 (accessed 7 December 2017). Showing a general lack of knowledge, he apparently had to retract this, although it is still accessible on his website. Barfi, 'AQAP's Soft Power Strategy'. While Wahhabi clerics had historically treated Zaydis in a slightly milder way than other Shias, they were still the subject of fierce attacks. See Ismail, *Saudi Clerics*, 63, for a discussion of a refutation of the Zaydiyya by Shaykh Mamduh al-Harbi.

151. A famous reply was written by the Alawite cleric Abd al-Rahman al-Khayyir and published with a brief introductory statement by Abdul Rahman al-Eryani, a Zaydi and former Yemeni judge under the Imamate, then long-term political prisoner for his support of the reform movement, and subsequently Yemeni president from 1967 until 1974, during which time he sought to bring about a reconciliation between monarchists and republicans. When he was driven out of power in 1974, he moved to Syria, which likely explains his letter to al-Khayyir. Stéphane Valter, 'La réplique à Ibn Baz (1912–1999) de ʿAbd al-Rahman al-Hayyir (1904–1986)', *Bulletin d'études orientales* 55 (2003), 299–383.

152. He also reacted to other fatwas and books that criticised the Zaydiyya, some going as far as declaring it *kufr*. In the introduction, he states that he thought

it was necessary to tackle the whole argument head on, not just the specific fatwas, and therefore starts his critique with a repudiation of Muhammad Ibn Abd al-Wahhab's famous book *kashf al-shubuhat fi al-tawhid* on the notion of *kufr*. He then moves on to tackle the different arguments of Ibn Baz to substantiate his fatwa against the Zaydiyya. Badr al-Din ibn Amir al-Din ibn al-Husayn al-Hawthi al-Husayni, *Al-Ijaz fi al-Radd 'Ala Fatawa al-Hijaz* (Sana: Maktabat al-Yaman al-Kubra, 1979), 21. It is briefly discussed in Barak A. Salmoni, Bryce Loidolt, and Madeleine Wells, *Regime and Periphery in Northern Yemen: The Huthi Phenomenon* (Santa Monica, CA: RAND, 2010), appendix C, which includes an annotated list of writings by Huthi leaders. On the notion of the visitation of shrines and the bowing (*ukuf*) in front of graves, al-Huthi argues that this is acceptable as long as it does not imply praying or worshipping the tomb, i.e. it does not need to be *shirk*. These points are also discussed by Samy Dorlian, *La mouvance zaydite dans le Yémen contemporain: Une modernisation avortée* (Paris: L'Harmattan, 2013), 163f. Ibn Abd al-Wahhab's booklet is reprinted by the Saudi government. See Muhammad ibn Abd al-Wahhab, *Kashf al-Shubuhat fi al-Tawhid* (Riyadh: Wizarat al-Shu'un al-Islamiyya wa-l-Da'wa wa-l-Irshad, 1419h). Al-Huthi pointed out that Ibn Baz's stance undermined official Saudi calls for Islamic unity. He used Hadith cited by Sunni authorities Bukhari and Muslim. Al-Husayni, *Al-Ijaz fi al-Radd*, 70; Dorlian, *La mouvance zaydite*, 163. Badr al-Din al-Huthi had moved from Dahyan, a religious scholarly community near Saada, to Marran in the 1950s. After 1962, he became a very influential local personality, carrying out many functions that would normally be done by a government. His son Hussain studied with him, as well as other local *ulama*, at the Mahad Ilmi in Saada and later at Sanaa University. Hamidi, 'Inscriptions of Violence', 167. See also Bonnefoy, *Salafism in Yemen*, 10ff.

153. Johnsen, *The Last Refuge*, 156. For more on the Huthi rebellion, see ibid., 144–59. A recording circulates online in which Muqbil al-Wadi relates Ibn Baz's views on Badr al-Din al-Huthi: https://www.youtube.com/watch?v=8UFkXaFbEkQ.

154. Mohammed Almahfali and James Root, 'How Iran's Islamic Revolution does, and does not, Influence Houthi Rule in Northern Yemen', *Sanaa Center*, 13 February 2020.

155. Hamidi, 'Inscriptions of Violence', 168f.

156. Hamad H. Albloshi, 'Ideological Roots of the Ḥūthī Movement in Yemen', *Journal of Arabian Studies* 6, 2 (2016), 143–62, 153–7. See also Abdullah Lux, 'Yemen's Last Zaydī Imām: The Shabāb al-Mu'min, the Malāzim, and "Ḥizb Allāh" in the Thought of Ḥusayn Badr al-Dīn al-Ḥūthī', *Contemporary Arab Affairs* 2, 3 (2009), 369–434.

157. Hamidi, 'Inscriptions of Violence', 167; Haykel, *Revival and Reform*, 227. See also James Robin King, 'Zaydī Revival in a Hostile Republic: Competing Identities, Loyalties and Visions of State in Republican Yemen', *Arabica* 59, 3–4 (2012), 404–45.

158. Including Ghadir Khumm (which had stopped after 1963) and the commemoration of Ali's arrival in Yemen. Ghadir Khumm was particularly controversial.

As we have seen earlier, it is held each year on the eighteenth day of Dhu al-Hijja and celebrates Ali's designation as the Prophet Muhammad's successor (who is said by the Shia to have announced this at Ghadir Khumm). The festival thus implicitly rejects the Caliphate of Abu Bakr and highlights the Alids' right to rule, which in the Yemeni context is often seen as a hint towards the Sayyids' right to rule. After clashes between the army and supporters of al-Huthi, however, the Ghadir ritual was prohibited again. Vom Bruck, *Islam*, 242. In 1992, local Salafis organised a campaign against the Ghadir festival to be organised in Razih. See Bonnefoy, *Salafism in Yemen*, 99; Shelagh Weir, 'A Clash of Fundamentalisms: Wahhabism in Yemen', *Middle East Report* 204 (1997), 22–3/26. See also Weir, *A Tribal Order: Politics and Law in the Mountains of Yemen* (Austin: University of Texas Press, 2007); Bernard Haykel, 'Recent Publishing Activity by the Zaidis in Yemen: A Select Bibliography', *Chroniques yéménites* 9 (2001), 225–7; Weir, 'A Zaydi Revival?', *Yemen Update* 36 (1995), 20–1. This also included setting up new publishing houses, such as the Maktabat Ahl al-Bayt in Saada. The first Zaydi books were only printed in the early twentieth century, many of them abroad, in particular in Cairo at *al-Manar* press. Messick, *The Calligraphic State*, 129. See also Muhammad ibn al-Qasim Huthi, *Al-Mawʿiza al-Hasana* (Saada: Maktabat Ahl al-Bayt, 1435h); Wachowski, *Sāda in Sanaʿāʾ*, 101.

CHAPTER 13

1. Tareq Y. Ismael and Jacqueline S. Ismael, *The Gulf War and the New World Order: International Relations of the Middle East* (Gainesville: University Press of Florida, 1994); Fred Halliday, *The Middle East in International Relations: Power, Politics and Ideology* (Cambridge: Cambridge University Press, 2005), 130–64; Raymond Hinnebusch, *The International Politics of the Middle East*, 2nd ed. (Manchester: Manchester University Press, 2015), 225–71.

2. Odd Arne Westad, *The Global Cold War: Third World Interventions and the Making of our Times* (Cambridge: Cambridge University Press, 2005).

3. Halawi, *A Lebanon Defied*, 1–14, esp. 1ff.; Robert Tomlinson, *Covering the Shiʿa: English Press Representation of the Lebanese Shiʿa 1975–1985* (Lanham: Lexington Books, 2018).

4. A decade after the Iranian Revolution, a well-known authority on Safavid Iran would, for example, open an edited volume, following up on a conference held in Israel on the revolution, with the question, 'Is Ithna Asharism Innately Revolutionary?'. Roger M. Savory, 'The Export of Ithnā ʿAsharī Shīʿism: Historical and Ideological Background', in: David Menashri (ed.), *The Iranian Revolution and the Muslim World* (Boulder, CO: Westview Press, 1990), 13–39, 14ff. A major overview of scholarship on Shiism and politics published in 1987 states that, '[w]hen they could, Shiʿis often rebelled; Islamic history is strewn with Shiʿi uprisings', thereby reiterating the state/Caliphate vs. Shii rebels dichotomy alluded to above, but not before adding that 'most of these failed dismally, and the few Shiʿi move-

ments which succeeded in seizing power soon lost their sense of higher purpose'. Martin Kramer, 'Introduction', in: Martin Kramer (ed.), *Shi'ism, Resistance, and Revolution* (Boulder, CO: Westview Press, 1987), 1–18, 2.

5. Faisal Devji, 'Imitatio Muhammadi: Khomeini and the Mystery of Citizenship', *Cultural Dynamics* 13, 3 (2001), 363–71.

6. Deepa Kumar, 'The Right Kind of "Islam": News Media Representations of US–Saudi Relations during the Cold War', *Journalism Studies* 19, 8 (2018), 1079–97.

7. Janet Afary and Kevin B. Anderson, *Foucault and the Iranian Revolution: Gender and the Seductions of Islamism* (Chicago: University of Chicago Press, 2005); Behrooz Ghamari-Tabrizi, *Foucault in Iran: Islamic Revolution after the Enlightenment* (Minneapolis: University of Minnesota Press, 2016). The revolution also led to a renewed interest in Shiism amongst Soviet Orientalists. Muriel Atkin, 'Soviet Attitudes toward Shi'ism and Social Protest', in: Juan R. I. Cole and Nikki R. Keddie (eds), *Shi'ism and Social Protest* (New Haven: Yale University Press, 1986), 275–301.

8. Halliday, *The Middle East*, 100. There were exceptions, of course, such as the Iran-Contra affair, weapons sales by France to Iran, and trade ties with Germany and other European countries. Trita Parsi, *Treacherous Alliance: The Secret Dealings of Israel, Iran, and the United States* (New Haven: Yale University Press, 2007).

9. Personal conversations, Karbala and Najaf, Iraq, 2018 and 2019; Wafa Amr, 'Shiite Shrines at Karbala, Najaf Show Blood, Battle Scars', *Associated Press*, 1 April 1991; 'Excerpts from 2 Statements by Bush on Iraq's Proposal for Ending Conflict', *New York Times*, 16 February 1991; Human Rights Watch, 'Endless Torment: The 1991 Uprising in Iraq and Its Aftermath', June 1992. In general, see Haddad, *Sectarianism in Iraq*, 65–86; Khoury, *Iraq in Wartime*, 124–45; Faleh A. Jabar, 'Why the Uprisings Failed', *Middle East Report* 176 (1992), 2–14; Keiko Sakai, 'The 1991 Intifadah in Iraq: Seen through Analyses of the Discourses of Iraqi Intellectuals', in: Keiko Sakai (ed.), *Social Protests and Nation-Building in the Middle East and Central Asia* (Chiba: Institute of Developing Economies, 2003), 157–72.

10. Tim Arango, 'A Long-Awaited Apology for Shiites, but the Wounds Run Deep', *New York Times*, 8 November 2011; Jon Meacham, *Destiny and Power: The American Odyssey of George Herbert Walker Bush* (New York: Random House, 2015); Paul Wolfowitz, 'The Gulf War Ended Too Soon: Bush Was Right Not to Go All the Way to Baghdad, but He Should Have Backed Shiite Rebels in Southern Iraq', *Wall Street Journal*, 12 August 2020.

11. This open addressing of sectarian division and the use of the terms 'Shia' and 'Kurd' in official discourse were a novelty. Davis, *Memories of State*, 242ff. It had long been argued that Saddam himself was the author of these articles, though that has been questioned. Haddad, *Sectarianism in Iraq*, 119–27; Helfont, *Compulsion in Religion*, 121–8.

12. Davis, *Memories of State*, 248. The line that the intifada was Iranian-inspired and partly carried out by Iranians was also pushed by Iraqi TV, which argued that the intifada was part of an American–Iranian conspiracy in cooperation with local 'traitors'. See https://www.youtube.com/watch?v=Z_APaniNgyI.

13. Haddad, *Sectarianism in Iraq*, 117–41; Helfont, *Compulsion in Religion*, 114–28. The regime also employed Shii tribes along the Iranian border to prevent infiltration from Iran, as part of a wider attempt to empower tribal chiefs (all the while marginalising Shii tribes). Baram, *Saddam Husayn*, 367n2; Haddad, *Sectarianism in Iraq*, 101; Amatzia Baram, 'Neo-Tribalism in Iraq: Saddam Hussein's Tribal Policies 1991–96', *International Journal of Middle East Studies* 29, 1 (1997), 1–31; Osman, *Sectarianism in Iraq*, 127. See also Lisa Blaydes, 'Rebuilding the Ba'thist State: Party, Tribe, and Administrative Control in Authoritarian Iraq, 1991–1996', *Comparative Politics* 53, 1 (2020), 1–23.

14. Davis, *Memories of State*, 248f.; Falih Abdul-Jabar, interview, cited in: Moslem, *Frieden im Islam*, 214; 'Saddam's Name Struck off Prophet's Lineage', *al-Jazeera*, 17 December 2003.

15. Jerry M. Long, *Saddam's War of Words: Politics, Religion, and the Iraqi Invasion of Kuwait* (Austin: University of Texas Press, 2004).

16. For background on the Naqshbandis, see Ramazan Aras, 'Naqshbandi Sufis and their Conception of Place, Time and Fear on the Turkish–Syrian Border and Borderland', *Middle Eastern Studies* 55, 1 (2019), 44–59. See also Elisheva Machlis, 'Reevaluating Sectarianism in Light of Sufi Islam: The Case-Studies of the Naqshbandiyya and Qadiriyya in Syria and Iraq', *Sociology of Islam* 7, 1 (2019), 22–40.

17. Helfont, *Compulsion in Religion*, 174–201; Helfont, 'Saddam and the Islamists: The Ba'thist Regime's Instrumentalization of Religion in Foreign Affairs', *Middle East Journal* 68, 3 (2014), 352–66. Speculation abounds, too, as to whether the regime already sensed that an invasion was looming and tried to foster ties between these groups to prepare for an eventual resistance. Joel Rayburn, *Iraq after America: Strongmen, Sectarians, Resistance* (Stanford: Hoover Institution Press, 2014), 101–9. See also Haddad, *Sectarianism in Iraq*, 103–9.

18. Haddad, *Sectarianism in Iraq*, 87–116; Haddad, 'Sectarian Relations before "Sectarianization" in Pre-2003 Iraq', in: Nader Hashemi and Danny Postel (eds), *Sectarianization: Mapping the New Politics of the Middle East* (London: Hurst, 2017), 101–22.

19. Haddad, *Sectarianism in Iraq*, 148; Davis, *Memories of State*, 261f.; Toby Dodge, 'Tracing the Rise of Sectarianism in Iraq after 2003', *LSE*, 13 September 2018.

20. See Jens-Uwe Rahe, 'Iraqi Shi'is in Exile in London', in: Faleh Abdul-Jabar (ed.), *Ayatollahs, Sufis and Ideologues: State, Religion and Social Movements in Iraq* (London: Saqi, 2002), 211–19; International Crisis Group, *Shiite Politics in Iraq: The Role of the Supreme Council* (Brussels: International Crisis Group, 2007), 5–9. For a powerful critique, see Juan Cole, 'The Iraqi Shiites: On the History of America's Would-be Allies', *Boston Review*, October/November 2003. See also the files in the Digital National Security Archive, 'Targeting Iraq, Part 1: Planning, Invasion, and Occupation, 1997–2004', https://proquest.libguides.com/dnsa/iraq97; interviews with Yousif al-Khoei and Ghanim Jawad, al-Khoei Foundation, London, 2008.

21. This can be seen in Graham E. Fuller and Rend Rahim Francke, *The Arab Shi'a: The Forgotten Muslims* (Basingstoke: Macmillan, 1999), but also in Nakash,

Reaching for Power, and Seyyed Vali Reza Nasr, *The Shia Revival: How Conflicts within Islam will Shape the Future* (New York: Norton, 2006). See also Juan R. I. Cole, 'The United States and Shi'ite Religious Factions in Post-Ba'thist Iraq', *Middle East Journal* 57, 4 (2003), 543–66. Since the invasion, moreover, countless writings explored the fate of Arab Shia and sectarian relations in Iraq. Excerpts of one of the most important studies of modern Iraqi history by the twentieth-century Iraqi sociologist Ali al-Wardi were, for example, translated into English and published with a foreword by an American soldier, explaining the value of al-Wardi's work for American soldiers and diplomats. The book is dedicated to 'Arlington Cemetery Section 60', a well-known military cemetery in Virginia where fallen US soldiers have been buried since the American Civil War. Al-Wardi's texts that were translated, and the American introductions, frame Iraqi history in terms of urban-rural, settled-tribal, and Sunni–Shia dichotomies. Ali al-Wardi, *Iraq in Turmoil: Historical Perspectives of Dr Ali al-Wardi, from the Ottoman Empire to King Feisal*, comp. by Youssef H. Aboul-Enein (Annapolis, MD: Naval Institute Press, 2012). The introduction to a translation of another of his books, *Study of the Nature of Iraqi Society*, emphasises the relevance of his writings for American policy-makers. Al-Wardi, *Understanding Iraq*. See also Fouad Jabir Kadhem al-Zurfi, 'Sectarianism in Iraq: A Critique by Ali al-Wardi', *Contemporary Arab Affairs* 7, 4 (2014), 510–25.

22. Sonoko Sunayama, *Syria and Saudi Arabia: Collaboration and Conflicts in the Oil Era* (London: Tauris, 2007); Eyal Ziser, *Asad's Legacy: Syria in Transition* (London: Hurst, 2001), 52–66.

23. Matthiesen, 'Shi'i Historians'. At the same time, they emphasised their belonging to the nation. Roel Meijer and Joas Wagemakers, 'The Struggle for Citizenship of the Shiites of Saudi Arabia', in: Brigitte Maréchal and Sami Zemni (eds), *The Dynamics of Sunni–Shia Relationships: Doctrine, Transnationalism, Intellectuals and the Media* (London: Hurst, 2013), 117–38.

24. Mamoun Fandy, 'From Confrontation to Creative Resistance: The Shia's Oppositional Discourse in Saudi Arabia', *Critique: Critical Middle Eastern Studies* 5, 9 (1996), 1–27; Laurence Louër, 'Shi'i Identity Politics in Saudi Arabia', in: Anh Nga Longva and Anne Sofie Roald (eds), *Religious Minorities in the Middle East: Domination, Self-Empowerment, Accommodation* (Leiden: Brill, 2012), 219–43.

25. Toby Matthiesen, 'Government and Opposition in the Middle East: The 1993 Negotiations between the Saudi Shia Opposition and King Fahd', in: Gabriele vom Bruck and Charles Tripp (eds), *Precarious Belongings: Being Shi'i in Non-Shi'i Worlds* (London: Centre for Academic Shia Studies, 2017), 377–417.

26. Munira Fakhro, 'The Uprising in Bahrain: An Assessment', in: Gary Sick and Lawrence Potter (eds), *The Persian Gulf at the Millennium: Essays in Politics, Economy, Security, and Religion* (Basingstoke: Macmillan, 1997), 167–88; Ute Meinel, *Die Intifada im Ölscheichtum Bahrain: Hintergründe des Aufbegehrens von 1994–98* (Münster: LIT, 2003).

27. Rieck, *The Shias of Pakistan*, 239–73; Vatanka, *Iran and Pakistan*, 200, 209f.

28. For background, see Madawi al-Rasheed, *Contesting the Saudi State: Islamic Voices from a New Generation* (Cambridge: Cambridge University Press, 2007); Lacroix, *Awakening Islam*; Mamoun Fandy, *Saudi Arabia and the Politics of Dissent* (Basingstoke: Macmillan, 1999); Thomas Hegghammer, *Jihad in Saudi Arabia: Violence and Pan-Islamism since 1979* (Cambridge: Cambridge University Press, 2010).

29. Iranian foreign minister Velayati and Prince Saud al-Faisal met secretly in Muscat in May 1989 for the first time since the breaking-off of diplomatic relations in April 1988. Banafsheh Keynoush, *Saudi Arabia and Iran: Friends or Foes?* (Basingstoke: Palgrave Macmillan, 2016); Marschall, *Iran's Persian Gulf Policy*; Fürtig, *Iran's Rivalry*; Dilip Hiro, *Cold War in the Islamic World: Saudi Arabia, Iran and the Struggle for Supremacy* (London: Hurst, 2018), 141–62; Matthiesen, 'Hizbullah al-Hijaz'; Bruce Riedel, 'Why Did It Take Saudi Arabia 20 Years to Catch Khobar Towers Bomber?', *al-Monitor*, 26 August 2015.

30. For the general discussion, see Emran Qureshi and Michael A. Sells (eds), *The New Crusades: Constructing the Muslim Enemy* (New York: Columbia University Press, 2003).

31. See US Secretary of State Condoleezza Rice's speech before AIPAC in 2005, https://www.youtube.com/watch?v=-sE8xivjkIY, as well as her 2006 comments made to Israeli Prime Minister Ehud Olmert, https://www.youtube.com/watch?v=rUpBLbPRm8M. The actual term was used in a speech she gave in Tel Aviv in June 2006 that swiftly gained notoriety.

32. Alex Strick van Linschoten and Felix Kuehn, *An Enemy We Created: The Myth of the Taliban/al-Qaeda Merger in Afghanistan, 1970–2010* (London: Hurst, 2012). But see also Jan-Peter Hartung, 'Between a Rock and a Hard Place: The Ṭālibān, Afghan Self-Determination, and the Challenges of Transnational Jihadism', *Die Welt des Islams* 56, 2 (2016), 125–52.

33. Ahmed, *Sectarian War*, xiii; Dorronsoro, 'Pakistan's Afghan Policy'; Halverson, *Theology*, ch. 5.

34. The Taliban had allegedly promised Hezb-i Wahdat that it would respect the party's demands for Shii communal law. Ibrahimi, *The Hazaras*, 197f. See also Mousavi, *The Hazaras*, 198–202; Ahmed Rashid, *Taliban: Militant Islam, Oil and Fundamentalism in Central Asia* (London: I. B. Tauris, 2001), 34f., 62ff., 67–75, 139.

35. Human Rights Watch, 'Afghanistan: The Massacre in Mazar-i Sharif', November 1998; Dorronsoro, 'Pakistan's Afghan Policy', 259, 264n18; Ibrahimi, *The Hazaras*, 198–208; Adnan Tabatabai, *Morgen in Iran: Die Islamische Republik im Aufbruch* (Hamburg: Körber-Stiftung, 2016), 127f.; Hazara.net, 'Massacre of Hazaras in Bamyan: September 1998–May 1999', https://www.hazara.net/persecution/bamyan.html; Vatanka, *Iran and Pakistan*, 217ff.

36. Rieck, *The Shias of Pakistan*, 249–63.

37. Ibid., 275–98; Nasr, 'The Rise of Sunni Militancy'.

38. Alexis Nicholson, 'Iran and the United States in Afghanistan: An International History, 1996–2002', *Oxford Middle East Review* 3, 1 (2019), 51–71; Ostovar, *Vanguard of the Imam*, 160f.

39. Nivi Manchanda, *Imagining Afghanistan: The History and Politics of Imperial Knowledge* (Cambridge: Cambridge University Press, 2020).

40. Monsutti, *War and Migration*, 68f., 94; Ibrahimi, *The Hazaras*, 213–27; Adlparvar, 'When Glass Breaks, It Becomes Sharper', 111–57; Hazara.net, 'The Conference in Bonn: A Step in the Right Direction', https://www.hazara.net/takeaction/bonn/bonn2.html; Melissa Kerr Chiovenda, 'Hazara Civil Society Activists and Local, National, and International Political Institutions', in: M. Nazif Shahrani (ed.), *Modern Afghanistan: The Impact of 40 Years of War* (Bloomington: Indiana University Press, 2018), 251–70. Separate personal status law courts for Shia were created in 2004. The Shia Personal Status Law was sponsored by the Afghan Shii cleric Asif Mohseni, who had been the founder of the Islamic Movement of Afghanistan. It was ratified by Hamid Karzai in 2009, but was then criticised for curtailing women's rights. Human Rights Watch, '"We Have the Promises of the World": Women's Rights in Afghanistan', 6 December 2009.

41. Ibrahimi, *The Hazaras*, 213, 233.

42. Shah Mahmoud Hanifi, 'Making Space for Shi'ism in Afghanistan's Public Sphere and State Structure', *Perspectives on History*, 1 July 2015.

43. *PBS Frontline*, '"An Axis of Evil": President George W. Bush: State of the Union Address', 29 January 2002.

44. Ostovar, *Vanguard of the Imam*, 161–5.

45. David Leigh and Richard Norton-Taylor, 'Iraqi Who Gave MI6 45-Minute Claim Says It Was Untrue', *Guardian*, 28 January 2004; *The Age*, 'Spy Chief Regrets "45 Minute" Iraq Weapons Claim', 17 September 2003. See also The National Archives, 'The Iraq Inquiry: The Report', 6 July 2016, https://webarchive.nationalarchives.gov.uk/20171123122743/; http://www.iraqinquiry.org.uk/the-rep; Philip Robins, 'The War for Regime Change in Iraq', in: Louise Fawcett (ed.), *International Relations of the Middle East*, 3rd ed. (Oxford: Oxford University Press, 2013), 304–20; Frank P. Harvey, *Explaining the Iraq War: Counterfactual Theory, Logic and Evidence* (Cambridge: Cambridge University Press, 2012).

46. Quoted in: 'A Letter from Saddam Hussein to the Iraqi People and the Arab Nation', *Memri.org*, 1 May 2003. See also Nassima Neggaz, 'Sectarianization and Memory in the Post-Saddam Middle East: The 'Alāqima', *British Journal of Middle Eastern Studies* 49, 1 (2022), 159–76, 172f.

47. Marc Lynch, *Voices of the New Arab Public: Iraq, al-Jazeera, and Middle East Politics Today* (New York: Columbia University Press, 2006). For the original notion of the public sphere, see Jürgen Habermas, *Strukturwandel der Öffentlichkeit: Untersuchungen zu einer Kategorie der bürgerlichen Gesellschaft* (Neuwied: Luchterhand, 1962).

48. Ahmed K. al-Rawi, 'The US Influence in Shaping Iraq's Sectarian Media', *International Communication Gazette* 75, 4 (2013), 374–91; Khaled Hroub, 'The Role of the Media in the Middle Eastern Sectarian Divide', in: Eduardo López Busquets (ed.), *Sunni and Shia: Political Readings of a Religious Dichotomy* (Cordoba: Casa Árabe, 2014), 37–47, 41ff. For case studies of Sunni and Shii TV channels, see Khaled Hroub (ed.), *Religious Broadcasting in the Middle East* (New York: Columbia University Press, 2012).

49. Two of the most infamous sites are http://www.dd-sunnah.net; https://gift2shias.com/about-2. For a collection of anti-Shii books, see section 'al-Radd 'ala al-Rafida' on https://www.noor-book.com. For a discussion, see Isaac Hasson, *Contemporary Polemics between Neo-Wahhabis and Post-Khomeinist Shiites* (Washington, DC: Hudson Institute, 2009). See also Hroub, 'The Role of the Media', 38.

50. Helfont, *Compulsion in Religion*, 227ff.; Joby Warrick, *Black Flags: The Rise of ISIS* (London: Bantam, 2015); George Michael, 'The Legend and Legacy of Abu Musab al-Zarqawi', *Defence Studies* 7, 3 (2007), 338–57; Guido Steinberg, *Der nahe und der ferne Feind: Die Netzwerke des islamistischen Terrors* (Munich: C. H. Beck, 2005), 217–35.

51. This was the title of a message he released in mid-May 2005. Osman, *Sectarianism in Iraq*, 64, 96f.; Steinberg, 'Jihadi-Salafism', 111.

52. Tim Jacoby and Nassima Neggaz, 'Sectarianism in Iraq: The Role of the Coalition Provisional Authority', *Critical Studies on Terrorism* 11, 3 (2018), 478–500.

53. Cole, 'The United States'.

54. In exile in Lebanon, he had married Leila Osseiran, daughter of the long-time MP and speaker of the Lebanese parliament Adil Osseiran. The speaker of the Lebanese parliament was under Lebanon's sectarian power-sharing agreement also a Shii.

55. Juan R. I. Cole, 'Struggles over Personal Status and Family Law in Post-Baathist Iraq', in: Kenneth M. Cuno and Manisha Desai (eds), *Family, Gender, and Law in a Globalizing Middle East and South Asia* (Syracuse: Syracuse University Press, 2009), 105–25.

56. David Romano, 'Iraq's Descent into Civil War: A Constitutional Explanation', *Middle East Journal* 68, 4 (2014), 547–66, 549; Matthijs Bogaards, 'Iraq's Constitution of 2005: The Case against Consociationalism "Light"', *Ethnopolitics* 20, 2 (2021), 186–202; Toby Dodge and Renad Mansour, 'Sectarianization and De-Sectarianization in the Struggle for Iraq's Political Field', *Review of Faith & International Affairs* 18, 1 (2020), 58–69; Tareq Y. Ismael and Jacqueline S. Ismael, 'The Sectarian State in Iraq and the New Political Class', *International Journal of Contemporary Iraqi Studies* 4, 3 (2010), 339–56; Feisal Amin Rasoul al-Istrabadi, 'Sectarian Visions of the Iraqi State: Irreconcilable Differences?', in: Susan H. Williams (ed.), *Social Difference and Constitutionalism in Pan-Asia* (New York: Cambridge University Press, 2014), 195–229; Larry Jay Diamond, *Squandered Victory: The American Occupation and the Bungled Effort to Bring Democracy to Iraq* (New York: Times, 2005).

57. Juan R. I. Cole, *The Ayatollahs and Democracy in Contemporary Iraq* (Amsterdam: Amsterdam University Press, 2006). They would fall out amongst themselves, but would agree on the continuation of the political system as such. Toby Dodge, 'The Failure of Peacebuilding in Iraq: The Role of Consociationalism and Political Settlements', *Journal of Intervention and Statebuilding* 15, 4 (2021), 459–475. See also Dodge, *Iraq: From War to a New Authoritarianism* (Abingdon: Routledge, 2017). For discussions in American government circles on what a

boycott by Sunnis would mean for Iraq, including recommendations to delay the elections, see Bob Woodward, *State of Denial* (New York: Simon & Schuster, 2006), 370–6.

58. Tareq Y. Ismael and Max Fuller, 'The Disintegration of Iraq: The Manufacturing and Politicization of Sectarianism', *International Journal of Contemporary Iraqi Studies* 2, 3 (2009), 443–73.

59. Reidar Visser, 'The Territorial Aspect of Sectarianism in Iraq: The Case of Anbar', in: Brigitte Maréchal and Sami Zemni (eds), *The Dynamics of Sunni–Shia Relationships: Doctrine, Transnationalism, Intellectuals and the Media* (London: Hurst, 2013), 83–97; Visser, *Basra, the Failed Gulf State: Separatism and Nationalism in Southern Iraq* (Münster: LIT, 2005); Visser, *Shi'i Separatism in Iraq: Internet Reverie or Real Constitutional Challenge?* (Oslo: Norwegian Institute of International Affairs, 2005).

60. Interviews with Shii scholarly families, Najaf, Iraq, 2018; Ghattas, *Black Wave*; Corboz, *Guardians of Shi'ism*. For background on the Sunni insurgency, see also Steinberg, *Der nahe und der ferne Feind*, 199–217.

61. Steinberg, 'Jihadi-Salafism', 110f., albeit with the mistake highlighted and rectified by Michot, 'Ibn Taymiyya's Critique'. It is indeed telling that the official translation of the State Department would get such a major matter wrong, indicating quite a profound unawareness of some of the language associated with Shiism. US Department of State, 'Zarqawi Letter', February 2004, https://2001–2009.state.gov/p/nea/rls/31694.htm. See also Haykel, 'Al-Qa'ida and Shiism', 194.

62. Simon Wolfgang Fuchs, 'Von Schiiten lernen: Der Reiz des Martyriums für sunnitische Gruppen in Pakistan und Afghanistan', *Behemoth* 12, 1 (2019), 52–68; Assaf Moghadam, 'Motives for Martyrdom: Al-Qaida, Salafi Jihad, and the Spread of Suicide Attacks', *International Security* 33, 3 (2008/9), 46–78; Moghadam, *The Globalization of Martyrdom: Al-Qaeda, Salafi Jihad, and the Diffusion of Suicide Attacks* (Baltimore: Johns Hopkins University Press, 2008).

63. N.a., 'The Rāfidah: From Ibn Saba' to the Dajjāl', *Dabiq* 13 (1437h), 32–45.

64. Shmuel Bar and Yair Minzili, 'The Zawahiri Letter and the Strategy of al-Qaeda', *Current Trends in Islamist Ideology* 3 (2006), 38–51. He argued in the letter, according to a translation by ISIL: 'If attacking some of the heads of the Shia is necessary [as you claim], then why do you attack the laymen of the Shia? Doesn't this lead to their false beliefs taking root deeper in their hearts, whereas the obligation upon us is to speak to them with da'wah and clarify and convey the truth to them so that they might be guided to it? Will the mujāhidīn ever be able to kill all the Shia of Iraq? Did any Islamic state in history ever try to do so? Why are the laymen of the Shia killed despite them being excused due to their ignorance? And what would we have supposedly lost if we had not targeted the Shia? [...] And do our brothers forget that both we and Iran are in need of each other not harming one another during this era in which the Americans target us both?' The letter was released by the US, claiming to have obtained it during a raid in Iraq. While the authenticity of the letter

was questioned immediately, it was later largely assumed to be authentic. IS seems to believe the letter was real, as it engages its arguments, refuting them to bolster its own argument that the Shia are the main enemy of the true Muslims. N.a., 'The Rāfidah'. For the English translation and the Arabic original of the letter, see Combating Terrorism Center, 'Zawahiri's Letter to Zarqawi', https://ctc.usma.edu/harmony-program/zawahiris-letter-to-zarqawi-original-language-2/.

65. See, for example, this interview with al-Zawahiri, in which he laments that the revolution failed to live up to its pan-Islamic aims and had become too narrowly Shii-focused. He also lists the failure of Iran to support numerous Sunni Jihadi movements and the doctrinal flaws of Shiism. Ayman al-Zawahiri, 'Mawqifuna min Iran', al-Ansar, April 1995. Much has been made of alleged ties between al-Qaeda and Iran, usually in documents released by the US that should therefore be seen critically. After the US invasion of Afghanistan, some leading AQ militants may have entered Iran, where they were put under house arrest. Adam Goldman, Eric Schmitt, Farnaz Fassihi, and Ronen Bergman, 'Al-Qaeda's No. 2, Accused in U.S. Embassy Attacks, was Killed in Iran', New York Times, 13 November 2020. The US also released an alleged AQ memo detailing that it downgraded its anti-Shiism in return for cooperation with Iran. The letter is translated here: Nelly Lahoud, 'Iran and al-Qa'ida: The View from Abbottabad', New America, 7 September 2018. I owe knowledge of this letter to Raphaël Lefèvre. Interestingly, despite detailing some communication in this regard and alleged Iranian efforts to receive reassurances that AQ would not target Shii holy sites, especially in Iraq, the alleged AQ document refers to Shia with the denigrating term al-rafida throughout. Other files captured in Bin Laden's compound, too, show a negative attitude towards Iran and Shiism. One of the documents seems to suggest that Bin Laden's acceptance of al-Zarqawi's network into the al-Qaeda umbrella in late 2014 was a concession to Iran to try to rein in al-Zarqawi's anti-Shii attacks. Even if that was the case, which is doubtful, it was not successful. Thomas Joscelyn, 'The al-Qaeda-Iran Connection', Foundation for Defense of Democracies, 8 August 2018; Joscelyn, 'No, it's not Surprising that Abu Muhammad al-Masri was Living in Iran', Foundation for Defense of Democracies, 19 November 2020; Nelly Lahoud, 'Iran through the Lens of al-Qaeda', Atlantic Council, 12 September 2018; Goldman et al., 'Al-Qaeda's No. 2'; Assaf Moghadam, Nexus of Global Jihad: Understanding Cooperation among Terrorist Actors (New York: Columbia University Press, 2017), 196–221; Fawaz A. Gerges, ISIS: A History (Princeton: Princeton University Press, 2017), 74–84.

66. Haykel, 'Al-Qa'ida and Shiism', 184–9.

67. Even al-Zarqawi's mentor and key Salafi ideologue Abu Muhammad al-Maqdisi stated that it was not accepted to excommunicate the Shia masses and attack their mosques and civilians. Haykel, 'Al-Qa'ida and Shiism', 195. He played a key role, however, in popularising the anti-Shiism inherent in Salafism in previous decades, and not least through his online activities. Ibid., 190–3. Al-Zarqawi

was also influenced by al-Albani. See also Nibras Kazimi, 'Zarqawi's Anti-Shi'a Legacy: Original or Borrowed?', *Current Trends in Islamist Ideology* 4 (2006), 53–72; International Crisis Group, *The Next Iraqi War? Sectarianism and Civil Conflict* (Brussels: International Crisis Group, 2006), 14ff.; Joas Wagemakers, 'Jihadi-Salafism in Jordan and the Syrian Conflict: Divisions Overcome Unity', *Studies in Conflict & Terrorism* 41, 3 (2018), 191–212; Abdullah bin Khaled al-Saud, 'The Spiritual Teacher and his Truants: The Influence and Relevance of Abu Mohammad al-Maqdisi', *Studies in Conflict & Terrorism* 41, 9 (2018), 736–54; Hassan Hassan, 'The Sectarianism of the Islamic State', in: Frederic Wehrey (ed.), *Beyond Sunni and Shia: The Roots of Sectarianism in a Changing Middle East* (Oxford: Oxford University Press, 2018), 39–59, 46f.; Guido Steinberg, *The Iraqi Insurgency: Actors, Strategies, and Structures* (Berlin: SWP, 2006); Steinberg, 'Jihadi-Salafism', 121–4; Steinberg, *Der nahe und der ferne Feind*, 222–8, 233ff.

68. Thomas Hegghammer, 'Global Jihadism after the Iraq War', *Middle East Journal* 60, 1 (2006), 11–32; Hegghammer, 'Saudis in Iraq: Patterns of Radicalization and Recruitment', *Cultures et Conflits* (2008), 1–14; Katherine Harvey, *A Self-Fulfilling Prophecy: The Saudi Struggle for Iraq* (London: Hurst, 2021); Nasr, *The Shia Revival*, 227f. See also Frederic Wehrey et al., *Saudi-Iranian Relations since the Fall of Saddam: Rivalry, Cooperation, and Implications for U.S. Policy* (Santa Monica, CA: RAND, 2009).

69. International Crisis Group, *In Their Own Words: Reading the Iraqi Insurgency* (Brussels: International Crisis Group, 2006); International Crisis Group, *Iraq after the Surge I: The New Sunni Landscape* (Brussels: International Crisis Group, 2008); Ahmed Hashim, *Iraq's Sunni Insurgency* (Abingdon: Routledge, 2009).

70. *MSNBC*, 'King Abdullah II of Jordan', 8 December 2004. Though for Jordan the rise of Salafi-Jihadis in Iraq led by the Jordanian al-Zarqawi must have been troubling, too. Juan R. I. Cole, 'A "Shiite Crescent"? The Regional Impact of the Iraq War', *Current History* 105, 687 (2006), 20–6. The idea was not new, however, and already discussed in the press in the 1980s. Seurat, *Syrie*, 44f. See also David Rigoulet-Roze, '"Arc sunnite" versus "Croissant chiite": Deux faces d'un même Janus conflictuel?', *Diploweb*, September 2007.

71. Deborah Amos, *Eclipse of the Sunnis: Power, Exile, and Upheaval in the Middle East* (New York: PublicAffairs, 2010). See this translation of a 2014 booklet written by a Lebanese Christian, called *Istihdaf Ahl al-Sunna* (Targeting Sunnis): Nabil Khalifé, *The Attempt to Uproot Sunni-Arab Influence: A Geo-Strategic Analysis of the Western, Israeli and Iranian Quest for Domination*, trans. by Joseph A. Kéchichian (Eastbourne: Sussex Academic Press, 2017). See also Nicolas Pelham, *A New Muslim Order: The Shia and the Middle East Sectarian Crisis* (London: Tauris, 2008); Nasr, *The Shia Revival*; Frederic Wehrey et al., *The Iraq Effect: The Middle East after the Iraq War* (Santa Monica, CA: RAND, 2010).

72. Patrick Cockburn, *Muqtada al-Sadr and the Battle for the Future of Iraq* (New York: Scribner, 2008); Pierre-Jean Luizard, 'The Sadrists in Iraq: Challenging the United States, the Marja'iyya and Iran', in: Sabrina Mervin (ed.), *The Shi'a Worlds and Iran* (London: Saqi, 2010), 255–80; Blaydes, *State of Repression*, 227ff., 255–63;

Roel Meijer, 'Muslim Politics under Occupation: The Association of Muslim Scholars and the Politics of Resistance in Iraq', *Arab Studies Journal* 13/4, 2/1 (2005/6), 92–112; Nicholas Krohley, *The Death of the Mehdi Army: The Rise, Fall and Revival of Iraq's Most Powerful Militia* (London: Hurst, 2015); Mark Etherington, *Revolt on the Tigris: The al-Sadr Uprising and the Governing of Iraq* (London: Hurst, 2005). For the later evolution of his trend, see Benedict Robin-D'Cruz and Renad Mansour, *Making Sense of the Sadrists: Fragmentation and Unstable Politics* (Philadelphia: Foreign Policy Research Institute, 2020); Benedict Robin-D'Cruz, 'Sadrists in the Public Sphere: An Ethnography of Political Shi'ism in Iraq', *Revue des mondes musulmans et de la Méditerranée* 145 (2019), 97–114.

73. Cole, *The Ayatollahs*; Caroleen Marji Sayej, *Patriotic Ayatollahs: Nationalism in Post-Saddam Iraq* (Ithaca, NY: Cornell University Press, 2018). Kalantari has written an important corrective to the quietist-activist binary in studies of the Shii clergy. Mohammad R. Kalantari, *The Clergy and the Modern Middle East: Shi'i Political Activism in Iran, Iraq and Lebanon* (London: I.B. Tauris, 2022). Iran, on the other hand, supported clerics that endorsed *velayat-e faqih* and tried to put them in a favourable position to eventually succeed al-Sistani. Hayder al-Khoei, 'Post-Sistani Iraq, Iran, and the Future of Shia Islam', *War on the Rocks*, 8 September 2016.

74. Harith Hasan al-Qarawee, 'The "Formal" Marja': Shi'i Clerical Authority and the State in Post-2003 Iraq', *British Journal of Middle Eastern Studies* 46, 3 (2019), 481–97. For some, expansion was too fast. Sadiq Abid, *An Examination of Heritage Protection and Conservation Practices in the Pilgrimage City of Najaf* (PhD, University of Sheffield, 2016).

75. Personal observations, Najaf and Karbala, Iraq, 2018/9.

76. Faraj Hattab Hamdan, *The Development of Iraqi Shi'a Mourning Rituals in Modern Iraq: The 'Ashurā Rituals and Visitation of al-Arb'ain* (MA, Arizona State University, 2012).

77. Robert F. Worth, 'Blast Destroys Shrine in Iraq, Setting off Sectarian Fury', *New York Times*, 22 February 2006. No group officially claimed responsibility, but Iraqi officials have blamed AQI. Radio Free Europe/Radio Liberty, 'Iraq: Bomber of Samarra Mosque Reportedly Captured', 28 June 2006. For more on Samarra, see Imranali Panjwani (ed.), *The Shi'a of Samarra: The Heritage and Politics of a Community in Iraq* (London: I. B. Tauris, 2012).

78. The Buratha Mosque in northern Baghdad is the second most important Shii mosque in the town (Ali is said to have dug a well at the site, and the mosque had already been razed to the ground under the Abbasids). It was destroyed by the Abbasid Caliph al-Muqtadir (r. 908–32) and rebuilt in 939/40. Osman, *Sectarianism in Iraq*, 59f.

79. In one case, for example, the Mahdi Army occupied a mosque they said had originally been built by Shia in 1980 but was then confiscated by the government and given to the Sunni *waqf* and run by a Sunni Imam. After 2003, that Imam refused to leave and restore ownership, and so, when tensions were running high after the Askari bombing, a local Shii cleric occupied the building

together with the Mahdi Army, changed its name from Saddam Hussein mosque to Imam Ali mosque, and started reciting the Shii call to prayer. Edward Wong, 'Shiite Militiamen Reclaim Mosque from the Sunnis', *New York Times*, 3 March 2006. See also Thabit Abdullah, *Dictatorship, Imperialism and Chaos: Iraq since 1989* (London: Zed, 2006), 115–18; Mushreq Abbas, 'Iraq's Sunni-Shiite Killings: When It's Based on a Name', *al-Monitor*, 24 September 2013.

80. Fanar Haddad, *Shia-Centric State-Building and Sunni Rejection in Post-2003 Iraq* (Washington, DC: Carnegie Endowment for International Peace, 2016). See also Ronen Zeidel, 'Between Aqalliya and Mukawin: Understanding Sunni Political Attitudes in Post-Saddam Iraq', in: Benjamin Isakhan (ed.), *The Legacy of Iraq: From the 2003 War to the 'Islamic State'* (Edinburgh: Edinburgh University Press, 2015), 97–109; Benjamin Isakhan, 'Shattering the Shia: A Maliki Political Strategy in Post-Saddam Iraq', in: Benjamin Isakhan (ed.), *The Legacy of Iraq: From the 2003 War to the 'Islamic State'* (Edinburgh: Edinburgh University Press, 2015), 67–81.

81. Saad Salloum, 'Fear of Extinction Pushes Basra's Christians to Isolation', *al-Monitor*, 17 November 2017; Internal Displacement Monitoring Centre, *Iraq: Sectarian Violence, Military Operations Spark New Displacement, as Humanitarian Access Deteriorates* (Geneva: Norwegian Refugee Council, 2006), 130f.; John Hagan, Joshua Kaiser, Anna Hanson, and Patricia Parker, 'Neighborhood Sectarian Displacement and the Battle for Baghdad: A Self-Fulfilling Prophecy of Fear and Crimes against Humanity in Iraq', *Sociological Forum* 30, 3 (2015), 675–97; Ashraf al-Khalidi and Victor Tanner, *Sectarian Violence: Radical Groups Drive Internal Displacement in Iraq* (Washington, DC: Brookings Institution/ University of Bern, 2006); Rhys Dubin, *The Power of Local Ties: Civilian Resistance to Sectarian Displacement in Iraq* (Sulaimani: Institute of Regional and International Studies, 2020); International Medical Corps, *Iraqis on the Move: Sectarian Displacement in Baghdad* (Santa Monica, CA: International Medical Corps, 2007); Adnan Abu Zeed, 'Anbar's Displaced Sunnis not Safe from Sectarianism', *al-Monitor*, 1 May 2015.

82. Michael Knights, 'The JRTN Movement and Iraq's Next Insurgency', *CTC Sentinel* 4, 7 (2011), 1–6; Rafid Fadhil Ali, 'Sufi Insurgent Groups in Iraq', *Jamestown Foundation*, 25 January 2008; CISAC Stanford, 'Jaysh Rijal al-Tariq al-Naqshbandia', https://cisac.fsi.stanford.edu/mappingmilitants/profiles/jrtn#_ftn7.

83. Fanar Haddad, 'Sectarian Relations in Arab Iraq: Contextualising the Civil War of 2006–2007', *British Journal of Middle Eastern Studies* 40, 2 (2013), 115–38. Haddad has argued that Shii anti-Sunnism is only in rare cases exclusionary to the extent that the Salafis exclude Shia from Islam and is often still couched in a mindset of numerical minority dealing with a majority. Fanar Haddad, 'Anti-Sunnism and Anti-Shiism: Minorities, Majorities and the Question of Equivalence', *Mediterranean Politics* 26, 4 (2021), 498–504. For an example of such anti-Sunni publications, see Wali al-Zamili, *Al-Wahhabiyya: Da'iyya al-Silm al-'Alami* (Beirut: Dar al-Nakhil, 2006). See also Hazim Saghiyya, *Nawasib wa Rawafid: Munaza'at al-Sunna wa-l-Shi'a fi al-'Alam al-Islami al-Yawm* (Beirut: Dar al-Saqi, 2009).

84. Though the status of Ismailis, Alawites, Druze, and other groups historically tied to Shiism remained ambiguous. The Amman Message, 'Summary', http://ammanmessage.com/?option=com_content&task=view&id=66&Itemid=42; Michaelle Browers, 'Official Islam and the Limits of Communicative Action: The Paradox of the Amman Message', *Third World Quarterly* 32, 5 (2011), 943–58; Stacey Gutkowski, 'We are the Very Model of a Moderate Muslim State: The Amman Messages and Jordan's Foreign Policy', *International Relations* 30, 2 (2016), 206–26; Joas Wagemakers, 'Sectarianism in the Service of Salafism: Shiites as a Political Tool for Jordanian Salafis', *British Journal of Middle Eastern Studies* 49, 2 (2022), 341–59.

85. It was organised by the Organisation of the Islamic Conference. The document opens with the following statement: 'The Muslim is he who professes his faith by bearing witness that there is no God but Allah and that Mohamed is His Prophet. These fundamental principles apply equally to the Sunnis and the Shiites without exception. The common grounds between the two schools of thought are many times more than areas of difference and their causes. Any differences between them are merely differences of opinion and interpretation and not essential differences of faith or on the substance of the Pillars of Islam. From the Islamic Shari'a viewpoint, no one follower of either school may excommunicate, hereticate, or in any other way cast aspersions on the faith and fidelity of a follower of the other school, on the grounds that God's Prophet (PBUH) said: "If ever one of you calls his brother: You infidel, one of them shall come out the infidel and bear the onus thereof!"' Organisation of the Islamic Conference, 'Makkah al-Mukarramah Declaration on the Iraqi Situation ("Mecca Document")', *Reliefweb*, 20 October 2006, http://reliefweb.int/report/iraq/makkah-al-mukarramah-declaration-iraqi-situation-mecca-document. It thus does not go into the details of the controversies between Sunni and Shia Islam or reopen past debates about them, but it does acknowledge Shia as Muslim and states that it is forbidden to excommunicate them, as some Sunni Jihadis, including some Saudis, have done. The meeting was thus highly symbolic, even though the highest-ranking clerics, such as Ali al-Sistani, did not attend (though they did send messages in support of the agreement).

86. A book published in Singapore in 2005 argued that the violent sectarian conflict, at the time raging mainly in Iraq, could force Sunnis and Shia to overcome their differences to forge unity so that Iraq 'may well become the witness to an everlasting Sunni-Shi'ite embrace'. Chandra Muzaffar, 'Foreword', in: Karim D. Crow and Ahmad Kazemi Moussavi, *Facing One Qiblah: Legal and Doctrinal Aspects of Sunni and Shi'ah Muslims* (Singapore: Pustaka Nasional, 2005), x.

87. Sagi Polka, 'Taqrib al-Madhahib: Qaradawi's Declaration of Principles Regarding Sunni-Shi'i Ecumenism', *Middle Eastern Studies* 49, 3 (2013), 414–29; Muhammad Qasim Zaman, 'Epilogue', in: Robert W. Hefner and Muhammad Qasim Zaman (eds), *Schooling Islam: The Culture and Politics of Modern Muslim Education* (Princeton: Princeton University Press, 2007), 242–68, 262ff.; Ebrahim Moosa, 'The Sunni Orthodoxy', *Critical Muslim* 10 (2014), 19–36, 19f.

88. Polka, 'Taqrib al-Madhahib', 424. The final conference statement by and large adopted these points, urging an end to proselytising by Sunnis and Shia in

countries where the other sect forms the majority and a stop to insulting the Companions of the Prophet. The Doha conference brought together key figures of both sides. Behnam Said, *Islamische Ökumene als Mittel der Politik: Aktuelle Tendenzen in der Annäherungsdebatte zwischen Sunna und Schia auf der Doha-Konferenz 2007* (Berlin: Klaus Schwarz, 2009).

89. He was reacting to a fatwa issued by Saudi cleric Abdallah bin Jibrin, who had declared that any assistance to *al-hizb al-rafidi* (the recreant/rejectionist sect) was prohibited. Polka, 'Taqrib al-Madhahib', 422f.

90. This was symbolised by the rise of the Hariri Foundation as a social service provider and the decline of the traditional social service and charity sector associated with the Sunni notables. Baumann, *Citizen Hariri*, 57–91, 117. For the notion of Gulf capital, see Adam Hanieh, *Capitalism and Class in the Gulf Arab States* (New York: Palgrave Macmillan, 2011); Hanieh, *Money, Markets, and Monarchies: The Gulf Cooperation Council and the Political Economy of the Contemporary Middle East* (Cambridge: Cambridge University Press, 2018).

91. Baumann, *Citizen Hariri*, 116; Melani Cammett, *Compassionate Communalism: Welfare and Sectarianism in Lebanon* (Ithaca: Cornell University Press, 2014); Bassel F. Salloukh, 'Taif and the Lebanese State: The Political Economy of a Very Sectarian Public Sector', *Nationalism and Ethnic Politics* 25, 1 (2019), 43–60; Nisreen Salti and Jad Chaaban, 'The Role of Sectarianism in the Allocation of Public Expenditure in Postwar Lebanon', *International Journal of Middle East Studies* 42, 4 (2010), 637–55. Attempts by civil society groups to challenge this system were deliberately undermined by sectarian elites. Janine A. Clark and Bassel F. Salloukh, 'Elite Strategies, Civil Society, and Sectarian Identities in Postwar Lebanon', *International Journal of Middle East Studies* 45, 4 (2013), 731–49.

92. Leenders, *Spoils of Truce*; Bassel F. Salloukh, 'Remaking Lebanon after Syria: The Rise and Fall of Proxy Authoritarianism', in: Holger Albrecht (ed.), *Contentious Politics in the Middle East: Political Opposition under Authoritarianism* (Gainesville: University Press of Florida, 2010), 205–28.

93. Bahout, 'The Unraveling of Taif', 144–7. For foreign policy under Bashar, see Bassel F. Salloukh, 'Demystifying Syrian Foreign Policy under Bashar al-Asad', in: Fred H. Lawson (ed.), *Demystifying Syria* (London: Saqi, 2009), 159–79; Bente Scheller, *The Wisdom of Syria's Waiting Game: Foreign Policy under the Assads* (London: Hurst, 2013).

94. Daher, *Hezbollah*, 89–94.

95. Volker Perthes, *Syria under Bashar al-Asad: Modernisation and the Limits of Change* (Oxford: Oxford University Press, 2004); Alan George, *Syria: Neither Bread nor Freedom* (London: Zed, 2003), 30–63.

96. Nicholas Blanford, *Killing Mr Lebanon: The Assassination of Rafik Hariri and its Impact on the Middle East* (London: I. B. Tauris, 2006); Daher, *Hezbollah*, 183–8; UN News, 'Lebanon: UN-Backed Tribunal Submits Indictment over Hariri Murder', 30 June 2011; Daher, 'Lebanon: UN-Backed Tribunal Sentences Hezbollah Militant in Hariri Assassination', 11 December 2020.

97. Andrew Arsan, *Lebanon: A Country in Fragments* (London: Hurst, 2018), 27–59.

98. Daher, *Hezbollah*, 188–99.

99. Ibid., 201–29; Morten Valbjørn and André Bank, 'Signs of a New Arab Cold War: The 2006 Lebanon War and the Sunni-Shi'i Divide', *Middle East Report* 242 (2007), 6–11; Valbjørn and Bank, 'The New Arab Cold War: Rediscovering the Arab Dimension of Middle East Regional Politics', *Review of International Studies* 38, 1 (2012), 3–24, 7ff.; Graham E. Fuller, 'The Hizballah–Iran Connection: Model for Sunni Resistance', *The Washington Quarterly* 30, 1 (2007), 139–50, 144ff.; Curtis R. Ryan, 'Saudi Sheik Issues Fatwa against Hezbollah', *UPI*, 21 July 2006; Neil MacFarquhar, 'Hezbollah's Prominence has Many Sunnis Worried', *New York Times*, 4 August 2006; Eli Lake, 'Leading Saudi Sheik Pronounces Fatwa against Hezbollah', *New York Sun*, 20 July 2006; Edward Wong, 'On Web, a Sunni-Shiite Split on Hezbollah', *New York Times*, 22 July 2006; Ismail, *Saudi Clerics*, 158f.

100. Steven Brooke, 'Sectarianism and Social Conformity: Evidence from Egypt', *Political Research Quarterly* 70, 4 (2017), 848–60; Rainer Brunner, 'Interesting Times: Egypt and Shiism at the Beginning of the Twenty-First Century', in: Meir Litvak and Ofra Bengio (eds), *The Sunna and Shi'a in History: Division and Ecumenism in the Muslim Middle East* (Basingstoke: Palgrave Macmillan, 2011), 223–41; Elizabeth Monier, 'Egypt, Iran, and the Hizbullah Cell: Using Sectarianism to "De-Arabize" and Regionalize Threats to National Interests', *Middle East Journal* 69, 3 (2015), 341–57; Joas Wagemakers, 'Anti-Shi'ism without the Shi'a: Salafi Sectarianism in Jordan', *Maydan*, 17 October 2016; Wagemakers, 'Making Sense of Sectarianism without Sects: Quietist Salafi anti-Shia Discourse in Jordan', *Mediterranean Politics* 26, 4 (2021), 518–23; Wagemakers, 'Sectarianism in the Service of Salafism'; Khalid Sindawi, 'Jordan's Encounter with Shiism', *Current Trends in Islamist Ideology* 10 (2010), 102–15.

101. Abdelhafidh Ghersallah, *Le chiisme en Algérie: De la conversion politique à la naissance d'une communauté religieuse* (Fribourg: Institut Religioscope, 2012); Jean-Pierre Tuquoi, 'WikiLeaks: Rabat a rompu ses relations avec l'Iran pour plaire à Ryad', *Le Monde*, 10 December 2010. Relations were restored in late 2014, after the election of the Rouhani government. While Morocco is dependent on aid and investments from the Gulf, its other main foreign policy priority is isolating Algeria and preventing recognition of the Western Sahara Polisario movement. Iran has good relations with Algeria, but does not recognise Polisario. For Morocco, maintaining relations with Iran is thus a way to isolate Polisario. Sophie Claudet, 'Why did Iran, Morocco Resume Relations?', *al-Monitor*, 25 January 2015. See also *Morocco World News*, 'Moroccan Islamists Warn against "Shia Threat" in Morocco', 17 March 2015; Mohammed Guenfoudi, 'Politicization of Moroccan Shiites? Between the State's Repression and the Internal Schism', *Moroccan Institute for Policy Analysis*, 5 February 2019.

102. For Palestinian Salafi attacks on Shiism, see Khaled Hroub, 'Salafi Formations in Palestine: The Limits of a De-Palestinised Milieu', in: Roel Meijer (ed.),

Global Salafism: Islam's New Religious Movement (London: Hurst, 2009), 221–43, 234f.; Legrain, 'The Shiite Peril'.

103. Bahout, 'The Unraveling of Taif', 149; Arsan, *Lebanon*, 61–98; Daher, *Hezbollah*, 239ff. In general for this period, see Bassel F. Salloukh et al., *The Politics of Sectarianism in Postwar Lebanon* (London: Pluto Press, 2015).

104. Bassel F. Salloukh, 'The Sectarianization of Geopolitics in the Middle East', in: Nader Hashemi and Danny Postel (eds), *Sectarianization: Mapping the New Politics of the Middle East* (London: Hurst, 2017), 35–52, 41ff.; Arsan, *Lebanon*, 99–104.

105. Hilal Khashan, 'The Rise and Growth of Hezbollah and the Militarization of the Sunni-Shiite Divide in Lebanon', *Middle East Institute*, 26 January 2016; Robert F. Worth and Nada Bakri, 'Sunni–Shiite Tensions out in the Open in Lebanon', *New York Times*, 18 May 2008.

106. Rabil, *Salafism in Lebanon*, 179–83.

107. Ibid., 191–212; Adham Saouli, 'Lebanon's Salafis: Opportunities and Constraints in a Divided Society', in: Francesco Cavatorta and Fabio Merone (eds), *Salafism after the Arab Awakening: Contending with People's Power* (London: Hurst, 2016), 43–60, 50–6.

108. Rola el-Husseini, 'Hezbollah and the Axis of Refusal: Hamas, Iran and Syria', *Third World Quarterly* 31, 5 (2010), 803–15.

109. Personal observations, Sayyida Zaynab, Syria, 2008. See also Paulo G. Pinto, 'Pilgrimage, Commodities, and Religious Objectification: The Making of Transnational Shi'ism between Iran and Syria', *Comparative Studies of South Asia, Africa and the Middle East* 27 (2007), 109–25. It also allowed for the development of Shii rituals and ideas unconstrained by the dominant thinking in Qom and Najaf. Edith Szanto, 'Challenging Transnational Shi'i Authority in Ba'th Syria', *British Journal of Middle Eastern Studies* 45, 1 (2018), 95–110; Szanto, 'Sayyida Zaynab in the State of Exception: Shi'i Sainthood as "Qualified Life" in Contemporary Syria', *International Journal of Middle East Studies* 44, 2 (2012), 285–99; Alessandro Cancian, *La Hawza 'Ilmiyya: E la formazione dell'élite religiosa nei collegi teologici dello sciismo duodecimano: Elementi dottrinali e indagine di campo* (PhD, University of Siena, 2005); Noor Zehra Zaidi, *Making Spaces Sacred: The Sayyeda Zaynab and Bibi Pak Daman Shrines and the Construction of Modern Shia Identity* (PhD, University of Pennsylvania, 2015).

110. For a debate in the early 1990s, see Stéphane Valter, *Islamité et identité: La réplique de ʿAlī Sulaymān al-Aḥmad aux investigations d'un journaliste syrien sur l'histoire de la communauté alaouite* (Damascus: Presses de l'Ifpo, 2015).

111. Yasser Tabbaa, 'Invented Pieties: The Rediscovery and Rebuilding of the Shrine of Sayyida Ruqayya in Damascus, 1975–2006', *Artibus Asiae* 67, 1 (2007), 95–112.

112. Myriam Ababsa, *Raqqa: Territoires et pratiques sociales d'une ville syrienne* (Damascus: Presses de l'Ifpo, 2009), ch. 6; Ababsa, 'Les mausolées invisibles: Raqqa, ville de pèlerinage chiite ou pôle etatique en Jazîra syrienne?', *Annales de Géographie* 110, 622 (2001), 647–64.

113. US Diplomatic Cable Released by Wikileaks: From Embassy Damascus to Secretary of State, *Influencing the SARG in the End of 2006*, 13 December 2006, 06DAMASCUS5399, https://wikileaks.org/cable/2006/12/06DAMAS CUS5399.html.

114. Pierret, 'Karbala'; Pierret, *Religion and State*, 207f. A good example is this book, which details Shii activity in Syria and lists Shii families, institutions, and settlements all across Syria. It especially focuses on Shii religious institutions founded in the past decades. 'Abd al-Rahman al-Hajj, *Al-Ba'ath al-Shi'i fi Suriyya, 1919–2007* (Beirut: Jusur lil-Tarjama wa-l-Nashr, 2017).

115. Von Maltzahn, *The Syria–Iran Axis*, 98–207.

116. See, in general, Khalid Sindawi, 'Al-Mustabsirūn, "Those Who Are Able to See the Light": Sunnī Conversion to Twelver Shī'ism in Modern Times', *Die Welt des Islams* 51, 2 (2011), 210–34.

117. In 2016, Alawite leaders dissociated themselves from Shiism, saying that they are a distinct branch of Islam and want to be treated as such. Caroline Wyatt, 'Syrian Alawites Distance Themselves from Assad', *BBC*, 3 April 2016.

118. Pinto, '"Oh Syria, God Protects You"', 197–200.

119. Pierret, *Religion and State*, 221 and passim; Pierret, 'al-Būṭī, Muḥammad Saʿīd Ramaḍān', *EI3*; Pinto, '"Oh Syria, God Protects You"', 192; Pinto, 'Sufism, Moral Performance and the Public Sphere in Syria', *Revue des mondes musulmans et de la Méditerranée* 115–16 (2006), 155–71; Annabelle Böttcher, 'L'élite feminine kurde de la Kaftariyya: Une confrérie Naqshbandi Damascène', in: Martin van Bruinessen and Joyce Blau (eds), *Islam des Kurdes* (Paris: INALCO, 1999), 125–39; Böttcher, *Official Sunni and Shi'i Islam in Syria* (Florence: European University Institute, 2002), 11; Andreas Christmann, 'Islamic Scholar and Religious Leader: A Portrait of Shaykh Muhammad Sa'id Ramadan al-Būti', *Islam and Christian–Muslim Relations* 9, 2 (1998), 149–69.

120. Paulo G. Pinto, 'Mystical Metaphors: Ritual, Symbols and Self in Syrian Sufism', *Culture and Religion* 18, 2 (2017), 90–109, 97f., 107; Pinto, 'Mystical Bodies/Unruly Bodies: Experience, Empowerment and Subjectification in Syrian Sufism', *Social Compass* 63, 2 (2016), 197–212.

121. Steven Heydemann, *Networks of Privilege in the Middle East: The Politics of Economic Reform Revisited* (New York: Palgrave Macmillan, 2004); Raymond Hinnebusch, 'Liberalization without Democratization in "Post-Populist" Authoritarian States: Evidence from Syria and Egypt', in: Nils A. Butenschon, Uri Davis, and Manuel Hassassian (eds), *Citizenship and the State in the Middle East: Approaches and Applications* (Syracuse: Syracuse University Press, 2000), 123–45; Thomas Pierret and Kjetil Selvik, 'Limits of "Authoritarian Upgrading" in Syria: Private Welfare, Islamic Charities, and the Rise of the Zayd Movement', *International Journal of Middle East Studies* 41, 4 (2009), 595–614; Raymond Hinnebusch, 'Syria: From "Authoritarian Upgrading" to Revolution?', *International Affairs* 88, 1 (2012), 95–113.

122. Lisa Wedeen, *Ambiguities of Domination: Politics, Rhetoric, and Symbols in Contemporary Syria* (Chicago: University of Chicago Press, 2015).

123. For the impact of the drought, see Myriam Ababsa, 'The End of a World: Drought and Agrarian Transformation in Northeast Syria (2007–2010)', in: Raymond Hinnebusch and Tina Zintl (eds), *Syria from Reform to Revolt: Political Economy and International Relations* (Syracuse: Syracuse University Press, 2015), 199–222; Marwa Daoudy, *The Origins of the Syrian Conflict: Climate Change and Human Security* (Cambridge: Cambridge University Press, 2020).

124. Afshin Shahi and Maya Vachkova, 'Eco-Sectarianism: From Ecological Disasters to Sectarian Violence in Syria', *Asian Affairs* 49, 3 (2018), 449–67.

125. US Diplomatic Cable Released by Wikileaks: From Embassy Damascus to Secretary of State, *Maximizing the Impact of Rami's Designation*, 31 January 2008, 08DAMASCUS70, https://wikileaks.org/plusd/cables/08DAMASCUS70_a. html. For background, see Haddad, *Business Networks*.

126. Hamidi, 'Inscriptions of Violence', 167.

127. Bonnefoy, *Salafism in Yemen*, 271.

128. International Crisis Group, *Yemen's al-Qaeda: Expanding the Base* (Brussels: International Crisis Group, 2017); Haykel, 'Al-Qa'ida and Shiism', 198.

129. Hamidi, 'Inscriptions of Violence', 165.

130. Minister of Interior Alimi apparently told the American embassy that US help had been decisive. US Diplomatic Cable Released by Wikileaks: From Embassy Sanaa to Secretary of State, *Royg Forces Kill Rebel Cleric al-Houthi in September 10 Raid*, 12 September 2004, 04SANAA2421, https://wikileaks.org/plusd/cables/04SANAA2421_a.html. The cave then became a shrine for Huthi supporters. Ghaith Abdul-Ahad, 'Diary: In Sanaa', *London Review of Books*, 21 May 2015; Safa al-Ahmad, 'Transcript: The Fight for Yemen', *PBS Frontline*, https://www.pbs.org/wgbh/frontline/film/fight-for-yemen/transcript/; al-Ahmad, 'The Rise of the Houthis', *BBC Documentary*, 21 March 2015, http://www.bbc.co.uk/news/world-middle-east-31994769.

131. See their website: http://www.ansarollah.com. They also established a TV channel, *al-Masira*, with offices in the Hizbullah-controlled Southern suburbs of Beirut.

132. The Commander of the First Armoured Division, Ali Mohsin, was officially leading the war in Saada, but many Yemenis thought that President Saleh was not giving him enough supplies to actually win the war to embarrass him and prevent him from becoming a rival to Saleh's son, Ahmad, whom Saleh was grooming as his successor. Ali Mohsin was also suspected of having Salafi sympathies and to be behind the recruiting of Salafi Jihadis for the war against the Huthis. Ginny Hill, *Yemen Endures: Civil War, Saudi Adventurism and the Future of Arabia* (London: Hurst, 2017), 189ff.; Marieke Brandt, 'The Irregulars of the Sa'ada War: "Colonel Sheikhs" and "Tribal Militias" in Yemen's Huthi Conflict (2004–2010)', in: Helen Lackner (ed.), *Why Yemen Matters: A Society in Transition* (London: Saqi, 2014), 105–22; Brandt, *Tribes and Politics in Yemen: A History of the Houthi Conflict* (London: Hurst, 2017); Helen Lackner, *Yemen in Crisis: Autocracy, Neo-Liberalism and the Disintegration of a State* (London: Saqi, 2017), 152–6.

133. For an in-depth study prepared for the US Defense Intelligence Agency that pays more attention to these factors and was made publicly available, see Barak A. Salmoni, Bryce Loidolt, and Madeleine Wells, *Regime and Periphery in Northern Yemen: The Huthi Phenomenon* (Santa Monica, CA: RAND, 2010). See also Stacey Philbrick Yadav, 'Sectarianization, Islamist Republicanism, and International Misrecognition in Yemen', in: Nader Hashemi and Danny Postel (eds), *Sectarianization: Mapping the New Politics of the Middle East* (London: Hurst, 2017), 185–98; Christopher Boucek, *War in Saada: From Local Insurrection to National Challenge* (Washington, DC: Carnegie Endowment for International Peace, 2010); Hamidi, 'Inscriptions of Violence', 172; vom Bruck, 'How the Past Casts its Shadows', 280–4.

134. Bonnefoy, *Salafism in Yemen*, 277. While the Yemeni Salafis around al-Wadi had essentially been apolitical and had rejected forming political parties (*hizbiyya*), a part of the movement became politicised, and Salafi militias from Dammaj fought against the Huthis on the government's side. Laurent Bonnefoy and Judit Kuschnitizki, 'Salafis and the "Arab Spring" in Yemen: Progressive Politicization and Resilient Quietism', *Arabian Humanities* 4 (2015).

135. Bonnefoy, *Salafism in Yemen*, 274; Hamidi, 'Inscriptions of Violence', 170; Lackner, *Yemen in Crisis*, 155.

136. US Diplomatic Cable Released by Wikileaks: From Embassy Sanaa to Secretary of State, *Iran in Yemen: Tehran's Shadow Looms Large, but Footprint Is Small*, 12 September 2009, 09SANAA1662, https://wikileaks.org/plusd/cables/09SANAA1662_a.html.

137. In 2009, a US diplomatic cable stated that 'no solid evidence has been shown of Hizballah activity in Sa'ada or of any desire on the part of the Huthis for such a partnership'. US Diplomatic Cable Released by Wikileaks: From Embassy Sanaa to Secretary of State, *Hizballah and the Houthis: Different Goals and Ideology*, 18 November 2009, 09SANAA2079, https://wikileaks.org/plusd/cables/09SANAA2079_a.html.

138. US Diplomatic Cable Released by Wikileaks: From Embassy Sanaa to Secretary of State, *Sa'ada Solution Requires More Thought, Fewer Weapons*, 11 November 2009, 09SANAA2052, https://wikileaks.org/plusd/cables/09SANAA2052_a.html. I thank Gabriele vom Bruck for this reference. See also *LobeLog*, 'Is Saudi Arabia's Assault on Yemen Just about Curtailing Iran's Influence?', 28 May 2015.

139. Samy Dorlian, 'Les reformulations identitaires du zaydisme dans leur contexte socio-politique contemporain', *Arabian Humanities* 15 (2008), 161–76. In some mosques in the North, Zaydi Imams were replaced with Sunni ones, Zaydi schools were refused licences, and Huthi demands that religious curricula in schools in Zaydi areas would conform to Zaydi teachings were refused. From Embassy Sanaa to Secretary of State, *Hizballah and the Houthis: Different Goals and Ideology*.

140. See Frederic Wehrey, *Sectarian Politics in the Gulf: From the Iraq War to the Arab Uprisings* (New York: Columbia University Press, 2014); Lawrence G. Potter (ed.), *Sectarian Politics in the Persian Gulf* (New York: Oxford University Press,

2014); Laurence Louër, 'The State and Sectarian Identities in the Persian Gulf Monarchies: Bahrain, Saudi Arabia, and Kuwait in Comparative Perspective', in: Lawrence G. Potter (ed.), *Sectarian Politics in the Persian Gulf* (New York: Oxford University Press, 2014), 117–42; Louër, *Transnational Shia Politics*, 243–63.

141. John E. Peterson, 'Bahrain: Reform, Promise and Reality', in: Joshua Teitelbaum (ed.), *Political Liberalization in the Persian Gulf* (London: Hurst, 2009), 157–85. See also Sajjad H. Rizvi, 'Shi'ism in Bahrain: Marja'iyya and Politics', *Orient* 4 (2009), 16–24.

142. In September 2006, a report by Dr Salah al-Bandar, a former adviser to the cabinet affairs minister, was published by the Gulf Centre for Democratic Development. Dubbed 'Bandargate', it claimed to provide documentary evidence of a regime plan to marginalise Shia political actors and alter the country's sectarian makeup by naturalising Sunnis. Zara al-Sitari, '"Al-Bander Report": Demographic Engineering in Bahrain and Mechanisms of Exclusion', *Bahrain Center for Human Rights*, 30 September 2006. See also Laurence Louër, 'The Political Impact of Labor Migration in Bahrain', *City & Society* 20, 1 (2008), 32–53; Jones, *Political Repression*. In general, see also Rizvi, 'Shi'ism in Bahrain'.

143. Toby Jones, 'The Iraq Effect in Saudi Arabia', *Middle East Report* 237 (2005), 20–5; Jones, 'Saudi Arabia's Not So New Anti-Shi'ism', *Middle East Report* 242 (2007), 29–32; Matthiesen, *The Other Saudis*, 166–96; Ismail, *Saudi Clerics*, 182–9.

144. Interviews with current and former MPs from various political trends, journalists and civil society figures, Kuwait, 2012; Madeleine Wells, 'Sectarianism, Authoritarianism, and Opposition in Kuwait', in: Nader Hashemi and Danny Postel (eds), *Sectarianization: Mapping the New Politics of the Middle East* (London: Hurst, 2017), 235–57, 242–52; Rivka Azoulay and Claire Beaugrand, 'Limits of Political Clientelism: Elites' Struggles in Kuwait Fragmenting Politics', *Arabian Humanities* 4 (2015); Wehrey, *Sectarian Politics*, 214–30.

145. Oliver Scharbrodt, 'Creating a Diasporic Public Sphere in Britain: Twelver Shia Networks in London', *Islam and Christian-Muslim Relations* 31, 1 (2020), 23–40; Shia.bs, 'Kuwaiti Rafidi Yasir al-Habib: Celebrating the Death of Aa'ishah al-Siddiqah', http://www.shia.bs/articles/ieuegxx-kuwaiti-rafidi-yasir-al-habib-celebrating-the-death-of-aaishah-al-siddiqah.cfm; Omar Shahid and Tamanna Ali, 'Meet the Controversial Cleric Threatening to Turn UK Muslims against Each Other', *VICE*, 10 May 2013; Matthijs van den Bos, 'The Promised Land of Fadak: Locating Religious Nationalism in Shiite Politics', *British Journal of Middle Eastern Studies* 49, 5 (2022), 769–91; Wehrey, *Sectarian Politics*, 230–4; https://alqtrah.com.

146. In 2016, Khamenei stated: 'Do not incite emotions of the Sunni community. Some people feel, in order to prove themselves as Shia, they need to insult Sunni figures. This goes against the mannerisms of the infallible imams. The fact, that there are TV stations launched to insult (Sunni figures) well, makes it crystal clear that they are funded by the British Treasury; this is British Shiism.' Khamenei.ir, 'No Shia is Allowed to Insult Sunnis: Ayatollah Khamenei', 20 September 2016.

147. See, for example, the rules laid out by Shaykh Salah al-Budayr, Imam and Khatib of the Prophet's Mosque: Islam Question & Answer, 'Islamic Guidelines for Visitors to the Prophet's Mosque', 13 February 2003, https://islamqa.info/en/36863.

148. They had arrived in Medina on 20 February to mark the anniversary of the death of Muhammad, which in 2009 fell on 24 February. On the same day, Shia commemorate the passing of Hasan, the second Imam. Pilgrims said that the religious police videotaped women in their group, affronting their piety and modesty. When a group of men, some of them husbands of the taped women, asked the police to destroy or hand over the tapes, the two sides clashed. Armed policemen confronted hundreds of protesters chanting slogans in reverence of Hussain. In the following days, the religious police arrested and injured dozens. According to Shii reports, many pilgrims gathered on the evening of 23 February to commemorate the death of Muhammad but were not let into the cemetery. They moved to the square between the cemetery and the mosque of the Prophet. There, they say, they were attacked by Sunnis exiting the mosque and by the religious police. Toby Matthiesen, 'The Shi'a of Saudi Arabia at a Crossroads', *MERIP*, 6 May 2009. The Saudi interior minister, Prince Nayif, pointed out that 'citizens have both rights and duties; their activities should not contradict the doctrine followed by the umma. This is the doctrine of Sunnis and our righteous forefathers. There are citizens who follow other schools of thought and the intelligent among them must respect this doctrine.' Amnesty International, 'Saudi Arabia Must Charge or Release Detained Dissident Cleric', 10 August 2012.

149. Matthiesen, *The Other Saudis*, 51, 161–5, 169, 197f.; Matthiesen, 'Government and Opposition'; Badr al-Ibrahim and Muhammad al-Sadiq, *Al-Hirak al-Shi'i fi al-Su'udiyya: Tasayyis al-Madhhab wa Madhhabat al-Siyyasa* (The Shia Movement in Saudi Arabia: The Politicisation of Confession and the Confessionalisation of Politics) (Beirut: al-Shabaka al-'Arabiyya li-l-Abhath wa-l-Nashr, 2013).

150. Matthiesen, 'The Shi'a of Saudi Arabia'.

151. Vatanka, *Iran and Pakistan*, 250–3; US Diplomatic Cable Released by Wikileaks: From Secretary of State to Embassy Abu Dhabi, *Secretary Clinton's April 7, 2009 Meeting with UAE Foreign Minister Sheikh Abdullah bin Zayed*, 9 April 2009, 09STATE34688, https://wikileaks.org/plusd/cables/09STATE34688_a.html.

152. Mohammad-Mahmoud Mohamedou, *A Theory of ISIS: Political Violence and the Transformation of the Global Order* (London: Pluto, 2018), 85f.

CHAPTER 14

1. See https://www.youtube.com/watch?v=jVCcYXVtT0g.

2. Salwa Ismail, 'The Syrian Uprising: Imagining and Performing the Nation', *Studies in Ethnicity and Nationalism* 11, 3 (2011), 538–49, 543; International Crisis Group, *Popular Protest in North Africa and the Middle East (VI): The Syrian People's Slow-Motion Revolution* (Brussels: International Crisis Goup, 2011), 2f.; Reinoud

Leenders, 'Collective Action and Mobilization in Dar'a: An Anatomy of the
Onset of Syria's Popular Uprising', *Mobilization: An International Quarterly* 17, 4
(2012), 419–34; Reinoud Leenders and Steven Heydemann, 'Popular Mobilization
in Syria: Opportunity and Threat, and the Social Networks of the Early Risers',
Mediterranean Politics 17, 2 (2012), 139–59.

3. For an overview of figures, see Daniel Finnbogason, Göran Larsson, and Isak
Svensson, 'Is Shia-Sunni Violence on the Rise? Exploring New Data on Intra-
Muslim Organised Violence 1989–2017', *Civil Wars* 21, 1 (2019), 25–53; Seung-
Whan Choi and Benjamin Acosta, 'Sunni Suicide Attacks and Sectarian Violence',
Terrorism and Political Violence 32, 7 (2020), 1371–90. See also Geneive Abdo, *The
New Sectarianism: The Arab Uprisings and the Rebirth of the Shi'a-Sunni Divide*
(New York: Oxford University Press, 2017), which includes a useful selection of
sectarian tweets from this period on pages 151–206.

4. For the original proposition of the term 'sectarianisation', see Nader Hashemi
and Danny Postel, 'Introduction: The Sectarianization Thesis', in: Nader Hashemi
and Danny Postel (eds), *Sectarianization: Mapping the New Politics of the Middle East*
(London: Hurst, 2017), 1–22. This resembles developments analysed in securi-
tisation theory as put forth by the Copenhagen School. See Barry Buzan, Ole
Wæver, and Jaap de Wilde, *Security: A New Framework for Analysis* (Boulder, CO:
Lynne Rienner, 1998). For an application to the Sunni–Shia question, see Toby
Matthiesen, *Sectarian Gulf: Bahrain, Saudi Arabia, and the Arab Spring that Wasn't*
(Stanford: Stanford University Press, 2013); Matthiesen, 'Sectarianization as
Securitization: Identity Politics and Counter-Revolution in Bahrain', in: Nader
Hashemi and Danny Postel (eds), *Sectarianization: Mapping the New Politics of the
Middle East* (London: Hurst, 2017), 199–214. For overviews of the different
approaches to sectarian politics, see Morten Valbjørn, 'Beyond the Beyond(s): On
the (Many) Third Way(s) beyond Primordialism and Instrumentalism in the
Study of Sectarianism', *Nations and Nationalism* 26, 1 (2020), 91–107; Valbjørn,
'Observing (the Debate on) Sectarianism: On Conceptualizing, Grasping and
Explaining Sectarian Politics in a New Middle East', *Mediterranean Politics* 26, 5
(2021), 612–34; Valbjørn, 'What's so Sectarian about Sectarian Politics? Identity
Politics and Authoritarianism in a New Middle East', *Studies in Ethnicity and
Nationalism* 19, 1 (2019), 127–49. See also Raymond Hinnebusch, 'The Sectarian
Revolution in the Middle East', *R/evolutions: Global Trends & Regional Issues* 4, 1
(2016), 120–52; Helle Malmvig, 'Coming in from the Cold: How We May Take
Sectarian Identity Politics Seriously in the Middle East without Playing to the
Tunes of Regional Power Elites', *POMEPS*, https://pomeps.org/coming-in-
from-the-cold-how-we-may-take-sectarian-identity-politics-seriously-in-the-
middle-east-without-playing-to-the-tunes-of-regional-power-elites;   May
Darwich and Tamirace Fakhoury, 'Casting the Other as an Existential Threat:
The Securitisation of Sectarianism in the International Relations of the Syria
Crisis', *Global Discourse* 6, 4 (2016), 712–32; Simon Mabon, 'Desectarianization:
Looking beyond the Sectarianization of Middle Eastern Politics', *Review of Faith*

& International Affairs 17, 4 (2019), 23–35. See also the outputs of the SEPAD project: https://www.sepad.org.uk.

5. F. Gregory Gause, *Beyond Sectarianism: The New Middle East Cold War* (Doha: Brookings Doha Center, 2014). Qatar and the United Arab Emirates (UAE), too, tried to influence transitions in Tunisia, Egypt, and Libya and expand their influence in, and relations with, Morocco and Algeria. Their rivalry became another important feature of post-2011 regional relations. Toby Matthiesen, 'Renting the Casbah: Gulf States' Foreign Policy towards North Africa since the Arab Uprisings', in: Kristian Coates Ulrichsen (ed.), *The Changing Security Dynamics of the Persian Gulf* (New York: Oxford University Press, 2018), 43–59. See also Marc Lynch, *The New Arab Wars: Uprisings and Anarchy in the Middle East* (New York: PublicAffairs, 2016).

6. Al-Rasheed, *Contesting the Saudi State*; Lacroix, *Awakening Islam*, 151–264; Fandy, *Saudi Arabia*. This was exemplified by Salman al-Awda and his embrace of the Arab Spring. In general, see Madawi al-Rasheed, *Muted Modernists: The Struggle over Divine Politics in Saudi Arabia* (London: Hurst, 2015); Toby Matthiesen, 'Saudi Arabia', in: Shadi Hamid and William McCants (eds), *Rethinking Political Islam* (Oxford: Oxford University Press, 2017), 118–31; Robert F. Worth, 'Leftward Shift by Conservative Cleric Leaves Saudis Perplexed', *New York Times*, 4 April 2014; Monika Bolliger, 'Islamische Kritik an der saudischen Regierung', *Neue Zürcher Zeitung*, 17 April 2012; Samuel Helfont, *The Sunni Divide: Understanding Politics and Terrorism in the Arab Middle East* (Philadelphia: Foreign Policy Research Institute, 2009).

7. There is an offshoot of the Islamic Jihad movement, al-Sabirin, that espoused Shiism, but it is denounced by other Palestinian factions, banned by the Hamas government in Gaza, and very small. Rasha Abou Jalal, 'Ex-Islamic Jihad Leader Launches New Armed Group in Gaza', *al-Monitor*, 10 June 2014.

8. Epitomised by quotes such as: 'The chain of resistance against Israel by Iran, Syria, Hezbollah, the new Iraqi government and Hamas passes through the Syrian highway. [...] Syria is the golden ring of the chain of resistance against Israel.' Ali Akbar Velayati, Senior Advisor for Foreign Affairs to Iran's Supreme Leader, 6 January 2012, quoted in: Jubin M. Goodarzi, *Iran and Syria at the Crossroads: The Fall of the Tehran-Damascus Axis?* (Washington, DC: Wilson Center, 2013), 1. Another, similar statement was: 'What is happening in Syria is not an internal issue, but a conflict between the axis of resistance and its enemies in the region and the world. Iran will not tolerate, in any form, the breaking of the axis of resistance, of which Syria is an intrinsic part.' Saeed Jalili, Head of Iran's Supreme National Security Council, 6 September 2012, quoted in: ibid.

9. Moncef Marzouki, 'Annual George Antonius Memorial Lecture: The Tunisian Revolution: Achievements and Disillusions', *Middle East Centre, University of Oxford*, 7 June 2018.

10. Amongst a vast literature on the topic, see Christopher Phillips, *The Battle for Syria: International Rivalry in the New Middle East* (New Haven: Yale University

Press, 2016), 3ff., 22–8, and passim; Fawaz A. Gerges, *Obama and the Middle East: The End of America's Moment?* (New York: Palgrave Macmillan, 2012); Seyyed Vali Reza Nasr, *The Dispensable Nation: American Foreign Policy in Retreat* (Melbourne: Scribe, 2013); Steven Simon, 'Turning Away from the Middle East', *New York Review of Books*, 8 April 2021; Marc Lynch, 'Obama and the Middle East: Rightsizing the U.S. Role', *Foreign Affairs*, September/October 2015; Marc Lynch and Amaney Jamal, 'Introduction: Shifting Global Politics and the Middle East', *POMEPS Studies* 34 (2019), 3–6.

11. Nicolas Dot-Pouillard, 'Iran and the Muslim Brotherhood: The Best of Enemies?', *Middle East Eye*, 4 July 2016. See also Hamid, 'The Lesser Threat'; Mohamed al-Araby, 'Identity Politics, Egypt and the Shia', *al-Ahram*, 25 April 2013. Other members of the Brotherhood and the Party for Justice and Development also stated that 'there is no place for Shiism in Egypt' and that 'al-Azhar is a bastion for the Sunni madhhab' that should not allow Shiism. Muslim Brotherhood Guidance Bureau (http://ikhwanonline.com/Article. aspx? ArtID=145152&SecID=211), quoted in: Human Rights Watch, 'Egypt: Lynching of Shia Follows Months of Hate Speech', 27 June 2013. See also Ahmed Hidji, 'How Do Egypt's Official Religious Authorities View Shiites?', *al-Monitor*, 12 August 2016; Marwa al-Asar, 'Persecution of Egypt's Shiites Continues', *al-Monitor*, 29 May 2015. In June 2013, a mob lynched four Shia, including the outspoken and controversial Egyptian Shii cleric Hasan Shehata, in a village on the outskirts of Cairo, after Salafi preachers had intensified their anti-Shia campaign in the village. Human Rights Watch, 'Egypt'. For earlier debates in the 2000s, see L. Azuri, 'Muslim Brotherhood Debates its Position on the Shi'a', *Memri.org*, 27 April 2009; Rainer Brunner, 'Shi'ite Doctrine iii. Imamite-Sunnite Relations since the Late 19th Century', *EIr*.

12. *Al-Khalij al-Jadid*, 'Tuqus Shi'iyya 'Alaniyya bi-Ba'd Masajid Misr li-Awwal Marra Mundhu al-Dawla al-Fatimiyya', 11 May 2016. Iranian overtures to al-Azhar, with proposals to establish research cooperation and the opening of al-Azhar institutes in Iran, were seen with deep suspicion by the Saudis. According to Saudi sources, Tantawi was in favour of this and agreed to admit Shia students to al-Azhar. See Saudi Ministry of Foreign Affairs Cables Released by Wikileaks, https://wikileaks.org/saudi-cables; Mohamed Hamama and Shady Zalat, 'Wikileaks: Saudi Arabia and Azhar on the "Shia Encroachment" in Egypt', *Mada Masr*, 9 July 2015. See also Lora Moftah, 'Saudi Arabia WikiLeaks: Egypt's Azhar Islamic Authority Denies Coordinating with Riyadh on Politics', *International Business Times*, 22 June 2015; Holly Dagres, 'The Shiite Scare in Egypt', *al-Monitor*, 11 April 2013.

13. My understanding of this is based on participant observations and interviews carried out during a research trip in Cairo just before the 2013 coup, including conversations with Egyptians of different political persuasions, journalists, and diplomats. In general, for Gulf policy towards North Africa, see Matthiesen, 'Renting the Casbah'.

14. For a timeline of events during the February–March 2011 protests, see International Crisis Group, *Popular Protests in North Africa and the Middle East (III): The Bahrain Revolt* (Brussels: International Crisis Group, 2011); Bahrain Independent Commission of Inquiry, 'Report of the Bahrain Independent Commission of Inquiry', 23 November 2011, 65–169, 171–217; Cortni Kerr and Toby Jones, 'A Revolution Paused in Bahrain', *MERIP*, 23 February 2011; Lin Noueihed and Alex Warren, *The Battle for the Arab Spring: Revolution, Counter-Revolution and the Making of a New Era* (New Haven: Yale University Press, 2012), 135–63. See also Alaa Shehabi and Marc Owen Jones (eds), *Bahrain's Uprising: Resistance and Repression in the Gulf* (London: Zed, 2015).

15. Toby Matthiesen, 'A "Saudi Spring?": The Shi'a Protest Movement in the Eastern Province 2011–2012', *Middle East Journal* 66, 4 (2012), 628–59.

16. Justin Gengler, 'The Political Economy of Sectarianism in the Gulf', *Carnegie Endowment for International Peace*, 29 August 2016; Madawi al-Rasheed, 'Sectarianism as Counter-Revolution: Saudi Responses to the Arab Spring', in: Nader Hashemi and Danny Postel (eds), *Sectarianization: Mapping the New Politics of the Middle East* (London: Hurst, 2017), 143–58; al-Rasheed, 'Sectarianism as Counter-Revolution: Saudi Responses to the Arab Spring', *Studies in Ethnicity and Nationalism* 11, 3 (2011), 513–26.

17. Robert F. Worth, 'Saudi's Lonely, Costly Bid for Sunni-Shiite Equality', *New York Times*, 14 March 2014.

18. Interviews with representatives of the Muslim Brotherhood and Salafis in Bahrain, 2011, and with representatives of Shii and Muslim Brotherhood political societies in Kuwait, 2012.

19. In the early protests, a sort of civil nationalism was on display, and parts of the opposition tried to establish a counter-hegemonic nationalist discourse. Adélie Chevée, 'From Suriyya al-Asad to Souriatna: Civic Nationalism in the Syrian Revolutionary Press', *Nations and Nationalism* 28, 1 (2022), 154–76; Kathrin Bachleitner and Toby Matthiesen, 'Introduction to Themed Section on "Belonging to Syria: National Identifications before and after 2011"', *Nations and Nationalism* 28, 1 (2022), 117–24.

20. Al-bab.com, 'Syria: Speech by Bashar al-Assad', 30 March 2011, https://al-bab.com/albab-orig/albab/arab/docs/syria/bashar_assad_speech_110330.htm; Robin Yassin-Kassab and Leila al-Shami, *Burning Country: Syrians in Revolution and War* (London: Pluto, 2016), 41f.

21. Leon T. Goldsmith, *Cycle of Fear: Syria's Alawites in War and Peace* (London: Hurst, 2015), 1–11; Yassin-Kassab and al-Shami, *Burning Country*, 47ff., 63–6; Salam Hafez, 'Syrian Alawite Professor Speaks Out', *Institute for War and Peace Reporting*, 17 November 2011; Carsten Wieland, 'Alawis in the Syrian Opposition', in: Michael Kerr and Craig Larkin (eds), *The Alawis of Syria: War, Faith and Politics in the Levant* (Oxford: Oxford University Press, 2015), 225–43; Samar Yazbek, *A Woman in the Crossfire: Diaries of the Syrian Revolution*, trans. by Max Weiss (London: Haus, 2012). See also Rasha Omran, 'The Sect as

Homeland', *Critical Muslim* 11 (2014); Omran, 'Syria with One Eye', *New York Review of Books*, 15 October 2016; Bruno Paoli, 'Et maintenant, on va où? Les alaouites à la croisée des destins', in: François Burgat and Bruno Paoli (eds), *Pas de printemps pour la Syrie: Les clés pour comprendre les acteurs et les défis de la crise (2011–2013)* (Paris: La Découverte, 2013), 124–43; Kheder Khaddour, 'The Alawite Dilemma', in: Friederike Stolleis (ed.), *Playing the Sectarian Card: Identities and Affiliations of Local Communities in Syria* (Beirut: Friedrich-Ebert-Stiftung, 2015), 11–26; Aziz Nakkash, *The Alawite Dilemma in Homs: Survival, Solidarity and the Making of a Community* (Berlin: Friedrich-Ebert-Stiftung, 2013); Fred H. Lawson, 'Why did the Syrian Uprising Become a Sectarian Conflict? A Provisional Synthesis', *Politics, Religion & Ideology* 21, 2 (2020), 216–31, 227f.; Nir Rosen, 'Ghosts in the Mosques', *al-Jazeera*, 30 September 2011; Rosen, 'Syria's Alawite Activists Stuck in the Middle', *al-Jazeera*, 8 March 2012; Christoph Sydow, 'Angst statt Treue: Assad und Syriens Alawiten', *Spiegel*, 19 September 2013; Naseef Naeem, 'Zum Abschuss freigegeben', *Zenith*, 24 September 2013.

22. Personal observations, Damascus, Syria, 2004–8; Kheder Khaddour, 'Assad's Officer Ghetto: Why the Syrian Army Remains Loyal', *Carnegie Middle East Center*, 4 November 2015.

23. Hicham Bou Nassif, '"Second-Class": The Grievances of Sunni Officers in the Syrian Armed Forces', *Journal of Strategic Studies* 38, 5 (2015), 626–49; Kheder Khaddour, 'Strength in Weakness: The Syrian Army's Accidental Resilience', *Carnegie Middle East Center*, 14 March 2016; Dorothy Ohl, Holger Albrecht, and Kevin Koehler, 'For Money or Liberty? The Political Economy of Military Desertion and Rebel Recruitment in the Syrian Civil War', *Carnegie Endowment for International Peace*, 24 November 2015; Aron Lund, 'Chasing Ghosts: The Shabiha Phenomenon', in: Michael Kerr and Craig Larkin (eds), *The Alawis of Syria: War, Faith and Politics in the Levant* (Oxford: Oxford University Press, 2015), 207–24; Fabrice Balanche, 'Géographie de la révolte syrienne', *Outre-Terre* 29, 3 (2011), 437–58. Ismail adds important nuances to Balanche's arguments. See Salwa Ismail, 'Urban Subalterns in the Arab Revolutions: Cairo and Damascus in Comparative Perspective', *Comparative Studies in Society and History* 55, 4 (2013), 865–94, 881–90; Ismail, *The Rule of Violence*, 171f., 179ff., 191ff.

24. Adam Baczko, Gilles Dorronsoro, and Arthur Quesnay, *Civil War in Syria: Mobilization and Competing Social Orders* (Cambridge: Cambridge University Press, 2018); Phillips, *The Battle for Syria*, 53ff., 161f.

25. Lawson, 'Why did the Syrian Uprising Become a Sectarian Conflict?', 225ff., 230.

26. In general, see Paulo G. Pinto, 'The Shattered Nation: The Sectarianization of the Syrian Conflict', in: Nader Hashemi and Danny Postel (eds), *Sectarianization: Mapping the New Politics of the Middle East* (London: Hurst, 2017), 123–42; Heiko Wimmen, 'The Sectarianization of the Syrian War', in: Frederic Wehrey (ed.), *Beyond Sunni and Shia: The Roots of Sectarianism in a Changing Middle East* (Oxford: Oxford University Press, 2018), 61–85; Baczko, Dorronsoro, and Quesnay, *Civil War in Syria*, 256–65; Lawson, 'Why did the Syrian Uprising Become a Sectarian Conflict?'; Reinoud Leenders, 'Repression Is Not "a Stupid

Thing": Regime Responses to the Syrian Uprising and Insurgency', in: Michael Kerr and Craig Larkin (eds), *The Alawis of Syria: War, Faith and Politics in the Levant* (Oxford: Oxford University Press, 2015), 245–73, 252–5. For the prisoners, see US Diplomatic Cable Released by Wikileaks: From Embassy Damascus to Secretary of State, *When Chickens Come Home to Roost: Syria's Proxy War in Iraq at Heart of 2008–09 Seidnaya Prison Riots*, 24 February 2010, 10DAMASCUS158, https://wikileaks.org/plusd/cables/10DAMASCUS158_a.html; *The Australian*, 'Political Prisoners Released amid Syrian Protests', 26 March 2011.

27. For a general account, see Charles R. Lister, *The Syrian Jihad: Al-Qaeda, the Islamic State and the Evolution of an Insurgency* (London: Hurst, 2015). See also Christopher Phillips, 'Sectarianism and Conflict in Syria', *Third World Quarterly* 36, 2 (2015), 357–76; Phillips, *The Battle for Syria*, 130f.

28. Nir Rosen, 'Among the Alawites', *London Review of Books*, 27 September 2012; Rosen, 'A Tale of Two Villages', *al-Jazeera*, 24 October 2011; Rosen, 'A Tale of Two Syrian Villages: Part Two', *al-Jazeera*, 26 October 2011.

29. Ismail, *The Rule of Violence*, 155f.

30. Line Khatib, 'Syria, Saudi Arabia, the U.A.E. and Qatar: The "Sectarianization" of the Syrian Conflict and Undermining of Democratization in the Region', *British Journal of Middle Eastern Studies* 46, 3 (2019), 385–403.

31. Phillips, *The Battle for Syria*, 108f.; Lefèvre, *Ashes of Hama*, 188ff.; Lefèvre, 'Syria', in: Shadi Hamid and William McCants (eds), *Rethinking Political Islam* (Oxford: Oxford University Press, 2017), 73–87; Aron Lund, 'Struggling to Adapt: The Muslim Brotherhood in a New Syria', *Carnegie Endowment for International Peace*, 7 May 2013.

32. Stéphane Lacroix, *Saudi Islamists and the Arab Spring* (London: LSE, 2014); Toby Matthiesen, *The Domestic Sources of Saudi Foreign Policy: Islamists and the State in the Wake of the Arab Uprisings* (Washington, DC: Brookings Institution, 2015); Raphaël Lefèvre, 'Saudi Arabia and the Syrian Brotherhood', *Middle East Institute*, 27 September 2013; Stéphane Lacroix, 'To Rebel or not to Rebel: Dilemmas among Saudi Salafis in a Revolutionary Age', in: Francesco Cavatorta and Fabio Merone (eds), *Salafism after the Arab Awakening: Contending with People's Power* (London: Hurst, 2016), 61–82, 64f.

33. Ian Black, 'Syria Crisis: Saudi Arabia to Spend Millions to Train New Rebel Force', *Guardian*, 7 November 2013; Aron Lund, 'Into the Tunnels: The Rise and Fall of Syria's Rebel Enclave in the Eastern Ghouta', *Century Foundation*, 21 December 2016; Aron Lund, 'The Syrian Rebel Who Tried to Build an Islamist Paradise', *Politico*, 31 March 2017; Khaled Yacoub Oweis, 'Insight: Saudi Arabia Boosts Salafist Rivals to al-Qaeda in Syria', *Reuters*, 1 October 2013.

34. See the speech by Zahran Alloush: https://web.archive.org/web/20150602232233/https://www.youtube.com/watch?v=nPLUhSy4vZ4. See also Joshua Landis, 'Zahran Alloush: His Ideology and Beliefs', *Syria Comment*, 15 December 2013; Aron Lund, 'The Death of Zahran Alloush', *Syria Comment*, 25 December 2015.

35. Weiss, 'Mosaic, Melting Pot, Pressure Cooker', 197–200. His two main publications on the subject are serious sociological studies of the topic: Burhan Ghaliun,

Nizam al-Ta'ifiyya: Min al-Dawla ila al-Qabila (Beirut: al-Markaz al-Thaqafi al-'Arabi, 1990); Ghaliun, *Al-Ma'sala al-Ta'ifiyya*. See also Zecca, 'The Ṭa'ifiyyah'.

36. This was Sadiq Jalal al-Azm. See, for example, his interviews with www.almo-don.com, 15 July 2016, and this interview with *Orient News*, https://www.youtube.com/watch?v=JzdWFCA-S-c.

37. Luke Harding and Martin Chulov, 'Moaz al-Khatib: Ex-Imam Charged with Uniting Syria's Opposition', *Guardian*, 12 November 2012; Phillips, *The Battle for Syria*, 115ff.

38. Yassin-Kassab and al-Shami, *Burning Country*, 108–46; Aaron Y. Zelin and Phillip Smyth, 'The Vocabulary of Sectarianism', *Foreign Policy*, 29 January 2014. Though there was also much competition between different Salafi networks. Thomas Pierret, 'Salafis at War in Syria: Logics of Fragmentation and Realignment', in: Francesco Cavatorta and Fabio Merone (eds), *Salafism after the Arab Awakening: Contending with People's Power* (London: Hurst, 2016), 137–68, 138; Pierret, 'Les salafismes dans l'insurrection syrienne: Des réseaux transnationaux à l'épreuve des réalités locales', *Outre-Terre* 44, 3 (2015), 196–215. See also Marc Lynch, 'Is There an Islamist Advantage at War?', *APSA MENA Politics Newsletter* 2, 1 (2019), 18–21; Barbara F. Walter, 'The Extremist's Advantage in Civil Wars', *International Security* 42, 2 (2017), 7–39.

39. Thomas Pierret, 'States Sponsors and the Syrian Insurgency: The Limits of Foreign Influence', in: Luigi Narbone, Agnès Favier, and Virginie Collombier (eds), *Inside Wars: Local Dynamics of Conflicts in Syria and Libya* (Florence: European University Institute, 2016), 22–8, 26. In general, see the chapters in Raymond Hinnebusch and Adham Saouli (eds), *The War for Syria: Regional and International Dimensions of the Syrian Uprising* (Abingdon: Routledge, 2020). For the general foreign policy of Qatar, see Kristian Coates Ulrichsen, *Qatar and the Arab Spring* (London: Hurst, 2014); Mehran Kamrava, *Qatar: Small State, Big Politics* (Ithaca: Cornell University Press, 2013).

40. Elizabeth Dickinson, *Playing with Fire: Why Private Gulf Financing for Syria's Extremist Rebels Risks Igniting Sectarian Conflict at Home* (Washington, DC: Brookings Institution, 2013).

41. Interviews with Kuwaiti Shii MPs, Kuwait, 2012. See also Sylvia Westall, 'Terror Case Opens up Kuwait's Sectarian Divisions', *Reuters*, 2 June 2016; Madeleine Wells, 'Sectarianism and Authoritarianism in Kuwait', *Washington Post*, 13 April 2015; Wells, 'Sectarianism, Authoritarianism, and Opposition in Kuwait', in: Nader Hashemi and Danny Postel (eds), *Sectarianization: Mapping the New Politics of the Middle East* (London: Hurst, 2017), 235–58.

42. Justin Gengler, 'Bahraini Salafis Fighting the Infidels Wherever They Find Them', *Religion and Politics in Bahrain*, 6 August 2012.

43. He died in 2016. The Syrian opposition and Sunni Islamic organisations, such as the International Union of Muslim Scholars headed by al-Qaradawi, hailed him as a key religious figure while downplaying his role in the rise of the ideological side of Sunni anti-Shiism and anti-Iranian sentiment. Hussein Ibish, 'The Legacy of Muhammad Sorour, Key Figure in Rise of Sunni Extremism', *Arab Gulf States*

Institute, 16 November 2016. See also Hassan Hassan, 'Muhammad Surur and the Normalisation of Extremism', *The National*, 13 November 2016. Interestingly, however, despite his role as a sort of Salafi godfather, he actually did not fund the most radical Salafi organisations in Syria, Ahrar al-Sham, Jabhat al-Nusra, or later IS, but rather supported a local militia in his native Deraa with whom he shared tribal ties. I thank Raphaël Lefèvre for these points.

44. Wesal and Safa TV channels are the most prominent amongst them. Toby Matthiesen, 'Sectarianism Comes Back to Bite Saudi Arabia', *Washington Post*, 18 November 2014. See the Twitter handle @Wesal_TV. See also Raihan Ismail, 'The Saudi 'Ulama and the Syrian Civil War', in: Amin Saikal (ed.), *The Arab World and Iran: A Turbulent Region in Transition* (New York: Palgrave Macmillan, 2016), 83–102; Abdo, *The New Sectarianism*, 76–9, 176–86; Pierret, *Religion and State*, 234–8.

45. Gerges, *ISIS*, 136f.; Haykel, 'Al-Qa'ida and Shiism', 196ff.

46. Haian Dukhan, 'Tribes and Tribalism in the Syrian Uprising', *Syria Studies* 6, 2 (2014), 1–28; Dukhan, *State and Tribes in Syria: Informal Alliances and Conflict Patterns* (London: Routledge, 2018), 127–58; Dukhan, 'The End of the Dialectical Symbiosis of National and Tribal Identities in Syria', *Nations and Nationalism* 28, 1 (2022), 141–53.

47. Pierret, 'Salafis', 140. After it had become one of the most powerful rebel brigades, Qatari-owned media tried to reposition it as 'moderate' and highlight its severing of ties to AQ. Al-Julani now said that normal Alawites, i.e. those who had not taken up arms and had not served the regime, would be spared. This was intended as a sign of moderation, but, given the large-scale association of Alawites with the state and the militarisation of the community, this reassured few Alawites. See also Aron Lund, *Syrian Jihadism* (Stockholm: Swedish Institute of International Affairs, 2012). See, amongst others, Daveed Gartenstein-Ross and Aymenn Jawad al-Tamimi, 'Druze Clues: Al-Nusra's Rebranding and What it Means for Syria', *Foreign Affairs*, 5 October 2015; *Ya Libnan*, 'Al-Qaeda Forces Druze of Idlib Syria to Destroy their Shrines and Convert', 19 March 2015; Aymenn Jawad al-Tamimi, 'Additional Notes on the Druze of Jabal al-Summaq', 6 October 2015; Waleed Rikab, 'The Plight of Syria's Druze Minority and U.S. Options', *Syria Comment*, 9 September 2015.

48. Ceren Lord, 'Rethinking the Justice and Development Party's "Alevi Openings"', *Turkish Studies* 18, 2 (2017), 278–96. At the same time, a Twelver Shii community in Turkey grew. It was largely made up of Azeri migrants to Turkish cities, who managed to establish Shii mosques and hold Shii processions fairly openly. They also established links with Alevis, although relations between the two were limited. Thierry Zarcone, 'Shi'isms under Construction: The Shi'a Community of Turkey in the Contemporary Era', in: Sabrina Mervin (ed.), *The Shi'a Worlds and Iran* (London: Saqi, 2010), 139–66.

49. Raoul Motika, 'Foreign Missionaries, Homemade Dissidents and Popular Islam: The Search for New Religious Structures in Azerbaijan', in: Rainer Brunner and Werner Ende (eds), *The Twelver Shia in Modern Times: Religious Culture & Political*

History (Leiden: Brill, 2001), 284–97; Sebastien Peyrouse, 'Shiism in Central Asia: The Religious, Political, and Geopolitical Factors', *Central Asia-Caucasus Analyst*, 20 May 2009; US Diplomatic Cable Released by Wikileaks: From Embassy Tashkent to Secretary of State, *Bukhara Activist: Better-Trained Imams Fending off Extremism*, 29 July 2008, 08TASHKENT878, https://wikileaks.org/plusd/cables/08TASHKENT878_a.html; US Diplomatic Cable Released by Wikileaks: From Embassy Tashkent to Secretary of State, *Ambassador-at-Large Hanford Meets with Uzbekistan's Religious Leaders*, 16 July 2007, 07TASHKENT1301, https://wikileaks.org/plusd/cables/07TASHKENT1301_a.html; Emil Souleimanov and Maya Ehrmann, 'The Rise of Militant Salafism in Azerbaijan and its Regional Implications', *Middle East Policy* 20, 3 (2013), 111–20; Brondz and Aslanova, 'Sunni-Shia Issue'; Dina Lisnyansky, 'Tashayu (Conversion to Shiism) in Central Asia and Russia', *Current Trends in Islamist Ideology* 8 (2009), 108–17; International Crisis Group, *Azerbaijan: Independent Islam and the State* (Brussels: International Crisis Group, 2008); Murad Ismayilov and Norman A. Graham (eds), *Turkish–Azerbaijani Relations: One Nation—Two States?* (Abingdon: Routledge, 2016); Balci and Goyushov, 'Changing Islam in Post-Soviet Azerbaijan', 202–7; Bayram Balci, 'Shi'ism in Post-Soviet Azerbaijan: Between Iranian Influence and Internal Dynamics', in: Sabrina Mervin (ed.), *The Shi'a Worlds and Iran* (London: Saqi, 2010), 167–92; Boris Pétric, 'The Ironis in Post-Soviet Uzbekistan: The Virtues of Mental Dissimulation (Taqiyya) in a Context of Sunnitization', in: Sabrina Mervin (ed.), *The Shi'a Worlds and Iran* (London: Saqi, 2010), 193–214; Dobroslawa Wiktor-Mach, *Religious Revival and Secularism in Post-Soviet Azerbaijan* (Berlin/Boston: De Gruyter, 2017), 106f., 156–64ff., 182–96, and passim. The influx of Azerbaijani workers into Russia, and proselytisation efforts, meant that the number of Shia in Russia grew as well (though they lacked institutional representation, as official Russian Muslim organisations are Sunni). Paul Goble, 'Who will Manage the 2 Million Shiites of Russia?', *Moscow Times*, 9 February 2010.

50. Ceren Lord, 'Sectarianized Securitization in Turkey in the Wake of the 2011 Arab Uprisings', *Middle East Journal* 73, 1 (2019), 51–72. An Alevi militia in turn vowed to defend the Gazi neighbourhood. *Halkin Sesi TV*, 'Statement of Gazi Cephe Militia', 8 September 2016; Mkrtich Karapetyan, 'The Alevi/Alawite Factor in Turkey–Syria Relations in the Light of the Syrian Crisis', *Journal of Liberty and International Affairs* 4, 3 (2018), 24–40; Cengiz Candar, 'Is Syria War Additional Spark to Alevi Protests in Turkey?', *al-Monitor*, 16 September 2013; Constanze Letsch, 'Syrian Conflict Brings Sectarian Tensions to Turkey's Tolerant Hatay Province', *Guardian*, 3 September 2013; Letsch, 'Turkey: Syria Conflict Heightens Alevi Tension', *Eurasianet*, 9 October 2013; Waldman and Caliskan, *The New Turkey*, 104f. There were also reports that Syria tried to mobilise Alawites in Turkey to upend Turkey's Syria policy, but these are difficult to verify. *Today's Zaman*, 'Group Tries to Recruit Hatay Alevis into Assad Army', 3 September 2012; Aymenn Jawad al-Tamimi, 'A Case Study of "the Syrian Resistance", a Pro-Assad Militia Force', *Syria Comment*, 22 September 2013.

51. Waldman and Caliskan, *The New Turkey*, 221–6.

52. Mark Mazzetti and Matt Apuzzo, 'U.S. Relies Heavily on Saudi Money to Support Syrian Rebels', *New York Times*, 23 January 2016. President Trump announced the phasing out of the programme in July 2017 after a meeting with Putin. Greg Jaffe and Adam Entous, 'Trump Ends Covert CIA Program to Arm Anti-Assad Rebels in Syria, a Move Sought by Moscow', *Washington Post*, 19 July 2017. See also Yehuda U. Blanga, 'Saudi Arabia's Motives in the Syrian Civil War', *Middle East Policy* 24, 4 (2017), 45–62.

53. Rougier, *The Sunni Tragedy*, 173–8; Rania Abouzeid, 'Opening the Weapons Tap: Syria's Rebels Await Fresh and Free Ammo', *Time*, 22 June 2012; Radwan Mortada, 'Exclusive: Inside Future Movement's Syria Arms Trade', *al-Akhbar*, 29 November 2012.

54. Bassel F. Salloukh, 'The Syrian War: Spillover Effects on Lebanon', *Middle East Policy* 24, 1 (2017), 62–78; Khashan, 'The Rise and Growth of Hezbollah'; Aurélie Daher, 'In the Wake of the Islamic State Threat: Repercussions on Sunni-Shi'i Competition in Lebanon', *Journal of Shi'a Islamic Studies* 8, 2 (2015), 209–35.

55. Can Kasapoğlu, 'Beyond Obama's Red Lines: The Syrian Arab Army and Chemical Warfare', *SWP Comment* 27 (2019), 1–4.

56. Phillip Smyth, *The Shiite Jihad in Syria and its Regional Effects* (Washington, DC: Washington Institute for Near East Policy, 2015); Suadad al-Salhy, 'Iraqi Shi'ites Flock to Assad's Side as Sectarian Split Widens', *Reuters*, 19 June 2013.

57. Jessica Lewis, Ahmed Ali, and Kimberly Kagan, 'Iraq's Sectarian Crisis Reignites as Shi'a Militias Execute Civilians and Remobilize', *Institute for the Study of War*, 1 June 2013.

58. For religious symbolism invoked in the war, see Maximilian Lakitsch, 'Islam in the Syrian War: Spotting the Various Dimensions of Religion in Conflict', *Religions* 9, 236 (2018), 1–17; Mark Tomass, *The Religious Roots of the Syrian Conflict: The Remaking of the Fertile Crescent* (Basingstoke: Palgrave Macmillan, 2016); Christopher Phillips and Morten Valbjørn, '"What Is in a Name?": The Role of (Different) Identities in the Multiple Proxy Wars in Syria', *Small Wars & Insurgencies* 29, 3 (2018), 414–33; Phillips, 'Sectarianism'; Ignacio Alvarez-Ossorio, 'The Sectarian Dynamics of the Syrian Conflict', *Review of Faith & International Affairs* 17, 2 (2019), 47–58; Christian C. Sahner, *Among the Ruins: Syria Past and Present* (London: Hurst, 2014).

59. Helle Malmvig, 'Allow Me This One Time to Speak as a Shi'i: The Sectarian Taboo, Music Videos and the Securitization of Sectarian Identity Politics in Hezbollah's Legitimation of its Military Involvement in Syria', *Mediterranean Politics* 26, 1 (2021), 1–24; Malmvig, 'Soundscapes of War: The Audio-Visual Performance of War by Shi'a Militias in Iraq and Syria', *International Affairs* 96, 3 (2020), 649–66; Bashir Saade, 'Hezbollah and its "Takfiri" Enemy in Syria: Rethinking Relationships between States and Non-State Actors', in: Rasmus Alenius Boserup, Waleed Hazbun, Karim Makdisi, and Helle Malmvig (eds), *New Conflict Dynamics: Between Regional Autonomy and Intervention in the Middle East and North Africa* (Copenhagen: Danish Institute for International Studies, 2017), 81–91; International Crisis Group, *Lebanon's Hizbollah Turns Eastward to Syria* (Brussels: International Crisis Group, 2014); International Crisis Group,

Hizbollah's Syria Conundrum (Brussels: International Crisis Group, 2017); Shoghig Mikaelian and Bassel F. Salloukh, 'Strong Actor in a Weak State: The Geopolitics of Hezbollah', in: Mehran Kamrava (ed.), *Fragile Politics: Weak States in the Greater Middle East* (New York: Oxford University Press, 2016), 119–43, 138–42; Adham Saouli, 'Hizbollah's Intervention in Syria: Causes and Consequences', in: Raymond Hinnebusch and Adham Saouli (eds), *The War for Syria: Regional and International Dimensions of the Syrian Uprising* (Abingdon: Routledge, 2020), 69–82; Marina Calculli, 'Hezbollah's Lebanese Strategy in the Syrian Conflict', in: Ioannis Galariotis and Kostas Ifantis (eds), *The Syrian Imbroglio: International and Regional Strategies* (Florence: European University Institute, 2017), 36–44; Zafer Kızılkaya, 'Hizbullah's Moral Justification of its Military Intervention in the Syrian Civil War', *Middle East Journal* 71, 2 (2017), 211–28; Aymenn Jawad al-Tamimi, 'Hizballah, the Jihad in Syria, and Commemorations in Lebanon', *Middle East Review of International Affairs* 19, 1 (2015), 8–36.

60. Rabil, *Salafism in Lebanon*, 213–33.

61. Saouli, 'Lebanon's Salafis', 57f.

62. Ali M. Latifi, 'How Iran Recruited Afghan Refugees to Fight Assad's War', *New York Times*, 30 June 2017; Human Rights Watch, 'Iran Sending Thousands of Afghans to Fight in Syria', 29 January 2016. Critics of the Syrian regime pointed to these foreign Shia fighters to undermine the regime. Amongst countless examples, see Justin Podur, 'The Afghans are Coming!', *Telesur*, 18 May 2017; Hashmatallah Moslih, 'Iran "Foreign Legion" Leans on Afghan Shia in Syria War', *al-Jazeera*, 22 January 2016; Reinoud Leenders and Antonio Giustozzi, 'Foreign Sponsorship of Pro-Government Militias Fighting Syria's Insurgency: Whither Proxy Wars?', *Mediterranean Politics* 27, 5 (2022), 614-43; Guido Steinberg, *The 'Axis of Resistance': Iran's Expansion in the Middle East is Hitting a Wall* (Berlin: SWP, 2021), 17–22.

63. Mona Mahmood and Martin Chulov, 'Syrian War Widens Sunni-Shia Schism as Foreign Jihadis Join Fight for Shrines', *Guardian*, 4 June 2013. See also Kristin Dailey, 'Iran Has More Volunteers for the Syrian War than it Knows What to Do With', *Foreign Policy*, 12 May 2016; Nils Wörmer, 'Assads afghanische Söldner: Der Einsatz der Fatemiyoun in Syrien', *Konrad-Adenauer-Stiftung*, 4 December 2018; Ali M. Latifi, '"Phantom Force": Young Afghans Fighting in Syria Face Uncertain Future', *Middle East Eye*, 26 September 2020. On a field trip to Najaf and Karbala, I bought biographies of Iranian 'martyrs in defence of the holy shrines of Sayyida Zaynab', on sale for pilgrims outside the shrines. They were published in Arabic and Persian by Dar al-Hadara al-Islamiyya, Beirut, 2018.

64. Zia ur-Rehman, 'Pakistan's Shia Mercenaries Return from Syria, Posing a Security Threat', *TRT World*, 2 March 2021. See also Jubin M. Goodarzi, *Iran and the Syrian and Iraqi Crises* (Washington, DC: Wilson Center, 2014); Goodarzi, *Iran and Syria: The End of the Road?* (Washington, DC: Wilson Center, 2015).

65. Eskandar Sadeghi-Boroujerdi, 'Strategic Depth, Counterinsurgency, and the Logic of Sectarianization: The Islamic Republic of Iran's Security Doctrine and

its Regional Implications', in: Nader Hashemi and Danny Postel (eds), *Sectarianization: Mapping the New Politics of the Middle East* (London: Hurst, 2017), 159–84; Arash Azizi, *The Shadow Commander: Soleimani, the US, and Iran's Global Ambitions* (London: Oneworld, 2020); International Institute for Strategic Studies, *Iran's Networks of Influence in the Middle East* (London: Routledge, 2020); Ostovar, *Vanguard of the Imam*, 204–19.

66. Tabatabai, *Morgen in Iran*, 48f., 68f.; *Associated Press*, 'Iranian Official Says at Least 400 Fighters Killed in Syria', 13 August 2016; Ostovar, *Vanguard of the Imam*. See also Narges Bajoghli, *Iran Reframed: Anxieties of Power in the Islamic Republic* (Stanford: Stanford University Press, 2019).

67. A Companion of the Prophet Muhammad, Hujr Ibn Adi, had been executed in 660 by the first Umayyad Caliph because of his support for the Shii cause. Khaled Keshk, 'The Historiography of an Execution: The Killing of Ḥujr b. 'Adī', *Journal of Islamic Studies* 19, 1 (2008), 1–35; Thomas Erdbrink and Hania Mourtada, 'Iran Warns Syrian Rebels after Report of Shrine Desecration', *New York Times*, 6 May 2013. Shia TV stations then broadcast a series on the life of Hujr. See Ahlulbayt.co.uk, 'Films: The Companion Hijr ibn Adi', https://ahlulbayt.co.uk/ondemand/films/The+Companion+Hijr+Ibn+Adi. Saudi writers criticised Iranian media for focusing on this and emphasised the many Sunni mosques being bombed. Sultan Alamer, 'Exhuming the Grave of Hujr ibn Adi: Iran and Hezbollah's Way of Fuelling Sectarianism in the Region', 7 December 2015, http://www.sultan-alamer.com/2015/12/07/hijr. A dedicated Shii militia vowed to 'defend' another shrine in the old city of Damascus. *Al-Jazeera*, 'ISIL Claims Deadly Blasts Near Sayeda Zeinab Shrine', 12 June 2016; *al-Jazeera*, 'Twin Bombings Kill Dozens in Damascus' Old City', 12 March 2017; Phillip Smyth, 'Hizballah Cavalcade: Al-Quwat al-Ja'afariyah & Liwa al-Sayyida Ruqayya: The Building of an "Islamic Resistance" in Syria', *Jihadology*, 28 September 2015. For other IS attacks on shrines in Syria, see Ballandalus, 'The Islamic State's (ISIS) Destruction of Shrines in Historical Perspective', 5 August 2014.

68. Josepha Wessels, 'Killing the Dispensables: Massacres Perpetrated in the Villages of Eastern Aleppo Province in 2013', *British Journal of Middle Eastern Studies* 49, 3 (2022), 463–85.

69. Pew Research Center, *Concerns about Islamic Extremism on the Rise in Middle East: Negative Opinions of al-Qaeda, Hamas and Hezbollah Widespread* (Washington, DC: Pew Research Center, 2014); Zogby Research Services, *Looking at Iran: How 20 Arab and Muslim Nations View Iran and its Policies* (Washington, DC: Zogby Research Services, 2012).

70. *Reuters*, 'Leading Sunni Muslim Cleric Calls for "Jihad" in Syria', 1 June 2013. 'There is no people's revolution in Bahrain but a sectarian one. [...] What is happening is not like what has happened in Egypt, Tunisia and Libya, but it is the empowerment of some factions via foreign forces on others; thereby it does not include the demands of all of the Bahraini people.' Mohamed Alarab, 'Qaradawi Says Bahrain's Revolution Sectarian', *al-Arabiya*, 19 March 2011.

71. Fanar Haddad, 'Can a "Sunni Spring" turn into an "Iraqi Spring"?', *Foreign Policy*, 7 January 2013; Renad Mansour, 'The Sunni Predicament in Iraq', *Carnegie Middle East Center*, 3 March 2016; Stephen Wicken, *Iraq's Sunnis in Crisis*, Middle East Security Report 11 (Washington: Institute for the Study of War, 2013).

72. Lawrence Joffe, 'Izzat Ibrahim al-Douri Obituary', *Guardian*, 29 October 2020. See also Aymenn Jawad al-Tamimi, 'The Naqshbandi Army's Current Situation in Iraq', 26 December 2014; https://alnakshabandia.net/army/our-approach/.

73. Adam Withnall, 'Iraq Crisis: Isis Declares its Territories a New Islamic State with "Restoration of Caliphate" in Middle East', *Independent*, 30 June 2014.

74. See, amongst others, Mohammed Hafez, 'The Crisis within Jihadism: The Islamic State's Puritanism vs. al-Qa'ida's Populism', *CTC Sentinel* 13, 9 (2020), 40–6. See also Patrick Cockburn, *The Rise of Islamic State: ISIS and the New Sunni Revolution* (London: Verso, 2015), 86ff., and passim for the sectarian dimension of IS's rise.

75. Benjamin Isakhan, 'The Islamic State Attacks on Shia Holy Sites and the "Shrine Protection Narrative": Threats to Sacred Space as a Mobilization Frame', *Terrorism and Political Violence* 32, 4 (2020), 724–48, 730.

76. The intense sectarian violence led to tensions between Sunni and Shii Turkmen. Dave van Zoonen and Khogir Wirya, *Turkmen in Tal Afar: Perceptions of Reconciliation and Conflict* (Erbil: Middle East Research Institute, 2017); BBC, 'Iraqi Turkmen Woman Recalls Horrors of IS Captivity', 16 October 2017.

77. This also applied to the Taliban. Cole Bunzel, 'Ideological Infighting in the Islamic State', *Perspectives on Terrorism* 13, 1 (2019), 12–21.

78. Several family members of his also joined IS. Cole Bunzel, 'The Caliphate's Scholar-in-Arms', *Jihadica*, 9 July 2014; Giorgio Cafiero, 'Meet the Likely Successor of Islamic State's Baghdadi', *al-Monitor*, 14 September 2016; Bill Law, 'Bahrain: The Islamic State Threat Within', *Middle East Eye*, 13 February 2015; Cole Bunzel, 'Bin'ali Leaks: Revelations of the Silent Mufti', *Jihadica*, 15 June 2015. Other Bahrainis, or descendants of Arabs working in the security sector in Bahrain, also went to Syria and joined IS. One of them grew up as the son of Syrian parents in Bahrain and then went to study Sharia in Saudi Arabia. He went to Syria to fight in 2012, later joined IS, and was motivated by his hatred of the *rafida*, the rejectionists, a hatred he internalised while in Bahrain and Saudi Arabia. Michael Weiss and Hassan Hassan, *ISIS: Inside the Army of Terror* (New York: Regan Arts, 2015), ix–xii. See also Justin Gengler, 'Sectarian Backfire? Assessing Gulf Political Strategy Five Years after the Arab Uprisings', *Middle East Institute*, 17 November 2015; Alaa Shehabi, 'Why is Bahrain Outsourcing Extremism?', *Foreign Policy*, 29 October 2014. The Bahrainis in IS in Iraq would, however, denounce and excommunicate the Bahraini Monarchy in 2014. Al-Lulua TV, 29 September 2014, https://www.youtube.com/watch?v=4koJWHe8Y4c.

79. See, amongst others, Cole Bunzel, *The Kingdom and the Caliphate: Duel of the Islamic States* (Washington, DC: Carnegie Endowment for International Peace, 2016); Toby Matthiesen, 'Sectarianism after the Saudi Mosque Bombings',

Washington Post, 29 May 2015; Matthiesen, 'The Islamic State Exploits Entrenched Anti-Shia Incitement', *Carnegie Endowment for International Peace*, 21 July 2015.

80. *BBC*, 'Dhaka Blasts: One Dead in Attack on Shia Ashura Ritual', 24 October 2015; *Reuters*, 'Suicide Bomb Attack on Afghan Shi'ite Mosque Kills 39, 80 Injured', 3 August 2018; *Independent*, 'Isis Claims Responsibility for Afghanistan Suicide Bombing that Killed 34 Students', 16 August 2018; *BBC*, 'Beirut Attacks: Suicide Bombers Kill Dozens in Shia Suburb', 12 November 2015.

81. Rori Donaghy, 'Saudi Crown Prince Accused of Silence on Sectarianism while Visiting Qatif', *Middle East Eye*, 27 May 2015.

82. See https://twitter.com/QatifDirect, in particular throughout 2015 and early 2016. See also Hassan al-Mustafa, 'Omran Mosque: The Traditional Shiite Fort in Qatif', *al-Arabiya*, 12 July 2016.

83. Jamal Khashoggi had long been outspoken against Iran and the rise of Shii political parties. In 2016, he wrote an article in *al-Hayat* entitled 'In the Defence of the Sunnis', in which he called on Sunni leaders, both Arab and Turkish, to finally overcome their fear of being too outwardly sectarian and take the side of the Sunnis wherever they are. See, for example, *al-Hayat*, 8 October 2016, https://web.archive.org/web/20170924015800/http://www.alhayat.com/opinion/Jamal-Khashoggi/17784575; tweet by Jamal Khashoggi, 7 October 2016, https://twitter.com/JKhashoggi/status/784497128978649088; Patrick Cockburn, 'Iraq Crisis: How Saudi Arabia Helped Isis Take Over the North of the Country', *Independent*, 14 July 2014. See also an email released by Wikileaks: Email from John Podesta to Hillary Clinton, 19 August 2014, https://wikileaks.org/podesta-emails/emailid/3774.

84. Interviews with former Iraqi officials, Karbala, Iraq, 2019.

85. See various articles by Renad Mansour on the topic, including Mansour, 'The Popularity of the Hashd in Iraq', *Carnegie Middle East Center*, 1 February 2016. See also Robert Tollast, 'Inside Iraq's Popular Mobilization Units', *National Interest*, 23 May 2016.

86. Inna Rudolf, 'The Sunnis of Iraq's "Shia" Paramilitary Powerhouse', *Century Foundation*, 13 February 2020.

87. Interview with an official in the Sunni Dar al-Ifta, Karbala, Iraq, 2019. In general, see Christopher Anzalone, 'In the Shadow of the Islamic State: Shi'i Responses to Sunni Jihadist Narratives in a Turbulent Middle East', in: Simon Staffell and Akil N. Awan (eds), *Jihadism Transformed: Al-Qaeda and Islamic State's Global Battle of Ideas* (New York: Oxford University Press, 2017), 157–82.

88. Phillip Smyth, 'Hizballah Cavalcade: What is the Liwa'a Abu Fadl al-Abbas (LAFA)? Assessing Syria's Shia "International Brigade" through their Social Media Presence', *Jihadology*, 15 May 2013. See also Smyth, 'Hizballah Cavalcade: From Najaf to Damascus and onto Baghdad: Iraq's Liwa Abu Fadl al-Abbas', *Jihadology*, 18 June 2014.

89. Interviews with former fighters in the Popular Mobilisation Forces, Najaf, Iraq, 2018.

90. The Twitter account of *Ahl al-Bayt*, for example, used this language to link the anti-IS campaign in Tikrit with repression against Shia in Bahrain. Alexandra Siegel, 'Twitter Wars: Sunni–Shia Conflict and Cooperation in the Digital Age', in: Frederic Wehrey (ed.), *Beyond Sunni and Shia: The Roots of Sectarianism in a Changing Middle East* (Oxford: Oxford University Press, 2018), 157–80, 170. For the controversy, see Juan Cole, 'Shiite Militias announce "Here I am, O Husayn" Campaign for Sunni Ramadi', 27 May 2015, https://www.juancole.com/2015/05/militias-announce-campaign.html. See also Younes Saramifar, 'Tales of Pleasures of Violence and Combat Resilience among Iraqi Shi'i Combatants Fighting ISIS', *Ethnography* 20, 4 (2019), 560–77.

91. Haddad, 'Anti-Sunnism and Anti-Shiism'.

92. Al-Khazali of Asaib Ahl al-Haqq. *Middle East Eye*, 'Shia Militia Leader Vows "Revenge for Hussein" in Mosul Battle', 14 October 2016.

93. See, for example, the tweet by Muhammad al-Barrak, 13 October 2016, https://twitter.com/mohamdalbarrak/status/786678214668251136.

94. Martin Chulov, 'From Tehran to Beirut: Shia Militias Aim to Firm up Iran's Arc of Influence', *Guardian*, 16 June 2017; Fabrice Balanche, 'The Iranian Land Bridge in the Levant: The Return of Territory in Geopolitics', *Telos*, 14 September 2018; Harith Hasan and Kheder Khaddour, 'The Transformation of the Iraqi-Syrian Border: From a National to a Regional Frontier', *Carnegie Middle East Center*, 31 March 2020.

95. Marc Lynch, Deen Freelon, and Sean Aday, 'Syria's Socially Mediated Civil War', *United States Institute of Peace*, 13 January 2014; Lynch, Freelon, and Aday, 'Syria in the Arab Spring: The Integration of Syria's Conflict with the Arab Uprisings, 2011–2013', *Research & Politics* 1, 3 (2014), 1–7; Siegel, 'Twitter Wars'; Marc Owen Jones, 'Automated Sectarianism and Pro-Saudi Propaganda on Twitter', *Exposing the Invisible*, 19 January 2017.

96. Toby Matthiesen, 'Transnational Diffusion between Arab Shia Movements', *POMEPS*, 9 June 2016; Marc Lynch, 'The Rise and Fall of the New Arab Public Sphere', *Current History* 114, 776 (2015), 331–6.

97. *Reuters*, 'Islamic State Bomb Attack on Afghan Hazara Protest in Kabul Kills at Least 61', *Telegraph*, 23 July 2016.

98. Human Rights Watch, 'Afghanistan's Shia Hazara Suffer Latest Atrocity: Insurgents' Increasing Threat to Embattled Minority', 13 October 2016.

99. Sune Engel Rasmussen and Aziz Ahmad Tassal, '"150,000 Americans Couldn't Beat Us": Taliban Fighters Defiant in Afghanistan', *Guardian*, 31 October 2017; Kersten Knipp, 'Tehran Buddies up to the Taliban', *Deutsche Welle*, 3 February 2021; Ali M. Latifi, '"Cold-Blooded": Taliban Accused of Executing Hazara People', *al-Jazeera*, 5 October 2021; *al-Jazeera*, 'Afghanistan: Dozens Killed in Suicide Bombing at Kunduz Mosque', 8 October 2021; *al-Jazeera*, 'Afghanistan: A Subdued Ashura under Taliban Rule', 19 August 2021; Mina Aldroubi, 'Ashura Processions Take Place in Afghanistan amid Taliban Takeover', *National News*, 19 August 2021; tweet by Ezzatullah Mehrdad, 17 August 2021, https://twitter.com/EzzatMehrdad/status/1427596817949155329?s=20; Hartung, 'Between a Rock and a Hard Place'.

100. Arif Rafiq, *Sunni Deobandi-Shiʻi Sectarian Violence in Pakistan: Explaining the Resurgence since 2007* (Washington, DC: Middle East Institute, 2014); Shahid Ali, 'The Specter of Hate and Intolerance: Sectarian–Jihadi Nexus and the Persecution of Hazara Shia Community in Pakistan', *Contemporary South Asia* 29, 2 (2021), 198–211. In 2017, a Pakistani court convicted a man to death for making comments about Aisha on social media. Imran Gabol, 'First Death Sentence Handed to Man for Blasphemy on Social Media', *Dawn*, 10 June 2017.

101. Srinivas Mazumdaru and Shamil Shams, 'Anti-Ismaili Attack Spotlights Pakistan's Intensifying Sectarian Violence', *Deutsche Welle*, 13 May 2015; Faisal Devji, 'The Anatomy of a Massacre', *Los Angeles Review of Books*, 27 May 2015; Devji, 'Why Playing for Pity in the Face of Islamic State's Atrocities is Counter-Productive', *Prospect*, 20 July 2017; Otared Haidar, 'Syrian Ismailis and the Arab Spring: Seasons of Death and White Carnations', in: Kenneth Scott Parker and Tony Emile Nasrallah (eds), *Middle Eastern Minorities and the Arab Spring: Identity and Community in the Twenty-First Century* (Piscataway: Gorgias Press, 2017), 147–74.

102. Jesse C. Reiff, 'When Ali Comes Marching Home: Shiʻa Foreign Fighters after Syria', *Studies in Conflict & Terrorism* 43, 11 (2020), 989–1010; ur-Rehman, 'Pakistan's Shia Mercenaries'; Ali M. Latifi, 'In Offering an Afghan Militia to Kabul, Iran's Zarif Causes Outrage', *Middle East Eye*, 23 December 2020; Latifi, '"Phantom Force"'.

103. Ali Khan Mahmudabad, 'Shia–Sunni Relations in India', *Live Encounters*, January 2014, https://liveencounters.net/january-2014/january/ali-khan-mahmudabad-shia-sunni-relations-in-india/. The root causes of a 2013 incident were primarily rivalling economic interests. Raphael Susewind, 'The "Wazirganj Terror Attack": Sectarian Conflict and the Middle Classes', *South Asia Multidisciplinary Academic Journal* 11 (2015), 1–17. Shia set up a separate personal law in January 2005 as a rival to the All India Muslim Personal Law Board, as Shia members on the latter did not feel they were being heard. Tapas Chakraborty and Rasheed Kidwai, '"Guest" Sadiq Tests Shia-Sunni Ties', *Telegraph India*, 15 March 2011.

104. Yoginder Sikand, 'Struggling against Sectarianism: Shia-Sunni Ecumenism', *Pakistan Christian Post*, 9 October 2008; *Shafaqna English*, 'Imam Fazlur Waizi Nadwi, Symbol of Shia-Sunni Unity, Passes Away in Lucknow', 14 January 2017; Mahan Abedin, 'Islam: Reviewing Shiite-Sunni Relations in India: An Interview with Seyed Mohammad Asgari', *Religioscope*, 12 January 2011. During a research trip in Delhi and Lucknow in 2019, I was informed of numerous Sunni–Shia joint initiatives, developed, not least, in the face of Hindu nationalism.

105. Fatemeh Aman, 'Iran Issues Rare Criticism of India over Kashmir', *Atlantic Council*, 30 August 2019; *Dawn*, 'Zarif Reaffirms Iran's Support for Kashmiris as Pakistan Continues Diplomatic Push to Highlight Issue', 3 September 2019.

106. Tolu Ogunlesi, 'Nigeria's Internal Struggles', *New York Times*, 23 March 2015; Isa, 'Sunni Literary Responses'.

107. Orji Sunday, 'Nigeria's Shia Protesters: A Minority at Odds with the Government', *al-Jazeera*, 22 April 2019. For more, see Varagur, *The Call*;

Alexander Thurston, 'Shi'ism and Anti-Shi'ism in Nigeria', *Maydan*, 15 May 2017; Thurston, 'Sectarian Triangles: Salafis, the Shi'a, and the Politics of Religious Affiliations in Northern Nigeria', *Politics and Religion* 14, 3 (2021), 484–511. See also https://www.islamicmovement.org/; Hakeem Onapajo, 'State Repression and Religious Conflict: The Perils of the State Clampdown on the Shi'a Minority in Nigeria', *Journal of Muslim Minority Affairs* 37, 1 (2017), 80–93.

108. See https://www.youtube.com/watch?v=-pD3Mts-Yb8; Mohammed Turki A. al-Sudairi, 'China as the New Frontier for Islamic Da'wah: The Emergence of a Saudi China-Oriented Missionary Impulse', *Journal of Arabian Studies* 7, 2 (2017), 225–46. See also Naser M. al-Tamimi, *China-Saudi Arabia Relations, 1990–2012: Marriage of Convenience or Strategic Alliance?* (Abingdon: Routledge, 2014); Niv Horesh (ed.), *Toward Well-Oiled Relations? China's Presence in the Middle East following the Arab Spring* (Basingstoke: Palgrave Macmillan, 2015).

109. Especially in Albania and Macedonia. See Arben Sulejmani (ed.), *A Light of Guidance: The Bektashi Community in the Balkans and around the World* (n.p.: n.p., 2015).

110. Haider, *Shi'i Islam*, conclusion.

111. Oliver Scharbrodt, 'A Minority within a Minority? The Complexity and Multilocality of Transnational Twelver Shia Networks in Britain', *Contemporary Islam* 13, 3 (2019), 287–305; Elvire Corboz, 'The al-Khoei Foundation and the Transnational Institutionalisation of Ayatollah al-Khu'i's Marja'iyya', in: Lloyd Ridgeon (ed.), *Shi'i Islam and Identity: Religion, Politics and Change in the Global Muslim Community* (London: I. B. Tauris, 2012), 93–112; Ridgeon, *Guardians of Shi'ism*; Liyakat Takim, *Shi'ism in America* (New York: NYU Press, 2009); Oliver Scharbrodt and Yafa Shanneik (eds), *Shi'a Minorities in the Contemporary World: Migration, Transnationalism and Multilocality* (Edinburgh: Edinburgh University Press, 2020).

112. Jessica Elgot, 'Shia and Sunni Tensions in Syria Threaten to Split British Muslim Community', *Huffington Post*, 29 June 2013; Marius Linge, 'Sunnite–Shiite Polemics in Norway', *FLEKS: Scandinavian Journal of Intercultural Theory and Practice* 3, 1 (2016), 1–18; Jelle Puelings, *Fearing a 'Shiite Octopus': Sunni-Shi'a Relations and the Implications for Belgium and Europe* (Ghent: Academia Press, 2010); Neil MacFarquhar, 'Iraq's Shadow Widens Sunni–Shiite Split in U.S.', *New York Times*, 4 February 2007.

113. Mariella Ourghi, 'Schiiten als Ungläubige: Zur situativen Kontingenz einer salafistischen Feindbildkonstruktion', in: Thorsten Gerald Schneiders (ed.), *Salafismus in Deutschland: Ursprünge und Gefahren einer islamisch-fundamentalistischen Bewegung* (Bielefeld: Transcript, 2014), 279–90; Susanne Olsson, 'Shia as Internal Others: A Salafi Rejection of the "Rejecters"', *Islam and Christian-Muslim Relations* 28, 4 (2017), 409–30; Stephen Castle, 'Deadly Mosque Arson in Belgium Attributed to Sunni-Shiite Friction', *New York Times*, 13 March 2012. See also Alina Isac Alak, 'The Sunni–Shi'a Conflict as Reflected in the Romanian Muslim Community', *Journal of Loss and Trauma* 20, 3 (2015), 207–13.

114. Martin Chulov and Kareem Shaheen, 'Sectarian Fighters Mass for Battle to Capture East Aleppo', *Guardian*, 29 September 2016.

115. Ahmed Rashid, 'Iran's Game in Aleppo', *New York Review of Books*, 1 December 2016.

116. It is impossible to independently verify figures. The opposition presented detailed figures to bolster these claims of sectarian engineering. A study published by a Saudi think tank headed by former Saudi intelligence chief Turki al-Faisal has made these allegations in some detail: Hussain Ibrahim Qutrib, *'Useful Syria' and Demographic Changes in Syria* (Riyadh: King Faisal Center for Research and Islamic Studies, n.d.).

117. Amounting to a few hundred thousand people, or between 1 and 2 per cent of Syria's population before the war, the community has undergone large-scale militarisation and a process of institutionalisation. Several militias and scout movements, especially in Damascus and Homs, have been set up, and a sectarian leadership structure modelled on the Lebanese example, the Supreme Islamic Jafari Council in Syria, was founded in 2012. It is headed by Sayyid Muhammad Ali al-Miski from Damascus, who has emerged as the public face of the community. In some of the Shii militias that are made up of Syrians and foreigners, divisions have emerged over the fact that apparently the Syrian militiamen are paid in Syrian pounds, which through devaluation has become almost worthless, and foreigners in dollars, which leads to stark imbalances in the remuneration of fighters and resentment amongst Syrian Shia fighters. Mohanad Hage Ali, 'The Shi'a Revival', *Carnegie Middle East Center*, 4 May 2017.

118. Rahaf Aldoughli, 'Departing "Secularism": Boundary Appropriation and Extension of the Syrian State in the Religious Domain since 2011', *British Journal of Middle Eastern Studies* 49, 2 (2022), 360–85; Aldoughli, 'Securitization as a Tool of Regime Survival: The Deployment of Religious Rhetoric in Bashar al-Asad's Speeches', *Middle East Journal* 75, 1 (2021), 9–32; Bachar Bakour, 'Regime or Revolution? The Dilemma of Syria's Religious Institutions: The Example of the Fatih Institute', *Politics, Religion & Ideology* 21, 2 (2020), 232–50; Jawad Qureshi, 'The Discourses of the Damascene Sunni Ulama during the 2011 Revolution', in: Line Khatib, Raphaël Lefèvre, and Jawad Qureshi, *State and Islam in Baathist Syria: Confrontation or Co-Optation?* (Boulder, CO: Lynne Rienner, 2012), 59–91.

119. Fanar Haddad, 'Iraq's Popular Mobilization Units: A Hybrid Actor in a Hybrid State', in: Adam Day (ed.), *Hybrid Conflict, Hybrid Peace: How Militias and Paramilitary Groups Shape Post-Conflict Transitions* (New York: United Nations University, 2020), 30–65; Renad Mansour, 'The "Hybrid Armed Actors" Paradox: A Necessary Compromise?', *War on the Rocks*, 21 January 2021; Toby Dodge, 'Understanding the Role of al-Hashd al-Shaabi in Iraq's National and Transnational Political Field', *POMEPS*, https://pomeps.org/understanding-the-role-of-al-hashd-al-shaabi-in-iraqs-national-and-transnational-political-field; Renad Mansour, *Networks of Power: The Popular Mobilization Forces and the State in Iraq* (London: Chatham House, 2021); Inna Rudolf, *From Battlefield to*

Ballot Box: Contextualising the Rise and Evolution of Iraq's Popular Mobilisation Units (London: International Centre for the Study of Radicalisation, 2018); Ibrahim al-Marashi, 'Iraq's Popular Mobilisation Units: Intra-Sectarian Rivalry and Arab Shi'a Mobilisation from the 2003 Invasion to Covid-19 Pandemic', *International Politics* 15, 4 (2021), 441–58.

120. Helen Lackner, 'The Change Squares of Yemen: Civil Resistance in an Unlikely Context', in: Adam Roberts, Michael J. Willis, Rory McCarthy, and Timothy Garton Ash (eds), *Civil Resistance in the Arab Spring: Triumphs and Disasters* (Oxford: Oxford University Press, 2015), 141–69; Laurent Bonnefoy, 'The Shabab, Institutionalized Politics and the Islamists in the Yemeni Revolution', in: Helen Lackner (ed.), *Why Yemen Matters: A Society in Transition* (London: Saqi, 2014), 87–104. For more on Islah, see Stacey Philbrick Yadav, *Islamists and the State: Legitimacy and Institutions in Yemen and Lebanon* (London: I. B. Tauris, 2013).

121. Khaled Fattah, 'Yemen's Sectarian Spring', *Carnegie Endowment for International Peace*, 11 May 2012. For more on the 2011–12 period in Yemen, see International Crisis Group, *Yemen: Enduring Conflicts, Threatened Transition* (Brussels: International Crisis Group, 2012).

122. Yadav, 'Sectarianization'; Sheila Carapico, 'Yemen between Revolution and Counter-Terrorism', in: Helen Lackner (ed.), *Why Yemen Matters: A Society in Transition* (London: Saqi, 2014), 29–49, 30.

123. Vom Bruck, 'How the Past Casts its Shadows', 276–80.

124. International Crisis Group, *The Huthis: From Saada to Sanaa* (Brussels: International Crisis Group, 2014).

125. See, for example, this booklet that listed the history of the Ansar Allah movement, the reasons why it managed to take Sanaa, and the options on the table for the GCC states: Dayf Allah Salih, *Tasawwur Huthi bi-Sha'n Saytarat al-Quwat al-Huthiyya 'ala Sana'a 2014* (Cairo: al-Maktab al-Arabi li-l-Maarif, 2015).

126. Toby Matthiesen and Sebastian Sons, 'The Yemen War in Saudi Media', *Muftah*, 20 July 2016.

127. 'The Houthis, unfortunately, are guided by mystical beliefs that power must be held by a specific dynasty. It is the same belief that concentrates power in the hands of the supreme leader of the Islamic Revolution in Iran and that brought the Houthis to war six times in the past decade against Yemen's central government.' Abdallah Y. al-Mouallimi, 'It's up to the Rebels to Stop Yemen's War', *New York Times*, 3 October 2017.

128. Remarks by Major General Ahmed Asiri, military advisor to Saudi Arabia's Minister of Defence and spokesman for the Saudi-led coalition in Yemen, European Council on Foreign Relations, London, 30 March 2017.

129. Thomas Juneau, 'Iran's Policy towards the Houthis in Yemen: A Limited Return on a Modest Investment', *International Affairs* 92, 3 (2016), 647–63; Samy Dorlian, 'The Sa'da War in Yemen: Between Politics and Sectarianism', *The Muslim World* 101, 2 (2011), 182–201; W. Andrew Terrill, 'Iranian Involvement in Yemen', *Orbis* 58, 3 (2014), 429–40; Elisabeth Kendall, *Iran's Fingerprints in Yemen: Real or Imagined?* (Washington, DC: Atlantic Council,

2017); Trevor Johnston et al., *Could the Houthis be the Next Hizballah? Iranian Proxy Development in Yemen and the Future of the Houthi Movement* (Santa Monica, CA: RAND, 2020); Hill, *Yemen Endures*, 194; Joost Hiltermann and April Longley Alley, 'The Houthis are not Hezbollah', *Foreign Policy*, 27 February 2017.

130. Anna Gordon and Sarah Parkinson, 'How the Houthis Became "Shi'a"', *MERIP*, 27 January 2018.

131. Peter Bergen, 'US Intercepts Multiple Shipments of Iranian Weapons Going to Houthis in Yemen', *CNN*, 29 October 2016.

132. Nonetheless, a Pakistani general was appointed as commander of a 41-nation, Saudi-led military alliance created to fight 'terrorism'. James M. Dorsey, 'Pakistan in the Hot Seat as General Takes Command of Saudi-Led Alliance', *The Turbulent World of Middle East Soccer*, 30 March 2017; *Dawn*, 'Raheel Sharif Will Become Controversial if He Leads Military Alliance: Abdul Qadir Baloch', 26 March 2017. Iran criticised the appointment, saying it might affect unity amongst Islamic countries. PTI, 'Iran not OK with Gen Raheel Sharif Heading Islamic Military Alliance', *Hindustan Times*, 4 April 2017. Pakistan also tried to mediate between Iran and Saudi Arabia. Kamal Alam, 'Asia's Quiet Superpower: Pakistan Army's Teetering Balance between Saudi Arabia and Iran', *Middle East Eye*, 21 February 2018.

133. UNICEF, 'Yemen Crisis', https://www.unicef.org/emergencies/yemen-crisis.

134. Toby Matthiesen, 'The World's Most Misunderstood Martyr', *Foreign Policy*, 8 January 2016. I have presented a paper, 'Nimr al-Nimr: The Making of a Shia Martyr', at the workshop 'Chiismes et politique au XXIe siècle: Militer, résister, gouverner' on 21–22 June 2016 at IREMAM in Aix-en-Provence and thank the participants of the workshop for their comments. See also *Newsweek*, 'Nimr al-Nimr: Anatomy of a Man', 13 January 2016.

135. Lee Fang and Zaid Jilani, 'After Executing Regime Critic, Saudi Arabia Fires up American PR Machine', *Intercept*, 4 January 2016. Dozens more Shia would be executed, some for allegedly attacking the police, others for spying for Iran. Simeon Kerr, 'Saudi Arabia Sentences 15 to Death on Spying for Iran Charges', *Financial Times*, 6 December 2016; Mohammad al-Sulami, 'Three Sentenced to Death for Firing at Police', *Arab News*, 1 December 2016.

136. N.a., 'Kill the Imāms of Kufr', *Dabiq* 13 (1437h), 6–8. It called upon lone wolves to attack those scholars, and one of the scholars the magazine had mentioned, Ayadh al-Qarni, was shot in March 2016 during a visit to a university in the Philippines. *Agence France-Presse*, 'Sheikh Aaidh al-Qarni, Saudi Preacher, Shot in Philippines', *Guardian*, 2 March 2016.

137. See, for example, this special issue dedicated to the Shia, particularly n.a., 'From the Pages of History: The Safawiyyah', and n.a., 'The Rāfidah: From Ibn Saba' to the Dajjāl', *Dabiq* 13 (1437h), 10–13 and 32–45, available at https://kyleorton.co.uk/wp-content/uploads/2017/11/dabiq-13-2016-01-19-the-rafidah.pdf. This special issue was even taken up by the mainstream media: Imogen Calderwood, 'ISIS Declares War on … Muslims: Latest Edition of Terror Group's

Magazine Calls for Shiites to be Targeted', *Daily Mail*, 21 January 2016. Al-Qaeda is frequently denounced in IS publications precisely because it did not target the Shia enough. See also Bunzel, *The Kingdom and the Caliphate*, 13.

138. For a discussion of contrasting positions of Sunni clerics towards the Arab uprisings, see Usaama al-Azami, *Islam and the Arab Revolutions: The Ulama between Democracy and Autocracy* (London: Hurst, 2021).

139. See, for example, *Shafaqna English*, 'Protest in India to Denounce Ayatollah Sheikh al-Nimr's Execution by Saudi Arabia', 2 January 2016.

140. Though it was not clear whether the street was officially renamed or not. Ian Black, 'Nimr al-Nimr Street, Tehran: Signpost for Troubled Iran-Saudi Ties', *Guardian*, 2 March 2016.

141. *Pars Today*, 'Leader Slams Silence of Muslim States on 2016 Hajj Tragedy', 7 September 2016; *Khamenei.ir*, 'Hajj Hijacked by Oppressors, Muslims Should Reconsider Management of Hajj: Ayatollah Khamenei', 5 September 2016.

142. Muhammad Mahdi al-Shirazi originally wanted the ideal Islamic state to be led by a group of senior clerics through consensus, or *shura al-fuqaha*, and not just by one cleric, as in Khomeini's political theory of *velayat-e faqih*. Both wanted clerics to rule, but Khomeini did not want others to challenge him or to defer to other senior clerics. Louër, *Transnational Shia Politics*, 97.

143. Arash Azizi, 'Iran Targets "MI6 Shiites"', *al-Monitor*, 29 April 2015.

144. Islamic Consultative Assembly News Agency, http://www.icana.ir/Fa/News/291568.

145. For a reconsideration of the notion of a Shii world with an Iranian core and other Shii communities related to it, see Morgan Clarke and Mirjam Künkler, 'De-Centring Shi'i Islam', *British Journal of Middle Eastern Studies* 45, 1 (2018), 1–17.

146. *Iranian Diplomacy*, 'Friday Prayers across Iran: Saudi-Bashing and Scandalous Salaries', 3 September 2016.

147. He argued that 'we must understand these are not Muslims, they are children of Magi and their hostility towards Muslims is an old one', referring to Iranians as Zoroastrians (Magi). Eric Randolph and Ian Timberlake, 'Iran-Saudi War of Words Heats up ahead of Hajj', *Agence France-Presse*, 7 September 2016.

148. Tweet by Mohammad Javad Zarif, 6 September 2016, https://twitter.com/JZarif/status/773206720353038336. See also Zarif, 'Let us Rid the World of Wahhabism', *New York Times*, 13 September 2016; Zarif, 'Saudi Arabia's Reckless Extremism', *New York Times*, 10 January 2016.

149. Marwa Osman, 'What is Wahhabism? Does ISIS Emerge from Wahhabism?', *Khamenei.ir*, 11 September 2016.

150. *Asharq al-Awsat*, 'Prince Turki al-Faisal, at the Paris Rally to Free Iran: The Muslim World Supports You Both in Heart and Soul', 9 July 2016.

151. Saeed Kamali Dehghan, 'Concern over UK-Based Iranian TV Channel's Links to Saudi Arabia', *Guardian*, 31 October 2018.

152. Dudoignon, *The Baluch, Sunnism and the State*, 1ff.; Chris Zambelis, 'The Evolution of the Ethnic Baluch Insurgency in Iran', *CTC Sentinel* 7, 3 (2014),

17–20; Scheherezade Faramarzi, *Iran's Sunnis Resist Extremism, but for How Long?* (Washington, DC: Atlantic Council, 2018).

153. *Khamenei.ir*, 'Enemies Trying to Infiltrate Decision Makers', 25 November 2015; *Khamenei.ir*, 'Attacking Sheikh Qassim will Provoke Fervent Bahrainis to Strike against Rulers', 17 August 2016. A small Shii militant group, Saraya al-Ashtar, named itself after a famous early military leader of Ali's armies. Al-Ashtar was the nickname of Malik Ibn al-Harith al-Nakha'i. L. Veccia Vaglieri, 'al-Ashtar', *EI2*. The choice of the name had strong sectarian and pro-Shii connotations, something previous Shii-led political movements in Bahrain had avoided (sporadic attacks targeted Bahraini security forces, almost exclusively staffed by Sunnis).

154. Richard Milne, 'Denmark Takes Tough Line with Saudi Arabia and Iran over Spying Claims', *Irish Times*, 3 February 2020; Sune Engel Rasmussen, 'Trial Exposes Iran-Saudi Battle in Europe', *Wall Street Journal*, 26 June 2020.

155. Charlie Savage and Scott Shane, 'Iranians Accused of a Plot to Kill Saudis' U.S. Envoy', *New York Times*, 11 October 2011.

156. In West Africa, for example, Shiism had spread since the 1970s through Shii migrant communities and the support of Iran. This was facilitated by a common hostility of Shiism and local Sufism to Salafi-Wahhabism and attempts to invoke Shiism's long history in North Africa. See references in Chapter 12 and Thomas Joassin, 'Algerian "Traditional" Islam and Political Sufism', in: Francesco Piraino and Mark J. Sedgwick (eds), *Global Sufism: Boundaries, Structures, and Politics* (London: Hurst, 2019), 209–24, 212ff.

157. The Saudis were hoping for much stronger commitments than the one made by Obama, when he stated that the US would protect its allies against invasions by a foreign country. In the Gulf, this was a reference to Iran, but the US would not be able to indefinitely support undemocratic regimes if they were threatened by internal instability. He argued that '[t]he biggest threats that they face may not be coming from Iran invading. It's going to be from dissatisfaction inside their own countries. Now disentangling that from real terrorist activity inside their country, how we sort that out, how we engage in the counterterrorism cooperation that's been so important to our own security— without automatically legitimizing or validating whatever repressive tactics they may employ—I think that's a tough conversation to have, but it's one that we have to have.' Thomas L. Friedman, 'Iran and the Obama Doctrine', *New York Times*, 5 April 2015; Nawaf Obaid, 'The Salman Doctrine: The Saudi Reply to Obama's Weakness', *National Interest*, 30 March 2016.

158. *Middle East Eye*, '"A Battle between Good and Evil": Donald Trump's Saudi Arabia Speech in Full', 22 May 2017.

159. Madawi al-Rasheed, 'The Saudi Leadership and Donald Trump? Two Sides of the Same Coin', *Middle East Eye*, 18 May 2017.

160. *Middle East Eye*, 'Qatar Launches Hacking Probe as Fake News Row Spreads across Gulf', 17 July 2017.

161. *Middle East Eye*, 'Iran Sends Five Plane Loads of Food as Kuwait Says Qatar "Ready" to Listen', 12 June 2017; Kristian Coates Ulrichsen, *Qatar and the Gulf Crisis* (London: Hurst, 2020).

162. Thomas Erdbrink, 'For Iran, Qatar Crisis is a Welcome Distraction', *New York Times*, 4 July 2017.

163. Qatari Ministry of Foreign Affairs, 'Qatar Announces Return of its Ambassador to Tehran', 23 August 2017, https://www.mofa.gov.qa/en/all-mofa-news/details/2017/08/23/qatar-announces-return-of-its-ambassador-to-tehran; Giorgio Cafiero, 'Iran's Role in Qatar's New Foreign Policy', *al-Monitor*, 30 August 2017.

164. *Al-Jazeera*, 'Iraq: Qatari "Ransom" Money with us, not Armed Groups', 11 June 2017; *Middle East Eye*, 'Hostage Qatari Royals "Used as Leverage" to End Syrian Sieges', 17 April 2017; *Middle East Eye,* 'Qatari Ransom for Kidnapped Royals Remains Unspent, Says Iraq', 12 June 2017. The boycott of Qatar, which Trump had endorsed, was to last until the end of Trump's presidency in late 2020.

165. Mansur al-Nuqaydan, 'Qatar wa Mashru'aha fi Da'm al-Wahhabiyya', in: *Al-Khalij wa-l-Rabi'a al-'Arabi: Al-Din wa-l-Siyyasa* (Dubai: al-Misbar, 2013), 153–69.

166. *Al-Arabiya*, 'Watch & Read: Mohammed bin Salman's Full Interview', 3 May 2017; *Associated Press*, 'Iran is Seeking "to Control Islamic World"', Says Saudi Arabian Prince', *Guardian*, 2 May 2017.

167. *Agence France-Presse*, 'Iran Says Trump Reaction to Isis Killings in Tehran was Repugnant', *Guardian*, 8 June 2017; Amanda Erickson, 'The Tehran Terrorist Attacks Targeted One of Iran's Most Sacred Spaces', *Washington Post*, 7 June 2017.

168. Zarif tweeted: 'Terror-sponsoring despots threaten to bring the fight to our homeland. Proxies attack what their masters despise most: the seat of democracy', in apparent reference to Saudi Arabia. Tweet by Mohammad Javad Zarif, 7 June 2017, https://twitter.com/JZarif/status/872543822525464577. A statement released by the IRGC after the attack also implicitly blamed Saudi Arabia and the US. Raf Sanchez, 'Iran's Revolutionary Guard Blames Saudi Arabia for Attacks in Tehran', *Telegraph*, 7 June 2017; Reza Haghighatnejad, 'Rouhani Fires Back at Trump and Saudi Arabia', *IranWire*, 23 May 2017.

169. Peter Baker and Michael D. Shear, 'To Trump, Human Rights Concerns are Often a Barrier to Trade', *New York Times*, 20 May 2017; Marc Owen Jones, 'From Hair Removal Products to Sectarianism: Propaganda Wars on the al-Awamiyya Hashtag', 15 May 2017; *Institute for Gulf Affairs*, 'Video Exposes Saudi Special Forces' Sectarian Doctrine', 8 August 2017. Several children also died during the siege. Alex MacDonald, 'Three-Year-Old Boy Dies amid Siege of Saudi Shia Town', *Middle East Eye*, 14 August 2017.

170. Ali Alaswad, 'It's No Coincidence that Bahrain's Bloodiest Day since 2011 Happened after Trump's Visit', *Middle East Eye*, 24 May 2017.

171. Tweet by Anwar Gargash, 3 December 2017, https://twitter.com/AnwarGargash/status/937328138471858176.

172. Nayef al-Rashid, 'Yemeni Minister: Iranian Houthi Militias Feel Defeat is Near', *Asharq al-Awsat*, 9 May 2018; *Asharq al-Awsat*, 'Yemen: Houthi Militias Kill, Injure Children in Marib', 12 August 2018.

173. Louis Imbert, 'Au Yémen, les houthistes seuls maîtres de Sanaa', *Le Monde*, 5 December 2017.

174. Peter Salisbury, 'Yemen's Future Looks Grim after Saleh Killing', *Chatham House*, 5 December 2017; April Longley Alley, 'The Killing of Former President Saleh Could Worsen Yemen's War', *International Crisis Group*, 6 December 2017.

175. But he warned that Jews had probably suffered more at the hands of Sunnis and that Israel should hedge its bets, i.e. not take sides in this conflict. Dore Gold, 'Shiites, Sunnis and Israel', *Israel Hayom*, 27 April 2012.

176. Rola el-Husseini, 'Political Exigency or Religious Affinity? Sectarianism in the Contemporary Arab World', *Mediterranean Politics* 26, 4 (2021), 491–7; Maren Koss, 'Flexible Resistance: How Hezbollah and Hamas are Mending Ties', *Carnegie Middle East Center*, 11 July 2018.

177. US Department of State, 'The Abraham Records', https://www.state.gov/the-abraham-accords/. For background, see Clive Jones and Yoel Guzansky, 'Israel's Relations with the Gulf States: Toward the Emergence of a Tacit Security Regime?', *Contemporary Security Policy* 38, 3 (2017), 398–419; Uzi Rabi and Chelsi Mueller, 'The Gulf Arab States and Israel since 1967: From "No Negotiation" to Tacit Cooperation', *British Journal of Middle Eastern Studies* 44, 4 (2017), 576–92.

178. Faleh A. Jabar, *The Iraqi Protest Movement: From Identity Politics to Issue Politics* (London: LSE Middle East Centre, 2018). See also the contributions to the special issue of *Studies in Ethnicity and Nationalism* 20, 2 (2020).

179. This quote is from Ali al-Amin: Al-amine.org, 'Transcript of Interview Conducted by al-Shorfa Website with Sayyid Ali al-Amin', 17 May 2013, http://www.al-amine.org; interview with the late Sayyid Hani Fahs, Beirut, Lebanon, 2013.

180. There has long been much critique from within the Shii community of the power-hungry Shii elites. See, for example, Hasan al-ʿAlawi, *Shiʿa al-Sulta wa Shiʿa al-ʿIraq: Siraʿ al-Ajnas* (London: Dar al-Zuraʾ, 2009).

181. Eskandar Sadeghi-Boroujerdi, 'Jailed Former Deputy Minister Claims Khamenei's Support for Assad has Provoked Shia-Sunni Conflict', *al-Monitor*, 15 February 2013.

182. Martin Chulov, 'Hezbollah Critic Lokman Slim Found Dead in Lebanon', *Guardian*, 4 February 2021.

183. Salloukh, 'The Sectarianization of Geopolitics', 39; Qassim Abdul-Zahra, 'Saudi Arabia Opens Iraq Embassy for First Time in Nearly 30 Years', *Independent*, 4 April 2019; Kristin Smith Diwan, 'Saudi Nationalism Raises Hopes of Greater Shia Inclusion', *Arab Gulf States Institute*, 3 May 2018; Abdul Hadi Habtor, 'Saudi Arabia Wants to Open an Embassy in Najaf, Iraq', *Asharq al-Awsat*, 15 August 2017; Erika Solomon, 'Sunni Saudi Arabia Courts an Ally in Iraq's Shia', *Financial Times*, 2 April 2018; interview with Shaykh Hasan

al-Saffar, *Sabq Online Newspaper*, 7 November 2021, https://sabq.org/bqzp29; Justin Gengler, 'Sectarianism from the Top Down or Bottom Up? Explaining the Middle East's Unlikely De-Sectarianization after the Arab Spring', *Review of Faith & International Affairs* 18, 1 (2020), 109–13; Mabon, 'Desectarianization'. See also Jeffrey Martini, Heather J. Williams, and William Young, *The Future of Sectarian Relations in the Middle East* (Santa Monica, CA: RAND, 2017).

184. The US also tried but failed to assassinate by drone strike an Iranian official in Yemen, Abdul Rida Shahlai, the commander of the Yemen division of Iran's Quds Force, near the Yemeni capital Sanaa. Alex Emmons, 'U.S. Strike on Iranian Commander in Yemen the Night of Suleimani's Assassination Killed the Wrong Man', *Intercept*, 10 January 2020.

185. Renad Mansour, 'Trump's Strikes Risk Upending Iraqi Politics', *Foreign Affairs*, 27 January 2020.

186. Toby Matthiesen, 'The Coronavirus in the Middle East', *Foreign Affairs*, 23 March 2020.

CONCLUSION

1. See also Thomas Pierret, 'Karbala in the Umayyad Mosque: Sunni Panic at the "Shiitization" of Syria in the 2000s', in: Brigitte Maréchal and Sami Zemni (eds), *The Dynamics of Sunni-Shia Relationships: Doctrine, Transnationalism, Intellectuals and the Media* (London: Hurst, 2013), 99–116; Paulo G. Pinto, '"Oh Syria, God Protects You": Islam as Cultural Idiom under Bashar al-Asad', *Middle East Critique* 20, 2 (2011), 189–205, 196–200; Pinto, 'Pilgrimage, Commodities, and Religious Objectification: The Making of Transnational Shi'ism between Iran and Syria', *Comparative Studies of South Asia, Africa and the Middle East* 27, 1 (2007), 109–25; Sahner, *Among the Ruins*, 13–30.

2. 'The Middle East is going through a transformation that will play out for a generation, rooted in conflicts that date back millennia.' Remarks of President Barack Obama, 12 January 2016, https://obamawhitehouse.archives.gov/the-press-office/2016/01/12/remarks-president-barack-obama-%E2%80%93-prepared-delivery-state-union-address. See also Karla Adam, 'Obama Ridiculed for Saying Conflicts in the Middle East "Date Back Millennia." (Some Don't Date Back a Decade.)', *Washington Post*, 13 January 2016; Nader Hashemi and Danny Postel, 'Introduction: The Sectarianization Thesis', in: Nader Hashemi and Danny Postel (eds), *Sectarianization: Mapping the New Politics of the Middle East* (London: Hurst, 2017), 1–22, 2.

3. Sectarian websites and TV stations, mostly anti-Shii, but increasingly also anti-Sunni, expanded their footprint in this heightened sectarian atmosphere. They also started translating polemics into the key languages across the Muslim world, as well as into European languages. For an analysis of the contents of one such website, see Göran Larsson, '"One Cannot Doubt the Potential Effect

of these Fatwas on Modern Muslim Society": Online Accusations of Disbelief and Apostasy: The Internet as an Arena for Sunni and Shia Muslim Conflicts', *Studies in Religion* 45, 2 (2016), 201–21; Jeffry R. Halverson, 'The Anti-Shiʿa Polemics of an Online Salafi-Jihadi: The Case of Nasir al-Qaʿida in Historical Perspective', *The Muslim World* 103, 4 (2013), 501–17.

4. A major survey of Muslim opinion in the early 2010s found that anti-Shii attitudes were most extreme in countries where Shiism was almost absent and that did not have much history of lived coexistence, but where Shiism and Iran were thus also no political threat, such as Morocco or Jordan. Many did not even see Shia as Muslims. At the same time, in countries such as Iraq and Lebanon, where people lived side by side, most accepted the other side as Muslim, but worried about the impact of sectarian tensions. Pew Research Center, *The World's Muslims: Unity and Diversity* (2012), ch. 5; Pew Research Center, *The World's Muslims: Religion, Politics and Society* (2013), ch. 5; Michael Lipka, 'The Sunni-Shia Divide: Where They Live, What They Believe and How They View Each Other', *PEW*, 18 June 2014, available at https://www.pewforum.org. I would like to thank colleagues in the *TOI: Bringing in the Other Islamists—Comparing Arab Shia and Sunni Islamism(s) in a Sectarianized Middle East* project, and Andrew Leber for bringing this dataset to my attention.

Bibliography

INTERVIEWS

Interview with Hasan al-Saffar, Qatif, Saudi Arabia, 2008.

Interviews with Shii clerics from various countries, over the period from 2008 to 2019.

Interviews with Yousif al-Khoei and Ghanim Jawad, al-Khoei Foundation, London, 2008.

Interviews with representatives of the Muslim Brotherhood and Salafis in Bahrain, 2011, and with representatives of Shii and Muslim Brotherhood political societies in Kuwait, 2012.

Interviews with current and former MPs from various political trends, journalists and civil society figures, Kuwait, 2012.

Interviews with Omani Shia, Muscat, Oman, February 2013.

Interview with Sayyid Hani Fahs, Beirut, Lebanon, 2013.

Interviews with Egyptians of different political persuasions, journalists, and diplomats, Cairo, 2013.

Interview with a Bahraini dissident involved in the 1981 Bahrain coup attempt, 2015.

Interview with an Arab Shii dissident based in Iran in 1980, London, 2017.

Interview with a former fighter of the Lebanese Forces, Beirut, 2018.

Interviews with former fighters in the Popular Mobilisation Forces, Najaf, Iraq, 2018.

Interview with a Lebanese Shii cleric, Beirut, 2018.

Interview with Murtada al-Qazwini, Karbala, Iraq, 2018.

Interviews with Shii clerics, Najaf, Iraq, 2018.

Interviews with Shii scholarly families, Najaf, Iraq, 2018.

Interview with a teacher in the Shii seminary (*hawza*) of Najaf, Najaf, Iraq, 2018.

Interviews with Ali Khan Mahmudabad and participants of Muharram, Mahmudabad, 2019.

Interviews at Dar al-Ulum Deoband, India, 2019.

Interview with a descendant of the Farangi Mahall family, Lucknow, 2019.

Interviews with former Iraqi officials, Karbala, Iraq, 2019.

Interview with an official in the Sunni Dar al-Ifta, Karbala, Iraq, 2019.

Interview with Suleiman, the Raja of Mahmudabad, Mahmudabad, 2019.

Interview with Talal Atrisi, Beirut, 2019.

JOURNALS

Dabiq
al-Irfan
Journal officiel de l'Etat des Alaouites
al-Manar
Oriente Moderno
The Muslim Review
Zeitschrift der Deutschen Morgenländischen Gesellschaft

WEBSITES

abu-hanefa.blogspot.com
ahlulbayt.co.uk/home
al-amine.org
al-bab.com
alhassanain.org
al-islam.org
almodon.com
alnakshabandia.net/army
alqtrah.com
ammanmessage.com
ansarollah.com
archive.org
archnet.org
armenian-genocide.org
australianislamiclibrary.org
aymennjawad.org
bahrainipolitics.blogspot.com
ballandalus.wordpress.com
binbaz.org.sa
binbaz.org.sa
bl.uk
censusindia.gov.in
cisac.fsi.stanford.edu/mappingmilitants
ctc.usma.edu
dante.princeton.edu/pdp
darulifta-deoband.com/en
darululoom-deoband.com/english
dd-sunnah.net
devletarsivleri.gov.tr
diploweb.com
discovery.nationalarchives.gov.uk
en.banglapedia.org

en.imam-khomeini.ir
en.wikishia.net
english.khamenei.ir
francearchives.fr
gerty.ncl.ac.uk
gift2shias.com/about-2
gulfinstitute.org
hazara.net
historians.org/perspectives
hrw.org
icana.ir
iiis.ir
iis.ac.uk
ikhwanonline.com
ilmway.com
imamreza.net
in.visitjordan.com
iqraonline.net
iranicaonline.org
isl.org.uk
islamansiklopedisi.org.tr
islamicmovement.org
islamqa.info
ismaili.net
jihadica.com
jihadology.net
joshualandis.com/blog (Syria Comment)
juancole.com
kashefalghtaa.com
kpsiaj.org
maktabah.org
mamluk.lib.uchicago.edu
mazaheb.urd.ac.ir
memri.org
mideastsoccer.blogspot.com
mofa.gov.qa
muqbel.net
muslimheritage.com
naqshbandi.org
news.un.org/en
nimatullahi.org
noor-book.com
pomeps.org
proquest.libguides.com/dnsa/iraqgate

qdl.qa/en
quran.com
reliefweb.int
reliefweb.int
salafi-dawah.com
sepad.org.uk
servat.unibe.ch
servat.unibe.ch/icl
shia.bs
simerg.com
sistani.org
state.gov
sultan-alamer.com
sunnionline.us
surour.net
syria.law
taghrib.org
taqrib.ir/fa
tarikhirani.ir
tatbir.org
tnfj.org.uk
twitter.com
un.int/lebanon
unicef.org
urd.ac.ir/fa
vam.ac.uk
web.archive.org
whitehouse.gov
wikileaks.org
wikishia.net
wipo.int/edocs/lexdocs/laws/en
worldcat.org
youtube.com

UNPUBLISHED PHDS

Abdullah, Darakhshan, *Religious Policy of the Sultans of Kashmir (1320–1586 A.D.)* (PhD, University of Kashmir, 1991).

Abid, Sadiq, *An Examination of Heritage Protection and Conservation Practices in the Pilgrimage City of Najaf* (PhD, University of Sheffield, 2016).

Adlparvar, Naysan, *'When Glass Breaks, It Becomes Sharper': De-Constructing Ethnicity in the Bamyan Valley, Afghanistan* (PhD, University of Sussex, 2015).

Alenezi, Fahaad J. M. M., *Usuli Shi'ism and State Approaches to Islamic Unity: The Ecumenical Movement in Post-Safavid Iran* (PhD, Durham University, 2009).

Altuğ, Seda, *Sectarianism in the Syrian Jazira: Community, Land and Violence in the Memories of World War I and the French Mandate (1915–1939)* (PhD, Utrecht University, 2011).

Arcak, Sine, *Gifts in Motion: Ottoman-Safavid Cultural Exchange, 1501–1618* (PhD, University of Minnesota, 2012).

Aslan, Rose, *From Body to Shrine: The Construction of Sacred Space at the Grave of 'Ali ibn Abi Talib in Najaf* (PhD, University of North Carolina, 2014).

Atiyah, Najla Wadih, *The Attitude of the Lebanese Sunnis towards the State of Lebanon* (PhD, University of London, 1973).

Atmaca, Metin, *Politics of Alliance and Rivalry on the Ottoman-Iranian Frontier: The Babans (1500–1851)* (PhD, University of Freiburg, 2013).

Babeair, Abdul-Wahab S., *Ottoman Penetration of the Eastern Region of the Arabian Peninsula, 1814–1841* (PhD, Indiana University, 1985).

Bahl, Christopher D., *Histories of Circulation: Sharing Arabic Manuscripts across the Western Indian Ocean, 1400–1700* (PhD, University of London, 2018).

Bailony, Reem, *Transnational Rebellion: The Syrian Revolt of 1925–1927* (PhD, University of California, 2015).

Banister, Mustafa, *The Abbasid Caliphate of Cairo (1261–1517): History and Tradition in the Mamluk Court* (PhD, University of Toronto, 2015).

Basu, P., *The Relations between Oudh and the East India Company from 1785 to 1801* (PhD, University of London, 1938).

Bayhom-Daou, Tamima, *The Imami Shii Conception of the Knowledge of Imam and the Sources of Religious Doctrine in the Formative Period: From Hisham b. al-Hakam (d. 179 A.H.) to Kulini (d. 329 A.H.)* (PhD, University of London, 1996).

Broadbridge, Anne F., *Mamluk Ideological and Diplomatic Relations with Mongol and Turkic Rulers of the Near East and Central Asia (658–807/1260–1405)* (PhD, University of Chicago, 2001).

Bunzel, Cole Michael, *Manifest Enmity: The Origins, Development, and Persistence of Classical Wahhābism (1153–1351/1741–1932)* (PhD, Princeton University, 2018).

Calder, Norman, *The Structure of Authority in Imami Shi'i Jurisprudence* (PhD, University of London, 1980).

Cancian, Alessandro, *La Hawza 'Ilmiyya: E la formazione dell'élite religiosa nei collegi teologici dello sciismo duodecimano: Elementi dottrinali e indagine di campo* (PhD, University of Siena, 2005).

Dann, Michael, *Contested Boundaries: The Reception of Shī'ite Narrators in the Sunnī Hadith Tradition* (PhD, Princeton University, 2015).

Davis, Craig, *Dara Shukuh and Aurangzib: Issues of Religion and Politics and Their Impact on Indo-Muslim Society* (PhD, Indiana University, 2002).

Dickson, Martin B., *Shah Tahmasb and the Uzbeks (The Duel for Khurasan with 'Ubayd Khan, 930–946/1524–1540)* (PhD, Princeton University, 1958).

Dockrat, M. A. E., *Between Orthodoxy and Mysticism: The Life and Works of Shaikh Muhammad ibn Tahir al-Fattani (914/1508–986/1578)* (PhD, University of South Africa, 2002).

Eliash, Joseph, *'Ali b. Abi Talib in Ithna-'Ashari Shii Belief* (PhD, University of London, 1966).

Fazel, Solaiman M., *Ethnohistory of the Qizilbash in Kabul: Migration, State, and a Shiʿa Minority* (PhD, Indiana University, 2017).

Fusfeld, Warren Edward, *The Shaping of Sufi Leadership in Delhi: The Naqshbandiyya Mujaddidiyya, 1750 to 1920* (PhD, University of Pennsylvania, 1981).

al-Gailani, Noorah, *The Shrine of ʿAbd al-Qādir al-Jīlānī in Baghdad & the Shrine of ʿAbd al-ʿAzīz al-Jīlānī in ʿAqra: Mapping the Multiple Orientations of Two Qādirī Sufi Shrines in Iraq* (PhD, University of Glasgow, 2016).

Gallagher, Amelia, *The Fallible Master of Perfection: Shah Ismail in the Alevi-Bektashi Tradition* (PhD, McGill University, 2004).

Ghofrani, Shayesteh, *Comparative Analysis of Wilāya in the Formative Period of Shiʿism and Sufism* (PhD, University of Exeter, 2014).

Gross, Max L., *Ottoman Rule in the Province of Damascus, 1860–1909* (PhD, Georgetown University, 1979).

Güngörürler, Selim, *Diplomacy and Political Relations between the Ottoman Empire and Safavid Iran, 1639–1722* (PhD, Georgetown University, 2016).

al-Habib, Mohammad, *The Formation of the Shiʿa Communities in Kuwait: Migration, Settlement and Contribution between 1880 and 1938* (PhD, University of London, 2017).

Hagemann, Hannah-Lena, *History and Memory: Khārijism in Early Islamic Historiography* (PhD, University of Edinburgh, 2014).

Hamm, Geoffrey, *British Intelligence and Turkish Arabia: Strategy, Diplomacy, and Empire, 1898–1918* (PhD, University of Toronto, 2012).

al-Hasan, Abd al-Latif Abd al-Rahman, *The Khulāṣat al-Ījāz of Shaykh al-Mufīd, Together with an Introductory Study of the Man and his Writings* (PhD, Manchester University, 1974).

al-Hassani, Jihad Taki Sadiq, *The Question of Imama, Political and Religious Authority, in Twelver Shiʿite Thought* (PhD, University of Manchester, 1979).

Heidari-Abkenar, Mohammad, *Die ideologische und politische Konfrontation Schia-Sunna am Beispiel der Stadt Rey des 10.-12. Jh. n. Chr.* (PhD, University of Cologne, 1992).

Hermann, Denis, *Aspects de l'Histoire Sociale et Doctrinale de l'Ecole Shaikhi au Cours de la Periode Qajar (1843–1911)* (PhD, École Pratique des Hautes Études, 2007).

Herzig, Edmund M., *The Armenian Merchants of New Julfa, Isfahan: A Study in Pre-Modern Asian Trade* (PhD, University of Oxford, 1991).

Hjortshoj, Keith, *Kerbala in Context: A Study of Muharram in Lucknow, India* (PhD, Cornell University, 1977).

Husted, Wayne R., *Shahid-i Salis Qazi Nurullah Shushtari: An Historical Figure in Shiʿite Piety* (PhD, University of Wisconsin-Madison, 1992).

al-Jamil, Tariq, *Cooperation and Contestation in Medieval Baghdad (656/1258–786/1384): Relationships Between Shīʿī and Sunnī Scholars in the Madīnat al-Salām* (PhD, Princeton University, 2004).

Kadhem, Fouad Jabir, *The Sacred and the Secular: The ʿUlama of Najaf in Iraqi Politics between 1950 and 1980* (PhD, University of Exeter, 2012).

Kaicker, Abhishek, *Unquiet City: Making and Unmaking Politics in Mughal Delhi, 1707–39* (PhD, Columbia University, 2014).

Karakaya-Stump, Ayfer, *Subjects of the Sultan, Disciples of the Shah: Formation and Transformation of the Kizilbash/Alevi Communities in Ottoman Anatolia* (PhD, Harvard University, 2008).

Kern, Karen M., *The Prohibition of Sunni-Shiʿi Marriages in the Ottoman Empire: A Study of Ideologies* (PhD, Columbia University, 1999).

Khan, Naveeda Ahmed, *Grounding Sectarianism: Islamic Ideology and Muslim Everyday Life in Lahore, Pakistan Circa 1920s/1990s* (PhD, Columbia University, 2003).

Khoury, Shaadi, *Instituting Renaissance: The Early Work of the Arab Academy of Science in Damascus, 1919–1930* (PhD, George Washington University, 2016).

Kohlberg, Etan, *The Attitude of the Imāmī-Shīʿīs to the Companions of the Prophet* (PhD, Oxford University, 1972).

Landis, Joshua M., *Nationalism and the Politics of Zaʿama: The Collapse of Republican Syria, 1945–1949* (PhD, Princeton University, 1997).

Lefèvre, Raphaël, *The 'Islamic Emirate' of North Lebanon: The Rise and Fall of the Tawheed Movement in Tripoli, 1982–1985* (PhD, University of Cambridge, 2016).

El-Moctar, Mohamed, *The Crusades' Impact on Sunni-Shiʿa Relations* (PhD, Texas Tech University, 2011).

Farhat, May, *Islamic Piety and Dynastic Legitimacy: The Case of the Shrine of ʿAlī b. Mūsā al-Ridā in Mashhad (10th–17th Century)* (PhD, Harvard University, 2002).

Husayn, N. A., *The Memory of ʿAlī b. Abī Tālib in Early Sunni Thought* (PhD, Princeton University, 2016).

Jacobs, Adam, *Sunni and Shii Perceptions, Boundaries and Affiliations in Late Timurid and Early Safawid Persia: An Examination of Historical and Quasi-Historical Narratives* (PhD, University of London, 1999).

Lee, Jonathan Leonard, *The New Year's Festivals and the Shrine of Ali ibn Abi Talib Sy Mazar-i-Sharif, Afghanistan* (PhD, University of Leeds, 1999).

Leiser, Gary La Viere, *The Restoration of Sunnism in Egypt: Madrasas and Mudarrisun 495–647/1101–1249* (PhD, University of Pennsylvania, 1976).

MacEoin, Denis M., *From Shaykhism to Babism: A Study in Charismatic Renewal in Shiʿi Islam* (PhD, University of Cambridge, 1979).

Mansour, Mansour Hasan, *The Spread and the Domination of the Maliki School of Law in North and West Africa, Eighth–Fourteenth Century* (PhD, University of Illinois Chicago, 1981).

Masad, Mohammad Ahmad, *The Medieval Islamic Apocalyptic Tradition: Divination, Prophecy and the End of Time in the 13th Century Eastern Mediterranean* (PhD, Washington University, 2008).

al-Nafeesi, Abdullah Fahad, *The Role of the Shīʿah in the Political Development of Modern Iraq (1914–1921)* (PhD, University of Cambridge, 1971).

Neggaz, Nassima, *The Falls of Baghdad in 1258 and 2003: A Study in Sunnī-Shīʿī Clashing Memories* (PhD, Georgetown University, 2013).

Nöldeke, Arnold, *Das Heiligtum al-Husains zu Kerbelâ* (PhD, University of Erlangen, 1909).

Pages, Meriem, *The Image of the Assassins in Medieval European Texts* (PhD, University of Massachusetts Amherst, 2007).

Pampus, Karl-Heinz, *Die theologische Enzyklopädie Biḥār al-Anwār des Muḥammad Bāqir al-Maǧlisī, 1037–1110 A.H. = 1627–1699 A.D.: Ein Beitrag zur Literaturgeschichte der Šīʿa in der Safawidenzeit* (PhD, University of Bonn, 1970).

Preckel, Claudia, *Islamische Bildungsnetzwerke und Gelehrtenkultur im Indien des 19. Jahrhunderts: Muḥammad Ṣiddīq Ḥasan Khān (st. 1890) und die Entstehung der Ahl-e Ḥadīth-Bewegung in Bhopal* (PhD, Ruhr University Bochum, 2005).

Rajkowski, W. W., *Early Shiʿism in Iraq* (PhD, University of London, 1955).

Rudd, Jeffery A., *Abdallah bin al-Husayn: The Making of an Arab Political Leader, 1908–1921* (PhD, University of London, 1993).

Ruprecht, Adrian P., *De-Centering Humanitarianism: The Red Cross and India, c. 1877–1939* (PhD, University of Cambridge, 2017).

Al Sarhan, Saud Saleh, *Early Muslim Traditionalism: A Critical Study of the Works and Political Theology of Aḥmad ibn Ḥanbal* (PhD, University of Exeter, 2011).

Shah, Amjad Hussain, *The Concept of Ijmāʿ in Imāmī Shīʿī Uṣūl al-Fiqh* (PhD, University of Edinburgh, 1999).

al-Shaibi, Kamil M., *Studies in the Interaction of Sufism and Shiism to the Rise of the Safawids* (PhD, University of Cambridge, 1961).

Stanfield-Johnson, Rosemary, *Mirza Makhdum Sharifi: A 16th-Century Sunni Ṣadr at the Safavid Court* (PhD, New York University, 1992).

Thaver, Tehseen, *Ambiguity, Hermeneutics, and the Formation of Shiʿi Identity in al-Sharif al-Radi's (d. 1015 CE) Qur'an Commentary* (PhD, University of North Carolina at Chapel Hill, 2013).

Thobie, Jacques, *Les intérêts économiques, financiers et politiques français dans la partie asïatique de l'empire Ottoman de 1895 à 1914*, 3 Vols (PhD, University of Lille, 1973).

Tholib, Udjang, *The Reign of the Caliph al-Qādir Billāh (381/991–422/1031)* (PhD, McGill University, 2002).

Üstün, Ismail Safa, *Heresy and Legitimacy in the Ottoman Empire in the Sixteenth Century* (PhD, University of Manchester, 2009).

van Caldenborgh, P. P. T. W., *Savage Human Beasts or the Purest Arabs? The Incorporation of the Alawi Community into the Syrian State during the French Mandate Period (1918–1946)* (PhD, Radboud University, 2005).

Voss, Gregor, *'Alawīya oder Nusairīya?': Schiitische Machtelite und sunnitische Opposition in der Syrischen Arabischen Republik: Untersuchung zu einer islamisch-politischen Streitfrage* (PhD, University of Hamburg, 1987).

Wagner, Steven B., *British Intelligence and Policy in the Palestine Mandate, 1919–1939* (PhD, University of Oxford, 2014).

Wilhite, Vincent Steven, *Guerilla War, Counterinsurgency, and State Formation in Ottoman Yemen* (PhD, Ohio State University, 2003).

Yildirim, Riza, *Turkomans between Two Empires: The Origins of the Qizilbash Identity in Anatolia, 1447–1514* (PhD, Bilkent University, 2008).

Zaidi, Noor Zehra, *Making Spaces Sacred: The Sayyeda Zaynab and Bibi Pak Daman Shrines and the Construction of Modern Shia Identity* (PhD, University of Pennsylvania, 2015).

al-Zekri, Muhammad A., *The Religious Encounter between Sufis and Salafis of East Arabia: Issue of Identity* (PhD, University of Exeter, 2004).

UNPUBLISHED MASTERS

Hairi, Abdulhadi, *Naṣīr al-Dīn Ṭūsī: His Supposed Political Role in the Mongol Invasion of Baghdad* (MA, McGill University, 1968).

Hamdan, Faraj Hattab, *The Development of Iraqi Shi'a Mourning Rituals in Modern Iraq: The 'Ashurā Rituals and Visitation of al-Arb'ain* (MA, Arizona State University, 2012).

Luca, Ana Maria, *Sectarian Conflict and Sunni Islamic Radicalization in Tripoli, Lebanon* (MA, Lebanese American University, 2015).

al-Sada, Reem Ahmad M., *The Introduction of Shaykh Ibn 'Abd al-Wahhāb's Doctrine in Qatar: Religion and Politics in the Writings of Shaykh Qāsim al-Thānī (1827–1913)* (MA, Hamad Bin Khalifa University, 2019).

REPORTS

Bahrain Independent Commission of Inquiry, 'Report of the Bahrain Independent Commission of Inquiry', 23 November 2011.

'"Al-Bander Report": Demographic Engineering in Bahrain and Mechanisms of Exclusion', *Bahrain Center for Human Rights*, 30 September 2006.

Human Rights Watch, 'Endless Torment: The 1991 Uprising in Iraq and Its Aftermath', June 1992.

Human Rights Watch, 'Afghanistan: The Massacre in Mazar-i Sharif', November 1998.

Human Rights Watch, '"We Have the Promises of the World": Women's Rights in Afghanistan', 6 December 2009.

Human Rights Watch, 'Egypt: Lynching of Shia Follows Months of Hate Speech', 27 June 2013.

Human Rights Watch, 'Indonesia: Ensure Safe Return Home of Evicted Shia Villagers: Government Capitulation to Militants Sets Dangerous Precedent', 30 June 2013.

Human Rights Watch, 'Iran Sending Thousands of Afghans to Fight in Syria', 29 January 2016.

Human Rights Watch, 'Afghanistan's Shia Hazara Suffer Latest Atrocity: Insurgents' Increasing Threat to Embattled Minority', 13 October 2016.

Immigration and Refugee Board of Canada, 'Pakistan: Whether Benazir Bhutto is a Shia; whether her Father, Z.A. Bhutto, was a Shia; and whether her Husband, Asif Ali Zardari is a Shia', 25 March 2002.

Internal Displacement Monitoring Centre, *Iraq: Sectarian Violence, Military Operations Spark New Displacement, as Humanitarian Access Deteriorates* (Geneva: Norwegian Refugee Council, 2006).

International Crisis Group, *In Their Own Words: Reading the Iraqi Insurgency* (Brussels: International Crisis Group, 2006).

International Crisis Group, *The Next Iraqi War? Sectarianism and Civil Conflict* (Brussels: International Crisis Group, 2006).

International Crisis Group, *Shiite Politics in Iraq: The Role of the Supreme Council* (Brussels: International Crisis Group, 2007).

International Crisis Group, *Azerbaijan: Independent Islam and the State* (Brussels: International Crisis Group, 2008).

International Crisis Group, *Iraq after the Surge I: The New Sunni Landscape* (Brussels: International Crisis Group, 2008).

International Crisis Group, *Popular Protests in North Africa and the Middle East (III): The Bahrain Revolt* (Brussels: International Crisis Group, 2011).

International Crisis Group, *Popular Protest in North Africa and the Middle East (VI): The Syrian People's Slow-Motion Revolution* (Brussels: International Crisis Goup, 2011).

International Crisis Group, *Yemen: Enduring Conflicts, Threatened Transition* (Brussels: International Crisis Group, 2012).

International Crisis Group, *The Huthis: From Saada to Sanaa* (Brussels: International Crisis Group, 2014).

International Crisis Group, *Lebanon's Hizbollah Turns Eastward to Syria* (Brussels: International Crisis Group, 2014).

International Crisis Group, *Hizbollah's Syria Conundrum* (Brussels: International Crisis Group, 2017).

International Crisis Group, *Yemen's al-Qaeda: Expanding the Base* (Brussels: International Crisis Group, 2017).

International Medical Corps, *Iraqis on the Move: Sectarian Displacement in Baghdad* (Santa Monica, CA: International Medical Corps, 2007).

International Institute for Strategic Studies, *Iran's Networks of Influence in the Middle East* (London: Routledge, 2020).

al-Khalidi, Ashraf, and Victor Tanner, *Sectarian Violence: Radical Groups Drive Internal Displacement in Iraq* (Washington, DC: Brookings Institution/University of Bern, 2006).

Martini, Jeffrey, Heather J. Williams, and William Young, *The Future of Sectarian Relations in the Middle East* (Santa Monica, CA: RAND, 2017).

Pew Research Center, *The World's Muslims: Unity and Diversity* (Washington, DC: Pew Research Center, 2012).

Pew Research Center, *The World's Muslims: Religion, Politics and Society* (Washington, DC: Pew Research Center, 2013).

Pew Research Center, *Concerns about Islamic Extremism on the Rise in Middle East: Negative Opinions of al-Qaeda, Hamas and Hezbollah Widespread* (Washington, DC: Pew Research Center, 2014).

The National Archives, 'The Iraq Inquiry: The Report', 6 July 2016, https://webarchive.nationalarchives.gov.uk/20171123122743/http://www.iraqinquiry.org.uk/the-rep.

The World War I Document Archive, 'The King-Crane Commission Report, August 28, 1919', https://wwi.lib.byu.edu/index.php/The_King-Crane_Report.

Zogby Research Services, *Looking at Iran: How 20 Arab and Muslim Nations View Iran and its Policies* (Washington, DC: Zogby Research Services, 2012).

BIBLIOGRAPHY ENTRIES

Oxford Bibliographies Online (abbreviated as *OBi*)

Newman, Andrew J., 'Safavids'.
Newman, Andrew J., 'Shiʻi Islam'.
Peterson, Daniel, 'Zaydiyya'.
Rajani, Kumail, 'Hadith: Shiʻi'.
Riggs, Robert, 'Shiʻi Shrine Cities'.
Ruffle, Karen, 'Muharram'.

Christian-Muslim Relations 600–1500 (abbreviated as *CMR*)

Thomas, David, 'Kitāb al-milal wa-l-niḥal'.

Christian-Muslim Relations 1500–1900 (abbreviated as *CMR2*)

Gori, Alessandro, 'Al-barq al-Yamānī fī l-fatḥ al-ʻUthmānī'.

ENCYCLOPEDIA ENTRIES

Encyclopædia Britannica (abbreviated as *EBr*)

Afsaruddin, Asma, and Seyyed Hossein Nasr, "Alī'.
Editors of Encyclopaedia Britannica, 'Levant'.

Encyclopædia Iranica (abbreviated as *EIr*)

Abisaab, Rula, 'Karaki'.
Algar, Hamid, 'Āqā Khan'.
Algar, Hamid, 'Astarābādī, Fażlallāh'.
Algar, Hamid, 'Barāq Bābā'.
Algar, Hamid, 'Bektāšīya'.
Algar, Hamid, 'Borūjerdī, Ḥosayn Ṭabāṭabāʾī'.
Algar, Hamid, 'Caliphs and the Caliphate, as Viewed by the Shiʻites of Persia'.
Algar, Hamid, 'Dahabīya'.
Algar, Hamid, 'Emām-e Jomʻa'.
Algar, Hamid, 'Iran ix. Religions in Iran (2) Islam in Iran (2.3) Shiʻism in Iran since the Safavids'.
Algar, Hamid, 'Jaʻfar al-Ṣādeq iii. And Sufism'.
Algar, Hamid, 'Jāmi ii. And Sufism'.
Algar, Hamid, 'Khomeini'.
Algar, Hamid, 'Kobrawiya ii. The Order'.
Amanat, Abbas, 'Constitutional Revolution i. Intellectual Background'.
Amanat, Abbas, 'Fatḥ-ʻAlī Shah Qājār'.
Amir-Moezzi, Mohammad Ali, 'Šahrbānu'.
Amitai, R., 'Gāzān Khan, Maḥmūd'.
Ansari, N. H., 'Bayram Khan'.
Anthony, Sean W., 'Nawbaḵti Family'.
Arjomand, Said Amir, 'Gayba'.

Aslan, Rose, 'Najaf'.

Babaie, Sussan, with Robert Haug, 'Isfahan x. Monuments (3) Mosques'.

Balland, D., 'Ašraf Ḡilzay'.

Bar-Asher, Meir M., 'Exegesis ii. In Shiʻism'.

Bosworth, C. E., 'Āl-e Afrāsīāb (1)'.

Bosworth, C. E., 'Maḥmud b. Sebüktegin'.

Bosworth, C. E., and S. Blair, 'Astarābād'.

Boyce, Mary, 'Bībī Shahrbānū'.

Bregel, Yuri, 'Abu'l-Khayrids'.

Brunner, Rainer, 'Majlesi, Moḥammad-Bāqer'.

Brunner, Rainer, 'Shiʻite Doctrine ii. Hierarchy in the Imamiyya'.

Brunner, Rainer, 'Shiʻite Doctrine iii. Imamite-Sunnite Relations since the Late 19th Century'.

Busse, H., ''Abbās Mīrzā Qajar'.

Calmard, J., ''Abbās b. 'Alī b. Abū Ṭāleb'.

Calmard, J., 'Ḏu'l-Faqār'.

Casari, Mario, 'Italy ii. Diplomatic and Commercial Relations'.

Cole, Juan, 'Conversion iii. to Imami Shiʻism in India'.

Cronin, Stephanie, 'Army v. Qajar Period'.

Cunha, Joao Teles e, 'Portugal i. Relations with Persia in the Early Modern Age (1500–1750)'.

De Laugier de Beaureceuil, S., ''Abdallāh Anṣārī'.

De Planhol, Xavier, 'Mazār-e Šarif'.

De Planhol, Xavier, and J. A. Kechichian, 'Bahrain'.

Durand-Guédy, David, 'Malekšāh'.

Eaton, Richard M., 'India vi. Political and Cultural Relations (13th–18th Centuries)'.

Eaton, Richard M., N. H. Ansari, and S. H. Qasemi, 'Bengal'.

Fleischer, C., 'Alqās Mīrzā'.

Floor, Willem, 'Dutch-Persian Relations'.

'Foẓūlī, Moḥammad'.

Ghereghlou, Kioumars, 'Esmāʻil II'.

Ghereghlou, Kioumars, 'Maḵdum Šarifi Širāzi'.

Glassen, Erika, 'Bedlīsī, Šaraf-al-Dīn Khan'.

Gleave, Robert, 'Jaʻfar al-Ṣādeq ii. Teachings'.

Hermansen, Marcia, 'Dehlavī, Šāh Walī-Allāh Qoṭb-al-Dīn Aḥmad Abu'l-Fayyāż'.

Howard, I. K. A., 'Ahl-e Bayt'.

Jackson, Peter, 'Jalayerids'.

Kazemi-Moussavi, A., 'Hadith ii. In Shiʻism'.

Khazeni, Arash, Alessandro Monsutti, and Charles M. Kieffer, 'Hazāra'.

Kohlberg, Etan, ''Alī b. Abī Ṭāleb ii. 'Alī as Seen by the Community'.

Kohlberg, Etan, 'Beḥār al-Anwār'.

Lane, George E., 'Ṭusi, Naṣir-al-Din i. Biography'.

Litvak, Meir, 'Iraq x. Shiʻites of Iraq'.

Litvak, Meir, 'Kazemayn'.

Madelung, Wilferd, "Abd-al-Ḥamīd b. Abu'l-Ḥadīd'.

Madelung, Wilferd, "Abd-al-Jalīl Rāzī'.

Madelung, Wilferd, 'Āl-e Bāvand'.

Madelung, Wilferd, "Alī al-Reżā'.

Madelung, Wilferd, 'Badā".

Madelung, Wilferd, 'Ḥasan b. 'Ali b. Abi Ṭāleb'.

Manz, Beatrice F., 'Gowhar-Šād Āgā'.

Marchinkowski, M. Ismail, 'Southeast Asia ii. Shi'ites in'.

Matthee, Rudi, 'Iraq iv. Relations in the Safavid Period'.

Matthee, Rudi, 'Safavid Dynasty'.

Mcchesney, Robert D., 'Central Asia vi. In the 16th–18th Centuries'.

Mcchesney, Robert D., and A. H. Tarzi, 'Fayż Moḥammad Kāteb'.

Melville, Charles, 'Čobān'.

Milani, Mohsen M., and Eir, 'Hostage Crisis'.

Mojtabā'ī, Fatḥ-Allāh, 'Dabestān-e Maḏāheb'.

Monzavi, 'A.-N., "Abaqāt al-Anwār'.

Nagel, Tilman, 'Buyids'.

O'Kane, Bernard, 'Domes'.

Özgüdenli, Osman G., 'Ottoman-Persian Relations i. Under Sultan Selim I and Shah Esmā'il I'.

Pellat, Ch., 'Abū Lo'lo'a'.

Perry, John, 'Karim Khan Zand'.

Perry, John, 'Zand Dynasty'.

Poonawala, I. K., "Alī b. Abī Ṭāleb i. Life'.

Qasemi, Sharif Husain, 'Fatḥ-Allāh Šīrāzī, Sayyed Mīr'.

Quiring-Zoche, R., 'Aq Qoyunlū'.

Rizvi, Sajjad H., 'Isfahan School of Philosophy'.

Roemer, H. R., 'Ḥosayn Bāyqarā'.

Schmidtke, Sabine, 'Ḥelli, Ḥasan b. Yusof b. Moṭahhar'.

Sheikh-ol-Islami, M. J., 'Aḥmad Shah Qājār'.

Simpson, Marianna S., 'Ebrāhīm Mīrzā'.

Soucek, Priscilla, 'Behzād, Kamāl-al-Dīn'.

Spuler, Bertold, 'Central Asia v. In the Mongol and Timurid Periods'.

Tarzi, Amin H., 'Dōst Moḥammad Khan'.

Tucker, Ernest, 'Nāder Shah'.

Tucker, Ernest, 'Ottoman-Persian Relations ii. Afsharid and Zand Periods'.

Zysow, Aron, 'Ejtehād in Shi'ism'.

Zysow, Aron, 'Karrāmiya'.

Encyclopædia Islamica (abbreviated as *EIs*)

Bahramian, Ali, and Rahim Gholami, 'al-Baqī''.

Encyclopaedia of Islam (abbreviated as *EI*)

Madelung, Wilferd, 'Imama'.

Massignon, Louis, 'Nuṣairī'.
Massignon, Louis, et al., 'Taṣawwuf'.
Nyberg, H. S., 'al-Muʿtazila'.
Wensinck, A. J., 'Sunna'.

Encyclopaedia of Islam 2 (abbreviated as *EI2*)
'Ahl al-Sunna'.
Algar, Hamid, "Atabāt'.
Algar, Hamid, 'Kubrā'.
Algar, Hamid, 'Naḳshband'.
Algar, Hamid, 'Niʿmat-Allāhiyya'.
Algar, Hamid, 'Nūrbakhshiyya'.
Algar, Hamid, and K. A. Nizami, 'Naḳshbandiyya'.
Amir-Moezzi, Mohammad Ali, 'al-Ṭūsī'.
Bazmee Ansari, A. S., 'Djahāngīr'.
Bosworth, C. E., 'al-Ṭabarī'.
Bosworth, C. E., 'Toghrïl (I) Beg'.
Boyle, J. A., 'Ibn al-Alḳamī'.
Bowen, H., and C. E. Bosworth, 'Niẓām al-Mulk'.
Buhl, F., A. T. Welch, Annemarie Schimmel, A. Noth, and T. Ehlert, 'Muḥammad'.
Buhl, F., C. E. Bosworth, and M. Lavergne, 'Ṭarābulus (or Aṭrābulus) al-Shām'.
Burton-Page, J., 'Ḥaydarābād'.
Cahen, Cl., 'Buwayhids or Būyids'.
Calmard, J., 'Marʿashis'.
Calmard, J., "Tabarru''.
Canard, M., 'Ḥamdānids'.
Caskel, W., "Abd al-Ḳays'.
Chaumont, E., 'al-Shāfiʿī'.
Chaumont, E., 'al-Shāfiʿiyya'.
Cottart, N., 'Mālikiyya'.
Crone, Patricia, "Uthmāniyya'.
Daiber, H., and F. J. Ragep, 'al-Ṭūsī, Naṣīr al-Dīn'.
Davies, C. Collin, 'Akbar'.
Davison, R. H., 'Tanẓīmāt'.
Djebli, Moktar, 'Nahdj al-Balāgha'.
Duri, A., 'Baghdad'.
Ende, W., 'Muḥibb al-Dīn al-Khaṭīb'.
Ende, W., 'Rashīd Riḍā'.
Gardet, L., and J. Berque, 'Djamāʿa'.
Geoffroy, E., 'al-Suyūṭī'.
Geoffroy, E., et al., 'Ṭarīḳa'.
Gimaret, D., 'Muʿtazila'.
Gleave, Robert, 'Khums'.
Goldziher, I., C. van Arendonk, and A. S. Tritton, 'Ahl al-Bayt'.

Haarmann, U., 'Khundjī'.

Hartmann, Angelika, 'al-Nāṣir Li-Dīn Allāh'.

Havemann, A., 'Naḳīb al-Ashrāf'.

Hawting, G. R., 'al-Mukhtār b. Abī 'Ubayd'.

Heffening, W., 'Mut'a'.

Heffening, W., and J. Schacht, 'Ḥanafiyya'.

Hinds, M., 'Miḥna'.

Hinds, M., 'Mu'āwiya I'.

Hodgson, M. G. S., "Abd Allāh b. Saba".

Hodgson, M. G. S., 'Dja'far al-Ṣādiḳ'.

Hodgson, M. G. S., 'Ghulāt'.

Honigmann, E., and C. E. Bosworth, 'al-Nadjaf'.

Juynboll, G. H. A., and D. W. Brown, 'Sunna'.

Kennedy, H., 'al-Mutawakkil 'Alā 'llāh'.

Khān, Ẓafarul-Islām, 'Nadwat al-'Ulamā".

Kohlberg, E., 'Mūsā al-Kāẓim'.

Laoust, Henri, 'al-Barbahārī'.

Laoust, Henri, 'Ibn 'Abd al-Wahhāb'.

Laoust, Henri, 'Ibn Baṭṭa, 'Ubayd Allāh b. Muḥammad Abū 'Abd Allāh al-'Ukbari'.

Laoust, Henri, 'Ibn Kathir'.

Laoust, Henri, 'Ibn Taymiyya'.

Lecker, M., 'Ṣiffīn'.

Lewis, B., "Abbāsids'.

Lewis, B., "Alids'.

Lewis, B., 'Ḥashīshiyya'.

Leisten, T., 'Turba'.

Luft, P., 'Musha'sha".

Madelung, Wilferd, 'al-Mahdī'.

Madelung, Wilferd, 'al-Ukhaydir'.

Madelung, Wilferd, 'Zaydiyya'.

Madelung, Wilferd, 'Zayd b. 'Alī b. al-Ḥusayn'.

Madelung, Wilferd, 'Imāma'.

Madelung, Wilferd, 'Makramids'.

Madelung, Wilferd, 'Shī'a'.

Manz, Beatrice F., 'Shāh Rukh'.

Manz, Beatrice F., 'Tīmūr Lang'.

Meri, J. W., et al., 'Ziyāra'.

Nasr, S. H., 'Ithnā 'Ashariyya'.

Northedge, A., 'Sāmarrā".

Omar, F., 'Hārūn al-Rashīd'.

Pellat, Ch., 'al-Mash 'Alā 'l-Khuffayn'.

Pellat, Ch., 'al-Mas'ūdī'.

Peskes, Esther, and W. Ende, 'Wahhābiyya'.

Rentz, G., 'al-Qatif'.

Sauvaget, J., 'Ḥalab'.

Schacht, J., 'Umm al-Walad'.

Shinar, P., and W. Ende, 'Salafiyya'.

Smith, J. M., 'Djalāyir, Djalāyirid'.

Sourdel, D., A. K. S. Lambton, F. de Jong, and P. M. Holt, 'Khalīfa'.

Sümer, F., 'Ḳarā-Ḳoyunlu'.

Ursinus, M. O. H., 'Millet'.

van Arendonk, C., and J. Schacht, 'Ibn Ḥadjar al-Haytamī'.

Veccia Vaglieri, L., "ʿAlī b. Abī Ṭālib'.

Veccia Vaglieri, L., 'Ghadīr ḥumm'.

Veccia Vaglieri, L., 'Ibn Abi 'l-Ḥadīd'.

Veccia Vaglieri, L., 'al-Ashtar'.

Veccia Vaglieri, L., '(al-)Ḥusayn b. ʿAlī b. Abī Ṭālib'.

Waardenburg, J. D. J., M. A. Jazayery, J. M. Landau, 'Madjmaʿ ʿIlmī'.

Watt, W. Montgomery, 'Abū Bakr'.

Watt, W. Montgomery, 'Aḳīda'.

Watt, W. Montgomery, 'al-Ghazālī'.

Encyclopaedia of Islam 3 (abbreviated as *EI3*)

Ahmed, Asad Q., 'Dars-i Niẓāmī'.

Allouche, Adel, 'Amasya, Treaty of'.

Amir-Moezzi, Mohammad Ali, 'Badā'''.

Amir-Moezzi, Mohammad Ali, 'Ghadīr Khumm'.

Athamina, Khalil, 'Abū Bakr'.

Atmaca, Metin, 'Bidlisī, Sharaf Din' (forthcoming).

Bellino, Francesca, 'Dhū l-Faqār'.

Benchekroun, Chafik T., 'Idrīsids'.

Bernheimer, Teresa, "ʿAlī l-Hādī'.

Borrut, Antoine, "ʿAbdallāh b. Muʿawiya'.

Ende, Werner, 'Baqīʿ al-Gharqad'.

Daftary, Farhad, "ʿAlids'.

Daftary, Farhad, 'Assassins'.

Donohue, John J., "ʿAḍud al-Dawla'.

Eddé, Anne-Marie, 'Ibn Abī Ṭayyi''.

Ende, Werner, 'al-Amīn, Muḥsin'.

Fischel, Roy S., 'Aḥmadnagar'.

Fischel, Roy S., 'Niẓām Shāhīs'.

Gleave, Robert M., "ʿAlī b. Abī Ṭālib'.

Goto, Yukako, 'Kār Kiyā dynasty'.

Hachmeier, Klaus, 'Bahā' al-Dawla'.

Haykel, Bernard, 'al-Amīr, Muḥammad b. Ismāʿīl'.

Hermansen, Marcia, "ʿAbd al-Raḥīm Dihlawī'.

Holtzman, Livnat, 'Aḥmad b. Ḥanbal'.

Hoover, Jon, 'Creed'.

Hutton, Deborah S., "Ādil Shāhīs'.

Katz, Marion H., 'Concubinage, in Islamic law'.
Keshani, Hussein, 'Imāmbāra'.
Mallett, Alex, "Ammār, Banū (Syria)'.
Masud, Muhammad Khalid, 'Anglo-Muhammadan law'.
McGregor, Richard J., 'Grave visitation/worship'.
Melchert, Christopher, 'al-Barbahārī'.
Mervin, Sabrina, "Āmil, Jabal'.
Mirza, Younus Y., 'Ibn Kathīr, 'Imād al-Dīn'.
Moin, A. Azfar, 'Dabistān-i madhāhib'.
Munt, Harry, 'Fadak'.
Nölle-Karimi, Christine, 'Herat art and architecture'.
Peskes, Esther, 'Daḥlān, Aḥmad b. Zaynī'.
Pierret, Thomas, 'al-Būṭī, Muḥammad Saʿīd Ramaḍān'.
Preckel, Claudia, 'Ahl-i Ḥadīth'.
Qutbuddin, Tahera, 'Ibn Abī l-Ḥadīd'.
Rippin, Andrew, 'Abrogation'.
Rowe, T. Jack, 'Kubraviyya'.
Streusand, Douglas E., 'Akbar'.
Streusand, Douglas E., 'Bayrām Khān'.
Subtelny, Maria E., 'Ḥusayn Vāʿiẓ Kāshifī'.
Subtelny, Maria E., 'Sulṭān Ḥusayn Bāyqarā'.
vom Bruck, Gabriele, 'al-Kibsī family'.
Weismann, Itzchak, 'al-Kawākibī, 'Abd al-Raḥmān'.
Weismann, Itzchak, 'Jān-i Jānān, Maẓhar'.

Encyclopaedia of the Qurʾān (abbreviated as *EQur*)
Martin, Richard C., 'Createdness of the Qurʾān'.

Islâm Ansiklopedisi
Khalid Zafarullah Daudi, 'Ihsan Ilâhî Zahîr'.

Oxford Encyclopedia of Islam and Law (abbreviated as *EIL*)
Burak, G., 'Madhhab'.

Oxford Encyclopedia of the Islamic World (abbreviated as *EIW*)
Humphrey, Michael, 'Ḥarakāt al-Tawḥīd al-Islāmī'.

Stanford Encyclopedia of Philosophy (abbreviated as *EPhil*)
Chittick, William, 'Ibn ʿArabî'.

BOOKS AND ARTICLES

Ababsa, Myriam, 'Les mausolées invisibles: Raqqa, ville de pèlerinage chiite ou pôle etatique en Jazîra syrienne?', *Annales de Géographie* 110, 622 (2001), 647–64.

Ababsa, Myriam, *Raqqa: Territoires et pratiques sociales d'une ville syrienne* (Damascus: Presses de l'Ifpo, 2009).

Ababsa, Myriam, 'The End of a World: Drought and Agrarian Transformation in Northeast Syria (2007–2010)', in: Raymond Hinnebusch and Tina Zintl (eds), *Syria from Reform to Revolt: Political Economy and International Relations* (Syracuse: Syracuse University Press, 2015), 199–222.

Abbas, Hassan, *The Prophet's Heir: The Life of 'Alī ibn Abī Ṭālib* (New Haven: Yale University Press, 2021).

Abbasi, Rushain, 'Did Premodern Muslims Distinguish the Religious and Secular? The Dīn–Dunyā Binary in Medieval Islamic Thought', *Journal of Islamic Studies* 31, 2 (2020), 185–225.

Abdallah, Ssekamanya Siraje, 'Ibn Taymiyyah on the Hadith of the 73 Sects', *Jurnal Akidah & Pemikiran Islam* 7, 1 (2006), 35–62.

Abd-Allah, Umar F., *The Islamic Struggle in Syria* (Berkeley: Mizan Press, 1983).

Abdelnasser, Walid M., 'Islamic Organizations in Egypt and the Iranian Revolution of 1979: The Experience of the First Few Years', *Arab Studies Quarterly* 19, 2 (1997), 25–39.

Abdi, Kamyar, 'The Name Game: The Persian Gulf, Archaeologists, and the Politics of Arab–Iranian Relations', in: Philip L. Kohl, Mara Kozelsky, and Nachman Ben-Yehuda (eds), *Selective Remembrances: Archaeology in the Construction, Commemoration, and Consecration of National Pasts* (Chicago: University of Chicago Press, 2007), 206–43.

Abdo, Geneive, *The New Sectarianism: The Arab Uprisings and the Rebirth of the Shi'a-Sunni Divide* (New York: Oxford University Press, 2017).

Abdullah, Thabit, *Dictatorship, Imperialism and Chaos: Iraq since 1989* (London: Zed, 2006).

Abdulsater, Hussein Ali, *Shi'i Doctrine, Mu'tazili Theology: Al-Sharif al-Murtada and Imami Discourse* (Edinburgh: Edinburgh University Press, 2017).

al-'Abidin, Muhammad Surur Zayn, *Ahwal Ahl al-Sunna fi Iran* (n.p.: n.p., 2006, first published in 1990).

al-'Abidin, Muhammad Surur Zayn, *Wa Ja'a Dawr al-Majus: Al-Ab'ad al-Tarikhiyya wa-l-'Aqa'idiyya wa-l-Siyyasiyya li-l-Thawra al-Iraniyya*, 10th ed. (n.p.: n.p., 2008).

Abisaab, Rula Jurdi, 'The Ulama of Jabal 'Āmil in Safavid Iran, 1501–1736: Marginality, Migration and Social Change', *Iranian Studies* 27, 1–4 (1994), 103–22.

Abisaab, Rula Jurdi, 'History and Self-Image: The 'Amili Ulema in Syria and Iran (Fourteenth to Sixteenth Centuries)', in: H. E. Chehabi, *Distant Relations: Iran and Lebanon in the Last 500 Years* (London: I. B. Tauris, 2006), 62–95.

Abisaab, Rula Jurdi, 'The Cleric as Organic Intellectual: Revolutionary Shi'ism in the Lebanese Hawzas', in: H. E. Chehabi, *Distant Relations: Iran and Lebanon in the Last 500 Years* (London: I. B. Tauris, 2006), 231–58.

Abisaab, Rula Jurdi, *Converting Persia: Religion and Power in the Safavid Empire*, 2nd ed. (London: I. B. Tauris, 2015).

Abisaab, Rula Jurdi, and Malek Hassan Abisaab, *The Shi'ites of Lebanon: Modernism, Communism, and Hizbullah's Islamists* (Syracuse: Syracuse University Press, 2014).

Abou-Zahab, Mariam, 'The Regional Dimensions of Sectarian Conflict in Pakistan', in: Christophe Jaffrelot (ed.), *Pakistan: Nationalism without a Nation?* (New Delhi: Manohar, 2002), 115–30.

Abou-Zahab, Mariam, 'Sectarianism as Substitute Identity: Sunnis and Shias in Central and South Punjab', in: Soofia Mumtaz, Jean-Luc Racine, and Imran Anwar Ali (eds), *Pakistan: The Contours of State and Society* (Oxford: Oxford University Press, 2002), 77–95.

Abou-Zahab, Mariam, 'The Sunni–Shia Conflict in Jhang (Pakistan)', in: Imtiaz Ahmed and Helmut Reifeld (eds), *Lived Islam in South Asia: Adaptation, Accommodation and Conflict* (New Delhi: Social Science, 2004), 135–48.

Abou-Zahab, Mariam, 'The Politicization of the Shia Community in Pakistan in the 1970s and 1980s', in: Alessandro Monsutti, Silvia Naef, and Farian Sabahi (eds), *The Other Shiites: From the Mediterranean to Central Asia* (Bern: Peter Lang, 2007), 97–114.

Abou-Zahab, Mariam, 'Salafism in Pakistan: The Ahl-e Hadith Movement', in: Roel Meijer (ed.), *Global Salafism: Islam's New Religious Movement* (London: Hurst, 2009), 126–42.

Abou-Zahab, Mariam, 'Between Pakistan and Qom: Shi'a Women's Madrasas and New Transnational Networks', in: Sabrina Mervin (ed.), *The Shi'a Worlds and Iran* (London: Saqi, 2010), 303–20.

Abou-Zahab, Mariam, '"It's Just a Sunni-Shia Thing": Sectarianism and Talibanism in the FATA (Federally Administered Tribal Areas) of Pakistan', in: Brigitte Maréchal and Sami Zemni (eds), *The Dynamics of Sunni–Shia Relationships: Doctrine, Transnationalism, Intellectuals and the Media* (London: Hurst, 2013), 179–92.

Abrahamian, Ervand, 'The Crowd in the Persian Revolution', *Iranian Studies* 2, 4 (1969), 128–50.

Abrahamian, Ervand, 'The Causes of the Constitutional Revolution in Iran', *International Journal of Middle East Studies* 10, 3 (1979), 381–414.

Abrahamian, Ervand, *A History of Modern Iran* (Cambridge: Cambridge University Press, 2008).

Abu-Amr, Ziad, *Islamic Fundamentalism in the West Bank and Gaza: Muslim Brotherhood and Islamic Jihad* (Bloomington: Indiana University Press, 1994).

Abu-Husayn, Abdul-Rahim, *The View from Istanbul: Ottoman Lebanon and the Druze Emirate* (London: I. B. Tauris, 2003).

Abu-Manneh, Butrus, 'The Naqshbandiyya-Mujaddidiyya in the Ottoman Lands in the Early 19th Century', *Die Welt des Islams* 22, 1/4 (1982), 1–36.

Abu-Manneh, Butrus, 'Shaykh Ahmad Ziya al-Din al-Gümüshhanevi and the Ziyai-Khalidi Suborder', in: F. de Jong (ed.), *Shī'a Islam, Sects and Sufism: Historical Dimensions, Religious Practice and Methodological Considerations* (Utrecht: M. Th. Houtsma, 1992), 105–17.

Abu-Manneh, Butrus, 'Salafiyya and the Rise of the Khālidiyya in Baghdad in the Early Nineteenth Century', *Die Welt des Islams* 43, 3 (2003), 349–72.

Abu-Manneh, Butrus, 'Sheikh Murād al-Bukhārī and the Expansion of the Naqshbandī-Mujaddidī Order in Istanbul', *Die Welt des Islams* 53, 1 (2013), 1–25.

Abū-Miḥnaf, *Der Tod des Ḥusein ben ʿAlī und die Rache: Ein historischer Roman aus dem Arabischen* (Göttingen: Dieterich, 1883).

Abu-Munshar, Maher Y., 'Fāṭimids, Crusaders and the Fall of Islamic Jerusalem: Foes or Allies?', *Al-Masāq* 22, 1 (2010), 45–56.

Abu'l Fazl, *The Aín-i Akbari*, Vol. 1, trans. by H. Blochmann (Calcutta: Asiatic Society, 1873).

Abu'l Fazl, *The History of Akbar*, ed./trans. by Wheeler M. Thackston, 8 Vols (Cambridge, MA: Harvard University Press, 2015–22).

Acharya, Amitav, and Barry Buzan, *The Making of Global International Relations: Origins and Evolution of IR at its Centenary* (Cambridge: Cambridge University Press, 2019).

Adam, Volker, 'Auf der Suche nach Turan: Panislamismus und Panturkismus in der aserbaidschanischen Vorkriegspresse', in: Raoul Motika and Michael Ursinus (eds), *Caucasia between the Ottoman Empire and Iran, 1555–1914* (Wiesbaden: Reichert, 2000), 189–205.

Adam, Volker, 'Why Do They Cry? Criticisms of Muḥarram Celebrations in Tsarist and Socialist Azerbaijan', in: Rainer Brunner and Werner Ende (eds), *The Twelver Shia in Modern Times: Religious Culture & Political History* (Leiden: Brill, 2001), 114–34.

Adamiyat, Fereydoun, *Bahrein Islands: A Legal and Diplomatic Study of the British-Iranian Controversy* (New York: F. A. Praeger, 1955).

Adang, Camilla, Maribel Fierro, and Sabine Schmidtke (eds), *Ibn Ḥazm of Cordoba: The Life and Works of a Controversial Thinker* (Leiden: Brill, 2013).

Addleton, Jonathan S., *Undermining the Centre: The Gulf Migration and Pakistan* (Karachi: Oxford University Press, 1992).

Adib-Moghaddam, Arshin, *The International Politics of the Persian Gulf: A Cultural Genealogy* (London: Routledge, 2006).

Adib-Moghaddam, Arshin, *Iran in World Politics: The Question of the Islamic Republic* (Oxford: Oxford University Press, 2010).

Adib-Moghaddam, Arshin, *A Critical Introduction to Khomeini* (Cambridge: Cambridge University Press, 2014).

al-Adjdad, Sayyed Mohammad Hossein Manzoor, 'The Naqīb of Ray Alids and His Support of Scientists', *Iranian Studies* 41, 4 (2008), 529–35.

Afary, Janet, *The Iranian Constitutional Revolution: Grassroots Democracy, Social Democracy, and the Origins of Feminism* (New York: Columbia University Press, 1996).

Afary, Janet, and Kevin B. Anderson, *Foucault and the Iranian Revolution: Gender and the Seductions of Islamism* (Chicago: University of Chicago Press, 2005).

Afkhami, Gholam Reza, *The Life and Times of the Shah* (Berkeley: University of California Press, 2009).

Afsaruddin, Asma, *Excellence and Precedence: Medieval Islamic Discourse on Legitimate Leadership* (Leiden: Brill, 2002).

Afsaruddin, Asma, 'The Epistemology of Excellence: Sunni-Shiʿi Dialectics on Legitimate Leadership', in: Gudrun Krämer and Sabine Schmidtke (eds), *Speaking for Islam: Religious Authorities in Muslim Societies* (Leiden: Brill, 2006), 49–69.

Afsaruddin, Asma, *The First Muslims: History and Memory* (Oxford: Oneworld, 2007).

Agha, Hussein J., and Ahmad S. Khalidi, *Syria and Iran: Rivalry and Cooperation* (London: Pinter/Chatham House, 1995).

Aghaie, Kamran Scot, *The Martyrs of Karbala: Shi'i Symbols and Rituals in Modern Iran* (Seattle: University of Washington Press, 2004).

Ahmad, Feroz, 'Ottoman Perceptions of the Capitulations 1800–1914', *Journal of Islamic Studies* 11, 1 (2000), 1–20.

al-Ahmad, Fu'ad, *Al-Shaykh Hasan 'Ali al-Badr al-Qatifi* (Beirut: Mu'assasat al-Baqi' li-Ihya' al-Turath, 1991).

Ahmad, Imtiaz, 'The Shia-Sunni Dispute in Lucknow, 1905–1980', in: Milton Israel and Narendra K. Wagle (eds), *Islamic Society and Culture: Essays in Honour of Professor Aziz Ahmad* (New Delhi: Manohar, 1983), 335–50.

Ahmad, Muhammad Basheer, *The Administration of Justice in Medieval India: A Study in Outline of the Judicial System under the Sultans and the Badshahs of Delhi Based Mainly upon Cases Decided by Medieval Courts in India between 1206–1750 A. D.* (Allahabad: Aligarh Historical Research Institute, 1941).

Ahmad, Sayyid (ed.), *Tuzuk-i Jahangiri* (Aligarh, 1864).

Ahmed, Chanfi, *West African 'Ulama' and Salafism in Mecca and Medina: Jawab al-Ifriqi, the Response of the African* (Leiden: Brill, 2015).

Ahmed, Khaled, *Sectarian War: Pakistan's Sunni-Shia Violence and Its Links to the Middle East* (Oxford: Oxford University Press, 2011).

Ahmed, Shahab, *What is Islam? The Importance of Being Islamic* (Princeton: Princeton University Press, 2015).

Ahmed, Shahab, *Before Orthodoxy: The Satanic Verses in Early Islam* (Cambridge, MA: Harvard University Press, 2017).

Ahmed, Sharif Uddin, *Dacca: A Study in Urban History and Development* (London: Routledge, 2018).

al-Ahsa'i, Muhammad al-'Abd al-Qadir al-Ansari, *Tuhfat al-Mustafid bi-Tarikh al-Ahsa' fi al-Qadim wa-l-Jadid*, 2 Vols (Riyadh: Matabi' al-Riyyad, 1960).

Aigle, Denise, 'The Mongol Invasions of Bilad al-Sham by Ghazan Khan and Ibn Taymiyah's Three "Anti-Mongol" Fatwas', *Mamluk Studies Review* 11, 2 (2007), 89–120.

Aigle, Denise, *The Mongol Empire between Myth and Reality: Studies in Anthropological History* (Leiden: Brill, 2014).

Ajami, Fouad, *The Vanished Imam: Musa al-Sadr and the Shia of Lebanon* (Ithaca: Cornell University Press, 1986).

Akbarnezhad, Mahdi, 'Criticism of Ibn Taymiyya's View Concerning Imam Mahdi (P.b.u.h.)', *Iranian Journal for the Quranic Sciences & Tradition* 42, 1 (2009), 25–42.

Akhavi, Shahrough, *Religion and Politics in Contemporary Iran: Clergy-State Relations in the Pahlavi Period* (Albany: SUNY Press, 1980).

Akhtar, Iqbal, 'Negotiating the Racial Boundaries of Khoja Caste Membership in Late Nineteenth-Century Colonial Zanzibar (1878–1899)', *Journal of Africana Religions* 2, 3 (2014), 297–316.

al-'Akri, 'Abd al-Nabi, *Al-Tanzimat al-Yasariyya fi al-Jazira wa-l-Khalij al-'Arabi* (Beirut: Dar al-Kunuz al-Adabiyya, 2003).

Aksan, Virginia H., *Ottoman Wars, 1700–1870: An Empire Besieged* (Harlow: Pearson, 2007).

Alagha, Joseph, *The Shifts in Hizbullah's Ideology: Religious Ideology, Political Ideology and Political Program* (Amsterdam: Amsterdam University Press, 2006).

Alagha, Joseph, *Hizbullah's Documents: From the 1985 Open Letter to the 2009 Manifesto* (Amsterdam: Amsterdam University Press, 2011).

Alagha, Joseph, *Hizbullah's Identity Construction* (Amsterdam: Amsterdam University Press, 2011).

Alagha, Joseph, 'Ideological Tensions between Hizbullah and Jihadi Salafism: Mutual Perceptions and Mutual Fears', in: Brigitte Maréchal and Sami Zemni (eds), *The Dynamics of Sunni-Shia Relationships: Doctrine, Transnationalism, Intellectuals and the Media* (London: Hurst, 2013), 61–82.

Alak, Alina Isac, 'The Sunni-Shi'a Conflict as Reflected in the Romanian Muslim Community', *Journal of Loss and Trauma* 20, 3 (2015), 207–13.

Alam, Muzaffar, *The Crisis of Empire in Mughal North India: Awadh and the Punjab, 1707–48* (New Delhi: Oxford University Press, 1986).

Alam, Muzaffar, 'Trade, State Policy and Regional Change: Aspects of Mughal-Uzbek Commercial Relations, c. 1550–1750', *Journal of the Economic and Social History of the Orient* 37, 3 (1994), 202–27.

Alam, Muzaffar, 'The Pursuit of Persian: Language in Mughal Politics', *Modern Asian Studies* 32, 2 (1998), 317–49.

Alam, Muzaffar, *The Languages of Political Islam: India 1200–1800* (London: Hurst, 2004).

Alam, Muzaffar, 'The Mughals, the Sufi Shaikhs and the Formation of the Akbari Dispensation', *Modern Asian Studies* 43, 1 (2009), 135–74.

Alam, Muzaffar, and Sanjay Subrahmanyam, *Writing the Mughal World: Studies on Culture and Politics* (New York: Columbia University Press, 2011).

Alatas, Syed Farid, 'The Ṭariqat al-'Alawiyyah and the Emergence of the Shi'i School in Indonesia and Malaysia', *Oriente Moderno* 18, 2 (1999), 322–39.

Alatas, Syed Farid, 'Salafism and the Persecution of Shi'ites in Malaysia', *Middle East Institute*, 30 July 2014.

Alavi, Seema, *Muslim Cosmopolitanism in the Age of Empire* (Cambridge, MA: Harvard University Press, 2015).

Alavi, Seema, 'Slaves, Arms, and Political Careering in Nineteenth-Century Oman', in: Eric Tagliacozzo, Helen F. Siu, and Peter C. Perdue (eds), *Asia Inside Out: Itinerant People* (Cambridge, MA: Harvard University Press, 2019), 179–200.

al-'Alawi, Hasan, *Shi'a al-Sulta wa Shi'a al-'Iraq: Sira' al-Ajnas* (London: Dar al-Zura', 2009).

Albergoni, Gianni, and Genviève Bédoucha, 'Hiérarchie, médiation, et tribalisme en Arabie du Sud: La hijra yéménite', *L'Homme* 31, 118 (1991), 7–36.

Albloshi, Hamad H., 'Ideological Roots of the Ḥūthī Movement in Yemen', *Journal of Arabian Studies* 6, 2 (2016), 143–62.

Albrecht, Sarah, *Dār al-Islām Revisited: Territoriality in Contemporary Islamic Legal Discourse on Muslims in the West* (Leiden: Brill, 2018).

Aldoughli, Rahaf, 'Revisiting Ideological Borrowings in Syrian Nationalist Narratives: Sati al-Husri, Michel 'Aflaq and Zaki al-Arsuzi', *Syria Studies* 8, 1 (2016), 7–39.

Aldoughli, Rahaf, 'Interrogating the Constructions of Masculinist Protection and Militarism in the Syrian Constitution of 1973', *Journal of Middle East Women's Studies* 15, 1 (2019), 48–74.

Aldoughli, Rahaf, 'Departing "Secularism": Boundary Appropriation and Extension of the Syrian State in the Religious Domain since 2011', *British Journal of Middle Eastern Studies* 49, 2 (2022), 360–85.

Aldoughli, Rahaf, 'Securitization as a Tool of Regime Survival: The Deployment of Religious Rhetoric in Bashar al-Asad's Speeches', *Middle East Journal* 75, 1 (2021), 9–32.

Aldrick, Judy, *The Sultan's Spymaster: Peera Dewjee of Zanzibar* (Naivasha: Old Africa Books, 2015).

Alexander, Claire, Joya Chatterji, and Annu Jalais, *The Bengal Diaspora: Rethinking Muslim Migration* (London: Routledge, 2016).

Alexander, David G., 'Dhū'l-Faqār and the Legacy of the Prophet, Mīrāth Rasūl Allāh', *Gladius* 19, 1 (1999), 157–87.

Algar, Hamid, *Religion and the State in Iran, 1785–1906: The Role of the Ulama in the Qajar Period* (Berkeley: University of California Press, 1969).

Algar, Hamid, 'The Revolt of Agha Khan Mahallati and the Transference of the Ismaili Imamate to India', *Studia Islamica* 29 (1969), 55–81.

Algar, Hamid, 'Some Observations on Religion in Safavid Persia', *Iranian Studies* 7, 1–2 (1974), 287–93.

Algar, Hamid, 'The Naqshbandī Order: A Preliminary Survey of its History and Significance', *Studia Islamica* 44 (1976), 123–52.

Algar, Hamid, 'Shi'ism and Iran in the Eighteenth Century', in: Thomas Naff and Roger Owen (eds), *Studies in Eighteenth Century Islamic History* (Carbondale: Southern Illinois University Press, 1977), 288–302.

Algar, Hamid, 'Participation by Iranian Diplomats in the Masonic Lodges of Istanbul', in: Th. Zarcone and F. Zarinebaf (eds), *Les Iraniens d'Istanbul* (Paris: Institut Français de Recherches en Iran/Institut Français d'Études Anatoliennes, 1993), 33–44.

Algar, Hamid, 'Naqshbandis and Safavids: A Contribution to the Religious History of Iran and her Neighbours', in: Michel M. Mazzaoui (ed.), *Safavid Iran & Her Neighbors* (Salt Lake City: University of Utah Press, 2003), 7–48.

Algar, Hamid, *Jami* (Oxford: Oxford University Press, 2013).

Algar, Hamid, 'Review of "Politics, Poetry and Sufism in Medieval Iran: New Perspectives on Jāmī's Salāmān va Absāl" by Chad G. Lingwood', *Journal of Islamic Studies* 27, 1 (2016), 54–65.

Alhaj, Wissam, Nicolas Dot-Pouillard, and Eugénie Rébillard, *De la théologie à la libération? Histoire du Jihad islamique palestinien* (Paris: La Découverte, 2014).

Alhasan, Hasan Tariq, 'The Role of Iran in the Failed Coup of 1981: The IFLB in Bahrain', *Middle East Journal* 65, 4 (2011), 603–17.

Ali, Shahid, 'The Specter of Hate and Intolerance: Sectarian-Jihadi Nexus and the Persecution of Hazara Shia Community in Pakistan', *Contemporary South Asia* 29, 2 (2021), 198–211.

Ali, Syed Ameer, *The Personal Law of the Mahommedans (According to All the Schools) Together with a Comparative Sketch of the Law of Inheritance among the Sunnis and the Shias* (London: W. H. Allen, 1880).

Ali, Syed Ameer, *A Short History of the Saracens: Being a Concise Account of the Rise and Decline of the Saracenic Power and of the Economic, Social and Intellectual Development of the Arab Nation from the Earliest Times to the Destruction of Bagdad, and the Expulsion of the Moors from Spain* (London: Macmillan, 1921).

Ali, Syed Ameer, *Mahommedan Law: Compiled from Authorities in the Original Arabic*, Vol. 2 (Calcutta and Simla: Thacker, Spink & Co., 1929).

Alkan, Necati, 'Fighting for the Nuṣayrī Soul: State, Protestant Missionaries and the 'Alawīs in the Late Ottoman Empire', *Die Welt des Islams* 52, 1 (2012), 23–50.

Alkan, Necati, 'The Ottoman Policy of "Correction of Belief(s)"', in: Vefa Erginbaş (ed.), *Ottoman Sunnism: New Perspectives* (Edinburgh: Edinburgh University Press, 2019), 166–92.

Alkan, Necati, *Non-Sunni Muslims in the Late Ottoman Empire: State and Missionary Perceptions of the Alawis* (London: I.B. Tauris, 2022).

Allawi, Ali A., *Faisal I of Iraq* (New Haven: Yale University Press, 2014).

Allen, Charles, 'The Hidden Roots of Wahhabism in British India', *World Policy Journal* 22, 2 (2005), 87–93.

Allen, Terry, *Ayyubid Architecture* (Occidental, CA: Solipsist Press, 1999).

Allison, Christine, '"Unbelievable Slowness of Mind": Yezidi Studies, from Nineteenth to Twenty-First Century', *Journal of Kurdish Studies* 6 (2008), 1–23.

Allouche, Adel, *The Origins and Development of the Ottoman-Safavid Diplomatic Conflict, 906–966/1500–1555* (Berlin: Klaus Schwarz, 1983).

Allouche, Adel, 'The Establishment of Four Chief Judgeships in Fāṭimid Egypt', *Journal of the American Oriental Society* 105, 2 (1985), 317–20.

Alpher, Yossi, *Periphery: Israel's Search for Middle East Allies* (Lanham: Rowman & Littlefield, 2015).

al-Alusi, Mahmud Shukri, *Sabb al-'Adhab 'ala man Sabba al-Ashab*, ed. by 'Abdallah al-Bukhari (Riyadh: Adua' al-Salaf, 1997).

Alvandi, Roham, *Nixon, Kissinger, and the Shah: The United States and Iran in the Cold War* (New York: Oxford University Press, 2014).

Alvarez-Ossorio, Ignacio, 'The Sectarian Dynamics of the Syrian Conflict', *Review of Faith & International Affairs* 17, 2 (2019), 47–58.

Alvi, Sajida S., 'Religion and State during the Reign of Mughal Emperor Jahāngīr (1605–27): Nonjuristical Perspectives', *Studia Islamica* 69 (1989), 95–119.

Alvi, Sajida S., *Perspectives on Mughal India: Rulers, Historians, 'Ulamā and Sufis* (Oxford: Oxford University Press, 2012).

Amanat, Abbas, *Pivot of the Universe: Nasir al-Din Shah Qajar and the Iranian Monarchy, 1831–1896* (Berkeley: University of California Press, 1997).

Amanat, Abbas, *Resurrection and Renewal: The Making of the Babi Movement in Iran, 1844–1850* (Ithaca: Cornell University Press, 1989).

Amanat, Abbas, 'Meadow of the Martyrs: Kāshifī's Persianization of the Shi'i Martyrdom Narrative in Late Tīmūrid Herat', in: Farhad Daftary and Josef W. Meri (eds), *Culture and Memory in Medieval Islam: Essays in Honour of Wilferd Madelung* (London: I. B. Tauris/Institute of Ismaili Studies, 2003), 250–75.

Amanat, Abbas, *Iran: A Modern History* (New Haven: Yale University Press, 2017).

Amil, Mahdi, *Fi al-Dawla al-Ta'ifiyya* (Beirut: Dar al-Farabi, 2003, first published 1986).

Amil, Mahdi, *Madkhal ila Naqd al-Fikr al-Ta'ifi: Al-Qadiyya al-Filastiniyya fi Idiyulujiyyat al-Burjwaziyya al-Lubnaniyya* (Beirut: Dar al-Farabi, 1989).

al-'Amili, Muhsin al-Hussayni, *Al-Husun al-Mani'a fi Radd ma Awradahu Sahib al-Manar fi Haqq al-Shi'a* (Damascus: Matba'a al-Islah, 1327/1909).

al-Amin, Muhsin, *Mustadrakat A'yan al-Shi'a: Haqqaqahu wa Akhrajahu Hasan al-Amin*, 11 Vols (Beirut: Dar al-Ta'arruf li-l-Matbu'at, 1986).

al-Amin, Muhsin, *Autobiographie d'un clerc chiite du Ǧabal 'Āmil: Tiré de: Les notables chiites (A'yān al-Šī'a)*, trans. by Sabrina Mervin (Damascus: Presses de l'Ifpo, 1998).

al-Amin, Muhsin, *Al-Shahid Zayd ibn 'Ali wa-l-Zaydiyya* (Beirut: Dar al-Murtada, 2003).

Amini, Nowrouz, and Sayyed Reza Mo'addab, 'Attitude of al-Tabari, Ibn Kathir, and Tha'alibi towards Commentatorial Hadiths of Ahl al-Bayt', *Iranian Journal for the Quranic Sciences & Tradition* 46, 1 (2013), 21–50.

Amirahmadi, Hooshang, 'Iranian-Saudi Arabian Relations since the Revolution', in: Hooshang Amirahmadi and Nader Entessar (eds), *Iran and the Arab World* (London: Macmillan, 1993), 139–60.

Amir-Moezzi, Mohammad Ali, *The Divine Guide in Early Shi'ism: The Sources of Esotericism in Islam*, trans. by David Streight (New York: State University of New York Press, 1994).

Amir-Moezzi, Mohammad Ali, 'Shahrbānū, princesse sassanide et épouse de l'imam Ḥusayn: De l'Iran préislamique à l'Islam shiite', *Comptes rendus des séances de l'Académie des Inscriptions et Belles-Lettres* 146, 1 (2002), 255–85.

Amir-Moezzi, Mohammad Ali, 'Al-Shaykh al-Mufīd (m. 413/1022) et la question de la falsification du Coran', *Rivista Degli Studi Orientali* 87, 1 (2014), 155–76.

Amir-Moezzi, Mohammad Ali, *The Silent Qur'an and the Speaking Qur'an: Scriptural Sources of Islam Between History and Fervor* (New York: Columbia University Press, 2016).

Amir-Moezzi, Mohammad Ali (and Christian Jambet), *What is Shi'i Islam? An Introduction* (Abingdon: Routledge, 2018).

Amir-Moezzi, Mohammad Ali, *Ali, le secret bien gardé: Figures du premier Maître en spiritualité shi'ite* (Paris: CNRS Editions, 2020).

Amirpur, Katajun, *Khomeini: Der Revolutionär des Islams* (Munich: C. H. Beck, 2021).

Amitai, Reuven, *Mongols and Mamluks: The Mamluk-Ilkhanid War, 1260–1281* (Cambridge: Cambridge University Press, 1995).

Amitai, Reuven, 'Ghazan, Islam and Mongol Tradition: A View from the Mamlūk Sultanate', *Bulletin of the School of Oriental and African Studies* 59, 1 (1996), 1–10.

Amitai, Reuven, 'The Mongol Occupation of Damascus in 1300: A Study of Mamluk Loyalties', in: Michael Winter and Amalia Levanoni (eds), *The Mamluks in Egyptian and Syrian Politics and Society* (Leiden: Brill, 2004), 21–41.

Amitai, Reuven, 'The Resolution of the Mongol-Mamluk War', in: Reuven Amitai and Michal Biran (eds), *Mongols, Turks, and Others: Eurasian Nomads and the Sedentary World* (Leiden: Brill, 2005), 359–90.

Amitai, Reuven, *Holy War and Rapprochement: Studies in the Relations between the Mamluk Sultanate and the Mongol Ilkhanate (1260–1335)* (Turnhout: Brepols, 2013).

Amitai, Reuven, 'Hülegü and his Wise Men: Topos or Reality?', in: Judith Pfeiffer (ed.), *Politics, Patronage and the Transmission of Knowledge in 13th–15th Century Tabriz* (Leiden: Brill, 2013), 13–34.

Amoretti, Biancamaria Scarcia, 'Una polemica religiosa tra "ulamâ" di Mashad e "ulamâ" uzbechi nell anno 977/1588–1589', *Annali dell'Istituto orientale di Napoli* 14 (1964), 647–71.

Amoretti, Biancamaria Scarcia, 'Religion in the Timurid and Safavid Periods', in: Peter Jackson and Lawrence Lockhart (eds), *The Cambridge History of Iran*, Vol. 6 (Cambridge: Cambridge University Press, 1986), 610–55.

Amoretti, Biancamaria Scarcia, 'Shi'a Devotion to the Ahl al-Bayt in Historical Perspective', in: Chiara Formichi and R. Michael Feener (eds), *Shi'ism in Southeast Asia: 'Alid Piety and Sectarian Constructions* (London: Hurst, 2015), 17–29.

Amoretti, Biancamaria Scarcia, and Laura Bottini (eds), *The Role of the Sadat/Asraf in Muslim History and Civilization* (Naples: Istituto per l'Oriente C. A. Nallino, 1999).

Amos, Deborah, *Eclipse of the Sunnis: Power, Exile, and Upheaval in the Middle East* (New York: PublicAffairs, 2010).

al-'Amri, Husayn b. 'Abdullah, *The Yemen in the 18th and 19th Centuries: A Political and Intellectual History* (London: Ithaca, 1985).

Anderson, Benedict, *Imagined Communities: Reflections on the Origin and Spread of Nationalism* (London: Verso, 1991).

Anderson, Michael, 'Islamic Law and the Colonial Encounter in British India', in: David Arnold and Peter Robb (eds), *Institutions and Ideologies: A SOAS South Asia Reader* (Richmond: Curzon, 1993), 165–85.

Anjum, Ovamir, 'Sufism Without Mysticism? Ibn Qayyim al-Ğawziyyah's Objectives in Madāriğ al-Sālikīn', in: Caterina Bori and Livnat Holtzman (eds), *A Scholar in the Shadow: Essays in the Legal and Theological Thought of Ibn al-Qayyim al-Jawziyya* (Rome: Herder, 2010), 161–88.

Anooshahr, Ali, *Turkestan and the Rise of Eurasian Empires: A Study of Politics and Invented Traditions* (Oxford: Oxford University Press, 2018).

Ansari, Ali M. (ed.), *Iran's Constitutional Revolution of 1906: Narratives of the Enlightenment* (London: Gingko Library, 2016).

Ansari, Hassan, *L'imamat et l'Occultation selon l'imamisme: Etude bibliographique et histoire des textes* (Leiden: Brill, 2017).

Ansari, Hassan, and Sabine Schmidtke, *Studies in Medieval Islamic Intellectual Traditions* (Atlanta: Lockwood Press, 2017).

Ansari, Hassan, Sabine Schmidtke, and Jan Thiele, 'Zaydī Theology in Yemen', in: Sabine Schmidtke (ed.), *The Oxford Handbook of Islamic Theology* (Oxford: Oxford University Press, 2016), 473–93.

Anscombe, Frederick F., *The Ottoman Gulf: The Creation of Kuwait, Saudi Arabia, and Qatar* (New York: Columbia University Press, 1997).

Anscombe, Frederick F., *State, Faith, and Nation in Ottoman and Post-Ottoman Lands* (Cambridge: Cambridge University Press, 2014).

Anthony, Sean, *The Caliph and the Heretic: Ibn Saba' and the Origins of Shī'ism* (Leiden: Brill, 2012).

Antonius, George, *The Arab Awakening: The Story of the Arab National Movement* (London: Hamish Hamilton, 1938).

Anzalone, Christopher, 'In the Shadow of the Islamic State: Shi'i Responses to Sunni Jihadist Narratives in a Turbulent Middle East', in: Simon Staffell and Akil N. Awan (eds), *Jihadism Transformed: Al-Qaeda and Islamic State's Global Battle of Ideas* (New York: Oxford University Press, 2017), 157–82.

Appadurai, Arjun, *Fear of Small Numbers: An Essay on the Geography of Anger* (Durham: Duke University Press, 2006).

Aras, Ramazan, 'Naqshbandi Sufis and their Conception of Place, Time and Fear on the Turkish–Syrian Border and Borderland', *Middle Eastern Studies* 55, 1 (2019), 44–59.

Arjomand, Said Amir, 'The Shi'ite Hierocracy and the State in Pre-Modern Iran: 1785–1890', *European Journal of Sociology* 22, 1 (1981), 40–78.

Arjomand, Said Amir, *The Shadow of God and the Hidden Imam: Religion, Political Order, and Societal Change in Shi'ite Iran from the Beginning to 1890* (Chicago: University of Chicago Press, 1984).

Arjomand, Said Amir, 'The Clerical Estate and the Emergence of a Shi'ite Hierocracy in Safavid Iran: A Study in Historical Sociology', *Journal of the Economic and Social History of the Orient* 28, 2 (1985), 169–219.

Arjomand, Said Amir, 'The Crisis of the Imamate and the Institution of Occultation in Twelver Shiism: A Sociohistorical Perspective', *International Journal of Middle East Studies* 28, 4 (1996), 491–515.

Arjomand, Said Amir, 'Political Ethic and Public Law in the Early Qajar Period', in: Robert Gleave (ed.), *Religion and Society in Qajar Iran* (London: Routledge, 2004), 21–40.

Arjomand, Said Amir, *The Turban for the Crown: The Islamic Revolution in Iran* (New York: Oxford University Press, 1988).

Arminjon Hachem, Constance, *Chiisme et État: Les clercs à l'épreuve de la modernité* (Paris: CNRS Editions, 2013).

Arminjon Hachem, Constance, *Les droits de l'homme dans l'Islam shi'ite: Confluences et lignes de partage* (Paris: Les Éditions du Cerf, 2017).

Arminjon Hachem, Constance, *Une brève histoire de la pensée politique en Islam contemporain* (Geneva: Labor et Fides, 2017).

Arsan, Andrew, *Interlopers of Empire: The Lebanese Diaspora in Colonial French West Africa* (London: Hurst, 2014).

Arsan, Andrew, *Lebanon: A Country in Fragments* (London: Hurst, 2018).

Arsuzi-Elamir, Dalal, *Arabischer Nationalismus in Syrien: Zakī al-Arsūzī und die arabisch-nationale Bewegung an der Peripherie Alexandretta/Antakya, 1930–1938* (Münster: LIT, 2003).

Asad, Talal, *Formations of the Secular: Christianity, Islam, Modernity* (Stanford: Stanford University Press, 2003).

Asatryan, Mushegh, *Controversies in Formative Shiʿi Islam: The Ghulat Muslims and their Beliefs* (London: I.B. Tauris, 2017).

al-ʿAskari, al-ʿAllama al-Sayyid Murtada, *Maʿalim al-Madrasatayn*, Vol. 2 (Tehran: Muʾassasat al-Baʿatha, 1405/1985).

Aslanian, Sebouh D., *From the Indian Ocean to the Mediterranean: The Global Trade Networks of Armenian Merchants from New Julfa* (Berkeley: University of California Press, 2010).

Assmann, Jan, *Das kulturelle Gedächtnis: Schrift, Erinnerung und politische Identität in frühen Hochkulturen* (Munich: C. H. Beck, 1997).

Assmann, Jan, 'Communicative and Cultural Memory', in: Astrid Erll and Ansgar Nünning (eds), *Cultural Memory Studies: An International and Interdisciplinary Handbook* (Berlin: De Gruyter, 2008), 109–18.

Ataie, Mohammad, 'Revolutionary Iran's 1979 Endeavor in Lebanon', *Middle East Policy* 20, 2 (2013), 137–57.

Ataie, Mohammad, 'Exporting the Iranian Revolution: Ecumenical Clerics in Lebanon', *International Journal of Middle East Studies* 53, 4 (2021), 672–90.

Atçıl, Abdurrahman, *Scholars and Sultans in the Early Modern Ottoman Empire* (Cambridge: Cambridge University Press, 2016).

Atçıl, Abdurrahman, 'The Safavid Threat and Juristic Authority in the Ottoman Empire during the 16th Century', *International Journal of Middle East Studies* 49, 2 (2017), 295–314.

Ateş, Sabri, 'Bones of Contention: Corpse Traffic and Ottoman-Iranian Rivalry in Nineteenth-Century Iraq', *Comparative Studies of South Asia, Africa and the Middle East* 30, 3 (2010), 512–32.

Ateş, Sabri, *Ottoman-Iranian Borderlands: Making a Boundary, 1843–1914* (Cambridge: Cambridge University Press, 2015).

Atkin, Muriel, *Russia and Iran, 1780–1828* (Minneapolis: University of Minnesota Press, 1980).

Atkin, Muriel, 'Soviet Attitudes toward Shiʿism and Social Protest', in: Juan R.I. Cole and Nikki R. Keddie (eds), *Shiʿism and Social Protest* (New Haven: Yale University Press, 1986), 275–301.

Atmaca, Metin, 'Review: I. Mahmud-Nadir Şah Mektuplaşmaları, 3 Numaralı Nâme-i Hümâyûn Defteri (Istanbul: Osmanli Arşivi Daire Başkanlığı Yayınları, 2014)', *Journal of the Ottoman and Turkish Studies Association* 2, 2 (2015), 424–6.

Atmaca, Metin, 'Contesting the Politics of Sectarianism: Naqshbandi-Khalidi Sufis on the Ottoman-Iranian Frontier and Their Relations with Shiʿa and Non-Muslims', paper presented at the *ACRPS Winter School on Communitarianism, Sectarianism, and the State*, Doha Institute, Qatar, 4–14 January 2020.

Atmaca, Metin, 'Negotiating Political Power in the Early Modern Middle East: Kurdish Emirates between the Ottoman Empire and Iranian Dynasties (Sixteenth to Nineteenth Centuries)', in: Hamit Bozarslan, Cengiz Gunes, and Veli Yadirgi (eds), *The Cambridge History of the Kurds* (Cambridge: Cambridge University Press, 2021), 45–72.

Atmaca, Metin, 'The Road to Sèvres: Kurdish Elites' Quest for Self-Determination after World War I', *International Journal of Conflict and Violence* 16 (2022), forthcoming.

Aubin, Jean, *Matériaux pour la biographie de Shāh Ni'matullāh Walī Kermānī* (Tehran: Institut Franco-Iranien, 1956).

Aubin, Jean, 'Etudes safavides: I. Šāh Ismāʿil et les notables de l'Iraq persan', *Journal of the Economic and Social History of the Orient* 2, 1 (1959), 37–81.

Aubin, Jean, 'Les sunnites du Larestán et la chute des Safavides', *Revue des études islamiques* 33 (1965), 151–71.

Auch, Eva-Maria, *Muslim, Untertan, Bürger: Identitätswandel in gesellschaftlichen Transformationsprozessen der muslimischen Ostprovinzen Südkaukasiens (Ende 18.-Anfang 20. Jh.): Ein Beitrag zur vergleichenden Nationalismusforschung* (Wiesbaden: Reichert, 2004).

Avery, Peter, 'Nadir Shah and the Afsharid Legacy', in: P. Avery, G. Hambly, and C. Melville (eds), *The Cambridge History of Iran*, Vol. 7 (Cambridge: Cambridge University Press, 1991), 1–62.

Avez, Renaud, *L'Institut français de Damas au Palais Azem (1922–1946): À travers les archives* (Damascus: Institut Français de Damas, 1993).

Awad, Abdul Aziz M., 'The Gulf in the Seventeenth Century', *Bulletin (British Society for Middle Eastern Studies)* 12, 2 (1985), 123–34.

Awada, Hassan, 'Le Liban et le flux islamiste', *Social Compass* 35, 4 (1988), 645–73.

Axworthy, Michael, *The Sword of Persia: Nader Shah, from Tribal Warrior to Conquering Tyrant* (London: I. B. Tauris, 2006).

Axworthy, Michael, 'The Army of Nader Shah', *Iranian Studies* 40, 5 (2007), 635–46.

Axworthy, Michael, *Revolutionary Iran: A History of the Islamic Republic* (Oxford: Oxford University Press, 2013).

Axworthy, Michael, 'The Awkwardness of Nader Shah: History, Military History, and Eighteenth-Century Iran', in: Michael Axworthy (ed.), *Crisis, Collapse, Militarism and Civil War: The History and Historiography of 18th Century Iran* (Oxford: Oxford University Press, 2018), 43–60.

Ayalon, David, 'Studies on the Transfer of the ʿAbbāsid Caliphate from Baġdād to Cairo', *Arabica* 7, 1 (1960), 41–59.

Ayalon, David, 'The Great Yāsa of Chingiz Khān: A Re-Examination (Part C1)', *Studia Islamica* 36 (1972), 113–58.

Ayata, Sencer, 'Patronage, Party, and State: The Politicization of Islam in Turkey', *Middle East Journal* 50, 1 (1996), 40–56.

Aydin, Cemil, *The Idea of the Muslim World: A Global Intellectual History* (Cambridge, MA: Harvard University Press, 2017).

Ayoub, Mahmoud, *Redemptive Suffering in Islam: A Study of the Devotional Aspects of 'Ashura' in Twelver Shiism* (The Hague: Mouton, 1978).

al-Aʿzam, Walid, *Al-Khumayniyya: Warithat al-Harakat al-Haqida wa-l-Afkar al-Fasida* (Amman: Dar ʿAmmar, 1988).

al-Azami, Usaama, *Islam and the Arab Revolutions: The Ulama between Democracy and Autocracy* (London: Hurst, 2021).

Azarbadegan, Zeinab, 'Imagined Geographies, Re-Invented Histories: Ottoman Iraq as Part of Iran', *Journal of the Ottoman and Turkish Studies Association* 5, 1 (2018), 115–41.

El-Azhari, Taef, *Zengi and the Muslim Response to the Crusades: The Politics of Jihad* (London: Routledge, 2016).

Aziz, Muhammad Ali, *Religion and Mysticism in Early Islam: Theology and Sufism in Yemen* (London: I. B. Tauris, 2011).

Azizi, Arash, *The Shadow Commander: Soleimani, the US, and Iran's Global Ambitions* (London: Oneworld, 2020).

Azoulay, Rivka, 'The Politics of Shi'i Merchants in Kuwait', in: Steffen Hertog, Giacomo Luciani, and Marc Valeri (eds), *Business Politics in the Middle East* (London: Hurst, 2013), 67–99.

Azoulay, Rivka, and Claire Beaugrand, 'Limits of Political Clientelism: Elites' Struggles in Kuwait Fragmenting Politics', *Arabian Humanities* 4 (2015).

Azzam, Abdel Rahman, *Saladin: The Triumph of the Sunni Revival* (Cambridge: Islamic Texts Society, 2014).

Azzam, Abdel Rahman, 'Sources of the Sunni Revival: Nizam u-Mulk & the Nizamiyya: An 11th Century Response to Sectarianism', *The Muslim World* 106, 1 (2016), 97–108.

Baack, Lawrence J., *Undying Curiosity: Carsten Niebuhr and the Royal Danish Expedition to Arabia (1761–1767)* (Stuttgart: Franz Steiner, 2014).

Babaie, Sussan, *Isfahan and its Palaces: Statecraft, Shi'ism and the Architecture of Conviviality in Early Modern Iran* (Edinburgh: Edinburgh University Press, 2008).

Babaie, Sussan, 'Nader Shah, the Delhi Loot, and the 18th-Century Exotics of Empire', in: Michael Axworthy (ed.), *Crisis, Collapse, Militarism and Civil War: The History and Historiography of 18th Century Iran* (Oxford: Oxford University Press, 2018), 215–34.

Babajanov, Bakhtiyar, 'La naqshbandiyya sous les premiers Sheybanides', *Cahiers d'Asie centrale* 3/4 (1997), 69–90.

Babayan, Kathryn, 'The Safavid Synthesis: From Qizilbash Islam to Imamite Shi'ism', *Iranian Studies* 27, 1/4 (1994), 135–61.

Babayan, Kathryn, *Mystics, Monarchs, and Messiahs: Cultural Landscapes of Early Modern Iran* (Cambridge, MA: Harvard University Press, 2002).

Babur, Zahir ud-Din Muhammad, *The Baburnama: Memoirs of Babur, Prince and Emperor*, trans./ed. by Wheeler M. Thackston (New York: Modern Library, 2002).

Bachleitner, Kathrin, and Toby Matthiesen, 'Introduction to Themed Section on "Belonging to Syria: National Identifications before and after 2011"', *Nations and Nationalism* 28, 1 (2022), 117–24.

Bacqué-Grammont, Jean-Louis, *Les Ottomans, les Safavides et leurs voisins: Contribution à l'histoire des relations internationales dans l'Orient islamique de 1514 à 1524* (Istanbul: Nederlands Historisch-Archeologisch Instituut te Istanbul, 1987).

Bacqué-Grammont, Jean-Louis, 'Les Ottomans et les Safavides dans la première moitié du XVIe siècle', in: *Convegno sul tema: La Shī'a nell'Impero Ottomano (Roma, 15 aprile 1991)* (Rome: Accademia Nazionale dei Lincei, 1993), 7–24.

Baczko, Adam, Gilles Dorronsoro, and Arthur Quesnay, *Civil War in Syria: Mobilization and Competing Social Orders* (Cambridge: Cambridge University Press, 2018).

Badakhchani, S. J., 'Introduction', in: S. J. Badakhchani (ed.), *Shi'i Interpretations of Islam: Three Treatises on Islamic Theology and Eschatology* (London: I. B. Tauris/ Institute of Ismaili Studies, 2010), 1–21.

al-Badauni, 'Abdul Qadir, *Muntakhab al-Tawarikh*, 3 Vols (Calcutta: Asiatic Society, 1898–1925).

Badeeb, Saeed M., *Saudi-Iranian Relations, 1932–1982* (London: Centre for Arab and Iranian Studies, 1993).

al-Baghdadi, Abu Mansur 'Abd al-Kahir ibn Tahir, *Moslem Schisms and Sects (Al-Fark Bain al-Firak), Being the History of the Various Philosophic Systems Developed in Islam, Part I*, trans. by Kate Chambers Seelye (New York: Columbia University Press, 1919).

Bagley, Frank, 'The Azhar and Shi'ism', *The Muslim World* 50, 2 (1960), 122–9.

Bahout, Joseph, *Les entrepreneurs syriens: Économie, affaires et politique* (Beirut: Presses de l'Ifpo, 1994).

Bahout, Joseph, 'The Unraveling of Taif: The Limits of Sect-Based Power-Sharing in Lebanon', in: Frederic Wehrey (ed.), *Beyond Sunni and Shia: The Roots of Sectarianism in a Changing Middle East* (Oxford: Oxford University Press, 2018), 135–56.

al-Bahrani, 'Ali al-Biladi, *Anwar al-Badrayn fi Tarajim 'Ulama' al-Qatif wa-l-Ahsa' wa-l-Bahrayn* (Beirut: Dar al-Murtada, 1991).

al-Bahrani, Muhammad 'Ali bin Ahmad bin 'Abbas al-Tajir, *Muntazzam al-Durrayn fi Tarajim 'Ulama' wa Udaba' al-Ahsa' wa-l-Qatif wa-l-Bahrayn*, 3 Vols. (Qom/Beirut: Mu'assasa Tayyiba li–Ihya' al-Turath, 2009).

al-Bahrani, Yusuf bin Ahmad, *Lu'lu'at al-Bahrayn fi al-Ijazat wa Tarajim Rijal al-Hadith* (Najaf: Matba'a al-'Uthman, 1966).

Bailey, Clinton, 'Lebanon's Shi'is after the 1982 War', in: Martin Kramer (ed.), *Shi'ism, Resistance, and Revolution* (Boulder, CO: Westview Press, 1987), 219–36.

Baillie, D. C., *Census of India, 1891*, Vol. 16 (Allahabad: North-Western Provinces and Oudh Government Press, 1894).

Baillie, John, *A Digest of Mohummudan Law: According to the Tenets of the Twelve Imams (by a Native Jurist) Extended, so as to Comprize the Whole of the Imameea Code of Jurisprudence* (Calcutta: Honourable Company's Press, 1805).

Baillie, Neil B. E., *A Digest of Moohummudan Law on the Subjects to which it is Usually Applied by British Courts of Justice in India* (London: Smith, Elder & Co., 1865).

Baines, Jervoise A., *General Report on the Census of India, 1891* (London: Eyre & Spottiswoode, 1893).

Bajoghli, Narges, *Iran Reframed: Anxieties of Power in the Islamic Republic* (Stanford: Stanford University Press, 2019).

Baker, Christine D., *Medieval Islamic Sectarianism* (Bradford: Arc Medieval Press, 2019).

Bakikhanov, 'Abbas Qoli Aqa, *The Heavenly Rose-Garden: A History of Shirvan and Daghestan*, trans./annot. by Willem Floor and Hasan Javadi (Washington, DC: Mage, 2009).

Bakour, Bachar, 'Regime or Revolution? The Dilemma of Syria's Religious Institutions: The Example of the Fatih Institute', *Politics, Religion & Ideology* 21, 2 (2020), 232–50.

Balabanlilar, Lisa, *Imperial Identity in the Mughal Empire: Memory and Dynastic Politics in Early Modern South and Central Asia* (London: I. B. Tauris, 2012).

Balanche, Fabrice, *La région alaouite et le pouvoir syrien* (Paris: Karthala, 2006).

Balanche, Fabrice, 'Les Alaouites: Une secte au pouvoir', *Outre-Terre* 2, 14 (2006), 73–96.

Balanche, Fabrice, 'Géographie de la révolte syrienne', *Outre-Terre* 29, 3 (2011), 437–58.

Balanche, Fabrice, '"Go to Damascus, my Son": Alawi Demographic Shifts under Ba'ath Party Rule', in: Michael Kerr and Craig Larkin (eds), *The Alawis of Syria: War, Faith and Politics in the Levant* (Oxford: Oxford University Press, 2015), 79–106.

Balci, Bayram, 'Between Sunnism and Shiism: Islam in Post-Soviet Azerbaijan', *Central Asian Survey* 23, 2 (2004), 205–17.

Balci, Bayram, 'Shi'ism in Post-Soviet Azerbaijan: Between Iranian Influence and Internal Dynamics', in: Sabrina Mervin (ed.), *The Shi'a Worlds and Iran* (London: Saqi, 2010), 167–92.

Balci, Bayram, and Altay Goyushov, 'Changing Islam in Post-Soviet Azerbaijan and its Weighting on the Sunnite-Shiite Cleavage', in: Brigitte Maréchal and Sami Zemni (eds), *The Dynamics of Sunni-Shia Relationships: Doctrine, Transnationalism, Intellectuals and the Media* (London: Hurst, 2013), 193–213.

Baldry, John, 'Imam Yahya and the Yamani Uprising of 1904–1907', *Abr-Nahrain* 18 (1978–9), 33–73.

Ballaster, Ros, *Fabulous Orients: Fictions of the East in England 1662–1785* (New York: Oxford University Press, 2005).

Baltacıoğlu-Brammer, Ayşe, 'The Formation of Kızılbaş Communities in Anatolia and Ottoman Responses, 1450s–1630s', *International Journal of Turkish Studies* 20, 1/2 (2014), 21–47.

Baltacıoğlu-Brammer, Ayşe, 'One Word, Many Implications: The Term 'Kızılbaş' in the Early Modern Ottoman Context', in: Vefa Erginbaş (ed.), *Ottoman Sunnism: New Perspectives* (Edinburgh: Edinburgh University Press, 2019), 47–70.

Baltacıoğlu-Brammer, Ayşe, '"Those Heretics Gathering Secretly…": Qizilbash Rituals and Practices in the Ottoman Empire according to Early Modern Sources', *Journal of the Ottoman and Turkish Studies Association* 6, 1 (2019), 39–60.

Baltacıoğlu-Brammer, Ayşe, 'The Emergence of the Safavids as a Mystical Order and their Subsequent Rise to Power in the Fourteenth and Fifteenth Centuries', in: Rudi Matthee (ed.), *The Safavid World* (London: Routledge, 2021).

Baltacıoğlu-Brammer, Ayşe, 'Neither Victim nor Accomplice: The Kızılbaş as Borderland Actors in the Early Modern Ottoman Realm', in: Tijana Krstić and Derin Terzioğlu (eds), *Historicizing Sunni Islam in the Ottoman Empire, c. 1450–c. 1750* (Leiden: Brill, 2021), 423–50.

Baqir, Muhammad, *Advice on the Art of Governance: Mauʿiẓah-i Jahāngīrī of Muḥammad Bāqir Najm-i Sānī: An Indo-Islamic Mirror for Princes*, trans. by Sajida S. Alvi (Albany: SUNY Press, 1989).

Bar, Shmuel, and Yair Minzili, 'The Zawahiri Letter and the Strategy of al-Qaeda', *Current Trends in Islamist Ideology* 3 (2006), 38–51.

Baram, Amatzia, 'Neo-Tribalism in Iraq: Saddam Hussein's Tribal Policies 1991–96', *International Journal of Middle East Studies* 29, 1 (1997), 1–31.

Baram, Amatzia, 'Religious Extremism and Ecumenical Tendencies in Modern Iraqi Shi'ism', in: Meir Litvak and Ofra Bengio (eds), *The Sunna and Shi'a in History: Division and Ecumenism in the Muslim Middle East* (Basingstoke: Palgrave Macmillan, 2011), 105–23.

Baram, Amatzia, *Saddam Husayn and Islam, 1968–2003: Ba'thi Iraq from Secularism to Faith* (Washington, DC: Woodrow Wilson Center Press, 2014).

Baramova, Maria, 'Non-Splendid Isolation: The Ottoman Empire and the Thirty Years' War', in: Olaf Asbach and Peter Schröder (eds), *The Ashgate Research Companion to the Thirty Years' War* (Farnham: Ashgate, 2014), 115–24.

Bar-Asher, Meir M., *Scripture and Exegesis in Early Imāmī Shiism* (Leiden: Brill, 1999).

Bar-Asher, Meir M., 'Introduction', in: Farhad Daftary and Gurdofarid Miskinzoda (eds), *The Study of Shi'i Islam: History, Theology and Law* (London: I. B. Tauris, 2014), 78–94.

Barfi, Barak, 'AQAP's Soft Power Strategy in Yemen', *CTC Sentinel* 3, 11–12 (2010), 1–5.

Barkey, Karen, *Empire of Difference: The Ottomans in Comparative Perspective* (Cambridge: Cambridge University Press, 2008).

Barnett, Richard B., *North India between Empires: Awadh, the Mughals, and the British, 1720–1801* (Berkeley: University of California Press, 1980).

Barthold, Vasilii Vladimirovitch, *Four Studies on the History of Central Asia*, Vol. 2 (Leiden: Brill, 1963).

Bashir, Shahzad, *Messianic Hopes and Mystical Visions: The Nūrbakhshīya between Medieval and Modern Islam* (Columbia, SC: University of South Carolina Press, 2003).

Bashkin, Orit, 'The Iraqi Afghanis and 'Abduhs: Debate over Reform among Shi'ite and Sunni "Ulama" in Interwar Iraq', in: Meir Hatina (ed.), *Guardians of Faith in Modern Times: 'Ulama' in the Middle East* (Leiden: Brill, 2008), 141–69.

Bashkin, Orit, *The Other Iraq: Pluralism and Culture in Hashemite Iraq* (Stanford: Stanford University Press, 2008).

Batatu, Hanna, *The Old Social Classes and the Revolutionary Movements of Iraq: A Study of Iraq's Old Landed and Commercial Classes and of its Communists, Ba'thists, and Free Officers* (Princeton: Princeton University Press, 1978).

Batatu, Hanna, 'Some Observations on the Social Roots of Syria's Ruling, Military Group and the Causes for its Dominance', *Middle East Journal* 35, 3 (1981), 331–44.

Batatu, Hanna, 'Syria's Muslim Brethren', *Middle East Report* 110 (1982), 12–20/34/36.

Batatu, Hanna, *Syria's Peasantry, the Descendants of its Lesser Rural Notables, and Their Politics* (Princeton, NJ: Princeton University Press, 1999).

Baumann, Hannes, *Citizen Hariri: Lebanon's Neoliberal Reconstruction* (London: Hurst, 2016).

Bausani, A., 'Religion in the Saljuq Period', in: J. A. Boyle (ed.), *The Cambridge History of Iran*, Vol. 5 (Cambridge: Cambridge University Press, 1968), 283–302.

Bausani, A., 'Religion under the Mongols', in: J. A. Boyle (ed.), *The Cambridge History of Iran*, Vol. 5 (Cambridge: Cambridge University Press, 1968), 538–49.

Bayat, Asef, and Bahman Baktiari, 'Revolutionary Iran and Egypt: Exporting Inspirations and Anxieties', in: Nikki R. Keddie and Rudolph P. Matthee (eds), *Iran and the Surrounding World: Interactions in Culture and Cultural Politics* (Seattle: University of Washington Press, 2002), 305–26.

Bayat, Mangol, *Mysticism and Dissent: Socioreligious Thought in Qajar Iran* (Syracuse: Syracuse University Press, 1982).

Bayhom-Daou, Tamima, 'The Imam's Knowledge and the Quran According to al-Faḍl b. Shādhān al-Nīsābūrī (d. 260 A.H./874 A.D.)', *Bulletin of the School of Oriental and African Studies* 64, 2 (2001), 188–207.

Bayhom-Daou, Tamima, *Shaykh Mufid* (Oxford: Oneworld, 2005).

Bayhom-Daou, Tamima, 'Al-Ma'mūn's Alleged Apocalyptic Beliefs: A Reconsideration of the Evidence', *Bulletin of the School of Oriental and African Studies* 71, 1 (2008), 1–24.

Bayly, Christopher A., *Rulers, Townsmen and Bazaars: North Indian Society in the Age of British Expansion, 1770–1870* (Cambridge: Cambridge University Press, 1983).

Bayly, Christopher A., 'The Pre-History of "Communalism"? Religious Conflict in India, 1700–1860', *Modern Asian Studies* 19, 2 (1985), 177–203.

Bayly, Christopher A., *Empire and Information: Intelligence Gathering and Social Communication in India, 1780–1870* (Cambridge: Cambridge University Press, 1996).

Bayly, Christopher A., *The Birth of the Modern World, 1780–1914: Global Connections and Comparisons* (Oxford: Blackwell, 2004).

Bayly, Christopher A., *Recovering Liberties: Indian Thought in the Age of Liberalism and Empire* (Cambridge: Cambridge University Press, 2012).

Bayly, Christopher A., 'Hodgson, Islam, and World History in the Modern Age', in: E. Burke III and R. J. Mankin (eds), *Islam and World History: The Ventures of Marshall Hodgson* (Chicago: University of Chicago Press, 2018), 38–54.

Bayly, Martin J., *Taming the Imperial Imagination: Colonial Knowledge, International Relations, and the Anglo-Afghan Encounter, 1808–1878* (Cambridge: Cambridge University Press, 2016).

Bayly, Susan, *Caste, Society and Politics in India from the Eighteenth Century to the Modern Age* (Cambridge: Cambridge University Press, 1999).

Bazantay, Pierre, *Les états du Levant sous mandat français: La pénétration de l'enseignement dans le sandjak autonome d'Alexandrette* (Beirut: Imprimerie catholique, 1935).

Bazzaz, Sahar, 'The Discursive Mapping of Sectarianism in Iraq: The "Sunni Triangle" in the Pages of The New York Times', in: Sahar Bazzaz, Yota Batsaki, and Dimiter Angelov (eds), *Imperial Geographies in Byzantine and Ottoman Space* (Washington, DC: Center for Hellenic Studies, 2013), 245–61.

Bdaiwi, Ahab, 'Some Remarks on the Confessional Identity of the Philosophers of Shiraz: Ṣadr al-Dīn al-Dashtakī (d. 903/1498) and his Students Mullā Shams al-Dīn al-Khafrī (942/1535) and Najm al-Dīn Maḥmūd al-Nayrīzī (948/1541)', *Ishraq* 5 (2014), 61–85.

Beben, Daniel, 'Remembering Saladin: The Crusades and the Politics of Heresy in Persian Historiography', *Journal of the Royal Asiatic Society* 28, 2 (2018), 231–53.

Behrooz, Maziar, *Rebels with a Cause: The Failure of the Left in Iran* (London: I. B. Tauris, 1999).

Bell, Gertrude L., *Review of the Civil Administration of Mesopotamia* (London: H. M. Stationery Office, 1920).

Bellamy, James A., 'Sources of Ibn Abī 'l-Dunyā's Kitāb Maqtal Amīr al-Mu'minīn 'Alī', *Journal of the American Oriental Society* 104, 1 (1984), 3–19.

Bellér-Hann, Ildikó, *Community Matters in Xinjiang, 1880–1949: Towards a Historical Anthropology of the Uyghur* (Leiden: Brill, 2008).

Bengio, Ofra, and Meir Litvak (eds), *The Sunna and Shiʿa in History: Division and Ecumenism in the Muslim Middle East* (Basingstoke: Palgrave Macmillan, 2011).

Beránek, Ondřej, and Pavel Ťupek, *The Temptation of Graves in Salafi Islam: Iconoclasm, Destruction and Idolatry* (Edinburgh: Edinburgh University Press, 2018).

Berkey, Jonathan P., *The Formation of Islam: Religion and Society in the Near East, 600–1800* (Cambridge: Cambridge University Press, 2003).

Berkey, Jonathan P., 'Mamluk Religious Policy', *Mamluk Studies Review* 13, 2 (2009), 6–22.

Bernhardsson, Magnus T., 'Gertrude Bell and the Antiquities Law of Iraq', in: Paul Collins and Charles Tripp (eds), *Gertrude Bell and Iraq: A Life and Legacy* (Oxford: Oxford University Press, 2017), 241–55.

Bernheimer, Teresa, 'The Revolt of 'Abdallāh b. Muʿāwiya, AH 127–130: A Reconsideration through the Coinage', *Bulletin of the School of Oriental and African Studies* 69, 3 (2006), 381–93.

Bernheimer, Teresa, *The 'Alids: The First Family of Islam, 750–1200* (Edinburgh: Edinburgh University Press, 2013).

Bernheimer, Teresa, 'Shared Sanctity: Some Notes on Ahl al-Bayt Shrines in the Early Ṭālibid Genealogies', *Studia Islamica* 108, 1 (2013), 1–15.

Bethencourt, Francisco, *The Inquisition: A Global History, 1478–1834* (Cambridge: Cambridge University Press, 2009).

Beydoun, Ahmad, *Identité confessionnelle et temps social chez les historiens libanais contemporains* (Beirut: Université Libanaise, 1984).

Bezhan, Faridullah, 'Nationalism, not Islam: The "Awaken Youth" Party and Pashtun Nationalism', in: Nile Green (ed.), *Afghanistan's Islam: From Conversion to the Taliban* (Oakland, CA: University of California Press, 2017), 163–85, 165, 173.

Bhagat, Ram B., 'Census and Caste Enumeration: British Legacy and Contemporary Practice in India', *Genus* 62, 2 (2006), 119–34.

Bhutto, Benazir, *Daughter of Destiny: An Autobiography* (London: Simon & Schuster, 1989).

Bianchi, Robert, *Guests of God: Pilgrimage and Politics in the Islamic World* (Oxford: Oxford University Press, 2004).

Biddulph, J., *Tribes of the Hindoo Koosh* (Calcutta: Office of the Superintendent of Government, 1880).

Biglari, Mattin, '"Captive to the Demonology of the Iranian Mobs": U.S. Foreign Policy and Perceptions of Shi'a Islam during the Iranian Revolution, 1978–79', *Diplomatic History* 40, 4 (2016), 579–605.

Bill, James A., and John Alden Williams, *Roman Catholics and Shi'i Muslims: Prayer, Passion, and Politics* (Chapel Hill, NC: University of North Carolina Press, 2002).

Binbaş, İlker Evrim, *Intellectual Networks in Timurid Iran: Sharaf al-Dīn 'Alī Yazdī and the Islamicate Republic of Letters* (Cambridge: Cambridge University Press, 2016).

Binbaş, İlker Evrim, 'The Jalayirid Hidden King and the Unbelief of Shāh Mohammad Qara Qoyunlu', *Journal of Persianate Studies* 12, 2 (2020), 206–36.

al-Bindari, Muhammad, *Al-Tashayyu' bayna Mafhum al-A'imma wa-l-Mafhum al-Farisi* (Amman: Dar 'Ammar, 1988).

Birge, John Kingsley, *The Bektashi Order of Dervishes* (London: Luzac Oriental, 1994, 1937).

Bishara, Azmi, *Sectarianism without Sects* (London: Hurst, 2021).

Black, Anthony, *The History of Islamic Political Thought: From the Prophet to the Present* (New York: Routledge, 2001).

Blackburn, Richard, *Journey to the Sublime Porte: The Arabic Memoir of a Sharifian Agent's Diplomatic Mission to the Ottoman Imperial Court in the Era of Suleyman the Magnificent: The Relevant Text from Quṭb al-Dīn al-Nahrawālī's al-Fawā'id al-Sanīyah fī al-Riḥlah al-Madanīyah wa al-Rūmīyah* (Beirut: Orient-Institut/Würzburg: Ergon, 2005).

Blair, Sheila S., 'The Epigraphic Program of the Tomb of Uljaytu at Sultaniyya: Meaning in Mongol Architecture', *Islamic Art* 2 (1987), 43–96.

Blair, Sheila S., 'An Amulet from Afsharid Iran', *Journal of the Walters Art Museum* 59 (2001), 85–102.

Blanche, Charles-Isidore, 'Études sur la Syrie: L'ansarié Kaïr-Beik', *Revue européenne* 2, 12 (1860), 384–402, 582–601.

Blanford, Nicholas, *Killing Mr Lebanon: The Assassination of Rafik Hariri and Its Impact on the Middle East* (London: I. B. Tauris, 2006).

Blanford, Nicholas, *Warriors of God: Inside Hezbollah's Thirty-Year Struggle against Israel* (New York: Random House, 2011).

Blanga, Yehuda U., 'Saudi Arabia's Motives in the Syrian Civil War', *Middle East Policy* 24, 4 (2017), 45–62.

Blank, Jonah, *Mullahs on the Mainframe: Islam and Modernity among the Daudi Bohras* (Chicago: University of Chicago Press, 2001).

Blaydes, Lisa, *State of Repression: Iraq under Saddam Hussein* (Princeton: Princeton University Press, 2018).

Blaydes, Lisa, 'Rebuilding the Ba'thist State: Party, Tribe, and Administrative Control in Authoritarian Iraq, 1991–1996', *Comparative Politics* 53, 1 (2020), 1–23.

Blichfeldt, Jan-Olaf, *Early Mahdism: Politics and Religion in the Formative Period of Islam* (Leiden: Brill, 1985).

Blumi, Isa, *Rethinking the Late Ottoman Empire: A Comparative Social and Political History of Albania and Yemen, 1878–1918* (Istanbul: Isis Press, 2003).

Boberg, Dorl, *Ägypten, Nagd und der Higaz: Eine Untersuchung zum religiös-politischen Verhältnis zwischen Ägypten und den Wahhabiten, 1923–1936, anhand von in Kairo veröffentlichten pro- und antiwahhabitischen Streitschriften und Presseberichten* (Bern: Peter Lang, 1991).

Bockholt, Philip, *Weltgeschichtsschreibung zwischen Schia und Sunna: Ḫvāndamīrs Ḥabīb as-Siyar im Handschriftenzeitalter* (Leiden: Brill, 2021).

Bogaards, Matthijs, 'Iraq's Constitution of 2005: The Case against Consociationalism "Light"', *Ethnopolitics* 20, 2 (2021), 186–202.

Boghardt, Lori Plotkin, *Kuwait amid War, Peace and Revolution: 1979–1991 and New Challenges* (Basingstoke: Palgrave Macmillan, 2006).

Bohdan, Siarhei, '"They were Going Together with the Ikhwan": The Influence of Muslim Brotherhood Thinkers on Shiʻi Islamists during the Cold War', *Middle East Journal* 74, 2 (2020), 243–62.

Böhme, Eric, *Die Außenbeziehungen des Königreiches Jerusalem im 12. Jahrhundert* (Berlin: De Gruyter, 2019).

Boivin, Michel, 'The Ismaʻili-Isna ʻAshari Divide among the Khojas: Exploring Forgotten Judicial Data from Karachi', *Journal of the Royal Asiatic Society* 24, 3 (2014), 381–96.

Bokova, Lenka, 'Le traité du 4 mars 1921 et la formation de l'État du Djebel druze sous le Mandat français', *Revue des mondes musulmans et de la Méditerranée* 48–9 (1988), 213–22.

Bokova, Lenka, 'La Révolution française dans le discours de l'insurrection syrienne contre le mandat français (1925–1927)', *Revue des mondes musulmans et de la Méditerranée* 52–3 (1989), 207–17.

Bokova, Lenka, 'Les Druzes dans la révolution syrienne de 1925 à 1927', *Guerres mondiales et conflits contemporains* 153 (1989), 91–104.

Bonacina, Giovanni, *The Wahhabis Seen through European Eyes (1772–1830): Deists and Puritans of Islam* (Leiden: Brill, 2015).

Boneschi, Paulo, 'Une fatwà du Grand Muftī de Jérusalem Muḥammad ʾAmīn al-Ḥusaynī sur les ʻAlawītes', *Revue de l'histoire des religions* 122 (1940), 42–54.

Boneschi, Paulo, 'Une fatwà du Grand Muftī de Jérusalem Muḥammad ʾAmīn al-Ḥusaynī sur les ʻAlawītes (Deuxième article)', *Revue de l'histoire des religions* 122 (1940), 134–52.

Bonnefoy, Laurent, 'Biography: Muqbil ibn Hadi al-Wadiʻi: Founder of Salafism in Yemen', in: Roel Meijer (ed.), *Global Salafism: Islam's New Religious Movement* (London: Hurst, 2009), 431–2.

Bonnefoy, Laurent, 'How Transnational is Salafism in Yemen?', in: Roel Meijer (ed.), *Global Salafism: Islam's New Religious Movement* (London: Hurst, 2009), 321–41.

Bonnefoy, Laurent, *Salafism in Yemen: Transnationalism and Religious Identity* (London: Hurst, 2011).

Bonnefoy, Laurent, 'The Shabab, Institutionalized Politics and the Islamists in the Yemeni Revolution', in: Helen Lackner (ed.), *Why Yemen Matters: A Society in Transition* (London: Saqi, 2014), 87–104.

Bonnefoy, Laurent, and Judit Kuschnitizki, 'Salafis and the "Arab Spring" in Yemen: Progressive Politicization and Resilient Quietism', *Arabian Humanities* 4 (2015).

Bori, Caterina, 'Ibn Taymiyya (14th to 17th Century): Transregional Spaces of Reading and Reception', *The Muslim World* 108 (2018), 87–123.

Bori, Caterina, and Livnat Holtzman (eds), *A Scholar in the Shadow: Essays in the Legal and Theological Thought of Ibn al-Qayyim al-Jawziyya* (Rome: Herder, 2010).

Borrut, Antoine, 'Remembering Karbalā': The Construction of an Early Islamic Site of Memory', *Jerusalem Studies in Arabic and Islam* 42 (2015), 249–82.

Bosworth, C. E., 'Sanawbari's Elegy on the Pilgrims Slain in the Carmathian Attack on Mecca (317/930): A Literary-Historical Study', *Arabica* 19, 3 (1972), 222–39.

Bosworth, C. E., 'Farrukhī's Elegy on Maḥmūd of Ghazna', *Iran* 29 (1991), 43–9.

Böttcher, Annabelle, 'L'élite feminine kurde de la Kaftariyya: Une confrérie Naqshbandi Damascène', in: Martin van Bruinessen and Joyce Blau (eds), *Islam des Kurdes* (Paris: INALCO, 1999), 125–39.

Böttcher, Annabelle, *Official Sunni and Shi'i Islam in Syria* (Florence: European University Institute, 2002).

Boucek, Christopher, *War in Saada: From Local Insurrection to National Challenge* (Washington, DC: Carnegie Endowment for International Peace, 2010).

Bou-Nacklie, N. E., 'Les Troupes Spéciales: Religious and Ethnic Recruitment, 1916–46', *International Journal of Middle East Studies* 25, 4 (1993), 645–60.

Boyce, Mary, 'Bībī Shahrbānū and the Lady of Pārs', *Bulletin of the School of Oriental and African Studies* 30, 1 (1967), 30–44.

Brandt, Marieke, 'The Irregulars of the Sa'ada War: "Colonel Sheikhs" and "Tribal Militias": in Yemen's Huthi Conflict (2004–2010)', in: Helen Lackner (ed.), *Why Yemen Matters: A Society in Transition* (London: Saqi, 2014), 105–22.

Brandt, Marieke, *Tribes and Politics in Yemen: A History of the Houthi Conflict* (London: Hurst, 2017).

Braude, Benjamin, 'Foundation Myths of the Millet System', in: Benjamin Braude and Bernard Lewis (eds), *Christians and Jews in the Ottoman Empire: The Functioning of a Plural Society* (New York: Holmes & Meier, 1982), 69–88.

Braudel, Fernand, *The Mediterranean and the Mediterranean World in the Age of Philip II*, 2 Vols (New York: Harper & Row, 1973).

Braudel, Fernand, *The Mediterranean in the Ancient World* (London: Allen Lane, 2001).

Braudel, Fernand, *Memory and the Mediterranean* (New York: Knopf, 2001).

Brennan, Lance, 'A Case of Attempted Segmental Modernization: Rampur State, 1930–1939', *Comparative Studies in Society and History* 23, 3 (1981), 350–81.

Brigaglia, Andrea, 'A Contribution to the History of the Wahhabi Da'wa in West Africa: The Career and the Murder of Shaykh Ja'far Mahmoud Adam (Daura, ca. 1961/1962–Kano 2007)', *Islamic Africa* 3, 1 (2012), 1–23.

Brinkmann, Stefanie, 'Ein Mangel an Quellen oder fehlendes Interesse? Zum späten Einstieg der deutschen Schia-Forschung', *Orient* 50, 4 (2009), 25–43.

Broadbridge, Anne F., 'Apostasy Trials in Eighth/Fourteenth Century Egypt and Syria: A Case Study', in: J. Pfeiffer and S. A. Quinn (eds), *History and Historiography of Post-Mongol Central Asia and the Middle East: Studies in Honor of John E. Woods* (Wiesbaden: Harrassowitz, 2006), 363–82.

Broadbridge, Anne F., *Kingship and Ideology in the Islamic and Mongol Worlds* (Cambridge: Cambridge University Press, 2008).

Brodkin, E. I., 'The Struggle for Succession: Rebels and Loyalists in the Indian Mutiny of 1857', *Modern Asian Studies* 6, 3 (1972), 277–90.

Brondz, Ilia, and Tahmina Aslanova, 'Sunni-Shia Issue in Azerbaijan', *Voice of the Publisher* 5, 1 (2019), 1–11.

Bronson, Rachel, *Thicker than Oil: America's Uneasy Partnership with Saudi Arabia* (Oxford: Oxford University Press, 2006).

Brooke, Steven, 'Sectarianism and Social Conformity: Evidence from Egypt', *Political Research Quarterly* 70, 4 (2017), 848–60.

Browers, Michaelle, 'Official Islam and the Limits of Communicative Action: The Paradox of the Amman Message', *Third World Quarterly* 32, 5 (2011), 943–58.

Brown, Jonathan A. C., *The Canonization of al-Bukhārī and Muslim: The Formation and Function of the Sunnī Ḥadīth Canon* (Leiden: Brill, 2007).

Brown, Jonathan A. C., *Hadith: Muhammad's Legacy in the Medieval and Modern World*, 2nd ed. (Oxford: Oneworld, 2017).

Browne, E. G., *A Literary History of Persia*, Vol. 4 (Cambridge: Cambridge University Press, 1928).

Brunner, Rainer, *Die Schia und die Koranfälschung* (Würzburg: Ergon, 2001).

Brunner, Rainer, *Islamic Ecumenism in the 20th Century: The Azhar and Shiism between Rapprochement and Restraint* (Leiden: Brill, 2004).

Brunner, Rainer, 'La question de la falsification du Coran dans l'exégèse chiite duodécimaine', *Arabica* 52, 1 (2005), 1–42.

Brunner, Rainer, '"Then I was Guided": Some Remarks on Inner-Islamic Conversions in the 20th and 21st Centuries', *Orient* 50, 4 (2009), 6–15.

Brunner, Rainer, 'Interesting Times: Egypt and Shiism at the Beginning of the Twenty-First Century', in: Meir Litvak and Ofra Bengio (eds), *The Sunna and Shi'a in History: Division and Ecumenism in the Muslim Middle East* (Basingstoke: Palgrave Macmillan, 2011), 223–41.

Brunner, Rainer, 'Sunnis and Shiites in Modern Islam: Politics, Rapprochement and the Role of Al-Azhar', in: Brigitte Maréchal and Sami Zemni (eds), *The Dynamics of Sunni–Shia Relationships: Doctrine, Transnationalism, Intellectuals and the Media* (London: Hurst, 2013), 25–38.

Brunner, Rainer, 'Die Schia', in: Rainer Brunner (ed.), *Islam: Einheit und Vielfalt einer Weltreligion* (Stuttgart: W. Kohlhammer, 2016), 310–37.

Brunner, Rainer, and Werner Ende, 'Preface', in: Rainer Brunner and Werner Ende (eds), *The Twelver Shia in Modern Times: Religious Culture & Political History* (Leiden: Brill, 2001), ix–xx.

Brunschvig, Robert, 'Les usul al-fiqh imamites a leur stade ancien (Xe et XIe siècles)', in: Centre de Recherches d'Histoire des Religions Strasbourg (ed.), *Le shī'isme imâmite: Colloque de Strasbourg (6–9 mai 1968)* (Paris: Presses Universitaires de France, 1970), 201–13.

Bsheer, Rosie, *Archive Wars: The Politics of History in Saudi Arabia* (Palo Alto, CA: Stanford University Press, 2020).

Buchta, Wilfried, *Die iranische Schia und die islamische Einheit 1979–1996* (Hamburg: Deutsches Orient-Institut, 1997).

Buchta, Wilfried, *Schiiten* (Munich: Diederichs, 2004).

Buehler, Arthur F., 'The Naqshbandiyya in Tīmūrid India: The Central Asian Legacy', *Journal of Islamic Studies* 7, 2 (1996), 208–28.

Buehler, Arthur F., 'Overlapping Currents in Early Islam: The Sufi Shaykh and Shī'ī Imam', *Journal of the History of Sufism* 3 (2001), 1–20.

Buehler, Arthur F., 'Aḥmad Sirhindī: A 21st-Century Update', *Der Islam* 86, 1 (2011), 122–41.

Bulliet, Richard, *The Patricians of Nishapur: A Study in Medieval Islamic Social History* (Cambridge, MA: Harvard University Press, 1972).

Bulliet, Richard, 'The Political-Religious History of Nishapur in the Eleventh Century', in: D. S. Richards (ed.), *Islamic Civilisation 950–1150* (Oxford: Cassirer, 1973), 71–91.

Bulloch, John, and Harvey Morris, *The Gulf War: Its Origins, History and Consequences* (London: Methuen London, 1989).

Bulmuş, Birsen, *Plague, Quarantines and Geopolitics in the Ottoman Empire* (Edinburgh: Edinburgh University Press, 2012).

Bunbury, N. L. St Pierre, *A Brief History of the Hazara Pioneers (Indian Army): 1904 to 1933* (n.p./n.d., possibly London: 1949).

Bunzel, Cole, 'The Caliphate's Scholar-in-Arms', *Jihadica*, 9 July 2014.

Bunzel, Cole, 'Bin'ali Leaks: Revelations of the Silent Mufti', *Jihadica*, 15 June 2015.

Bunzel, Cole, *The Kingdom and the Caliphate: Duel of the Islamic States* (Washington, DC: Carnegie Endowment for International Peace, 2016).

Bunzel, Cole, 'Ideological Infighting in the Islamic State', *Perspectives on Terrorism* 13, 1 (2019), 12–21.

Burak, Guy, 'Faith, Law and Empire in the Ottoman "Age of Confessionalization" (Fifteenth to Seventeenth Centuries): The Case of "Renewal of Faith"', *Mediterranean Historical Review* 28, 1 (2013), 1–23.

Burak, Guy, *The Second Formation of Islamic Law: The Hanafi School in the Early Modern Ottoman Empire* (Cambridge: Cambridge University Press, 2015).

Burke, Edmund, 'A Comparative View of French Native Policy in Morocco and Syria, 1912–1925', *Middle Eastern Studies* 9, 2 (1973), 175–86.

Burke, Edmund, 'Islamic History as World History: Marshall Hodgson, "The Venture of Islam"', *International Journal of Middle East Studies* 10, 2 (1979), 241–64.

Burke, Edmund, *The Ethnographic State: France and the Invention of Moroccan Islam* (Oakland, CA: University of California Press, 2014).

Burke, Edmund, and Robert J. Mankin, 'The Ventures of Marshall G. S. Hodgson', in: Edmund Burke and Robert J. Mankin (eds), *Islam and World History: The Ventures of Marshall Hodgson* (Chicago: University of Chicago Press, 2018), 1–15.

Burn, R., *Census of India, 1901*, Vol. 16 (Allahabad: North-Western Provinces and Oudh Government Press, 1902).

Burns, Ross, *Aleppo: A History* (Abingdon: Routledge, 2017).

Burton, Richard Francis, *Personal Narrative of a Pilgrimage to al-Madinah and Meccah*, 2 Vols (London: Tylston and Edwards, 1893).

Busse, Heribert, *Chalif und Großkönig: Die Buyiden im Irak (945–1055)* (Beirut/ Wiesbaden: Franz Steiner, 1969).

al-Bustani, Butrus, *The Clarion of Syria: A Patriot's Call against the Civil War of 1860*, trans. by Jens Hanssen and Hicham Safieddine (Oakland: University of California Press, 2019).

Buzan, Barry, Ole Wæver, and Jaap de Wilde, *Security: A New Framework for Analysis* (Boulder, CO: Lynne Rienner, 1998).

Buzpinar, S. Tufan, 'Abdulhamid II and Sayyid Fadl Pasha of Hadramawt: An Arab Dignitary's Ambitions (1876–1900)', *Osmanlı Araştırmaları/Journal of Ottoman Studies* 13 (1993), 227–39.

Cagaptay, Soner, *Islam, Secularism and Nationalism in Modern Turkey: Who is a Turk?* (London: Routledge, 2006).

Cahen, Claude, 'Une chronique chiite au temps des Croisades', *Comptes rendus des séances de l'Académie des Inscriptions et Belles-Lettres* 79, 3 (1935), 258–69.

Cahen, Claude, 'Le problème du shī'isme dans l'Asie mineure turque préottomane', in: Centre de Recherches d'Histoire des Religions Strasbourg (ed.), *Le shî'isme imâmite: Colloque de Strasbourg (6–9 mai 1968)* (Paris: Presses Universitaires de France, 1970), 115–29.

Calabrese, John, *Revolutionary Horizons: Regional Foreign Policy in Post-Khomeini Iran* (New York: St Martin's Press, 1994).

Calabrese, Erminia Chiara, *Militer au Hezbollah: Ethnographie d'un engagement dans la banlieue sud de Beyrouth* (Paris: Karthala/IFPO, 2016).

Calculli, Marina, 'Hezbollah's Lebanese Strategy in the Syrian Conflict', in: Ioannis Galariotis and Kostas Ifantis (eds), *The Syrian Imbroglio: International and Regional Strategies* (Florence: European University Institute, 2017), 36–44.

Çalışır, M. Fatih, 'Decline of a "Myth": Perspectives on the Ottoman "Decline"', *The History School* 9 (2011), 37–60.

Calmard, Jean, 'Le chiisme imamite en Iran à l'époque seldjoukide d'après le Kitab al-Naqd', *Le monde Iranien et l'Islam: Sociétés et cultures* 1 (1971), 43–66.

Calmard, Jean, 'Muharram Ceremonies and Diplomacy: A Preliminary Study', in: Edmund Bosworth and Carole Hillenbrand (eds), *Qajar Iran: Political, Social and Cultural Change, 1800–1925* (Edinburgh: Edinburgh University Press, 1983), 213–28.

Calmard, Jean, 'Shi'i Rituals and Power II. The Consolidation of Safavid Shi'ism: Folklore and Popular Religion', in: Charles Melville (ed.), *Safavid Persia: The History and Politics of an Islamic Society* (London: I. B. Tauris, 1996), 139–90.

Calmard, Jean, 'Le chiisme imamite sous les Ilkhans', in: Denise Aigle (ed.), *L'Iran face à la domination mongole* (Tehran: Institut Français de Recherche en Iran, 1997), 261–92.

Cammett, Melani, *Compassionate Communalism: Welfare and Sectarianism in Lebanon* (Ithaca: Cornell University Press, 2014).

Campanini, Massimo, 'In Defence of Sunnism: Al-Ghazālī and the Seljuqs', in: Christian Lange and Songül Mecit (eds), *The Seljuqs: Politics, Society and Culture* (Edinburgh: Edinburgh University Press, 2011), 228–39.

Canbakal, Hülya, 'An Exercise in Denominational Geography in Search of Ottoman Alevis', *Turkish Studies* 6, 2 (2005), 253–71.

Canbakal, Hülya, 'The Ottoman State and Descendants of the Prophet in Anatolia and the Balkans (c. 1500–1700)', *Journal of the Economic and Social History of the Orient* 52, 3 (2009), 542–78.

Canfield, Robert L., *Faction and Conversion in a Plural Society: Religious Alignments in the Hindu Kush* (Ann Arbor: University of Michigan, 1973).

Carapico, Sheila, 'Yemen between Revolution and Counter-Terrorism', in: Helen Lackner (ed.), *Why Yemen Matters: A Society in Transition* (London: Saqi, 2014), 29–49.

Carroll, Lucy, 'Application of the Islamic Law of Succession: Was the Propositus a Sunnī or a Shīʿī?', *Islamic Law and Society* 2, 1 (1995), 24–42.

Casale, Giancarlo, 'Imperial Smackdown: The Portuguese between Imamate and Caliphate in the Persian Gulf', in: Rudi Matthee and Jorge Flores (eds), *Portugal, the Persian Gulf, and Safavid Persia* (Leuven: Peeters, 2011), 177–90.

Casale, Giancarlo, 'The Islamic Empires of the Early Modern World', in: J. Bentley, S. Subrahmanyam, and M. Wiesner-Hanks (eds), *The Cambridge World History*, Vol. 6 (Cambridge: Cambridge University Press, 2015), 323–44.

Caskel, Werner, 'Eine "unbekannte" Dynastie in Arabien', *Oriens* 2, 1 (1949), 66–71.

Catafago, J., 'Die drei Messen der Nossairier', *Zeitschrift der Deutschen Morgenländischen Gesellschaft* 2, 3 (1848), 388–94.

Çetinsaya, Gökhan, 'Rethinking Nationalism and Islam: Some Preliminary Notes on the Roots of "Turkish-Islamic Synthesis" in Modern Turkish Political Thought', *The Muslim World* 89, 3–4 (1999), 350–76.

Çetinsaya, Gökhan, 'The Caliph and Mujtahids: Ottoman Policy towards the Shiite Community of Iraq in the Late Nineteenth Century', *Middle Eastern Studies* 41, 4 (2005), 561–74.

Çetinsaya, Gökhan, *Ottoman Administration of Iraq, 1890–1908* (London: Routledge, 2006).

Çetinsaya, Gökhan, 'The Ottoman View of the Shiite Community of Iraq in the Late Nineteenth Century', in: Alessandro Monsutti, Silvia Naef, and Farian Sabahi (eds), *The Other Shiites: From the Mediterranean to Central Asia* (New York: Peter Lang, 2008), 19–40.

Chaib, Kinda, 'Hezbollah Seen through its Images: The Representation of the Martyr', in: Sabrina Mervin (ed.), *The Shi'a Worlds and Iran* (London: Saqi, 2010), 115–35.

Chalabi, Tamara, *The Shi'is of Jabal ʿAmil and the New Lebanon: Community and Nation-State, 1918–1943* (New York: Palgrave Macmillan, 2006).

Chamberlain, Michael, *Knowledge and Social Practice in Medieval Damascus, 1190–1350* (Cambridge: Cambridge University Press, 1994).

Chatterjee, Nandini, 'Reflections on Religious Difference and Permissive Inclusion in Mughal Law', *Journal of Law and Religion* 29, 3 (2014), 396–415.

Chatterjee, Nandini, *Negotiating Mughal Law: A Family of Landlords across Three Indian Empires* (Cambridge: Cambridge University Press, 2020).

Chehab, Hafez, 'Reconstructing the Medici Portrait of Fakhr al-Din al-Ma'ani', *Muqarnas* 11 (1994), 117–24.

Chehabi, Houchang E., *Iranian Politics and Religious Modernism: The Liberation Movement of Iran under the Shah and Khomeini* (London: Tauris, 1990).

Chehabi, Houchang E., 'The Anti-Shah Opposition and Lebanon', in: H. E. Chehabi, *Distant Relations: Iran and Lebanon in the Last 500 Years* (London: I. B. Tauris, 2006), 180–98.

Chehabi, Houchang E., *Distant Relations: Iran and Lebanon in the Last 500 Years* (London: I. B. Tauris, 2006).

Chehabi, Houchang E., 'Iran and Iraq: Intersocietal Linkages and Secular Nationalisms', in: Abbas Amanat and Farzin Vejdani (eds), *Iran Facing Others: Identity Boundaries in a Historical Perspective* (London: Palgrave, 2012), 193–218.

Chehabi, Houchang E., 'The Islamic Republic of Iran and the Muslim World', in: *Iranian Influences in Oecumenic Cultural Exchanges* (Seoul: Korean Association of Central Asian Studies, 2013), 77–84.

Chehabi, Houchang E., 'South Africa and Iran in the Apartheid Era', *Journal of Southern African Studies* 42, 4 (2016), 687–709.

Chehabi, Houchang E., and Majid Tafreshi, 'Musa Sadr and Iran', in: H. E. Chehabi, *Distant Relations: Iran and Lebanon in the Last 500 Years* (London: I. B. Tauris, 2006), 137–61.

Chelkowski, Peter J. (ed.), *Ta'ziyeh: Ritual and Drama in Iran* (New York: NYU Press, 1979).

Chevée, Adélie, 'From Suriyya al-Asad to Souriatna: Civic Nationalism in the Syrian Revolutionary Press', *Nations and Nationalism* 28, 1 (2022), 154–76.

Chiovenda, Melissa Kerr, 'Hazara Civil Society Activists and Local, National, and International Political Institutions', in: M. Nazif Shahrani (ed.), *Modern Afghanistan: The Impact of 40 Years of War* (Bloomington: Indiana University Press, 2018), 251–70.

Choi, Seung-Whan, and Benjamin Acosta, 'Sunni Suicide Attacks and Sectarian Violence', *Terrorism and Political Violence* 32, 7 (2020), 1371–90.

Christmann, Andreas, 'Islamic Scholar and Religious Leader: A Portrait of Shaykh Muhammad Sa'id Ramadan al-Būti', *Islam and Christian-Muslim Relations* 9, 2 (1998), 149–69.

Chubin, Shahram, and Charles Tripp, *Iran and Iraq at War* (London: I. B. Tauris, 1988).

Cilardo, Agostino, *The Early History of Ismaili Jurisprudence: Law under the Fatimids* (London: I. B. Tauris/Institute of Ismaili Studies, 2012).

Cipa, H. Erdem, *The Making of Selim: Succession, Legitimacy, and Memory in the Early Modern Ottoman World* (Bloomington: Indiana University Press, 2017).

Clancy-Smith, Julia, 'Islam and the French Empire in North Africa', in: David Motadel (ed.), *Islam and the European Empires* (Oxford: Oxford University Press, 2014), 90–111.

Clark, Janine A., and Bassel F. Salloukh, 'Elite Strategies, Civil Society, and Sectarian Identities in Postwar Lebanon', *International Journal of Middle East Studies* 45, 4 (2013), 731–49.

Clarke, Morgan, and Mirjam Künkler, 'De-Centring Shi'i Islam', *British Journal of Middle Eastern Studies* 45, 1 (2018), 1–17.

Clayer, Nathalie, *Mystiques, état et société: Les Halvetis dans l'aire balkanique de la fin du XVe siècle à nos jours* (Leiden: Brill, 1994).

Clayer, Nathalie, 'The Bektashi Institutions in Southeastern Europe: Alternative Muslim Official Structures and their Limits', *Die Welt des Islams* 52, 2 (2012), 183–203.

Clayer, Nathalie, 'The Pilgrimage to Mount Tomor in Albania: A Changing Sacred Place in a Changing Society', in: Tsypylma Darieva, Thede Kahl, and Svetoslava Toncheva (eds), *Sakralität und Mobilität im Kaukasus und in Südosteuropa* (Vienna: Verlag der Österreichischen Akademie der Wissenschaften, 2017), 125–42.

Clemow, F. G., 'The Shiah Pilgrimage and the Sanitary Defences of Mesopotamia and the Turco-Persian Frontier', *The Lancet* 188, 4853 (1916), 441–3.

Cleveland, William L., *Islam against the West: Shakib Arslan and the Campaign for Islamic Nationalism* (Austin: University of Texas Press, 1985).

Cleveland, William L., *The Making of an Arab Nationalist: Ottomanism and Arabism in the Life and Thought of Sati' al-Husri* (Princeton: Princeton University Press, 1971).

Cleveland, William L., 'The Role of Islam as Political Ideology in the First World War', in: Edward Ingram (ed.), *National and International Politics in the Middle East* (London: Frank Cass, 1986), 84–101.

Cockburn, Patrick, *Muqtada al-Sadr and the Battle for the Future of Iraq* (New York: Scribner, 2008).

Cockburn, Patrick, *The Rise of Islamic State: ISIS and the New Sunni Revolution* (London: Verso, 2015).

Cole, Juan R. I., 'Rashid Rida on the Bahá'í Faith: A Utilitarian Theory of the Spread of Religions', *Arab Studies Quarterly* 5, 3 (1983), 276–91.

Cole, Juan R. I., 'Shi'i Clerics in Iraq and Iran, 1722–1780: The Akhbari-Usuli Conflict Reconsidered', *Iranian Studies* 18, 1 (1985), 3–34.

Cole, Juan R. I., '"Indian Money" and the Shi'i Shrine Cities of Iraq, 1786–1850', *Middle Eastern Studies* 22, 4 (1986), 461–80.

Cole, Juan R. I., 'Rival Empires of Trade and Imami Shiism in Eastern Arabia, 1300–1800', *International Journal of Middle East Studies* 19, 2 (1987), 177–203.

Cole, Juan R. I., *Roots of North Indian Shi'ism in Iran and Iraq: Religion and State in Awadh, 1722–1859* (Berkeley: University of California Press, 1988).

Cole, Juan R. I., 'Casting Away the Self: The Mysticism of Shaykh Ahmad al-Ahsa'i', in: Rainer Brunner and Werner Ende (eds), *The Twelver Shia in Modern Times: Religious Culture & Political History* (Leiden: Brill, 2001), 25–37.

Cole, Juan R. I., 'Printing and Urban Islam in the Mediterranean World, 1890-1920', in: Leila Tarazi Fawaz and C. A. Bayly (eds), *Modernity and Culture: From the Mediterranean to the Indian Ocean* (New York: Columbia University Press, 2002), 344–64.

Cole, Juan R. I., 'Shaikh al-Ra'is and Sultan Abdülhamid II: The Iranian Dimension of Pan-Islam', in: Israel Gershoni, Hakan Erdem, and Ursula Wokoeck (eds), *Histories of the Modern Middle East: New Directions* (Boulder, CO: Lynne Rienner, 2002), 167–85.

Cole, Juan R. I., 'The Iraqi Shiites: On the History of America's Would-be Allies', *Boston Review*, October/November 2003.

Cole, Juan R. I., 'A "Shiite Crescent"? The Regional Impact of the Iraq War', *Current History* 105, 687 (2006), 20–6.

Cole, Juan R. I., *Napoleon's Egypt: Invading the Middle East* (New York: Palgrave Macmillan, 2007).

Cole, Juan R. I., 'Struggles over Personal Status and Family Law in Post-Baathist Iraq', in: Kenneth M. Cuno and Manisha Desai (eds), *Family, Gender, and Law in a Globalizing Middle East and South Asia* (Syracuse: Syracuse University Press, 2009), 105–25.

Cole, Juan R. I., *Sacred Space and Holy War: The Politics, Culture and History of Shi'ite Islam* (London: I. B. Tauris, 2002).

Cole, Juan R. I., 'The United States and Shi'ite Religious Factions in Post-Ba'thist Iraq', *Middle East Journal* 57, 4 (2003), 543–66.

Cole, Juan R. I., *The Ayatollahs and Democracy in Contemporary Iraq* (Amsterdam: Amsterdam University Press, 2006).

Cole, Juan R. I., 'British Policy toward the Iraqi Shiites during World War I', *Journal of Contemporary Iraq & the Arab World* 15, 3 (2021), 285–304.

Cole, Juan R. I., and Moojan Momen, 'Mafia, Mob and Shiism in Iraq: The Rebellion of Ottoman Karbala 1824–1843', *Past & Present* 112, 1 (1986), 112–43.

Coll, Steve, *Ghost Wars: The Secret History of the CIA, Afghanistan and Bin Laden, from the Soviet Invasion to September 10, 2001* (New York: Penguin, 2004).

Collins, Paul, and Charles Tripp, 'Introduction', in: Paul Collins and Charles Tripp (eds), *Gertrude Bell and Iraq: A Life and Legacy* (Oxford: Oxford University Press, 2017), 1–21.

Commins, David, *Islamic Reform: Politics and Social Change in Late Ottoman Syria* (Oxford: Oxford University Press, 1990).

Commins, David, *The Wahhabi Mission and Saudi Arabia* (London: I. B. Tauris, 2006).

Commins, David, *Islam in Saudi Arabia* (London: I. B. Tauris, 2015).

Conduit, Dara, *The Muslim Brotherhood in Syria* (New York: Cambridge University Press, 2019).

Conermann, Stephan, 'Carsten Niebuhr und das orientalistische Potential des Aufklärungsdiskurses – oder: Ist das Sammeln von Daten unverdächtig?', in: J. Wiesehöfer and S. Conermann (eds), *Carsten Niebuhr (1733–1815) und seine Zeit: Beiträge eines interdisziplinären Symposiums vom 7.-10. Oktober 1999 in Eutin* (Stuttgart: Franz Steiner, 2002), 403–32.

Cook, Michael, 'Max Weber und islamische Sekten', in: Wolfgang Schluchter (ed.), *Max Webers Sicht des Islams: Interpretation und Kritik* (Frankfurt am Main: Suhrkamp, 1987), 334–41.

Cook, Michael, 'The Historians of Pre-Wahhābī Najd', *Studia Islamica* 76 (1992), 163–76.

Cook, Michael, 'On the Origins of Wahhābism', *Journal of the Royal Asiatic Society* 2, 2 (1992), 191–202.

Cook, Michael, *Commanding Right and Forbidding Wrong in Islamic Thought* (Cambridge: Cambridge University Press, 2000).

Cook, Michael, 'Written and Oral Aspects of an Early Wahhābī Epistle', *Bulletin of the School of Oriental and African Studies* 78, 1 (2015), 161–78.

Cooley, John K., 'Iran, the Palestinians, and the Gulf', *Foreign Affairs* 57, 5 (1979), 1017–34.

Cooper, Andrew Scott, *The Fall of Heaven: The Pahlavis and the Final Days of Imperial Iran* (New York: Henry Holt, 2016).

Cooperson, Michael, *Classical Arabic Biography: The Heirs of the Prophets in the Age of al-Ma'mūn* (Cambridge: Cambridge University Press, 2000).

Corbin, Henry, *En Islam Iranien: Aspects spirituels et philiosophiques*, 4 Vols (Paris: Gallimard, 1971).

Corboz, Elvire, 'The al-Khoei Foundation and the Transnational Institutionalisation of Ayatollah al-Khu'i's Marja'iyya', in: Lloyd Ridgeon (ed.), *Shi'i Islam and Identity: Religion, Politics and Change in the Global Muslim Community* (London: I. B. Tauris, 2012), 93–112.

Corboz, Elvire, *Guardians of Shi'ism: Sacred Authority and Transnational Family Networks* (Edinburgh: Edinburgh University Press, 2015).

Corboz, Elvire, 'Khomeini in Najaf: The Religious and Political Leadership of an Exiled Ayatollah', *Die Welt des Islams* 55, 2 (2015), 221–48.

Cornell, Svante E., and M. K. Kaya, 'Political Islam in Turkey and the Naqshbandi-Khalidi Order', *Current Trends in Islamist Ideology* 19 (2015), 39–62.

Corrado, Monica, *Mit Tradition in die Zukunft: Der taǧdīd-Diskurs in der Azhar und ihrem Umfeld* (Würzburg: Ergon, 2011).

Crawford, Michael, *Ibn 'Abd al-Wahhab* (London: Oneworld, 2014).

Crawford, Michael, 'Religion and Religious Movements in the Gulf, 1700–1971', in: John Peterson (ed.), *The Emergence of the Gulf States: Studies in Modern History* (London: Bloomsbury, 2016), 43–84.

Crawford, Michael, and William Henry Dyke Facey, "Abd Allāh al-Sa'ūd and Muḥammad 'Alī Pasha: The Theatre of Victory, the Prophet's Treasures, and the Visiting Whig, Cairo 1818', *Journal of Arabian Studies* 7, 1 (2017), 44–62.

Crews, Robert D., *For Prophet and Tsar: Islam and Empire in Russia and Central Asia* (Cambridge, MA: Harvard University Press, 2006).

Crone, Patricia, *Medieval Islamic Political Thought* (Edinburgh: Edinburgh University Press, 2004).

Crone, Patricia, 'Mawālī and the Prophet's Family: An Early Shī'ite View', in: Monique Bernards and John Abdallah Nawas (eds), *Patronate and Patronage in Early and Classical Islam* (Leiden: Brill, 2005), 167–94.

Crone, Patricia, *From Arabian Tribes to Islamic Empire: Army, State and Society in the Near East c.600–850* (Aldershot: Ashgate, 2008).

Crone, Patricia, and Michael Cook, *Hagarism: The Making of the Islamic World* (Cambridge: Cambridge University Press, 1977).

Crone, Patricia, and Martin Hinds, *God's Caliph: Religious Authority in the First Centuries of Islam* (Cambridge: Cambridge University Press, 1986).

Cronin, Stephanie, 'Conscription and Popular Resistance in Iran, 1925–1941', in: Erik J. Zürcher (ed.), *Arming the State: Military Conscription in the Middle East and Central Asia, 1775–1925* (London: I. B. Tauris, 1999), 145–68.

Cronin, Stephanie, 'The Left in Iran: Illusion and Disillusion', *Middle Eastern Studies* 36, 3 (2000), 231–43.

Cronin, Stephanie (ed.), *Reformers and Revolutionaries in Modern Iran: New Perspectives on the Iranian Left* (London: Routledge, 2004).

Cronin, Stephanie, 'Building a New Army: Military Reform in Qajar Iran', in: Roxane Farmanfarmaian (ed.), *War and Peace in Qajar Persia: Implications Past and Present* (London: Routledge, 2008), 47–87.

Cummings, Sally N., and Raymond Hinnebusch (eds), *Sovereignty after Empire: Comparing the Middle East and Central Asia* (Edinburgh: Edinburgh University Press, 2011).

Cunha, Joao Teles e, 'The Eye of the Beholder: The Creation of a Portuguese Discourse on Safavid Iran', in: Rudi Matthee and Jorge Flores (eds), *Portugal, the Persian Gulf and Safavid Persia* (Leuven: Peeters, 2011), 11–50.

Currie, P. M., *The Shrine and Cult of Muʿīn al-Dīn Chishtī of Ajmer* (Oxford: Oxford University Press, 1989).

Curry, John, *The Transformation of Muslim Mystical Thought in the Ottoman Empire: The Rise of the Halveti Order, 1350–1650* (Edinburgh: Edinburgh University Press, 2010).

Curry, John, 'Some Reflections on the Fluidity of Orthodoxy and Heterodoxy in an Ottoman Sunni Context', in: Vefa Erginbaş (ed.), *Ottoman Sunnism: New Perspectives* (Edinburgh: Edinburgh University Press, 2019), 193–210.

Dabashi, Hamid, 'Philosopher/Vizier Khwāja Naṣīr al-Dīn al-Ṭūsī and the Ismaʿilis', in: Farhad Daftary (ed.), *Mediaeval Ismaʿili History and Thought* (Cambridge: Cambridge University Press, 1996), 231–45.

Dabashi, Hamid, *Shiʿism: A Religion of Protest* (Cambridge, MA: Belknap Press, 2011).

Dabashi, Hamid, *Theology of Discontent: The Ideological Foundation of the Islamic Revolution in Iran*, 2nd ed. (London: Routledge, 2017).

Daftary, Farhad, 'Professor Asaf A. A. Fyzee (1899–1981)', *Arabica* 31, 3 (1984), 327–30.

Daftary, Farhad, 'Naṣir al-Dīn al-Ṭūsī and the Ismailis of the Alamūt Period', in: N. Pourjavady and Z. Vesel (eds), *Naṣir al-Dīn Ṭūsi: Philosophe et savant du XIIIe siècle* (Tehran: Institut Français de Recherche en Iran, 2000), 59–67.

Daftary, Farhad, 'Husayni, Shah Tahir b. Radi al-Din (d. 956 AH/1549 CE)', *Institute of Ismaili Studies* (2006), https://iis.ac.uk/encyclopaedia-articles/husayni-shah-tahir-b-radi-al-din-d-956-ah-1549-ce.

Daftary, Farhad, 'The "Order of the Assassins": J. von Hammer and the Orientalist Misrepresentations of the Nizari Ismailis', *Iranian Studies* 39, 1 (2006), 71–81.

Daftary, Farhad, *The Ismailis: Their History and Doctrines*, 2nd ed. (Cambridge: Cambridge University Press, 2007).

Daftary, Farhad, 'Religious Identity, Dissimulation and Assimilation: The Ismaili Experience', in: Yasir Suleiman (ed.), *Living Islamic History: Studies in Honour of Professor Carole Hillenbrand* (Edinburgh: Edinburgh University Press, 2010), 47–61.

Daftary, Farhad, *Ismaili History and Intellectual Traditions* (Abingdon: Routledge, 2018).

d'Aguilers, Raimond, *Le 'Liber' de Raymond d'Aguilers*, ed. by J. H. Hill and L. L. Hill (Paris: P. Geuthner, 1969).

Daher, Aurélie, 'In the Wake of the Islamic State Threat: Repercussions on Sunni-Shiʿi Competition in Lebanon', *Journal of Shiʿa Islamic Studies* 8, 2 (2015), 209–35.

Daher, Aurélie, *Hezbollah: Mobilisation and Power* (London: Hurst, 2019).

Daher, Massoud, 'The Lebanese Leadership at the Beginning of the Ottoman Period: A Case Study of the Ma'n Family', in: Peter Sluglett and Stefan Weber (eds), *Syria and Bilad al-Sham under Ottoman Rule: Essays in Honour of Abdul Karim Rafeq* (Leiden: Brill, 2010), 323–45.

Dahlan, Ahmad b. Zayni b. Ahmad, *Al-Durar al-Saniyya fi l-Radd 'ala-l-Wahhabiyya* (Cairo: n.p., 1299h/1882).

Dahlan, Malik R., *The Hijaz: The First Islamic State* (London: Hurst, 2018).

Dakake, Maria, 'Hiding in Plain Sight: The Practical and Doctrinal Significance of Secrecy in Shi'ite Islam', *Journal of the American Academy of Religion* 74, 2 (2006), 324–55.

Dakake, Maria, *The Charismatic Community: Shi'ite Identity in Early Islam* (Albany: SUNY Press, 2007).

al-Dakhil, Khalid, *Al-Wahhabiyya: Bayn al-Shirk wa Tasaddu'a al-Qabila* (Beirut: al-Shabaka al-'Arabiyya li-l-Abhath wa-l-Nashr, 2013).

Dakhli, Leyla, *Une génération d'intellectuels arabes: Syrie et Liban, 1908–1940* (Paris: Karthala/IISMM, 2009).

Dakhli, Leyla, 'L'expertise en terrain colonial: Les orientalistes et le mandat français en Syrie et au Liban', *Matériaux pour l'histoire de notre temps* 3, 99 (2010), 20–7.

Dale, Stephen F., *Indian Merchants and Eurasian Trade, 1600–1750* (Cambridge: Cambridge University Press, 1994).

Dale, Stephen F., 'The Legacy of the Timurids', *Journal of the Royal Asiatic Society* 8, 1 (1998), 43–58.

Dale, Stephen F., 'India under Mughal Rule', in: D. Morgan and A. Reid (eds), *The New Cambridge History of Islam*, Vol. 3 (Cambridge: Cambridge University Press, 2010), 266–314.

Dale, Stephen F., *The Muslim Empires of the Ottomans, Safavids, and Mughals* (Cambridge: Cambridge University Press, 2010).

Dale, Stephen F., *Babur: Timurid Prince and Mughal Emperor, 1483–1530* (Cambridge: Cambridge University Press, 2018).

Dalrymple, William, *The Anarchy: The East India Company, Corporate Violence, and the Pillage of an Empire* (London: Bloomsbury, 2019).

Daneshgar, Majid, 'The Study of Persian Shi'ism in the Malay-Indonesian World: A Review of Literature from the Nineteenth Century Onwards', *Journal of Shi'a Islamic Studies* 7, 2 (2014), 191–229.

Daoudy, Marwa, *The Origins of the Syrian Conflict: Climate Change and Human Security* (Cambridge: Cambridge University Press, 2020).

Darwich, May, and Tamirace Fakhoury, 'Casting the Other as an Existential Threat: The Securitisation of Sectarianism in the International Relations of the Syria Crisis', *Global Discourse* 6, 4 (2016), 712–32.

Davari, Mahmood T., *The Political Thought of Ayatollah Murtaza Mutahhari: An Iranian Theoretician of the Islamic State* (London: Routledge, 2005).

Davidson, Christopher, *After the Sheikhs: The Coming Collapse of the Gulf Monarchies* (London: Hurst, 2012).

Davis, Eric, *Memories of State: Politics, History, and Collective Identity in Modern Iraq* (Berkeley: University of California Press, 2005).

Dawisha, Adeed, *Arab Nationalism in the Twentieth Century: From Triumph to Despair* (Princeton: Princeton University Press, 2003).

Dawisha, Adeed, *Iraq: A Political History* (Princeton: Princeton University Press, 2013).

al-Darura, ʿAli bin Ibrahim, *Tarikh al-Ihtilal al-Burtughali li-l-Qatif 1521–1572* (Abu Dhabi: Majmaʿ al-Thaqafi, 2001).

de Bruijn, J. T. P., 'Iranian Studies in the Netherlands', *Iranian Studies* 20, 2/4 (1987), 161–77.

de Goeje, Michael Jan, *Mémoire sur les Carmathes du Bahraïn et les Fatimides* (Leiden: Brill, 1886).

de Jong, Frederick, 'Problems Concerning the Origins of the Qizilbash in Bulgaria: Remnants of the Safaviyya?', in: *Convegno sul tema: La Shīʿa nell'Impero Ottomano (Roma, 15 aprile 1991)* (Rome: Accademia Nazionale dei Lincei, 1993), 203–24.

de Smet, Daniel, 'La translation du "raʾs al-Husayn" au Caire fatimide', in: Urbain Vermeulen and J. van Steenbergen (eds), *Egypt and Syria in the Fatimid, Ayyubid and Mamluk Eras* (Leuven: Peeters, 1995), 29–44.

Deringil, Selim, 'The Struggle against Shiʿism in Hamidian Iraq: A Study in Ottoman Counter-Propaganda', *Die Welt des Islams* 30 (1990), 45–62.

Deringil, Selim, 'The Invention of Tradition as Public Image in the Late Ottoman Empire, 1808 to 1908', *Comparative Studies in Society and History* 35, 1 (1993), 3–29.

Deringil, Selim, *The Well-Protected Domains: Ideology and the Legitimation of Power in the Ottoman Empire* (London: I. B. Tauris, 1998).

Detalle, Michel-Pierre, and Renaud Detalle, 'L'Islam vu par Carsten Niebuhr, voyageur en Orient (1761–1767)', *Revue de l'histoire des religions* 225, 4 (2008), 487–543.

Detalle, Renaud (ed.), *Tensions in Arabia: The Saudi-Yemeni Fault Line* (Baden-Baden: SWP-Conflict Prevention Network/Nomos, 1999).

Devji, Faisal, 'Imitatio Muhammadi: Khomeini and the Mystery of Citizenship', *Cultural Dynamics* 13, 3 (2001), 363–71.

Devji, Faisal, *Landscapes of the Jihad: Militancy, Morality, Modernity* (London: Hurst, 2005).

Devji, Faisal, *Muslim Zion: Pakistan as a Political Idea* (London: Hurst, 2013).

Devji, Faisal, 'The Idea of Ismailism', *Critical Muslim* 10 (2014), 51–62.

Devji, Faisal, 'The Problem of Muslim Universality', in: Edmund Burke and Robert J. Mankin (eds), *Islam and World History: The Ventures of Marshall Hodgson* (Chicago: University of Chicago Press, 2018), 145–64.

Diamond, Larry Jay, *Squandered Victory: The American Occupation and the Bungled Effort to Bring Democracy to Iraq* (New York: Times, 2005).

Dib, Kamal, 'Predator Neoliberalism: Lebanon on the Brink of Disaster', *Contemporary Arab Affairs* 13, 1 (2020), 3–22.

Dickinson, Elizabeth, *Playing with Fire: Why Private Gulf Financing for Syria's Extremist Rebels Risks Igniting Sectarian Conflict at Home* (Washington, DC: Brookings Institution, 2013).

al-Din, Mayssoun Zein, *Religion als politischer Faktor? Eine Untersuchung am Beispiel der Frage des politischen Konfessionalismus in Libanon* (Baden-Baden: Nomos, 2010).

al-Din, Sayyid Abd al-Husain Sharaf, *The Right Path* (Blanco: Zahra/Peermohammed Ebrahim Trust, 1983).

al-Din, Sayyid Abd al-Husain Sharaf, *Al-Muraja'at: A Shi'i-Sunni Dialogue* (Beirut: Imam Husayn Islamic Foundation, 1994).

Dirks, Nicholas B., *Castes of Mind: Colonialism and the Making of Modern India* (Princeton: Princeton University Press, 2001).

Djalili, Mohammad-Reza, *Diplomatie Islamique: Stratégie Internationale du Khomeynisme* (Paris: Presses Universitaires de France, 1989).

Djebli, Moktar, *Les invasions mongoles en Orient vécues par un savant médiéval arabe Ibn Abi l-Hadid al-Mada'ini (1190–1258), extrait du Sharh Nahj al-Balagha* (Paris: L'Harmattan, 1995).

Dodge, Bayard, 'The Fatimid Legal Code', *The Muslim World* 50, 1 (1960), 30–8.

Dodge, Toby, *Inventing Iraq: The Failure of Nation-Building and a History Denied* (London: Hurst, 2003).

Dodge, Toby, 'Intervention and Dreams of Exogenous Statebuilding: The Application of Liberal Peacebuilding in Afghanistan and Iraq', *Review of International Studies* 39, 5 (2013), 1189–1212.

Dodge, Toby, *Iraq: From War to a New Authoritarianism* (Abingdon: Routledge, 2017).

Dodge, Toby, 'Tracing the Rise of Sectarianism in Iraq after 2003', *LSE*, 13 September 2018.

Dodge, Toby, 'The Failure of Peacebuilding in Iraq: The Role of Consociationalism and Political Settlements', *Journal of Intervention and Statebuilding* 15, 4 (2021), 459–475.

Dodge, Toby, 'Understanding the Role of al-Hashd al-Shaabi in Iraq's National and Transnational Political Field', *POMEPS*, 2020.

Dodge, Toby, and Renad Mansour, 'Sectarianization and De-Sectarianization in the Struggle for Iraq's Political Field', *Review of Faith & International Affairs* 18, 1 (2020), 58–69.

Don Juan of Persia (formerly Oruj Beg Bayat), *Relaciones de Don Juan de Persia*, trans. as *Don Juan of Persia: A Shi'ah Catholic, 1560–1604* (London: Routledge, 1926).

Donohue, John J., *The Buwayhid Dynasty in Iraq 334H./945 to 403H./1012: Shaping Institutions for the Future* (Leiden: Brill, 2003).

Dorlian, Samy, *La mouvance zaydite dans le Yémen contemporain: Une modernisation avortée* (Paris: L'Harmattan, 2013).

Dorlian, Samy, 'Les reformulations identitaires du zaydisme dans leur contexte socio-politique contemporain', *Arabian Humanities* 15 (2008), 161–76.

Dorlian, Samy, 'The Sa'da War in Yemen: Between Politics and Sectarianism', *The Muslim World* 101, 2 (2011), 182–201.

Dorronsoro, Gilles, 'Pakistan's Afghan Policy', in: Soofia Mumtaz, Jean-Luc Racine, and Imran Anwar Ali (eds), *Pakistan: The Contours of State and Society* (Oxford: Oxford University Press, 2002), 251–65.

Douglas, Fedwa Malti, 'Controversy and Its Effects in the Biographical Tradition of al-Khaṭīb al-Baghdādī', *Studia Islamica* 46 (1977), 115–31.

Doumato, Eleanor Abdella, 'Manning the Barricades: Islam According to Saudi Arabia's School Texts', *Middle East Journal* 57, 2 (2003), 230–47.

Douwes, Dick, 'Reorganizing Violence: Traditional Recruitment Patterns and Resistance against Conscription in Ottoman Syria', in: Erik J. Zürcher (ed.), *Arming the State: Military Conscription in the Middle East and Central Asia, 1775–1925* (London: I. B. Tauris, 1999), 111–27.

Douwes, Dick, *The Ottomans in Syria: A History of Justice and Oppression* (London: I. B. Tauris, 2000).

Douwes, Dick, 'Migration, Faith and Community: Extra-Local Linkages in Coastal Syria', in: Peter Sluglett and Stefan Weber (eds), *Syria and Bilad al-Sham under Ottoman Rule: Essays in Honour of Abdul Karim Rafeq* (Leiden: Brill, 2010), 483–95.

Douwes, Dick, 'Modern History of the Nizari Ismailis of Syria', in: Farhad Daftary (ed.), *A Modern History of the Ismailis: Continuity and Change in a Muslim Community* (London: I. B. Tauris, 2011), 19–44.

Douwes, Dick, and Norman N. Lewis, 'The Trials of Syrian Ismailis in the First Decade of the 20th Century', *International Journal of Middle East Studies* 21, 2 (1989), 215–32.

Drayton, Richard, and David Motadel, 'Discussion: The Futures of Global History', *Journal of Global History* 13, 1 (2018), 1–21.

Drechsler, Andreas, *Geschichte der Stadt Qom im Mittelalter (650–1350)* (Berlin: Klaus Schwarz, 1999).

Dresch, Paul, *Tribes, Government, and History in Yemen* (Oxford: Clarendon, 1989).

Dresch, Paul, *A History of Modern Yemen* (Cambridge: Cambridge University Press, 2000).

Dressler, Markus, *Die civil religion der Türkei: Kemalistische und alevitische Atatürk-Rezeption im Vergleich* (Würzburg: Ergon, 1999).

Dressler, Markus, *Die alevitische Religion: Traditionslinien und Neubestimmungen* (Würzburg: Ergon, 2002).

Dressler, Markus, 'Inventing Orthodoxy: Competing Claims for Authority and Legitimacy in the Ottoman-Safavid Conflict', in: Hakan T. Karateke and Maurus Reinkowski (eds), *Legitimizing the Order: The Ottoman Rhetoric of State Power* (Leiden: Brill, 2005), 151–73.

Dressler, Markus, *Writing Religion: The Making of Turkish Alevi Islam* (Oxford: Oxford University Press, 2013).

Drysdale, Alasdair, 'Ethnicity in the Syrian Officer Corps: A Conceptualization', *Civilisations* 29, 3–4 (1979), 359–74.

Drysdale, Alasdair, 'The Syrian Political Elite, 1966–1976: A Spatial and Social Analysis', *Middle Eastern Studies* 17, 1 (1981), 3–30.

D'Souza, Rohan, 'Crisis before the Fall: Some Speculations on the Decline of the Ottomans, Safavids and Mughals', *Social Scientist* 30, 9/10 (2002), 3–30.

Dubin, Rhys, *The Power of Local Ties: Civilian Resistance to Sectarian Displacement in Iraq* (Sulaimani: Institute of Regional and International Studies, 2020).

Dudoignon, Stéphane A., 'Zahedan vs. Qom? L'émergence du Baloutchistan d'Iran comme foyer de droit hanafite, sous la monarchie Pahlavi', in: Denise Aigle, Isabelle Charleux, Vincent Goossaert, and Roberte N. Hamayon (eds), *Miscellanea Asiatica: Mélanges en l'honneur de Françoise Aubin* (Sankt Augustin: Institute Monumenta Serica, 2010), 271–315.

Dudoignon, Stéphane A., 'Sunnites and Shiites in Iran since 1979: Confrontations, Exchanges, Convergences', in: Brigitte Maréchal and Sami Zemni (eds), *The Dynamics of Sunni–Shia Relationships: Doctrine, Transnationalism, Intellectuals and the Media* (London: Hurst, 2013), 141–61.

Dudoignon, Stéphane A., *The Baluch, Sunnism and the State in Iran: From Tribal to Global* (London: Hurst, 2017).

Dueck, Jennifer M., *The Claims of Culture at Empire's End: Syria and Lebanon under French Rule* (Oxford: Oxford University Press, 2010).

Dukhan, Haian, 'Tribes and Tribalism in the Syrian Uprising', *Syria Studies* 6, 2 (2014), 1–28.

Dukhan, Haian, *State and Tribes in Syria: Informal Alliances and Conflict Patterns* (London: Routledge, 2018).

Dukhan, Haian, 'The End of the Dialectical Symbiosis of National and Tribal Identities in Syria', *Nations and Nationalism* 28, 1 (2022), 141–53.

Dupont, Anne-Laure, 'The Ottoman Revolution of 1908 as Seen by al-Hilâl and al-Manâr: The Triumph and Diversification of the Reformist Spirit', in: Christoph Schumann (ed.), *Liberal Thought in the Eastern Mediterranean: Late 19th Century until the 1960s* (Leiden: Brill, 2008), 123–46.

Dupont, M. Félix, 'Mémoire sur les mœurs et les cérémonies religieuses des Nesserié, connus en Europe sous le nom d'Ausari', *Journal Asiatique* 5 (1824), 129–39.

Durrer, Antonia, *Die Kreuzfahrerherrschaften des 12. und 13. Jahrhunderts zwischen Integration und Segregation: Zeitgenössische und moderne Stimmen im Vergleich* (Ostfildern: Jan Thorbecke, 2016).

Dussaud, René, *Histoire et religion des Nosairîs* (Paris: É. Bouillon, 1900).

Eaton, Richard M., *The Sufis of Bijapur, 1300–1700: Social Rules of Sufis in Medieval India* (Princeton: Princeton University Press, 1978).

Eaton, Richard M., *The Rise of Islam and the Bengal Frontier, 1204–1760* (Berkeley: University of California Press, 1993).

Eaton, Richard M., *India in the Persianate Age, 1000–1765* (Berkeley: University of California Press, 2019).

Eaton, Richard M., and Phillip B. Wagoner, *Power, Memory, Architecture: Contested Sites on India's Deccan Plateau, 1300–1600* (New Delhi: Oxford University Press, 2014).

Eberhard, Elke, *Osmanische Polemik gegen die Safawiden im 16. Jahrhundert nach arabischen Handschriften* (Freiburg: Klaus Schwarz, 1970).

Eddé, Anne-Marie, 'Sunnites et Chiites à Alep sous le règne d'al-Salih Isma'il (569–77/1174–81): Entre conflits et réconciliations', in: Carole Hillenbrand (ed.), *Syria in Crusader Times: Conflict and Co-Existence* (Edinburgh: Edinburgh University Press, 2019), 197–210.

Edwards, David B., 'The Evolution of Shi'i Political Dissent in Afghanistan', in: Juan R. I. Cole and Nikki R. Keddie (eds), *Shi'ism and Social Protest* (New Haven: Yale University Press, 1986), 201–29.

Ehteshami, Anoushiravan, and Raymond A. Hinnebusch, *Syria and Iran: Middle Powers in a Penetrated Regional System* (London: Routledge, 1997).

Eich, Thomas, 'Abū l-Hudā, the Rifā'iya and Shiism in Ḥamīdian Iraq', *Der Islam* 80, 1 (2003), 142–52.

El Shamsy, Ahmed, *The Canonization of Islamic Law: A Social and Intellectual History* (Cambridge: Cambridge University Press, 2015).

Eliash, J., 'The Šī'ite Qur'ān: A Reconsideration of Goldziher's Interpretation', *Arabica* 16 (1969), 15–24.

Eliash, J., 'On the Genesis and Development of the Twelver-Shii Three-Tenet Shahadah', *Der Islam* 47 (1971), 265–72.

Eligür, Banu, *The Mobilization of Political Islam in Turkey* (Cambridge: Cambridge University Press, 2010).

Elisséeff, Nikita, *Nūr ad-Dīn: Un grand prince musulman de Syrie au temps des Croisades (511–569 H./118–1174)*, 3 Vols (Damascus: Institut Français de Damas, 1967).

Elling, Rasmus Christian, *Minorities in Iran: Nationalism and Ethnicity after Khomeini* (New York: Palgrave Macmillan, 2013).

Elsie, Robert, *The Albanian Bektashi: History and Culture of a Dervish Order in the Balkans* (London: I. B. Tauris, 2019).

Emadi, Hafizullah, 'Exporting Iran's Revolution: The Radicalization of the Shiite Movement in Afghanistan', *Middle Eastern Studies* 31, 1 (1995), 1–12.

Emadi, Hafizullah, 'The End of Taqiyya: Reaffirming the Religious Identity of Ismailis in Shughnan, Badakhshan: Political Implications for Afghanistan', *Middle Eastern Studies* 34, 3 (1998), 103–20.

Emre, Side, *Ibrahim-i Gulshani and the Khalwati-Gulshani Order: Power Brokers in Ottoman Egypt* (Leiden: Brill, 2017).

Enayat, Hamid, 'Iran: Khumayni's Concept of the "Guardianship of the Jurisconsult"', in: James P. Piscatori (ed.), *Islam in the Political Process* (Cambridge: Cambridge University Press, 1983), 160–80.

Enayat, Hamid, *Modern Islamic Political Thought: The Response of the Shi'i and Sunni Muslims to the Twentieth Century*, 2nd ed.(London: I. B. Tauris, 2005).

Ende, Werner, *Arabische Nation und islamische Geschichte: Die Umayyaden im Urteil arabischer Autoren des 20. Jahrhunderts* (Beirut/Wiesbaden: Orient-Institut/Franz Steiner, 1977).

Ende, Werner, 'The Flagellations of Muharram and the Shiʿite ʿUlama', *Der Islam* 55, 1 (1978), 19–36.

Ende, Werner, 'Ehe auf Zeit (mutʿa) in der innerislamischen Diskussion der Gegenwart', *Die Welt des Islams* 20 (1980), 1–43.

Ende, Werner, 'Eine schiitische Kontroverse über Naql al-Ǧanāʾiz', *Zeitschrift der Deutschen Morgenländischen Gesellschaft* 4 (1980), 217–8.

Ende, Werner, 'Iraq in World War I: The Turks, the Germans, and the Shiʿite Mujtahids' Call for Jihad', in: Rudolph Peters (ed.), *Proceedings of the Ninth Congress of the Union Européenne des Arabisants et Islamisants: Amsterdam, 1st to 7th Septembre 1978* (Leiden: Brill, 1981), 57–71.

Ende, Werner, 'Sunniten und Schiiten im 20. Jahrhundert', *Saeculum* 36 (1985), 187–200.

Ende, Werner, 'Sunni Polemical Writings on the Shiʿa and the Iranian Revolution', in: David Menashri (ed.), *The Iranian Revolution and the Muslim World* (Boulder, CO: Westview Press, 1990), 219–32.

Ende, Werner, 'The Nakhawila, a Shiʿite Community in Medina: Past and Present', *Die Welt des Islams* 37, 3 (1997), 264–348.

Ende, Werner, 'Der schiitische Islam', in: Werner Ende and Udo Steinbach (eds), *Der Islam in der Gegenwart*, 5th ed. (Munich: C. H. Beck, 2005), 70–98.

Ende, Werner, 'Zwischen Annäherung und Konflikt: Schiiten und Sunniten in Geschichte und Gegenwart', in: John D. Patillo-Hess (ed.), *Islam: Dialog und Kontroverse* (Vienna: Löcker, 2007), 73–84.

Ende, Werner, 'Success and Failure of a Shiite Modernist: Muhammad ibn Muhammad Mahdi al-Khalisi (1890–1963)', in: Alessandro Monsutti, Silvia Naef, and Farian Sabahi (eds), *The Other Shiites: From the Mediterranean to Central Asia* (Bern: Peter Lang, 2008), 231–44.

Ende, Werner, '"Teilhaber an dem einen Vaterland": Die Petition saudischer Schiiten vom 30. April 2003', in: Markus Ritter, Ralph Kauz, and Birgitt Hoffmann (eds), *Iran und iranisch geprägte Kulturen: Studien zum 65. Geburtstag von Bert G. Fragner* (Wiesbaden: Ludwig Reichert, 2008), 336–44.

Ende, Werner, 'Schiitische Tendenzen bei sunnitischen Sayyids aus Ḥaḍramaut: Muḥammad b. ʿAqīl al-ʿAlawī (1863–1931)', *Der Islam* 50, 1 (2009), 82–97.

Ende, Werner, 'Steine des Anstoßes: Das Mausoleum der Ahl al-Bayt in Medina', in: H. Biesterfeldt and V. Klemm (eds), *Differenz und Dynamik im Islam: Festschrift für Heinz Halm zum 70. Geburtstag* (Würzburg: Ergon, 2012), 181–200.

Entessar, Nader, 'The Lion and the Sphinx: Iranian-Egyptian Relations in Perspective', in: Hooshang Amirahmadi and Nader Entessar (eds), *Iran and the Arab World* (Basingstoke: Macmillan, 1993), 161–79.

Enthoven, R. E., *Census of India, 1901*, Vol. 9 (Bombay: Government Central Press, 1902).

Ephrat, Daphna, *A Learned Society in a Period of Transition: The Sunni ʿUlama' of Eleventh-Century Baghdad* (Albany: SUNY Press, 2000).

Ephrat, Daphna, 'The Seljuqs and the Public Sphere in the Period of Sunni Revivalism: The View from Baghdad', in: Christian Lange and Songül Mecit (eds), *The Seljuqs: Politics, Society and Culture* (Edinburgh: Edinburgh University Press, 2011), 139–56.

Erginbaş, Vefa, 'Problematizing Ottoman Sunnism: Appropriation of Islamic History and Ahl al-Baytism in Ottoman Literary and Historical Writing in the Sixteenth Century', *Journal of the Economic and Social History of the Orient* 60, 5 (2017), 614–46.

Erginbaş, Vefa, 'Reappraising Ottoman Religiosity in the Last Decades of the Sixteenth Century: Mustafa Darir's Siret and its Alid Content', in: Vefa Erginbaş (ed.), *Ottoman Sunnism: New Perspectives* (Edinburgh: Edinburgh University Press, 2019), 71–89.

Ernst, Carl W., and Bruce B. Lawrence, *Sufi Martyrs of Love: The Chishti Order in South Asia and Beyond* (New York: Palgrave Macmillan, 2002).

Erskine, Stuart, *King Faisal of Iraq: An Authorised and Authentic Study* (London: Hutchinson, 1933).

Erturk, Omer F., 'The Myth of Turkish Islam: The Influence of Naqshbandi-Gümüşhanevi Thought in Turkish Islamic Orthodoxy', *British Journal of Middle Eastern Studies* 49, 2 (2022), 223–47.

Eschraghi, Armin, 'Promised One (mawʿūd) or Imaginary One (mawhūm)? Some Notes on Twelver Shīʿī Mahdī Doctrine and its Discussion in Writings of Bahāʾ Allāh', in: Orkhan Mir-Kasimov (ed.), *Unity in Diversity: Mysticism, Messianism and the Construction of Religious Authority in Islam* (Leiden: Brill, 2013), 111–35.

Escovitz, J. H., '"He was the Muḥammad ʿAbduh of Syria": A Study of Ṭāhir al-Jazāʾirī and his Influence', *International Journal of Middle East Studies* 18 (1986), 293–310.

Eskander, Saad B., 'Gertrude Bell and the Formation of the Iraqi State: The Kurdish Dimension', in: Paul Collins and Charles Tripp (eds), *Gertrude Bell and Iraq: A Life and Legacy* (Oxford: Oxford University Press, 2017), 215–38.

Esposito, John L. (ed.), *The Iranian Revolution: Its Global Impact* (Miami: Florida International University Press, 1990).

Etherington, Mark, *Revolt on the Tigris: The al-Sadr Uprising and the Governing of Iraq* (London: Hurst, 2005).

Faath, Sigrid, (ed.), *Rivalitäten und Konflikt zwischen Sunniten und Schiiten in Nahost* (Berlin: DGAP, 2010).

Fadhil Ali, Rafid, 'Sufi Insurgent Groups in Iraq', *Jamestown Foundation*, 25 January 2008.

Fahmy, Khaled, *All the Pasha's Men: Mehmed Ali, his Army and the Making of Modern Egypt* (Cairo: American University in Cairo Press, 2002).

Fakhro, Munira, 'The Uprising in Bahrain: An Assessment', in: Gary Sick and Lawrence Potter (eds), *The Persian Gulf at the Millennium: Essays in Politics, Economy, Security, and Religion* (Basingstoke: Macmillan, 1997), 167–88.

Fandy, Mamoun, 'From Confrontation to Creative Resistance: The Shia's Oppositional Discourse in Saudi Arabia', *Critique: Critical Middle Eastern Studies* 5, 9 (1996), 1–27.

Fandy, Mamoun, *Saudi Arabia and the Politics of Dissent* (Basingstoke: Macmillan, 1999).

Farah, Caesar E., *The Politics of Interventionism in Ottoman Lebanon, 1830–1861* (London: I. B. Tauris, 2000).

Farah, Caesar E., *The Sultan's Yemen: Nineteenth-Century Challenges to Ottoman Rule* (London: I. B. Tauris, 2002).

Faramarzi, Scheherezade, *Iran's Sunnis Resist Extremism, But for How Long?* (Washington, DC: Atlantic Council, 2018).

Farha, Mark, 'Searching for Sectarianism in the Arab Spring: Colonial Conspiracy or Indigenous Instinct?', *The Muslim World* 106, 1 (2016), 8–61.

Farha, Mark, *Lebanon: The Rise and Fall of a Secular State under Siege* (Cambridge: Cambridge University Press, 2019).

Farhadi, A. G. Ravan, *Abdullah Ansari of Herat: An Early Sufi Master* (Abingdon: Routledge, 2013).

Farhat, May, 'Shi'i Piety and Dynastic Legitimacy: Mashhad under the Early Safavid Shahs', *Iranian Studies* 47, 2 (2014), 201–16.

Faroqhi, Suraiya, *Der Bektaschi-Orden in Anatolien (vom späten fünfzehnten Jahrhundert bis 1826)* (Vienna: Institut für Orientalistik der Universität Wien, 1981).

Faroqhi, Suraiya, 'Conflict, Accommodation and Long-Term Survival: The Bektashi Order and the Ottoman State', in: Alexandre Popovic and Gilles Veinstein (eds), *Bektachiyya: Études sur l'ordre mystique des Bektachis et les groupes relevant de Hadji Bektach* (Istanbul: Isis Publications, 1995), 171–84.

Faroqhi, Suraiya, *Geschichte des Osmanischen Reiches* (Munich: C. H. Beck, 2006).

Faroqhi, Suraiya, 'Trade between the Ottomans and Safavids: The Acem Tüccari and Others', in: Willem Floor and Edmund Herzig (eds), *Iran and the World in the Safavid Age* (London: I. B. Tauris, 2012), 237–52.

Faroqhi, Suraiya, *Pilgrims and Sultans: The Hajj under the Ottomans*, 2nd ed. (London: I. B. Tauris, 2014).

Farquhar, Michael, *Circuits of Faith: Migration, Education, and the Wahhabi Mission* (Stanford: Stanford University Press, 2017).

Farzaneh, Mateo Mohammad, *The Iranian Constitutional Revolution and the Clerical Leadership of Khurasani* (Syracuse: Syracuse University Press, 2015).

Fattah, Hala M., *The Politics of Regional Trade in Iraq, Arabia, and the Gulf, 1745–1900* (Albany: SUNY Press, 1997).

Fattah, Hala M., 'Islamic Universalism and the Construction of Regional Identity in Turn-of-the-Century Basra: Sheikh Ibrahim al-Haidari's Book Revisited', in: Leila Tarazi Fawaz and C. A. Bayly (eds), *Modernity and Culture: From the Mediterranean to the Indian Ocean* (New York: Columbia University Press, 2002), 112–29.

Fattah, Hala M., '"Wahhabi" Influences, Salafi Responses: Shaikh Mahmud Shukri and the Iraqi Salafi Movement, 1745–1930', *Journal of Islamic Studies* 14, 2 (2003), 127–48.

Fawaz, Leila Tarazi, *An Occasion for War: Civil Conflict in Lebanon and Damascus in 1860* (London: Centre for Lebanese Studies/I. B. Tauris, 1994).

Feener, R. Michael, and Chiara Formichi, 'Debating "Shi'ism" in the History of Muslim Southeast Asia', in: Chiara Formichi and R. Michael Feener (eds), *Shi'ism in Southeast Asia: 'Alid Piety and Sectarian Constructions* (London: Hurst, 2015), 3–16.

Fernée, Tadd, *Enlightenment and Violence: Modernity and Nation-Making* (New Delhi: Sage, 2014).

Ferris, Jesse, *Nasser's Gamble: How Intervention in Yemen Caused the Six-Day War and the Decline of Egyptian Power* (Princeton: Princeton University Press, 2013).

Fieldhouse, David K., *Western Imperialism in the Middle East, 1914–1958* (Oxford: Oxford University Press, 2006).

Fildis, Ayse Tekdal, 'Roots of Alawite-Sunni Rivalry in Syria', *Middle East Policy* 19, 2 (2012), 148–56.

Findley, Carter, 'The Tanzimat II', in: R. Kasaba (ed.), *The Cambridge History of Turkey*, Vol. 4 (Cambridge: Cambridge University Press, 2008), 9–37.

Findly, Ellison Banks, *Nur Jahan: Empress of Mughal India* (Oxford: Oxford University Press, 1993).

Finkel, Caroline, *Osman's Dream: The Story of the Ottoman Empire, 1300–1923* (London: John Murray, 2006).

Finnbogason, Daniel, Göran Larsson, and Isak Svensson, 'Is Shia-Sunni Violence on the Rise? Exploring New Data on Intra-Muslim Organised Violence 1989–2017', *Civil Wars* 21, 1 (2019), 25–53.

Finster, Barbara, 'An Outline of the History of Islamic Religious Architecture in Yemen', *Muqarnas* 9 (1992), 124–47.

Firishta, Muhammad, *Ferishta's History of Dekkan, from the First Mahummedan Conquests*, trans./ed. by Jonathan Scott, 2 Vols (Cambridge: Cambridge University Press, 2013).

Firro, Kais M., *A History of the Druzes* (Leiden: Brill, 1992).

Firro, Kais M., 'The Attitude of the Druzes and 'Alawis vis-à-vis Islam and Nationalism in Syria and Lebanon', in: Krisztina Kehl-Bodrogi, Barbara Kellner-Heinkele, and Anke Otter-Beaujean (eds), *Syncretistic Religious Communities in the Near East: Collected Papers of the International Symposium 'Alevism in Turkey and Comparable Syncretistic Religious Communities in the Near East in the Past and Present', Berlin, 14–17 April 1995* (Leiden: Brill, 1997), 87–99.

Firro, Kais M., *Inventing Lebanon: Nationalism and the State under the Mandate* (London: I. B. Tauris, 2003).

Firro, Kais M., 'Ethnicizing the Shi'is in Mandatory Lebanon', *Middle Eastern Studies* 42, 5 (2006), 741–59.

Firro, Kais M., 'The Shi'is in Lebanon: Between Communal 'Asabiyya and Arab Nationalism, 1908–21', *Middle Eastern Studies* 42, 4 (2006), 535–50.

Firro, Kais M., *Metamorphosis of the Nation (al-Umma): The Rise of Arabism and Minorities in Syria and Lebanon, 1850–1940* (Brighton: Sussex Academic Press, 2009).

Fischer, Michael M. J., *Iran: From Religious Dispute to Revolution* (Cambridge, MA: Harvard University Press, 1980).

Fisher, Michael H., 'British Expansion in North India: The Role of the Resident in Awadh', *Indian Economic & Social History Review* 18, 1 (1981), 69–82.

Fisher, Michael H., 'Political Marriage Alliances at the Shi'i Court of Awadh', *Comparative Studies in Society and History* 25, 4 (1983), 593–616.

Fisher, Michael H., 'The Imperial Coronation of 1819: Awadh, the British and the Mughals', *Modern Asian Studies* 19, 2 (1985), 239–77.

Fitzherbert, Teresa, 'Religious Diversity under Ilkhanid Rule c. 1300 as Reflected in the Freer Bal'amī', in: Linda Komaroff (ed.), *Beyond the Legacy of Genghis Khan* (Leiden: Brill, 2006), 390–406.

Flannery, John M., *The Mission of the Portuguese Augustinians to Persia and Beyond (1602–1747)* (Leiden: Brill, 2013).

Flaskerud, Ingvild, *Visualizing Belief and Piety in Iranian Shi'ism* (London: Continuum, 2010).

Fleischer, Cornell H., *Bureaucrat and Intellectual in the Ottoman Empire: The Historian Mustafa Ali (1541–1600)* (Princeton: Princeton University Press, 1986).

Fleischer, Cornell H., 'The Lawgiver as Messiah: The Making of the Imperial Image in the Reign of Süleymân', in: Gilles Veinstein (ed.), *Soliman le magnifique et son temps* (Paris: La Documentation française, 1992), 159–77.

Floor, Willem, *The Afghan Occupation of Safavid Persia, 1721–1729* (Paris: Association pour l'Avancement des Études Iraniennes, 1998).

Floor, Willem, 'The ṣadr or Head of the Safavid Religious Administration, Judiciary and Endowments and Other Members of the Religious Institution', *Zeitschrift der Deutschen Morgenländischen Gesellschaft* 150 (2000), 461–500.

Floor, Willem, 'The Economic Role of the Ulama in Qajar Persia', in: Linda Walbridge (ed.), *The Most Learned of the Shi'a: The Institution of the Marja' Taqlid* (Oxford: Oxford University Press, 2001), 53–81.

Floor, Willem, *The Persian Gulf: The Rise of the Gulf Arabs: The Politics of Trade on the Persian Littoral, 1747–1792* (Washington, DC: Mage, 2007).

Floor, Willem, *Guilds, Merchants, and Ulama in Nineteenth-Century Iran* (Washington, DC: Mage, 2009).

Floor, Willem, *The Persian Gulf: The Rise and Fall of Bandar-e Lengeh: The Distribution Center for the Arabian Coast, 1750–1930* (Washington, DC: Mage, 2010).

Floor, Willem, *The Persian Gulf: Bandar Abbas: The Natural Trade Gateway of Southeast Iran* (Washington, DC: Mage, 2011).

Floor, Willem, and Hasan Javadi, 'The Role of Azerbaijani Turkish in Safavid Iran', *Iranian Studies* 46, 4 (2013), 569–81.

Flores, Jorge, 'Solving Rubik's Cube: Hormuz and the Geopolitical Challenges of West Asia, c. 1592–1622', in: Rudi Matthee and Jorge Flores (eds), *Portugal, the Persian Gulf and Safavid Persia* (Leuven: Peeters, 2011), 191–215.

Flores, Jorge, *Unwanted Neighbours: The Mughals, the Portuguese, and their Frontier Zones* (Oxford: Oxford University Press, 2018).

Foley, Sean, 'The Naqshbandiyya-Khalidiyya, Islamic Sainthood, and Religion in Modern Times', *Journal of World History* 19, 4 (2008), 521–45.

Foley, Sean, 'Temporal and Spiritual Power in Nineteenth-Century Ottoman Politics: Shaykh Khalid, Gürcü Necib Pasha and the Naqshbandiyya-Khalidiyya', *Türkiyat Araştırmaları* 9 (2008), 227–44.

Foltz, Richard, 'The Central Asian Naqshbandī Connections of the Mughal Emperors', *Journal of Islamic Studies* 7, 2 (1996), 229–39.

Fontana, Maria Vittoria, *Iconografia dell'Ahl al-Bayt: Immagini di arte persiana del XII al XX secolo* (Naples: Istituto Universitario Orientale, 1994).

Formichi, Chiara, 'From Fluid Identities to Sectarian Labels: A Historical Investigation of Indonesia's Shiʿi Communities', *Al-Jāmiʿah: Journal of Islamic Studies* 52, 1 (2014), 101–26.

Formichi, Chiara, 'Shaping Shiʿa Identities in Contemporary Indonesia between Local Tradition and Foreign Orthodoxy', *Die Welt des Islams* 54 (2014), 212–36.

Formichi, Chiara, 'Violence, Sectarianism, and the Politics of Religion: Articulations of Anti-Shiʿa Discourses in Indonesia', *Indonesia* 98 (2014), 1–27.

Formichi, Chiara, and R. Michael Feener (eds), *Shiʿism in Southeast Asia: ʿAlid Piety and Sectarian Constructions* (London: Hurst, 2015).

Fortna, Benjamin C., *Imperial Classroom: Islam, the State, and Education in the Late Ottoman Empire* (Oxford: Oxford University Press, 2002).

Fragner, Bert G., *Die Persophonie: Regionalität, Identität und Sprachkontakt in der Geschichte Asiens* (Berlin: Das Arabische Buch, 1999).

Francesca, Ersilia (ed.), *Ibadi Theology: Rereading Sources and Scholarly Works* (Hildesheim: Georg Olms, 2015).

Frangie, Samer, 'Theorizing from the Periphery: The Intellectual Project of Mahdi ʿAmil', *International Journal of Middle East Studies* 44, 3 (2012), 465–82.

Franke, Patrick, *Göttliche Karriere eines syrischen Hirten: Sulaimān Muršid (1907–1946) und die Anfänge der Muršidiyya* (Berlin: Klaus Schwarz, 1994).

Frankl, P. J. L., and K. Jopp, 'Lieutenant Jopp's Report on a Visit to Hufuf, 1257/1841', *New Arabian Studies* 1 (1993), 215–27.

Franzén, Johan, *Red Star over Iraq: Iraqi Communism before Saddam* (London: Hurst, 2011).

Freer, Courtney Jean, *Rentier Islamism: The Influence of the Muslim Brotherhood in Gulf Monarchies* (New York: Oxford University Press, 2018).

Freitag, Sandria B., *Collective Action and Community: Public Arenas and the Emergence of Communalism in North India* (Berkeley: University of California Press, 1989).

Freitag, Ulrike, 'Scholarly Exchange and Trade: Muhammad Husayn Nasif and his Letters to Christiaan Snouck Hurgronje', in: Michael Kemper and Ralf Elger (eds), *The Piety of Learning: Islamic Studies in Honor of Stefan Reichmuth* (Leiden: Brill, 2017), 292–300.

Friar Alexander of Malabar, 'The Story of the Sack of Ispahan by the Afghans in 1722', *Journal of the Royal Central Asian Society* 23, 4 (1936), 643–53.

Friedlaender, Israel, 'The Heterodoxies of the Shiites in the Presentation of Ibn Hazm', *Journal of the American Oriental Society* 29 (1908), 1–183.

Friedman, Jeremy, 'The Enemy of my Enemy: The Soviet Union, East Germany, and the Iranian Tudeh Party's Support for Ayatollah Khomeini', *Journal of Cold War Studies* 20, 2 (2018), 3–37.

Friedman, Yaron, 'Ibn Taymiyya's Fatāwā against the Nuṣayrī-ʿAlawī Sect', *Der Islam* 82, 2 (2005), 349–63.

Friedman, Yaron, *The Shī'īs in Palestine: From the Medieval Golden Age until the Present* (Leiden: Brill, 2020).

Friedman, Yaron, 'Musa al-Sadr and the Missing Fatwa Concerning the 'Alawi Religion', *British Journal of Middle Eastern Studies* (online, 2022).

Friedmann, Yohanan, *Shaykh Ahmad Sirhindi: An Outline of His Thought and a Study of His Image in the Eyes of Posterity* (Montreal: McGill University, 1971).

Fuccaro, Nelida, 'Ethnicity, State Formation, and Conscription in Postcolonial Iraq: The Case of the Yazidi Kurds of Jabal Sinjar', *International Journal of Middle East Studies* 29, 4 (1997), 559–80.

Fuccaro, Nelida, 'Communalism and the State in Iraq: The Yazidi Kurds, c. 1869–1940', *Middle Eastern Studies* 35, 2 (1999), 1–26.

Fuccaro, Nelida, 'Mapping the Transnational Community: Persians and the Space of the City in Bahrain, c. 1869–1937', in: Madawi al-Rasheed (ed.), *Transnational Connections and the Arab Gulf* (London: Routledge, 2005), 39–58.

Fuccaro, Nelida, 'Between Imara, Empire and Oil: Saudis in the Frontier Society of the Persian Gulf', in: Madawi al-Rasheed (ed.), *Kingdom without Borders: Saudi Political, Religious and Media Frontiers* (London: Hurst, 2008), 39–64.

Fuccaro, Nelida, *Histories of City and State in the Persian Gulf: Manama since 1800* (Cambridge: Cambridge University Press, 2009).

Fuccaro, Nelida, 'Knowledge at the Service of the British Empire: The Gazetteer of the Persian Gulf, Oman and Central Arabia', in: Inga Brandell, Marie Carlson, and Önver A. Cetrez (eds), *Borders and the Changing Boundaries of Knowledge* (Istanbul: Swedish Research Institute in Istanbul, 2015), 17–34.

Fuchs, Simon Wolfgang, 'Faded Networks: The Overestimated Saudi Legacy of Anti-Shi'i Sectarianism in Pakistan', *Global Discourse* 9, 4 (2019), 703–15.

Fuchs, Simon Wolfgang, *In a Pure Muslim Land: Shi'ism between Pakistan and the Middle East* (Chapel Hill: University of North Carolina Press, 2019).

Fuchs, Simon Wolfgang, 'Third Wave Shi'ism: Sayyid 'Arif Husain al-Husaini and the Islamic Revolution in Pakistan', *Journal of the Royal Asiatic Society* 24, 3 (2014), 493–510.

Fuchs, Simon Wolfgang, 'The Long Shadow of the State: The Iranian Revolution, Saudi Influence, and the Shifting Arguments of Anti-Shi'i Sectarianism in Pakistan', in: Laurence Louër and Christophe Jaffrelot (eds), *Pan-Islamic Connections: Transnational Networks between South Asia and the Gulf* (London: Hurst, 2017), 217–32.

Fuchs, Simon Wolfgang, 'Von Schiiten lernen: Der Reiz des Martyriums für sunnitische Gruppen in Pakistan und Afghanistan', *Behemoth* 12, 1 (2019), 52–68.

Fuller, Graham E., *The 'Center of the Universe': The Geopolitics of Iran* (Boulder, CO: Westview Press, 1991).

Fuller, Graham E., and Rend Rahim Francke, *The Arab Shi'a: The Forgotten Muslims* (Basingstoke: Macmillan, 1999).

Fuller, Graham E., 'The Hizballah-Iran Connection: Model for Sunni Resistance', *The Washington Quarterly* 30, 1 (2007), 139–50.

Fürtig, Henner, *Der irakisch-iranische Krieg, 1980–1988: Ursachen, Verlauf, Folgen* (Berlin: Akademie, 1992).

Fürtig, Henner, *Iran's Rivalry with Saudi Arabia between the Gulf Wars* (Reading: Ithaca, 2002).

Fyzee, Asaf A. A., *The Ismaili Law of Wills* (London: Oxford University Press, 1933).

Fyzee, Asaf A. A., *A Shiʿite Creed: A Translation of Risālatu l-Iʿtiqādāt of Muḥammad b. ʿAlī ibn Bābawayhi al-Qummī, Known as Shaykh Ṣadūq* (Bombay: Oxford University Press, 1942).

Fyzee, Asaf A. A., *Outlines of Muhammadan Law* (New Delhi: Oxford University Press, 1974).

Gallagher, Amelia, 'Shah Ismaʿil's Poetry in the Silsilat al-Nasab-i Safawiyya', *Iranian Studies* 44, 6 (2011), 895–911.

Gandelot, Ludovic, 'Islam Shia Ithna Asheri et Migrations: Chez les Khojas, 1860–1925', in: Michel Boivin (ed.), *Les Ismaéliens d'Asie du sud: Gestion des héritages et productions identitaires* (Paris: L'Harmattan, 2007), 199–219.

García, E., J. Cutillas, and R. Matthee (eds), *The Spanish Monarchy and Safavid Persia in the Early Modern Period: Politics, War and Religion* (Valencia: Albatros, 2016).

Gause, F. Gregory, *Saudi-Yemeni Relations: Domestic Structures and Foreign Influence* (New York: Columbia University Press, 1990).

Gause, F. Gregory, *Oil Monarchies: Domestic and Security Challenges in the Arab Gulf States* (New York: Council on Foreign Relations Press, 1994).

Gause, F. Gregory, *The International Relations of the Persian Gulf* (Cambridge: Cambridge University Press, 2010).

Gause, F. Gregory, *Beyond Sectarianism: The New Middle East Cold War* (Doha: Brookings Doha Center, 2014).

Gause, F. Gregory, 'Revolution and Threat Perception: Iran and the Middle East', *International Politics* 52, 5 (2015), 637–45.

Gay, Denis, *Les Bohra de Madagascar: Religion, commerce et échanges transnationaux dans la construction de l'identité ethnique* (Zurich: LIT, 2009).

Gelvin, James L., *Divided Loyalties: Nationalism and Mass Politics in Syria at the Close of Empire* (Berkeley: University of California Press, 1998).

Gelvin, James L., *The Modern Middle East: A History*, 4th ed. (New York: Oxford University Press, 2016).

Gengler, Justin J., 'Royal Factionalism, the Khawalid, and the Securitization of "the Shīʿa Problem" in Bahrain', *Journal of Arabian Studies* 3, 1 (2013), 53–79.

Gengler, Justin J., 'Understanding Sectarianism in the Persian Gulf', in: Lawrence G. Potter (ed.), *Sectarian Politics in the Persian Gulf* (London: Hurst, 2013), 31–66.

Gengler, Justin J., *Group Conflict and Political Mobilization in Bahrain and the Arab Gulf: Rethinking the Rentier State* (Bloomington: Indiana University Press, 2015).

Gengler, Justin J., 'Sectarianism from the Top Down or Bottom Up? Explaining the Middle East's Unlikely De-Sectarianization after the Arab Spring', *Review of Faith & International Affairs* 18, 1 (2020), 109–13.

George, Alan, *Syria: Neither Bread nor Freedom* (London: Zed, 2003).

Georgeon, François, *Abdülhamid II: Le sultan calife (1876–1909)* (Paris: Fayard, 2003).

Gerges, Fawaz A., *The Far Enemy: Why Jihad Went Global* (Cambridge: Cambridge University Press, 2005).

Gerges, Fawaz A., *Obama and the Middle East: The End of America's Moment?* (New York: Palgrave Macmillan, 2012).

Gerges, Fawaz A., *ISIS: A History* (Princeton: Princeton University Press, 2017).

Gerges, Fawaz A., *Making the Arab World: Nasser, Qutb, and the Clash that Shaped the Middle East* (Princeton, NJ: Princeton University Press, 2018).

Ghaliun, Burhan, *Al-Ma'sala al-Ta'ifiyya wa Mushkila al-Aqalliyyat* (The Sectarian Question and the Problem of Minorities) (Beirut: Dar al-Tali'a, 1979).

Ghaliun, Burhan, *Nizam al-Ta'ifiyya: Min al-Dawla ila al-Qabila* (Beirut: al-Markaz al-Thaqafi al-'Arabi, 1990).

Ghamari-Tabrizi, Behrooz, *Foucault in Iran: Islamic Revolution after the Enlightenment* (Minneapolis: University of Minnesota Press, 2016).

Ghanem, Aghiad, *Les Alaouites de Turquie dans les relations turco-syriennes: Une diplomatie de résilience* (Paris: L'Harmattan, 2017).

Ghareeb, Edmund A., and Beth Dougherty, *Historical Dictionary of Iraq* (Oxford: Scarecrow Press, 2004).

al-Ghariri, Sami, *Al-Zaydiyya: Bayn al-Imamiyya wa Ahl al-Sunna* (Qom: Dar al-Kitab al-Islami, 2006).

Ghattas, Kim, *Black Wave: Saudi Arabia, Iran, and the Forty-Year Rivalry that Unravelled Culture, Religion, and Collective Memory in the Middle East* (New York: Henry Holt, 2020).

Ghereghlou, Kioumars, 'A Safavid Bureaucrat in the Ottoman World: Mirza Makhdum Sharifi Shirazi and the Quest for Upward Mobility in the İlmiye Hierarchy', *Osmanlı Araştırmaları/Journal of Ottoman Studies* 53 (2019), 153–94.

Ghersallah, Abdelhafidh, *Le chiisme en Algérie: De la conversion politique à la naissance d'une communauté religieuse* (Fribourg: Institut Religioscope, 2012).

Gholsorkhi, Shohreh, 'Ismail II and Mirza Makhdum Sharifi: An Interlude in Safavid History', *International Journal of Middle East Studies* 26, 3 (1994), 477–88.

Ghubash, Hussein, *Oman: The Islamic Democratic Tradition* (London: Routledge, 2006).

Gibb, H. A. R., 'Notes on the Arabic Materials for the History of the Early Crusades', *Bulletin of the School of Oriental and African Studies* 7, 4 (1935), 739–54.

Gilli-Elewy, Hend, 'Al-awādi al-ğāmia: A Contemporary Account of the Mongol Conquest of Baghdad, 656/1258', *Arabica* 58, 5 (2001), 353–71.

Gimaret, Daniel, *La doctrine d'al-Ash'ari* (Paris: Editions du CERF, 1990).

Giunchi, Elisa, 'The Reinvention of Sharī'a under the British Raj: In Search of Authenticity and Certainty', *Journal of Asian Studies* 69, 4 (2010), 1119–42.

Glassen, Erika, 'Muharram-Ceremonies ('Azâdârî) in Istanbul at the End of the XIXth and the Beginning of the XXth Century', in: Th. Zarcone and F. Zarinebaf (eds), *Les Iraniens d'Istanbul* (Paris: Institut Français de Recherches en Iran/Institut Français d'Études Anatoliennes, 1993), 113–29.

Gleave, Robert, *Inevitable Doubt: Two Theories of Shi'i Jurisprudence* (Leiden: Brill, 2000).

Gleave, Robert, 'Between Ḥadīth and Fiqh: The "Canonical" Imāmī Collections of Akhbār', *Islamic Law and Society* 8, 3 (2001), 350–82.

Gleave, Robert, 'Jihad and Religious Legitimacy in the Early Qajar State', in: Robert Gleave (ed.), *Religion and Society in Qajar Iran* (London: Routledge, 2004), 41–70.

Gleave, Robert, 'Recent Research into the History of Early Shi'ism', *History Compass* 7 (2009), 1593–605.

Gleave, Robert, 'Shi'i Jurisprudence during the Seljuq Period: Rebellion and Public Order in an Illegitimate State', in: Christian Lange and Songül Mecit (eds), *The Seljuqs: Politics, Society and Culture* (Edinburgh: Edinburgh University Press, 2011), 205–27.

Gleave, Robert, *Islam and Literalism: Literal Meaning and Interpretation in Islamic Legal Theory* (Edinburgh: Edinburgh University Press, 2012).

Gleave, Robert, 'Muhammad Taqi al-Majlisi and Safavid Shi'ism: Akhbarism and Anti-Sunni Polemic during the Reigns of Shah 'Abbas the Great and Shah Safi', *Iran* 55, 1 (2017), 24–34.

Göbel, Karl-Heinrich, *Moderne schiitische Politik und Staatsidee nach Taufiq al-Fukaiki, Muhammad Gawad Mugniya, Ruhulläh Humaini (Khomeyni)* (Opladen: Leske, 1984).

Gölbaşı, Edip, 'Turning the "Heretics" into Loyal Muslim Subjects: Imperial Anxieties, the Politics of Religious Conversion, and the Yezidis in the Hamidian Era', *The Muslim World* 103, 1 (2013), 3–23.

Goldberg, Jacob, 'The 1913 Saudi Occupation of Hasa Reconsidered', *Middle Eastern Studies* 18, 1 (1982), 21–9.

Goldberg, Jacob, 'The Origins of British-Saudi Relations: The 1915 Anglo-Saudi Treaty Revisited', *The Historical Journal* 28, 3 (1985), 693–703.

Goldberg, Jacob, 'Captain Shakespear and Ibn Saud: A Balanced Reappraisal', *Middle Eastern Studies* 22, 1 (1986), 74–88.

Goldberg, Jacob, 'The Shi'i Minority in Saudi Arabia', in: Juan R. I. Cole and Nikki R. Keddie (eds), *Shi'ism and Social Protest* (New Haven: Yale University Press, 1986), 230–46.

Goldberg, Jacob, 'Saudi Arabia and the Iranian Revolution: The Religious Dimension', in: David Menashri (ed.), *The Iranian Revolution and the Muslim World* (Boulder, CO: Westview Press, 1990), 155–70.

Goldsmith, Leon T., '"God Wanted Diversity": Alawite Pluralist Ideals and their Integration into Syrian Society 1832–1973', *British Journal of Middle Eastern Studies* 40, 4 (2013), 392–409.

Goldsmith, Leon T., *Cycle of Fear: Syria's Alawites in War and Peace* (London: Hurst, 2015).

Goldziher, Ignaz, *Beiträge zur Literaturgeschichte der Śi'â und der sunnitischen Polemik* (Vienna: Karl Gerold's Sohn, 1874).

Goldziher, Ignaz, *Muhammedanische Studien*, 2 Vols (Halle: Max Niemeyer, 1889/90).

Goldziher, Ignaz, 'Das Prinzip der "takijja" Im Islam', *Zeitschrift der Deutschen Morgenländischen Gesellschaft* 60, 1 (1906), 213–26.

Goldziher, Ignaz, *Vorlesungen über den Islam*, 1st ed. (Heidelberg: Carl Winter, 1910).

Goldziher, Ignaz, *Streitschrift des Gazali gegen die Batinijja-Sekte* (Leiden: Brill, 1916).

Goldziher, Ignaz, *Die Richtungen der islamischen Koranauslegung: An der Universität Upsala gehaltene Olaus-Petri-Vorlesungen* (Leiden: Brill, 1920).

Goldziher, Ignaz, *Vorlesungen über den Islam*, 2nd ed. (Heidelberg: Carl Winter, 1925).

Gommans, Jos J. L., *The Rise of the Indo-Afghan Empire, c. 1710–1780* (Leiden: Brill, 1994).

Gonnella, Julia, *Islamische Heiligenverehrung im urbanen Kontext am Beispiel von Aleppo (Syrien)* (Berlin: Klaus Schwarz, 1995).

Goodarzi, Jubin M., *Syria and Iran: Diplomatic Alliance and Power Politics in the Middle East* (London: I. B. Tauris, 2006).

Goodarzi, Jubin M., *Iran and Syria at the Crossroads: The Fall of the Tehran-Damascus Axis?* (Washington, DC: Wilson Center, 2013).

Goodarzi, Jubin M., *Iran and the Syrian and Iraqi Crises* (Washington, DC: Wilson Center, 2014).

Goodarzi, Jubin M., *Iran and Syria: The End of the Road?* (Washington, DC: Wilson Center, 2015).

Gooptu, Nandini, *The Politics of the Urban Poor in Early Twentieth-Century India* (Cambridge: Cambridge University Press, 2001).

Gordon, Anna, and Sarah Parkinson, 'How the Houthis Became "Shi'a"', *MERIP*, 27 January 2018.

Gorton, T. J., *Renaissance Emir: A Druze Warlord at the Court of the Medici* (Northampton, MA: Interlink, 2014).

Goudarzi, Masoumeh Rad, and Sediqeh Nazarpour, 'The Separation of Bahrain from Iran', in: Mansoureh Ebrahimi, Masoumeh Rad Goudarzi, and Kamaruzaman Yusoff (eds), *The Dynamics of Iranian Borders: Issues of Contention* (Cham: Springer, 2019), 95–114.

Grabar, Oleg, 'The Earliest Islamic Commemorative Structures, Notes and Documents', *Ars Orientalis* 6 (1966), 7–46.

Grabar, Oleg, 'The Earliest Islamic Commemorative Structures, Notes and Documents', in: *Jerusalem: Constructing the Study of Islamic Art*, Vol. 4 (Aldershot: Ashgate, 2005), 65–110.

Grady, Standish Grove, *A Manual of the Mahommedan Law of Inheritance and Contract, Comprising the Doctrines of the Soonee and Sheea Schools, and Based upon the Text of Sir W. H. Macnaghten's Principles and Precedents, Together with the Decisions of the Privy Council and High Courts of the Presidencies in India* (London: W. H. Allen, 1869).

Gramlich, Richard, 'Pol und Scheich im heutigen Derwischtum der Schia', in: Centre de Recherches d'Histoire des Religions Strasbourg (ed.), *Le shî'isme imâmite: Colloque de Strasbourg (6–9 mai 1968)* (Paris: Presses Universitaires de France, 1970), 175–82.

Gramlich, Richard, *Die schiitischen Derwischorden Persiens*, Vol. 3 (Wiesbaden: Deutsche Morgenländische Gesellschaft/Franz Steiner, 1981).

Green, Nile (ed.), *The Persianate World: The Frontiers of a Eurasian Lingua Franca* (Berkeley: University of California Press, 1997).

Green, Nile, *Indian Sufism since the Seventeenth Century: Saints, Books and Empires in the Muslim Deccan* (London: Routledge, 2006).

Green, Nile, *Bombay Islam: The Religious Economy of the West Indian Ocean, 1840–1915* (Cambridge: Cambridge University Press, 2011).

Green, Nile, *Sufism: A Global History* (Chichester: Wiley-Blackwell, 2012).

Green, Nile, 'Introduction: Afghanistan's Islam: A History and its Scholarship', in: Nile Green (ed.), *Afghanistan's Islam: From Conversion to the Taliban* (Oakland, CA: University of California Press, 2017), 1–37.

Grehan, James, *Twilight of the Saints: Everyday Religion in Ottoman Syria and Palestine* (New York: Oxford University Press, 2014).

Gribble, J. D. B., *History of the Deccan* (New Delhi: Rupa, 2002).

Gribetz, Arthur, *Strange Bedfellows: Mutʿat al-nisāʾ and mutʿat al-ḥajj: A Study Based on Sunnī and Shīʿī Sources of tafsīr, ḥadīth and fiqh* (Berlin: Klaus Schwarz, 1994).

Griffel, Frank, *Apostasie und Toleranz im Islam: Die Entwicklung zu al-Ġazālīs Urteil gegen die Philosophie und die Reaktionen der Philosophen* (Leiden: Brill, 2000).

Griffel, Frank, 'Toleration and Exclusion: Al-Shāfiʿī and al-Ghazālī on the Treatment of Apostates', *Bulletin of the School of Oriental and African Studies* 64, 3 (2001), 339–54.

Grigoriadis, Ioannis N., *Instilling Religion in Greek and Turkish Nationalism: A 'Sacred Synthesis'* (Basingstoke: Palgrave Macmillan, 2012).

Guenther, Alan, 'Hanafi Fiqh in Mughal India: The Fatāwá-i ʿĀlamgīrī', in: Richard M. Eaton (ed.), *India's Islamic Traditions, 711–1750* (New Delhi: Oxford University Press, 2003), 207–30.

Guest, John S., *Survival among the Kurds: A History of the Yezidis* (London: Kegan Paul, 1993).

Güngörürler, Selim, 'Ottoman Archival Documents on the Shrines of Karbala, Najaf, and the Hejaz (1660s–1720s): Endowment Wars, the Spoils System, and Iranian Pilgrims', *Journal of the Economic and Social History of the Orient* 64 (2021), 897–1032.

Gunny, Ahmad, *Images of Islam in Eighteenth-Century Writings* (London: Grey Seal, 1996).

Gupta, Radhika, 'Experiments with Khomeini's Revolution in Kargil: Contemporary Shiʿa Networks between India and West Asia', *Modern Asian Studies* 48, 2 (2014), 370–98.

Gutkowski, Stacey, 'We Are the Very Model of a Moderate Muslim State: The Amman Messages and Jordan's Foreign Policy', *International Relations* 30, 2 (2016), 206–26.

Guyard, Stanislas, 'Le Fetwa d'Ibn Taymiyah sur les Noṣairis', *Journal Asiatique* 18 (1871), 158–98.

Haarmann, Ulrich, 'Staat und Religion in Transoxanien im frühen 16. Jahrhundert', *Zeitschrift der Deutschen Morgenländischen Gesellschaft* 124, 2 (1974), 332–69.

Haarmann, Ulrich, 'Yeomanly Arrogance and Righteous Rule: Fażl Allāh b. Rūzbihān Khunjī and the Mamluks of Egypt', in: K. Eslami (ed.), *Iran and Iranian Studies: Essays in Honor of Iraj Afshar* (Princeton: Zagros, 1998), 109–24.

Habermas, Jürgen, *Strukturwandel der Öffentlichkeit: Untersuchungen zu einer Kategorie der bürgerlichen Gesellschaft* (Neuwied: Luchterhand, 1962).

Habib, Irfan, 'The Political Role of Shaikh Ahmad Sirhindi and Shah Waliullah', *Proceedings of the Indian History Congress* 23 (1960), 209–23.

Habib, Irfan, *The Agrarian System of Mughal India 1556–1707*, 3rd ed. (New Delhi: Oxford University Press, 2013).

Habib, John S., *Ibn Saʾud's Warriors of Islam: The Ikhwan of Najd and Their Role in the Creation of the Saʾudi Kingdom, 1910–1930* (Leiden: Brill, 1978).

Habib, John S., 'Wahhabi Origins of the Contemporary Saudi State', in: Mohammed Ayoob and Hasan Kosebalaban (eds), *Religion and Politics in Saudi Arabia: Wahhabism and the State* (London: Lynne Rienner, 2008), 57–73.

Haddad, Bassam, *Business Networks in Syria: The Political Economy of Authoritarian Resilience* (Stanford: Stanford University Press, 2011).

Haddad, Fanar, *Sectarianism in Iraq: Antagonistic Visions of Unity* (London: Hurst, 2011).

Haddad, Fanar, 'Can a "Sunni Spring" turn into an "Iraqi Spring?"', *Foreign Policy*, 7 January 2013.

Haddad, Fanar, 'Sectarian Relations and Sunni Identity in Post-Civil War Iraq', in: Lawrence G. Potter (ed.), *Sectarian Politics in the Persian Gulf* (London: Hurst, 2013), 67–115.

Haddad, Fanar, 'Sectarian Relations in Arab Iraq: Contextualising the Civil War of 2006–2007', *British Journal of Middle Eastern Studies* 40, 2 (2013), 115–38.

Haddad, Fanar, 'Secular Sectarians', *Middle East Institute*, 17 June 2014.

Haddad, Fanar, *Shia-Centric State-Building and Sunni Rejection in Post-2003 Iraq* (Washington, DC: Carnegie Endowment for International Peace, 2016).

Haddad, Fanar, 'Sectarian Relations before "Sectarianization" in Pre-2003 Iraq', in: Nader Hashemi and Danny Postel (eds), *Sectarianization: Mapping the New Politics of the Middle East* (London: Hurst, 2017), 101–22.

Haddad, Fanar, '"Sectarianism" and Its Discontents in the Study of the Middle East', *Middle East Journal* 71, 3 (2017), 363–82.

Haddad, Fanar, 'Anti-Sunnism and Anti-Shiism: Are They the Same Thing?', *Middle East Institute, National University of Singapore*, 9 April 2018.

Haddad, Fanar, 'Anti-Sunnism and Anti-Shiism: Minorities, Majorities and the Question of Equivalence', *Mediterranean Politics* 26, 4 (2021), 498–504.

Haddad, Fanar, 'Iraq's Popular Mobilization Units: A Hybrid Actor in a Hybrid State', in: Adam Day (ed.), *Hybrid Conflict, Hybrid Peace: How Militias and Paramilitary Groups Shape Post-Conflict Transitions* (New York: United Nations University, 2020), 30–65.

Haddad, Fanar, 'Sectarian Identity and National Identity in the Middle East', *Nations and Nationalism* 26 (2020), 123–137.

Haddad, Fanar, *Understanding 'Sectarianism': Sunni-Shi'a Relations in the Modern Arab World* (London: Hurst, 2020).

Haddad, Mahmoud, 'Arab Religious Nationalism in the Colonial Era: Rereading Rashīd Riḍā's Ideas on the Caliphate', *Journal of the American Oriental Society* 117, 2 (1997), 253–77.

Haeri, Shahla, *Law of Desire: Temporary Marriage in Shi'i Iran* (Syracuse, NY: Syracuse University Press, 1989).

Hafez, Mohammed, 'The Crisis within Jihadism: The Islamic State's Puritanism vs. al-Qa'ida's Populism', *CTC Sentinel* 13, 9 (2020), 40–6.

Hagan, John, Joshua Kaiser, Anna Hanson, and Patricia Parker, 'Neighborhood Sectarian Displacement and the Battle for Baghdad: A Self-Fulfilling Prophecy of Fear and Crimes against Humanity in Iraq', *Sociological Forum* 30, 3 (2015), 675–97.

Hagler, Aaron, 'Sapping the Narrative: Ibn Kathir's Account of the Shūrā of 'Uthman in Kitab al-Bidaya wa-l-Nihaya', *International Journal of Middle East Studies* 47, 2 (2015), 303–21.

Haidar, Otared, 'Syrian Ismailis and the Arab Spring: Seasons of Death and White Carnations', in: Kenneth Scott Parker and Tony Emile Nasrallah (eds), *Middle Eastern Minorities and the Arab Spring: Identity and Community in the Twenty-First Century* (Piscataway: Gorgias Press, 2017), 147–74.

al-Haidari, Ibrahim, *Zur Soziologie des schiitischen Chiliasmus* (Freiburg im Breisgau: Klaus Schwarz, 1975).

Haider, Najam, *The Origins of the Shī'a: Identity, Ritual, and Sacred Space in Eighth-Century Kūfa* (Cambridge: Cambridge University Press, 2014).

Haider, Najam, *Shi'i Islam: An Introduction* (Cambridge: Cambridge University Press, 2014).

Haider, Najam, *The Rebel and the Imam in Early Islam: Explorations in Muslim Historiography* (Cambridge: Cambridge University Press, 2019).

Haig, Wolseley, 'The Religion of Ahmad Shah Bahmani', *Journal of the Royal Asiatic Society* 1 (1924), 73–80.

Hairi, Abdul-Hadi, 'Why did the 'Ulamā Participate in the Persian Constitutional Revolution of 1905–1909?', *Die Welt des Islams* 17, 1/4 (1976–7), 127–54.

Hairi, Abdul-Hadi, *Shī'ism and Constitutionalism in Iran: A Study of the Role Played by the Persian Residents of Iraq in Iranian Politics* (Leiden: Brill, 1977).

Hairi, Abdul-Hadi, 'The Legitimacy of the Early Qajar Rule as Viewed by the Shi'i Religious Leaders', *Middle Eastern Studies* 24, 3 (1988), 271–86.

al-Hajj, 'Abd al-Rahman, *Al-Ba'ath al-Shi'i fi Suriyya, 1919–2007* (Beirut: Jusur lil-Tarjama wa-l-Nashr, 2017).

Hakim, Carol, *The Origins of the Lebanese National Idea, 1840–1920* (Berkeley: University of California Press, 2013).

Hakken, B. D., 'Sunni-Shia Discord in Eastern Arabia', *The Muslim World* 23 (1933), 302–5.

Halawi, Majed, *A Lebanon Defied: Musa al-Sadr and the Shi'a Community* (Boulder, CO: Westview Press, 1992).

Halbwachs, Maurice, *La topographie légendaire des Évangiles en Terre Sainte: Étude de memoire collective* (Paris: Presses Universitaires de France, 1941).

Halbwachs, Maurice, *On Collective Memory* (Chicago: University of Chicago Press, 1992).

Halevi, Leor, *Muhammad's Grave: Death Rites and the Making of Islamic Society* (New York: Columbia University Press, 2007).

Halevi, Leor, *Modern Things on Trial: Islam's Global and Material Reformation in the Age of Rida, 1865–1935* (New York: Columbia University Press, 2019).

Hallaq, Wael B., 'Was the Gate of Ijtihad Closed?', *International Journal of Middle East Studies* 16, 1 (1984), 3–41.

Halliday, Fred, 'Iranian Foreign Policy since 1979: Internationalism and Nationalism in the Islamic Revolution', in: Juan R. I. Cole and Nikki R. Keddie (eds), *Shi'ism and Social Protest* (New Haven, CT: Yale University Press, 1986), 88–107.

Halliday, Fred, *Revolution and Foreign Policy: The Case of South Yemen, 1967–1987* (Cambridge: Cambridge University Press, 1990).

Halliday, Fred, *Revolution and World Politics: The Rise and Fall of the Sixth Great Power* (Basingstoke: Macmillan, 1999).

Halliday, Fred, *The Middle East in International Relations: Power, Politics and Ideology* (Cambridge: Cambridge University Press, 2005).

Halm, Heinz, *Kosmologie und Heilslehre der frühen Ismāʿīlīya: Eine Studie zur islamischen Gnosis* (Wiesbaden: Franz Steiner, 1978).

Halm, Heinz, *Die islamische Gnosis: Die extreme Schia und die ʿAlawiten* (Zurich: Artemis, 1982).

Halm, Heinz, *Das Reich des Mahdi: Der Aufstieg der Fatimiden 875–973* (Munich: C.H. Beck, 1991) (Engl. Transl.: *The Empire of the Mahdi: The Rise of the Fatimids* (Leiden: Brill, 1996).

Halm, Heinz, *The Fatimids and Their Traditions of Learning* (London: I. B. Tauris, 2001).

Halm, Heinz, *Die Schiiten* (Munich: C. H. Beck, 2005).

Halm, Heinz, *Kalifen und Assassinen: Ägypten und der Vordere Orient zur Zeit der ersten Kreuzzüge 1074–1171* (Munich: C. H. Beck, 2014).

Halm, Heinz, *Die Assassinen: Geschichte eines islamischen Geheimbundes* (Munich: C. H. Beck, 2017).

Halverson, Jeffry R., *Theology and Creed in Sunni Islam: The Muslim Brotherhood, Ashʿarism, and Political Sunnism* (New York: Palgrave Macmillan, 2010).

Halverson, Jeffry R., 'The Anti-Shiʿa Polemics of an Online Salafi-Jihadi: The Case of Nasir al-Qaʿida in Historical Perspective', *The Muslim World* 103, 4 (2013), 501–17.

Hammada, Rashid, *ʿAsifa Fawq Miyah al-Khalij: Qissa Awwal Inqilab ʿAskari fi al-Bahrayn 1981* (London: al-Safa li-l-Nashr wa-l-Tawziʿ, 1990).

Hammada, Saʿdun, *Tarikh al-Shiʿa fi Lubnan*, 2 Vols, 2nd ed. (Beirut: Dar al-Khayyal, 2013).

Hamdani, Sumaiya A., 'The Dialectic of Power: Sunni-Shiʿi Debates in Tenth-Century North Africa', *Studia Islamica* 90 (2000), 5-21.

Hamdani, Sumaiya A., *Between Revolution and State: The Path to Fatimid Statehood: Qadi al-Nuʿman and the Construction of Fatimid Legitimacy* (London: I. B. Tauris, 2006).

Hamid, Shadi, 'The Lesser Threat: How the Muslim Brotherhood Views Shias and Shiism', *Mediterranean Politics* 26 (2021), 511–517.

Hamidi, Ayman, 'Inscriptions of Violence in Northern Yemen: Haunting Histories, Unstable Moral Spaces', *Middle Eastern Studies* 45, 2 (2009), 165–87.

Hamilton, Lillias A., *Die Tochter des Wesirs: Eine Erzählung aus dem Hazara-Krieg (Afghanistan, 1887–1893)* (Bubendorf: Bibliotheca Afghanica, 2000).

Hanieh, Adam, *Capitalism and Class in the Gulf Arab States* (New York: Palgrave Macmillan, 2011).

Hanieh, Adam, *Money, Markets, and Monarchies: The Gulf Cooperation Council and the Political Economy of the Contemporary Middle East* (Cambridge: Cambridge University Press, 2018).

Hanifi, Shah Mahmoud, *Connecting Histories in Afghanistan: Market Relations and State Formation on a Colonial Frontier* (Stanford: Stanford University Press, 2011).

Hanioğlu, M. Şükrü, *A Brief History of the Late Ottoman Empire* (Princeton: Princeton University Press, 2008).

Hanioğlu, M. Şükrü, 'Contract or Treaty? The Da'an Agreement of 1911 and the Limits on Imam Yahya's Authority', *Journal of Arabian Studies* 8, 1 (2018), 25–46.

Hanne, Eric J., *Putting the Caliph in his Place: Power, Authority and the Late Abbasid Caliphate* (Madison, WI: Farleigh Dickinson University Press, 2007).

Hansen, Thorkild, *Arabia Felix: The Danish Expedition of 1761–1767* (London: Collins, 1964).

Hanssen, Jens, *Fin de Siècle Beirut: The Making of an Ottoman Provincial Capital* (Oxford: Clarendon Press, 2005).

Haqqi, Halifa, and Ida Mujtahidah, 'International Political Analysis on the Second Committee of Hejaz', in: M. F. Mujahidin et al. (eds), *Proceeding: International Conference on Middle East and South East Asia (ICoMS) 2016* (Surakarta: Sebelas Maret University, 2016), 134–45.

al-Harawi, 'Ali ibn Abi Bakr, *A Lonely Wayfarer's Guide to Pilgrimage: 'Alī ibn Abī Bakr al-Harawī's Kitāb al-Ishārāt ilā Ma'rifat al-Ziyārāt*, trans. by Josef W. Meri (Princeton: Darwin Press, 2004).

Harawi, Muhammad Yusuf Riyazi, *'Ayn al-Waqayi': Tarikh-i Afghanistan dar Salha-yi 1207–1324*, ed. by Muhammad Asif Fikrat (Tehran: Bunyad-i Mawqufat-i Duktur Mahumd Afshar Yazdi, 1990).

Hardinge, Arthur Henry, *A Diplomatist in the East* (London: J. Cape, 1928).

Harik, Judith, 'Hizballah's Public and Social Services and Iran', in: H. E. Chehabi, *Distant Relations: Iran and Lebanon in the Last 500 Years* (London: I. B. Tauris, 2006), 259–86.

Haroon, Sana, *Frontier of Faith: Islam in the Indo-Afghan Borderland* (New York: Columbia University Press, 2007).

Harris, Christina Phelps, 'The Persian Gulf Submarine Telegraph of 1864', *Geographical Journal* 135, 2 (1969), 169–90.

Harris, William, *Lebanon: A History, 600–2011* (Oxford: Oxford University Press, 2012).

Harrow, Leonard, 'Notes on Catholic-Shi'i Relations during the Safavid Period', *Journal of Eastern Christian Studies* 63, 1–2 (2011), 99–121.

Hart, Fuchsia, 'Pictorial Narration of the Battle of Karbala in Qajar Iran: A Combined Art Historical and Anthropological Approach', *Iran Namag* 1, 4 (2017), 4–22.

Hartmann, Angelika, *An-Nasir li-Din Allah: Politik, Religion, Kultur in der späten Abbasidenzeit* (Berlin: De Gruyter, 1975).

Hartung, Jan-Peter, 'The Nadwat al-'Ulama': Chief Patron of Madrasa Education in India and a Turntable to the Arab World', in: Jan-Peter Hartung and Helmut Reifeld (eds), *Islamic Education, Diversity and National Identity: Dīnī Madāris in India Post 9/11* (New Delhi: Sage, 2006), 135–57.

Hartung, Jan-Peter, *A System of Life: Mawdudi and the Ideologisation of Islam* (New York: Oxford University Press, 2014).

Hartung, Jan-Peter, 'Between a Rock and a Hard Place: The Ṭālibān, Afghan Self-Determination, and the Challenges of Transnational Jihadism', *Die Welt des Islams* 56, 2 (2016), 125–52.

Harvey, Frank P., *Explaining the Iraq War: Counterfactual Theory, Logic and Evidence* (Cambridge: Cambridge University Press, 2012).

Harvey, Katherine, *A Self-Fulfilling Prophecy: The Saudi Struggle for Iraq* (London: Hurst, 2021).

al-Hasan, Hamza, *Al-Shiʿa fi al-Mamlaka al-ʿArabiyya al-Suʿudiyya*, 2 Vols (Beirut: Muʾassasat al-Baqiʿ li-Ihyaʾ al-Turath, 1993).

Hasan, Mushirul, 'Traditional Rites and Contested Meanings: Sectarian Strife in Colonial Lucknow', *Economic and Political Weekly* 31, 9 (1996), 543–50.

Hashemi, Nader, and Danny Postel, 'Introduction: The Sectarianization Thesis', in: Nader Hashemi and Danny Postel (eds), *Sectarianization: Mapping the New Politics of the Middle East* (London: Hurst, 2017), 1–22.

Hashim, Ahmed, *Iraq's Sunni Insurgency* (Abingdon: Routledge, 2009).

Hassan, Hassan, 'The Sectarianism of the Islamic State', in: Frederic Wehrey (ed.), *Beyond Sunni and Shia: The Roots of Sectarianism in a Changing Middle East* (Oxford: Oxford University Press, 2018), 39–59.

Hassan, Mona, *Longing for the Lost Caliphate: A Transregional History* (Princeton: Princeton University Press, 2017).

Hassaniyan, Allan, *Kurdish Politics in Iran: Crossborder Interactions and Mobilisation since 1947* (Cambridge: Cambridge University Press, 2021).

Hasson, Isaac, *Contemporary Polemics between Neo-Wahhabis and Post-Khomeinist Shiites* (Washington, DC: Hudson Institute, 2009).

Hathaway, Jane, 'The Forgotten Icon: The Sword Zülfikâr in its Ottoman Incarnation', *Turkish Studies Association Journal* 27, 1–2 (2003), 1–14.

Hathaway, Jane, *A Tale of Two Factions: Myth, Memory, and Identity in Ottoman Egypt and Yemen* (Albany: SUNY Press, 2003).

Hathaway, Jane, 'The Mawzaʿ Exile at the Juncture of Zaydi and Ottoman Messianism', *Association for Jewish Studies Review* 29, 1 (2005), 111–28.

Hathaway, Jane, 'The Forgotten Province: A Prelude to the Ottoman Era in Yemen', in: David J. Wasserstein and Ami Ayalon (eds), *Mamluks and Ottomans: Studies in Honour of Michael Winter* (London: Routledge, 2006), 195–205.

Hatina, Meir, 'Debating the "Awakening Shiʿa": Sunni Perceptions of the Iranian Revolution', in: Meir Litvak and Ofra Bengio (eds), *The Sunna and Shiʿa in History: Division and Ecumenism in the Muslim Middle East* (Basingstoke: Palgrave Macmillan, 2011), 203–21.

Haugbolle, Sune, *War and Memory in Lebanon* (New York: Cambridge University Press, 2010).

Hawwa, Saʿid, *Al-Khumayniyya: Shudhudh fi al-ʿAqaʾid wa Shudhudh fi al-Mawaqif* (Amman: Dar ʿAmmar, 1987).

Hawwa, Saʿid, *Hadhihi Tajribati wa Hadhihi Shahadati* (Cairo: Maktabat Wahba, 1987).

Hawting, Gerald R., *The First Dynasty of Islam: The Umayyad Caliphate AD 661–750*, 2nd ed. (London: Routledge, 2000).

Hayakawa, Hideaki, 'What does Antisectarianism Oppose? Lebanese Communists' Debates on Sectarianism, 1975–1981', *British Journal of Middle Eastern Studies* (published online, 1 September 2021).

Haydar, Afak, 'The Politicization of the Shias and the Development of the Tehrik-e-Nifaz-e-Fiqh-e-Jafaria in Pakistan', in: Charles H. Kennedy (ed.), *Pakistan: 1992* (Boulder, CO: Westview Press, 1993), 75–93.

Haydar, Rustum, *Mudhakkirat Rustum Haydar: Haqqaqaha wa Kataba laha Muqaddima 'an Sirat Rustum Haydar wa Maqtalihi Najda Fathi Safwa* (Beirut: al-Dar al-'Arabiyya li-l-Mawsu'at, 1988).

Haydari, Ibrahim, 'The Rituals of Ashura: Genealogy, Functions, Actors and Structures', in Faleh A. Jabar (ed.), *Ayatollahs, Sufis and Ideologues: State, Religion and Social Movements in Iraq* (London: Saqi, 2002), 101–13.

Hayes, Edmund, 'Alms and the Man: Fiscal Sectarianism in the Legal Statements of the Shi'i Imams', *Journal of Arabic and Islamic Studies* 17 (2017), 280–98.

Hayes, Edmund, *Agents of the Hidden Imam: Forging Twelver Shi'ism, 850–950 CE* (Cambridge: Cambridge University Press, 2022).

Haykel, Bernard, 'Al-Shawkâni and the Jurisprudential Unity of Yemen', *Revue des mondes musulmans et de la Méditerranée* 67 (1993), 53–65.

Haykel, Bernard, 'A Zaydi Revival?', *Yemen Update* 36 (1995), 20–1.

Haykel, Bernard, 'Rebellion, Migration or Consultative Democracy? The Zaydis and their Detractors in Yemen', in: R. Leveau, F. Mermier, and U. Steinbach (eds), *Le Yémen contemporain* (Paris: Karthala, 1999), 193–201.

Haykel, Bernard, 'Recent Publishing Activity by the Zaidis in Yemen: A Select Bibliography', *Chroniques yéménites* 9 (2001), 225–7.

Haykel, Bernard, *Revival and Reform in Islam: The Legacy of Muhammad al-Shawkani* (Cambridge: Cambridge University Press, 2003).

Haykel, Bernard, 'On the Nature of Salafi Thought and Action', in: Roel Meijer (ed.), *Global Salafism: Islam's New Religious Movement* (London: Hurst, 2009), 33–57.

Haykel, Bernard, 'Al-Qa'ida and Shiism', in: Assaf Moghadam and Brian Fishman (eds), *Fault Lines in Global Jihad: Organizational, Strategic, and Ideological Fissures* (London: Routledge, 2011), 184–202.

Hazara Encyclopaedia Foundation, *Hazara Encyclopaedia*, Vol. 1 (Kabul: Hazara Encyclopaedia Foundation, 2019).

Hazara, Fayz Muhammad Katib, *The History of Afghanistan: Fayż Muḥammad Kātib Hazārah's Sirāj al-Tawārīkh*, 3 Vols (Leiden: Brill, 2013).

Hazelton, Lesley, *After the Prophet: The Epic Story of the Shia-Sunni Split in Islam* (New York: Doubleday, 2009).

Heard-Bey, Frauke, *Die arabischen Golfstaaten im Zeichen der islamischen Revolution* (Bonn: Forschungsinstitut der Deutschen Gesellschaft für Auswärtige Politik, 1983).

Heern, Zackery, *The Emergence of Modern Shi'ism: Islamic Reform in Iraq and Iran* (London: Oneworld, 2015).

Heern, Zackery, 'One Thousand Years of Islamic Education in Najaf: Myth and History of the Shi'i Ḥawza', *Iranian Studies* 50, 3 (2017), 415–38.

Hegghammer, Thomas, 'Global Jihadism after the Iraq War', *Middle East Journal* 60, 1 (2006), 11–32.

Hegghammer, Thomas, 'Saudis in Iraq: Patterns of Radicalization and Recruitment', *Cultures et Conflits* (2008), 1–14.

Hegghammer, Thomas, *Jihad in Saudi Arabia: Violence and Pan-Islamism since 1979* (Cambridge: Cambridge University Press, 2010).

Hegghammer, Thomas, *The Caravan: Abdallah Azzam and the Rise of Global Jihad* (Cambridge: Cambridge University Press, 2020).

Hegghammer, Thomas, and Stéphane Lacroix, 'Rejectionist Islamism in Saudi Arabia: The Story of Juhayman al-'Utaybi Revisited', *International Journal of Middle East Studies* 39, 1 (2007), 103–22.

Heidemann, Stefan, *Das Aleppiner Kalifat (A.D. 1261): Vom Ende des Kalifates in Bagdad über Aleppo zu den Restaurationen in Kairo* (Leiden: Brill, 1994).

Heidemann, Stefan, 'Numismatics', in: Chase F. Robinson (ed.), *The New Cambridge History of Islam*, Vol. 1 (Cambridge: Cambridge University Press, 2010), 648–63.

Heine, Peter, 'Die Imam-Kurse der deutschen Wehrmacht im Jahre 1944', in: Gerhard Höpp (ed.), *Fremde Erfahrungen: Asiaten und Afrikaner in Deutschland, Österreich und in der Schweiz bis 1945* (Berlin: Das Arabische Buch, 1996), 229–38.

Helfont, Samuel, *The Sunni Divide: Understanding Politics and Terrorism in the Arab Middle East* (Philadelphia: Foreign Policy Research Institute, 2009).

Helfont, Samuel, 'Saddam and the Islamists: The Ba'thist Regime's Instrumentalization of Religion in Foreign Affairs', *Middle East Journal* 68, 3 (2014), 352–66.

Helfont, Samuel, *Compulsion in Religion: Saddam Hussein, Islam, and the Roots of Insurgencies in Iraq* (New York: Oxford University Press, 2018).

Hellot, Florence, 'Tentatives missionnaires auprès des musulmans de Perse et dans les montagnes kurdes (sur les marges de l'Empire ottoman et de la Perse, avant la Première Guerre mondiale)', in: Bernard Heyberger and Rémy Madinier (eds), *L'Islam des marges: Mission chrétienne et espaces périphériques du monde musulman, XVI–XXe siècles* (Paris: IISMM/Karthala, 2011), 145–205.

Henley, Alexander D. M., *Religious Authority and Sectarianism in Lebanon* (Washington, DC: Carnegie Endowment for International Peace, 2016).

Hermann, Denis, 'Aspectos de la penetración del shiismo en Irán durante los periodos ilkhâní y timurí: El éxito político de los movimientos sarbedâr, mar'ashi y musha'sha'yân', *Estudios de Asia y Africa* 39, 3 (2004), 673–709.

Hermann, Denis, 'La instauración del shiismo como religión de Estado en Irán bajo los safávidas: Del shiismo qizilbāsh al shiismo imamita', *Estudios de Asia y África* 41, 3 (2006), 439–72.

Hermann, Denis, 'Shiism, Sufism and Sacred Space in the Deccan: Counter-Narratives of Saintly Identity in the Cult of Shah Nur', in: Alessandro Monsutti, Silvia Naef, and Farian Sabahi (eds), *The Other Shiites: From the Mediterranean to Central Asia* (Bern: Peter Lang, 2008), 195–218.

Hermann, Denis, and Mathieu Terrier (eds), *Shi'i Islam and Sufism: Classical Views and Modern Perspectives* (London: I.B. Tauris/Institute of Ismaili Studies, 2019).

Hermann, Denis, and Mathieu Terrier, 'Introduction: New Perspectives on Imami Shi'i–Sufi Relations in the Modern and Pre-Modern Periods', in: Denis Hermann and Mathieu Terrier(eds), *Shi'i Islam and Sufism: Classical Views and Modern Perspectives* (London: I. B. Tauris/Institute of Ismaili Studies, 2020), 1–24.

Hermann, Denis, and Omid Rezai, 'Le rôle du VAQF dans la formation de la communauté Shaykhi Kermani à l'époque Qājār (1259-1324/1843-1906)', *Studia Iranica* 36, 1 (2007), 87–131.

Hermann, Rainer, *Kulturkrise und konservative Erneuerung: Muḥammad Kurd 'Alī (1876–1953) und das geistige Leben in Damaskus zu Beginn des 20. Jahrhunderts* (Frankfurt am Main: Peter Lang, 1990).

Hernandez, Rebecca, *The Legal Thought of Jalāl al-Dīn al-Suyūṭī: Authority and Legacy* (Oxford: Oxford University Press, 2017).

Hertog, Steffen, *Princes, Brokers, and Bureaucrats: Oil and the State in Saudi Arabia* (Ithaca, NY: Cornell University Press, 2010).

Heyberger, Bernard, 'Peuples "sans loi, sans foi, ni prêtre": Druzes et nusayrîs de Syrie découverts par les missionnaires catholiques (XVIIe–XVIIIe siècles)', in: Bernard Heyberger and Rémy Madinier (eds), *L'Islam des marges: Mission chrétienne et espaces périphériques du monde musulman, XVI–XXe siècles* (Paris: IISMM/Karthala, 2011), 45–80.

Heydemann, Steven, *Networks of Privilege in the Middle East: The Politics of Economic Reform Revisited* (New York: Palgrave Macmillan, 2004).

Higgins, Patricia J., 'Minority-State Relations in Contemporary Iran', in: Ali Banuazizi and Myron Weiner (eds), *The State, Religion, and Ethnic Politics: Pakistan, Iran, and Afghanistan* (Syracuse: Syracuse University Press, 1986), 167–97.

Hill, Ginny, *Yemen Endures: Civil War, Saudi Adventurism and the Future of Arabia* (London: Hurst, 2017).

Hillenbrand, Carole, *The Crusades: Islamic Perspectives* (Edinburgh: Edinburgh University Press, 1999).

Hillenbrand, Carole, 'The Shi'is of Aleppo in the Zengid Period: Some Unexploited Textual and Epigraphic Evidence', in: H. Biesterfeldt and V. Klemm (eds), *Difference and Dynamism in Islam: Festschrift for Heinz Halm on his 70th Birthday* (Würzburg: Ergon, 2012), 163–79.

al-Hilli, Hasan b. Yusuf 'al-Allama', *Al-Bâbu 'l-Ḥâdî, 'Ashar: A Treatise on the Principles of Shî'ite Theology*, trans. by William McElwee Miller (London: Royal Asiatic Society, 1928).

al-Hilli, Hasan b. Yusuf 'al-Allama', *Sharh Minhaj al-Karama fi Ma'rifat al-Imama*, ed. by S. Ali al-Milani (Qom: Dar al-Hijra, 1997).

Hinds, Martin, 'Kufan Political Alignments and their Background in the Mid-Seventh Century A.D.', *International Journal of Middle East Studies* 2, 4 (1971), 346–67.

Hinds, Martin, 'The Murder of the Caliph 'Uthmān', *International Journal of Middle East Studies* 3, 4 (1972), 450–69.

Hinds, Martin, 'The Ṣiffīn Arbitration Agreement', *Journal of Semitic Studies* 17 (1972), 93–113.

Hinds, Martin, 'The Banners and Battle Cries of the Arabs at Siffin', in: Jere Bacharach, Lawrence I. Conrad, and Patricia Crone (eds), *Studies in Early Islamic History* (Princeton: Darwin Press, 1996), 97–142.

Hinnebusch, Raymond, 'Liberalization without Democratization in "Post-Populist" Authoritarian States: Evidence from Syria and Egypt', in: Nils A. Butenschon, Uri Davis, and Manuel Hassassian (eds), *Citizenship and the State in the Middle East: Approaches and Applications* (Syracuse: Syracuse University Press, 2000), 123–45.

Hinnebusch, Raymond, 'Syria: From "Authoritarian Upgrading" to Revolution?', *International Affairs* 88, 1 (2012), 95–113.

Hinnebusch, Raymond, *The International Politics of the Middle East*, 2nd ed. (Manchester: Manchester University Press, 2015).

Hinnebusch, Raymond, 'Syria's Alawis and the Ba'ath Party', in: Michael Kerr and Craig Larkin (eds), *The Alawis of Syria: War, Faith and Politics in the Levant* (Oxford: Oxford University Press, 2015), 107–24.

Hinnebusch, Raymond, 'The Sectarian Revolution in the Middle East', *R/evolutions: Global Trends & Regional Issues* 4, 1 (2016), 120–52.

Hinnebusch, Raymond, 'The Sectarianization of the Middle East: Transnational Identity Wars and Competitive Interference', memo prepared for the workshop 'Transnational Diffusion and Cooperation in the Middle East and North Africa', held 8–9 June 2016 in Hamburg, Germany.

Hinnebusch, Raymond, and Adham Saouli (eds), *The War for Syria: Regional and International Dimensions of the Syrian Uprising* (Abingdon: Routledge, 2020).

Hiro, Dilip, *Cold War in the Islamic World: Saudi Arabia, Iran and the Struggle for Supremacy* (London: Hurst, 2018).

Hirschkind, Charles, *The Ethical Soundscape: Cassette Sermons and Islamic Counterpublics* (New York: Columbia University Press, 2006).

al-Hirz, Muhammad 'Ali, 'Al-Qada' al-Ja'fari fi al-Ahsa", *al-Waha* 20 (2001), 19–38.

al-Hirz, Muhammad 'Ali, 'Malamih min al-Haya al-'Ilmiyya fi 'Asr al-Shaykh al-Ahsa'i (1210-1241 A.H.)', *al-Waha* 50 (2008), 62–78.

al-Hirz, Muhammad 'Ali, *Ahsa'iyyun Muhajirun* (Beirut: Dar al-Mahajja al-Bayda', 2010).

Hitti, Philip K., *History of the Arabs* (London: Macmillan, 1937).

Hjortshoj, Keith Guy, 'Shi'i Identity and the Significance of Muharram in Lucknow, India', in: Martin Kramer (ed.), *Shi'ism, Resistance, and Revolution* (Boulder, CO: Westview Press, 1987), 289–309.

Hobsbawm, Eric J., *Nations and Nationalism since 1780: Programme, Myth, Reality*, 2nd ed. (Cambridge: Cambridge University Press, 1992).

Hodgson, Marshall G. S., 'How did the Early Shi'a Become Sectarian?', *Journal of the American Oriental Society* 75, 1 (1955), 1–13.

Hodgson, Marshall G. S., *The Secret Order of Assassins: The Struggle of the Early Nizārī Ismā'īlīs against the Islamic World* (Philadelphia: University of Pennsylvania Press, 1955).

Hodgson, Marshall G. S., 'Al-Darazî and Ḥamza in the Origin of the Druze Religion', *Journal of the American Oriental Society* 82, 1 (1962), 5–20.

Hodgson, Marshall G. S., 'The Ismāʿīlī State', in: J. A. Boyle (ed.), *The Cambridge History of Iran*, Vol. 5 (Cambridge: Cambridge University Press, 1968), 422–82.

Hodgson, Marshall G. S., *The Venture of Islam*, 3 Vols (Chicago: University of Chicago Press, 1974–7).

Hoffman, Valerie J., 'Devotion to the Prophet and His Family in Egyptian Sufism', *International Journal of Middle East Studies* 24, 4 (1992), 615–37.

Hoffman, Valerie J., 'Ibadi Muslim Scholars and the Confrontation with Sunni Islam in Nineteenth- and Early Twentieth-Century Zanzibar', *Bulletin of the Royal Institute for Inter-Faith Studies* 7, 1 (2005), 91–118.

Hoffman, Valerie J., *The Essentials of Ibadi Islam* (New York: Syracuse University Press, 2012).

Hoffman, Valerie J., 'Ibāḍism: History, Doctrines, and Recent Scholarship', *Religion Compass* 9 (2015), 297–307.

Hoffmann, Friedhelm, *Die syro-palästinensische Delegation am Völkerbund und Šakīb Arslān in Genf 1921–1936/46* (Zurich: LIT, 2010).

Holden, David, and Richard Johns, *The House of Saud* (London: Sidgwick and Jackson, 1981).

Hollister, John Norman, *The Shiʿa of India* (London: Luzac & Co., 1953).

Holmes Katz, Marion, *The Birth of the Prophet Muhammad: Devotional Piety in Sunni Islam* (Abingdon: Routledge, 2007).

Holtzman, Livnat, 'Accused of Anthropomorphism: Ibn Taymiyya's Miḥan as Reflected in Ibn Qayyim al-Jawziyya's al-Kāfiya al-Shāfiya', *The Muslim World* 106 (2016), 561–87.

Homerin, Th. Emil, 'Ibn Taymiyya's al-Ṣūfiyah wa-al-Fuqarāʾ', *Arabica* 32 (1985), 219–44.

Honegger, Claudia (ed.), *M. Bloch, F. Braudel, L. Febvre u. a.: Schrift und Materie der Geschichte: Vorschläge zur systematischen Aneignung historischer Prozesse* (Frankfurt am Main: Suhrkamp, 1977).

Honegger, Claudia, *Die Hexen der Neuzeit: Studien zur Sozialgeschichte eines kulturellen Deutungsmusters* (Frankfurt am Main: Suhrkamp, 1978).

Hoover, Jon, *Ibn Taymiyya's Theodicy of Perpetual Optimism* (Leiden: Brill, 2007).

Hopkins, Ben D., *The Making of Modern Afghanistan* (Basingstoke: Palgrave Macmillan, 2008).

Hopkins, Ben D., 'Race, Sex and Slavery: "Forced Labour" in Central Asia and Afghanistan in the Early 19th Century', *Modern Asian Studies* 42, 4 (2008), 629–71.

Horesh, Niv (ed.), *Toward Well-Oiled Relations? China's Presence in the Middle East Following the Arab Spring* (Basingstoke: Palgrave Macmillan, 2015).

Hourani, Albert, *Minorities in the Arab World* (London: Oxford University Press, 1947).

Hourani, Albert, 'Ottoman Reform and the Politics of Notables', in: William R. Polk and Richard L. Chambers (eds), *Beginnings of Modernization in the Middle East: The Nineteenth Century* (Chicago: University of Chicago Press, 1968), 41–68.

Hourani, Albert, 'Rashid Rida and the Sufi Orders: A Footnote to Laoust', *Bulletin d'études orientales* 29 (1977), 231–41.

Hourani, Albert, 'Sufism and Modern Islam: Mawlana Khalid and the Naqshbandi Order', in: Albert Hourani (ed.), *The Emergence of the Modern Middle East* (London: Macmillan, 1981), 75–89.

Hourani, Albert, *Arabic Thought in the Liberal Age, 1798–1939*, 2nd ed. (Cambridge: Cambridge University Press, 1983).

Hourani, Albert, 'From Jabal 'Amil to Persia', in: H. E. Chehabi, *Distant Relations: Iran and Lebanon in the Last 500 Years* (London: I. B. Tauris, 2006), 51–61.

Hourani, Albert, and Nadim Shehadi (eds), *The Lebanese in the World: A Century of Emigration* (London: I. B. Tauris, 1992).

Houston, Chloë, '"Thou Glorious Kingdome, Thou Chiefe of Empires": Persia in Early Seventeenth-Century Travel Literature', *Studies in Travel Writing* 13, 2 (2009), 141–52.

Houston, Chloë, 'Turning Persia: The Prospect of Conversion in Safavid Iran', in: Lieke Stelling, Harald Hendrix, and Todd Richardson (eds), *The Turn of the Soul: Representations of Religious Conversion in Early Modern Art and Literature* (Leiden: Brill, 2012), 85–107.

al-Houthi, Yahya bin al-Hussein, *Sublime Answers to the Iraqi's Questions* (*Al-Jawāb ar-Rāqi 'ala al-Masā'il al-Irāqi*), available at https://www.scribd.com/document/ 36214491/الجواب-الراقي.

Howard, I. K. A., 'The Development of the Adhan and Iqama of the Salat in Early Islam', *Journal of Semitic Studies* 26 (1981), 219–28.

Howard, I. K. A., 'Shī'ī Theological Literature', in: M. Young, J. Latham, and R. Serjeant (eds), *Religion, Learning and Science in the 'Abbasid Period* (Cambridge: Cambridge University Press, 1990), 16–32.

Howarth, Toby, *The Twelver Shi'a as a Muslim Minority in India: Pulpit of Tears* (London: Routledge, 2005).

Hroub, Khaled, 'Salafi Formations in Palestine: The Limits of a De-Palestinised Milieu', in: Roel Meijer (ed.), *Global Salafism: Islam's New Religious Movement* (London: Hurst, 2009), 221–43.

Hroub, Khaled (ed.), *Religious Broadcasting in the Middle East* (New York: Columbia University Press, 2012).

Hroub, Khaled, 'The Role of the Media in the Middle Eastern Sectarian Divide', in: Eduardo López Busquets (ed.), *Sunni and Shia: Political Readings of a Religious Dichotomy* (Cordoba: Casa Árabe, 2014), 37–47.

Humphrey, Michael, *Islam, Sect and State: The Lebanese Case* (Oxford: Centre for Lebanese Studies, 1989).

Hurvitz, Nimrod, 'Muhibb al-Din al-Khatib's Semitic Wave Theory and Pan-Arabism', *Middle Eastern Studies* 29, 1 (1993), 118–34.

Husain, Afzal, 'Liberty and Restraint: A Study of Shiaism in the Mugial Nobility', *Proceedings of the Indian History Congress* 42 (1981), 275–88.

Husain, Afzal, 'Accommodation and Integration: Shi'as in the Mughal Nobility', *Proceedings of the Indian History Congress* 69 (2008), 211–24.

Husain, Wahed, *Administration of Justice during the Muslim Rule in India: With a History of the Origin of the Islamic Legal Institutions* (Calcutta: University of Calcutta, 1934).

Husayn, Nebil A., 'The Rehabilitation of 'Alī in Sunnī Ḥadīth and Historiography', *Journal of the Royal Asiatic Society* 29, 4 (2019), 565–83.

Husayn, Nebil A., 'Aḥkām Concerning the Ahl al-Bayt', *Islamic Law and Society* 27, 3 (2020), 145–84.

Husayn, Nebil A., *Opposing the Imam: The Legacy of the Nawasib in Islamic Literature* (Cambridge: Cambridge University Press, 2021).

al-Husayni, Badr al-Din ibn Amir al-Din ibn al-Husayn al-Hawthi, *Al-Ijaz fi al-Radd 'Ala Fatawa al-Hijaz* (Sana: Maktabat al-Yaman al-Kubra, 1979).

Husayni, Ishaq Musa, *The Moslem Brethren: The Greatest of Modern Islamic Movements* (Beirut: Khayat, 1956).

al-Husri, Abu Khaldun Sati, *Mudhakkirati fi al-Iraq*, Vol. 1 (Beirut: Dar al-Tali'a, 1967).

al-Hussayni, Abdallah (ed.), *Al-Judhur al-Tarikhiyya li-l-Nusayriyya al-'Alawiyya* (Cairo: Dar al-I'tisam, 1980).

Hussayni, Kamyar Sadaqat Thamar, *Shi'ahshinasi-i Ahl-i Sunnat va Chalishha-yi Fararuy-i An dar Dawran-i pas az Inqilab-i Islami-i Iran* (Tehran: World Forum for the Proximity of Islamic Schools of Thought, 2012).

el-Husseini, Rola, 'Resistance, Jihad, and Martyrdom in Contemporary Lebanese Shi'a Discourse', *Middle East Journal* 62, 3 (2008), 399–414.

el-Husseini, Rola, 'Hezbollah and the Axis of Refusal: Hamas, Iran and Syria', *Third World Quarterly* 31, 5 (2010), 803–15.

el-Husseini, Rola, 'Political Exigency or Religious Affinity? Sectarianism in the Contemporary Arab World', *Mediterranean Politics* 26, 4 (2021), 491–7.

Huthi, Muhammad ibn al-Qasim, *Al-Maw'izah al-Hasanah* (Saada: Maktabat Ahl al-Bayt, 1435h).

Hyder, Syed Akbar, *Reliving Karbala: Martyrdom in South Asian Memory* (Oxford: Oxford University Press, 2006).

Ibn Abd al-Wahhab, Muhammad, *Al-Radd 'ala al-Rafida* (Sanaa: Dar al-Athar, 2006).

Ibn al-Adim, Kamal Eddin, *Zubdat al-Halab fi Ta'rikh Halab*, 3 Vols (Damascus: Institut Français de Damas, 1951–68).

Ibn al-Athir, 'Izzal-Din, *The Annals of the Saljuq Turks: Selections from al-Kāmil fi'l-Ta'rīkh of 'Izz al-Dīn Ibn al-Athīr*, trans. by D. S. Richards (London: Routledge, 2002).

Ibn al-Athir, 'Izzal-Din, *The Chronicle of Ibn al-Athīr for the Crusading Period from al-Kāmil fi'l-Ta'rīkh*, trans. by D. S. Richards, 3 Vols (Aldershot: Ashgate, 2005–8).

Ibn Battuta, *The Travels of Ibn Battuta, AD 1325–1354*, Vol. 4, trans./ed. by H. A. R. Gibb and C. F. Beckingham (London: Hakluyt Society, 1994).

Ibn Bishr, *'Unwan al-Majd fi Tarikh Najd*, 2 Vols (Riyadh: Maktaba al-Riyyad al-Haditha, n.d., likely facsimile from the 1980s).

Ibn Ishaq, *Das Leben des Propheten*, trans. by Gernot Rotter (Kandern: Spohr, 1999).

Ibn Ishaq, *Al-Sira al-Nabawiyya li-Ibn Hisham* (Beirut: Mu'assasat al-Ma'arif, 2005).

Ibn Khaldun, *The Muqaddimah: An Introduction to History*, trans. by Franz Rosenthal (Princeton: Princeton University Press, 2015).

Ibn Munqidh, Usamah, *An Arab-Syrian Gentleman and Warrior in the Period of the Crusades: Memoirs of Usāmah ibn Munqidh (Kitāb al-Iʿtibār)*, trans. by Philip K. Hitti (New York: Columbia University Press, 1929).

Ibn Munqidh, Usamah, *Usâma ibn Munqidh: Ein Leben im Kampf gegen Kreuzritterheere*, trans. by Gernot Rotter (Lenningen: Edition Erdmann, 2004).

Ibn Ruzbahan, Fazl Allah, *Persia in A.D. 1478–1490, Turkmenica 12*, trans. by Vladimir Minorsky and John E. Woods (London: Royal Asiatic Society, 1992).

Ibn Taymiyya, Ahmad, *Minhaj al-Sunna al-Nabawiyya fi Naqd Kalam al-Shiʿa wa-l-Qadariyya* (The Way of the Prophetic Sunna in the Criticism of the Words of the Shia and the Qadiriyya), 4 Vols (Cairo: Bulaq, 1903–5); and 9 Vols (Riyadh: Imam Mohammad Ibn Saud Islamic University, 1991–).

Ibn Taymiyya, Ahmad, *The Madinan Way: The Soundness of the Basic Premises of the School of the People of Madina* (Norwich: Bookwork, 2000).

Ibrahim, Ahmed Fekry, *Pragmatism in Islamic Law: A Social and Intellectual History* (Syracuse, New York: Syracuse University Press, 2015).

al-Ibrahim, Badr, and Muhammad al-Sadiq, *Al-Hirak al-Shiʿi fi al-Suʿudiyya: Tasayyis al-Madhhab wa Madhhabat al-Siyyasa* (The Shia Movement in Saudi Arabia: The Politicisation of Confession and the Confessionalisation of Politics) (Beirut: al-Shabaka al-ʿArabiyya li-l-Abhath wa-l-Nashr, 2013).

Ibrahim, Ferhad, *Konfessionalismus und Politik in der arabischen Welt: Die Schiiten im Irak* (Münster: LIT, 1997).

Ibrahim, Fuʾad, *Al-Faqih wa-l-Dawla: Tatawwur al-Fikr al-Siyyasi al-Shiʿi* (Beirut: Dar al-Kunuz al-Adabiyya, 1998).

Ibrahim, Fuʾad, *The Shiʿis of Saudi Arabia* (London: Saqi, 2006).

Ibrahimi, Niamatullah, *The Hazaras and the Afghan State: Rebellion, Exclusion and the Struggle for Recognition* (London: Hurst, 2017).

Ilahi, Shereen, 'Sectarian Violence and the British Raj: The Muharram Riots of Lucknow', *India Review* 6, 3 (2007), 184–208.

Ilhan, Mehmet Mehdi, 'The Katif District (Liva) during the First Few Years of Ottoman Rule: A Study of the 1551 Ottoman Cadastral Survey', *Belleten (Türk Tarih Kurumu)* 51, 200 (1987), 780–98.

Imam, S. M. A., 'The Orientalists', *The Muslim Review* 39, 4/5 (1952), 91–4, and 6/7 (1952), 130–2.

Imber, Colin H., 'The Persecution of the Ottoman Shiʿites according to the Mühimme Defterleri, 1565–1585', *Der Islam* 56 (1979), 245–73.

Imber, Colin H., 'The Ottoman Dynastic Myth', *Turcica* 19 (1987), 7–27.

Imber, Colin H., *Ebu's-Suʿud: The Islamic Legal Tradition* (Stanford: Stanford University Press, 1997).

Imbert, Frédéric, 'L'Islam des pierres: L'expression de la foi dans les graffiti arabes des premiers siècles', *Revue des mondes musulmans et de la Méditerranée* 129 (2011), 57–78.

İnalcik, Halil, 'The Emergence of the Ottomans', in: P. M. Holt, Ann K. S. Lambton, and Bernard Lewis (eds), *The Cambridge History of Islam*, Vol. 1A (Cambridge: Cambridge University Press, 1977), 263–92.

India Census Commissioner, *Report on the Census of British India, Taken on the 17th February 1881*, Vol. 1 (London: Eyre & Spottiswoode, 1883).

Ingram, Brannon D., *Revival from Below: The Deoband Movement and Global Islam* (Oakland: University of California Press, 2018).

Ioannides, Chris P., 'The PLO and the Islamic Revolution in Iran', in: Augustus R. Norton and Martin H. Greenberg (eds), *The International Relations of the Palestine Liberation Organization* (Carbondale: Southern Illinois University Press, 1989), 74–108.

Iqbal, Muhammad, *The Development of Metaphysics in Persia: A Contribution to the History of Muslim Philosophy* (Lahore: Bazm-i-Iqbal, 1959).

Irwin, Robert, 'Der Islam und die Kreuzzüge 1096–1699', in: Jonathan Riley-Smith (ed.), *Illustrierte Geschichte der Kreuzzüge* (Frankfurt am Main: Campus, 1999), 251–98.

Isa, Kabiru Haruna, 'Sunni Literary Responses to the Spread of Shia Ideology in Northern Nigeria', *Studies in African Languages and Cultures* 52 (2018), 113–30.

Isakhan, Benjamin, 'Shattering the Shia: A Maliki Political Strategy in Post-Saddam Iraq', in: Benjamin Isakhan (ed.), *The Legacy of Iraq: From the 2003 War to the 'Islamic State'* (Edinburgh: Edinburgh University Press, 2015), 67–81.

Isakhan, Benjamin, 'The Islamic State Attacks on Shia Holy Sites and the "Shrine Protection Narrative": Threats to Sacred Space as a Mobilization Frame', *Terrorism and Political Violence* 32, 4 (2020), 724–48.

Ismaeel, Saeed, *The Difference between the Shee'ah and the Muslims* (US Office, World Assembly of Muslim Youth, 1995).

Ismael, Tareq Y., *The Rise and Fall of the Communist Party of Iraq* (Cambridge: Cambridge University Press, 2008).

Ismael, Tareq Y., and Jacqueline S. Ismael, *The Gulf War and the New World Order: International Relations of the Middle East* (Gainesville: University Press of Florida, 1994).

Ismael, Tareq Y., and Jacqueline S. Ismael, 'The Sectarian State in Iraq and the New Political Class', *International Journal of Contemporary Iraqi Studies* 4, 3 (2010), 339–56.

Ismael, Tareq Y., and Jacqueline S. Ismael, 'Entrenching Sectarianism: How Chilcot Sees Iraq', *International Journal of Contemporary Iraqi Studies* 11, 1–2 (2017), 23–46.

Ismael, Tareq Y., and Max Fuller, 'The Disintegration of Iraq: The Manufacturing and Politicization of Sectarianism', *International Journal of Contemporary Iraqi Studies* 2, 3 (2009), 443–73.

Ismail, Raihan, *Saudi Clerics and Shī'a Islam* (New York: Oxford University Press, 2016).

Ismail, Raihan, 'The Saudi 'Ulama and the Syrian Civil War', in: Amin Saikal (ed.), *The Arab World and Iran: A Turbulent Region in Transition* (New York: Palgrave Macmillan, 2016), 83–102.

Ismail, Raihan, *Rethinking Salafism: The Transnational Networks of Salafi 'Ulama in Egypt, Kuwait, and Saudi Arabia* (New York: Oxford University Press, 2021).

Ismail, Salwa, 'The Syrian Uprising: Imagining and Performing the Nation', *Studies in Ethnicity and Nationalism* 11, 3 (2011), 538–49.

Ismail, Salwa, 'Urban Subalterns in the Arab Revolutions: Cairo and Damascus in Comparative Perspective', *Comparative Studies in Society and History* 55, 4 (2013), 865–94.

Ismail, Salwa, *The Rule of Violence: Subjectivity, Memory and Government in Syria* (Cambridge: Cambridge University Press, 2018).

Ismayilov, Murad, and Norman A. Graham (eds), *Turkish–Azerbaijani Relations: One Nation—Two States?* (Abingdon: Routledge, 2016).

Israeli, Raphael, 'Is there Shi'a in Chinese Islam?', *Institute of Muslim Minority Affairs Journal* 9, 1 (1988), 49–66.

al-Istrabadi, Feisal Amin Rasoul, 'Sectarian Visions of the Iraqi State: Irreconcilable Differences?', in: Susan H. Williams (ed.), *Social Difference and Constitutionalism in Pan-Asia* (New York: Cambridge University Press, 2014), 195–229.

Izzati, Abu l-Fadl, *An Introduction to Shi'i Islamic Law and Jurisprudence with an Emphasis on the Authority of Human Reason as a Source of Law According to Shi'i and Persian Law* (Tehran/Lahore: University of Tehran/Ashraf Press, 1974).

Jabar, Faleh A., 'Why the Uprisings Failed', *Middle East Report* 176 (1992), 2–14.

Jabar, Faleh A., *The Shi'ite Movement in Iraq* (London: Saqi, 2003).

Jabar, Faleh A., *The Iraqi Protest Movement: From Identity Politics to Issue Politics* (London: LSE Middle East Centre, 2018).

Jackson, Peter, 'The Mongols and the Faith of the Conquered', in: Reuven Amitai and Michal Biran (eds), *Mongols, Turks, and Others: Eurasian Nomads and the Sedentary World* (Leiden: Brill, 2005), 245–90.

Jackson, Peter, *The Mongols and the West, 1221–1410* (Harlow: Pearson/Longman, 2005).

Jackson, Peter, 'Muslim India: The Delhi Sultanate', in: D. Morgan and A. Reid (eds), *The New Cambridge History of Islam*, Vol. 3 (Cambridge: Cambridge University Press, 2010), 100–27.

Jackson, Peter, *The Mongols and the Islamic World: From Conquest to Conversion* (New Haven: Yale University Press, 2017).

Jackson, Simon, '"What is Syria Worth?": The Huvelin Mission, Economic Expertise and the French Project in the Eastern Mediterranean, 1918–1922', *Monde(s)* 2, 4 (2013), 83–103.

Jacob, Harold F., *Kings of Arabia: The Rise and Set of the Turkish Sovranty in the Arabian Peninsula* (London: Mills & Boon, 1923).

Jacoby, Tim, and Nassima Neggaz, 'Sectarianism in Iraq: The Role of the Coalition Provisional Authority', *Critical Studies on Terrorism* 11, 3 (2018), 478–500.

Jacquot, Paul, *L'état des Alaouites: Terre d'art, de souvenirs, et de mystère* (Beirut: Imprimerie catholique, 1929).

al-Jad'an, al-Shaykh Salih, *Ayatallah al-Shaykh Muhammad 'Ali al-'Amri: Sira wa 'Ita'* (n.p.: n.p., 2011).

Jader, Adel S. al-Abdul, 'The Origin of Key Shi'ite Thought Patterns in Islamic History', in: Yasir Suleiman (ed.), *Living Islamic History: Studies in Honour of Professor Carole Hillenbrand* (Edinburgh: Edinburgh University Press, 2010), 1–13.

Ja'fariyan, Rasul, *Ukdhubat tahrif al-Qur'an bayn al-Shi'a wa-l-Sunna* (Tehran: Mu'awaniyyat al-'Alaqat al-Duwaliyya fi Munazzama al-I'lam al-Islami, 1985).

Ja'fariyan, Rasul, 'Die vorgebliche Rolle von Hwâǧa Nasîr ad-Dîn at-Tûsî bei dem Fall von Bagdad', *Spektrum Iran* 3 (1990), 30–53.

Ja'fariyan, Rasul, *Din va Siyasat dar Dawrah-yi Safavi* (Qom: Ansariyan, 1370/1991–2).

Ja'fariyan, Rasul, *Tarikh-i Tashayyu' dar Iran: Az Aghaz ta Qarn-i Dahum-i Hijri*, 2 Vols (Qom: Ansariyan, 1375/1996–7).

Ja'fariyan, Rasul, *Chahardah Safarnamah-i Hajj-i Qajar-i Digar* (Tehran: Ilm, 2013).

Ja'fariyan, Rasul, 'The Alleged Role of Khawajah Nasir al-Din al-Tusi in the Fall of Baghdad', *Al-Islam.org*, https://www.al-islam.org/al-tawhid/vol8-n2/alleged-role-khawajah-nasir-al-din-al-tusi-fall-baghdad/alleged-role-khawajah.

Jafri, Saiyid Naqi Husain, 'A Modernist View of Madrasa Education in Late Mughal India', in: Jan-Peter Hartung and Helmut Reifeld (eds), *Islamic Education, Diversity and National Identity: Dīnī Madāris in India Post 9/11* (New Delhi: Sage, 2006), 39–55.

Jafri, Saiyid Zaheer Husain, *Awadh from Mughal to Colonial Rule: Studies in the Anatomy of a Transformation* (New Delhi: Gyan, 2016).

Jafri, Syed Husain Mohammad, *The Origins and Early Development of Shi'a Islam* (London: Longman, 1979).

Jahangir, *The Jahangirnama: Memoirs of Jahangir, Emperor of India*, trans. by Wheeler M. Thackston (New York: Oxford University Press, 1999).

Jalal, Ayesha, *The Sole Spokesman: Jinnah, the Muslim League, and the Demand for Pakistan* (Cambridge: Cambridge University Press, 1985).

Jalalzai, Musa Khan, *The Sunni-Shia Conflict in Pakistan* (Lahore: Book Traders, 1998).

Jamal, 'Abd al-Muhsin Yusuf, *Lamahat min Tarikh al-Shi'a fi al-Kuwayt: Al-Fitra min Nasha'at al-Kuwayt ila al-Istiqlal* (Kuwait: Dar al-Naba' lil-Nashr, 2005).

Jamali, Fadil, 'Theological Colleges of Najaf', *The Muslim World* 50, 1 (1960), 15–22.

al-Jamil, Tariq, 'Ibn Taymiyya and Ibn al-Mutahhar al-Hilli: Shi'i Polemics and the Struggle for Religious Authority in Medieval Islam', in: Yossef Rapoport and Shahab Ahmed (eds), *Ibn Taymiyya and his Times* (Oxford: Oxford University Press, 2010), 229–46.

Jansen, Johannes J. G., 'Echoes of the Iranian Revolution in the Writings of Egyptian Muslims', in: David Menashri (ed.), *The Iranian Revolution and the Muslim World* (Boulder, CO: Westview Press, 1990), 207–18.

Jarrar, Maher, 'Some Aspects of Imami Influence on Early Zaydite Theology', in: Rainer Brunner, Monika Gronke, Jens P. Laut, and Ulrich Rebstock (eds), *Islamstudien ohne Ende: Festschrift für Werner Ende* (Würzburg: Deutsche Morgenländische Gesellschaft/Ergon, 2002), 201–23.

Jarrar, Maher, 'Al-Manṣūr bi-Llāh's Controversy with Twelver Šī'ites Concerning the Occultation of the Imam in his Kitāb al-'Iqd al-tamīn', *Arabica* 59, 3–4 (2012), 319–31.

Jessup, Henry Harris, *Fifty-Three Years in Syria*, 2 Vols (New York: Fleming H. Revell, 1910).

Jiwa, Shainool, *Towards a Shi'i Mediterranean Empire: Fatimid Egypt and the Founding of Cairo* (London: I. B. Tauris, 2009).

Joassin, Thomas, 'Algerian "Traditional" Islam and Political Sufism', in: Francesco Piraino and Mark J. Sedgwick (eds), *Global Sufism: Boundaries, Structures, and Politics* (London: Hurst, 2019), 209–24.

Johnsen, Gregory D., *The Last Refuge: Yemen, al-Qaeda, and the Battle for Arabia* (London: Oneworld, 2013).

Johnson, Michael, *Class and Client in Beirut: The Sunni Muslim Community and the Lebanese State, 1840–1985* (London: Ithaca, 1986).

Johnston, Trevor, et al., *Could the Houthis be the Next Hizballah? Iranian Proxy Development in Yemen and the Future of the Houthi Movement* (Santa Monica, CA: RAND, 2020).

Jones, Clive, and Yoel Guzansky, 'Israel's Relations with the Gulf States: Toward the Emergence of a Tacit Security Regime?', *Contemporary Security Policy* 38, 3 (2017), 398–419.

Jones, Justin, 'The Local Experiences of Reformist Islam in a "Muslim" Town in Colonial India: The Case of Amroha', *Modern Asian Studies* 43, 4 (2009), 871–908.

Jones, Justin, *Shi'a Islam in Colonial India: Religion, Community and Sectarianism* (Cambridge: Cambridge University Press, 2012).

Jones, Justin, 'Shi'ism, Humanity and Revolution in Twentieth Century India: Selfhood and Politics in the Husainology of 'Ali Naqi Naqvi', *Journal of the Royal Asiatic Society* 24, 3 (2014).

Jones, Justin, '"The Pakistan that is Going to be Sunnistan": Indian Shi'i Responses to the Pakistan Movement', in: Ali Usman Qasmi and Megan Eaton Robb (eds), *Muslims against the Muslim League: Critiques of the Idea of Pakistan* (Cambridge: Cambridge University Press, 2017), 350–80.

Jones, Justin, and Ali Usman Qasmi (eds), *The Shi'a in Modern South Asia: Religion, History and Politics* (Cambridge University Press, 2015).

Jones, Marc Owen, *Political Repression in Bahrain* (Cambridge: Cambridge University Press, 2020).

Jones, Toby, 'Seeking a "Social Contract" for Saudi Arabia', *Middle East Report* 228 (2003), 42–8.

Jones, Toby, 'Violence and the Illusion of Reform in Saudi Arabia', *Middle East Report Online*, 13 November 2003.

Jones, Toby, 'The Iraq Effect in Saudi Arabia', *Middle East Report* 237 (2005), 20–5.

Jones, Toby, 'Rebellion on the Saudi Periphery: Modernity, Marginalization, and the Shi'a Uprising of 1979', *International Journal of Middle East Studies* 38, 2 (2006), 213–33.

Jones, Toby, 'Saudi Arabia's not so New Anti-Shi'ism', *Middle East Report* 242 (2007), 29–32.

Jones, Toby, *Embattled in Arabia: Shi'is and the Politics of Confrontation in Saudi Arabia* (Combating Terrorism Center at West Point, 2009).

Jones, Toby, *Desert Kingdom: How Oil and Water Forged Modern Saudi Arabia* (Cambridge, MA: Harvard University Press, 2010).

al-Juhany, Uwaidah M., *Najd before the Salafi Reform Movement: Social, Political and Religious Conditions during the Three Centuries Preceding the Rise of the Saudi State* (Reading: Ithaca, 2002).

Juneau, Thomas, 'Iran's Policy towards the Houthis in Yemen: A Limited Return on a Modest Investment', *International Affairs* 92, 3 (2016), 647–63.

Kadhim, Abbas, *Reclaiming Iraq: The 1920 Revolution and the Founding of the Modern State* (Austin: University of Texas Press, 2012).

Kadhim, Abbas, *The Hawza under Siege: A Study in the Ba'th Party Archive* (Boston: Boston University Institute for Iraqi Studies, 2013).

Kafadar, Cemal, *Between Two Worlds: The Construction of the Ottoman State* (Berkeley: University of California Press, 1996).

Kaicker, Abhishek, *The King and the People: Sovereignty and Popular Politics in Mughal Delhi* (Oxford: Oxford University Press, 2020).

Kaiser, Thomas, 'The Evil Empire? The Debate on Turkish Despotism in Eighteenth-Century French Political Culture', *Journal of Modern History* 72, 1 (2000), 6–34.

Kakar, M. Hasan, *The Pacification of the Hazaras of Afghanistan* (New York: Afghanistan Council/Asia Society, 1973).

Kakar, M. Hasan, *Government and Society in Afghanistan: The Reign of Amir Abd al-Rahman Khan* (Austin: University of Texas Press, 1979).

Kakar, M. Hasan, *Afghanistan: The Soviet Invasion and the Afghan Response, 1979–1982* (Berkeley: University of California Press, 1995).

Kalantari, Mohammad R., *The Clergy and the Modern Middle East: Shi'i Political Activism in Iran, Iraq and Lebanon* (London: I. B. Tauris, 2022).

Kamaly, Hossein, *God and Man in Tehran: Contending Visions of the Divine from the Qajars to the Islamic Republic* (New York: Columbia University Press, 2018).

Kamran, Tahir, and Amir Khan Shahid, 'Shari'a, Shi'as and Chishtiya Revivalism: Contextualising the Growth of Sectarianism in the Tradition of the Sialvi Saints of the Punjab', *Journal of the Royal Asiatic Society* 24, 3 (2014), 477–92.

Kamrava, Mehran, *Revolution in Iran: The Roots of Turmoil* (London: Routledge, 1990).

Kamrava, Mehran, *Qatar: Small State, Big Politics* (Ithaca: Cornell University Press, 2013).

Kane, Eileen M., *Russian Hajj: Empire and the Pilgrimage to Mecca* (Ithaca: Cornell University Press, 2015).

Kantz Feder, Rachel, 'Fatima's Revolutionary Image in Fadak fi al-Ta'rikh (1955): The Inception of Muhammad Baqir al-Sadr's Activism', *British Journal of Middle Eastern Studies* 41, 1 (2014), 79–96.

Kaptein, N. J. G., *Muhammad's Birthday Festival: Early History in the Central Muslim Lands and Development in the Muslim West until the 10th/16th Century* (Leiden: Brill, 1993).

Kara, Cem, *Grenzen überschreitende Derwische: Kulturbeziehungen des Bektaschi-Ordens 1826–1925* (Göttingen: Vandenhoeck & Ruprecht, 2019).

Kara, Seyfeddin, 'The Collection of the Qur'ān in the Early Shī'ite Discourse: The Traditions Ascribed to the Fifth Imām Abū Ja'far Muḥammad al-Bāqir', *Journal of the Royal Asiatic Society* 26, 3 (2016), 375–406.

Kara, Seyfeddin, *In Search of Alī ibn Abī Tālib's Codex: History and Traditions of the Earliest Copy of the Qur'ān* (Berlin: Gerlach Press, 2018).

Karakaya-Stump, Ayfer, 'Documents and "Buyruk" Manuscripts in the Private Archives of Alevi Dede Families: An Overview', *British Journal of Middle Eastern Studies* 37, 3 (2010), 273–86.

Karakaya-Stump, Ayfer, 'The Forgotten Dervishes: The Bektashi Convents in Iraq and Their Kizilbash Clients', *International Journal of Turkish Studies* 16, 1/2 (2011), 1–24.

Karakaya-Stump, Ayfer, 'The Vefā'iyye, the Bektashiyye and Genealogies of "Heterodox" Islam in Anatolia: Rethinking the Köprülü Paradigm', *Turcica* 44 (2012–3), 279–300.

Karamustafa, Ahmed T., *God's Unruly Friends: Dervish Groups in the Islamic Middle Period 1200–1550* (Salt Lake City: University of Utah Press, 1994).

Karamustafa, Ahmed T., *Sufism: The Formative Period* (Edinburgh: Edinburgh University Press, 2007).

Karapetyan, Mkrtich, 'The Alevi/Alawite Factor in Turkey–Syria Relations in the Light of the Syrian Crisis', *Journal of Liberty and International Affairs* 4, 3 (2018), 24–40.

Karimi, Ali, 'The Bazaar, the State, and the Struggle for Public Opinion in Nineteenth-Century Afghanistan', *Journal of the Royal Asiatic Society* 30, 4 (2020), 613–33.

Karolewski, Janina, 'What Is Heterodox about Alevism? The Development of Anti-Alevi Discrimination and Resentment', *Die Welt des Islams* 48, 3/4 (2008), 434–56.

Kartomi, Margaret, 'Tabut: A Shia Ritual Transplanted from India to Sumatra', in: David P. Chandler and Merle C. Ricklefs (eds), *Nineteenth and Twentieth Century Indonesia: Essays in Honour of Professor J. D. Legge* (Clayton: Monash University, 1986), 141–62.

Kasapoğlu, Can, 'Beyond Obama's Red Lines: The Syrian Arab Army and Chemical Warfare', *SWP Comment* 27 (2019), 1–4.

Al Kashif al-Ghita, 'Abd al-Rida, *Al-Anwar al-Hussayniyya wa-l-Sha'a'ir al-Islamiyya* (Bombay: Hur Printing, 1346h).

Al Kashif al-Ghita, Muhammad al-Hussayn, *Asl al-Shi'a wa Usuliha*, 7th ed. (Najaf: al-Matba'a al-Haydariyya, 1950).

Al Kashif al-Ghita, Muhammad al-Hussayn, *Le Shi'isme: Origins et principes* (Beirut: Albouraq, 2007).

Al Kashif al-Ghita, Muhammad al-Hussayn, *Naqd Fatawa al-Wahhabiyya* (Qom: Mu'assasat Al al-Bayt li-Ihya' al-Turath, 1416/1995).

Kassam, Zayn, and Bridget Blomfield, 'Remembering Fatima and Zaynab: Gender in Perspective', in: Farhad Daftary, Amyn B. Sajoo, and Shainool Jiwa (eds), *The Shi'i World: Pathways in Tradition and Modernity* (London: I. B. Tauris, 2015), 211–28.

Kastritsis, Dimitris, *The Sons of Bayezid: Empire Building and Representation in the Ottoman Civil War of 1402–13* (Leiden: Brill, 2007).

Katouzian, Homa, *The Persians: Ancient, Medieval, and Modern Iran* (London: Yale University Press, 2009).

Katzman, Kenneth, *The Warriors of Islam: Iran's Revolutionary Guard* (Boulder, CO: Westview Press, 1993).

Kaufman, Asher, 'Between Palestine and Lebanon: Seven Shi'i Villages as a Case Study of Boundaries, Identities, and Conflict', *Middle East Journal* 60, 4 (2006), 685–706.

Kazimi, Nibras, 'Zarqawi's Anti-Shi'a Legacy: Original or Borrowed?', *Current Trends in Islamist Ideology* 4 (2006), 53–72.

Kedar, Benjamin Z., 'Some New Light on the Composition Process of William of Tyre's Historia', in: Susan B. Edgington and Helen J. Nicholson (eds), *Deeds Donebeyond the Sea: Essays on William of Tyre, Cyprus and the Military Orders Presented to Peter Edbury* (Aldershot: Ashgate, 2014), 3–11.

Keddie, Nikki R., 'Religion and Irreligion in Early Iranian Nationalism', *Comparative Studies in Society and History* 4, 3 (1962), 265–95.

Keddie, Nikki R., *Religion and Rebellion in Iran: The Tobacco Protest of 1891–1892* (London: Cass, 1966).

Keddie, Nikki R., *Sayyid Jamāl ad-Dīn 'al-Afghānī': A Political Biography* (Berkeley: University of California Press, 1972).

Keddie, Nikki R., *Modern Iran: Roots and Results of Revolution* (New Haven, CT: Yale University Press, 2006).

Keddie, Nikki R., and Rudolph P. Matthee (eds), *Iran and the Surrounding World: Interactions in Culture and Cultural Politics* (University of Washington Press, 2002).

Kedourie, Elie, 'The Iraqi Shi'is and their Fate', in: Martin Kramer (ed.), *Shi'ism, Resistance, and Revolution* (Boulder, CO: Westview Press, 1987), 135–57.

Kedourie, Elie, 'Anti-Shiism in Iraq under the Monarchy', *Middle Eastern Studies* 24, 2 (1988), 249–53.

Kehl-Bodrogi, Krisztina, *Kizilbas/Aleviten: Untersuchungen über eine esoterische Glaubensgemeinschaft in Anatolien* (Berlin: Klaus Schwarz, 1988).

Kelidar, Abbas, 'The Shii Imami Community and Politics in the Arab East', *Middle Eastern Studies* 19, 1 (1983), 3–16.

Kelly, J. B., 'The Persian Claim to Bahrain', *International Affairs* 33, 1 (1957), 51–70.

Kemalpashazade (Ahmad ibn Suleiman ibn Kamal), 'Fatwa/Epistle Concerning the Qizilbash (1513/1514)', in: Adel Allouche, *The Origins and Development of the Ottoman-Safavid Conflict, 906–966/1500–1555* (Berlin: Klaus Schwarz, 1983), 170–3.

Kendall, Elisabeth, *Iran's Fingerprints in Yemen: Real or Imagined?* (Washington, DC: Atlantic Council, 2017).

Kennedy, Hugh, *The Early Abbasid Caliphate: A Political History* (London: Routledge, 2015).

Kennedy, Hugh, *Caliphate: The History of an Idea* (New York: Basic Books, 2016).

Kennedy, Hugh, *The Prophet and the Age of the Caliphates: The Islamic Near East from the 6th to the 11th Century*, 2nd ed. (Harlow: Pearson, 2004).

Kern, Karen M., *Imperial Citizen: Marriage and Citizenship in the Ottoman Frontier Provinces of Iraq* (Syracuse: Syracuse University Press, 2011).

Kerr, Cortni, and Toby Jones, 'A Revolution Paused in Bahrain', *MERIP*, 23 February 2011.

Kerr, Malcolm, *The Arab Cold War: Gamal 'Abd al-Nasir and his Rivals, 1958–1970*, 3rd ed. (London: Oxford University Press, 1971).

Kerr, Michael, and Craig Larkin (eds), *The Alawis of Syria: War, Faith and Politics in the Levant* (Oxford: Oxford University Press, 2015).

Keshk, Khaled, *The Historian's Mu'awiya: The Depiction of Mu'awiya in the Early Islamic Sources* (Saarbrücken: VDM Verlag Dr. Müller, 2008).

Keshk, Khaled, 'The Historiography of an Execution: The Killing of Ḥujr b. 'Adī', *Journal of Islamic Studies* 19, 1 (2008), 1–35.

Keshk, Khaled, 'How to Frame History', *Arabica* 56, 4/5 (2009), 381–99.

Keynoush, Banafsheh, *Saudi Arabia and Iran: Friends or Foes?* (Basingstoke: Palgrave Macmillan, 2016).

Khaddour, Kheder, 'The Alawite Dilemma', in: Friederike Stolleis (ed.), *Playing the Sectarian Card: Identities and Affiliations of Local Communities in Syria* (Beirut: Friedrich-Ebert-Stiftung, 2015), 11–26.

Khadduri, Majid, 'Iran's Claim to the Sovereignty of Bahrayn', *American Journal of International Law* 45, 4 (1951), 631–47.

Khalaf, Samir, *Civil and Uncivil Violence in Lebanon: A History of the Internationalization of Communal Conflict* (New York: Columbia University Press, 2002).

Khalfoui, Mouez, 'Together but Separate: How Muslim Scholars Conceived of Religious Plurality in South Asia in the Seventeenth Century', *Bulletin of the School of Oriental and African Studies* 74, 1 (2011), 87–96.

Khalidi, Tarif, 'Shaykh Ahmad ʿArif az-Zain and al-ʿIrfān', in: Marwan R. Buheiry (ed.), *Intellectual Life in the Arab East, 1890–1939* (Beirut: American University of Beirut, 1981), 110–24.

Khalidi, Umar, 'The Shiʿites of the Deccan: An Introduction', *Rivista degli Studi Orientali* 64, 1/2 (1990), 5–16.

Khalifé, Nabil, *The Attempt to Uproot Sunni-Arab Influence: A Geo-Strategic Analysis of the Western, Israeli and Iranian Quest for Domination*, trans. by Joseph A. Kéchichian (Eastbourne: Sussex Academic Press, 2017).

Khalil, Muhammad Mahmud, *Tarikh al-Khalij wa Sharq al-Jazira al-ʿArabiyya al-Musamma Iqlim Bilad al-Bahrayn fi Zill Hukm al-Duwaylat al-ʿArabiyya 469–963 A.H./1076–1555* (Cairo: Maktaba Madbuli, 2006).

Khalili, Laleh, '"Standing with my Brother": Hizbullah, Palestinians, and the Limits of Solidarity', *Comparative Studies in Society and History* 49, 2 (2007), 276–303.

Khalilzad, Zalmay, 'The Iranian Revolution and the Afghan Resistance', in: Martin Kramer (ed.), *Shiʿism, Resistance, and Revolution* (Boulder, CO: Westview Press, 1987), 257–73.

al-Khalisi, Muhammad ibn Muhammad Mahdi, *La vie de l'ayatollah Mahdî al-Khâlisî* (Paris: La Martinière, 2005).

Khan, Adil Hussain, *From Sufism to Ahmadiyya: A Muslim Minority Movement in South Asia* (Bloomington: Indiana University Press, 2015).

Khan, Ahmad Raza, *Majmūʿa-yi Risaʾil-i Radd-i Ravafiz: Radd al-Rafaza: Al-Adillat al-Taʿina: Risala-yi Taʿziyadari/Tasnif Imam Ahmad Raza Qadiri Barelvi* (Lahore: Markazi Majlis-i Riza, 1986).

Khan, Ansar Zahid, 'Ismailism in Multan and Sind', *Journal of the Pakistan Historical Society* 23 (1975), 36–57.

Khan, Hasan Ali, *Constructing Islam on the Indus: The Material History of the Suhrawardi Sufi Order, 1200–1500 AD* (Cambridge: Cambridge University Press, 2016).

Khan, M.S., 'The Early History of Zaydi Shiʿism in Daylaman and Gilan', *Zeitschrift der Deutschen Morgenländischen Gesellschaft* 125 (1975), 301–14.

Khan, Mohammad Ali, *Speech by the Hon'ble Raja Sir Mohammad Ali Mohammad Khan, Khan Bahadur, of Mahmudabad, President of the All-India Moslem League, 30 December 1917, Calcutta* (Calcutta: Statesman Press, n.d.).

Khan, Mohammad Amir Ahmad, *Presidential Address Delivered by Raja Mohammad Amir Ahmad Khan of Mahmudabad at the Bombay Presidency Muslim League Conference, Hubli, 24–25 May 1940* (Lucknow: Lucknow Publishing House, n.d.).

Khan, Muhammad Amir Ahmad (Ali Khan Mahmudabad), 'Shia–Sunni Relations in India', *Live Encounters*, January 2014, https://liveencounters.net/january-2014/january/ali-khan-mahmudabad-shia-sunni-relations-in-india/.

Khan, Muhammad Amir Ahmad (Ali Khan Mahmudabad), 'Local Nodes of a Transnational Network', in: Justin Jones and Ali Usman Qasmi (eds), *The Shi'a in Modern South Asia: Religion, History and Politics* (Cambridge: Cambridge University Press, 2015), 57–79.

Khan, Muhammad Amir Ahmad (Ali Khan Mahmudabad), *Poetry of Belonging: Muslim Imaginings of India 1850–1950* (New Delhi: Oxford University Press, 2020).

Khan, Muin-ud-din Ahmad, *History of the Fara'idi Movement in Bengal, 1818–1906* (Karachi: Pakistan Historical Society, 1965).

Khan, Reyaz Ahmad, 'Jahangir on Shias and Sunnis in Majalis-i Jahangiri', *Proceedings of the Indian History Congress* 72 (2011), 302–7.

Khan, Reyaz Ahmad, 'Naqib Khan: Secretary to Emperors Akbar and Jahangir', *Proceedings of the Indian History Congress* 74 (2013), 240–4.

Khatib, Line, 'Syria, Saudi Arabia, the U.A.E. and Qatar: The "Sectarianization" of the Syrian Conflict and Undermining of Democratization in the Region', *British Journal of Middle Eastern Studies* 46, 3 (2019), 385–403.

al-Khatib, Muhibb al-Din, *Al-Khutut al-'Arida*, 3rd ed. (Qatar: n.p., 1386/1966).

al-Khatib, Muhibb al-Din, *Şiilik (Imamiyye-Isnaaşeriyye) dini esaslarının görünen çizgileri* (n.p., n.d.).

Khashan, Hilal, 'The Rise and Growth of Hezbollah and the Militarization of the Sunni-Shiite Divide in Lebanon', *Middle East Institute*, 26 January 2016.

Khaÿat, Henri Michel, 'The Šī'ite Rebellions in Aleppo in the 6th A. H./12th A. D. Century', *Rivista degli Studi Orientali* 46, 3/4 (1971), 167–95.

al-Khoei, Hayder, 'Post-Sistani Iraq, Iran, and the Future of Shia Islam', *War on the Rocks*, 8 September 2016.

al-Khoei, Yousif, 'The Marja and the Survival of a Community: The Shia of Medina', in: Linda Walbridge (ed.), *The Most Learned of the Shi'a: The Institution of the Marja' Taqlid* (Oxford: Oxford University Press, 2001), 247–50.

Khomeini, Sayyid Ruhullah Musawi, *Islamic Government: Governance of the Jurist*, trans. by Hamid Algar (Institute for the Compilation and Publication of the Works of Imam Khomeini, n.d.).

Khomeini, Sayyid Ruhullah Musawi, *Islam and Revolution: Writings and Declarations of Imam Khomeini*, trans. by Hamid Algar (Berkeley: Mizan Press, 1981).

Khoury, Dina Rizk, 'Who is a True Muslim? Exclusion and Inclusion among Polemicists of Reform in Nineteenth-Century Baghdad', in: Virginia H. Aksan and Daniel Goffman (eds), *The Early Modern Ottomans: Remapping the Empire* (Cambridge: Cambridge University Press, 2007), 256–74.

Khoury, Dina Rizk, *Iraq in Wartime: Soldiering, Martyrdom, and Remembrance* (Cambridge: Cambridge University Press, 2013).

Khoury, Gérard D., 'Robert de Caix et Louis Massignon', in: Peter Sluglett and Nadine Méouchy (eds), *The British and French Mandates in Comparative Perspectives* (Leiden: Brill, 2004), 165–83.

Khoury, Gérard D., *Une tutelle coloniale: Le mandat français en Syrie et au Liban: Écrits politiques de Robert de Caix* (Paris: Belin, 2006).

Khoury, Philip S., 'Factionalism among Syrian Nationalists during the French Mandate', *International Journal of Middle East Studies* 13, 4 (1981), 441–69.

Khoury, Philip S., *Urban Notables and Arab Nationalism: The Politics of Damascus, 1860–1920* (Cambridge: Cambridge University Press, 1983).

Khoury, Philip S., *Syria and the French Mandate: The Politics of Arab Nationalism, 1920–1945* (Princeton: Princeton University Press, 1987).

al-Khunayzi, ʿAli Abu al-Hasan ibn Hasan bin Mahdi, *Al-Daʿwa al-Islamiyya ila Wahdat Ahl al-Sunna wa-l-Imamiyya*, 2 Vols (Beirut: Dar al-Fikr, 1956).

al-Khurasan, Salah, *Hizb al-Daʿwa al-Islamiyya: Haqaʾiq wa Wathaʾiq: Fusul min Tajriba al-Haraka al-Islamiyya fi al-ʿIraq Khilala 40 ʿAman* (Damascus: al-Muʾassasa al-ʿArabiyya li-l-Dirasat wa-l-Buhuth al-Istiratijiyya, 1999).

Khuri, Fuad I., *Tribe and State in Bahrain: The Transformation of Social and Political Authority in an Arab State* (Chicago: University of Chicago Press, 1980).

Khuri, Fuad I., *Imams and Emirs: State, Religion and Sects in Islam* (London: Saqi, 1990).

Khuri-Makdisi, Ilham, 'Ottoman Arabs in Istanbul, 1860–1914: Perceptions of Empire, Experiences of the Metropole through the Writings of Aḥmad Fāris al-Shidyāq, Muḥammad Rashīd Riḍā, and Jirjī Zaydān', in: Sahar Bazzaz, Yota Batsaki, and Dimiter Angelov (eds), *Imperial Geographies in Byzantine and Ottoman Space* (Washington, DC: Center for Hellenic Studies, 2013), 254–97.

Khusraw, Nāṣir-i, *Nāser-e Khosraw's Book of Travels (Safarnāma)*, trans. by W. M. Thackston, Jr. (Albany, NY: Bibliotheca Persica, 1986).

Khwandamir, 'Genghis Khan's Progeny who Ruled Autonomously and Independently in Iran', in: *Classical Writings of the Medieval Islamic World: Persian Histories of the Mongol Dynasties*, trans. by Wheeler M. Thackston, Vol. 2 (London: I. B. Tauris, 2012), 53–139.

Khwandamir, 'The History of the Reign of Sultan Husayn Mirza', in: *Classical Writings of the Medieval Islamic World: Persian Histories of the Mongol Dynasties*, trans. by Wheeler M. Thackston, Vol. 2 (London: I. B. Tauris, 2012), 403–520.

Kia, Chad, *Art, Allegory and the Rise of Shiʿism in Iran, 1487–1565* (Edinburgh: Edinburgh University Press, 2019).

Kia, Mehrdad, 'Pan-Islamism in Late Nineteenth-Century Iran', *Middle Eastern Studies* 32, 1 (1996), 30–52.

Kienle, Eberhard, *Baʿth v. Baʿth: The Conflict between Syria and Iraq, 1968–1989* (London: I.B. Tauris, 1990).

Kieser, Hans-Lukas, *Der verpasste Friede: Mission, Ethnie und Staat in den Ostprovinzen der Türkei, 1839–1923* (Zurich: Chronos, 2000).

Kieser, Hans-Lukas, 'Muslim Heterodoxy and Protestant Utopia: The Interactions between Alevis and Missionaries in Ottoman Anatolia', *Die Welt des Islams* 41, 1 (2001), 89–111.

Kieser, Hans-Lukas, 'The Anatolian Alevis' Ambivalent Encounter with Modernity in Late Ottoman and Early Republican Turkey', in: Alessandro Monsutti, Silvia Naef, and Farian Sabahi (eds), *The Other Shiites: From the Mediterranean to Central Asia* (Bern: Peter Lang, 2008), 41–57.

King, James Robin, 'Zaydī Revival in a Hostile Republic: Competing Identities, Loyalties and Visions of State in Republican Yemen', *Arabica* 59, 3–4 (2012), 404–45.

Kingston, Paul W. T., *Reproducing Sectarianism: Advocacy Networks and the Politics of Civil Society in Postwar Lebanon* (Albany, NY: SUNY Press, 2013).

Kister, Meir Jacob, '"Shaʿbān is My Month...": A Study of an Early Tradition', in: Joshua Blau, Shlomo Pines, Meir Jacob Kister, and Shaul Shaked (eds), *Studia Orientalia Memoriae David Hartwig Baneth Dedicate* (Jerusalem: Magnes Press/ Institute of Asian and African Studies, 1979), 15–37.

Kızılkaya, Zafer, 'Hizbullah's Moral Justification of its Military Intervention in the Syrian Civil War', *Middle East Journal* 71, 2 (2017), 211–28.

Klausen, Jytte, *The Cartoons that Shook the World* (New Haven: Yale University Press, 2009).

Klemm, Verena, 'Die vier Sufarāʾ des Zwölften Imām: Zur formativen Periode der Zwölferšīʿa', *Die Welt des Orients* 15 (1984), 126–43.

Knights, Michael, 'The JRTN Movement and Iraq's Next Insurgency', *CTC Sentinel* 4, 7 (2011), 1–6.

Knysh, Alexander D., *Ibn ʿArabi in the Later Islamic Tradition: The Making of a Polemical Image in Medieval Islam* (Albany: SUNY Press, 1999).

Knysh, Alexander D., *Islamic Mysticism: A Short History* (Leiden: Brill, 2000).

Kohlberg, Etan, 'Some Notes on the Imamite Attitude to the Quran', in: S. M. Stern, Albert Habib Hourani, and Vivian Brown (eds), *Islamic Philosophy and the Classical Tradition* (Columbia: University of South Carolina Press, 1972), 209–24.

Kohlberg, Etan, 'Some Imāmī-shīʿī Views on Taqiyya', *Journal of the American Oriental Society* 95, 3 (1975), 395–402.

Kohlberg, Etan, 'The Development of the Imāmī Shīʿī Doctrine of Jihād', *Zeitschrift der Deutschen Morgenländischen Gesellschaft* 126, 1 (1976), 64–86.

Kohlberg, Etan, 'From Imāmiyya to Ithnā-ʿAshariyya', *Bulletin of the School of Oriental and African Studies* 39, 3 (1976), 521–34.

Kohlberg, Etan, 'Some Zaydi Views on the Companions of the Prophet', *Bulletin of the School of Oriental and African Studies* 39, 1 (1976), 91–8.

Kohlberg, Etan, 'The Term "Rāfida" in Imāmī Shīʿī Usage', *Journal of the American Oriental Society* 99, 4 (1979), 677–9.

Kohlberg, Etan, 'Barāʾa in Shīʿī Doctrine', *Jerusalem Studies in Arabic and Islam* 7 (1986), 139–75.

Kohlberg, Etan, 'Western Studies of Shiʿa Islam', in: Martin Kramer (ed.), *Shiʿism, Resistance, and Revolution* (Boulder, CO: Westview Press, 1987), 31–44.

Kohlberg, Etan, 'Imam and Community in the Pre-Ghayba Period', in: Said Amir
    Arjomand (ed.), *Authority and Political Culture in Shi'ism* (Albany: SUNY Press,
    1988), 25–53.
Kohlberg, Etan, *Belief and law in Imami Shi'ism* (Aldershot: Variorum, 1991).
Kohlberg, Etan, 'Some Imami Shi'i Views on the Sahaba', in: Etan Kohlberg (ed.),
    Belief and Law in Imami Shi'ism (Aldershot: Variorum, 1991), 143–75.
Kohlberg, Etan, '"Ali b. Musa ibn Tawus and his Polemic against Sunnism', in:
    Bernard Lewis and Friedrich Niewöhner (eds), *Religionsgespräche im Mittelalter*
    (Wiesbaden: Harrassowitz, 1992), 325–50.
Kohlberg, Etan, *A Medieval Muslim Scholar at Work: Ibn Tawus and his Library* (Leiden:
    Brill, 1992).
Kohlberg, Etan, 'Taqiyya in Shī'ī Theology and Religion', in: H. G. Kippenberg and
    G. G. Stroumsa (eds), *Secrecy and Concealment: Studies in the History of Mediterranean
    and Near Eastern Religions* (Leiden: Brill, 1995), 347–80.
Kohlberg, Etan, 'Shī'ī Views of the Death of the Prophet Muḥammad', in: Rotraud
    Hansberger, M. Afifi al-Haytham, and Charles Burnett (eds), *Medieval Arabic Thought:
    Essays in Honour of Fritz Zimmermann* (London: Warburg Institute, 2012), 77–86.
Kohlberg, Etan, 'Introduction: Shi'i Hadith', in: Farhad Daftary and Gurdofarid
    Miskinzoda (eds), *The Study of Shi'i Islam: History, Theology and Law* (London:
    I. B. Tauris, 2014), 165–79.
Kohlberg, Etan, and Mohammad Ali Amir-Moezzi (ed. and trans.), *Revelation and
    Falsification: The Kitāb al-Qirā'āt of Aḥmad b. Muḥammad al-Sayyārī* (Leiden:
    Brill, 2009).
Köprülü, Mehmed Fuad, *Islam in Anatolia after the Turkish Invasion: Prolegomena*,
    ed./trans. by Gary Leiser (Salt Lake City: University of Utah Press, 1993).
Kornrumpf, Hans-Jürgen, 'Untersuchungen zum Bild ʿAlīs und des frühen Islams
    bei den Schiiten (nach dem Nahǧ al-Balāġa des Šarīf ar-Raḍī)', *Der Islam* 45, 1
    (1969), 2–63, and *Der Islam* 45, 2 (1969), 261–98.
Korom, Frank J., *Hosay Trinidad: Muharram Performances in an Indo-Caribbean Diaspora*
    (Philadelphia: University of Pennsylvania Press, 2003).
Kostiner, Joseph, 'Shi'i Unrest in the Gulf', in: Martin Kramer (ed.), *Shi'ism,
    Resistance, and Revolution* (Boulder, CO: Westview Press, 1987), 173–86.
Kozlowski, Gregory C., *Muslim Endowments and Society in British India* (Cambridge:
    Cambridge University Press, 1985).
Kraemer, Joel L., *Humanism in the Renaissance of Islam: The Cultural Revival during the
    Buyid Age*, 2nd ed. (Leiden: Brill, 1992).
Kramer, Martin, *Islam Assembled: The Advent of the Muslim Congresses* (New York:
    Columbia University Press, 1986).
Kramer, Martin, 'Introduction', in: Martin Kramer (ed.), *Shi'ism, Resistance, and
    Revolution* (Boulder, CO: Westview Press, 1987), 1–18.
Kramer, Martin, 'Islam's Enduring Feud', *Middle East Contemporary Survey* 11
    (1987), 153–79.
Kramer, Martin, 'Syria's Alawis and Shi'ism', in: Martin Kramer (ed.), *Shi'ism,
    Resistance, and Revolution* (Boulder, CO: Westview Press, 1987), 237–54.

Kramer, Martin, 'Redeeming Jerusalem: The Pan-Islamic Premise of Hizballah', in: David Menashri (ed.), *The Iranian Revolution and the Muslim World* (Boulder, CO: Westview Press, 1990), 105–30.

Kramer, Martin, *Arab Awakening and Islamic Revival: The Politics of Ideas in the Middle East* (New Brunswick, NJ: Transaction, 1996).

Krämer, Gudrun, *Geschichte des Islam* (Munich: C. H. Beck, 2005).

Krämer, Gudrun, *Hasan al-Banna* (Oxford: Oneworld, 2010).

Krawietz, Birgit, and Georges Tamer (eds), *Islamic Theology, Philosophy and Law: Debating Ibn Taymiyya and Ibn Qayyim al-Jawziyya* (Berlin: De Gruyter, 2013).

Krohley, Nicholas, *The Death of the Mehdi Army: The Rise, Fall and Revival of Iraq's Most Powerful Militia* (London: Hurst, 2015).

Krokus, Christian, *The Theology of Louis Massignon: Islam, Christ, and the Church* (Washington, DC: Catholic University of America Press, 2017).

Krstić, Tijana, 'Illuminated by the Light of Islam and the Glory of the Ottoman Sultanate: Narratives of Conversion to Islam in the Age of Confessionalization', *Comparative Studies in Society and History* 51, 1 (2009), 35–63.

Krstić, Tijana, *Contested Conversions to Islam: Narratives of Religious Change in the Early Modern Ottoman Empire* (Stanford: Stanford University Press, 2011).

Krstić, Tijana, 'From Shahāda to 'Aqīda: Conversion to Islam, Catechisation and Sunnitisation in Sixteenth-Century Ottoman Rumeli', in: A. C. S. Peacock (ed.), *Islamisation: Comparative Perspectives from History* (Edinburgh: Edinburgh University Press, 2017), 296–314.

Kruse, Hans, 'Takfir und Ǧihād bei den Zaiditen des Jemen', *Die Welt des Islams* 23/4 (1984), 424–57.

Krusiński, Judas Thaddaeus, *The History of the Revolution of Persia: Taken from the Memoirs of Father Krusinski* (Dublin: S. Powell, 1729).

Kubba, Muhammad Mahdi, *Mudhakkirat fi Samim al-Ahdath, 1918–1958* (Beirut: Dar al-Tali'a, 1965).

Kuehn, Thomas, *Empire, Islam, and Politics of Difference: Ottoman Rule in Yemen, 1849–1919* (Leiden: Brill, 2011).

Kugle, Scott Alan, 'Framed, Blamed and Renamed: The Recasting of Islamic Jurisprudence in Colonial South Asia', *Modern Asian Studies* 35, 2 (2001), 257–313.

Kugle, Scott Alan, *When Sun Meets Moon: Gender, Eros, and Ecstasy in Urdu Poetry* (Chapel Hill: University of North Carolina Press, 2016).

Kuiper, Matthew J., *Da'wa and Other Religions: Indian Muslims and the Modern Resurgence of Global Islamic Activism* (Abingdon: Routledge, 2017).

Kumar, Deepa, 'The Right Kind of "Islam": News Media Representations of US-Saudi Relations during the Cold War', *Journalism Studies* 19, 8 (2018), 1079–97.

Künkler, Mirjam, and Roja Fazaeli, 'The Life of Two Mujtahidahs: Female Religious Authority in Twentieth-Century Iran', in: Masooda Bano and Hilary E. Kalmbach (eds), *Women, Leadership, and Mosques: Changes in Contemporary Islamic Authority* (Leiden: Brill, 2012), 127–60.

Kupferschmidt, Uri M., 'The General Muslim Congress of 1931 in Jerusalem', *Asian and African Studies* 12 (1978), 123–57.

Kurzman, Charles, *The Unthinkable Revolution in Iran* (Cambridge, MA: Harvard University Press, 2004).

Kwarten, Leo, *Why the Saudi Shiites Won't Rise Up Easily* (Conflicts Forum, 2009).

Lacey, Robert, *Inside the Kingdom: Kings, Clerics, Modernists, Terrorists and the Struggle for Saudi Arabia* (London: Penguin, 2009).

Lackner, Helen, *A House Built on Sand: A Political Economy of Saudi Arabia* (London: Ithaca, 1978).

Lackner, Helen (ed.), *Why Yemen Matters: A Society in Transition* (London: Saqi, 2014).

Lackner, Helen, 'The Change Squares of Yemen: Civil Resistance in an Unlikely Context', in: Adam Roberts, Michael J. Willis, Rory McCarthy, and Timothy Garton Ash (eds), *Civil Resistance in the Arab Spring: Triumphs and Disasters* (Oxford: Oxford University Press, 2015), 141–69.

Lackner, Helen, *Yemen in Crisis: Autocracy, Neo-Liberalism and the Disintegration of a State* (London: Saqi, 2017).

Lacroix, Stéphane, 'Between Islamists and Liberals: Saudi Arabia's New "Islamo-Liberal" Reformists', *Middle East Journal* 58, 3 (2004), 345–65.

Lacroix, Stéphane, 'Islamo-Liberal Politics in Saudi Arabia', in: Paul Aarts and Gerd Nonneman (eds), *Saudi Arabia in the Balance: Political Economy, Society, Foreign Affairs* (New York: NYU Press, 2005), 35–56.

Lacroix, Stéphane, 'Between Revolution and Apoliticism: Nasir al-Din al-Albani and His Impact on the Shaping of Contemporary Salafism', in: Roel Meijer (ed.), *Global Salafism: Islam's New Religious Movement* (London: Hurst, 2009), 58–80.

Lacroix, Stéphane, *Awakening Islam: The Politics of Religious Dissent in Contemporary Saudi Arabia* (Cambridge, MA: Harvard University Press, 2011).

Lacroix, Stéphane, *Saudi Islamists and the Arab Spring* (London: LSE, 2014).

Lacroix, Stéphane, 'To Rebel or Not to Rebel: Dilemmas among Saudi Salafis in a Revolutionary Age', in: Francesco Cavatorta and Fabio Merone (eds), *Salafism after the Arab Awakening: Contending with People's Power* (London: Hurst, 2016), 61–82.

Lakitsch, Maximilian, 'Islam in the Syrian War: Spotting the Various Dimensions of Religion in Conflict', *Religions* 9, 236 (2018), 1–17.

Lala, Ismail, *Knowing God: Ibn ʿArabī and ʿAbd al-Razzāq al-Qāshānī's Metaphysics of the Divine* (Leiden: Brill, 2019).

Lalani, Arzina R., *Early Shīʿī Thought: The Teachings of Imam Muḥammad al-Bāqir* (London: I. B. Tauris/Institute of Ismaili Studies, 2000).

Lambton, Ann K. S., 'A Reconsideration of the Position of the Marjaʿ al-Taqlīd and the Religious Institution', *Studia Islamica* 20 (1964), 115–35.

Lambton, Ann K. S., 'A Nineteenth Century View of Jihād', *Studia Islamica* 32 (1970), 181–92.

Lambton, Ann K. S., *State and Government in Medieval Islam: An Introduction to the Study of Islamic Political Theory: The Jurists* (Oxford: Oxford University Press, 1981).

Lammens, Henri, 'Voyage au pays des Nosairis', *Revue de l'Orient chrétien* 4, 1 (1899), 572–90.

Lammens, Henri, 'Voyage au pays des Nosairis', *Revue de l'Orient chrétien* 5 (1900), 99–117, 303–18, 423–44.

Lammens, Henri, 'Les Nosairis furent-ils chrétiens? A propos d'un livre récent', *Revue de l'Orient chrétien* 6 (1901), 33–50.

Lammens, Henri, 'Les Nosairis dans le Liban', *Revue de l'Orient Chrétien* 7 (1902), 452–77.

Lammens, Henri, 'Le "triumvirat" Aboû Bakr, 'Omar et Aboû 'Obaida', *Mélanges de la Faculté orientale de l'Université St. Joseph de Beyrouth* 4 (1910), 113–44.

Landau, Jacob M., *The Politics of Pan-Islam: Ideology and Organization* (Oxford: Clarendon Press, 1990).

Lane, Edward William, *An Account of the Manners and Customs of the Modern Egyptians* (London: J. M. Dent, 1923).

Lane, George, *Early Mongol Rule in Thirteenth-Century Iran: A Persian Renaissance* (London: RoutledgeCurzon, 2003).

Lange, Christian, *Paradise and Hell in Islamic Traditions* (Cambridge: Cambridge University Press, 2016).

Langer, Robert, and Udo Simon, 'The Dynamics of Orthodoxy and Heterodoxy: Dealing with Divergence in Muslim Discourses and Islamic Studies', *Die Welt Des Islams* 48, 3/4 (2008), 273–88.

Laoust, Henri, *Le califat dans la doctrine de Rašīd Riḍā: Traduction annotée d'al-Ḫilāfa au al-imāma al-'uẓmā (Le califat ou l'Imāma suprême)* (Beirut: n.p., 1938).

Laoust, Henri, *Essai sur les doctrines sociales et politiques de Taki-d-Din Ahmad b. Taimiya, canoniste hanbalite, né à Harrān en 661/1262, mort à Damas en 728/1328* (Cairo: Institut Français d'Archéologie Orientale, 1939).

Laoust, Henri, 'Remarques sur les Expéditions du Kasrawan sous les Premiers Mamluks', *Bulletin du Musée de Beyrouth* 4 (1940), 93–115.

Laoust, Henri, 'Ibn Kathir historien', *Arabica* 2 (1955), 42–88.

Laoust, Henri, *La profession de foi d'Ibn Baṭṭa* (Damascus: Institut Français de Damas, 1958).

Laoust, Henri, 'Le Hanbalisme sous le califat de Bagdad', *Revue des études islamiques* 27 (1959), 67–128.

Laoust, Henri, 'La classification des sectes dans le Farq d'al-Baghdadi', *Revue des études islamiques* 29 (1961), 19–59.

Laoust, Henri, 'La classification des sectes dans l'hérésiographie ash'arite', in: George Makdisi (ed.), *Arabic and Islamic Studies in Honor of Hamilton A. R. Gibb* (Leiden: Brill, 1965), 377–86.

Laoust, Henri, *Les schismes dans l'Islam: Introduction à une étude de la religion musulmane* (Paris: Payot, 1965).

Laoust, Henri, 'La critique du Sunnisme dans la Doctrine d'al-Hilli', *Revue des études islamiques* 34 (1966), 35–60.

Laoust, Henri, 'L'hérésiographie musulmane sous les Abbassides', *Cahiers de civilisation médiévale* 10, 38 (1967), 157–78.

Laoust, Henri, 'Les agitations religieuses à Baghdad aux IVe et Ve siècles de l'Hégire', in: D. S. Richards (ed.), *Islamic Civilisation 950–1150* (Oxford: Cassirer, 1973), 169–86.

Laoust, Henri, 'Les fondaments de l'Imamat dans le Minhaj d'al-Hilli', *Revue des études islamiques* 46 (1978), 3–55.

Laoust, Henri, *Comment définir le sunnisme et le chiisme* (Paris: Librairie orientaliste Paul Geuthner, 1979).

Lapidus, Ira M., *A History of Islamic Societies*, 2nd ed. (Cambridge: Cambridge University Press, 2002).

Larsson, Göran, '"One Cannot Doubt the Potential Effect of these Fatwas on Modern Muslim Society": Online Accusations of Disbelief and Apostasy: The Internet as an Arena for Sunni and Shia Muslim Conflicts', *Studies in Religion* 45, 2 (2016), 201–21.

Latour, Bruno, *We Have Never Been Modern* (Cambridge, MA: Harvard University Press, 1993).

Lauzière, Henri, 'The Construction of Salafiyya: Reconsidering Salafism from the Perspective of Conceptual History', *International Journal of Middle East Studies* 42, 3 (2010), 369–89.

Lauzière, Henri, *The Making of Salafism: Islamic Reform in the Twentieth Century* (New York: Columbia University Press, 2015).

Lav, Daniel, *Radical Islam and the Revival of Medieval Theology* (Cambridge: Cambridge University Press, 2012).

Lawson, Fred Haley, *Bahrain: The Modernization of Autocracy* (Boulder, Co.: Westview Press, 1989).

Lawson, Fred Haley, 'Why Did the Syrian Uprising Become a Sectarian Conflict? A Provisional Synthesis', *Politics, Religion & Ideology* 21, 2 (2020), 216–31.

Leenders, Reinoud, 'Collective Action and Mobilization in Dar'a: An Anatomy of the Onset of Syria's Popular Uprising', *Mobilization: An International Quarterly* 17, 4 (2012), 419–34.

Leenders, Reinoud, *Spoils of Truce: Corruption and State-Building in Postwar Lebanon* (Ithaca: Cornell University Press, 2012).

Leenders, Reinoud, 'Repression Is Not 'a Stupid Thing': Regime Responses to the Syrian Uprising and Insurgency', in: Michael Kerr and Craig Larkin (eds), *The Alawis of Syria: War, Faith and Politics in the Levant* (Oxford: Oxford University Press, 2015), 245–73.

Leenders, Reinoud, and Antonio Giustozzi, 'Foreign Sponsorship of Pro-Government Militias Fighting Syria's Insurgency: Whither Proxy Wars?', *Mediterranean Politics* 27, 5 (2022), 614–43.

Leenders, Reinoud, and Steven Heydemann, 'Popular Mobilization in Syria: Opportunity and Threat, and the Social Networks of the Early Risers', *Mediterranean Politics* 17, 2 (2012), 139–59.

Leezenberg, Michiel, 'Between Assimilation and Deportation: The Shabak and the Kakais in Northern Iraq', in: Krisztina Kehl-Bodrogi, Barbara Kellner-Heinkele, and Anke Otter-Beaujean (eds), *Syncretistic Religious Communities in the Near East: Collected Papers of the International Symposium 'Alevism in Turkey and Comparable Syncretistic Religious Communities in the Near East in the Past and Present', Berlin, 14–17 April 1995* (Leiden: Brill, 1997), 155–74.

Lefèvre, Corinne, *Pouvoir impérial et élites dans l'Inde moghole de Jahāngīr (1605–1627)* (Paris: Les Indes Savantes, 2017).

Lefèvre, Raphaël, *Ashes of Hama: The Muslim Brotherhood in Syria* (London: Hurst, 2013).

Lefèvre, Raphaël, *The Roots of Crisis in Northern Lebanon* (Washington, DC: Carnegie Endowment for International Peace, 2014).

Lefèvre, Raphaël, 'The Syrian Muslim Brotherhood's Alawi Conundrum', in: Michael Kerr and Craig Larkin (eds), *The Alawis of Syria: War, Faith and Politics in the Levant* (Oxford: Oxford University Press, 2015), 125–37.

Lefèvre, Raphaël, 'Syria', in: Shadi Hamid and William McCants (eds), *Rethinking Political Islam* (Oxford: Oxford University Press, 2017), 73–87.

Lefèvre, Raphaël, *Jihad in the City: Militant Islam and Contentious Politics in Tripoli* (Cambridge: Cambridge University Press, 2021).

LeGall, Dina, *A Culture of Sufism: Naqshbandīs in the Ottoman World, 1450–1700* (Albany: SUNY Press, 2013).

Legrain, Jean-François, 'The Shiite Peril in Palestine: Between Phobias and Propaganda', in: Brigitte Maréchal and Sami Zemni (eds), *The Dynamics of Sunni-Shia Relationships: Doctrine, Transnationalism, Intellectuals and the Media* (London: Hurst, 2013), 41–60.

Leichtman, Mara A., 'Shi'i Islamic Cosmopolitanism and the Transformation of Religious Authority in Senegal', *Contemporary Islam* 8, 3 (2014), 261–83.

Leichtman, Mara A., *Shi'i Cosmopolitanisms in Africa: Lebanese Migration and Religious Conversion in Senegal* (Bloomington: Indiana University Press, 2015).

Lelyveld, David, *Aligarh's First Generation: Muslim Solidarity in British India* (Princeton: Princeton University Press, 1978).

Lenfant, Arnaud, 'L'évolution du salafisme en Syrie au XXe siècle', in: Bernard Rougier (ed.), *Qu'est-ce que le salafisme?* (Paris: Presses Universitaires de France, 2008), 161–78.

Lenk, Titus, 'Die SS-Mullah-Schule und die Arbeitsgemeinschaft Turkestan in Dresden', *Zukunft braucht Erinnerung*, 12 November 2006, http://www.zukunft-braucht-erinnerung.de/die-ss-mullah-schule-und-die-arbeitsgemeinschaft-turkestan-in-dresden/.

LeStrange, Guy, *Palestine under the Moslems: A Description of Syria and the Holy Land from A.D. 650 to 1500* (London: Alexander P. Watt, 1890).

LeThomas, Catherine, *Les écoles chiites au Liban: Construction communautaire et mobil-isation politique* (Paris: Karthala, 2012).

Lev, Yaacov, 'The Fāṭimid Imposition of Ismāʿīlism on Egypt (358–386/969–996)', *Zeitschrift der Deutschen Morgenländischen Gesellschaft* 138, 2 (1988), 313–25.

Lev, Yaacov, *State and Society in Fatimid Egypt* (Leiden: Brill, 1991).

Lev, Yaacov, *Saladin in Egypt* (Leiden: Brill, 1999).

Leverrier, Ignace, 'L'Arabie Saoudite, le pélerinage et l'Iran', *Cahiers d'études sur la Méditerranée orientale et le monde turco-iranien* 22 (1996), 111–47.

Lewental, D. Gershon, '"Saddam's Qadisiyyah": Religion and History in the Service of State Ideology in Baʿthi Iraq', *Middle Eastern Studies* 50, 6 (2014), 891–910.

Lewis, Bernard, *The Assassins: A Radical Sect in Islam* (London: Weidenfeld & Nicolson, 1967).

Lewis, Bernard, 'The Shi'a in Islamic History', in: Martin Kramer (ed.), *Shi'ism, Resistance, and Revolution* (Boulder, CO: Westview Press, 1987), 21–30.

Lewis, Kevin James, *The Counts of Tripoli and Lebanon in the Twelfth Century: Sons of Saint-Gilles* (London: Routledge, 2017).

Lewis, Norman N., 'The Isma'ilis of Syria Today', *Journal of the Royal Central Asian Society* 39, 1 (1952), 69–77.

Lewis, Norman N., *Nomads and Settlers in Syria and Jordan, 1800–1980* (Cambridge: Cambridge University Press, 1987).

Lewisohn, Leonard (ed.), *The Heritage of Sufism*, 3 Vols (Oxford: Oneworld, 1999).

Lia, Brynjar, *The Society of the Muslim Brothers in Egypt: The Rise of an Islamic Mass Movement, 1928–1942* (Reading: Ithaca, 1998).

Lia, Brynjar, 'The Islamist Uprising in Syria, 1976–82: The History and Legacy of a Failed Revolt', *British Journal of Middle Eastern Studies* 43, 4 (2016), 541–59.

Linge, Marius, 'Sunnite-Shiite Polemics in Norway', *FLEKS: Scandinavian Journal of Intercultural Theory and Practice* 3, 1 (2016), 1–18.

Lingwood, Chad G., *Politics, Poetry and Sufism in Medieval Iran: New Perspectives on Jāmī's Salāmān va Absāl* (Leiden: Brill, 2013).

Lisnyansky, Dina, 'Tashayu (Conversion to Shiism) in Central Asia and Russia', *Current Trends in Islamist Ideology* 8 (2009), 108–17.

Lister, Charles R., *The Syrian Jihad: Al-Qaeda, the Islamic State and the Evolution of an Insurgency* (London: Hurst, 2015).

Little, Donald Presgrave, *An Introduction to Mamluk Historiography: An Analysis of Arabic Annalistic and Biographical Sources for the Reign of al-Malik an-Nāṣir Muḥammad ibn Qalā'ūn* (Wiesbaden: Franz Steiner, 1970).

Little, Donald Presgrave, 'The Historical and Historiographical Significance of the Detention of Ibn Taymiyya', *International Journal of Middle East Studies* 4, 3 (1973), 311–27.

Little, Donald Presgrave, 'Did Ibn Taymiyya Have a Screw Loose?', *Studia Islamica* 41 (1975), 93–111.

Little, Donald Presgrave, 'Coptic Conversion to Islam under the Baḥrī Mamlūks, 692–755/1293–1354', *Bulletin of the School of Oriental and African Studies* 39, 3 (1976), 552–69.

Little, Donald Presgrave, 'Religion under the Mamluks', *The Muslim World* 73 (1983), 165–81.

Litvak, Meir, *Shi'i Scholars of Nineteenth-Century Iraq: The 'Ulama' of Najaf and Karbala'* (Cambridge: Cambridge University Press, 1998).

Litvak, Meir, 'A Failed Manipulation: The British, the Oudh Bequest and the Shī'ī 'Ulamā' of Najaf and Karbalā'', *British Journal of Middle Eastern Studies* 27, 1 (2000), 68–89.

Litvak, Meir, 'The Finances of the Ulama Communities of Najaf and Karbala, 1796–1904', *Die Welt des Islams* 40, 1 (2000), 41–66.

Litvak, Meir, 'Money, Religion and Politics: The Oudh Bequest in Najaf and Karbala', 1850–1903', *International Journal of Middle East Studies* 33, 1 (2001), 1–21.

Litvak, Meir, '"More Harmful than the Jews": Anti-Shi'i Polemics in Modern Radical Sunni Discourse', in: Mohammad Ali Amir-Moezzi, Meir M. Bar-Asher, and Simon Hopkins (eds), *Le shī'isme imāmite quarante ans après: Hommage à Etan Kohlberg* (Turnhout: Brepols, 2009), 293–314.

Llewellyn-Jones, Rosie, *Engaging Scoundrels: True Tales of Old Lucknow* (New Delhi: Oxford University Press, 2000).

Llewellyn-Jones, Rosie, *The Last King in India: Wajid Ali Shah, 1822–1887* (London: Hurst, 2014).

Llewellyn-Jones, Rosie, 'The British Raj and the British Mandate in Iraq', *Asian Affairs* 46, 2 (2015), 270–9.

Lobmeyer, Hans Günter, *Islamismus und sozialer Konflikt in Syrien* (Berlin: Das Arabische Buch, 1990).

Lobmeyer, Hans Günter, *Opposition und Widerstand in Syrien* (Hamburg: Deutsches Orient-Institut, 1995).

Lockhart, Laurence, *Nadir Shah: A Critical Study Based Mainly upon Contemporary Sources* (London: Luzac, 1938).

Lockhart, Laurence, *The Fall of the Safavi Dynasty and the Afghan Occupation of Persia* (Cambridge: Cambridge University Press, 1958).

Lockman, Zachary, *Contending Visions of the Middle East: The History and Politics of Orientalism* (Cambridge: Cambridge University Press, 2004).

Lockman, Zachary, *Field Notes: The Making of Middle East Studies in the United States* (Stanford: Stanford University Press, 2016).

Lodhi, Maleeha, 'Pakistan's Shia Movement: An Interview with Arif Hussaini', *Third World Quarterly* 10, 2 (1988), 806–17.

Lokhandwalla, S. T., 'Islamic Law and Ismaili Communities (Khojas and Bohras)', *Indian Economic & Social History Review* 4, 2 (1967), 155–76.

Long, David E., 'The Impact of the Iranian Revolution on the Arabian Peninsula and the Gulf States', in: John L. Esposito (ed.), *The Iranian Revolution: Its Global Impact* (Miami: Florida International University Press, 1990), 100–15.

Long, Jerry M., *Saddam's War of Words: Politics, Religion, and the Iraqi Invasion of Kuwait* (Austin: University of Texas Press, 2004).

Longrigg, Stephen H., *Syria and Lebanon under French Mandate* (London: Oxford University Press, 1958).

Lord, Ceren, 'Between Islam and the Nation: Nation-Building, the Ulama and Alevi Identity in Turkey', *Nations and Nationalism* 23, 1 (2017), 48–67.

Lord, Ceren, 'Rethinking the Justice and Development Party's "Alevi Openings"', *Turkish Studies* 18, 2 (2017), 278–96.

Lord, Ceren, *Religious Politics in Turkey: From the Birth of the Republic to the AKP* (Cambridge: Cambridge University Press, 2018).

Lord, Ceren, 'Sectarianized Securitization in Turkey in the Wake of the 2011 Arab Uprisings', *Middle East Journal* 73, 1 (2019), 51–72.

Lorimer, John Gordon, *Gazetteer of the Persian Gulf, 'Omān, and Central Arabia*, 6 Vols (Farnsborough: Gregg, 1970).

Löschner, Harald, *Die dogmatischen Grundlagen des šī'itischen Rechts: Eine Untersuchung zur modernen imāmitischen Rechtsquellenlehre* (Cologne: Carl Heymanns, 1971).

Louër, Laurence, 'The Political Impact of Labor Migration in Bahrain', *City & Society* 20, 1 (2008), 32–53.

Louër, Laurence, *Transnational Shia Politics: Religious and Political Networks in the Gulf* (London: Hurst, 2008).

Louër, Laurence, 'Shi'i Identity Politics in Saudi Arabia', in: Anh Nga Longva and Anne Sofie Roald (eds), *Religious Minorities in the Middle East: Domination, Self-Empowerment, Accommodation* (Leiden: Brill, 2012), 219–43.

Louër, Laurence, 'The State and Sectarian Identities in the Persian Gulf Monarchies: Bahrain, Saudi Arabia, and Kuwait in Comparative Perspective', in: Lawrence G. Potter (ed.), *Sectarian Politics in the Persian Gulf* (New York: Oxford University Press, 2014), 117–42.

Louër, Laurence, *Sunnis and Shi'a: A Political History* (Princeton: Princeton University Press, 2020).

Lucas, Scott C., *Constructive Critics, Ḥadīth Literature, and the Articulation of Sunnī Islam* (Leiden: Brill, 2004).

Lüdke, Tilman, *Jihad Made in Germany: Ottoman and German Propaganda and Intelligence Operations in the First World War* (Münster: LIT, 2005).

Luesink, Anja W. M., 'The Iranian Community in Cairo at the Turn of the Century', in: Th. Zarcone and F. Zarinebaf (eds), *Les Iraniens d'Istanbul* (Paris: Institut Français de Recherches en Iran/Institut Français d'Études Anatoliennes, 1993), 193–200.

Luizard, Pierre-Jean, 'Les confréries soufies en Irak arabe aux dix-neuvième et vingtième siècles face au chiisme duodécimain et au wahhabisme', in: F. de Jong and B. Radtke (eds), *Islamic Mysticism Contested: Thirteen Centuries of Controversies and Polemics* (Leiden: Brill, 1999), 283–309.

Luizard, Pierre-Jean, 'Shaykh Muhammad al-Khalisi (1890–1963) and his Political Role in Iraq and Iran in the 1910s/20s', in: Rainer Brunner and Werner Ende (eds), *The Twelver Shia in Modern Times: Religious Culture & Political History* (Leiden: Brill, 2001), 223–35.

Luizard, Pierre-Jean, *La formation de l'Irak contemporain: Le rôle politique des ulémas chiites à la fin de la domination ottomane et au moment de la construction de l'État irakien* (Paris: CNRS Editions, 2002).

Luizard, Pierre-Jean, 'The Sadrists in Iraq: Challenging the United States, the Marja'iyya and Iran', in: Sabrina Mervin (ed.), *The Shi'a Worlds and Iran* (London: Saqi, 2010), 255–80.

Lund, Aron, *Syrian Jihadism* (Stockholm: Swedish Institute of International Affairs, 2012).

Lund, Aron, 'Chasing Ghosts: The Shabiha Phenomenon', in: Michael Kerr and Craig Larkin (eds), *The Alawis of Syria: War, Faith and Politics in the Levant* (Oxford: Oxford University Press, 2015), 207–24.

Lux, Abdullah, 'Yemen's Last Zaydī Imām: The Shabāb al-Mu'min, the Malāzim, and 'Ḥizb Allāh' in the Thought of Ḥusayn Badr al-Dīn al-Ḥūthī', *Contemporary Arab Affairs* 2, 3 (2009), 369–434.

Lyde, Samuel, *The Ansyreeh and Ismaeleeh: A Visit to the Secret Sects of Northern Syria, with a View to the Establishment of Schools* (London: Hurst and Blackett, 1853).

Lyde, Samuel, *The Asian Mystery: Illustrated in the History, Religion, and Present State of the Ansaireeh or Nusairis of Syria* (London: Longman, Green & Co., 1860).

Lynch, Marc, *The New Arab Wars: Uprisings and Anarchy in the Middle East* (New York: PublicAffairs, 2016).

Lynch, Marc, *Voices of the New Arab Public: Iraq, al-Jazeera, and Middle East Politics Today* (New York: Columbia University Press, 2006).

Lynch, Marc, 'The Rise and Fall of the New Arab Public Sphere', *Current History* 114, 776 (2015), 331–6.

Lynch, Marc, 'Is There an Islamist Advantage at War?', *APSA MENA Politics Newsletter* 2, 1 (2019), 18–21.

Lynch, Marc, and Amaney Jamal, 'Introduction: Shifting Global Politics and the Middle East', *POMEPS Studies* 34 (2019), 3–6.

Lynch, Marc, Deen Freelon, and Sean Aday, 'Syria in the Arab Spring: The Integration of Syria's Conflict with the Arab Uprisings, 2011–2013', *Research & Politics* 1, 3 (2014), 1–7.

Maalouf, Amin, *Der Heilige Krieg der Barbaren: Die Kreuzzüge aus der Sicht der Araber* (Munich: DTV, 2004).

Maalouf, Amin, *The Crusades through Arab Eyes* (London: Saqi, 2006).

Mabon, Simon, 'Desectarianization: Looking beyond the Sectarianization of Middle Eastern Politics', *Review of Faith & International Affairs* 17, 4 (2019), 23–35.

MacCulloch, Diarmaid, *A History of Christianity: The First Three Thousand Years* (London: Allen Lane, 2009).

MacEvitt, Christopher H., *The Crusades and the Christian World of the East: Rough Tolerance* (Philadelphia: University of Pennsylvania Press, 2008).

Machlis, Elisheva, 'A Shi'a Debate on Arabism: The Emergence of a Multiple Communal Membership', *British Journal of Middle Eastern Studies* 40, 2 (2013), 95–114.

Machlis, Elisheva, *Shi'i Sectarianism in the Middle East: Modernisation and the Quest for Islamic Universalism* (London: I. B. Tauris, 2014).

Machlis, Elisheva, 'Al-Wefaq and the February 14 Uprising: Islam, Nationalism and Democracy—the Shi'i-Bahraini Discourse', *Middle Eastern Studies* 52, 6 (2016), 978–95.

Machlis, Elisheva, 'Reevaluating Sectarianism in Light of Sufi Islam: The Case-Studies of the Naqshbandiyya and Qadiriyya in Syria and Iraq', *Sociology of Islam* 7, 1 (2019), 22–40.

Mackerras, Colin, 'Han-Muslim and Intra-Muslim Social Relations in Northwestern China', *Nationalism and Ethnic Politics* 4, 1–2 (1998), 28–46.

Macnaghten, W. H., *Principles and Precedents of Moohummudan Law: Being a Compilation of Primary Rules Relative to the Doctrine of Inheritance (Including the Tenets of the Schia Sectaries), Contracts and Miscellaneous Subjects* (Calcutta: Church Mission Press, 1825).

al-Madani, Muhammad Muhammad (ed.), *Da'wa al-Taqrib min Khilal Risala al-Islam* (Cairo: Dar al-Taqrib, 1966).

Madelung, Wilferd, 'Das Imamat in der frühen ismailitischen Lehre', *Der Islam* 37 (1961), 43–135.

Madelung, Wilferd, *Der Imam al-Qāsim ibn Ibrāhīm und die Glaubenslehre der Zaiditen* (Berlin: Walter de Gruyter, 1965).

Madelung, Wilferd, 'Bemerkungen zur imamitischen Firaq-Literatur', *Der Islam* 43 (1967), 37–52.

Madelung, Wilferd, 'Early Sunni Doctrine Concerning Faith as Reflected in the "Kitāb al-Imān" of Abū 'Ubayd al-Qāsim b. Sallām (d. 224/839)', *Studia Islamica* 32 (1970), 233–54.

Madelung, Wilferd, 'Imamism and Mu'atazilite Theology', in: Centre de Recherches d'Histoire des Religions Strasbourg (ed.), *Le shî'isme imâmite: Colloque de Strasbourg (6–9 mai 1968)* (Paris: Presses Universitaires de France, 1970), 13–30.

Madelung, Wilferd, 'The Origins of the Controversy Concerning the Creation of the Qur'ān', in: J. M. Barral (ed.), *Orientalia Hispanica: Sive studia F. M. Pareja octogenaria dicata* (Leiden: Brill, 1974), 504–25.

Madelung, Wilferd, 'The Minor Dynasties of Northern Iran', in: R. N. Frye (ed.), *The Cambridge History of Iran*, Vol. 4 (Cambridge: Cambridge University Press, 1975), 198–249.

Madelung, Wilferd, 'Aš-Šahrastānīs Streitschrift gegen Avicenna und ihre Widerlegung durch Naṣīr ad-Dīn at-Ṭūsī', in: Albert Dietrich (ed.), *Akten des VII. Kongresses für Arabistik und Islamwissenschaft Göttingen, 1974* (Göttingen: Vandenhoeck & Ruprecht, 1976), 250–9.

Madelung, Wilferd, 'Some Notes on Non-Ismā'īlī Shiism in the Maghrib', *Studia Islamica* 44 (1976), 87–97.

Madelung, Wilferd, 'The Sources of Ismā'īlī Law', *Journal of Near Eastern Studies* 35, 1 (1976), 29–40.

Madelung, Wilferd, 'Shi'i Attitudes toward Women as Reflected in "fiqh"', in: Afaf Lutfi al-Sayyid-Marsot (ed.), *Society and the Sexes in Medieval Islam* (Malibu, CA: Undena, 1979), 69–79.

Madelung, Wilferd, 'The Shiite and Kharijite Contribution to Pre-Ash'arite Kalam', in: Parviz Morewedge (ed.), *Islamic Philosophical Theology* (Albany: SUNY Press, 1979), 120–39.

Madelung, Wilferd, 'A Treatise of the Sharīf al-Murtaḍā on the Legality of Working for the Government (Mas'ala Fī 'l-'Amal Ma'a 'l-Sulṭān)', *Bulletin of the School of Oriental and African Studies* 43, 1 (1980), 18–31.

Madelung, Wilferd, 'Shi'ite Discussions on the Legality of the Kharaj', in: Rudolf Peters (ed.), *Proceedings of the Ninth Congress of the Union Européenne des Arabisants et Islamisants* (Leiden: Brill, 1981), 193–202.

Madelung, Wilferd, 'Authority in Twelver Shiism in the Absence of the Imam', in: G. Makdisi, D. Sourdel, and J. Sourdel-Thomine (eds), *La notion d'autorité au moyen âge* (Paris: Presses Universitaires de France, 1982), 163–73.

Madelung, Wilferd, *Arabic Texts Concerning the History of the Zaydī Imāms of Ṭabaristān, Daylamān and Gīlān* (Beirut/Wiesbaden: Orient-Institut der Deutschen Morgenländischen Gesellschaft/Franz Steiner, 1987).

Madelung, Wilferd, *Religious Trends in Early Islamic Iran* (Albany: SUNY Press, 1988).

Madelung, Wilferd, 'The Hashimiyyat of al-Kumayt and Hashimi Shi'ism', *Studia Islamica* 70 (1989), 5–26.

Madelung, Wilferd, 'The Origins of the Yemenite Hijra', in: Alan Jones (ed.), *Arabicus Felix, Luminosus Brittanicus: Essays in Honour of A. F. L. Beeston on his Eightieth Birthday* (Reading: Ithaca, 1991), 25–44.

Madelung, Wilferd, 'The Fatimids and the Qarmaṭīs of Baḥrayn', in: Farhad Daftary (ed.), *Mediaeval Isma'ili History and Thought* (Cambridge: Cambridge University Press, 1996), 21–74.

Madelung, Wilferd, *The Succession to Muḥammad: A Study of the Early Caliphate* (Cambridge: Cambridge University Press, 1997).

Madelung, Wilferd, "Abd Allah b. 'Abbas and Shi'ite Law', in: U. Vermeulen and J. M. F. van Reeth (eds), *Law, Christianity and Modernism in Islamic Society: Proceedings of the Eighteenth Congress of the Union Européenne des Arabisants et Islamisants Held at the Katholieke Universiteit Leuven* (Leuven: Peeters, 1998), 13–26.

Madelung, Wilferd, 'The Religious Policy of the Fatimids toward their Sunni Subjects in the Maghrib', in Marianne Barrucand (ed.), *L'Egypte Fatimide: Son art et son histoire* (Paris: Presses de l'Université de Paris-Sorbonne, 1999), 97–104.

Madelung, Wilferd, 'Zaydī Attitudes to Sufism', in: F. deJong and B. Radtke (eds), *Islamic Mysticism Contested: Thirteen Centuries of Controversies and Polemics* (Leiden: Brill, 1999), 124–44.

Madelung, Wilferd, 'Nasir al-Din Tusi's Ethics: Between Philosophy, Shi'ism and Sufism' (London: *Institute of Ismaili Studies*, 2011).

Madelung, Wilferd, 'Shi'ism in the Age of the Rightly-Guided Caliphs', in: Sabine Schmidtke (ed.), *Studies in Medieval Shi'ism* (Aldershot: Ashgate, 2012), 9–18.

Madelung, Wilferd, 'Introduction: History and Historiography', in: Farhad Daftary and Gurdofarid Miskinzoda (eds), *The Study of Shi'i Islam: History, Theology and Law* (London: I. B. Tauris, 2014), 3–16.

Madelung, Wilferd, and Paul E. Walker, *An Ismaili Heresiography: The 'Bāb al-Shayṭān' from Abū Tammām's' Kitāb al-Shajara* (Leiden: Brill, 1998).

Madelung, Wilferd, and Paul E. Walker (eds), *The Advent of the Fatimids: A Contemporary Shi'i Witness: An Edition and English Translation of Ibn al-Haytham's Kitab al-Munazarat* (London: I. B. Tauris/Institute of Ismaili Studies, 2000).

Madoeuf, Anna, 'Mulids of Cairo: Sufi Guilds, Popular Celebrations, and the "Roller-Coaster Landscape" of the Resignified City', in: Diane Singerman and Paul Amar (eds), *Cairo Cosmopolitan: Politics, Culture, and Urban Space in the New Globalized Middle East* (Cairo: American University in Cairo Press, 2006), 465–87.

Mahdjoub, Mohammad-Dja'far, 'The Evolution of Popular Eulogy of the Imams among the Shi'a', in: Said Amir Arjomand (ed.), *Authority and Political Culture in Shi'ism* (Albany: SUNY Press, 1988), 54–79.

Mahendrarajah, Shivan, 'The Sarbadars of Sabzavar: Re-Examining their 'Shi'a' Roots and Alleged Goal to "Destroy Khurasanian Sunnism"', *Journal of Shi'a Islamic Studies* 5, 4 (2012), 379–402.

Maheshwari, Shriram, *The Census Administration under the Raj and After* (New Delhi: Concept, 1996).

Mahmood, Saba, *Religious Difference in a Secular Age: A Minority Report* (Princeton: Princeton University Press, 2015).

Makdisi, George, *Ibn 'Aqil et la résurgence de l'Islam traditionaliste au XIe siècle, Ve siècle de l'Hégire* (Damascus: Institut Français de Damas, 1963).

Makdisi, George, 'Sunni Revival', in: D. S. Richards (ed.), *Islamic Civilisation 950–1150* (Oxford: Cassirer, 1973), 155–68.

Makdisi, George, 'The Hanbali School and Sufism', *Humaniora Islamica* 2 (1974), 61–72.

Makdisi, George, 'Ibn Taymīya: A Ṣūfī of the Qādiriyya Order', *American Journal of Arabic Studies* 1 (1974), 118–29.

Makdisi, George, 'Les rapports entre Calife et Sultan à l'époque Saljuqide', *International Journal of Middle East Studies* 6, 2 (1975), 228–36.

Makdisi, George, *Ibn 'Aqil: Religion and Culture in Classical Islam* (Edinburgh: Edinburgh University Press, 1997).

Makdisi, Ussama Samir, *The Culture of Sectarianism: Community, History, and Violence in Nineteenth-Century Ottoman Lebanon* (Berkeley, CA: University of California Press, 2000).

Makdisi, Ussama Samir, 'Ottoman Orientalism', *American Historical Review* 107, 3 (2002), 768–96.

Makdisi, Ussama Samir, 'Revisiting Sectarianism', in: Thomas Scheffler (ed.), *Religion between Violence and Reconciliation* (Beirut: Orient-Institut, 2002), 179–91.

Makdisi, Ussama Samir, *Artillery of Heaven: American Missionaries and the Failed Conversion of the Middle East* (Ithaca: Cornell University Press, 2008).

Makdisi, Ussama Samir, *Faith Misplaced: The Broken Promise of U.S.-Arab Relations, 1820–2001* (New York: PublicAffairs, 2010).

Makdisi, Ussama Samir, 'Diminished Sovereignty and the Impossibility of "Civil War" in the Modern Middle East', *American Historical Review* 120, 5 (2015), 1739–52.

Makdisi, Ussama Samir, 'Understanding 1860 in an Ottoman and Global Context', in: Dima de Clerck, Carla Eddé, Naila Kaidbey, and Souad Slim (eds), *Histoires et mémoires d'un conflit* (Beirut: USJ, 2015), 25–32.

Makdisi, Ussama Samir, *Age of Coexistence: The Ecumenical Frame and the Making of the Modern Arab World* (Oakland: University of California Press, 2019).

al-Makki, Qutb al-Din al-Nahrawali, *Lightning over Yemen: A History of the Ottoman Campaign 1569–71*, trans. by Clive Smith (London: I. B. Tauris, 2002).

Maktabi, Rania, 'The Lebanese Census of 1932 Revisited: Who Are the Lebanese?', *British Journal of Middle Eastern Studies* 26, 2 (1999), 219–41.

Mal-Allah, Muhammad, *Mawqif al-Khumayni min Ahl al-Sunna* (Cairo: al-Muslim Publishing House, 1982).

Malcolm, Noel, *Agents of Empire: Knights, Corsairs, Jesuits and Spies in the Sixteenth-Century Mediterranean World* (New York: Oxford University Press, 2015).

Malešević, Siniša, 'Nationalisms and the Orthodox Worlds', *Nations and Nationalism* 26, 3 (2020), 544–52.

Malik, Jamal, *Islamische Gelehrtenkultur in Nordindien: Entwicklungsgeschichte und Tendenzen am Beispiel von Lucknow* (Leiden: Brill, 1997).

Malik, Jamal, *Islam in South Asia: A Short History* (Leiden: Brill, 2008).

al-Maliki, Ibn Sabbagh, *Al-Fusul al-Muhimma fi Ma'rifat al-A'imma* (Cairo: Dar al-Hadith, 2001).

Mallat, Chibli, *Aspects of Shi'i Thought from the South of Lebanon: Al-'Irfan, Muhammad Jawad Mughniyya, Muhammad Mahdi Shamseddin, Muhammad Husain Fadlallah* (Oxford: Centre for Lebanese Studies, 1988).

Mallat, Chibli, 'Religious Militancy in Contemporary Iraq: Muhammad Baqer as-Sadr and the Sunni-Shia Paradigm', *Third World Quarterly* 10, 2 (1988), 699–729.

Mallat, Chibli, *The Renewal of Islamic Law: Muhammad Baqer as-Sadr, Najaf, and the Shi'i International* (Cambridge: Cambridge University Press, 1993).

Mallat, Chibli, 'Shi'ism and Sunnism in Iraq: Revisiting the Codes', *Arab Law Quarterly* 8, 2 (1993), 141–59.

Mallat, Chibli, *Introduction to Middle Eastern Law* (Oxford: Oxford University Press, 2007).

Malmvig, Helle, 'Coming in from the Cold: How We May Take Sectarian Identity Politics Seriously in the Middle East without Playing to the Tunes of Regional Power Elites', *POMEPS*, 2015.

Malmvig, Helle, 'Soundscapes of War: The Audio-Visual Performance of War by Shi'a Militias in Iraq and Syria', *International Affairs* 96, 3 (2020), 649–66.

Malmvig, Helle, 'Allow Me This One Time to Speak as a Shi'i: The Sectarian Taboo, Music Videos and the Securitization of Sectarian Identity Politics in Hezbollah's Legitimation of its Military Involvement in Syria', *Mediterranean Politics* 26, 1 (2021), 1–24.

Manchanda, Nivi, *Imagining Afghanistan: The History and Politics of Imperial Knowledge* (Cambridge: Cambridge University Press, 2020).

Mandaville, Jon E., 'The Ottoman Province of al-Hasā in the Sixteenth and Seventeenth Centuries', *Journal of the American Oriental Society* 90, 3 (1970), 486–513.

al-Mani', Saleh, 'The Ideological Dimension in Saudi-Iranian Relations', in: Jamal S. al-Suwaida (ed.), *Iran and the Gulf: A Search for Stability* (Abu Dhabi: Emirates Center for Strategic Studies and Research, 1996), 158–74.

Mann, Michael, *The Sources of Social Power: The Rise of Classes and Nation-States, 1760–1914* (Cambridge: Cambridge University Press, 1993).

Mansour, Renad, 'The Popularity of the Hashd in Iraq', *Carnegie Middle East Center*, 1 February 2016.

Mansour, Renad, 'The Sunni Predicament in Iraq', *Carnegie Middle East Center*, 3 March 2016.

Mansour, Renad, 'Trump's Strikes Risk Upending Iraqi Politics', *Foreign Affairs*, 27 January 2020.

Mansour, Renad, 'The "Hybrid Armed Actors" Paradox: A Necessary Compromise?', *War on the Rocks*, 21 January 2021.

Mansour, Renad, *Networks of Power: The Popular Mobilization Forces and the State in Iraq* (London: Chatham House, 2021).

Manucci, Niccolao, *Storia do Mogor or Mogul India, 1653–1708*, trans. by William Irvine, Vol. 2 (London: John Murray, 1907).

Manz, Beatrice Forbes, *The Rise and Rule of Tamerlane* (Cambridge: Cambridge University Press, 1989).

Manz, Beatrice Forbes, *Power, Politics and Religion in Timurid Iran* (Cambridge: Cambridge University Press, 2007).

Maʿoz, Moshe, *Ottoman Reform in Syria and Palestine, 1840–1861: The Impact of the Tanzimat on Politics and Society* (Oxford: Clarendon Press, 1968).

Marashi, Afshin, *Nationalizing Iran: Culture, Power, and the State, 1870–1940* (Seattle: University of Washington Press, 2008).

al-Marashi, Ibrahim, 'Iraq's Popular Mobilisation Units: Intra-Sectarian Rivalry and Arab Shiʿa Mobilisation from the 2003 Invasion to Covid-19 Pandemic', *International Politics* 15, 4 (2021), 441–458.

al-Marashi, Ibrahim, and Sammy Salama, *Iraq's Armed Forces: An Analytical History* (Abingdon: Routledge, 2008).

Marchand, Suzanne L., *German Orientalism in the Age of Empire: Religion, Race, and Scholarship* (Cambridge: Cambridge University Press, 2010).

Marcinkowski, Christoph, 'Aspects of Shiʿism in Contemporary Southeast Asia', *The Muslim World* 98, 1 (2008), 36–71.

Marcinkowski, Christoph, *Shiʿite Identities: Community and Culture in Changing Social Contexts* (Münster: LIT, 2010).

Mardin, Şerif, *Religion and Social Change in Modern Turkey: The Case of Bediüzzaman Said Nursi* (Albany: SUNY Press, 1989).

Margariti, Roxani Eleni, *Aden and the Indian Ocean Trade: 150 Years in the Life of a Medieval Arabian Port* (Chapel Hill: University of North Carolina Press, 2007).

Margoliouth, D. S., 'Review: صبح الاعسللقلقسندى Volumes XI–XIV', *Journal of the Royal Asiatic Society of Great Britain & Ireland* 53, 2 (1921), 294.

Markiewicz, Christopher, 'Europeanist Trends and Islamicate Trajectories in Early Modern Ottoman History', *Past & Present* 239, 1 (2018), 265–81.

Marr, Phebe, *The Modern History of Iraq* (Boulder, CO: Westview Press, 1985).

Marschall, Christin, *Iran's Persian Gulf Policy: From Khomeini to Khatami* (London: Routledge Curzon, 2003).

Marshall, P. J., *Bengal: The British Bridgehead: Eastern India 1740–1828* (Cambridge: Cambridge University Press, 1988).

Marsham, Andrew, *Rituals of Islamic Monarchy: Accession and Succession in the First Muslim Empire* (Edinburgh: Edinburgh University Press, 2009).

Martin, Vanessa, *Islam and Modernism: The Iranian Revolution of 1906* (London: Tauris, 1989).

Martin, Vanessa, *Creating an Islamic State: Khomeini and the Making of a New Iran* (London: I. B. Tauris, 2000).

Marx, Anthony W., *Faith in Nation: Exclusionary Origins of Nationalism* (Oxford: Oxford University Press, 2003).

Masalha, N., 'Faisal's Pan-Arabism, 1921–33', *Middle Eastern Studies* 27, 4 (1991), 679–93.

Masarwa, Alev, 'Der Irak: Identitätskonzepte im Wandel', in: Rüdiger Robert, Daniela Schlicht, and Shazia Saleem (eds), *Kollektive Identitäten im Nahen und Mittleren Osten: Studien zum Verhältnis von Staat und Religion* (Münster: Waxmann, 2010), 335–58.

Masarwa, Alev, *Bildung, Macht, Kultur: Das Feld des Gelehrten Abū t̲-T̲anā' al-Ālūsī (1802–1854) im spätosmanischen Bagdad* (Würzburg: Ergon, 2011).

Masid, Muhammad Khalid, 'Fatwa Advice on Proper Muslim Names', in: Barbara D. Metcalf (ed.), *Islam in South Asia in Practice* (Princeton: Princeton University Press, 2009), 339–51.

Massignon, Louis, 'Mutanabi devant le siècle ismaélien de l'Islam', in: *Al Mutanabbî: Recueil publié à l'occasion de son millénaire* (Beirut: Institut Français de Damas, 1936), 1–17.

Massignon, Louis, *The Passion of al-Hallāj: Mystic and Martyr of Islam*, trans. by Herbert Mason, 4 Vols (Princeton: Princeton University Press, 1972–86).

Masters, Bruce, *Christians and Jews in the Ottoman Arab World: The Roots of Sectarianism* (Cambridge: Cambridge University Press, 2001).

Masters, Bruce, 'The Establishment of the Melkite Catholic Millet in 1848 and the Politics of Identity in Tanzimat Syria', in: Peter Sluglett and Stefan Weber (eds), *Syria and Bilad al-Sham under Ottoman Rule: Essays in Honour of Abdul Karim Rafeq* (Leiden: Brill, 2010), 455–73.

Masuzawa, Tomoko, *The Invention of World Religions: Or, How European Universalism was Preserved in the Language of Pluralism* (Chicago: University of Chicago Press, 2005).

Mather, Yassamine, and David Mather, 'The Islamic Republic and the Iranian Left', *Critique: Journal of Socialist Theory* 30, 1 (2002), 179–91.

Matthee, Rudi, 'The Egyptian Opposition on the Iranian Revolution', in: Juan R. I. Cole and Nikki R. Keddie (eds), *Shi'ism and Social Protest* (New Haven: Yale University Press, 1986), 247–74.

Matthee, Rudi, 'Administrative Stability and Change in Late-17th-Century Iran: The Case of Shaykh Ali Khan Zanganah (1669–89)', *International Journal of Middle East Studies* 26, 1 (1994), 77–98.

Matthee, Rudi, 'Anti-Ottoman Politics and Transit Rights: The Seventeenth-Century Trade in Silk between Safavid Iran and Muscovy', *Cahiers du Monde Russe* 35, 4 (1994), 739–61.

Matthee, Rudi, 'Unwalled Cities and Restless Nomads: Firearms and Artillery in Safavid Iran', in: Charles Melville (ed.), *Safavid Persia: The History and Politics of an Islamic Society* (London: I. B. Tauris, 1996), 389–416.

Matthee, Rudi, 'Anti-Ottoman Concerns and Caucasian Interests: Diplomatic Relations between Iran and Russia, 1587–1639', in: Michel M. Mazzaoui (ed.), *Safavid Iran & Her Neighbors* (Salt Lake City: University of Utah Press, 2003), 101–28.

Matthee, Rudi, 'The Safavid-Ottoman Frontier: Iraq-i Arab as Seen by the Safavids', *International Journal of Turkish Studies* 9, 1–2 (2003), 157–73.

Matthee, Rudi, 'Blinded by Power: The Rise and Fall of Fath 'Alī Khān Dāghestānī, Grand Vizier under Shāh Solṭān Ḥoseyn Ṣafavī (1127/1715–1133/1720)', *Studia Iranica* 33 (2004), 179–219.

Matthee, Rudi, 'Between Arabs, Turks and Iranians: The Town of Basra, 1600–1700', *Bulletin of the School of Oriental and African Studies* 69, 1 (2006), 53–78.

Matthee, Rudi, 'Was Safavid Iran an Empire?', *Journal of the Economic and Social History of the Orient* 53, 1/2 (2010), 233–65.

Matthee, Rudi, *Persia in Crisis: Safavid Decline and the Fall of Isfahan* (London: I. B. Tauris, 2012).

Matthee, Rudi, 'The Ottoman-Safavid War of 986–998/1578–90: Motives and Causes', *International Journal of Turkish Studies* 20, 1–2 (2014), 1–20.

Matthee, Rudi, 'The Decline of Safavid Iran in Comparative Perspective', *Journal of Persianate Studies* 8, 2 (2015), 276–308.

Matthee, Rudi, 'Nader Shah in Iranian Historiography: Warlord or National Hero?', *Institute for Advanced Study*, 2018, https://www.ias.edu/ideas/2018/matthee-nader-shah.

Matthee, Rudi, 'Introduction', in: Giovanni-Tommaso Minadoi, *The War between the Turks and the Persians: Conflict and Religion in the Safavid and Ottoman Worlds* (London: I. B. Tauris, 2019), vii–xiv.

Matthee, Rudi, 'Safavid Iran and the "Turkish Question" or How to Avoid a War on Multiple Fronts', *Iranian Studies* 52, 3–4 (2019), 513–42.

Matthiesen, Toby, 'Hizbullah al-Hijaz: A History of the Most Radical Saudi Shi'a Opposition Group', *Middle East Journal* 64, 2 (2010), 179–97.

Matthiesen, Toby, 'A "Saudi Spring?": The Shi'a Protest Movement in the Eastern Province 2011–2012', *Middle East Journal* 66, 4 (2012), 628–59.

Matthiesen, Toby, *Sectarian Gulf: Bahrain, Saudi Arabia, and the Arab Spring that Wasn't* (Stanford: Stanford University Press, 2013).

Matthiesen, Toby, 'Syria: Inventing a Religious War', *New York Review of Books*, 12 June 2013.

Matthiesen, Toby, 'The Local and the Transnational in the Arab Uprisings: The Protests in Saudi Arabia's Eastern Province', in: May Seikaly and Khawla Matar (eds), *The Silent Revolution: The Arab Spring and the Gulf States* (Berlin: Gerlach Press, 2014), 105–43.

Matthiesen, Toby, 'Migration, Minorities, and Radical Networks: Labour Movements and Opposition Groups in Saudi Arabia, 1950–1975', *International Review of Social History* 59, 3 (2014), 473–504.

Matthiesen, Toby, 'Mysticism, Migration and Clerical Networks: Ahmad al-Ahsa'i and the Shaykhis of al-Ahsa, Kuwait and Basra', *Journal of Muslim Minority Affairs* 34, 4 (2014), 386–409.

Matthiesen, Toby, *The Domestic Sources of Saudi Foreign Policy: Islamists and the State in the Wake of the Arab Uprisings* (Washington, DC: Brookings Institution, 2015).

Matthiesen, Toby, *The Other Saudis: Shiism, Dissent and Sectarianism* (Cambridge: Cambridge University Press, 2015).

Matthiesen, Toby, 'Shi'i Historians in a Wahhabi State: Identity Entrepreneurs and the Politics of Local Historiography in Saudi Arabia', *International Journal of Middle East Studies* 47, 1 (2015), 25–45.

Matthiesen, Toby, 'Transnational Diffusion between Arab Shia Movements', *POMEPS*, 9 June 2016.

Matthiesen, Toby, 'Government and Opposition in the Middle East: The 1993 Negotiations between the Saudi Shia Opposition and King Fahd', in: Gabriele vom Bruck and Charles Tripp (eds), *Precarious Belongings: Being Shiʿi in Non-Shiʿi Worlds* (London: Centre for Academic Shia Studies, 2017), 377–417.

Matthiesen, Toby, 'Saudi Arabia', in: Shadi Hamid and William McCants (eds), *Rethinking Political Islam* (Oxford: Oxford University Press, 2017), 118–31.

Matthiesen, Toby, 'Sectarianization as Securitization: Identity Politics and Counter-Revolution in Bahrain', in: Nader Hashemi and Danny Postel (eds), *Sectarianization: Mapping the New Politics of the Middle East* (London: Hurst, 2017), 199–214.

Matthiesen, Toby, 'Renting the Casbah: Gulf States' Foreign Policy towards North Africa since the Arab Uprisings', in: Kristian Coates Ulrichsen (ed.), *The Changing Security Dynamics of the Persian Gulf* (New York: Oxford University Press, 2018), 43–59.

Matthiesen, Toby, 'Saudi Arabia and the Cold War', in: Madawi al-Rasheed (ed.), *Salman's Legacy: The Dilemmas of a New Era in Saudi Arabia* (London: Hurst, 2018), 217–33.

Matthiesen, Toby, 'The Shiʿa of Saudi Arabia at a Crossroads', *MERIP*, 6 May 2009.

Matthiesen, Toby, 'The Cold War and the Communist Party of Saudi Arabia, 1975–1991', *Journal of Cold War Studies* 22, 3 (2020), 32–62.

Matuz, Josef, 'Vom Übertritt osmanischer Soldaten zu den Safawiden', in: Ulrich Haarmann and Peter Bachmann (eds), *Die islamische Welt zwischen Mittelalter und Neuzeit: Festschrift für Hans Robert Roemer zum 65. Geburtstag* (Beirut/Wiesbaden: Orient-Institut/Steiner, 1979), 402–15.

Maurer, Michael, *Konfessionskulturen: Die Europäer als Protestanten und Katholiken* (Paderborn: Ferdinand Schöningh, 2019).

Maxwell, Alexander, 'Primordialism for Scholars who Ought to Know Better: Anthony D. Smith's Critique of Modernization Theory', *Nationalities Papers* 48, 5 (2020), 826–42.

May, Pierre, *L'Alaouite: Ses croyances, ses moeurs, les Cheikhs, les lois de la tribu et les chefs* (Beirut: Imprimerie catholique, 1931).

Mayer, Ann E., 'Review: 'The Origins of the Safawids: Shiism, Sufism, and the Ghulat' by Michel M. Mazzaoui', *Iranian Studies* 8, 4 (1975), 268–77.

Mayeur-Jaouen, Catherine, 'Les débuts d'une revue néo-salafiste: Muḥibb al-Dîn al-Khaṭîb et al-Fatḥ de 1926 à 1928', *Revue des mondes musulmans et de la Méditerranée* 95–8 (2002), 227–55.

Mazzaoui, Michel M., *The Origins of the Safawids: Shiism, Sufism, and the Ghulat* (Wiesbaden: Franz Steiner/Freiburger Islamstudien, 1972).

McCabe, Ina Baghdiantz, *Orientalism in Early Modern France: Eurasian Trade, Exoticism, and the Ancien Régime* (New York: Berg, 2008).

McCarthy, Rory, *Inside Tunisia's al-Nahda: Between Politics and Preaching* (Cambridge: Cambridge University Press, 2018).

McChesney, Robert D., *Waqf in Central Asia: Four Hundred Years in the History of a Muslim Shrine, 1480–1889* (Princeton: Princeton University Press, 1991).

McChesney, Robert D., "'Barrier of Heterodoxy"? Rethinking the Ties between Iran and Central Asia in the 17th Century', in: Charles Melville (ed.), *Safavid Persia: The History and Politics of an Islamic Society* (London: I. B. Tauris, 1996), 231–67.

McChesney, Robert D., *Kabul under Siege: Fayz Muhammad's Account of the 1929 Uprising* (Princeton: Markus Wiener, 1999).

McChesney, Robert D., 'The Central Asian Hajj-Pilgrimage in the Time of the Early Modern Empires', in: Michel M. Mazzaoui (ed.), *Safavid Iran & Her Neighbors* (Salt Lake City, UT: University of Utah Press, 2003), 129–56.

McChesney, Robert D., 'Islamic Culture and the Chinggisid Restoration: Central Asia in the Sixteenth and Seventeenth Centuries', in: D. Morgan and A. Reid (eds), *The New Cambridge History of Islam,* Vol. 3 (Cambridge: Cambridge University Press, 2010), 239–65.

McChesney, Robert D., "'The Bottomless Inkwell": The Life and Perilous Times of Fayz Muhammad 'Katib' Hazara', in: Nile Green (ed.), *Afghan History through Afghan Eyes* (London: Hurst, 2015), 97–129.

McDermott, Martin J., *The Theology of al-Shaikh al-Mufid (d. 413/1022)* (Beirut: Dar el-Machreq, 1978).

MacDonald, Duncan B., *Development of Muslim Theology, Jurisprudence, and Constitutional Theory* (London: Routledge, 1903).

McDowall, David, *A Modern History of the Kurds* (London: I. B. Tauris, 2007).

McHugo, John, *A Concise History of Sunnis and Shi'is* (London: Saqi, 2017).

McMahon, Sean F., *The Discourse of Palestinian–Israeli Relations: Persistent Analytics and Practices* (New York: Routledge, 2010).

McNeill, William H., *The Age of Gunpowder Empires, 1450–1800* (Washington, DC: American Historical Association, 1989).

al-Mdaires, Falah Abdullah, *Islamic Extremism in Kuwait: From the Muslim Brotherhood to al-Qaeda and Other Islamist Political Groups* (Abingdon: Routledge, 2010).

Meacham, Jon, *Destiny and Power: The American Odyssey of George Herbert Walker Bush* (New York: Random House, 2015).

Meer Hassan Ali, B., *Observations on the Mussulmauns of India: Descriptive of their Manners, Customs, Habits, and Religious Opinions, Made during a Twelve Years' Residence in their Immediate Society*, 2 Vols (London: Parbury, Allen & Co., 1832).

Mehta, N. C., 'An Unpublished Testament of Babur', *The Twentieth Century* (1936), 339–44.

Meijer, Roel, 'Muslim Politics under Occupation: The Association of Muslim Scholars and the Politics of Resistance in Iraq', *Arab Studies Journal* 13/4, 2/1 (2005/6), 92–112.

Meijer, Roel, and Joas Wagemakers, 'The Struggle for Citizenship of the Shiites of Saudi Arabia', in: Brigitte Maréchal and Sami Zemni (eds), *The Dynamics of Sunni–Shia Relationships: Doctrine, Transnationalism, Intellectuals and the Media* (London: Hurst, 2013), 117–38.

Meinel, Ute, *Die Intifada im Ölscheichtum Bahrain: Hintergründe des Aufbegehrens von 1994–98* (Münster: LIT, 2003).

Mektuplaşmaları, I. *Mahmud-Nadir Şah, 3 Numaralı Nâme-i Hümâyûn Defteri* (Istanbul: Osmanli Arşivi Daire Başkanlığı Yayınları, 2014).

Melchert, Christopher, 'Religious Policies of the Caliphs from al-Mutawakkil to al-Muqtadir, A H 232–295/A D 847–908', *Islamic Law and Society* 3, 3 (1996), 316–42.

Melchert, Christopher, *The Formation of the Sunni Schools of Law, 9th–10th Centuries C.E.* (Leiden: Brill, 1997).

Melchert, Christopher, 'The Ḥanābila and the Early Sufis', *Arabica* 48, 3 (2001), 352–67.

Melchert, Christopher, *Ahmad ibn Hanbal* (Oxford: Oneworld, 2006).

Melchert, Christopher, 'Renunciation (Zuhd) in the Early Shi'i Tradition', in: Farhad Daftary and Gurdofarid Miskinzoda (eds), *The Study of Shi'i Islam: History, Theology and Law* (London: I. B. Tauris, 2014), 271–94.

Meleady, Conor, '"Far from the Orthodox Road": Conceptualizing the Shi'a in the Nineteenth-Century Official Mind', in: Justin Quinn Olmstead (ed.), *Britain in the Islamic World: Imperial and Post-Imperial Connections* (Basingstoke: Palgrave Macmillan, 2019), 57–85.

Mélikoff, Irène, 'L'origine sociale des premiers Ottomans', in: Elizabeth Zachariadou (ed.), *The Ottoman Emirate (1300–1389)* (Rethymno: Crete University Press, 1993), 135–44.

Mélikoff, Irène, *Hadji Bektach: Un mythe et ses avatars: Genèse et évolution du soufisme populaire en Turquie* (Leiden: Brill, 1998).

Melville, Charles, 'The Itineraries of Sultan Öljeitü, 1304–16', *Iran* 28 (1990), 55–70.

Melville, Charles, 'Pādshāh-i Islām: The Conversion of Sultan Maḥmūd Ghāzān Khān', *Pembroke Papers* 1 (1990), 159–77.

Melville, Charles, 'The Year of the Elephant: Mamluk-Mongol Rivalry in the Hejaz in the Reign of Abu Sa'id (1317–1335)', *Studia Iranica* 21, 2 (1992), 197–214.

Melville, Charles, '"Sometimes by the Sword, Sometimes by the Dagger": The Role of the Ismailis in Mamluk-Mongol Relations in the 8th/14th Century', in: Farhad Daftary (ed.), *Mediaeval Isma'ili History and Thought* (Cambridge: Cambridge University Press, 1996), 247–63.

Melville, Charles, 'Shah 'Abbas and the Pilgrimage to Mashhad', in: Charles Melville (ed.), *Safavid Persia: The History and Politics of an Islamic Society* (London: I. B. Tauris, 1996), 191–229.

Melville, Charles, 'The Itineraries of Shahrukh b. Timur (1405–47)', in: David Durand-Guédy (ed.), *Turko-Mongol Rulers, Cities and City Life* (Leiden: Brill, 2013), 285–315.

Melville, Charles, 'New Light on Shah 'Abbas and the Construction of Isfahan', *Muqarnas* 33, 1 (2016), 155–76.

Melville, Firuza, 'Hilali and Mir 'Ali: Sunnis among the Shi'is, or Shi'is among the Sunnis between the Shaybanids, Safavids and the Mughals', *Iran* 59, 2 (2021), 245–62.

Melvin-Koushki, Matthew, 'Early Modern Islamicate Empire: New Forms of Religiopolitical Legitimacy', in: Armando Salvatore, Roberto Tottoli, and Babak Rahimi (eds), *The Wiley-Blackwell History of Islam* (Hoboken: Wiley-Blackwell, 2018), 353–75.

Melvin-Koushki, Matthew, 'Khunjī Iṣfahānī, Faẓl Allāh b. Rūzbihān (1455–1521): Sulūk al-Mulūk' (forthcoming, published on Academia).

Membrado, Mojan, 'L'impact des missionnaires chrétiens du début du XXe siècle sur l'étude d'une communauté initiatique kurde: Les 'Fidèles de Vérité' (Ahl-e Haqq)', in: Bernard Heyberger and Rémy Madinier (eds), *L'Islam des marges: Mission chrétienne et espaces périphériques du monde musulman, XVI–XXe siècles* (Paris: IISMM/Karthala, 2011), 207–29.

Membrè, Michele, *Mission to the Lord Sophy of Persia (1539–1542)*, trans. by A. H. Morton (London: School of Oriental and African Studies, 1993).

Menashri, David (ed.), *The Iranian Revolution and the Muslim World* (Boulder, CO: Westview Press, 1990).

Méouchy, Nadine, 'La réforme des juridictions religieuses en Syrie et au Liban (1921–1939): Raisons de la puissance mandataire et raisons des communautés', in: Pierre-Jean Luizard (ed.), *Le choc colonial et l'Islam: Les politiques religieuses des puissances colonials en terres d'Islam* (Paris: La Découverte, 2006), 359–82.

Merali, Amaan, 'Legitimising Authority: A Muslim Minority under Ottoman Rule', in: Amyn B. Sajoo (ed.), *The Sharīʿa: History, Ethics and Law* (London: I. B. Tauris, 2018), 153–71.

Merali, Amaan, 'Fear and Violence in Late Ottoman Syria: The Ismaʿilis and the School of Agriculture', *Diyâr* 1, 1 (2020), 58–83.

Meri, Josef, *The Cult of Saints among Muslims and Jews in Medieval Syria* (Oxford: Oxford University Press, 2002).

Mervin, Sabrina, 'Sayyida Zaynab, Banlieue de Damas ou nouvelle ville sainte chiite?', *Cahiers d'études sur la Méditerranée orientale et le monde turco-iranien* 22, 1 (1996), 149–62.

Mervin, Sabrina, *Un réformisme chiite: Ulémas et lettrés du Ǧabal ʿĀmil (actuel Liban-Sud) de la fin de l'Empire ottoman à l'indépendance du Liban* (Paris: Karthala, 2000).

Mervin, Sabrina, 'The Clerics of Jabal 'Amil and the Reform of Religious Teaching in Najaf since the Beginning of the 20th Century', in: Rainer Brunner and Werner Ende (eds), *The Twelver Shia in Modern Times: Religious Culture & Political History* (Leiden: Brill, 2001), 79–86.

Mervin, Sabrina, 'Quelques jalons pour une histoire du rapprochement (taqrîb) des alaouites vers le chiisme', in: Rainer Brunner, Monika Gronke, Jens P. Laut, and Ulrich Rebstock (eds), *Islamstudien ohne Ende: Festschrift für Werner Ende* (Würzburg: Deutsche Morgenländische Gesellschaft/Ergon, 2002), 281–8.

Mervin, Sabrina, 'L'"entité alaouite", une création française', in: Pierre-Jean Luizard (ed.), *Le choc colonial et l'Islam: Les politiques religieuses des puissances colonials en terres d'Islam* (Paris: La Découverte, 2006), 343–58.

Mervin, Sabrina, 'Des nosayris aux ja'farites: Le processus de "chiitisation" des alaouites', in: Baudouin Dupret (ed.), *La Syrie au present: Reflets d'une société* (Paris: Sindbad, 2007), 359–64.

Mervin, Sabrina, 'Ashura: Some Remarks on Ritual Practices in Different Shiite Communities (Lebanon and Syria)', in: Alessandro Monsutti, Silvia Naef, and Farian Sabahi (eds), *The Other Shiites: From the Mediterranean to Central Asia* (Bern: Peter Lang, 2008), 137–47.

Mervin, Sabrina, *Le Hezbollah, état des lieux* (Paris: Sindbad, 2008).

Mervin, Sabrina, 'Normes religieuses et loi du silence: Le mariage temporaire chez les chiites du Liban', in: Barbara Drieskens (ed.), *Les métamorphoses du mariage au Moyen-Orient* (Beirut: Presses de l'Ifpo, 2008), 47–58.

Mervin, Sabrina (ed.), *The Shi'a Worlds and Iran* (London: Saqi, 2010).

Mervin, Sabrina, 'On Sunnite-Shiite Doctrinal and Contemporary Geopolitical Tensions', in: Brigitte Maréchal and Sami Zemni (eds), *The Dynamics of Sunni-Shia Relationships: Doctrine, Transnationalism, Intellectuals and the Media* (London: Hurst, 2013), 11–24.

Mesbahi, Mohammad, 'Dynamic Quietism and the Consolidation of the ḥawza 'ilmīyya of Qum during the Pahlavi Era', *British Journal of Middle Eastern Studies* (online, 2021).

Mesbahi, Mohiaddin, 'The USSR and the Iran–Iraq War: From Brezhnev to Gorbachev', in: Farhang Rajaee (ed.), *The Iran–Iraq War: The Politics of Aggression* (Gainesville: University Press of Florida, 1993), 69–102.

Meserve, Margaret, 'The Sophy: News of Shah Ismail Safavi in Renaissance Europe', *Journal of Early Modern History* 18 (2014), 579–608.

Messick, Brinkley, *The Calligraphic State: Textual Domination and History in a Muslim Society* (Berkeley: University of California Press, 1993).

Metcalf, Barbara D., *Islamic Revival in British India: Deoband, 1860–1900* (Princeton: Princeton University Press, 1982).

Métral, Jean, 'Robert Montagne et les études ethnographiques françaises dans la Syrie sous mandat', in: Peter Sluglett and Nadine Méouchy (eds), *The British and French Mandates in Comparative Perspectives* (Leiden: Brill, 2004), 217–34.

Michael, George, 'The Legend and Legacy of Abu Musab al-Zarqawi', *Defence Studies* 7, 3 (2007), 338–57.

Michael, Thomas, 'Ibn Taymiyya's Sharḥ on the Futūḥ al-Ghayb of 'Abd al-Qādir al-Jīlānī', *Hamdard Islamicus* 4, 2 (1981), 3–12.

Michot, Yahya M., *Muslims under Non-Muslim Rule* (Oxford: Interface, 2006).

Michot, Yahya M., 'Ibn Taymiyya's "New Mardin Fatwa": Is Genetically Modified Islam (GMI) Carcinogenic?', *The Muslim World* 101, 2 (2011), 130–81.

Michot, Yahya M., 'Ibn Taymiyya's Critique of Shī'ī Imāmology: Translation of Three Sections of his Minhaj al-Sunna', *The Muslim World* 104, 1–2 (2014), 109–49.

Mikaelian, Shoghig, and Bassel F. Salloukh, 'Strong Actor in a Weak State: The Geopolitics of Hezbollah', in: Mehran Kamrava (ed.), *Fragile Politics: Weak States in the Greater Middle East* (New York: Oxford University Press, 2016), 119–43.

al-Milani, Ali al-Hussayni (ed.), *Khalasa 'Abaqat al-Anwar fi Imamat A'imat al-Athar*, 6 Vols (Tehran: Mu'assassat al-Ba'atha, 1404h).

Minault, Gail, *The Khilafat Movement: Religious Symbolism and Political Mobilization in India* (New York: Columbia University Press, 1982).

Minawi, Mostafa, *The Ottoman Scramble for Africa: Empire and Diplomacy in the Sahara and the Hijaz* (Stanford: Stanford University Press, 2016).

Minorsky, V., 'Jihān-Shāh Qara-Qoyunlu and his Poetry (Turkmenica, 9)', *Bulletin of the School of Oriental and African Studies* 16, 2 (1954), 271–97.

Minorsky, V., 'The Poetry of Shāh Ismā'īl I', *Bulletin of the School of Oriental and African Studies* 10, 4 (1942), 1006–29.

Mir-Hosseini, Ziba, 'Inner Truth and Outer History: The Two Worlds of the Ahl-i Haqq of Kurdistan', *International Journal of Middle East Studies* 26, 2 (1994), 267–85.

Mir-Hosseini, Ziba, 'Redefining the Truth: Ahl-i Haqq and the Islamic Republic of Iran', *British Journal of Middle Eastern Studies* 21, 2 (1994), 211–28.

Mir-Hosseini, Ziba, 'Breaking the Seal: The New Face of the Ahl-e Haqq', in: Krisztina Kehl-Bodrogi, Barbara Kellner-Heinkele, and Anke Otter-Beaujean (eds), *Syncretistic Religious Communities in the Near East: Collected Papers of the International Symposium 'Alevism in Turkey and Comparable Syncretistic Religious Communities in the Near East in the Past and Present', Berlin, 14–17 April 1995* (Leiden: Brill, 1997), 175–94.

Mir-Kasimov, Orkhan, *Words of Power: Ḥurūfī Teachings between Shi'ism and Sufism: The Original Ḥurūfī Doctrine of Faḍl Allāh Astarābādī* (London: I. B. Tauris/Institute of Ismaili Studies, 2015).

al-Mirshid, 'Abbas Mirza, and 'Abd al-Hadi al-Khawaja', *Al-Tanzimat wa-l-Jama'iyyat al-Siyyasiyya fi al-Bahrayn* (Bahrain: Faradis lil-Nashr wa-l-Tawzi', 2008).

Mirza, Humayun, *From Plassey to Pakistan: The Family History of Iskander Mirza, the First President of Pakistan* (Lahore: Ferozsons, 2000).

Mirza, Nasseh Ahmad, *Syrian Ismailism: The Ever Living Line of the Imamate, AD 1100–1260* (Richmond: Curzon, 1997).

Mirza, Shireen, 'Travelling Leaders and Connecting Print Cultures: Two Conceptions of Twelver Shi'i Reformism in the Indian Ocean', *Journal of the Royal Asiatic Society* 24, 3 (2014), 455–75.

Mirza, Shireen, 'Waqf and Urban Space: Production of Minority Identity in Hyderabad's Old City', in: Jyotirmaya Tripathy and Sudarsan Padmanabhan (eds.), *Becoming Minority: How Discourses and Policies Produce Minorities in Europe and India* (Los Angeles: Sage, 2014), 293–313.

Mishal, Shaul, and Ori Goldberg, *Understanding Shiite Leadership: The Art of the Middle Ground in Iran and Lebanon* (Cambridge: Cambridge University Press, 2015).

Mitchell, Colin Paul, 'Sister Shi'a States? Safavid Iran and the Deccan in the 16th Century', *Deccan Studies* 2, 2 (2004), 44–72.

Mitchell, Colin Paul, *The Practice of Politics in Safavid Iran: Power, Religion and Rhetoric* (London: I. B. Tauris, 2009).

Mitchell, Colin Paul, 'Two Tales of One City: Herat under the Early Modern Empires of the Timurids and Safavids', in: Eric Nelson and Jonathan Wright (eds), *Layered Landscapes: Early Modern Religious Space across Faiths and Cultures* (Abingdon: Routledge, 2017), 207–22.

Mitchell, Richard P., *The Society of the Muslim Brothers* (Oxford: Oxford University Press, 1993).

Mitha, Farouk, *Al-Ghazali and the Ismailis: A Debate on Reason and Authority in Medieval Islam* (London: I. B. Tauris/Institute of Ismaili Studies, 2001).

Mizrahi, Jean-David, 'La France et sa politique de mandat en Syrie et au Liban (1920–1939)', in: Nadine Méouchy (ed.), *France, Syrie et Liban 1918–1946: Les ambiguïtés et les dynamiques de la relation mandataire* (Damascus: Presses de l'Ifpo, 2002), 35–71.

Moaddel, Mansoor, 'Shi'i Political Discourse and Class Mobilization in the Tobacco Movement of 1890–1892', *Sociological Forum* 7, 3 (1992), 447–68.

Moazzen, Maryam, *Formation of a Religious Landscape: Shi'i Higher Learning in Safavid Iran* (Leiden: Brill, 2018).

el-Moctar, Mohamed, 'Saladin in Sunni and Shi'a Memories', in: Nicholas Paul and Suzanne Yeager (eds), *Remembering the Crusades: Myth, Image, and Identity* (Baltimore: Johns Hopkins University Press, 2012), 197–214.

el-Moctar, Mohamed, 'Defensive Jihad: Islamization of the Turks and Turkification of Islam', *İnönü University International Journal of Social Sciences* 6, 1 (2017), 1–21.

Modarressi, Seyyed Hossein, *An Introduction to Shī'ī Law: A Bibliographical Study* (London: Ithaca Press, 1984).

Modarressi, Seyyed Hossein, *Crisis and Consolidation in the Formative Period of Shi'ite Islam: Abū Ja'far ibn Qiba al-Rāzī and his Contribution to Imāmite Shī'ite Thought* (Princeton: Darwin Press, 1993).

Modarressi, Seyyed Hossein, 'Early Debates on the Integrity of the Qur'ān: A Brief Survey', *Studia Islamica* 77 (1993), 5–39.

Moghadam, Assaf, 'Mayhem, Myths, and Martyrdom: The Shi'a Conception of Jihad', *Terrorism and Political Violence* 19, 1 (2007), 125–43.

Moghadam, Assaf, *The Globalization of Martyrdom: Al-Qaeda, Salafi Jihad, and the Diffusion of Suicide Attacks* (Baltimore: Johns Hopkins University Press, 2008).

Moghadam, Assaf, 'Motives for Martyrdom: Al-Qaida, Salafi Jihad, and the Spread of Suicide Attacks', *International Security* 33, 3 (2008/9), 46–78.

Moghadam, Assaf, *Nexus of Global Jihad: Understanding Cooperation among Terrorist Actors* (New York: Columbia University Press, 2017).

Mohamedou, Mohammad-Mahmoud, *A Theory of ISIS: Political Violence and the Transformation of the Global Order* (London: Pluto, 2018).

Mohseni, Shahbaz, 'Der sunnitische Islam im Iran', *Spektrum Iran* 30, 3 (2017), 71–82.

Moin, A. Azfar, 'Partisan Dreams and Prophetic Visions: Shi'i Critique in al-Masudi's History of the Abbasids', *Journal of the American Oriental Society* 127, 4 (2007), 415–28.

Moin, A. Azfar, 'Peering through the Cracks in the Baburnama: The Textured Lives of Mughal Sovereigns', *Indian Economic & Social History Review* 49, 4 (2012), 493–526, 501–4.

Moin, Baqer, *Khomeini: Life of the Ayatollah* (London: I. B. Tauris, 1999).

Mokhberi, Susan, *The Persian Mirror: Reflections of the Safavid Empire in Early Modern France* (Oxford: Oxford University Press, 2019).

Mol, Arnold Yasin, Majid Daneshgar, and Faisal Ahmad Shah, 'Ashura in the Malay-Indonesian World: The Ten Days of Muharram in Sumatra as Depicted by Nineteenth-Century Dutch Scholars', *Journal of Shi'a Islamic Studies* 8, 4 (2015), 491–505.

Molé, Marijan, 'Les Kubrawiya entre sunnisme et shiisme aux huitième et neuvième siècles de l'hégire', *Revue des études islamiques* 29 (1961), 61–142.

Momen, Moojan, 'The Trial of Mullā 'Alī Basṭāmī: A Combined Sunnī-Shī'ī Fatwā against the Bāb', *Iran* 20 (1982), 113–43.

Momen, Moojan, *An Introduction to Shi'i Islam: The History and Doctrines of Twelver Shi'ism* (New Haven: Yale University Press, 1985).

Momen, Moojan, 'Millennialism and Violence: The Attempted Assassination of Nasir al-Din Shah of Iran by the Babis in 1852', *Nova Religio* 12, 1 (2008), 57–82.

Monier, Elizabeth, 'Egypt, Iran, and the Hizbullah Cell: Using Sectarianism to "De-Arabize" and Regionalize Threats to National Interests', *Middle East Journal* 69, 3 (2015), 341–57.

Monserrate, Antonio, *The Commentary of Father Monserrate, S. J., on his Journey to the Court of Akbar*, trans. by John S. Hoyland (London: H. Milford/Oxford University Press, 1922).

Monshi, Eskandar Beg, *History of Shah 'Abbās the Great (Tārīkh-e 'Ālamārā-ye 'Abbāsī)*, trans. by Roger M. Savory, 3 Vols (Boulder, CO: Westview Press, 1978–86).

Monsutti, Alessandro, *War and Migration: Social Networks and Economic Strategies of the Hazaras of Afghanistan* (London: Routledge, 2005).

Monsutti, Alessandro, 'Image of the Self, Image of the Other: Social Organization and the Role of "Ashura" among the Hazaras of Quetta (Pakistan)', in: Alessandro Monsutti, Silvia Naef, Farian Sabahi (eds), *The Other Shiites: From the Mediterranean to Central Asia* (Bern: Peter Lang, 2007).

Monsutti, Alessandro, 'Islamism among the Shi'a of Afghanistan: From Social Revolution to Identity-Building', in: Sabrina Mervin (ed.), *The Shi'a Worlds and Iran* (London: Saqi, 2010), 45–62.

Montenegro, Silvia, "Alawi Muslims in Argentina: Religious and Political Identity in the Diaspora', *Contemporary Islam* 12 (2018), 23–38.

Moosa, Ebrahim, 'The Sunni Orthodoxy', *Critical Muslim* 10 (2014), 19–36.

Moosa, Matti, *Extremist Shiites: The Ghulat Sects* (Syracuse: Syracuse University Press, 1987).

Moosvi, Shireen, 'The Conversations of Jahangir 1608–11: Table Talk on Religion', *Proceedings of the Indian History Congress* 68 (2007), 326–31.

Mordtmann, J. H., 'Sunnitisch-schiitische Polemik im 17. Jahrhundert', *Mitteilungen des Seminars für orientalische Sprachen an der Friedrich-Wilhelms-Universität zu Berlin* 29 (1926), 112–29.

Morimoto, Kazuo, 'The Formation and Development of the Science of Talibid Genealogies in the 10th & 11th Century Middle East', *Oriente Moderno* 18, 2 (1999), 541–70.

Morimoto, Kazuo, 'The Earliest 'Alid Genealogy for the Safavids: New Evidence for the Pre-dynastic Claim to Sayyid Status', *Iranian Studies* 43, 4 (2010), 447–69.

Morimoto, Kazuo (ed.), *Sayyids and Sharifs in Muslim Societies: The Living Links to the Prophet* (Abingdon: Routledge, 2012).

Morimoto, Kazuo, 'An Enigmatic Genealogical Chart of the Timurids: A Testimony to the Dynasty's Claim to Yasavi-'Alid Legitimacy?', *Oriens* 44, 1–2 (2016), 145–78.

Morimoto, Kazuo, 'Sayyid Ibn 'Abd al-Ḥamīd: An Iraqi Shi'i Genealogist at the Court of Özbek Khan', *Journal of the Economic and Social History of the Orient* 59 (2016), 661–94.

Morrison, Robert G., *Islam and Science: The Intellectual Career of Nizam al-Din al-Nisaburi* (New York: Routledge, 2007).

Mortel, Richard, 'Zaydi Shi'ism and the Ḥasanid Sharifs of Mecca', *International Journal of Middle East Studies* 19, 4 (1987), 455–72.

Mortel, Richard, 'The Ḥusaynid Amirate of Madīna during the Mamlūk Period', *Studia Islamica* 80 (1994), 97–123.

Morton, Nicholas, 'The Saljuq Turks' Conversion to Islam: The Crusading Sources', *Al-Masāq* 27, 2 (2015), 109–18.

Moslem, Majid S., *Frieden im Islam: Die Instrumentalisierung des Islam im irakisch-iranischen Krieg* (Berlin: Klaus Schwarz, 2005).

Mostashari, Firouzeh, *On the Religious Frontier: Tsarist Russia and Islam in the Caucasus* (London: I. B. Tauris, 2017).

Motadel, David, 'Qajar Shahs in Imperial Germany', *Past & Present* 213, 1 (2011), 191–235.

Motadel, David, 'Iran and the Aryan Myth', in: Ali M. Ansari (ed.), *Perceptions of Iran: History, Myths and Nationalism from Medieval Persia to the Islamic Republic* (London: I. B. Tauris, 2014), 119–45.

Motadel, David (ed.), *Islam and the European Empires* (Oxford: Oxford University Press, 2014).

Motadel, David, *Islam and Nazi Germany's War* (Cambridge, MA: Harvard University Press, 2014).

Motika, Raoul, 'Foreign Missionaries, Homemade Dissidents and Popular Islam: The Search for New Religious Structures in Azerbaijan', in: Rainer Brunner and Werner Ende (eds), *The Twelver Shia in Modern Times: Religious Culture & Political History* (Leiden: Brill, 2001), 284–97.

Motika, Raoul, 'Islam in Post-Soviet Azerbaijan', *Archives de sciences sociales des religions* 46, 115 (2001), 111–24.

Mottahedeh, Roy P., 'The Shu'ûbîyah Controversy and the Social History of Early Islamic Iran', *International Journal of Middle East Studies* 7, 2 (1976), 161–82.

Mottahedeh, Roy P., *Loyalty and Leadership in an Early Islamic Society* (Princeton: Princeton University Press, 1980).

Motzki, Harald, *The Origins of Islamic Jurisprudence: Meccan Fiqh Before the Classical Schools* (Leiden: Brill, 2002).

Mousavi, Sayed A., *The Hazaras of Afghanistan: An Historical, Cultural, Economic and Political Study* (Richmond: Curzon, 1998).

Mousavian, Seyed Hossein, and Shahir Shahidsaless, *Iran and the United States: An Insider's View of the Failed Past and the Road to Peace* (New York: Bloomsbury, 2014).

al-Mudayris, Falah 'Abdallah, *Al-Haraka al-Shi'iyya fi al-Kuwayt* (Kuwait: Dar al-Qurtas, 1999).

al-Mudayris, Falah 'Abdallah, *Al-Harakat wa-l-Jama'at al-Siyyasiyya fi al-Bahrayn 1937–2002* (Beirut: Dar al-Kunuz al-Adabiyya, 2004).

Mughniyya, Muhammad Jawad, *Al-Fiqh 'ala al-Madhahib al-Khamsa: Al-Ja'fari, al-Hanafi, al-Maliki, al-Shafi'i, al-Hanbali*, 6th ed. (Beirut: Dar al-'Ilm li-l-Mallayyin, 1979).

Mughniyya, Muhammad Jawad, *Hadhihi hiya al-Wahhabiyya* (Tehran: Munazzamat al-'Ilam al-Islami, 1987).

Mukherjee, Soumen, 'Universalising Aspirations: Community and Social Service in the Isma'ili Imagination in Twentieth-Century South Asia and East Africa', *Journal of the Royal Asiatic Society* 24, 3 (2014), 435–53.

Mukherjee, Soumen, *Ismailism and Islam in Modern South Asia: Community and Identity in the Age of Religious Internationals* (Cambridge: Cambridge University Press, 2017).

Mulder, Stephennie, 'The Mausoleum of Imam al-Shafi'i', *Muqarnas* 23 (2006), 15–46.

Mulder, Stephennie, 'Abdülhamid and the 'Alids: Ottoman Patronage of "Shi'i" Shrines in the Cemetery of Bāb al-Ṣaghīr in Damascus', *Studia Islamica* 108, 1 (2013), 16–47.

Mulder, Stephennie, *The Shrines of the 'Alids in Medieval Syria: Sunnis, Shi'is and the Architecture of Coexistence* (Edinburgh: Edinburgh University Press, 2014).

al-Mulk, Nizam, *The Book of Government or Rules for Kings: The Siyar al-Muluk or Siyasat-Nama of Nizam al-Mulk*, trans. by Hubert Darke (London: Routledge and Kegan Paul, 1978).

Munir, Muhammad Ahmad, and Brian Wright, 'Fatwās of 'Abd al-Ḥayy of Farangī Maḥall and Their Role in the Formation of Sunnī Identity in British India', *Journal of Islamic Thought and Civilization* 11, 2 (2021), 20–43.

Murray, Williamson, and Kevin M. Woods, *The Iran–Iraq War: A Military and Strategic History* (Cambridge: Cambridge University Press, 2014).

Musa, Mohd Faizal, 'The Malaysian Shi'a: A Preliminary Study of their History, Oppression, and Denied Rights', *Journal of Shi'a Islamic Studies* 6, 4 (2013), 411–63.

al-Muslim, Muhammad Sa'id, *Sahil al-Dhahab al-Aswad: Dirasa Tarikhiyya Insaniyya li-Mintaqat al-Khalij al-'Arabi*, 2nd ed. (Beirut: Manshurat Dar Maktabat al-Haya, 1962).

Muwahidah, Siti Sarah, 'For the Love of Ahl al-Bayt: Transcending Sunni-Shi'i Sectarian Allegiance', *Journal of Shi'a Islamic Studies* 9, 3 (2016), 327–58.

Muzaffar, Chandra, 'Foreword', in: Karim D. Crow and Ahmad Kazemi Moussavi, *Facing One Qiblah: Legal and Doctrinal Aspects of Sunni and Shi'ah Muslims* (Singapore: Pustaka Nasional, 2005).

N.a., *Correspondence between Sir Henry McMahon, G.C.M.G., G.C.V.O., K.C.I.E., C.S.I., His Majesty's High Commissioner at Cairo, and the Sherif Hussein of Mecca, July 1915–March 1916* (London: HM Stationery Office, 1939).

N.a., *Al-Tasawwuf fi al-Su'udiyya wa-l-Khalij* (Dubai: Markaz al-Misbar li-l-Dirasat wa-l-Buhuth, 2011).

Naaman, Abdallah, *Les Alawites: Histoire mouvementée d'une communauté mystérieuse* (Paris: Éditions Érick Bonnier, 2017).

Nadjmabadi, Shahnaz, 'The Arab Presence on the Iranian Coast of the Persian Gulf', in: Lawrence G. Potter (ed.), *The Persian Gulf in History* (New York: Palgrave Macmillan, 2009), 129–45.

Naef, Silvia, 'Aufklärung in einem schiitischen Umfeld: Die libanesische Zeitschrift al-'Irfān', *Die Welt des Islams* 36, 3 (1996), 365–78.

Nafi, Basheer M., 'The General Islamic Congress of Jerusalem Reconsidered', *The Muslim World* 86, 3–4 (1996), 243–72.

Nafi, Basheer M., 'Abu al-Thana' al-Alusi: An Alim, Ottoman Mufti, and Exegete of the Qur'an', *International Journal of Middle East Studies* 34, 3 (2002), 465–94.

Nafi, Basheer M., 'A Teacher of Ibn 'Abd al-Wahhāb: Muḥammad Ḥayāt al-Sindī and the Revival of Asḥāb al-Ḥadīth's Methodology', *Islamic Law and Society* 13, 2 (2006), 208–41.

Nafi, Basheer M., 'Salafism Revived: Nu'mān al-Alūsī and the Trial of Two Aḥmads', *Die Welt des Islams* 49, 1 (2009), 49–97.

Nagar, Richa, 'Religion, Race, and the Debate over Mut'a in Dar es Salaam', *Feminist Studies* 26, 3 (2000), 661–90.

Nagle, Shane, 'Confessional Identity as National Boundary in National Historical Narratives: Ireland and Germany Compared', *Studies in Ethnicity and Nationalism* 13, 1 (2013), 38–56.

Nahouza, Namira, *Wahhabism and the Rise of the New Salafists: Theology, Power and Sunni Islam* (London: I. B. Tauris, 2018).

Naji, 'Abd al-Jabar, *Al-Tashayi' wa-l-Istishraq: 'Ard Naqdi Muqarin li-Dirasat al-Mustashriqin 'an al-'Aqida al-Shi'iyya wa A'imatiha* (Beirut: al-Jamal, 2011).

Nakash, Yitzhak, 'An Attempt to Trace the Origin of the Rituals of 'Āshūrā'', *Die Welt des Islams* 33, 2 (1993), 161–81.

Nakash, Yitzhak, 'The Conversion of Iraq's Tribes to Shiism', *International Journal of Middle East Studies* 26, 3 (1994), 443–63.

Nakash, Yitzhak, *The Shi'is of Iraq*, 2nd ed. (Princeton: Princeton University Press, 2003).

Nakash, Yitzhak, *Reaching for Power: The Shi'a in the Modern Arab World* (Princeton: Princeton University Press, 2006).

Nakhleh, Emile A., *Bahrain: Political Development in a Modernizing Society* (Lanham: Lexington Books, 1976).

al-Nakhli, Hasan bin Marzuq Rija' al-Sharimi, *Al-Nakhawila (al-Nakhliyyun) fi al-Madina al-Munawwara: Al-Takwin al-Ijtima'i wa-l-Thaqafi* (Beirut: Mu'assasat al-Intishar al-'Arabi, 2012).

Nakkash, Aziz, *The Alawite Dilemma in Homs: Survival, Solidarity and the Making of a Community* (Berlin: Friedrich-Ebert-Stiftung, 2013).

Napier, W. F. P., *The Conquest of Scinde: With Some Introductory Passages in the Life of Major-General Sir Charles James Napier* (Cambridge: Cambridge University Press, 2012).

Naqavi, Sadiq, *The Iran–Deccan Relations* (Hyderabad: Bab-ul-Ilm Society, 1994).

an-Nasafi, Abu Hafs, *Pillar of the Creed of the Sunnites: Being a Brief Exposition of their Principal Tenets* (London: James Madden & Co., 1843).

al-Nasiri, al-Shaykh Ahmad al-ʿAmari, *Qabilat Bani Khalid fi al-Tarikh* (Beirut: Dar al-Rafidayn li-l-Tibaʿa wa-l-Nashr wa-l-Tawziʿ, 2009).

Nasr, Seyyed Hossein, 'Shiʿism and Sufism: Their Relationship in Essence and in History', *Religious Studies* 6, 3 (1970), 229–42.

Nasr, Seyyed Hossein, 'SUFISM', in: R. N. Frye (ed.), *The Cambridge History of Iran*, Vol. 4 (Cambridge: Cambridge University Press, 1975), 442–63.

Nasr, Seyyed Hossein, and M. Mutahhari, 'The Religious Sciences', in: R. N. Frye (ed.), *The Cambridge History of Iran*, Vol. 4 (Cambridge: Cambridge University Press, 1975), 464–80.

Nasr, Seyyed Hossein, Hamid Dabashi, and Seyyed Vali Reza Nasr (eds), *Shiʿism: Doctrines, Thought, and Spirituality* (Albany: SUNY Press, 1988).

Nasr, Seyyed Hossein, Hamid Dabashi, and Seyyed Vali Reza Nasr (eds.), *Expectation of the Millennium: Shiʿism in History* (Albany: SUNY Press, 1989).

Nasr, Seyyed Vali Reza, *Mawdudi and the Making of Islamic Revivalism* (Oxford: Oxford University Press, 1996).

Nasr, Seyyed Vali Reza, 'International Politics, Domestic Imperatives, and Identity Mobilization: Sectarianism in Pakistan, 1979–1998', *Comparative Politics* 32, 2 (2000), 171–90.

Nasr, Seyyed Vali Reza, 'The Rise of Sunni Militancy in Pakistan: The Changing Role of Islamism and the Ulama in Society and Politics', *Modern Asian Studies* 34, 1 (2000), 139–80.

Nasr, Seyyed Vali Reza, 'Islam, the State and the Rise of Sectarian Militancy in Pakistan', in: Christophe Jaffrelot (ed.), *Pakistan: Nationalism without a Nation?* (New Delhi: Manohar, 2002), 85–114.

Nasr, Seyyed Vali Reza, *The Shia Revival: How Conflicts within Islam Will Shape the Future* (New York: Norton, 2006).

Nasr, Seyyed Vali Reza, *The Dispensable Nation: American Foreign Policy in Retreat* (Melbourne: Scribe, 2013).

Nassif, Hicham Bou, '"Second-Class": The Grievances of Sunni Officers in the Syrian Armed Forces', *Journal of Strategic Studies* 38, 5 (2015), 626–49.

Navias, Martin S., and E. R. Hooton, *Tanker Wars: The Assault on Merchant Shipping during the Iran-Iraq Conflict 1980–1988* (London: I. B. Tauris, 1996).

Nawas, John Abdallah, *Al-Maʾmun, the Inquisition, and the Quest for Caliphal Authority* (Atlanta, GA: Lockwood Press, 2015).

al-Nawbakhti, Abi Muhammad al-Hasan ibn Musa, *Kitāb Firaq al-Shīʿa* (The Sects of the Shia) (Istanbul: Matbaʿat al-Dawlah/Deutsche Morgenländische Gesellschaft, 1931).

al-Nawbakhti, Abi Muhammad al-Hasan ibn Musa, *Les sectes shiites*, annot. by M. Javad Mashkour (Tehran: n.p., 1980).

Nawid, Senzil K., *Religious Response to Social Change in Afghanistan, 1919–29: King Aman-Allah and the Afghan Ulama* (Costa Mesa: Mazda, 1999).

Nayeem, M. A., *External Relations of the Bijapur Kingdom, 1489–1686 A.D.: A Study in Diplomatic History* (Hyderabad: Bright, 1974).

Nayeem, M. A., *The Heritage of the Qutb Shahis of Golconda and Hyderabad* (Hyderabad: Hyderabad Publishers, 2006).

Necipoğlu, Gülru, *The Age of Sinan: Architectural Culture in the Ottoman Empire* (London: Reaktion, 2010).

Neep, Daniel, *Occupying Syria under the French Mandate: Insurgency, Space and State Formation* (Cambridge: Cambridge University Press, 2012).

Neggaz, Nassima, 'The Many Deaths of the Last 'Abbāsid Caliph al-Mustaʿṣim bi-llāh (d. 1258)', *Journal of the Royal Asiatic Society* 30, 4 (2020), 585–612.

Neggaz, Nassima, 'Al-Karkh: The Development of an Imāmī-Shīʿī Stronghold in Early Abbasid and Būyid Baghdad (132–447/750–1055)', *Studia Islamica* 114, 3 (2020), 265–315.

Neggaz, Nassima, 'Sectarianization and Memory in the Post-Saddam Middle East: The 'Alāqima', *British Journal of Middle Eastern Studies* 49, 1 (2022), 159–76.

Neuwirth, Angelika, *Der Koran als Text der Spätantike* (Frankfurt am Main: Verlag der Weltreligionen, 2010).

Nevo, Joseph J., 'Religion and National Identity in Saudi Arabia', *Middle Eastern Studies* 34, 3 (1998), 34–53.

Newman, Andrew J., 'The Myth of the Clerical Migration to Safavid Iran: Arab Shiite Opposition to 'Ali al-Karaki and Safawid Shiism', *Die Welt des Islams* 33 (1993), 66–112.

Newman, Andrew J., 'Sufism and Anti-Sufism in Safavid Iran: The Authorship of the "Hadiqat al-Shi'a" Revisited', *Iran* 37 (1999), 95–108.

Newman, Andrew J., *The Formative Period of Twelver Shīʿism: Ḥadīth as Discourse between Qum and Baghdad* (Abingdon: Routledge, 2000).

Newman, Andrew J., 'Fayd al-Kashani and the Rejection of the Clergy/State Alliance: Friday Prayer as Politics in the Safavid Period', in: Linda Walbridge (ed.), *The Most Learned of the Shiʿa: The Institution of the Marjaʿ Taqlid* (Oxford: Oxford University Press, 2001), 34–52.

Newman, Andrew J., *Safavid Iran: Rebirth of a Persian Empire* (London: I. B. Tauris, 2006).

Newman, Andrew J., 'The Vezir and the Mulla: A Late Safavid Period Debate on Friday Prayer', *Eurasian Studies* 5, 1–2 (2006), 237–70.

Newman, Andrew J., *Twelver Shi`ism: Unity and Diversity in the Life of Islam, 632 to 1722* (Edinburgh: Edinburgh University Press, 2013).

Newman, Andrew J., '"Minority Reports": Twelver Shiʿi Disputation and Authority in the Buyid Period', in: Farhad Daftary and Gurdofarid Miskinzoda (eds), *The Study of Shiʿi Islam: History, Theology and Law* (London: I. B. Tauris, 2014), 433–52.

Newman, Andrew J., 'Of Mullas, Manuscripts, and Migration: Aspects of Twelver Shiʿi Community Life in the 18th Century', in: Michael Axworthy (ed.), *Crisis, Collapse, Militarism and Civil War: The History and Historiography of 18th Century Iran* (Oxford: Oxford University Press, 2018), 105–24.

Newman, Andrew J., 'The Limits of "Orthodoxy"? Notes on the Anti-Abū Muslim Polemic of Early 11th/17th-Century Iran', in: Denis Hermann and Mathieu Terrier (eds), *Shiʿi Islam and Sufism: Classical Views and Modern Perspectives* (London: I. B. Tauris/Institute of Ismaili Studies, 2019), 65–119.

Nicholson, Alexis, 'Iran and the United States in Afghanistan: An International History, 1996–2002', *Oxford Middle East Review* 3, 1 (2019), 51–71.

Niebuhr, Carsten, *Travels through Arabia and Other Countries in the East*, 2 Vols (Edinburgh: R. Morison & Son, 1792).

Nieger, Colonel, 'Choix de Documents sur le Territoire des Alaouites (Pays des Noseiris)', *Revue du Monde Musulman* 49 (1922), 1–69.

Nielsen, Jorgen S., 'Sultan al-Ẓāhir Baybars and the Appointment of Four Chief Qāḍīs, 663/1265', *Studia Islamica* 60 (1984), 167–76.

Nieuwenhuis, Tom, *Politics and Society in Early Modern Iraq: Mamluk Pashas, Tribal Shayks and Local Rule between 1802 and 1831* (The Hague: M. Nijhoff, 1982).

Nimier, Alain, *Les Alaouites* (Paris: Asfar, 1987).

Nischan, Bodo, *Lutherans and Calvinists in the Age of Confessionalism* (Aldershot: Ashgate, 1999).

Nizami, Moin Ahmad, *Reform and Renewal in South Asian Islam: The Chishti-Sabris in 18th–19th Century North India* (New Delhi: Oxford University Press, 2017).

Noelle-Karimi, Christine, *State and Tribe in Nineteenth-Century Afghanistan: The Reign of Amir Dost Muhammad Khan (1826–1863)* (London: Curzon, 1997).

Noelle-Karimi, Christine, *The Pearl in its Midst: Herat and the Mapping of Khurasan (15th–19th Centuries)* (Vienna: Verlag der Österreichischen Akademie der Wissenschaften, 2014).

Nöldeke, Theodor, *Geschichte des Qorâns* (Göttingen: Dieterichsche Buchhandlung, 1860).

Nöldeke, Theodor, 'Zur Ausbreitung des Schiitismus', *Der Islam* 13, 1–2 (1923), 70–81.

Nonneman, Gerd, *Iraq, the Gulf States & the War* (London: Ithaca Press, 1986).

Nora, Pierre, and Lawrence D. Kritzman (eds), *Realms of Memory: The Construction of the French Past*, 3 Vols (New York: Columbia University Press, 1996–8).

Norris, H. T., *Popular Sufism in Eastern Europe: Sufi Brotherhoods and the Dialogue with Christianity and 'Heterodoxy'* (London: Routledge, 2006).

Norton, Augustus Richard, *Amal and the Shiʿa: Struggle for the Soul of Lebanon* (Austin: University of Texas Press, 1987).

Norton, Augustus Richard, 'Ritual, Blood, and Shiite Identity: Ashura in Nabatiyya, Lebanon', *The Drama Review* 49, 4 (2005), 140–55.

Noueihed, Lin, and Alex Warren, *The Battle for the Arab Spring: Revolution, Counter-Revolution and the Making of a New Era* (New Haven: Yale University Press, 2012).

al-Nuʿman, Qadi, *Daʿāʾim al-Islam*, ed. by A. A. A. Fyzee, 2 Vols (Cairo: Dar al-Maʿarif, 1951/60).

Numani, Shibli, *Al-Farooq: The Life of Omar the Great* (Lahore: Muhammad Ashraf, 1939).

al-Nuqaydan, Mansur, 'Qatar wa Mashruʿaha fi Daʿm al-Wahhabiyya', in: *Al-Khalij wa-l-Rabiʿa al-ʿArabi: Al-Din wa-l-Siyyasa* (Dubai: al-Misbar, 2013), 153–69.

Nuraniyah, Navhat, *The Anti-Shiʿa Movement in Indonesia* (Jakarta: Institute for Policy Analysis of Conflict, 2016).

Obermeyer, Gerald J., 'Al-Iman and al-Imam: Ideology and State in Yemen', in: Marwan R. Buheiry (ed.), *Intellectual Life in the Arab East, 1890–1939* (Beirut: American University of Beirut, 1981), 178–92.

Ocak, Ahmet Yasar, 'Les milieux soufis dans les territoires du Beylicat Ottoman et le probleme des "Abdalan-i Rum" (1300–1389)', in: Elizabeth Zachariadou (ed.), *The Ottoman Emirate (1300–1389)* (Rethymno: Crete University Press, 1993), 145–58.

Oldenburg, Veena Talwar, *The Making of Colonial Lucknow, 1856–1877* (Princeton: Princeton University Press, 1984).

Olesen, Niels Henrik, *Culte des saints et pèlerinages chez Ibn Taymiyya (661/1263–728/1328)* (Paris: Paul Geuthner, 1991).

Olson, Robert W., *The Siege of Mosul and Ottoman-Persian Relations, 1718–1743* (Bloomington: Indiana University Press, 1975).

Olson, Robert W., *The Ba'th and Syria, 1947 to 1982: The Evolution of Ideology, Party, and State, from the French Mandate to the Era of Hafiz al-Asad* (Princeton, NJ: Kingston Press, 1982).

Olsson, Susanne, 'Shia as Internal Others: A Salafi Rejection of the "Rejecters"', *Islam and Christian-Muslim Relations* 28, 4 (2017), 409–30.

O'Mahony, Anthony, Timothy Wright, and Mohammad Ali Shomali (eds), *A Catholic-Shi'a Dialogue: Ethics in Today's Society* (Bishop's Stortford: Melisende, 2008).

Omissi, David, 'Britain, the Assyrians and the Iraq Levies, 1919–1932', *Journal of Imperial and Commonwealth History* 17, 3 (1989), 301–22.

Omran, Rasha, 'The Sect as Homeland', *Critical Muslim* 11 (2014).

Onapajo, Hakeem, 'State Repression and Religious Conflict: The Perils of the State Clampdown on the Shi'a Minority in Nigeria', *Journal of Muslim Minority Affairs* 37, 1 (2017), 80–93.

Onley, James, 'Transnational Merchants in the Nineteenth-Century Gulf: The Case of the Safar Family', in: Madawi al-Rasheed (ed.), *Transnational Connections and the Arab Gulf* (London: Routledge, 2005), 59–89.

Onley, James, *The Arabian Frontier of the British Raj: Merchants, Rulers, and the British in the Nineteenth-Century Gulf* (Oxford: Oxford University Press, 2007).

Ortayli, Ilber, 'Les Groupes Hétérodoxes et l'Administration Ottomane', in: Krisztina Kehl-Bodrogi, Barbara Kellner-Heinkele, and Anke Otter-Beaujean (eds), *Syncretistic Religious Communities in the Near East: Collected Papers of the International Symposium 'Alevism in Turkey and Comparable Syncretistic Religious Communities in the Near East in the Past and Present', Berlin, 14–17 April 1995* (Leiden: Brill, 1997), 205–11.

Ortayli, Ilber, 'The Policy of the Sublime Porte towards Naqshbandis and Other Tariqas during the Tanzimat', in: Elisabeth Özdalga (ed.), *Naqshbandis in Western and Central Asia: Change and Continuity* (Istanbul: Swedish Research Institute, 1999), 67–72.

Osman, Khalil, *Sectarianism in Iraq: The Making of State and Nation since 1920* (Abingdon: Routledge, 2015).

Osman, Rawand, *Female Personalities in the Qur'an and Sunna: Examining the Major Sources of Imami Shi'i Islam* (Abingdon: Routledge, 2015).

Osterhammel, Jürgen, *Die Entzauberung Asiens: Europa und die asiatischen Reiche im 18. Jahrhundert* (Munich: C. H. Beck, 1998).

Osterhammel, Jürgen, *Die Verwandlung der Welt: Eine Geschichte des 19. Jahrhunderts* (Munich: C. H. Beck, 2011).

Osterhammel, Jürgen, *Unfabling the East: The Enlightenment's Encounter with Asia* (Princeton: Princeton University Press, 2018).

Ostovar, Afshon, *Vanguard of the Imam: Religion, Politics, and Iran's Revolutionary Guards* (New York: Oxford University Press, 2016).

Ott, Ursula, *Transoxanien und Turkestan zu Beginn des 16. Jahrhunderts: Das Mihmān-nāma-yi Buḫārā des Faḍlallāh b. Rūzbihān Ḫungī* (Freiburg im Breisgau: Klaus Schwarz, 1974).

Otter-Beaujean, Anke, 'Stellenwert der Buyruk-Handschriften im Alevitum', in: Krisztina Kehl-Bodrogi, Barbara Kellner-Heinkele, and Anke Otter-Beaujean (eds), *Syncretistic Religious Communities in the Near East: Collected Papers of the International Symposium 'Alevism in Turkey and Comparable Syncretistic Religious Communities in the Near East in the Past and Present', Berlin, 14–17 April 1995* (Leiden: Brill, 1997), 213–26.

Ouahes, Idir, *Syria and Lebanon under the French Mandate: Cultural Imperialism and the Workings of Empire* (London: I. B. Tauris, 2018).

Ourghi, Mariella, 'Schiiten als Ungläubige: Zur situativen Kontingenz einer salafistischen Feindbildkonstruktion', in: Thorsten Gerald Schneiders (ed.), *Salafismus in Deutschland: Ursprünge und Gefahren einer islamisch-fundamentalistischen Bewegung* (Bielefeld: Transcript, 2014), 279–90.

Overton, Keelan (ed.), *Iran and the Deccan: Persianate Art, Culture, and Talent in Circulation, 1400–1700* (Bloomington: Indiana University Press, 2020).

Owen, Roger, *The Middle East in the World Economy, 1800–1914* (London: I. B. Tauris, 1993).

Özbaran, Salih, 'Ottomans and the India Trade in the Sixteenth Century: Some New Data and Reconsiderations', *Oriente Moderno* 25, 86 (2006), 173–9.

Özcan, Azmi, *Pan-Islamism: Indian Muslims, the Ottomans and Britain (1877–1924)* (Leiden: Brill, 1997).

Özervarlı, M. Sait, 'Between Tension and Rapprochement: Sunni-Shi'ite Relations in the Pre-Modern Ottoman Period, with a Focus on the Eighteenth Century', *Historical Research* 90, 249 (2017), 526–42.

Palgrave, William Gifford, *Personal Narrative of a Year's Journey through Central and Eastern Arabia* (London: Macmillan, 1868).

Pall, Zoltan, *Lebanese Salafis between the Gulf and Europe: Development, Fractionalization and Transnational Networks of Salafism in Lebanon* (Amsterdam: Amsterdam University Press, 2013).

Pall, Zoltan, *Kuwaiti Salafism and its Growing Influence in the Levant* (Washington, DC: Carnegie Endowment for International Peace, 2014).

Pall, Zoltan, 'Between Ideology and International Politics: The Dynamics and Transformation of a Transnational Islamic Charity', in: Philip Fountain, Robin Bush, and R. Michael Feener (eds), *Religion and the Politics of Development* (Basingstoke: Palgrave Macmillan, 2015), 177–200.

Pandey, Gyanendra, *The Construction of Communalism in Colonial North India* (Oxford: Oxford University Press, 1990).

Panjwani, Imranali (ed.), *The Shi'a of Samarra: The Heritage and Politics of a Community in Iraq* (London: I. B. Tauris, 2012).

Paoli, Bruno, 'Et maintenant, on va où? Les alaouites à la croisée des destins', in: François Burgat and Bruno Paoli (eds), *Pas de printemps pour la Syrie: Les clés pour comprendre les acteurs et les défis de la crise (2011–2013)* (Paris: La Découverte, 2013), 124–43.

Parry, Jonathan, *Promised Lands: The British and the Ottoman Middle East* (Princeton: Princeton University Press, 2022).

Parsi, Trita, *Treacherous Alliance: The Secret Dealings of Israel, Iran, and the United States* (New Haven: Yale University Press, 2007).

Parsons, Laila, *The Commander: Fawzi al-Qawuqji and the Fight for Arab Independence 1914–1948* (London: Saqi, 2017).

Patton, Walter M., *Ahmed Ibn Hanbal and the Mihna: A Biography of the Imam Including an Account of the Mohammedan Inquisition Called the Mihna, 218–234 AH* (Leiden: Brill, 1897).

Paul, Jürgen, *Die politische und soziale Bedeutung der Naqšbandiyya in Mittelasien im 15. Jahrhundert* (Berlin: De Gruyter, 1991).

Peacock, A. C. S., *Early Seljūq History: A New Interpretation* (London: Routledge, 2010).

Pedersen, Susan, *The Guardians: The League of Nations and the Crisis of Empire* (Oxford: Oxford University Press, 2015).

Peirce, Leslie P., *Morality Tales: Law and Gender in the Ottoman Court of Aintab* (Berkeley: University of California Press, 2003).

Pelham, Nicolas, *A New Muslim Order: The Shia and the Middle East Sectarian Crisis* (London: Tauris, 2008).

Pellat, Charles, 'Masʿūdī et l'Imāmisme', in: Centre de Recherches d'Histoire des Religions Strasbourg (ed.), *Le shīʿisme imâmite: Colloque de Strasbourg (6–9 mai 1968)* (Paris: Presses Universitaires de France, 1970), 69–80.

Pellat, Charles, 'Notice sur la vie et les travaux de Henri Laoust, membre de l'Académie [note biographique]', *Comptes rendus des séances de l'Académie des Inscriptions et Belles-Lettres* 130, 3 (1986), 502–18.

Pelsaert, Francisco, *Jahangir's India: The 'Remonstrantie' of Francisco Pelsaert* (Cambridge: Heffer, 1925).

Pemble, John, *The Raj, the Indian Mutiny, and the Kingdom of Oudh, 1801–1859* (New Delhi: Oxford University Press, 1979).

Pennington, Brian K., *Was Hinduism Invented? Britons, Indians, and the Colonial Construction of Religion* (Oxford: Oxford University Press, 2005).

Perry, John R., *Karim Khan Zand: A History of Iran, 1747–1779* (Chicago: University of Chicago Press, 1979).

Perry, John R., 'The Zand Dynasty', in: P. Avery, G. Hambly, and C. Melville (eds), *The Cambridge History of Iran*, Vol. 7 (Cambridge: Cambridge University Press, 1991), 63–103.

Perry, John R., 'The Historical Role of Turkish in Relation to Persian of Iran', *Iran & the Caucasus* 5 (2001), 193–200.

Perthes, Volker, *Staat und Gesellschaft in Syrien, 1970–1989* (Hamburg: Deutsches Orient-Institut, 1990).

Perthes, Volker, *Syria under Bashar al-Asad: Modernisation and the Limits of Change* (Oxford: Oxford University Press, 2004).

Peskes, Esther, *Muhammad b. ʿAbdalwahhab (1703–92) im Widerstreit: Untersuchungen zur Rekonstruktion der Frühgeschichte der Wahhābīya* (Beirut: Franz Steiner, 1993).

Peters, F. E. (ed.), *Judaism, Christianity, and Islam: The Classical Texts and their Interpretation*, 3 Vols (Princeton: Princeton University Press, 1990–1).

Peters, F. E., *The Hajj: The Muslim Pilgrimage to Mecca and the Holy Places* (Princeton: Princeton University Press, 1994).

Petersen, Andrew, *Bones of Contention: Muslim Shrines in Palestine* (Basingstoke: Palgrave Macmillan, 2018).

Petersen, Erling L., "Ali and Mu'awiyah: The Rise of the Umayyad Caliphate, 656–661', *Acta Orientalia* 23 (1959), 157–96.

Petersen, Erling L., 'Studies on the Historiography of the 'Ali-Mu'awiya Conflict', *Acta Orientalia* 27 (1963), 83–118.

Petersen, Erling L., *Ali and Muawiya in Early Arabic Tradition* (Aarhus: Odense University Press, 1974).

Peterson, John E., *Yemen: The Search for a Modern State* (Baltimore: Johns Hopkins University Press, 1982).

Peterson, John E., 'Bahrain: Reform, Promise and Reality', in: Joshua Teitelbaum (ed.), *Political Liberalization in the Persian Gulf* (London: Hurst, 2009), 157–85.

Pétric, Boris, 'The Ironis in Post-Soviet Uzbekistan: The Virtues of Mental Dissimulation (Taqiyya) in a Context of Sunnitization', in: Sabrina Mervin (ed.), *The Shi'a Worlds and Iran* (London: Saqi, 2010), 193–214.

Petrushevsky, I. P., *Islam in Iran*, trans. by Hubert Evans (Albany: SUNY Press, 1985).

Peyrouse, Sebastien, 'Shiism in Central Asia: The Religious, Political, and Geopolitical Factors', *Central Asia-Caucasus Analyst*, 20 May 2009.

Pfeiffer, Judith, 'Conversion Versions: Sultan Öljeytü's Conversion to Shi'ism (709/1309) in Muslim Narrative Sources', *Mongolian Studies* 22 (1999), 35–67.

Pfeiffer, Judith, 'Twelver Shi'ism as State Religion in Mongol Iran: An Abortive Attempt, Recorded and Remembered', *Pera-Blätter* 11 (1999), 3–38.

Pfeiffer, Judith, 'Reflections on a "Double Rapprochement": Conversion to Islam among the Mongol Elite during the Early Ilkhanate', in: Linda Komaroff (ed.), *Beyond the Legacy of Genghis Khan* (Leiden: Brill, 2006), 369–89.

Pfeiffer, Judith, '"Faces Like Shields Covered with Leather": Keturah's Sons in the Post-Mongol Islamicate Eschatological Traditions', in: İlker Evrim Binbaş and Nurten Kılıç-Schubel (eds), *Horizons of the World: Festschrift for İsenbike Togan* (Istanbul: İthaki, 2011), 556–94.

Pfeiffer, Judith, 'Confessional Ambiguity vs. Confessional Polarization: Politics and the Negotiation of Religious Boundaries in the Ilkhanate', in: Judith Pfeiffer (ed.), *Politics, Patronage and the Transmission of Knowledge in 13th–15th Century Tabriz* (Leiden: Brill, 2014), 129–68.

Philby, H. St John, *Sa'udi Arabia* (London: Benn, 1955).

Phillips, Christopher, 'Sectarianism and Conflict in Syria', *Third World Quarterly* 36, 2 (2015), 357–76.

Phillips, Christopher, *The Battle for Syria: International Rivalry in the New Middle East* (New Haven: Yale University Press, 2016).

Phillips, Christopher, and Morten Valbjørn, '"What is in a Name?": The Role of (Different) Identities in the Multiple Proxy Wars in Syria', *Small Wars & Insurgencies* 29, 3 (2018), 414–33.

Pierce, Matthew, 'Ibn Shahrashub and Shi'a Rhetorical Strategies in the 6th/12th Century', *Journal of Shi'a Islamic Studies* 5, 4 (2012), 441–54.

Pierce, Matthew, *Twelve Infallible Men: The Imams and the Making of Shi'ism* (Cambridge, MA: Harvard University Press, 2016).

Pierret, Thomas, 'Karbala in the Umayyad Mosque: Sunni Panic at the "Shiitization" of Syria in the 2000s', in: Brigitte Maréchal and Sami Zemni (eds), *The Dynamics of Sunni-Shia Relationships: Doctrine, Transnationalism, Intellectuals and the Media* (London: Hurst, 2013), 99–116.

Pierret, Thomas, *Religion and State in Syria: The Sunni Ulama from Coup to Revolution* (Cambridge: Cambridge University Press, 2013).

Pierret, Thomas, 'Les salafismes dans l'insurrection syrienne: Des réseaux transnationaux à l'épreuve des réalités locales', *Outre-Terre* 44, 3 (2015), 196–215.

Pierret, Thomas, 'Salafis at War in Syria: Logics of Fragmentation and Realignment', in: Francesco Cavatorta and Fabio Merone (eds), *Salafism after the Arab Awakening: Contending with People's Power* (London: Hurst, 2016), 137–68.

Pierret, Thomas, 'States Sponsors and the Syrian Insurgency: The Limits of Foreign Influence', in: Luigi Narbone, Agnès Favier, and Virginie Collombier (eds), *Inside Wars: Local Dynamics of Conflicts in Syria and Libya* (Florence: European University Institute, 2016), 22–8.

Pierret, Thomas, and Kjetil Selvik, 'Limits of "Authoritarian Upgrading" in Syria: Private Welfare, Islamic Charities, and the Rise of the Zayd Movement', *International Journal of Middle East Studies* 41, 4 (2009), 595–614.

Pietsch, Andreas, and Barbara Stollberg-Rilinger (eds), *Konfessionelle Ambiguität: Uneindeutigkeit und Verstellung als religiöse Praxis in der Frühen Neuzeit* (Gütersloh: Gütersloher Verlagshaus, 2013).

Pinault, David, *The Shiites: Ritual and Popular Piety in a Muslim Community* (New York: St Martin's, 1992).

Pinault, David, *Horse of Karbala: Muslim Devotional Life in India* (New York: Palgrave Macmillan, 2001).

Pink, Johanna, 'Where Does Modernity Begin? Muhammad al-Shawkani and the Tradition of Tafsīr', in: Johanna Pink and Andreas Görke (eds), *Tafsir and Intellectual History: Exploring the Boundaries of a Genre* (Oxford: Oxford University Press/ Institute of Ismaili Studies, 2014), 323–60.

Pinto, Paulo G., 'Sufism, Moral Performance and the Public Sphere in Syria', *Revue des mondes musulmans et de la Méditerranée* 115–16 (2006), 155–71.

Pinto, Paulo G., 'Pilgrimage, Commodities, and Religious Objectification: The Making of Transnational Shi'ism between Iran and Syria', *Comparative Studies of South Asia, Africa and the Middle East* 27, 1 (2007), 109–25.

Pinto, Paulo G., '"Oh Syria, God Protects You": Islam as Cultural Idiom under Bashar al-Asad', *Middle East Critique* 20, 2 (2011), 189–205.

Pinto, Paulo G., 'Mystical Bodies/Unruly Bodies: Experience, Empowerment and Subjectification in Syrian Sufism', *Social Compass* 63, 2 (2016), 197–212.

Pinto, Paulo G., 'Mystical Metaphors: Ritual, Symbols and Self in Syrian Sufism', *Culture and Religion* 18, 2 (2017), 90–109.

Pinto, Paulo G., 'The Shattered Nation: The Sectarianization of the Syrian Conflict', in: Nader Hashemi and Danny Postel (eds), *Sectarianization: Mapping the New Politics of the Middle East* (London: Hurst, 2017), 123–42.

Piscatori, James P. (ed.), *Islamic Fundamentalisms and the Gulf Crisis* (Chicago: American Academy of Arts and Sciences, 1991).

Piscatori, James P., 'Managing God's Guests: The Pilgrimage, Saudi Arabia and the Politics of Legitimacy', in: Paul Dresch and James P. Piscatori (eds), *Monarchies and Nations: Globalisation and Identity in the Arab States of the Gulf* (London: I. B. Tauris, 2005), 222–45.

Piscatori, James P., 'Imagining Pan-Islam', in Shahram Akbarzadeh and Fethi Mansouri (ed.), *Islam and Political Violence: Muslim Diaspora and Radicalism in the West* (London: I.B. Tauris, 2007), 27–38.

Piscatori, James P., and Amin Saikal, *Islam beyond Borders: The Umma in World Politics* (Cambridge: Cambridge University Press, 2019).

Piscatori, James P., and Dale Eickelman, *Muslim Politics* (Princeton: Princeton University Press, 2004).

Pistor-Hatam, Anja, "Āšūrā in Istanbul: Religiöse Feierlichkeiten als Ausdruck persisch-schiitischen Selbstverständnisses am Ende des 19. Jahrhunderts', *Die Welt des Islams* 38, 1 (1998), 95–119.

Pistor-Hatam, Anja, 'Pilger, Pest und Cholera: Die Wallfahrt zu den Heiligen Stätten im Irak als gesundheitspolitisches Problem im 19. Jahrhundert', *Die Welt des Islams* 31, 2 (1991), 228–45.

Playfair, Sir Robert Lambert, *History of Arabia Felix or Yemen from the Commencement of the Christian Era to the Present Time: Including an Account of the British Settlement of Aden* (Bombay: Education Society's Press, 1859).

Podeh, Elie, *The Politics of National Celebrations in the Arab Middle East* (Cambridge: Cambridge University Press, 2011).

Pohl-Schöberlein, Monika, *Die schiitische Gemeinschaft des Südlibanon (Ǧabal ʿĀmil) innerhalb des libanesischen konfessionellen Systems* (Berlin: Klaus Schwarz, 1986).

Poladi, Hassan, *The Hazāras* (Lahore: Mughal, 1989).

Polka, Sagi, 'Taqrīb al-Madhahib: Qaradawi's Declaration of Principles Regarding Sunni-Shi'i Ecumenism', *Middle Eastern Studies* 49, 3 (2013), 414–29.

Poonawala, Ismail K., 'The Evolution of al-Qadi al-Nu'man's Theory of Ismaili Jurisprudence as Reflected in the Chronology of his Works on Jurisprudence', in: Farhad Daftary and Gurdofarid Miskinzoda (eds), *The Study of Shi'i Islam: History, Theology and Law* (London: I. B. Tauris, 2014), 295–351.

Posch, Walter, *Osmanisch-safavidische Beziehungen (1545–1550): Der Fall Alḳâs Mîrzâ* (Wien: Österreichische Akademie der Wissenschaften, 2013).

Potter, Lawrence G. (ed.), *Sectarian Politics in the Persian Gulf* (New York: Oxford University Press, 2014).

Pourjavady, Nasrollah, 'Opposition to Sufism in Twelver Shiism', in: F. deJong and B. Radtke (eds), *Islamic Mysticism Contested: Thirteen Centuries of Controversies and Polemics* (Leiden: Brill, 1999), 614–23.

Pouzet, Louis, *Damas au VIIe/XIIIe siècle: Vie et structures religieuses d'une métropole islamique* (Beirut: Dar el-Machreq, 1988).

Powers, David S., 'Orientalism, Colonialism, and Legal History: The Attack on Muslim Family Endowments in Algeria and India', *Comparative Studies in Society and History* 31, 3 (1989), 535–71, 554–7.

Prasad, Rajendra, *India Divided* (New Delhi: Penguin, 2010).

Prasad, Y. D., 'The Aga Khan as a British Imperial Agent during World War I', *Proceedings of the Indian History Congress* 39, 2 (1978), 946–53.

Preckel, Claudia, 'Screening Siddiq Hasan Khan's (1832–1890) Library: The Use of Hanbali Literature in 19th-Century Bhopal', in: Birgit Krawietz, Georges Tamer, and Alina Kokoschka (eds), *Islamic Theology, Philosophy and Law: Debating Ibn Taymiyya and Ibn Qayyim al-Jawziyya* (Berlin: De Gruyter, 2013), 162–219.

Procházka-Eisl, Gisela, and Stephan Procházka, *The Plain of Saints and Prophets: The Nusayri-Alawi Community of Cilicia (Southern Turkey) and its Sacred Places* (Wiesbaden: Harrassowitz, 2010).

Prokop, Michaela, 'The War of Ideas: Education in Saudi Arabia', in *Saudi Arabia in the Balance: Political Economy, Society, Foreign Affairs*, ed. Paul Aarts and Gerd Nonneman (Washington Square, NY: New York University Press, 2005), 57–81.

Provence, Michael, *The Great Syrian Revolt and the Rise of Arab Nationalism* (Austin: University of Texas Press, 2005).

Provence, Michael, 'Ottoman Modernity, Colonialism, and Insurgency in the Interwar Arab East', *International Journal of Middle East Studies* 43, 2 (2011), 205–25.

Provence, Michael, 'French Mandate Counterinsurgency and the Repression of the Great Syrian Revolt', in: Cyrus Schayegh and Andrew Arsan (eds), *The Routledge Handbook of the History of the Middle East Mandates* (London: Routledge, 2015), 136–51.

Provence, Michael, *The Last Ottoman Generation and the Making of the Modern Middle East* (Cambridge: Cambridge University Press, 2017).

Puelings, Jelle, *Fearing a 'Shiite Octopus': Sunni-Shi'a Relations and the Implications for Belgium and Europe* (Ghent: Academia Press, 2010).

Puin, Gerd-R., 'The Yemeni Hijrah Concept of Tribal Protection', in: Tarif Khalidi (ed.), *Land Tenure and Social Transformation in the Middle East* (Beirut: American University of Beirut Press, 1984), 483–94.

Purohit, Teena, *The Aga Khan Case: Religion and Identity in Colonial India* (Cambridge, MA: Harvard University Press, 2012).

Pursley, Sara, *Familiar Futures: Time, Selfhood, and Sovereignty in Iraq* (Stanford: Stanford University Press, 2019).

al-Qadi, Wadad, 'Abu Hayyan al-Tawhidi: A Sunni Voice in the Shi'i Century', in: Farhad Daftary and Josef W. Meri (eds), *Culture and Memory in Medieval Islam: Essays in Honour of Wilferd Madelung* (London: I. B. Tauris/Institute of Ismaili Studies, 2003), 128–59.

al-Qarawee, Harith Hasan, 'The "Formal" Marja': Shi'i Clerical Authority and the State in Post-2003 Iraq', *British Journal of Middle Eastern Studies* 46, 3 (2019), 481–97.

Qasim, Na'im, *Hizbullah: The Story from Within* (London: Saqi, 2005).

Qasim, Na'im, *Hizbullah: Al-Manhaj, al-Tajruba, al-Mustaqbal*, 4th ed. (Beirut: Dar al-Hadi, 2008).

Qazvini, 'Abd al-Jalil ibn Abi al-Hasan, *Kitab al-Naqd ma'ruf beh ba'd mathalib al-Nawasib fi Naqd 'ba'd fada'ih al-Rawwafid'* (Tehran: n.p., 1952).

Qazwini, Amir Muhammad, *Al-Islam wa-l-Alusi* (Kuwait: Dar al-Tali'a, 1977).

al-Qazwini, Muhammad Mahdi al-Kazimi, *Kitab Minhaj al-Shari'a fi al-Radd 'ala Ibn Taymiyya*, 2 Vols (Najaf: al-Matba'a al-'Alawiyya, 1929–30).

al-Qazzaz, Ayad, 'Power Elite in Iraq, 1920-1958: A Study of the Cabinet', *The Muslim World* 61, 4 (1971), 267–83.

Quandt, William B., *Saudi Arabia in the 1980s: Foreign Policy, Security, and Oil* (Washington: Brookings Institution, 1981).

Querry, Amédée, *Droit musulman: Recueil de lois concernant les musulmans schyites*, 2 Vols (Paris: Imprimerie nationale, 1871/2).

Quinn, S., 'Iran under Safavid Rule', in: D. Morgan and A. Reid (eds), *The New Cambridge History of Islam*, Vol. 3 (Cambridge: Cambridge University Press, 2010), 201–38.

Quinn, S., *Shah 'Abbas: The King Who Refashioned Iran* (London: Oneworld, 2015).

Qureshi, Emran, and Michael A. Sells (eds), *The New Crusades: Constructing the Muslim Enemy* (New York: Columbia University Press, 2003).

Qureshi, I. H., 'India under the Mughals', in: P. M. Holt, Ann K. S. Lambton, and Bernard Lewis (eds), *The Cambridge History of Islam*, Vol. 2A (Cambridge: Cambridge University Press, 1977), 35–63.

Qureshi, Jawad, 'The Discourses of the Damascene Sunni Ulama during the 2011 Revolution', in: Line Khatib, Raphaël Lefèvre, and Jawad Qureshi, *State and Islam in Baathist Syria: Confrontation or Co-Optation?* (Boulder, CO: Lynne Rienner, 2012), 59–91.

Qureshi, Naeem M., *Pan-Islam in British Indian Politics: A Study of the Khilafat Movement, 1918–1924* (Leiden: Brill, 1999).

Qutrib, Hussain Ibrahim, *'Useful Syria' and Demographic Changes in Syria* (Riyadh: King Faisal Center for Research and Islamic Studies, n.d.).

Rabi, Uzi, *Yemen: Revolution, Civil War and Unification* (London: I. B. Tauris, 2015).

Rabi, Uzi, and Chelsi Mueller, 'The Gulf Arab States and Israel since 1967: From "No Negotiation" to Tacit Cooperation', *British Journal of Middle Eastern Studies* 44, 4 (2017), 576–92.

Rabil, Robert G., *Salafism in Lebanon: From Apoliticism to Transnational Jihadism* (Washington, DC: Georgetown University Press, 2014).

Rabinovich, Itamar, 'The Compact Minorities and the Syrian State, 1918–45', *Journal of Contemporary History* 14, 4 (1979), 693–712.

Rabinovich, Itamar, and Gitta Yaffe, 'An Anthropologist as a Political Officer: Evans-Pritchard, the French and the Alawis', in: Haim Shamir (ed.), *France and Germany in an Age of Crisis, 1900–1960: Studies in Memory of Charles Bloch* (Leiden: Brill, 1990), 177–89.

Rafeq, Abdul-Karim, 'New Light on the 1860 Riots in Ottoman Damascus', *Die Welt des Islams* 28, 1/4 (1988), 412–30.

Rafeq, Abdul-Karim, 'Craft Organization, Work Ethics, and the Strains of Change in Ottoman Syria', *Journal of the American Oriental Society* 111, 3 (1991), 495–511.

Rafeq, Abdul-Karim, 'Craft Organizations and Religious Communities in Ottoman Syria', in: *Convegno sul tema: La Shī'a nell'Impero Ottomano (Roma, 15 aprile 1991)* (Rome: Accademia Nazionale dei Lincei, 1993), 25–56.

Rafiq, Arif, *Sunni Deobandi-Shi'i Sectarian Violence in Pakistan: Explaining the Resurgence since 2007* (Washington, DC: Middle East Institute, 2014).

Rahe, Jens-Uwe, 'Iraqi Shi'is in Exile in London', in: Faleh Abdul-Jabar (ed.), *Ayatollahs, Sufis and Ideologues: State, Religion and Social Movements in Iraq* (London: Saqi, 2002), 211–19.

Rahimi, Babak, *Theater State and the Formation of Early Modern Public Sphere in Iran: Studies on Safavid Muharram Rituals, 1590–1641 CE* (Leiden: Brill, 2011).

Rahnema, Ali, *An Islamic Utopian: A Political Biography of Ali Shariati* (London: I. B. Tauris, 1998).

Ramadan, Tariq, *Aux sources du renouveau musulman: D'al-Afghani à Hassan al-Banna, un siècle de réformisme islamique* (Paris: Bayard/Centurion, 1998).

Ramazani, Rouhollah K., 'The Settlement of the Bahrain Dispute', *Indian Journal of International Law* 12, 1 (1972), 1–14.

Ramazani, Rouhollah K., *Revolutionary Iran: Challenge and Response in the Middle East* (Baltimore: Johns Hopkins University Press, 1986).

Ramazani, Rouhollah K., 'Shi'ism in the Persian Gulf', in: Juan R. I. Cole and Nikki R. Keddie (eds), *Shi'ism and Social Protest* (New Haven: Yale University Press, 1986), 30–54.

Ramazani, Rouhollah K., 'Iran's Export of the Revolution: Politics, Ends, and Means', in: John L. Esposito (ed.), *The Iranian Revolution: Its Global Impact* (Miami: Florida International University Press, 1990), 40–62.

Ramusack, Barbara N., *The Indian Princes and their States* (Cambridge: Cambridge University Press, 2004).

Randjbar-Daemi, Siavush, 'Building the Islamic State: The Draft Constitution of 1979 Reconsidered', *Iranian Studies* 46, 4 (2013), 641–63.

Randjbar-Daemi, Siavush, *The Quest for Authority in Iran: A History of the Presidency from Revolution to Rouhani* (London: I. B. Tauris, 2017).

Randjbar-Daemi, Siavush, 'The Tudeh Party of Iran and the Peasant Question, 1941–53', *Middle Eastern Studies* 56, 6 (2020), 969–87.

Rapoport, Yossef, 'Legal Diversity in the Age of Taqlīd: The Four Chief Qāḍīs under the Mamluks', *Islamic Law and Society* 10, 2 (2003), 210–28.

Rapoport, Yossef, 'Ibn Taymiyya on Divorce Oaths', in: Michael Winter and Amalia Levanoni (eds), *The Mamluks in Egyptian and Syrian Politics and Society* (Leiden: Brill, 2004), 191–217.

al-Rasheed, Madawi, *Politics in an Arabian Oasis: The Rashidi Tribal Dynasty* (London: I. B. Tauris, 1991).

al-Rasheed, Madawi, 'The Shia of Saudi Arabia: A Minority in Search of Cultural Authenticity', *British Journal of Middle Eastern Studies* 25, 1 (1998), 121–38.

al-Rasheed, Madawi, *A History of Saudi Arabia* (Cambridge: Cambridge University Press, 2002).

al-Rasheed, Madawi, *Contesting the Saudi State: Islamic Voices from a New Generation* (Cambridge: Cambridge University Press, 2007).

al-Rasheed, Madawi, *Muted Modernists: The Struggle over Divine Politics in Saudi Arabia* (London: Hurst, 2015).

al-Rasheed, Madawi, 'Saudi Arabia and the 1948 Palestine War: Beyond Official History', in: Eugene L. Rogan and Avi Shlaim (eds), *The War for Palestine: Rewriting the History of 1948*, 2nd ed. (Cambridge: Cambridge University Press, 2007), 228–47.

al-Rasheed, Madawi, 'Sectarianism as Counter-Revolution: Saudi Responses to the Arab Spring', *Studies in Ethnicity and Nationalism* 11, 3 (2011), 513–26.

al-Rasheed, Madawi, 'Sectarianism as Counter-Revolution: Saudi Responses to the Arab Spring', in: Nader Hashemi and Danny Postel (eds), *Sectarianization: Mapping the New Politics of the Middle East* (London: Hurst, 2017), 143–58.

Rashid, Ahmed, *Taliban: Militant Islam, Oil and Fundamentalism in Central Asia* (London: I. B. Tauris, 2001).

Rashid, Ahmed, 'Iran's Game in Aleppo', *New York Review of Books*, 1 December 2016.

al-Rassi, Qasim b. Ibrahim, *Anthropomorphism and Interpretation of the Qur'ān in the Theology of al-Qāsim ibn Ibrāhīm: Kitāb al-Mustarshid*, trans./ed. by Binyamin Abrahamov (Leiden: Brill, 1996).

Ra'uf, 'Adil, *Al-'Amal al-Islami fi al-'Iraq bayn al-Marji'iyya wa-l-Hizbiyya: Qira'a Naqdiyya li-Masirat Nisf Qarn (1950–2000)* (Damascus: al-Markaz al-'Iraqi li-l-I'lam wa-l-Dirasat, 2000).

al-Rawi, Ahmed Khalid, 'The Campaign of Truth Program: US Propaganda in Iraq during the Early 1950s', in: Philip E. Muehlenbeck (ed.), *Religion and the Cold War: A Global Perspective* (Nashville: Vanderbilt University Press, 2012), 113–38.

al-Rawi, Ahmed Khalid, 'The US Influence in Shaping Iraq's Sectarian Media', *International Communication Gazette* 75, 4 (2013), 374–91.

Rayburn, Joel, *Iraq after America: Strongmen, Sectarians, Resistance* (Stanford: Hoover Institution Press, 2014).

Razoux, Pierre, *The Iran-Iraq War* (Cambridge, MA: Harvard University Press, 2015).

Reeves, Peter, 'Lucknow Politics: 1920–47', in: Violette Graff (ed.), *Lucknow: Memories of a City* (New Delhi: Oxford University Press, 1999), 213–26.

Reiff, Jesse C., 'When Ali Comes Marching Home: Shi'a Foreign Fighters after Syria', *Studies in Conflict & Terrorism* 43, 11 (2020), 989–1010.

Reinhard, Wolfgang, 'Zwang zur Konfessionalisierung? Prolegomena zu einer Theorie des konfessionellen Zeitalters', *Zeitschrift für historische Forschung* 10, 3 (1983), 257–77.

Reinhart, A. Kevin, 'On Sunni Sectarianism', in: Yasir Suleiman (ed.), *Living Islamic History: Studies in Honour of Professor Carole Hillenbrand* (Edinburgh: Edinburgh University Press, 2010), 209–25.

Reinkowski, Maurus, *Ottoman 'Multiculturalism'? The Example of the Confessional System in Lebanon* (Beirut: Orient-Institut der Deutschen Morgenländischen Gesellschaft, 1999).

Reinkowski, Maurus, *Die Dinge der Ordnung: Eine vergleichende Untersuchung über die osmanische Reformpolitik im 19. Jahrhundert* (Berlin: De Gruyter, 2005).

Reissner, Johannes, *Ideologie und Politik der Muslimbrüder Syriens: Von den Wahlen 1947 bis zum Verbot unter Adīb aš-Šīšaklī 1952* (Freiburg: K. Schwarz, 1980).

Reissner, Johannes, 'Kerbela 1802: Ein Werkstattbericht zum "islamischen Fundamentalismus"', als es ihn noch nicht gab', *Die Welt des Islams* 28, 1/4 (1988), 431–44.

Rekhess, Elie, 'The Iranian Impact on the Islamic Jihad Movement in the Gaza Strip', in: David Menashri (ed.), *The Iranian Revolution and the Muslim World* (Boulder, CO: Westview Press, 1990), 189–206.

Reland, Adriaan, *De religione Mohammedica libri duo* (Utrecht: Willem Broedelet, 1717).

Rentz, George, 'The Wahhabis', in: A. J. Arberry (ed.), *Religion in the Middle East: Three Religions in Concord and Conflict*, Vol. 2 (Cambridge: Cambridge University Press, 1969), 270–84.

Resconi, Stefano, 'Dante e gli Sciiti: L'Alì di "Inf.", XXVIII, alla luce delle possibili fonti', *Rivista di Studi Danteschi* 2 (2016), 365–88.

Rezaee Haftador, Hasan, and Fatemeh Sarvi, 'Criticism of Ethan Kohlberg's View on the Distortion of the Quran', *Iranian Journal for the Quranic Sciences & Tradition* 46, 1 (2013), 73–87.

Rezavi, Syed Ali Nadeem, 'The Shia Muslims', in: J. S. Grewal (ed.), *Religious Movements and Institutions in Medieval India* (New Delhi: Oxford University Press, 2006), 280–95.

Rezavi, Syed Ali Nadeem, 'Religious Disputations and Imperial Ideology: The Purpose and Location of Akbar's Ibadatkhana', *Studies in History* 24, 2 (2008), 195–209.

Rezavi, Syed Ali Nadeem (ed.), *Fathpur Sikri Revisited* (New Delhi: Oxford University Press, 2013).

Rezavi, Syed Ali Nadeem, 'The State, Shia's and Shi'ism in Medieval India', *Studies in People's History* 4, 1 (2017), 32–45.

Rice, Edward, *Captain Sir Richard Francis Burton: The Secret Agent Who Made the Pilgrimage to Mecca, Discovered the Kama Sutra, and Brought the Arabian Nights to the West* (New York: Scribner, 1990).

Richard, Francis, 'Catholicisme et Islam chiite au "grand siècle": Autour de quelques documents concernant les Missions catholiques en Perse au XVIIème siècle', *Euntes Docete* 33, 3 (1980), 339–403.

Richard, Yann, *Shi'ite Islam: Polity, Ideology, and Creed* (Oxford: Blackwell, 1995).

Rida, Muhammad Rashid, *Al-Wahhabiyyun wa-l-Hijaz* (Cairo: Matba'at al-Manar, 1344/1925).

Rida, Muhammad Rashid, *Al-Sunna wa-l-Shi'a aw al-Wahhabiyya wa-l-Rafida: Haqa'iq Diniyya Ta'rihiyya Ijtima'iyya Islahiyyya*, 2nd ed. (Cairo: Dar al-Manar, 1947).

Rida, Muhammad Rashid, *Maqalat al-Shaykh Rashid Rida al-Siyyasiyya*, 5 Vols (Beirut: Dar Ibn Arabi, 1994).

Rieck, Andreas, *Unsere Wirtschaft: Eine gekürzte kommentierte Übersetzung des Buches Iqtisaduna von Muhammad Baqir as-Sadr* (Berlin: Klaus Schwarz, 1984).

Rieck, Andreas, *Die Schiiten und der Kampf um den Libanon: politische Chronik 1958–1988* (Hamburg: Deutsches Orient-Institut, 1989).

Rieck, Andreas, 'The Nurbakhshis of Baltistan: Crisis and Revival of a Five Centuries Old Community', *Die Welt des Islams* 35, 2 (1995), 159–88.

Rieck, Andreas, 'The Struggle for Equal Rights as a Minority: Shia Communal Organizations in Pakistan, 1948–1968', in: Rainer Brunner and Werner Ende (eds), *The Twelver Shia in Modern Times: Religious Culture & Political History* (Leiden: Brill, 2001), 268–83.

Rieck, Andreas, *The Shias of Pakistan: An Assertive and Beleaguered Minority* (London: Hurst, 2015).

Riexinger, Martin, *Sana'ullah Amritsari (1868–1948) und die Ahl-i-Hadis im Punjab unter britischer Herrschaft* (Würzburg: Ergon, 2004).

Riexinger, Martin, 'Gammelt had eller nutidskonflikter? Et moyenne durée-perspektiv på aktuelle sekteriske konflikter', *TIFO: Tidsskrift for Islamforskning (Islamic Studies Journal)* 13, 1 (2019), 87–111.

Rippin, Andrew, 'What Defines a (Pre-Modern) Shi'i Tafsīr? Notes towards the History of the Genre of Tafsīr in Islam, in the Light of the Study of the Shi'i Contribution', in: Farhad Daftary and Gurdofarid Miskinzoda (eds), *The Study of Shi'i Islam: History, Theology and Law* (London: I. B. Tauris, 2014), 95–112.

Risso, Patricia, *Oman and Muscat: An Early Modern History* (London: Croom Helm, 1986).

Ritter, Markus, *Moscheen und Madrasabauten in Iran 1785–1848: Architektur zwischen Rückgriff und Neuerung* (Leiden: Brill, 2005).

Rizvi, Kishwar, *The Safavid Dynastic Shrine: Architecture, Religion and Power in Early Modern Iran* (London: I. B. Tauris, 2011).

Rizvi, Saiyid Athar Abbas, *Muslim Revivalist Movements in Northern India in the Sixteenth and Seventeenth Centuries* (Agra: Agra University, 1965).

Rizvi, Saiyid Athar Abbas, *Religious and Intellectual History of Muslims in Akbar's Reign: With Special Reference to Abu'l Fazl (1556–1605)* (New Delhi: Munshiram Manoharlal, 1975).

Rizvi, Saiyid Athar Abbas, *A History of Sufism in India*, 2 Vols (New Delhi: Munshiram Manoharlal, 1978/83).

Rizvi, Saiyid Athar Abbas, *Shāh Walī-Allāh and His Times: A Study of Eighteenth Century Islam, Politics, and Society in India* (Canberra: Marifat, 1980).

Rizvi, Saiyid Athar Abbas, *Shah 'Abd al-'Aziz: Puritanism, Sectarian Polemics and Jihad* (Canberra: Marifat, 1982).

Rizvi, Saiyid Athar Abbas, *A Socio-Intellectual History of the Isnā 'Asharī Shī'īs in India*, 2 Vols (Canberra: Marifat, 1986).

Rizvi, Sajjad H., 'A Sufi Theology Fit for a Shī'ī King: The Gawhar-i Murād of 'Abd al-Razzāq Lāhījī (d. 1072/1661–2)', in: A. Shihadeh (ed.), *Sufism and Theology* (Edinburgh: Edinburgh University Press, 2007), 83–98.

Rizvi, Sajjad H., 'Faith Deployed for a New Shi'i Polity in India: The Theology of Sayyid Dildar 'Ali Nasirabadi', *Journal of the Royal Asiatic Society* 24, 3 (2014), 363–80.

Rizvi, Sajjad H., 'Faith Deployed for a New Shi'i Polity in India', in: Justin Jones and Ali Usman Qasmi (eds), *The Shi'a in Modern South Asia: Religion, History and Politics* (Cambridge: Cambridge University Press, 2015), 12–35.

Rizvi, Sajjad H., 'Sayyid Ni'mat Allāh al-Jazā'irī and his Anthologies: Anti-Sufism, Shi'ism and Jokes in the Safavid World', *Die Welt des Islams* 50 (2010), 224–42.

Rizvi, Sajjad H., 'Shī'i Polemics at the Mughal Court: The Case of Qāẓi Nūrullāh Shūshtarī', *Studies in People's History* 4, 1 (2017), 53–67.

Rizvi, Sajjad H., 'Shi'ism in Bahrain: Marja'iyya and Politics', *Orient* 4 (2009), 16–24.

Rizvi, Syed Najmul Raza, 'Shi'a Madaris of Awadh: Historical Development and Present Situation', in: Jan-Peter Hartung and Helmut Reifeld (eds), *Islamic Education, Diversity and National Identity: Dīnī Madāris in India Post 9/11* (New Delhi: Sage, 2006), 104–31.

Roberts, Nicholas E., 'Making Jerusalem the Centre of the Muslim World: Pan-Islam and the World Islamic Congress of 1931', *Contemporary Levant* 4, 1 (2019), 52–63.

Robin-D'Cruz, Benedict, 'Sadrists in the Public Sphere: An Ethnography of Political Shi'ism in Iraq', *Revue des mondes musulmans et de la Méditerranée* 145 (2019), 97–114.

Robin-D'Cruz, Benedict, and Renad Mansour, *Making Sense of the Sadrists: Fragmentation and Unstable Politics* (Philadelphia: Foreign Policy Research Institute, 2020).

Robins, Philip, 'The War for Regime Change in Iraq', in: Louise Fawcett (ed.), *International Relations of the Middle East*, 3rd ed. (Oxford: Oxford University Press, 2013), 304–20.

Robinson, Chase F., *Islamic Historiography* (Cambridge: Cambridge University Press, 2003).

Robinson, Francis, 'Technology and Religious Change: Islam and the Impact of Print', *Modern Asian Studies* 27, 1 (1993), 229–51.

Robinson, Francis, 'Ottomans-Safavids-Mughals: Shared Knowledge and Connective Systems', *Journal of Islamic Studies* 8, 2 (1997), 151–84.

Robinson, Francis, 'The British Empire and the Muslim World', in: R. Louis and J. Brown (eds), *The Oxford History of the British Empire*, Vol. 4 (Oxford: Oxford University Press, 1999), 398–420.

Robinson, Francis, 'The Emergence of Lucknow as a Major Political Centre, 1899–1923', in: Violette Graff (ed.), *Lucknow: Memories of a City* (New Delhi: Oxford University Press, 1999), 196–212.

Robinson, Francis, *The 'Ulama of Farangi Mahall and Islamic Culture in South Asia* (New Delhi: Permanent Black, 2001).

Robinson, Francis, 'Global History from an Islamic Angle', in: James Belich, John Darwin, Margret Frenz, and Chris Wickham (eds), *The Prospect of Global History* (Oxford: Oxford University Press, 2016), 127–45.

Robinson, Francis, *Jamal Mian: The Life of Maulana Jamaluddin Abdul Wahab of Farangi Mahall, 1919–2012* (Karachi: Oxford University Press, 2017).

Rocalve, Pierre, *Louis Massignon et l'Islam* (Damascus: Institut Français de Damas, 1993).

Roded, Ruth, 'Bint al-Shati's Wives of the Prophet: Feminist or Feminine?', *British Journal of Middle Eastern Studies* 33, 1 (2006), 51–66.

Roemer, H. R., 'Die Safawiden: Ein orientalischer Bundesgenosse des Abendlandes im Türkenkampf', *Saeculum* 4 (1953), 27–44.

Roemer, H. R., 'The Jalayirids, Muzaffarids and Sarbardārs', in: P. Jackson and L. Lockhart (eds), *The Cambridge History of Iran*, Vol. 6 (Cambridge: Cambridge University Press, 1986), 1–40.

Roemer, H. R., 'The Safavid Period', in: P. Jackson and L. Lockhart (eds), *The Cambridge History of Iran*, Vol. 6 (Cambridge: Cambridge University Press, 1986), 189–350.

Roemer, H. R., 'The Successors of Tīmūr', in: P. Jackson and L. Lockhart (eds), *The Cambridge History of Iran*, Vol. 6 (Cambridge: Cambridge University Press, 1986), 98–146.

Roemer, H. R., 'The Türkmen Dynasties', in: P. Jackson and L. Lockhart (eds), *The Cambridge History of Iran*, Vol. 6 (Cambridge: Cambridge University Press, 1986), 147–88.

Roemer, H. R., 'Timur in Iran', in: P. Jackson and L. Lockhart (eds), *The Cambridge History of Iran*, Vol. 6 (Cambridge: Cambridge University Press, 1986), 42–97.

Roff, William R., 'Customary Law, Islamic Law, and Colonial Authority: Three Contrasting Case Studies and their Aftermath', *Islamic Studies* 49, 4 (2010), 455–62.

Rogan, Eugene L., *Frontiers of the State in the Late Ottoman Empire: Transjordan, 1850–1921* (Cambridge: Cambridge University Press, 1999).

Rogan, Eugene L., 'Sectarianism and Social Conflict in Damascus: The 1860 Events Reconsidered', *Arabica* 51, 4 (2004), 493–511.

Rogan, Eugene L., *The Arabs: A History* (London: Allen Lane, 2009).

Rogerson, Barnaby, *The Heirs of the Prophet Muhammad: Islam's First Century and the Origins of the Sunni–Shia Schism* (New York: Overlook, 2007).

Romano, David, 'Iraq's Descent into Civil War: A Constitutional Explanation', *Middle East Journal* 68, 4 (2014), 547–66.

Rosiny, Stephan, *Islamismus bei den Schiiten im Libanon: Religion im Übergang von Tradition zur Moderne* (Berlin: Das Arabische Buch, 1996).

Rosiny, Stephan, '"The Tragedy of Fāṭima al-Zahrā"' in the Debate of Two Shiite Theologians in Lebanon', in: Rainer Brunner and Werner Ende (eds), *The Twelver Shia in Modern Times: Religious Culture & Political History* (Leiden: Brill, 2001), 207–19.

Rossi, Ettore, 'La Stampa nel Yemen', *Oriente Moderno* 18, 10 (1938), 568–80.

Rota, Giorgio, *Under Two Lions: On the Knowledge of Persia in the Republic of Venice (ca. 1450–1797)* (Vienna: Verlag der Österreichischen Akademie der Wissenschaften, 2009).

Rougier, Bernard, *The Sunni Tragedy in the Middle East: Northern Lebanon from al-Qaeda to ISIS* (Princeton: Princeton University Press, 2015).

Roussel, Cyril, *Les Druzes de Syrie: Territoire et mobilité* (Beirut: Presses de l'Ifpo, 2011).

Roy, Olivier, *Islam and Resistance in Afghanistan* (Cambridge: Cambridge University Press, 1986).

Roy, Olivier, 'The Taliban: A Strategic Tool for Pakistan', in: Christophe Jaffrelot (ed.), *Pakistan: Nationalism without a Nation?* (New Delhi: Manohar, 2002), 149–59.

Roy, Olivier, 'The Impact of the Iranian Revolution on the Middle East', in: Sabrina Mervin (ed.), *The Shi'a Worlds and Iran* (London: Saqi, 2010), 29–44.

Rubiés, Joan-Pau, 'Oriental Despotism and European Orientalism: Botero to Montesquieu', *Journal of Early Modern History* 9, 1–2 (2005), 109–80.

Rubin, Avi, *Ottoman Nizamiye Courts: Law and Modernity* (New York: Palgrave Macmillan, 2011).

Rubin, Barnett R., *The Search for Peace in Afghanistan: From Buffer State to Failed State* (New Haven: Yale University Press, 1995).

Rubin, Barry M., *Islamic Fundamentalism in Egyptian Politics* (London: Macmillan, 1990).

Rudolf, Inna, *From Battlefield to Ballot Box: Contextualising the Rise and Evolution of Iraq's Popular Mobilisation Units* (London: International Centre for the Study of Radicalisation, 2018).

Rudolf, Inna, 'The Sunnis of Iraq's "Shia" Paramilitary Powerhouse', *Century Foundation*, 13 February 2020.

Ruffle, Karen G., *Gender, Sainthood, and Everyday Practice in South Asian Shi'ism* (Chapel Hill: University of North Carolina Press, 2011).

Ruggles, D. Fairchild, *Tree of Pearls: The Extraordinary Architectural Patronage of the 13th-Century Egyptian Slave-Queen Shajar al-Durr* (Oxford: Oxford University Press, 2020).

Rumaihi, Muhammad G., *Bahrain: Social and Political Change since the First World War* (London: Bowker/Centre for Middle Eastern and Islamic Studies of the University of Durham, 1976).

Russell, Malcolm B., *The First Modern Arab State: Syria under Faysal, 1918–1920* (Minneapolis: Bibliotheca Islamica, 1985).

Russell, William Howard, *My Diary in India, in the Year 1858–9* (Cambridge: Cambridge University Press, 2011).

Ryad, Umar, 'A Printed Muslim "Lighthouse" in Cairo: Al-Manār's Early Years, Religious Aspiration and Reception (1898–1903)', *Arabica* 56, 1 (2009), 27–60.

Ryad, Umar, 'Islamic Reformism and Great Britain: Rashid Rida's Image as Reflected in the Journal al-Manār in Cairo', *Islam and Christian-Muslim Relations* 21, 3 (2010), 263–85.

Rycaut, Paul, *The History of the Present State of the Ottoman Empire: Containing the Maxims of the Turkish Polity, the Most Material Points of the Mahometan Religion, Their Sects and Heresies, Their Convents and Religious Votaries: Their Military Discipline, with an Exact Computation of Their Forces Both by Sea and Land: Illustrated with Divers Pieces of Sculpture Representing the Variety of Habits amongst the Turks: In Three Books* (London: John Starkey and Henry Brome, 1668).

Saade, Bashir, *Hizbullah and the Politics of Remembrance: Writing the Lebanese Nation* (Cambridge: Cambridge University Press, 2016).

Saade, Bashir, 'Hezbollah and its "Takfiri" Enemy in Syria: Rethinking Relationships between States and Non-State Actors', in: Rasmus Alenius Boserup, Waleed Hazbun, Karim Makdisi, and Helle Malmvig (eds), *New Conflict Dynamics: Between Regional Autonomy and Intervention in the Middle East and North Africa* (Copenhagen: Danish Institute for International Studies, 2017), 81–91.

Saad-Ghorayeb, Amal, *Hizbu'llah: Politics and Religion* (London: Pluto, 2002).

Sabahi, Farian, 'Iran, Iranian Media and Sunnite Islam', in: Brigitte Maréchal and Sami Zemni (eds), *The Dynamics of Sunni-Shia Relationships: Doctrine, Transnationalism, Intellectuals and the Media* (London: Hurst, 2013), 163–77.

Sabari, Simha, *Mouvements populaires à Bagdad à l'époque 'Abbasside* (Paris: Libraire d'Amérique et d'Orient, 1981).

Sachedina, Abdulaziz Abdulhussein, *Islamic Messianism: The Idea of the Mahdi in Twelver Shi'ism* (Albany: SUNY Press, 1981).

Sachedina, Abdulaziz Abdulhussein, *The Just Ruler (al-Sultān al-'Ādil) in Shī'ite Islam: The Comprehensive Authority of the Jurist in Imamite Jurisprudence* (Oxford: Oxford University Press, 1988).

Sadeghi, Zohreh, *Fatima von Qum: Ein Beispiel für die Verehrung heiliger Frauen im Volksglauben der Zwölfer-Schia* (Berlin: Klaus Schwarz, 1996).

Sadeghi-Boroujerdi, Eskandar, 'Strategic Depth, Counterinsurgency, and the Logic of Sectarianization: The Islamic Republic of Iran's Security Doctrine and its Regional Implications', in: Nader Hashemi and Danny Postel (eds), *Sectarianization: Mapping the New Politics of the Middle East* (London: Hurst, 2017), 159–84.

Sadeghi-Boroujerdi, Eskandar, *Revolution and its Discontents: Political Thought and Reform in Iran* (Cambridge: Cambridge University Press, 2019).

Sadleir, George Forster, and Patrick Ryan, *Diary of a Journey across Arabia from el-Khatif in the Persian Gulf, to Yambo in the Red Sea, during the Year 1819* (Bombay: Education Society's Press, 1866).

al-Sadr, Muhammad Baqir, *Principles of Islamic Jurisprudence: According to Shi'i Law* (London: Islamic College for Advanced Studies Press, 2003).

Saeedullah, *The Life and Works of Muhammad Siddiq Hasan Khan, Nawab of Bhopal: 1248–1307/1832–1890* (Lahore: Ashraf, 1973).

Saffari, Said, 'The Legitimation of the Clergy's Right to Rule in the Iranian Constitution of 1979', *British Journal of Middle Eastern Studies* 20, 1 (1993), 64–82.

al-Safi, 'Ala', *Al-Shaykh Muhammad Taqi al-Shirazi al-Ha'iri wa Dawrihi al-Siyyasi min 'am 1918–1920* (Karbala: Dar al-Kafil, 2019).

Safi, Omid, *The Politics of Knowledge in Premodern Islam: Negotiating Ideology and Religious Inquiry* (Chapel Hill: University of North Carolina Press, 2006).

Saghiyya, Hazim, *Nawasib wa Rawafid: Munaza'at al-Sunna wa-l-Shi'a fi al-'Alam al-Islami al-Yawm* (Beirut: Dar al-Saqi, 2009).

Şahin, Kaya, *Empire and Power in the Reign of Süleyman: Narrating the Sixteenth-Century Ottoman World* (Cambridge: Cambridge University Press, 2013).

Sahner, Christian C., *Among the Ruins: Syria Past and Present* (London: Hurst, 2014).

Sahner, Christian C., *Christian Martyrs under Islam: Religious Violence and the Making of the Muslim World* (Princeton: Princeton University Press, 2018).

Said, Behnam, *Islamische Ökumene als Mittel der Politik: Aktuelle Tendenzen in der Annäherungsdebatte zwischen Sunna und Schia auf der Doha-Konferenz 2007* (Berlin: Klaus Schwarz, 2009).

Said, Edward W., *Orientalism* (New York: Pantheon Books, 1978).

Sakai, Keiko, 'Modernity and Tradition in the Islamic Movements in Iraq: Continuity and Discontinuity in the Role of the Ulama', *Arab Studies Quarterly* 23, 1 (2001), 37–53.

Sakai, Keiko, 'The 1991 Intifadah in Iraq: Seen through Analyses of the Discourses of Iraqi Intellectuals', in: Keiko Sakai (ed.), *Social Protests and Nation-Building in the Middle East and Central Asia* (Chiba: Institute of Developing Economies, 2003), 157–72.

Salamandra, Christa and Leif Stenberg (eds), *Syria from Reform to Revolt: Culture, Society and Religion* (Syracuse: Syracuse University Press, 2015).

Salati, Marco, 'La Lu'lu'a al-Bahrayn fi l-ijâza li-qurratay al-'ayn di Shaykh Yûsuf b. Ahmad al-Bahrânî (1107–1186/1695–1772): Per lo studio della shî'a di Bahrayn', *Annali di Ca' Foscari* 28, 3 (1989), 111–45.

Salati, Marco, 'Ricerche sullo sciismo nell'Impero ottomano: Il viaggio di Zayn al-Din al-Shahid al-Thani a Istanbul al tempo di Solimano il Magnifico (952/1545)', *Oriente Moderno* 9 (1990), 81–92.

Salati, Marco, *Ascesa e caduta di una famiglia di Ašrāf sciiti di Aleppo: I Zuhrāwī o Zuhrāzāda, 1600–1750* (Rome: Istituto per l'Oriente C. A. Nallino, 1992).

Salati, Marco, 'Toleration, Persecution and Local Realities: Observations on the Shiism in the Holy Places and the Bilâd al-Shâm (16th-17th Centuries)', in: *Convegno sul tema: La Shī'a nell'Impero Ottomano (Roma, 15 aprile 1991)* (Rome: Accademia Nazionale dei Lincei, 1993), 121–48.

Salati, Marco, 'A Shiite in Mecca: The Strange Case of Mecca-Born Syrian and Persian Sayyid Muhammad Haydar (d. 1139/1727)', in: Rainer Brunner and Werner Ende (eds), *The Twelver Shia in Modern Times: Religious Culture & Political History* (Leiden: Brill, 2001), 3–24.

Salati, Marco, 'Shiism in Ottoman Syria: A Document from the Qadi-Court of Aleppo (963/1555 A.D.)', *Eurasian Studies* 1, 1 (2002), 77–84.

Salati, Marco, 'Tre documenti sull'uso della ǧizyah nella Aleppo ottomana del XVII secolo', *Oriente Moderno* 94, 1 (2014), 176–85.

Salati, Marco, 'Shiite Survival in Ottoman Aleppo: The Endowment Deed of Ahmad and Baha' al-Din al-Zuhrawi (1066/1656) (Aleppo Court Records, Vol. 3, pp. 788–790)', *Eurasian Studies* 14, 1 (2016), 205–30.

Saleh, Alam, and Hendrik Kraetzschmar, 'Politicized Identities, Securitized Politics: Sunni-Shi'a Politics in Egypt', *Middle East Journal* 69, 4 (2015), 545–62.

Saleh, Mohammad Waleed Abid, 'Of Arab Issues in the Letters of al-Mufti Muhammad Habib al-Obeidi to International Bodies and Western Leaders', *Al Malweah for Archaeological and Historical Studies* 7, 20 (2020), 133–62.

Saleh, Walid A., *The Formation of the Classical Tafsīr Tradition: The Qurʾān Commentary of al-Thaʿlabī (d. 427/1035)* (Leiden: Brill, 2004).

Salehi, Nasrollah, 'Les fatwas des ulémas persans de Najaf et Kerbala', in: Oliver Bast (ed.), *La Perse et la grande guerre* (Tehran: Institut Français de Recherche en Iran, 2002), 157–76.

Saliba, George, 'Horoscopes and Planetary Theory: Ilkhanid Patronage of Astronomers', in: Linda Komaroff (ed.), *Beyond the Legacy of Genghis Khan* (Leiden: Brill, 2006), 357–68.

Salibi, Kamal S., 'The Maronites of Lebanon under Frankish and Mamluk Rule (1099–1516)', *Arabica* 4, 3 (1957), 288–303.

Salibi, Kamal S., *Maronite Historians of Medieval Lebanon* (New York: AMS Press, 1959).

Salibi, Kamal S., 'The Buḥturids of the Garb: Mediaeval Lords of Beirut and of Southern Lebanon', *Arabica* 8, 1 (1961), 74–97.

Salih, Dayf Allah, *Tasawwur Huthi bi-Sha'n Saytarat al-Quwat al-Huthiyya 'ala Sana'a 2014* (Cairo: al-Maktab al-Arabi li-l-Maarif, 2015).

Salih, Shakeeb, 'The British-Druze Connection and the Druze Rising of 1896 in the Hawran', *Middle Eastern Studies* 13, 2 (1977), 251–7.

al-Salimi, Abdulrahman, 'Ibadi Studies and Orientalism', in: Angeliki Ziaka (ed.), *On Ibadism* (Hildesheim: Georg Olms, 2013), 23–34.

Salisbury, Edward E., 'Translation of Two Unpublished Arabic Documents, Relating to the Doctrines of the Ismâ'ilis and Other Bâṭinian Sects, with an Introduction and Notes', *Journal of the American Oriental Society* 2 (1851), 257–324.

Salisbury, Edward E., 'Notice of كتاب الباكورة السليمانية في كشف اسرار الديانة النصرية تأليف سليمان افندى الاذني The Book of Sulaimân's First Ripe Fruit, Disclosing the Mysteries of the Nusairian Religion', *Journal of the American Oriental Society* 8 (1866), 227–308.

Salloukh, Bassel F., 'Demystifying Syrian Foreign Policy under Bashar al-Asad', in: Fred H. Lawson (ed.), *Demystifying Syria* (London: Saqi, 2009), 159–79.

Salloukh, Bassel F., 'Remaking Lebanon after Syria: The Rise and Fall of Proxy Authoritarianism', in: Holger Albrecht (ed.), *Contentious Politics in the Middle East: Political Opposition under Authoritarianism* (Gainesville: University Press of Florida, 2010), 205–28.

Salloukh, Bassel F., 'The Arab Uprisings and the Geopolitics of the Middle East', *The International Spectator* 48, 2 (2013), 32–46.

Salloukh, Bassel F., 'The Geopolitics of the Struggle for Syria', *e-International Relations*, 23 September 2013.

Salloukh, Bassel F., 'Sect Supreme: The End of Realist Politics in the Middle East', *Foreign Affairs*, 14 July 2014.

Salloukh, Bassel F., et al., *The Politics of Sectarianism in Postwar Lebanon* (London: Pluto Press, 2015).

Salloukh, Bassel F., 'The Architecture of Sectarianization in Lebanon', in: Nader Hashemi and Danny Postel (eds), *Sectarianization: Mapping the New Politics of the Middle East* (London: Hurst, 2017), 215–34.

Salloukh, Bassel F., 'The Sectarianization of Geopolitics in the Middle East', in: Nader Hashemi and Danny Postel (eds), *Sectarianization: Mapping the New Politics of the Middle East* (London: Hurst, 2017), 35–52.

Salloukh, Bassel F., 'The Syrian War: Spillover Effects on Lebanon', *Middle East Policy* 24, 1 (2017), 62–78.

Salloukh, Bassel F., 'Taif and the Lebanese State: The Political Economy of a Very Sectarian Public Sector', *Nationalism and Ethnic Politics* 25, 1 (2019), 43–60.

Salmoni, Barak A., Bryce Loidolt, and Madeleine Wells, *Regime and Periphery in Northern Yemen: The Huthi Phenomenon* (Santa Monica, CA: RAND, 2010).

Salti, Nisreen, and Jad Chaaban, 'The Role of Sectarianism in the Allocation of Public Expenditure in Postwar Lebanon', *International Journal of Middle East Studies* 42, 4 (2010), 637–55.

Samin, Nadav, *Of Sand or Soil: Genealogy and Tribal Belonging in Saudi Arabia* (Princeton, NJ: Princeton University Press, 2016).

al-Sana'ani, al-Imam al-Amir Muhammad ibn Isma'il, *The Purification of Tawhid from the Filth of Deviation* (Birmingham: Dar as-Sunnah, 2009).

Sander, Paul, *Zwischen Charisma und Ratio: Entwicklungen in der frühen imāmitischen Theologie* (Berlin: Klaus Schwarz, 1994).

Sanders, Paula, *Ritual, Politics, and the City in Fatimid Cairo* (Albany: SUNY Press, 1994).

Sanyal, Usha, *Ahmad Riza Khan Barelwi: In the Path of the Prophet* (Oxford: Oneworld, 2005).

Saouli, Adham, 'Lebanon's Salafis: Opportunities and Constraints in a Divided Society', in: Francesco Cavatorta and Fabio Merone (eds), *Salafism after the Arab Awakening: Contending with People's Power* (London: Hurst, 2016), 43–60.

Saouli, Adham, 'Hizbollah's Intervention in Syria: Causes and Consequences', in: Raymond Hinnebusch and Adham Saouli (eds), *The War for Syria: Regional and International Dimensions of the Syrian Uprising* (Abingdon: Routledge, 2020), 69–82.

Saramifar, Younes, 'Tales of Pleasures of Violence and Combat Resilience among Iraqi Shi'i Combatants Fighting ISIS', *Ethnography* 20, 4 (2019), 560–77.

Sarasin, Willhelm, *Das Bild Alis bei den Historikern der Sunna* (Basel: M. Werner-Riehm, 1907).

al-Sarhan, Saud, 'The Saudis as Managers of the Hajj', in: Eric Tagliacozzo and Shawkat M. Toorawa (eds), *The Hajj: Pilgrimage in Islam* (New York: Cambridge University Press, 2016), 196–212.

Sariyannis, Marinos, *A History of Ottoman Political Thought up to the Early Nineteenth Century* (Leiden: Brill, 2018).

Sarkar, Jadunath, *History of Aurangzib: Based on Original Sources*, 5 Vols (Calcutta: M. C. Sarkar, 1919–28).

Sarkar, Jadunath, 'Bengal under Murshid Quli Khan', in: Jadunath Sarkar (ed.), *The History of Bengal*, Vol. 2 (Dhaka: BRPC, 1943), 397–421.

Sassoon, Joseph, *Saddam Hussein's Ba'th Party: Inside an Authoritarian Regime* (Cambridge: Cambridge University Press, 2011).

Satia, Priya, 'Developing Iraq: Britain, India and the Redemption of Empire and Technology in the First World War', *Past & Present* 197, 1 (2007), 211–55.

al-Saud, Abdullah bin Khaled, 'The Spiritual Teacher and His Truants: The Influence and Relevance of Abu Mohammad al-Maqdisi', *Studies in Conflict & Terrorism* 41, 9 (2018), 736–54.

Sauvaget, J., 'Deux sanctuaires chiites d'Alep', *Syria* 9, 4 (1928), 320–7.

Savarkar, Vinayak Damodar, *Essentials of Hindutva* (n.p.: n.p., 1923).

Savory, Roger M., 'A 15th-Century Ṣafavid Propagandist at Harāt', in: D. Sinor (ed.), *The American Oriental Society, Middle West Branch Semi-Centennial Volume* (Bloomington: Indiana University Press, 1969), 189–97.

Savory, Roger M., 'The Export of Ithnā 'Asharī Shī'ism: Historical and Ideological Background', in: David Menashri (ed.), *The Iranian Revolution and the Muslim World* (Boulder, CO: Westview Press, 1990), 13–39.

Sayed, Linda, 'Education and Reconfiguring Lebanese Shi'i Muslims into the Nation-State during the French Mandate, 1920–43', *Die Welt des Islams* 59, 3–4 (2019), 282–312.

Sayej, Caroleen Marji, *Patriotic Ayatollahs: Nationalism in Post-Saddam Iraq* (Ithaca, NY: Cornell University Press, 2018).

Sayfo, Omar, 'From Kurdish Sultan to Pan-Arab Champion and Muslim Hero: The Evolution of the Saladin Myth in Popular Arab Culture', *Journal of Popular Culture* 50 (2017), 65–85.

Schäbler, Birgit, *Aufstände im Drusenbergland: Ethnizität und Integration einer ländlichen Gesellschaft Syriens vom Osmanischen Reich bis zur staatlichen Unabhängigkeit, 1850–1949* (Gotha: Perthes, 1996).

Schacht, Joseph, *The Origins of Muhammadan Jurisprudence* (Oxford: Clarendon Press, 1953).

Schacht, Joseph, *An Introduction to Islamic Law* (Oxford: Oxford University Press, 1964).

Scharbrodt, Oliver, 'The Salafiyya and Sufism: Muḥammad ʿAbduh and his Risālat al-Wāridāt (Treatise on Mystical Inspirations)', *Bulletin of the School of Oriental and African Studies* 70, 1 (2007), 89–115.

Scharbrodt, Oliver, 'The Qutb as Special Representative of the Hidden Imam: The Conflation of Shii and Sufi Vilayat in the Niʿmatullahi Order', in: D. Hermann and S. Mervin (eds), *Courants et dynamiques chiites à l'époque moderne (XVIIIe–XXe siècles)* (Beirut: Orient Institute Beirut, 2010), 33–49.

Scharbrodt, Oliver, 'A Minority within a Minority? The Complexity and Multilocality of Transnational Twelver Shia Networks in Britain', *Contemporary Islam* 13, 3 (2019), 287–305.

Scharbrodt, Oliver, 'Creating a Diasporic Public Sphere in Britain: Twelver Shia Networks in London', *Islam and Christian-Muslim Relations* 31, 1 (2020), 23–40.

Scharbrodt, Oliver, 'Contesting Ritual Practices in Twelver Shiism: Modernism, Sectarianism and the Politics of Self-Flagellation (taṭbīr)', *British Journal of Middle Eastern Studies* (online, 2022).

Scharbrodt, Oliver, and Yafa Shanneik (eds), *Shiʿa Minorities in the Contemporary World: Migration, Transnationalism and Multilocality* (Edinburgh: Edinburgh University Press, 2020).

Schayegh, Cyrus, *The Middle East and the Making of the Modern World* (Cambridge, MA: Harvard University Press, 2017).

Schayegh, Cyrus, and Andrew Arsan, 'Introduction', in: Cyrus Schayegh and Andrew Arsan (eds), *The Routledge Handbook of the History of the Middle East Mandates* (London: Routledge, 2015), 1–23.

Scheller, Bente, *The Wisdom of Syria's Waiting Game: Foreign Policy under the Assads* (London: Hurst, 2013).

Scherberger, Max, 'The Confrontation between Sunni and Shiʿi Empires: Ottoman-Safavid Relations between the Fourteenth and the Seventeenth Century', in: Ofra Bengio and Meir Litvak (eds), *The Sunna and Shiʿa in History: Division and Ecumenism in the Muslim Middle East* (New York: Palgrave Macmillan, 2011), 51–67.

Schielke, Samuli, 'Policing Ambiguity: Muslim Saints-Day Festivals and the Moral Geography of Public Space in Egypt', *American Ethnologist* 35, 4 (2008), 539–52.

Schilling, Heinz, 'Confessionalization: Historical and Scholarly Perspectives of a Comparative and Interdisciplinary Paradigm', in: John M. Headley, Hans

J. Hillerbrand, and Anthony J. Papalas (eds), *Confessionalization in Europe, 1555–1700: Essays in Honor and Memory of Bodo Nischan* (Aldershot: Ashgate, 2004), 21–35.

Schimmel, Annemarie, *Mystical Dimensions of Islam* (Chapel Hill, NC: University of North Carolina Press, 1975).

Schimmel, Annemarie, *Islam in the Indian Subcontinent* (Leiden: Brill, 1980).

Schmidtke, Sabine, *The Theology of al-ʿAllama al-Ḥilli (d. 726/1325)* (Berlin: Klaus Schwarz, 1991).

Schmidtke, Sabine, *Theologie, Philosophie und Mystik im zwölferschiitischen Islam des 9./15. Jahrhunderts: Die Gedankenwelten des Ibn Abi Gumhur al-Ahsai* (Leiden: Brill, 2000).

Schmidtke, Sabine, 'Review of "Islamic Legal Orthodoxy: Twelver Shiite Responses to the Sunni Legal System" by Devin J. Stewart', *Iranian Studies* 37, 1 (2004), 123–6.

Schmidtke, Sabine, 'The History of Zaydī Studies: An Introduction', *Arabica* 59, 3–4 (2012), 185–99.

Schmidtke, Sabine, and Jan Thiele, *Preserving Yemen's Cultural Heritage: The Yemen Manuscript Digitization Project* (Sanaa: Botschaft der Bundesrepublik Deutschland/ Deutsches Archäologisches Institut, 2011).

Schofield, Richard, 'Narrowing the Frontier: Mid-Nineteenth Century Efforts to Delimit and Map the Perso-Ottoman Border', in: Roxane Farmanfarmaian (ed.), *War and Peace in Qajar Persia: Implications Past and Present* (London: Routledge, 2008), 149–73.

Schölch, Alexander, 'Der arabische Osten im neunzehnten Jahrhundert: 1800–1914', in: Ulrich Haarmann, *Geschichte der arabischen Welt*, 4th ed. (Munich: C. H. Beck, 2001), 365–431.

Schulze, Kirsten E., *Israel's Covert Diplomacy in Lebanon* (Basingstoke: Macmillan, 1998).

Schulze, Reinhard, *Islamischer Internationalismus im 20. Jahrhundert: Untersuchungen zur Geschichte der Islamischen Weltliga* (Leiden: Brill, 1990).

Schulze, Reinhard, *Geschichte der islamischen Welt: Von 1900 bis zur Gegenwart* (Munich: C. H. Beck, 2016).

Schwinges, Rainer Christoph, *Kreuzzugsideologie und Toleranz: Studien zu Wilhelm von Tyrus* (Stuttgart: Anton Hiersemann, 1977).

Scott, James C., *Seeing Like a State: How Certain Schemes to Improve the Human Condition Have Failed* (New Haven: Yale University Press, 1998).

Seale, Patrick, *Asad of Syria: The Struggle for the Middle East* (Berkeley: University of California Press, 1988/95).

Sedgwick, Mark J. R., 'Saudi Sufis: Compromise in the Hijaz, 1925–40', *Die Welt des Islams* 37, 3 (1997), 349–68.

Serjeant, Robert B., 'The Zaydis', in: A.J. Arberry (ed.), *Religion in the Middle East: Three Religions in Concord and Conflict*, Vol. 2 (Cambridge: Cambridge University Press, 1969), 285–301.

Serjeant, Robert B., 'The Interplay between Tribal Affinities and Religious (Zaydi) Authority in Yemen', *al-Abhath* 30 (1982), 11–50.

Setton, Kenneth M., *The Papacy and the Levant (1204–1571)*, 4 Vols (Philadelphia: American Philosophical Society, 1976–84).

Seurat, Michel, 'Le rôle de Lyon dans l'installation du mandat français en Syrie: Intérêts économiques et culturels, luttes d'opinion (1915–1925)', *Bulletin d'études orientales* 31 (1979), 129–65.

Seurat, Michel, *Syrie: L'état de barbarie* (Paris: Presses Universitaires de France, 2012).

Şeyhun, Ahmet, *Islamist Thinkers in the Late Ottoman Empire and Early Turkish Republic* (Leiden: Brill, 2014).

Sezgin, Ursula, *Abū Miḥnaf: Ein Beitrag zur Historiographie der umaiyadischen Zeit* (Leiden: Brill, 1971).

Shaery-Eisenlohr, Roschanack, *Shiʿite Lebanon: Transnational Religion and the Making of National Identities* (New York: Columbia University Press, 2008).

Shah, Mustafa (ed.), *Tafsir: Interpreting the Qur'an*, Vol. 1 (Abingdon: Routledge, 2013), 41–4.

Shahi, Afshin, and Maya Vachkova, 'Eco-Sectarianism: From Ecological Disasters to Sectarian Violence in Syria', *Asian Affairs* 49, 3 (2018), 449–67.

Shahidi, Hamideh, 'Religious Politics of Sultan Husain Bayqara (A Case Study: The Impact on Shiʿism)', *Historical Studies of Islam* 8, 29 (2016), 61–82.

Shahin, Emad Eldin, *Through Muslim Eyes: Muhammad Rashid Rida and the West* (Herndon, VA: International Institute of Islamic Thought, 1994).

Shah-Kazemi, Reza, *Justice and Remembrance: Introducing the Spirituality of Imam ʿAli* (London: I. B. Tauris/Institute of Ismaili Studies, 2006).

Shahmoradi, S. M., M. Moradian, and A. Montazerolghaem, 'The Religion of the Kara Koyunlu Dynasty: An Analysis', *Asian Culture and History* 5, 2 (2013), 95–103.

Shahrani, Nazif M., 'State Building and Social Fragmentation in Afghanistan: A Historical Perspective', in: Ali Banuazizi and Myron Weiner (eds), *The State, Religion, and Ethnic Politics: Pakistan, Iran, and Afghanistan* (Syracuse, NY: Syracuse University Press, 1986), 23–74.

al-Shahrastani, Abu al-Fath Ibn ʿAbd al-Karim, *Religionspartheien und Philosophen-Schulen*, trans. by Theodor Haarbrücker, 2 Vols (Halle: Schwetschke, 1850–1).

al-Shaibi, Kamil M., *Sufism and Shiʿism* (Surbiton: LAAM, 1991).

Shakeb, M. Z. A., *Relations of Golkonda with Iran: Diplomacy, Ideas, and Commerce, 1518–1687* (Delhi: Primus, 2017).

Shakely, Farhad, 'The Naqshbandi Shaikhs of Hawraman and the Heritage of Khalidiyya-Mujaddidiyya in Kurdistan', *International Journal of Kurdish Studies* 19, 1–2 (2005), 119–35.

al-Shakhs, Hashim Muhammad, *Aʿlam Hajar min al-Madiyyin wa-l-Muʿasirin*, 4 Vols (Beirut: Muʾassasat Umm al-Qura li-l-Tahqiq wa-l-Nashr, 1996–2006).

Shakman Hurd, Elizabeth, 'Politics of Sectarianism: Rethinking Religion and Politics in the Middle East', *Middle East Law and Governance* 7 (2015), 61–75.

Shaltut, Mahmoud, 'The Introduction of the Story of Taqreeb', in: *Two Historical Documents* (Cairo: Dar al-Taqreeb, 1963), 3–13.

Shaltut, Mahmoud, 'The Official Councel (Fatwa) Given by His Eminence on the Validity of Worshipping According to the Doctrine of the Imamite Shiʿâ', in: *Two Historical Documents* (Cairo: Dar al-Taqreeb, 1963), 14–16.

Shama, Nael, *Egyptian Foreign Policy from Mubarak to Morsi: Against the National Interest* (London: Routledge, 2014).

Shanahan, Rodger, *The Shi'a of Lebanon: Clans, Parties and Clerics* (London: I. B. Tauris, 2005).

Shanahan, Rodger, 'Malaysia and its Shi'a "Problem"', *Middle East Institute*, 25 July 2014.

Shankland, David, *The Alevis in Turkey: The Emergence of a Secular Islamic Tradition* (London: RoutledgeCurzon, 2003).

Shankland, David, 'Are the Alevis Shi'ite?', in: Lloyd Ridgeon (ed.), *Shi'i Islam and Identity: Religion, Politics and Change in the Global Muslim Community* (London: I. B. Tauris, 2012), 210–28.

Shanneik, Yafa, 'Remembering Karbala in the Diaspora: Religious Rituals among Iraqi Shii Women in Ireland', *Religion* 45, 1 (2015), 89–102.

Sharafi, Mitra, *Law and Identity in Colonial South Asia: Parsi Legal Culture, 1772–1947* (New York: Cambridge University Press, 2014).

Sharar, Abdul Halim, *Lucknow: The Last Phase of an Oriental Culture* (New Delhi: Oxford University Press, 1994).

Shariati, Ali, *Hajj* (Bedford, OH: Free Islamic Literature, 1977).

Shariati, Ali, *Fatima is Fatima*, trans. by Laleh Bakhtiar (Tehran: Shariati Foundation, 1981).

Shariati, Ali, 'Red Shi'ism (the Religion of Martyrdom) vs. Black Shi'ism (the Religion of Mourning)', *Iran Chamber*, http://www.iranchamber.com/personalities/ashariati/works/red_black_shiism.php.

Sharma, Sri Ram, *The Religious Policy of the Mughal Emperors* (Bombay: H. Milford/ Oxford University Press, 1940).

Sharon, Moshe, *Black Banners from the East: The Establishment of the Abbasid State: Incubation of a Revolt* (Jerusalem: Magnes Press, 1983).

Shaw, Stanford J., *Between Old and New: The Ottoman Empire under Sultan Selim III, 1789–1807* (Cambridge, MA: Harvard University Press, 1971).

Shaw, Stanford J., *History of the Ottoman Empire and Modern Turkey: Reform, Revolution, and Republic: The Rise of Modern Turkey, 1808–1975* (Cambridge: Cambridge University Press, 1977).

Shaw, Stanford J., 'Iranian Relations with the Ottoman Empire in the Eighteenth and Nineteenth Centuries', in: P. Avery, G. Hambly, and C. Melville (eds), *The Cambridge History of Iran*, Vol. 7 (Cambridge: Cambridge University Press, 1991), 295–313.

El-Shazly, Nadia El-Sayed, *The Gulf Tanker War: Iran and Iraq's Maritime Swordplay* (Houndmills: Macmillan, 1998).

Shea, David, and Anthony Troyer (trans.), *The Dabistán or School of Manners*, 2 Vols (Paris: Oriental Translation Fund, 1843).

Shehabi, Alaa, and Marc Owen Jones (eds), *Bahrain's Uprising: Resistance and Repression in the Gulf* (London: Zed, 2015).

al-Shehabi, Omar, *Contested Modernity: Sectarianism, Nationalism, and Colonialism in Bahrain* (London: Oneworld, 2019).

Sheikh, Samira, 'Aurangzeb as Seen from Gujarat: Shi'i and Millenarian Challenges to Mughal Sovereignty', *Journal of the Royal Asiatic Society* 28, 3 (2018), 557–81.

Shields, Sarah D., *Fezzes in the River: Identity Politics and European Diplomacy in the Middle East on the Eve of World War II* (New York: Oxford University Press, 2011).

Shlaim, Avi, 'Israel, the Great Powers, and the Middle East Crisis of 1958', *Journal of Imperial and Commonwealth History* 27, 2 (1999), 177–92.

Shlaim, Avi, *The Iron Wall: Israel and the Arab World*, 2nd ed. (London: Penguin, 2014).

Shodhan, Amrita, 'Legal Formulation of the Question of Community: Defining the Khoja Collective', *Indian Social Science Review* 1, 1 (1999), 137–51.

Shorrock, William I., *French Imperialism in the Middle East: The Failure of Policy in Syria and Lebanon, 1900–1914* (Madison: University of Wisconsin Press, 1976).

Shurreef, Jaffur, and G. A. Herklots, *Qanoon-e-Islam: Or, the Customs of the Moosulmans of India, Comprising a Full and Exact Account of Their Various Rites and Ceremonies, from the Moment of Birth till the Hour of Death* (London: Parbury, Allen & Co., 1832).

Shushtari, Nurullah Ibn Abdallah, *Kitab-i Mustatab-i Majalis al-Muminin*, 2 Vols (Tehran: Kitabfurush-i Islamiyya, 1998/99).

Siddiqi, Muhammad Suleman, 'Sufi-State Relationship under the Bahmanids (A.D. 1348–1538)', *Rivista degli Studi Orientali* 64, 1/2 (1990), 71–96.

Siddiqui, Sohaira, *Law and Politics under the Abbasids: An Intellectual Portrait of al-Juwayni* (Cambridge: Cambridge University Press, 2019).

Sidorko, Clemens P., '"Kampf den ketzerischen Qizilbash!": Die Revolte des Haggi Da'ud (1718–1728)', in: Raoul Motika and Michael Ursinus (eds), *Caucasia between the Ottoman Empire and Iran, 1555–1914* (Wiesbaden: Reichert, 2000), 133–45.

Siebenga, Rianne, 'Picturing Muharram: Images of a Colonial Spectacle, 1870–1915', *South Asia: Journal of South Asian Studies* 36, 4 (2013), 626–43.

Siegel, Alexandra, 'Twitter Wars: Sunni-Shia Conflict and Cooperation in the Digital Age', in: Frederic Wehrey (ed.), *Beyond Sunni and Shia: The Roots of Sectarianism in a Changing Middle East* (Oxford: Oxford University Press, 2018), 157–80.

Simpson, Marianna S., *Sultan Ibrahim Mirza's Haft Awrang: A Princely Manuscript from Sixteenth-Century Iran* (New Haven: Yale University Press, 1997).

Sindawi, Khalid, 'Are There any Shi'ite Muslims in Israel?', *Journal of Holy Land and Palestine Studies* 7, 2 (2008), 183–99.

Sindawi, Khalid, 'The Shiite Turn in Syria', *Current Trends in Islamist Ideology* 8 (23 June 2009), 82–107.

Sindawi, Khalid, 'Jordan's Encounter with Shiism', *Current Trends in Islamist Ideology* 10 (2010), 102–15.

Sindawi, Khalid, 'Al-Mustabsirūn, "Those Who Are Able to See the Light": Sunnī Conversion to Twelver Shī'ism in Modern Times', *Die Welt des Islams* 51, 2 (2011), 210–34.

Sirriyeh, Elizabeth, 'Rashid Rida's Autobiography of the Syrian Years, 1865–1897', *Arabic & Middle Eastern Literature* 3, 2 (2000), 179–94.

Sivan, Emmanuel, 'Sunni Radicalism in the Middle East and the Iranian Revolution', *International Journal of Middle East Studies* 21, 1 (1989), 1–30.

Skare, Erik, *A History of Palestinian Islamic Jihad: Faith, Awareness, and Revolution in the Middle East* (Cambridge: Cambridge University Press, 2021), 129–39.

Skocpol, Theda, 'Rentier State and Shi'a Islam in the Iranian Revolution', *Theory and Society* 11, 3 (1982), 265–83.

Slight, John, *The British Empire and the Hajj: 1865–1956* (Cambridge, MA: Harvard University Press, 2015).

Sluglett, Peter, 'The Mandates: Some Reflections on the Nature of the British Presence in Iraq (1914–1932) and the French Presence in Syria (1918–1946)', in: Peter Sluglett and Nadine Méouchy (eds), *The British and French Mandates in Comparative Perspectives* (Leiden: Brill, 2004), 103–27.

Sluglett, Peter, *Britain in Iraq: Contriving King and Country*, 2nd ed. (London: I. B. Tauris, 2007).

Sluglett, Peter, 'The British, the Sunnis and the Shi'is: Social Hierarchies of Interaction under the British Mandate', *International Journal of Contemporary Iraqi Studies* 4, 3 (2010), 257–73.

Sluglett, Peter, 'Sectarianism in Recent Iraqi History: What It Is and What It Isn't', in: Imranali Panjwani (ed.), *The Shi'a of Samarra: The Heritage and Politics of a Community in Iraq* (London: I.B. Tauris, 2012), 143–61.

Sluglett, Peter, 'Shi'i Actors in Post-Saddam Iraq: Partisan Historiography', in: Jordi Tejel, Peter Sluglett, Riccardo Bocco, and Hamit Bozarslan (eds), *Writing the History of Iraq: Historiographical and Political Challenges* (London: World Scientific Publishing/Imperial College London Press, 2012), 289–304.

Sluglett, Peter, and Marion Farouk-Sluglett, 'Some Reflections on the Sunni/Shi'i Question in Iraq', *Bulletin (British Society for Middle Eastern Studies)* 5, 2 (1978), 78–87.

Smith, Anthony D., *Chosen Peoples: Sacred Sources of National Identity* (Oxford: Oxford University Press, 2003).

Smith, Anthony D., *Ethno-Symbolism and Nationalism: A Cultural Approach* (London: Routledge, 2009).

Smith Diwan, Kristin, 'Saudi Nationalism Raises Hopes of Greater Shia Inclusion', *Arab Gulf States Institute in Washington*, 3 May 2018.

Smith, John Masson, *The History of the Sarbadar Dynasty 1336–1381 A.D. and Its Sources* (The Hague: Mouton, 1970).

Smith, Peter, *The Babi and Baha'i Religions: From Messianic Shi'ism to a World Religion* (Cambridge: Cambridge University Press, 1987).

Smyth, Phillip, 'Hizballah Cavalcade: What is the Liwa'a Abu Fadl al-Abbas (LAFA)? Assessing Syria's Shia "International Brigade" through their Social Media Presence', *Jihadology*, 15 May 2013.

Smyth, Phillip, 'Hizballah Cavalcade: From Najaf to Damascus and onto Baghdad: Iraq's Liwa Abu Fadl al-Abbas', *Jihadology*, 18 June 2014.

Smyth, Phillip, *The Shiite Jihad in Syria and its Regional Effects* (Washington, DC: Washington Institute for Near East Policy, 2015).

Smyth, Phillip, 'Hizballah Cavalcade: Al-Quwat al-Ja'afariyah & Liwa al-Sayyida Ruqayya: The Building of an "Islamic Resistance" in Syria', *Jihadology*, 28 September 2015.

Sobhani, Jafar, *Doctrines of Shi'i Islam: A Compendium of Imami Beliefs and Practices*, trans. by Reza Shah-Kazemi (London: I. B. Tauris/Institute of Ismaili Studies, 2001).

Sohoni, Pushkar, 'Patterns of Faith: Mosque Typologies and Sectarian Affiliation in the Kingdom of Ahmadnagar', in: David J. Roxburgh (ed.), *Envisioning Islamic Art and Architecture: Essays in Honor of Renata Holod* (Leiden: Brill, 2014), 109–26.

Sohoni, Pushkar, *The Architecture of a Deccan Sultanate: Courtly Practice and Royal Authority in Late Medieval India* (London: I. B. Tauris, 2018).

Sohrweide, H., 'Der Sieg der Safaviden in Persien und seine Rückwirkungen auf die Schiiten Anatoliens im 16. Jahrhundert', *Der Islam* 41 (1965), 95–223.

el-Solh, Raghid K., 'Lebanese Arab Nationalists and Consociational Democracy during the French Mandate Period', in: Christoph Schumann (ed.), *Liberal Thought in the Eastern Mediterranean: Late 19th Century until the 1960s* (Leiden: Brill, 2008), 217–36.

Somel, Selçuk Akşin, *The Modernization of Public Education in the Ottoman Empire, 1839–1908: Islamization, Autocracy, and Discipline* (Leiden: Brill, 2001).

Soucek, Svat, 'Arabistan or Khuzistan', *Iranian Studies* 17, 2–3 (1984), 195–213.

Souleimanov, Emil, and Maya Ehrmann, 'The Rise of Militant Salafism in Azerbaijan and its Regional Implications', *Middle East Policy* 20, 3 (2013), 111–20.

Spellberg, Denise A., *Politics, Gender, and the Islamic Past: The Legacy of 'A'isha bint Abi Bakr* (New York: Columbia University Press, 1994).

Sprenger, Aloys (comp.), *A Catalogue of the Arabic, Persian and Hindustany Manuscripts: Of the Libraries of the King of Oudh*, Vol. 1 (Calcutta: 1854; reprint Osnabrück: 1979).

Sreberny-Mohammadi, Annabelle, and Ali Mohammadi, *Small Media, Big Revolution: Communication, Culture, and the Iranian Revolution* (Minneapolis: University of Minnesota Press, 1994).

Srivastava, Ashirbadi Lal, *The First Two Nawabs of Awadh*, 2nd ed. (Agra: Shiva Lal Agarwala, 1954).

Stanfield-Johnson, Rosemary, 'Sunni Survival in Safavid Iran: Anti-Sunni Activities during the Reign of Tahmasp I', *Iranian Studies* 27, 1/4 (1994), 123–33.

Stanfield-Johnson, Rosemary, 'The Tabarra'iyan and the Early Safavids', *Iranian Studies* 37, 1 (2004), 47–71.

Stark, Ulrike, *An Empire of Books: The Naval Kishore Press and the Diffusion of the Printed Word in Colonial India* (Ranikhet: Permanent Black, 2007).

Steensgaard, Niels, *The Asian Trade Revolution: The East India Companies and the Decline of the Caravan Trade* (Chicago: University of Chicago Press, 1975).

Steinberg, Guido, 'The Shiites in the Eastern Province of Saudi Arabia (al-Ahsa') 1913–1953', in: Rainer Brunner and Werner Ende (eds), *The Twelver Shia in Modern Times: Religious Culture & Political History* (Leiden: Brill, 2001), 236–54.

Steinberg, Guido, *Religion und Staat in Saudi-Arabien: Die wahhabitischen Gelehrten 1902–1953* (Würzburg: Ergon, 2002).

Steinberg, Guido, *Der nahe und der ferne Feind: Die Netzwerke des islamistischen Terrors* (Munich: C. H. Beck, 2005).

Steinberg, Guido, *The Iraqi Insurgency: Actors, Strategies, and Structures* (Berlin: SWP, 2006).

Steinberg, Guido, 'Wahhabi 'Ulama and the State in Saudi Arabia, 1927', in: Camron Michael Amin, Benjamin C. Fortna, and Elizabeth Brown Frierson (eds), *The Modern Middle East: A Sourcebook for History* (Oxford: Oxford University Press, 2006), 57–61.

Steinberg, Guido, 'Jihadi-Salafism and the Shi'is: Remarks about the Intellectual Roots of Anti-Shi'ism', in: Roel Meijer (ed.), *Global Salafism: Islam's New Religious Movement* (London: Hurst, 2009), 107–25.

Steinberg, Guido, 'The Wahhabiyya and Shi'ism, from 1744/45 to 2008', in: Ofra Bengio and Meir Litvak (eds), *The Sunna and Shi'a in History: Division and Ecumenism in the Muslim Middle East* (New York: Palgrave Macmillan, 2011), 163–82.

Steinberg, Guido, *The 'Axis of Resistance': Iran's Expansion in the Middle East is Hitting a Wall* (Berlin: SWP, 2021).

Stellhorn Mackensen, Ruth, 'Moslem Libraries and Sectarian Propaganda', *American Journal of Semitic Languages and Literatures* 51, 2 (1935), 83–113.

Stenersen, Anne, *Al-Qaida in Afghanistan* (Cambridge: Cambridge University Press, 2017).

Stephens, Julia, 'The Phantom Wahhabi: Liberalism and the Muslim Fanatic in Mid-Victorian India', *Modern Asian Studies* 47, 1 (2013), 22–52.

Stephens, Julia, *Governing Islam: Law, Empire, and Secularism in Modern South Asia* (Cambridge: Cambridge University Press, 2018).

Steppat, Fritz, 'Islamisch-fundamentalistische Kritik an der Staatskonzeption der Islamischen Revolution in Iran', in: Hans Roemer and Albrecht Noth (eds), *Studien zur Geschichte und Kultur des Vorderen Orients: Festschrift für Bertold Spuler zum siebzigsten Geburtstag* (Leiden: Brill, 1981), 443–52.

Stern, S. M., 'Ismā'īlī Propaganda and Fatimid Rule in Sind', *Islamic Culture* 23/4 (1949), 289–307.

Stern, S. M., 'The Early Ismā'īlī Missionaries in North-West Persia and in Khurāsān and Transoxania', *Bulletin of the School of Oriental and African Studies* 23, 1 (1960), 56–90.

Stewart, Devin J., 'Notes on the Migration of 'Āmilī Scholars to Safavid Iran', *Journal of Near Eastern Studies* 55, 2 (1996), 81–103.

Stewart, Devin J., 'Popular Shiism in Medieval Egypt: Vestiges of Islamic Sectarian Polemics in Egyptian Arabic', *Studia Islamica* 84 (1996), 35–66.

Stewart, Devin J., *Islamic Legal Orthodoxy: Twelver Shiite Responses to the Sunni Legal System* (Salt Lake City: University of Utah Press, 1998).

Stewart, Devin J., 'The Genesis of the Akhbārī Revival', in: Michel M. Mazzaoui (ed.), *Safavid Iran & Her Neighbors* (Salt Lake City: University of Utah Press, 2003), 169–93.

Stewart, Devin J., 'An Episode in the 'Amili Migration to Safavid Iran: Husayn b. 'Abd al-Samad al-'Amili's Travel Account', *Iranian Studies* 39, 4 (2006), 481–508.

Stewart, Devin J., 'The Ottoman Execution of Zayn al-Dīn al-'Āmilī', *Die Welt des Islams* 48, 3/4 (2008), 289–347.

Stewart, Devin J., 'Ibn al-Nadīm's Ismā'īlī Contacts', *Journal of the Royal Asiatic Society* 19, 1 (2009), 21–40.

Stewart, Devin J., 'Polemics and Patronage in Safavid Iran: The Debate on Friday Prayer during the Reign of Shah Tahmasb', *Bulletin of the School of Oriental and African Studies* 72, 3 (2009), 425–57.

Stewart, Devin J., 'The Historical Roles of Jihād in Sunnī-Shīʿī Relations', *Journal of the Middle East and Africa* 12, 2 (2021), 127–56.

Stickel, Farida, *Zwischen Chiliasmus und Staatsräson: Religiöser Wandel unter den Ṣafaviden* (Berlin: De Gruyter, 2019).

Stookey, Robert W., *Yemen: The Politics of the Yemen Arab Republic* (Boulder, CO: Westview Press, 1978).

Strauss, Eduard, 'L'inquisition dans l'état mamlouk', *Rivista degli Studi Orientali* 25 (1950), 11–26.

Strauss, Johann, 'Sii ne demekdir? Ein türkisches Traktat über die Schia aus dem Jahre 1925', in: Rainer Brunner, Monika Gronke, Jens P. Laut, and Ulrich Rebstock (eds), *Islamstudien ohne Ende: Festschrift für Werner Ende* (Würzburg: Deutsche Morgenländische Gesellschaft/Ergon, 2002), 471–84.

Streusand, Douglas E., *Islamic Gunpowder Empires: Ottomans, Safavids, and Mughals* (Boulder, CO: Westview Press, 2011).

Strick van Linschoten, Alex, and Felix Kuehn, *An Enemy We Created: The Myth of the Taliban/al-Qaeda Merger in Afghanistan, 1970–2010* (London: Hurst, 2012).

Strobl, Staci, 'From Colonial Policing to Community Policing in Bahrain: The Historical Persistence of Sectarianism', *International Journal of Comparative and Applied Criminal Justice* 35, 1 (2011), 19–37.

Strobl, Staci, *Sectarian Order in Bahrain: The Social and Colonial Origins of Criminal Justice* (Lanham: Lexington, 2018).

Strothmann, Rudolf, 'Die Literatur der Zaiditen', *Islam* 1 (1910), 354–68.

Strothmann, Rudolf, 'Die Literatur der Zaiditen', *Islam* 2 (1911), 49–78.

Strothmann, Rudolf, *Das Staatsrecht der Zaiditen* (Strasbourg: Karl J. Trübner, 1912).

Strothmann, Rudolf, *Kultus der Zaiditen* (Strasbourg: Karl J. Trübner, 1912).

Strothmann, Rudolf, 'Das Problem der literarischen Persönlichkeit Zaid b. ʿAli', *Der Islam* 13 (1923), 1–52.

Strothmann, Rudolf, *Die Zwölfer-Schīʿa: Zwei religionsgeschichtliche Charakterbilder aus der Mongolenzeit* (Leipzig: Otto Harrassowitz, 1926).

Subrahmanyam, Sanjay, 'Un Grand Dérangement: Dreaming an Indo-Persian Empire in South Asia, 1740–1800', *Journal of Early Modern History* 4, 3–4 (2000), 337–78.

Subtelny, Maria E., 'The Cult of Abdullah Ansari under the Timurids', in: Alma Giese and J. Christoph Bürgel (eds), *Gott ist schön und Er liebt die Schönheit: Festschrift für Annemarie Schimmel zum 7. April 1992 dargebracht von Schülern, Freunden und Kollegen* (Bern: Peter Lang, 1994), 377–406.

Subtelny, Maria E., *Timurids in Transition: Turko-Persian Politics and Acculturation in Medieval Iran* (Leiden: Brill, 2007).

Subtelny, Maria E., 'Tamerlane and his Descendants: From Paladins to Patrons', in: D. Morgan and A. Reid (eds), *The New Cambridge History of Islam*, Vol. 3 (Cambridge: Cambridge University Press, 2010), 169–200.

Subtelny, Maria E., and Anas B. Khalidov, 'The Curriculum of Islamic Higher Learning in Timurid Iran in the Light of the Sunni Revival under Shāh-Rukh', *Journal of the American Oriental Society* 115, 2 (1995), 210–36.

al-Sudairi, Mohammed Turki A., 'China as the New Frontier for Islamic Daʿwah: The Emergence of a Saudi China-Oriented Missionary Impulse', *Journal of Arabian Studies* 7, 2 (2017), 225–46.

Sulejmani, Arben (ed.), *A Light of Guidance: The Bektashi Community in the Balkans and around the World* (n.p.: n.p., 2015).

Suleman, Fahmida (ed.), *People of the Prophet's House: Artistic and Ritual Expressions of Shiʿi Islam* (London: Azimuth/Institute of Ismaili Studies, 2015),

Sunayama, Sonoko, *Syria and Saudi Arabia: Collaboration and Conflicts in the Oil Era* (London: Tauris, 2007).

Susewind, Raphael, 'The "Wazirganj Terror Attack": Sectarian Conflict and the Middle Classes', *South Asia Multidisciplinary Academic Journal* 11 (2015), 1–17.

al-Subayʿi, 'Abdallah ibn Nasir, *Al-Qadaʾ wa-l-Awqaf fi al-Ahsaʾ wa-l-Qatif wa Qatar Athnaʾ al-Hukm al-ʿUthmani al-Thani 1871–1913* (Riyadh: Matabiʿ al-Jumʿa al-Iliktruniyya, 1999).

al-Subhani, Jaʿfar (ed.), *Hiwarat ʿIlmiyya bayna al-ʿAlamayn al-Sayyid Muhsin al-Amin al-ʿAmili wa-l-Sayyid Muhammad Rashid Rida* (Qom: Muʾassasat al-Imam al-Sadiq, 2017).

al-Suwaydi, Abdullah ibn Husain, 'Muʾtamar al-Najaf (The Najaf Conference)', https://ar.wikisource.org/wiki/%D9%85%D8%A4%D8%AA%D9%85%D8%B1_%D8%A7%D9%84%D9%86%D8%AC%D9%81.

al-Suyuti, Jalal al-Din, *History of the Caliphs*, trans. by Major H. S. Jarrett (Calcutta: Asiatic Society, 1881).

Szanto, Edith, 'Sayyida Zaynab in the State of Exception: Shiʿi Sainthood as "Qualified Life" in Contemporary Syria', *International Journal of Middle East Studies* 44, 2 (2012), 285–99.

Szanto, Edith, 'Challenging Transnational Shiʿi Authority in Baʿth Syria', *British Journal of Middle Eastern Studies* 45, 1 (2018), 95–110.

Tabaar, Mohammad Ayatollahi, *Religious Statecraft: The Politics of Islam in Iran* (New York: Columbia University Press, 2018).

Tabar, Paul, 'Ashura in Sydney: A Transformation of a Religious Ceremony in the Context of a Migrant Society', *Journal of Intercultural Studies* 23, 3 (2002), 285–305.

al-Tabari, *The History of al-Tabari*, Vol. 6, *Muhammad at Mecca*, trans. by Montgomery Watt and M. V. McDonald (Albany: SUNY Press, 1988).

al-Tabari, *The History of al-Tabari*, Vol. 16, *The Community Divided*, trans. by Adrian Brockett (Albany: SUNY Press, 1997).

al-Tabari, *The History of al-Tabari*, Vol. 17, *The First Civil War*, trans. by G. R. Hawting (Albany: SUNY Press, 1997).

al-Tabari, *The History of al-Tabari*, Vol. 19, *The Caliphate of Yazid b. Muʿawiyah A.D. 680–683/A.H. 60–64*, trans. by I. K. A. Howard (Albany: SUNY Press, 1990).

Tabatabai, Adnan, *Morgen in Iran: Die Islamische Republik im Aufbruch* (Hamburg: Körber-Stiftung, 2016).

Tabbaa, Yasser, *The Transformation of Islamic Art during the Sunni Revival* (Seattle: University of Washington Press, 2001).

Tabbaa, Yasser, 'Review of "The Shrines of the 'Alids in Medieval Syria" by Stephennie Mulder', *Shii Studies Review* 1, 1–2 (2017), 265–71.

Tabbaa, Yasser, 'Invented Pieties: The Rediscovery and Rebuilding of the Shrine of Sayyida Ruqayya in Damascus, 1975–2006', *Artibus Asiae* 67, 1 (2007), 95–112.

Tabbaa, Yasser, and Sabrina Mervin, *Najaf, the Gate of Wisdom: History, Heritage and Significance of the Holy City of the Shiʿa* (Paris: UNESCO, 2014).

Tagliacozzo, Eric, 'The Dutch Empire and the Hajj', in: David Motadel (ed.), *Islam and the European Empires* (Oxford: Oxford University Press, 2014), 73–89.

Takeyh, Ray, *Guardians of the Revolution: Iran and the World in the Age of the Ayatollahs* (Oxford: Oxford University Press, 2009).

Takeyh, Ray, *The Last Shah: America, Iran, and the Fall of the Pahlavi Dynasty* (New Haven: Yale University Press, 2021).

Takim, Liyakat A., 'From Bidʿa to Sunna: The Wilāya of ʿAlī in the Shīʿī Adhān', *Journal of the American Oriental Society* 120, 2 (2000), 166–77.

Takim, Liyakat A., *The Heirs of the Prophet: Charisma and Religious Authority in Shiʿite Islam* (Albany: SUNY Press, 2006).

Takim, Liyakat A., *Shiʿism in America* (New York: NYU Press, 2009).

Talhamy, Yvette, 'The Nusayri Leader Ismaʿil Khayr Bey and the Ottomans (1854–58)', *Middle Eastern Studies* 44, 6 (2008), 895–908.

Talhamy, Yvette, 'The Syrian Muslim Brothers and the Syrian-Iranian Relationship', *Middle East Journal* 63, 4 (2009), 561–80.

Talhamy, Yvette, 'The Fatwas and the Nusayri/Alawis of Syria', *Middle Eastern Studies* 46, 2 (2010), 175–94.

Talhamy, Yvette, 'American Protestant Missionary Activity among the Nusayris (Alawis) in Syria in the Nineteenth Century', *Middle Eastern Studies* 47, 2 (2011), 215–36.

Talhamy, Yvette, 'Conscription among the Nusayris ('Alawis) in the Nineteenth Century', *British Journal of Middle Eastern Studies* 38, 1 (2011), 23–40.

Talhamy, Yvette, 'The Nusayri and Druze Minorities in Syria in the Nineteenth Century: The Revolt against the Egyptian Occupation as a Case Study', *Middle Eastern Studies* 48, 6 (2012), 973–95.

Talmon-Heller, Daniella, 'The Shaykh and the Community: Popular Hanbalite Islam in 12th–13th Century Jabal Nablus and Jabal Qasyūn', *Studia Islamica* 79 (1994), 103–20.

Talmon-Heller, Daniella, *Islamic Piety in Medieval Syria: Mosques, Cemeteries and Sermons under the Zangids and Ayyubids (1146–1260)* (Leiden: Brill, 2007).

al-Tamimi, Aymenn Jawad, 'Hizballah, the Jihad in Syria, and Commemorations in Lebanon', *Middle East Review of International Affairs* 19, 1 (2015), 8–36.

al-Tamimi, Naser M., *China-Saudi Arabia Relations, 1990–2012: Marriage of Convenience or Strategic Alliance?* (Abingdon: Routledge, 2014).

Taner, Melis, *Caught in a Whirlwind: A Cultural History of Ottoman Baghdad as Reflected in Its Illustrated Manuscripts* (Brill: Leiden, 2019).

Tanielian, Melanie S., *The Charity of War: Famine, Humanitarian Aid, and World War I in the Middle East* (Stanford: Stanford University Press, 2018).

Tapper, Richard, *Frontier Nomads of Iran: A Political and Social History of the Shahsevan* (Cambridge: Cambridge University Press, 1997).

Taqui, Roshan, *Lucknow 1857: The Two Wars at Lucknow. The Dusk of an Era* (Lucknow: New Royal Book, 2019).

al-Tarabulsi, 'Ali al-Ibrahim, *Al-Tashayyu' fi Tarablus wa Bilad al-Sham: Adwa' 'ala Dawlat Bani 'Ammar* (Beirut: Dar al-Saqi, 2007).

Tarzi, Amin, 'Islam, Shari'a, and State Building under 'Abd al-Rahman Khan', in: Nile Green (ed.), *Afghanistan's Islam: From Conversion to the Taliban* (Oakland, CA: University of California Press, 2017), 129–44.

Tauber, Eliezer, 'Rashid Rida as Pan-Arabist before World War I', *The Muslim World* 79, 2 (1989), 102–12.

Tauber, Eliezer, 'Rashid Rida and Faysal's Kingdom in Syria', *The Muslim World* 85, 3–4 (1995), 235–45.

Tauber, Eliezer, 'Rashid Rida's Political Attitudes during World War I', *The Muslim World* 85, 1-2 (1995), 107–21.

Tauber, Eliezer, *The Formation of Modern Syria and Iraq* (London: Cass, 1995).

Tavassoli, Sasan, *Christian Encounters with Iran: Engaging Muslim Thinkers after the Revolution* (London: I. B. Tauris, 2011).

Tawil, Muhammad Amin Ghalib, *Tarikh al-'Alawiyyin* (Latakia: Matba'at al-Taraqqi, 1924).

Taylor, Christopher S., 'Reevaluating the Shi'i Role in the Development of Monumental Islamic Funerary Architecture: The Case of Egypt', *Muqarnas* 9 (1992), 1–10.

Taylor, Christopher S., *In the Vicinity of the Righteous: Ziyāra and the Veneration of Muslim Saints in Late Medieval Egypt* (Leiden: Brill, 1999).

Teitelbaum, Joshua, *Holier than Thou: Saudi Arabia's Islamic Opposition* (Washington: Washington Institute for Near East Policy, 2000).

Teitelbaum, Joshua, *The Rise and Fall of the Hashemite Kingdom of Arabia* (London: Hurst, 2001).

Teitelbaum, Joshua, 'Sunni vs. Shiite in Saudi Arabia', *Jerusalem Issue Briefs* 10, 23, 16 January 2011.

Teitelbaum, Joshua, 'Hashemites, Egyptians and Saudis: The Tripartite Struggle for the Pilgrimage in the Shadow of Ottoman Defeat', *Middle Eastern Studies* 56, 1 (2020), 36–47.

Tejel Gorgas, Jordi, *Le mouvement kurde de Turquie en exil: Continuités et discontinuités du nationalisme kurde sous le mandat français en Syrie et au Liban (1925–1946)* (Bern: Peter Lang, 2007).

Tendler Krieger, Bella, 'The Rediscovery of Samuel Lyde's Lost Nuṣayrī Kitāb al-Mashyakha (Manual for Shaykhs)', *Journal of the Royal Asiatic Society* 24, 1 (2014), 1–16.

Terrill, W. Andrew, 'Iranian Involvement in Yemen', *Orbis* 58, 3 (2014), 429–40.

Terzioğlu, Derin, 'The Imperial Circumcision Festival of 1582: An Interpretation', *Muqarnas* 12 (1995), 84–100.

Terzioğlu, Derin, 'Sunna-Minded Sufi Preachers in Service of the Ottoman State: The Nasīhatnāme of Hasan Addressed to Murad IV', *Archivum Ottomanicum* 27 (2010), 243–59.

Terzioğlu, Derin, 'Sufis in the Age of State-Building and Confessionalization', in: Christine Woodhead (ed.), *The Ottoman World* (London: Routledge, 2012), 86–99.

Terzioğlu, Derin, 'How to Conceptualize Ottoman Sunnitization: A Historiographical Discussion', *Turcica* 44 (2012–13), 301–38.

Terzioğlu, Derin, 'Where 'Ilm-i Ḥāl Meets Catechism: Islamic Manuals of Religious Instruction in the Ottoman Empire in the Age of Confessionalization', *Past & Present* 220, 1 (2013), 79–114.

Tétreault, Mary Ann, *Stories of Democracy: Politics and Society in Contemporary Kuwait* (New York: Columbia University Press, 2000).

Tezcan, Baki, 'Lost in Historiography: An Essay on the Reasons for the Absence of a History of Limited Government in the Early Modern Ottoman Empire', *Middle Eastern Studies* 45, 3 (2009), 477–505.

Thackston, Wheeler M. (comp./trans.), *A Century of Princes: Sources on Timurid History and Art* (Cambridge, MA: Agha Khan Program for Islamic Architecture, 1989).

Thiele, Jan, *Kausalität in der mu'tazilitischen Kosmologie: Das Kitab al-Mu'aththirāt wa-miftaḥ al-muškilāt des Zayditen al-Ḥasan ar-Raṣṣāṣ (st. 584/1188)* (Leiden: Brill, 2011).

Thiele, Jan, *Theologie in der jemenitischen Zaydiyya: Die naturphilosophischen Überlegungen des al-Ḥasan ar-Raṣṣāṣ* (Leiden: Brill, 2013).

Thiollet, Helene, 'Migration as Diplomacy: Labor Migrants, Refugees, and Arab Regional Politics in the Oil-Rich Countries', *International Labor and Working-Class History* 79 (2011), 103–21.

Thomas, David, and Alexander Mallett (eds), *Christian-Muslim Relations: A Bibliographical History*, Vol. 4 (Leiden: Brill, 2012).

Thomas, Martin C., 'French Intelligence-Gathering in the Syrian Mandate, 1920-40', *Middle Eastern Studies* 38, 1 (2002), 1–32.

Thomaz, Luis Filipe F. R., 'Iranian Diaspora and the Deccan Sultanates in India: A Study of Sixteenth Century Portuguese Sources', *Studies in History* 30, 1 (2014), 1–42.

Thompson, Elizabeth F., 'Rashid Rida and the 1920 Syrian-Arab Constitution: How the French Mandate Undermined Islamic Liberalism', in: Cyrus Schayegh and Andrew Arsan (eds), *The Routledge Handbook of the History of the Middle East Mandates* (London: Routledge, 2015), 244–57.

Thompson, Elizabeth F., *How the West Stole Democracy from the Arabs: The Syrian Arab Congress and the Destruction of its Historic Liberal-Islamic Alliance* (London: Grove Press, 2020).

Thomsen, Christiane M., *Burchards Bericht über den Orient: Reiseerfahrungen eines staufischen Gesandten im Reich Saladins 1175/1176* (Berlin: De Gruyter, 2018).

Thurlkill, Mary F., *Chosen among Women: Mary and Fatima in Medieval Christianity and Shi'ite Islam* (Notre Dame, IN: University of Notre Dame Press, 2008).

Thurston, Alexander, *Salafism in Nigeria: Islam, Preaching, and Politics* (Cambridge: Cambridge University Press, 2016).

Thurston, Alexander, 'Sectarian Triangles: Salafis, the Shi'a, and the Politics of Religious Affiliations in Northern Nigeria', *Politics and Religion* 14, 3 (2021), 484–511.

Tibawi, Abdul Latif, *American Interests in Syria, 1800–1901: A Study of Educational, Literary and Religious Work* (Oxford: Clarendon Press, 1966).

Tibi, Bassam, *Vom Gottesreich zum Nationalstaat: Islam und panarabischer Nationalismus* (Frankfurt: Suhrkamp, 1987).

El-Tobgui, Carl Sharif, *Ibn Taymiyya on Reason and Revelation: A Study of Dar' ta'āruḍ al-'aql wa-l-naql* (Leiden: Brill, 2020).

Tomass, Mark, *The Religious Roots of the Syrian Conflict: The Remaking of the Fertile Crescent* (Basingstoke: Palgrave Macmillan, 2016).

Tomlinson, Robert, *Covering the Shi'a: English Press Representation of the Lebanese Shi'a 1975–1985* (Lanham: Lexington Books, 2018).

Tomsen, Peter, *The Wars of Afghanistan: Messianic Terrorism, Tribal Conflicts, and the Failures of Great Powers* (New York: PublicAffairs, 2011).

Tor, Deborah, 'An Historiographical Re-examination of the Appointment and Death of 'Ali al-Rida', *Der Islam* 78, 1 (2001), 103–28.

Traboulsi, Fawwaz, *A History of Modern Lebanon* (London: Pluto, 2007).

Traboulsi, Samer, 'An Early Refutation of Muḥammad ibn 'Abd al-Wahhāb's Reformist Views', *Die Welt des Islams* 42, 3 (2002), 373–415.

Trausch, Tilmann, *Abbildung und Anpassung: Das Türkenbild in safawidischen Chroniken des 16. Jahrhunderts* (Berlin: Klaus Schwarz, 2008).

Trautmann, Thomas R., *Aryans and British India* (Berkeley: University of California Press, 1997).

Trégan, François-Xavier, 'Appréhensions et méthodes dans un systéme mandataire: Le cas de la participation des États du Levant à l'Exposition coloniale internationale de Paris, 1931', in: Nadine Méouchy (ed.), *France, Syrie et Liban 1918–1946: Les ambiguïtés et les dynamiques de la relation mandataire* (Damascus: Presses de l'Ifpo, 2002), 91–103.

Trégan, François-Xavier, 'Approche des saviors de l'Institut français de Damas: À la recherche d'un temps mandataire', in: Peter Sluglett and Nadine Méouchy (eds), *The British and French Mandates in Comparative Perspectives* (Leiden: Brill, 2004), 235–47.

Trimingham, J. Spencer, *The Sufi Orders in Islam* (Oxford: Oxford University Press, 1971).

Tripp, Charles, *A History of Iraq* (Cambridge: Cambridge University Press, 2000).

Troeller, Gary, 'Ibn Sa'ud and Sharif Husain: A Comparison in Importance in the Early Years of the First World War', *The Historical Journal* 14, 3 (1971), 627–33.

Trofimov, Yaroslav, *The Siege of Mecca: The Forgotten Uprising* (London: Allen Lane, 2007).

Truschke, Audrey, *Aurangzeb: The Life and Legacy of India's Most Controversial King* (Palo Alto: Stanford University Press, 2017).

Tucker, Ernest, 'Nadir Shah and the Ja'fari Madhhab Reconsidered', *Iranian Studies* 27, 1/4 (1994), 163–79.

Tucker, Ernest, 'The Peace Negotiations of 1736: A Conceptual Turning Point in Ottoman-Persian Relations', *Turkish Studies Association Bulletin* 20, 1 (1996), 16–37.

Tucker, Ernest, *Nadir Shah's Quest for Legitimacy in Post-Safavid Iran* (Gainesville: University Press of Florida, 2006).

Tucker, William F., *Mahdis and Millenarians: Shi'ite Extremists in Early Muslim Iraq* (Cambridge: Cambridge University Press, 2008).

Turner, Colin, *Islam without Allah? The Rise of Religious Externalism in Safavid Iran* (Richmond: Curzon, 2000).

al-Tusi, Shaykh al-Ta'ifa al-Imam Abu Jafar Muhammad b. al-Hasan, *Fihrist Kutub al-Shī'a*, ed. by Aloys Sprenger (Calcutta: 1848).

al-Tusi, Shaykh al-Ta'ifa al-Imam Abu Jafar Muhammad b. al-Hasan, *Kitab al-Khilaf*, Vols 1 and 2 (Qom: Mu'assasat al-Nashr al-Islami, 1407/1987).

Tyerman, Christopher, *The World of the Crusades: An Illustrated History* (New Haven: Yale University Press, 2019).

Ulrichsen, Kristian Coates, 'The British Occupation of Mesopotamia, 1914–1922', *Journal of Strategic Studies* 30, 2 (2007), 349–77.

Ulrichsen, Kristian Coates, *Qatar and the Arab Spring* (London: Hurst, 2014).

Ulrichsen, Kristian Coates, *Qatar and the Gulf Crisis* (London: Hurst, 2020).

Um, Nancy, *The Merchant Houses of Mocha: Trade and Architecture in an Indian Ocean Port* (Seattle: University of Washington Press, 2009).

al-'Umar, Nasir ibn Sulayman, *Waqi' al-Rafida fi Bilad al-Tawhid* (n.p., available at http://ar.islamway.net/book/3165).

al-'Utaybi, Maryam bint Khalaf, *Al-Ahsa' wa-l-Qatif fi 'Ahd al-Dawla al-Su'udiyya al-Thaniyya (1245–1288 AH)* (Beirut: Jadawel, 2012).

al-'Uthaymin, 'Abdallah al-Salih, *Tarikh al-Mamlaka al-'Arabiyya al-Su'udiyya*, 9th ed., 2 Vols, Vol. 1 (Riyadh: Obeikan, 1998).

al-'Uthaymin, 'Abdallah al-Salih, *Muhammad ibn 'Abd al-Wahhab: The Man and his Works* (London: I. B. Tauris, 2009).

al-Uzri, 'Abd al-Karim, *Tarikh fi Dhikrayat: Al-'Iraq 1930–1958* (Beirut: n.p., 1982).

Vahabzadeh, Peyman, *A Guerrilla Odyssey: Modernization, Secularism, Democracy, and the Fadai Period of National Liberation in Iran, 1971–1979* (Syracuse: Syracuse University Press, 2010).

Valbjørn, Morten, and André Bank, 'Signs of a New Arab Cold War: The 2006 Lebanon War and the Sunni-Shi'i Divide', *Middle East Report* 242 (2007), 6–11.

Valbjørn, Morten, 'What's so Sectarian about Sectarian Politics? Identity Politics and Authoritarianism in a New Middle East', *Studies in Ethnicity and Nationalism* 19, 1 (2019), 127–49.

Valbjørn, Morten, 'Beyond the Beyond(s): On the (Many) Third Way(s) beyond Primordialism and Instrumentalism in the Study of Sectarianism', *Nations and Nationalism* 26, 1 (2020), 91–107.

Valbjørn, Morten, 'Observing (the Debate on) Sectarianism: On Conceptualizing, Grasping and Explaining Sectarian Politics in a New Middle East', *Mediterranean Politics* 26, 5 (2021), 612–634.

Valbjørn, Morten, and André Bank, 'The New Arab Cold War: Rediscovering the Arab Dimension of Middle East Regional Politics', *Review of International Studies* 38, 1 (2012), 3–24.

Valeri, Marc, 'High Visibility, Low Profile: The Shiʿa in Oman under Sultan Qaboos', *International Journal of Middle East Studies* 42, 2 (2010), 251–68.

Vali, Abbas, *Kurds and the State in Iran: The Making of Kurdish Identity* (London: I. B. Tauris, 2014).

Valter, Stéphane, 'La réplique à Ibn Baz (1912–1999) de ʿAbd al-Rahman al-Hayyir (1904–1986)', *Bulletin d'études orientales* 55 (2003), 299–383.

Valter, Stéphane, *Islamité et identité: La réplique de ʿAlī Sulaymān al-Aḥmad aux investigations d'un journaliste syrien sur l'histoire de la communauté alaouite* (Damascus: Presses de l'Ifpo, 2015).

Valter, Stéphane, *Norm and Dissidence: Egyptian Shiʿa between Security Approaches and Geopolitical Stakes* (Doha: Center for International and Regional Studies, 2019).

van Arendonk, Cornelis, *De Opkomst van het Zaidietische Imamaat in Yemen* (Leiden: Brill, 1919).

van Arendonk, Cornelis, *Les débuts de l'imamat zaidite au Yémen*, trans. by Jacques Ryckmans (Leiden: Brill, 1960).

van Bruinessen, Martin, 'Kurds, Turks and the Alevi Revival in Turkey', *Middle East Report* 200 (1996), 7–10.

van Bruinessen, Martin, '"Aslını inkar eden haramzadedir!": The Debate on the Ethnic Identity of the Kurdish Alevis', in: Krisztina Kehl-Bodrogi, Barbara Kellner-Heinkele, and Anke Otter-Beaujean (eds), *Syncretistic Religious Communities in the Near East: Collected Papers of the International Symposium 'Alevism in Turkey and Comparable Syncretistic Religious Communities in the Near East in the Past and Present', Berlin, 14–17 April 1995* (Leiden: Brill, 1997), 1–23.

van Bruinessen, Martin, 'A Kızılbash Community in Iraqi Kurdistan: The Shabak', *Les annales de l'autre Islam* 5 (1998), 185–96.

van Bruinessen, Martin, 'Between Dersim and Dâlahû: Reflections on Kurdish Alevism and the Ahl-i Haqq Religion', in: Shahrokh Raei (ed.), *Islamic Alternatives: Non-Mainstream Religion in Persianate Societies* (Wiesbaden: Harrassowitz, 2017), 65–93.

van Bruinessen, Martin, 'Faylis, Kurds and Lurs: Ambiguity on the Frontier of Iran and Iraq: An Overview of the Literature', Conference Paper, 12 April 2018.

van Bruinessen, Martin, 'Muslims of the Dutch East Indies and the Caliphate Question', *Studia Islamika* 2, 3 (1995), 115–40.

van Bruinessen, Martin, 'Najmuddin al-Kubra, Jumadil Kubra and Jamaluddin al-Akbar: Traces of Kubrawiyya Influence in Early Indonesian Islam', *Bijdragen tot de Taal-, Land- en Volkenkunde* 150, 2 (1994), 305–29.

van Bruinessen, Martin, 'Nationalismus und religiöser Konflikt: Der kurdische Widerstand im Iran', in: Kurt Greussing (ed.), *Religion und Politik im Iran* (Frankfurt am Main: Syndikat, 1981), 372–409.

van Bruinessen, Martin, 'Vom Osmanismus zum Separatismus: Religiöse und ethnische Hintergründe der Rebellion des Scheich Said', in: Jochen Blaschke and Martin van Bruinessen (eds), *Islam und Politik in der Türkei* (Berlin: Edition Parabolis, 1989), 109–65.

van Bruinessen, Martin, 'The Naqshbandi Order in Seventeenth-Century Kurdistan', in: Marc Gaborieau, Alexandre Popovic, and Thierry Zarcone (eds), *Naqshbandis: Cheminements et situation actuelle d'un ordre mystique musulman* (Paris: Éditions Isis, 1990), 337–60.

van Dam, Nikolaos, *The Struggle for Power in Syria: Sectarianism, Regionalism, and Tribalism in Politics, 1961–1978* (London: Croom Helm, 1979).

van Dam, Nikolaos, 'Middle Eastern Political Clichés: "Takriti" and "Sunni Rule" in Iraq; "Alawi Rule" in Syria: A Critical Appraisal', *Orient* 21, 1 (1980), 42–57.

van Dam, Nikolaos, *The Struggle for Power in Syria: Politics and Society under Asad and the Ba'th Party*, 4th ed. (London: I. B. Tauris, 2011).

van den Boogert, Maurits H., *The Capitulations and the Ottoman Legal System: Qadis, Consuls and Beratlıs in the 18th Century* (Leiden: Brill, 2005).

van den Bos, Matthijs, *Mystic Regimes: Sufism and the State in Iran, from the Late Qajar Era to the Islamic Republic* (Leiden: Brill, 2002).

van den Bos, Matthijs, 'The Balance of Ecumenism and Sectarianism: Rethinking Religion and Foreign Policy in Iran', *Journal of Political Ideologies* 23, 1 (2018), 30–53.

van den Bos, Matthijs, 'The Promised Land of Fadak: Locating Religious Nationalism in Shiite Politics', *British Journal of Middle Eastern Studies* 49, 5 (2022), 769–91.

van Dijk, Cornelis, *The Netherlands Indies and the Great War, 1914–1918* (Leiden: Brill, 2007).

van Eijk, Esther, *Family Law in Syria: Patriarchy, Pluralism and Personal Status Codes* (London: I. B. Tauris, 2016).

van Ess, Josef, 'Ibn Kullāb und die Miḥna', *Oriens* 18/9 (1965/6), 97–142.

van Ess, Josef, *Theologie und Gesellschaft im 2. und 3. Jahrhundert Hidschra: Eine Geschichte des religiösen Denkens im frühen Islam*, 6 Vols (Berlin: De Gruyter, 1991–5).

van Ess, Josef, *Der Eine und das Andere: Beobachtungen an islamischen häresiographischen Texten*, 2 Vols (Berlin: De Gruyter, 2011).

van Ess, Josef, 'Sunniten und Schiiten: Staat, Recht und Kultus', in: Hinrich Biesterfeldt (ed.), *Kleine Schriften by Josef van Ess* (Leiden: Brill, 2018), 556–69.

van Zoonen, Dave, and Khogir Wirya, *Turkmen in Tal Afar: Perceptions of Reconciliation and Conflict* (Erbil: Middle East Research Institute, 2017).

Varagur, Krithika, *The Call: Inside the Global Saudi Religious Project* (New York: Columbia Global Reports, 2020).

Vassiliev, Alexei, *The History of Saudi Arabia* (London: Saqi, 2000).

Vatanka, Alex, *Iran and Pakistan: Security, Diplomacy and American Influence* (London: I. B. Tauris, 2015).

Veccia Vaglieri, Laura, 'Il conflitto 'Ali-Mu'awiya e la secessione kharigita riesaminati alla luce di fonti ibadite', *Annali dell'Istituto Universitario Orientale di Napoli* NS4 (1952), 1–94.

Veccia Vaglieri, Laura, 'Sulla origine della denominazione Sunniti', in: *Studi Orientalistici in onore di Giorgio Levi della Vida*, Vol. 2 (Rome: Istituto per l'Oriente, 1956), 573–85.

Verdeil, Chantal, 'Une "révolution sociale dans la montagne": La conversion des Alaouites par les jésuites dans les années 1930', in: Bernard Heyberger and Rémy Madinier (eds), *L'Islam des marges: Mission chrétienne et espaces périphériques du monde musulman, XVI–XXe siècles* (Paris: IISMM/Karthala, 2011), 81–105.

Verghese, Ajay, *The Colonial Origins of Ethnic Violence in India* (Stanford: Stanford University Press, 2016).

Vermeulen, Urbain, 'Some Remarks on a Rescript of an-Nāṣir Muḥammad b. Qalā'ūn on the Abolition of Taxes and the Nuṣayris (Mamlaka of Tripoli, 717/1317)', *Orientalia Lovaniensia Periodica* 1 (1970), 195–201.

Vermeulen, Urbain, 'The Rescript against the Shī'ites and Rāfiḍites of Beirut, Ṣaidā and District (764 A.H./1363 A.D.)', *Orientalia Lovaniensia Periodica* 4 (1973), 169–75.

Vikør, Knut, *Between God and the Sultan: A History of Islamic Law* (London: Hurst, 2005).

Vilozny, Roy, 'Some Remarks on Ibn Taymiyya's Acquaintance with Imāmī Shī'ism in Light of his Minhāj al-Sunna al-Nabawiyya', *Der Islam* 97, 2 (2020), 456–75.

Virani, Shafique N., *The Ismailis in the Middle Ages: A History of Survival, a Search for Salvation* (Oxford: Oxford University Press, 2007).

Virani, Shafique N., 'Taqiyya and Identity in a South Asian Community', *Journal of Asian Studies* 70, 1 (2011), 99–139.

Vitalis, Robert, *America's Kingdom: Mythmaking on the Saudi Oil Frontier*, 2nd ed. (London: Verso, 2009).

Visser, Reidar, *Basra, the Failed Gulf State: Separatism and Nationalism in Southern Iraq* (Münster: LIT, 2005).

Visser, Reidar, *Shi'i Separatism in Iraq: Internet Reverie or Real Constitutional Challenge?* (Oslo: Norwegian Institute of International Affairs, 2005).

Visser, Reidar, 'Ethnicity, Federalism, and the Idea of Sectarian Citizenship in Iraq: A Critique', *International Review of the Red Cross* 89, 868 (2007), 809–22.

Visser, Reidar, 'The Western Imposition of Sectarianism on Iraqi Politics', *Arab Studies Journal* 15/6, 2/1 (2007/8), 83–99.

Visser, Reidar, 'The Sectarian Master Narrative in Iraqi Historiography: New Challenges since 2003', in: Jordi Tejel, Peter Sluglett, Riccardo Bocco, and Hamit Bozarslan (eds), *Writing the Modern History of Iraq: Historiographical and Political Challenges* (Hackensack: World Scientific, 2012), 47–59.

Visser, Reidar, 'The Territorial Aspect of Sectarianism in Iraq: The Case of Anbar', in: Brigitte Maréchal and Sami Zemni (eds), *The Dynamics of Sunni-Shia Relationships: Doctrine, Transnationalism, Intellectuals and the Media* (London: Hurst, 2013), 83–97.

Vogel, Frank E., *Islamic Law and Legal System: Studies of Saudi Arabia* (Leiden: Brill, 2000).

Voll, J. O., 'Muḥammad Ḥayyā al-Sindī and Muḥammad ibn 'Abd al-Wahhab: An Analysis of an Intellectual Group in Eighteenth-Century Madīna', *Bulletin of the School of Oriental and African Studies* 38, 1 (1975), 32–9.

Voll, J. O., 'Hadith Scholars and Tarīqahs: An Ulama Group in the 18th Century Haramayn and their Impact in the Islamic World', *Journal of Asian and African Studies* 15, 3 (1980), 264–73.

Voll, J. O., 'Renewal and Reform in Islamic History: Tajdid and Islah', in: John L. Esposito (ed.), *Voices of Resurgent Islam* (New York: Oxford University Press, 1983), 32–47.

Voll, J. O., "Abdallah ibn Salim al-Basri and 18th Century Hadith Scholarship', *Die Welt des Islams* 42, 3 (2002), 356–72.

vom Bruck, Gabriele, 'Disputing Descent-Based Authority in the Idiom of Religion: The Case of the Republic of Yemen', *Die Welt des Islams* 38, 2 (1998), 149–91.

vom Bruck, Gabriele, *Islam, Memory, and Morality in Yemen: Ruling Families in Transition* (New York: Palgrave Macmillan, 2005).

vom Bruck, Gabriele, 'Regimes of Piety Revisited: Zaydī Political Moralities in Republican Yemen', *Die Welt des Islams* 50 (2010), 185–223.

vom Bruck, Gabriele, 'How the Past Casts its Shadows: Struggles for Ascendancy in Northern Yemen in the Post-Salih Era', in: Gabriele vom Bruck and Charles Tripp (eds), *Precarious Belongings: Being Shi'i in Non-Shi'i Worlds* (London: Centre for Academic Shia Studies, 2017), 257–332.

von Denffer, D., 'Mut'a: Ehe oder Prostitution? Beitrag zur Untersuchung einer Institution des šī'itischen Islam', *Zeitschrift der Deutschen Morgenländischen Gesellschaft* 128 (1978), 299–325.

von Grunebaum, Gustave E., *Modern Islam: The Search for Cultural Identity* (Berkeley: University of California Press, 1962).

von Kremer, Alfred, *Culturgeschichtliche Streifzüge auf dem Gebiete des Islams* (Leipzig: F. A. Brockhaus, 1873).

von Kremer, Alfred, *Die Nationalitätsidee und der Staat* (Vienna: Carl Ronegen, 1885).

von Maltzahn, Nadia, *The Syria-Iran Axis: Cultural Diplomacy and International Relations in the Middle East* (London: I. B. Tauris, 2013).

von Palombini, Barbara, *Bündniswerben abendländischer Mächte um Persien 1453–1600* (Wiesbaden: Franz Steiner, 1968).

Vorhoff, Karin, '"Let's Reclaim our History and Culture!": Imagining Alevi Community in Contemporary Turkey', *Die Welt des Islams* 38, 2 (1998), 220–52.

Wachowski, Markus, *Sāda in Ṣana'ā': Zur Fremd- und Eigenwahrnehmung der Prophetennachkommen in der Republik Jemen* (Berlin: Klaus Schwarz, 2004).

al-Wadi'i, Abi 'Abd al-Rahman Muqbil ibn Hadi, *al-Ilhad al-Khumayni fi Ard al-Haramayn*, 2nd ed. (Sanaa: Dar al-Athar, 2000).

Wagemakers, Joas, 'Anti-Shi'ism without the Shi'a: Salafi Sectarianism in Jordan', *Maydan*, 17 October 2016.

Wagemakers, Joas, 'Jihadi-Salafism in Jordan and the Syrian Conflict: Divisions Overcome Unity', *Studies in Conflict & Terrorism* 41, 3 (2018), 191–212.

Wagemakers, Joas, 'Making Sense of Sectarianism without Sects: Quietist Salafi anti-Shia Discourse in Jordan', *Mediterranean Politics* 26, 4 (2021), 518–23.

Wagemakers, Joas, 'Sectarianism in the Service of Salafism: Shiites as a Political Tool for Jordanian Salafis', *British Journal of Middle Eastern Studies* 49, 2 (2022), 341–59.

al-Wahbi, 'Abd al-Karim bin 'Abdallah al-Munif, *Banu Khalid wa 'Alaqatuhum bi-Najd, 1669–1794* (n.p.: Dar Thaqif li-l-Nashr wa-l-Ta'lif, 1989).

al-Wahhab, Muhammad ibn Abd, *Kashf al-Shubuhat fi al-Tawhid* (Riyadh: Wizarat al-Shu'un al-Islamiyya wa-l-Da'wa wa-l-Irshad, 1419h).

Walbridge, Linda, 'The Counterreformation: Becoming a Marja' in the Modern World', in Linda Walbridge (ed.), *The Most Learned of the Shi'a: The Institution of the Marja' Taqlid* (Oxford: Oxford University Press, 2001), 230–46.

Walbridge, Linda, 'Introduction: Shi'ism and Authority': in Linda Walbridge (ed.), *The Most Learned of the Shi'a: The Institution of the Marja' Taqlid* (Oxford: Oxford University Press, 2001), 3–13.

Waldman, Simon A., and Emre Caliskan, *The New Turkey and its Discontents* (London: Hurst, 2016).

Walker, Paul E., 'Al-Maqrizi and the Fatimids', *Mamluk Studies* 7, 2 (2003), 83–97.

Walker, Paul E., 'The Responsibilities of Political Office in a Shi'i Caliphate and the Delineation of Public Duties under the Fatimids', in: Asma Afsaruddin (ed.), *Islam, the State, and Political Authority: Medieval Issues and Modern Concerns* (New York: Palgrave Macmillan, 2011), 93–110.

Walt, Stephen M., *Revolution and War* (Ithaca: Cornell University Press, 1996).

Walter, Barbara F., 'The Extremist's Advantage in Civil Wars', *International Security* 42, 2 (2017), 7–39.

Wang, Jianping, 'The Opposition of a Leading Akhund to Shi'a and Sufi Shaykhs in Mid-Nineteenth-Century China', *Cross-Currents: East Asian History and Culture Review* 3, 2 (2015), 518–41.

Wansbrough, John, *Quranic Studies: Sources and Methods of Scriptural Interpretation* (Oxford: Oxford University Press, 1977).

Wansbrough, John, *The Sectarian Milieu: Content and Composition of Islamic Salvation History* (Oxford: Oxford University Press, 1978).

al-Wardani, Salih, *Al-Haraka al-Islamiyya fi Misr: Ru'iya Waqi'iyya li-Rihlat al-Sab'inat* (Cairo: al-Bidaya, 1986).

al-Wardani, Salih, *Al-Shi'a fi Misr: Min al-Imam 'Ali hatta al-Imam al-Khumayni* (Cairo: Maktabat Madbuli al-Saghir, 1993).

al-Wardani, Salih, *Misr wa Iran: Sira' al-Amn wa-l-Siyyasa* (Cairo: Maktaba Nakhrush, 1995).

al-Wardani, Salih, *Ahl al-Sunna: Sha'b Allah al-Mukhtar wa Dirasa fi Fasad 'Aqa'id Ahl al-Sunna* (Cairo: Kanuta, 1997).

al-Wardani, Salih, *'Aqa'id al-Sunna wa 'Aqa'id al-Shi'a: Al-Taqarub wa-l-Taba'ud* (Beirut: al-Ghadir, 1999).

al-Wardani, Salih, *Al-Khud'a: Rihlati min al-Sunna ila al-Shi'a* (Cairo: al-Hadaf, 2001).

al-Wardani, Salih, *Azmat al-Haraka al-Islamiyya al-Mu'asira: Min al-Hanabila ila Taliban* (Cairo: al-Hadaf, 2002).

al-Wardi, 'Ali, *Dirasa fi Tabi'a al-Mujtam'a al-'Iraqi* (Baghdad: Matba'a al-'Ani, 1965).

al-Wardi, 'Ali, *Lamahat Ijtima'iyya min Tarikh al-'Iraq al-Hadith*, Vol. 2 (Baghdad: Matba'at al-Irshad, 1971).

al-Wardi, Ali, *Soziologie des Nomadentums: Studie über die iraqische Gesellschaft* (Neuwied: Luchterhand, 1972).

al-Wardi, Ali, *Understanding Iraq: Society, Culture, and Personality*, trans. by Fuad Baali (Lewiston, NY: Lampeter/Edwin Mellen Press, 2008).

al-Wardi, Ali, *Iraq in Turmoil: Historical Perspectives of Dr. Ali al-Wardi, from the Ottoman Empire to King Feisal*, comp. by Youssef H. Aboul-Enein (Annapolis, MD: Naval Institute Press, 2012).

Warrick, Joby, *Black Flags: The Rise of ISIS* (London: Bantam, 2015).

Wasella, Jürgen, *Vom Fundamentalisten zum Atheisten: Die Dissidentenkarriere des Abdallah al-Qasimi (1907–1996)* (Stuttgart: Klett, 1997).

Watenpaugh, Keith D., '"Creating Phantoms": Zaki al-Arsuzi, the Alexandretta Crisis, and the Formation of Modern Arab Nationalism in Syria', *International Journal of Middle East Studies* 28, 3 (1996), 363–89.

Watenpaugh, Keith D., *Being Modern in the Middle East: Revolution, Nationalism, Colonialism, and the Arab Middle Class* (Princeton: Princeton University Press, 2006).

Watson, Oliver, 'Pottery under the Mongols', in: Linda Komaroff (ed.), *Beyond the Legacy of Genghis Khan* (Leiden: Brill, 2006), 325–45.

Watt, W. Montgomery, 'Shi'ism under the Umayyads', *Journal of the Royal Asiatic Society* 92, 3–4 (1960), 158–72.

Watt, W. Montgomery, 'The Reappraisal of Abbasid Shiism', in George Makdisi (ed.), *Arabic and Islamic Studies in Honor of Hamilton A.R. Gibb* (Leiden: Brill, 1965), 638–54.

Watt, W. Montgomery, *Islamic Creeds: A Selection* (Edinburgh: Edinburgh University Press, 1994).

Weber, Max, *Schriften 1894–1922*, ed. by Dirk Kaesler (Stuttgart: Alfred Kröner, 2002).

Wedeen, Lisa, *Ambiguities of Domination: Politics, Rhetoric, and Symbols in Contemporary Syria* (Chicago: University of Chicago Press, 2015).

DeWeese, Devin, 'The Eclipse of the Kubravīyah in Central Asia', *Iranian Studies* 21, 1/2 (1988), 45–83.

DeWeese, Devin, *Islamization and Native Religion in the Golden Horde: Baba Tükles and Conversion to Islam in Historical and Epic Tradition* (University Park: Penn State University Press, 1994).

DeWeese, Devin, 'The Mashā'ikh-i Turk and the Khojagān: Rethinking the Links between the Yasavī and Naqshbandī Sufi Traditions', *Journal of Islamic Studies* 7, 2 (1996), 180–207.

DeWeese, Devin, 'Foreword', in: Mehmed Fuad Köprülü, *Early Mystics in Turkish Literature*, ed./trans. by Gary Leiser and Robert Dankoff (London: Routledge, 2006).

DeWeese, Devin, 'Succession Protocols and the Early Khwajagani Schism in the Maslak al-'Ārifīn', *Journal of Islamic Studies* 22, 1 (2011), 1–35.

Wehrey, Frederic, *The Forgotten Uprising in Eastern Saudi Arabia* (Washington, DC: Carnegie Endowment for International Peace, 2013).

Wehrey, Frederic, *Sectarian Politics in the Gulf: From the Iraq War to the Arab Uprisings* (New York: Columbia University Press, 2014).

Wehrey, Frederic, et al., *Saudi-Iranian Relations since the Fall of Saddam: Rivalry, Cooperation, and Implications for U.S. Policy* (Santa Monica, CA: RAND, 2009).

Wehrey, Frederic, et al., *The Iraq Effect: The Middle East after the Iraq War* (Santa Monica, CA: RAND, 2010).

Weineck, Benjamin, 'Fabricating the Great Mass: Heresy and Legitimate Plurality in Harputlu İshak Efendi's Polemics against the Bektaşi Order', in:Vefa Erginbaş (ed.), *Ottoman Sunnism: New Perspectives* (Edinburgh: Edinburgh University Press, 2019), 146–65.

Weir, Shelagh, 'A Clash of Fundamentalisms: Wahhabism in Yemen', *Middle East Report* 204 (1997), 22–3/26.

Weir, Shelagh, *A Tribal Order: Politics and Law in the Mountains of Yemen* (Austin: University of Texas Press, 2007).

Weismann, Itzchak, 'Sa'id Hawwa and Islamic Revivalism in Ba'thist Syria', *Studia Islamica* 85 (1997), 131–54.

Weismann, Itzchak, 'The Naqshbandiyya-Khalidiyya and the Salafi Challenge in Iraq', *Journal of the History of Sufism* 4 (2004), 229–40.

Weismann, Itzchak, *The Naqshbandiyya: Orthodoxy and Activism in a Worldwide Sufi Tradition* (London: Routledge, 2007).

Weismann, Itzchak, 'Genealogies of Fundamentalism: Salafi Discourse in Nineteenth-Century Baghdad', *British Journal of Middle Eastern Studies* 36, 2 (2009), 267–80.

Weismann, Itzchak, *Taste of Modernity: Sufism and Salafiyya in Late Ottoman Damascus* (Leiden: Brill, 2001).

Weiss, Max, '"Don't Throw Yourself Away to the Dark Continent": Shi'i Migration to West Africa and the Hierarchies of Exclusion in Lebanese Culture', *Studies in Ethnicity and Nationalism* 7, 1 (2007), 46–63.

Weiss, Max, 'Institutionalizing Sectarianism: The Lebanese Ja'fari Court and Shi'i Society under the French Mandate', *Islamic Law and Society* 15, 3 (2008), 371–407.

Weiss, Max, 'The Historiography of Sectarianism in Lebanon', *History Compass* 7, 1 (2009), 141–54.

Weiss, Max, *In the Shadow of Sectarianism: Law, Shi'ism, and the Making of Modern Lebanon* (Cambridge, MA: Harvard University Press, 2010).

Weiss, Max, 'Practicing Sectarianism in Mandate Lebanon: Shi'i Cemeteries, Religious Patrimony, and the Everyday Politics of Difference', *Journal of Social History* 43, 3 (2010), 707–33.

Weiss, Max, 'Community, Sect, Nation: Colonial and Social Scientific Discourses on the Alawis in Syria during the Mandate and Early Independence Periods', in: Michael Kerr and Craig Larkin (eds), *The Alawis of Syria: War, Faith and Politics in the Levant* (Oxford: Oxford University Press, 2015), 63–75.

Weiss, Max, 'Mosaic, Melting Pot, Pressure Cooker: The Religious, the Secular, and the Sectarian in Modern Syrian Social Thought', in: Jens Hanssen and Max Weiss (eds), *Arabic Thought against the Authoritarian Age: Towards an Intellectual History of the Present* (Cambridge: Cambridge University Press, 2018), 181–202.

Weiss, Michael, and Hassan Hassan, *ISIS: Inside the Army of Terror* (New York: Regan Arts, 2015).

Wellhausen, Julius, *Die religiös-politischen Oppositionsparteien im alten Islam* (Berlin: Weidmannsche Buchhandlung, 1901).

Wellhausen, Julius, *Das arabische Reich und sein Sturz* (Berlin: Georg Reimer, 1902).

Wells, Madeleine, 'Sectarianism, Authoritarianism, and Opposition in Kuwait', in: Nader Hashemi and Danny Postel (eds), *Sectarianization: Mapping the New Politics of the Middle East* (London: Hurst, 2017), 235–58.

Wensinck, A. J., *The Muslim Creed: Its Genesis and Historical Development* (Cambridge: Cambridge University Press, 1932).

Wenzlhuemer, Roland, *Connecting the Nineteenth-Century World: The Telegraph and Globalization* (Cambridge: Cambridge University Press, 2013).

Wessels, Josepha, 'Killing the Dispensables: Massacres Perpetrated in the Villages of Eastern Aleppo Province in 2013', *British Journal of Middle Eastern Studies* 49, 3 (2022), 463–485.

Westad, Odd Arne, *The Global Cold War: Third World Interventions and the Making of our Times* (Cambridge: Cambridge University Press, 2005).

Wetzel, Dietmar J., *Maurice Halbwachs* (Konstanz: UVK, 2009).

Weulersse, Jacques, *Le pays des Alaouites*, 2 Vols (Tours: Arrault & Co., 1940).

Wheeler, Brannon, 'The Ancient Authority of the Imam and Mahdi in Imami Shi'i Scholarship', in: *Community, State, History and Changes: Festschrift for Ridwan al-Sayyid on his Sixtieth Birthday* (Beirut: al-Shabaka al-'Arabiyya li-l-Abhath wa-l-Nashr, 2011), 137–74.

White, Benjamin T., *The Emergence of Minorities in the Middle East: The Politics of Community in French Mandate Syria* (Edinburgh: Edinburgh University Press, 2011).

Wicken, Stephen, *Iraq's Sunnis in Crisis* (Washington: Institute for the Study of War, 2013).

Wickens, G. M., 'Nasir ad-Din Tusi on the Fall of Baghdad: A Further Study', *Journal of Semitic Studies* 7, 1 (1962), 23–35.

Wieland, Carsten, 'Alawis in the Syrian Opposition', in: Michael Kerr and Craig Larkin (eds), *The Alawis of Syria: War, Faith and Politics in the Levant* (Oxford: Oxford University Press, 2015), 225–43.

Wiktor-Mach, Dobroslawa, *Religious Revival and Secularism in Post-Soviet Azerbaijan* (Berlin/Boston: De Gruyter, 2017).

Wiley, Joyce N., *The Islamic Movement of Iraqi Shi'as* (Boulder, CO: Lynne Rienner, 1992).

Wilkinson, John C., *Ibâdism: Origins and Early Development in Oman* (Oxford: Oxford University Press, 2010).

Wilkinson, Luke, 'Troubled Beginnings: The First Decade of Hizbullah's Interaction with Pan-Islamic Ideas', *MENAF*, 13 March 2020.

William of Tyre, *A History of Deeds Done beyond the Sea*, 2 Vols (New York: Columbia University Press, 1943).

Williams, J. Charles, *The Report on the Census of Oudh*, Vol. 1 (Lucknow: Oudh Government Press, 1869).

Williams, Wesley, 'Aspects of the Creed of Imam Ahmad ibn Hanbal: A Study of Anthropomorphism in Early Islamic Discourse', *International Journal of Middle East Studies* 34, 3 (2002), 441–63.

Williamson, Graham, 'The Turko-Persian War of 1821–1823: Winning the War but Losing the Peace', in: Roxane Farmanfarmaian (ed.), *War and Peace in Qajar Persia: Implications Past and Present* (London: Routledge, 2008), 88–109.

Willis, John, 'Debating the Caliphate: Islam and Nation in the Work of Rashid Rida and Abul Kalam Azad', *International History Review* 32, 4 (2010), 711–32.

Willis, John, 'Governing the Living and the Dead: Mecca and the Emergence of the Saudi Biopolitical State', *American Historical Review* 122, 2 (2017), 346–70.

Wilson, Arnold T., *Loyalties: Mesopotamia, 1914–1917* (London: Oxford University Press, 1930).

Wimmen, Heiko, 'The Sectarianization of the Syrian War', in: Frederic Wehrey (ed.), *Beyond Sunni and Shia: The Roots of Sectarianism in a Changing Middle East* (Oxford: Oxford University Press, 2018), 61–85.

Winder, R. Bayly, *Saudi Arabia in the Nineteenth Century* (London: Macmillan, 1965).

Windler, Christian, *Missionare in Persien: Kulturelle Diversität und Normenkonkurrenz im globalen Katholizismus (17.-18. Jahrhundert)* (Cologne: Böhlau, 2018).

Wing, Patrick, *The Jalayirids: Dynastic State Formation in the Mongol Middle East* (Edinburgh: Edinburgh University Press, 2016).

Wink, André, 'III. "Al-Hind" India and Indonesia in the Islamic World-Economy, c. 700–1800 A.D.', *Itinerario* 12, 1 (1988), 33–72.

Wink, André, *Al-Hind: The Making of the Indo-Islamic World. Early Medieval India and the Expansion of Islam 7th–11th Centuries* (Leiden: Brill, 1991).

Wink, André, *Akbar* (Oxford: Oneworld, 2009).

Wink, André, 'The Early Expansion of Islam in India', in: D. Morgan and A. Reid (eds), *The New Cambridge History of Islam*, Vol. 3 (Cambridge: Cambridge University Press, 2010), 78–99.

Winter, Michael, 'Egypt and Syria in the Sixteenth Century', in: Stephan Conermann and Gül Şen (eds), *The Mamluk-Ottoman Transition: Continuity and Change in Egypt and Bilād al-Shām in the Sixteenth Century* (Göttingen: Vandenhoeck & Ruprecht, 2016), 33–56.

Winter, Stefan, 'La revolte alaouite de 1834 contre l'occupation egyptienne: Perceptions alaouites et lecture ottomane', *Oriente Moderno* 79, 3 (1999), 60–71.

Winter, Stefan, 'Shams al-Dīn Muḥammad ibn Makkī "al-Shahīd al-Awwal" (d. 1384) and the Shi'ah of Syria', *Mamluk Studies Review* 3 (1999), 149–82.

Winter, Stefan, *The Shiites of Lebanon under Ottoman Rule, 1516–1788* (Cambridge: Cambridge University Press, 2010).

Winter, Stefan, 'The Kizilbaş of Syria and Ottoman Shiism', in: Christine Woodhead (ed.), *The Ottoman World* (London: Routledge, 2011), 171–83.

Winter, Stefan, 'The Alawis in the Ottoman Period', in: Michael Kerr and Craig Larkin (eds), *The Alawis of Syria: War, Faith and Politics in the Levant* (Oxford: Oxford University Press, 2015), 49–62.

Winter, Stefan, *A History of the 'Alawis: From Medieval Aleppo to the Turkish Republic* (Princeton: Princeton University Press, 2016).

Wolf, Anne M., *Political Islam in Tunisia: The History of Ennahda* (London: Hurst, 2017).

Wood, Simon A., *Christian Criticisms, Islamic Proofs: Rashid Rida's Modernist Defence of Islam* (Oxford: Oneworld, 2006).

Woods, John E., *The Aqquyunlu: Clan, Confederation, Empire*, 2nd ed. (Salt Lake City: University of Utah Press, 1999).

Woodward, Bob, *State of Denial* (New York: Simon & Schuster, 2006).

Wortabet, John, *Researches into the Religions of Syria: Or Sketches, Historical and Doctrinal, of its Religious Sects, Drawn from Original Sources* (London: James Nisbet, 1860).

Wright, Lawrence, *The Looming Tower: Al-Qaeda's Road to 9/11* (London: Allen Lane, 2006).

Wright, Robin B., *Sacred Rage: The Crusade of Modern Islam* (London: Andre Deutsch, 1986).

Yadav, Stacey Philbrick, *Islamists and the State: Legitimacy and Institutions in Yemen and Lebanon* (London: I. B. Tauris, 2013).

Yadav, Stacey Philbrick, 'Sectarianization, Islamist Republicanism, and International Misrecognition in Yemen', in: Nader Hashemi and Danny Postel (eds), *Sectarianization: Mapping the New Politics of the Middle East* (London: Hurst, 2017), 185–98.

Yaffe-Schatzmann, Gitta, 'Alawi Separatists and Unionists: The Events of 25 February 1936', *Middle Eastern Studies* 31, 1 (1995), 28–38.

Yaffe-Schatzmann, Gitta, and Uriel Dann, 'Suleiman al-Murshid: Beginnings of an Alawi Leader', *Middle Eastern Studies* 29, 4 (1993), 624–40.

Yakoubi, Myriam, 'Gertrude Bell's Perception of Faisal I of Iraq and the Anglo-Arab Romance', in: Paul Collins and Charles Tripp (eds), *Gertrude Bell and Iraq: A Life and Legacy* (Oxford: Oxford University Press, 2017), 187–213.

Yapp, M. E., 'The Revolutions of 1841-2 in Afghanistan', *Bulletin of the School of Oriental and African Studies* 27, 2 (1964), 333–81.

Yarbrough, Luke, 'Medieval Sunni Historians on Fatimid Policy and Non-Muslim Influence', *Journal of Medieval History* 45, 3 (2019), 331–46.

Yarshater, Ehsan, 'The Qajar Era in the Mirror of Time', *Iranian Studies* 34, 1/4 (2001), 187–94.

Yassini, Ayman, *Religion and State in the Kingdom of Saudi Arabia* (Boulder, CO: Westview Press, 1985).

Yassin-Kassab, Robin, and Leila al-Shami, *Burning Country: Syrians in Revolution and War* (London: Pluto, 2016).

Yavuz, Hakan, 'The Matrix of Modern Turkish Islamic Movements: The Naqshbandī Sufi Order', in: Elisabeth Özdalga (ed.), *Naqshbandis in Western and Central Asia: Change and Continuity* (Istanbul: Swedish Research Institute, 1999), 129–46.

Yavuz, Hakan, *Islamic Political Identity in Turkey* (Oxford: Oxford University Press, 2003).

Yavuz, Hakan, *Secularism and Muslim Democracy in Turkey* (Cambridge: Cambridge University Press, 2009).

Yaycioglu, Ali, *Partners of the Empire: The Crisis of the Ottoman Order in the Age of Revolutions* (Stanford: Stanford University Press, 2017).

Yazbek, Samar, *A Woman in the Crossfire: Diaries of the Syrian Revolution*, trans. by Max Weiss (London: Haus, 2012).

Yazbeck, Natacha, 'The Karbalization of Lebanon: Karbala as Lieu de Mémoire in Hezbollah's Ashura Narrative', *Memory Studies* 11, 4 (2018), 469–82.

Yazdani, Mina, 'The Confessions of Dolgoruki: Fiction and Masternarrative in Twentieth-Century Iran', *Iranian Studies* 44, 1 (2011), 25–47.

Yazdani, Mina, 'The Confessions of Dologoruki: The Crisis of Identity and the Creation of a Master Narrative', in: Abbas Amanat and Farzin Vejdani (eds), *Iran Facing Others: Identity Boundaries in a Historical Perspective* (London: Palgrave, 2012), 243–64.

Yazdi, Majid, 'Patterns of Clerical Political Behavior in Postwar Iran, 1941–53', *Middle Eastern Studies* 26, 3 (1990), 281–307.

Yildirim, Riza, 'An Ottoman Prince Wearing a Qizilbash Tāj: The Enigmatic Career of Sultan Murad and Qizilbash Affairs in Ottoman Domestic Politics, 1510–1513', *Turcica* 43 (2011), 91–119.

Yildirim, Riza, 'Shī'itisation of the Futuwwa Tradition in the Fifteenth Century', *British Journal of Middle Eastern Studies* 40, 1 (2013), 53–70.

Yildirim, Riza, 'Sunni Orthodox vs Shi'ite Heterodox? A Reappraisal of Islamic Piety in Medieval Anatolia', in: A. C. S. Peacock, Bruno DeNicola, and Sara Nur Yıldız (eds), *Islam and Christianity in Medieval Anatolia* (Burlington: Ashgate, 2015), 287–307.

Yildirim, Riza, 'The Rise of the "Religion and State" Order: Re-Confessionalisation of State and Society in the Early Modern Ottoman Empire', in: Vefa Erginbaş (ed.), *Ottoman Sunnism: New Perspectives* (Edinburgh: Edinburgh University Press, 2019), 12–46.

Yildirim, Riza, 'The Safavid-Qizilbash Ecumene and the Formation of the Qizilbash-Alevi Community in the Ottoman Empire, c. 1500–c. 1700', *Iranian Studies* 52, 3–4 (2019), 449–83.

Yılmaz, Hüseyin, *Caliphate Redefined: The Mystical Turn in Ottoman Political Thought* (Princeton: Princeton University Press, 2018).

Yılmaz, Yasir, 'Confessionalization or a Quest for Order? A Comparative Look at Religion and State in the Seventeenth-Century Ottoman, Russian, and Habsburg Empires', in: Vefa Erginbaş (ed.), *Ottoman Sunnism: New Perspectives* (Edinburgh: Edinburgh University Press, 2019), 90–120.

Yisraeli, Sarah, *The Remaking of Saudi Arabia: The Struggle between King Saud and Crown Prince Faysal, 1953–1962* (Tel Aviv: Moshe Dayan Center for Middle Eastern and African Studies, 1997).

Yürekli, Zeynep, *Architecture and Hagiography in the Ottoman Empire: The Politics of Bektashi Shrines in the Classical Age* (Abingdon: Routledge, 2012).

Yürekli, Zeynep, 'The Sword Dhū'l-Faqār and the Ottomans', in: Fahmida Suleman (ed.), *People of the Prophet's House: Artistic and Ritual Expressions of Shi'i Islam* (London: Azimuth Editions/Institute of Ismaili Studies, 2015), 163–72.

Yusoff, Maulana Muhammad 'Asri, *Syiah Rafidhah: Di Antara Kecuaian 'Ulama' dan Kebingungan Ummah* (n.p.: DarulKautsar.net, n.d.).

Zabad, Ibrahim, *Middle Eastern Minorities: The Impact of the Arab Spring* (Abingdon: Routledge, 2017).

Zaheer, Ehsan Elahi, *Qadiyaniat: An Analytical Survey* (Lahore: Idara Tarjuman al-Sunnah, 1972).

Zaheer, Ehsan Elahi, *Al-Shi'a wa-l-Sunna* (Lahore: Idara Tarjuman al-Sunnah, 1975).

Zaheer, Ehsan Elahi, *Al-Babiyya: 'Ard wa Naqd* (Lahore: Idara Tarjuman al-Sunnah, 1981).

Zaman, Muhammad Qasim, *Religion and Politics under the Early 'Abbasids: The Emergence of the Proto-Sunnī Elite* (Leiden: Brill, 1997).

Zaman, Muhammad Qasim, 'Sectarianism in Pakistan: The Radicalization of Shi'i and Sunni Identities', *Modern Asian Studies* 32, 3 (1998), 689–716.

Zaman, Muhammad Qasim, 'Epilogue', in: Robert W. Hefner and Muhammad Qasim Zaman (eds), *Schooling Islam: The Culture and Politics of Modern Muslim Education* (Princeton: Princeton University Press, 2007), 242–68.

Zaman, Muhammad Qasim, 'Tradition and Authority in Deobandi Madrasas of South Asia', in: Robert W. Hefner and Muhammad Qasim Zaman (eds), *Schooling Islam: The Culture and Politics of Modern Muslim Education* (Princeton: Princeton University Press, 2007), 61–86.

Zaman, Muhammad Qasim, 'Political Power, Religious Authority, and the Caliphate in Eighteenth-Century Indian Islamic Thought', *Journal of the Royal Asiatic Society* 30, 2 (2020), 313–40.

Zambelis, Chris, 'The Evolution of the Ethnic Baluch Insurgency in Iran', *CTC Sentinel* 7, 3 (2014), 17–20.

al-Zamili, Wali, *Al-Wahhabiyya: Da'iyya al-Silm al-'Alami* (Beirut: Dar al-Nakhil, 2006).

Zamir, Meir, 'Faisal and the Lebanese Question, 1918–20', *Middle Eastern Studies* 27, 3 (1991), 404–26.

Zarcone, Thierry, 'La situation du Chi'isme à Istanbul à la fin du XIXe et au début du XXe siècle', in: Th. Zarcone and F. Zarinebaf (eds), *Les Iraniens d'Istanbul* (Paris: Institut Français de Recherches en Iran/Institut Français d'Études Anatoliennes, 1993), 97–111.

Zarcone, Thierry, 'Shi'isms under Construction: The Shi'a Community of Turkey in the Contemporary Era', in: Sabrina Mervin (ed.), *The Shi'a Worlds and Iran* (London: Saqi, 2010), 139–66.

Zarinebaf, Fariba, 'Qizilbash "Heresy" and Rebellion in Ottoman Anatolia during the Sixteenth Century', *Anatolia Moderna* 7 (1997), 1–15.

Zarinebaf, Fariba, 'Rebels and Renegades on the Ottoman-Iranian Frontier', in: Abbas Amanat and Farzin Vejdani (eds), *Iran Facing Others: Identity Boundaries in a Historical Perspective* (London: Palgrave, 2012), 79–97.

Zarinebaf, Fariba, 'Azerbaijan between Two Empires: A Contested Borderland in the Early Modern Period (Sixteenth-Eighteenth Centuries)', *Iranian Studies* 52, 3–4 (2019), 299–337.

Zawadowski, G., 'Note sur l'origine magique de Dhoû-l-Faqâr', *En Terre d'Islam* 1 (1943), 36–40.

Zecca, Valentina, 'The Ṭā'ifiyyah or Sectarianism in Syria: Theoretical Considerations and Historical Overview', *Oriente Moderno* 98, 1 (2018), 33–51.

Zeidel, Ronen, 'Between Aqalliya and Mukawin: Understanding Sunni Political Attitudes in Post-Saddam Iraq', in: Benjamin Isakhan (ed.), *The Legacy of Iraq: From the 2003 War to the 'Islamic State'* (Edinburgh: Edinburgh University Press, 2015), 97–109.

Zia-Ebrahimi, Reza, 'Self-Orientalization and Dislocation: The Uses and Abuses of the "Aryan" Discourse in Iran', *Iranian Studies* 44, 4 (2011), 445–72.

Zia-Ebrahimi, Reza, '"Arab Invasion" and Decline, or the Import of European Racial Thought by Iranian Nationalists', *Ethnic and Racial Studies* 37, 6 (2014), 1043–61.

Zia-Ebrahimi, Reza, *The Emergence of Iranian Nationalism: Race and the Politics of Dislocation* (New York: Columbia University Press, 2016).

Zisser, Eyal, 'The Alawis, Lords of Syria: From Ethnic Minority to Ruling Sect', in: Ofra Bengio and Gabriel Ben-Dor (eds), *Minorities and the State in the Arab World* (Boulder, CO: Lynne Rienner, 1999), 129–45.

Zisser, Eyal, *Asad's Legacy: Syria in Transition* (London: Hurst, 2001).

Zubaida, Sami, 'Contested Nations: Iraq and the Assyrians', *Nations and Nationalism* 6, 3 (2000), 363–82.

Zubaida, Sami, 'The Fragments Imagine the Nation: The Case of Iraq', *International Journal of Middle East Studies* 34, 2 (2002), 205–15.

Zubaida, Sami, 'Communalism and Thwarted Aspirations of Iraqi Citizenship', *Middle East Report* 237 (2005), 8–11.

Zubaida, Sami, 'Sectarian Violence as Jihad', in: Elisabeth Kendall and Ewan Stein (eds), *Twenty-First Century Jihad: Law, Society and Military Action* (London: I. B. Tauris, 2015), 141–8.

Zulkifli, *The Struggle of the Shi'is in Indonesia* (Canberra: ANU Press, 2013).

Zulkifli, 'Qom Alumni in Indonesia: Their Role in the Shi'i Community', in: Masooda Bano and Keiko Sakurai (eds), *Shaping Global Islamic Discourses: The Role of al-Azhar, al-Medina and al-Mustafa* (Edinburgh: Edinburgh University Press, 2015), 117–41.

Zürcher, Erik-Jan, *Jihad and Islam in World War I: Studies on the Ottoman Jihad on the Centenary of Snouck Hurgronje's 'Holy War Made in Germany'* (Leiden: Leiden University Press, 2016).

al-Zurfi, Fouad Jabir Kadhem, 'Sectarianism in Iraq: A Critique by Ali al-Wardi', *Contemporary Arab Affairs* 7, 4 (2014), 510–25.

Zygulski, Zdzislaw, *Ottoman Art in the Service of the Empire* (New York: NYU Press, 1992).

NEWS SOURCES

Agence France-Presse
al-Ahram
al-Akhbar
al-Arabiya
al-Araby
al-Jazeera
al-Khalij al-Jadid
al-Monitor
al-Sharq al-Awsat
Arab News
Asharq al-Awsat
Associated Press
BBC
Bloomberg
CBN
CNN
Daily Mail
Dawn
Deutsche Welle
Egypt Today
Eurasianet
Financial Times
Foreign Affairs
Foreign Broadcast Information Service (FBIS)
Foreign Policy
Guardian
Gulf News
Haaretz
Halkin Sesi TV
Hindustan Times
Huffington Post
ICANA
Independent
India Legal
Institute for War and Peace Reporting
Intercept
International Business Times
Iranian Diplomacy
IranWire
Irish Times
Israel Hayom

Le Monde
Le Monde Diplomatique
Live Encounters
LobeLog
London Review of Books
Los Angeles Review of Books
Mada Masr
Maydan
Middle East Eye
Morocco World News
Moscow Times
MSNBC
Muftah
Neue Zürcher Zeitung
New York Review of Books
New York Sun
New York Times
Newsweek
openDemocracy
Orient News
Pakistan Christian Post
Pars Today
PBS Frontline
Politico
Prospect
Religioscope
Reuters
RFE/RL
Sabq Online Newspaper
Shafaqna English
Spiegel
Telegraph
Telegraph India
Telesur
Telos
The Age
The Australian
The National
The National Interest
Time Magazine
Times of India
Today's Zaman
TRT World

UPI
VICE
Voice of America
Wall Street Journal
War on the Rocks
Washington Post
Ya Libnan
Zenith

THINK TANK PUBLICATIONS

Arab Gulf States Institute in Washington
Atlantic Council
Carnegie Endowment for International Peace
Carnegie Middle East Center
Century Foundation
Chatham House
Foundation for Defense of Democracies
Institute for Gulf Affairs
Institute for the Study of War
International Crisis Group
International Institute for Strategic Studies
Jamestown Foundation
Middle East Institute
Middle East Research and Information Project
Middle East Research Institute
Moroccan Institute for Policy Analysis
New America
Pew Research Center
Sanaa Center
United States Institute of Peace

Index